ESSENTIALS OF Fifth Edition
Psychology

STEPHEN L. FRANZOI

Publisher and Marketing Manager: Richard Schofield

Managing Editor: Joyce Bianchini

Project Research and Development: Jenefier Winchell

Production Manager: Janai Bryand

Cover and Interior Design: Esther Scannell

Typesetting Manager: Rhonda Minnema

Proofreader: Anne Schofield

Pre-Production Coordinator: Tommi Morgenthal

Permissions Coordinator: Christine Davies

Photo Researcher: Jacquelyn Wein

For information, address BVT Publishing, LLC, P.O. Box 492831, Redding, CA 96049-2831

Some ancillaries, including electronic and print components, may not be available to customers outside the United States.

Hardcover ISBN: 978-1-61882-693-0

Softcover ISBN: 978-1-61882-694-7

Loose Leaf ISBN: 978-1-61882-695-4

eBook ISBN: 978-1-61882-697-8

Photo Credits: Cover: *Shutterstock*. Interior Section: Journey of Discovery, *iStock*; Section Review, *iStock*; Psychological Applications, *Shutterstock*; Self Discovery, *Shutterstock*. Table of Contents: page v, *Shutterstock*; page vi, *iStock*; page vii, *Shutterstock*; page viii, *iStock*; page ix, *Shutterstock*; page ix, *iStock*; page x, *iStock*; page xi, *iStock*; page xii, *iStock*; page xiii, *Shutterstock*.

BVT Publishing
Better textbooks, better prices
www.BVTPublishing.com

To the women in my life, Cheryl, Amelia, and Lillian;

To my parents, Lou and Joyce;

And to my brother and sister, Randy and Susie:

Together, and singly, they influence the essential elements of my life.

Brief Contents

Table *of* Contents

Chapter Three

Human Development   89

Chapter Four

Sensation and Perception   145

Chapter Five

Consciousness   199

Chapter Six
Learning   241

Chapter Seven
Memory   281

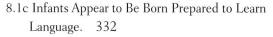

Chapter Eight

Language, Thinking, and Intelligence   327

Chapter Nine

Motivation and Emotion   391

Chapter Ten

Personality   443

Chapter Thirteen

Stress, Coping, and Health   563

List *of* Vignettes

EXPLORING CULTURE & DIVERSITY

SELF-DISCOVERY QUESTIONNAIRE

CLOSER LOOK

Preface

Why do I describe psychology as a discovery experience? Much of my reasoning is very personal: My own study of psychology, including my career in this scientific discipline, has been a true journey of discovery. Growing up in a small town did not offer many opportunities to learn about the social sciences. However, during my first year in college, I was introduced to psychology and became hooked. I spent the following summer reading a stack of psychology books. After my sophomore year I began conducting research. As you will learn when reading Chapter 1, one of my more interesting undergraduate research projects involved studying the followers of a religious cult. Since then, I am repeatedly reminded that the science of psychology is a valuable way to understand behavior and the process of living on this planet.

What can I offer you as an enticement to read this book? Well, are you interested in becoming more competent in dealing with future life events? Psychology involves the "study of the mind." As such, introductory psychology offers you the hope that course material will help you better understand not only other people but also yourself. Seeking such knowledge is a distinguishing feature of young adulthood, and the college experience is specifically designed to foster this quest. In writing this text, I sought to bring to these pages that same message of hope and discovery that infuses the entire field of psychology. Does this sort of journey interest you?

I have written this text in a way that introduces you to the science of psychology as a journey of discovery, undertaken both by researchers in their search for knowledge over the past century, and by students over the course of the term. I explain how psychology has expanded our understanding of how people think, feel, and behave, while also motivating you to apply this knowledge to better understand yourself and others. By regularly encouraging you to consider how psychological knowledge relates to your own life, I place your learning experience within a personally relevant context that will help you remember course material, while also fostering self-insights that can be applied to your daily living.

The history of psychology is infused with compelling stories of how researchers' intense interest in learning about the nature of human and animal behavior led them on a journey of discovery that eventually culminated in important new knowledge. The fundamental difference between our personal journeys of discovery and the journeys of discovery found in psychology is that the vehicle employed in the latter journeys is the scientific method. Throughout *Essentials of Psychology*, I present discovery stories in psychology so that you appreciate both the human element and the ever-evolving nature of scientific knowledge and insight.

Following Chapter 1's introduction to psychology—which covers the field's history, areas of specialization, and research methodology—we examine the subject matter spanning the entire field of psychology. Each chapter also includes boxes that discuss selected studies in detail. This emphasis on the scientific enterprise encourages a healthy, scientific skepticism of the many, often contradictory, commonsense truisms we learn from others.

One last thing I would like to mention about the stories you will read in this book is that some of them involve personal disclosures about me and my friends and family. Because I am asking you to take this discovery journey with me, I think it is only fair that I share some of my life experiences as they relate to chapter topics. I hope you enjoy these stories and that, in turn, you begin to consider how psychological knowledge can help you understand some of your own past and unfolding life stories.

Encouraging Self-Discovery

While encouraging you to analyze the scientific journey of discovery in psychology, the text also facilitates a personal journey of discovery by including more than 30 Self-Discovery questionnaires that ask you to consider how the specific text material relates to your life. Many of these "Self-Discovery" questionnaires include self-report surveys that researchers currently use to study the selected self-discovery topic, and the results of studies employing them are part of the text material. Thus, as you learn about various psychological theories and relevant research findings, you also learn something about yourself.

Applying Psychology to Everyday Experiences

Beyond self-report questionnaires, I also present a Psychological Applications section at the end of each chapter that demonstrates how psychology can be applied to your life. In these sections, you learn how the theories and research in a particular chapter can be applied to real-world settings. Topics covered in the "Psychological Application" sections include: developing critical thinking skills, learning how to exercise self-control in your academic and personal life, improving everyday memory, encouraging your creativity, coping with jealousy, and many others.

Encouraging Critical Thinking

You can develop an understanding of yourself and others by reading astrological predictions, internalizing the varied messages of popular culture, and uncritically accepting the advice and "wisdom" of friends, family, and (yes!) college professors. Yet, what is the value of this understanding if it is not subjected to critical cognitive analysis? Critical evaluation is an important component of *Essentials of Psychology*. Throughout the text, critical thinking is facilitated by numerous Closer Look boxes that examine specific chapter topics in greater detail and encourage you to ponder and analyze the research and theory underlying each topic. Each chapter also features Journey of Discovery questions, which require critical analyses of current discussion topics. Possible answers to these questions are provided in the appendix of the print version of the text and are "clickable" in the online version. Strategically placed Info-bits in each chapter provide additional information on selected topics. Critical thinking is also encouraged by the questions frequently posed in the main body of the text, inviting you to guess a study's hypotheses, results, or alternative interpretations of findings. Questions that appear in the captions of figures, tables, and photos inspire further analysis of text material. Last, but certainly not least, are the end-of-chapter Practice Quiz questions. These questions test your knowledge of various topics and the end-of-text answers provide immediate feedback on the extent of your understanding.

Recognizing the Diversity and Unity of People

Integrated within this book's journey of discovery theme is the encouragement to recognize the ways in which people are both similar to, and different from, one another. *Essentials of Psychology* tells the story of the science of psychology in such a way that you will recognize the "yin-yang" of unity and diversity whether you are trying to understand the thoughts, emotions, and behavior of your college roommates or those of people

from other cultures. This emphasis on diversity can be seen most clearly in the numerous Exploring Culture & Diversity boxes found throughout the book.

The text not only analyzes how culture and our individual developmental experiences influence the way we think, feel, and behave, but also examines how humans, as a species, often respond similarly to their physical and social surroundings. The "yin" in this diversity-unity analysis is the sociocultural perspective, while the "yang" is the evolutionary perspective. The text explains that the culture of a people is based on their relationship with the environment, and the evolution of our species is a story of how we have adapted to our surroundings. Thus, just as our bodies and brains are products of evolutionary forces, so, too, is our culture. Yet, cultural change occurs much more rapidly than genetic change. This is why the world's cultures vary greatly, despite little meaningful genetic variation among cultural groups.

Two belief systems that explain how individuals relate to their groups, and that are important to understanding the psychology of human behavior, are individualism and collectivism. Individualism is a philosophy of life stressing the priority of personal goals over group goals, a preference for loose-knit social relationships, and a desire to be relatively independent of others' influence. In contrast, collectivism is a philosophy of life stressing the priority of group needs over individual needs, a preference for tightly knit social relationships, and a willingness to submit to the influence of one's group. Although we know that cultures differ in their individualist-collectivist orientations, we do not know whether one is better than the other in any ultimate evolutionary sense. *Essentials of Psychology* periodically examines how the psychology of people from different cultures differs due to their individualist-collectivist bents. For those chapter topics where the individualist-collectivist analysis is not especially relevant, other more relevant cultural factors are highlighted.

New to the Fifth Edition

The fifth edition of *Essentials of Psychology* has a great deal of new content, including many new photos, figures, and cartoons, as well as more than 400 new references. Other significant changes in this new edition include:

Chapter 1
- Expanded coverage of positive psychology
- Expanded coverage of evolutionary psychology

Chapter 2

- Expanded coverage of the specialized abilities of the two hemispheres
- New coverage of sensitive periods in development

Chapter 3

- Expanded coverage of parenting style
- Expanded coverage of self-esteem
- Expanded coverage of adolescence
- New research on emerging adulthood and Generation Next
- New research on the prevalence of the mid-life crisis
- New coverage of culture and ageism
- Expanded coverage of Alzheimer's disease
- Expanded coverage of wisdom development

Chapter 4

- New discussion of bottom-up versus top-down processing

Chapter 5

- New coverage of mindfulness
- Expanded coverage of why we sleep
- Expanded coverage of dream theories

Chapter 6

- New coverage of mirror neurons and observational learning
- Expanded coverage of violence depicted in music lyrics and music videos

Chapter 7

- Reorganized chapter content
- Expanded coverage of the neural basis of memory

Chapter 8

- More information on the neural basis of insight
- Increased coverage of multiple intelligences
- New information on group-based differences in IQ scores

Chapter 9

- New section on how friends and family influence people's body weight
- Increased coverage of sexual scripts and date rape
- Increased coverage of social rejection
- Increased coverage of gender and decoding emotional expressions

Chapter 10

- Expanded coverage of the neuroscience of psychoanalytic theory
- New research on the Five-Factor Model
- New section on positive psychology and character strengths
- New coverage of the Jungian-based Myers-Briggs Type Indicator
- Increased coverage of the biological basis of personality
- New research on the personality trait of self-monitoring

Chapter 11

- Complete chapter re-organization based on the *DSM* revision
- New research on prevalence of psychological disorders worldwide
- New research on social anxiety disorder
- Increased coverage of depression
- Increased coverage of suicide risk
- New research on dissociative identity disorder
- Substantially revised coverage of schizophrenia
- Substantially revised coverage of personality disorders

Chapter 12

- New section on deep brain stimulation

Chapter 13

- Increased coverage of stress
- New research on the benefits of stress
- Increased coverage of the psychology of happiness

Chapter 14

- New research on cognitive dissonance

Pedagogical Aids

Essentials of Psychology enhances learning with the following pedagogical devices:

1. Each chapter opens with a chapter outline.

2. Short-sentence headings compactly summarize the content of chapter sections and facilitate recall of text topics.

3. A bulleted summary at the end of each major chapter section reviews the section's most important concepts.

4. Beautifully rendered, four-color illustrations throughout the text clarify and enhance chapter concepts.

5. Key terms and concepts are highlighted and defined on first appearance. Key terms are also defined in the text margins and listed in alphabetical order with page references at the end of each chapter. A glossary at the end of the book presents all of the definitions alphabetically.

6. Journey of Discovery Questions within each chapter require critical analyses of current discussion topics. Possible answers are found online, as well as in the appendix at the end of the book.

7. Info-bits briefly describe the results from psychological studies that enhance text material.

8. Quotes from famous individuals in other fields illustrate text material.

9. Self-Discovery questionnaires, Exploring Culture & Diversity boxes, and Closer Look vignettes enhance your understanding of a variety of topics. See the List of Vignettes on page xiii.

10. Psychological Applications sections help you to apply each chapter's psychological concepts to real-world situations.

11. Suggested websites at the end of each chapter provide online sources that you can access to obtain a better understanding of chapter material.

12. Review Questions at the end of each chapter allow you to check your comprehension of the chapter's major concepts.

APA Principles for Quality Undergraduate Education in Psychology

The APA Board of Educational Affairs (BEA) has developed a set of principles and recommendations for creating a world-class educational system that provides students with

- the workplace skills needed in the information age

- a solid academic background that prepares them for advanced study in a wide range of fields

- the knowledge, skills and values they will need to enter and succeed in the workforce and thrive in their daily lives.

These principles and recommendations are available at www.apa.org/education/undergrad/principles.aspx. Please visit www.BVTPublishing.com/APA to see how *Essentials of Psychology,* fifth edition, supports all of these principles.

Acknowledgments

While writing this text, many people provided me with invaluable assistance and understanding. I first want to thank my family for not only supporting my writing efforts and forgiving my memory lapses during this time, but also providing me with wonderful examples of psychological principles that I have used throughout the text. I also apologize to my daughters, Amelia and Lillian, for any future embarrassment I may cause them by retelling some of their life experiences in the book!

I owe a big debt of gratitude to the students in my introductory psychology courses at Marquette University, who are the first ones exposed to my new stories of the psychological journey of discovery. I would also like to thank the numerous family members, friends, acquaintances, and strangers who allowed me to take their photos for use in the book.

There are a number of people I would like to warmly thank at BVT Publishing. First, I would like to thank Publisher and Marketing Manager Richard Schofield for seeing the value of this project and providing the necessary resources to bring it to fruition. While completing this fifth edition, I worked with Managing Editor Joyce Bianchini, Project Research and Development Manager Jenefier Winchell, Production Manager Janai Bryand, Cover and Interior Design Manager Esther Scannell, Typesetting Manager Rhonda Minnema, Proofreader Anne Schofield, and Pre-Production Coordinator Tommi Morgenthal. All seven of these talented people did a great job coordinating and organizing numerous book tasks, of which many I wasn't even aware!

Numerous reviewers, who obviously care very much about psychology and the art and craft of teaching, generously provided feedback during the writing of this text. I would like to thank:

Paul Bell, Colorado State University

Wayne Briner, University of Nebraska at Kearney

Sheila Brownlow, Catawba College

Trey Buchanan, Wheaton College

Adam Butler, University of Northern Iowa

Robert Caldwell, Michigan State University

Jorge Conesa, Everett Community College

James R. Cook, University of North Carolina–Charlotte

Tom Copeland, Hardin Simmons University

Wendy Domjan, University of Texas–Austin

Natalie Dove, Purdue University

Carol Edwards, Purdue University North Central

Ron Faulk, St. Gregory's University

Gary D. Fisk, Georgia Southwestern State University

Donelson R. Forsyth, Virginia Commonwealth University

Susan M. Frantz, Highline Community College

Traci Giuliano, Southwestern University

Wind Goodfriend, Purdue University

Judith Harackiewicz, University of Wisconsin–Madison

Robert M. Hessling, University of Wisconsin–Milwaukee

Deborah E. Horn, Blinn College

Neil Levens, Indiana University of Pennsylvania

Scott F. Madey, Shippensburg University

Michael Major, Loyola University of New Orleans

Michael S. Ofsowitz, University of Maryland, European Division

Daniel Osherton, Rice University

Maria Pagano, New York City College of Technology

Debra L. Palmer, University of Wisconsin–Stevens Point

Ellen Peters, University of Oregon

Laura Richardson, University of Guam

Alan Searleman, St. Lawrence University

Robert R. Sinclair, Portland State University

Jason S. Spiegelman, Community College of Baltimore County

Leland Swenson, Loyola Marymount University

Alan Swinkels, St. Edward's University

Kris Vasquez, Alverno College

Lona Whitmarsh, Fairleigh Dickinson University

Bob Wildblood, Indiana University, Kokomo

Brian T. Yates, American University

And Finally …

I welcome your comments and feedback. The prospect of being able to develop a robust exchange of ideas with current users, both students and faculty, is truly exciting. You can reach me at stephen.franzoi@marquette.edu.

Very best wishes,
Steve Franzoi

About *the* Author

Stephen L. Franzoi is a Professor of Psychology at Marquette University in Milwaukee, Wisconsin. Born and raised in Iron Mountain, Michigan, Dr. Franzoi is proud to call himself a "Yooper" (a native of the Upper Peninsula of Michigan, or U.P.). Dr. Franzoi received his BS in both psychology and sociology from Western Michigan University and his MA and PhD from the University of California at Davis; he was also a postdoctoral fellow at Indiana University before joining Marquette's faculty. Dr. Franzoi has served as assistant editor of *Social Psychology Quarterly* and associate editor of *Social Problems*. Professor Franzoi has taught introductory psychology courses for more than 30 years, and in 2013 was honored with the Marquette University Teaching Excellence Award. He is an active researcher in the area of physical appearance and body esteem. Over the years, Dr. Franzoi has discussed his research in many popular media outlets, including *The New York Times, USA Today, National Public Radio,* and the *Oprah Winfrey Show.* He and Cheryl Figg are the proud parents of Amelia and Lillian. In his spare time, he enjoys relaxing with his family, bicycling, making wine, and playing bocce ball.

Supplements *and* Resources

Instructor Supplements

A complete teaching package is available for instructors who adopt this book. This package includes an **online lab**, **instructor's manual**, **test bank**, **course management software**, and **PowerPoint™ slides**.

BVT*Lab*	An online lab is available for this textbook at www.BVTLab.com, as described in the BVT*Lab* section below.
Instructor's Manual	A comprehensive manual provides chapter overviews, key terms and definitions, learning objectives, lecture suggestions, discussion questions, and in-class activities.
Test Bank	An extensive test bank is available to instructors in both hard copy and electronic form. Each chapter has 120 to 150 multiple choice questions ranked by difficulty and style, as well as 20 written-answer questions. Each question is referenced to the appropriate section of the text to make test creation quick and easy.
Course Management Software	BVT's course management software, Respondus, allows for the creation of tests and quizzes that can be downloaded directly into a wide variety of course management environments such as Blackboard, Web CT, Desire2Learn, ANGEL, E-Learning, eCollege, Canvas, Moodle, and others.
PowerPoint Slides	A set of PowerPoint slides includes about 30 slides per chapter, comprising a chapter overview, learning objectives, slides covering all key topics, key figures and charts, as well as summary and conclusion slides.

Student Resources

Student resources are available for this textbook at www.BVTLab.com. These resources are geared toward students needing additional assistance as well as those seeking complete mastery of the content. The following resources are available:

Practice Questions	Students can work through hundreds of practice questions online. Questions are multiple choice or true/false in format, and are graded instantly for immediate feedback.
Flashcards	BVT*Lab* includes sets of flashcards for each chapter that reinforce the key terms and concepts from the textbook.
Chapter Summaries	A convenient and concise chapter summary is available as a study aid for each chapter.
Study Guide	A thorough and practical student study guide includes chapter overviews, key terms, learning objectives, multiple choice and true/false practice questions, as well as discussion questions. The study guide is available in both printed and online (printable) form.
Chapter Quiz Rationales	Detailed rationales are available to explain all of the end-of-chapter quiz answers.
PowerPoint Slides	All instructor PowerPoints are available for convenient lecture preparation and for students to view online for a study recap.

BVT*Lab*

BVT*Lab* is an affordable online lab for instructors and their students. It includes an online classroom with grade book and chat room, a homework grading system, extensive test banks for quizzes and exams, and a host of student study resources.

Course Setup	BVT*Lab* has an easy-to-use, intuitive interface that allows instructors to quickly set up their courses and grade books, and to replicate them from section to section and semester to semester.
Grade Book	Using an assigned passcode, students register themselves into the grade book; and all homework, quizzes, and tests are automatically graded and recorded.
Chat Room	Instructors can post discussion threads to a class forum and then monitor and moderate student replies.
Student Resources	All student resources for this textbook are available in BVT*Lab* in digital form.
eBook	A web-based eBook is available within the lab for easy reference during online classes, homework, and study sessions.

Even if a class is not taught in the lab, students are always welcome to login as a guest and explore the many student resources described above.

TEXTBOOK +

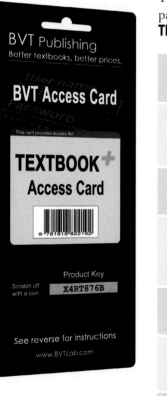

The most complete and affordable package for this textbook is **TEXTBOOK** +. This package is available at BVTLab.com, or in campus bookstores (via an access card). **TEXTBOOK** + includes the following:

Textbook	The choice of a loose-leaf, black and white textbook or a full-semester textbook loan is included with **TEXTBOOK** +. Textbook purchase options are also available at a discount.
eBook	An online eBook is included for convenience while doing homework and studying. This eBook can be printed (some restrictions apply). An advanced, downloadable eBook is also available.
BVT*Lab*	Complete access to all features of the lab, for both instructor and student, is included in **TEXTBOOK** +. Instructors can pick and choose what features of the lab they wish to use.
Student Resources	All of the student resources are included in **TEXTBOOK** +, including practice quizzes, flashcards, chapter summaries, study guide (eBook/printable), chapter-quiz rationales, and PowerPoint slides.
Homework Grading	Even if instructors do not wish to teach within the lab, they can use it to grade homework or to monitor student progress on practice quizzes.
Extended 6-year Edition Cycle	Professors adopting **TEXTBOOK** + may qualify to lock in 6-year availability of the edition they adopt, including full support of all ancillary materials and resources.
6-year Price Freeze	Professors adopting **TEXTBOOK** + may qualify to lock in the current net price for up to 6 years.

BVT also offers a paperless version of **TEXTBOOK**➕, which provides even more cost savings to students. It includes everything listed above except the physical textbook. Those students who decide they would like a physical product as well can either print the pages they want, or purchase any of the available printed formats at a significant discount.

Customization

BVT's Custom Publishing Division can help you modify this book's content to satisfy your specific instructional needs. The following are examples of customization:

- Rearrangement of chapters to follow the order of your syllabus

- Deletion of chapters not covered in your course

- Addition of paragraphs, sections, or chapters you or your colleagues have written for this course

- Editing of the existing content, down to the word level

- Customization of the accompanying student resources and online lab

- Addition of handouts, lecture notes, syllabus, etc.

- Incorporation of student worksheets into the textbook

All of these customizations will be professionally typeset to produce a seamless textbook of the highest quality, with an updated table of contents and index to reflect the customized content.

Chapter One

Psychology as a Science

Chapter Outline

Quest—An act or instance of seeking; an adventurous journey.

The theme of this book is that both the science of psychology and your own life are journeys of discovery. Throughout your life you will undertake many quests, and a large number of these will be hopelessly doomed to fail. Others, however, will be fabulously successful due to a combination of factors, including good planning, skill, effort, fortunate circumstances, and the help of others. Certainly, one very important lesson in life is to learn to recognize the difference between the foolish quests and the profound ones. Perhaps an even more important lesson is that it is absolutely essential to undertake quests regularly, because in such quests— both the large and the small variety—you develop new ways of looking at yourself and the world. With this thought in mind, let's begin.

My personal and professional journey of discovery in psychology began when I was an undergraduate student, like you.

Since the beginning of the twentieth century, people's innate desire to understand themselves—and the human condition—has found a new avenue toward the answer: the scientific method.

—Jacqueline Swartz,
contemporary Canadian
journalist

The followers of Guru Maharaji Ji believed that this 16-year-old leader of the Divine Light Mission was "Lord of the Universe." How did they respond when the guru's mother proclaimed that he was no longer the Perfect Master?

© Bettmann/CORBIS

Besides taking psychology courses, I also began conducting psychological studies. One of my more interesting undergraduate studies involved an investigation of the members of a very curious and popular religious cult. Allow me to describe this study by briefly transporting you back in time to the fall of 1974.

It was a pleasantly mild Midwest day in Kalamazoo, Michigan. I sat across from Dave, a young and energetic man of 21, in a small, two-story house that was the residence, or ashram, of the local Divine Light Mission. This was a red-letter day for me as an aspiring psychologist, and I wanted to be careful how I asked the question foremost in my mind. The Divine Light Mission was a neo-Hindu religious movement from India that had been receiving much national attention during the past few years. For two months I had visited the ashram, administering personality tests to its members. I was trying to understand why so many people were attracted to this new Eastern religion. Dave had been a devoted member for more than two years, despite the protests of his family. I was a senior in college with aspirations for graduate study in psychology. Now I had the opportunity, with Dave's help, to observe some classic psychological principles in operation.

That year, the Divine Light Mission claimed a worldwide membership of 6 million, with about 80,000 located in the United States. The leader of this new religious movement was a 16-year-old boy from India named Guru Maharaj Ji, hailed by his disciples (who were called Premies) as being "Lord of the Universe" and "Divine Incarnation." Premies believed that this young boy was about to usher in the New Age of Peace; and followers were promised salvation if they received the "Knowledge," which was described as being infinite and therefore unexplainable.

Although Guru Maharaj Ji touted himself as a divine entity, he very much enjoyed earthly pleasures such as expensive cars, airplanes, motorcycles, townhouses and mansions staffed with servants, and many Batman comic books and squirt guns as well. What allowed the young guru to live in such luxury were thousands of unpaid Premies, like Dave, who worked at a host of enterprises, including ten Divine Sales thrift stores, a "Cleanliness Is Next To Godliness" janitorial service, and a vegetarian restaurant in New York City. In addition to the income generated by these businesses, all new members' financial assets were routinely funneled into the mission's accounts upon joining, as was any income earned from worldly jobs.

Which brings me back to why I was sitting across from Dave in the ashram. The previous day, Guru Maharaj Ji had skipped town and eloped with his secretary. Upon learning of this youthful, and decidedly ungodlike, flight of spontaneous passion, his mother had publicly pronounced that Guru Maharaj Ji was no longer the Perfect Master. Instead, she angrily proclaimed that his older brother was the new divine incarnation. Within one day's time, members of the religious movement were being told to believe that Guru Maharaj Ji had gone from being the Perfect Master of their 6-million-member mission to being spiritually "grounded" by his "Holy Mother." How would Dave and the other members of the Kalamazoo ashram make sense of this turn of events? After all, they had paid a high price to gain admission to this religious cult that promised them divine salvation. Yet now the Mission that was their life's work was in danger of crumbling. Had Dave begun questioning the spirituality of his guru and his own commitment to the Divine Light Mission?

Dave's reply was immediate and unwavering. He told me that these recent events were all part of the

Perfect Master's plan of ushering in the New Age of Peace. If anything, Dave stated, Guru Maharaj Ji was now more in his thoughts than before; and he was even more certain that the New Age would be dawning soon.

Does Dave's strengthened conviction in the face of troubling evidence to the contrary surprise you? Was his reaction different from what you might expect from a normal person? Was it irrational? Was Dave suffering from some sort of mental illness?

Because I had been exposed to research and theories within psychology, I did not think that Dave's thinking reflected a psychological disorder. Instead, I strongly suspected that his far-fetched rationalizations were more similar to the normal and all-too-ordinary thoughts of someone caught in a very uncomfortable psychological position. Years ago, psychologist Leon Festinger (1957) had outlined a theory to explain how our need to maintain consistency between our beliefs can often lead to irrational behavior. That is, if people hold two thoughts that are inconsistent ("I've paid a high price to follow Guru Maharaj Ji" and "Guru Maharaj Ji is a spiritual fraud"), an internal conflict will be created that people will try to reduce or eliminate. The greater their investment in particular beliefs (for example, "Guru Maharaj Ji is a god and worthy of my devotion"), the more difficult it is for people to reject their beliefs. Known as the theory of cognitive dissonance, Festinger's ideas provided an explanation for how normally rational individuals can engage in some rather odd forms of thought and behavior while trying to justify their past actions.

For me, studying the Divine Light Mission represented one of the first of many scientific journeys of discovery that I have undertaken as a psychologist during the past four decades. Many of you reading this textbook will feel a similar intensity of interest in learning about the science of psychology. For others, whose passions burn for different life pursuits, this text, and the course in which it is offered, can still provide valuable knowledge that will serve you well while following other desires.

A journey of a thousand miles starts from beneath one's feet.

—Lao-Tzu, Chinese philosopher, sixth century BC

At its heart, the science of psychology is a journey of discovery undertaken both by researchers in their search for knowledge over the past 100-odd years and by you, the student, over the course of the term. Throughout this text, as you learn how psychology has expanded our understanding of the ways people think, feel, and behave (the discipline's journey of discovery), I will encourage you to apply this knowledge to better understand yourself and others (your own journey of discovery).

Wheresoever you go, go with all your heart.

—Confucius, Chinese philosopher, 551–479 BC

1.1 **What Is Psychology?**

A basic necessity for any successful journey is knowing how to read the road signs; and for you, the reader of this textbook, this means understanding the terminology. Throughout this book, I define important concepts that will help you navigate your understanding of the discipline of psychology.

1.1a   Psychology Is the Scientific Study of Mental Processes and Behavior.

The term psychology comes from the Greek words *psyche*, meaning "mind," and *logos*, meaning "study." In its broadest sense, **psychology** is the scientific study of mental processes and behavior. This means that psychologists are interested in using scientific methods (see Section 1.3) to understand how we and other living creatures think, feel, and act.

People often confuse psychology with **psychiatry**, which is a branch of medicine concerned with the diagnosis and treatment of psychological disorders and that is

Psychology The scientific study of mental processes and behavior

Psychiatry A branch of medicine concerned with the diagnosis and treatment of psychological disorders. (The roughly comparable specialty area in psychology is known as clinical psychology.)

Wilhelm Wundt, the founder of psychology

Structuralism An early theory in psychology that sought to identify the components of the conscious mind

William James, the first major American psychologist

Functionalism An early approach to psychology that studied how the conscious mind helps humans survive and successfully adapt to their environment

Sigmund Freud, the founder of psychoanalysis

practiced by physicians. Psychology also deals with the diagnosis and treatment of such disorders (see Chapter 11), but this interest represents only one area of specialization in a discipline that has a much broader scope than psychiatry (see Section 1.2g). Whereas psychiatrists have completed medical school and obtained an MD (doctor of medicine), psychologists have completed graduate school in psychology and obtained a PhD (doctor of philosophy) or, in some cases, a Psy.D. (doctor of psychology).

1.1b Early Pioneers Established Paths for Later Discoveries.

Most historians identify Wilhelm Wundt (pronounced "Vill-helm Voont," 1832–1920) as the "world's first psychologist." In 1879, Wundt established the first institute for research in experimental psychology at the University of Leipzig in Germany (Kim, 2009). Over the next 40 years, more than 100 students obtained doctoral degrees studying psychological topics under his supervision (Fernberger, 1933). Wundt's research focused on the study of consciousness; and his method for studying the mind was known as *introspection*, a research technique in which trained observers would report on the contents of their own immediate states of consciousness. His model of consciousness, which his student Edward Titchener later named **structuralism**, sought to identify the components of the conscious mind. Wundt's influence on the first generation of psychologists was so great that most contemporary psychologists can probably trace their historical lineage back to him.

Beyond Europe's shores, in the United States, the first American psychologist to exert a guiding influence on the young science of psychology was William James (1842–1910). Although both James and Wundt studied consciousness, James's desire was to understand how the mind affects what people do, rather than to merely identify its components. In addition, his approach to psychology had very little to do with laboratory studies and relied heavily, instead, on his own rich ideas and eloquent writing (Hoffman & Thelen, 2010). Because of James's interest in how the conscious mind helps humans survive and successfully adapt to their environment—that is, how the mind functions—his approach to psychology came to be called **functionalism**. In 1890, James published a brilliant two-volume text entitled *Principles of Psychology,* which today is still considered a classic among classics. Unlike Wundt, James had a relatively small group of students. Among them, however, were such luminaries as Mary Calkins (1863–1930), pioneer in memory research; Edward Thorndike (1874–1949), who investigated trial-and-error animal learning; and Robert Woodworth (1869–1962), a pioneer in motivation and drive theory. In Chapter 9, Section 9.5d, we will explore James's theory of emotion.

Journey of Discovery

At the beginning of the twentieth century, Hermann Ebbinghaus (1850–1909), one of psychology's pioneers, stated that "Psychology has a long past, but only a short history." What do you think he meant by this statement?

The third prominent founder of psychology was Sigmund Freud (1856–1939), an Austrian physician trained as a neurologist. Actually, because Freud was a physician, his proper title is "psychiatrist" and not "psychologist." Despite this technicality, psychology claims him as an important founder of one of the early schools of thought in the discipline. Instead of working in the lab (like Wundt) or teaching at the university (like James), Freud developed his approach to psychology through clinical practice. Based on his work with patients who suffered from ailments that had no known physical causes, Freud developed a theory that all human behavior is determined by hidden or unconscious motives and desires that are sexual in nature. This approach to psychology, which Freud called **psychoanalysis**, influenced the study of such diverse topics as dreams, childhood development, aggression, sexuality, creativity, motivation, personality, and led to the development of psychotherapy. In Chapter 10, Section 10.2, we will examine Freud's theory of personality and its influence on contemporary psychological theories.

Just as psychoanalysis is closely associated with Sigmund Freud, **behaviorism** is intimately intertwined with John Watson (1878–1958). This American's research with rats, dogs, and other animals caused him to question the mainstream view in psychology that the structure, content, and function of the mind were the proper focus of scientific inquiry. Instead, Watson (1913) asserted that psychology should study observable behavior rather than hidden psychological processes. Watson's radical behaviorism struck a responsive chord among many American psychologists who shared his impatience with what they considered to be the "fuzziness" of the other scientific approaches within psychology. Underlying behaviorism was a philosophy known as *logical positivism,* which contended that all knowledge should be expressed in terms that can be verified empirically or through direct observation. These new psychologists sought to describe, explain, predict, and control behavior. Behaviorism dominated psychology in North America from the 1920s through the 1950s.

Journey of Discovery

Consider the four early pioneers in psychology: Wundt, James, Freud, and Watson. What contribution did each make to our understanding of thinking and behavior?

I am actually not at all a man of science, not an observer, not an experimenter, not a thinker. I am by temperament not but a conquistador—an adventurer, if you want it translated—with all the curiosity, daring, and tenacity of a man of this sort.

—Sigmund Freud, 1856–1939

Psychoanalysis An approach to psychology that studies how the unconscious mind shapes behavior

Behaviorism An approach to psychology that studies observable behavior rather than hidden mental processes; also referred to as the *behavioral perspective*

John Watson, the founder of behaviorism

Wikimedia Commons

1.1c Women and Ethnic Minorities Faced Discrimination as Pioneers in Psychology.

During the first 75 years of psychology's existence, women and minorities were generally excluded from graduate education due to the prejudice and discrimination of the time (Minton, 2000). Those who were fortunate enough to be granted the opportunity to pursue a career in psychology often had a substandard environment in which to conduct their research (Furumoto & Scarborough, 2002). Even with such impediments, many women and ethnic minorities made valuable contributions to the development of psychology.

A good example of the prejudice and discrimination faced by women comes from the career of Mary Calkins, who completed all requirements for a PhD at Harvard University in 1895. William James described her dissertation defense as "the most brilliant examination for the PhD that we have had at Harvard." Yet, despite a unanimous recommendation by James and her other professors, Calkins's doctorate was denied because the university did not grant degrees to women. Indeed, when James first allowed Calkins to enroll in his seminar, the male students walked out in protest—leaving Calkins as the sole student with her professor! So how did Harvard University respond to this brilliant woman's attempt

Mary Calkins, the first female president of the American Psychological Association

Archives of the History of American Psychology— The University of Akron

Margaret Washburn, the first woman to receive a PhD in psychology

Kenneth and Mamie Clark's scientific findings that racial segregation had a negative impact on Black children's self-concept were instrumental in shaping the U.S. Supreme Court's 1954 decision to integrate the nation's educational institutions.

George Sanchez (1906–1972), early pioneer in educational and cultural psychology

to be recognized as an equal among her peers? The college offered Calkins a PhD from its "sister college," Radcliffe; however, she declined, stating that accepting it would mean that she also accepted the college's discriminatory policies. Pursuing the few career paths open to her, Calkins became a non-PhD professor at the all-female Wellesley College. There, she established one of the first psychology laboratories in the United States, pioneered research in short-term memory, and in 1905 became the first woman president of the American Psychological Association (Madigan & O'Hara, 1992). Remarkably, Harvard has repeatedly resisted efforts to grant Calkins the degree she earned more than more than a century ago, with the last effort being rejected in 2002.

The first woman to actually receive her doctorate in psychology was Margaret Washburn (1871–1939) from Cornell University in 1894. During her distinguished career, Washburn was a research pioneer in comparative psychology and served as president of the American Psychological Association in 1921. Like Calkins, but unlike most of her male colleagues, Washburn never married because a woman's decision to marry generally required her not to work outside the home.

Similar obstacles also impeded the careers of ethnic minorities (Schultz & Schultz, 2000). The first African American to receive a PhD in psychology was Gilbert Jones, who obtained his degree from the University of Jena in Germany in 1901. Thirty-two years later, Inez Prosser, after teaching many years with a master's degree, became the first African American woman to receive her doctorate in psychology from the University of Cincinnati. Despite the discrimination faced by African Americans during these early years, many made significant contributions to this budding science. For example, in 1920 the structural psychologist J. Henry Alston discovered how we sense heat and cold from our skin receptors (see Chapter 4, Section 4.4b). In the field of social psychology, Kenneth Clark and Mamie Phipps Clark's ground-breaking research in the 1930s and 1940s on the self-concept of Black children provided the scientific justification for the United States Supreme Court to end the practice of racially segregated education. In 1971, Kenneth Clark became the first African American elected president of the American Psychological Association.

Hispanic psychologists have also made many important contributions. For example, George Sanchez was an influential educational and cultural psychologist who was a civil rights advocate and an early critic of using culturally biased psychological tests in assessing Mexican American children. Similarly, John Garcia pioneered research on taste aversion in the 1960s (see Chapter 6, Section 6.1d).

Today, in the United States, about half of all psychologists holding doctoral degrees are women; they make up almost three-fourths of all the new PhDs, and they now outnumber men as members of the American Psychological Association by almost 2 to 1 (American Psychological Association, 2008). Moreover, members of ethnic minority groups now account for about 23 percent of graduate students in psychology master's degree and doctoral programs. Similar diversity trends are found in Canada.

Despite these advances, more work is needed. For example, although the majority of new doctorates in psychology today are women, men are still far more likely than women to hold the most powerful positions of authority in university psychology departments. It is also true that there are still far too few ethnic minorities in the discipline compared to their numbers in the general population. As an example, although Latinos make up about 13 percent of the U.S. population, fewer than 8 percent of graduate school students and only about 1 percent of psychology practitioners and psychology full professors are Latino (Dingfelder, 2005). Similar patterns are found among African Americans. Thus, although

BVT *Lab*

Flashcards are available
for this chapter at
www.BVTLab.com.

women and ethnic minorities have begun to share more of the center stage with their White male colleagues, the twenty-first century awaits a more diverse cast of characters in this ever-changing science. Some of you reading this textbook will be part of this new generation of psychologists. What would you do to encourage this greater diversity without unfairly limiting the opportunities of young White men?

Section
REVIEW

- Psychology is the scientific study of mental processes and behavior.

- Wilhelm Wundt and structuralism sought to identify the components of the conscious mind.

- William James and functionalism studied how the conscious mind helps humans survive and successfully adapt to their environment.

- Sigmund Freud and psychoanalysis studied how the unconscious mind shapes behavior.

- John Watson and behaviorism considered only observable behaviors to be legitimate topics of scientific inquiry.

- Despite discrimination, women and ethnic minorities made valuable contributions to the development of psychology.

1.2 Contemporary Perspectives and Areas of Specialization

Of the early schools of psychology, only psychoanalysis and behaviorism have survived as contemporary perspectives, and even they have been significantly altered from their original form. Let us now briefly examine seven contemporary perspectives within psychology that shape current psychological theory and research, and their applications in everyday settings.

1.2a *The Psychoanalytic and Behaviorist Perspectives Still Influence Theory and Research.*

Many psychoanalysts today downplay Freud's emphasis on sexual drives and emphasize, instead, cultural experiences in explaining personality. Despite this shift in focus, the unconscious mind and early childhood experiences are still central areas of attention within this perspective. Yet, many contemporary psychoanalysts, influenced by Erik Erikson's (1902–1994) writings, have rejected Freud's view that personality development, for all practical purposes, is complete by age 5. Instead, contemporary psychoanalysis generally accepts Erikson's (1980) view that personality continues to be shaped and changed throughout life. Erikson's work is discussed in Chapter 3.

The central figure shaping contemporary behaviorism was B. F. Skinner (1904–1990), who stressed the role of consequences in controlling behavior. His research, which is discussed in Chapter 6, found that people and other animals tend to repeat behaviors that are followed by positive consequences and avoid behaviors that bring negative consequences. For example, if you are rewarded for being helpful, you are likely to repeat such actions in the future; however, you are unlikely to do so if your helpfulness is punished. In addition, this psychological perspective played a key role in insisting that psychologists precisely define and objectively measure the concepts they study. Although behaviorism does not exert the influence over psychology that it once enjoyed, you will recognize its footprints throughout this text as you examine various psychological topics.

1.2b Humanistic Psychology and Positive Psychology Highlight Personal Growth.

Humanistic psychology An approach to psychology that emphasizes human beings' innate capacity for personal growth and their ability to consciously make choices

Arising out of the dissatisfaction of many psychologists with both the psychoanalytic and the behavioristic views of human nature, a third force exerted its influence on psychology in the 1950s. **Humanistic psychology** emphasizes people's innate capacity for personal growth and their ability to consciously make choices. Carl Rogers (1902–1987) and Abraham Maslow (1908–1970) were the primary architects of this perspective; and both contended—like William James before them—that psychology should study people's unique subjective mental experience of the world. In the 1960s, humanistic psychology served as the intellectual inspiration of the *human potential movement,* which became a loosely knit social movement striving to help individuals achieve their full human potential. Both within psychology and throughout the larger culture, humanistic psychology has had a broad impact by stressing the important role that positive life experiences play in people's lives.

Although the humanistic approach has been criticized for being the least scientifically based of all contemporary perspectives within psychology, its emphasis on conscious experience and the essential goodness of people has promoted the scientific study of previously neglected topics, such as self-awareness, love, helping behavior, and positive personality growth—all issues that we will explore in this text.

Positive psychology A new scientific approach to studying optimal human functioning that asserts that the normal functioning of human beings cannot be accounted for in purely negative (or problem-focused) terms

Within the past ten years, a new psychological perspective called *positive psychology,* which is a direct descendant of the humanistic perspective, has emerged. **Positive psychology** is a scientific approach to studying optimal human functioning that asserts the normal functioning of human beings cannot be accounted for within purely negative (or problem-focused) frames of reference. Because this new perspective is more firmly grounded in rigorous scientific methodology than is the traditional humanistic perspective, positive psychology may be in a better position to shape the future direction of psychology. Researchers who identify themselves as positive psychologists are currently studying what it means to be a well-adapted person and what makes people happy and optimistic in their daily living (McNulty & Fincham, 2012; Ong & Dulmen, 2007). For example, when does an optimistic view of life help you overcome hurdles to success, and when does it cause you to overlook impending failure? Teaching people to avoid harmful self-deceptions while still maintaining a sense of realistic optimism about life is one of the goals of positive psychology.

1.2c Cognitive Psychology Focuses on How the Mind Organizes and Interprets Experiences.

Cognitive psychology An approach to psychology that attempts to understand behavior by studying how the mind organizes perceptions, processes information, and interprets experiences

Accompanying the criticism of behaviorism by humanistic theorists was the fact that laboratory research was finding some interesting phenomena difficult to explain without reintroducing the concept of consciousness. In the 1960s, when this evidence had reached a sufficient "critical mass," the theoretical center of gravity in psychology shifted from behaviorism to cognitive psychology. The word *cognitive* comes from the Latin for "to know." **Cognitive psychology** is a psychological approach that attempts to understand behavior by studying how the mind organizes perceptions, processes information, and interprets experiences (Bargh & Mosella, 2008). For example, how do you remember a new friend's phone number? While serving on a jury, how do you decide whether a defendant is guilty or innocent? Cognitive theories provide insights into these kinds of mental processes. Two of the principal leaders of this cognitive revolution in psychology were George Miller, who made important discoveries in human memory, and Ulric Neisser, who coined the term "cognitive psychology" and wrote one of the first books in the field.

The ascendancy of cognitive psychology coincided with the development of a new form of technology, namely, the computer. Cognitive psychologists argued that the mind was like a computer, in that it receives input from the environment, which it then transforms, stores, and later retrieves using a host of "programs," ultimately leading to specific response outputs. The computer is not only a useful metaphor for the mind. As new generations of computers are developed to actually work like the human brain, they have become invaluable subjects of study, simulating human thought. Today, behaviorist John Watson's description of the brain as "a black box forever mysterious" is no longer true, thanks largely to the discoveries of cognitive psychologists. This perspective provides valuable insights into many of the topics we will examine throughout this text.

1.2d The Neuroscience Perspective Focuses on the Nervous System.

In recent years, as new techniques and instruments have been developed to examine the brain and how it reacts under different circumstances, psychologists have become increasingly interested in biological mechanisms (Hasselmo, 2012). The resulting attempts to understand behavior and mental processes by examining the nervous system have come to be known as the **neuroscience perspective**. In its study of how the brain communicates with itself and other body organs, as well as its attempt to understand elementary biochemical processes, this approach to psychology is focused on the most precise microscopic levels of analysis.

Neuroscience perspective An approach to psychology that attempts to understand behavior and mental processes by examining the nervous system

Although neuroscientists do study humans, they conduct a good deal of their research using animals with simpler brains, hoping that the knowledge gained in these studies will lead to greater understanding of the brain's building blocks. For example, in attempting to better understand memory loss in Alzheimer's disease (the most common form of dementia in the elderly), a researcher might graft tissue from the brains of rat fetuses into the brains of elderly rats. If such a procedure improves the older rats' memory, this finding may provide a crucial clue to curing this disease in humans. Chapter 2 introduces you to some of the discoveries uncovered by this neuroscience approach.

1.2e Evolutionary Psychology Studies How Behavior Is Shaped by Natural Selection.

Fueled by the growing belief in the social sciences that behavior is at least partly influenced by the effects of *evolution,* a perspective known as **evolutionary psychology** is increasingly being incorporated into psychological theories (Al-Shawaf & Buss, 2011). Yet, what is evolution? The evolutionary perspective is partly based on the writings of biologist Charles Darwin (1809–1882), who theorized that changes in the population of a species occur over many generations due to the interaction of environmental and biological variables.

Evolutionary psychology An approach to psychology based on the principle of natural selection

According to evolutionary theory, living organisms struggle to survive; and within each species, a great deal of competition and biological variation occurs among individuals (Darwin, 1859). Those individuals with genetic traits best adapted for survival in their environment will produce more offspring; as a result, their numbers will increase in frequency in the population. As the environment changes, however,

Natural selection The process by which organisms with inherited traits best suited to the environment reproduce more successfully than less well-adapted organisms over a number of generations, which leads to evolutionary changes

Evolution The genetic changes that occur in a species over generations due to natural selection

It may metaphorically be said that natural selection is daily and hourly scrutinising ... the slightest variations; rejecting those that are bad, preserving and adding up all that are good; silently and insensibly working, whenever and wherever opportunity offers, at the improvement of each organic being in relation to its organic and inorganic conditions of life. We see nothing of these slow changes in progress, ... we see only that the forms of life are now different from what they formerly were.

—Charles Darwin, 1859, *On the Origin of Species*, pp. 90–91

other members of the species possessing traits better suited to the new conditions will flourish, a process called **natural selection**. In this way, the environment selects which genetic traits are passed on to future generations (see Figure 1-1). As natural selection continues and the features best suited for survival change again and again, the result is **evolution**, a term that refers to the gradual genetic changes that occur in a species over generations. Reproduction is central to natural selection; the essence of the natural selection process is that the characteristics of some individuals allow them to produce more offspring than others. For example, in an environment that is mostly frigid and snowy, mammals that have a lot of insulating fur are more likely to survive and reproduce than are those with less fur. Similarly, animals that look white are more likely than darker-appearing members of their species to blend in with the snow. This may protect them from predators or make them more stealthy hunters of prey (see the accompanying photo of a polar bear). Thus, this "whiteness" will lead to more offspring being produced. The result of this natural selection process is that mammals from many species living in a frigid and snowy environment will have thick, white fur covering their bodies.

In summarizing the evolutionary process, keep in mind that it is ongoing. Every species on the planet is undergoing some sort of evolution, even though the speed of the process differs substantially across species. Species that experience a great deal of change in their environment evolve faster than those that live in stable environments. Also keep in mind that individual organisms do not evolve—populations evolve. Individuals play a role in evolution by interacting with the environment and having their genes screened by natural selection. Thus, individuals contribute to a change in their species' population by their own successes or failures in reproducing. Over many generations, the accumulated effects of literally thousands or even millions of individuals' reproductive successes and failures lead to evolution of the species (Barrett et al., 2002). The specific role that genes play in reproduction will be discussed more fully in Chapter 2, Section 2.4a.

FIGURE 1-1

How Natural Selection Works

Environments are always undergoing changes. Throughout these changes, those organisms in a species that possess genetic traits which allow them to best adapt to the changes are most likely to survive, reproduce, and pass their genes on to the next generation. This is the reason that evolutionary theorists contend that it is the environment that "selects" which traits will be passed on to future generations. The result of this natural selection process is evolution.

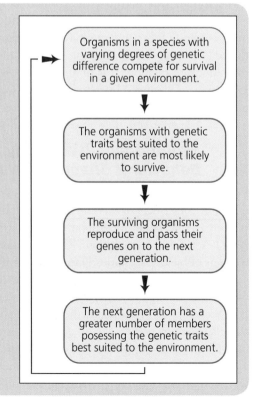

Organisms in a species with varying degrees of genetic difference compete for survival in a given environment.

↓

The organisms with genetic traits best suited to the environment are most likely to survive.

↓

The surviving organisms reproduce and pass their genes on to the next generation.

↓

The next generation has a greater number of members posessing the genetic traits best suited to the environment.

Shutterstock

According to natural selection, animals that live in very cold and snowy environments will be more likely to survive and reproduce if their fur provides both insulating warmth and camouflage so that they blend in with the snow. Why doesn't the fur of zoo-housed polar bears turn darker to better match their zoo environment?

INFO-BIT Some historians trace the scientific concept of evolution back 2,500 years to the Greek philosopher Anaximander, who contended that life arose in water and that simpler life-forms preceded more complex ones. However, the more influential Greek philosopher Aristotle held that species are fixed and do not evolve. Aristotle's views, combined with the Judeo-Christian beliefs that God created the earth and all species, and they are only about 6,000 years old, dominated scientific and intellectual debate until the mid-1800s. To what degree has your own thinking been shaped by these contrasting views?

Journey of Discovery

By *evolution,* do we mean the changes observed in a single member
of a species or the changes in the species as a whole?

1.2f The Sociocultural Perspective Studies How Behavior Is Shaped by Social and Cultural Forces.

While the evolutionary perspective examines how the behavior of humans and other living creatures is shaped due to inherited genes, the **sociocultural perspective** emphasizes the role that social and cultural factors play in explaining behavior (Kirschner & Martin, 2010). **Culture** is the total lifestyle of people from a particular social grouping, including all the ideas, symbols, preferences, and material objects that they share. It is a shared system of ideas about the nature of the world and consists of rules governing how people should think, feel, and act within this world.

Many countries contain a number of distinct cultures. For example, in the United States you can identify many cultural heritages—among them Native American,

Sociocultural perspective An approach to psychology that emphasizes social and cultural influences on behavior

Culture The total lifestyle of people from a particular social grouping, including all the ideas, symbols, preferences, and material objects they share

According to dynamic systems theory, new forms of behavior emerge through the interactions between people's biology and their culture and physical environment.

Hispanic, European, African, Asian, and Middle Eastern. In analyzing culture, it's important to understand that lifestyle changes over time. Thus, Native American culture today is not the same as Native American culture in the 1800s or even in the mid-1900s. This attention to social and cultural factors as a means to explain human thought and behavior is a central element in many psychological theories.

Are the sociocultural and evolutionary perspectives compatible? Yes, say a growing number of psychologists who believe that these cultural and evolutionary forces operate simultaneously in shaping behavior (Buss & Schmitt, 2011). They argue that a culture is based on its people's relationship with the environment, and that the evolution of our species is a story of how we have adapted to our environment. Thus, just as our bodies and brains are a product of evolutionary forces, so too is our culture. Yet, culture change occurs much more rapidly than genetic change. This is why there is a great deal of variation between the world's cultures, but little meaningful genetic variation between cultural groups.

In this textbook, the evolutionary perspective will provide insight into how we, as a species, got to where we are with our biological structure and behavioral traits. The sociocultural perspective, on the other hand, will suggest how culture can either reinforce or attempt to change these evolutionary-based tendencies and patterns. This idea that new forms of behavior emerge from the interactions between people's biology and their culture and physical environment is referred to as **dynamic systems theory** (Hickman et al., 2011; Van Geert & Steenbeek, 2010). Essentially, this theory proposes that life is shaped by a set of vigorously active components or factors; therefore, a full understanding of living creatures, including humans, must take into account how those factors shape the life course of both individuals and entire species (see Exploring Culture & Diversity 1.1).

Dynamic systems theory The idea that new forms of behavior emerge from the interactions between people's biology and their culture and physical environment

Exploring CULTURE & DIVERSITY 1.1

Do Cultures Differ in How Members Relate to Their Groups?

One aspect of culture that has a great deal of importance to the understanding of the psychology of human behavior is the belief system concerning how individuals relate to their groups (Triandis, 1989, 1995). The human species has evolved within a social group sphere. One of the fundamental dilemmas we have faced throughout our existence is that each individual's inherent desire to pass her or his genes on to the next generation pushes

TABLE 1-1   Differences Between Collectivist and Individualist Cultures

Collectivist Cultures	Individualist Cultures
Identity is given by one's group.	Identity is achieved by one's own striving.
Individuals are socialized to be emotionally dependent on their social group, and conformity is valued.	Individuals are socialized to be emotionally independent of their social group, and independence is valued.
Personal and group goals are generally consistent; when inconsistent, group goals have priority.	Personal and group goals are often inconsistent; when inconsistent, personal goals have priority.
Trust is placed in group decisions.	Trust is placed in individual decisions.

the individual toward selfish, self-serving actions that can potentially threaten the survival of the individual's group, and thus the individual's own survival. Somehow through the process of natural selection, we have struck a delicate balance between these conflicting tendencies. Today, the cultural belief systems known as *individualism* and *collectivism* are products of this evolutionary-based tension between the desire to selfishly maximize one's reproductive fitness and the need to cooperate with others in order to survive (Kågitçibasi, 1994; Oyserman et al., 2002).

Individualism is a philosophy of life characterized by stressing the priority of personal goals over group goals, a preference for loosely knit social relationships, and a desire to be relatively free of others' influence. In contrast, **collectivism** is a philosophy of life characterized by the priority of group needs over individual needs, a preference for tightly knit social relationships, and a willingness to submit to the influence of one's group (Hornsey et al., 2006; Tower et al., 1997). Table 1-1 lists some of the differences between these two philosophies of life. Collectivism is considered the older of the two philosophies because it focuses on the type of thinking and behavior that affords the most protection for people who live in the type of highly threatening environments that have historically confronted all human groups until fairly recently (Singelis et al., 1995). Individualism is a much more recent philosophy of life because it develops among people who inhabit relatively safe environments where their survival is less dependent on maintaining strong group ties. This liberation from immediate physical threats reduces the importance of survival-focused values and gives higher priority to freedom of choice (Inglehart & Oyserman, 2004). Currently, 70 percent of the world's population live in cultures with a collectivist orientation.

Although we know that cultures differ in their individualist-collectivist orientations, we do not know whether one is better than the other in any ultimate evolutionary sense. In this text, we periodically examine how the psychology of people from different cultures differs due to their individualist-collectivist bents. For example, in the chapter on human development (Chapter 3), you will discover that within collectivist societies, child-rearing practices tend to emphasize conformity, obedience, and knowing one's proper place, whereas within more individualist societies, independence and self-reliance are stressed (Peterson et al., 2005). One consequence of these differing views is that in an individualist society, people develop a belief in their own uniqueness and diversity. This sense of individuality is nurtured and fostered within the educational system, and its manifestation is considered to be a sign of maturity. In a collectivist society, on the other hand, uniqueness and individual differences are often seen only as impediments to proper self-growth. Instead, the person becomes most meaningful and complete when she or he is closely identified with—not independent of—the group.

Individualism A philosophy of life characterized by the priority of personal goals over group goals, a preference for loosely knit social relationships, and a desire to be relatively autonomous of others' influence

Collectivism A philosophy of life characterized by the priority of group needs over individual needs, a preference for tightly knit social relationships, and a willingness to submit to the influence of one's group

Wikimedia Commons

Seventy percent of the world's population live in collectivist societies. How might the thinking and behavior of these Japanese schoolchildren differ from those of children in the United States, Canada, and Europe?

1.2g Psychology's Subfields Tend to Have Either a Research or Application Emphasis.

Now that you have learned something about the different schools of thought within psychology, you might be wondering who employs psychologists and what they do in these jobs. About one-fourth of all psychologists who received their PhDs during the past 25 years are employed at colleges, universities, or institutes where they teach and conduct research in their areas of specialization (see Figure 1-2). Their goals are to acquire psychological knowledge through scientific methods and to teach this knowledge to students. Seven areas of specialization for these research psychologists are as follows:

1. **Neuroscience** (also called *psychobiology, biopsychology, physiological psychology*) focuses on behavior by examining physiological processes, especially those occurring in the brain. Neuroscientists/psychobiologists are increasingly investigating the genetic bases of thought and action.

2. **Developmental psychology** focuses on how people mature and change physically, cognitively, and socially throughout the life span, from conception to old age.

3. **Experimental psychology** focuses on basic psychological processes such as sensation, perception, learning, motivation, emotion, and states of consciousness. Keep in mind, however, that psychologists in every area of psychology use experiments.

4. **Comparative psychology** focuses on similarities and differences in the physiology, behavior, and abilities of different species, including humans.

5. **Cognitive psychology** focuses on all aspects of thinking, including problem solving, decision making, memory, reasoning, and language.

6. **Personality psychology** focuses on the consistent and distinct ways in which people think, feel, and behave, including how these characteristics originated and developed.

7. **Social psychology** focuses on how people think about and influence one another in social settings, including how the social settings and the cultural beliefs of the individuals shape the interaction.

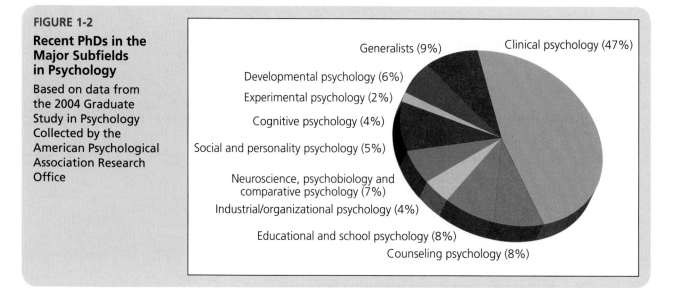

FIGURE 1-2

Recent PhDs in the Major Subfields in Psychology

Based on data from the 2004 Graduate Study in Psychology Collected by the American Psychological Association Research Office

Generalists (9%)
Clinical psychology (47%)
Developmental psychology (6%)
Experimental psychology (2%)
Cognitive psychology (4%)
Social and personality psychology (5%)
Neuroscience, psychobiology and comparative psychology (7%)
Industrial/organizational psychology (4%)
Educational and school psychology (8%)
Counseling psychology (8%)

In addition to psychologists within these seven areas, two-thirds of the psychologists who received their PhDs during the past ten years have careers in specialty areas where they use existing psychological knowledge to solve and prevent problems (see Figure 1-2). These **applied psychologists** most often work in mental health centers, schools, industries, governmental agencies, or private practice; some also work at colleges and universities. Four major applied specialties are as follows:

Applied psychologists
Psychologists who use existing psychological knowledge to solve and prevent problems

1. *Clinical psychology* focuses on diagnosing and treating people with psychological disorders, such as depression and schizophrenia, as well as seeks to determine the causes for these disorders.

2. *Counseling psychology* focuses on diagnosing and treating people with personal problems that do not involve psychological disorders. It includes marriage counseling, social skills training, and career planning.

3. *Industrial/organizational psychology* focuses on ways to select, motivate, and evaluate employees, as well as improving the management structure and working conditions.

4. *Educational and school psychology* focuses on assessing and treating both students and the educational environment in order to facilitate children's learning and adjustment in school.

Section REVIEW

- Of the early schools of psychology, only psychoanalysis and behaviorism survived as contemporary perspectives.

- The humanistic perspective and positive psychology emphasize human beings' capacity for personal growth and their ability to consciously make choices.

- The cognitive perspective attempts to understand behavior by studying how the mind organizes perceptions, processes information, and interprets experiences.

- The neuroscience perspective attempts to understand behavior by examining physiological processes, especially those occurring in the brain.

- The evolutionary perspective assumes that all species have evolved in ways that maximize the chances of their genes being passed on to their offspring.

- The sociocultural perspective emphasizes social and cultural influences on behavior.

- Seven primary areas of specialization for research psychologists include: neuroscience, developmental psychology, experimental psychology, comparative psychology, cognitive psychology, personality psychology, and social psychology.

- Four primary areas of specialization for applied psychologists include: clinical psychology, counseling psychology, industrial/organizational psychology, and educational and school psychology.

1.3 Scientific Methods in Psychology

When you were a child, did you ever try building something that came with a set of plans? I remember making my first model airplane—and being so excited about getting it to look like the image on the box that I ignored the directions and simply slapped the pieces together as fast as my little fingers would allow. Of course, employing such a slapdash method did not lead to a very pleasing final result. Through such experiences, I gradually learned the value of designing a plan of action when undertaking projects. This basic lesson is what the rest of this chapter is about. That is, in order for psychologists to effectively study the mind and behavior, they must employ scientific methods to carefully plan and execute their research projects.

1.3a *Scientific Methods Minimize Error and Lead to Dependable Generalizations.*

When conducting research, psychologists employ **scientific methods**, which consist of a set of procedures used to gather, analyze, and interpret information in a way that minimizes error and leads to dependable generalizations. By *generalizations*, I mean statements that apply to members of a group as a whole, rather than to specific members.

In research, a **sample** is a group of subjects who are selected to participate in a given study, whereas a **population** consists of all the members of an identifiable group from which a sample is drawn. The closer a sample is in representing the population, the greater the confidence researchers have in generalizing their findings beyond the sample. Researchers have the most confidence that their sample is an accurate representation of the population when everyone in the population has an equal chance of being selected for the sample. Such **random selection** of participants, although highly desirable, is not always possible. For instance, in studying the effects of using cell-phones while driving a motor vehicle, it would be impossible to design a study in which every driver in the United States had an equal chance of being included in the sample.

Beyond sample selection, how might you employ the scientific method to understand the personalities of your research participants? Often, psychologists use well-established, highly structured questionnaires in their research. For example, in my study of religious cult members described in the chapter-opening story, instead of simply asking these people questions that I thought of at the moment, I asked them all to respond to the same set of questions that other researchers had previously developed to measure specific aspects of personality. I then compared, using a series of statistical computations, their responses to one another as well as to those of other young adults who were not cult members. These statistical analyses allowed me to determine whether these groups differed from one another, and if so, how.

Based on my brief description of scientific methodology, you can see that the guidelines psychologists follow when conducting research are far more stringent than those typically employed in everyday thinking. Psychologists also approach the study of the mind by engaging in **critical thinking**, which is the process of deciding what to believe and how to act based on a careful evaluation of the evidence. An important aspect of critical thinking is ruling out alternative explanations. Can a hypnotized person be induced to commit murder? Is there compelling evidence that psychics can predict future events? Can subliminal tapes improve memory and increase self-esteem? These are a few of the fascinating questions we will examine in our journey of discovery, and we will do so while using critical thinking skills. The "Psychological Applications" section at the end of this chapter discusses how you can develop critical

---

Scientific methods A set of procedures used in science to gather, analyze, and interpret information in a way that reduces error and leads to dependable generalizations

Sample A group of subjects selected to participate in a research study

Population All the members of an identifiable group from which a sample is drawn

Random selection A procedure for selecting a sample of people to study in which everyone in the population has an equal chance of being chosen

Critical thinking The process of deciding what to believe and how to act based on careful evaluation of the evidence

thinking skills to aid you in your journey. In the meantime, let's examine the research process itself and then scrutinize more thoroughly the structure of the various scientific methods psychologists use in their research.

1.3b   The Research Process Unfolds in a Series of Stages.

For psychologists to effectively study the mind and behavior, they must carefully plan and execute their research projects, employing scientific methods. This process occurs in a series of four sequential stages, which are summarized in Figure 1-3.

The first stage involves selecting a topic and reviewing past research. Scientists get their ideas from many sources. Inspiration could come from someone else's research, from an incident in the daily news, or from some personal experience in the researcher's life. After selecting a topic, researchers need to search the scientific literature to determine whether prior investigations exist. The findings from these previous studies generally shape the course of the current investigation. Today, psychologists can vastly accelerate literature searches by using a number of computer-based programs that catalog even the most recently published studies. Keeping abreast of other colleagues' discoveries and insights is a necessity during all stages in the research process. For this reason, searching the research literature may be thought of as a never-ending endeavor.

The second stage involves developing a theory and hypotheses. A **theory** is an organized system of ideas that seeks to explain why two or more events are related. Put simply, a theory provides a picture of reality concerning some phenomena. What makes a good theory depends on a number of factors, some of which are listed in

Theory An organized system of ideas that seeks to explain why two or more events are related

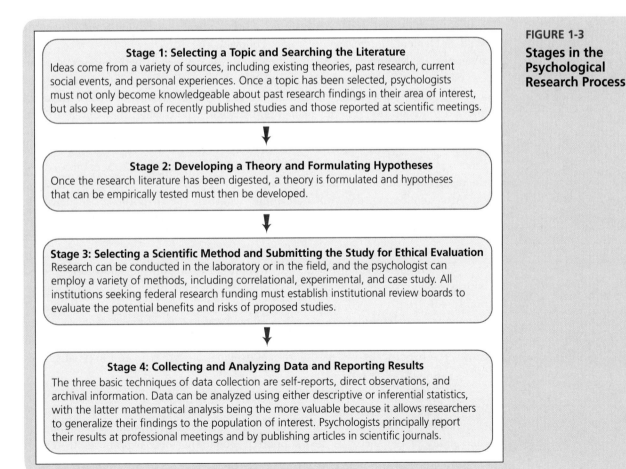

FIGURE 1-3

Stages in the Psychological Research Process

Stage 1: Selecting a Topic and Searching the Literature
Ideas come from a variety of sources, including existing theories, past research, current social events, and personal experiences. Once a topic has been selected, psychologists must not only become knowledgeable about past research findings in their area of interest, but also keep abreast of recently published studies and those reported at scientific meetings.

Stage 2: Developing a Theory and Formulating Hypotheses
Once the research literature has been digested, a theory is formulated and hypotheses that can be empirically tested must then be developed.

Stage 3: Selecting a Scientific Method and Submitting the Study for Ethical Evaluation
Research can be conducted in the laboratory or in the field, and the psychologist can employ a variety of methods, including correlational, experimental, and case study. All institutions seeking federal research funding must establish institutional review boards to evaluate the potential benefits and risks of proposed studies.

Stage 4: Collecting and Analyzing Data and Reporting Results
The three basic techniques of data collection are self-reports, direct observations, and archival information. Data can be analyzed using either descriptive or inferential statistics, with the latter mathematical analysis being the more valuable because it allows researchers to generalize their findings to the population of interest. Psychologists principally report their results at professional meetings and by publishing articles in scientific journals.

TABLE 1-2   What Makes a Good Theory?
Predictive accuracy: Can the theory reliably predict behavior?
Internal coherence: Are there logical inconsistencies between any of the theoretical ideas?
Economy: Does the theory contain only what is necessary to explain the phenomenon in question?
Fertility: Does the theory generate research, and can it be used to explain a wide variety of behaviors?

One of the most serious problems confronting psychology is that of connecting itself with life. ... Theory that does not someway affect life has no value.

—Lewis Terman, U.S. psychologist, 1877–1959

Hypothesis An educated guess or prediction about the nature of things based upon a theory

Table 1-2 (Higgins, 2004). The most salient factor is a theory's *predictive accuracy*. In other words, can it reliably predict behavior? A second factor is that it should have *internal coherence*—there shouldn't be any logical inconsistencies or unexplained coincidences among the theoretical principles and concepts. A third characteristic of a good theory is that it should be *economical*, meaning that it includes the minimum number of principles or concepts necessary to adequately explain and predict the phenomena in question. Finally, a fourth and equally important quality in a good theory is *fertility*—the ability to generate sufficient interest in other scientists so that the theory is tested and extended to a wide variety of behavior.

The way that scientists determine the predictive accuracy of a theory is by formulating hypotheses. A **hypothesis** is an educated guess or prediction about the nature of things based upon a theory—it is the logical implication of the theory. The researcher asks, "If the theory is true, what observations would we expect to make in our investigation?" An example of a hypothesis developing from a theory is William Dement's interest in dreaming. Following the discovery by other researchers (Aserinsky & Kleitman, 1953) that dreaming was associated with periods of rapid eye movement (REM sleep), Dement (1960) developed a theory that dreaming was a fundamental requirement for all humans. He hypothesized that if people were not allowed to dream over a series of nights (by waking them when they entered REM sleep), they would experience some kind of pressure to increase their "dream time" on subsequent nights. This hypothesis was a logical extension of Dement's theory that there was something basic in our need to dream (refer to Chapter 5, Section 5.2d, for the results of Dement's research).

After collecting data to determine whether the hypothesis successfully predicts the outcome of the study, researchers reevaluate the theory. Was the research hypothesis supported by the data, which thereby support the validity of the theory? If the data do not support the study's hypothesis, the theory needs revising. Although results that do not support stated hypotheses are often greeted with disappointment by researchers, great discoveries often follow such disappointment. In this regard, psychologist William McGuire contends that the task of science is "not the dull and easy job of showing that a fixed hypothesis is right or wrong in a given context. Science has the more exciting task of discovering in what senses the hypotheses and its theoretical explanations are true and in what senses false" (McGuire, 1999, p. 407).

The research process reflects a cyclical relationship between a theory and a testable hypothesis (see Figure 1-4), with the data from a research study providing the evidence to support or refute the hypothesis. If the research hypothesis is supported, the validity of the theory is also supported, generating new hypotheses to test in future research. If the hypothesis is not supported, the theory's validity is questioned,

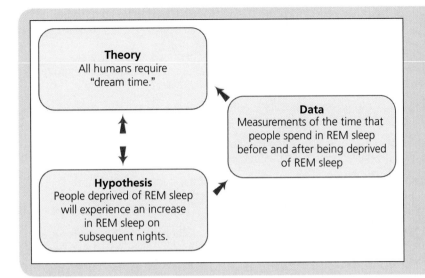

FIGURE 1-4 The Theory-Hypothesis Relationship

There is a cyclical relationship between a theory and a hypothesis, with the data from a research study providing the evidence to support or reject the hypothesis. If the hypothesis is supported, the validity of the theory is also supported, generating new hypotheses to test in future research. If the research hypothesis is not supported, the validity of the theory is questioned, prompting a revision of the theory. From the revised theory, new hypotheses are developed that are then tested in another round of studies.

prompting a revision of the theory. From the revised theory, new hypotheses are developed that are then tested in another set of empirical studies. Scientists who can think "outside the box" of their own theories and entertain alternative explanations for their hypotheses are the most likely candidates to advance scientific knowledge.

The third research stage involves selecting a scientific method and obtaining approval to conduct the study. In all scientific methods, psychologists seek to determine the nature of the relationship between two or more factors, called *variables* because they are things that can be measured and that can vary. When scientists describe a variable, they do so by using an **operational definition**, which is a very precise description of how a variable in a study is measured. For example, when studying hunger, scientists often operationally define this variable as "the beginning of stomach contractions," and they use specialized instruments to measure when those contractions begin. This precise and concrete definition of hunger provides other psychologists with the necessary information concerning what was measured in the study, and it also allows them to repeat the same scientific procedures in future studies.

Operational definition A scientist's precise description of how a variable has been quantified so that it can be measured

Each scientific method has its advantages and disadvantages, and we will examine these in greater detail in Sections 1.3c through 1.3e. After settling upon the method by which data will be collected, researchers must present their proposed study to an *institutional review board (IRB)*, which monitors and evaluates all research involving both human and animal subjects (Fisher et al., 2012). To guard against harm to participants, the guidelines followed by IRBs focus on the *risk/benefit ratio*, which weighs the potential risks to those participating in a study against the benefits that the study may have for advancing knowledge about humanity (Hayes, 2002; Rice, 2011). In assessing proposed studies involving human participants, priority is always given to the welfare of the participants over any potential benefits of the research. Table 1-3 lists some of the guidelines followed when conducting research involving human participants (American Psychological Association, 2010).

IRBs also evaluate animal research, which accounts for about 5 percent of all research published in psychology journals (Kiple & Ornelas, 2001). The vast majority of these studies involve little more than slightly modifying the environment of animals and observing how these changes affect their behavior. A minority of studies, however, involve painful and dangerous experimental procedures that would never be attempted on human participants. For example, research investigating the effect of drugs on brain function or the treatment of

TABLE 1-3 Guidelines for Conducting Research with Human Participants

In assessing proposed studies involving human subjects, priority is always given to ensuring their welfare over any potential benefits of the research. The guidelines also urge researchers to do the following:

1. Provide enough information to possible participants about the activities they will perform in the study so that the participants can freely give their *informed consent*.

2. Be truthful whenever possible. *Deception* should be used only when absolutely necessary and when adequate debriefing is provided.

3. Allow participants the *right to decline* to be a part of the study and the right to discontinue their participation at any point without this decision resulting in any negative consequences (for example, not receiving full payment for their participation).

4. *Protect participants* from both physical and psychological harm. If participants suffer any undesirable consequences, the researcher must do as much as possible to remove the damaging effects.

5. Ensure that any information provided by individual participants is kept *confidential*.

6. *Debrief* individuals once they have completed their participation. Explain all aspects of the research, attempt to answer all questions and resolve any negative feelings, and make sure they realize that their participation contributes to better scientific understanding.

brain disorders and brain damage often begins with animal studies. This research has helped explain the causes of human mental illness and has facilitated the development of effective treatments. Animal research has also contributed greatly to explanations of how the brain works, as well as to the discovery of basic principles of perception, motivation, and learning (Swanson, 2004).

Virtually all scientists who conduct animal research state that they support the humane treatment of animals, but they deny that animals have the same rights as people. Instead, they contend that every advance in science must sooner or later be tried on a living creature. If animals are not substituted for humans in studies that pose significant health risks, then we must either (1) place human participants at serious risk in these studies or (2) simply abandon the research altogether. Because neither of these options is acceptable to most people, animal research continues, as does the debate (Bateson, 2011). Table 1-4 lists some myths and facts about animal research.

 Journey of Discovery

For every dog or cat used in a laboratory experiment, 10,000 dogs and cats are abandoned by their owners (Miller, 1985). When these abandoned animals are brought to local humane societies and are not adopted, should they be made available as subjects for scientific research? Upon what values would you base your decision?

Finally, the fourth research stage involves collecting and analyzing data and reporting results. There are three basic techniques of data collection: (1) *self-reports,* (2) *direct observations,* and (3) *archival information.* Collecting data using self-reports allows researchers to measure important subjective states such as people's perceptions, emotions, or attitudes. However, because people may not always be able to

TABLE 1-4   Some Myths and Facts About Animal Research

Myth: Most animal research is unnecessary.
Fact: This may have been partly true 30 years ago when, for example, psychology students regularly used laboratory rats in their courses to better understand well-documented principles of learning. Today, however, strong economic pressures weigh against the unnecessary use of animals in research. The extremely limited funds available to conduct animal research minimize the possibility that animals will be used for such trivial purposes.

Myth: Other research methods can be used so that animals are not needed in behavioral research.
Fact: In most cases, no good alternatives exist. For example, computerized models of complex behavior still do not truly mimic actual behavior.

Myth: Most research animals are dogs, cats, and nonhuman primates.
Fact: Dogs and cats account for less than 1 percent of the total number of animal subjects. The same is true of nonhuman primates. Nearly 90 percent of the animals used in research are rats, mice, and other rodents.

Myth: Most animals in research suffer great pain and distress.
Fact: The vast majority of behavioral and biomedical research (over 90 percent) does not cause pain or significant distress to the animal. In only 6 percent of experiments are anesthesia or painkillers withheld. In such instances, researchers withhold pain relief because it would interfere with the objectives of the research (for example, studying the effects of pain).

Myth: Animal research benefits only humans.
Fact: Animal research benefits both humans and animals. For example, knowledge of animal sexual and feeding behavior has helped save a number of species from extinction. Further, insights gained through animal research on taste aversion have been used by both ranchers and conservationists to condition animal predators in the wild to avoid killing livestock and endangered species (see Chapter 6, Section 6.1d).

accurately describe these internal states, many researchers prefer to directly observe people's behavior, recording its quantity and direction of change over time. Finally, researchers will sometimes examine existing documents, or archives, to gather information. These accumulated records come from a wide variety of sources (for example, census information, court records, newspaper articles) and can provide researchers with a great deal of valuable information.

Once the data have been collected, the researcher must analyze them. Such data analysis generally requires extensive knowledge of statistical procedures and computer software packages. The two basic kinds of statistics employed by psychologists are descriptive and inferential. **Descriptive statistics** simply summarize and describe the behavior or characteristics of a particular sample of participants in a study; **inferential statistics** move beyond mere description to make inferences about the larger population from which the sample was drawn. Inferential statistics are used to estimate the likelihood that a difference found in the groups studied would also be found if everyone in the population participated in the study. Psychologists generally accept a difference as statistically significant if the likelihood of it having occurred by chance is less than 1 in 20—that is, a probability of less than 5 percent (Nickerson, 2000). Because one of the main objectives of psychological research is to generalize research findings to the population of interest, inferential statistics are the more valued type of statistic. See Closer Look 1-1 for an explanation of how data from multiple studies can be analyzed using statistical techniques.

Descriptive statistics
Numbers that summarize and describe the behavior or characteristics of a particular sample of participants in a study

Inferential statistics
Mathematical analyses that are used to determine whether the data support or do not support the research hypothesis

What Is Meta-Analysis?

Repeating a previous study's scientific procedures using different participants in an attempt to duplicate the findings is known as **replication**. Replication is important in advancing scientific knowledge because the findings from a single study are far less convincing than the same findings from a series of related studies. Yet what happens when studies are repeated numerous times and the results often differ? If, for example, seven studies find that one type of psychotherapy is effective in treating depression, while four studies find that it is ineffective, what conclusions should be drawn?

In the past, researchers often used the "majority rules" approach to resolve such controversies. That is, they merely counted up the number of studies that found or did not find a particular psychological effect and then concluded that the effect existed if it occurred in the majority of studies. During the past 20 years, researchers have increasingly relied on a more sophisticated comparison procedure called *meta-analysis* to better assess the findings from numerous studies (Card, 2012). **Meta-analysis** is the use of statistical techniques to sum up a body of similar studies in order to objectively estimate the reliability and overall size of the effect. Because many studies may find small differences that do not reach statistical levels of significance between groups, meta-analysis can determine whether these small effects are indeed "real" or merely measurement error.

Replication Repeating a previous study's scientific procedures using different participants in an attempt to duplicate the findings

Meta-analysis The use of statistical techniques to sum up a body of similar studies in order to objectively estimate the reliability and overall size of the effect

The last task in the fourth stage of the research process is to report results. By informing fellow scholars of their discoveries, researchers build upon and refine one another's work, and the understanding of psychology is enriched. Yet, others do not uncritically accept a psychologist's research findings. At scientific conventions where research is often first reported and in scientific journals where studies are ultimately published, all stages in the research process are scrutinized for possible errors and oversights. It is through such critical analysis that psychological knowledge is advanced.

1.3c Description Is the Goal of Observational Research.

To understand behavior so that it can be predicted and controlled, a scientist must first describe it accurately. Scientific methods that have description as their primary goal fall under the category of observational research (Rustin, 2011). Within this category are the methods of *naturalistic observation, participant observation*, and *case study.*

Naturalistic Observation

Naturalistic observation A scientific method that describes how people or animals behave in their natural environment

Naturalistic observation is a method that investigates behavior in its natural environment (Crabtree & Miller, 1992; Schnicker et al., 2011). Settings for such research range from day-care centers, where developmental psychologists might record the play behavior of children, to the jungles of Africa, where comparative psychologists might study how a troop of baboons defends itself against predators. In all such naturalistic studies, behavior is merely observed and recorded—it is not manipulated.

One example of a naturalistic observation study was Robert Levine and Ara Norenzayan's (1999) analysis of the pace of everyday life in 31 cultures. Some of the data they collected were measurements of people's average walking speed on city sidewalks, the speed at which postal clerks responded to a simple request, and the accuracy of clocks in public settings. Notice that these measurements simply involved the researchers observing how people behaved in their natural surroundings. Their findings indicated that the pace of life was faster in colder and more economically productive cultures (such as Switzerland and Japan) than in those that were hotter and less economically energetic (such as Mexico and Indonesia).

Naturalistic observation involves studying behavior in its natural environment, such as the daily behavior of residents in an urban setting. What are some advantages of this research method?

Participant Observation

Another type of observational method is **participant observation**. Here, as in naturalistic observation, a researcher records behavior as it occurs in its natural environment—but does so as a participant of the group being studied. One of the chief benefits of this research strategy is that it allows investigators to get closer to what they are studying than does any other method.

> **Participant observation** A descriptive scientific method in which a group is studied from within by a researcher who records behavior as it occurs in its natural environment

An excellent example of this method was Leon Festinger's study of a doomsday cult in the 1950s (Festinger et al., 1956). The leader of the cult, Mrs. Keetch, claimed that aliens from outer space had told her the world would come to an end on a specific date, December 21. She also stated that the only survivors of this catastrophe would be members of her group. When Festinger and his coworkers learned of Mrs. Keetch, they became interested in measuring the psychological changes that would occur within the group when the doomsday came and passed with the world still intact. To accomplish this task, these researchers infiltrated the group as participant observers and began describing its dynamics over a period of several weeks. This descriptive study was one of the first tests of a very influential theory in psychology called *cognitive dissonance theory* (see Chapter 14, Section 14.2c).

The following are four advantages of both naturalistic and participant observation research:

1. Researchers are able to watch behavior in its "wholeness," providing the full context in which to understand it.

2. Researchers are able to record rare events that may never occur in a controlled laboratory environment.

3. Researchers are able to systematically record events that were previously observed only by nonscientists.

4. Researchers are able to observe events that would be too risky, dangerous, or unethical to create in the laboratory.

Despite these benefits, there are also some problems in using naturalistic and participant observation methods. First, because of the absence of control that researchers have in such studies, conclusions must be drawn very carefully. Second, researchers must be mindful that their participation in, or even observation of, events can significantly alter the participants' behavior and thus taint the data. Although researchers assume that after a period of time those who are being observed become accustomed to the researchers' presence, it is difficult to evaluate to what degree this actually occurs. Finally, observational methods pose the most ethical problems involving invasion of others' privacy—more than any other scientific method.

The case study method produces a more detailed analysis of a subject than does any other method, but what are two of its disadvantages?

Case study A descriptive scientific method involving in-depth analysis of a single subject, usually a person

Case Study

Another form of observational research is a **case study**, which involves an in-depth analysis of a single subject (Dunbar-Hall, 2011). This method of inquiry is common in clinical work, where psychotherapists provide an extensive description of a person suffering from a particular psychological disorder to illustrate the factors that lead to and influence it. Sigmund Freud's work is perhaps the most famous example of this method. The advantage of the case study is that it produces a more detailed analysis of a person than any other method. One disadvantage is that researchers must be extremely cautious in generalizing from a single case to the population as a whole. Another problem is that this method often depends on people's memories of the past, which all too often are both selective and inaccurate (see Chapter 7, Section 7-3d).

1.3d Correlational Research Is Used to Analyze the Nature of the Relationship Between Variables.

Correlational research Research designed to examine the nature of the relationship between two or more naturally occurring variables

Besides simply describing a phenomenon under study, often psychologists also want to know whether two or more variables are related; and if so, how strongly. When changes in one variable relate to changes in another variable, we say that they *correlate*. **Correlational research** assesses the nature of the relationship between two or more variables that are not controlled by the researcher. The importance of correlational research for psychologists is *prediction*: It allows psychologists to predict a change in one variable by knowing the value of another variable.

Using Surveys When Conducting Correlational Research

Survey A structured set of questions or statements given to a group of people to measure their attitudes, beliefs, values, or behaviors

Although studying the relationships among variables can be done by directly observing behavior, it is often accomplished by asking people carefully constructed questions. A **survey** is a structured sets of questions or statements given to a group of people to measure their attitudes, beliefs, values, or behavioral tendencies (Nestor & Schutt, 2012). Obtaining information using surveys is generally relatively easy; however, its main disadvantage is that it relies on people's self-reports, which are often faulty. My Divine Light Mission study involved the use of surveys.

Surveys are often used to gather information on behavior or other psychological processes that are difficult, if not impossible, to observe directly. For example, imagine that you are a psychologist interested in learning the degree to which people pay attention to their private thoughts and feelings, and the degree to which they disclose these private thoughts and feelings to others. You might ask them to complete a survey questionnaire similar to the one in Self-Discovery Questionnaire 1-1, which measures both the personality trait known as *private self-consciousness* and the behavioral tendency to *self-disclose*. Before reading further, spend a few minutes answering these items and check how your responses compare with those of other adults.

SELF-DISCOVERY 1-1
Questionnaire

How Do Psychologists Measure Self-Consciousness and Self-Disclosure Tendencies?

Measuring Private Self-Consciousness

Items on the Self-Consciousness Scale (SCS) (Fenigstein et al., 1975) measure the personality trait of private self-consciousness. To obtain information on the degree to which you attend to your own private thoughts and feelings, read each item below and then indicate how well each statement describes you, using the following response scale:

0 = extremely uncharacteristic (not at all like me)
1 = uncharacteristic (somewhat unlike me)
2 = neither characteristic nor uncharacteristic
3 = characteristic (somewhat like me)
4 = extremely characteristic (very much like me)

____ 1. I'm always trying to figure myself out.

____ 2. Generally, I'm not very aware of myself.*

____ 3. I reflect about myself a lot.

____ 4. I'm often the subject of my own fantasies.

____ 5. I never scrutinize myself.*

____ 6. I'm generally attentive to my inner feelings.

____ 7. I'm constantly examining my motives.

____ 8. I sometimes have the feeling that I'm off somewhere watching myself.

____ 9. I'm alert to changes in my mood.

____ 10. I'm aware of the way my mind works when I work through a problem.

The two items with an asterisk (*) are reverse-scored; that is, for these items, a lower rating actually indicates a greater tendency to attend to private thoughts and feelings. Before summing the items, recode those with an asterisk so that 0 = 4, 1 = 3, 3 = 1, and 4 = 0. To calculate your private self-consciousness score, simply add up your responses to the 10 items. The average, or mean, score for college students on private self-consciousness is about 26. The higher your score is above this value, the greater is your tendency to reflect upon your private thoughts and feelings compared to the average American college

student. The lower your score is below this value, the less likely is your tendency to regularly engage in this sort of private self-awareness compared to other students.

Measuring the Tendency to Self-Disclose

Items on The Self-Disclosure Scale (Miller et al., 1983) measure one's willingness to self-disclose. To obtain information on your self-disclosure tendencies, indicate for the topics listed below the degree to which you have disclosed to a close romantic partner, using the following scale:

Discussed not at all 0 1 2 3 4 Discussed fully and completely

____ 1. My personal habits

____ 2. Things I have done that I feel guilty about

____ 3. Things I wouldn't do in public

____ 4. My deepest feelings

____ 5. What I like and dislike about myself

____ 6. What is important to me in life

____ 7 What makes me the person I am

____ 8. My worst fears

____ 9. Things I have done that I am proud of

____ 10. My close relationships with other people

Total Score

You can determine your overall self-disclosure score by adding up the scores in the column. The higher the score, the greater is your willingness to self-disclose.

Sources: SCS: From "Public and Private Self-Consciousness: Assessment and Theory" by Allan Fenigstein, Michael F. Scheier, and Arnold H. Buss in *Journal of Consulting and Clinical Psychology,* 1975, 43, 522–527 (Table 1, p. 524). Copyright © 1975 by the American Psychological Association. Adapted with permission. Self-Disclosure Scale: From "Openers: Individuals Who Elicit Intimate Self-Disclosure" by L. C. Miller, J. H. Berg, and R. L. Archer in *Journal of Personality and Social Psychology,* 1983, 44, pp. 1234–1244 (Table 2, p. 1236). Copyright © 1983 by the American Psychological Association. Adapted with permission.

If you simply used survey data to determine how people compare on various personality and behavioral measures, this type of research would involve observational methods in which description is the primary goal. However, returning to our example, imagine that you are interested in discovering whether there is a relationship between private self-consciousness and willingness to self-disclose. That is, do people who regularly attend to their private thoughts and feelings disclose this private side of themselves more than those who do not habitually self-reflect? Now, you are seeking information on whether these two variables are *correlated*. That is, can you predict whether people are likely to self-disclose based on their level of private self-consciousness, or vice versa? In correlational research, as in observational research, you would not try to influence how much time people in your study actually spent thinking about themselves. Instead, you would merely gather information on how often they attended to their own thoughts and feelings, and the degree to which they self-disclosed to others.

The Correlation Coefficient

Correlation coefficient (*r*) A statistical measure of the direction and strength of the linear relationship between two variables, which can range from −1.00 to +1.00

Correlational research aids in prediction by providing information on the *direction* and *strength* of the relationship between two variables. The direction of the relationship between variable A and variable B tells the researcher how they are related (positively or negatively). The strength of the relationship can be thought of as the degree of accuracy with which you can predict the value of one variable by knowing the value of the other variable. The direction and strength of the relationship between two variables are described by the statistical measure known as the **correlation coefficient (*r*)**. This correlation coefficient can range from −1.00 to +1.00.

Returning to the example of self-consciousness and self-disclosure, a correlation at or very near zero indicates the absence of a *linear relationship* between these two variables. This zero correlation may mean one of two things: (1) regularly self-reflecting has no association with self-disclosing, or (2) there is a *curvilinear relationship* between self-reflection and self-disclosing. One can easily determine the meaning of a zero correlation by plotting the pairing of these two variables on a graph, as is illustrated in Figure 1-5. In marked contrast to a zero correlation, one that is near +1.00 would suggest that people who regularly attend to their private thoughts and feelings are much more likely to self-disclose than those who engage in little self-reflection. In contrast, a correlation near −1.00 indicates that those who regularly self-reflect are much less likely to self-disclose to others than those who engage in little self-reflection.

Regarding the strength of a relationship, researchers seldom find a perfect or near perfect (*r* = +1.00 or *r* = −1.00) correlation between variables. For example, a study investigating the relationship between young adults' private self-consciousness and their degree of self-disclosure to their romantic partners found a correlation of .36 for men and a correlation of .20 for women (Franzoi et al., 1985). Due to the direction of the correlation, you might predict that men with a high level of private self-consciousness would be more likely to self-disclose to their romantic partners than men with a low level of private self-consciousness. For women, you would make the same prediction, but you would be less confident due to this correlation's lower strength.

Although these correlations might seem small, in social science research correlations seldom exceed .60. Correlations of .50 to .60 are regarded as strong, those between .30 and .50 are moderately strong, and those below .30 or .20 are considered rather weak. The reason correlations rarely exceed .60 is that many variables determine human behavior. In the example of self-disclosing to someone, many variables will influence people's degrees of self-disclosure. In addition to the disclosers' own levels

FIGURE 1-5   Graphing the Relationship Between Variable X and Variable Y

The points on the graphs represent a pairing of variable X with variable Y for each participant in the study. As you can see in the curvilinear relationship graph, the zero correlation is hiding a meaningful relationship, one in which both high and low levels of X are associated with high levels of Y, but moderate levels of X are associated with low levels of Y. Can you think of variables that would have a curvilinear relationship? In addition to the direction of the relationship between variable X and variable Y, correlations can have different values. The greater the scatter of values on the graph, the lower the correlation. A perfect correlation occurs when all the values fall on an imaginary straight line.

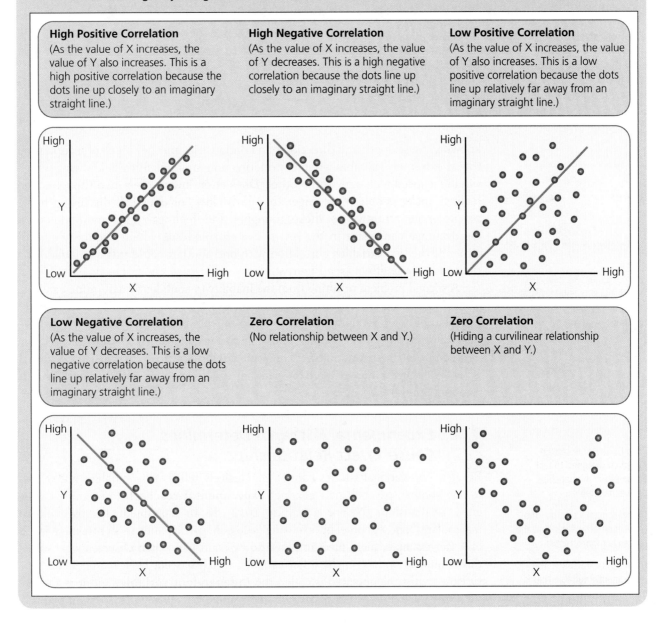

of private self-consciousness, we must consider their partners' willingness to listen, the closeness of the relationship, and the amount of time they actually spend together. Furthermore, even if researchers could isolate all the important variables that influence self-disclosing, because of the nature of our subject—humans with minds of their own—it's unlikely they would be able to predict with perfect reliability people's actions.

The major disadvantage of the correlational study is that it cannot definitively determine the cause of the relationship between two variables. That is, besides

FIGURE 1-6 Difficulties in Determining Causation from Correlation

People who are high in private self-consciousness (PSC) are more willing self-disclosers than those low in PSC. Thus, you might conclude that being high in PSC causes increased self-disclosing in people (arrow 1). However, an alternative explanation is that the act of regular self-disclosing causes an increase in people's level of PSC (arrow 2). What is this methodological problem of correlation interpretation called? Now look at arrow 3. What if parental upbringing or inherited genes were causing the changes in both PSC and self-disclosing? What sort of correlation problem would this example illustrate?

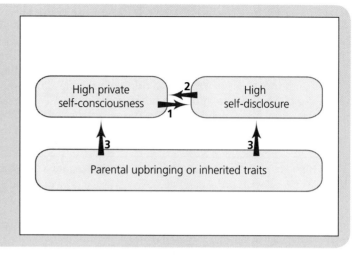

knowing the strength and direction of a relationship, another piece of information that is extremely valuable when conducting an empirical study is knowing which variable caused a change in the other. Does attending to their own thoughts and feelings make people more eager to self-disclose, or does self-disclosing make people more attentive to these thoughts and feelings? This methodological disadvantage can result in the *reverse-causality problem,* which occurs whenever either of the two variables correlated with one another could just as plausibly be the cause or the effect (see Figure 1-6).

A second problem resulting from the inability to confidently determine causality is that it is possible that a third, unmeasured variable causes changes in both variables under study. This is known as the *third-variable problem* (see Figure 1-6 again). Regarding our previous example, it's possible that what looks like a positive correlation between private self-consciousness and self-disclosing is really an illusion because it is really another variable—perhaps parental upbringing or inherited traits—that is causing both those changes.

1.3e Experimental Research Determines Cause-Effect Relationships.

Because correlational studies cannot conclusively tell us *why* variables are related to one another, psychologists conduct **experimental research** to examine cause-effect relationships (Nestor & Schutt, 2012). In an experiment, the psychologist manipulates one variable by exposing research participants to contrasting levels of it (for example, high, medium, low, no exposure) and then observes what effect this manipulation has on the other variable, which has not been manipulated. The variable that is manipulated is called the **independent variable**, and it is the one the experimenter is testing as the possible cause of any changes that might occur in the other variable. The variable whose changes are considered to be the effect of the manipulated changes in the independent variable is called the **dependent variable**. Once participants have been exposed to the independent variable, their behavior is carefully monitored to determine whether the dependent variable changes in the predicted fashion with different levels of the independent variable. If it does, the experimenter concludes that the independent variable is the cause of the changes in the dependent variable.

A key feature of most experiments is that participants are randomly assigned to the different levels of the independent variable. In such a **random assignment**, the

Experimental research Research designed to test cause-effect relationships between variables

Independent variable The experimental variable that the researcher manipulates

Dependent variable The experimental variable that is measured because it is believed to depend on the manipulated changes in the independent variable

Random assignment Placement of research participants into experimental conditions in a manner that guarantees that all have an equal chance of being exposed to each level of independent variable

experimenter, by some random procedure, decides which participants are exposed to which level of the independent variable. Due to this procedure, the experimenter can be reasonably confident that the participants in the different experimental conditions don't differ from one another.

Some of the better-known experiments in psychology are Albert Bandura's Bobo doll studies, in which he and his colleagues studied whether children would imitate the behavior of an aggressive adult (Bandura et al., 1961). In one of these experiments, a child was first brought into a room to work on an art project. In another part of the room, an adult who was a *confederate*—meaning she was an accomplice of the experimenter—was playing quietly with some Tinker Toys. Near these toys were a mallet and a Bobo doll, which is a big, inflatable clownlike toy that is weighted down so that when it is pushed or punched down it will bounce back to an upright position. With half of the children in the study, the adult, after playing with the Tinker Toys for a minute, stood up, walked over to the Bobo doll, and began to attack it. She punched the doll, kicked it, hit it with the mallet, and even sat on it. As she pummeled the clown doll, she yelled out, "Sock him in the nose! ... Kick him! ... Knock him down!" With the other children, the adult simply played quietly and nonaggressively with her toys for ten minutes.

In Bandura's study, the independent variable (remember, that is the variable that is manipulated) was the aggressiveness of the adult's play behavior. After witnessing either the aggressive or nonaggressive adult confederate, each child was led into another room filled with many interesting toys. However, before the child could play with them, the experimenter aroused frustration by saying that these were her best toys and she must "save them for the other children." The child was then led to a third room, containing both aggressive and nonaggressive toys, including a Bobo doll. What children did in this third room was the essential question of the study, for their level of aggressive play here was the dependent variable. The children who had observed the aggressive adult were in what is called the **experimental condition**, which is the condition where participants are exposed to different levels of the independent variable (in this case, the adult's aggression). In contrast, the children who had observed the nonaggressive adult were in what is called the **control condition**, which is the condition where participants are not exposed to the independent variable. Because the only difference between the experimental and control conditions in this study was whether or not the children had been exposed to an aggressive adult (the independent variable), any subsequent differences in the children's aggression (the dependent variable) could be explained as being caused by the manipulation of the independent variable.

So what happened in the third room? Children in the control condition tended to play nonaggressively with the toys, whereas those in the experimental condition tended to beat up the Bobo doll, often shouting the same things at the clown as the previous aggressive adult. Based on this experiment and others like it, Bandura concluded that observing adult aggression could teach children to act more aggressively themselves. Figure 1-7 provides an overview of the elements in an experiment, using Bandura's study as an example.

Recently, some psychologists have begun using *virtual environment technology (VET)*, in which they create a virtual research environment using a computer (Schmelter et al., 2009). Once this simulated reality is created, research participants wearing virtual reality equipment are "immersed" in the setting. A commonly used piece of virtual reality equipment is a head-mounted or binocular-style device that allows an individual to view 3-D images and to "walk" through the virtual environment. Although this type of simulated environment is completely controlled by the experimenter—even more than the traditional laboratory setting—it has a

Experimental condition The condition in an experiment whereby participants are exposed to different levels of the independent variable

Control condition The condition in an experiment in which participants are not exposed to the independent variable

FIGURE 1-7

The Basic Elements in an Experiment

As illustrated in the Bandura study, the power of experimental research is based on treating the experimental and control groups exactly alike except for the manipulation of the independent variable. Any later observed differences in the dependent variable between the two groups can then be confidently attributed to the effects of the independent variable.

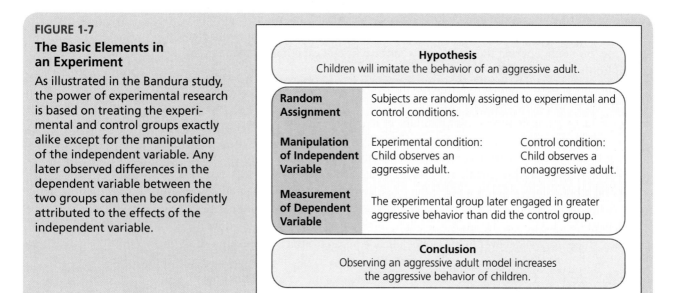

Hypothesis
Children will imitate the behavior of an aggressive adult.

Random Assignment	Subjects are randomly assigned to experimental and control conditions.	
Manipulation of Independent Variable	Experimental condition: Child observes an aggressive adult.	Control condition: Child observes a nonaggressive adult.
Measurement of Dependent Variable	The experimental group later engaged in greater aggressive behavior than did the control group.	

Conclusion
Observing an aggressive adult model increases the aggressive behavior of children.

very "real-world" feel to it. Studies employing virtual environment technology suggest that participants behave relatively naturally in such settings (Waller et al., 2002). Although still in its infancy, virtual environment technology is currently being used to study such topics as conformity, eyewitness testimony, effects of violent video games, and simulated weightlessness. As this technology improves, psychologists hope to involve senses beyond sight and hearing, as well as to improve the ways people can interact with the virtual creations they encounter. This technology is not meant to replace traditional laboratory studies but instead is meant to provide another research vehicle that psychologists can use in their journey of discovery.

Journey of Discovery

What role should values play in science? Is it possible or desirable to separate values from science?

Now that you have learned about the different scientific methods that psychologists use, which is best? Actually, what I hope you take from this overview is that there is no one best method for all research settings. In each investigation, the psychologist must decide what method would provide the best test of the hypotheses under consideration. The best overall strategy for psychologists to take is a multimethod approach—employing different methods to study the same topic, thereby capitalizing on each method's strengths and controlling for its weaknesses.

Shutterstock

Should psychologists use their scientific knowledge about the harmful effects of television violence to influence social decisions? Will the knowledge you gain by studying psychology influence how you raise your own children?

1.3f *There Are No "Final Truths" in Science.*

In the United States, an increasing number of school boards are in the grip of a controversy concerning whether *creation science* should be taught in science classes as an alternative explanation to evolutionary theory. The core of this argument involves what qualifies as a scientific theory. Advocates of creation science (sometimes referred to as *creationism* or *intelligent design*) reject evolution and adhere to a Bible-based explanation of God creating the world in seven days (Evans, 2001). Some followers of creation science proclaim a more literal interpretation of the Bible's creation story than do others. *Young earth creationists* believe in the book of Genesis's literal 7-day creation story, while *old earth creationists* believe that the seven days should be interpreted as figurative lengths of time. Whatever their differences concerning how much time passed while God created life, all creationists assert that their explanation is at least as scientifically based as evolutionary theory. My purpose here is not to judge the validity of the Bible's creation story. Instead, I would like to pose the following question: Based on your understanding of the scientific method, does creation science have a legitimate claim on being referred to as a scientific theory?

Let's review what constitutes a scientific theory. A *theory* is an organized system of ideas that seeks to explain why two or more events are related. To qualify as a scientific theory, an explanation must be testable by the methods of science. The explanation must also be *falsifiable,* meaning that it must be possible to find fault with, or disconfirm, the explanation. If no one can think of a test that would falsify an explanation, then the explanation is not a scientific theory—even if it is true. "God exists" is a statement that cannot be tested because there is no conceivable experiment or observation that would falsify it. Belief in God's existence is a matter of faith, not science. Likewise, the statement "God created life" is not falsifiable. Therefore, creationism does not qualify as a scientific theory (Perakh, 2004). In 1987, the U.S. Supreme Court agreed with this assessment and ruled that creationism is religion, not science, and cannot be advocated as a scientific theory in public school classrooms (*Edwards v. Auguillard*).

As already noted, creationism stands sharply opposed to evolutionary theory. Why does the theory of evolution qualify as a scientific theory? The simple answer is that this theory is falsifiable. Tests can determine whether or not evolutionary theory is correct as it currently stands (actually, there is more than one theory of evolution), and these tests can be carried out. Current and past evolutionary theories have all been subjected to these tests, and the general principles of evolutionary theory have been repeatedly supported. Based on this wealth of evidence, virtually all scientists express strong confidence in the overall theory. Likewise, many religious organizations have concluded that evolutionary theory is not inconsistent with descriptions of creation and the origin of the human species. Many members of these religious organizations could be classified as *theistic evolutionists:* They believe that evolution is an accurate explanation of how organisms change over time, but they also believe in a God who is both personal and concerned about his (or her) creation (which is different from a Deist God who isn't concerned). Their first belief rests on the findings of science, while their second belief rests on their religious faith, which is beyond the bounds of science.

The vast majority of Americans, including many scientists, believe that God created the universe and life on this planet (Deckman, 2002). This belief in theistic evolution does not necessarily contradict or otherwise stand in opposition to scientific explanations of evolution. Perhaps one way to approach science and religion is in the following manner, suggested by Roman Catholic Pope Pius X:

BVT *Lab*

Improve your test scores. Practice quizzes are available at **www.BVTLab.com**.

... science is entirely concerned with the reality of phenomena, into which faith does not enter at all; faith on the contrary concerns itself with the divine reality which is entirely unknown to science ..[T]here can never be any dissension between faith and science, for if each keeps on its own ground they can never meet and therefore never be in contradiction.

—Pius X, Roman Catholic Pope, 1835–1914

In summary, it is important to understand that truth in science is never final. Scientific theories are explanations of how things in the world are related to one another and how they operate. They are logically constructed and reconfigured from careful observations and testable hypotheses. You can have such overwhelming data supporting your theory that you have very strong confidence that it accurately explains the phenomena in question; at the core of the scientific journey of discovery, however, is the assumption that any theory can be modified or completely discarded tomorrow. Thus, if you seek to understand the human mind using the scientific method, it is a mistake to believe that any theory can achieve a "final truth."

Section REVIEW

- Scientific methods help psychologists gather, analyze, and interpret information in a way that reduces error and leads to dependable generalizations.

- The process of scientific inquiry occurs in stages:
    - Stage 1 involves selecting a topic and searching the research literature.
    - Stage 2 involves developing theories and hypotheses.
    - Stage 3 involves selecting a scientific method and submitting a proposed study for ethical evaluation.
    - Stage 4 involves collecting and analyzing data, and reporting results.

- Observational research describes behavior as it occurs in its natural setting.

- Correlational research assesses the direction and strength of the relationship between two or more variables.

- Experimental research involves manipulation of one or more independent variables to determine what effect this has on nonmanipulated dependent variables.

- A basic assumption in science is that any theory can be modified or completely discarded in the light of new evidence.

How Can You Develop Critical Thinking Skills?

In this last section of Chapter 1, I discuss the kinds of critical thinking skills that not only are necessary in conducting scientific research but also are important in making you both a wise consumer of psychological knowledge and a capable decision maker in your own journey of discovery.

What Is Critical Thinking?

When my oldest daughter, Amelia, was 9 years old, I took her to a toy store so that she could pick out a new bicycle for her birthday present. The colors, names, and styles of the bikes were clearly aimed at steering girls and boys toward different choices. Yet, Amelia ignored these gender labels and tested all the bikes. At the end of this process, she knew which bike felt the best riding-wise—the blue Huffy Hyper Force boy's bike. She also knew, however, that if she picked a boy's bike, some of the neighborhood kids would tease her. Amelia realized she could avoid the negative comments by picking her second choice, the pink Barbie Fashion Fun girl's bike. All this she explained to me as we stood in the store scanning the array of possibilities before us. Perhaps she was hoping that I would draw upon that mystical "father knows best" wisdom that I had sometimes alluded to and simply tell her which bike to choose. Instead, I said, "Amelia, this is your decision. Think about what's most important to you." After carefully evaluating the evidence and weighing the possible consequences of her two choices, she picked the Hyper Force boy's bike.

This Amelia example illustrates an important type of problem-solving skill known as *critical thinking*. As defined earlier in the chapter, critical thinking is the process of deciding what to believe and how to act based on a careful evaluation of the evidence. In picking a bike, Amelia could have uncritically followed the color designations and bike styles that her culture designates for girls; instead, she decided that these gender labels unnecessarily restricted her choices. By challenging the assumption that a bike's color and style restricted who could ride it, Amelia could now entertain many more bike possibilities. Once she had gathered her own information by riding all the bikes, she also could have ignored the evidence of her senses and chosen the gender-appropriate but less rider-worthy bike. Again, based on careful reflection of her options, she made her choice. That is one hallmark of critical thinking.

What if Amelia had decided, after going through this entire process, that the benefits of the better-riding boy's bike were not enough to justify the social hassles associated with it? Would this decision to pick the girl's bike not be based on critical thinking? The answer is no. The choice is not what determines whether critical thinking took place. Rather, it is the type of cognitive process that one engages in that is crucial. What we know is that thinking critically about the arguments that you make to yourself, or that others make to you, can greatly improve your own decision making (Anderson, 1993; McBride et al., 2002).

Guidelines for Critical Thinking

The following are some general guidelines on how to think critically:

1. *Be willing to ask questions.* Knowledge begins with questioning the nature of things. Think of the process of questioning as a sign of inquisitiveness, not as a lack of intelligence.

2. *Analyze assumptions.* Instead of passively accepting assumptions as facts, think about possible exceptions and contradictions.

3. *Examine the evidence.* Instead of accepting a conclusion without evidence, ask for and analyze the evidence that supports and contradicts the various positions.

4. *Be cautious of emotional decisions.* Although there is certainly nothing wrong with being emotionally involved with a particular decision, avoid basing your decision on what you would like to be true rather than what you know to be true.

5. *Avoid oversimplifying issues.* It can be comforting to make simple generalizations about complex events, but resisting glib explanations provides the opportunity for creative complexity.

6. *Tolerate ambiguity.* By rejecting simple answers, you must learn to develop a tolerance for ambiguity. Don't be afraid to admit that you don't know the correct answer when the evidence suggests not one correct solution, but many possible ones.

Critical thinking can be fostered through many activities, but the study of psychology is particularly helpful in promoting this type of cognitive activity (Haw, 2011). In fact, when researchers examined the reasoning ability of graduate students in psychology and chemistry, they found that as the two groups advanced through graduate school, the psychology students became better at analyzing everyday events, while the chemistry students showed no improvement (Lehman et al., 1988).

One of the likely reasons that psychology promotes critical thinking is that students of psychology learn a great deal about how the mind works, including the many biases and errors that are obstacles to intelligent thinking. In this instance, knowledge really is power. Hopefully, one of the benefits of taking this course is that your increased knowledge of how people think and behave will allow you to make more intelligent decisions in your everyday life.

Using Critical Thinking While Reading This Textbook

Although greater knowledge of psychology may ultimately benefit future decision making, one of your more immediate concerns may be how critical thinking can improve your study skills in college. This is certainly a legitimate concern. Let me briefly describe how you can use a critical thinking strategy known as PRQR while reading the textbook.

The PRQR Technique

Before reading each chapter, *preview* (P) the material by first reading the chapter-opening story and outline, as well as the section summaries and "Journey of Discovery" questions. This will provide you with a general understanding of what you are about to read so that you can better organize the text material in memory. Next, *read* (R) an entire chapter section; and as you do, ask *questions* (Q) that focus your attention on the topics. Regularly ask yourself how the text material supports or calls into question any prior beliefs you may have had on the topic. Further, how can the material you are reading help you better understand your own life and events in your world? In writing this text, I attempted to facilitate your critical thinking by regularly asking you questions within the main body of the text and in the captions accompanying the tables, figures, and photographs. Finally, once you have read the chapter, *review* (R) the material so that the information is more securely stored in memory.

In addition to this reading technique, I recommend that you read text material before your professor talks about it in lecture. By staying slightly ahead of lecture content, you will better comprehend and remember the material presented in class because you already have information in memory upon which you can "hang" the new lecture material. Also, spend time answering the "Journey of Discovery" questions contained within each chapter. These focused questions encourage you to analyze psychological concepts, provide alternative explanations for research findings, and explore the implications of the text material.

In summary, to be an efficient consumer of psychological knowledge and a capable decision maker in your everyday activities, you need to be willing to exercise your mind like athletes exercise their bodies. You must condition yourself to actively question and scrutinize not only course material but also life events. If you learn to think critically, you will retain something of value long after this textbook and your psychology course are distant memories.

> *We do not live to think, but, on the contrary, we think in order that we may succeed in surviving.*
>
> —José Ortega y Gasset, Spanish philosopher, 1883–1955

Suggested Websites

Today in the History of Psychology

http://www.cwu.edu/~warren/today.html

This site contains a collection of dates and brief descriptions of over 3,100 events in the history of psychology. Type in any day of the year and find out what happened on that day.

American Psychological Association

http://www.apa.org

This official APA site provides access to many APA-sponsored websites related to various psychological issues.

Association for Psychological Science

http://www.psychologicalscience.org

This official website of the APS provides access to many psychology-related websites and APS journals.

Psychology Web Links by Topic

http://www.socialpsychology.org/psylinks.htm

This is the general psychology link on the Social Psychology Network, which has more than 5,000 links to psychology topics. The Psychology Subject Areas list provides important information on the various subdisciplines in psychology.

Animal Welfare Information Center

http://www.nal.usda.gov/awic

This website provides information on the ethical treatment of animals in government-sponsored research programs.

Critical Thinking and Psychology Links

http://www.mcckc.edu/longview/ctac/psychlink.htm

This website contains exercises for promoting critical thinking in psychology.

Key Terms

Applied psychologists, 17
Behaviorism, 7
Case study, 26
Cognitive psychology, 10
Collectivism, 15
Control condition, 31
Correlation coefficient (r), 28
Correlational research, 26
Critical thinking, 18
Culture, 13
Dependent variable, 30
Descriptive statistics, 23
Dynamic systems theory, 14
Evolutionary psychology, 11
Evolution, 12

Experimental condition, 31
Experimental research, 30
Functionalism, 6
Humanistic psychology, 10
Hypothesis, 20
Independent variable, 30
Individualism, 15
Inferential statistics, 23
Meta-analysis, 24
Naturalistic observation, 24
Natural selection, 12
Neuroscience perspective, 11
Operational definition, 21
Participant observation, 25
Population, 18

Positive psychology, 10
Psychiatry, 5
Psychoanalysis, 7
Psychology, 5
Random assignment, 30
Random selection, 18
Replication, 24
Sample, 18
Scientific methods, 18
Sociocultural perspective, 13
Structuralism, 6
Survey, 26
Theory, 19

Review Questions

1. In what year was the first institute for research in experimental psychology opened?
   a. 1879
   b. 1890
   c. 1921
   d. 1940
   e. 1960

2. Which of the following is true of William James?
   a. He wrote a classic book, titled Principles of Psychology.
   b. He wanted to understand how the mind affects what people do rather than merely identifying its components.
   c. He did very little lab work; rather, he relied on his ideas and writings.
   d. His approach to psychology became known as functionalism.
   e. All of the above

3. Which of the following is true of Sigmund Freud?
   a. He contended that our personality matures slowly but surely over the years.
   b. He emphasized the study of the conscious experience.
   c. He had no direct experience working with patients.
   d. He was technically a psychiatrist, not a psychologist.
   e. He is closely associated with behaviorism.

4. Which of the following founders of psychology believed psychology should study observable behavior rather than hidden psychological processes?
   a. Sigmund Freud
   b. William James
   c. John Watson
   d. Wilhelm Wundt
   e. Max Wertheimer

5. Of the four early schools of psychology discussed in the chapter, which perspective(s) survived as (a) contemporary perspective(s)?
   a. psychoanalysis
   b. behaviorism
   c. structuralism
   d. functionalism
   e. a and b

6. Who were considered the architects of the perspective that emphasized people's innate capacity for personal growth and their ability to make choices?
   a. William James and Wilhelm Wundt
   b. Carl Rogers and Abraham Maslow
   c. Mary Calkins and Mamie Phipps Clark
   d. Sigmund Freud and B. F. Skinner
   e. None of the above

7. Which of the following is true of the cognitive perspective?
   a. It emphasized the essential goodness of people.
   b. It coincided with the development of the computer.
   c. It is the least scientifically based of the contemporary perspectives.
   d. It promoted the scientific study of love.
   e. None of the above

8. Which of the following is true of the neuroscience perspective?
   a. A good deal of its research is done on humans.
   b. It does not believe that research on animals can benefit humans.
   c. It is focused on the most precise microscopic levels of analysis.
   d. It is based on the writings of the biologist Charles Darwin.
   e. All of the above

9. Which of the following statements is true?
   a. Evolutionary factors along with social and cultural factors can help explain human thought and behavior.
   b. The sociocultural and evolutionary perspectives are not compatible.
   c. Genetic change occurs more rapidly than cultural changes.
   d. There is a great deal of genetic variation among cultural groups.
   e. All of the above

10. Which of the following statements is true?
    a. Thirty percent of the world's population lives in cultures with a collectivist orientation.
    b. The cultural belief system of individualism is older than collectivism.
    c. From an evolutionary perspective, individualism is better than collectivism.
    d. All of the above
    e. None of the above

11. Which of the following is an applied specialty?
    a. clinical psychology
    b. counseling psychology
    c. industrial psychology
    d. school psychology
    e. all of the above

12. Dement's claim that there is something basic in our need to dream would be considered a

    _____.
    a. hypothesis
    b. theory
    c. case study
    d. correlational coefficient
    e. topic selection

13. Which of the following applies to institutional review boards (IRBs)?
    a. They monitor and evaluate research proposals involving only human subjects.
    b. They focus on risk/benefit ratio.
    c. They never allow participants to be deceived about a study's true purpose.
    d. They claim that human psychological research is a high-risk activity.
    e. a and b

14. Which of the following statements is true of animal research?
    a. Most animal research is unnecessary.
    b. Other methods could be used so that animals are not needed in behavioral research.
    c. Nearly 90 percent of animals used in research are rodents.
    d. Ninety percent of behavioral and biomedical research causes pain and significant distress to animals.
    e. Animals do not benefit from animal research.

15. Which of the following statements is true?
    a. Descriptive statistics are a more valued type of statistic than inferential statistics.
    b. A difference is considered statistically significant if the likelihood of it having occurred by mere chance is less than 1 in 5.
    c. Contemporary psychology does not require extensive knowledge of statistics.
    d. Meta-analysis is the technique of counting the number of studies that find or do not find a particular effect.
    e. Reporting results is an important stage of research.

16. All but which of the following are advantages of naturalistic research and participant observation research?
    a. There is an absence of control.
    b. They provide a full context for behavior.
    c. The opportunity to record events is difficult to replicate in a laboratory.
    d. They can observe events too risky to create in a laboratory.
    e. They can record events previously only observed by nonscientists.

17. Correlational studies cannot determine the cause of the relationship between two variables because of which of the following?
    a. the third-variable problem
    b. the reverse-causality problem
    c. research correlation rarely exceeds .60
    d. all of the above
    e. a and b

18. In Bandura's Bobo doll study, the level of aggressive play of the child in the third room was which of the following?
    a. the experimental condition
    b. the control condition
    c. the dependent variable
    d. the independent variable
    e. the random assignment

19. Considering the Amelia example, which of the following choices illustrates critical thinking?
    a. buying the boy's bike
    b. buying the girl's bike
    c. not buying a bike at all
    d. asking her dad's advice
    e. none of the above

20. Which of the following does the PRQR technique suggest you do?
    a. Preview the material by first reading the chapter-opening story and outline.
    b. Read an entire section.
    c. Ask questions that focus your attention on the topics.
    d. Review the material so that the information is more securely stored in memory.
    e. All of the above

Chapter Two

Neurological and Genetic Bases of Behavior

Chapter Outline

It's like waking up, sort of like waking up in the world. You're waking, trying to push things together yourself, reaching back. And you wonder at times yourself just, well, what it is and what it isn't. (Hilts, 1995, p. 239)

Have you ever had the experience of waking from a dream feeling disoriented, not quite sure where you were or what was happening? If so, then perhaps you can relate in some small way to the life of an extraordinary man—Henry Molaison.

My own brain is to me the most unaccountable of machinery—always buzzing, humming, soaring, roaring, diving, and then buried in mud. And why? What's this passion for?

—Virginia Woolf, British novelist, 1882–1941

At the age of 16, Henry experienced his first major grand mal epileptic seizure. By age 27 he was having as many as 11 seizures per week and was unable to hold a job or live on his own. Faced with a future filled with such incapacitating convulsions, Henry decided to have a radical operation that his doctors believed would cure his epilepsy. Following his mother's advice, on an August morning in 1953 and at the age of 27, Henry underwent the procedure.

Henry's physician drilled two holes into Henry's skull above the eyes and inserted metal spatulas into the holes to lift the frontal lobes of the brain slightly. With the front of the brain raised, the physician next inserted a silver straw deep into Henry's brain and sucked out a fist-sized piece of it that contained nearly the entire mass of the *hippocampus* and the regions leading up to it. What is all the more horrifying about this procedure is that Henry was awake the entire time, since he was anesthetized only on his scalp. Because the brain has no sensory receptors, Henry felt no pain.

The surgery did indeed diminish Henry's epileptic seizures, but it had an additional unintended consequence—Henry lost his memories. Prior to this surgery, no one realized that the hippocampus is a part of the brain that plays a critical role in memory (see Section 2.3b). Henry was now a man with a memory frozen in time. His memories of people and events prior to his surgery were intact. Yet now, when Henry stopped thinking about something that had just happened to him, the memory disappeared, as if it never occurred (Corkin, 1984). Commenting on Henry's sorry state of mind, his physician sadly noted, "Guess what, I tried to cut out the epilepsy of a patient, but took his memory instead! What a trade!" (Hilts, 1995, p. 100).

In describing his state of mind in the years following surgery, Henry said it was like perpetually waking from a dream and not knowing what day it was or what he should be doing on that day. With this confusion came a tug of fear and concern. As he confided on one occasion to the scientists who were studying him:

> *Right now, I'm wondering, have I done or said anything amiss? You see, at this moment everything looks clear to me, but what happened just before? That's what worries me.* (Hilts, 1995, p. 138)

Until his death in 2008 at the age of 82, Henry Molaison remained ignorant of all the changes and advances in the world around him. Not only did he not know that his mother and father had died or that people had walked on the moon, but he also had no realization that his tragic life circumstances had dramatically increased the scientific community's understanding of the neuropsychology of memory. Indeed, over the years, Brenda Milner and other neuroscientists learned a great deal about the functioning of the human brain by studying Henry and other people like him whose brains have been damaged in some manner (Milner et al., 1968; Penfield & Milner, 1968).

The brain comprises only about 2 percent of your total body weight, yet it controls most of the complex aspects of your behavior and mental life. Evidence of the brain's importance is demonstrated by the fact that it uses more energy than any other human organ, accounting for up to 20 percent of the body's total energy consumption (Breedlove et al., 2007). In this chapter, we continue our journey of discovery by examining this most marvelous organ. Yet before analyzing the brain's larger structures and functions, we first need to examine the complex network of nerve cells, or *neurons*, that account for all human thought and action. After investigating the basic structure and function of these nerve cells, we will see how they are organized in our *central nervous system* and *peripheral nervous system* (Woolsey et al., 2008). Finally, we will end our analysis of the biology of behavior by examining its genetic basis.

Wikimedia Commons

After brain surgery in 1953 accidently removed Henry Molaison's ability to create new memories, scientists learned a great deal about how the brain creates memories by studying him over the next 50 years.

2.1 The Neuron

The nervous system has specialized cells, called **neurons**, which send and receive information throughout the body. They are the nervous system's building blocks. One of the first persons to discover that neurons were separate and distinct units—and not simply a thick clump of cell matter—was Spanish neuroanatomist Santiago Ramón y Cajal (1852–1934). The amazing thing about Cajal's discovery was that he made it while working in a makeshift laboratory in his attic and using a $25 microscope and a single box of slides! His resulting theory on how the brain processes information earned him the Nobel Prize for Physiology and Medicine in 1906.

2.1a Neurons Are the Nervous System's Building Blocks.

Today we know that the human nervous system contains anywhere from 90 to 180 billion neurons, roughly equal to the number of stars in our galaxy. Approximately 98.8 percent of these neurons reside within the brain, with the remaining 1.2 percent (over 1 billion neurons) distributed throughout the spinal cord (Nicholls et al., 2012). On average, each neuron transmits information to tens of thousands of other neurons, which means that there are trillions of different neural connections in the brain. Although these elementary units of the nervous system come in hundreds of shapes and sizes, researchers have identified three basic types:

1. **Sensory neurons** detect stimuli inside the body (for example, a headache or strained muscle) or in the world (for example, another person's voice). They send this information from sensory receptors to the brain, usually by way of the spinal cord.

2. Going in the opposite direction, **motor neurons** send commands from the brain to glands, muscles, and organs, directing them to do, cease, or inhibit something.

3. Finally, the vast majority of neurons are **interneurons**, those that connect neurons to one another. One of their most important functions is to link the sensory neurons' input signals with the motor neurons' output signals.

2.1b A Neuron Consists of a Soma, Dendrites, and an Axon.

Neurons have different functions, but most share common structural features. As illustrated in Figure 2-1, neurons have three basic parts. The central part of the neuron is the **soma**, which is the Latin word for "body." This cell body contains the *nucleus*, or control center of the neuron, and other components of the cell that preserve and nourish it. Attached to the soma are branchlike extensions, known as **dendrites** (the Greek word for "trees"), which receive information from other neurons and bring it to the soma. As previously noted, each neuron may have hundreds or thousands of dendrites. After integrating this information, the soma transmits it to a tubelike extension called an **axon** (Greek for "axle"), which carries the information from the soma to the other end of the axon in the form of an electrochemical impulse (Rutishauser, 2008). Axons can range in length from 1/32 of an inch to more than 3 feet. To give you some idea of the relative size and length of the soma, dendrites, and axon of some of the longer neurons, visualize a tennis ball with a number of shoelaces attached to one side of it and a thin rope 14 miles long attached to the other side. The tennis ball is the soma, the shoelaces are the dendrites, and the long rope is the axon.

Neurons Specialized cells in the nervous system that send and receive information

[The neuron is] the aristocrat among the structures of the body, with its giant arms stretched out like the tentacles of an octopus to the provinces on the frontier of the outside world, to watch for the constant ambushes of physical and chemical forces.

—Santiago Ramón y Cajal, Spanish scientist credited with discovering the neuron, 1852–1934,

Sensory neurons Neurons that send information from sensory receptors to the brain, usually by way of the spinal cord

Motor neurons Neurons that send commands from the brain to glands, muscles, and organs to do, cease, or inhibit something

Interneurons Neurons that connect the sensory neurons' input signals with the motor neurons' output signals

Soma The cell body of the neuron which contains the nucleus and other components that preserve and nourish it

Dendrites Branchlike extensions of the soma that receive information from other neurons

Axon An extension of the soma that sends information in the form of electrochemical impulses to other neurons

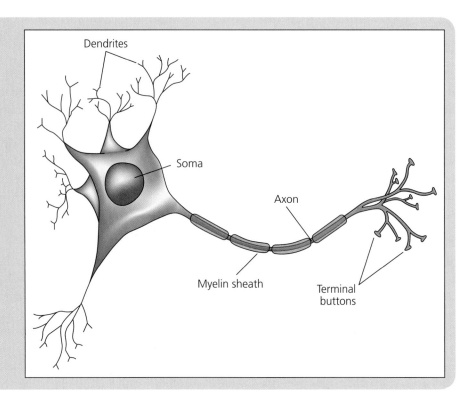

FIGURE 2-1

Structure of a Neuron

The primary components of the specialized cell known as the neuron are the soma, dendrites, and axon. The soma contains the nucleus of the cell, the dendrites receive information from other neurons, and the axon passes this information to other neurons. Do you know the range in length of our axons?

Dendrites

Soma

Axon

Myelin sheath

Terminal buttons

Myelin sheath A protective coating of fatty material around an axon that hastens the transmission of the electrochemical charge

Many axons are covered with a protective coating of fatty cells known as a **myelin sheath** that hastens the transmission of the electrochemical charge. In certain diseases, such as multiple sclerosis, the myelin sheath is slowly destroyed, causing impairment to brain-to-muscle communication and the loss of muscle control (Moll et al., 2011).

INFO-BIT

Scientists believe that the myelin sheath developed in humans as our brains evolved and became larger, making it necessary for information to travel faster over longer distances in the nervous system. Part of the reason children cannot learn and respond as quickly as adults in many cognitive and motor tasks is that their axons have not yet been fully covered by these neural speed-enhancing fatty cells. Neural axons in regions of the brain involved in abstract thinking may not become fully covered with myelin until a person reaches the age of 20!

At the end of each axon are branches with knoblike tips called *terminal buttons* that closely approach, but do not touch, the dendrites of other neurons. The space between the axon's terminal buttons and the dendrites is less than a millionth of an inch wide and is known as the synaptic cleft. The entire area composed of the terminal button of one neuron, the *synaptic cleft*, and the dendrite of another neuron is known as the **synapse**, which in Greek means "to clasp." In Section 2.1d, you will see how neurons communicate at this synapse through a complex process of electrical and chemical (electrochemical) changes.

Synapse The entire area composed of the terminal button of one neuron, the synaptic cleft, and the dendrite of another neuron

This brief outline of the neuron's structure is greatly simplified. In fact, there are some neurons with many axons and some without any axons at all. In addition, some neurons do not synapse on dendrites, but instead do so on axons or somas. Despite these exceptions, in general, dendrites receive information from other neurons and pass it through the soma, and then along the axon to the dendrites of other neurons at the synapses. In this capacity as the receiver, integrator, and transmitter of neural information, the neuron truly earns its reputation as the workhorse of the nervous system.

One last important point is worth mentioning. Santiago Cajal also discovered that the brain and spinal cord are not solid masses of neurons. Nerve tissue throughout the body is composed of two kinds of cells: neurons and supporting **glial cells** (*glial* in Greek means "glue"), which supply the neurons with support, nutrients, and insulation. Glial cells have no axons or dendrites. If you think of the brain as a house, then the glial cells are the floors, walls, and supporting beams, while the neurons are the electrical wiring. In essence, the glial cells hold the brain together while the neurons send and receive information throughout the brain structure. The myelin sheath that covers most axons is made up of glial cells. Glial cells also help form the *blood-brain barrier*, which is a semipermeable membrane-like mechanism that prevents certain chemicals in the bloodstream from reaching the brain. Interestingly, there are ten times more glial cells in the nervous system than there are neurons, although they are much smaller than neurons and constitute about half the brain's total mass (Zhang et al., 2012). Now that you understand the makeup of neurons and their supporting glial cells, let's examine how information travels within a single neuron.

2.1c A Neuron Is in Either a Resting or a Firing State.

A neuron is always in either a resting or a firing state—there is no in-between condition. Whether or not the neuron fires an electrochemical impulse depends on whether the combined stimulation received by the dendrites exceeds a certain minimum intensity, or *threshold*. If the threshold is exceeded, the neuron's membrane transmits an electrochemical impulse. If the threshold is not exceeded, nothing happens. This effect is known as the *all-or-none law*.

One useful way to think about a neuron is that it is like a liquid-filled balloon surrounded by a slightly different kind of liquid. The axon part of this "balloon" is stretched to form a very long, thin tube. A neuron's electrochemical impulse results from positively and negatively charged particles, called *ions*, moving back and forth through specialized pores, referred to as *ion channels*, in the axon's membrane walls. The important ions in the inside and outside liquids are positively charged sodium and potassium ions and negatively charged chlorine ions. When the neuron is in a resting state, the ions floating inside the axon are mostly negatively charged, whereas those outside the axon's membrane are mostly positively charged. The reason there are more negative ions inside is that, in its resting state, the cell membrane of the axon resists the passage of positive sodium ions through its ion channels into the cell. In this stable resting state, there is a tiny negative electrical charge—about one-twentieth of a volt, or –70 millivolts—within the axon, making it a storehouse of potential energy (Koester, 1995). When the inactive neuron is in this chemical balancing state—more positive ions outside of the membrane and more negative ions inside—its tiny electrical charge is known as the **resting potential**.

How is this resting potential changed? As previously stated, in its resting state the axon's cell membrane does not allow positive ions through its gates. Yet, just as the negative pole of a magnet attracts the positive pole of another magnet (an event called *polarization*), the negative ions inside the axon attract positive ions along the external wall of the cell membrane. As illustrated in Figure 2-2, when a neuron receives sufficient stimulation through its dendrites from other neurons, the neural membrane nearest where the axon emerges from the soma opens its gates, allowing the clustered positive sodium ions to rush in. For an instant, the charge inside this part of the axon

BVT *Lab*

Flashcards are available for this chapter at www.BVTLab.com.

Glial cells Non-neuron cells that supply the neurons with support, nutrients, and insulation

Resting potential The stable, negative charge of an inactive neuron

FIGURE 2-2

Structure and Operation of the Neuron

When the combined stimulation received by the dendrites exceeds a certain minimum intensity, or threshold, an electrochemical impulse is transmitted down the axon. This impulse results from positively and negatively charged ions moving back and forth through the axon's membrane walls. How does the diameter of the axon and the myelin sheath covering it affect the speed of the impulse?

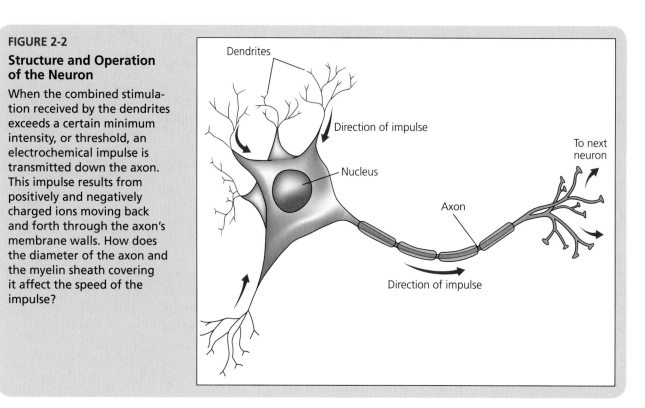

Action potential The brief shift in a neuron's electrical charge that travels down the axon

switches from negative to positive (an event known as *depolarization*), eliminating the resting potential and sending a brief electrochemical charge or impulse down to the next section of the axon farther away from the soma. This electrical disturbance—which transpires in about one-thousandth of a second—is called the **action potential** and is analogous to a pulse of electricity traveling along a wire. As soon as the resting potential has been eliminated, the axon membrane gates in this area again open; this time, however, they pump the positive sodium ions back out, restoring the positive-outside and negative-inside polarization. At the same time this is transpiring, the action potential has traveled farther down the axon, causing the gates there to open in the next axonal section so that it too depolarizes, setting off a domino-like chain reaction down the entire length of the axon (Nicholls et al., 2012).

This flood of electrically charged ions in and out of each section of the axon constitutes the neural impulse—which, you remember, was all started by stimulation to threshold at the dendrite side of the neuron. In different neurons, the speed of the impulse varies from 2 to over 200 miles per hour, but its speed is always constant within a given neuron. The larger the diameter of the axon is and the more myelin surrounding its outer surface, the faster the impulse. Although this neural impulse speed may seem fast, consider that the speed of an electric current passing through a wire is 3 million times faster. The fact that electrical wire transmission is so much faster than neural impulse speed explains why we can build machines that respond faster than our bodies.

Neurons not only differ in the speed at which the impulse moves down the axon but also in their potential rate of firing. Some neurons can reachieve their action potential within milliseconds after firing and can fire as many as 1,000 times per second. Other neurons take a great deal longer to recover their action potential. Thus, while it is true that a bright light or a loud sound causes a higher rate of firing in neurons than a less intense stimulation, some neurons will not fire as rapidly as others due to their slow recovery rate.

2.1d *Neurons Communicate with One Another by Releasing Chemicals.*

Now that you understand the basic operation of a single neuron, how do the billions of neurons in the nervous system work together to coordinate the body's activities? To explore this process, you need to examine how neural impulses get from one neuron to another.

As noted earlier (see Section 2.1b), at the end of each axon are *terminal buttons* that closely approach, but do not touch, the dendrites of other neurons. Most of these terminal buttons contain a number of tiny round sacs called *synaptic vesicles*. When an action potential arrives at the axon's terminal buttons, it causes these vesicles to release varying amounts of chemical messengers, called **neurotransmitters**, which travel across the synaptic cleft. As the neurotransmitters arrive at the receiving neuron's dendrites—within 1/10,000 of a second of being released by the synaptic vesicles—they fit into *receptor sites* like keys fit into locks. Just as specific keys can fit into only specific kinds of locks, each kind of neurotransmitter has a unique chemical configuration that allows it to fit into only one specific type of receptor site on the dendrites of the receiving neuron. This neural communication process, which is known as *synaptic transmission*, is illustrated in Figure 2-3.

Once a neurotransmitter fits into a receptor site, it unlocks tiny channels that permit either positively or negatively charged ions to enter the receiving dendrite, which affects the probability that the neuron will fire. *Excitatory messages* increase the probability of an action potential, and *inhibitory messages* reduce the likelihood of neural firing. Because the dendrites of a neuron receive both excitatory and inhibitory messages simultaneously from different receptor sites, whether or not the neuron fires will depend on which type of message is in greater abundance. If a neuron receives many more excitatory than inhibitory messages, it will fire. However, if the number of inhibitory messages is greater than that of the excitatory ones, the neuron will remain in a resting state.

What happens to the neurotransmitters after they lock into the receptor sites and either excite or inhibit the firing of the dendrites of the receiving neuron? This is an important question. If the neurotransmitters are not quickly removed from the synaptic cleft, they will block the transmission of any additional signals to the receiving neuron other than their own excitatory or inhibitory messages. The primary way the synapse is cleared is by taking the neurotransmitters back into the terminal buttons from which they came, repackaging them into new synaptic vesicles, and using them again. This recycling process, which is called *reuptake*, is also used on many of the neurotransmitters that fail to reach the receptor sites (Ago et al., 2005). When not recycled, neurotransmitters are broken down and removed from the synaptic cleft by enzymes in a process called *enzyme deactivation* (see Figure 2-3).

The emerging knowledge of how neurotransmitters function in the brain has enabled scientists to develop drugs that are structurally similar to naturally occurring neurotransmitters. When such a drug is ingested into the body and reaches the appropriate receptor site in the brain, it may cause an action potential, just as the real neurotransmitter would do. Similarly, another drug may mimic a neurotransmitter that blocks the same receptor site, thus reducing the likelihood of neural transmission at the synapse. Still other drugs reduce the amount of the neurotransmitter that is recycled into the terminal buttons in the reuptake process, which keeps the neurotransmitter active in the synapse longer, thus increasing or decreasing the probability of neural transmission (Davis, 2006). One such drug that delays the reuptake of the neurotransmitter serotonin is Prozac, which is widely used in treating depression (see Chapter 12, Section 12.7b).

Neurotransmitters Chemical messengers released by the synaptic vesicles that travel across the synaptic cleft that either excite or inhibit adjacent neurons

FIGURE 2-3

Synaptic Transmission

The axon's terminal buttons house synaptic vesicles that contain chemical messengers called neurotransmitters. Neurotransmitters travel across the synaptic cleft to the receiving neuron's dendrites, where they fit into receptor sites and deliver either excitatory or inhibitory messages. Excitatory messages increase the likelihood of an action potential, whereas inhibitory messages decrease this likelihood. After delivering their messages, neurotransmitters are either repackaged into new synaptic vesicles (reuptake), or they are broken down by enzymes and removed from the synaptic cleft (enzyme deactivation).

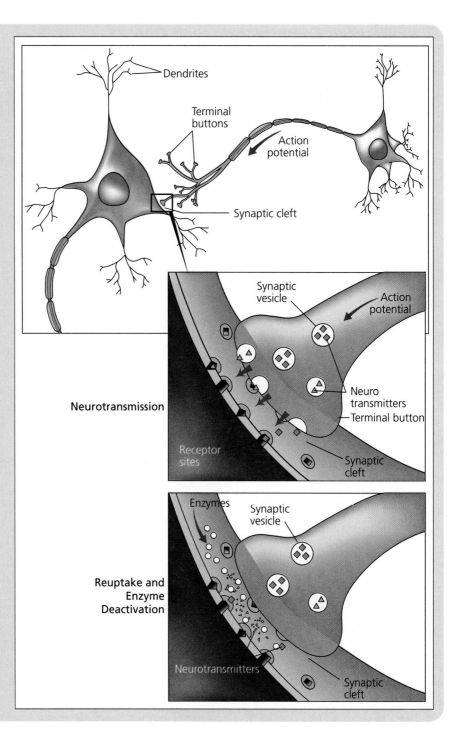

Acetylcholine (ACh) A neurotransmitter involved in muscle contraction and memory formation

To date, about 75 neurotransmitters have been identified, but neuroscientists believe that many more will be discovered in the future (Shigematsu et al., 2008). One of the most prominent neurotransmitters identified so far is **acetylcholine (ACh)**, which is an excitatory transmitter found throughout the nervous system. ACh is the chemical key that transmits excitatory messages to our skeletal muscles. Its continuing presence at the appropriate receptor sites enables us not only to walk, talk, and blink our eyes, but also to breathe. If it is prevented from reaching receptor sites or too much of it floods the synapses between motor neurons and muscles, the results can be disastrous. For example, the botulin bacterium, a poison found in improperly processed food, blocks the ACh receptors, which leads to respiratory paralysis and suffocation. In contrast, the venom from a black widow spider—if of sufficient dosage—causes these same receptors to be flooded, triggering severe muscle contractions, convulsions, and even heart failure. Besides its central role in the functioning of skeletal muscles, ACh also appears to play a critical role in cognition and the formation of new memories (Hasselmo & Bower, 1993). Researchers believe that the memory loss exhibited in the degenerative brain disorder known as *Alzheimer's disease*—which afflicts 11 percent of people over the age of 65—is caused by a sharp reduction in the supply of this neurotransmitter (Karim et al., 2011).

Another important neurotransmitter is **dopamine (DA)**, which is involved in controlling large muscle movements as well as influencing pleasure and motivation. Such pleasurable activities as eating, drinking, and having sex are associated with activation of dopamine receptors (Wang et al., 2003). Too much or too little dopamine in the brain results in a wide variety of debilitating effects, ranging from jerky muscle movements to psychotic hallucinations. Researchers have found that degeneration of dopamine-producing neurons in the brain causes *Parkinson's disease*, a disorder affecting many elderly adults. The main symptoms of this disease are uncontrollable tremors, slowness of movement, altered body posture, and depressed mood (Rao et al., 1992). When Parkinson's disease patients are given the L-dopa drug, their brains convert it to dopamine; this helps them regain control over their muscles (Parkinson Study Group, 2002). Another potentially useful treatment for Parkinson's disease is transplanting fetal tissue into the brains of Parkinson's disease patients. Researchers hope that the transplanted healthy fetal tissue will produce dopamine, thereby reducing patients' motor problems. Initial studies suggest that such transplants can help people regain the ability to walk and perform everyday activities (O'Keeffe et al., 2008).

Dopamine (DA) A neurotransmitter that promotes and facilitates movement as well as influencing thought and emotion

Although the destruction of the brain's dopamine-producing system appears to be the cause of Parkinson's disease, increasing evidence shows that an overactive central dopamine system may be the root cause of *schizophrenia*, a psychological disorder we will examine more closely in Chapter 11, Section 11.2d. Drugs that block the reception of dopamine have proven effective in reducing schizophrenic symptoms in those suffering from this disorder (Murray et al., 2008). Unfortunately, because these drugs reduce dopamine levels in several brain areas, their long-term use sometimes produces symptoms similar to those of Parkinson's disease.

One group of neurotransmitters that is important in the experience of pleasure and the control of pain are chemical substances known as **endorphins** (Pert, 2002). The brain produces endorphins in response to injury and many forms of physical stress, such as intense exercise and the labor of childbirth. During such times of bodily stress, the increase in endorphins not only temporarily provides the body with a natural painkiller, but also may explain the state of euphoria many runners experience following a strenuous workout, as well as the pain-reducing effects of *acupuncture*, an ancient Chinese medical technique that involves inserting needles into the body.

Endorphins A family of neurotransmitters that are similar to morphine and that play an important role in the experience of pleasure and control of pain

Another neurotransmitter that is involved in a number of psychological processes is **serotonin**. This chemical messenger is especially important in regulating emotional states, aggression, appetite, and sleep onset. Depressed and anxious moods, aggressiveness, and food cravings are associated with low levels of serotonin in the brain (Paulus & Mintz, 2012). As previously mentioned, drugs that keep serotonin active in the synapse longer by blocking reuptake are used to elevate depressed moods, as well as to inhibit violence and overeating. Research also indicates that increasing the body's levels of *tryptophan*, the amino acid needed by the brain for synthesis of serotonin, facilitates sleep induction (Hartman, 1978). Because milk is a good source of tryptophan, grandma's advice to drink a glass of milk before going to bed may be the ticket to a good night's rest.

Serotonin A neurotransmitter that is important in regulating emotional states, sleep cycles, dreaming, aggression, and appetite

TABLE 2-1   Major Neurotransmitters

Neurotransmitters	Involved In
Acetylcholine (ACh)	Walking, talking, breathing
Dopamine (DA)	Large muscle movement, pleasure, motivation, schizophrenia
Endorphins	Pain suppression, pleasure
Epinephrine	Blood pressure, heart rate
GABA (gamma-amino-butyric acid)	Relaxation, anxiety
Norepinephrine (NE)	Stress, wakefulness, mood
Serotonin	Sleep, arousal, depression, schizophrenia

As you will discover in later chapters, other neurotransmitters play important roles in controlling aggression, sexual activity, blood pressure, sleep cycles, and food and water intake, as well as learning and immune responses (see Table 2-1). The mysteries of neurotransmitter functioning revealed to date will no doubt be overshadowed by the discoveries yet to come as neuroscientists continue their studies of these key factors in synaptic transmission.

Section **REVIEW**

- Neurons are specialized cells in the nervous system that send and receive information throughout the body.
- The soma is the central part of the neuron.
- Dendrites are branchlike extensions at one end of the soma that receive electrical impulses from other neurons.
- The axon is a tubelike extension at the other end of the soma that carries impulses to other neurons.
- A neuron fires if it receives many more excitatory than inhibitory messages from other neurons.
- Neurotransmitters are chemicals that deliver excitatory or inhibitory messages to neurons.
- Some of the more important neurotransmitters are acetylcholine, dopamine, endorphins, and serotonin.

2.2 Neural and Hormonal Systems

Now that we have examined the structure and function of neurons, let's inspect the structure and function of the nervous system that neurons combine to form. The nervous system is our body's primary information system and is divided into two major portions, the *central nervous system* and the *peripheral nervous system* (Figure 2-4).

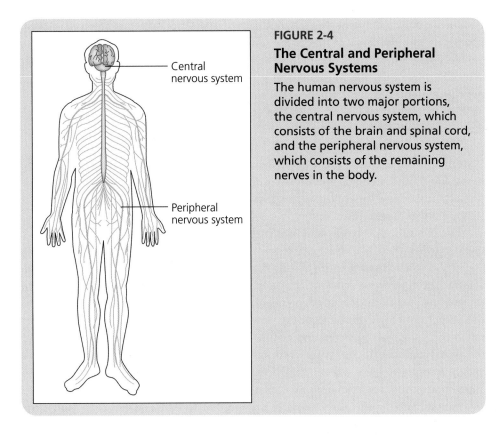

FIGURE 2-4

The Central and Peripheral Nervous Systems

The human nervous system is divided into two major portions, the central nervous system, which consists of the brain and spinal cord, and the peripheral nervous system, which consists of the remaining nerves in the body.

Central nervous system

Peripheral nervous system

One thing you will notice as you study these two divisions is that they also consist of a series of systems of twos. In addition to exploring the nervous system, we will explore a second communication system within the body that is interconnected with the nervous system, namely, the *endocrine system*.

2.2a *The Peripheral Nervous System Connects the Brain and Spinal Cord with Body Organs and Tissues.*

The **peripheral nervous system** consists of all the nerves located outside the brain and spinal cord. Its function is to connect the brain and spinal cord with the organs and tissues of the body. It accomplishes this task by conducting neural impulses into and out of the central nervous system.

Because the peripheral nervous system is made up of a network of nerves, you might be wondering whether nerves are the same thing as neurons. The answer is no. While a neuron is a single cell, a **nerve** is a bundle of axons from many neurons that are routed together in the peripheral nervous system. Just as a single telephone line from your home is bundled together with thousands of other users' lines to form a telephone cable, so too are thousands of axons from many neurons bundled together to form a single nerve. Due to their sheer number, many neurons in this bundle could be destroyed without adversely affecting nerve function; however, the destruction of the entire nerve—for example, the optic nerve controlling vision—would certainly be much more problematic.

The peripheral nervous system is also composed of two major divisions: the somatic nervous system and the autonomic nervous system. The **somatic nervous system** transmits commands to the voluntary skeletal muscles by way of the *motor neurons* and receives sensory information from the muscles and the skin by way of the *sensory neurons* (refer back to Section 2.1). The commands to the skeletal muscles

Peripheral nervous system That portion of the nervous system containing all the nerves outside the brain and spinal cord

Nerve A bundle of axons from many neurons that are routed together in the peripheral nervous system

Somatic nervous system A division of the peripheral nervous system that transmits commands to the voluntary skeletal muscles and receives sensory information from the muscles and skin

control our movement, whereas the messages received from the muscles and the skin provide us with the sense of touch, the sense of position in our surroundings, and the perception of temperature and pain. If you are reading these words on the computer screen, for example, the movement of your eyes is being controlled by the somatic nervous system. Likewise, your ability to actually *see* the words and *feel* the book (or the "mouse," if you are reading this online) in your hands is aided by this same division of the peripheral nervous system.

Autonomic nervous system A division of the peripheral nervous system that controls the movement of nonskeletal muscles, such as the heart and lung muscles, over which people have little or no voluntary control

The word *autonomic* means "self-governing." Thus, the **autonomic nervous system** commands movement of involuntary, nonskeletal muscles—such as the heart, lungs, and stomach muscles—over which we have little or no control. The primary function of this self-governing system is to maintain *homeostasis*, the body's steady state of normal functioning.

Sympathetic nervous system The part of the autonomic nervous system that activates the body's energy resources to deal with threatening situations

Parasympathetic nervous system The part of the autonomic nervous system that acts to conserve and maintain the body's energy resources

The autonomic nervous system is further divided into two separate branches—the *sympathetic* and *parasympathetic systems* (Figure 2-5)—which tend to work in opposition to each other in regulating many of our body functions. In general, the **sympathetic nervous system** activates the body's energy resources to deal with threatening situations. If something angers or frightens you, the sympathetic system will prepare you for "fight or flight" by slowing your digestion, accelerating your heart rate, raising your blood sugar, and cooling your body with perspiration. In contrast, the **parasympathetic nervous system** acts to conserve and maintain the body's energy resources. Thus, when the threat ceases, parasympathetic nerves slow the autonomic system back down to its normal levels of functioning.

In summarizing this discussion, it is important to emphasize that although the sympathetic and parasympathetic systems produce opposite effects, together they keep the nervous system as a whole in a steady state of normal functioning. In this case, opposites are indeed attractive... to our overall health.

2.2b *The Spinal Cord Connects the Peripheral Nervous System to the Brain.*

Central nervous system That portion of the nervous system located in the bony central core of the body and consisting of the brain and spinal cord

Cerebrospinal fluid A clear, cushioning fluid secreted by the brain and circulated inside and around the brain and spinal cord

The **central nervous system** is that portion of the nervous system located in the bony central core of the body and consists of the brain and spinal cord. Besides being encased in bone and swaddled in three protective membranes (called *meninges*), the central nervous system is further cushioned and shielded from injury by a clear solution known as **cerebrospinal fluid**, which is secreted by the brain.

INFO-BIT The protective cerebrospinal fluid, which circulates inside and around the brain and spinal cord, has a specific gravity that is slightly greater than that of the brain, allowing the brain to literally float inside the skull. In this floating state, the brain's 3-pound "air weight" is reduced to only a few ounces, significantly reducing the pressure it exerts on the spinal cord. The importance of the cerebrospinal fluid in supporting and cushioning the brain is dramatically demonstrated when patients have it drained away during brain surgery. Until the brain replenishes this fluid, the patients suffer terrible headaches and experience intense pain whenever they move their heads abruptly.

Spinal cord The slender, tube-shaped part of the central nervous system that extends from the base of the brain down the center of the back and made up of a bundle of nerves

The **spinal cord**, which is a bundle of nerves the thickness of a pencil, connects the brain to the rest of the body through the peripheral nervous system. Encased within the vertebrae of the spinal column and bathed in cerebrospinal fluid, the nerves of the spinal cord transmit information from sensory neurons up to the brain and from the brain down to motor neurons that initiate movement. Every voluntary

FIGURE 2-5

The Dual Functions of the Autonomic Nervous System

The sympathetic and parasympathetic divisions of the autonomic nervous system often stimulate opposite effects in the body's organs. The sympathetic nervous system prepares your body for action, while the parasympathetic nervous system calms the body. Can you explain how these two systems respond to threat?

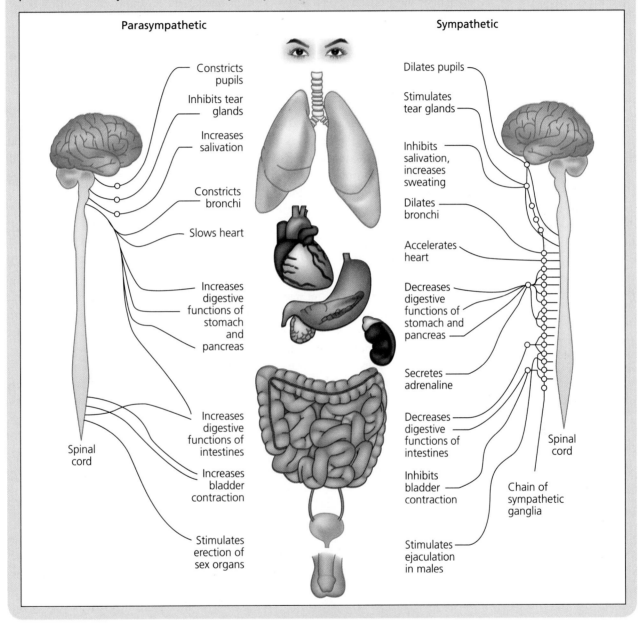

action, such as walking and moving one's arms, requires a message from the brain to the spinal cord and from the spinal cord to the muscles.

The spinal cord extends from the base of the brain to slightly below the waist. By and large, the upper segments of the spinal cord control the upper parts of the body, while the lower segments control the lower body. If a segment of the spinal cord is ever severed, the person loses all sensation and muscle control below the injury. Some 11,000 Americans injure their spinal cords each year. The higher up the spine an injury occurs, the greater the extent of paralysis. Thus, when the late actor Christopher Reeve—who played the role of Superman in several 1970/80s films—severed his spinal cord just below the base of his neck in a horse-riding accident, he not only lost the ability to breathe on his own and to move any part of his body below the injury point but also lost feeling in these areas as well. When such injuries occur, the central nervous system cannot repair itself. However, recent advances in medical science provide hope that the neural circuitry of the spinal cord can be regenerated. With the benefit of these advances, Reeve recovered some sensation and muscle control below his injury prior to his death in 2004.

In addition to transmitting information to and from the brain, the spinal cord controls some automatic, involuntary responses to sensory stimuli called reflexes. **Reflexes**, of which the *knee-jerk response* is one example, involve no interaction with the brain. Thus, when you accidentally place your hand on a hot stove and immediately pull it away, your ability to respond so quickly is because your action involves no thinking—that is, no input from the brain. The pain message does continue traveling up the spinal cord to the brain, so that within a second you will respond with a cry of pain; the action of removing your hand from the burner, however, is achieved by the spinal nerves. Such quick reflexive responses by the spinal cord enable the body to avoid serious injury.

Reflexes Automatic, involuntary responses to sensory stimuli

2.2c *The Endocrine System Communicates by Secreting Hormones.*

The **endocrine system** is interconnected with—but not actually part of—the nervous system. It consists of a network of glands in various parts of the body that secrete chemical messengers, known as **hormones**, directly into the bloodstream (see Table 2-2). Because the blood carries these hormones throughout the body, and because the membrane of every cell has receptors for one or more hormones, these chemical messengers have a direct effect on many different body activities and organs, including the brain. Hormones affecting the brain influence our interest in food, aggression, and sex. However, unlike neural impulses that rely on electro-chemical transmission and can be measured in thousandths of a second, hormonal

Endocrine system A network of glands in various parts of the body that secrete hormones directly into the bloodstream

Hormones Chemical signals, secreted into the blood by the endocrine glands, that help regulate bodily activities

TABLE 2-2   Major Endocrine Glands and Some of Their Hormones

Gland	Hormone	Effects
Pituitary gland	Growth hormone	Stimulates growth (especially of bones) and metabolic functions
	Oxytocin	Stimulates contraction of uterus and mammary gland cells, and may possibly promote prosocial behavior
Thyroid gland	Thyroxin	Stimulates and maintains metabolic processes
Adrenal glands	Epinephrine and norepinephrine	Increase metabolic activities and blood glucose and constrict certain blood vessels
Gonads (male testes and female ovaries)	Androgens (males), estrogens (females)	Support male sperm formation, stimulate female uterine lining growth, and stimulate development and maintenance of secondary sex characteristics, such as chest hair growth in men and breast development in women

communications traveling through the bloodstream often take minutes to reach their destinations. Although the endocrine system generally affects bodily organs more slowly than the nervous system does, the effects of hormonal stimulation typically have a longer duration than those of neurotransmitters. Besides regulating body activities, hormones also organize the nervous system and body tissues at certain stages of development. Puberty is perhaps the most noticeable time in life when hormones trigger important physical changes.

The most influential endocrine gland is the **pituitary gland**, a pea-sized structure located in the base of the brain and controlled by a nearby brain area called the *hypothalamus* (see Section 2.3b). The pituitary is often referred to as the "master gland" because it releases about ten different hormones that stimulate and regulate the rest of the endocrine system. The pituitary gland also releases another hormone that influences growth. At puberty, the pituitary gland increases its secretion of this *growth hormone*, which acts directly on bone and muscle tissue to produce the adolescent growth spurt (Zhou et al., 2005). Throughout life, growth hormone also plays an important role in tissue repair and muscle growth. However, in adulthood, the pituitary gland produces less and less growth hormone each year, and this depletion is thought to contribute to body aging. Because growth hormone helps bone, cartilage, and muscle tissues grow and regenerate following injury, abuse of this hormone in performance-enhancing drugs has become a serious problem in both amateur and professional sports (Bollmann et al., 2007).

Another hormone released by the pituitary gland is *oxytocin*, which causes the uterus to contract during childbirth and the mammary glands to produce milk. When a mother begins nursing her infant, the hypothalamus signals the pituitary gland to produce oxytocin, which results in the "let down" of milk into the nipple. Surprisingly, men also have significant amounts of oxytocin in their bodies, but for what purpose? Besides the role it plays in childbirth and nursing, animal research indicates that this hormone also influences social and sexual behavior, as well as parental behavior (Norman et al., 2012). Animals with higher levels of oxytocin more strongly desire companionship, are more sexually active, and take better care of their young than do

Pituitary gland The body's "master" gland, located in the base of the brain, whose hormones stimulate and regulate the rest of the endocrine system

Human growth hormone performance-enhancing drugs increase the growth of bone, cartilage, and muscles, therefore giving a competitive advantage to users. Such use can cause dangerous side effects—including heart damage, arthritis, diabetes, and impotence.

those with lower levels (Young, 2002). A possible implication of these findings is that oxytocin is an *affiliative hormone*, promoting prosocial behavior in both humans and other animals, regardless of their sex.

Other notable glands in the endocrine system are the *thyroid gland*, the *adrenal glands*, and the *gonads* (see Table 2-2). The **thyroid gland**, located just below the larynx in the neck, produces the hormone *thyroxin*, which controls metabolism—that is, the rate at which the food we eat is transformed into energy. People with an underactive thyroid—a condition known as *hypothyroidism*—tend to be lethargic and depressed, whereas those with an overactive thyroid tend to be very excitable, be easily agitated, and have short attention spans.

The **adrenal glands**, located near the kidneys, secrete *epinephrine* (also called *adrenaline*) and *norepinephrine* (also called *noradrenaline*) when you feel anxious or threatened. These hormones complement and enhance the effects of the sympathetic nervous system, thus making the heart beat faster, slowing digestion, and increasing the rate at which the body uses energy. Interestingly, epinephrine and norepinephrine also act as neurotransmitters, stimulating neural firing in the sympathetic nervous system. The fact that epinephrine and norepinephrine levels remain high following stressful events explains why it takes considerable time to calm down from such experiences.

Finally, the **gonads** are the two sex glands (Hagenauer et al., 2011). The two male gonads are called *testes*, and they produce sperm cells. The two female gonads are known as *ovaries*, and they produce ova, or eggs.

In men, the testes secrete male sex hormones called *androgens*, which are the body's natural anabolic steroids. Androgens are important in muscle and bone growth, the enhancement of sexual arousal, and in the development of male secondary sexual characteristics such as hair growth on the face and body and the deepening of the voice. The most important androgen is *testosterone*, which is also secreted by the adrenal glands in both women and men. A number of well-known male and female athletes have been accused of using artificial steroids that act like testosterone by adding muscle weight and increasing strength. While these drugs enhance performance, they are extremely dangerous because they can cause cancer, heart damage, strokes, and violent behavior.

In women, the ovaries secrete *estrogen* and *progesterone*, two hormones that balance each other in the body. Both hormones are important in the development of secondary sex characteristics such as enlarged breasts and widened hips. They also regulate women's menstrual and reproductive cycles. Progesterone is essential during pregnancy, not only because it ensures the normal functioning of the mother's placenta, but also because it passes into the developing fetus' circulatory system where it is converted into other useful hormones.

Thyroid gland The gland located just below the larynx in the neck that controls metabolism

Adrenal glands Two glands, located near the kidneys, that secrete epinephrine and norepinephrine, which activate the sympathetic nervous system

Gonads The two sex glands, called ovaries in females and testes in males

Section REVIEW

- The central nervous system consists of the brain and spinal cord.

- The peripheral nervous system encompasses all the nerves outside the central nervous system.

- The two major divisions of the peripheral nervous system are: the somatic nervous system (transmits commands to the voluntary skeletal muscles by way of the motor neurons and receives sensory information from the muscles and the skin by way of the sensory neurons) and the autonomic nervous system (controls movement of involuntary, nonskeletal muscles, such as the heart and lung muscles).

- The autonomic nervous system is divided into two separate parts: the sympathetic system, which activates the body's energy resources in threatening situations, and the parasympathetic system, which conserves and maintains the body's energy resources.

- The endocrine system is a network of glands throughout the body that manufactures and secretes hormones directly into the bloodstream.

2.3 The Brain

Imagine how Henry Molaison's life would have been different had he undergone medical treatment today rather than in the 1950s, when neuroscientists knew so little about the brain. One primary reason we now know so much more about brain function is that contemporary neuroscientists have the ability to eavesdrop on the brain without causing it harm (Moses & Stiles, 2002). In this section of the chapter, before exploring specific brain regions, let us examine the different technologies used to study the brain.

2.3a *Modern Technology Measures the Brain's Electrical Activity, Structure, Blood Flow, and Chemistry.*

Technological advances now allow researchers to use *brain-imaging techniques* that provide pictures—or scans—of this body organ. These techniques generate "maps" of the brains of living people by examining their electrical activity, structure, blood flow, and chemistry (Roth et al., 2008).

The most widely used technique is the **electroencephalograph (EEG)**, which records "waves" of electrical activity in the brain by using metal electrodes placed on a person's scalp (Roche-Labarbe et al., 2008). EEG measurement has provided researchers with invaluable information on brain functioning, especially in the areas of sleep, different states of awareness, and brain disease. The one drawback of the EEG is that it measures the overall electrical activity of many different areas of the brain at once, making it difficult to pinpoint the exact location of specific brain wave activity. However, although it is difficult to determine exactly *where* an electrical event is taking place in the brain, the EEG is very good at determining *when* it happens. The technological cousin of the EEG is the *magnetoencephalogram (MEG)*, which records magnetic fields instead of electrical activity.

A more revealing look at the functioning brain is obtained by the **computerized axial tomography (CAT) scan**, which takes thousands of X-ray photographs of the brain while the person lies very still on a table with her or his head in the middle of a doughnut-shaped ring. A computer combines these many X-ray images to construct a cross-sectional brain picture. CAT scans are particularly helpful in detecting brain abnormalities, such as swelling and enlargement of certain areas.

Another brain-imaging technique is **magnetic resonance imaging (MRI)**, which produces 3-dimensional images of the brain's soft tissues by detecting magnetic activity from nuclear particles in brain molecules. MRI provides greater accuracy in the diagnosis of diseases of the brain than does the CAT scan, and this has led to some ground-breaking discoveries. For example, as we will discuss more fully in Chapter 11, Section 11.2d, MRI researchers have found that there may be an association between enlarged ventricles (hollow, fluid-filled cavities) in the brain and schizophrenic disorders (Suddath et al., 1990).

Electroencephalograph (EEG) A brain-imaging technique that records "waves" of electrical activity in the brain using metal electrodes placed on a person's scalp.

Computerized axial tomography (CAT) scan A brain-imaging technique that combines thousands of X-ray brain photographs to construct a cross-sectional picture of the brain

Magnetic resonance imaging (MRI) A brain-imaging technique that produces three-dimensional images of the brain's soft tissues by detecting magnetic activity from nuclear particles in brain molecules

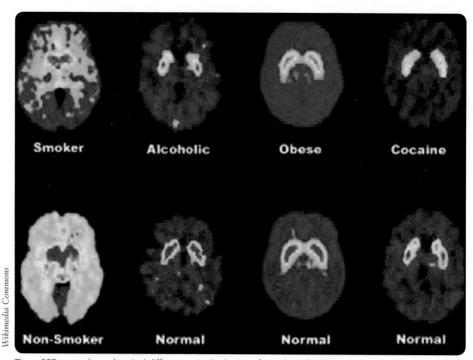

These PET scans show chemical differences in the brains of people with addiction disorders (top row) and non-addicts (bottom row). Addicts have fewer than average dopamine receptors in their brains, so that weaker dopamine signals are sent between cells.

Positron emission tomography (PET) scan A brain-imaging technique that measures, over several minutes, the average amount of neural activity in different brain regions by showing each region's consumption of the sugar glucose, the brain's chemical fuel

Unlike CAT or MRI scans, which document the brain's structure, the **positron emission tomography (PET) scan** measures the amount of brain *activity*. Neural activity in different brain regions is measured by showing each region's consumption of glucose, a sugar that is the brain's chemical fuel. These readings are obtained by injecting a person with a safe level of radioactive glucose liquid and then monitoring its consumption in the brain. PET scans can reveal which parts of the brain are most active in such tasks as talking or listening to others, reading, listening to music, and solving math problems. Thus, this technique has been especially useful in revealing localization of brain function.

One disadvantage of the PET scan is that the picture of brain activity it provides is an average of the activity that occurs over several minutes. Another disadvantage is that it exposes people to small amounts of radioactivity, thus making extensive scanning somewhat risky. A newer technology, called **functional magnetic resonance imaging (fMRI)**, does not suffer from these drawbacks (Chen et al., 2007). It can produce a picture of neural activity averaged over seconds, not minutes; and it measures fluctuations in naturally occurring blood oxygen levels, not fluctuations in ingested radioactive glucose. The images produced by fMRI scans are also much sharper than those in PET scans; thus, they can be used to identify much smaller brain structures.

Functional magnetic resonance imaging (fMRI) A brain-imaging technique that measures, over a few seconds, the average neural activity in different brain regions by showing fluctuations in blood oxygen levels

As you see, these brain-imaging techniques are providing researchers with the means to make new discoveries about our most important body organ. Improvements in neuroscientists' ability to "peek" into the brain provide them with the necessary information to better prevent the type of surgical calamity experienced by Henry Molaison. However, the ability to measure the workings of the human brain is also raising growing concerns about how such technology might be abused by tapping into people's private thoughts without their consent. Closer Look 2-1 introduces the new field of *neuroethics*.

Is Privacy an Issue in Brain Imaging?

Would you be concerned if brain-imaging techniques could "read" people's minds and determine their sexual orientation, their degree of racial prejudice, or their truthfulness when answering specific questions? Is this possibility purely science fiction? Maybe not. Brain-imaging studies have found that certain areas of the brain are more active when people lie (Lee et al., 2002; Priori et al., 2008). Scientists are now trying to determine whether this knowledge can be used to produce an effective lie detector that would outperform the conventional polygraph machine (see Chapter 9, Closer Look 9-1).

Another brain-imaging study was able to detect unconscious racism among White Americans (O'Connor et al., 2000). In this research, White college students who had previously stated that they held no conscious racial prejudice toward Blacks were shown photos of familiar or unfamiliar Black and White faces. When viewing unfamiliar Black faces as compared to unfamiliar White faces, brain scans indicated greater activation of the amygdala, the brain area associated with fear and emotional learning. No heightened amygdala activity occurred when viewing familiar Black faces. These findings suggest that, despite not consciously reporting any negative attitudes toward African Americans, these White students perhaps unknowingly felt some level of fear and negativity toward Black people. Similar findings have also been obtained from Black students when they viewed photos of White faces (Hart et al., 2000). One possible implication of these studies is that brain-imaging technology may one day be able to peel back the surface of human thought and emotion and reveal "unconscious racism."

Are there dangers in employing such methods? Some experts think so. Privacy issues raised by brain imaging are becoming an important topic of discussion in the new field of *neuroethics* (Coch, 2007). Arthur Caplan, director of the University of Pennsylvania's Center for Bioethics, states that the need to discuss brain privacy is urgent (C. Goldberg, 2003): "If you were to ask me what the ethical hot potato of this coming century is, I'd say

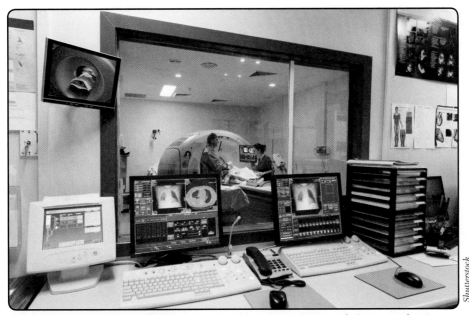

Modern brain-imaging technology provides important information on how specific brain areas function. Although such advances will help neurosurgeons avoid the mistakes made during Henry Molasion's brain surgery in 1953, what are some of the ethical concerns raised by these technological advances?

it's new knowledge of the brain, its structure and function." Although the current media focus is on genetic privacy, Caplan contends that most people feel a greater need for privacy in regard to their brains than their genes, because brain activity is more associated with the immediate "here and now" than is genetic functioning.

Today, the automobile-sized MRI machines used to create brain images cost approximately $3 million and thus are much too expensive to be used by most nonscientists or nonmedical personnel. However, certain well-funded marketing research firms are using these machines to try to determine consumers' unconscious preferences for certain products. There have also been recent scientific advances that increase the likelihood that brain imaging technology will one day be able to detect brain activity from afar. For example, scientists have already demonstrated the ability to remotely detect brain activity from a distance of about three feet (Farahany, 2008). While scientific limitations to usable remote brain scanning still exist, it is very possible that these will be overcome in the not-too-distant future.

Does it concern you that police officers and airport security personnel may one day be remotely examining your brain activity so that they better understand your current emotional and cognitive states? Would this be an unacceptable invasion of your privacy, or just the price you would be willing to pay to live in a more safe and secure world? If the brain privacy debate follows the same path as the genetic privacy debate, new laws may soon be proposed to protect the public from the misuse of this fascinating and powerful new technology.

2.3b *Three Major Brain Regions Are the Hindbrain, Midbrain, and Forebrain.*

The names for the three major brain regions—*hindbrain, midbrain,* and *forebrain*—come from their physical arrangement in the developing human embryo. In the embryo, the central nervous system begins its development as a long, hollow *neural tube,* but within five weeks, this tubular cluster of neurons changes its shape into these three distinct regions (see Figure 2-6). The forebrain is the farthest forward, near where the face will develop. The midbrain comes next, just above the hindbrain, which is near the back of what will become the neck. The remainder of the neural tube develops into the spinal cord. This section of the chapter first briefly describes each of these major brain regions and then focuses attention on that part of the forebrain that dominates the rest of the brain, namely, the *cerebral cortex.*

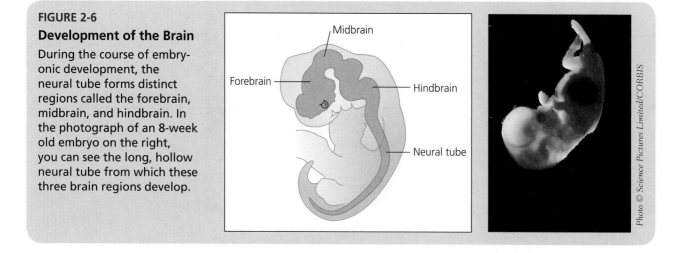

FIGURE 2-6

Development of the Brain

During the course of embryonic development, the neural tube forms distinct regions called the forebrain, midbrain, and hindbrain. In the photograph of an 8-week old embryo on the right, you can see the long, hollow neural tube from which these three brain regions develop.

Photo © Science Pictures Limited/CORBIS

You have probably heard the following statement many times: "We use only 10 percent of our brains." Based on what you have learned about brain functioning, do you think this statement is true? In pondering the merits of this expression, consider another type of human functioning: athletic performance. Do athletes use only 10 percent of their muscles when competing?

The Hindbrain

Figure 2-7 shows that directly above the spinal cord is the **hindbrain**, consisting of the medulla, pons, and cerebellum (Mendoza & Foundas, 2008). The **medulla**, which looks like a swelling at the top of the spinal cord, controls our breathing, heart rate, swallowing, and digestion. It also allows us to maintain an upright posture. Besides controlling these functions, the medulla is the place in the brain where the nerves from the left side of our body cross over to the right side of the brain and the nerves from the right side of our body cross over to the left side of the brain. (Yes! We are cross-wired!) The **pons**, located just above the medulla, is concerned with sleep and arousal. Behind the medulla and pons is the **cerebellum** (meaning *little brain*), which not only is important in the regulation and coordination of body movement but also appears to play a role in learning. Damage to this area of the brain results in jerky and poorly coordinated muscle functioning, and also causes severe disturbances in balance, gait, speech, and the control of eye movement. The cerebellum is also one of the first brain structures affected by alcohol, which explains why intoxicated individuals are uncoordinated and have slurred speech.

Hindbrain Region of the brain above the spinal cord that contains the medulla, the pons, and the cerebellum

Medulla A part of the hindbrain that controls breathing, heart rate, swallowing, and digestion, and allows us to maintain an upright posture

Pons A part of the hindbrain that is concerned with sleep and arousal

Cerebellum A part of the hindbrain that regulates and coordinates basic motor activities and may also play a role in learning

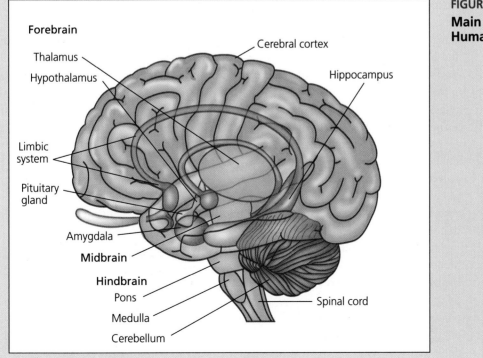

FIGURE 2-7

Main Parts of the Human Brain

Forebrain
- Thalamus
- Hypothalamus
- Cerebral cortex
- Hippocampus
- Limbic system
- Pituitary gland
- Amygdala

Midbrain

Hindbrain
- Pons
- Medulla
- Cerebellum
- Spinal cord

The Midbrain

Midbrain The region of the brain above the hindbrain that contains the reticular formation

Reticular formation A part of the midbrain involved in the regulation and maintenance of consciousness

The **midbrain** (see Figure 2-7) is a small neural area located above the hindbrain. The most important structure in the midbrain is the **reticular formation**, a finger-shaped network of neurons involved in the regulation and maintenance of consciousness, including sleep. Actually, the reticular formation extends into the hindbrain, where it makes up a portion of the pons. When you are startled by a loud noise, it is the reticular formation that causes your heightened state of arousal. Likewise, when you sleep through familiar sounds in your surroundings, it again is the reticular formation that filters out these background noises. The reticular formation's ability to respond to incoming stimuli can be shut down. This is exactly the function of anesthetics used in surgery. *Anesthetics* are chemicals that prevent certain "locks" from being opened at the synaptic level. Also, if the reticular formation is damaged, a permanent coma can result.

The Forebrain

Forebrain Region of the brain above the midbrain that contains the thalamus, the hypothalamus, and the limbic system

Thalamus A part of the forebrain that is the brain's sensory relay station, sending messages from the senses to higher parts of the brain

Hypothalamus A part of the forebrain involved in regulating basic biological processes, such as eating, drinking, sexual activity, emotion, and a stable body temperature

As we move up past the first two brain regions, we come to the most interesting—and the most evolutionarily recent—region, namely, the **forebrain**. The forebrain allows us to engage in complex emotional reactions, cognitive processes, and movement patterns. It consists of such important structures as the *thalamus, hypothalamus,* and *limbic system*. On top of these structures is the *cerebral cortex*, the most complex part of the brain.

The **thalamus**, looking like a joined pair of eggs, is the brain's sensory relay station, sorting and sending messages from the eyes, ears, tongue, and skin to the cerebral cortex. The thalamus, working closely with the reticular formation, also plays an important role in the control of sleep and wakefulness.

The **hypothalamus** (*hypo* means "beneath") is located under the thalamus and is less than one-tenth its size (less than 1 cubic centimeter). One of its most important functions is acting as the control center of the autonomic nervous system, meaning that it controls that part of the nervous system governing the involuntary muscles (see Section 2.2a). As the control center, the hypothalamus ensures that the autonomic nervous system provides *homeostasis*, which is the maintenance of a constant internal body state. Your relatively steady body temperature, blood pressure, and body fluid volume are a result of the hypothalamus coordinating the autonomic regulatory activities of the body. Another important function of the hypothalamus is providing a critical link between the central nervous system and the endocrine system. As discussed in Section 2.2c, by exercising control over the release of hormones from the endocrine system's pituitary gland, the hypothalamus influences hormone release by other glands throughout the body. Last, but not least, this small brain structure also regulates several motivated behaviors, including eating, drinking, and sexual activity. In addition, it plays an important role in the experience of emotion, stress, and pleasurable reward; and it is strongly affected by certain addictive drugs, such as cocaine. All in all, this is one cubic centimeter of the brain that you cannot function without.

Limbic system A part of the forebrain consisting of structures that influence fear and aggression (amygdala) and the acquisition and consolidation of new information in memory (hippocampus)

A series of interrelated doughnut-shaped neural structures, located at the border of the brain's older parts and the soon-to-be-discussed *cerebral cortex*, is the **limbic system**. Its two main structures are the *amygdala* and *hippocampus*. The amygdala (which means "almond" in Greek) consists of two almond-shaped neural clusters that influence fear and aggression. Damage to—or electrical stimulation of—this part of the brain can result in either intense fear or uncontrollable rage, depending on what part of the amygdala is activated (Fanselow & Poulos, 2005).

Such damage can also short-circuit these feelings. For example, monkeys with destroyed amygdalas lose their fear of natural predators. The other limbic structure, the hippocampus, is central in the acquisition and consolidation of new information in memory (Suchan et al., 2008). This is exactly the part of the brain that was surgically removed in Henry Molaison to control his seizures, leaving him unable to form new memories. Although acquiring new memories is no longer possible with such damage, acquisition of *implicit* memories—those outside of conscious awareness—is not affected (Cohen et al., 1985). Thus, Henry was able to learn new skills, such as reading mirror writing or solving mazes and puzzles—but he was not able to remember having done so!

As you have learned, many vital functions are controlled and regulated by the hindbrain, midbrain, and selected parts of the forebrain. Yet, despite the complexity of these different brain areas, what sets us apart from all other animals and makes us "humans" is the forebrain structure known as the *cerebral cortex*, which is the subject of Section 2.3c.

INFO-BIT Would it surprise you to learn that about 200,000 neurons in your brain die each day of your life? It's true. Fortunately, because you were born with so many neurons and because some neurons are replenished, you will lose only about 6 percent of your original supply over 80 years (Dowling, 1992).

2.3c   *The Cerebral Cortex Is the Crowning Achievement of Human Evolution.*

There are five different primate groups: prosimians, new-world monkeys, old-world monkeys, apes, and hominids. *Homo sapiens* (or humans) are the only surviving species of the hominid line (Tattersall, 2007). Today, our nearest living relatives are the great apes, which include chimpanzees, bonobos, gorillas, and orangutans. According to existing fossil records, hominids and apes diverged, 6–10 million years ago, in their evolutionary lineage when hominids became bipedal—that is, developed the habit of walking on two legs (Lemonick & Dorfman, 2002). The evolved ability of our hominid ancestors to walk erect was an important environmental adaptation because the upright posture allowed them to explore a much larger expanse of territory and secure many new resources.

Besides the ability to walk erect, the second important adaptation in the evolution of the human species was the increase in brain size (Eccles, 1989). When scientists first studied the evolution of the human brain, they assumed that brain size was closely related to intellectual capacity. However, this assumption quickly ran into problems (Harvey & Krebs, 1990). First, although humans believed themselves to be the most intelligent of all creatures, their brains of about 1,350 grams weighed far less than those of less intelligent species, such as elephants (8,000 grams). Second, adult human brains vary between 1,000 and 2,000 grams, but there is no indication that the "heavy brainers" are more intelligent than the "light brainers." Another approach was to examine brain weight as a percentage of total body weight. Although this formula

Shutterstock

Humans (*Homo sapiens*) are the only surviving species of the hominids. Around 8 million years ago, hominids began walking on two legs and diverged from gorillas, bonobos, orangutans, and chimpanzees in their evolutionary lineage. Why was walking upright an important evolutionary adaptation?

resulted in humans leaping ahead of elephants (2.33 percent versus 0.20 percent), they were now outdistanced by the shrew (3.33 percent), which is a mouse-sized mammal related to the mole.

Instead of comparing brain weight, researchers began to compare the evolution of different brain regions. Of all the brain regions studied, the most dramatic differences between humans and other animals can be seen in the relative sizes of the brain stem—which includes the hindbrain and midbrain—and the cerebral cortex. As previously discussed, the brain stem regulates basic life processes, such as heart rate, respiration, digestion, and sleep. In contrast, the **cerebral cortex**, located in the uppermost portion of the forebrain, is the "thinking" center of the brain, coordinating and integrating all other brain areas into a fully functioning unit. Its name is derived from two Latin words—*cerebrum*, meaning "brain," and *cortex*, meaning "bark." Basically, the cerebral cortex is the part of the brain that looks like the bark of a tree.

The surface of the cerebral cortex has a gray appearance because it primarily contains gray nerve cell bodies and unmyelinated fibers. Although it is only one-eighth of an inch thick, this densely packed system of interneurons is mostly responsible for our ability to plan, reason, remember, speak, and analyze ourselves. Right below this thin layer of *gray matter* is *white matter*, consisting mostly of the axons of the cortical neurons (Seldon, 2005). They appear white because the axons are covered and insulated by the white myelin sheath discussed in Section 2.1b.

As you can see in Figure 2-7, the cortex of humans has a great number of *convolutions* (folds), allowing a greater volume of it to fit into the skull cavity. Indeed, if you were able to unfold the cortex, it would cover four sheets of typing paper. In comparison, a chimpanzee's flattened cortex would cover only one sheet, a monkey's would cover a postcard, and a rat's would cover a postage stamp (Calvin, 1996). The relative sizes of the cerebral cortex and brain stem of species with different evolutionary ages indicate that most of the growth has occurred in the cerebral cortex (Parker et al., 2000). Not only do humans have a larger cerebral cortex than other species, but also a human's cerebral cortex has a great deal more convolutions. About 90 percent of our cerebral cortex evolved relatively recently (Kaas, 2008).

Cerebral cortex The largest structure in the forebrain; largely responsible for higher-order mental processes

INFO-BIT   Mammals are about ten times brainier than reptiles and amphibians. Two orders of mammals have significantly larger brains than the rest: primates and toothed whales. Among the primates, the brain of a human is three times bigger than that of an ape of the same body size (Lewin, 1993).

As the size of the cerebral cortex increased in our hominid ancestors, the brain required more oxygen to keep it alive. By examining the imprint left by the brain's blood vessels on the inside surface of our ancestors' fossilized skulls, paleontologists have been able to observe the evolution of this blood supply to the brain. What they discovered was a dramatic increase in the number of blood vessels supplying oxygen to the brain from our early hominid ancestors to modern-day *Homo sapiens*. As the number of oxygen-delivering blood vessels increased, our ancestors exhibited increased brain growth, which in turn required even more oxygen to be carried by the blood to the brain. This cycle continued, and today we have large brains with a complex and very dense network of surrounding blood vessels.

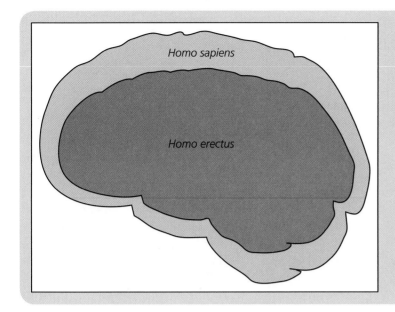

FIGURE 2-8

The Hominid Brain

Based on molded casts of the inside surface of fossilized skulls, scientists are able to compare the size and shape of our modern-day brains (Homo sapiens) with those of Homo erectus, a hominid that became extinct about 300,000 years ago.

Figure 2-8 compares the size and shape of the brain of *Homo erectus*, a hominid that became extinct about 300,000 years ago, with the modern human brain (Parker et al., 2000). Although 20 percent smaller than our brains, the *erectus* brain has the characteristic football shape found in the more recent hominids (Neanderthals and *Homo sapiens*). This modern look was primarily caused by an expansion of two regions of the cerebral cortex: the *occipital lobe* at the back of the brain and the *frontal lobe* at the front of the brain (see Section 2.3d). Evolutionary scientists believe that the expansion of these two brain lobes of the cortex was associated with our hominid ancestors' increasing reliance on sight and complex thinking to survive in their environment. The football shape of the modern human brain has a more bloated look than the *erectus* brain, largely due to the evolutionary expansion of the parietal lobe, which, among other things, is important in perceiving the spatial layout of the environment and effectively moving through it (Joseph, 2000).

2.3d The Cerebral Cortex Consists of Specialized Regions, or Lobes.

The cerebral cortex is divided into two rounded halves, called the **cerebral hemispheres**. These hemispheres are connected at the bottom by the **corpus callosum**, a thick band of over 200 million white nerve fibers that transmit information between the two hemispheres (Figure 2-9). As mentioned earlier, our brain is cross-wired, meaning that the right hemisphere controls movement and feeling of the left side of the body and the left hemisphere controls the right side of the body.

Both hemispheres can be divided into four major sections called *lobes*: the frontal, parietal, temporal, and occipital (see Figure 2-10). Thus, you have a right and a left lobe of each of these hemispheric divisions. These lobes are not distinct, independent parts of the cortex but are convenient regions, instead, named for the bones of the skull covering them.

The **occipital lobes**, located at the back of the cerebral hemispheres, are the visual regions of the brain. Here, we experience shapes, color, and motion in our world. Damage to the occipital lobes can cause blindness, even if our eyes and optic nerves are healthy. The **parietal lobes**, situated in front of the occipital lobes, are

I was taught that the human brain was the crown glory of evolution so far, but I think it's a very poor scheme for survival.

—Kurt Vonnegut, Jr., science fiction author, 1922–2007

What made this brain of mine, do you think? Not the need to move my limbs; for a rat with half my brain moves as well as I.

—George Bernard Shaw, Irish dramatist and socialist, 1856–1950

Cerebral hemispheres The two main parts of the cerebral cortex: the left and right hemispheres

Corpus callosum A thick band of nerve fibers connecting the right and left cerebral hemispheres that transmits information between them

Occipital lobes One of the four major sections of the cerebral cortex, located at the back of each cerebral hemisphere and primarily responsible for visual processing

Parietal lobes One of the four major sections of the cerebral cortex, situated in front of the optical lobe in each cerebral hemisphere and involved in touch sensation and in monitoring the body's position in space

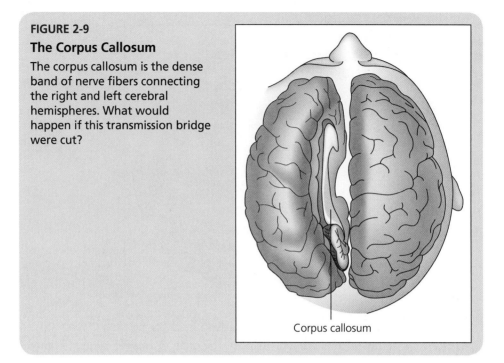

FIGURE 2-9

The Corpus Callosum

The corpus callosum is the dense band of nerve fibers connecting the right and left cerebral hemispheres. What would happen if this transmission bridge were cut?

Corpus callosum

Temporal lobes One of the four major sections of the cerebral cortex, located below the parietal lobe and near the temple in each cerebral hemisphere; important in audition and language

Frontal lobes One of the four major sections of the cerebral cortex, situated in the front of each cerebral hemisphere and behind the forehead; involved in the coordination of movement and higher mental processes

involved in touch sensation and in the monitoring of the body's position in space. Damage to these brain regions can destroy people's sense of touch, making it impossible for them to feel objects placed in their hands. The **temporal lobes** are located below the parietal lobes, near the temples (hence, the name). These regions of the cerebral hemispheres are important in audition (hearing) and language. Damage to what is called *Wernicke's area* in the left temporal lobe can cause difficulty understanding what words and sentences mean. People with such damage may speak smoothly and expressively, but their sentences consist merely of "word salad," which is meaningless words strung together. Finally, the largest lobes in the human brain are the **frontal lobes**, which are situated in the front of the cerebral hemispheres, just behind the forehead. These regions of the cerebral cortex are involved in the coordination of movement and higher mental processes, such as planning, social skills, and abstract thinking (Goldberg, 2001).

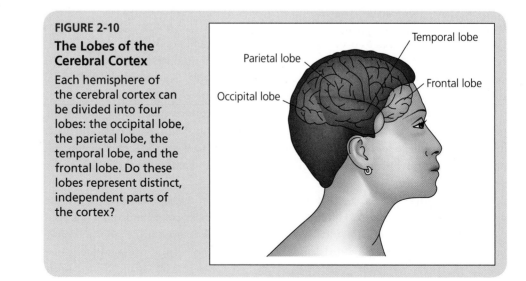

FIGURE 2-10

The Lobes of the Cerebral Cortex

Each hemisphere of the cerebral cortex can be divided into four lobes: the occipital lobe, the parietal lobe, the temporal lobe, and the frontal lobe. Do these lobes represent distinct, independent parts of the cortex?

Parietal lobe

Temporal lobe

Occipital lobe

Frontal lobe

Damage to the frontal lobes can result in dramatic personality changes, as was first discovered in 1848 when a Vermont railroad worker named Phineas Gage suffered severe damage to this area of his brain. While using an iron tamping rod to pack gunpowder into a boulder, Gage accidentally ignited the gunpowder, rocketing the tamping rod up into his left cheek, through the frontal lobe of his brain, and out the top of his head. Unbelievably, Gage survived this accident and was pronounced cured in less than two months. Yet, despite his outward recovery, Gage no longer possessed the same personality. Before the accident, he was a friendly, popular, hardworking, and emotionally mature adult. Following the accident, he was irresponsible, disrespectful, profane, and unable to control his own impulses. The sort of dramatic alteration seen in Gage's personality is common among people with frontal lobe damage.

In later studies of patients with similar frontal damage, researchers have found that these patients not only tend to be unable to make sound decisions in their personal lives but also lack the ability to experience strong emotions (Shamay-Tsoory, 2007). Although these people might well have been warm, loving, considerate, and responsible individuals prior to their illness or accident, they are now uniformly cold, distant, inconsiderate, and irresponsible. Although these declines in reasoning and emotional abilities do not affect their basic attention, memory, intelligence, and language ability, these people are no longer who they once were.

This link between the frontal lobes and emotional expression was further explored in an interesting set of studies conducted by Richard Davidson and his colleagues (Henriques & Davidson, 1990; Tomarken et al., 1990). Testing both infants and adults, they found that the left frontal lobe governs more positive feelings, while the right frontal lobe controls more negative moods, even as early as 10 months of age. They also discovered that people with more active left frontal lobes tend to be happier and more cheerful, optimistic, sociable, and self-confident than those with more active right frontal lobes. Table 2-3 lists some of the effects of damage to the frontal lobes, as well as the other lobes.

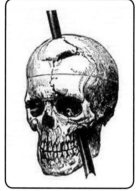

Wikimedia Commons

Using measurements of Phineas Gage's skull and modern neuroimaging techniques, Hanna Damasio and her coworkers (1994) reconstructed Gage's accident and the likely path taken by the metal tamping rod as it traveled through his brain.

2.3e The Right and Left Cerebral Hemispheres Function Differently.

Although the right and left hemispheres of the brain look very much alike, they make different contributions to our mental lives. The term **cerebral lateralization** refers to the degree to which the right or left hemisphere controls various cognitive and behavioral functions. Much of what we now know about these different functions has come about by studying people who have undergone a very rare and unique surgical procedure.

Cerebral lateralization The degree to which the right or left hemisphere controls various cognitive and behavior functions

TABLE 2-3 Possible Consequences of Damage to Different Areas of the Cerebral Cortex

Damaged Area	Effects
Occipital Lobes	Blindness
Parietal Lobes	Loss of touch sensation
Temporal Lobes	Inability to understand the meaning of words and sentences
Frontal Lobes	Dramatic personality changes; inability to plan and reason

BVT *Lab*

Visit www.BVTLab.com
to explore the student
resources available for
this chapter.

What would happen if the lobes of the cerebral cortex were healthy, but the right and left hemispheres could not transmit information to each other through the bundle of nerves that make up the corpus callosum? This was the question asked by psychologists Roger Sperry (1964, 1968) and Michael Gazzaniga (1970, 1989) when they began studying *split-brain* patients. In most cases, these were patients in whom the nerves of the corpus callosum had been surgically cut in a now-outmoded treatment for severe epileptic seizures. The technique was drastic, but the patients did improve rapidly; and their personality and behavior did not undergo major changes. However, now these patients had two brain hemispheres, acting more or less independently. What Sperry and Gazzaniga discovered was that these patients essentially had two minds.

The practical problem with a severed corpus callosum for split-brain patients is that sometimes one hemisphere will initiate a behavior that conflicts with the other hemisphere's intentions. Now, without a direct line of communication between the right and left hemispheres, each has its own separate and private sensations, perceptions, and impulses to act. For example, shortly following surgery, split-brain patients were often surprised to find that while dressing, their right hands (controlled by the left hemisphere) would reach for one article of clothing only to be brushed aside by their left hands (controlled by the right hemisphere), which had a different choice in mind. Despite these occasional hemispheric conflicts, split-brain patients generally behave normally (Iaccino, 1993).

When split-brain patients have been studied in the laboratory, certain interesting effects have provided scientists with a clearer understanding of the right and left hemispheres' abilities (Walsh, 2000). For example, in one experiment, Gazzaniga (1967) had split-brain participants stare at a dot while the word *HEART* was flashed across their visual field, with *HE* in the left visual field of each eye (which is processed by the right hemisphere) and *ART* in the right visual field (which is processed by the left hemisphere). The word could be seen for only about 150 milliseconds, providing insufficient time for the eyes to move and process the entire word in each hemisphere. Participants were asked first to report verbally what they saw and then to indicate with their left hands what they saw. When people with an intact corpus callosum performed this task, the right and left hemispheres passed the different information between them and the word *HEART* was seen and reported. Yet, with split-brain persons, something very interesting occurred. As depicted in Figure 2-11, split-brain individuals said they saw the word *ART*, but their left hands pointed to the word *HE*.

In another task in this same study, when the word *PENCIL* was flashed in their right visual field, the split-brain participants could easily read aloud the word—but not when it was flashed in their left visual field. What Gazzaniga discovered was that the right hemisphere did perceive and comprehend the word *PENCIL*, but the participants could not verbalize what they saw. However, using the left hand—which was controlled by the right hemisphere—the split-brain participants could easily pick out a pencil from a host of unseen objects.

Further research on the intact brain using brain-imaging techniques examined in greater detail the question of cerebral lateralization (Berninger et al., 2002; Federmeier & Kutas, 2002). Although generalizations should be made with caution, it appears that the right hemisphere is superior to the left in completing visual and spatial tasks, recognizing nonlinguistic sounds (such as music and environmental noise), identifying faces, and perceiving and expressing emotions (Ewbank et al., 2008). In contrast, the left hemisphere excels at using language, employing logic,

FIGURE 2-11   **Testing the Split Brain**

When the word HEART flashes across the visual field of split-brain patients, they verbally report seeing the portion of the word transmitted to their left hemispheres (ART). However, when asked to indicate with their left hands what they saw, they point to the portion of the word transmitted to their right hemispheres (HE).

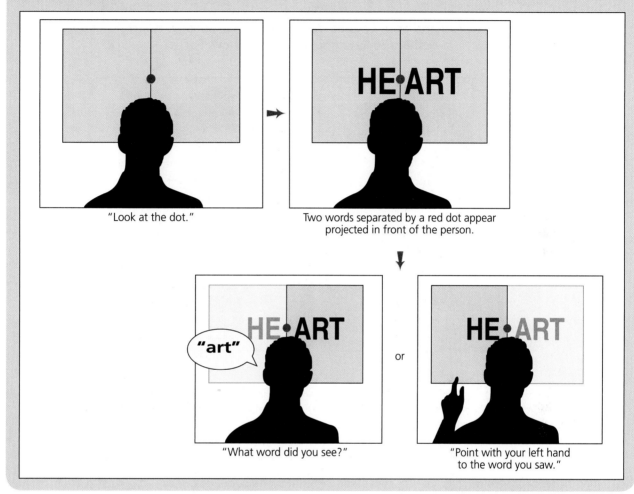

"Look at the dot."

Two words separated by a red dot appear projected in front of the person.

"What word did you see?"   or   "Point with your left hand to the word you saw."

and providing explanations for events (Cappelletti et al., 2008). Indeed, Gazzaniga (1988) describes the left hemisphere as being the brain's "interpreter," always striving to assign some rational meaning to behavior, even when there is none. Thus, when reading a map, listening to music, looking for a friend in a crowd, or laughing and crying at life's ups and downs, it's likely that there is more neural firing occurring in your right hemisphere than in your left hemisphere. By contrast, when talking on the phone, balancing your checkbook, or explaining to your parents why you need extra money for your spring vacation, your left hemisphere is probably the most active.

Having made the case that each of the two hemispheres appears to be more in control of certain functions than the other, it is important to add that these different specialized abilities are almost always relative differences, not absolute differences (Reuter-Lorenz & Miller, 1998). That is, whatever the task we work on, both hemispheres are activated to some extent (see Self-Discovery Questionnaire 2-1).

SELF-DISCOVERY 2-1
Questionnaire

Do You and Your Friends Use Different Patterns of Brain Activity to Recognize One Another's Faces?

Shutterstock

Which of these faces looks happier to you?

Like most people, you probably perceive the face in photo (b), with the smile on the left side, as the happier face. This is because most people more accurately recognize visual stimuli presented to the left visual field, which is processed first in the right hemisphere. Exercises like this one suggest that the right hemisphere generally plays a larger role in recognition of facial expression than the left hemisphere (Levy, Heller, Banich, & Burton, 1983). Of course, because virtually everybody has an intact corpus callosum, after a very brief interval, both hemispheres will share this information. Yet until they do, the right hemisphere will exert greater influence in recognizing facial features.

Is right-hemisphere dominance for facial expression true for everyone? No. Some people fail to show a left visual field advantage, while others actually demonstrate an advantage for the right visual field. To demonstrate individual differences in the lateralization of brain function, ask as many people as possible to complete this exercise. Are there any of them who do not show this right-hemisphere preference?

2.3f There May Be Sex Differences in Hemispheric Organization.

Try two simple tasks. First, mentally run through the alphabet and count as quickly as possible the number of letters, including the letter e, that when silently pronounced contain the sound "ee." Next, and again as quickly as possible, mentally count the number of letters that contain curves when they are printed as capitals. Writing or speaking out loud is not permitted.

Which task was harder for you: counting sounds or counting curves? Your answer may partly depend on whether you are a woman or a man (Hall et al., 2008). Women tend to be more accurate and slightly faster in the sound task, and men tend to do better in the shape task, which suggests that there are sex differences in verbal and spatial abilities (Kimura, 1992). Because language abilities are more associated with the left hemisphere and spatial abilities are more closely aligned with right-hemisphere functioning, researchers wondered whether women and men differ in hemispheric dominance.

If the cerebral hemispheres function somewhat differently in women and men, it is likely that these differences will be reflected in the effects of brain injury. Support for this reasoning comes from studies of damage to the left hemisphere following stroke. A stroke causes damage to the brain by starving it of needed oxygen when its blood supply is temporarily interrupted. Men are three times more likely than women to develop **aphasia**, which is the inability to recognize or express language (McGlone, 1978). Some studies suggest that the reason women are less susceptible to aphasia is that their brains are more *bilateralized* for language—that is, they are more likely than men to use both hemispheres for this cognitive function (Reuter-Lorenz & Miller, 1998). For instance, when women and men were asked to process and compare sounds, PET scans indicated that an area of the left hemisphere was activated in both sexes. However, in a majority of the women—but in none of the men—the same area in the right hemisphere was also activated (Shaywitz et al., 1995). This study's finding that women's language functions are less likely to be located solely in the left hemisphere of the brain (less lateralized) may explain why women experience fewer language deficits than men when their left hemispheres are damaged by stroke. It may also partly explain why women tend to be less adept at spatial tasks than men. Put simply, because the right hemisphere tends to control spatial functioning, and because women are more likely than men to also use part of this hemisphere for language functioning, this bilaterality in language function may result in less proficient processing of spatial tasks (Sanders et al., 2002). In assessing these possible sex differences, we need to keep in mind not only that they appear to be very small but also that the similarities in brain function between women and men far outweigh the differences (Rogers, 2001).

Aphasia The inability to recognize or express language as a result of damage to brain tissue, such as after a stroke

What might explain these differences? One possibility is that evolutionary pressures played a decisive role. (Levy, 1972). Because our species evolved with women being principally responsible for raising the young, verbal bilateralization may have given them a more developed communication system that fostered their survival. In contrast, because men have historically been more involved in the hunting and gathering of food and other resources, having male spatial functioning clearly separate from verbal functioning in the brain may also have benefited their survival. Although this different hemispheric arrangement between women and men may no longer provide any survival value for us, we still inherit and exhibit these biological differences because there is considerable "lag time" in the genetic changes that occur in a species when environmental changes occur.

Despite the fact that there is evidence of sex differences in brain organization, no one knows what these differences mean for the general abilities and behavior of women and men in their daily lives (Hoptman & Davidson, 1994). It is also true that culture profoundly shapes people's skills and interests. Consistent with *dynamic systems theory* (see Chapter 1, Section 1.2f), research finds that the different manner in which girls and boys are typically socialized often has an important impact on what specific abilities are nurtured. The greater verbal abilities of females today, for example, may have nothing at all to do with evolutionary factors and more to do with the fact that girls typically receive greater encouragement to talk during infancy and early childhood (Brody & Hall, 1993; Lewis & Weintraub, 1979). It is possible that this relatively high amount of verbal attention given to girls may foster greater elaboration of neural interconnections in certain areas of the brain.

2.3g Left-Brain and Right-Brain Descriptors of People Are Too Simplistic.

Beyond possible sex differences in cerebral lateralization, a number of popular writers claim that people can be identified as being "left-brainers" or "right-brainers." Books with such titles as *Educating the Right Brain* and *Drawing on the Right Side of the Brain* give advice on how to increase creative thinking by both tapping into unused right-brain potential and suppressing left-brain activity. Is this sound advice?

As previously discussed, the left hemisphere exerts a greater influence on verbal skills such as reading, writing, math, and logic, while the right hemisphere exercises greater control over nonverbal activities such as spatial tasks, music, art, and face recognition. Yet does this imply that some people are logical and scientific because they rely mostly on their left hemispheres ("left-brainers"), while others are creative and artistic because they mostly use their right hemispheres ("right-brainers")? Despite the simplistic appeal of this description of brain functioning, there is no sound evidence that individuals significantly differ in their sheer reliance on one hemisphere over the other (Springer & Deutsch, 1998). Books making such claims are based on the incorrect assumption that various cognitive functions are completely localized within the left and right hemispheres. Yet, what you have learned in this chapter is that while certain tasks may activate one hemisphere somewhat more than the other, both hemispheres are involved in the completion of any task a person might perform. This literal "side-by-side" exchange of information is the hallmark of the healthy brain (Gazzaniga, 2000). Thus, the ideas that a given person significantly relies more on one hemisphere than on the other and that you can train yourself to activate and suppress hemispheric functioning remain interesting, but wholly unconfirmed, hypotheses. Given this cautionary reminder, Figure 2-12 lists the different abilities generally associated with one hemisphere more than another, as well as their shared general functions.

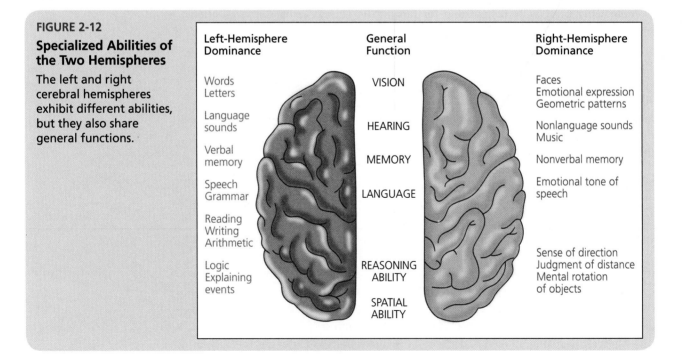

FIGURE 2-12

Specialized Abilities of the Two Hemispheres

The left and right cerebral hemispheres exhibit different abilities, but they also share general functions.

Left-Hemisphere Dominance	General Function	Right-Hemisphere Dominance
Words / Letters	VISION	Faces / Emotional expression / Geometric patterns
Language sounds	HEARING	Nonlanguage sounds / Music
Verbal memory	MEMORY	Nonverbal memory
Speech / Grammar	LANGUAGE	Emotional tone of speech
Reading / Writing / Arithmetic		
Logic / Explaining events	REASONING ABILITY	Sense of direction / Judgment of distance / Mental rotation of objects
	SPATIAL ABILITY	

2.3h The Brain Can Alter Its Neural Connections.

What happens when one part of the brain is severely damaged or destroyed? Are the cognitive functions associated with that brain area lost forever? The answers to these questions are partly being found by following the remarkable lives of children who have undergone a *hemispherectomy*—having one of their cerebral hemispheres surgically removed to control life-threatening epileptic seizures (Kossoff et al., 2003). Although this surgery may appear even more foolhardy than the procedure performed on Henry Molaison 60 years ago, we now know a great deal more about how the brain functions because of the advances made in neuroscience. Specifically, we understand that although normal functioning is not possible without a hippocampus, it is possible to live a relatively normal life following the loss of an entire cerebral hemisphere (Lettori et al., 2008). For example, in the case of hemispherectomy of the left cerebral hemisphere, although half the skull is now filled with nothing but cerebrospinal fluid, the only visible effects of the operation are often a slight limp, limited use of one of the hands and arms, no right peripheral vision in either eye, and some language deficits (Curtiss et al., 2001). In fact, brain scans indicate that the remaining healthy hemisphere takes over many of the functions of the removed hemisphere (Rossini & Pauri, 2000; Swerdlow, 1995).

The brain is wider than the sky.
—Emily Dickinson, U.S. poet, 1830–1886

This transferring of neural function is probably due to the accelerated growth of dendrites that provide the connections between neurons. Just like other children with normal brains, these children's production of dendrites is at a peak level from about age 4 to age 10. Besides neural connections being caused by inherited growth patterns, they are also fostered by environmental challenges, which is exactly why children who undergo this procedure are pushed so hard during their weekly speech and language therapy sessions. As more connections are made among the billions of neurons in their remaining brain regions, the end result is a better-functioning brain. Indeed, children who have had one of their brain hemispheres removed have later earned college degrees and are currently leading successful and productive lives as adults (Battro, 2001; Vining et al., 1997).

The extraordinary recovery of these children from such a dramatic loss of brain tissue demonstrates what neuroscientists call **plasticity**—the remarkable flexibility of the brain to alter its neural connections (Bryck & Fisher, 2012). Through such *collateral growth* (Figure 2-13), branches from the axons of nearby healthy neurons grow into the pathways previously occupied by the axons of damaged neurons. The ability to transfer brain functions from one part of the brain to the other is highest in childhood, during the peak years of dendrite growth (Liegeois & Morgan, 2012). Yet, it is also true that limited transfer of function can occur in older adults when certain brain areas are destroyed by strokes or accidents. (See Self-Discovery Questionnaire 2-2.)

Plasticity The ability of the brain to alter its neural connections following damage

Journey of Discovery

After limbs have been amputated, amputees often feel excruciating pain in the area of their lost limb. How might the brain's plasticity play a role in this pain?

SELF-DISCOVERY 2-2
Questionnaire

How Can You Keep Your Brain Healthy as You Age?

Scientists once believed that brain structures ceased any positive physical development by early adulthood. Yet, this thinking changed following a series of studies that suggested a very different developmental pattern. In this research, rats with an age equivalent to that of 75 human years were moved from the impoverished physical environment in which they had lived all their lives (bare cage, simple food containers) to an enriched environment (spacious home, interesting playthings). By the time they reached the equivalent of 90 human years, these rats showed significant increases in brain growth and synaptic interconnections (Diamond, 1988). These findings, which mirror the results of studies with baby rats, adult monkeys, and other species, suggest that environmental enrichment significantly enhances brain functioning, even among the elderly (Gould, Reeves, Graziano, & Gross, 1999).

Today we know that the mature brain generates new neurons every day, especially in enriched environments. Research also indicates that older adults' brains can achieve a fairly substantial transfer of function after suffering strokes or brain damage due to accidents (Di Lazzaro et al., 2008). The lesson here is simple, yet profound: Exercising the brain at all stages of life increases its ability to adapt to and overcome life's challenges and hard knocks.

Neuroscientific research suggests the following lifelong strategies to maintain a healthy brain at any age:

1. *Avoid harmful substances.* Drug abuse and alcohol abuse damage brain cells.

2. *Exercise on a regular basis.* People who engage in strenuous physical activity throughout their lives are not only more likely to stay physically healthy but also more likely to maintain high cognitive functioning. Further, elderly adults who do not exercise can enhance their cognitive vitality by engaging in some form of aerobic fitness training. The type of exercise that has the greatest benefit for brain longevity is that requiring complex motor skills and focused attention, rather than the repetition of simple motor skills. Thus, playing tennis or soccer might be better for your brain than simply doing jumping jacks or running on a treadmill.

3. *Eat sensibly.* Dietary factors are associated with the incidence of stroke, which is the largest single cause of brain disabilities. Decrease the intake of saturated fat, and eat more fruits and vegetables. Overeating also harms the brain. Elderly adults who overeat—consume 2,100 to 6,000 calories a day—are twice as likely to have mild cognitive impairment as those who eat fewer than 1,500 calories daily.

Shutterstock

"Use it or lose it!" Staying mentally active by reading regularly or doing crossword puzzles keeps the brain strong.

4. *Get adequate sleep.* Sleep deprivation and interrupted sleep harms the brain and the body. The average length of sleep for North American and European adults today is less than 7.5 hours, about 20 percent lower than what it was a hundred years ago. Middle-aged and elderly adults who don't sleep well—waking up more than five times each hour—are more likely to have deposits of protein in their brain related to Alzheimer's disease.

5. *Challenge yourself mentally.* When it comes to the brain, the old adage "Use it or lose it" really does apply. Staying mentally active by reading regularly and learning new skills strengthens neural connections much like regular physical exercise strengthens the heart.

6. *Wear your seat belt and bike helmet.* Motor vehicle accidents account for up to half of all brain injuries. Head injury is the most common cause of death in bicycle crashes, accounting for 62 percent of all bicycle-related deaths.

Finally, advances in neuroscience also raise the possibility that in the not-so-distant future, drugs developed for treating brain disease could be prescribed for healthy people looking to enhance their cognitive performance (Fauber, 2004). For example, Alzheimer's drugs might be given to air traffic controllers or other workers in highly skilled jobs to improve attention and memory. Yet such possibilities raise serious ethical issues. Should we permit the use of memory enhancement drugs by healthy people? Would the use of such drugs be permissible by physicians who need to operate on patients at peak cognitive efficiency? Should we allow students to take these drugs to help them study for exams? What are the dangers in using drugs to enhance the brain's cognitive efficiency?

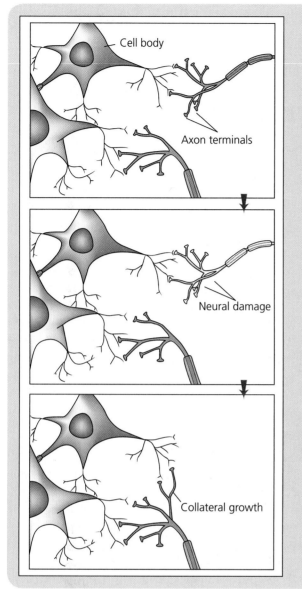

FIGURE 2-13

Collateral Growth

The brain's plasticity is demonstrated by the way in which neural connections are altered when neurons are damaged. This collateral growth is highest in childhood, when dendrite growth is at its peak.

- Some of the more commonly used technological devices to examine the brain's electrical activity, structure, blood flow, and chemistry are the electroencephalograph (EEG), computerized axial tomography (CAT), magnetic resonance imaging (MRI), positron emission tomography (PET), and functional magnetic resonance imaging (fMRI).

- There are three major brain regions: the hindbrain, located above the spinal cord and consisting of the medulla, pons, and cerebellum; the midbrain, which contains the reticular formation and is located above the hindbrain; and the forebrain, which consists of the thalamus, hypothalamus, limbic system, and cerebral cortex and is located above the midbrain.

- The cerebral cortex, which is divided into two rounded halves called the cerebral hemispheres, coordinates and integrates all other brain areas and is mostly responsible for our ability to plan, reason, remember, speak, and analyze ourselves.

- The left and right cerebral hemispheres are both divided into four major sections: frontal lobe, parietal lobe, temporal lobe, and occipital lobe.

- The right hemisphere is superior to the left in completing visual and spatial tasks, recognizing nonlinguistic sounds, identifying faces, and perceiving and expressing emotions.

- The left hemisphere excels at using language, employing logic, and providing explanations for events.

- Women's brains may be less lateralized—less likely to have various brain functions located in only one of the hemispheres—than men's brains.

- The brain can alter its neural connections to compensate for damage.

2.4 Genetic Influences on Behavior

Having examined the neural basis of human functioning, let us now turn our attention to the influence of genetics on human functioning. The primary question I want to address in this section of the chapter is how the visible and measurable traits (**phenotype**) of an organism reflect its underlying genetic composition (**genotype**).

Phenotype The visible and measurable traits of an organism

Genotype The underlying genetic composition of an organism

2.4a *The Basic Biochemical Unit of Inheritance Is the Gene.*

In 2003, geneticists completed the Human Genome Project, which identified 99.99 percent of the genetic material in humans. Because every person has a unique genetic pattern, researchers do not expect to ever reach 100 percent. *Genome* is the term used to describe the total genetic information in the cells of a particular species. The focus of the Human Genome Project was the **gene**, the biochemical unit of inheritance that provides instructions for how every activity in every cell of our body should be carried out.

Gene The basic biochemical unit of inheritance that is located on and transmitted by chromosomes

What sort of instructions do genes provide to the body's cells? Gene instructions concern the production of *proteins*, which regulate the body's physiological processes and the expression of phenotypic traits (for example, body build, intelligence, athletic ability). Proteins are the building blocks of life. As an example, consider how a gene instructs a liver cell to remove excess cholesterol from the bloodstream. The gene instructs the cell to make a particular protein (a receptor protein), and it is this protein that removes the cholesterol from the blood. The cholesterol molecules are then transported into the cell and processed by other proteins.

Genes are located on and transmitted by **chromosomes** that are threadlike structures found in every cell of the body, with the exception of red blood cells. All chromosomes contain strands of the molecule **deoxyribonucleic acid**, commonly known as DNA, which in turn contains thousands of different genes, located at fixed positions. Figure 2-14 depicts our genetic building blocks, breaking down the human body from its 100 trillion cells to the genes that provide them with instructions on protein production.

Chromosomes Threadlike structures carrying genetic information that are found in every cell of the body

Deoxyribonucleic acid (DNA) The complex molecular strands of a chromosome that contain thousands of different genes, located at fixed positions

One of the most surprising early findings of the Human Genome Project is that humans have only about 30,000 genes, not many more than a worm (18,000) and less than a rice plant (40,000). This discovery highlights the fact that human complexity is not solely due to the number of genes we possess, but is largely determined by the

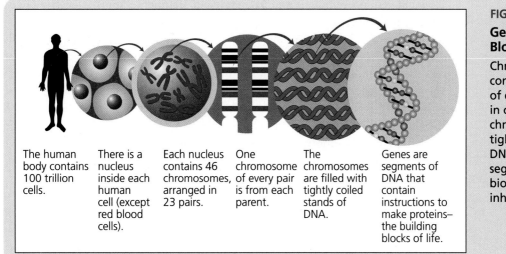

FIGURE 2-14

Genetic Building Blocks

Chromosomes are contained in the nucleus of each of the cells in our bodies. Each chromosome contains tightly coiled strands of DNA. Genes are DNA segments that are the biochemical units of inheritance.

The human body contains 100 trillion cells.

There is a nucleus inside each human cell (except red blood cells).

Each nucleus contains 46 chromosomes, arranged in 23 pairs.

One chromosome of every pair is from each parent.

The chromosomes are filled with tightly coiled stands of DNA.

Genes are segments of DNA that contain instructions to make proteins—the building blocks of life.

many different ways that genes interact with one another (Drayna, 2006; Johnston & Edwards, 2002). By understanding how genes function and interact with one another, scientists may soon be able to identify genes that cause cancer, diabetes, and heart disease.

When comparing the genes of different species, counting the sheer number of total genes is less important than determining how many genes the species share. This is because the structural similarity of DNA between species provides scientists with important clues concerning how closely related the species are on the evolutionary tree. For example, humans and chimpanzees share 98 percent of the same DNA structure, humans and gorillas share a bit less than 98 percent, and humans' and monkeys' DNA similarity is only about 90 percent. Coupled with the fossil record studies of these species, the DNA evidence indicates that monkeys diverged from humans much earlier in their evolutionary past than did chimps and gorillas.

Humans are unusual among primates because we have much less genetic variability within our species than do chimpanzees, gorillas, and other apes (Gagneux et al., 1999). These findings strongly suggest that not long ago in human evolution our ancestors experienced a severe reduction in their population due to disease, famine, or some other disaster. The best estimates are that this brush with extinction occurred about 70,000 years ago, with the number of early humans shrinking to as low as 2,000 (Schmid, 2008). The effective result of this massive population loss was that a large part of our within-species genetic variability was lost. Genetic testing of humans around the world indicates that the great majority of the existing overall genetic variation in humans is represented by individual diversity within populations, not across populations (Fish, 2002). This finding has important implications in understanding the concept of "race" as a distinguishing feature in the human population, a topic that we will examine in Section 2.4d.

All humans possess 99.9 percent of the same genes. This is why we have the capacity to do many of the same things, such as walking, talking, and engaging in abstract thought (Plomin & Crabbe, 2000). Despite this genetic similarity, there also is a great deal of genetic variation across individuals in that final one-tenth of 1 percent of genetic material. As you have already discovered in the Chapter 1, Section 1.2e discussion of the evolutionary process, the genetic makeup of organisms not only determines their ability to survive in their environment but also influences their ability to reproduce and pass their genes on to the next generation.

Sex chromosomes Threadlike structures carrying genetic information that are found in every cell of the body

How did you inherit your particular genotype? Putting it simply, each sperm cell of a human male and egg cell of a human female contains 23 chromosomes. Upon the union of your father's sperm and your mother's egg at conception, all body cells that developed from this new cell (called the *zygote*) contained 46 chromosomes, or 23 pairs. Each of these body cells contained your genetic blueprint, or genotype, with half the genetic material coming from each parent. Among the 23 chromosomal pairs, one pair, known as the **sex chromosomes**, determined your sex. You inherited an X chromosome from your mother and either an X or a Y chromosome from your father. XX pairings result in the embryo developing female physical characteristics, whereas XY pairings lead to male physical characteristics. Because it is only the father's sex chromosome that varies, it is your father's genetic contribution that determined your sex.

Fraternal twins Twins who develop from the union of two separate sperm and eggs; also known as *dizygotic twins*

Identical twins Twins who develop from the union of the same egg and sperm, and thus share exactly the same genotype; also known as *monozygotic twins*

Just as you share 50 percent of the same genes with each of your parents, you also share that same percentage with your brothers and sisters. This is true even for **fraternal twins** (also known as *dizygotic twins*), who develop in the womb from the union of two separate sperms and eggs. The exception to this rule, of course, is **identical twins** (also called *monozygotic twins*), who develop from the union of the same egg and sperm. Identical twins share exactly the same genotype. Although identical twins are identical genetically, they may not express these identical genes in identical ways. That is, their phenotype may not be identical. Environmental factors, such as stress and nutrition, can actually cause certain genes to become activated or deactivated, resulting in even identical twins not having the same *active* genetic makeup (Lytton & Gallagher, 2002). Thus, the interaction of genotype (our underlying genetic composition) with the environment can produce changes in our phenotype (our visible and measurable traits).

2.4b Both Heredity and Environment Can Influence Physical and Behavioral Traits.

Behavior genetics The study of how the genotype and the environment of an organism influence its behavior

The field of **behavior genetics** studies how the genotype and the environment of an organism influence its behavior (Sémon et al., 2005). One example of how heredity and environment can influence phenotype is obesity, a condition afflicting many adults (Thorpe & Day, 2008). In understanding obesity, overeating is certainly an important cause of weight gain, but some people can consume many calories without gaining a pound (Rodin, 1981). Research suggests that obesity is partly related to the number and size of fat cells in the body, with the number being determined by our genes and the size being determined by our eating habits (Grinker, 1982). When people overeat beyond their bodily needs, the number of fat cells does not increase, but the size of the fat cells does.

Adoption and twin studies indicate that heredity is an important factor in determining both how many fat cells you have and how efficiently you utilize your intake of calories (Bouchard et al., 1990; Stunkard et al., 1990). Some people are born with an overabundance of fat cells, while others are born with a tendency to burn excess calories by turning them into muscle tissue rather than fat. Thus, regardless of whether they are raised together or apart, identical twins—whose genes are the same—have virtually the same weight. In contrast, the weight of fraternal twins—whose genes are different—differs greatly. In addition, the body size of children adopted from birth resembles more the body size of their biological parents, who each provide 50 percent of the children's genes, than that of their adoptive parents. This example illustrates that both heredity and environment can influence a specific phenotypic characteristic, namely, body size. The nature of the gene-environment interaction is still not clearly understood. What is clear, however, is that neither genes nor environment alone can account for how we live our lives.

2.4c *Molecular Genetics Seeks to Identify Specific Genes That Influence Behavior.*

While behavior genetics has focused on determining the degree to which genes influence behavior, a relatively new area in the biological sciences is **molecular genetics**, which seeks to identify the *specific genes* that influence behavior. One hope is that discoveries in molecular genetics will provide cures for genetically influenced disorders. Many diseases are caused by *mutations*, which are chemical changes in the DNA sequence of a gene (Benet-Pagès et al., 2005).

Most research in molecular genetics has been conducted using nonhuman genomes, such as those of the fruit fly, the roundworm, and the laboratory mouse (Meikle et al., 2005). These animals, with simpler genetic construction, provide useful models for developing and testing the procedures needed for studying the much more complex human genome. The results of this work have already yielded valuable knowledge that has helped geneticists identify single genes associated with a number of diseases and age-related disorders, such as cystic fibrosis, colon cancer, and hearing loss. Research is also under way to discover the mechanisms for diseases caused by several genes or by single genes interacting with environmental factors (Ertekin-Taner et al., 2005). By identifying the genes and their proteins associated with disease susceptibility and the aging process, scientists will be better able to design more effective therapies and preventive measures. For example, researchers have identified a gene that prevents the regeneration of inner ear cells critical to hearing (Sage et al., 2005). If geneticists discover how to "turn off" this gene, they can potentially reverse hearing loss among the elderly. Investigators are also attempting to identify genes that play a role in various psychological disorders, learning disabilities, and other health problems such as diabetes and alcoholism.

Molecular genetics The subdiscipline in biology that studies the molecular structure and function of genes to determine how they influence behavior

Ethical Concerns Raised by Genetic Testing

Genetic tests can now determine the risk that people might have for specific diseases. The most common test is conducted on newborn infants to screen them for abnormal or missing gene products (Patenaude, 2005). Four million newborns undergo such testing each year in the United States. Genetic testing of fetuses in the mother's womb is also increasingly common, especially when there is a risk of bearing a child with genes associated with mental retardation or severe birth defects. Do you perceive any dangers that might result from such prenatal screening?

One danger is that these tests can easily determine the sex of a fetus. Parents in such countries as China and India—which place a much higher value on male babies than female babies—have used prenatal genetic testing to abort pregnancies involving undesirable female fetuses. Estimates are that millions of such sex-selective abortions have already been carried out, which will probably lead to future male-female population imbalances in these countries (Das Gupta & Mari Bhat, 1997).

Adult genetic testing also raises serious ethical issues (Gaivoronskaia & Solem, 2004). For example, if testing reveals that an individual has an inherited risk for colon cancer, early-onset Alzheimer's disease, or a specific psychological disorder, should family members be informed that they might be at risk? This question has generated concerns within the medical community regarding the conflict between the physician's ethical obligations to respect the privacy of genetic information versus the potential liabilities resulting from the physician's failure to notify at-risk relatives. The failure to warn family members about hereditary disease risks has already resulted in at least three lawsuits in the United States (Offit et al., 2004).

Cloning The process of making
a genetically identical organism
through nonsexual means

Another related concern involves the dangers in releasing genetic information to persons and organizations outside the family of those tested. For example, if a family has an inherited gene that makes them highly likely to develop a specific disease, this information could affect their future employability and insurability if it became public knowledge. That is, such results could be misused by employers and insurers, discriminating between those identified as low risk and high risk (Raithatha & Smith, 2004).

The Ethics of Cloning

Ethical concerns have also been raised about **cloning**, which is the process of making a genetically identical organism through nonsexual means. Actually, cloning refers to three very different procedures that have very different goals.

Embryo cloning is a medical technique that duplicates the process that nature uses to produce twins or triplets. One or more cells are removed from a fertilized embryo and encouraged to develop into duplicate embryos. This procedure has been performed for many years on different animal species, but only very limited experimentation has been done on humans.

Adult DNA cloning, or *reproductive cloning*, is a technique used to produce a duplicate of an existing animal. To date, this technique has been used to clone such mammals as mice, sheep, cats, cows, and horses. In reproductive cloning, the DNA from a female egg is removed and replaced with the DNA from a cell removed from an adult animal. Then the fertilized egg is implanted in a womb and allowed to develop into a new animal. Animal studies reveal that such cloning can produce severe genetic defects. For this reason alone, there are very serious ethical concerns about human cloning. Many countries have specifically outlawed this procedure.

Finally, *therapeutic cloning*, or *biomedical cloning*, is a procedure in which *stem cells*—which are immature cells from which all mature cells develop—are removed from a pre-embryo so that tissue or a whole organ can be produced. The goal of therapeutic cloning is to produce a healthy copy of a sick person's tissue or organ, and it is vastly superior to relying on organ transplants from other people (Civin et al., 2005). Although the ethical issues surrounding the use of stem cells are not as readily apparent as those involving human cloning, some people argue that embryonic stem cells represent a human life and that this life is destroyed in therapeutic cloning (Tsai, 2005). This is an ongoing debate that brings up the question of when life begins.

As you see, unlocking the mysteries of the human genome carries both great rewards and risks, as well as mind-boggling ethical concerns. In the coming years, the advances in molecular genetics and the controversies surrounding how to use this new knowledge will undoubtedly have a significant impact on our lives. Stay tuned.

2.4d *Controversies Surround Genetic Explanations of Certain Sex and Race Differences.*

For more than a century, there has been an ongoing debate in psychology and other sciences concerning whether certain cognitive and behavioral differences found between women and men, as well as those between different racial groups (see Chapter 8, Section 8.4c), are caused by genetic factors or life experiences (the old *nature-nurture debate*). In this text we will examine the research surrounding these group-based comparisons (for example, see Section 2.3f in this chapter). To help you better understand the complexities in the various debates concerning genetic determinants of group differences in thought and action, I want to introduce you to a few important concepts and issues.

What Is the Difference Between Sex and Gender?

The terms *sex* and *gender* are often used interchangeably. However, to better understand what it means to be female and male, a growing number of psychologists believe that distinctions should be made between these two concepts (Lippa, 2005). In this text, **sex** refers to the biological status of being female or male, and **gender** refers to the meanings that societies and individuals attach to being female and male. Put simply, sex is a matter of genetic construction, and gender is a matter of cultural construction (Yoder, 1999). Sex is something we *are*, whereas gender is something we *do* with the help and encouragement of others.

Sex The biological state of being female or male

Gender The meanings that societies and individuals attach to being female and male

People are often confused about the distinction between sex and gender because the two concepts are generally thought of as going together—that is, female equals feminine, and male equals masculine. Yet behaviors or interests considered masculine in one culture may be defined as feminine in others (Zinn et al., 2000). For instance, in certain North African societies, decorating and beautifying the face and body is a sign of masculinity, not femininity. Similarly, within cultures, beliefs about gender transform over time. For instance, in contemporary North American culture, it is now acceptable—even encouraged—for girls to participate in sports that were previously designated only for boys. Among adults, women are now much more actively involved in careers outside the household (a masculine domain), and men are more involved in child care (a feminine domain) than in previous generations. Gender is not fixed—it is constantly changing and being redefined.

Because sex is biologically based and gender is culturally based, when research finds that men and women actually behave differently, we often ask whether this difference is due to sex (biology) or to gender (culture). This is not an idle question. If someone labels the behavior in question a *sex difference*, the implication is that the cause of the difference is rooted in human biology rather than in social or cultural factors. In contrast, when people talk about *gender differences*, the implication is that these differences do not stem from biology but develop, instead, in the course of socialization as boys and girls learn about appropriate gender-based attitudes, roles, and behaviors.

As discussed in Section 2.4a, men and women differ biologically in a number of ways. The most basic sex difference is that males carry the chromosomal pattern XY, and females carry the pattern XX. This important difference at the chromosomal level produces differences in female and male anatomy and physical appearance. For instance, a newborn male has a penis and testicles, whereas a newborn female has a vagina and ovaries. At puberty, a male develops a prominent Adam's apple, while a female's breasts enlarge. Although the changes associated with puberty occur well after birth, no one would seriously argue that boys have been taught how to grow an Adam's apple or that girls learn how to grow breasts. These particular differences are due to biological factors—that is, they are sex differences and are not due to cultural experience.

Beyond these identifiable biological differences in chromosome pattern and anatomy, it is extremely difficult, if not impossible, to currently conclude that differences in the way women and men think, feel, and act are clearly due to sex or gender. As already discussed, psychologists with a biological or evolutionary orientation emphasize biological factors in explaining such differences, whereas psychologists with a sociocultural orientation weigh in with cultural explanations. Yet the point that many psychologists often make when the issue of genetics is discussed is that even in those instances when genetics influences behavioral differences between men and women, these biologically based differences can be greatly increased or decreased due to social forces.

How great are the differences between women and men in their psychological functioning? This is an issue we will address throughout this text. As a preliminary answer, I can tell you that research conducted over the past 30 years indicates there are many more similarities than differences. Across a wide variety of cognitive skills, psychological motives, and social behaviors, men and women do not differ from one another. Thus, despite cultural stereotypes to the contrary, women and men are remarkably alike in much of their psychological functioning. Reflecting these scientific findings, in this text I do not use the misleading term *opposite sex* when comparing one sex with the other but instead use the more appropriate term *other sex*.

Does Race Tell Us Anything Useful about How People Differ Genetically?

The *Oxford English Dictionary* defines race as "a group of persons connected by a common descent; a subdivision of species." Consistent with this definition, many people believe that Caucasians, Blacks, Asians, and Hispanics make up biologically distinct races. Often underlying this common belief in race categorization is the assumption that greater genetic similarity exists among the members of each race than between the races. However, are two people categorized as Black more genetically similar than a Black person and an Asian person, or a Caucasian person and a Hispanic person?

Analysis of fossilized skull fragments found in Ethiopia, a country in eastern Africa, has led scientists to estimate that the very first modern-looking human beings emerged about 195,000 years ago (McDougall et al., 2005). This research, coupled with fossil evidence from other scientists and genetic analysis of contemporary human populations throughout the world, strongly suggests that it was these first modern *Homo sapiens* in eastern Africa who eventually populated the rest of the planet (Stringer, 2003). Thus, all humans are related, and our common ancestors came from Africa. What then is the biological significance of race?

When early humans migrated to different areas of the planet, they often encountered physical environments vastly different from those in eastern Africa. Over the course of thousands of generations, human populations that were geographically separated from one another gradually began to differ in their physical appearance due to the effects of natural selection. For example, the dark skin of early humans in Africa offered protection against the intense ultraviolet light in the region. Too much ultraviolet light penetrating the skin not only causes skin cancer but also, more importantly, breaks down folic acid in the body, which can cause anemia and deadly birth defects. Thus, in this region of the world—and in other areas close to the equator—darker-skinned humans were better adapted to their surroundings and more likely to produce healthy offspring than those with light skin. However, those humans who had migrated to northern Europe and northern North America lived in parts of the world with much less sunlight. In these new surroundings, they needed much lighter skin in order to take in more ultraviolet light for the production of vitamin D, which is essential for absorbing calcium to build strong bones and teeth. Here, light skin provided an advantage over dark skin (Jablonski, 1998). Lighter-skinned humans produced more vitamin D than those with darker skin, and they were ultimately more successful in surviving and reproducing.

Also due to natural selection, humans who migrated to very cold climates gradually became shorter and more round, because this body type lost less heat and thus was better adapted to the frigid environment. In very hot climates, taller, thinner body frames were advantageous because they dispersed heat more effectively so that the body stayed cooler. Large, circular nostrils and broad noses also helped disperse extra heat among people living

Shutterstock

These three individuals identify themselves as Asian, Black, and Caucasian, respectively. Genetic studies reveal that these three persons may be more similar to one another genetically than to many members of their own "race."

in hot climates, while smaller, noncircular nostrils and more projecting noses helped warm the incoming air for people living in cold climates.

The superficial physical differences resulting from this migration of early humans to different world regions are what many of us now rely on when designating a person's race. Yet almost all anthropologists and many geneticists agree that the concept of race is purely a social construct and has very little to do with who is actually genetically similar to whom (Smedley & Smedley, 2005). For example, DNA research demonstrates that genetically, all humans—regardless of skin color, facial features, and other surface distinctions—are basically identical. Any person's race accounts for less than one-fourth of 1 percent of her or his genetic makeup (Ossorio & Duster, 2005). The genetic differences that account for these evolutionary-based adaptations in physical appearance probably involve only a few hundred of the billions of nucleotides in a person's DNA.

Would it surprise you to learn that greater genetic diversity exists among the different human populations in Africa than among the different populations in Asia, Europe, and North and South America? Would you also be surprised to learn that non-African populations are more genetically similar to many African populations than the African populations are to each other? This means that if you identify yourself as African American, it is entirely possible that you are genetically more similar to a randomly chosen person who is White, Hispanic, or Asian than you are to another African American who is not a direct blood relative. This is because the human species has spent most of its 195,000-year existence in Africa; and as mentioned in Chapter 8, Section 8.1a, many human populations in Africa have been physically separated from each other longer than they have been separated from the human populations in other parts of the world. Thus, more genetic differences exist between the indigenous peoples of Africa than between them and non-Africans.

Given this scientific fact, what exactly does the race of a person tell us about his or her genetic makeup? As previously mentioned, it tells us very little: 99.76 percent of our genetic makeup has nothing to do with race. However, does the less than one-fourth of 1 percent genetic difference account for any differences other than the superficial physical characteristics we use in making racial classifications in the first place? This question is currently being studied and intensely discussed in the scientific community. In the meantime, we can cast aside the *Oxford English Dictionary* definition of race. What we call "races" are not biologically distinct from one another, and thus are definitely not subspecies in the human population. Biologically, there is only one race: the human race.

Section
REVIEW

- Genes are the biochemical units of inheritance located on and transmitted by chromosomes, which are threadlike structures found in human body cells containing strands of DNA.

- The field of behavior genetics studies how an organism's genetic makeup and environment influence its behavior.

- The field of molecular genetics studies how specific genes influence behavior, and the application of this knowledge has raised many ethical concerns.

- When differences in thinking and action are found between women and men or between people from different racial groups, genetically based researchers and socioculturally based researchers offer very different explanations of these differences.

PSYCHOLOGICAL
applications

If You Are Left-Handed, Is Your Brain Organized
Differently from That of a Right-Hander?

Are you a "lefty" or a "righty?" Actually, people rarely use the same hand for all manual activities. Instead, one hand tends to be preferred for more tasks than the other. One of the most commonly employed questionnaires to assess a person's direction and degree of handedness is the *Edinburgh Handedness Inventory* (Oldfield, 1971), reproduced in Table 2-4. Before reading further, complete this questionnaire to determine your laterality quotient

If you are predominantly left-handed, you are among the 7–8 percent minority of people who live in a right-handed world (Iaccino, 1993). Put simply, our world is designed for right-handers. Indeed, powerful cultural pressures are often brought to bear on many natural left-handers to use their right hands (Coren & Halpern, 1991). For example, many tools, materials, and equipment—such as power saws, can openers, fishing reels, bowling balls, scissors, and school desks—are designed for right-handed persons.

There is a great deal of evidence that handedness is substantially determined by our biology. For example, when the human figures depicted in more than 1,000 drawings, paintings, and engravings spanning thousands of years are analyzed regarding their handedness, 90 percent are right-handers (Coren, 1989). Likewise, ultrasound studies of fetal

TABLE 2-4   What Is Your Direction and Degree of Handedness?

Instructions: Consider each of the 10 activities listed below and indicate which hand you prefer using when engaged in each of these different tasks by placing an "x" in either the "left" or the "right" box.

	Left	Right
1. Writing	☐	☐
2. Drawing	☐	☐
3. Throwing	☐	☐
4. Using scissors	☐	☐
5. Using a toothbrush (brushing your teeth)	☐	☐
6. Using a knife (without a fork)	☐	☐
7. Using a spoon	☐	☐
8. Using a broom (upper hand)	☐	☐
9. Striking a match (hand holding the match)	☐	☐
10. Opening a box (lid)	☐	☐

Scoring: Once hand preferences for all 10 activities have been identified, your laterality quotient is found by subtracting the number of left x's from right x's and then multiplying by 10. The quotient's range extends from +100 for extreme right-handedness to –100 for extreme left-handedness, with 0 representing ambidextrous activity (that is, equal use of both hands). About 50 percent of right-handers who completed this questionnaire had laterality quotients greater than 80, while 50 percent of left-handers had quotients less than –76. What these findings indicate is that (1) people tend to exhibit a preference for one hand over the other rather than being ambidextrous, and (2) right-handers are more strongly hand dominant than left-handers.

Source: Reprinted from Neuropsychologia, 9, R. C. Oldfield, "The assessment and analysis of handedness: The Edinburgh Inventory", pp. 97–114, Copyright 1971, with permission from Elsevier.

thumb-sucking indicate the same percentage of left-right hand preferences, further suggesting that handedness may be an inherited trait (Hepper et al., 1990). Yet, one problem with a simple genetic explanation of handedness is that 54 percent of the children of two left-handed parents are right-handed (Coren, 1992). What we know about genetics would lead us to expect more left-handed children in this case. Even more troublesome is the fact that identical twins are no more likely to prefer the same hand than are fraternal twins (Coren & Halpern, 1991; Sicotte et al., 1999).

Faced with these problems, some genetic theorists have proposed that handedness is related to the lateralization of the brain. They argue that although there may be no specific gene for left- or right-handedness, there is a dominant gene responsible for the development of speech in the left hemisphere; and it is this gene that also predisposes people toward right-handedness (Annett, 1985). Support for this view comes from studies indicating that although over 95 percent of right-handers have speech localized to the left hemisphere, only about 65 percent of left-handers show this same pattern (Loring et al., 1990; Springer & Deutsch, 1998). The remaining 35 percent of left-handers tend to process speech using either the right hemisphere or both hemispheres. These findings suggest that, for left-handers, the two hemispheres are less specialized than they are for right-handers. Due to this difference, left-handers experience less language loss following damage to either hemisphere and recover more quickly than right-handers because their healthy hemisphere is better equipped to assume the speech functions (Provins, 1997).

Another explanation for the development of left-handedness is that prenatal hormonal imbalances or birth stress causes neurological disturbances in the left hemisphere, which in turn causes the right hemisphere to become dominant, thus causing them to favor their left

Shutterstock

Most tools in our culture are designed for right-handed persons, often forcing left-handers to adapt and use their nondominant hand for most tasks. Many left-handers initially learn a new activity, such as golf, with right-handed tools.

hands (Coren & Halpern, 1991). There is also evidence that left-handers are more likely to be gifted and creative individuals (Benbow & Stanley, 1983). Indeed, the incidence of left-handedness is much higher in artists than in the population as a whole (Mebert & Michel, 1980). Although the meaning of these findings is still unclear, it certainly poses problems for any hypothesis that left-handedness is caused by some sort of cognitive defect.

Suggested Websites

Society for Neuroscience

http://apu.sfn.org

This official website for the Society for Neuroscience provides brochures and newsletters on a number of relevant topics.

Neurosciences on the Internet

http://www.neuroguide.com

This website provides a wealth of information on the brain and nervous system. You will find facts on brain disorders and neurosurgery, as well as the disciplines of psychology and psychiatry.

Brain Model Tutorial

http://pegasus.cc.ucf.edu/~Brainmd1/brain.html

This is a teaching website devoted to the various parts and functions of the brain.

The Whole Brain Atlas

http://www.med.harvard.edu/AANLIB/home.html

This website, produced by the Harvard Medical School, provides a great deal of information and animated graphics of the brain, neuroimaging techniques, and brain disorders, such as strokes and Alzheimer's.

Key Terms

Acetylcholine (ACh), 48
Action potential, 46
Adrenal glands, 56
Aphasia, 71
Autonomic nervous system, 52
Axon, 43
Behavior genetics, 78
Central nervous system, 52
Cerebellum, 61
Cerebral cortex, 64
Cerebral hemispheres, 65
Cerebral lateralization, 67
Cerebrospinal fluid, 52
Chromosomes, 76
Cloning, 80
Computerized axial tomography (CAT) scan, 57
Corpus callosum, 65
Dendrites, 43
Deoxyribonucleic acid (DNA), 76
Dopamine (DA), 49
Electroencephalograph (EEG), 57
Endocrine system, 54
Endorphins, 49

Forebrain, 62
Fraternal twins, 78
Frontal lobes, 66
Functional magnetic resonance imaging (fMRI), 58
Gender, 81
Gene, 76
Genotype, 76
Glial cells, 45
Gonads, 56
Hindbrain, 61
Hormones, 54
Hypothalamus, 62
Identical twins, 78
Interneurons, 43
Limbic system, 62
Magnetic resonance imaging (MRI), 57
Medulla, 61
Midbrain, 62
Molecular genetics, 79
Motor neurons, 43
Myelin sheath, 44
Nerve, 51
Neurons, 43
Neurotransmitters, 47

Occipital lobes, 65
Parasympathetic nervous system, 52
Parietal lobes, 65
Peripheral nervous system, 51
Phenotype, 76
Pituitary gland, 55
Plasticity, 73
Pons, 61
Positron emission tomography (PET) scan, 58
Reflexes, 54
Resting potential, 45
Reticular formation, 62
Sensory neurons, 43
Serotonin, 49
Sex chromosomes, 78
Sex, 81
Soma, 43
Somatic nervous system, 51
Spinal cord, 52
Sympathetic nervous system, 52
Synapse, 44
Temporal lobes, 66
Thalamus, 62
Thyroid gland, 56

Review Questions

1. Which of the following does story of Henry Molasion illustrate?
    a. The hippocampus is responsible for emotional expression.
    b. The brain has sensory receptors.
    c. The brain is a complex organ that scientists are only beginning to understand.
    d. Neurons account for all human thoughts and action.
    e. None of the above

2. All the following make up a synapse except the _____.
    a. myelin sheath
    b. terminal button
    c. synaptic cleft
    d. dendrite of another neuron
    e. a and b

3. Which of the following statements is true?
    a. Neurons never synapse on somas.
    b. Neurons receive, integrate, and transmit information to the nervous system.
    c. The brain and spinal cord are solid masses of neurons.
    d. Glial cells make up a very small percentage of the brain's mass.
    e. b and d

4. Which of the following is true of the speed of neuron impulses?
    a. It is always constant within a given neuron.
    b. It can vary.
    c. It increases with the diameter of the axon.
    d. It is slower than an electrical impulse.
    e. All of the above

5. For which of the following do neuroscientists believe that neurotransmitters such as ACh, DA, and endorphins are responsible?
    a. convulsions and severe muscle contractions
    b. cognition and the formation of new memories
    c. influences on thought and emotion
    d. a and b
    e. a, b, and c

6. What causes a neuron to fire?
    a. dendrites
    b. inhibitory neurotransmitters
    c. a flood of electrically charged ions that exceeds the threshold
    d. a and b
    e. a, b, and c

7. The peripheral nervous system consists of which of the following?
    a. somatic and endocrine systems
    b. somatic, sympathetic, and parasympathetic nervous systems
    c. brain and spinal cord
    d. b and c
    e. none of the above

8. The autonomic nervous system plays a part in which of the following bodily functions?
    a. blood pressure, heart rate
    b. digestion
    c. breathing
    d. all of the above
    e. a and b

9. Which of the following statements is true?
    a. The central nervous system cannot repair itself.
    b. All body actions require interaction between the brain and spinal cord.
    c. If a section of the spinal cord is severed, a person loses all sensation and muscle control above the injury.
    d. None of the above
    e. a and c

10. The hindbrain is involved in controlling which of the following?
    a. breathing, heart rate, swallowing, and digestion
    b. sleep and arousal
    c. learning and body movement
    d. all of the above
    e. b and c

11. If I am unable to remember new skills, which region of my brain is likely damaged?
    a. occipital lobe
    b. parietal lobe
    c. temporal lobe
    d. none of the above
    e. a and c

12. Which of the following statements is true?
    a. Women's brains tend to be more bilateralized for language.
    b. Women tend to be less adept at spatial tasks than men.
    c. Similarities in brain function between men and women far outweigh any differences.
    d. All of the above
    e. a and b

13. Which of the following is true about brain functioning?
    a. The brain cannot function without both of the cerebral hemispheres.
    b. The brain cannot function if there is damage to the cerebellum.
    c. The brain cannot function with a cut corpus callosum.
    d. All of the above
    e. None of the above

14. Which of the following statements is true?
    a. You receive half of your genetic blueprint from each parent.
    b. Of all the human genes, 50 percent are identical in all humans.
    c. There are chromosomes in every cell of the body.
    d. The environment does not influence phenotype.
    e. All of the above

15. If you wanted to study the blood flow or chemical makeup of the brain, you would use a(an) _____.
    a. EEG
    b. CAT scan or MRI
    c. PET scan
    d. fMRI
    e. c and d

16. Which of the following diseases may result from too much or too little of a neurotransmitter?
    a. Parkinson's disease
    b. schizophrenia
    c. botulism
    d. all of the above
    e. none of the above

Chapter Three

Human Development

Chapter Outline

Psychological Applications: *Using Effective Tutoring Strategies to Facilitate Cognitive Development*

W hen I was in fourth grade, there was a period of time where I spent a good deal of the school day leaning forward so that I put almost all my weight on the front right leg of my desk. Why? Because that desk leg was balancing on top of a lump of coal about the size of my fist. I had found the lump of coal on the school playground. While Mrs. Rahm talked about math, science, and U.S. history, I earnestly pressed down on that black rock at my feet. Why? Because I had a plan. In the latest issue of Superman comics, the Man of Steel had taken a piece of coal, squeezed it in his superhand for a few seconds, and transformed it into a valuable diamond. I knew I was no Superman, but I also knew I was only 9 years old and had a lot of years left in me. If the Man of Steel could use his superhuman strength to turn a lump of coal into a precious diamond in only a few seconds, then maybe I could do the same thing if I desk-pressured my coal from now until high school graduation. So at the end of each school day, I would pull my project out from under that desk leg and inspect it carefully, looking for any signs of crystal growth.

Old age lives minutes slowly, hours quickly; childhood chews hours and swallows minutes.

—Malcolm de Chazal,
Mauritian author, 1902–1981

Needless to say, I never witnessed any mineral transformation during Mrs. Rahm's class that year. Yet, while that lump of coal remained essentially unchanged, the child sitting in the desk above it was undergoing many transformations. Indeed, every child in that classroom was changing and becoming something different during the course of that school year. Some of these changes could be attributed to the "mind pressure" that Mrs. Rahm exerted on us every school day, while other transformations were due to "peer pressure," "parental pressure," and, yes, the "biological pressure" changing us from within. Unlike the hands of Superman, which can take sole credit for turning coal into diamond, in the real world the development of a child is the result of many forces working simultaneously. **Development** is the systematic physical, cognitive, and social changes in the individual that occur between conception and death. In our journey of discovery concerning human development, it is our job to analyze these forces so that we better understand their role in shaping, not only who we are now, but also who we will become.

Development The systematic physical, cognitive, and social changes in the individual that occur between conception and death

3.1 Physical and Prenatal Development

Look at the period at the end of this sentence. That's approximately the single-cell size of all human beings shortly after conception. Compare that dot to your current size. How did such an incredible transformation take place? Don't look to Superman for an answer to this question; instead, let's go back to before you were even a dot.

3.1a *Prenatal Development Occurs in Three Stages.*

Every month, an egg is released by one of a woman's two ovaries and travels down to her fallopian tubes. During this time period, if she has sexual intercourse with a man without the use of birth control, and if any of his seminal fluid is deposited into her vagina, she could become pregnant. During sexual intercourse, a man ejaculates between 200 and 500 million sperm into a woman's vagina; however, only a few thousand will actually complete the 6- or 7-inch journey to the fallopian tubes. If the egg is present and one of the sperm successfully fertilizes it, a new cell is formed. If all goes well, about 38 weeks later a baby is born. During that period of time, the many changes that transform the fertilized egg into a newborn baby are known as **prenatal development**.

Prenatal development The many changes that transform a fertilized egg into a newborn baby

 **INFO-BIT**

Consistent with gender stereotypes, biologists once described male sperm as the active participant in conception, with the female egg being passive. Today we know that conception is more accurately described as the egg "grabbing" the sperm rather than the sperm "penetrating" the egg.

Germinal Stage

As you recall from Chapter 2, Section 2.4a, in humans, each male sperm cell and female egg cell contains 23 chromosomes. When the sperm fertilizes the egg, this new cell, the zygote, contains 46 chromosomes, or 23 pairs, with half the genetic material coming from each parent. The zygote travels down the fallopian tubes toward the uterus, dividing into an ever-more-complex multicelled ball every 12 hours. On rare occasions, the zygote splits into two separate clusters that will eventually become identical (monozygotic) twins. Fraternal (dizygotic) twins develop when two eggs are released by the ovaries and fertilized by different sperm cells. This **germinal stage** lasts two weeks, from conception until the zygote implants itself in the wall of the uterus. By the end of the second week, the zygote is about 1 millimeter in diameter and consists of a few thousand cells.

Germinal stage The first two weeks of prenatal development, from conception until the zygote implants itself in the wall of the uterus

Embryonic Stage

Mainly due to abnormalities in the chromosomes, about 30 percent of all zygotes are spontaneously aborted (Plomin et al., 1997). If the zygote successfully embeds itself in the uterine wall, this living tissue is considered to be an embryo. The **embryonic stage** lasts from the third week through the eighth week of prenatal development. During this stage, the head develops before the rest of the body, and arms and legs develop before hands and feet. Between the fourth and eighth weeks, the gonads of the genetically male embryos secrete the hormone testosterone; this stimulates the development of male sex organs. Otherwise, the embryo develops into a female. By the end of the eighth week, the embryo has facial features, fingers, toes, and a functioning heart that pumps blood—yet it still is only an inch long and weighs a tenth of an ounce!

Embryonic stage The second stage of prenatal development, lasting from the third week through the eighth week of pregnancy

Fetal Stage

The last and longest stage in prenatal development is the **fetal stage**, which extends from the ninth week after conception until birth. In the third month, identifiable sex organs appear, bones and muscles develop, and the fetus begins to move. At four months, the fetus is large enough (4–8 ounces) for the mother to feel its movements. By the seventh month, all the major organs are working, and the fetus has a chance of surviving outside the womb, though not without enormous high-tech medical intervention. Premature babies born this early have trouble breathing because their lungs are not fully developed, and they also cannot adequately regulate their body temperature because insulating body fat doesn't form until the eighth month.

Fetal stage The last and longest stage in prenatal development, extending from the ninth week after conception until birth

3.1b *The Fetus Can Be Harmed by Parental and Environmental Factors.*

Among the risk factors that can harm a developing fetus are a parent's age, maternal nutrition, and harmful environmental agents (Montgomery, 2008).

Parental Age and Maternal Nutrition

The ages of both the mother and the father can affect prenatal development. The safest ages for women to bear children are from about age 17 to age 35. Mothers younger and older than this age range run a greater risk that spontaneous abortions will occur due to chromosome abnormalities or that their babies will be born with birth defects. For men entering their 30s and 40s, there is a slightly greater risk that a damaged sperm will fertilize an egg and cause genetic abnormalities.

Because the mother is the fetus's only source of nutrition, her diet is extremely important to its health and development. Inadequate maternal nutrition can cause premature births, underweight babies, higher infant mortality, and, in some cases, permanent intellectual deficits (Huffman et al., 2001; Tamaru et al., 2011). Such negative effects are most likely to happen when the malnutrition occurs during the last three months of pregnancy, for this is the time when the fetus gains most of its weight and new brain cells are rapidly growing.

Teratogens

Teratogen Any disease, drug, or other noxious agent that causes abnormal prenatal development

A **teratogen**—which in Greek means "monster maker"—is any disease, drug, or other noxious agent that causes abnormal prenatal development (Howell et al., 2008). Many drugs administered during pregnancy can pose serious risks to the developing fetus, especially during the first three months of development. Table 3-1 lists several drugs that are known teratogens.

TABLE 3-1   Teratogenic Drugs and Their Consequences on Prenatal Development

Drug	Potential Consequences
Alcohol	Heavy drinking can cause fetal alcohol syndrome (facial deformities, heart damage, mental retardation), while moderate drinking may cause small cognitive deficits
Aspirin	Deficits in intelligence, attention, and motor skills
Antibiotics	Cataracts, retarded skeletal growth, and premature delivery
Anticonvulsants	Heart problems and cleft palate
Caffeine	Premature births, lower birth weight, abnormal reflexes, and decreased muscle tone
Cocaine and heroin	Retarded growth, brain damage, sluggishness, poor attention span, and heart abnormalities
Codeine, morphine, and methadone	Addicted baby, withdrawal symptoms (fever, tremors, convulsions, breathing problems)
Marijuana	Lower birth weight and less motor control
Nicotine	Increased risk of attention deficit hyperactivity disorder, conduct disorders, learning disabilities, chronic respiratory problems, and sudden infant death syndrome
Thalidomide	Abnormalities in arms and legs
Tranquilizers (other than thalidomide)	May produce respiratory distress in newborns

One commonly used drug that is dangerous to a fetus is alcohol. Women who drink large quantities of alcohol while pregnant are 30 percent more likely to give birth to babies with **fetal alcohol syndrome**, which is characterized by mental retardation, motor deficits, and heart problems (Mattson et al., 2011). Children with fetal alcohol syndrome also suffer from facial deformities, such as a small head, a short nose, and widely spaced eyes. Because of evidence indicating that even small amounts of alcohol may cause minor cognitive deficits, most medical experts recommend that expectant mothers drink no alcohol at all during pregnancy.

Nicotine is another widely available drug that poses a serious danger to a developing fetus. Tobacco use during pregnancy is a leading cause of abnormal fetal development. The primary danger of nicotine is that it interferes with normal brain development and is associated with later attention deficit hyperactivity disorder, conduct disorders, and learning disabilities (Slotkin, 2008). Further, these nicotine-induced neurological alterations that occur prior to birth affect the brain's reward systems, which increase the susceptibility of nicotine addiction in later life.

Besides drugs, maternal infections such as rubella (German measles), chicken pox, mumps, and syphilis are another class of teratogens that can be hazardous to the fetus (Isada & Grossman, 1991). Two sexually transmitted diseases, *genital herpes* and *acquired immune deficiency syndrome (AIDS),* are especially dangerous. Genital herpes is typically transmitted to newborns during the birth process when they come into contact with their mothers' genital lesions. Herpes can cause blindness, serious brain damage, paralysis, and even death to the newborn. For these reasons, mothers with active herpes have cesarean deliveries to avoid infecting their babies through contact with the vaginal tract. Of even greater concern to the fetus is AIDS, the fatal disease caused by the human immunodeficiency virus (HIV). AIDS can be transmitted prenatally if the virus passes through the *placenta,* which is the thick membrane that passes nutrition and oxygen from the mother to the fetus. The disease also can be transmitted during birth, when there may be an exchange of blood between the mother and newborn as the umbilical cord separates from the placenta, or after birth, when the virus may be passed through the mother's milk during breast feeding. Of the 30 percent of babies who contract the HIV virus from their infected mothers, few live longer than three years if not treated with antiviral drugs (Nakiyingi et al., 2003).

Fetal alcohol syndrome Physical and cognitive abnormalities in children that result when pregnant women consume large quantities of alcohol

3.1c   *Neurons in an Infant's Brain Compete for Survival.*

The brain develops its incredible complexity through two simple but powerful processes: (1) producing way more brain cells than can possibly survive, and (2) creating a fierce competition between these cells for survival. Both of these processes begin prior to birth (Capone & Kaufmann, 2008). The surviving neurons are responsible for creating complex connections of neural networks that are the keys to learning specific skills.

As discussed in Chapter 2, Section 2.1, the basic unit of the nervous system is the neuron, or brain cell. You might be surprised to learn that when you were a 6-month-old fetus, you had more than twice as many brain cells as you do now, and your brain produced about 250,000 new neurons per minute (Sowell et al., 2004). In fact, you reached your maximum brain-cell density three months before you were born! This is the process of overproduction. During those final months, your brain was pruned of unnecessary neurons. This commenced the process of neural competition and elimination, which persisted during infancy and early childhood, because as you grew, the billions of neurons were shaped by your environment (Cicchetti, 2002). Each sight, sound, and touch you experienced activated and strengthened specific neurons and their connections, while other neurons that were not regularly

FIGURE 3-1

Neural Network Growth During Infancy

As we mature during infancy and interact with our environment, the neural connections in our brains grow bushier in appearance because they are becoming increasingly complex. Depicted here are neurons in an infant's cerebral cortex during the first 15 months of life.

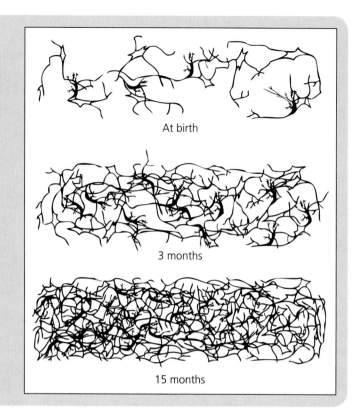

At birth

3 months

15 months

activated grew weak and died (see Figure 3-1). This use-it-or-lose-it principle in brain development operates throughout life, even during advanced age, but there are specific *sensitive periods* during the first five to ten years of life when the human brain is more easily able to make these neural connections. Humans have sensitive periods for acquiring certain abilities most easily, such as language, discrimination of sensory stimuli, and mental modeling of the environment. However, once the sensitive period for a particular ability is past, the development of the brain has progressed beyond the point at which the neural connections necessary for easy learning can be efficiently made. Then, learning of that ability is much more difficult, requiring much more effort. Sensitive periods and the accompanying brain "sculpting" also occur among other animals, including insects (Kolb & Whishaw, 1998; Strausfeld, 2001). This means that although the brains of many animals are programmed by genetics, they are more specifically shaped by life experiences.

Neural development during the early years of life causes the brain's weight to balloon from three-quarters of a pound to about two and a third pounds by age 4. Most of this added mass is due to (1) the growth of new dendrites that increase the connections between neurons, and (2) the growth of the protective coating of fatty cells—known as the *myelin sheath*—around neural axons. To understand the importance of brain growth for the overall development of the individual, consider this fact: Although the rest of a newborn's body weighs only about 5 percent of what it will weigh as an adult, its brain is already 25 percent of its adult weight. By age 2, the brain has reached 75 percent of its adult weight, whereas the body has only grown to 20 percent. At age 5, the brain/body adult percentages are 90 percent and 35 percent, respectively. The most likely reason the brain grows so much more quickly than the rest of the body is that it plays a major role in coordinating the physical and perceptual development of the body as a whole.

BVT Lab

Flashcards are available for this chapter at www.BVTLab.com.

Brain development proceeds in stages, generally from back to front. During the first few months of infancy, the area at the back of the brain (the hindbrain) that is developing the most is the cerebellum, which is important in regulating and coordinating basic motor activities such as sucking and swallowing. Between 6 and 8 months of age, greater neurological maturity in the temporal lobes of the cerebral cortex (located in the middle-side of the brain) prepares children for language acquisition. Finally, in late adolescence, neurological development in the frontal cortex allows teenagers to engage in the type of abstract thinking so crucial for complex scientific and moral reasoning. In essence, brain development provides the necessary neurological underpinnings for our social and cognitive development (Quinn et al., 2006). The capacity to be skilled in many different areas is literally shaped by the interaction of inherited potential and early life experiences (refer to *reaction range* in Chapter 8, Section 8.4b). Thus, how you spend your time during infancy and childhood, including the nutrition you receive and the infections you endure, will have a profound impact on your adult neural wiring and complexity (Qin et al., 2004).

3.1d *Physical Growth and Motor Development Occur Hand in Hand.*

Although the brain grows faster than the rest of the body, infant body growth is by no means slow. During the first year of life, the body almost triples in weight (from about 7 pounds to 20 pounds) and increases in length by about one-third (from about 20 inches to 29 inches). After this initial surge, the rate of childhood growth slows to about 2 to 3 inches and 4 to 7 pounds per year. Middle childhood is a time when bones continue to grow and harden, and muscles grow in strength. The height of a child is largely determined by heredity, with tall parents generally having tall children and short parents generally having short children (Plomin, 1984).

Accompanying the physical growth of the body is motor deve (Murray et al., 2006). Basic motor skills develop from the head downward to the trunk and legs. As depicted in Figure 3-2, infants in North American culture lift their heads at about 2 months of age. By 6 months, they can sit up without support; and by the end of the first year they begin walking. Although this pattern is mirrored in many other cultures, variations do occur (Wu et al., 2008). For example, at 10 months of age—when North American infants are only beginning to learn how to stand alone—Ugandan infants are already walking. One possible explanation for this cultural difference is that in Uganda, babies are carried upright on their mother's backs, which helps to develop their trunk and leg muscles at a faster rate than occurs in most North American infants (Bril, 1986).

Newborns enter the world with a number of reflexes. (See Closer Look 3-1 and Table 3-2.) As mentioned in Chapter 2, Section 2.2b, a *reflex* is an automatic, involuntary response to sensory stimuli. Some reflexes are called *survival reflexes* because they are essential for survival; others are known as *primitive reflexes* because they are believed to be holdovers from our evolutionary history that have outlived their usefulness. Examples of survival reflexes are the eye-blink reflex, which protects us from bright lights and foreign objects, and the sucking reflex, which allows us to receive necessary nourishment. The swimming reflex, which is an active movement of the arms and legs and an involuntary holding of the breath when immersed in water, is an example of a primitive reflex. Table 3-2 lists some reflexes that are easily observed in normal newborns. Many of these reflexes—such as the rooting, grasping, and Babinski reflexes—eventually disappear; others—such as the eye-blink, pupillary, and breathing reflexes—are permanent.

FIGURE 3-2 Motor Development

Infants' motor skills develop from the head downward to the trunk and legs. This chart identifies when the average child in North American culture develops different motor skills. Why might it be that there are cultural differences in the ages at which some motor skills develop?

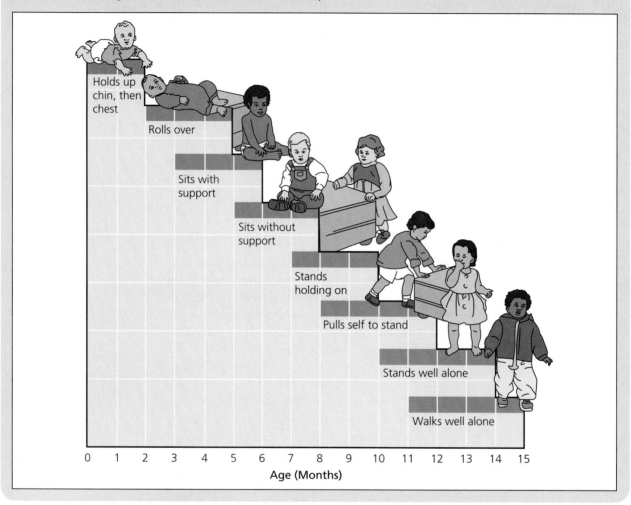

Holds up chin, then chest

Rolls over

Sits with support

Sits without support

Stands holding on

Pulls self to stand

Stands well alone

Walks well alone

0   1   2   3   4   5   6   7   8   9   10   11   12   13   14   15

Age (Months)

Closer LOOK   *3-1*

Are the Senses Functional Prior to Birth?

William James (see Chapter 1, Section 1.1b) once described a newborn's perceptual world as being a "blooming, buzzing confusion" of sights, sounds, and other sensations with no distinguishing patterns. Is his description accurate?

Audition

There is evidence that even before birth—during the final two months of pregnancy—the fetus is capable not only of hearing sounds but of recognizing them as well. These facts were uncovered due to an ingenious series of studies conducted by Anthony DeCasper and his colleagues. In the most famous of these studies, the researchers had 16 women read aloud Dr. Seuss's *The Cat in the Hat* twice a day during the last six weeks of their pregnancy (DeCasper & Spence, 1986). Three days after birth, the babies sucked on artificial nipples that activated a tape recording of their mothers' voice reading either the

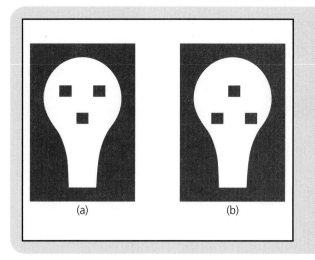

FIGURE 3-3

Newborns' Preference for Faces

In studies of newborns, when shown stimulus (a) and stimulus (b), babies spent almost twice as much time looking at stimulus (a), which mimics the facial features of a human (Mondloch et al., 1999). Why might this apparent innate ability to attend to the human face foster an infant's survival?

familiar Dr. Seuss story or some other unfamiliar story. Thirteen of the 16 babies sucked to hear a tape of their mother reading *The Cat in the Hat* but not to hear the other story. Similarly, DeCasper and his colleagues found that newborn infants preferred their mother's voice or a heartbeat to an unfamiliar male voice (DeCasper & Fifer, 1980; DeCasper & Sigafoos, 1983). These studies indicate not only that hearing is functional prior to birth but also that learning begins in the womb. That is, the newborns were already capable of distinguishing one pattern of sounds (mother's voice) from another pattern of sounds.

Vision

The vision of newborns is not as well developed as hearing, but they can follow slowly moving objects; and within a day they begin to show a preference for their mother's face. Although newborns can see, they cannot see very clearly (Courage & Adams, 1990). By 6 months of age, as the visual cortex in the back of the brain and retina in the back of the eye mature, infants' vision improves so that it approaches normal adult levels.

Newborns are particularly attentive to facial features (see Figure 3-3). Faces and objects with qualities similar to faces are attended to more than are other objects (Mondloch et al., 1999). In fact, a number of studies have found that newborns exposed to an adult making a happy, sad, or surprised face are able to imitate the corresponding expression (Meltzoff & Moore, 1989). How might imitating facial gestures help infants survive? One possibility is that infants' attentiveness to their mothers' faces and even their imitation of the mothers' facial gestures help to establish an emotional bond between the two, making it more likely that the newborn will be nurtured and protected.

Taste and Smell

At birth, infants have the ability to both taste and smell, making positive and negative facial expressions in response to various odors and preferring sweetness to other tastes (Bartoshuk & Beauchamp, 1994). This sweet tooth persists during childhood; and for some people, sweets remain the top-ranking taste throughout life. Regarding smell, babies can discriminate not only between various odors but also, within six days of birth, can recognize their mother's scent from that of other women (MacFarlane, 1975). In addition, they prefer the breast odor of a nursing female to that of a non-nursing female (Makin & Porter, 1989).

Touch

As will be discussed in Chapter 4, Section 4.4b, touch consists of several senses: temperature, pain, and pressure. The sense of touch is functional well before birth, although pain receptors may be less developed than the other skin senses (Porter et al., 1988). Infants' sensitivity to touch explains why they can be comforted by being rocked and held.

As you can see from this brief overview, William James's description of the newborn's perceptual world was very much mistaken. Today we know that infant perception is not a meaningless jumble, but rather a number of sensations can be meaningfully perceived.

Shutterstock

TABLE 3-2 Reflexes of the Newborn Baby

Reflexes	Developmental Course	Significance
Survival Reflexes		
Breathing reflex	Permanent	Provides oxygen and expels carbon dioxide
Eye-blink reflex	Permanent	Protects eyes from bright lights and foreign objects
Pupillary reflex (constriction and dilation of pupils due to the amount of light)	Permanent	Protects eyes from bright lights and adapts vision to darkness
Rooting reflex (turning of cheek in direction of a touch in search of something to suck on)	Gradually weakens during the first six months of life	Orients child to mother's breast
Sucking reflex (sucking on anything placed in the mouth)	Gradually modified by experience	Allows child to receive nourishment
Swallowing reflex	Permanent, but modified by experience	Allows child to receive nourishment and protects against choking
Primitive Reflexes		
Babinski reflex (splaying outward and then inward of toes)	Disappears within the first year of life	Presence at birth and later disappearance indicate normal neurological development
Grasping reflex (curling of fingers around objects that touch the palm)	Disappears by fourth month of life	Presence at birth and later disappearance indicate normal neurological development
Moro or "startle" reflex (throwing arms out and arching of back due to loud noise or sudden movement of baby's head)	Disappears by seventh month of life but is replaced by adult startle reflex	Presence at birth and later disappearance indicate normal neurological development
Swimming reflex (active movement of arms and legs and involuntarily holding of breath when immersed in water)	Disappears by sixth month of life	Presence at birth and later disappearance indicate normal neurological development
Stepping reflex (walking movements when held upright so that feet just touch the ground)	Disappears by second month of life	Presence at birth and later disappearance indicate normal neurological development

- Human development involves the physical, cognitive, and social changes that take place in a person from conception to death.

- Prenatal development consists of three stages: the zygote, embryonic, and fetal stages.

- Possible risk factors during the fetal stage include parental age, maternal nutrition, and teratogens.

- As the brain grows, some neurons are strengthened through repeated stimulation, while others weaken and die.

- Infants are born with a number of reflexes.

- Basic motor skills soon develop from the head downward to the trunk and legs.

- Prior to birth, the fetus is capable of hearing sounds and being sensitive to touch.

- Newborns can both taste and smell, but they do not see as clearly as normal-sighted people.

3.2 Social Development

Although physical and perceptual development provide us with the necessary biological infrastructure to survive in the world, there is more to survival than simple biology. In this section, we examine some of the social and cultural forces that shape our essential humanity, beginning with the development of an emotional attachment to our caregivers.

3.2a *Attachment Is a Basic Need.*

Attachment is the strong emotional bond a young child forms with its primary caregiver; it is considered to be the cornerstone for all other relationships in a child's life (Mercer, 2006). This bond is not unique to humans; it can also be observed in most species of birds and mammals (Graves & Hennesy, 2000; Mason, 1997). Based on his analysis of both orphaned children and other species, British psychiatrist John Bowlby (1969, 1988) proposed that attachment is part of many species' genetic heritage; and its evolutionary function is to keep immature animals close to their parents so that they are protected from predators.

Attachment The strong emotional bond a young child forms with its primary caregiver

The Development of Attachment

In many species, an important ingredient in developing attachment is receiving *contact comfort*—that is, direct contact with soft objects (Harlow & Harlow, 1962; Harlow & Zimmermann, 1959). This is why toddlers enjoy stroking and being stroked by their parents. It also explains why children often clutch or stroke soft objects when they feel anxious or tired (Passman & Weisberg, 1975). As a youngster, my daughter

FIGURE 3-4

Contact comfort is found in many species. For example, when placed in an environment with both a soft terry cloth "mother" and a wire-mesh "mother," infant rhesus monkeys overwhelmingly preferred the cloth one. Likewise, when my daughter Lillian could not find her favorite blanket, she found a suitable soft substitute. How is contact comfort related to security needs?

Source: Harlow monkey photo courtesy of Harlow Primate Laboratory. Baby on package of diapers photo courtesy of Figzoi

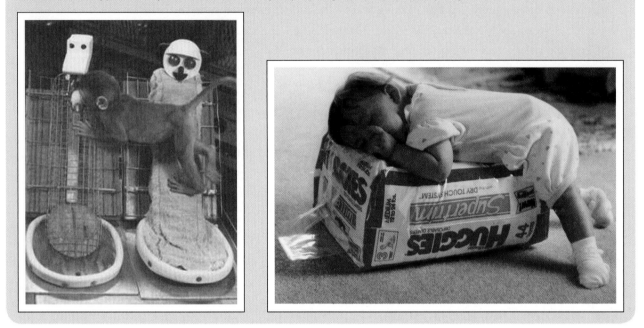

Lillian always needed her favorite blanket to hold close to her body and rub between her fingers when settling down for a nap. One afternoon, she apparently could not find this most cherished object as fatigue settled in and thus chose a convenient substitute—an unopened bag of disposable diapers (see Figure 3-4). When loved ones are not available, children bond to other cuddly objects.

Newborn humans are equipped with a number of attachment behaviors—such as smiling, cooing, and clinging—to which adults seem to naturally respond with care and attention. Because newborn babies' attachment behaviors are not directed toward a specific person, they not only will coo, smile, and cling to their caregivers but also will engage in these behaviors in response to strangers and even inanimate objects. If adults do not respond to the infants' attachment behaviors, these bonding signals decrease in frequency (Ainsworth et al., 1978). Infants' initial attachment bond usually is with their mothers because mothers provide most of the early care.

Between the ages of 3 and 6 months, infants show a clear preference for their primary caregivers but do not yet become upset when separated from them. In contrast, between 7 and 9 months, the child forms an attachment bond toward a specific caregiver and usually becomes extremely upset following separation. The fear and distress that infants display when separated from their primary caregiver, known as **separation anxiety**, usually persist until they are about age 2 or 3. Also during this time, children develop a fear of strangers, called **stranger anxiety**. Stranger anxiety develops at about 6 or 7 months of age, peaks at about 1 year, and gradually subsides during the second year. Neither separation anxiety nor stranger anxiety is unique to Western culture; both are found throughout the world.

Separation anxiety The fear and distress that infants display when separated from their primary caregiver

Stranger anxiety The fear and distress that infants often display when approached by an unfamiliar person

Individual Differences in Attachment Style

As infants mature and interact with their parents, they develop either optimistic or pessimistic beliefs about human relationships (Moss et al., 2004). Children with parents who are nurturing and sensitively responsive to their needs tend to develop a *secure attachment* style characterized by a belief that they are worthy of others' love and that people can be trusted to care for them. In marked contrast, children with parents who are inattentive to their needs tend to develop an *insecure attachment* style characterized by a belief that they are unworthy love objects and that others cannot be relied upon. Attachment style remains quite stable throughout childhood unless the family experiences a major disruption, such as divorce, illness, or death.

About 65 percent of children in the United States are securely attached, while the remaining 35 percent have an insecure attachment style (M. Lamb et al., 1992). Secure attachment promotes psychological adjustment and health, while insecure attachment typically fosters problematic social relationships. Infants who are securely attached at 1 year of age tend to mature into popular, independent, socially skilled, and self-assured children (Rackett & Holmes, 2010). In contrast, insecurely attached infants tend to become children who lack curiosity, perform poorly in school, and are emotionally withdrawn. They also often exhibit contradictory social behavior, sometimes initiating social contact but then unexpectedly spurning others' social advances. This vacillating pattern of approach-avoidance invites social rejection from peers, which then serves to confirm the child's original sense of insecurity and distrust about the world outside (Bureau et al., 2006).

Despite the sharply contrasting consequences of secure and insecure attachment, these findings by no means imply that secure attachment makes a child invulnerable to later problems in life or that insecure attachment dooms one to a life of loneliness and misery. Instead, the research suggests that children with a secure attachment history have an understanding of themselves ("I am worthy of love") and their relationship with others ("People can be trusted") that makes it easier for them to form satisfying social attachments than for those who have an insecure attachment history.

3.2b Parental Responsiveness, Initial Temperament, and Culture Shape Attachment Style.

A number of factors influence children's attachment style toward their parents. Three of the more important factors are the parents' behavior toward the child, the child's inborn temperament, and the family's culture.

Parental Responsiveness

Parents who are sensitively responsive to their children's needs and emotional signals, and provide a great deal of contact comfort, tend to foster secure attachment (Aird, 2008). In feeding, for example, they pay attention to the infant's verbal and nonverbal behavior to determine when to start and stop. They also respond promptly to the baby's cries and behave affectionately when holding her or him. In marked contrast, parents of infants who show insecure attachment pay less attention to their infants' moods and respond more on the basis of their own needs and desires (Pederson et al., 1990). For example, they will feed the baby when it is convenient for them to do so, and they will cuddle the baby when they themselves desire contact comfort but will avoid the baby at other times. Mothers with insecurely attached babies seem to derive less pleasure from contact comfort and will often refuse to console their babies when they are crying.

Temperament

Another factor that influences the quality of the parent-child attachment is the initial temperament of the newborn. About two-thirds of all infants can be classified into three broad temperamental patterns. Infants with an *easygoing temperament* generally react positively to new situations or stimuli, such as people or toys; and they have regular sleeping and eating patterns. *Slow-to-warm-up* infants often have a low activity level, withdraw from new situations, and only adapt gradually. Infants with a *difficult temperament* tend to react to new situations by crying or fussing, and they have irregular sleeping and eating patterns. The remaining one-third of infants do not fit clearly into any of these three temperamental categories and are considered to have an *average* temperament.

Temperament appears to be significantly shaped by inherited biological factors and is remarkably stable (Donnellan et al., 2008). It is also true that temperament can influence the quality of parent-child interactions. Infants who develop a secure attachment style tend to be naturally easygoing, while those who develop an insecure attachment style are more likely to be rather difficult. Of the two factors, most studies suggest that parental responsiveness has a greater impact than the child's temperament in shaping the quality of the attachment (Rosen & Rothbaum, 1993; Seifer et al., 1996). For example, in one experiment, Dutch researchers randomly assigned 6- to 9-month-old temperamentally difficult babies to one of two conditions. In the experimental condition, mothers received training in how to respond sensitively to their child's needs, whereas in the control condition they received no training. When the children reached the age of 1 year, 68 percent of those in the experimental condition were securely attached—right at the national average—while only 28 percent in the control condition were securely attached.

Culture

Culture also appears to significantly shape the nature of attachment (Rothbaum et al., 2000). For example, both U.S. and German children, who are raised in individualist cultures, are far more likely than Japanese children, who are raised in a collectivist culture, to develop a type of insecure attachment style characterized by avoiding intimacy with the mother (Cole, 1992). These cultural differences in attachment are probably partly due to different views on how to raise children and on the importance of having close-knit family interactions. Parents in the United States and Germany try to foster independence at an earlier age; thus, they discourage their children from staying near them and are more likely to give the children toys or food when they cry rather than picking them up. In contrast, Japanese parents do not promote independence; thus, they rarely leave their children alone and quickly pick them up when they cry.

Another consideration when studying attachment is that in certain ethnic groups in North America (for example, Hispanic and Filipino families) and in various cultures around the world (for example, Israeli kibbutzim and the Hausa culture in Nigeria), the existence of extended families results in many people sharing in the rearing of a child. In such instances, the child develops attachments to many people, without adverse consequences (Lynch, 1994). Figure 3-5 summarizes some of the possible causes of children's attachment styles.

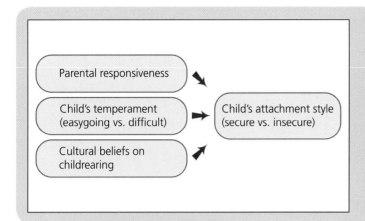

FIGURE 3-5

Possible Causes of Children's Attachment Style

Whether a child develops a secure or insecure attachment style is determined by a variety of factors, including parental responsiveness, the child's temperament, and cultural beliefs on childrearing. Parents who are sensitively responsive to their children's needs tend to foster secure attachment, and easygoing infants tend to develop secure attachment. Cultures that encourage close, intimate family ties tend to promote higher levels of secure attachment.

3.2c Children Can Handle Parental Separation Under Certain Conditions.

The notion of multiple caregivers raises the question of what effect day care has on the formation of attachment. A related question is whether the physical separation of one parent from the child, caused by divorce, disrupts the attachment process.

Day Care and Attachment

With only 20 percent of infants and toddlers in the United States being regularly cared for by their parents during the day, an important question is whether they are negatively affected by being placed into day-care programs (National Research Council and Institute of Medicine, 2003). Employing meta-analysis (See Chapter 1, Closer Look 1-1), researchers examined the overall effects of day care versus maternal care across 59 studies and found no overall differences between children who stayed home and those who attended day care (Erel et al., 2000). However, this analysis did find that children in day care were somewhat more likely to exhibit an insecure attachment style if they started attending after two and a half years of age rather than earlier. This finding suggests that placing children in day care may be emotionally disruptive and require more adjustment only when their attachment behaviors are well established. Thus, when working parents expose their children to day care prior to the toddler years, no ill effects on child development occur. Finally, numerous studies reveal that in choosing day-care programs, the key criterion is "high-quality" care (Badanes et al., 2012; Ghazvini & Mullis, 2002). Table 3-3 lists the important characteristics of high-quality day-care programs.

In evaluating the effects that day care has on children's development, it is important to keep in mind that these effects are significantly influenced by the quality of care children receive from their parents when at home (Marshall, 2004). Children who attend high quality day-care programs are most likely to develop strong language, cognitive, and social skills when they also receive high quality care at home. Children's social and intellectual development suffers when parents are neglectful.

Divorce and Attachment

A little over half of all marriages in the United States end in divorce; in China its occurrence is less than 15 percent. Yet, regardless of how common it is, divorce generally negatively affects the children involved. For example, a meta-analysis of over 90 studies indicates that children of divorce feel less emotionally secure and

TABLE 3-3   Characteristics of High-Quality Day-Care Programs

- A low child-to-caregiver ratio:
  - 3-to-1 infant-to-adult ratio
  - 3-to-1 toddler-to-adult ratio
  - 8-to-1 preschooler-to-adult ratio

- Caregivers who are warm, emotionally expressive, and responsive to children

- Caregivers who have a college education

- Age-appropriate planned activities

- Low staff turnover so that children feel comfortable and can emotionally bond with their caregivers

Longitudinal study Research in which the same people are restudied and retested over time

grow up feeling less happy than those who come from intact families (Amato & Keith, 1991). Further, a 23-year **longitudinal study** of more than 17,000 infants born in Great Britain in 1958 found that parental divorce had a moderate, long-term negative impact on the mental health of about 12 percent of the children after they grew up (Chase-Lansdale et al., 1995). Some studies find that the emotional turmoil surrounding divorce has a greater impact on younger children than on their older peers. Despite these potential negative consequences, children of divorce tend to be psychologically healthier than children who come from conflict-ridden, two-parent families (Sroufe & McIntosh, 2011). In fact, the emotional stress experienced by children from troubled intact families can often be substantially reduced by the termination of the marriage.

Self-concept The "theory" or "story" that a person constructs about herself or himself through social interaction

Socialization Learning the ways of a given society or group well enough to be able to function according to its rules

Self-awareness A psychological state in which you focus on yourself as an object of attention

3.2d   Self-Concept Is the Primary Social Achievement of Childhood.

While the primary social achievement of infancy is attachment, the primary social achievement of childhood is **self-concept**, which is the "theory" or "story" that a person constructs about herself or himself through social interaction (Baumeister, 2005). Self-concept is a product of a larger social psychological process known as **socialization**, which involves learning the ways of a given society or group well enough to be able to function according to its rules. Socialization occurs throughout life, but societies are especially attentive to educating the young. Self-concept development is at the very core of this socialization process because it involves internalizing socially approved attitudes, values, and beliefs so they become guidelines for understanding our social world and ourselves. How does self-concept develop?

Self-Awareness Development

Stop reading for a moment and think about those personal aspects of which you are most proud and those of which you are least proud. In doing this, you engaged in **self-awareness**, a psychological state in which you focus on yourself as an object of attention. To have a self-concept, you must be able to engage in self-awareness; newborn infants do not yet possess this ability, however. Instead, the development of self-awareness occurs at the

Shutterstock

The ability of children to recognize their own image in a mirror is evidence that they have developed self-awareness.

SELF-DISCOVERY 3-1
Questionnaire

Who Am I?

The Twenty Statements Test

On a sheet of paper, write the numbers 1–20 down the left column of the page. Now, list up to 20 different responses to the question "Who Am I?" by beginning each sentence with the statement "I am." Respond as if you were giving the answers to yourself, not to someone else. When finished, evaluate your responses according to a commonly used classification scheme (see Hartley, 1970) by coding each response into one of the following four categories:

1. **Physical self-descriptions**: This is where you identify yourself in terms of physical qualities that do not imply social interaction (for example, "I am a male;" "I am a brunette;" "I am overweight").

2. **Social self-descriptions**: This is where you identify yourself in terms of social roles, institutional memberships, or other socially defined statuses ("I am a student." "I am a daughter." "I am a Muslim.").

3. **Attributive self-descriptions:** This is where you identify yourself in terms of psychological/physiological states or traits ("I am intelligent." "I am assertive." "I am boring.").

4. **Global self-descriptions:** This is where you identify yourself in a manner that is so comprehensive or vague that it doesn't distinguish you from any other person (for example, "I am a human being;" "I am alive;" "I am me").

Code each response into one of these four categories. Which category occurs most frequently for you? Cross-cultural research finds that people in individualist cultures write more attributive self-descriptions, which highlight their differences with other people, whereas collectivists write more social self-descriptions, which highlight their connections to their social groups. Why might this be so?

---

same time as children's brains are experiencing a rapid growth of *spindle neurons*—which are not present at birth—in the frontal lobe of the cerebral cortex. Spindle neurons facilitate self-awareness and other intelligent behavior.

Psychologists first discovered that self-awareness develops well after birth by unobtrusively placing a spot of rouge on babies' noses and then placing the babies in front of a mirror (Lewis & Brooks, 1978). If babies have mental images of their own faces and can recognize their mirror images as their own, they should notice the rouge mark and reach for or wipe their noses rather than the nose of the mirror image. When tested in this manner, infants between 9 and 12 months treat their mirror image as if it were another child, showing no interest in the unusual rouge spot. Yet, those around 18 months exhibit self-recognition—and thus, self-awareness ability—by consistently staring in the mirror and touching the mysterious spot on their own noses, not the one in the mirror. Recognizing the image in the mirror as their own, they realize that they look different from how they looked before. Based on such studies, it appears that self-awareness develops at about 18 months of age (Amsterdam, 1972; Butterworth, 1992).

Parenting Style and Self-Esteem Development

Once children engage in self-awareness, they begin to develop a self-concept. Before reading further, go to Self-Discovery Questionnaire 3-1 and spend a few minutes answering the question "Who Am I?" Check your responses again after reading the rest of Section 3.2d.

SELF-DISCOVERY 3-2
Questionnaire

Self-Esteem Scale

Instructions: Read each item below, and then indicate how well each statement describes you, using the following response scale:

0 = extremely uncharacteristic (not at all like me)
1 = uncharacteristic (somewhat unlike me)
2 = neither characteristic nor uncharacteristic
3 = characteristic (somewhat like me)
4 = extremely characteristic (very much like me)

1. On the whole, I am satisfied with myself.

2. At times, I think I am no good at all.*

3. I feel that I have a number of good qualities.

4. I am able to do things as well as most other people.

5. I feel I do not have much to be proud of.*

6. I certainly feel useless at times.*

7. I feel that I'm a person of worth, at least on an equal plane with others.

8. I wish I could have more respect for myself.*

9. All in all, I am inclined to feel that I am a failure.*

10. I take a positive attitude toward myself.

Directions for scoring: Half of the self-esteem items are reverse-scored; that is, for these items, a lower rating actually indicates a higher level of self-esteem. Before summing all 10 items to find out your total self-esteem score, recode those with an asterisk (*) so that 0 = 4, 1 = 3, 3 = 1, and 4 = 0. Your total self-esteem score can range from 0 to 40, with a higher score indicating a higher level of self-esteem. Scores greater than 20 indicate generally positive attitudes toward the self, while those below 20 indicate generally negative self-attitudes.

Source: From Conceiving the Self by Morris Rosenberg. Reprinted by permission.

Self-esteem A person's overall evaluation of his or her self-concept.

Self-concept is not a dispassionate self-theory but consists, rather, of numerous evaluations of self as being good, bad, or mediocre. This evaluation of the self-concept is called **self-esteem**. In the early years, children's self-concepts display little organization and little negativity, and they have not yet developed a recognizable sense of self-esteem (Harter, 1988). During middle childhood, however, children have the cognitive maturity to integrate others' evaluations of them and their own self-assessments into a global sense of self-esteem (Marsh et al., 1991). A number of studies indicate that high self-esteem individuals generally are more happy and optimistic, and they tend to take greater achievement risks in their lives than those with low self-esteem (Swann et al., 2007). Before reading further, spend a few minutes completing the self-esteem scale in Self-Discovery Questionnaire 3-2.

Given our previous discussion of attachment, it shouldn't surprise you to learn that children with high self-esteem and healthy control over their emotions tend to come from families where parents are warmly expressive toward their children (DeHart et al., 2006; Dennis, 2006). Yet parental warmth encompasses only half the equation when analyzing parents' influence on children's self-esteem.

Cross-cultural research indicates that children need love combined with a set of boundaries to structure their behavior. This correct combination of *parental responsiveness* and *parental control* is best provided by a specific parenting style. Children who develop high self-esteem and self-confidence usually have **authoritative parents**—parents who are warm, responsive, and involved in their children's lives. Authoritative parents exert control over their children, not merely by imposing rules and consistently enforcing them, but also by allowing their children a fair amount of freedom to make their own decisions within the rules. Authoritative

Authoritative parent Parent who sets rules for proper conduct for her or his children, consistently enforces those rules, yet allows the children a fair amount of freedom

parents also discuss with their children the rationale behind their family rules and decisions (Baumrind, 1991; Querido et al., 2002).

In contrast, **authoritarian parents** impose many rules, demand strict obedience, and harshly punish their children for rule breaking or even questioning their decisions. By demanding unquestioning obedience, authoritarian parents smother their children's initiative and judgment, which has a negative effect on their self-esteem. Children of authoritarian parents tend to be relatively passive, moody, fearful, and withdrawn.

Instead of demanding strict obedience to rules, **permissive parents** teach their children that adult rules are unimportant, often allowing their children to set their own rules. Permissive parents provide their children with very little adult structure or supervision, make few demands, and often submit to their desires. By ignoring the fact that children often need to receive direction and guidance from adults, permissive parents produce children who often lack the self-discipline to achieve goals in their lives. While children of permissive parents are generally happier than children of authoritarian parents, the failures that often result from their immaturity and lack of self-discipline undermine their self-confidence and self-esteem.

The detrimental effect that authoritarian parenting has on children's self-esteem is most apparent in Caucasian-American families, where this parental style is often used to "break the child's will." However, in many ethnic-minority families, greater value is placed on authoritarian parenting as a positive socialization tool (Lynch, 1994; Parke & Buriel, 1998). For example, Chinese-American parents use authoritarian discipline to "train" (chiao shun) and "govern" (guan) children so that they will know what is expected of them (Chao, 1992). In such a cultural context, authoritarian parenting is not associated with lower self-esteem or lower levels of achievement (Steinberg et al., 1992).

Self-Concept and Culture

Our self-concept is not only shaped by loved ones but also molded by culture. As discussed in Chapter 1, Section 1.2f, the United States, Canada, and many Northern European cultures cultivate *individualism,* a philosophy of life stressing the importance of the individual over the group (Oyserman & Lee, 2008). In this cultural belief system, the person is thought of as being independent and having unique attributes. In contrast, many Asian, African, and Central and South American cultures nurture *collectivism,* an older philosophy of life stressing the priority of group needs over individual needs (Inglehart & Oyserman, 2004). Collectivist cultures tend to value similarity and conformity rather than uniqueness and independence. About 70 percent of the world's population live in cultures with a collectivist orientation.

These two contrasting cultural perspectives concerning people's relationship to groups within society lead to important differences in the way children are socialized. Within collectivist societies childrearing practices emphasize being obedient and knowing one's proper place. In collectivist China, for example, educational theories and practices focus on shaping children's personalities to best meet societal needs and goals (Greenfield, 1994). Consistent with this upbringing, when asked to describe their self-concepts, people from collectivist cultures primarily list their **social roles**—clusters of socially defined expectations that people in given situations are supposed to fulfill, such as the role of son, daughter, student, or employee. In contrast, individualist societies encourage independence and self-reliance, and children develop a belief in their own uniqueness and diversity. When individualists describe their self-concepts, they tend to identify themselves in terms of personal

Authoritarian parent Parent who imposes many rules, demands strict obedience, and harshly punishes his or her children for rule breaking or even questioning the parent's decisions

Permissive parent A parent who allows his/her children to set their own rules, makes few demands, and submits to the children's desires

Social roles Clusters of socially defined expectations that people in given situations are supposed to fulfill, such as the role of son, daughter, student, or employee

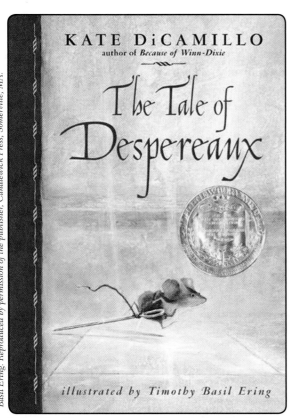

In *The Tale of Despereaux*, a mouse doesn't behave like all the other mice, and his unique behavior makes him a hero. How does this story reflect individualist values? How might such stories shape children's values and beliefs?

attributes and psychological characteristics, such as outgoing, kind, and jealous (Kanagawa et al., 2001). How do your responses to the "Who Am I?" test in Self-Discovery Questionnaire 3-1 correspond to this cultural pattern?

North American culture socializes children to value independence and self-reliance, and children develop a belief in their own uniqueness and diversity. A book that illustrates how individualist cultures socialize children to value independence and uniqueness is *The Tale of Despereaux* (DiCamillo, 2003). The main character in this book is a mouse named Despereaux who doesn't look or act like all the other mice. When brought before the Mouse Council for not acting like all the other mice, he refuses to change and is banished to the dungeon. After many trials and hardships, Despereaux uses all his unique skills and independent nature to save the human princess from the collective rats. For this, Despereaux earns glory, fame, and friendship. Such stories convey values that are different from children's literature in collectivist cultures, which stresses fulfilling group goals, doing one's duty, and bringing pride to one's family, not one's self.

Table 3-4 outlines how cultural differences regarding individualism-collectivism may influence self-concept (Peterson et al., 2005). In addition, Exploring Culture & Diversity 3-1 discusses how different culturally based childrearing practices in the United States may have different effects on children's self-concept and self-esteem.

TABLE 3-4   Differences Between Collectivist and Individualist Cultures

Collectivist	Individualist
Identity is based in the social system and given by one's group.	Identity is based in the individual and achieved by one's own striving.
People are socialized to be emotionally dependent on organizations and institutions.	People are socialized to be emotionally independent of organizations and institutions.
Personal and group goals are generally consistent; and when inconsistent, group goals get priority.	Personal and group goals are often inconsistent; and when inconsistent, personal goals get priority.
People explain others' social behavior as being more determined by social norms and roles than by personal attitudes.	People explain others' social behavior as being more determined by personal attitudes than by social norms and roles.
Emphasis is on belonging to organizations and other groups.	Emphasis is on individual initiative, individual achievement, and leadership.
Trust is placed in group decisions.	Trust is placed in individual decisions.

Journey of Discovery

If you were to tell someone to "just be yourself," what would that mean to a person from an individualist culture? What would it mean to a person from a collectivist culture?

Exploring CULTURE & DIVERSITY 3.1

Are There Cultural Differences in What Determines Self-Esteem?

Several studies demonstrate that, among African American and Caucasian American children, high self-esteem is associated with competitiveness (Peplau & Taylor, 1997; Rosenberg, 1965). In other words, children's feelings of self-worth are likely to be bolstered if they adopt a competitive approach to others. This orientation conforms to the individualist values of mainstream American culture. Yet, in contrast to this association, researchers have found that among second-generation Mexican American children, high self-esteem is associated with cooperativeness, not competitiveness (DeVoe, 1977; Kagan & Knight, 1979). For these children, their parents teach them to value and conform to the cooperative cultural norms of their collectivist Mexican homeland. For them, the growth and enhancement of self-concept and self-esteem do not appear to depend on a competitive comparison process with others. This same research indicates that as Mexican American children become more acculturated to mainstream American culture, this association between cooperativeness and self-esteem weakens. These findings and additional studies suggest that as Mexican American youth strive to "fit in" to the larger American society, they adopt a more competitive approach to life.

3.2e Children Learn the "Right Way" to Think about Gender.

Masculinity A set of attributes, behaviors, and social roles culturally defined as being typical of or appropriate to males

Femininity A set of attributes, behaviors, and social roles culturally defined as being typical of or appropriate to females

As discussed in Chapter 2, Section 2.4d, *gender* refers to the meanings that societies and individuals attach to being female and male. Parents often perceive their newborns through these gendered lenses, describing their daughters as finer featured, more delicate, and less strong than their sons (Karraker et al., 1995; Raffaelli & Ontai, 2004). Often accompanying gender-based distinctions are different values placed on these personal qualities. While **masculinity** is a set of attributes, behaviors, and social roles culturally defined as being typical of or appropriate to males, **femininity** is a set of attributes, behaviors, and social roles culturally defined as being typical of or appropriate to females. In our society and in most societies around the globe, masculinity is more highly valued than femininity.

Ambivalent Sexism and Gender Roles

In understanding why masculinity is more highly valued than femininity, it is important to realize that virtually all societies in the world are *patriarchal*, meaning they are

Francis Tipton Hunter, Sleeping Infant, ca. 1920, pastel on paperboard, 16 X 13.5 inches

"Is it a boy or a girl?" In cultures throughout the world, this is often the first question asked about a newborn. Once answered, people are much more confident in assessing the infant's temperament, strength, and future interests and abilities.

organized so that men have the power to dominate and control women (Neely, 2008). To sustain this male dominance, patriarchal societies have developed a set of beliefs, norms, and values—referred to as *sexism*—that justify this control (Krefting, 2003). The basic storyline of sexist beliefs is that while women have important virtues, they are fragile and inferior to men, and thus need to be controlled, protected, and provided for by the stronger sex.

Despite the dominance that men traditionally exert over women, there is a great deal of intimacy in male-female relationships. Men and women both depend on the other sex as parents, spouses, and sexual/romantic partners; and they both receive rewards in these complementary social roles. Historically, this intimacy has resulted in men idealizing women in traditional feminine roles. They cherish these women and want to protect them because these traditional relationships fulfill their dual desires for social dominance and intimacy. However, these same men are often hostile toward women who "step out" of their traditional roles and compete with men for the more socially valued and powerful masculine roles in society (Fowers & Fowers, 2010). Peter Glick and Susan Fiske (1996) contend that the positive yet patronizing attitudes toward women who conform to traditional gender roles (benevolent sexism), combined with the negative attitudes toward women who do not conform to traditional gender roles (hostile sexism), serve to both maintain gender inequality and represent the "two sides of sexism" referred to as **ambivalent sexism**.

Although *hostile sexism* is easily recognized by most people as negative and harmful to women, *benevolent sexism* is often not recognized as a problem. Yet the majority of people who endorse benevolent sexism feel positively toward women only when they conform to feminine gender roles, or "how women should be." This "gentle" form of sexism motivates chivalrous acts that many women welcome, such as a man's offer to carry heavy boxes or to pay for the meal while on a date. Although such actions are well intentioned, they reinforce not only the belief that men should take care of and provide for women's needs but also that men should have the higher-status and better-paying jobs in society so that they can take care of women.

Gender Identity and Gender Socialization

Shortly after children begin engaging in self-awareness—by age 2—they develop an understanding of themselves as being either a boy or a girl (Katz, 1986). This knowledge is called **gender identity**, and it is one of the basic elements in self-concept (Rustemeyer & Fischer, 2007). Once children identify with the girl or boy label, they strive to act in ways consistent with this identity (Aitchison, 2007). Instead of being passively shaped by gender beliefs in the culture, they become active participants in socializing themselves. In this process of gender socialization, children learn to differentiate a wide variety of objects, activities, games, careers, and even basic personality traits as either "natural" or "unnatural" for them based on their gender identity. They also quickly recognize the different value placed on masculine and feminine behaviors and activities.

In societies where gender expectations are clearly defined and rigidly enforced by adults—such as in Afghanistan, Brazil, or Saudi Arabia—a great deal of consistency is seen in how boys and girls model appropriate behavior. By contrast, in societies where gender is more flexibly defined—such as in Canada, Great Britain, or the United States—the child's own gender role tends to have a more distinct quality. However, even in the United States and Canada, a great deal of gender conformity pressure is exerted by children themselves. In learning the "right way" to think about gender, children often segregate themselves into boy and girl play groups, adopt a fairly rigid set of gender rules, and punish one another for violating these rules (Letendre, 2007;

Our nation has had a long and unfortunate history of sex discrimination…rationalized by an attitude of "romantic paternalism" which, in practical effect, put women not on a pedestal, but in a cage.

—William Joseph Brennan, Jr., U.S. Supreme Court Justice, 1906–1997

Ambivalent sexism Sexism directed against women based on both positive and negative attitudes (benevolence and hostility) rather than uniform dislike

Gender identity The knowledge that one is a male or a female and the internalization of this fact into one's self-concept

Maccoby, 1990). Such gender monitoring is at its height during early childhood. During the later elementary years, this gender inflexibility often decreases as children become more aware of nontraditional gender views and exhibit greater cognitive complexity. Despite this tendency toward greater gender flexibility in later childhood, however, traditional gender expectations significantly shape many adolescent and adult social relationships (see Sections 3.6a and 3.6b).

3.2f Erikson Developed a Stage Model of Social Development.

One theorist who was an important influence on social scientists studying attachment and early social development was Erik Erikson (1902–1994), a psychoanalyst who believed that people's social development occurs in identifiable stages. According to Erikson, each stage is marked by a crisis or conflict related to a specific developmental task. The more successfully people overcome these crises, the better chance they have to develop in a healthy manner (Erikson, 1950). Table 3-5 summarizes this eight-stage theory of psychosocial development.

Developing a sense of *trust versus mistrust* is the crisis of the first psychosocial stage, which corresponds to our previous discussion of attachment (refer back to

Erik Erikson, a neo-Freudian whose personality theory encompasses the entire life span

TABLE 3-5 Erikson's Stages of Psychosocial Development

Psychosocial Stage	Crisis	Description of Crisis
Infancy (birth–1 year)	Trust vs. mistrust	If basic needs are met, infants develop a sense of trust. If these needs are not adequately satisfied, infants develop a mistrust of others.
Toddlerhood (1–2 years)	Autonomy vs. shame and doubt	If toddlers can control their own actions and act independently, they develop a sense of autonomy. If they fail, they experience shame and doubt their own abilities.
Preschool (3–5 years)	Initiative vs. guilt	If preschoolers can get what they want while acting responsibly, they develop a sense of initiative. If their impulses are not kept in check by a sense of guilt, they become undisciplined. If they are made to feel overly guilty, this will inhibit their initiative.
Elementary school (6–12 years)	Industry vs. inferiority	If children master the knowledge and skills necessary for adult life, they develop a sense of competence. If they are unable to achieve competence, they feel inferior and develop low self-esteem.
Adolescence (13–18 years)	Identity vs. role confusion	Teenagers struggle to develop a sense of identity by experimenting with different roles and integrating them into a single identity. If they fail to develop their own personal identity, they become confused about who they are.
Young adulthood (19–45 years)	Intimacy vs. isolation	If young adults successfully develop close relationships, they gain a sense of intimacy. If they are unable to develop such relationships, they feel socially isolated.
Middle adulthood (46–65 years)	Generativity vs. stagnation	If the middle-aged believe that they are contributing to the world and the next generation, they develop a sense of generativity. If they fail to do so, they experience a sense of stagnation.
Late adulthood (66 years and up)	Integrity vs. despair	If the elderly have successfully managed the previous crises in their lives, they will feel a sense of integrity. If they regret many of their life choices, they will feel a sense of despair.

Section 3.2b) and occurs during the first year of life. Trust is established when an infant's basic needs for comfort, food, and warmth are met. If these needs are not adequately satisfied, the infant develops a mistrust of others.

The second crisis, *autonomy versus shame and doubt,* occurs during the second year of life. Here, toddlers attempt to control their own actions and act independently. If successful, they develop a feeling of confidence or sense of autonomy; if they fail or are restrained too severely, they may experience shame and doubt their own abilities.

During the third stage of development, which occurs between the ages of 3 and 5 (the preschool years), children struggle with *initiative versus guilt.* This stage deals with learning how to initiate plans, set goals, and attain them without breaking rules of proper behavior. If children can successfully get what they want while acting responsibly, this increases their initiative. Trouble arises, however, when initiative and guilt are not properly balanced. If children's impulses are not adequately kept in check by a sense of guilt over social transgressions—as is common in permissive parenting—they become undisciplined. In contrast, if children are made to feel overly guilty—as is common in authoritarian parenting—this will inhibit their initiative.

Between the ages of 6 and 12, children face the conflict of *industry versus inferiority,* where they attempt to master the knowledge and intellectual skills necessary for adult life. Children who are successful in this type of learning develop a sense of competence and achievement, while those who do poorly feel inferior and develop low self-esteem.

During adolescence (ages 13 to 18), children face the most crucial stage in Erikson's theory: *identity versus role confusion* (Erikson, 1968). Although knowing who you are and where you're headed is a lifelong task, adolescence is the first time that individuals make a concerted effort to consciously form their own identity or self-concept. One of the primary ways teenagers create their identity is by experimenting with many different roles—the nonconformist, the obedient son or daughter, the thrill-seeker, and so forth. Through such experimentation, adolescents gradually construct a theory about who they are that prepares them for adulthood. Often, this identity is an integration of many of the roles with which they previously experimented and serves as a guide for future life choices. According to Erikson, if adolescents cannot settle upon an identity, they suffer role confusion and may feel "lost."

The sixth psychosocial stage involves the struggle with the main crisis of young adulthood, *intimacy versus isolation* (ages 19 to 45). Intimacy refers to sharing that which is inmost with others (McAdams, 1988). As we learned earlier in our review of research on attachment (see Section 3.2a), those who do not feel a sense of security and trust in their social relationships have a difficult time achieving intimacy. Erikson contends that without close, loving relationships, people will live in emotional isolation.

During middle adulthood (ages 46 to 65), the person faces the crisis of the seventh stage, namely, *generativity versus stagnation.* For middle-aged adults, generativity involves teaching and nurturing the next generation, as well as creating something of substance in the world of work. Those who fail to contribute and produce something that they feel is worthy of their efforts experience a sense of stagnation or lack of purpose in their lives.

Finally, during the last stage in psychosocial development (ages 66 and on), Erikson believes that the crisis revolves around the issue of *integrity versus despair.* As elderly adults look back on their lives, they ask themselves, "Did my life have meaning?" If they have successfully managed the crises in the previous seven stages, they will feel a sense of integrity (Holman, 2001). However, if they regret many of their important life choices, they will likely experience a sense of despair. Research among the elderly has found that developing intimacy with children, especially one's own grandchildren, provides protection against the despair some people experience in this last stage of life (Oswald et al., 2007).

There are three things extremely hard: Steel, a diamond, and to know one's self.

—Benjamin Franklin, U.S. statesman and scientist, 1706–1790

One of the primary strengths of Erikson's theory is its ability to draw connections between important psychosocial developments throughout a person's life (Friedman, 2001). For example, as predicted by Erikson's theory and confirmed by attachment researchers, failing to develop a sense of trust in one's caregivers early in life can have a detrimental effect on one's ability to develop satisfying romantic relationships in adulthood (Hazan & Shaver, 1987; Mikulincer & Erev, 1991).

In addition to the stage connections, Erikson's highlighting of the identity search in adolescence has generally been supported, although research also indicates two important qualifications. First, identity development is not reserved solely for the adolescent years, but rather continues at least into young adulthood (Hill, 1993). Second, as Erikson himself readily admitted, his theory best describes psychosocial development in Western industrialized cultures and does not accurately depict development in nonindustrialized or collectivist societies. Indeed, the need to search for one's identity is a foreign notion for most collectivists because one's identity is often simply provided by the social group (Kroger, 1996). Although this criticism has merit, some social scientists argue that as the world becomes more globalized and industrialized, young members of collectivist cultures may increasingly adopt individualist values from the West, including the notion of personal identity search (Arnett, 2002; Stevenson & Zusho, 2002). If this is true, Erikson's analysis of identity crisis may now have more relevance for people around the world than it did when he first developed his theory in the middle of the twentieth century.

Section REVIEW

- Attachment is the primary social achievement of infancy.

- Infants who receive tender and loving care develop secure attachment, which fosters psychological adjustment and health.

- Infants who receive neglectful or abusive care develop insecure attachment, which fosters problematic social relationships.

- Self-concept is the paramount social achievement of childhood, and it is predicated on the development of self-awareness.

- Collectivist cultures foster group-oriented self-concepts, whereas individualist cultures foster self-focused self-concepts.

- Children are socialized within cultures in which both positive and negative attitudes (benevolence and hostility) are expressed toward women.

- Gender identity is one of the basic elements in self-concept.

- Erikson's theory of psychosocial development explains the social conflicts encountered in eight life stages.

3.3 Cognitive Development

Cognition is the activity of knowing and the processes through which knowledge is acquired and problems are solved. How does cognition, or thinking, emerge and develop in the mind of a child? For a good start in answering this question, let's turn to the pioneering work of Jean Piaget, the person to have the single most important impact on developmental psychology.

Jean Piaget (1896–1980).

3.3a Piaget's Theory of Cognitive Development Has Four Distinct Stages.

Eighty years ago, young Swiss psychologist Jean Piaget (1896–1980) was intrigued by the fact that children of different ages made different kinds of mistakes while solving problems. Based on his observations, he argued that children are not like "little adults" who simply know less; instead they think about the world in a very different way. Piaget's subsequent research led him to conclude that as children mature, they move through four chronological cognitive stages, each distinguished by a qualitatively different type of thinking, and each building upon the stages preceding it (see Table 3-6). Perhaps influenced by his culture's individualist beliefs concerning self-reliance, Piaget also conceived of cognitive development as being a relatively solitary process, something children achieved by actively interacting with the world. Later in this chapter (see Section 3.3c), you will be introduced to a theorist from a collectivist culture, who proposed a more "group-oriented" view of cognitive development.

Schemas

Schema An organized pattern of thought or behavior that people use to understand and interpret information

According to Piaget, children's cognitive development is made possible because they organize their thoughts and behavior into understandable patterns, called **schemas**, to better adapt to their environment. A schema is an organized pattern of thought or behavior that people use to understand and interpret information. For example, when teaching my daughters how to play "catch," I had them hold out their arms about six inches apart and then gently tossed them a stuffed bear. When it landed on their arms, they pulled it to their chests—mission accomplished. By repeating this activity, they developed a schema for "catching."

Assimilation and Accommodation

Assimilation The process of absorbing new information into existing schemas

Accommodation The process of changing existing schemas in order to absorb new information

In using schemas, people's acquisition of knowledge occurs through the two complementary processes of assimilation and accommodation (Piaget & Inhelder, 1969). **Assimilation** is the process of absorbing new information into existing schemas, while **accommodation** is the process of changing existing schemas in order to absorb new information. Once my daughters learned how to catch a stuffed bear, I began throwing other things to them: a beach ball, a pillow, and a ping-pong ball. For the beach ball and pillow, they were able to use their bear-catching schema

TABLE 3-6   Piaget's Stages of Cognitive Development

Typical Age Range	Description of Stage	Developmental Phenomena
Birth–2 years	*Sensorimotor:* Experiencing the world through actions (grasping, looking, touching, and sucking)	• Object permanence • Stranger anxiety
2–6 years	*Preoperational:* Representing things with words and images but no logical reasoning	• Egocentrism • Pretend play • Animistic thinking • Language
7–11 years	*Concrete operational:* Thinking logically about concrete events; understanding concrete analogies and performing arithmetical operations	• Conservation • Mathematical transformations
11 years through adulthood	*Formal operational:* Using abstract reasoning	• Abstract logic

quite nicely, so they engaged in assimilation. However, trying to assimilate the ping-pong ball into the bear-catching schema didn't work—it fell right between their outstretched arms. So they had to accommodate—they adjusted their catching posture, using their cupped hands more than their outstretched arms to cradle the ball. Throughout life, the major dilemma in learning and problem solving is whether one will attempt to assimilate new information into existing schemas or change those knowledge structures so that the new information can be better handled and understood. Generally, people first try to assimilate; but if that fails, they use accommodation in an attempt to deal with the situation.

There are two ways of meeting difficulties. You alter the difficulties or you alter yourself to meet them.

—Phyllis Bottome, English author, 1884–1963

Sensorimotor Stage

As you can see from Table 3-6, the first stage in Piaget's theory of cognitive development is the **sensorimotor stage** (birth to age 2), a period of time where infants develop the ability to coordinate their sensory input with their motor actions. One of the major accomplishments at this stage is the development of **object permanence**, which is the realization that an object continues to exist even if you can't see it or touch it. For infants who lack a schema for object permanence, out of sight is quite literally out of mind. Although Piaget's research suggested that children do not exhibit memory for hidden objects prior to 8 months, later studies indicated that infants as young as 3 or 4 months have at least some understanding of object permanence (Baillargeon & DeVos, 1991; Diamond, 1985).

One quick and easy way to determine whether infants have a clear understanding of object permanence is to try to engage them in a game of peek-a-boo. If they wait for your face to emerge from behind your hands, out of sight is definitely not out of mind for them; they have the capacity to retain a mental image of you in their minds. Piaget stated that object permanence marks the beginning of *representational thought*, which is the ability to use mental imagery and other symbolic systems, such as language. It also is associated with the onset of separation anxiety (refer back to Section 3.2a). Babies who cry when their mothers leave them are demonstrating that they have a schema for object permanence—they know she exists when she is out of sight, and this knowledge creates anxiety.

Sensorimotor stage The first stage in Piaget's theory of cognitive development (birth to age 2), in which infants develop the ability to coordinate their sensory input with their motor actions

Object permanence The realization that an object continues to exist even if you can't see it or touch it

Preoperational Stage

Between the ages of around 2 to 6, children are in the **preoperational stage**, a maturational period marked by the full emergence of representational thought, which started at the end of the sensorimotor stage. Not only do they think in terms of language, but they also begin to engage in make-believe play, in which they act out familiar activities, such as eating or sleeping. This stage is called *preoperational* because children have difficulty performing what Piaget called *operations*, which are mental manipulations of objects that are reversible. For example, a preoperational child might know that adding 7 plus 2 equals 9 but find that of no value in trying to figure out its reverse, namely, what 9 minus 2 equals.

Another important limitation of preoperational thinking is **egocentrism**, which is the tendency to view the world from one's own perspective without recognizing that others may have different viewpoints. Piaget demonstrated preoperational egocentrism in his famous *three-mountains problem* (Piaget & Inhelder, 1956). In this task, children were seated at a table with three model mountains like those depicted in Figure 3-6 and with a doll sitting in another chair opposite to them. When asked to choose a picture that corresponded to the doll's view of the mountains, preoperational children often chose the picture depicting their own view instead.

Preoperational stage The second stage in Piaget's theory of cognitive development (ages 2 to 7), marked by the full emergence of representational thought

Egocentrism The tendency to view the world from one's own perspective without recognizing that others may have different points of view

FIGURE 3-6

The Three-Mountains Problem

In the three-mountains problem, preoperational children typically do not understand that the doll "sees" the mountains from a perspective different from their own. This is an example of egocentrism.

What does the doll see?

Although preoperational children are not egocentric in every situation, they are much more likely to make egocentric mistakes than older children. This is why 3-year-olds might play hide-and-seek by simply closing their eyes. As far as they're concerned, they've found a pretty good hiding place because they can't see a thing!

Another distinctive characteristic of the preoperational stage is *animistic thinking,* which refers to children's belief that inanimate (meaning "nonliving") objects—such as dolls, chairs, and the moon and the sun—have motives, feelings, and intentions. For example, when Piaget asked a child if the sun moved, the child answered, "Yes when one walks, it goes too." When asked if the sun was alive, the child said, "Of course, otherwise it wouldn't follow us; it couldn't shine" (Piaget, 1972a, p. 215).

One additional limitation at this stage can be traced back to our earlier discussion of preoperational children's difficulty in reversing operations. Due to this inability to reverse thinking, children do not understand **conservation**, which is the understanding that certain physical properties of an object remain unchanged despite superficial changes in its appearance. A 5-year-old, Jason, illustrated his lack of understanding of conservation when I poured each of us the same amount of soda into two identical glasses and then poured his soda into a third glass that was wider than the other two.

> **Conservation** The understanding that certain physical properties of an object remain unchanged despite superficial changes in the object's appearance

After pouring the same amount of soda into two identical glasses:

S.F.: "Do I have more soda than you? Do you have more soda than me? Or do we have the same amount of soda?"

Jason: "We've both got the same."

S.F.: "OK, now I'm going to take your soda and pour it into here [wider glass]. Now, look at your soda. Do I have more soda than you? Do you have more soda than me? Or do we have the same amount of soda?"

Jason: "You've got more than me."

S.F.: "Why is that?"

Jason: "Because it's put into a bigger glass, so my soda is lower."

S.F.: "Can you make it so that we have the same amount of soda?"

Jason: "Just pour it back into the first glass."

After pouring the soda back into the original glass:

S.F.: "Do we have the same amount again?"

Jason: "Yes."

Jason's inability to mentally reverse the operation of pouring contributed to his inability to understand the conservation of liquid. Another factor that hindered Jason's ability to understand the conservation of liquid was that he paid attention to only one feature of the liquid in the glass—its height. Like other preoperational children, Jason engaged in *centration*, which is the tendency to focus (or center) on one feature of an object and ignore other relevant features. By noticing only the height of the liquid in the glass—which was lower than the original—and not noticing that the glass's width was greater, Jason falsely concluded that he had lost some soda in the transfer. Preoperational children have difficulty with conservation tasks because they not only cannot reverse operations, but they also tend to pay attention to only one feature of the object. Figure 3-7 lists a number of conservation tasks that preoperational children have difficulty performing.

Do you see something that egocentrism and centration have in common? In egocentrism, children see things from only one perspective (their own), and in centration, children consider only one feature of an object. Thus, in both mental activities, when judging reality, preoperational children can think about events or objects in only one way.

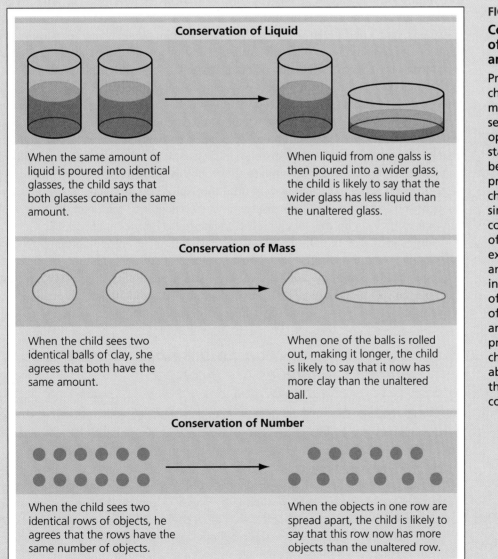

Conservation of Liquid

When the same amount of liquid is poured into identical glasses, the child says that both glasses contain the same amount.

When liquid from one galss is then poured into a wider glass, the child is likely to say that the wider glass has less liquid than the unaltered glass.

Conservation of Mass

When the child sees two identical balls of clay, she agrees that both have the same amount.

When one of the balls is rolled out, making it longer, the child is likely to say that it now has more clay than the unaltered ball.

Conservation of Number

When the child sees two identical rows of objects, he agrees that the rows have the same number of objects.

When the objects in one row are spread apart, the child is likely to say that this row now has more objects than the unaltered row.

FIGURE 3-7

Conservation of Liquid, Mass, and Number

Preoperational children cannot mentally reverse a sequence of events (an operation) back to the starting point. Further, because of centration, preoperational children cannot simultaneously consider two features of an object (for example, the height and width of liquid in a glass). As a result of these problems of reversibility and centration, preoperational children are not yet able to comprehend the principle of conservation.

Concrete Operational Stage

Concrete operational stage
The third stage in Piaget's theory of cognitive development (ages 7 to 11), a time when children can perform mental operations on tangible objects or events and gradually engage in logical reasoning

Around age 7, children advance to what Piaget called the **concrete operational stage**, a time in which they can perform mental operations and gradually begin to engage in logical reasoning. During this stage, children develop an understanding of the principle of conservation, usually first in relation to number and liquid (ages 6–7), followed by mass and length (ages 7–8), and finally area (ages 8–10). Piaget called this stage *concrete operational* because children's thinking and their use of logic are limited to concrete reality, not abstract or hypothetical concepts. When concrete operational children cannot yet directly experience something, they have difficulty thinking about it. For example, ask a 7-year-old to explain the concept of friendship. Instead of defining it abstractly, by saying that it is the emotional attachment we have toward someone based on affection, she or he is likely to say that "friendship is when you play with someone." The concrete operational child understands friendship only from actual everyday experiences.

Formal Operational Stage

Formal operational stage The fourth and final stage in Piaget's theory of cognitive development (ages 11 and beyond), during which a person is able to reason abstractly and make predictions about hypothetical situations

The **formal operational stage**, beginning sometime around age 11 or later, is the fourth and final stage in Piaget's theory of cognitive development. Here, early adolescents are able to reason abstractly and make predictions about hypothetical situations, much like a scientist does. Whereas problem solving in earlier stages often tends to use trial-and-error methods, formal operational thinking involves much more systematic and reflective strategies. A demonstration of these different problem-solving modes was provided in one of Piaget's own experiments (Inhelder & Piaget, 1958). In this study, youngsters were presented with several flasks containing clear liquids and told that their task was to determine which liquid combinations would produce a blue liquid. Concrete operational children haphazardly poured one liquid in with another, trying to stumble upon the correct solution. In contrast, formal operational children tended to step back and contemplate their choices prior to acting, and then they kept track of each liquid combination until they solved the problem. Such reflective thought and abstract reasoning are necessary for teenagers to competently study such subjects as philosophy, theology, politics, and science (Renner et al., 1990).

Although Piaget initially believed that all children eventually attained formal operations sometime during adolescence, later research found that many older adolescents and even some adults have yet to attain this ability (Piaget, 1972b). For example, only 25 percent of all first-year college students and 50 percent of all college students are at the formal operational stage (McKinnon, 1976).

3.3b *Some of Piaget's Conclusions About Children's Mental Capabilities Are Incorrect.*

No theory comes close to matching the impact that Piaget's cognitive developmental theory has had on the field of developmental psychology, and numerous studies have supported many of Piaget's central propositions (Gopnik, 1996; Lourenço & Machado, 1996). Yet, despite Piaget's continuing influence, certain aspects of his theory have been disproven.

Theory of mind The commonsense knowledge about other people's mental states that allows one to understand or predict their behavior in specific situations

First, it appears that children are more cognitively advanced and adults are less cognitively sophisticated than outlined by Piaget (Thomas, 2001). For example, although still egocentric, preschoolers develop a **theory of mind**, meaning a theory of other people's mental states—their beliefs, feelings, and desires—that allows them to predict how others will behave in specific situations (Flavell, 1999). The understanding that other people have knowledge and beliefs different from one's own is a major accomplishment for children and it appears to coincide with the maturation of the brain's frontal lobes. With a theory of mind, children can engage in much more sophisticated social interactions, ranging from empathy to manipulation (Leslie et al., 2005).

Second, cross-cultural research also suggests that cognitive development is more influenced by social and environmental factors than Piaget thought (Gauvain et al., 2011). For example, in nomadic societies where quantifying objects is not very important, the development of the conservation of number occurs later than in Western cultures (Dasen, 1994). In contrast, the fact that these nomadic societies move frequently from place to place probably explains why their children's *spatial abilities*—the ability to orient themselves in their environment—develop more rapidly.

Perhaps the most serious criticism of the theory is that cognitive development doesn't occur in the sequential manner Piaget described; that is, children do not progress through qualitatively distinct stages of thinking. Instead, an increasing number of researchers contend that mental growth is more accurately characterized by continuous and gradual changes that are less distinct from one another than Piaget described (Case, 1992). Further, it is also now known that people who have the ability to engage in formal operations often will fall back on concrete operational reasoning when they are dealing with an unfamiliar task (Flavell, 1992). Thus, just because you progress to a more sophisticated type of thinking doesn't mean that you will engage in that type of thinking in all instances.

Despite these criticisms, most developmental psychologists agree that Piaget has generally outlined an accurate view of many of the significant changes that occur in mental functioning with increasing childhood maturation. They also credit Piaget with highlighting the fact that children are not passive creatures merely being molded by environmental forces, but that they are actively involved in their own cognitive growth. Not only has Piaget's work advanced our understanding of childhood development, but also his insights have profoundly influenced how and what we teach our children in elementary and secondary schools.

3.3c *Vygotsky's Theory of Cognitive Development Stresses Instruction and Guidance.*

One implication of Piaget's theory for educators is that children's level of cognitive development should first be determined so they can be taught material appropriate to that level. According to Piaget, trying to accelerate children's learning beyond their current stage of mental functioning is not just a waste of time; it can also undermine their confidence due to the sure failure they will experience. Standing in sharp contrast to this view is the work of Russian psychologist Lev Vygotsky (1896–1934). Perhaps influenced by his culture's collectivist beliefs concerning cooperation or its Marxist beliefs emphasizing the role of experience, Vygotsky argued that children's mental development can be accelerated if they are given instruction and guidance by someone who is more mentally mature (Veresov, 2005). Where Piaget stressed the biological limits of learning due to age, Vygotsky emphasized how social environmental factors can assist and nurture cognitive development (Gredler & Shields, 2008; Vygotsky, 1986). Whereas Piaget conceived of cognitive development proceeding "from the inside out" and being relatively asocial, Vygotsky viewed it as proceeding "from the outside in" and being inherently social (Cornejo, 2001; Karpov, 2005; Matusov & Hayes, 2000).

BVT *Lab*

Visit **www.BVTLab.com** to explore the student resources available for this chapter.

Private Speech and Internalization

Private speech Overt language that is not directed to others but, rather, is self-directed

According to Vygotsky, learning occurs through the social instrument of language (Langford, 2005). Children listen to people, observe their actions, and then internalize this knowledge and make it their own through private speech. **Private speech** is part of a larger cognitive process, known as **internalization**, in which people absorb knowledge from their social surroundings. Internalization is one of the key mechanisms through which children's environments influence their cognitive development (Kyjonkova & Lacinova, 2010).

Internalization A process of cognition in which people absorb knowledge from their social surroundings

Zone of Proximal Development

Zone of proximal development (ZPD) The cognitive range between what a child can do on her or his own and what the child can do with the help of adults or more-skilled children

In assessing cognitive development, Vygotsky maintained that children's **zone of proximal development (ZPD)** needs to be identified. The ZPD is the cognitive range between what a child can do on her or his own and what the child can do with the help of adults or more-skilled children. The lower limit of the ZPD is the level of problem solving the child can successfully accomplish working alone, whereas the upper limit of the ZPD is the child's untapped cognitive capacity—which is realized only through working closely with an instructor. According to Vygotsky, one of the most important jobs of educators is identifying each child's ZPD and then pushing each of them toward that upper limit (DeVries, 2000). Once the child can problem-solve alone at that upper limit, it becomes the foundation for a new and more-advanced ZPD.

Private speech plays an important role in reaching the upper limit of the ZPD. By engaging in cooperative dialogues with their instructors, children can incorporate their instructors' language into their own private speech and later use this speech when working on the task alone (Berk, 1994). By internalizing the instructor's language and making it their own, children become less dependent on direct assistance regarding the task at hand. The use of private speech to work at the upper limit of the ZPD is employed not only by children but by adults as well. For example, the next time you study for an exam, try to catch yourself incorporating your instructor's language into your own w. According to Vygotsky, engaging in this internal dialogue is an essential part of the learning process at all age levels.

Although Vygotsky's theory of cognitive development has profoundly shaped Russian and Eastern European developmental psychology since the 1920s, his work remained relatively unknown in the West until the easing of international tensions between the East and the West in the late 1980s and the dismantling of the Soviet Union in the early 1990s (Eun, 2010; Kozulin, 2009). However, since then his ideas have helped psychologists and educators in the West better understand how learning new cognitive skills is often very much a social activity (see the "Psychological Applications" section at the end of the chapter).

3.3d *The Information-Processing Approach Examines Age-Related Differences in How Information Is Organized and Manipulated.*

Another perspective on cognitive development is the *information-processing approach,* which examines age-related changes in the way information is processed, stored, and actively manipulated (Torbeyns et al., 2004). According to this perspective, a number of important changes occur in children's information-processing systems that directly affect their ability to learn. For example, the speed of processing information increases throughout childhood as some abilities become more automatic. This increase in performance speed appears to be due to the maturation of the brain.

As the brain matures, children also become less easily distracted. Because humans' information-processing capacities are rather limited (refer to Chapter 7, section 7.1c), this increasing ability to focus attention greatly aids learning.

The types of memory strategies children employ change with age as well. Prior to age 5, most children do not use any memory strategies. At the age of 5, however, children develop the ability to use rehearsal to remember information, but they use it much less frequently than older children. Older children also employ more complex rehearsal strategies, such as categorization and imagery (Alexander & Schwanenflugel, 1994).

One reason older children employ more sophisticated memory strategies than younger children is because they have developed **metacognition**, an awareness and understanding of their own cognitive processes. Cognitive psychologists believe that this ability to "think about thinking" allows older children and adults to acquire new and more complex strategies for increasing their cognitive efficiency (Moses & Chandler, 1992).

Metacognition An awareness and understanding of one's own cognitive processes

The information-processing approach is not necessarily incompatible with either Piaget's or Vygotsky's theories of cognitive development. In fact, some theorists have combined the insights from all three perspectives into what are called *neo-Piagetian* theories. These theories tend to view development as occurring gradually, with later cognitive structures developing from earlier ones due to children's interaction with their environment (Kail, 2007). As continuing studies provide us with a better understanding of the child's developing mind, it is likely that Jean Piaget's work will still serve as the fundamental springboard for new theories.

Section REVIEW

- According to Piaget, children move through the following four cognitive stages: sensorimotor, preoperational, concrete operational, and formal operational.

- Vygotsky believed that by instructing children within their zone of proximal development and encouraging internalization of knowledge, mental development could be pushed beyond the cognitive limits proposed by Piaget.

- The information-processing approach examines age-related changes in the way information is processed, stored, and actively manipulated.

3.4 Moral Development

Consider the following hypothetical situation:

> In Europe, a woman is dying from a special kind of cancer. The one drug that the doctors think might save her is a form of radium recently discovered by a local druggist. The drug is expensive to make, costing $200; and the druggist is charging 10 times his cost, or $2,000, for a small dose. The sick woman's husband, Heinz, goes to everyone he knows asking to borrow money to buy the drug, but he is able to scrape together only $1,000. He tells the druggist that his wife is dying and asks the druggist to lower the price or let him pay the balance later, but the druggist says, "No, I discovered the drug, and I'm going to make money from it." In desperation, Heinz breaks into the druggist's office and steals the drug for his wife.

Do you agree or disagree with Heinz's course of action? What are the reason(s) for your answer?

3.4a *Kohlberg Identified Three Levels of Moral Development.*

According to Lawrence Kohlberg (1981, 1984), the reasons you give concerning the correctness of Heinz's behavior—and not simply your agreement or disagreement—provide insights into your level of moral development. Influenced by Piaget's theory of cognitive development, Kohlberg maintained that people pass through three levels of moral development, each containing two stages. Each successive level involves a less egocentric and more mature analysis of moral choices (refer to Figure 3-8).

At level one, **preconventional morality**, children's sense of moral reasoning centers on avoiding punishment (Stage 1) or seeking concrete rewards (Stage 2). Due to their egocentrism, people operating at the preconventional level focus on how their moral choices will affect them and not others. Thus, a preconventional person might reason either that Heinz should not steal the drug because he could end up in jail or that he should steal the drug because his wife might make him something nice.

Many children begin to engage in **conventional morality** as they cognitively mature and become more aware of others' perspectives and the conventions of society. Here, people define what is right and wrong in terms of societal norms and laws, and they are motivated to conform to these rules in order to gain the approval or avoid the disapproval of others. According to Kohlberg, most people will remain at

Preconventional morality The first level of moral reasoning in Kohlberg's theory of moral development; characterized by avoiding punishment and seeking rewards

Conventional morality The second level of moral reasoning in Kohlberg's theory of moral development that is characterized by conforming to societal norms and laws

FIGURE 3-8

Kohlberg's Levels of Moral Development

According to Kohlberg, we move through six stages of moral development, reflecting three different levels of moral reasoning. Each successive level represents a more mature analysis of moral choices. Which level are you on?

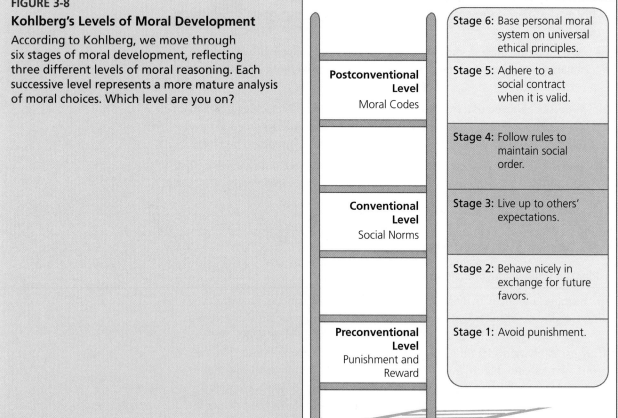

this level of moral reasoning the rest of their lives, basing their moral choices either on seeking acceptance and approval of others (Stage 3) or conforming to authority to maintain the official social order (Stage 4). The reason Kohlberg considered social-order conformity more advanced than interpersonal approval-seeking is that stage 4 reasoning is based on attention to rules made by representatives of the larger society rather than merely by a person's immediate peer group. In the Heinz dilemma, a person at the stage 4 conventional level might argue that Heinz should not steal the drug because it is illegal.

Postconventional morality involves moving beyond mere acceptance of interpersonal norms and societal rules to basing moral judgments on abstract principles and values that may conflict with self-interest and contemporary thinking. A basic requirement of postconventional moral reasoning is the ability to engage in formal operational thought. Yet, to attain this third level of moral development, abstract thinkers must base their moral decisions either on democratically agreed upon individual rights (Stage 5) or on universal ethical principles (Stage 6). An adult at stage 6 might say that Heinz should steal the drug because saving a life is a principle that is more important than any law.

Postconventional morality
The third and final level of moral reasoning in Kohlberg's theory of moral development; characterized by making moral judgments based on abstract universal principles

3.4b *Culture Shapes Moral Reasoning.*

Although Kohlberg asserted that his stage theory described moral development throughout the world, subsequent findings from cross-cultural studies suggest this is not so. As with self-concept development, the development of moral reasoning is influenced by whether a culture has an individualist or collectivist orientation. A number of studies confirm that children in diverse societies progress from the preconventional to the conventional levels, but that the postconventional level is typically reached only by people raised in individualist cultures, where personal rights and privileges take priority over those of the group (Al-Ansari, 2002; Snarey, 1985). Based on these findings, critics claim that Kohlberg's theory is not equipped to explain the development of moral reasoning in collectivist societies.

Whereas Kohlberg's individualist theory of moral development considers the abstract principles of individual rights and social justice as the basis for the most "mature" moral reasoning, the religious and philosophical teachings from collectivist China and India, for example, emphasize social cohesion and group welfare (Miller, 2007). Here, morality is associated with an adherence to many rules and fits most closely with Kohlberg's conventional morality. Yet why should those cultures that emphasize social harmony and the good of the group ahead of the good of the individual be labeled as having a less sophisticated sense of morality? Cross-cultural research teaches us that moral development may vary considerably from society to society, and that what stands for mature moral reasoning in one culture may not be recognized as such in another culture.

Besides possible cross-cultural distinctions in moral reasoning, several early studies employing Kohlberg's theory found that women were often classified at a lower level of moral reasoning than men. Do these findings suggest that women are less sophisticated moral thinkers than men? Carol Gilligan (1982, 1990)

Facing the threat of extermination by Nazis during WWII, more than 2,000 Jews living in Albania were sheltered in the homes of their Muslim neighbors who were following their moral code of *besa*, which means *keeping the promise.* Albania, like many collectivist cultures, has a history of placing greater value on the collective care of others in their moral reasoning than on individual rights.

While men represent powerful activity as assertion and aggression, women in contrast portray acts of nurturance as acts of strength.
—Carol Gilligan, b. 1946

asserted that these findings had nothing to do with any deficiencies in female moral reasoning. Instead, Gilligan proposed that these gender differences reflected the fact that Kohlberg's theory emphasizes values more often held by men, such as independence and rationality, while deemphasizing values more associated with women, such as concern for others and belonging. She proposed that females in many cultures, including our North American culture, are socialized to analyze moral dilemmas based on these values. According to Gilligan, the end result of these different value orientations is that women's moral reasoning is more influenced by a desire to relieve distress and promote social welfare, and that men's moral reasoning is more influenced by a desire to uphold individual rights and privileges. Reflecting their different viewpoints, Gilligan's approach is often referred to as the *care perspective* on moral development, while Kohlberg's approach is referred to as the *justice perspective*.

The findings from a number of studies provide limited support for certain aspects of Gilligan's gender-based critique of Kohlberg's theory, but this research does not directly contradict his theory (Berkowitz et al., 2006). It does appear that the manner in which men and women are socialized often results in their having different views on how they should approach social relationships, which might influence their moral reasoning (Dunn, 2006). Throughout the world, men are more likely than women to value and seek *social power* over others and to view social relationships in terms of social dominance (Dambrun et al., 2004; Sidanius et al., 2000). In contrast, women are more likely than men to value and seek *social connectedness* with others and to view social relationships in terms of emotional sharing (Cross & Gore, 2004; Taylor et al., 2000). How might this affect moral reasoning?

Consistent with Gilligan's caring perspective, when making moral judgments, women may be more likely than men to take into account the social connectedness of people. However, having stated this possibility, it is important to note that a meta-analysis of the findings from many different studies has not found systematic gender differences in moral development (Jaffee & Hyde, 2000). Instead, evidence indicates that most women and men, as well as boys and girls, consider both justice and caring values when making moral judgments.

In summary, while Gilligan's assertion that men and women have markedly different styles of moral reasoning appears questionable, her work and the insights from cross-cultural studies have led to the realization that Kohlberg's theory is incomplete. Adult moral reasoning appears to be characterized by considerations of both justice and caring, with culture shaping the degree to which moral judgments also take into account the welfare of the larger group (Dawson et al., 2002; Turiel, 2006).

Section REVIEW

- According to Kohlberg, people pass through three levels of moral development, with each successive level being a less egocentric and more mature analysis of moral choices.

- Questions remain concerning how well Kohlberg's stages accurately describe moral development in both women and members of collectivist cultures.

3.5 Adolescence and Emerging Adulthood

Are you an adult or an adolescent? If you are between the ages of 16 and 22, you may not know the answer to this question. In a very real sense, adolescence and adulthood are a states of mind and social labels.

3.5a Adolescence Is a Bridge Between Childhood and Adulthood.

Adolescence, as a recognized stage in life, is a relatively recent phenomenon (Ben-Amos, 1994; Nelson et al., 2004). Most societies have always viewed young people as needing instruction and time to develop. However, as societies industrialized, they had a greater need for workers with more specialized skills. To adequately train these workers, it was necessary to extend education beyond puberty and to delay adulthood—hence **adolescence**, the transition period or "bridge" between childhood and adulthood (see Figure 3-9). In preindustrialized societies, such as the Sambia of Papua, New Guinea, or many African hunter-gatherer tribes, there is little need for this transition period (Turnbull, 1989). Instead, following sometimes painful and demanding ritualistic ceremonies, children are ushered into adulthood and expected to take on the responsibilities associated with their new social status. For such groups, there is no adolescence.

Adolescence The transition period between childhood and adulthood

In North American culture, instead of going through one rite of passage after which everyone recognizes you as an adult, you go through many formal and informal rituals that make you more "adultlike." Adolescence is a time when you are en route to becoming an adult, and people differ on when they arrive at the adult designation (Lerner & Steinberg, 2004). In this culture, the length of the adolescent period has gradually increased over the past 40 years, partly due to society's emphasis on attending college (Eccles et al., 2003).

Developmental psychologists often describe three separate age ranges, or phases, of adolescence. Each phase reflects a different level of maturity. The phase of *early adolescence* is the range of about 11 to 14 years, *middle adolescence* refers to teens that are about 15 to 17 years old, and those 18 or older are known to be in *late adolescence*. The social life that adolescents experience becomes increasingly complex as they move through these phases. Early adolescence is the time when many physical,

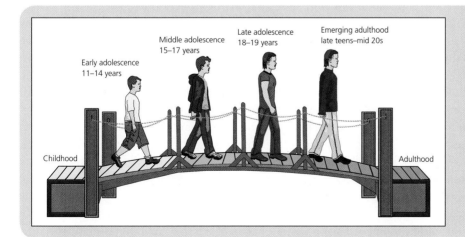

Childhood — Early adolescence 11–14 years — Middle adolescence 15–17 years — Late adolescence 18–19 years — Emerging adulthood late teens–mid 20s — Adulthood

FIGURE 3-9

The Bridge Between Childhood and Adulthood

For many people in industrialized societies, the time period between childhood and adulthood is a transition period where they learn how to become an adult.

mental, and emotional changes begin; and it also is the time when teens begin to actively let go of childhood behavior and try to act older. This desire to be judged as older increases during middle and late adolescence when most adolescents are given more adult responsibilities.

Because there are no clear rules on when adolescence begins or ends, many developmental psychologists now contend that the age period from the late teens to the mid-twenties deserves to be identified as another developmental stage, namely, **emerging adulthood**. This is a stage of life when a person is relatively free from many adult responsibilities and expectations. One consequence of this extension of the adolescent period is that today's youth are marrying at a later average age than past generations. For example, in 1960, the average age for getting married was 23 for men and 20 for women. Today, those averages have increased by about 5 years.

A national survey found that most Americans consider people "grown up" after they finish school, get a full-time job, and start raising and supporting a family (National Opinion Research Center, 2003). Interestingly, "getting married" and "having children" were ranked last in importance, especially among young adult respondents. With the economic downturn experienced in the United States and abroad during the past decade, an increasing number of young adults have come back home to live with their parents after living independently. By returning home, these young adults—often referred to as the *Boomerang Generation*—do not complete some of the culturally defined steps of full adulthood (Mitchell, 2006).

Emerging adulthood A stage of life for some individuals from the late teens to the mid-twenties when they are relatively free from adult responsibilities and expectations

3.5b *Puberty Signals Important Physical Changes and New Neural Wiring.*

Most people would agree that adolescence begins at the onset of **puberty**, when the pituitary gland's increased secretion of the growth hormone triggers a growth spurt lasting about two years. Children vary a great deal on when they experience this growth spurt; however, in North America, girls generally start at about 10 years of age, and boys begin at 13 (Bragmen et al., 2011). Accompanying height and weight gains is the maturation of both the primary and the secondary sex characteristics. **Primary sex characteristics** are the reproductive organs; **secondary sex characteristics** are the nonreproductive physical features that distinguish the two sexes from one another. Examples of developing secondary sex characteristics in pubescent females are breast enlargement, a widening of the hips, and an increase in fat deposits. In adolescent males, facial hair, deeper voices, and greater upper-body strength are some of the more noticeable secondary sex characteristics that develop. For both sexes, two unwelcomed physical changes caused by growth hormones are an increase in body odor and the development of acne, or pimples. Figure 3-10 lists the average sequence of puberty for the two sexes.

Recent studies suggest the possibility that family conflict can influence the timing of puberty in girls. For example, in a longitudinal study of elementary school children who were monitored as they progressed through middle school, researchers have found that girls living in families with greater marital conflict and less parental support tend to start puberty earlier than other girls (Ellis & Essex, 2007). Although more research is needed to fully understand these findings, some psychologists contend that evolutionary forces may explain this relationship between sexual maturation and stress (Ellis & Boyce, 2008; Tither & Ellis, 2008). According to this reasoning, children who grow up in a stressful and possibly even dangerous family and social environment have a better chance of passing their genes on to the next generation if they reach sexual maturity earlier.

Puberty The growth period of sexual maturation, during which a person becomes capable of reproducing

Primary sex characteristics The body organs that make sexual reproduction possible

Secondary sex characteristics The non-reproductive physical features that distinguish the two sexes from one another

FIGURE 3-10   Sequences of Puberty in Adolescent Females and Adolescent Males

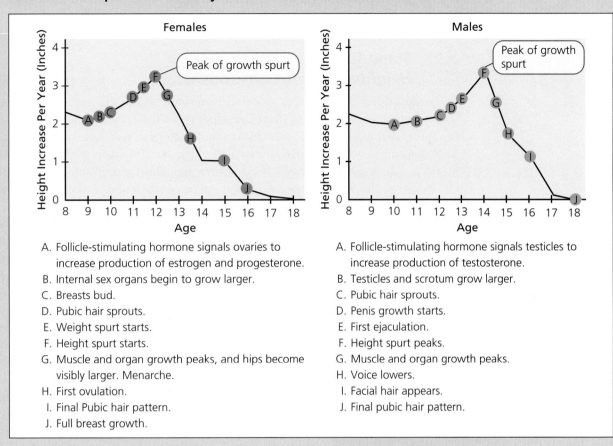

Females

A. Follicle-stimulating hormone signals ovaries to increase production of estrogen and progesterone.
B. Internal sex organs begin to grow larger.
C. Breasts bud.
D. Pubic hair sprouts.
E. Weight spurt starts.
F. Height spurt starts.
G. Muscle and organ growth peaks, and hips become visibly larger. Menarche.
H. First ovulation.
 I. Final Pubic hair pattern.
J. Full breast growth.

Males

A. Follicle-stimulating hormone signals testicles to increase production of testosterone.
B. Testicles and scrotum grow larger.
C. Pubic hair sprouts.
D. Penis growth starts.
E. First ejaculation.
F. Height spurt peaks.
G. Muscle and organ growth peaks.
H. Voice lowers.
 I. Facial hair appears.
J. Final pubic hair pattern.

Puberty and Brain Function

The hormonal changes that characterize puberty also influence brain function. The adrenal glands—located near the kidneys—release testosterone-like hormones that attach themselves to receptor sites throughout the brain and directly influence the neurotransmitters serotonin and dopamine, which play an important role in regulating mood and excitability (Blakemore et al., 2010). Two results of this hormone-induced chain of events are that adolescents' emotions easily reach a flash point; they are now more motivated to seek out intense experiences that will thrill, scare, and generally excite them (Paus, 2005). Unfortunately, the brain regions that inhibit risky, impulsive behavior are still maturing, so there often is an insufficient internal brake on teenagers' sensation-seeking desires and roller-coaster emotions (L. Steinberg, 2007).

Where in the brain does this internal brake reside? The primary area is the prefrontal lobe of the cerebral cortex, which is responsible for complicated cognitive activities, such as planning, decision making, goal setting, and metacognition (see Chapter 2, Section 2.3d). However, while the adolescent brain is undergoing hormonal assault, the prefrontal cortex is not quite ready to rein in or redirect the resulting emotions and thrill-seeking desires (Sebastian et al., 2008). Precisely at this time, the prefrontal cortex is experiencing a new phase of brain cell elimination and rewiring based on the use-it-or-lose-it principle. This pruning of unnecessary neuronal connections eventually results in much more efficient and more focused information processing and a prefrontal cortex that can serve as a reliable internal brake on runaway emotions and impulsive actions. In the meantime, developmental psychologists recommend that parents serve as the external brake while the adolescent brain is in this new phase of development.

3.5c *Some Teenagers Experience Heightened Self-Consciousness.*

At the same time adolescents are physically maturing, they are also further developing reasoning abilities and thinking in greater depth about their place in the social world. In a sense, during adolescence, a cognitive-emotional "push-pull" takes place. On one hand, the emergence of formal operational thinking gives teenagers greater capability for deep thinking; on the other hand, however, they must often learn to cope with new emotions that may sidetrack cognition into egocentrism and self-consciousness (Artar, 2007).

One way that adolescents' self-consciousness is manifested is through the **imaginary audience**, a belief that other people are constantly focusing on the adolescents' thoughts, feelings, and behaviors (Poulsen, 2010). For example, a teenager may be so convinced that everyone will notice a minor blemish on his face, or the fact that he is infatuated with a particular person, that he may actually refuse to leave the house until he believes this unwanted attention has subsided.

Being so self-absorbed often results in the development of the **personal fable**, which is the tendency for teenagers to believe that no one has ever felt or thought as they do (Elkind & Bowen, 1979). Thus, teenagers in love may believe that no one has ever felt the intense emotions they feel; and when relationships end, they may believe that no one can understand what they are going through—least of all their parents.

Although developmental psychologists once believed that almost all adolescents experienced heightened self-consciousness and social anxiety, it now appears that this is not the case. Teenagers are generally more aware of and concerned about being scrutinized by others than are younger children, but many adolescents experience little social anxiety. Instead, adolescence is the time when the emergence of formal operational thinking may lead to the development—or at least the recognition—of individual differences in self-consciousness and social anxiety, with these differences often extending into adulthood (Frankenberger, 2000).

Despite self-consciousness concerns in some teenagers, in most areas of their lives, adolescents are as well adjusted as children and adults, with about 80 percent reporting that they are relatively happy (Arnett, 1999). The problematic areas involve conflicts with parents and risky behavior. Compared to younger children, teenagers have more arguments with their parents, which the teens often spark by engaging in dangerous activities, such as drug use, reckless driving, and unprotected sex. Fortunately, as adolescents mature, they become more sophisticated in their social judgments, and as a result, parent-child conflicts and risky behavior decrease in frequency.

Imaginary audience Adolescents' belief that their thoughts, feelings, and behavior are constantly being focused on by other people

Personal fable The tendency for adolescents to believe that their experiences and feelings are unique

Shutterstock

How does the imaginary audience heighten self-consciousness?

3.5d Ethnic Identity Development Often Occurs During Adolescence.

As discussed in Section 3.2f, one of the challenges of adolescence is developing a personal identity that prepares you for adult challenges. Yet what happens if you live in a society where the ethnic group to which you belong is devalued by the larger culture? In such circumstances, your search for personal identity may also encompass a search for **ethnic identity**, which is your sense of personal identification with a particular ethnic group (Cross & Cross, 2008). In a very real sense, ethnic identity is a state of mind, and acquiring it often requires considerable effort.

Sociologist Jean Phinney (1993) describes ethnic identity formation as typically occurring in three stages (see Table 3-7). In stage 1, the *unexamined ethnic identity stage,* you have not examined ethnic identity issues and may have incorporated negative ethnic stereotypes from the dominant culture into your own self-concept. One consequence of internalizing these derogatory social beliefs into your self-concept is that you are likely to experience low self-esteem and feelings of inadequacy (Clark & Clark, 1939; Phinney & Kohatsu, 1997). In contrast to those who are ignorant of ethnicity issues, some people in stage 1 may have been exposed to positive ethnic attitudes from others but have simply not incorporated them into their self-concepts.

In stage 2, *ethnic identity search,* a personal experience with prejudice or your more general search for personal identity may kindle an interest in your ethnicity. Whatever the initial spark, this stage often entails an intense period of searching, in which you passionately consume ethnic literature and participate in cultural events. During stage 2, you may also develop an *oppositional identity,* in which you actively reject the values of the dominant culture and denigrate members of the dominant group. While in this oppositional stance, anything associated with the dominant group is typically perceived as evil and/or worthless, whereas anything associated with your own ethnic group is declared superior and highly valued (Carter, 2003).

The third and final stage of this process is a deeper understanding and appreciation of your ethnicity—what Phinney labels *achieved ethnic identity.* Confidence and security in a newfound ethnic identity allow you to feel a deep sense of ethnic pride along with a new understanding of your own place in the dominant culture. You are able to identify and internalize those aspects of the dominant culture that are acceptable and stand against those that are oppressive. In this manner, the development of a positive ethnic identity not only functions to protect you from continuing intolerance but also allows you to use this positive social identity to pursue mainstream goals and participate in mainstream life.

A number of studies support Phinney's view of the mental-health benefits of ethnic identity development, among them being high self-esteem and a stable self-concept (Phinney et al., 1997; Phinney & Kohatsu, 1997). These findings indicate that it is our commitment and attitudes toward our ethnic group, rather than the evaluations of our group by the larger society, that influence our self-esteem. Such positive ethnic identities can short-circuit the negative effects that prejudice can inflict on self-esteem.

Ethnic identity A person's sense of personal identification with a particular ethnic group

A race of people is like an individual man; until it uses its own talent, takes pride in its own history, expresses its own culture, affirms its own selfhood, it can never fulfill itself.

—Malcolm X, U.S. Muslim and Black nationalist, 1925–1965

Shutterstock

For many minority youth, their exploring and seeking to understand the meaning of ethnicity is an additional dimension in personal identity development. How does an achieved ethnic identity prepare a person for the challenges of adult life?

TABLE 3-7   Stages in Ethnic Identity Formation

Stage 1 *Unexamined ethnic identity:* Lack of exploration of ethnicity, due to lack of interest or due to having merely adopted other people's opinions of ethnicity

Stage 2 *Ethnic identity search:* Involvement in exploring and seeking to understand the meaning of ethnicity for oneself, often sparked by some incident that focused attention on one's minority status in the dominant culture

Stage 3 *Achieved ethnic identity:* Clear and confident sense of one's own ethnicity; able to identify and internalize those aspects of the dominant culture that are acceptable and stand against those that are oppressive

Section REVIEW

- Adolescence is a fairly recent social construction marking a gradual transition into adulthood; an even more recent transition stage between adolescence and adulthood is emerging adulthood, which involves few adult responsibilities and expectations.

- Adolescence is a time of significant physical changes, including growth spurts and the maturation of primary and secondary sex characteristics.

- Adolescence is characterized by more complex thinking, heightened self-focus, and, for some teenagers, a heightened sense of self-consciousness and social anxiety.

- Minority adolescents who successfully complete ethnic identity development tend to have higher self-esteem and more stable self-concepts than those who do not develop an ethnic identity.

3.6 Adulthood

The psychological study of human development was once devoted almost exclusively to infancy, childhood, and adolescence. Today, developmental psychologists investigate the entire spectrum of our life's journey. Many of the physical, cognitive, and social changes that take place in adulthood differ from those that occur earlier in life (Eccles et al., 2008).

What is an adult? A child blown up by age.

—Simone de Beauvoir, French writer and feminist, 1908–1986

3.6a   *Friendship Is an Important Emotional Bond Throughout Life.*

Beyond the intimacy of family relationships, friendships provide important sources of social and emotional support throughout life (Perlman, 2007). However, largely due to competing time demands, adults typically have fewer friends than do adolescents.

Gender Differences in Friendship Patterns

Both men and women value friendship, but a number of studies find gender differences in the friendship patterns of North Americans from childhood through adulthood (Johnson et al., 2007; Zarbatany et al., 2007). The most notable gender difference involves the level of emotional expressiveness within same-sex friendships. Put simply, women's friendships are more intimate and involve more emotional sharing than men's friendships. There is one important exception to this finding: Same-sex friendships of gay men are as intimate as those of lesbians (Nardi & Sherrod, 1994). What is it about gender socialization that leads to less friendship intimacy among heterosexual males?

As discussed in Section 3.2e, socializing boys and men in North American culture to conform to heterosexual masculinity results in them valuing masculine traits related to power and control, while devaluing feminine traits related to the expression of tenderness and vulnerability. This narrowly and rigidly defined perspective on manhood especially denigrates male homosexuality because it is perceived to be the antithesis of masculinity. For a man to express warmth, nurturance, or caring toward another man is often interpreted as an indication of homosexuality, which was once also falsely considered a sign of psychological maladjustment (see Chapter 9, Section 9.3e). Thus, many heterosexual men believe that to be masculine requires them to avoid acting in ways that might indicate homosexuality, including expressing warmth, tenderness, and affection in friendships with other men. In contrast, gay men do not feel similarly constrained in expressing intimacy to their gay friends. Although many gay men are justifiably wary of expressing affection toward one another in public because of anti-gay prejudice, no such anxiety exists in the gay community. As a result, their same-sex friendships are more intimate than those of heterosexual males.

This conception of masculinity as not encompassing tenderness and affection in male friendships is a fairly recent historical development in Western culture, and one not shared by many non-Western societies. As we move through the twenty-first century, changes in gender roles may eventually lead men to feeling less constrained in their expression of tenderness and affection toward other men. Until that time, however, male heterosexual friendships will generally lack the emotional intensity and gratification of the average female friendship.

Cross-Sex Friendships

Many young adults have friends of the other sex. In these *cross-sex friendships*, individuals gravitate toward the "intimacy mean"—that is, men tend to be more emotionally open with their female friends than they are with their male friends, while women are not as intimate with their male friends as they are with their female friends (Monsour, 1997). Generally, heterosexual men believe their female friends provide more emotional support and security than their male friends, but not as much as women with whom they are romantically involved. In contrast, women do not perceive their cross-sex friendships as being that intimate, and they are likely to turn to female friends for highly personal interaction (P. H. Wright & Scanlon, 1991).

A common problem in cross-sex friendships is sexual tension. One-fourth of cross-sex friendship failures are due to romantic and/or sexual desires, with men being more likely than women to experience such desires (Bleske-Rechek & Buss, 2001). In fact, men are much more likely than women to identify the potential of having sex with their other-sex friends as one of the major benefits of such friendships. This gender difference may occur because men tend not only to view sex as the primary means of achieving intimacy with women but also to misinterpret

Shutterstock

In cross-sex friendships, why are men often more emotionally open and self-disclosing than they are with their male friends?

certain signs of affection (for example, physical touching) as indicating sexual desire (Haselton & Buss, 2000). In the workplace, concerns about coworkers misinterpreting friendliness as romantic or sexual interest are often a barrier to establishing cross-sex friendships (Elsesser & Peplau, 2006).

Overall, the research suggests that cross-sex friendships (1) can be an important source of intimacy for both men and women, (2) may be more highly valued by men than by women, and (3) raise issues of sexuality that often have to be managed and negotiated to sustain such a relationship over time.

3.6b   *Parenting and Job Responsibilities Can Conflict.*

Most adults devote tremendous time and effort to pursuing careers and/or raising or otherwise mentoring children (generativity). Despite increasing gender equity, young women are still more likely than young men to receive mixed messages concerning their ability to juggle these dual responsibilities. Such mixed messages occur because career opportunities often conflict with the traditional feminine role of child nurturer. Due to this conflict, young women are more likely than young men to believe that their plans for work and family are interdependent, with a great deal of trade-off necessary to balance both roles.

All women do not experience this fear of conflict between occupational and family goals, however. For example, women who have internalized feminist beliefs concerning gender equality generally expect that future conflicts between family and career goals will be negotiated and resolved with one's partner (Yoder et al., 2007). Further, women who have witnessed their own mothers balancing family and work obligations are less likely to perceive a family-career conflict. This is especially true among African American women attending college because they are much more likely to have mothers who have worked outside the household than White, Hispanic, or Asian American women (Willson, 2003).

In contrast to women, young men generally view work and family decisions as independent issues. This is so because in industrialized societies, many generations of fathers have spent long periods of time away from their families, resulting in many fathers being emotionally distant from their children. Despite this absent-father tendency, many men today are becoming more involved in the care of their children than their fathers were, largely because over two-thirds of all mothers are now working outside the household (Fagerskiold, 2008). Yet, even with increasing father involvement, mothers in all ethnic groups continue to have far more direct physical contact with infants (holding, hugging, and kissing them) and to spend far more time with their children than fathers do (Lamb et al., 1987; Wyche, 1993). In addition, women still perform two-thirds of household work, or about 15 more hours each week of childcare and housework than do men (Steil, 1994). This imbalance in the sharing of household chores is smaller within African American, Mexican American, and Puerto Rican dual-earner families than it is within Caucasian families; but even here, the men's contributions are still not equal to those of the women (Herrera & DelCampo, 1995; Saracho & Spodek, 2007). In fact, the only household in which a woman's romantic partner shares chores and childcare equally is a lesbian household (Kurdek, 1995). These statistics suggest that although modern society has succeeded in encouraging women to expand their social responsibilities outside the household, it has failed to adequately encourage men to expand their responsibilities within the household.

What are the possible societal benefits of expanding the male gender role to include greater household and child-care responsibilities? Research suggests that when families have actively involved and caring fathers, everyone benefits. The children exhibit higher cognitive and social skills than children of less involved fathers; working mothers' stress levels decrease; the fathers gain greater confidence in their parenting abilities; and the couple's happiness with each other increases (Atkinson, 1995; Callaghan, 2005).

Journey of Discovery

Why do you think it might be easier to encourage women to expand their gender roles to include "work outside the household" than it is to encourage men to expand their gender roles to include "domestic child-care" responsibilities?

3.6c Most Adults Do Not Experience a Midlife Crisis.

Developmental psychologists often have described the years between 40 and 50 as a time when many adults experience a **midlife crisis**, which is a stressful period when adults review and reevaluate their lives (Strenger, 2009). As already mentioned, Erikson described this crisis as being triggered by a feeling that life lacks meaning or purpose. Other psychologists suggest that people's realization that they are growing older and moving closer to the end of life causes the midlife crisis.

Midlife crisis A stressful period when adults review and reevaluate their lives

Most Americans believe that many adults experience a midlife crisis. However, recent studies find that fewer than 10 percent of adults have psychological crises related to their age or aging (Freund & Ritter, 2009). Researchers do find evidence that many middle-aged adults spend time reflecting on and reassessing their lives. However, this self-reflection seldom is related to the sort of psychological distress that is popularly labeled a "midlife crisis."

Most middle aged adults do not experience a midlife crisis.

What about the empty nest syndrome where middle-aged parents become depressed when their last child leaves home? Is this evidence for the midlife crisis? The reality is that most parents experience a sense of relief, not depression, when their last child departs. Empty-nest parents can now pursue their own interests while their children do likewise.

It is not true that the midlife crisis is a complete myth. After all, about one out of ten middle-aged adults do struggle with an age-related crisis. The average age at which this crisis begins is 46. For men, midlife crises last about three to ten years, while for women they tend to last two to five years. However, for most adults, entering middle age is just one more of life's many transitions.

3.6d The Body Begins a Slow Process of Physical Decline After Early Adulthood.

Aging is the progressive deterioration of the body that culminates in death. People can age in at least two ways. *Chronological age* is the number of years you have lived, while *functional age* is a measure of how well you can physically and mentally function in your surroundings. Chronological age and functional age are not always in

Aging The progressive deterioration of the body that culminates in death

sync. For example, some 50-year-olds function like a typical 35-year-old, while other 50-year-olds function like a typical 60-year-old.

During adolescence and young adulthood, the body operates at its peak efficiency and strength. Beginning in the 20s, however, it starts to burn calories at a slower rate, causing many people to add extra pounds to their frame. Hearing also declines somewhat by the late 20s, especially for high-pitched tones. By the 30s and 40s, outward signs of aging become much more noticeable, with hair thinning and becoming gray, wrinkles developing, and visual acuity declining. A less noticeable aging effect is the loss of bone mass, which not only makes bones weaker and more brittle but also can actually cause them to compress slightly. Due to bone compression in the spinal column and changes in posture, by the age of 70, people have shrunk 1 to 2 inches.

Menopause The ending of menstruation

The most significant biological sign of aging in women is **menopause**, which is the ending of menstruation. The time of onset of menopause varies, but it usually occurs within a few years of age 50 and is accompanied by a reduction in the hormone *estrogen.* The most consistently reported sign of menopause is the *hot flash,* which is a sensation of heat in the upper torso and face that lasts for a few minutes. Many women going through menopause with the uncomfortable symptoms of hot flashes and night sweating have undergone *hormone-replacement therapy,* which involves taking prescription drugs to artificially boost female hormones to their premenopause levels. Although hormone-replacement therapy is often effective in alleviating the negative effects of menopause, extended use of these drugs (lasting more than a couple of years) may have long-term negative consequences, such as doubling the risk of developing Alzheimer's disease and other cognitive problems later in life (Gerhardsson et al., 2011). Based on these findings, most women who take hormone-replacement drugs should do so for less than two years.

Old age is the most unexpected of all the things that happen to a man.

—Leon Trotsky, Russian revolutionary, 1879–1940

Although menopause increases the risk of depression among women (Bromberger et al., 2011), it is also true that over two-thirds of American women who have experienced menopause generally feel better after going through "the change" than they have for years (Goode, 1999).

Unlike women, middle-aged men do not experience a cessation of fertility or even a sharp drop in sex hormones. However, they do undergo a more gradual reduction in sperm count, testosterone level, and overall sex drive, which can cause depression, insomnia, and impotence (Harris, 2011). They also tend to suffer an earlier decline in hearing and smell than women (Steinberg, 1995).

Aging and the Brain

Regarding physical changes in the brain, people begin losing neurons at an accelerated rate after the age of 50, so that at death they may have 5 percent or so less brain mass than they had in young adulthood (Espeseth et al., 2008). Women's brains shrink more slowly than men's, which may be one reason why they live an average of four years longer than men worldwide, and nearly seven years longer in the United States and Canada. The most neural loss occurs in the association areas of the cortex, which are involved with thought, or in the brain stem, which controls basic physiological functions. This neural death in old age, combined with reduced blood flow to the brain and decreased levels of important neurotransmitters, can result in a significant loss of cognitive skill.

Although we experience increased neural loss in later adulthood, there is more to the aging brain than deterioration. Just as the brains of children can alter their neural connections following injury (refer to Chapter 2, Section 2.3h), as more neurons die during advancing age, the dendrites of surviving neurons can grow longer and bushier and take over many of the dead neurons' functions. In addition, researchers studying humans and other animals have discovered that throughout life the brain has the ability to generate a significant number of new neurons every day to partly replace dead neurons (Gould et al., 2000). This means that at the same time the aging brain is degenerating, it also exhibits remarkable *plasticity*. The aging brain is not as flexible as the young brain; however, if adults live in an enriched environment—that is, one that is intellectually stimulating—they may show little evidence of intellectual decline through their 70s.

Why Do We Age?

You might be wondering why we don't live forever. Let's consider this question from an evolutionary perspective. According to evolutionary theorists, all species are designed to live long enough to reproduce. The basic biochemical units that are maintained by natural selection are the genes, not the individuals who carry the genes. From this perspective, our bodies are really no more than disposable vehicles for replicating the information in our genes. Reproduction of genes is the most important function of the body, and natural selection may even favor a gene that causes cancer later in life if it makes us more fertile during our young adult years. Thus, from an evolutionary perspective, whether we live or die after reproducing is not important unless our survival or death will benefit the ability of the next generation to reproduce its own genes. So, in the large scheme of life, it might not make much evolutionary sense for us to live that far beyond our reproductive years.

If our deaths make evolutionary sense, what specifically causes the aging process that culminates in death? Biologists offer a host of theories but no conclusive answers. One set of theories proposes that aging is programmed into our genes (Hayflick, 1965). According to this view, each time a cell copies itself by dividing in half, the chromosomes—which carry genetic information—are copied incompletely. After many such cell divisions (on average, about 50), these copying errors accumulate to the point where the cell can no longer divide. Another set of theories compares the body to a machine that wears out due to constant use (Arking, 1998). According to one theory from this perspective, body cells gradually wear out after years of damage due to a variety of factors, including stress, toxins, and radiation. When young, our bodies are able to repair much of this damage, but not all the repairs are accurate or complete. After many years, these faulty and incomplete repairs weaken the ability of cells to both copy and repair themselves, resulting in eventual death.

Regardless of which theory ultimately proves to be the best explanation for the aging process, one of the biggest existing challenges for elderly adults is deciding how to adjust to these physical changes. According to the **activity theory of aging**, keeping physically and mentally active is important in managing the aging process (Benyamini & Lomranz, 2004). In support of this theory, numerous studies find that people age with differing degrees of success. Those who both age successfully and live longer tend to have an optimistic outlook on life, a high degree of curiosity, and a sense of personal control over important aspects of their lives

Activity theory of learning A theory that keeping physically and mentally active is important for life satisfaction in late adulthood

Despite negative cultural views about growing old, most elderly adults lead happy, productive lives. Have you ever expressed negative opinions about aging and the elderly?

(Andrews et al., 2002; Benyamini & Roziner, 2008). Whenever you see elderly persons doing volunteer work for social service organizations you are observing this sort of productive aging. As an increasing number of Baby Boomers enter "old age," it is highly likely that there will be increasing instances of people witnessing those who shatter negative aging stereotypes.

3.6e   *Certain Intellectual Abilities Increase While Others Decrease as We Age.*

Despite the physical toll of aging, our mental skills remain fully functional throughout most of our adult lives. In fact, longitudinal studies of the intellectual abilities of about 5,000 people in the Seattle, Washington, area over the past 50 years indicate that general intellectual abilities gradually increase until the early 40s and then remain fairly stable until the mid-60s (Schaie, 1996). The abilities that show the most improvement during adulthood are verbal ability, mathematical ability, and reasoning (Kaufman et al., 1996). The only ability that declines between age 25 and the early 40s is perceptual speed—the ability to quickly and accurately perform a task such as deciding whether two website addresses are identical.

Around the age of 65 or so, a small percentage of adults experience a slight decline in intellectual abilities requiring rapid manipulation of ideas, abstract problem solving, and rigorous mental effort (Friedman et al., 2008). This decline appears to be largely due to the continued deterioration of the brain's mental processing speed. However, the reduced neural processing speed of older adults does not generally adversely affect their ability to reason through everyday problems, understand mathematical concepts, or learn new information.

Dementia and Alzheimer's Disease

Although neurological decline is a natural part of the aging process, some elderly adults suffer brain damage that causes *dementia,* a condition of declining mental abilities, especially memory (Karim et al., 2011). Dementia is most likely to occur among adults older than 65 years, and stroke, a tumor, long-term alcohol abuse, or certain diseases often cause the brain damage. The most common cause of dementia is **Alzheimer's disease**, which is a progressive and irreversible disorder that destroys areas of the brain that control thought, memory, and language (Levinoff et al., 2006). Individuals with Alzheimer's disease have problems doing things they used to be able to do, such as balancing their checkbook, driving a car safely, or preparing meals. They often have problems finding the right words to use in conversation and become confused when given too many things to do at once (Nygard, 2004). Alzheimer's disease may also cause personality changes, with sufferers becoming aggressive, paranoid, or depressed.

Neuroscientists still do not know what causes Alzheimer's disease, but there is some evidence of a genetic risk factor (Lee et al., 2008). At this time there is no known cure. Studies indicate that people with Alzheimer's disease develop large tangles of twisted fibers inside the brain's neurons and dense protein plaques around the neurons. Some researchers believe that the tangles and plaques disrupt communication between neurons and slowly kill these brain cells. The tangles and plaques begin forming first in areas important for learning and memory and then slowly spread to other brain regions (Bondi et al., 2008).

The number of people with Alzheimer's disease doubles every five years beyond age 65. Current estimates are that about 4.5 million Americans suffer from this type of dementia, with the costs for care exceeding $100 billion.

Alzheimer's disease A progressive and irreversible brain disorder that strikes older people, causing memory loss and other symptoms

Wisdom Development in Later Life

Despite the devastating toll that brain disorders like Alzheimer's disease can inflict upon elderly adults and their families, the vast majority of older adults still have the ability to use the knowledge they have accumulated throughout life to critically analyze complex life events (Baltes & Mayer, 2001). In fact, growing old can be associated with high levels of **wisdom**, which is expert knowledge and judgment about important, difficult, and uncertain questions associated with the meaning and conduct of life (Brown, 2005). Wisdom grows as people learn to think flexibly to solve problems in various social contexts. An important factor in wisdom development is the guidance of mentors who already possess wisdom (Baltes & Staudinger, 2000).

Longitudinal studies suggest that the personal qualities typically associated with wisdom do not begin to peak until people reach their late 50s or 60s. Although childhood experiences do not predict later wisdom, early adulthood experiences do appear to influence the development of wisdom. Those who are most likely later in life to develop personal qualities associated with wisdom have open and complex personalities as young adults, and they choose careers that deal with psychological or spiritual issues (Ardelt, 2009; Helson & Srivastava, 2002). These findings suggest that wisdom is most likely to develop among people who are unusually receptive to new ideas and complex issues (see Chapter 1, "Psychological Applications") and who choose careers that require a great deal of reflective thinking about human nature. Additional cross-cultural research suggests that while Western cultures emphasize cognitive or intellectual qualities in defining wisdom, Eastern cultures place more emphasis on emotional and communal qualities (Yang, 2008). Despite these differences, in all cultures wisdom involves heightened concern for the collective good.

Wisdom Expert knowledge and judgment about important, difficult, and uncertain questions associated with the meaning and conduct of life

Even the seasons form a great circle in their changing, and always come back again to where they were. The life of a person is a circle from childhood to childhood and so it is in everything where power moves.

—Black Elk, Native American, 1863–1950

Everything has an end.

—East-African Masai saying

3.6f People Differ in How They Cope with Dying.

The most inescapable thing in life is death. Perhaps it is this knowledge that gives life its meaning. Yet, how do people typically cope with their own impending death and the loss of loved ones?

Are There Psychological Stages of Dying?

As discussed in Section 3.2f, Erikson asserted that awareness of impending death triggers the final psychological crisis in life (integrity versus despair). Based on interviews with terminally ill patients, Elisabeth Kübler-Ross (1969, 1981) developed a 5-stage theory of how people approach their own death: First, they experience *denial* that they are going to die; then *anger* ("Why me?"); followed by *bargaining* with God for an extension or second chance; next, *depression* when the illness can no longer be denied and what will be lost sinks in; and finally, *acceptance* of the inevitable.

Although Kübler-Ross's theory generated interest in the psychology of dying when it was first proposed over 30 years ago, researchers have found little evidence that people generally follow this 5-stage sequence (Konisberg, 2011). For instance, counter to the theory, people who are old do not typically view death with a good deal of fear and anger (Wass et al., 1978–1979). Additionally, there is no empirical evidence that terminally ill people become calmer or happier as death approaches. Also, how people approach death varies a good deal according to their culture, and these differences are not addressed in Kübler-Ross's theory (Coppola & Trotman, 2002). Thus, despite this theory's appeal, it does not adequately account for people's differing reactions toward death. At best, it may describe how some people who are dying at a relatively young age cope with death. Yet, even among this age group, many people do not follow the stages as outlined by Kübler-Ross (Bowes et al., 2002).

Communicating with the Dying Person

Unfortunately, the health-care system's emphasis on diagnosing and curing illnesses often results in medical professionals largely neglecting the psychological and spiritual needs of dying persons (Kaut, 2002). Family members also often find it hard to bring up end-of-life issues with those facing terminal illnesses. Because of this reality, many people often die feeling emotionally isolated. Despite the fact that some people believe it is best not to discuss death and the terminal circumstances of the illness with a dying person, research indicates that open discussion and disclosure of dying are almost always beneficial (Kalish, 1985; Wright & Flemons, 2002).

Spirituality and Meaningfulness

Spirituality provides a sense of meaning, hope, and purpose to many people (Kim et al., 2011; Leak 2007). As death approaches, many people find solace in religion or in other spiritual beliefs. Spirituality can be a source of strength and comfort as a person nears death, but it can also trigger distress and despair if the individual feels abandoned or punished by God. One factor that determines whether spirituality provides comfort near the end of life is whether such beliefs increase people's perceptions of control (Jackson & Bergeman, 2011).

Consistent with Erikson's idea that the final crisis involves a search for meaning in one's life, studies suggest that the people who have the most difficulty coming to grips with their impending death are those who believe they have nothing meaningful to grasp onto in their lives (Breitbart et al., 2000). For example, one study interviewed 241 cancer patients, who had less than three months to live, about their lives and spiritual beliefs (McClain et al., 2003). As death approached, those who felt they had led productive lives weren't immune to depression, but they were protected from the deepest despair experienced by those who found little meaning in their lives. Further, belief in an afterlife correlated with less hopelessness and with less desire to hasten death through suicide. This reluctance to hasten death among those with religious faith appears to be due to the belief that the power to end life is held by God, not by humans.

Most of us have an impact on many different people, shaping who they become as individuals. This legacy we build ensures that we will continue to live in their minds following death.

Every person must ultimately find their own personal meaning in life, but you are not alone in this search. I began this chapter by relating an incident from my childhood in which I earnestly tried to turn a lump of coal into a diamond. It is the "pressure" applied to you by those with whom you interact throughout your life that transforms you into what you ultimately become. Their life force shapes you, as yours in turn shapes them. Whether you believe in an afterlife or not, in death, your life story goes on living. Those who loved you and others who knew you carry within their minds memories of you. Each day of your life, you are building a legacy of memories for them as well. In this sense, your life extends beyond your death.

Section REVIEW

- Male-male friendships are not as intimate as female-female friendships, except among gay men; cross-sex friendships gravitate toward the "intimacy mean."

- Women are more likely than men to experience conflict between their family and career roles.

- Only about one out of ten adults struggle with a midlife crisis.

- Aging is the progressive deterioration of the body that culminates in death. Keeping physically and mentally active is important in managing the aging process.

- If adults regularly engage in intellectually stimulating activities, they may show little evidence of intellectual decline through their 70s.

- A stage model of dying does not adequately describe most people's end-of-life experiences.

- People who have the most difficulty dealing with their own impending death are those who lack meaning in their lives.

Using Effective Tutoring Strategies to Facilitate Cognitive Development

In tutoring students, effective teachers pay attention to each child's zone of proximal development, which is the cognitive range between what the child can do on his own and what he can achieve through guided collaboration.

When Zinacanteco Mexican girls learn traditional weaving skills from more experienced women in their community, they first spend most of their time simply watching the women weave. Next, the girls begin to weave by cooperating with their teachers, starting with easy activities and then progressing to more challenging tasks. At each stage of learning, their teachers provide the girls with just the right amount of instruction to successfully complete the task (Greenfield & Lave, 1982). This example of informal learning is typical of how tutors play a crucial role in the learning of new skills. To better understand how tutoring figures into cognitive development and what tutoring strategies are most effective, let's take a second look at the work of the Russian psychologist Lev Vygotsky.

Tutoring and the Zone of Proximal Development

As discussed in Section 3.3c, one of Vygotsky's central concepts is the zone of proximal development (ZPD), which is the cognitive range between what people can do on their own and what they can achieve through guided collaboration with those who already have the knowledge and skills. In teaching a young would-be weaver her craft, a more experienced adult first assesses the child's cognitive range of weaving skills— her weaving ZPD—and then slowly moves her from the lower limit to the upper limit of that range. The upper limit of the girl's ZPD can be reached only through working closely with her tutor; yet once this upper limit is reached, it becomes the lower limit for a more challenging ZPD.

There is no one single "best" strategy in tutoring, but research indicates that the most effective instructors are those who combine general and specific interventions according to the learner's progress (Wood et al., 1976). In this two-pronged tutoring approach, the teacher begins with general instructions and stays at that level of advice until the learner runs into difficulties. The teacher then switches to a more specific type of instruction or demonstration. An example of this combined instruction strategy is the way my wife often teaches social studies to her fourth grade class. First, she gives students general instructions, telling them to read that day's lesson and then answer a series of questions at the end. If any students have problems answering the questions, her instructions become more specific: Preread the questions before reading the lesson; look for bold-faced words in the reading related to question material. This two-pronged style allows children considerable latitude in making their own learning choices, while still providing careful guidance when they reach the upper limits of their abilities.

In assisting the learner, effective tutors engage in their own problem solving: They modify their approach based on how the learner responds to instruction (Rogoff, 1990). Good tutors also provide instruction that involves one extra operation or decision beyond the level at which their instructees are currently performing so that they are pushed to the upper limit of their ZPD. In trying to determine whether learners are "stuck" on a task, observant tutors will not only listen to what learners say but also closely monitor their nonverbal behavior, such as pauses, sighs, and nervous laughter (Fox, 1988).

Obstacles to Effective Tutoring

One complicating factor that all tutors must bear in mind is that their tutoring should never so dominate the lesson that it demotivates the learner, causing him or her to lose interest in the task altogether (Deci et al., 1993). This problem generally occurs when the tutor attempts to exercise control over a task that is within the learner's ability to perform—that is, at the lower limit of the learner's ZPD. For example, in trying to teach a child how to play a new computer game, a parent might take over the entire operation of the game instead of simply providing occasional hints. Before the parent realizes what he has done, his child has lost interest and is off doing something else.

Shutterstock

Another potential problem faced by tutors is trying to teach a skill to someone who is not interested in learning it. A prime example of such reluctant learning occurs in the arena of household chores (Goodnow, 1988). Am I mistaken, or didn't all of us learn in childhood that if we acted wholly incompetent at, say, washing the dishes or sweeping the floor, our parents would do it themselves? At that young age, we already intuitively grasped Vygotsky's notion of ZPD and were banking on our parents believing that these chores were so beyond our current skill levels that even guided collaboration was fruitless!

Suggested Websites

Attachment Theory

http://www.johnbowlby.com

This website provides information on Bowlby-Ainsworth attachment research.

Birth Psychology

http://www.birthpsychology.com

This is a website devoted to information on life before birth, birth traumas, and literature on birth psychology.

American Academy of Child and Adolescent Psychiatry

http://www.aacap.org

This website offers information about adoption, bedwetting, teenage suicide, divorce, and other developmental issues.

The Jean Piaget Society

http://www.piaget.org

This is a website covering Piaget's life and theory, with student links and information about the society.

Kohlberg's Theory of Moral Development

http:// web.cortland.edu/andersmd/KOHL/CONTENT.HTML

This is a website with information about Kohlberg's theory, including applications.

Adult Development & Aging

http://apadiv20.phhp.ufl.edu/apadiv20_1104.html

This is an APA-related student website for Division 20, which is the APA division devoted to the psychology of adult development and aging.

Key Terms

Accommodation, 116
Activity theory of learning, 137
Adolescence, 127
Aging, 135
Alzheimer's disease, 138
Ambivalent sexism, 112
Assimilation, 116
Attachment, 101
Authoritarian parent, 109
Authoritative parent, 108
Concrete operational stage, 120
Conservation, 118
Conventional morality, 124
Development, 92

Egocentrism, 117
Embryonic stage, 93
Emerging adulthood, 128
Ethnic identity, 131
Femininity, 111
Fetal alcohol syndrome, 95
Fetal stage, 93
Formal operational stage, 120
Gender identity, 112
Germinal stage, 93
Imaginary audience, 130
Internalization, 122
Longitudinal study, 106
Masculinity, 111

Menopause, 136
Metacognition, 123
Midlife crisis, 135
Object permanence, 117
Permissive parent, 109
Personal fable, 130
Postconventional morality, 125
Preconventional morality, 124
Prenatal development, 92
Preoperational stage, 117
Primary sex characteristics, 128
Puberty, 128
Schema, 116

Review Questions

1. Which of the following statements is true of a zygote?
   a. It is created at conception.
   b. It contains 46 cells.
   c. It spontaneously aborts 10 percent of the time.
   d. It is developed during the longest stage of prenatal development.
   e. It can survive outside the womb.

2. Which of the following is true of a child's brain?
   a. It has fewer nerve cells than an adult brain.
   b. It is not shaped by environment.
   c. It is 75 percent of its adult weight by age 2.
   d. It does not grow new dendrites.
   e. None of the above

3. Which of the following statements is true of physical growth and motor development of children?
   a. Motor development is not affected by culture.
   b. Basic motor skills develop from the legs up.
   c. Reflexes are permanent.
   d. There is a surge in height and weight during middle childhood.
   e. Primitive reflexes have outlived their usefulness.

4. There is evidence to support which of the following?
   a. The fetus is not capable of recognizing sounds.
   b. Newborns can see very clearly.
   c. Infants prefer sour tastes to sweet.
   d. The sense of touch is not functional before birth.
   e. None of the above

5. Which of these characteristics has been attributed to securely attached babies?
   a. invulnerablity to later problems in life
   b. lack of curiosity
   c. increased popularity
   d. increased independence and social skill
   e. c and d

6. Which of the following is supported by studies on attachment style?
   a. Temperament is not significantly shaped by inherited biological factors.
   b. Parenting style has a greater impact than the child's temperament.
   c. Attachment style is not shaped by culture.
   d. Multiple attachments can cause adverse consequences.
   e. All of the above

7. Which of the following statements is supported by studies?
   a. The quality of day care is irrelevant when considering impact on attachment.
   b. Children who come from conflict-ridden, two-parent families tend to be psychologically healthier than children of divorce.
   c. Mothers in all ethnic groups spend more time with their children than fathers.
   d. There is no long-term impact on children of divorce.
   e. None of the above

8. The study by Lewis and Brooks that put babies in front of a mirror with rouge on their noses illustrates the concept of _____.
   a. attachment
   b. self-awareness
   c. contact comfort
   d. self-esteem
   e. temperament

9. Studies have indicated that children with high self-esteem tend to have _____ parents.
   a. authoritarian
   b. permissive
   c. authoritative
   d. all types of
   e. There have been no such studies.

10. What term is used by psychologists for children's identification of themselves as male or female?
    a. gender schema
    b. gender identity
    c. sexual identity
    d. sexual orientation
    e. gender orientation

11. According to Erikson, the crisis that occurs when a person discerns whether he or she has contributed or produced something worthy of his or her efforts is called _____ versus _____.
    a. trust, mistrust.
    b. autonomy, shame and doubt.
    c. initiative, guilt.
    d. competence, inferiority.
    e. generativity, stagnation.

12. Piaget's three-mountain problem demonstrated which of the following notions?
    a. object permanence
    b. representational thought
    c. egocentrism
    d conservation
    e. assimilation

13. Which of the following is true of Vygotsky's theory of cognitive development?
    a. The cognitive development stage should first be determined so that children can be taught material appropriate to that level.
    b. Children's mental development cannot be accelerated.
    c. Cognitive development is relatively asocial.
    d. Learning occurs through the social instrument of language.
    e. Internal dialogue is detrimental to the learning process.

14. Which of the following statements is true of aging?
    a. The body operates at its peak efficiency during a person's late 20s.
    b. Middle-aged men experience a cessation of fertility in their 50s.
    c. Older brains can form new neural connections to replace those they lose.
    d. No studies have been done on how people cope with their impending death.
    e. Research indicates that open discussion and disclosure of dying is rarely beneficial.

15. Which of the following is a reason why teens often engage in risky behavior?
    a. General intelligence actually dips slightly in adolescence.
    b. Teens have a desire to "test out" their new bodies.
    c. Brain areas that control impulsive behavior are underdeveloped.
    d. The so-called "fear neurons" conduct impulses more slowly in teens.
    e. Risky behavior is an evolutionary strategy to attract the opposite sex.

16. In Phinney's (1993) research on ethnic identity formation, she found which of the following in relation to self-esteem?
    a. Evaluation of our group by the larger society is the most influential factor on our self-esteem.
    b. Our commitment and attitudes toward our ethnic group are most influential on our self-esteem.
    c. Ethnic identity is not as important as was originally thought in the development of self-esteem.
    d. Our self-esteem is more drastically damaged when we identify with members of our ethnic group.
    e. None of the above is correct.

17. To which of the following does the term ethnic identity refer?
    a. the characteristics, such as skin color, associated with ethnicity
    b. an individual's personal feeling of belonging to an ethnic group
    c. stereotypes associated with particular races
    d. the unique cultural practices of ethnic subgroups
    e. the performance of behaviors designed to show that one is "keeping it real"

Chapter Four

Sensation and Perception

Chapter Outline

Psychological Applications: *Can You Improve Your Memory and Self-Esteem through Subliminal Persuasion?*

On April 26, 2003, 27-year-old Aron Ralston planned a one-day training excursion in Utah's Canyonlands National Park. His goal was to go canyoneering, which involves scrambling, climbing, and rappelling up the sheer sides of canyons. After pedaling his bike into the park, Aron entered Bluejohn Canyon and began scaling its walls. When Aron was at the height of 60 feet and inside a 3-foot-wide slot, an 800-pound boulder shifted and pinned his right arm to the rocky surface. For three days, this former mechanical engineer used

We live on the leash of our senses.

—Diane Ackerman, American poet, b. 1948

Aron Ralston amputated his own arm after it became pinned by an 800-pound boulder while he was climbing canyon walls in Utah's Canyonlands National Park.

Wikimedia Commons

all his skills to try to free his arm, including vainly looping ropes around the boulder and rigging a pulley system with his climbing gear. Nothing worked, and he had used up all his food and water. What could he do?

Because of his remote location, Aron knew there was little hope of rescue and that only drastic action could save him. So he decided to cut off his pinned arm. He practiced applying a tourniquet using a climbing cord and came up with a plan for cutting through the bone with his pocketknife. First he cut off his crushed forearm just below the elbow. "It occurred to me I could break my bones," Aron later said. "I was able to first snap the radius and then within another few minutes snap the ulna at the wrist and from there, I had the knife out and applied the tourniquet and went to task. It was a process that took about an hour."

How was he able to cope with the blinding pain while cutting through his own flesh and bone? "I'm not sure how I handled it," Aron later said. "I felt pain and I coped with it. I moved on." After freeing himself from the boulder, Aron fashioned a tourniquet around his partially severed limb, crawled through the canyon, and then rappelled to the canyon floor. With blood seeping from his wound, he walked six miles until he came upon some hikers, who notified nearby rescuers. Following surgeries and rehabilitation, Aron resumed his outdoor adventures.

Although few of us will ever have to deal with the type of life-threatening dilemma presented to Aron, experiencing and managing pain is a natural part of life, as well as one of the topics of this chapter. We continue our journey of discovery in psychology by examining the two interrelated processes of sensation and perception. **Sensation** is the process that detects stimuli from our bodies and our environment, whereas **perception** is the process that organizes those stimuli into meaningful objects and events (d'Ydewalle, 2000; Ross, 2000).

Normally, we experience sensation and perception as one process, but they can be distinguished. For example, look at Figure 4-1. Initially, you may have a hard time seeing anything meaningful—that is, you may sense different shapes but perceive no meaningful pattern. In fact, some of you will give up before organizing these visual sensations into a coherent set of objects. This process of building a perceptual experience from smaller pieces of information is known as **bottom-up processing**. In the brain, bottom-up processing involves data being relayed from lower levels of mental processing to higher levels of processing, from the bottom-up (Lenartowicz et al., 2011). Bottom-up processing will be the primary focus of the first part of this chapter when we examine sensory processes.

Perception can also occur through **top-down processing**—where perception of the whole is based on our memories, experiences, and expectations, which shape our perception of smaller sensory features of a stimulus (Jensen & Mathewson, 2011). Top-down processing will be the primary focus of the second half of this chapter when we examine perceptual processes. Look again at Figure 4-1. When informed that these assortment of black lines depict a horse and rider, you are now more likely to perceive the expected image, based on your past experience with similar images. Similarly, try to decipher the following sentence:

Fou_sc_re an_ s_ven _ears ag_ o_r fa_hers s_t fo_th on th_s cont_n_nt a n_w na_ion, c_nce_ved _n Lib_rt_ a_d d_d_cated to th_ pr_p_sit_on th_t a_l men ar_ cre_t_d eq_al.

Sensation The process that detects stimuli from our bodies and our environment

Perception The process that organizes sensations into meaningful objects and events

Bottom-up processing The idea that perception is a process of building a perceptual experience from smaller pieces of information

Top-down processing The idea that perception of the whole is based on our memories, experiences, and expectations, which shape our perception of smaller sensory features of a stimulus

FIGURE 4-1

Sensation and Perception

Detecting the different shapes in this figure involves the process of sensation, but seeing a meaningful image involves the process of perception. Which process did you experience first, sensation or perception? Is this noticeable delay in sensory and perceptual processing a common occurrence in your everyday life?

Can you read the preceding sentence with many letters missing? If perception was based simply on bottom-up processing, you shouldn't be able to understand this sentence. However, the fact that you probably were able to identify the first sentence of Abraham Lincoln's *Gettysburg Address* is due to top-down processing where your perception of these missing-letter words was based on your understanding of both the English language and American history.

We begin our analysis of these two interrelated processes by examining some basic principles that apply to all sensory systems. Next we will discuss the six senses of *vision*, *audition* (hearing), *olfaction* (smell), *gustation* (taste), *touch*, and *proprioception* (the sense of body position and movement). From there, we will examine how the brain organizes sensations into perceptions.

4.1 Basic Principles of Sensation

Can you sometimes overhear others' quiet conversations when you are considerably distant from them? Do you sometimes "tune out" distracting sensations around you? These are the sorts of questions of interest to the field of **psychophysics**, the study of how physical stimuli are translated into psychological experience (Baumann, 2008).

Psychophysics The study of how physical stimuli are translated into psychological experience

4.1a Our Sensory Receptors Convert Energy from Stimuli into Neural Impulses.

While typing this sentence, I am eating a handful of peanut M & Ms. I can hear their crunch while chewing, and I know that this sound is a response to vibrations in the air, or *sound waves*. I am also noticing a sweet taste, which I know is a response to the dissolving chemicals in my mouth. I can even faintly smell the aroma of chocolate, which is a response to molecules in the air that I am inhaling through my nose. I also feel the last three M & Ms in my hand, which is a response to their physical pressure on my skin. Finally, I see that these remaining candies are colored red, blue, and brown, which is a response to the light waves reflecting from their surfaces.

One thing to understand about this experience—and others like it—is that sound, light, and other kinds of stimuli from our surroundings cannot travel through our nerves to the brain. Instead, our sensory receptors convert the energy from these various stimuli into neural impulses. This conversion process, which is a very basic aspect of bottom-up processing, is called **transduction**; and it takes place at

Transduction The process by which our sensory organs convert a stimulus's physical properties into neural impulses

TABLE 4-1   The Stimuli and Sensory Receptors for Each Primary Sense

Sense	Stimulus	Sensory Receptors
Vision	Light waves	Light-sensitive rods and cones in the retina of the eye
Hearing	Sound waves	Pressure-sensitive hair cells in the cochlea of the inner ear
Taste	Molecules dissolved in fluid on the tongue	Taste cells in the taste buds of the tongue
Smell	Molecules dissolved in fluid on mucus membranes in the nose	Sensitive ends of olfactory neurons in the mucus membranes
Touch	Pressure on the skin	Sensitive ends of touch neurons in the skin

structures called *sensory receptors*. Following transduction, connecting neurons in the sensory receptors send this information to the brain. The brain then processes these neural impulses into what we experience.

One important fact to remember is that you can be aware of a stimulus in your environment only if you have sensory receptors that can transduce it. Human beings cannot see X-rays or hear very-high-frequency tones, and we cannot taste certain chemicals because we do not have sensory receptors that can convert these stimuli into neural impulses. These stimuli are just as real as those that we can transduce, but they are not a part of our sensory experience. Table 4-1 lists the stimuli and sensory receptors for each sense.

4.1b Our Senses Vary in Their Sensitivity Thresholds

German scientist Gustav Fechner (1801–1887), who was a pioneer in psychophysics, introduced the term **absolute threshold** to explain instances of detecting minimal stimuli (Fechner, 1966). An absolute threshold is the lowest level of intensity of a given stimulus that a person can detect half the time. Psychologists measure absolute thresholds by presenting a stimulus (for example, a light or a sound) to a person at different intensities and determining what is the lowest level detectable 50 percent of the time. Some examples of absolute thresholds for various senses are listed in Table 4-2.

Absolute threshold The lowest level of intensity of a given stimulus that a person can detect half the time

TABLE 4-2   Examples of Absolute Thresholds

Stimulus	Absolute Threshold
Vision	A candle seen at 30 miles on a dark, clear night
Hearing	The tick of a watch at 20 feet under quiet conditions
Taste	One teaspoon of sugar in 2 gallons of water
Smell	One drop of perfume diffused into a 3-room apartment
Touch	The wing of a fly falling on your cheek from a distance of 0.5 inch

Source: Adapted from Galanter, 1962.

A number of studies have found that the absolute threshold for a given sense varies between people (Rabin & Cain, 1986). For instance, due to the damaging effects that tobacco smoke has on nasal cavities, smokers or people regularly exposed to tobacco smoke have a less sensitive sense of smell than nonsmokers (Richardson & Zucco, 1989). As people age, their absolute thresholds for all senses increase, which means that greater stimulation is necessary to detect stimuli (Schiffman, 1997; Stevens, 1989).

The assumption underlying the absolute threshold concept is that there is a minimum intensity level at which a stimulus is consistently detected. However, according to **signal-detection theory**, the detection of a stimulus is also influenced by the observer's decision-making strategy or criterion (King-Smith, 2005; Swets, 1992). Consistent with the notion of top-down processing, two important factors that shape this decision making are (1) the observer's expectations about the probability that the stimulus will occur and (2) the rewards and costs associated with detecting or not detecting the stimulus (Harder et al., 1989). For example, suppose you were looking for shooting stars on a night in which you mistakenly thought there was a meteor shower. Due to your false expectation, you probably would detect fainter, fleeting flashes of light in the sky than if you expected no meteor shower. Detecting these flashes might also be affected by how important this task was to you. If astronomy was your favorite hobby, you might "see" more flashes than if stargazing was merely a lark.

One major contribution of signal-detection theory is that it points out that we do not have a single absolute threshold for a given sense. Whether or not we perceive a particular stimulus depends on the situation, and what expectations and motives we bring to it. Such knowledge is important because many signal-detection tasks carry life-and-death implications. Consider the task of a medical technician who is screening numerous X-rays every hour for possible signs of disease. Are those faint markings on the lungs normal, or do they indicate the early stages of cancer? Studies demonstrate that when people try to judge whether a faint stimulus is present or absent, their vigilance diminishes after about 30 minutes, due to fatigue. Although such fatigue effects won't cause any serious consequences when looking for shooting stars, they could prove disastrous in the medical lab.

Besides detecting a weak stimulus, we often must detect changes in the intensity of a stimulus or discriminate between two similar stimuli. The smallest difference between two stimuli that can be detected half the time is known as the **difference threshold** (also called the *just-noticeable difference*, or *jnd*). For example, what is the minimum amount of difference that you can detect in the sweetness of two soft drinks?

In 1834, Ernst Weber (1795–1878), Fechner's brother-in-law, discovered that the amount of change in stimulation necessary to produce a just-noticeable difference is a constant proportion of the original stimulus. The size of the difference threshold depends on the intensity of the stimuli being compared (Laming, 1985; Norwich, 1987). A weak or small stimulus does not require much change before you notice that the stimulus has changed, but a strong or large stimulus requires a proportionately greater change before you notice the change. For example, you will easily notice the weight difference when holding a 1-pound bag versus a 2-pound bag but will not notice a difference between a 100-pound bag and a 101-pound bag. According to **Weber's law**, to be noticed as different, two stimuli must differ by

Signal-detection theory The theory that explains how detection of a stimulus is influenced by observers' expectations

Difference threshold The smallest difference between two stimuli that can be detected half the time; also called *just-noticeable difference*, or *jnd*

Weber's law The principle that to be noticed as different, two stimuli must differ by a constant minimum percentage rather than by a constant amount

Weber's law states that a weak stimulus does not require much change before a person notices that it has changed, but a stronger stimulus requires a proportionately greater change before it is noticed. When power lifting, you would notice a weight difference after about 3 percent of the current weight is either added or taken away.

TABLE 4-3	Difference Thresholds: How Much Must a Stimulus Change to Be Noticeable?
Stimulus	**Amount of Average Necessary Change**
Sound frequency	0.3 percent
Light brightness	2.0 percent
Weight heftiness	3.0 percent
Odor concentration	7.0 percent
Pressure intensity	14.0 percent
Taste concentration	20.0 percent

a constant minimum percentage rather than by a constant amount. The smallest noticeable change in weight is about 3 percent. Thus, you would need to add two more pounds to the 101-pound bag to reach the difference threshold.

As you can see from Table 4-3, the values of these proportions vary a great deal for the different senses. Although you can detect a change in sound frequency of 0.3 percent (one-third of 1 percent), it requires a 7 percent increase to detect a difference threshold in smell, and a whopping 20 percent increase to detect a difference in taste! This means that your sense of hearing is much more sensitive than your sense of taste.

4.1c *Our Sensory Receptors Adapt to Unchanging Stimuli.*

During my first year in graduate school, I attended City College of New York and rode the subway to school each day. At first, the noise was so distracting that I not only had difficulty reading but also, invariably, came home with a headache. Yet, within a few days, the subway noise appeared to diminish; and I was comfortably reading and headache-free when riding it. This example illustrates **sensory adaptation**, the tendency for our sensory receptors to have decreasing responsiveness to stimuli that continue without change. The most common explanation for sensory adaptation is that it is caused by our nerve cells firing less frequently after high levels of stimulation (Rajimehr et al., 2004; Yamaguchi et al., 2004).

From an evolutionary perspective, sensory adaptation makes sense. Animals that tune out constant unchanging stimuli that provide no new information should be better able to detect more useful information for survival. However, sensory adaptation is occasionally disadvantageous. For example, while tuning out subway noises increased my ability to study for exams, I sometimes didn't hear the conductor call out my stop, causing me to arrive late for class!

Auditory adaptation occurs much more slowly than adaptation to odors, tastes, and skin sensations (Scharf, 1983). For example, we adapt to smells very quickly, with the perceived magnitude of odor decay occurring at the rate of about 2.5 percent each second (Cain, 1978). Within one minute, odor adaptation is essentially complete, and the perceived magnitude of the smell is about 30 percent of the initial magnitude. We still smell it, but not as intensely. Try a little demonstration on yourself. Place a substance with a strong odor—perhaps an onion, perfume, or shaving lotion—near your nose for a few minutes. Its odor will seem less intense over time. Next, remove the substance for five minutes and then smell it again. Now it should smell as strong as it did when you first smelled it.

Sensory adaptation The tendency for our sensory receptors to show decreasing responsiveness to stimuli that continue without change

- Stimuli must be transduced into neural impulses to be understood by the brain.

- Absolute threshold is the lowest level of intensity of a given stimulus that a person can detect half the time.

- According to signal-detection theory, detection of a stimulus is influenced by both stimulus intensity and the observer's decision-making strategy.

- Difference threshold is the smallest difference between two stimuli that can be detected half the time.

- Sensory adaptation refers to our sensory receptors' decreasing responsiveness to an unchanging stimulus.

4.2 Vision

Because scientific inquiry has discovered more about the visual system than any of the other senses, I not only examine this sense first but also later use the visual system to explain the major principles of perception.

4.2a *We See Only a Narrow Band of Electromagnetic Radiation.*

Light is a form of energy known as *electromagnetic energy*. This energy is all around us and travels in waves of different lengths and intensities, created by the vibration of electrically charged particles. A **wavelength** is the distance between two peaks of adjacent waves. Our eyes can detect the wavelengths of *visible light*, which range from 400 to 750 nanometers, with a nanometer being one-billionth of a meter. Within this range of visible light, the colors we see are determined by the size of the wavelength (refer to Figure 4-2). The shorter wavelengths are experienced as violet, the intermediate ones as blue, green, and yellow, and the longer ones as red. Other forms of electromagnetic energy that our eyes cannot detect because they

Wavelength The distance between two peaks of adjacent waves

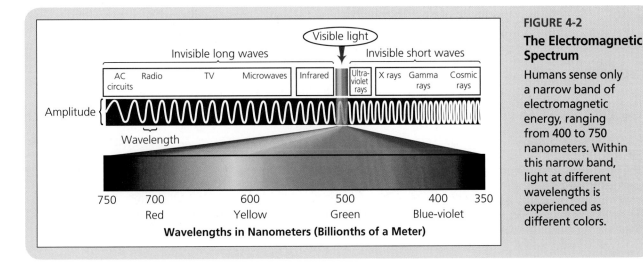

FIGURE 4-2

The Electromagnetic Spectrum

Humans sense only a narrow band of electromagnetic energy, ranging from 400 to 750 nanometers. Within this narrow band, light at different wavelengths is experienced as different colors.

FIGURE 4-3

Major Structures of the Human Eye

Light first passes through the cornea, pupil, and lens and is then focused on the retina at the back of the eye. The point of sharpest vision on the retina is the fovea.

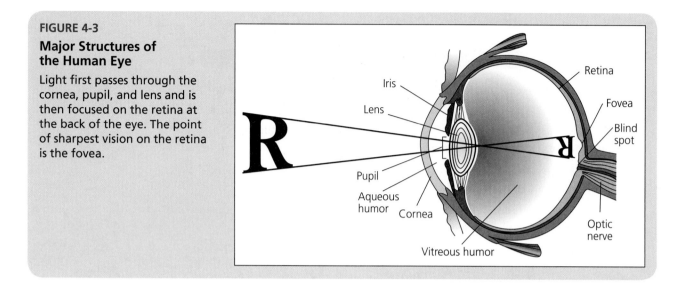

fall outside this 400- to 750-nanometer range are radio, infrared, ultraviolet, and X-ray radiation.

4.2b *Light Passes Through the Cornea, Pupil, and Lens Before Focusing on the Retina.*

Light enters the eye through the cornea, a clear membrane covering the front of the eyeball (see Figure 4-3). The cornea bends the light falling on its surface just enough to focus it at the back of the eye. From the **cornea**, light passes through a pocket of fluid known as the *aqueous humor*, which carries oxygen and other nutrients to the cornea and lens. Next, light passes through a hole in the *iris*, called the **pupil**. The **iris** is a ring of muscles that functions much like the diaphragm of a camera. As illustrated in Figure 4-4, in dim light, muscle fibers in the iris dilate (open) the pupil, letting in more light, while in bright light the pupil constricts, letting in less light. Pupil size is affected not only by light. When psychologically aroused or interested in something, your pupils dilate (Hess, 1975).

After passing through the pupil, light enters a clear, elastic, disc-shaped structure called the **lens**, which refocuses the light with the aid of muscles attached to it. A clear image of distant objects is achieved by these muscles stretching and flattening the lens, while relaxing the lens and making it more spherical results in a clear image of near objects. Because the lens changes shape without any willful action, people often mistakenly assume that everything, near and far, is always in focus. To demonstrate to yourself that this is not the case, close one eye and look at a distant object; and then, while still focusing on this object, begin moving a pencil toward you

Cornea A clear membrane covering the front of the eyeball that aids in visual acuity by bending light that falls on its surface

Pupil A hole in the center of the iris that regulates how much light enters the eye

Iris A ring of muscles in the eye that range in color from light blue to dark brown

Lens An elastic, disc-shaped structure that focuses light

FIGURE 4-4

Light Adaptation by the Eye

The black spots in the middle of these two eyeballs show how small and large the pupil becomes when you are in bright light (*a*) and darkness (*b*).

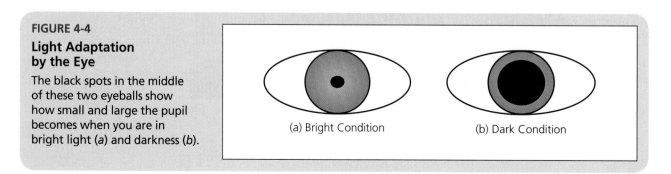

(a) Bright Condition   (b) Dark Condition

while paying attention to—but not focusing on—the pencil point. As the pencil gets closer, notice that the point becomes blurred and appears to be doubled. When the pencil is about 12 inches away, focus on the point; you will notice that the faraway object becomes blurred. As you move the pencil to within a couple of inches of your eyes, you will no longer be able to bring the point into focus because the lens has reached its maximum curvature and cannot get any fatter. This distance at which your lens can no longer accommodate to bring the pencil point into focus is called the *near point*. As you get older (past the age of 45), the distance of the near point will increase because aging causes a reduction in the elasticity of the lens.

After being focused by the lens, light travels through the *vitreous humor*, which is a clear jellylike liquid that occupies the space behind the lens, and is then projected onto a light-sensitive surface at the back of the eye known as the **retina** (Mills & Catania, 2004). As people age, the vitreous humor inside their eyes may thicken, causing tiny clumps of cells to form and float around. If you have these "floaters," you can actually see them; they look like specks, strands, webs, or other shapes. Actually, what you see are the shadows of these floating cells and fibers projected on the retina. One of the best ways to see floaters is to close your eyes while looking at a light source, and then watch for tiny strands, dots, or squiggles to float through your field of vision. A similar effect can often be achieved by keeping your eyes open and looking at a blank white background. In almost all cases, floaters are normal and perfectly harmless eye events. However, seeing floaters accompanied by flashes of light or peripheral vision loss could indicate a serious medical condition, such as diabetes, retinal hemorrhage, or the beginning stages of retinal detachment.

Besides the minor annoyance of floaters, abnormalities in the cornea's outer membrane wall and abnormalities in the lens can affect *visual acuity*, which is the sharpness of the visual image at the retina. *Myopia*, or nearsightedness—decreased acuity for distant objects—occurs when the cornea and lens focus the image in front of the retina. In contrast, *hyperopia*, or farsightedness—blurred vision for near objects—occurs when the eye focuses the image on a point beyond the retina. These eye defects affect many people, but they can be easily corrected by wearing glasses or contact lenses that alter the eye's focus. More modern medical procedures, such as laser surgery, can also restore visual acuity by shaving off minute portions of the cornea and restoring proper curvature so that light striking the eye is bent correctly.

Returning to our discussion of the retina, would it surprise you to learn that it is actually a piece of the brain that migrates to the eye during early fetal development (Gregory, 1998)? Below its outer layer of cells resides a layer of sensory receptors, called *photoreceptors*, which convert incoming light into neural impulses (Greenstein et al., 2004). There are two basic kinds of photoreceptors: **rods** and **cones** (see Figure 4-5). The rods, located at the edges of the retina, are extremely sensitive to light and are central to the detection of patterns of black, white, and gray. The rods function best under low-light conditions and, thus, are most useful at night. In contrast to the rods, the cones require much more light to be activated and play a key role in color vision. Most cones are concentrated in a small area near the center of the retina known as the **fovea**, which is the area of central focus. A human retina contains about 125 million rods and 7 million cones (Pugh, 1988). As you would expect, animals that are most active at night, such as owls and

Retina A light-sensitive surface at the back of the eye

Rods Receptor neurons in the eye located at the edges of the retina that are sensitive to the brightness of light

Cones Receptor neurons in the eye, located near the center of the retina, which mediate color vision

Fovea The retina's area of central focus

When viewing a scene similar to this on a moonlit night, your world looks relatively colorless because only your rod photoreceptors are functioning under these low-light conditions. Your color-sensitive cone photoreceptors are not sufficiently stimulated by night light.

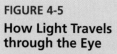

FIGURE 4-5

How Light Travels through the Eye

When light passes through the eye and falls on the retina, it passes through several layers of cells before striking and activating sensory receptors called photoreceptors. The two different kinds of photoreceptors are rods and cones. The rods detect patterns of black, white, and gray, whereas the cones play a key role in color vision. When activated, rods and cones send neural impulses to bipolar cells that, in turn, activate the ganglion cells (Chen et al., 2004). The ganglion cells' axons converge to form the optic nerve, which sends information to the brain.

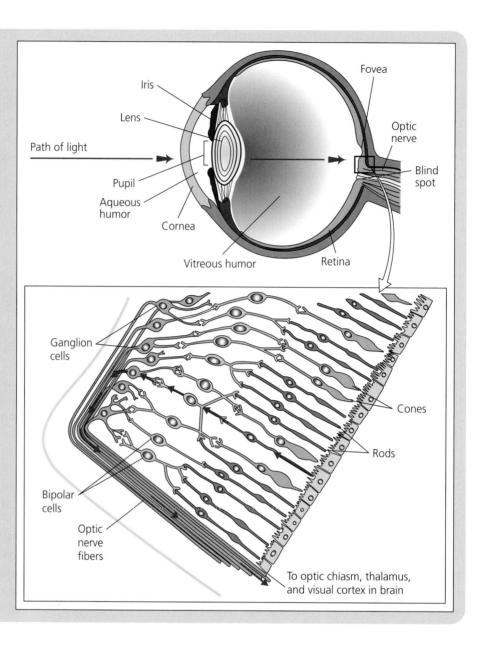

Optic nerve The bundle of nerve cells that carries information from the retina to the brain

Blind spot The area on the retina where the optic nerve leaves the eye; contains no receptor cells

rats, have all-rod eyes, whereas daytime animals, such as lizards and chipmunks, have mostly cone-dominant retinas (Tansley, 1965; Wagner, 2001).

When light reaches the back of the eye and strikes the retina, it actually passes through several layers of cells below the retina's surface before reaching the rods and cones. Once activated by this light energy, the rods and cones generate neural signals that activate adjacent *bipolar cells*, which in turn activate neighboring *ganglion cells* (see Figure 4-5). The axons of the ganglion cells converge like the strands of a rope to form the **optic nerve**, which carries information from the retina to the brain. Before the information is sent on to the brain, however, a great deal of complex information processing takes place in the retina (Slaughter, 1990). This processing occurs in the bipolar and ganglion cells, where information from the rods and cones is integrated and compressed so that it can be more easily transmitted along the optic nerve.

The portion of the retina where the optic nerve leaves the eye contains no rods or cones, which means that images falling there are not seen (Ramachandran, 1992). This area is called the **blind spot** in the field of vision. One reason you are not more aware of your blind spot is that when an image falls on the blind spot of one eye, it

FIGURE 4-6

The Blind Spot

You can experience your own blind spot by closing your right eye and lining up the cross with your left eye. Slowly move your head back and forth. When the image is between 6 and 18 inches away from your eye, the image of the happy face falls on your blind spot and disappears from sight.

falls on the receptors of the other—thus you still detect the image. Another reason you don't often perceive the blind spot, even with one-eyed vision, is that it is located off to the side of your visual field; thus objects near this area are never in sharp focus. Finally, perhaps the most important reason that you are not aware of the blind spot is that your visual system somehow "fills in" the place where the image disappears. Thus, when you try the blind spot demonstration in Figure 4-6, the place where the happy face used to be isn't replaced by a "hole" or by "nothingness," but rather by the white surrounding it.

4.2c Visual Information Is Transmitted to Both Brain Hemispheres.

After they leave the eyes, the axons of the ganglion cells that make up the optic nerve separate, and half of them cross to the other side of the head at the *optic chiasm* (pronounced "KYE-az-um"), which is at the bottom of the brain. As illustrated in Figure 4-7, the axons from the right side of each eye are connected to the right hemisphere of the brain and those from the left side of each eye are connected to the left hemisphere. Thus, visual information in a person's *left visual field*, which is the area to the left of the person, will go to the right hemisphere, while the exact opposite will be true for information in the person's *right visual field*. This splitting and crossing over of the optic nerve is important because it ensures that signals from both eyes go to both brain hemispheres.

A short distance after leaving the optic chiasm, the optic nerve fibers diverge along two pathways. Eighty percent of the nerve fibers are connected to the lateral geniculate nucleus of the thalamus, while most of the rest of the nerve fibers are attached to the *superior colliculus* in the midbrain. The superior colliculus is the evolutionarily older of the two brain structures and is the primary area for visual processing in less developed animals, like frogs. In humans, the superior colliculus is involved in controlling eye movements. In contrast to this more primitive brain structure, the lateral geniculate nucleus is a kidney-bean-shaped cluster of neurons that performs much more detailed visual analysis. Six different layers of cells in the *lateral geniculate nucleus* not only organize information about color and other aspects of the visual field reaching it from the retina, but they also create a "map" of visual space in the retina where each location on the lateral geniculate nucleus corresponds to a location on the retina (Mollon, 1990).

FIGURE 4-7

The Brain's Visual Pathways

Information from the right half of the visual field strikes the left side of each retina and is sent by the optic nerve to the left cerebral hemisphere. Information from the left half of the visual field strikes the right side of each retina and is sent to the right cerebral hemisphere. After reaching the optic chiasm, a minor pathway goes to the superior colliculus in the midbrain, but the major visual pathway is to the lateral geniculate nucleus of the thalamus. From there, visual information is sent to the occipital lobe, or visual cortex (Dow, 2002).

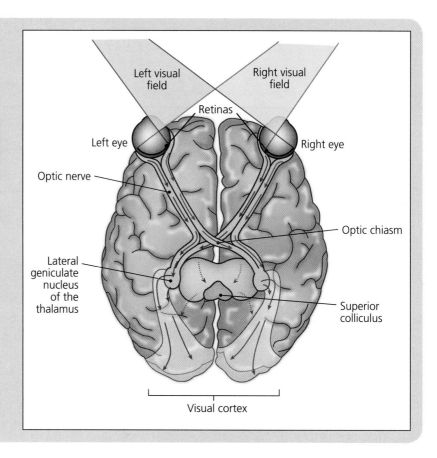

From the lateral geniculate nucleus, visual information is sent to areas in the occipital lobe that make up the visual cortex. To understand how cells in the visual cortex communicate with one another, in the late 1950s David Hubel and Tortsen Wiesel placed microelectrodes in this area of a cat's brain to record action potentials from individual neurons. To stimulate action potentials, the researchers projected spots of light onto a screen with a slide projector, but they were initially unable to get the neurons to fire with any regularity. Then, quite by accident, as they were inserting a glass slide containing a spot stimulus into their projector, a neuron began firing like crazy. What Hubel and Wiesel discovered was that the rapid neural firing was in response, not to the image of the spot, but to the image of the straight edge of the slide as it moved downward on the projector screen! They proposed that cells in the visual cortex known as **feature detectors** respond only to a highly specific *feature* or characteristic of a visual stimulus, such as a straight edge, an angle, movement of a spot, or brightness (Hubel & Wiesel, 1965a, 1965b). This information is then passed on to other cells that in turn respond only to more complex features. Through this interaction among many types of visual neurons, each responsible for specific tasks, our brain is provided with the basic building blocks of visual perception that it then assembles into a meaningful whole (Hubel, 1996; Jiang et al., 2002; Rolls & Deco, 2002). This groundbreaking research by Hubel and Wiesel earned them the Nobel Prize in physiology in 1981.

Feature detectors Cells in the visual cortex that respond only to a highly specific feature of a visual stimulus, such as a straight edge, an angle, movement of a spot, or brightness

4.2d *Colors Are Created in Our Visual System.*

What does it really mean when we say that a leaf is green? Does the leaf actually possess the color we perceive? The answer is "no." An object appears as a particular color because it absorbs certain wavelengths of light and reflects others. The color green is not actually *in* the leaf, nor is it in the light waves reflected from it. Instead, the color resides in our own visual system. The leaf absorbs all the wavelengths of light except those that *evoke* the sensation of green in our minds. There is nothing inherently "blue" about short wavelengths or "red" about long wavelengths. These wavelengths are simply energy. Colors are *created* by our nervous system in response to these wavelengths.

Because the experience of colors is created by the nervous system, species differ in what they see when looking at the same object (Smith et al., 2002). For example, although honeybees have trichromatic vision like us, their three kinds of color receptors are spread out over a much wider band of the spectrum than our own; thus, they are sensitive to light in the ultraviolet range (Menzel & Backhaus, 1989). Pigeons have color vision based on five kinds of receptors (*pentachromatic* vision)—thus they undoubtedly see the world differently than do we (Varela et al., 1993). Astonishingly, our difference threshold for colors is so low that the average person can discriminate about 2 million different colors (Abramov & Gordon, 1994; Gouras, 1991).

Artists construct their paintings so that when light strikes them, the paintings' surfaces absorb certain wavelengths of light and reflect others. In our eyes, this light is converted into neural impulses and sent to the brain for further processing. Thus, the colors that we perceive are a creation of our nervous system. Most of us can agree on the different colors that we see in our world because our visual systems operate in roughly the same manner.

4.2e Both Trichromatic Theory and Opponent-Process Theory Explain Color Vision.

Any color can be created by combining the light wavelengths of three primary colors—red, green, and blue (Hunt, 1998). Combining red, green, and blue lights makes white light. This mixing of different light wavelengths is known as *additive color mixing* because the process adds wavelengths and thus increases light. In contrast, when you mix paint pigments, you are *subtracting* wavelengths from the reflected light. Each color you mix in absorbs (or subtracts) more wavelengths, resulting in fewer being reflected back. The colors that result when you mix pigments are different from the colors that result when you combine the primary colors of light. Magenta, cyan, and yellow are called the primary pigments. In *subtractive color mixing*, combining magenta, cyan, and yellow pigments result in no light waves being reflected—and you see black. Figure 4-8 illustrates these two types of color mixing.

To explain how our visual system causes us to experience this color mixing, two nineteenth-century scientists—first, the English physician Thomas Young (1773–1829) and later the German physiologist Hermann von Helmholtz (1821–1894)—hypothesized that the retina has three types of color receptors and that differing sensitivities to the different light waves are associated with these three primary colors. According to what came to be called the Young-Helmholtz **trichromatic theory**, light of a particular wavelength stimulates these three types of receptors to different degrees; and the resulting pattern of neural activity among these receptors results in color perception (Finger & Wade, 2002).

Trichromatic theory A theory of color perception proposing that three types of color receptors in the retina produce the primary color sensations of red, green, and blue

More than 100 years after the trichromatic theory was offered as an explanation for color vision, George Wald verified the existence of three different types of cones in the retina (Brown & Wald, 1964; Wald, 1964), a discovery that earned him a Nobel Prize. As trichromatic theory proposed, each cone is most sensitive to a particular wavelength of light. Long-wavelength cones (L-cones) are most sensitive to wavelengths of about 555 nanometers, which are perceived as red. Middle-wavelength

FIGURE 4-8   Additive and Subtractive Color Mixing

(*Left*) The three primary light colors—red, green, and blue—combine to create all the other colors of light. Mixing light of different wavelengths involves *additive color mixing* because the process adds wavelengths and thus increases light. (*Right*) Mixing color pigments in paint involves *subtractive color mixing* because the process subtracts wavelengths of reflected light and thus decreases light. Magenta, cyan, and yellow are the primary pigments. Paint with any of these colors absorbs one primary color of light and reflects the other two.

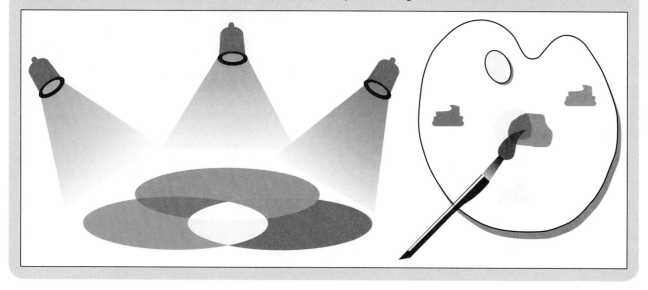

cones (M-cones) produce the sensation of green and are most sensitive to wavelengths of about 525 nanometers. Finally, short-wavelength cones (S-cones), which produce the sensation of blue, are most sensitive to wavelengths of about 450 nanometers. By combining different stimulation levels from these three kinds of cones, our visual system produces a multitude of different color sensations.

Color blindness A deficiency in the ability to distinguish among colors

The trichromatic theory provides a partial explanation for **color blindness**, which is a deficiency in the ability to distinguish among colors (see Figure 4-9 in Self-Discovery Questionnaire 4-1). Approximately 1 in 50 people is color-blind, with about 90 percent of these being male because the defect is genetic and carried on the X chromosome. A male who inherits the trait on his single X chromosome will be color-blind, but a female must inherit the trait on both of her X chromosomes to be color-blind.

Actually, the term *color blindness* is misleading because most people classified as color-blind are *dichromats*—they can see two primary colors but are insensitive to the third because the cone that is sensitive to that color is nonfunctional (Gouras, 1991; Ladd-Franklin, 1929). In contrast, only about 10 people out of 1 million have the rare form of color blindness where they have no functioning cones. These *monochromats* see everything in shades of white, gray, and black. Thus, while the relatively rare monochromats are truly color-blind, *color deficiency* is a more accurate term to describe the much more prevalent dichromats.

Afterimages Visual images that persist after a stimulus has been removed

Opponent-process theory A theory proposing that color perception depends on receptors that make opposing responses to three pairs of color

At roughly the same time that Helmholtz was championing the trichromatic theory, German physiologist Ewald Hering (1834–1918) proposed a competing theory. His ideas were sparked by the observation of **afterimages**, which are visual images that persist after a stimulus has been removed (Figure 4-10). Pointing out that the trichromatic theory could not explain this visual phenomenon, Hering proposed a theory that could, namely, his **opponent-process theory**. This theory argues that all colors are derived from three opposing color processes: black-white, red-green, and

SELF-DISCOVERY 4-1
Questionnaire

Are You Color-Blind?

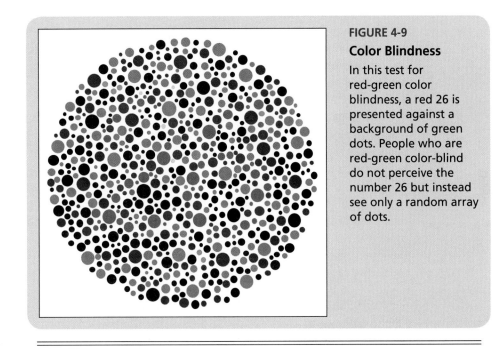

FIGURE 4-9

Color Blindness

In this test for red-green color blindness, a red 26 is presented against a background of green dots. People who are red-green color-blind do not perceive the number 26 but instead see only a random array of dots.

blue-yellow. The black-white opponent process determines the brightness of what we see, while the other two processes determine color perception. Stimulation of one color inhibits its opposing color. When stimulation stops, the opposing color is seen as an afterimage.

A century after Hering proposed his theory, research by Russell de Valois and his colleagues (1966) supported its basic propositions. After leaving the cones, visual information is processed in terms of the opposing colors by certain bipolar and ganglion cells in the retina and certain cells in the thalamus, which are collectively

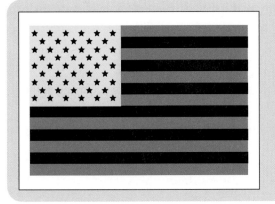

FIGURE 4-10

Afterimage

Gaze steadily for about a minute at the lower right corner of the yellow field of stars, and then look at the white space beside the flag. What do you see? The "Old Glory" you see is composed of the complementary colors in your visual system. Why do these colors reverse in this manner?

known as *opponent cells*. These opponent cells respond to light at one end of the spectrum with an increase in nerve firing and to light at the other end of the spectrum with an inhibition of spontaneous activity. Opponent cells that are inhibited from firing by a particular wavelength (which we experience as a particular color) produce a burst of firing as soon as that wavelength is removed. Similarly, cells that fire in response to a particular wavelength stop firing when that wavelength is removed (de Valois & Jacobs, 1984; Zrenner et al., 1990). The end result of this inhibition and firing of opponent cells is that we experience *negative afterimages* due to a "rebound effect" in opponent cells.

Opponent-process theory explains why people who are color-blind to red are also color-blind to green. The opponent-process cells responsible for perceiving red are also responsible for perceiving green. Thus, when these opponent cells are nonfunctional, a person cannot perceive red *or* green. The same is true for those opponent cells responsible for blue-yellow perception.

Although Hering formulated his theory in opposition to trichromatic theory, research indicates that *both* theories accurately represent the process of color perception, but at two different stages in the visual process. In the first stage of color processing, the trichromatic theory explains how the retina's red, green, and blue color-sensitive cone receptors match the wavelength of the light stimulus. In the second stage, the opponent-process theory explains how opponent cells in both the retina and in the thalamus of the brain are either stimulated or inhibited from firing by wavelengths of varying sizes. Put more simply, trichromatic theory explains most of the visual processing occurring in the eye, and opponent-process theory explains the processing occurring between the eye and the brain.

> *The best work of artists in any age is the work of innocence liberated by technical knowledge. The laboratory experiments that led to the theory of pure color equipped the impressionists to paint nature as if it had only just been created.*
>
> —Nancy Hale, U.S. writer, 1908–1989

Section REVIEW

- Light is a form of electromagnetic energy that passes through the cornea, pupil, and lens and then is projected onto the retina.

- Below the retina's surface reside two kinds of photoreceptors: rods, which function best under low-light conditions, and cones, which require much more light to be activated and play a key role in color vision.

- Rods and cones generate neural signals that activate adjacent bipolar cells, which activate ganglion cells.

- Behind the eyes, ganglion cell axons of the optic nerve separate, with half crossing to the other side of the head at the optic chiasm.

- Most optic nerve fibers run to the lateral geniculate nucleus, which performs detailed visual analysis.

- The experience of color is created by our nervous system in response to different wavelengths of light.

- Trichromatic theory explains most of the visual processing occurring in the eye.

- Opponent-process theory explains visual processing occurring between the eye and the brain.

4.3 Hearing

Stop reading for a minute, look around, and notice what your sense of vision tells you about your surroundings. Next, close your eyes, listen carefully, and notice what your sense of hearing, or **audition**, tells you.

When I did this exercise, looking around my den I noticed my computer screen, my desk, a lamp, an antique clock, a phone, two windows, and many stacks and shelves of books and journal articles. When I closed my eyes and listened, my experience changed dramatically. Now I noticed the clock ticking, the computer fan whirring, the robins in our yard chirping, and the geese in the nearby woods honking. I also heard the soft rustle of my daughter's papers as she did her homework in the kitchen and the sound of a plane flying high overhead. Although these sensations were present when I looked around the room, I had not noticed them.

This exercise demonstrates that hearing is an important, though sometimes unrecognized, sense (Plack, 2005). From an evolutionary perspective, hearing was essential for our ancestors' survival, helping them detect the approach of predatory animals, locate food, and communicate with others (Nathan, 1982). Yet, how exactly does hearing take place?

Audition The sense of hearing

4.3a *Sound Waves Are the Stimuli for Hearing.*

Sound depends on a wave of pressure created when an object vibrates. The vibration causes molecules in an elastic medium—such as air, water, or solid material—to move together and apart in a rhythmic fashion. Like ripples on a pond, these pulsations move away from the vibrating object as **sound waves**, growing weaker as they travel farther from their source. Although sound waves weaken with increased distance, their speed remains constant, about 1,070 feet (or 330 meters) per second in air and about 4,724 feet (or 1,440 meters) per second in water. The number of sound waves that pass a given point in 1 second is the sound's *frequency*. Sound frequency is measured in *Hertz (Hz)*, which is named after the nineteenth-century German physicist Heinrich Hertz (1857–1894). One Hz equals one cycle per second. The physical quality of sound frequency roughly corresponds to the psychological experience of *pitch*. Although people are most sensitive to sounds at frequencies between 2,000 and 5,000 Hz (Gulick et al., 1989), young adults can typically hear tones with frequencies as low as 20 Hz and as high as 20,000 Hz (Gelfand, 1981). As people age, their lower limit of hearing changes very little; however, the upper range falls steadily from adolescence onward.

The height of a sound wave is its *amplitude* and corresponds to the psychological experience of the loudness of a sound. Amplitude is measured in *decibels (dB)*. The greater the amplitude is, the louder the sound, with perceived loudness doubling about every 10 decibels (Stevens, 1955). By definition, 0 dB is the minimal detectable sound for normal hearing. A whisper has amplitude of about 20 dB, normal conversation occurs at about 60 dB, and a jet aircraft taking off nearby has amplitude of about 140 dB. Exposure to sounds over 120 dB, such as a shotgun blast or a jet aircraft motor, can be painful and may cause hearing damage (Henry, 1984). Prolonged exposure to sounds over 90 dB—such as those found in industrial settings, subway trains, and rock concerts—can contribute to permanent hearing loss. Table 4-4 provides examples of some common sounds and their danger levels.

One of the annoyances of modern-day living is widespread exposure to excess noise. Noise levels above 65 dB not only are irritating, but can also cause sleep disturbances in all age groups and learning deficits in children (Bullinger et al., 1999). For example, in one recent study investigating the effects of aircraft noise on children's

Sound waves Pressure changes in a medium (air, water, solids) caused by the vibrations of molecules

TABLE 4-4   Decibel Level of Some Common Sounds

Decibels	Source	Exposure Danger
180	Space shuttle launch	Hearing loss certain within 150 feet of launch pad
140	Shotgun blast, jet aircraft engine	Any exposure dangerous
120	Sandblaster, thunderclap	Immediate danger
100	Heavy auto traffic, lawn mower	2 hours or longer
60	Normal conversation	No danger
40	Quiet office	No danger
30	Quiet library	No danger
20	Soft whisper	No danger
0	Minimal detectable sound	No danger

cognitive development, researchers tested German children living near the old and new sites of the Munich International Airport (Hygge et al. 2002). The impending closing and opening of the two airports located in different areas of the city provided researchers with the opportunity to observe how the exposure to and elimination of loud airport noise affected children's attention, reading ability, long-term memory, and speech perception. Children were tested three times: once before and twice after the airport switch over. Following the switch, children living near the now-closed airport showed improvements in all four cognitive areas; and children living near the new airport—where noise levels were now high—experienced deficits in all areas. These findings provide strong evidence that chronic exposure to noise levels above 65 dB can adversely affect children's cognitive development. It further suggests that these deficits can be reversed if children are removed from their noisy surroundings.

Most sounds are actually a combination of many different waves of different frequencies. This *complexity* corresponds to the psychological experience of *timbre*. Just as we can differentiate the sounds of different musical instruments because of the different frequencies of sound they blend together, we can also recognize the voices of different people over the telephone due to their unique sound-frequency blending. To experience a simple example of timbre perception, first clap your hands together while holding them flat, and then clap them again when they are cupped. Cupped hand-clapping produces a greater combination of low-frequency sound waves than flat hand-clapping—thus, it is a more complex sound.

INFO-BIT   The amplitude of sound waves generated by iPods and other mobile digital music players can get as high as 120 decibels, which is comparable to the sound level produced by a sandblasting machine. At these levels, you risk hearing damage after 7 1/2 minutes of exposure. How do you know if your iPod volume is too loud? Experts recommend that your music is too loud if (1) someone 3 feet away in an elevator can hear your music or (2) you need to turn down your music to hear someone talking directly to you.

4.3b *The Auditory System Consists of the Outer Ear, Middle Ear, and Inner Ear.*

The evolution of the modern mammalian ear can be traced back to the primitive internal ears found in some types of fish that consist of a system of looping passages filled with fluid (Békésy, 1960; Stebbins, 1980). Mammals, birds, and some reptiles have a more complex system of looping passages that contain a **cochlea** (pronounced COKE-lee-ah), a coiled, fluid-filled tube in the inner ear that contains hairlike auditory receptor cells. The ears of mammals have three small bones to transmit vibrations to the cochlea, whereas the ears of birds and reptiles have only one bone (Hackett & Kaas, 2003).

You hear a bell ringing because your ears respond to sound waves generated by the metal gong striking the bell's sides. How do the frequency, amplitude, and complexity of the sound waves generated by the bell affect what you hear?

Operation of the Ear

The ear can be divided into three major parts: the *outer ear*, *middle ear*, and *inner ear* (see Figure 4-11). The most visible part of the outer ear is the *pinna*, which is the skin-covered cartilage visible from the outside. Only mammals have pinnae, and their funnel shape is useful for channeling sound waves to the other part of the outer ear known as the *auditory canal*. This passageway is about an inch long, and as sound waves resonate in the auditory canal, their amplification is doubled.

At the end of the auditory canal is a thin, flexible membrane, known as the **eardrum**, which vibrates in sequence with the sound waves. Beyond the eardrum is the middle ear. As the eardrum vibrates, it sets in motion those three tiny, interconnected bones—the hammer, anvil, and stirrup—known collectively as *ossicles*. The ossicles, which are the tiniest bones in the body, further amplify the sound waves two or three times before transmitting them to the liquid-filled inner ear.

The main parts of the inner ear are the *oval window*, *cochlea*, and *organ of Corti*. The stirrup is attached to the oval window, which is a thin membrane that transmits the sound waves from the stirrup to the cochlea. As mentioned earlier, the cochlea is a coiled, fluid-filled tube. The vibrations of the oval window cause pressure waves in the cochlear fluid. Running down the middle of the cochlea is a rubberlike membrane, known as the *basilar membrane*, which moves in a wavelike fashion in response to these pressure waves. Lying on top of the basilar membrane is the organ of Corti, which contains 16,000–20,000 receptors for hearing, called *hair cells*. When movement of the basilar membrane stimulates these hair cells, this stimulation triggers action potentials in bundles of sensory neurons forming the *auditory nerve*, which transmits auditory information to the brain. Which of the hair cells are stimulated determines which neurons fire and how rapidly they fire, and the resulting pattern of firing determines the sort of sound we hear.

Perceiving the Location of a Sound

The ability to locate objects in space solely on the basis of the sounds they make is known as **sound localization.** People with only one functioning ear have difficulty accurately locating sounds. To experience this auditory fact, close your eyes and ask

Cochlea The coiled, fluid-filled tube in the inner ear that contains the hairlike auditory receptors

Eardrum A thin, flexible membrane at the end of the auditory canal that vibrates in sequence with sound waves

Sound localization The ability to locate objects in space solely on the basis of the sounds they make

FIGURE 4-11

The Human Ear

The outer ear directs sounds to the eardrum. From there, the bones of the middle ear (hammer, anvil, and stirrup) greatly amplify the sound through the oval window to the inner ear. The vibrations of the oval window cause pressure waves in the cochlear fluid, which, in turn, cause the basilar membrane to move, bending the hair cells on its surface. This stimulation triggers action potentials in the bundles of sensory neurons that form the auditory nerve, which then sends information to the brain.

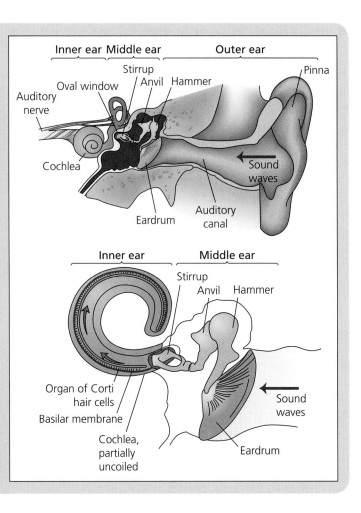

a friend to make a noise from somewhere in the room. Point to your friend's location and then open your eyes to determine your accuracy. Next, place your index finger in one ear and repeat this exercise. The reason two ears are better than one is that sounds coming from points other than those equidistant between your two ears reach one ear slightly before they reach the other. Sounds reaching the closer ear may also be slightly more intense because the head blocks some of the sound waves reaching the ear on the other side of the head (Getzmann, 2003). Because your ears are only about 6 inches apart, the time lag for the sound reaching the farthest ear is extremely short; thus, the different intensities of the sounds are extremely small. Yet even such small differences provide your auditory system with sufficient information to locate the sound (Middlebrooks & Green, 1991; Phillips & Brugge, 1985).

4.3c Different Theories Explain Different Aspects of Pitch Perception.

How does the auditory system convert sound waves into perceptions of pitch? Like our understanding of color perception, our current understanding of pitch perception is based on two theories that were once considered incompatible.

Place theory *A theory that pitch is determined by which place along the cochlea's basilar membrane is most activated*

Place theory contends that we hear different pitches because different sound waves trigger the hair cells on different portions, or *places*, of the cochlea's basilar membrane. The brain detects the frequency of a tone according to which place along the membrane is most activated. Place theory was first proposed by Herman von Helmholtz (1863), the codeveloper of trichromatic color theory, and later tested and refined by Hungarian scientist Georg von Békésy (1947, 1957), who won a Nobel Prize for this work in 1961. Békésy's research indicated that high-frequency tones trigger the greatest activity at the beginning of the cochlea's basilar membrane, where the oval window is located.

Although place theory explains how we hear high-frequency tones, it cannot account for how we perceive very low-frequency tones. The problem is that at very low frequencies, the entire basilar membrane vibrates uniformly; thus no one place is more activated than another. One theory that can explain the perception of low-frequency tones is **frequency theory**, which was first proposed by English physicist Ernest Rutherford (1861–1937) in 1886. According to frequency theory, the basilar membrane vibrates at the same frequency as the incoming sound wave, which in turn triggers neural impulses to the brain at this same rate. Thus, a sound wave of 800 Hz will set the basilar membrane vibrating 800 times per second, which will cause neurons to fire at 800 times per second.

One important problem with frequency theory is that individual neurons cannot fire more than 1,000 times per second. Because of this fact, frequency theory cannot explain people perceiving sounds with frequencies above 1,000 Hz. A revision of frequency theory, namely, psychologist Ernest Wever's **volley theory**, contends that neurons work in groups and alternate firing, thus achieving a combined frequency of firing well above 1,000 times per second (Wever, 1949; Wever & Bray, 1937). Studies indicate that such alternate firing of groups of auditory nerves can generate volleys of up to 5,000 impulses per second (Zwislocki, 1981).

Based on what we now know, it appears that place theory, frequency theory, and volley theory account for different aspects of pitch perception. Place theory best explains high-frequency sounds, whereas frequency theory can best explain the perception of low-frequency sounds. For sounds between 1,000 and 5,000 Hz, pitch perception seems to be best explained by volley theory, which is a revision of frequency theory.

4.3d *There Are Two General Types of Hearing Impairment.*

Hearing impairment is one of the most common birth defects, occurring in about 3 in 1,000 newborns. Hearing loss that is present at birth is called *congenital hearing loss* (Tabaee et al., 2004). Genetic factors are believed to cause about half of all congenital hearing-loss cases, but infections during pregnancy, such as rubella (German measles), herpes, or syphilis, are also known causes (Beasley & Amedee, 2001).

Millions of adults have some degree of hearing impairment, ranging from mild to severe. Because the process of loss is gradual, individuals who have this disorder may not realize that their hearing is diminishing. Older adults are the age group most affected by this condition, with high-pitched sounds being the most difficult to hear (Marcincuk & Roland, 2002). About 33 percent of adults between the ages of 65 and 75 years have some degree of hearing loss, with this figure rising to at least 50 percent among those older than 75 years (Bagai et al., 2006). Individuals who are hearing impaired may experience several of the following symptoms:

1. Conversations are difficult to understand, especially when there is background noise.

2. The higher pitches of women's voices are harder to hear than the lower pitches of men's voices.

3. Certain sounds seem annoying or overly loud.

4. A ringing, roaring, or hissing sound may occur in one or both ears.

When music fails to agree to the ear, to soothe the ear and the heart and the senses, then it has missed its point.

—Maria Callas, Greek soprano, 1923–1977

Frequency theory A theory that pitch is determined by the frequency with which the basilar membrane vibrates

Volley theory A theory of pitch stating that neurons work in groups and alternate firing, thus achieving a combined frequency corresponding to the frequency of the sound wave

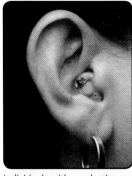

Individuals with conductive hearing loss often wear digital hearing aids, which are worn just inside the outer ear. Implantable hearing devices are also available.

The damage that causes hearing impairment involves defects in one or more areas of the auditory system (Beasley & Amedee, 2001). Abnormalities with the mechanical system that carries sound waves to the cochlea cause conductive hearing loss. These middle ear problems often involve a punctured eardrum or reduced functioning of the tiny bones making up the ossicles. Whatever the cause, the result is that the middle ear is less able to send sound waves to the inner ear. A common treatment for conductive hearing loss is digital hearing aids, which are tiny instruments worn just inside the outer ear. Hearing aids amplify vibrations for frequencies that are troublesome—usually high frequencies—and compress sound so that soft sounds are amplified. Because the effectiveness of these external hearing aids is sometimes diminished due to perspiration in the outer ear and noise distortion, implantable hearing aids employing more advanced technology are increasingly common. One such device consists of a micro-magnet that is surgically placed on a segment of the tiny bones in the middle ear with an external sound processor that uses electromagnetic waves instead of air pressure to amplify volume (Hough et al., 2002).

The more common type of hearing impairment is *sensorineural hearing loss*, or nerve deafness. This condition involves a defect in the neural mechanisms that create nerve impulses in the inner ear or send them to the auditory cortex. Problems in the auditory cortex can also result in this type of hearing loss. Most sensorineural hearing loss occurs because hair cells in the cochlea are damaged by disease, injury, or aging (Oghalai, 2005; Singh & Selesnick, 2005). We are born with about 50,000 inner-ear hair cells, but the number gradually declines over time. Unlike birds and sharks that can regenerate lost hair cells, humans do not have this ability.

Currently, the only means of restoring hearing in some people with nerve deafness is a *cochlear implant*, which bypasses damaged or missing hair cells to send electrical signals through an array of electrodes within the cochlea (Gantz & Turner, 2003; Hallberg et al., 2005). The implant actually consists of three separate parts: headpiece, speech processor, and receiver. The headpiece contains a microphone and transmitter and is worn just behind the ear. It picks up sounds and sends them to the cell-phone-sized processor that fits in a pocket or is worn on a belt. The processor converts sounds into electronic signals that are sent to the receiver, which is a small disc about the size of a quarter that is surgically implanted as far into the cochlea as possible. The receiver sends the sound signals to the brain (Debener et al., 2008). About 60,000 people in the world have received cochlear implants. Young children born with hearing loss are the best candidates for this device, although some older adults with profound or severe hearing loss are beginning to receive these implants as well (Pisoni, 2008). Besides mechanical remedies, many people with hearing loss rely upon lip reading and sign language.

Researchers have discovered that susceptibility to age-related hearing loss is due to defects that develop in several genes, which, in turn, destroy inner-ear hair cells (Noben-Trauth et al., 2003). Recently, studies with genetically modified mice and guinea pigs have found that deleting a specific gene permits the growth of new hair cells (Kawamoto et al., 2003; Sage et al., 2005). These findings provide invaluable insights into the genetics of hearing and increase the possibility that one day medical science will be able to regenerate lost hair cells and thereby restore hearing in those suffering from nerve deafness.

- Frequency refers to the number of sound waves that pass a given point in one second, and corresponds to the experience of pitch.

- Amplitude is the height of a sound wave and corresponds to the experience of loudness.

- Complexity is the extent to which a sound is composed of different frequencies and corresponds to the experience of timbre.

- Sound localization is the ability to locate objects in space due to the sounds they make.

- Place theory best explains high-frequency sounds.

- Frequency theory best explains low-frequency sounds.

- Volley theory best explains intermediate sounds.

- Conductive hearing loss involves abnormalities in the mechanical system that carries sound waves to the cochlea.

- Sensorineural hearing loss, or nerve deafness, involves a defect in the neural mechanisms that create nerve impulses in the inner ear or send them to the auditory cortex.

4.4 Your Other Senses

Through natural selection, animals come to possess the sensory mechanisms they need to survive in their specific environment. This is why animals that inhabit similar environments have similar sensory mechanisms. Our own human senses share the most similarity to those species that are our closest cousins on the evolutionary tree, namely, other primates (Hodos & Butler, 2001). Like all primates, we primarily rely on our vision, with hearing being our distant second sense. These two sensory systems are classified as *higher senses* in humans, meaning they are extremely important to our survival. In contrast, the senses of taste, smell, touch, and proprioception are classified as *minor senses* because they are not considered as crucial to sustaining life.

4.4a *Smell and Taste Represent "Far" and "Near" Chemical Senses.*

As life evolved from the sea to the land, two anatomically separate chemical sensory mechanisms developed. These two distinct senses—namely, taste and smell—came to serve different functions. The sense of taste became a "near" sense, providing the last check on the acceptability of food, while the sense of smell became a "far" sense, able to detect stimuli from a much farther distance.

Smell

Olfaction is the sense of smell, and its stimuli are airborne molecules. When you smell fresh-brewed coffee (see Figure 4-12), you are sensing molecules that have left the coffee and traveled through the air to your nose. These molecules then enter your nasal passages and reach tiny receptor cells at the top of the nasal cavity. These

Olfaction The sense of smell

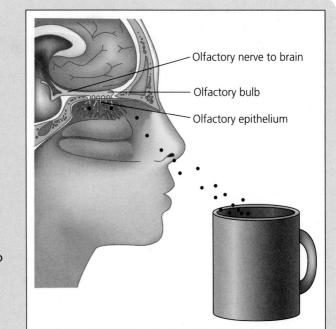

FIGURE 4-12

The Olfactory System

Odor molecules in the air travel up the nasal passages to the receptor cells on the olfactory epithelium where they are trapped and dissolved in the olfactory mucus. Receptor cells then send neural impulses to the olfactory bulb. From there, this information travels to the primary olfactory cortex in the frontal lobes.

Olfactory nerve to brain

Olfactory bulb

Olfactory epithelium

Olfactory epithelium A thin layer of tissue at the top of the nasal cavity that contains the olfactory receptor cells

olfactory receptors are located on a thin, dime-sized, mucus-coated layer of tissue known as the **olfactory epithelium**. The odor molecules from the coffee are then trapped and dissolved in the mucus of the epithelium, and this causes the olfactory receptor cells to transmit a neural impulse directly to the olfactory bulb at the base of the brain. From here, the signals are processed before being sent to the *primary olfactory cortex*, which is located in the frontal lobes (Dade et al., 2002; McLean & Shipley, 1992). Olfaction is the only sensation that is not relayed through the thalamus on its way to the cortex. Once your brain has processed the airborne molecules, you appreciate the coffee's wonderful fragrance.

INFO-BIT   Studies of various languages around the world reveal that between two-thirds and three-fourths of all words applying to the senses describe the two higher senses, vision and audition (Wilson, 1997).

Humans have hundreds of different types of olfactory receptor cells, with each type responding to only a limited family of odor molecules (DiLorenzo & Youngentob, 2003; Ressler et al., 1994). This large number of different types of receptors stands in sharp contrast to the three basic receptors involved in vision. Although we do not yet know exactly how the brain processes all the different types of olfactory information, scientists estimate that together these receptors allow us to distinguish among about 4,000 to 10,000 different smells (Malnic et al., 1999). The range of this smell estimate is so broad because no one has ever attempted to precisely measure the smells in the world that humans can detect (Gilbert, 2008).

Having so many types of olfactory receptors may mean that a great deal of the processing necessary for odor perception occurs in the nose itself. Despite the staggering number of odors that we can distinguish, for some unknown reason, we have a hard time correctly identifying and attaching names to specific odors. Thus, you may have a hard time correctly distinguishing the smell of smoke from that of soap.

Numerous studies indicate that we are drawn toward perfumelike fragrances, such as those of flowers and many food substances, and repulsed by foul and sulfurous odors (Miller, 1997). This suggests that our olfactory systems evolved to help us distinguish things that are poisonous from those that are edible. Cross-cultural studies further suggest that the smells we pay most attention to are those that help us survive in our immediate surroundings (Classen et al., 1994). For example, the Dassanetch people of southwestern Ethiopia are especially sensitive to the smells associated with their principal livelihood, raising cattle (Almagor, 1987). They identify the time of year by predictable changes in surrounding smells, such as the odors of decay and burning during the dry season and the fresh smell of new plant growth during the rainy season. Further, the smell of everything associated with cattle is considered good, and the Dassanetch go out of their way to highlight those valued smells. Women smear liquid butter—*ghee*—on their bodies to ensure fertility and attract suitors, while men do the same with cow manure!

Olfactory sensitivity is substantially determined by the number of receptors in the epithelium. Animals with more receptors than other animals have much keener senses of smell. Whereas we humans have about 10 million olfactory receptors, dogs have an astounding 200 million receptors, putting us at the lower end of the scale of smell sensitivity. The olfactory systems of many animals also have specialized receptors to detect airborne chemicals known as **pheromones**, which are released by other members of the same species. Once detected, these pheromones directly affect the animal's behavior. Many species rely on pheromones to communicate their territorial boundaries, social status, and readiness to sexually reproduce (Luo et al., 2003).

Do we humans emit and detect pheromones? If so, how might this shape our behavior? In the late 1960s, Martha McClintock, a college student, tried to answer these questions by conducting a scientific investigation into the folk notion that women who live in the same dorm develop synchronized menstrual periods. Her survey of fellow students found that as women spent more time together, their menstrual cycles became more synchronized. In addition, McClintock discovered that women who spent a lot of time with men had shorter and more regular cycles (McClintock, 1971). Inspired by her undergraduate research, McClintock became a biopsychologist and has devoted her career to investigating the existence and possible function of human pheromones. She and her colleagues have discovered that pheromone-like chemicals are secreted in blood, sweat, armpit hair, and semen, and that at least some of these chemical substances may unconsciously influence sexual attraction (Jacob et al., 2001; Jacob & McClintock, 2000). For example, recent studies have found that heterosexual women and homosexual men exhibit an involuntary sexual response when exposed to the male pheromone *androstadien*, but they are not aroused by the female pheromone *estratetraen* (Savic et al., 2005, 2007). However, despite such discoveries, scientists are still unsure about whether humans possess sexual attractant pheromones. Even if such substances exist, it is extremely unlikely that they will be found to have the sort of direct effect on sexual behavior that is found among many animal species because the human sexual response is much more complex than that of most other animals (see Chapter 9, Section 9.3). Rather than directly producing sexual attraction, it is much more likely that human sexual attractant pheromones would affect a person's mood and emotional states, which in turn would affect how the person interacts with other people (Cutler et al., 1998).

Pheromones Airborne chemicals that are released by animals and detected by other animals using specialized receptors and that affect the behavior of other animals of the same species

Although human behavior is not as strongly shaped by olfactory information as the behavior of other species, we do have the ability to identify people by their olfactory cues. For example, based on the smell of breath, hands, and clothing, people are reasonably accurate in detecting another person's sex (Doty et al., 1982; Wallace, 1977). Further, at least one study has found that blindfolded mothers can identify with close to 95 percent accuracy the clothing worn by their own children by smell alone (Porter & Moore, 1981). Similarly, breast-feeding infants quickly learn to identify their mother's odor from that of other breast-feeding women (Porter, 1991). Although these studies suggest that humans as a group have a good deal of smell sensitivity, women's sensitivity is much higher than that of men's—brain scans taken while people are smelling objects find that odors trigger more olfactory activation in women than in men (Yousem et al., 1999; Yousem et al., 2001).

Finally, odors can also evoke memories and feelings associated with past events (Richardson & Zucco, 1989). For example, the smell of freshly cut grass or the scent of a specific perfume can mentally transport us back to a time in our lives when these odors were associated with specific events.

Taste

Gustation The sense of taste

Taste buds Sensory receptor organs located on the tongue and inside the mouth and throat that contain the receptor cells for taste

As mentioned earlier, taste, or **gustation**, is a near sensation occurring when a substance makes contact with specialized receptor cells in the mouth and throat (Cacchione, 2008). About 50 to 150 of these receptor cells are contained in each of the 10,000 **taste buds** that are primarily located on the tongue (Margolskee, 1995). Some taste buds are also in the throat, on the insides of the cheeks, and on the roof of the mouth. The taste buds on the surface of the tongue are grouped together in structures called *papillae*, which in Latin means "pimple." Because of their constant contact with the chemicals they are designed to sense—as well as their exposure to bacteria, dirt, and dry air—the receptor cells wear out and die within 10 days (Pfaffmann, 1978). Fortunately, new cells emerge at the edge of the taste bud and migrate inward toward the center, replacing the old cells. Although this cycle of death and replacement of taste cells operates throughout our lives, it occurs more slowly in the elderly, which is one reason their taste sensitivity becomes less acute (Cowart, 1981).

When these taste cells absorb chemicals dissolved in saliva, they trigger neural impulses that are transmitted to one of two brain areas. One pathway involves information first being sent to the thalamus and then to the primary gustatory cortex, where taste identification occurs. The second pathway leads to the limbic system and allows you to quickly respond to a taste prior to consciously identifying it, such as when you reflexively spit out sour milk (Sekuler & Blake R., 1994).

In contrast to our olfactory system's ability to distinguish among about 10,000 different smells, our taste receptors can detect only a handful of taste sensations (Classen, 1993; Laing et al., 1993). The five most familiar taste sensations are sweetness (mostly sugars), sourness (mostly acids), saltiness (mostly salts), bitterness (mainly chemicals that have no food value or are toxic), and umami (a savory taste common in fermented and aged foods). However, most taste experiences are complex and result from the combined effects of receptor cells in the mouth and nose, which produce the different flavors you experience.

Has anyone ever told you that the taste buds sensitive to sweetness are on the front of your tongue and the taste buds for saltiness and sourness are on the sides? If so, don't believe them. As depicted in Figure 4-13, this popular belief that the taste buds on different areas of the tongue detect different tastes is based on a mistranslation of a German paper that was written more than 100 years ago. To

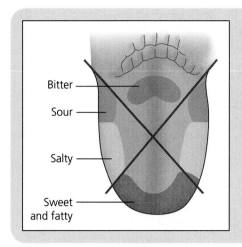

FIGURE 4-13

The Tongue Map Myth

Contrary to popular belief, different areas of the tongue are not more sensitive to one of the four primary tastes. All taste buds can detect all types of tastes.

Bitter

Sour

Salty

Sweet and fatty

set the record straight, all your taste buds detect all taste qualities. Despite this fact, makers of expensive wine glasses still falsely claim that their different-shaped glasses will direct specific types of wine onto the areas of the tongue that will make that wine taste the best.

Although the taste of a particular substance depends on whether one or more of the five basic taste sensations are activated, the flavor of this substance is a combination of both its smell and its taste (DiLorenzo & Youngentob, 2003). The important role that olfaction plays in the flavor experience was demonstrated by one study in which some research participants were allowed to both taste and smell substances placed on their tongues, while others were only allowed to taste them. Although over half the taste-smell participants were able to correctly identify chocolate, root beer, cherry, coffee, and garlic, less than 3 percent of the taste-only group could accurately identify those flavors (Mozell et al., 1969). To personally experience the role that olfaction plays in flavor perception, pinch your nostrils closed before approaching a particular food. Then place the food in your mouth and swish it around while paying attention to the flavor. Next, release your nostrils, open your mouth slightly, and breathe in gently through both your mouth and your nose. You should experience a significant increase in the food's flavor.

INFO-BIT About 25 percent of people have a very large number of taste buds. These "supertasters" are extremely sensitive to bitter compounds, and they also perceive saccharin and sucrose as sweeter than other people do (Pickering & Robert, 2006). Due to this hypersensitivity, supertasters may face a higher cancer risk if they find broccoli and other veggies that carry cancer-preventing vitamins too bitter to stomach. On the positive side, supertasters' discriminating palates may lead to lower risk for obesity.

4.4b Touch Is Determined by the Skin Senses— Pressure, Temperature, and Pain.

Every living thing has a "skin" of some sort that defines its boundaries with the environment, and every living thing has a sense of touch. Indeed, the skin is the largest sensory organ, with the average adult having more than 2 square yards of skin receptors covering her or his body. Our sense of touch is actually a combination of three skin senses: *pressure*, *temperature*, and *pain* (Klatzky & Lederman, 2008).

Although the 5 million sense receptors in our skin consist of a variety of types, like our taste receptors, there is no one type of skin receptor that produces a specific sensory experience. Instead, it appears that the skin's sensory experiences are due to the pattern of stimulation of nerve impulses reaching the somatosensory cortex of the brain (Hsiao et al., 2003).

 **INFO-BIT** Neuroscientists have identified a special set of thin nerves in humans that are especially sensitive to the soft touches generated by tender caresses and reassuring hugs but not to rough touches, pinches, or jabs (Olausson et al., 2002). These nerves stimulate the same brain areas activated by romantic love and sexual arousal and appear to provide the emotional aspects of touch. Researchers speculate that these nerves may have evolved to guide humans toward tenderness and nurturing behavior.

Pressure

Although the entire body is sensitive to pressure, most of the cells in the somatosensory cortex are devoted to processing neural impulses coming from the fingers, lips, face, tongue, and genitals because these areas of the skin have the greatest concentration of receptors. That's why you are so much more sensitive to objects that come into contact with these skin areas than those contacting other regions.

Try the following exercise. First, touch your two index fingers together. Most people report about equal pressure intensity from both fingertips. Now lightly touch one fingertip repeatedly to your upper lip. Most people report sensations mostly on the lip and little or none from the fingertip. The reason your lip is more pressure sensitive than your finger when these two skin areas touch has to do with the relative lengths of their neural pathways to the brain. When touched simultaneously, neural impulses from the lip reach the brain 1 millisecond faster than those coming from the finger. Apparently, even when two places on the skin are being equally stimulated, the impulses that reach the brain first dictate where the sensation will be primarily experienced.

Temperature

The skin contains two kinds of temperature receptors, one sensitive to warm and the other to cold. In 1920, the structural psychologist J. Henry Alston discovered that the sensation of "hot" is triggered by the simultaneous stimulation of both the warm and the cold receptors (Alston, 1920). He demonstrated this phenomenon by intertwining two metal pipes, one containing cold water and the other containing warm water. When people grasped these two braided pipes, they quickly pulled away because they felt the sensation of intense heat. Of course, their skin was not actually scalded; Alston's unusual apparatus had simply fooled these people's brains into feeling intense heat. However, when you accidentally touch a hot stove with your fingers, the resulting sensation of intense heat in your fingers is correctly warning you about imminent harm to your skin.

Although temperature sensations depend on which type of receptor is stimulated, whether more warm or cold receptors are stimulated will depend on the difference between the temperature of the skin and that of the object you are feeling. This is why washing your hands in 60°F water feels warm after coming in from the cold, but feels cool when in a hot environment.

Pain

The chapter-opening story described how Aron Ralston cut off his own arm to save his life. What is so remarkable about Aron's actions is that he performed this self-surgery while ignoring all of his body's built-in defenses against the self-infliction of pain. Although pain is an unpleasant experience, it is important to survival because it serves as a warning system that signals danger and the risk of injury (Wall, 2000). In order to save his life, Aron had to largely ignore this sensory warning system.

Pain can also force people to cope appropriately with an injury by inducing them both to seek treatment and to be still to promote healing. The importance of this sense is dramatically demonstrated by those rare individuals who are born with insensitivity to pain due to improperly functioning nerve pathways that normally transmit pain signals to the brain (Sternbach, 1963). In one such case, a woman called Ms. C died at the age of 29 from massive infections caused by a lifetime of abrasion and unhealed injury (Melzack & Wall, 1982a).

Pain is induced through tissue damage or intense stimulation of sensory receptors (Gatchel & Turk, 1999). Light that is too bright, noises that are too loud, or pressure that is too great will trigger the pain experience. Yet overstimulation can sometimes occur without eliciting pain, as demonstrated when you eat something that is too sweet for your sense of taste. The too-sweet substance has certainly overstimulated your taste receptors, but there is no pain.

The sensation of pain appears to originate in *free nerve endings* in the skin, around muscles, and in internal organs. When intense stimuli cause cell and tissue damage, the damaged cells release chemicals—including a neurotransmitter called *substance P* (for pain)—that stimulate the free nerve endings, which in turn transmit pain signals to the brain (Beyer et al., 1991). People with the previously discussed rare disorder that makes them insensitive to pain have extremely low levels of substance P in or near the nerve endings (Pearson et al., 1982). Normal individuals do not experience pain in those areas of the body that have no free nerve endings, such as the cerebral cortex.

Two distinct peaks of pain are experienced upon suffering an injury, differing in quality and separated in time. For example, when you sprain your ankle or pound your thumb with a hammer, you experience what is known as *double pain* (Cooper et al., 1986; Willis, 1985). The first is a sharp, stinging pain caused by large-diameter nerve fibers (called *L-fibers*) in the spinal cord that transmit pain information very quickly to the brain, while the second is a dull or burning pain arising from small-diameter and slower-operating nerve fibers (called *S-fibers*) in the spinal cord. These small, slower-operating S-fibers transmit most pain signals (Coderre et al., 2003).

The most widely accepted theory of pain is Ronald Melzack and Patrick Wall's (1982b) **gate-control theory**, which proposes that the L-fibers and S-fibers open and close "gateways" for pain in the spinal cord. According to this theory, the fast-transmitting, large L-fibers not only carry information about sharp pain to the brain but also carry information about most other forms of tactile stimulation. Once their information is transmitted to the brain, they close the pain gate by inhibiting the firing of neurons with which they synapse. The thin, slower-transmitting S-fibers, which carry information about dull and burning pain to the brain, also synapse with these same neurons; thus, their pain information may arrive at a closed gate due to the faster operation of the L-fibers. When this happens, the pain information from the S-fibers cannot be sent to the brain.

Gate-control theory explains why rubbing, massaging, or even pinching a bruised or sore muscle can ease the pain. These actions activate the large and fast-transmitting L-fibers, which then close the pain gate to the stimuli transmitted by the thin and

Gate control theory A theory of pain perception proposing that small and large nerve fibers open and close "gateways" for pain in the spinal cord

Shutterstock

When you hit your thumb with a hammer, you experience double pain. First, you feel a sharp, stinging pain caused by large-diameter nerve fibers (L-fibers) in the spinal cord that quickly transmit pain information to the brain. Second, you feel a dull or burning pain caused by small-diameter and slower-operating nerve fibers (S-fibers) in the spinal cord.

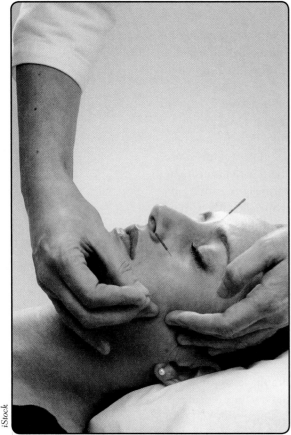

Acupuncture, which means "needle piercing," is the ancient Chinese medical practice of inserting very fine needles into the skin to stimulate specific areas in the body. Research suggests that acupuncture releases pain-reducing endorphins and is effective in easing pain.

slower-operating S-fibers. Because most pain information is transmitted by the S-fibers, blocking these signals significantly reduces the pain experience. This also explains why placing ice on a sprained ankle eases pain. The ice not only reduces swelling but also, by triggering cold messages transmitted by the L-fibers, closes the gate on the S-fibers' pain signals.

Besides explaining normal pain, gate-control theory can account for the type of pain that Aron and other amputees experience long after their limb has been removed. This *phantom limb pain* occurs when an amputee feels pain in a missing limb (Gagliese & Katz, 2000; Melzack, 1992). How could Aron feel pain in his missing arm when the pain receptors in the skin no longer existed? According to gate-control theory, when L-fibers are destroyed by amputation, the pain gates remain open, which permits random neural stimulation at the amputation site to trigger the experience of pain in the missing limb (Melzack, 1973).

Research indicates that the brain can also send messages to the spinal cord to close the pain gate, thus preventing pain messages from reaching the brain (Melzack, 1986; Whitehead & Kuhn, 1990). In such instances, the brain's messengers are a class of substances known as *endorphins*. As discussed in Chapter 2, Section 2.1d, endorphins are the body's natural defense against pain, and are released following an injury. The analgesic effects of endorphins helped Aron perform the self-surgery necessary to save his life, despite the pain it was causing him. Drugs such as morphine bind with endorphin receptors in the brain and greatly reduce

Acupuncture An ancient Chinese healing technique in which needles are inserted into the skin at specific points, stimulating the release of pain-reducing endorphins

the subjective experience of pain. Apparently, the ancient Chinese healing and pain-reducing technique of **acupuncture**, in which long, thin needles are inserted into the skin at specific points, stimulates the release of endorphins (Wang & Audette, 2008). Recent controlled clinical trials demonstrate that acupuncture is effective in alleviating pain caused by dental extractions, headaches, and degenerative arthritis of the knee (Argo et al., 2005; Backer et al., 2008). Similarly, a more modern pain-relief procedure, known as *transcutaneous electrical nerve stimulation (TENS)*, electrically stimulates painful body regions and also stimulates the release of endorphins (He et al., 2005; Radhakrishnan & Sluka, 2005; Stener-Victorin et al., 2004). Self-Discovery Questionnaire 4-2 discusses some psychological techniques for reducing pain.

4.4c *The Proprioceptive Senses Detect Body Movement and Location.*

Proprioceptive senses Two additional sources of sensory information that detect body position and movement

In addition to the traditional five senses of vision, hearing, smell, taste, and touch, there are two additional sources of sense information, called **proprioceptive senses**, which detect body position and movement (Mercier et al., 2008). One type of proprioception, the *kinesthetic sense*, provides information about the movement and location of body parts with respect to one another. Kinesthetic information comes from receptors in muscles, joints, and ligaments (Gandevia et al., 1992). Without this

SELF-DISCOVERY 4-2
Questionnaire

Can You Use Psychology to Reduce Pain?

Brain scans of people experiencing pain suggest that their psychological response to pain is most associated with the frontal lobes of the cerebral cortex, which controls emotional expression and self-control (Duquette et al., 2008). More than any of our other senses, our experience of pain can be significantly influenced by a variety of psychological factors (Kotzer, 2000; Turk & Winter, 2006). For example, diverting people's attention away from painful stimulation to some other stimulus, such as soothing music or a pleasant image ("Imagine yourself on a warm, sunny beach") is an effective strategy to alleviate pain (Fernandez & Turk, 1989; McCaul & Malott, 1984). Recognizing the benefits of distraction, dentists and other health-care workers provide music, videos, and a constant flow of conversation while performing painful procedures in order to divert a patient's attention away from the source of the pain.

Another psychological technique to reduce pain is to give someone a *placebo*, which is an inert substance that the person believes will produce a particular effect, such as pain relief. Studies indicate that up to 35 percent of patients with chronic pain get relief from taking placebos (Weisenberg, 1977). The reason these patients feel less pain is that, unlike those who do not experience relief, their brains produce higher levels of endorphins in response to the placebos (Lipman et al., 1990). Quite literally, their brains are "fooled" into releasing pain-relieving chemicals because they expect pain relief from the fictitious drug in the placebos!

---

feedback about where our body parts are located, we would have trouble performing any voluntary movement. You sometimes experience partial disruption of your kinesthetic sense when your leg "falls asleep" and you have trouble walking, or when a dentist numbs your jaw and talking and chewing become problematic.

Journey of Discovery

Based on what you know about your vestibular sense,
why do you think it is difficult to walk in a straight line
after spinning yourself around on a swing?

Another type of proprioception, the *vestibular sense* (or equilibrium), provides information on the position of the body in space—especially the head—by sensing gravity and motion (Highstein et al., 2004). Vestibular sense information comes from tiny, hairlike receptors located in the fluid-filled vestibular sacs and the semicircular canals of the inner ear, above the cochlea (refer back to Figure 4-10). Whenever the head moves, these receptors send messages through a part of the auditory cortex that is not involved in hearing; and this information helps us maintain our balance. Perhaps you recall how much fun it used to be—and maybe still is—to twirl yourself around on a swing at the park until you were silly with dizziness. What happened was that when you stopped twirling, the fluid in your semicircular canals and your vestibular receptors did not immediately return to a normal state; and thus you experienced the illusion of spinning while standing still. The vestibular imbalance caused by this twirling exercise is very similar to the vestibular imbalance caused by drunkenness.

- Humans have at least 100 different types of olfactory receptor cells, with each type responding to only a limited family of odor molecules.

- Most taste receptors are located on the tongue, in bumps called papillae.

- Humans detect five primary tastes: sweet, sour, salty, bitter, and umami.

- The skin is the largest sensory organ.

- Touch is a combination of three skin senses: pressure, temperature, and pain.

- Pain is induced through tissue damage or intense stimulation of sensory receptors.

- According to gate-control theory, small and large nerve fibers open and close "gateways" for pain in the spinal cord.

- The following two proprioceptive senses detect body position and movement:

  — The kinesthetic sense provides information about the movement and location of body parts with respect to one another.

  — The vestibular sense provides information about the position of the body in space by sensing gravity and motion.

4.5 Perception

As defined at the beginning of the chapter, perception is the process that organizes sensations into meaningful objects and events. For some of our senses, such as taste and smell, the distinction between sensation and perception is so fine that it is virtually impossible to distinguish one from the other. For others, such as hearing and vision, psychologists have been able to make sufficiently clear distinctions between these two processes so that greater insight has been gained into how we assign meaning to sensory stimuli.

4.5a   Sensory Stimuli Are Organized into a Gestalt.

In the summer of 1910 while gazing out the window of a moving train, German psychologist Max Wertheimer noticed that close, stationary objects—such as fences, trees, and buildings—appeared to race in the opposite direction of the train, while distant objects—such as mountains and clouds—seemed to slowly move along with the train. Wertheimer became so enthralled with understanding the psychological origins of what later came to be called *motion parallax* that he began conducting experiments that ultimately led to the development of a new school of thought in psychology, **Gestalt psychology**, which studies how the mind actively organizes stimuli into coherent wholes. According to Gestalt psychologists, our perceptions are to be understood, not as the mind passively responding to a cluster of individual sensations, but rather as the mind actively organizing sensory stimuli into a coherent whole, or **gestalt**.

Gestalt psychology The approach to psychology that studies how the mind actively organizes stimuli into meaningful wholes

Gestalt An organized and coherent whole

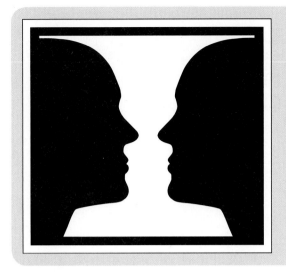

FIGURE 4-14
Reversible Figure and Ground
Can you keep the "white vase" in mind without the "black faces" intruding? Because the stimuli here are ambiguous, the figure-ground relationship continually reverses, changing what you perceive. This exercise nicely illustrates how the same stimulus can trigger more than one perception.

Form Perception

Form perception is the process by which sensations are organized into meaningful shapes and patterns. One basic rule of form perception, the **figure-ground relationship**, states that when people focus on an object in their perceptual field, they automatically distinguish it from its surroundings (see Figure 4-14). What they focus on is the *figure*, and everything else becomes the *ground*. For example, the words you are reading are the figures in your perceptual field, while the white surrounding the text is the ground. When there are not enough cues to reliably distinguish a figure from its ground, it is difficult to perceive the sought-after object. The blending of objects into their surroundings is the basic principle behind camouflage (Regan & Beverley, 1984).

The figure-ground relationship applies to all the senses, not just vision. For example, I can distinguish the sound of my daughters' singing voices against the ground of the rest of the school chorus, the taste of cinnamon in pumpkin pie, and the smell of barbecued chicken at a county fair. In all instances, I perceive one object as the figure and the other sensory information as the background.

Once we distinguish figure from ground, we must next organize the figure into a meaningful form. To give meaning to these sensations, Gestalt psychologists identified the following additional principles, known collectively as the **laws of grouping** (see Figure 4-15), that describe how people group discrete stimuli together into a meaningful whole:

- *Similarity*   We group together stimuli that are similar.

- *Proximity*   We group nearby stimuli together.

- *Continuity*   We perceive the contours of straight or curving lines as continuous, flowing patterns.

- *Connectedness*   We perceive objects that are uniform and linked as a single unit.

- *Closure*   We close the gaps in a figure and perceive it as a whole.

- *Common Fate*   We perceive objects moving together in the same direction (sharing a "common fate") as belonging to a single group.

Form perception The process by which sensations are organized into meaningful shapes and patterns

Figure-ground relationship The Gestalt principle that, when people focus on an object in their perceptual field, they automatically distinguish it from its surroundings

Laws of grouping Simple gestalt principles describing how people tend to group discrete stimuli together into a meaningful whole

FIGURE 4-15

Gestalt Laws of Grouping

There are many ways to perceive the objects shown here, but people tend to organize them into groups based on specific perceptual "laws."

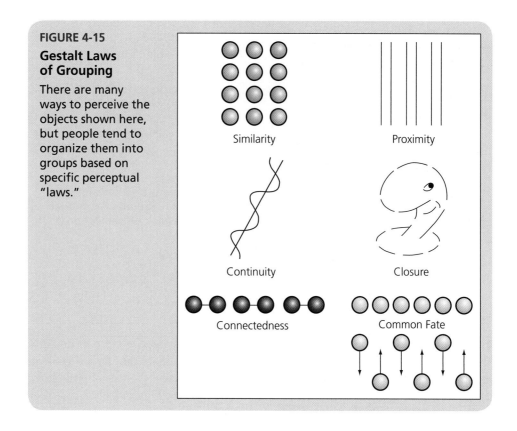

Depth Perception

Depth perception The ability to perceive objects three-dimensionally

Binocular cues Depth cues that require information from both eyes

In addition to organizing sensations into meaningful shapes and patterns, another aspect of visual perception involves organizing sensations in terms of the distance they are from us. To judge distance, our brains must transform the 2-dimensional images that fall on our retinas into 3-dimensional perceptions. This ability to perceive objects 3-dimensionally is known as **depth perception** and depends on the use of both *binocular cues* and *monocular cues* (Jacobs, 2002).

Binocular cues are depth cues that require information from both eyes. Because our eyes are about three inches apart, they receive slightly different images on their retinas when looking at the same scene. This degree of difference between the two images—which is greater when objects are closer to us—is known as the binocular cue of retinal disparity. Our brains automatically fuse these two images into one and use the cue of *retinal disparity* to judge the distance of objects (Genovesio & Ferraina, 2004; Harwerth et al., 2003). You can see the difference between the views of your eyes by holding both forefingers vertically in front of you, one at a distance of six inches and the other at arm's length. Now alternately close each eye while looking at both fingers. Notice that the closer finger appears to move farther side to side than the farther finger. If you focus on one finger with both eyes, you will see two images of the other finger. Stereoscopes and 3-D movies create the illusion of depth by presenting to each eye slightly different views of the same image.

In the late 1800s, photographers created stereo pictures that mimicked the slightly different images seen by the two eyes. When viewers looked into a stereoscope, each eye saw only one of the two images and perceived a three-dimensional view of the scene. The stereoscope provided solid evidence that the visual system treats retinal disparity as a depth cue, regardless of whether the disparity is produced by real or simulated images of a scene.

Another binocular distance cue is *convergence*, which is the degree the eyes turn inward as an object gets closer. By receiving information on the angle of convergence from the muscles of your eyes, your brain automatically calculates the distance at which you are focusing. The eyestrain you experience after staring at a near object for a long time, such as a book or computer terminal, is caused by continuous convergence (Tyrrell & Leibowitz, 1990).

While binocular cues result from both eyes working together, **monocular cues** are depth cues that require information from only one eye. Some of the more important monocular cues—some of which are illustrated in Figures 4-16 and 4-17—are as follows (Andre & Owens, 2003; Todd & Norman, 2003):

- *Interposition* When one object partially blocks our view of another, we perceive the partially obscured object as more distant.

- *Familiar size* When we see a familiar object, we perceive it as near or distant based on the size of its retinal image. Familiar objects that cast small retinal images are perceived as distant, while familiar objects that make large retinal images are perceived as near.

- *Relative size* If we assume that two objects are similar in size, we perceive the object with the larger retinal image as being closer.

- *Height in the field of view* When we see objects, those closer to the horizon are perceived as farther away. This means that objects on the ground (below the horizon) are perceived as farther away when higher in our field of view, while aerial objects (above the horizon) are perceived as farther away when lower in our field of view. This depth cue is also called *relative elevation* or *relative height*.

- *Texture gradients* When we see a change in the surface texture of objects from coarse, distinct features to fine, indistinct features, we perceive increasing distance.

- *Atmospheric blur* When we see objects that appear hazy, we perceive them as farther away than sharp, clear objects. This cue is also called *atmospheric perspective* or *aerial perspective*.

Monocular cues Depth cues that require information from only one eye

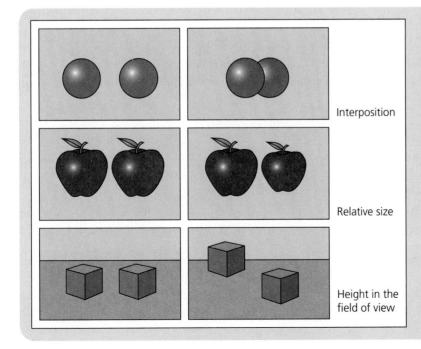

Interposition

Relative size

Height in the field of view

FIGURE 4-16

Monocular Cues

Monocular cues are depth cues that require information from only one eye. Close one eye and test this depth perception principle for yourself.

FIGURE 4-17   The Monocular Cues of Texture Gradients, Atmospheric Blur, Linear Perspective, and Light and Shadow

(*a*) Due to texture gradients, objects are perceived to be more distant as their surface texture becomes less distinct. (*b*) Due to atmospheric blur, objects that appear hazy are judged to be farther away than sharp, clear objects. (*c*) Due to linear perspective, we perceive the converging of seemingly parallel lines as indicating increasing distance. (*d*) The relative brightness cue suggests that when an object reflects more light to our eyes than another object, the brighter objects must be closer.

(a)

(b)

(c)

(d)

- *Linear perspective*   When we see the converging of what we assume are parallel lines, we perceive this convergence as indicating increasing distance.

- *Light and shadow*   When objects reflect more light to our eyes than other objects, we perceive the brighter objects as closer to us. Further, when we see different degrees of light and shadow on a single object, this provides clues about the object's orientation relative to us and its three-dimensional shape. This cue is also called *relative brightness*.

- *Motion parallax*   When we move our head sideways, objects at different distances appear to move in different directions and at different speeds.

The eye sees only what the mind is prepared to comprehend.

—Henri Bergson, French philosopher, 1859–1941

The monocular cue of *motion parallax* deals with movement (Ichikawa & Saida, 2002; Ujike & Ono, 2001). *Parallax* means a change in position, so motion parallax is a change in the position of an object caused by motion. It was Wertheimer's attention to this perceptual phenomenon that led to the founding of Gestalt psychology. The next time you ride in a car, bus, or train, experience what Wertheimer experienced by

Norman Badgley Wilson, Cattle in a Landscape, 1930, oil on canvas, 24 x 36 inches.

FIGURE 4-18

Several monocular cues are evident in this painting by Indiana artist Norman Badgley Wilson. Can you identify where Wilson has used the monocular cues of interposition, familiar size, texture gradients, and atmospheric blur to depict three dimensions on the flat surface of his canvas?

focusing on a distant object to your side. Notice how the speed and direction of motion depend on distance. Closer objects appear to speed by in the opposite direction of your own movement, while farther objects seem to move more slowly and in your same direction. It is this motion parallax that causes many children to believe that the moon or clouds they see through their side windows are actually following them.

When artists use monocular cues to create a 3-dimensional look in their paintings, the monocular cues are called *pictorial cues* (Zimmer, 2006). Prior to the Renaissance, which occurred in Europe from the fourteenth through the sixteenth centuries, artists did not understand how to use the full range of monocular cues. As a result, their paintings often looked two-dimensional and unrealistic. Figure 4-18 depicts a painting by the twentieth-century Indiana artist Norman Badgley Wilson that utilizes a number of pictorial cues to convey varying degrees of depth in a country scene.

What we see depends mainly on what we look for.

—Sir John Lubbock, English naturalist, 1834–1913

Perceptual Constancy

Thus far, you have learned how we organize sensations into meaningful shapes and patterns, and how we also organize them in space. A third aspect of perceptual organization involves **perceptual constancy**, which is the tendency to perceive objects as relatively stable despite continually changing sensory information. Once we form a stable perception of an object, we can recognize it from almost any distance, angle, and level of illumination.

There are various forms of perceptual constancy. *Color constancy* is the tendency to perceive objects as having consistent color under different conditions of illumination (Lotto & Purves, 2002). Research indicates that color constancy works best when an object is surrounded by objects of many colors, suggesting that our brain perceives color partly based on computations of the light reflected by an object relative to the light reflected by surrounding objects (Land, 1986; Pokorny et al., 1991). *Size constancy* is the tendency to perceive objects as stable in size despite changes in the size of their retinal images when we view them from different distances. This form of perceptual constancy explains why you don't perceive people approaching you from a distance as little people who are mysteriously growing in stature before your eyes. Likewise, *shape constancy* is the tendency to perceive an object as the same shape no matter from what angle we view it. Thus, when you look at your hand, this book, or a door from different angles, you still perceive it as retaining its original shape despite changes in the shape of its retinal image.

Perceptual constancy The tendency to perceive objects as relatively stable despite continually changing sensory information

FIGURE 4-19
What Kind of a Duck Is This?

Now that you have seen the duck, look again at this drawing, but now see the rabbit.

Source: Illustration from Mind Sights by Roger Shepard, Copyright © 1990 by Roger Shepard. Reprinted by permission of Henry Holt and Company, LLC.

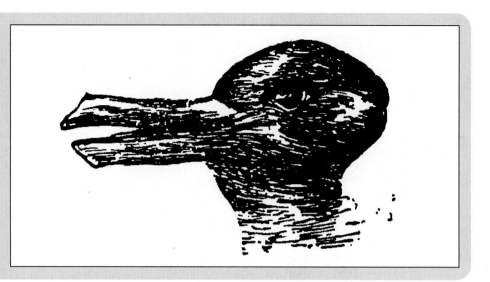

Perceptual sets Expectations that create a tendency to interpret sensory information in a particular way

4.5b Perceptual Sets Shape Interpretations of Sensory Stimuli.

Just as expectations can influence whether we detect the presence of a stimulus (refer back to Section 4.1a), the expectations we bring to a situation can also influence *how* we perceive the stimulus object. These expectations, known as **perceptual sets**, create a tendency to interpret sensory information in a particular way, due to top-down processing. For example, look at the drawing of the duck in Figure 4-19 and then read the figure caption. Based on your initial expectation of seeing a duck, you most likely organized the stimuli in this drawing so that your expectation was realized. Yet, now ask a friend to look at this same drawing (cover up the caption), but tell them to "look at the rabbit." This is a demonstration of how people can develop different perceptions of the same stimuli based on the situational contexts that create different perceptual sets.

Perceptual set can also be influenced by culture. For example, look at Figure 4-20a. Most of you will see a rather confusing pattern of black shapes that may look somewhat like a boot. However, when you look at Figure 4-20b, most of you readily perceive the word FLY in the white spaces. Your experience with the English language causes you to focus attention on the white spaces of Figure 4-20b, while the black regions serve as background. Yet, if you were a native Chinese, you would readily perceive the white spaces in Figure 4-20a as depicting the Chinese calligraphic character for the word FLY, and it would be Figure 4-20b that would likely look confusing (Coren et al., 1987).

Perceptual sets can certainly influence how we interpret stimuli in our world. For example, as a cost-saving measure during White House parties, former President Richard Nixon occasionally instructed waiters to refill empty bottles of fine and expensive wine with cheaper and lower-quality brands. Nixon was counting on the expensive bottle's label creating a perceptual set of fine taste in his guests. Later brain scan studies backed up Nixon's thinking. In one such study, when people tasted $5 wine but were told that it cost $45, the area of their brains responsible for pleasant experiences became more active; and they rated the wine tastier than when they drank the same wine but were told its true $5 price (Kringelbach et al., 2003).

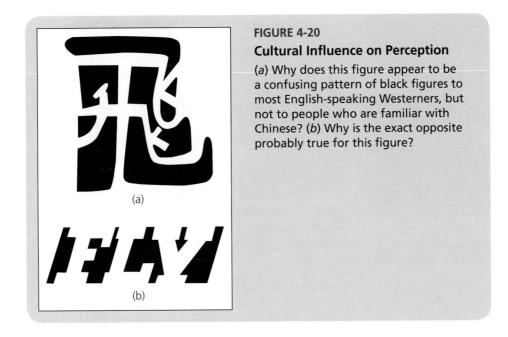

FIGURE 4-20
Cultural Influence on Perception
(a) Why does this figure appear to be a confusing pattern of black figures to most English-speaking Westerners, but not to people who are familiar with Chinese? (b) Why is the exact opposite probably true for this figure?

This study demonstrates that expectations, or top-down processing, can influence taste experience and associated neural activity. The psychological phenomenon of perceptual set is yet another illustration that what we perceive is much more than just a matter of detecting sensory stimuli in the world (bottom-up processing); perception also has to do with what's going on in our minds (top-down processing).

4.5c Perceptual Illusions Represent a Misperception of Physical Reality.

Because perception depends on how the perceiver interprets sensory stimuli, errors or misperceptions are bound to occur (Glover & Dixon, 2002; Logvinenko et al., 2002). For example, have you ever been sitting behind the driver's wheel of a parked car when the car parked next to you began to back up, and you mistakenly perceived your car moving forward? I know that when this happens to me, I slam on my brakes before realizing that I have just experienced a **perceptual illusion** called **induced movement**. The reason we sometimes experience perceptual illusions is because we misapply one or more of the perceptual principles previously examined in this chapter (see Section 4.5a). In the case of induced movement, it is the misapplication of the principle of motion parallax. That is, instead of your movement forward causing close objects to appear as though they are moving backward, the movement backward of the car close to you makes you feel like you are moving forward.

Because vision is our dominant sense, we know more about *visual* illusions than any other sensory misperceptions. Thus, in this section, the type of perceptual illusions we will focus on will be mostly of the visual variety. Yet, let me mention one *auditory* illusion I am hearing right now as I type this sentence. As mentioned previously, I have an antique clock in my den. Although I know it is making a steady click-click-click-click sound as the pendulum swings back and forth, what I more often hear is an accented CLICK-click-CLICK-click. The reason for this auditory illusion is that people tend to group the steady clicks of a clock into patterns of two clicks, with one of the clicks—usually the first—being misperceived as slightly louder than the other.

Perceptual illusion A misperception of physical reality, often due to the misapplication of perceptual principles

Induced movement The illusory movement of a stationary object caused by the movement of another nearby object

However, no two people see the external world in exactly the same way. To every separate person a thing is what he thinks it is—in other words, not a thing, but a think.

—Penelope Fitzgerald, British author, b. 1960

The ancient Greeks built the Parthenon in Athens to look perfectly symmetrical, but it is not. The designers understood and used some basic principles of visual illusions. If it had been built with perfect right angles, it would have looked crooked and ready to fall down.

Wikimedia Commons

Humans have recognized and used many of the basic principles of perceptual illusions for thousands of years. For example, in 447 BC when the ancient Greeks were designing the Parthenon in Athens, they used a variety of visual tricks to make the temple appear perfectly symmetrical, which it is not. To compensate for the illusion of concavity created by parallel lines, the Parthenon's columns lean inward slightly, and there is a bulge in the middle of the temple's base so that each column looks straight (see photo on this page). Cultural upbringing can affect whether you experience certain visual illusions. Check out Exploring Culture & Diversity 4-1 to learn how perceptual illusions differ cross-culturally.

Exploring CULTURE & DIVERSITY 4-1

Do Perceptual Illusions Differ Cross-Culturally?

Müeller-Lyer illusion A perceptual illusion in which the perceived length of a line is influenced by placing inward- or outward-facing wings on the ends of the line

The most famous and extensively studied illusion is the **Müeller-Lyer illusion** shown in Figure 4-21 (van Doorn et al., 2007). Notice that the vertical line *b* to the right appears longer than line *a* to the left. Yet, if you measure the lines with a ruler, you will find that they are equal in length. The generally accepted explanation for this illusion is that it is due to the misapplication of size constancy (Gregory, 1998; Nijhawan, 1991). That is, because figure *a* bears a likeness to the outside corner of a building and figure *b* resembles the inside corner of a room, the vertical line *b* appears farther away than the vertical line *a*. As a result of this distance cue, the application of size constancy enlarges the perceived length of *b* relative to *a*. Interestingly, cross-cultural research indicates that the Müeller-Lyer illusion is most likely to occur in cultures where straight lines, right angles, and rectangles are common design elements in buildings (Segall et al., 1966, 1990). People who live in curved buildings without straight lines and right angles, such as the Zulu of southeastern Africa, are much less susceptible to this particular perceptual illusion.

The Japanese psychologist Kazunori Morikawa (2003) demonstrated that the popularity of high-cut bathing suits is at least partly due to the fact that they make a woman's legs look longer than a conventional bathing suit. This fashion effect is simply an application of the Müeller-Lyer illusion. How so? Figure 4-22a depicts the "low-cut" look of a conventional bathing suit, whereas Figure 4-22b depicts the "high-cut" look. Don't the legs in figure *b* look longer, even though we know they are not?

FIGURE 4-21

The Müller-Lyer Illusion

In the Müller-Lyer illusion, lines of equal length are perceived as unequal. Research indicates that this illusion is more commonly experienced in cultures where straight lines, right angles, and rectangles are common building-design elements. What monocular distance cue is misapplied in this illusion?

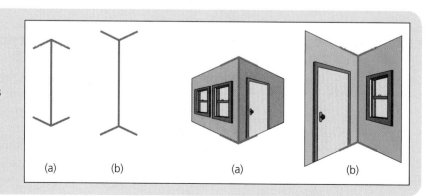

(a)   (b)   (a)   (b)

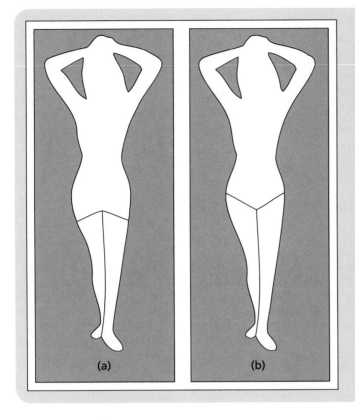

FIGURE 4-22

High-Cut Bathing Suits and the Müeller-Lyer Illusion

Fashion designers rely on the Müeller-Lyer illusion to make women's legs appear longer, and thus more attractive, when they wear high-cut bathing suits (*b*) rather than low-cut bathing suits (*a*). Is it possible that this misperception of these two women's leg lengths will occur more often in cultures where straight lines, right angles, and rectangles are common building-design elements?

(a)   (b)

Just as in the Müeller-Lyer illusion, the misperception of distance cues by people in carpentered cultures causes the perceptual illusion of the Ames Room. Designed by Adelbert Ames and depicted in Figure 4-23, this room is built with a trapezoidal rear

FIGURE 4-23 The Ames Room

(a) Why does the man in the right corner of the Ames Room look like a giant? (b) This perceptual illusion is created by having viewers look into the room through a peephole, with one eye. When viewed through the peephole, this room looks like a normal rectangular room—despite the fact that this room has a trapezoidal rear wall, a left window that is larger than the right window, and a sloping floor and ceiling. This illusion occurs because people on the right fill more of the space between the floor and ceiling; and because peephole viewers assume that when two objects are the same distance from them, the object that produces the larger image on their retinas is larger in size than the object that produces a smaller retinal image.

David Wells/The Image Works

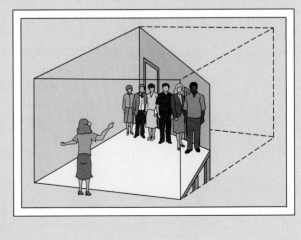

FIGURE 4-24

The Ponzo Illusion

Although the two horizontal lines are the same length, our experience tells us that a more distance object can create the same-sized retinal image only if it is larger. What monocular distance cue is being misapplied here?

wall, different-sized windows, and a sloping floor and ceiling. When viewed through a peephole with one eye, this room appears to have a normal rectangular shape. The man standing to the right (the near corner) appears disproportionately large because we judge his size based on the incorrect assumption that he is the same distance away as the person in the far left corner. Even more interesting is what we mistakenly perceive when people in the room walk to the opposite corner. When they cross the room from right to left they appear to shrink before our very eyes, while they are transformed from "little people" to giants as they move from left to right!

Another perceptual illusion caused by the misapplication of size constancy is the **Ponzo illusion** depicted in Figure 4-24. Most people see the line on top as longer than the one on the bottom (Oyama & Goto, 2007). As in the Müeller-Lyer illusion, these two lines cast the same-sized retinal image; thus, the illusion occurs due to the top line appearing farther away than the bottom line because people misapply the monocular distance cue of linear perspective. This illusion is also less likely to be experienced by people who live in cultures where they aren't exposed to many straight lines and right angles (Deregowski, 1989; Segall et al., 1966).

Ponzo illusion A perception illusion in which the perceived lengths of horizontal lines are influenced by their placement between vertical converging lines that serve as distance cues

Stroboscopic movement The illusion of movement produced by a rapid pattern of stimulation on different parts of the retina

The most important visual illusion you experience when watching movies and playing video games is **stroboscopic movement**, the illusion of movement produced by a rapid pattern of stimulation on different parts of the retina (Anstis, 1978). In motion pictures, stroboscopic movement is created by rapidly passing a series of still pictures (or film frames) past a light source, which projects these images onto a screen. As we watch these rapidly changing images, the memory of each lasts just long enough in our minds until the next one appears (see Figure 4-25). For this illusion of movement to occur, a film frame must replace the previous one 24 times per second. During the early days of motion pictures, the frame rate was only 16 per second, resulting in jerky and disjointed movement and a noticeable flickering of light. In television and video games, the static frames change about 30 times per second, resulting in the perception of fluid movement.

When stroboscopic movement is combined with the nineteenth-century technology of stereoscope photography, the visual illusion offered by 3-D movies is created (McCarthy, 1992). Early black-and-white 3-D movies from the 1950s were filmed from two slightly different angles, and the two images were later projected onto the theater screen with different-colored filters (red or blue) placed in front of each projector (McGee, 1989). So that each eye could receive a different view of the same scene, moviegoers wore special glasses with one red and one blue lens. The red lens washed out the red image, and the blue lens washed out the blue image. As previously described (see Section 4.5a), as their brains merged these two images into

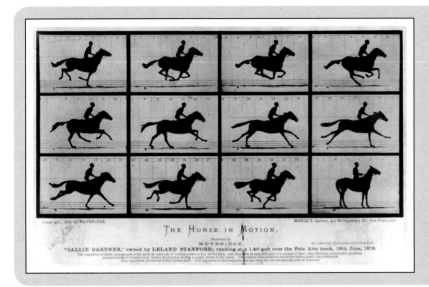

FIGURE 4-25

Stroboscopic Movement

Motion picture film consists of a series of still photographs. Presenting the pictures, one at a time in quick succession, creates the illusion of movement. Why do silent movies from the 1920s have a noticeable flickering of light and jerky images, while the movement seen in contemporary movies is fluid and realistic in appearance?

Source: Image Select/Art Resource, NY.

one, and applied the cue of retinal disparity, the audience experienced 3-dimensional movie vision. Later 3-D movies used different types of polarized light that allowed color to be depicted.

The modern-day version of the 3-D movie is the *virtual environment*, in which a person can experience 3-D images and sounds while wearing a head visor (Aznar-Casanova et al., 2008). The visor sends clear, full wraparound 3-D images to each eye, and the ears receive digital stereo sound. The images and sounds transmitted by the visor are controlled by a computer that takes into account the head movements of the wearer. Thus, whenever the wearer's head turns, the scene shifts accordingly. As discussed in Chapter 1, Section 1.3e, psychologists are beginning to use virtual environment technology in their research to increase the realism of laboratory experiments. Likewise, some clinical psychologists employ this technology when treating clients who suffer from certain phobic disorders (see Chapter 11, Section 11.2a).

Outside of psychology, virtual environment visors and helmets not only are used to train airline pilots, police officers, surgeons, and soldiers in their various environments but also are quickly becoming an integral part of the equipment used by gamers. One troubling fact about most virtual-environment computer games is that they involve violence. As noted in Chapter 1, Section 1.3e, psychological research suggests that watching aggression on television and in movies appears to increase people's own aggressive tendencies. Yet, when people play virtual-environment computer games, such as MechWarrior, Doom, and F-15 Strike Eagle, they are not merely observing violence—they are actively participating in simulated aggression. What effect does this more active participation in violent media events have on people's later aggression? Despite denials from the videogame industry, a meta-analysis of 33 videogame studies involving over 3,000 participants found that high levels of videogame violence are associated with heightened aggression in the real world among young adults and children (Anderson & Bushman, 2001; Barlett et al., 2008).

Finally, one last illusion that is affected by the perception of depth is the **moon illusion**, in which the moon appears to be about one and one-half times larger when near the horizon than when high in the sky (the same illusion also occurs for the sun). Of course, we know that the moon does not actually shrink as it rises in the sky, and the retinal size of the horizon moon and zenith moon is exactly the same, as represented by Figure 4-26a. We also know that the earth's atmosphere does not

Art has a double face, of expression and illusion, just like science has a double face: the reality of error and the phantom of truth.

—René Daumal, French poet, 1908–1944

Moon illusion A perceptual illusion in which the moon appears to be larger when near the horizon than when high in the sky

(a)   (b)

magnify the visual appearance of the horizon moon. Yet if you have ever watched the moon rise from the horizon to the night sky, you know that it does appear to decrease in size, as represented in Figure 4-26b. What causes this illusion?

One of the oldest and best-known explanations of the moon illusion is the *apparent-distance theory*, which contends that the illusion is caused by the two monocular depth cues of interposition and height in the field of view, combined with the misapplication of the principle of size constancy. According to this theory, when we see the moon near the horizon, it is often partially covered by buildings or trees that provide distance cues (interposition) that the moon is relatively far away. These distance cues are absent when the moon is high on the horizon because it is almost always unobstructed. Regarding height in the field of view, when the moon is closer to the horizon, we perceive it as farther away than when it is higher in our visual field. Thus, apparent-distance theory states that these two monocular cues cause us to mistakenly perceive the horizon moon as farther away than the moon that is high in the sky. If we perceive the horizon moon as farther away than the zenith moon, we implicitly conclude that this "distant low moon" must be larger than the "near high moon" (Kaufman & Rock, 1962). The problem with apparent-distance theory, however, is that when people are asked to judge which moon appears to be closer (Coren & Aks, 1990; Kim, 2008), most report that the horizon moon looks closer, not farther away! Of course, this directly contradicts apparent-distance theory.

So, is there any solution to the moon illusion puzzle? Not yet. Some scientists believe that the primary cause of this illusion is the moon's appearance near objects of known size (Hershenson, 1982, 2003). According to this explanation, when seen near the horizon next to trees, buildings, and mountains, the size of the moon in the sky appears rather large in relation to these known-size objects. In contrast, when seen high overhead the moon doesn't seem very big because there is nothing with which to compare it. As you might expect, this explanation also has its critics; and they offer their own solutions to this perceptual puzzle. And so it goes. The most accurate statement I can make to you at this time regarding the moon illusion is that it is a very complicated illusion, and there is still widespread disagreement as to its causes (Acosta, 2004; McCready, 1999; Ross & Plug, 2002).

4.5d Certain Aspects of Perception Are Innate, and Others Are Learned.

The principles of Gestalt psychology describe how we transform sensory information into meaningful perceptions. Gestalt psychologists believe that we are born with these principles for organizing sensory information. Yet, to what extent is perception based on inborn abilities versus experience-based learning?

The Visual Cliff

To study the ability to perceive depth, Eleanor Gibson and Richard Walk (1960) designed the *visual cliff*. This apparatus consists of a glass-covered tabletop with a "shallow" checkerboard on one end and a "deep" checkerboard on the other end that appears to drop off like a cliff (see Figure 4-27). When infants between ages 6 and 14 months were placed on the middle of this table, their mothers were instructed to try to coax them into crawling to one side or the other. Although the mothers had little problem getting their children to crawl toward them on the shallow end, most refused to crawl past the visual cliff onto the deep end (Walk & Gibson, 1961). It's possible that by the time they learned to crawl, these children had also learned to perceive depth, yet newborn animals that can walk the day they're born—such as lambs, chicks, kittens, pigs, and rats—also avoid the deep end of the visual cliff (Walk, 1981). In addition, later studies using the visual cliff found that when younger noncrawling infants were physically moved from the shallow end of the table to the deep end, their heart rates slowed down, which is a typical reaction when people try to orient themselves in new situations (Campos et al., 1970). In other words, although these younger babies may not have known precisely how to react, they did *perceive* something different between the shallow and deep ends of the table. Together, these findings suggest that infants develop depth perception shortly after birth, but that

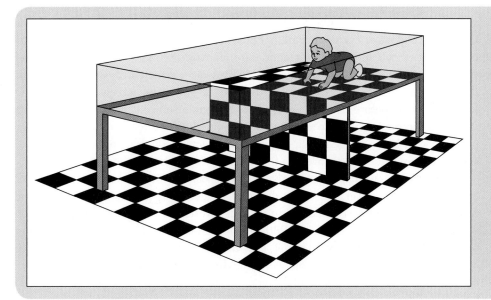

FIGURE 4-27

The Visual Cliff

The visual cliff consists of a glass-covered tabletop with a "shallow" checkerboard on one end and a "deep" checkerboard on the other end that appears to drop off like a cliff. Most 6-month-old infants won't crawl across the "deep" side.

fear and avoidance of dangerous depths may develop only after they learn to crawl and obtain first-hand experience with the dangers of height.

Newly "Sighted" People and Animals

Further evidence that some perceptual abilities are inborn comes from case histories of people who have gained sight after a lifetime of blindness. Most gained their vision by having *cataracts*—clouded lenses that allow only diffused light to enter the eye—surgically removed. Following this procedure, these newly sighted individuals could distinguish figure from ground, scan objects, perceive colors, and follow moving objects with their eyes (Gregory, 1998). Unfortunately, they often could not recognize objects until they touched them.

Seeking to study this same phenomenon under more controlled conditions, Tortsen Wiesel (1982) either stitched closed the eyelids of newborn kittens and monkeys or placed goggles over their eyes that enabled them to see only diffused light. Following infancy, when these visual impairments were removed, the animals exhibited perceptual limitations similar to those observed in the human cataract patients. Further studies with cats found that the first three months of life are a critical period in the development of their ability to detect horizontal and vertical lines (Hirsch & Spinelli, 1970; Mitchell, 1980). If kittens don't get the necessary exposure to these visual stimuli, they experience a permanent deficit in visual perception even after years of living in a normal environment. Together, these studies suggest that although certain aspects of visual perception may be inborn, others require experience-based learning during critical periods in infancy. If this critical period is missed, certain perceptual deficits cannot be corrected through later learning.

4.5e   *There Is Little Scientific Evidence for Extrasensory Perception.*

Besides the types of perception already discussed, some people believe that we can also perceive events in the world without using the normal sensory receptors. This **extrasensory perception (ESP)** is a controversial topic within psychology, with only a minority of psychologists believing in its possible existence (Hoppe, 1988; Hyman, 1994). The field that studies ESP and other paranormal phenomena is known as **parapsychology**.

Parapsychologists study a variety of extrasensory abilities. Mental telepathy is the alleged ability to perceive others' thoughts, whereas clairvoyance is the alleged ability to perceive objects or events that are not physically present. For example, telepathists might claim they can "read" your mind, and clairvoyants might claim they can find your lost jewelry. Unlike telepathy and clairvoyance, which involve perception of things in the present, precognition is the alleged ability to perceive events in the future—that is, before they happen. Thus, you might consult a fortune-teller who claims to use precognition to reveal an impending love interest in your life. Finally, psychokinesis is the alleged ability to control objects through mental manipulation, such as causing a chair to move or a flipped coin to land either "heads" or "tails."

One of the main reasons why the scientific community is skeptical about ESP claims is that whenever one study discovers evidence of paranormal abilities, the findings often cannot be replicated in subsequent research (Alcock et al., 2003; Bosch et al., 2006). For example, in the 1930s, parapsychologist J. B. Rhine designed a set of cards with each containing distinct, easy-to-recall symbols on one side (see Figure 4-28). When research participants were asked repeatedly to guess which of the five symbols was on the other side of a "target" card presented to them, Rhine (1934)

Extrasensory perception (ESP) The ability to perceive events without using normal sensory receptors

Parapsychology The field that studies ESP and other paranormal phenomena

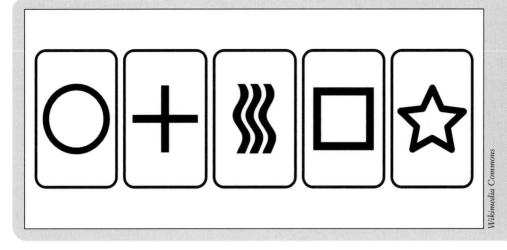

Wikimedia Commons

FIGURE 4-28

In the 1930s, parapsychologist J. B. Rhine designed a special set of cards with easy-to-recall symbols as a way to test paranormal abilities. How might you design an ESP experiment using these cards to test participants' abilities at mental telepathy?

reported that they were able to successfully do so with a frequency significantly better than chance. Had researchers in other laboratories successfully reproduced these findings, the scientific community might have been suitably impressed. Unfortunately for Rhine and parapsychology, other researchers could not replicate these impressive findings. Further, careful examination of Rhine's methods revealed that some of his participants might have been able to identify cards by their warped edges and stains. More recently, scientists tested the ESP ability of almost 28,000 people by asking them to guess the outcome of four random electronic coin tosses. With such a large sample size, this study had the statistical power to detect the possible existence of even a very small ESP effect. However, the results found no evidence of ESP ability (Wiseman & Greening, 2002).

INFO-BIT Between 1978 and 1985, the leading psychics identified by the *National Enquirer* made 486 predictions about the future, but only two came true, which means they were wrong more than 99.5 percent of the time (Strentz, 1986)!

What about the widely held belief that psychics are successful at helping various government agencies uncover hidden or secret information, such as aiding the police in solving crimes or uncovering spy plots? Regarding psychic ability in crime solving, it appears that almost all the successful collaborations between psychics and police departments occur in fictional stories, such as the TV show *Medium*. When police departments in the 50 largest cities in the United States were surveyed, 65 percent reported never having used psychics; and of the remaining 35 percent that had used psychics on a crime case, not one police department had found it helpful (Sweat & Durm, 1993). Additional studies comparing the success rates of psychics, college students, and experienced crime detectives in solving test crime cases—those previously solved in actual police investigations—have found that the psychics are no more successful than the students and detectives (Lucas, 1985; Reiser, 1982). Similar disappointing results have occurred when psychics have been tested in the clandestine world of intelligence gathering. After 20 years of testing "psychic spies," the Central Intelligence Agency concluded in a 1995 report that no reliable evidence supported any ESP claims (Hyman, 1996).

Despite the fact that there are many competent researchers studying psychic phenomena (e.g., Bem, 2011), flawed research methodology and outright fraud by people claiming psychic abilities have been persistent problems in parapsychology since its inception. In one famous case, the alleged psychic and magician Uri Geller claimed to be able to bend spoons using psychokinesis. However, closer inspection by another trained magician revealed that Geller's powers were well short of anyone's definition of miraculous (Randi, 1980). Like any good magician, he used sleight-of-hand techniques to distract people's attention and then quickly bent the spoons using normal physical force!

Although there is little evidence to indicate that ESP is a viable means of gathering information about our world, over half of all American, Canadian, and British adults believe in its existence (Blackmore, 1997; Newport & Strausberg, 2001). Popular culture fosters such beliefs, with fictional television shows and movies depicting people with fantastic paranormal powers. Buoyed by this supportive cultural climate, psychic hotlines take in over $1 billion per year, mostly from low-income persons who are seeking special insight into their lives (Nisbet, 1998). Without exception, the evidence upon which laypersons base their beliefs comes from anecdotal accounts, not scientific studies. These accounts could simply be due to unusual coincidences, exaggerated gossip, or—as we have seen—outright fraud. Until the phenomenon known as ESP can be reliably replicated in carefully controlled scientific studies, it will remain only a highly speculative "extra sense" to most practitioners of science.

Section
REVIEW

- *Form perception* is the process by which sensations are organized into meaningful shapes and patterns.

- *Figure-ground relationship* is a Gestalt principle stating that when people focus on an object or "figure" in their perceptual field, they automatically distinguish it from its surroundings.

- *Depth perception* is the ability to perceive objects 3-dimensionally.

- *Perceptual constancy* is the tendency to perceive objects as relatively stable despite continually changing sensory information.

- *Perceptual set* refers to the expectations an observer brings to a situation that influence what is perceived.

- *Perceptual illusion* is a misperception of physical reality due to the misapplication of perceptual principles.

- Certain aspects of visual perception may be inborn, whereas others require experience-based learning during critical periods in infancy.

- *Extrasensory perception* is the ability to perceive events without using normal sensory receptors. There is no reliable scientific evidence that this type of perception exists.

PSYCHOLOGICAL
applications

Can You Improve Your Memory and Self-Esteem Through Subliminal Persuasion?

As discussed earlier in Section 4.1b, there are many events that we do not consciously experience because they are below our absolute threshold. Although we are not consciously aware of these stimuli, can they still influence our behavior? Stimulation just below the absolute threshold of conscious awareness is known as *subliminal stimulation*. **Subliminal perception** is the processing of such information (Ruys & Stapel, 2008). As with extrasensory perception, many astounding claims have been made over the years about the powerful influence that subliminal messages can have on our minds and actions. For example, popular author Wilson Bryan Key warns about the dangers that cleverly hidden subliminal messages can have on our lives (Key, 1989). As Key states:

> **Subliminal perception** The processing of information that is just below the absolute threshold of conscious awareness

> Every person ... has been victimized and manipulated by the use of subliminal stimuli directed into his unconscious mind by the mass merchandisers of media. The techniques are in widespread use by media, advertising and public relations agencies, industrial and commercial corporations, and by the Federal government itself. (Key, 1973, p. 1)

The views expressed by Key are widely held by the American public, and thus, it isn't surprising that many companies are trying to profit from this cultural belief in the power of subliminal stimulation (Zanot et al., 1983). Today, in stores throughout the country, you can buy subliminal audiotapes to improve memory, stop smoking, lose weight, or increase self-esteem. Is there any evidence that such tapes are effective? Should you spend your money on such products?

Although numerous studies have found that people can respond to stimuli without being aware that they are doing so (Eimer & Schlaghecken, In Press; Katkin et al., 2001), there is no convincing evidence that subliminal persuasion influences consumer behavior (Trappey, 1996). Yet what about people who have used subliminal tapes and swear that their lives have been changed? Isn't this evidence that subliminal persuasion can be effective at least some of the time?

This was the question that Anthony Greenwald and his colleagues (1991) were interested in answering when they conducted a study of such self-help tapes. Participants were first pretested for their level of self-esteem and memory-recall ability and then given an audiotape containing various pieces of classical music. The tape manufacturers claimed that embedded within these self-help tapes were subliminal messages designed either to increase self-esteem (for example, "I have high self-worth and high self-esteem") or to increase memory (for example, "My ability to remember and recall is increasing daily"). Half the tapes were purposely mislabeled by the researchers, leading the participants who received them to believe they had a memory tape when they really had a self-esteem tape, or vice versa. The rest of the tapes, with correct labels, were distributed to the remaining participants. During the next five weeks, these volunteers listened at home daily to their respective tapes. After this exposure period, they again were given self-esteem and memory tests and were also asked whether they believed the tapes had been effective. The test results indicated no self-esteem or memory increases; the subliminal tapes were utterly ineffective. Despite these null findings, however, participants who thought they had received the self-esteem tape tended to believe their self-esteem had increased; and those who thought they had received the memory tape believed their memory had improved. This was true even if they had received a mislabeled tape!

These results, combined with other subliminal tape studies, suggest that whatever benefits people derive from such self-help products have little to do with the content of

Shutterstock

Although subliminal self-help tapes and CDs do not improve memory or increase self-esteem, they continue to do a brisk business. Why do you think people believe in their effectiveness?

Placebo effect A situation in which people experience some change or improvement from an empty, fake, or ineffectual treatment

the subliminal messages (Merikle & Skanes, 1992; Moore, 1995). Instead, people's expectations (the **placebo effect**), combined with their economic and psychological investment ("I invested a lot of time and money in this tape; it must be good!"), appear to be the sole influence operating here.

Before we dismiss the possibility that subliminal persuasion can influence people's everyday attitudes and behavior, we should consider that there are some studies, conducted under carefully controlled laboratory conditions, which have successfully manipulated people's attitudes and behavior using subliminal stimuli (Stapel & Koomen, 2006; Weisbuch et al., 2003). For example, in a series of experiments, participants who were repeatedly exposed to subliminal stimuli (abstract geometric figures or people's faces) later expressed greater liking for those stimuli (Bornstein, Leone, & Galley, 1987). In another study, participants who were subliminally exposed to achievement-oriented words (*strive, succeed, master*) while completing a "word search" puzzle were more likely to continue working on the puzzle task when signaled to stop than those in the control group (Bargh & Churchland, 1999). These findings suggest that it may be possible for a stimulus subliminally embedded in an advertisement to influence buyers' preferences. Additional research suggests that advertisers may be able to subliminally persuade people who are already motivated to actually purchase specific products over others (Karremans et al., 2006).

The caveat to this possibility is that there are some important differences between the laboratory environment where these results were obtained and the real world where people would normally receive subliminal messages. In the carefully controlled settings where these subliminal effects have been found, participants paid a great deal of attention to the experimental stimuli. In watching the average media advertisement, people are considerably less attentive. Due to the viewer's wandering eye, it is much less likely that a subliminal stimulus embedded in an ad would be unconsciously processed. A second reason to doubt that these effects would occur outside the lab is that the duration of most of these subliminal effects appears to be very short, perhaps lasting only a few seconds. If the subliminal effects last only a short time, they are unlikely to influence product purchases. Thus, although it is not beyond the realm of possibility that practitioners of persuasion could at some time in the future develop clever subliminal techniques that influence the thinking and behavior of the general public, there are no known effective techniques at the present time. Future research will determine the actual potential use—and abuse—of subliminal procedures in persuasion.

Suggested Websites

Sensation and Perception Jeopardy

http://www.uni.edu/walsh/jeopardy.html

This website, prepared by Professor Linda Walsh at the University of Northern Iowa, tests your knowledge of sensation and perception using the "Jeopardy" game show format.

Grand Illusions

http://www.grand-illusions.com

This website has many optical and sensory illusions and interactive demonstrations and puzzles.

Key Terms

Review Questions

1. Which of the following statements is true?
   a. To determine absolute threshold, a stimulus must be detectable 90 percent of the time.
   b. We have many thresholds for a given sense.
   c. Our sense of taste is more sensitive than hearing.
   d. Sensory adaptation occurs with vision without any special equipment.
   e. None of the above

2. Which of the following types of energy can our eyes detect?
   a. radio
   b. ultraviolet and infrared
   c. X-ray radiation
   d. none of the above
   e. a and c

3. Pupil size is affected by _____.
   a. light
   b. psychological arousal
   c. interest
   d. all of the above
   e. a and b

4. Which of the following animals have all-rod eyes?
   a. lizards and chipmunks
   b. rats
   c. bears
   d. owls
   e. b and d

5. Which of the following statements is true?
   a. Visual information in the right visual field goes to the left hemisphere of the brain.
   b. Visual information in the left visual field goes to the right hemisphere of the brain.
   c. Axons from the right eye are all connected to the right hemisphere of the brain.

   d. The optic nerve is the retina's area of central focus.
   e. a and b

6. Which of the following is true of color?
   a. Color is energy.
   b. Color is created by our nervous system.
   c. Color is the same for humans and animals.
   d. a and b
   e. All of the above

7. The theory that best explains color blindness is the _____ theory.
   a. trichromatic
   b. opponent-process
   c. vision
   d. a and b
   e. None of the above

8. The main parts of the inner ear include which of the following?
   a. oval window, cochlea, and organ of Corti
   b. hammer, anvil, and stirrup
   c. pinna, cochlea, and basilar membrane
   d. basilar membrane, oval window, and hammer
   e. None of the above

9. What theory best explains how we can hear sounds at frequencies of 5,000 Hz?
    a. volley
    b. place
    c. frequency
    d. a and b
    e. None of the above

10. Which of the following statements is true?
    a. Sensitivity to sweet and salty substances is strongest along the sides of the tongue.
    b. If your L-fibers are destroyed, you will be insensitive to pain.
    c. The inner ear is responsible only for our sense of hearing.
    d. Our tongue is the largest sensory organ.
    e. None of the above

11 Which of the following statements is true?
    a. Our sense of smell is as refined as that of a cat or dog.
    b. Our ears appear to have evolved from our sense of touch.
    c. We cannot recognize each other from body odor alone.
    d. All of the above
    e. None of the above

12. Which of the areas of the skin has the greatest concentration of receptors?
    a. fingers, lips, face, tongue, and genitals
    b. fingers, lips, bottom of feet, and genitals
    c. toes, elbows, and eyes
    d. knees, wrists, and neck
    e. None of the above

13. On which of the following principles is Gestalt psychology based?
    a. Our mind responds to individual sensations.
    b. Our mind actively organizes stimuli into a whole.
    c. motion parallax
    d. a and b
    e. None of the above

14. Depth perception depends on which of the following?
    a. binocular cues
    b. monocular cues
    c. convergence
    d. retinal disparity
    e. All of the above

15. To fool the brain into seeing in three dimensions, 3-D movies rely on which of the following?
    a. monocular cues
    b. retinal disparity
    c. amplitude
    d. a and b
    e. None of the above

16. How have scientists tried to determine what aspects of perception are innate?
    a. by studying human infants
    b. by studying newborn animals
    c. by studying blind people whose eyesight was surgically restored
    d. All of the above
    e. a and c only

Chapter Five

Consciousness

Chapter Outline

Psychological Applications: *How Can You Deal with Sleep Disorders?*

The discovery that changed the course of sleep research from a relatively mundane area of inquiry into an intensely exciting journey occurred in 1952. Graduate student Eugene Aserinsky, who worked as a research assistant in the sleep lab of Nathaniel Kleitman at the University of Chicago, was hovering over his sleeping eight-year-old son, Armond. The young boy had electrodes taped to his head, near his eyes. These electrodes were connected to an *electroencephalograph*, which is a machine that measures the level of electrical activity in the brain. Something strange was happening. About every 90 minutes, Armond's eyes began darting about behind his closed lids. Aserinsky was deeply puzzled because these seemingly searching eye movements had all the characteristics associated with someone who was wide awake! How could this be happening? Wasn't sleep the time when the brain was supposed to be quiet and resting?

Adding further mystery to this event was the fact that when Aserinsky awakened his son during one of these eye-movement episodes, Armond reported that he was having a dream!

The next day when Aserinsky excitedly told

Conscious and unconscious experiences do not belong to different compartments of the mind; they form a continuous scale of gradations, of degrees of awareness.

—Arthur Koestler, British author and political activist, 1905–1983

Kleitman about his observations, the skeptical professor phoned the machine's manufacturer and was told by the chief technical expert that the inexperienced graduate student must have done something to the machine to make it spew out such nonsense. Upon hearing this indictment of his competency, Aserinsky's career flashed before his eyes. Later, recounting this dark moment in his life, Aserinsky (1996) stated, "If I had a suicidal nature, this would have been the time. I was married; I had a child; I'd been in universities for twelve years with no degree to show for it. I'd already spent a couple of years horsing around on this. I was absolutely finished."

Luckily, Aserinsky's mentor did not "pull the plug" on Aserinsky's research or career. By waking people who were producing these fast, jerky eye movements, Aserinsky and Kleitman (1953) ascertained that dreams are a characteristic feature of this active stage of sleep. As we continue our psychological journey of discovery through the landscape of consciousness, we will explore the inner world of sleep. In addition, we will search for answers to questions about other areas of consciousness. For example, can you recall ever being surprised by unusual states of awareness that occurred while you were awake? When labeling one state of mind an unusual or altered state, how well do you really understand the state with which you are comparing it? Are these normal and altered states the same for everyone, or do you inhabit your own unique experiential world? Luckily for us, researchers have explored these areas of consciousness, and their discoveries will become ours as we follow their footprints in this part of our journey.

5.1 The Nature of Consciousness

Despite the fact that almost everyone would agree that consciousness is highly important for our survival, scientists and philosophers argue about its essential characteristics (Robinson, 2008; Stamos, 2008).

5.1a Consciousness Is Subjective, Selective, Divided, Continuous, Changing, and Consists of Many Levels.

Consciousness Awareness of yourself and your environment

Consciousness is your awareness of yourself and your environment. Such consciousness is highly complex. It is *subjective*—you cannot share it with another person; it is selective—you can be aware of some things while ignoring others; it is *divided*—you can pay attention to two different things at once; it is *continuous*—each moment of consciousness blends into the next moment; it is *changing*—what you are aware of now will normally shift to awareness of other things within seconds; and it is made up of *many levels*—from an alert and focused awareness to the relative stupor of deep sleep. These qualities of consciousness allow human beings to negotiate a complex social world (Butler, 2008).

Subjectivity

Each of us has our own conscious experiences. We can discuss with others what we see, hear, feel, and think: but we cannot directly share these experiences—our consciousness is unique. Because psychologists cannot directly observe others' consciousness, they have devised objective methods that *infer* what conscious experiences are occurring, through careful observation. For example, by simultaneously measuring people's brain activity and obtaining self-reports from them, psychologists try to identify different states of consciousness.

Selective Attention

Focused awareness on a single stimulus to the exclusion of all others is known as **selective attention**, and it is one of the defining characteristics of consciousness (Fox et al., 2011). In reading this chapter, you are employing selective attention. Yet, while you are ignoring all the background noise around you, certain stimuli will find it easier than others to penetrate your concentration (see Closer Look 5-1). For instance, you may be able to ignore another person in the room, but what if that person turns toward you with a threatening expression on her face? You are likely to take notice because we automatically divert our attention to threatening faces (Mogg & Bradley, 1999). This ability to override attentional focus and notice signs of impending danger is a useful trait and undoubtedly was of great survival value to our human ancestors.

Selective attention Focused awareness on a single stimulus to the exclusion of all others

How Do Psychologists Study Selective Attention?

One way that psychologists study selective attention in the laboratory is through dichotic listening tasks. They place earphones on research participants and deliver different messages to each ear simultaneously but instruct participants to listen to only one of the messages. To ensure they do this, psychologists ask participants to repeat the message, a process known as *shadowing*. Typically in such studies, participants are able to completely ignore the nonshadowed information in the other ear (Cherry, 1953). Participants are usually so good at shadowing the message that if it is switched between the two ears, they continue to shadow it, following the content rather than the ear. However, if the participant's name is mentioned in the nonshadowed message or if it contains sexually explicit words, she or he is likely to notice this at least some of the time (Wood & Cowan, 1995).

Although participants in most shadowing studies show no ability to recall or recognize any of the nonshadowed information, they do appear to process it to some degree (Nisbett & Wilson, 1977). For example, if the word "Wisconsin" is part of the unattended message, the person may not remember it but may be more likely to say "Madison" when asked to name a state capital than someone for whom "Wisconsin" was not part of the unattended message. Similarly, less time will be needed to answer the question "What state is known as the 'Dairy State'?"

Neurologically, selective attention is possible because of the brain's ability to separate different signals from each other. At the neural level, the brain appears to reconfigure itself in a way that temporarily alters how certain specialized neurons respond to incoming sensory information (Seiler et al., 2011; Yantis, 2008). In the absence of focused attention, these specialized neurons respond to many different sensory stimuli. However, when your attention becomes focused on specific stimuli in your perceptual world, these neurons respond more sensitively to this specific incoming information.

Talking on your cell phone in a noisy room is a particularly challenging selective attention task. The reason it is so difficult is that, when you're talking on a phone, the mouthpiece not only sends your voice and any background noise to the person to

FIGURE 5-1 **An Effective Technique to Use Your Cell Phone in a Noisy Room**

When trying to use your cell phone in a noisy room, your brain has difficulty selectively attending to your caller's voice because it appears to be coming from the same location as the room noise. Placing your thumb over the cell phone mouthpiece significantly improves your ability to hear your caller. How does this listening strategy capitalize on a basic principle of selective attention?

whom you are speaking, it also mixes these sounds with the voice signal it receives from the other phone. As depicted in Figure 5-1, if you are holding your cell phone to your left ear, you hear your caller's voice mixed in with your own room noise. In such a situation, your brain has difficulty selectively attending to your caller's voice because it appears to be coming from the same location as the room noise. Trying to hear better by putting your finger in your right ear is not a good solution because it doesn't solve the selective attention problem in your left ear. There is a better solution, which capitalizes on your brain's ability to separate different noises from each other when they come from different locations (Aamodt & Wang, 2008). Simply place your thumb over the mouthpiece of your cell phone. With no room noise now being sent to your left ear, your brain can tune out the room noise in your right ear and selectively attend to your caller's voice in your left ear. The result is that you can now hear your caller much better.

Divided Attention

Divided attention Attention that is split and simultaneously focused on different stimuli

The evidence that some unattended messages are processed suggests that it is possible to attend to different stimuli at the same time (Pereira-Pasarin & Rajaram, 2011). You demonstrate such **divided attention**—which is a third characteristic of consciousness—when you get dressed in the morning while listening to music or talking to someone. Performing these tasks simultaneously is relatively easy because at least one of them is so well learned that you can do it automatically (Schneider, 1985). How can you simultaneously listen to a lecture and take notes when both tasks require substantial attention? Research suggests that you can divide your attention with a good deal of success in such instances because each task requires different brain resources. In listening to the lecturer's words, your primary attentional resources are devoted to perceiving this incoming stimulus, while other resources handle notetaking.

The divided attention that occurs when driving a car while talking on or texting with a cell phone creates distractions and increases the likelihood of accidents and traffic fatalities.

Although we can engage in both selective and divided attention, we sometimes risk our health and safety when performing two or more tasks at once. For example, there are over 300 million cell-phone users in the United States, and 85 percent of them talk on their phones while driving a motor vehicle. A number of studies suggest that this sort of divided attention creates distractions and increases the risk of traffic accidents, even when using hands-free models (Beede & Kass, 2006; Neyens & Boyle, 2008; Strayer & Johnston, 2001). Listening to the radio or talking to a passenger while driving does not distract us to the same dangerous degree, yet texting while driving is even more distracting than simply talking on a cell phone (Cobb et al., 2010).

Research suggests that the upper limit of individual attentional abilities is determined by the efficiency of our nervous system. For example, as we age, our nervous system becomes less efficient, which weakens our ability to sustain attention, either the selective or the divided variety (Valeriani et al., 2003). Children who have *attention-deficit/hyperactivity disorder (ADHD)*, which appears to be biologically based, also are unable to concentrate for extended time periods. Still, among these children and among the elderly, strategies to improve attention can be learned, even in complex tasks (Mason et al., 2004).

The Stream of Consciousness

Psychologists have long recognized that consciousness is continuous and changing. Indeed, over 100 years ago, William James (1902–1985) described this continuous, altering flow of thoughts, feelings, and sensations as being a *stream of consciousness*. To understand James's viewpoint, reflect on your own awareness as you read these words. Are other things passing through your mind? Try to pay attention only to these words on the page. This is not easy because irrelevant thoughts often interrupt and distract you.

One interesting type of stream of consciousness is **daydreaming**, a relatively passive waking state in which attention is directed away from external stimuli to internal thoughts and imaginary situations (Smallwood, 2011). Almost everyone daydreams on a daily basis, yet daydream frequency and intensity decrease with age in adulthood. Despite the common belief that daydreaming is an inconsequential part of daily consciousness, at least one study estimated that college students spend about one-third of their waking hours daydreaming (Bartusiak, 1980). Although 95 percent of us admit to daydreaming about sex (Leitenberg & Henning, 1995), most daydreams deal with practical daily concerns and tasks, future goals, and interpersonal relationships.

BVT *Lab*

Flashcards are available for this chapter at www.BVTLab.com.

Daydreaming A relatively passive state of waking consciousness that involves turning attention away from external stimuli to internal thoughts and imaginary situations

Journey of Discovery

Because daydreaming involves thinking about internal thoughts and imaginary situations, what effect do you think television viewing might have on daydreaming? Do you think people who watch a lot of television would daydream more or less than those who watch little television? Why?

Why do we daydream? Several possibilities have been suggested. Fantasizing about actual people, events, or problems in our lives may help us formulate useful future plans of action. For example, imagining how to tell your professor that you slept through her exam may help when you actually explain the situation to her. Second, daydreams may help us regulate our behavior by either providing safe avenues to imaginatively act out certain desires or helping us consider the possible outcomes of our actions. For example, your fantasy of kissing your best friend's boyfriend or girlfriend may not only temporarily soothe your sexual desires but may, also, inhibit your acting on this impulse as you can imagine the damage it could cause to your friendship. Finally, when our external surroundings are providing insufficient stimulation, we may daydream as a way to escape boredom and stay mentally aroused. Perhaps this is why college students spend so much class time daydreaming!

One disadvantage of daydreaming is that we become much less attentive to our surroundings, and thus our effectiveness in the world is diminished (Cunningham et al., 2000). About 4 percent of the adult population daydreams so much that they are called **fantasy-prone personalities** (Cuper & Lynch, 2008; Lynn et al., 1996). Not surprisingly, due to the amount of time spent daydreaming and the intensity of these experiences, fantasy-prone individuals occasionally have trouble separating their daydreams from their memories of real events (Nickell, 1996). Although this habitual blending of fantasy with reality can sometimes indicate a dissociative psychological disorder (see Chapter 11, Section 11.2c), many frequent fantasizers are merely more creative and imaginative than most people (Singer et al., 2000).

Fantasy-prone personality A person who has regular, vivid fantasies and who sometimes cannot separate fantasy from reality

Levels of Consciousness

The final defining characteristic of consciousness is that it exists on many levels. Mental events that you are currently aware of are said to exist at the *conscious level*. For example, the sensations you feel when you squeeze your arm are at your conscious level of awareness. As already discussed, consciousness ebbs and flows. Daydreaming is a form of consciousness when we are less alert and present than normal. In contrast, **mindfulness** is a heightened state of awareness of the present moment (Hill & Updegraff, 2012). When you experience mindfulness while speaking to a friend, you are likely aware of how she looks, how she is reacting nonverbally, what she is saying, and also how you are reacting, feeling, and thinking. Some events are not currently at the conscious level but could become so with prompting. For instance, stop for a moment and recall what you were doing yesterday around noon. Although you probably were not thinking about the events surrounding your previous midday activities—they were at the *preconscious level*—they are now "on your mind." Finally, some mental events are not consciously available to us; they exist at the *unconscious level*. For example, you are not consciously aware of your brain regulating your various hormone levels. You are also generally unaware of most of the mental events that occur while you are sleeping (see Section 5.2). Many psychologists believe that some of these unconscious mental events—especially those involving unacceptable thoughts or urges—are actively kept out of consciousness (see Chapter 10, Section 10.2a). In this chapter, we will examine various levels of consciousness, including those identified as *altered states,* which are noticeably different from our "normal" state of consciousness (see Section 5.3).

Mindfulness A heightened state of awareness of the present moment

5.1b Consciousness May Provide Us with Survival Advantages.

According to the evolutionary principle of natural selection (see Chapter 1, Section 1.2e), members of a species with inborn traits most adaptive for survival in their environment will produce more offspring; as a result, their numbers will increase in frequency in the population. What advantage might the emergence of consciousness have given to our ancestors?

One possibility is that consciousness provided our ancestors with a mental representation of the world that allowed them to more effectively plan future activities

Evolution is an ascent towards consciousness.

—Pierre Teilhard de Chardin, French priest and cosmic evolutionist, 1881–1955

(Trupp, 2006). That is, by mentally manipulating events and reflecting on possible behavioral choices *before* acting, our ancestors were able to greatly reduce the sort of aimless and impulsive behavior that is likely to cause death. Another related explanation is that consciousness may have evolved as a means of categorizing and making sense of primitive emotions (Humphrey, 1992). According to this perspective, each of the primitive emotions came to be associated with a different state of consciousness, and, as a result, these states of consciousness provided our ancestors with information that aided their survival. For instance, the negative emotions caused by a snakebite or a fall from a tree became associated with a specific state of consciousness that led our ancestors to avoid similar situations in the future, thus lowering injury and death. Similarly, the positive emotions resulting from eating, drinking, and having sex became associated with states of consciousness that led our ancestors to seek out similar situations, which again benefited them. Although both explanations sound plausible, we currently have no way of knowing whether they accurately account for the emergence of consciousness.

Section **REVIEW**

- Consciousness is personal, selective, divided, continuous, changing, and consists of many levels.

- In daydreaming, attention is directed away from external stimuli to internal thoughts and imaginary situations.

- Consciousness and evolution may have allowed our ancestors to plan future activities and/or categorize and make sense of emotions.

5.2 Sleep

In addition to the awareness that we have of surroundings and ourselves while engaged in typical waking activities, we also regularly experience altered states of consciousness. An **altered state of consciousness** is an awareness of ourselves and our environment that is noticeably different from our normal state of consciousness. The most common altered state of consciousness is **sleep**, which is a nonwaking state of consciousness characterized by minimal physical movement and minimal responsiveness to one's surroundings. To understand this altered state of consciousness, in this section we examine the sleep-wake cycle, sleep stages, possible reasons for sleep, and different dream theories.

5.2a *Daily Body Rhythms Regulate Our Activities.*

While typing this sentence, I notice how tired I feel. It is almost midnight, and I am ready for a good night's sleep. Yet, as my day winds down, I know somewhere in the nearby woods, there is a great horned owl whose day is in full swing. Mammals can be classified into two categories based on their sleep cycles. *Diurnal mammals* are awake during the day and asleep at night, while *nocturnal mammals* are asleep during the day and awake at night. These sleep-wakefulness cycles have evolved because they permit a species the maximum adaptation to its environment.

The behavioral cycle of sleep and wakefulness that we naturally follow throughout our lives corresponds to physiological changes, such as body temperature, blood

Altered state of consciousness An awareness of oneself and one's environment that is noticeably different from the normal state of consciousness

Sleep A nonwaking state of consciousness characterized by minimal physical movement and minimal responsiveness to one's surroundings

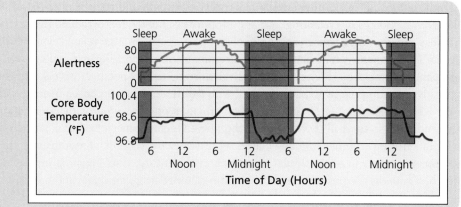

FIGURE 5-2

Circadian Rhythms

As you can see in the graph, as core body temperature changes, a person's level of alertness also changes. Based on this graph, what happens to your alertness as your core body temperature drops?

Circadian rhythms Internally generated behavior and physiological changes that occur on a daily bases

pressure, and hormone levels. Together, these daily behavioral and physiological changes are known as **circadian rhythms** (in Latin, *circa* means "about" and *diem* means "day"). Some of these circadian rhythms help to regulate the sleep-wake cycle. For instance, as you can see in Figure 5-2, body temperature rises in the early morning, peaks at midday, and then begins to drop one to two hours prior to sleep. Because body temperature influences feelings of arousal, you generally feel most alert late in the afternoon or early evening. Thus, if you've ever pulled an all-nighter, you probably felt most tired around 4:00 A.M. when your body temperature was lowest; you probably began to perk up, however, just before your normal waking time as your temperature began to rise.

One way that circadian rhythms have been studied is by eliminating any environmental cues that would indicate the time of day. This has been accomplished by isolating people in a lab without windows or clocks, or by having them live underground in specially built "houses." Findings from such studies initially suggested that in the absence of daylight and time cues, circadian rhythms drifted toward a 25-hour cycle (Welsh, 1993; Wever, 1979). Indeed, for almost 30 years, sleep researchers believed these findings meant that humans were off-kilter with the natural world! Then, researchers discovered that all the previous research testing the 25-hour-cycle hypothesis had inadvertently created the effect (Shanahan et al., 1999). In these studies, the artificial light that participants relied on to see while deprived of natural sunlight was sufficiently intense to reset their sleep-wake cycle. Further, because participants often left lights on well after the sun had set in the outside world, this caused their brains' circadian pacemaker to keep them alert and awake longer than normal. Over the course of many days, their sleep-wake cycle appeared to drift to 25 hours. However, when researchers subsequently reduced light levels, they discovered that participants' true circadian cycle was about 24 hours. This research provides a valuable lesson in the way that the scientific method is self-correcting. In the journey of discovery, scientists sometimes follow false paths, but the critical analysis that drives this search eventually reveals past missteps.

How does the brain reset this aspect of our biological clock? A small area of the hypothalamus known as the *suprachiasmatic nucleus (SCN)* and the hormone *melatonin,* which is produced by the pineal gland, appear to be crucial in readjusting the body's sleep-wake cycle (Bai et al., 2008; Blum et al., 2012). As the sun sets, special photoreceptors in the eye detect this decrease in available light (Wang et al., 2008). This information is then transmitted to the SCN, which responds by signaling the pineal gland to increase its production of the hormone **melatonin** by ten times its daily amount. As this melatonin "rush" enters the bloodstream, you experience drowsiness (Dowling et al., 2008; Okamura, 2008). Chronic insomniacs who receive

Melatonin A hormone produced by the pineal gland that induces drowsiness

synthetic forms of melatonin often sleep better and feel more alert within a month of taking the hormone (Livianos et al., 2012). This finding has led some researchers to refer to melatonin as "nature's sleeping pill."

The level of melatonin in your bloodstream continues to rise during the evening, peaking between 1:00 A.M. and 3:00 A.M. However, shortly before sunrise, the pineal gland stops producing melatonin, which soon causes you to become aroused from sleep. During the day, exposure to sunlight and other bright light continues to suppress your melatonin levels until dusk, when this cycle repeats itself. Thus, sunlight plays a crucial role in setting the SCN so your body operates on a 24-hour schedule.

Scientists have also isolated a gene in the SCN that, along with perhaps 10 other genes, actually controls this internal clock (Katzenberg et al., 1998). The discovery of this gene—which has been named "clock"—may eventually lead to more effective treatment of ailments related to disruptions in circadian rhythms, such as insomnia and depression.

Disruptions in circadian rhythms also occur when you travel by jet through a number of time zones. The severity of this jet lag depends on whether you fly westward or eastward (see Figure 5-3). When flying westward—say, from London to Detroit—your regular sleep cycle is pushed back five hours (a *phase delay*), so that your 24-hour day is stretched to 29 hours. The jet lag resulting from such east-west travel is easier to adjust to—and thus less severe—than eastward-induced jet lag. Why? Perhaps phase delays coincide with the tendency in modern times to habitually stretch out waking time to the limits of the 24-hour, 11-minute sleep-wake cycle. In contrast, flying eastward across five time zones results in your day being shortened to 19 hours (a *phase advance*), which not only is farther away from your natural 24-hour sleep-wake cycle, but also is inconsistent with your day-stretching habits. Consistent with this explanation, in the study depicted in Figure 5-3, travelers who flew eastward from Detroit to London had increased difficulty falling asleep following their arrival,

The only thing wrong with insomniacs is that they don't get enough sleep!

—W. C. Fields, American comedian and film actor, 1880–1946

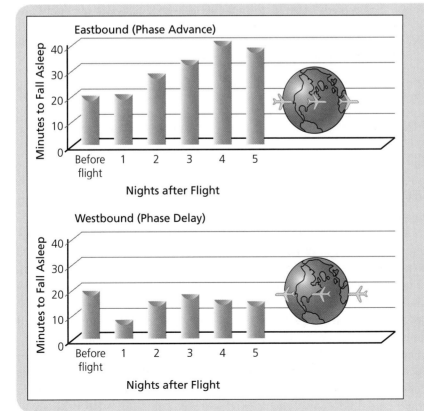

FIGURE 5-3

Circadian Rhythms and Jet Lag

The severity of jet lag depends on whether you fly eastward or westward. In one study, people who flew eastward through five time zones had increased difficulty falling asleep following their arrival, whereas travelers who flew westward through five time zones experienced no sleep difficulties (Nicholson et al., 1986).

while travelers who flew westward from London to Detroit experienced no sleep difficulties (Nicholson et al., 1986).

Shift workers, who work during their normal sleeping hours, experience a similar problem (Mikko et al., 2006). Of the 7 million Americans who work at night, 75 percent are regularly sleepy, and 20 percent have actually fallen asleep on the job—factors that lead directly to higher accident rates and lower productivity than any other work schedule (Smith et al., 1995). In an attempt to correct this work-related health problem, sleep researchers recommend that employers schedule workers on rotating shifts in a "clockwise" direction (from days to evenings to nights), so that changes are phase delays rather than phase advances (Waage et al., 2007). For example, if you were working an evening shift (4:00 p.m. to midnight), it would be easier for you to move forward to a night shift (midnight to 8:00 a.m.) rather than backward to a day shift (8:00 a.m. to 4:00 p.m.) because moving backward (a phase advance) forces you to try to sleep during the time you previously were working. Phase-delayed work schedules promote greater worker health, productivity, and satisfaction than phase-advanced schedules (Scott, 1994).

The readjustment of circadian rhythms can be sped up by light-treatment therapy. In such therapy, workers are exposed to bright lights mimicking the daylight sun during the first few days of their night shift. They are also exposed to eight hours of total darkness at home during the day (Bougrine et al., 1995). NASA ground personnel who worked on shifted schedules during two space shuttle missions reported better sleep, performance, and physical and emotional well-being if they received light-treatment therapy during the prelaunch week and during the mission itself (Stewart et al., 1995).

 **INFO-BIT**   Circadian rhythms perform many critical functions for a species. Monarch butterflies, the champions among long-distance butterfly travelers, rely upon a properly set circadian clock to guide them during their more than 2,000-mile migratory trek from the northeastern United States and eastern Canada to the mountains of central Mexico. Monarchs exposed to normal sunlight during development correctly fly southwest, the direction of their overwintering destination in Mexico. However, when scientists expose monarchs to different patterns of light and darkness during the time they are developing from caterpillar to butterfly, their circadian rhythms no longer provide them with accurate navigation cues (Mouritsen & Frost, 2002). These findings yield strong evidence indicating that monarchs use an internal, time-compensated sun compass to keep them on course during migration.

5.2b   There Are Distinct Stages of Sleep.

Just as circadian rhythms regulate your sleep-wake cycle, you also follow a biological rhythm during sleep. This was one of the important discoveries that followed in the wake of the 1952 discovery—described at the beginning of the chapter—that rapid eye movements occurred in predictable cycles during the course of a night's sleep. In sleep studies using electroencephalograms (EEGs), investigators such as Eugene Aserinsky and Nathaniel Kleitman (1953) discovered that at about every 90 or 100 minutes we cycle through distinct sleep stages, each associated with a different pattern of brain activity. These EEG brain wave patterns are depicted in Figure 5-4.

The two most common EEG patterns that people experience while awake are **beta waves**, associated with an active, alert, state of mind, and **alpha waves**, indicating relaxed wakefulness (Knyazev et al., 2006). However, when we are asleep, our brain wave patterns change and we experience two basic types of sleep. **NREM sleep**, or

Beta waves Very fast, low-amplitude brain waves associated with an active, alert state of mind

Alpha waves Fast, low-amplitude brain waves associated with a relaxed, wakeful state

NREM sleep Non-rapid-eye-movement sleep; which is a relatively inactive phase in the sleep cycle

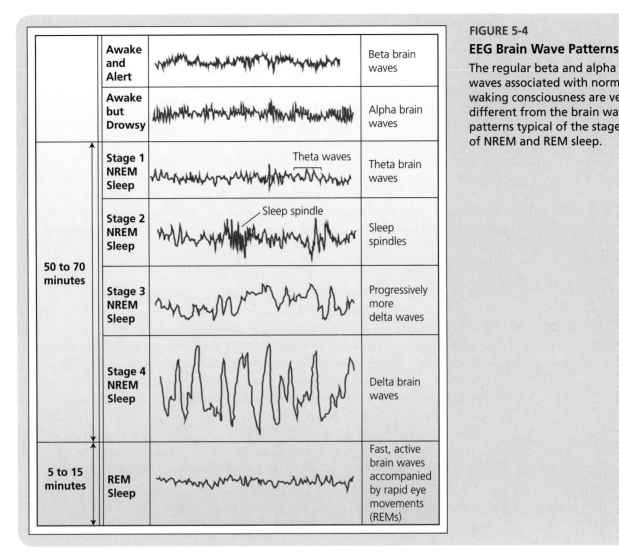

	Awake and Alert		Beta brain waves
	Awake but Drowsy		Alpha brain waves
50 to 70 minutes	Stage 1 NREM Sleep	Theta waves	Theta brain waves
	Stage 2 NREM Sleep	Sleep spindle	Sleep spindles
	Stage 3 NREM Sleep		Progressively more delta waves
	Stage 4 NREM Sleep		Delta brain waves
5 to 15 minutes	REM Sleep		Fast, active brain waves accompanied by rapid eye movements (REMs)

FIGURE 5-4

EEG Brain Wave Patterns
The regular beta and alpha waves associated with normal waking consciousness are very different from the brain wave patterns typical of the stages of NREM and REM sleep.

non-rapid-eye-movement sleep, is sometimes referred to as *quiet sleep* because our brain activity and other physiological functions slow down. In contrast, **REM sleep**, or rapid-eye-movement sleep, is often called *active sleep* because there is heightened brain and body activity. Let us more closely examine these two different types of sleep.

NREM Sleep

As you gradually enter the light sleep of *stage 1*, your alpha-wave EEG pattern changes to the smaller, more rapid, irregular **theta waves** (Vyazovskiy & Tobler, 2005). Stage 1 sleep, which is referred to as the *hypnogogic state*, is a transitional state between wakefulness and sleep usually lasting only a few minutes. Heart rate and breathing slow as body temperature drops and muscles begin to relax. What may be orchestrating this sleep induction is a very small cluster of brain cells—called *sleep-on neurons*—located at the base of the forebrain (Siegel, 2003). Typical experiences reported during stage 1 sleep are sensations of falling (hence the term "falling asleep") or floating, as well as visual and auditory hallucinations. You can be easily awakened during stage 1 sleep.

Stage 2 sleep lasts about 20 minutes and is characterized by **sleep spindles**, which are bursts of rapid, rhythmic brain-wave activity. Muscle tension is greatly

REM sleep A relatively active phase in the sleep cycle, characterized by rapid eye movements, in which dreaming occurs

Theta waves Irregular, low-amplitude brain waves associated with stage 1 sleep

Sleep spindles Bursts of rapid, rhythmic electrical activity in the brain characteristic of stage 2 sleep

reduced. Although sleeptalking can occur at any time during sleep, it is most likely to occur during stage 2.

In *stage 3*, you begin to move into the deeper form of *slow-wave sleep* in which your brain waves become higher in amplitude and slower in frequency. These **delta waves** become much more pronounced during the even deeper sleep of *stage 4*. It is difficult to arouse a person at this stage of the sleep cycle.

From the time you enter stage 1 and progress to stage 4, between 50 and 70 minutes usually passes. These first four stages make up *NREM sleep,* or non-rapid-eye-movement sleep. Now the sleep cycle reverses itself, and you move back up through the stages to stage 2 (where you spend about half your night). NREM sleep is often called "quiet sleep" because of the slow, regular breathing, the general absence of body movement, and the slow, regular brain activity exhibited in the EEG. Actually, the term "quiet sleep" is a bit misleading because snoring is most likely to occur during NREM sleep.

Delta waves Slow, high-amplitude brain waves most typical of stage 4 deep sleep

REM Sleep

As you can see in Figure 5-5, once you arrive back at stage 2, you do not fully enter stage 1; rather, you enter an entirely different kind of sleep. In this new stage, your brain waves become rapid, somewhat like waking alpha waves and stage 1 theta waves; your heart rate and breathing also increase; and your eyes begin darting back and forth behind your closed eyelids. This phase of "active sleep," which completes the sleep cycle, has come to be known for these quick eye movements and is called REM (rapid eye movement) sleep. What appear to be responsible for creating REM sleep are specialized neurons located in the pons at the base of the hindbrain, called *REM sleep-on neurons.* These neurons become very active during the REM sleep phase. You go through about four or five sleep cycles during the night, each lasting about 90 minutes. As also depicted in Figure 5-5, after the first few sleep cycles, you do not usually pass through all the sleep stages.

Why Do We Sleep?

Your body needs sleep and will malfunction without a sufficient amount (Lucidi et al., 2006). For example, after about 18 hours of wakefulness, your reaction time begins to

FIGURE 5-5

Stages of Sleep in the Nighttime Sleep Cycles

Most people follow rather consistent sleep cycles during the night, with each cycle lasting about 90 minutes and consisting of four NREM stages followed by REM sleep. Nightmares and other dreams occur during REM sleep, but sleepwalking and night terrors (see the "Psychological Applications" section at the end of the chapter) typically occur in stages 3 and 4, respectively. Based on this figure, what can you conclude about the duration of REM sleep as the night progresses?

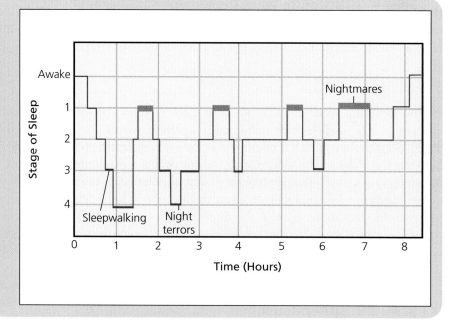

slow from a quarter second to half a second. You also experience bouts of *microsleep*, in which you momentarily tune out your surroundings. If you are reading a book, you will probably have to reread a paragraph when you tune back in; and if you are driving a car, the consequences can be deadly. Every year drowsy U.S. drivers are responsible for about 100,000 automobile accidents, resulting in 1,500 deaths and 71,000 injuries (Gupta, 2006). After 20 hours of wakefulness, your reaction time is equivalent to someone who is considered legally intoxicated (a blood alcohol content of 0.08), and your ability to remember things diminishes. Studies also suggest that children age 2 to 5 years who fail to get sufficient sleep at night or during daytime nap periods are at greater risk for behavior problems (Dement, 1999).

Although sleep is essential in maintaining health, sleep experts are not quite sure *why* we need to sleep. The **restorative theory of sleep** suggests that sleep allows the body to restore itself following the rigors of daily activity (Colrain, 2011). Research supporting this view finds that people sleep longer and spend more time in deep sleep (stages 3 and 4) after vigorous physical exercise (Vein et al., 1991). Testosterone levels depleted in males during the day are also restored during sleep. In addition, deep sleep promotes new cell growth by triggering the pituitary gland to release a growth hormone (see Chapter 2, Section 2.2c). As people advance from childhood to adulthood, less of this growth hormone is released, and they spend less time in deep sleep.

In contrast to the restorative theory, the **adaptive theory of sleep** contends that sleep is simply a product of our evolutionary heritage, preventing us from moving about and being injured (or eaten) during a time of the day (darkness) in which our bodies are not well adapted. Sleep also conserves energy for that part of the day (daylight) in which our bodies are most efficient. Thus, sleep may have been selected because of its value in promoting both physical safety and energy conservation (Webb, 1992). Today, although we no longer need sleep for the same reasons as our ancestors, sleep mechanisms still have a significant influence on our lives.

Which of these theories is the better explanation for why we sleep? It may well be that both the restorative theory and the safety/conservation theory provide part of the answer to this puzzle. Both are consistent with a finding across the animal species: Bigger animals generally need less sleep than smaller animals. Elephants, giraffes, horses, sheep, and the larger primates (including humans) sleep less than rats, mice, bats, squirrels, and cats do (Kuo et al., 2004; Siegel, 2003). Smaller animals not only are generally more vulnerable to attack from predators than larger animals but also have higher metabolic rates. *Metabolism*, which is the process of cells burning food to produce energy, generates extremely reactive chemicals (*free radicals*) that cause injury to cell membranes. Sleep slows metabolism, which may provide an opportunity for the body to repair the damage done by free radicals. Perhaps most importantly, sleep may give damaged neurons in the brain the time to become relatively inactive and deal with the free radicals.

Restorative theory of sleep A theory that sleep allows the body to restore itself following the rigors of daily activity

Adaptive theory of sleep A theory that sleep prevents us from moving about and being injured during a time of the day in which our bodies are not well adapted

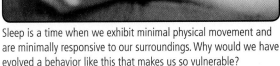

Sleep is a time when we exhibit minimal physical movement and are minimally responsive to our surroundings. Why would we have evolved a behavior like this that makes us so vulnerable?

Shutterstock

5.2c *Sleep Habits Vary Individually and Culturally.*

How much sleep you need partly depends on your age. The amount of time spent sleeping declines throughout the life cycle. Newborns sleep approximately 16 hours, children average between 9 and 12 hours, and adolescents average about 7.5 hours.

SELF-DISCOVERY 5-1
Questionnaire

Are You a Morning or a Night Person?

Respond to the following items by circling either "Day" or "Evening."

1. I prefer to work during the	Day	Evening
2. I enjoy leisure-time activities most during the	Day	Evening
3. I feel most alert during the	Day	Evening
4. I get my best ideas during the	Day	Evening
5. I have my highest energy during the	Day	Evening
6. I prefer to take classes during the	Day	Evening
7. I prefer to study during the	Day	Evening
8. I feel most intelligent during the	Day	Evening
9. I am most productive during the	Day	Evening
10. When I graduate, I would prefer to find a job with ___ hours.	Day	Evening

If you answered "Day" to eight or more items, you are probably a morning person. However, if you answered "Evening" to eight or more items, you are probably a night person.

Source: From "Day persons, night persons, and variability in hypnotic susceptibility" by B. Wallace in *Journal of Personality and Social Psychology*, 1993, 64, 827–833 (Appendix, p.833). Copyright © 1993 by the American Psychological Association. Adapted with permission.

Newborns and young children have the highest percentage of REM sleep, and many sleep experts believe that the heightened brain activity during REM sleep promotes the development of new neural pathways (Siegel, 2003). In adulthood, both the quantity and the quality of sleep usually decrease, especially among the elderly. Less time is spent in slow-wave stage 4 deep sleep and a greater proportion of stage 1 sleep occurs, resulting in more nighttime awakenings. Although stage 4 sleep declines, the percentage of REM sleep remains fairly constant throughout most adulthood, diminishing only in later life.

Besides these age-related sleep differences, we also differ in the times at which we typically go to sleep and awaken. Have you ever heard of "morning people" and "night people"? Morning people wake up early, with a good deal of energy and alertness, but are ready to retire before 10:00 P.M. Night people, on the other hand, stay up much later in the evening and have a hard time getting up early in the morning (Goel, 2011; Thoman, 1999). About 25 percent of us are night people, 25 percent are morning people, and the remaining 50 percent fall somewhere between these two extremes. These different sleep preferences are related to differences in circadian body temperatures, with genetics playing an important role in these sleep-wake variations (Hellman et al., 2010). Morning people's body temperatures quickly rise upon awakening and remain high until about 7:30 P.M. The body temperature of night people, in contrast, rises much more gradually when they wake, peaks at midday, and begins dropping only late in the evening. Not surprisingly, in one study, college students identified as morning people obtained better grades in early-morning classes than in evening classes. The opposite effect was found for students classified as night people (Guthrie et al., 1995). Complete the questionnaire in Self-Discovery Questionnaire 5-1 to determine whether you are more of a night person or a morning person.

Besides these individual differences in sleep patterns, cultural differences have also been documented. For example, in tropical cultures, midday naps—or *siestas*—are common because they allow people to avoid strenuous activity during the hottest time of the day. Interestingly, as these "siesta cultures" industrialize, they abandon this practice (Kribbs, 1993). This change in napping patterns is probably due to the greater comfort that can be achieved with air-conditioning, combined with the greater emphasis on productivity in industrialized settings.

With industrialization also comes less nighttime sleep. As with the gradual disappearance of napping in industrialized siesta cultures, the lower overall sleep time found in industrialized settings can undoubtedly be traced to the development of a stronger work ethic. Yet another related factor is electricity and its ability to literally light up the night and thereby extend the time people can be active and productive. People who live in cultures without electricity generally retire shortly after the sun sets and sleep about 10 hours. In contrast, the average length of sleep for North American and European adults is less than 7.5 hours, about 20 percent lower than what it was a hundred years ago (National Sleep Foundation, 2002). Because all humans still possess the physiology that evolved to fit the ecological niche of a hunter-gatherer culture, our lower sleeping average suggests that many of us are sleep deprived (Gander et al., 2006).

Lack of sufficient sleep is a common problem reported by college students, especially while studying for final exams. Yet, results from sleep-deprivation experiments indicate that people lose their ability to concentrate and think creatively after only a day of sleep deprivation (Dodds et al., 2011; McCoy & Strecker, 2011). These findings suggest that engaging in long hours of continuous studying before final exams may actually lower academic performance. If all-night studying cannot be avoided, however, research indicates that grabbing a few hours of naptime during the day can offset some of the negative effects of sleep deprivation. Remember this bit of information when preparing for your next exam! To determine whether you are getting enough sleep, answer the questionnaire in Self-Discovery Questionnaire 5-2.

5.2d *Dreaming Often Occurs During REM Sleep.*

As mentioned in Section 5.2b, at the end of each sleep cycle you enter REM sleep. The fact that the brain and other physiological functions are almost as active during REM sleep as in the waking state has led some to describe this phase of sleep as *paradoxical sleep.* Accompanying rapid eye movements is dreaming. A **dream** is a story-like sequence of visual images experienced during sleep. Eugene Aserinsky first discovered this association between rapid eye movement and dreaming when he awakened sleepers as their eyes darted about behind closed lids (see chapter-opening story). Subsequent research found that people awakened from REM sleep report dreaming 78 percent of the time versus only 14 percent of the time during NREM sleep (Schwartz & Maquet, 2002). This discovery led some researchers to speculate that sleepers moved their eyes as they "watched" their dream activities (Dement, 1978). The problem with this *scanning hypothesis,* however, is that most research has not found a strong correlation between rapid eye movement and dream content. Instead of dreaming causing rapid eye movement, it is more likely that both are caused by the brain's relatively high level of activation during REM sleep.

Although your ability to respond to external cues is diminished during REM sleep, it is not entirely absent. Research indicates that unexpected sounds or other sensory stimulation may be incorporated into dreams, thus allowing the dreamer to continue sleeping. For example, in one experiment, sleeping volunteers who were sprayed with a mist of water and then awakened were more likely to report dreams of being squirted by someone, experiencing a sudden rainfall, or standing under a leaking roof than were volunteers who were not sprayed (Dement & Wolpert, 1958).

One study comparing people's dream reports during REM sleep and NREM sleep found that aggressive social interactions were more characteristic of REM dreams, while dreamer-initiated friendliness was more characteristic of NREM dreams

Dream A story like sequence of vivid visual images experienced during sleep

Dreaming permits each and every one of us to be quietly and safely insane every night of our lives.

—William Dement, sleep researcher, b. 1928

SELF-DISCOVERY 5-2
Questionnaire

Are You Getting Enough Sleep?

Shutterstock

People differ in their sleeping needs. Complete this questionnaire and follow the accompanying instructions to assess and possibly improve your alertness and energy level.

Psychologist James Maas (1998) has developed the following questionnaire to measure people's sleep needs. To determine whether you might be suffering from sleep deprivation, answer true or false to the following items regarding your current life experiences.

	True	False
1. It's a struggle for me to get out of bed in the morning.	☐	☐
2. I need an alarm clock to wake up at the appropriate time.	☐	☐
3. Weekday mornings I hit the snooze bar several times to get more sleep.	☐	☐
4. I often sleep extra hours on weekend mornings.	☐	☐
5. I often need a nap to get through the day.	☐	☐
6. I have dark circles around my eyes.	☐	☐
7. I feel tired, irritable, and stressed out during the week.	☐	☐
8. I have trouble concentrating and remembering.	☐	☐
9. I feel slow with critical thinking, problem solving, and being creative.	☐	☐
10. I often fall asleep in boring meetings or lectures or in warm rooms.	☐	☐
11. I often feel drowsy while driving.	☐	☐
12. I often fall asleep watching TV.	☐	☐
13. I often fall asleep after heavy meals or after a low dose of alcohol.	☐	☐
14. I often fall asleep while relaxing after dinner.	☐	☐
15. I often fall asleep within five minutes of getting into bed.	☐	☐

If you answered "true" to three or more items, you probably are not getting enough sleep. Keep in mind that we differ in our individual sleep needs. If this questionnaire suggests that you may be sleep deprived, Maas recommends that you go to bed 15 minutes earlier every night for a week. Continue adding 15 more minutes each week until you are waking without the aid of an alarm clock and without feeling tired during the day. Encourage your family and friends to also try this exercise, and compare your experiences over the next few weeks to see if your daily alertness and energy level improve.

Source: From *The Sleep Advantage* by James B. Maas. Copyright © 1998 by James B. Maas. Used by permission of Villard Books, a division of Random House, Inc.

BVT *Lab*

Visit **www.BVTLab.com** to explore the student resources available for this chapter.

(McNamera et al., 2005). Why might REM sleep be associated with the emergence of aggressive social impulses, while cooperative social impulses are more likely to emerge during NREM sleep? At present, there is no good answer to this question, but these findings suggest that certain brain areas are more active than others during these two different sleep stages. Section 5.2e examines various theories that explain the cause or meaning of dreams.

How important is REM sleep? When participants in sleep studies are partially deprived of REM sleep by being awakened whenever they begin exhibiting rapid eye movements, they often report feeling more tired and spend more time in REM sleep the next night than those who are not deprived of REM sleep (Dement et al., 1966). This extra time spent in REM sleep following such deprivation is known as *REM rebound*. Although some sleep researchers once thought that REM sleep deprivation led to psychotic hallucinations, later research disproved this idea (Kryger et al., 2000). However, some studies have found that people who experience prolonged REM sleep deprivation exhibit poorer recall of recently learned material than those not deprived of REM sleep (Ishikawa et al., 2006; Mallick et al., 2008).

All mammals except the Australian anteater have REM sleep, as do some birds; fish, reptiles, and amphibians do not. It is possible that those animals that engage in REM sleep also have dreams, but it is unlikely that most of them possess the cognitive ability required to distinguish dream events from real events. This inability to separate the dream world from the real world would pose a serious threat to animals if they remembered their dreams upon awakening. For instance, what if your cat "Tabby" had a dream that a family of fat, juicy mice replaced the vicious dog next door? If Tabby remembered this dream, she would likely saunter over for a nutritious breakfast and quickly become the dear-departed Tabby. Thinking about Tabby's situation from an evolutionary perspective, it is plausible that animals that remembered their dreams as real events were less likely to survive to pass on their genes to the next generation.

As mentioned, REM sleep is greatest early in life, accounting for at least 50 percent of all sleep time in normal human newborns and as much as 80 percent among premature infants (Burnham et al., 2003). This finding suggests that prior to birth, REM sleep makes up virtually the entire mode of existence of the late-developing fetus. Within six months of birth, REM sleep declines to about 30 percent of all sleep time; and by early childhood, its 20 percent level remains unchanged until diminishing once again later in life.

5.2e No Consensus Exists on the Cause or Meaning of Dreams.

I'm at the ocean on a beautiful summer day, standing on a wooden pier jutting out from shore. The sky is a clear blue. I begin walking to the end of the pier where an old woman is sitting. When I reach her, I notice an unattended fishing pole nearby. As soon as I look at the pole, I realize a fish has taken the bait at the other end. Without thinking, I grab the pole and begin reeling in the line. About a quarter mile from shore, a huge beautiful blue fish jumps high out of the water. This is what is at the end of the line! I have to use all my strength to keep from being pulled into the ocean. The old woman gives me advice, but I am confident I know what I am doing. As I struggle with the fish, I learn about its life. After an hour of labor, I have the fish next to the pier. At the moment when I should get it in place to be hoisted up, a thought comes to me that what is important is the struggle, not the victory. I throw the pole down and the fish swims away. The woman looks up at me and nods. She knows too. I walk back to shore.

Perhaps like the college student who had this dream while preparing for an important exam, you too have pondered whether these sleep experiences are worth analyzing. The simple fact is that we all dream, whether we remember doing so or not. While dreaming, most people are not aware they are dreaming: The dream is experienced as "real." Exceptions to this rule are the 10 percent who occasionally are aware that they are dreaming while they are dreaming (Kunzendorf et al., 2006; LaBerge, 2007). This **lucid dream**, can be very enjoyable because the lucid dreamer is often able to shift the dream plot while it is in progress (Buzzi, 2011; Patrick & Durndell, 2004). One recent study suggests that individuals who have frequent lucid dreams are mentally healthier than non-lucid dreamers, but it is currently unclear why this might be so (Doll et al., 2009).

In some cultures, people believe you should be held accountable for your dreams. Thus, among the New Guinea Arapesh, if you hurt someone in your dreams, you must try to undo the harm in your waking life. In other cultures, dreams are believed to foretell the future. Although some people in Western cultures believe in precognitive dreams, most do not place such importance on the stories generated by our unconscious minds.

Dreams as Wish Fulfillment

The most famous dream theory in psychology is that proposed by Sigmund Freud (1900) and *psychoanalytic theory* (see Chapter 10, Section 10.2). According to Freud, dreams are disguised wishes originating in the unconscious mind. The dream that is remembered by the dreamer represents only the surface or **manifest content**. The true meaning of the dream—the "disguised" or **latent content**—is concealed from the dreamer because it would not only arouse great anxiety but also disrupt sleep. So dreams are constructed to express these wishes in a confusing symbolic manner so that the dreamer's peace of mind—and her or his sleep—is protected. In the student's "fish dream," the struggle with the fish is the manifest dream content, perhaps symbolically representing the student's attempt to better understand, but not destroy, some unconscious desire (the latent content) dredged up by his studies.

Dreams as Problem Solving

There is a good deal of research indicating that waking-life experiences are reflected in dreams (Pesant & Zadra, 2006). According to Rosalind Cartwright's (1977, 1989) **problem-solving theory**, dreams provide people with the opportunity to creatively solve their everyday problems because what we think about in dreams is not hampered by logic or realism. From this perspective, the fish dream might reflect the student's dawning recognition that he should be more confident in his own intellectual abilities and rely less on others' advice (the old woman in the dream). In support of problem-solving theory, studies of people going through a divorce find that their first dream of the night often occurs sooner, lasts longer, and is more emotional and story-like than it is for other people. Further, those who frequently dream about divorce-related problems tend to make a better adjustment to single life than those who did not dream much about their problems (Cartwright, 1991).

Brain-imaging studies provide empirical support for the idea that dreaming may help us solve daytime problems by freeing up our creative thinking (Barrett, 2010). For example, EEG studies indicate that neural activity in the prefrontal cortex is suppressed during REM sleep (Picchioni et al., 2011). It is possible that this diminished prefrontal cortex activity sufficiently lowers logical reasoning and reality testing so that creative problem solving becomes more likely. Beyond empirical

---

Lucid dream A dream in which the dreamer is aware of dreaming and is often able to change the plot of the dream

Manifest content The dream that is remembered by the dreamer

Latent content The true meaning of the dream that is concealed from the dreamer through the symbols that make up the manifest dream content

I do not know whether I was then a man dreaming I was a butterfly, or whether I am now a butterfly dreaming I am a man.

—Chuang-tzu, Chinese philosopher, 369–286 B.C.

Problem-solving theory A theory that dreaming provides the opportunity to creatively solve everyday problems because dreams are not hampered by logic or realism

findings, there are numerous historical anecdotes about people using dreams as a problem-solving strategy. For example, Paul McCartney claims that he created the melody for the Beatles' hit song "Yesterday" while dreaming. Similarly, one evening in 1857, the German chemist Friedrich Kekulé fell asleep in front of a fire while trying to solve the mystery of how the benzene molecule was constructed. In a dream, he saw the carbon atoms of the benzene molecule twisting and twining like snakes, when suddenly one of the snakes seized hold of its own tail. Upon awakening, he realized that the carbon atoms bonded with one another in a 'closed chain,' just like a snake biting its tail!

Dreams as Information Processing

In contrast to attributing dreams to unconscious wish-fulfillment or problem-solving attempts, the **off-line dream theory** contends that the cognitive processing that occurs during dreaming consolidates and stores information gathered during the day, thus allowing us to maintain a smaller and more efficient brain (McNaughton et al., 2003). The term *off-line* is a computer phrase, referring to the fact that computers need time when data are not being input but instead are being analyzed and stored into memory. According to the off-line theory, dreaming is the time when the brain— our computer—goes off-line to somehow integrate the new information from the day with our older memories and experiences (Kaechele, 2006).

Off-line dream theory A theory that the cognitive process of dreaming consolidates and stores information gathered during the day, thus allowing us to maintain a smaller and more efficient brain

Journey of Discovery

Have you ever had a dream that later seemed to come true? Many people who have had this experience, or who hear of it from a close friend or family member, believe that dreams can predict the future. What other potential explanations could there be for a dream that comes true?

Evidence that dreaming may indeed serve an integrating function and be instrumental to learning comes from research demonstrating that both humans and other animals spend more time in REM sleep after learning difficult material than after learning easy material, and if denied REM sleep, memory retention suffers. Additional studies suggest that REM sleep helps consolidate both perceptual and motor skill learning, emotional and factual memories, and complex cognitive learning (Strickgold, 2003; Walker & Stickgold, 2006). Some neuroscientists believe that if we didn't dream—that is, have off-line time—we would need much larger forebrains to handle our daily learning experiences. This may explain why the Australian anteater—the only known mammal that does not engage in REM sleep—has such a large forebrain compared with the rest of its brain (Hawkins, 1986).

Dreams As Interpreted Brain Activity

Although the previous theories support a belief that dreams fulfill wishes, solve problems, or maintain brain efficiency, J. Allan Hobson and Robert McCarley argue that dreaming has no particular significance other than as a by-product of brain activity. This **activation-synthesis theory** states that a dream is the forebrain's attempt to interpret the random neural activity initiated in the midbrain during sleep (Hobson, 1999). As you recall from Chapter 2, Section 2.3b, the uppermost portion of the forebrain is the brain's "thinking" center and consists of the left and right cerebral hemispheres. According to activation-synthesis theory, the more verbal left

Activation-synthesis theory A theory that dreaming is a by-product of random brain activity, which the forebrain weaves into a somewhat logical story

TABLE 5-1   Dream Theories

Theory	Explanation	Meaning of Dream	Is Meaning of Dream Hidden?
Psychoanalytic	Dreams are anxiety-producing wishes originating in the unconscious mind.	Latent content of dream reveals unconscious wishes.	Yes, by manifest content of dreams
Off-line	Dreaming consolidates and stores information input during the day, thus allowing us to maintain a smaller and more efficient brain for survival.	Previous day's experiences are reprocessed in dreams.	Not necessarily
Problem-solving	Dreams provide the opportunity to creatively solve everyday problems.	Possible solutions to everyday problems are signaled.	Not necessarily
Activation-synthesis	Dreams are the forebrain's attempt to interpret random neural activity.	Dream content is only vaguely related to the dreamer's life experiences; thus, there is little, if any, meaning in the dream.	No real meaning to hide

hemisphere strives to assign some rational meaning to behavior, even when there is none. It is just this sort of thinking that appears to be involved in creating the plots of our dreams. Similarly, the right hemisphere may help construct most of the dream's visual features. The resulting dream constructed from this random brain activity will have a personal touch unique to the dreamer because it is based on available memories, but the dream has no hidden meaning (Hobson et al., 1998).

The various dream theories discussed here are summarized in Table 5-1. Currently, researchers have not come to consensus concerning the cause or meaning of dreams. Yet, whatever the ultimate answer, all the theories agree that the specific content of dreams is associated with the life experiences of the dreamer. Supporting this view, numerous studies indicate that dreams reflect the daily concerns and interests of the dreamer (Domhoff, 2003). This may mean that exploring our unconscious world can help us better understand our conscious lives.

Section REVIEW

- Circadian rhythms closely align with the 24-hour rotation of the earth.
- Jet lag and shift work can disrupt normal circadian rhythms.
- Every 90 to 100 minutes, we cycle through distinct sleep stages.
- Sleep may provide time to restore the body and mind, as well as protect us from the dangers posed by engaging in nighttime activities.
- As people age, the quantity and quality of sleep decrease.
- Individuals and cultures differ in their sleeping patterns.
- REM sleep is where most dreaming occurs.
- Psychoanalytic dream theory asserts that dreams are disguised wishes originating in the unconscious.
- Problem-solving dream theory contends that dreaming is where we creatively solve everyday problems unencumbered by logic or realism.

- Off-line dream theory proposes that dreaming allows us to maintain a smaller and more efficient brain by consolidating and storing information gathered during the day.

- Activation-synthesis theory explains dreaming as the forebrain's attempt to interpret the random neural activity initiated in the midbrain during sleep.

5.3 Other Altered States of Consciousness

Sleep is our most familiar altered state of consciousness, and it is typically induced due to fatigue although it also can be facilitated by ingesting various drugs. Besides sleep, there are a wide variety of altered states that are induced by various means. In this section, we examine the altered states associated with *hypnosis, meditation,* and *drugs.*

5.3a *Hypnosis Has Been Practiced for Thousands of Years.*

Imagine that you attend a group demonstration of hypnosis. As you sit with others in an auditorium, the hypnotist begins talking:

> I want you to get comfortable and begin to relax. Ignore what is going on around you and pay attention only to my words … You can become hypnotized if you are willing to do what I tell you to do … Just do your best to pay close attention to my words, and let happen whatever you feel is going to take place. Let yourself relax … Sometimes you experience something very similar to hypnosis when driving along a stretch of highway, and your concentration becomes narrowed so that you don't notice landmarks along the road … As you continue to listen to my voice, your eyes are growing heavy … Heavy and tired … Droopy …You are beginning to feel drowsy and sleepy … Sleepy and drowsy … Relax … You're becoming more and more relaxed … and tired … Tired and sleepy … As your eyes become heavier, it's getting harder and harder to keep them open … They feel so heavy, like lead … You may feel you want to close them. That's all right … Let your eyes close as your muscles relax more and more.

During this *hypnotic induction,* although you may begin to feel tired, you probably won't fall asleep. Hypnosis was named after the Greek god of sleep, Hypnos, but the two altered states of hypnosis and sleep bear only a superficial resemblance to one another. Sleep is characterized by minimal responsiveness to one's surroundings, whereas **hypnosis** is a state of altered attention and awareness in which a person is unusually responsive to suggestions. In our culture, hypnosis is typically induced using suggestions for deep relaxation while the person being hypnotized remains relatively passive and motionless. However, this altered state can be achieved with many varied techniques, including *active alert induction,* as in inducing hypnosis while a person pedals a stationary bicycle (Gafner & Benson, 2003).

Various forms of hypnosis have been practiced for thousands of years. For example, in 2600 BC, the father of Chinese medicine, Wang Tai, described a hypnotic-like medical technique involving incantations and the passing of hands over patients. Similar descriptions of trance states appear in ancient Hindu and Egyptian medical writings (c.1600 BC). More recently, in the eighteenth century, Austrian physician Franz Anton Mesmer (1734–1815) used hypnosis—which he called *animal magnetism*—to restore the balance of supposed magnetic fluid in people's bodies, thus curing them of disease. In the nineteenth century, French neurologist

Hypnosis A psychological state of altered attention and awareness in which a person is unusually receptive to suggestions

Jean Marie Charcot (1825–1893) used hypnosis to treat hysteria. Interestingly, it was partly Sigmund Freud's lack of success in using hypnosis as a therapeutic tool in the treatment of psychological disorders that led him to develop psychoanalysis in the 1890s. Freud's rejection of hypnosis slowed the development of research and theory on this altered state of consciousness for many years.

What Are the Characteristic Features of Hypnosis?

The following features often characterize people's awareness when they are hypnotized (Gravitz, 2011):

- *Enriched fantasy:*   The hypnotized person can readily imagine situations dissociated from reality.

- *Cognitive passivity:*   Instead of planning actions, the hypnotized person waits for the hypnotist to suggest thoughts or actions.

- *Hyperselective attention:*   The hypnotized person will focus attention on the hypnotist's voice and ignore other stimuli. Even pain that a person would find unbearable during their normal waking state can be tolerated through the hypnotically induced focused attention.

- *Reduced reality testing:*   The hypnotized person tends to uncritically accept hallucinated experiences suggested by the hypnotist.

- *Posthypnotic amnesia:*   When instructed by the hypnotist, the hypnotized person will often forget all or most of what occurred during the hypnotic session. These memories are restored when the hypnotist gives a prearranged signal. Hypnotically induced amnesia does not appear to be due to deliberate thought suppression on the part of the hypnotized person.

What Are Common Misconceptions about Hypnosis?

Hypnosis has long been used as a form of entertainment, and this history has led to certain myths about the capabilities of the hypnotized person. A list follows of some of these misconceptions accompanied by the discoveries made by scientific research (Lynn & Kirsch, 2006; Musikantow, 2011):

- *Hypnotized people can be forced to violate their moral values.*   There is no evidence that hypnosis causes people to act against their will.

- *Memory is more accurate under hypnosis.*   Although hypnosis may help people to recall forgotten events, it often results in people recalling events that never happened.

- *While hypnotized, people are much stronger than normal.*   Hypnosis has no effect on strength.

- *Hypnosis acts like a truth serum, compelling people to avoid deception.*   Hypnotized people can lie and keep secrets if they so desire.

- *Hypnotized people can be age-regressed, thus allowing them to relive childhood experiences.*   Although hypnotized people may believe they have regressed to an earlier age, they typically display cognitive abilities far beyond those of a child.

Individual Differences in Hypnotizability

People differ in their **hypnotizability**, which is the degree to which they can enter a deep hypnotic state (Carvalho et al., 2008; Hilgard, 1965). Individuals who are highly hypnotizable have the ability to concentrate totally on material outside them and to become absorbed in imaginative activities (Kirsch & Braffman, 2001). Children are the most hypnotizable individuals, which is not surprising, given the fact that being able to engage freely in fantasy is an important predictor of hypnotizability.

Although the ability to suspend ordinary reality facilitates entrance into the hypnotic state, highly hypnotizable persons are not more gullible or more conforming than their less hypnotizable counterparts. Among adults, about 10 percent cannot be hypnotized at all, approximately 15 percent are very susceptible, and the rest fall somewhere in between (Barber, 2000). Research also indicates that hypnotizability is a fairly stable trait during adulthood (Piccione et al., 1989).

Hypnotizability The degree to which a person can enter a deep hypnotic state

INFO-BIT College students answered questions concerning their beliefs about hypnosis, and then either watched a stage hypnotist or attended a lecture on hypnosis. When questioned later, both groups were more likely to correctly believe that hypnotizability does not reflect lower intelligence. However, although those students who had heard the lecture were less likely to believe that a hypnotized person is robot-like and automatically acts on all suggestions, the reverse was true for those who had watched the stage hypnotist (Echterling & Whalen, 1995). Why might students who saw the stage hypnotist be more likely to believe such false descriptions of hypnosis?

5.3b *Some Psychologists Doubt that Hypnosis Is an Altered State.*

In contrast to the sleep state, the brain wave activity (EEG) of hypnotized individuals differs only slightly from that of their normal waking states (De Pascalis, 1999). This lack of any clear physiological difference between the normal and the hypnotic states has fueled suspicion that hypnosis is not really an altered state at all. One such "nonstate" theory proposes that the hypnotized person is simply playing a role (Barber, 1979). This *role-playing* explanation contends that hypnosis is a normal waking state in which suggestible people behave as they think hypnotized people are supposed to behave. The proponents of this view do not necessarily believe that hypnotized people are consciously faking an altered state. Instead they argue that because of the misguided cultural beliefs about the powers of hypnosis, people get caught up in the hypnotic role and often unwittingly confirm these beliefs by demonstrating hypnotic behavior (Gorassini, 1996).

In support of this role-playing interpretation of hypnosis, research indicates that people's responsiveness to hypnotic suggestions can be influenced by their expectations and their desire to please the hypnotist. For example, when individuals who previously exhibited low hypnotizability take *active training* programs to enhance their attitudes and expectations about hypnosis, they subsequently exhibit large gains in hypnotizability. These gains are much more likely to occur when rapport with trainers is high rather than low. Yet, merely liking one's trainer is generally not sufficient to increase hypnotizability. When persons with low hypnotizability were given *passive training,* in which their well-liked trainers told them that hypnotic responses just "happened by themselves," their level of hypnotizability did not increase (Spanos et al., 1989–1990).

Neodissociation theory A theory that hypnotized persons enter an altered state in which two streams of consciousness operate simultaneously, one actively responding to suggestions and the other passively observing what is going on

Despite evidence indicating that hypnosis is influenced by social expectations and a desire to please the hypnotist, many hypnosis researchers contend that there are enough special features of hypnosis to legitimately call it an altered state. For example, people who are hypnotized often report *dissociation* in consciousness, whereby they process perceptual information on two levels simultaneously (Hilgard, 1986, 1992). Based on this research, Ernest Hilgard proposed his **neodissociation theory**, which contends that the hypnotized person has two streams of consciousness operating at once. One stream responds to the hypnotist's suggestions, while the other stream, called the *hidden observer*, remains concealed from conscious awareness and merely observes what is going on.

Based on our previous discussion of selective and divided attention (see Section 5.1a), Hilgard's theory of a *divided consciousness* is not that unusual. While engaging in normal daily activities, you can literally split your attention. Sometimes, you might even engage in an activity without any memory of having done so. For instance, have you ever been so engrossed in dinner conversation that you forgot what your meal tasted like or that you even ate it? This common experience during the normal waking state is not that different from Hilgard's explanation of hypnosis.

This debate about hypnosis being an altered state is a matter of ongoing scientific inquiry. Although many of the more bizarre or peculiar effects observed during hypnosis might be explained by people's expectations about hypnosis and their desire to please the hypnotist, other effects—such as hypnotized patients being able to undergo surgery without pain (Hornyak & Green, 2000)—suggest a truly altered state of consciousness. Brain-imaging studies further indicate that when hypnotized individuals are exposed to normally painful experiences—such as having their hands immersed in a hot water bath—and are told to imagine pleasant sensations, not only do they report less pain, but also the suggestion alters activity in the brain areas associated with the emotional component of pain (Faymonville et al., 2000). An even more recent brain-imaging study has found evidence that hypnosis may prompt brain areas involved in voluntary movement to be unusually influenced by mental imagery (Cojan et al., 2009). This heightened influence may explain why hypnotists can induce body paralysis in people by having them imagine that a body part or the entire body is "too heavy to move." Together, these studies clearly suggest that something other than fakery is going on with hypnotized people.

However, even if hypnosis is ultimately determined to be a legitimate altered state, it should also be thought of as a product of common principles of social influence and an extension of ordinary splits in consciousness (Chaves, 1999). For our current purposes, we can safely conclude that the power of hypnosis does not reside in any mysterious qualities of the hypnotist, but in the mind of the hypnotized, instead.

5.3c *Meditation Provides Relaxation and Reduces Arousal.*

Meditation A variety of mental exercises that alter the normal flow of consciousness in order to enhance self-knowledge

Meditation refers to a variety of mental exercises that alter the normal flow of consciousness in order to enhance self-knowledge. Although some forms of meditation encourage emptying the mind of all content, more common forms of meditation—such as *Zen, transcendental meditation,* and *the relaxation response*—teach people to focus attention on a single sound, image, or object and effortlessly ignore any intruding sensations. Still other techniques emphasize body movement, such as the Sufi whirling dervishes, a religious brotherhood in Turkey that seeks mystic experiences through dance (Deikman, 2000). About eight percent of the population in the United States have tried or regularly practice some form of meditation; however, it is much more widely used in Asian cultures (Wootton, 2008). Many forms of meditation develop *mindfulness*, which is a heightened state of awareness of the present moment (see Section 5.1a). Further, regular practitioners of meditation score higher on measures of mindfulness than do non-meditators (Keune & Forintos, 2010).

Numerous studies find that meditation is effective in promoting relaxation and reducing physiological arousal (Kelly, 2008). Accomplished meditators exhibit high-amplitude alpha waves, reduced oxygen consumption, and slowed heart rate while meditating, all indicators of a deeply relaxed state (Ricard, 2011). During meditation, the hypothalamus—which is the brain's control center of the autonomic nervous system—reduces the sympathetic response while increasing the parasympathetic response; the result is relaxation. Simultaneously, meditation also engages brain areas responsible for higher-order thinking. Brain scans of experienced Buddhist meditators find that at the "peak" moment of their meditative state, their frontal lobes are highly active while their left parietal lobe becomes relatively inactive (Lazar et al., 2000; Newberg et al., 2001). The heightened activation of the frontal lobes makes sense because these brain areas are involved in focused attention, which is a defining characteristic of meditation. Similarly, the lowered activation of the left parietal lobe is understandable because this brain area is involved in keeping track of time and orienting us in physical space. During peak meditative states, people often experience a diminished awareness of the physical world, a sense of timelessness and infinity, and a profound feeling of communion with everyone and everything in existence. Additional research finds that very experienced Zen meditators have thicker brain tissue in the frontal lobes, which suggests that mediation might play a role in actually rewiring the brain (J. A. Grant et al., 2010).

Beyond fostering relaxation, research indicates that meditation can be an effective treatment for insomnia, anxiety, depression, chronic pain, and drug abuse (Evans et al., 2008; Morone et al., 2008). Other studies even suggest that meditation may increase longevity among the elderly by reducing the negative effects of cardiovascular disease and strengthening the immune system, especially in African Americans with high blood pressure (Davidson et al., 2003). Taken as a whole, it appears that regular meditation can enhance physical and psychological health beyond the benefits provided by simple relaxation alone (Wallace & Hodel, 2008). If you would like to try a simple meditative exercise, follow the instructions in Self-Discovery Questionnaire 5-3.

No one can see their reflection in running water. It is only in still water that we can see.

—Taoist proverb

5.3d Psychoactive Drug Use Can Lead to Dependence.

Psychoactive drugs—which are chemicals that modify mental processes and behavior—are often used to deliberately alter consciousness. Such drugs alter consciousness by attaching themselves to synaptic receptors, thereby either blocking or stimulating neural activity. Although psychoactive drugs are sometimes used in religious ceremonies, they are mostly taken for medicinal and recreational purposes. When people persist in taking drugs even when impaired behavior or social functioning results, this is known as **drug abuse**, or *substance dependence* (see Self-Discovery Questionnaire 5-4). Abuse of psychoactive drugs is one of our most serious and costly social problems, accounting for a third of all hospital admissions, a quarter of all deaths, and a majority of serious crimes. In the United States alone, its combined medical and social costs exceed $240 billion per year (Volkow & Li, 2007). One effect of drug abuse is **drug tolerance**, meaning that greater amounts of the drug are necessary to produce the same effect once produced by a smaller dose. For example, an infrequent drinker might become intoxicated after only two beers, but an alcoholic might have to consume two six-packs to experience the same effect.

Often accompanying tolerance is the development of *physical dependence*. A person who is physically dependent on a drug needs it to function normally. How do you determine whether someone is physically dependent? By withdrawing the

Psychoactive drugs Chemicals that modify mental processes and behavior

Drug abuse Persistence in drug use even when impaired behavior or social functioning results

Drug tolerance An effect of drug abuse in which greater amounts of the drug are necessary to produce the same effect once produced by a smaller dose

S E L F - D I S C O V E R Y 5-3
Q u e s t i o n n a i r e

How Can You Meditate?

Does meditation induce an altered state of
consciousness, or is it simply a form of relaxation?

To get some sense of what meditation is all about, try the following exercise derived from Herbert Benson's relaxation response (Benson, 1975; Benson & Klipper, 1988).

Sit quietly in a comfortable position, close your eyes, and relax your muscles. Choose some word or short phrase (a mantra) that you can focus your attention on. It should be something that is calming to you, such as "love," "serenity," or "I am at peace." Don't concentrate too hard on the mantra; it could become only a faint idea at times. As you repeat this mantra silently to yourself, breathe through your nose and pay attention to your breathing. Continue this exercise for 10 to 20 minutes and maintain a passive attitude throughout. When your attention is distracted away from your mantra, don't get upset, but simply and gently refocus your mind. If you find this to be a pleasant experience, practice it once or twice daily.

---

drug and watching for the appearance of unpleasant physical symptoms—known as *withdrawal symptoms*—as the body reacts to its absence. Among heroin addicts, for example, common withdrawal symptoms are chills, fever, diarrhea, and a runny nose. What makes it difficult for drug abusers to stop their abuse is that readministering the drug can terminate the symptoms of withdrawal.

Besides physical dependence, many drugs produce an immediate pleasurable effect that, through continued use, leads to *psychological dependence,* in which the person experiences intense mental and emotional desires for the drug. Many abused drugs cause both physical and psychological dependence. Importantly, psychological dependence can persist even when a person is no longer physically dependent on a drug.

5.3e *Depressants Slow Bodily Functions and Induce Relaxation.*

Depressants Psychoactive drugs that slow down—or depress—the nervous system and decrease mental and physical activity

The **depressants** are a class of psychoactive drugs that slow down—or depress—the nervous system and decrease mental and physical activity. In low doses, depressants induce a relaxed state, while in higher doses they induce sleep. Further, their effects are *additive,* meaning that taking different depressants at the same time, such as alcohol and sleeping pills, can amount to a dangerous overdose that can lead to death. All depressants are potentially physically addictive.

SELF-DISCOVERY 5-4
Questionnaire

Are You Abusing a Drug?

Instructions: Listed below are eight criteria that the American Psychiatric Association uses to diagnose drug abuse (also known as *substance dependence*). If three or more of the following criteria describe your own behavior, you may have a problem with substance abuse.

	Yes	*No*
1. The substance is often taken in larger amounts or over a longer period than intended.	☐	☐
2. There is a persistent desire or one or more unsuccessful efforts to cut down or control substance use.	☐	☐
3. A great deal of your time is spent in activities necessary to get the substance (for example, theft), taking the substance (for example, chain smoking), or recovering from its effects (for example, alcohol "hangovers").	☐	☐
4. You experience frequent intoxication or withdrawal symptoms when you are expected to fulfill obligations at work, school, or home, or when substance use is physically dangerous (for example, driving when intoxicated).	☐	☐
5. You give up or reduce in frequency important social, occupational, or recreational activities because of substance use.	☐	☐
6. You continue to use the drug despite recognizing its harmfulness to your life.	☐	☐
7. You need increased amounts of the drug (at least 50 percent more) to achieve the desired effect, and/or you experience a decreased effect with continued use of the same amount.	☐	☐
8. You often take the drug to relieve or avoid withdrawal symptoms.	☐	☐

Source: Adapted from the American Psychiatric Association (1994).

Alcohol

By far the most widely consumed and abused depressant in the world is alcohol. Besides slowing body functions, depressants like alcohol reduce a person's awareness of both internal and external stimuli. As blood alcohol levels rise, the brain becomes increasingly impaired. For example, as noted in Table 5-2, even at a blood alcohol level of 0.05 percent—which is below the level of legal intoxication—brain areas that control judgment and inhibitions are impaired, making it more likely that the person will act impulsively (Ito et al., 1996). Some researchers believe that this weakening of restraints, or *disinhibition,* is caused by an interruption of our ability to process and respond to the meaning of complex and subtle situational cues (Johnson et al., 2000; Steele & Josephs, 1988). For example, when provoked, people who are drunk are much less attentive than those who are sober to such inhibiting cues as the provocateur's intentions and the possible negative consequences of violence. This impairment of judgment partly explains why alcohol is the leading cause of domestic violence and highway deaths in the general population, and why college students who drink heavily are two to five times more likely to argue, fight, damage property, be injured, and engage in unplanned or unprotected sex (O'Farrell & Murphy, 1995).

How prevalent is alcohol use? In the United States, more than two-thirds of all adults consume alcohol at least occasionally. Of those adults, over 20 million frequently drink in excess, thus putting their health at risk, and about 7 million Americans are *alcoholics* (Cooper, 2000).

Alcoholism is defined as tolerance and physical dependence resulting from the prolonged abuse of alcohol. Among the health problems associated with chronic

Alcoholism Tolerance of and physical dependence on alcohol due to prolonged abuse of that substance

TABLE 5-2   Blood Alcohol Levels and Their Behavioral Effects

Blood Alcohol Level*	Behavioral Effects
0.05%	Lowered alertness, impaired judgment, release of inhibitions
0.10%	Slowed reaction time, impaired motor function, less caution
0.15%	Large, consistent increases in reaction time
0.20%	Marked depression in sensory and motor capability
0.25%	Severe motor disturbance, impairment of sensory perceptions
0.30%	In a stupor but still conscious, no comprehension of surrounding events
0.35%	Surgical anesthesia, minimal level to cause death
0.40%	Lethal dose for half of all adults

*In milligrams of alcohol per 100 milliliters of blood.

iStock

Over 20 million Americans frequently drink in excess, and about 7 million are alcoholics. At what blood alcohol level is the typical person cognitively impaired?

alcohol abuse are liver disease (*cirrhosis*), heart disease, stroke, memory loss, cancer, malnutrition, and loss of sexual interest (Yelena et al., 2002). People who start drinking at a younger age are more likely to abuse alcohol as adults (Grant & Dawson, 1997).

A survey of students at 119 U.S. college campuses found that almost 50 percent of the men and 40 percent of the women were *binge drinkers*, meaning that they consumed five or more drinks on a single occasion (Wechsler et al., 2002). Further, every year approximately 1,400 American college students die from alcohol-related causes, and another 150,000 students develop a health problem related to alcohol. Students who are most likely to binge-drink are those who strongly identify with campus groups that have social norms encouraging alcohol consumption (Elliott & Ainsworth, 2012; Johnston & White, 2003). Some of the campus groups most likely to foster binge drinking are fraternities and sororities, as well as groups composed of avid sports fans. White students are most likely to binge-drink, whereas African American students are least likely.

Although the health risks of alcohol certainly highlight the dangers of drug abuse, studies indicate that one possible long-term benefit of moderate alcohol consumption is reduced coronary heart disease (Fuchs et al., 1995). However, it must be emphasized that this potential health benefit is far outweighed by the risks associated with *heavy* drinking.

The proportion of men who have been physically violent toward their wives is at least four times higher among married men in treatment for alcoholism than among demographically similar nonalcoholic men (O'Farrell & Murphy, 1995).

Barbiturates and Tranquilizers

Like alcohol, **barbiturates** are powerful depressants that reduce anxiety and promote sleep. In milder doses these drugs produce relaxation, slight euphoria, and reduced inhibitions (Alexander et al., 2004). Physicians often prescribe barbiturates as a sleep aid, yet one of their side effects is that they greatly reduce REM sleep. Common prescription barbiturates include the drugs *Seconal* and *Nembutal.* Because barbiturates produce both physical and psychological dependence, their medical use has declined over the years; however, they are still widely abused through illegal drug markets. Even small doses of these drugs can prove fatal when mixed with alcohol.

Milder depressants that are similar to barbiturates are *tranquilizers,* which are often used to relieve anxiety (Shaywitz & Liebowitz, 2003). Common prescription tranquilizers are Xanax, Valium, Librium, and Equanil. Although they are chemically different from barbiturates, most tranquilizers are also extremely addictive and very dangerous when mixed with alcohol.

Barbiturates Powerful depressants that reduce anxiety and promote sleep, and in milder doses produce relaxation, slight euphoria, and reduced inhibitions

The Opiates

Another category of depressants is the **opiates** (also called *narcotics*), which include such drugs as *opium, morphine,* and *heroin* (Smith-Rohrberg et al., 2004). For centuries, opium extracted from poppy seeds has been used as a pain reliever because it mimics the effects of the brain's own naturally produced pain-relieving neurotransmitters, *endorphins* (see Chapter 2, Section 2.1d). Opiates not only depress the nervous system and relieve pain but also produce a relaxed, dreamlike state that is highly pleasurable (Chao & Nestler, 2004). However, such pleasure comes at a cost—users quickly develop a strong physical and psychological dependence, and their withdrawal symptoms are extremely intense and painful (Amato et al., 2004). The reason withdrawal symptoms are so severe is that opiates affect the brain's production of endorphins. Regular use of opiates overloads endorphin receptors within the brain, causing the brain to cease its endorphin production. When the drugs are withdrawn, the brain has an insufficient supply of these pain-relieving neurotransmitters; this is the primary cause of severe withdrawal symptoms.

The greatest danger in abusing opiates is overdosing, which can lead to respiratory failure and death. The abuse of opiate-based prescription painkillers, such as *OxyContin,* can cause hearing loss because the drug destroys the hair cells in the ear's cochlea (Aamodt & Wang, 2008). In 2001, right-wing radio personality Rush Limbaugh lost most of his hearing because of his drug addiction to OxyContin.

Opiates A category of depressant drugs, including opium, morphine, and heroine, that depress the nervous system, temporarily relieve pain, and produce a relaxed, dreamlike state

5.3f Stimulants Speed Up Bodily Functions.

Stimulants are drugs that speed up—or stimulate—the nervous system and increase mental and physical activity. All stimulants are at least mildly addictive—and most of us are somewhat addicted to at least one type of stimulant.

Stimulants Psychoactive drugs that speed up—or stimulate— the nervous system and increase mental and physical activity

Caffeine and Nicotine

Do you need a jolt of java in the morning to get yourself going? What happens when you do not have that morning cup of coffee? Habitual heavy caffeine users are physically dependent on the drug.

To cease smoking is the easiest thing I ever did. I ought to know because I've done it a thousand times.

—Mark Twain, U.S. author, 1835–1910

Are you a person who needs a cup of coffee in the morning to "get going" or a cigarette to curb your appetite or relieve stress? Because stimulants speed up bodily functions and reduce appetite (due to increased blood sugar), people often use them to stay awake, lose weight, enhance athletic performance, or elevate mood. Two of the most commonly used stimulant substances are *caffeine* and *nicotine*. Caffeine is found in coffee, tea, cocoa, and the cola nut (which is used to flavor cola beverages), while tobacco is the only natural source of nicotine.

Caffeine stimulates the cerebral cortex, which causes an increase in mental alertness and wakefulness (Lyvers et al., 2004). This increased alertness is partly caused by caffeine delaying the onset of boredom from repetitive tasks and enhancing the appeal of novel situations. Although moderate doses of caffeine can fight off drowsiness, large doses can make a person feel jittery and anxious and can cause insomnia. In addition, habitual heavy users of caffeine can become physically dependent, experiencing headaches and depression when deprived of the drug.

When inhaled through tobacco smoke, nicotine reaches the brain within seconds. There it stimulates various brain areas, including the frontal lobes, thalamus, hippocampus, and amygdala (Stein et al., 1998). Like caffeine, nicotine increases mental alertness and elevates heart rate, respiration, and blood pressure. Paradoxically, this stimulant also appears to have a calming effect on smokers, often relieving stress. In addition to these effects, nicotine reduces blood flow to the skin, causing a drop in skin temperature, which makes blushing less common in smokers than in nonsmokers. This reduced blood flow is probably why the skin of smokers tends to wrinkle and age faster than that of nonsmokers (Daniell, 1971). Nicotine also appears to produce a decrease in hand steadiness and fine motor control.

Prolonged use of tobacco—primarily in cigarettes, cigars, and chewing tobacco—is a serious health hazard, causing diseases in nearly every organ of the body (Carmona, 2004). It is also the single most important *preventable* risk to human health in developed countries and an important cause of premature death worldwide (Peto et al., 1992). Each year in the United States tobacco products are the cause of over 400,000 deaths. Further, among nonsmoking adults, exposure to secondary smoke doubles the risk of heart disease and increases the risk of lung cancer by 30 percent (Hauri et al., 2011). Such exposure also increases the risk of respiratory diseases and other health problems in nonsmoking children. Unfortunately for casual tobacco users, a greater percentage of them become addicted to this drug than do casual users of cocaine, morphine, or alcohol (Henningfield et al., 1995). Among adolescents, cigarette smoking is associated with increased likelihood of trying and becoming dependent on marijuana (Ream et al., 2008).

Fear of gaining weight is the primary reason many women give for not quitting smoking. Yet research indicates that women who exercise regularly while trying to "kick the habit" not only limit their weight gain but also are twice as likely to stop smoking and stay smoke-free as are nonexercisers (Marcus et al., 2003). Similar benefits are also likely for male smokers. When trying to quit, African American abstainers tend to have less severe withdrawal symptoms—such as irritability, difficulty concentrating, and restlessness—than Caucasians (Falck et al., 2008).

Cocaine and Amphetamines

Despite the associated health dangers, nicotine-laced tobacco products—and caffeine—are only mild stimulants. Much stronger stimulants are *cocaine* and *amphetamines* (also known as "speed"), which produce a sense of euphoria and can cause severe psychological and physical problems.

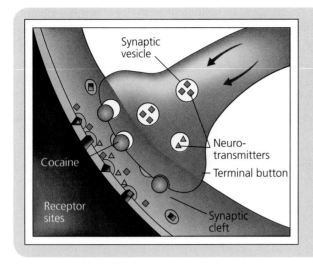

FIGURE 5-6

Effects of Cocaine on Neurotransmitters

Cocaine blocks the reuptake of neurotransmitters into the terminal buttons, causing them to remain in the synaptic cleft longer than normal. Their extended presence in the synaptic cleft creates the drug's stimulant effects.

Cocaine is one of the more widely abused illegal stimulant drugs (Baker et al., 2004). This stimulant is a natural substance that comes from the leaves of the coca bush, which grows in South America. When cocaine is smoked (*crack*), sniffed (*snorting*), or injected directly into the bloodstream (*mainlining*), users quickly experience a 15- to 30-minute "high" during which they feel energized, excited, happy, talkative, and confident. Cocaine activates the sympathetic branch of the autonomic nervous system, raising body temperature, heart rate, and breathing, while reducing the desire for food and sleep.

What causes the cocaine high? As depicted in Figure 5-6, in the brain's neurons, the drug blocks the repackaging of dopamine and norepinephrine neurotransmitters into the synaptic vesicles of the axon's terminal buttons, so the neurotransmitters remain in the synaptic cleft longer than normal (Bubar et al., 2003). Because these neurotransmitters are the chemical messengers for feelings of pleasure and heightened wakefulness, their extended presence in the synaptic cleft sets in motion a series of events that result in the cocaine high. However, because this high only lasts a short time, users often repeatedly ingest the drug as soon as the effects wear off. The fast-acting, yet short-duration, nature of this drug also may make it more addictive than many other drugs. Cocaine binges can last for hours or even days, causing the users to eventually reach a state of physical exhaustion, after which they require long periods of sleep. Although cocaine is not generally believed to create physical dependence, it often produces strong psychological dependence due to its highly pleasurable effects (Bonson et al., 2002).

Like cocaine, amphetamines activate the sympathetic nervous system and increase dopamine and norepinephrine activity, producing many cocainelike effects. Sometimes referred to as "uppers" or "speed," these synthetic stimulants have long been used by people to lose weight or stay awake for extended time periods. They also increase alertness and response speed. However, physicians rarely prescribe these drugs because they produce many negative side effects. For example, as a treatment for weight loss, amphetamine users quickly develop a tolerance to the appetite-suppressing effects of the drug, requiring increasingly higher doses to maintain these effects. Furthermore, such high dosage can cause insomnia, anxiety, heart problems, and even brain damage (Mintzer & Griffiths, 2003). As with cocaine, amphetamines are not generally physically addictive but do produce strong psychological dependence.

Habitual amphetamine and cocaine users often develop **stimulant-induced psychosis**, which is characterized by many of the symptoms seen in *schizophrenia*, a psychological disorder discussed in Chapter 11, Section 11.2d. One of the primary

Stimulant-induced psychosis
Schizophrenic-like symptoms that can occur following prolonged and excessive use of cocaine and amphetamines

symptoms of stimulant-induced psychosis is hallucinations—for example, hearing strange voices, seeing snow, or feeling bugs crawling on or under the skin (Adeyemo, 2002; Pezze et al., 2002). The sensation of these "cocaine bugs" is actually caused by the cocaine-induced spontaneous firing of sensory neurons. Other symptoms of stimulant-induced psychosis are depression, paranoia, teeth grinding, and repetitive behaviors.

INFO-BIT   Believe it or not, cocaine was once an ingredient in Coca-Cola. However, in 1906, the U.S. government outlawed cocaine, and the drug was dropped as an ingredient of this popular soft drink.

Ecstasy and Ritalin

One stimulant that has become popular among adolescents and young adults as an alternative to cocaine and amphetamines is "ecstasy," or MDMA, which is short for methylenedioxymethamphetamine. Taken as a pill, MDMA primarily affects the brain cells that produce serotonin, a neurotransmitter that is the body's primary regulator of mood (see Chapter 2, Section 2.1d). The massive release of serotonin by these cells may be responsible for the feelings of blissfulness and greater closeness to others that ecstasy users often experience, as well as for significant increases in their body temperature, heart rate, and blood pressure. MDMA also blocks serotonin reuptake, amplifying and extending serotonin's effects (Braun, 2001).

Although MDMA is not physically addictive, it is a dangerous drug (Fernandez-Castillo et al., 2012). When ecstasy users take several doses over the course of a few hours, the body's natural ability to control its temperature can be severely impaired. Dozens of deaths have occurred due to overheating when users have engaged in strenuous physical activity. Findings from animal and human studies also raise the possibility that MDMA use can cause permanent damage to the axons of the serotonin-containing brain cells, resulting in memory and concentration problems (Aamodt & Wang, 2008).

Another disturbing cultural trend has been the increased abuse of Ritalin (methylphenidate), a stimulant drug prescribed to treat attention-deficit/hyperactivity disorder (ADHD) in children. Ritalin is effective in treating the disorder because it decreases distractibility and improves concentration (Van der Oord et al., 2008). Yet, some adults—among them college students—who do not have the disorder ingest the drug to increase their concentration and productivity while working or studying for exams (Jasinski et al., 2008). They also develop a tolerance for the drug more quickly than do those with ADHD and experience withdrawal symptoms when the dosage is reduced.

5.3g Hallucinogens Induce Profoundly Altered States.

The psychoactive drugs that produce the most profound alterations in consciousness are the **hallucinogens** (also called *psychedelics*), which distort perception and generate sensory images without any external stimulation. As the name implies, these drugs often create *hallucinations*, which are sensations and perceptions that occur without any external stimulation. Although hallucinogens were once thought to mimic psychotic states of mind, careful analysis indicates that these drugs do not produce the same behavioral patterns observed in people suffering from psychotic episodes.

Hallucinogens Psychoactive drugs that distort perception and generate sensory images without any external stimulation

Many hallucinogenic drugs are naturally derived from plants, such as the peyote cactus that contains mescaline or the Mexican mushroom that contains *psilocybin*. These natural hallucinogens have been used for thousands of years in the religious rites of the Aztecs and other Mexican Indians and still today play an important role in the religious practices of the Native American Church of North America (Baruss, 2003). As a religious sacrament—similar to the bread and wine used in Christianity—members of the Native American Church seldom abuse these hallucinogens.

LSD

The most potent of the hallucinogenic drugs, **LSD** (technically known as *lysergic acid diethylamide*), is not found in nature but is a synthesized drug that is structurally similar to the neurotransmitter serotonin (see Chapter 2, Section 2.1d). Following its discovery in 1938 by Swiss chemist Albert Hoffman, LSD was sometimes given to patients in psychotherapy because its mind-expanding properties were thought to facilitate the recovery of repressed memories (Yensen & Dryer, 2007). During the 1960s, LSD became a recreational drug on college campuses, championed by former Harvard lecturer Timothy Leary, who believed that it could be used as a vehicle to spiritual discovery.

When taken orally, LSD'sfects are felt within 30 minutes to an hour and persist for about 10 to 12 hours. Although the physiological effects of LSD are minor—a slight increase in heart rate, blood pressure, blood glucose, and body temperature; dizziness; drowsiness; and nausea—the psychological effects are intense. The exact nature of the psychological experience is difficult to predict because it is influenced by a host of factors, including the user's personality and expectations, the persons with whom the user interacts during the LSD experience, and the setting in which the drug is administered. However, the principal psychological effects involve hallucinations and distortions. These effects are produced when the drug binds with the serotonin brain receptors associated with dreaming, causing users to experience a dreamlike state of mind while they are awake (Goodman, 2002). During this altered state, users may also experience a blending of sensory experiences known as *synesthesia,* in which colors are felt or heard, and sounds are seen. Subjective time is also altered, so that a few seconds might seem like many minutes; and people often feel detached from their bodies. For some, these experiences are enjoyable and even insightful; for others, they are unpleasant and even terrifying. Importantly, unpleasant experiences are relatively frequent, and *flashbacks*—recurrences of the drug's effects without the drug—occur in more than 15 percent of LSD users and can persist for months following the drug experience (Jaffe, 1990; Lerner et al., 2003). Most important, there is no way to predict how a person will react to the drug. Indeed, the same person may react positively during one experience and negatively during another.

LSD use is largely independent of the "party drugs" scene, which is perhaps not surprising because its effects—profound hallucinations and distortions of reality—are very unlikely to promote or enhance social interaction (Prepeliczay, 2003). Interestingly, LSD users do not become physically dependent on the drug, even after prolonged use. In fact, most people discontinue using LSD because they tire of it or have no further need for it. However, the lack of physical dependence does not mean that this is a "safe" drug. Although LSD has never been definitely linked to even one human overdose death, fatal accidents and suicides have occurred while people were under the drug's influence. For example, people have fallen to their deaths due to an LSD-induced belief that they could fly. On rare occasions, among individuals who have an existing tendency toward mental illness, LSD can trigger psychosis. For these reasons, LSD is considered a dangerous drug and should be avoided.

LSD A synthesized chemical that is the most potent of the hallucinogens; induces hallucinations, distortions, and a blending of sensory experiences

Marijuana

Marijuana A mild hallucinogen derived from the leafy material of the hemp, or Cannabis, plant; often induces a sense of giddiness or euphoria, as well as heightened sensitivity to various stimuli

Marijuana, which is sometimes classified as a mild hallucinogen, is a preparation of leafy material from the hemp, or *Cannabis,* plant. The earliest reference to marijuana is in a pharmacy book written in 2737 BC by the Chinese emperor Shen Nung, who called marijuana the "Liberator of Sin" due to its ability to induce a sense of giddiness or euphoria in users. This pleasurable effect probably accounts for the fact that marijuana continues to be the most frequently used illegal drug in the world. For example, 47 percent of American adults have tried it at least once, and about 3 percent are daily users (Kingery et al., 1999; Martin, 1995). Although its use is widespread, marijuana appears to be a "maturational drug" for most people, meaning that they begin using it during the exploratory years of adolescence and stop using it in early adulthood as they secure their career and family relationships (Mitchell et al., 1999).

THC The major psychoactive ingredient in marijuana

The major psychoactive ingredient in marijuana is **THC**, short for the complex organic molecule delta-9 tetrahydrocannabinol. THC is concentrated in the resin of the hemp plant, with most of the resin in the flowering tops (from which the stronger form of marijuana, known as *hashish,* is made), less in the leaves, and little in the stems. When smoked, THC is quickly absorbed into the blood and reaches the brain within seven seconds; however, when eaten in such foods as brownies or cookies, the effect is delayed. Marijuana is at most only mildly physically addictive, but some habitual users experience unpleasant withdrawal symptoms when they stop using the drug (Budney et al., 2001; Haney et al., 2003).

What are the effects of marijuana? Physiologically, it produces mild arousal in the form of increased heart rate and blood pressure, and dryness of the mouth and throat. Psychologically, users often experience an increased sense of well-being and relaxation, spontaneous laughter, and a heightened sensitivity to various stimuli, such as tastes, sounds, colors, and smells. In addition, people often experience a distortion of time and a disconnected flow of ideas, which may be caused by temporary impairment of short-term memory, leading users to confuse past, present, and future. Like alcohol, moderate marijuana use can impair coordination, attention, and reaction time and has been linked to accidents and traffic fatalities (Rahn & Hohmann, 2009; Earleywine, 2002). On the positive side, medical evidence indicates that the drug is effective in treating glaucoma, chronic pain, and nausea from cancer chemotherapy (Tramer et al., 2001). Although scientists are not yet certain what specific brain mechanisms are affected by marijuana, there are a class of *cannabinoid* receptor cells in the brain's hippocampus that are activated by THC, adjusting and enhancing mental activity and perhaps even altering pain perception (Vaidya et al., 2012). As of 2012, sixteen states in the U.S., plus the District of Columbia, have legalized marijuana for medical use due to its documented health and pain management benefits.

No clear understanding of the health consequences of long-term marijuana use has been achieved; however, research suggests that, as with tobacco, marijuana use

iStock

Marijuana can impair coordination, attention, and reaction time and has been linked to accidents and traffic fatalities. Why is it referred to as a "maturational drug"?

increases a person's susceptibility to throat and mouth cancers due to its high tar content (Budney et al., 2008). There also is sufficient evidence to recommend that the drug not be used during pregnancy due to possible negative prenatal effects (Willford et al., 2012). In addition, prolonged marijuana use appears to disrupt memory formation and weaken the body's immune system. Regarding possible psychological and social effects, consistent use of high quantities of marijuana does appear to have a negative effect on motivation and interpersonal skills, and thus may impede the normal development of adolescents and young adults (Martin, 1995).

As it now stands, although marijuana does not appear to be a "killer weed," it also is not a harmless substance. In addition, the more heavily individuals use marijuana, the greater the probability that they will use other drugs. Thus, the most serious danger of marijuana use may be related more to "drug-use proneness" than to the effects of the marijuana itself (McMillan et al., 2003).

Inhalants

The last category of psychoactive drugs are **inhalants**, which are chemicals whose vapors are breathed in to produce a mind-altering effect (Howard & Perron, 2009). The act of breathing in the vapors is called sniffing, bagging, huffing, or inhaling. Inhalants are absorbed into the lungs and quickly travel through the bloodstream causing an immediate, but short-lived, high. The effect is similar to alcohol intoxication, and it can cause vomiting, drowsiness, unconsciousness, and even death.

Four categories of inhalants include volatile solvents (such as gasoline and glue), aerosols (such as deodorant and hair sprays), gases (such as nitrous oxide found in whipping cream and butane lighters), and nitrites (used for heart patients). Inhalants are addictive. Long-term use can cause brain damage, muscle weakness, loss of smell or hearing, and depression (Collins et al., 2008). Table 5-3 lists the effects and the risks of physical and psychological dependence for the four types of psychoactive drugs.

5.3h *Biological and Sociocultural Factors Influence Drug Use.*

Twin studies provide evidence that drug abuse vulnerability may have a biological link (Malone et al., 2004). For example, the shared incidence of alcoholism is more common among identical twins than among fraternal twins. Similarly, twin studies in the United States and Scandinavia indicate a genetic contribution not only to risks of smoking and marijuana use but also to *resistance* to using these substances (Kendler et al., 2002). These findings suggest that the closer the genetic makeup between people, the more similar the drug use pattern (Clarke et al., 2008; Xuei et al., 2008).

In regards to personal or social factors, although personality problems do not predict drug use in adolescents, a teenager's degree of rebellion against parents and societal norms is a good predictor of drug use. Those teens who are religious, attend school regularly and get good grades, have good relationships with their parents, and do not break the law are least likely to drink alcohol and use other drugs (Wills et al., 2003). Rebellious adolescents, in contrast, often have closer emotional ties to their friends than to their parents; and these friends are also likely to be drug users. In this regard, peer pressure is a significant predictor of alcohol and other drug use among adolescents and young adults (Weitzman et al., 2003). The desire to "fit in" with friends who are using consciousness-altering drugs is often sufficient to prompt initial drug use. People who are most likely to conform in this manner are those who strongly desire acceptance from their friends (Johnston & White, 2003).

BVT Lab

Improve your test scores. Practice quizzes are available at www.BVTLab.com.

Inhalants Chemicals whose vapors can be breathed in to produce a mind-altering effect

TABLE 5-3   Psychoactive Drugs

Drug	Main Effects	Potential for Physical/Psychological Dependence
Depressants		
Alcohol	Relaxation, anxiety reduction, reduced inhibitions	High/High
Opiates ("narcotics")	Euphoria, relaxation, anxiety reduction, pain relief	High/High
Barbiturates and tranquilizers	Relaxation, mild euphoria, reduced inhibitions	High/High
Stimulants		
Caffeine	Alertness	Moderate/Moderate
Cocaine	Alertness, euphoria	Moderate to high/High
Nicotine	Alertness	High/Moderate
Amphetamines	Alertness, euphoria	Moderate to high/High
MDMA (Ecstasy)	Blissfulness, increased sociability	Low/Low
Ritalin	Increased concentration	Moderate/Moderate
Hallucinogens		
LSD	Hallucination, altered perceptions	Low/Low
Marijuana	Mild euphoria, relaxation, altered perceptions	Low/Moderate
Inhalants		
Volatile solvents, aerosols, and gases	Euphoria, drowsiness	Low/Moderate
Nitrites	Enhances sensation	Low/Moderate

Cultural factors also influence drug dependence. Numerous studies indicate that the poor and the less educated are more likely to abuse various drugs than are people who have more money and education (Caldwell et al., 2008). One explanation for these findings is that poor and undereducated people experience higher levels of stress than do those who are rich and well-schooled, while simultaneously having considerably less access to medical care for physical and psychological problems. For people who are living in such underprivileged circumstances, drug abuse becomes an ill-advised and destructive means of self-medication. One notable exception to this tendency is found in the African American community. A number of studies indicate that African Americans are less likely than White Americans to abuse alcohol, tobacco, and other psychoactive drugs (Wechsler et al., 2002). Why is this so, given the fact that African Americans as a group earn less money and are less educated than White Americans? In searching for answers, researchers have examined cultural traditions in the African American community that might protect people against substance abuse. One important tradition is religion. Many African Americans are members of evangelical religions, such as the Baptist faith, which forbid the use of drugs, including alcohol. At least one study has found that African American Baptists who attend church frequently are more likely to abstain from alcohol use than are comparable White American Baptists (Blazer et al., 2002). This greater adherence to their religion's antidrug social norm may partly explain the racial differences in drug abuse.

Cross-cultural studies find further support for the hypothesis that a culture's attitudes and beliefs about drug use are strong predictors of substance dependence. For example, *temperance cultures*—cultures that maintain activist approaches to combating drinking problems—consume less alcohol than nontemperance cultures (Levine, 1992). Further, alcohol consumption is more "socialized" in temperance cultures (Peele, 1996). That is, in such cultures alcohol is more likely to be integrated into mixed-sex social settings (such as family meals and cafés), whereas in nontemperance cultures it is more likely to be a part of male-dominated settings devoted exclusively to drinking (such as taverns). The drinking that occurs in these relatively isolated settings is much more likely to be excessive and lead to alcoholism than that which takes place in the more integrated social arenas.

Section REVIEW

- People differ in their hypnotizability, with children being the most hypnotizable.

- The role-playing explanation maintains that hypnosis is a normal waking state in which suggestible people behave as they think hypnotized people are supposed to behave.

- According to neodissociation theory, hypnosis is an altered state, with the hypnotized person having two streams of consciousness operating at once.

- Meditation may involve an altered state of consciousness, but skeptics claim that it simply leads to relaxation.

- Depressants induce a relaxed state when taken in low doses but induce sleep when taken in higher doses.

- Stimulants speed up the nervous system and increase mental and physical activity.

- The psychoactive drugs that produce the most profound alterations in consciousness are the hallucinogens.

- Inhalants are chemicals whose vapors are breathed in to produce a mind-altering effect.

- Drug abuse occurs when people persist in taking drugs even when impaired behavior or social functioning results.

- The poor and the less educated are more likely to abuse drugs than are people who have more money and education.

PSYCHOLOGICAL
applications

How Can You Deal with Sleep Disorders?

Problems related to sleep are among the most common psychological disorders, but they are often underdiagnosed and undertreated (Wickwire et al., 2008). In the United States alone, between 50 million to 70 million people suffer from some form of chronic sleep problem, accounting for about $50 billion a year in medical costs and lost labor. Some of the more common disorders of sleep are *night terrors, sleepwalking, narcolepsy, sleep apnea, and insomnia.*

> *When I woke up this morning, my girlfriend asked me, "Did you sleep well?" I said, "No, I made a few mistakes."*
>
> —Steven Wright, American comedian

Night Terrors

A type of sleep disorder most common among children between the ages of 3 and 8 is **night terror**, which is a panic attack that generally occurs during early-night stage 4 NREM sleep. Victims sit up in bed, let out a terrified scream, stare into space, and talk incoherently; however, they seldom wake up, and they recall little or nothing of the event the next morning. It is important to distinguish night terrors from the far more common *nightmares,* which are anxiety-arousing dreams that occur during REM sleep and are as likely to occur among adults as children. During childhood, this disorder is more common among boys, but in adulthood women and men experience it about equally. Night terrors often run in families, suggesting that they are genetically based (Schenck, 2007). Being overtired or over-stressed can often trigger night terrors. For example, Roger Federer, the world's top tennis player, had a night terror episode the night before one of his most important tennis matches. This disorder often requires no treatment, especially in children. The most effective treatment is maintaining a regular sleep schedule, getting adequate sleep, and reducing stress. In severe and persistent cases, this disorder can sometimes be treated with drugs.

Night terror A sleep disorder involving panic attacks that occur during early-night stage 4 NREM sleep

Sleepwalking

Sleepwalking, also known as *somnambulism,* is a sleep disorder in which a person arises and wanders about while remaining asleep. Like night terrors, sleepwalking occurs during early-night NREM sleep (Hughes, 2007). Thus, contrary to popular thinking, sleepwalkers are not acting out a dream. Also contrary to popular belief, it is not dangerous to wake a sleepwalker—although it may be difficult, due to the sleepwalker being in deep stage 4 sleep. Sleepwalkers typically do not recall their sleepwalking episodes the following day. This disorder is more common among children (10 percent) than adults (2 percent), and more common among boys than girls (Gunn & Gunn, 2007). Fortunately, because most children sleepwalk during the first hour or two after falling asleep, their still-awake parents can direct them back to bed. Adults who have night terrors also tend to sleepwalk, which suggests that the two disorders have some genetically related cause. Genetic factors play a role in 65 percent of sleepwalkers, with sleep deprivation and stress often being triggering events (Schenck, 2007). Drug therapy can reduce sleepwalking, but most children outgrow the problem.

Sleepwalking A sleep disorder in which a person arises and wanders about while remaining asleep

Narcolepsy

A more serious form of sleep disorder than the ones discussed thus far is **narcolepsy**, which is characterized by uncontrollable REM sleep attacks during normal waking hours (Shin et al., 2008). About 250,000 Americans—one in every thousand—suffer from this disorder. Narcolepsy can strike at any time, even when a person is driving a car or otherwise engaged in activities where inattentiveness is dangerous, but unconsciousness can be fatal. Fortunately, stimulant drugs can usually control the symptoms of this disorder. The cause of narcolepsy is unknown, but people who have the disorder in their families are 50 times more likely to develop it than others, which suggests that possible genetic factors underlie this disorder. Planned napping can reduce the frequency of narcoleptic episodes, as can the stimulant drug *modafinil* (Silber, 2001).

Narcolepsy A sleep disorder characterized by uncontrolled REM sleep attacks during normal waking hours

Sleep Apnea

Another disorder with a possible hereditary cause is **sleep apnea**, in which sleeping individuals briefly stop breathing several times an hour, interrupting their sleep without their knowledge (Walter et al., 2011). About 12 million Americans suffer from this disorder, with overweight men older than 40 being the most common victims (Ingbar & Gee, 1985). Apnea sufferers report daytime sleepiness, morning headaches, and even occasional heart and lung problems. The loss of sleep experienced by apnea sufferers has been shown to affect their waking reaction time, making them as slow to

Sleep apnea A sleep disorder in which a person repeatedly stops breathing during sleep

respond as someone who is legally intoxicated (Kayumov et al., 2000). Apnea may be treated by a number of methods, including weight loss, a change of sleeping positions, use of a nasal mask to increase air intake, hormone therapy, and even surgery to open constricted airways.

Insomnia

Daily hassles and stress often create sleep difficulties. What recommendations do sleep experts make for getting a good night's rest?

The most common sleep disorder is **insomnia**, which is the chronic inability to fall or stay asleep (Harvey & Tang, 2012). Approximately 30 percent of adults complain of insomnia to some degree, and it is a recurring problem for about 15 percent to 20 percent of the population (Pearson et al., 2006). The elderly and women are more likely to suffer from insomnia than the young and men (Kaeppler & Hohagen, 2003). Some of the more common causes of this disorder are daily hassles and life stress, physical illness or discomfort, loneliness, depression, jet lag, shifting work schedules, menopause, and drug abuse (Morin et al., 2003). Although many insomniacs rely on sleeping pills and alcohol to alleviate insomnia, both reduce REM sleep and can cause lowered moods the next day. Instead, sleep experts suggest the following guidelines for getting a good night's sleep (Irwin et al., 2006):

Insomnia A common sleep disorder characterized by the chronic inability to fall or stay asleep

1. Establish a solid circadian rhythm by going to bed and getting up on a regular schedule. Don't try to catch up by sleeping longer on the weekends.

2. Do not take naps during the day, especially after a bad night's sleep.

3. Relax before going to bed and get into the habit of setting up presleep rituals such as soft music or a warm bath. A warm bath not only is relaxing but also promotes deep sleep by raising your core body temperature.

4. Avoid computer activity just before bedtime. Staring into a bright screen can trick your circadian clock into functioning as if it is still daytime, which will throw off your sleep schedule.

5. Greatly reduce or eliminate entirely the use of coffee, tea, or other sources of caffeine during the entire day because it affects sleep. Also, avoid alcohol, nicotine, and chocolate in the late afternoon and evening. Instead, drink a glass of milk before retiring because it contains the sleep-inducing amino acid *tryptophan*.

6. Being very hungry or very full prior to retiring will disrupt sleep. Eating a light snack before going to bed will reduce nighttime restlessness and increase sleep time.

7. Regular exercise promotes slow-wave sleep, but do not exercise within three hours of bedtime because the arousing effect can delay sleep.

8. Condition yourself so you associate your bed with sleeping. Thus, don't use your bed for anything but sleep and sex.

9. If you're still awake, but relaxed, after about 20 minutes, stay in bed. If you're anxious, get out of bed and do something relaxing, such as listening to soothing music or reading. Return when you feel sleepy. Still maintain your regular waking time.

Suggested Websites

Center for Consciousness Studies

http://www.consciousness.arizona.edu

This website for the Center for Consciousness Studies at the University of Arizona offers online papers on consciousness as well as information on conferences, bibliographical references, and related websites.

National Institute on Drug Abuse

http://www.nida.nih.gov

This website provides valuable information and national statistics on drug use and related weblinks.

Sleepnet.com™

http://www.sleepnet.com

This website provides information on the psychology and physiology of sleep, including sleep disorders, dreams, and the addresses of sleep labs around the country.

Working (and Playing) with Dreams

http://www.rider.edu/users/suler/dreams.html

This website offers information on various theories and methods of dream interpretation.

Key Terms

Activation-synthesis theory, 219
Adaptive theory of sleep, 213
Alcoholism, 227
Alpha waves, 210
Altered state of
    consciousness, 207
Barbiturates, 229
Beta waves, 210
Circadian rhythms, 208
Consciousness, 202
Daydreaming, 205
Delta waves, 212
Depressants, 226
Divided attention, 204
Dream, 215
Drug abuse, 225
Drug tolerance, 225

Fantasy-prone personality, 206
Hallucinogens, 232
Hypnosis, 221
Hypnotizability, 223
Inhalants, 235
Insomnia, 239
Latent content, 218
LSD, 233
Lucid dream, 218
Manifest content, 218
Marijuana, 234
Meditation, 224
Melatonin, 208
Mindfulness, 206
Narcolepsy, 238
Neodissociation theory, 224
Night terror, 238

NREM sleep, 210
Off-line dream theory, 219
Opiates, 229
Problem-solving theory, 218
Psychoactive drugs, 225
REM sleep, 211
Restorative theory of sleep, 213
Selective attention, 203
Sleep, 207
Sleep apnea, 238
Sleep spindles, 211
Sleepwalking, 238
Stimulant-induced
    psychosis, 231
Stimulants, 229
THC
Theta waves, 211

Review Questions

1. According to the author, which of the following is true of consciousness?
    a. It can be shared with other people.
    b. It requires that you focus on one specific thing.
    c. It never changes.
    d. It has only one level.
    e. It is important for our survival.

2. Which of the following statements is true?
    a. Strategies to improve attention cannot be learned.
    b. Experience-sampling methods are used to study stream of consciousness.
    c. Research indicates few people daydream on a daily basis.
    d. There are no advantages to daydreaming.
    e. TV viewing appears to encourage more creative thinking.

3. Which of the following are diurnal mammals?
   a. humans
   b. owls
   c. bats
   d. opossum
   e. None of the above

4. Which of the following is true of the study of circadian rhythms?
   a. The study indicates that humans drift toward a 25-hour cycle.
   b. The study used natural light.
   c. The study provides a valuable lesson in the way the scientific method is self-correcting.
   d. The study discovered how to relieve insomnia.
   e. None of the above

5. Which part of the brain appears to be responsible for the body's sleep-wake cycle?
   a. hypothalamus
   b. suprachiasmatic nucleus
   c. pineal gland
   d. All of the above
   e. a and b

6. Which of the following statements is true about stages of sleep?
   a. You spend half your night at stage 1.
   b. It is difficult to arouse a person from sleep during stage 4.
   c. You go through only one sleep cycle a night.
   d. The first four stages make up REM sleep.
   e. Alpha waves are associated with an active, alert state of mind.

7. Which of the following statements describes a theory in this chapter about why we sleep?
   a. Sleep occurs due to the activation of the hippocampus in the brain.
   b. Sleep allows the body to restore itself.
   c. Children ages 2 to 5 who fail to get sufficient sleep at night or during naps have greater behavior problems.
   d. All of the above
   e. a and c

8. Which of the following statements is true of dreaming?
   a. Dreams occur only during REM sleep.
   b. You cannot respond to external cues while dreaming.
   c. REM sleep does not appear to be important.
   d. All animals have REM sleep.
   e. In humans, REM sleep is greatest early in life.

9. In the student's "fish dream," what would the latent content be?
   a. the struggle with the fish
   b. the old woman
   c. the lake
   d. letting the fish go
   e. None of the above

10. Which dream theory believes dreams have no particular significance other than that they are by-products of brain activity?
    a. off-line dream
    b. problem-solving
    c. psychoanalytic
    d. activation-synthesis
    e. None of the above

11. Which of the following statements is true of hypnosis?
    a. Brain wave activity under hypnosis is radically different from brain wave activity during normal waking states.
    b. Hypnosis compels people to avoid deception.
    c. Everyone is hypnotizable.
    d. A hypnotized person tends to uncritically accept hallucinated experiences suggested by the hypnotist.
    e. Hypnotized people can be forced to violate their moral values.

12. What has the research on meditation found?
    a. high-amplitude alpha waves in accomplished mediators while meditating
    b. It is useful in promoting relaxation.
    c. It reduces physiological arousal.
    d. a reduction in oxygen consumption, slower heart rate, and increased blood flow in the arms and forehead
    e. All of the above

13. The most widely consumed and abused depressant in the world is _____.
    a.   opium
    b.   alcohol
    c.   morphine
    d.   heroin
    e.   caffeine

14. Which of the following statements is true?
    a.   There are no naturally occurring hallucinogens.
    b.   LSD creates physical dependence after prolonged use.
    c.   Forty-seven percent of American adults have tried marijuana at least once.
    d.   Marijuana does not appear to have any negative effects when used in high quantities.
    e.   All drug users become addicted.

15. Which of the following is true of sleep disorders?
    a.   They are among the most common psychological disorders.
    b.   They do not occur in children under age 5.
    c.   They occur only during NREM sleep.
    d.   a and b
    e.   None of the above

Chapter Six

Learning

Chapter Outline

6.1 Classical Conditioning
- a Pavlov Stumbled upon Classical Conditioning.
- b Classical Conditioning Helps Animals Learn to Predict Events.
- c Other Stimuli Can Produce the Conditioned Response.
- d Animals Differ in What Responses Can Be Classically Conditioned.

6.2 Operant Conditioning
- a Operant Behavior Is Controlled by Consequences.
- b A Reinforcer Increases the Probability of Behavior.
- c Punishment Decreases the Probability of Behavior.
- d Different Reinforcement Schedules Lead to Different Learning.
- e Accidental Reinforcement Can Cause Superstitious Behavior.
- f Shaping Reinforces Closer Approximations to Desired Behavior.
- g Skinner Overlooked Genetic Predispositions and Cognitive Processes.

6.3 Observational Learning
- a Learning Often Occurs by Observing Others' Behavior.
- b Mirror Neurons Play a Role in Observational Learning.
- c We Often Learn Aggressive Behavior Through Observation.
- d Positive Social Modeling Can Counteract the Negative Influence of Aggressive Models.

Psychological Applications: *Learning How to Exercise Self-Control in Your Academic and Personal Life*

Dear Frederic,

Your very interesting letter has been read and discussed by mother and me. We naturally are deeply interested in your future … In no circumstances would we want to say or do anything to discourage you in following out your ambition …

On the other hand, we want to give you the benefit of our observation and experience. You will find that the world is not standing with outstretched arms to greet you just because you are emerging from a college— that the real rough and tumble world is not the world pictured by college professors who are constantly dealing with the theoretical and not the practical affairs of life. I am yet to be convinced that it is possible for you to make a living as a writer of fiction.

… Let's go slow and sure … Let us arrange some plan whereby you can support yourself, get married when the fever strikes you, have a good home life, and when these things are provided for, then go to it, and if your talents enable you to do something big and startle the world, no one of course will rejoice more than your mother and I, who have our whole life centered in you and your success.

With love,

Father

I am learning all the time. The tombstone will be my diploma.

—Eartha Kitt, U.S. actor and singer, 1927–2008

What do you want to do when *you* graduate? Fred wanted to be a famous writer. Following this letter from his father, Fred spent a year after college working on his writing skills. He even submitted samples of his writing to the poet Robert Frost, asking whether he should persevere in his chosen profession. Frost replied that the young man had twice as much talent as anyone else he had read that year, but that only Fred himself could know whether his future lay in writing. At the end of this yearlong odyssey, which Fred later called his "dark year," he was frustrated with writing and began casting about in search of an alternative career path. But what path should he choose?

The year was 1927. In his searching, Fred read psychologist John Watson's (1924) recently published book, *Behaviorism*. Watson presented a perspective on learning and the future of the young science of psychology that was novel for the time, in that his focus was not on people's internal states

Wikimedia Commons

B. F. Skinner, 1904–1990.

and unconscious drives but on the outward behavior that people exhibit. Fred had always been interested in observing the behavior of people, a useful talent for a writer; this approach to the human condition appealed to him. He applied and was accepted to Harvard University for graduate studies in psychology, where his own personal journey of

discovery quickly became wedded to psychology's scientific discovery journey.

Although Fred never "startled the world" with his fiction writing, his subsequent extensions and refinements of Watson's behaviorism rocked the field of psychology and made Fred one of the best-known psychologists of all time. Outside his circle of family and friends, people knew and referred to Fred by his formal name, Burrhus Frederic ("B. F.") Skinner. Throughout his career, Skinner looked for ways in which his operant conditioning principles of learning (which are discussed in Section 6.2) could be used to improve daily life (Vargas, 2003).

In this segment of our journey of discovery, we will focus our attention on the psychology of **learning**, which psychologists define as a relatively permanent change in behavior that results from experience (Klein, 2012).

> **Learning** A relatively permanent change in behavior that results from experience

Learning can occur in a variety of ways, but we will review three basic learning perspectives: *classical conditioning*, *operant conditioning*, and *observational learning*. Classical conditioning is a type of learning in which one stimulus comes to serve as a signal for the occurrence of a second stimulus. Operant conditioning, the name for the type of conditioning Skinner investigated, is a form of learning in which we discover the consequences of behavior. Finally, observational learning deals with how we learn by observing the behaviors—and the behavioral consequences—of those around us.

> *Learning is a treasure that will follow its owner everywhere.*
> —Chinese proverb

6.1 Classical Conditioning

In science, as in other areas of life, researchers sometimes need time to realize that they have actually discovered a new scientific principle. Would you believe that one discovery that profoundly shaped the course of psychology was initially viewed only as an annoyance?

6.1a *Pavlov Stumbled upon Classical Conditioning.*

In 1904, Russian physiologist Ivan Pavlov (1849–1936) won the Nobel Prize for his research on digestion in dogs (Pavlov, 1897/1997). In conducting his studies, Pavlov

Wikimedia Commons

Ivan Pavlov, 1849–1936.

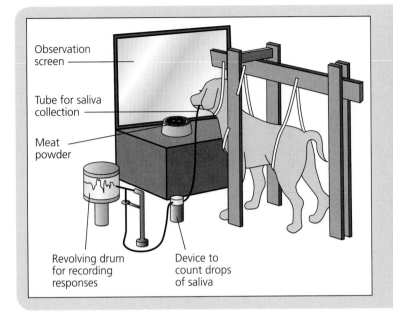

FIGURE 6-1

Pavlov's Apparatus for Studying Classical Conditioning in Dogs

Pavlov used a device similar to this in his experiments on classical conditioning. He restrained the dog in a harness and attached a tube to its salivary gland in order to accurately measure its salivation response. A ticking metronome often served as the conditioned stimulus (CS), and the meat powder was the unconditioned stimulus (UCS). In classical conditioning terms, what type of response does the saliva represent when it occurred due to the presentation of the meat powder? What type of response does the saliva represent when the metronome triggered it?

Observation screen

Tube for saliva collection

Meat powder

Revolving drum for recording responses

Device to count drops of saliva

would place meat powder on a dog's tongue to elicit reflexive salivation. One thing he noticed was that, over time, dogs began salivating *before* any food reached their mouths and even before they smelled the food. For example, they might salivate simply from seeing the food dish or merely from hearing the feeder's approaching footsteps. At first, Pavlov considered this phenomenon an irritating development because he could no longer control the beginning of the dog's salivation. However, his annoyance turned into excitement when he realized that he had stumbled upon a simple but important form of learning, which came to be known as classical conditioning.

Classical conditioning is a type of learning in which a neutral stimulus acquires the capacity to elicit a response after being paired with another stimulus that naturally elicits that response (Miller & Grace, 2003). In his experiments investigating classical conditioning, Pavlov would place a hungry dog in an apparatus similar to the one depicted in Figure 6-1. Just before injecting meat powder into the dog's mouth, Pavlov would present an initially neutral stimulus to the dog, such as the ticking of a metronome. At first, this ticking would produce no response in the dog. However, the food powder presented right after the ticking sound naturally triggered the dog's salivary reflex. Because this act of salivating was unlearned, Pavlov called it an **unconditioned response (UCR)**, and he called the food that elicited this automatic response an **unconditioned stimulus (UCS)**.

Classical conditioning A type of learning in which a neutral stimulus acquires the capacity to elicit a response after being paired with another stimulus that naturally elicits that response

Unconditioned response (UCR) In classical conditioning, the unlearned, automatic response to an unconditioned stimulus

Unconditioned stimulus (UCS) In classical conditioning, a stimulus that naturally and automatically elicits an unconditioned response

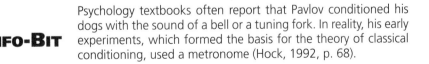

INFO-BIT Psychology textbooks often report that Pavlov conditioned his dogs with the sound of a bell or a tuning fork. In reality, his early experiments, which formed the basis for the theory of classical conditioning, used a metronome (Hock, 1992, p. 68).

Although the neutral stimulus initially had no effect on the dog, after several pairings of metronome and food, the dog began to salivate in response to the ticking alone. The dog had *learned* to associate the ticking with the presentation of the food powder (see Figure 6-2). This learned response was called the **conditioned response (CR)**, and the previously neutral stimulus that now triggered the CR was called the

Conditioned response (CR) In classical conditioning, the learned response to a previously neutral conditioned stimulus

FIGURE 6-2

Classical Conditioning

Before classical conditioning, the neutral stimulus of the ticking metronome presented just before the unconditioned stimulus of the meat powder does not trigger salivation. Instead, the unconditioned response of salivation occurs only when the unconditioned stimulus is presented. However, during conditioning, through repeated pairings of the neutral stimulus and unconditioned stimulus, the neutral stimulus becomes a conditioned stimulus. Now this conditioned stimulus produces a conditioned response.

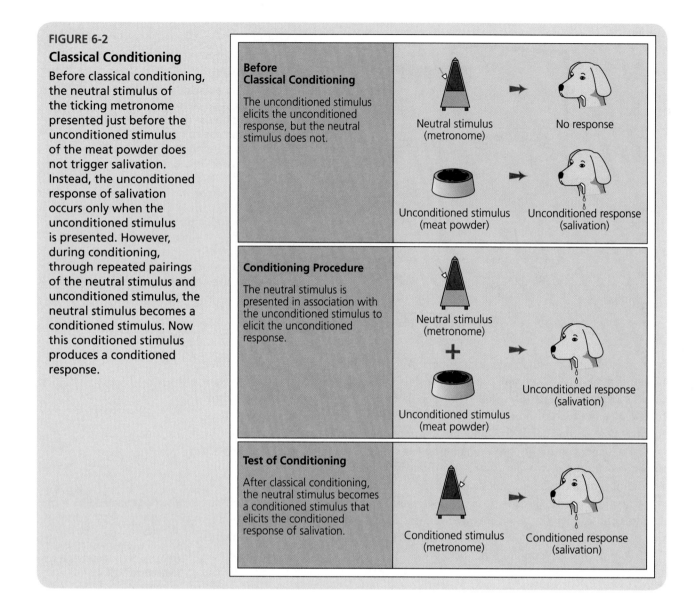

Before Classical Conditioning

The unconditioned stimulus elicits the unconditioned response, but the neutral stimulus does not.

Neutral stimulus (metronome)   No response

Unconditioned stimulus (meat powder)   Unconditioned response (salivation)

Conditioning Procedure

The neutral stimulus is presented in association with the unconditioned stimulus to elicit the unconditioned response.

Neutral stimulus (metronome)

Unconditioned stimulus (meat powder)   Unconditioned response (salivation)

Test of Conditioning

After classical conditioning, the neutral stimulus becomes a conditioned stimulus that elicits the conditioned response of salivation.

Conditioned stimulus (metronome)   Conditioned response (salivation)

Conditioned stimulus (CS) In classical condition, a previously neutral stimulus that, after repeated pairing with an unconditioned stimulus, comes to elicit a conditioned response

conditioned stimulus (CS). One way to remember the difference between stimuli and responses that are either unconditioned or conditioned is to think of these two terms in the following manner: *un*conditioned = *un*learned; conditioned = learned (see Self-Discovery Questionnaire 6-1).

Classical conditioning may not be what you think of as learning. For instance, you are not using classical conditioning principles to understand the important points in this chapter. The type of learning that goes on in classical conditioning is often considered unintentional and automatic—that is, you do not usually set out to learn an association, and you do not usually consciously elicit the conditioned response. Neither your pleasure (CR) upon seeing a good friend (CS) nor your anxiety (CR) upon hearing a dentist's drill (CS) is an intentionally learned response. They develop with no apparent effort on your part because both your friend's image and the drill noise have become associated with other stimuli that naturally evoke pleasure or pain. Similar effortless learning permeates our lives and profoundly affects our everyday behavior, but we often do not notice it because it is so automatic. Yet, is that all there is to classical conditioning?

SELF-DISCOVERY 6-1
Questionnaire

Can You Classically Condition Your Own Pupil Dilation and Eye Blinking?

Figzoi

To experience classical conditioning, try this exercise. First, look in a mirror under bright light conditions and notice the size of your pupils. Now, turn out the light for 30 seconds and then flick it back on while gazing into a mirror. Notice how much larger your pupils have become in response to the lack of light. This pupillary response to light is an example of an unconditioned response. Now do the same demonstration, but just before turning out the light, ring a bell. Repeat the pairing of the neutral stimulus (the bell) with the unconditioned stimulus (the darkness) at least 20 times. Then, with the lights on, ring the bell while watching your eyes closely in the mirror. You should see your eyes dilate slightly even though the unconditioned stimulus is not present. The previously neutral bell sound has become the conditioned stimulus, and your resulting pupil dilation is the conditioned response. Now you can truly say that classical conditioning does indeed ring a bell!

You can also classically condition your own eye blinking. As you may already know, a puff of air directed at your eye is an unconditioned stimulus that causes the reflexive unconditioned response of eye blinking. If you flash a light just before each puff of air, the light will soon become a conditioned stimulus that will cause eye blinking on its own (Lavond & Steinmetz, 2003). Following hundreds of studies investigating human classical eyeblink conditioning, scientists have discovered that the hippocampus in the brain is involved in the development of this conditioned response (Green & Woodruff-Pak, 2000; Orsini, Kim, Knapska, & Maren, 2011). They have also discovered that this same brain structure is damaged in the early stages of Alzheimer's disease and in the brain disorder known as autism. This knowledge is now being used to help diagnose autism and to identify individuals who might be at high risk for Alzheimer's disease. Early diagnosis of such serious medical disorders allows for more effective treatment that, in the case of Alzheimer's disease, can delay onset of the disease.

6.1b   Classical Conditioning Helps Animals Learn to Predict Events.

Although Pavlov asserted that classical conditioning was an essentially "mindless" process, most contemporary learning theorists believe it often involves quite a bit of "mindfulness" because, through the conditioning process, humans and other animals are learning to reliably predict upcoming events (Timberlake, 2004). First proposed by Robert Rescorla and Allan Wagner (1972), this general rule of classical conditioning states that a previously neutral stimulus will lead to a conditioned response whenever it provides the organism with *information* about the upcoming unconditioned stimulus. In other words, classical conditioning is a process by which organisms learn to expect the unconditioned stimulus based on the presentation of the conditioned stimulus. For example, in the original Pavlovian conditioning studies, if a metronome always ticked (CS) just before the presentation of food (UCS), the dog later began salivating (CR) whenever the metronome ticked (CS). Conditioning occurred because the ticking provided the dog with the information that food would soon be delivered. The conditioned stimulus became a *signal* that the unconditioned stimulus would soon appear. Similarly, whenever our dog Maizy hears the rustling of her food bag in our utility room, she becomes excited because she has learned that this sound predicts the appearance of food in her bowl.

This idea that classical conditioning involves a learning process by which humans and other animals acquire conditioned responses when one event reliably predicts, or *signals*, the appearance of another event greatly expands upon Pavlov's initial understanding of this type of learning. Instead of simply explaining basic, reflexlike responses, this revised conception of classical conditioning assumes that it often involves predicting the likely occurrence or nonoccurrence of future events (Asli & Flaten, 2012; Domjan, 2005).

Acquisition

Acquisition The initial stage of classical conditioning, during which a previously neutral stimulus begins to acquire the ability to elicit a conditioned response

The learned ability to predict what events might follow other events certainly aids survival for animals. Yet, how quickly and in what manner does the **acquisition**, or initial learning, of a conditioned response occur? Pavlov discovered that conditioned responses seldom occur at full strength right away (a phenomenon known as *one-trial learning*), but rather, gradually build up over a series of trials. Based on this finding, psychologists initially believed that the key to acquiring a conditioned response was the sheer *number* of CS-UCS pairings. However, subsequent research in other laboratories indicated that the *order* and *timing* of the CS-UCS pairings are also very important because they provide the animal with valuable information about the upcoming occurrence of the unconditioned stimulus (Buhusi & Schmajuk, 1999; Wasserman & Miller, 1997).

Regarding order of presentation, learning seldom occurs when the CS comes after the UCS (*backward conditioning*) or at the same time as the UCS (*simultaneous conditioning*). Instead, conditioning generally occurs only when the CS comes before the UCS (*forward conditioning*). This finding is consistent with the hypothesis that classical conditioning is biologically adaptive because it prepares the organism for good or bad events in the immediate future. As previously mentioned, the CS becomes a signal that a UCS is about to be presented. Prior to conditioning, the organism's response is dictated by the UCS appearing. However, after conditioning, the organism responds more quickly because it is now reacting to the earlier-occurring CS, not to the later-occurring UCS. These quicker conditioned responses often spell the difference between life and death. For example, as depicted in Figure 6-3, classical

FIGURE 6-3   **Avoiding a Predator's Attack Through Classical Conditioning**

As a learning technique, classical conditioning is biologically adaptive because it prepares the animal for good or bad events in the immediate future. Such prior conditioning helps animals respond more quickly to events. For example, when reacting to a lion attack, Chimp B's prior experiences with lions provided it with a quicker response than that of Chimp A.

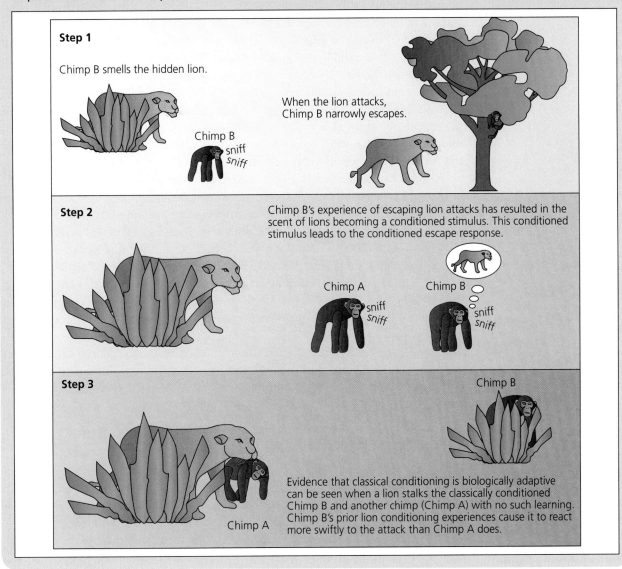

Step 1

Chimp B smells the hidden lion.

When the lion attacks, Chimp B narrowly escapes.

Chimp B
sniff
Sniff

Step 2

Chimp B's experience of escaping lion attacks has resulted in the scent of lions becoming a conditioned stimulus. This conditioned stimulus leads to the conditioned escape response.

Chimp A
sniff
Sniff

Chimp B
sniff
Sniff

Step 3

Chimp B

Evidence that classical conditioning is biologically adaptive can be seen when a lion stalks the classically conditioned Chimp B and another chimp (Chimp A) with no such learning. Chimp B's prior lion conditioning experiences cause it to react more swiftly to the attack than Chimp A does.

Chimp A

conditioning could help an animal react swiftly to a predator's impending attack. Animals having prior experience with predators are more likely to quickly respond when stimuli associated with the predator (its sight, sound, or smell, for instance) are presented. Through experience, the animals that have been conditioned to respond to stimuli preceding the UCS are most likely to survive. Can you think of instances in your own life when conditioned responses may foster your survival?

Besides presentation order, in most cases the UCS must follow the CS closely in time. In animal research, the most efficient CS-UCS interval is between 0.2 and 2 seconds. If the interval is longer, the CR is more difficult to establish because animals have difficulty recognizing it as a signal for the appearance of the UCS.

In addition to the presentation order and timing of the CS-UCS pairings, the *accuracy* with which the CS can predict the appearance of the UCS also determines whether a conditioned response is formed. If the UCS reliably follows the CS but also occurs when the CS is not present, a conditioned response is unlikely to develop. For example, in one experiment (Rescorla, 1968), rats were presented with a tone (CS), followed by a mild electric shock (UCS) that caused them to jump (UCR). In one condition, the shock was given only after the tone. Very quickly, these rats began displaying a fear response—freezing (CR)—after hearing the tone. In another condition, however, the shock was given both after the tone and during times when the tone had not been presented. These rats displayed little, if any, freezing in anticipation of the coming shock. Why do you think this group of rats did not become conditioned to the tone? No conditioning occurred because their ability to prepare for the UCS could not be accurately predicted by the sound of the tone. In other words, the tone was a poor signal of the coming shock; thus, the rats did not use it to predict the appearance of the shock. These findings are consistent with the previously stated rule that a stimulus will become "conditioned" whenever it signals to the organism that an unconditioned stimulus is about to occur.

Once a particular stimulus is recognized as a poor signal for an upcoming event, an animal can have difficulty learning a new association between the two stimuli. In a study similar to the preceding one, researchers first presented tones and shocks to rats in a random order so that the tone did not serve as a signal of an upcoming shock (Nakajima et al., 2000). Then the researchers changed the order of presentation so that a shock always followed the tone. Because the tone was now a signal, wouldn't you expect the rats to learn the association and freeze when they heard the tone? Interestingly, they did not. Having once learned that the tone provided no information, the animals had difficulty later detecting a real association, a phenomenon called *general learned irrelevance*.

Overall, research on the acquisition of conditioned responses tells us that organisms are not passive in this process. They actively seek information in their environment to establish when certain events (CS) predict the occurrence of other events (UCS).

Extinction and Spontaneous Recovery

What do you think happens when the CS no longer provides accurate information about the appearance of the UCS? In other words, what happens when the CS occurs repeatedly without the UCS? The answer is **extinction**, which is the gradual weakening and disappearance of the conditioned response (Kalmbach & Mauk, 2012). In Pavlov's experiments, when the ticking metronome (CS) was repeatedly presented to the dog without the delivery of food (UCS), the metronome gradually lost its ability to elicit salivation (CR). In cognitive terms, the dog learned that the CS was no longer useful in predicting the UCS (Lovibond, 2004).

Extinction In classical condition, the gradual weakening and disappearance of the conditioned response when the conditioned stimulus is repeatedly presented without being paired with the unconditioned stimulus

Cocaine is a stimulant drug (UCS) that naturally induces a sense of euphoria (UCR) in users (see Chapter 5, Section 5.3f), and this principle of extinction has been used to treat cocaine abuse. One problem that recovering drug users must overcome is the familiar reminders associated with their addiction. Anything repeatedly associated with past drug use—such as certain locations, smells, or objects— becomes a conditioned stimulus that can elicit a craving for the drug (Bonson et al., 2002; Miguens et al., 2008). Because drug addicts use money to obtain cocaine, in one treatment program, researchers attempted to weaken the conditioned link between money and cocaine-induced euphoria by asking addicts to engage in one of two activities under the guise of a "budgetary task" (M. E. Hamilton et al., 1997). One group of addicts was given $500 in cash to hold in their hands as they explained how they would spend it, while the other group was asked to merely imagine that they had the money. Those addicts who held the actual cash initially reported a stronger craving for cocaine after handling the money than the group who imagined the money. However, repeated exposure to the cash without it being associated with cocaine use gradually reduced drug craving, as would be expected due to extinction. These results suggest that applying the principle of extinction in drug treatment programs can enhance their effectiveness.

Although you undoubtedly remember instances when conditioned responses have become extinct in your own life, have you also noticed that occasionally a response that you thought was extinguished long ago reappears spontaneously when you happen to encounter the conditioned stimulus? This phenomenon, known as **spontaneous recovery**, is the reappearance of an extinguished response after a period of nonexposure to the conditioned stimulus (Thanellou & Green, 2011). For example, former soldiers who long ago overcame the panic attacks they experienced during combat may reexperience acute anxiety while viewing a movie containing graphic war scenes. The practical importance of spontaneous recovery is that even if you succeed in ridding yourself of a conditioned response, it may surprise you by reappearing later (Schmajuk & Larrauri, 2006).

Spontaneous recovery The reappearance of an extinguished response after a period of nonexposure to the conditioned stimulus

6.1c *Other Stimuli Can Produce the Conditioned Response.*

One observation Pavlov made while conditioning his dogs to salivate was that salivation triggered by the conditioned stimulus often generalized to other, similar stimuli. Pavlov called this phenomenon **stimulus generalization**. Such generalization often fosters an organism's survival, as when a bird that becomes sick after eating a poisonous Monarch butterfly avoids eating other orange and black insects. This reaction makes good adaptive sense: Things that look, taste, feel, or sound the same often share other important characteristics. The more similar that the new stimuli are to the original conditioned stimulus, the greater the likelihood of generalization. Stimulus generalization may explain why you sometimes respond very warmly or coldly to strangers who look like people for whom you previously developed either positive or negative conditioned responses. In such instances, you may not realize that your emotional response is caused by the power of stimulus generalization, but it nonetheless has an impact on your social life. Closer Look 6-1 describes a classic study in psychology that demonstrated how fear not only can become a classically conditioned response but also can be learned through stimulus generalization (Ryan et al., 2011).

Stimulus generalization In classical conditioning, the tendency for a conditioned response to be elicited by stimuli similar to the conditioned stimulus

Can Fear Be Learned Through Stimulus Generalization?

In 1920, John Watson, the founder of behaviorism (see Chapter 1, Section 1.1b), and his colleague, Rosalie Rayner, conducted the best-known study of stimulus generalization. Their subject was an eight-month-old boy whom they identified as "Little Albert B." During initial testing, Watson and Rayner presented Albert with a white rat, a rabbit, a monkey, a dog, masks with and without hair, and white cotton wool. The boy reacted with interest, but no fear.

Two months later, while Albert sat on a mattress placed on a table, the researchers presented him with the white rat. Just as Albert touched the rat, however, Watson made a loud noise behind him by striking a 4-foot steel bar with a hammer. This noise (the

John Watson and Rosalie Rayner classically conditioned Little Albert B. to fear white rats. Due to stimulus generalization, he also became fearful of other furry-looking objects. How does this research provide insight into the development of phobias? What are the ethical concerns raised by this study?

UCS) startled and frightened (the UCR) the toddler. During two sessions spaced one week apart, this procedure was repeated a total of seven times. Each time, the pairing of the rat and noise resulted in a fear response. Next, the rat alone was presented to Albert, without the noise. As I'm sure you've guessed, he reacted to the rat (the CS) with extreme fear (the CR). He cried, turned away, rolled over on one side away from the rat, and began crawling away so fast that he almost went over the edge of the table before the researchers caught hold of him! Five days later, Albert showed stimulus generalization to a white rabbit:

> Negative responses began at once. He leaned as far away from the animal as possible, whimpered, then burst into tears. When the rabbit was placed in contact with him, he buried his face in the mattress, then got up on all fours and crawled away, crying as he went. (Watson & Rayner, 1920, p. 6)

Besides to the rabbit, Albert's fear response also generalized to a dog, a white fur coat, Watson's own head of gray hair, and even a Santa Claus mask! These fear responses also occurred outside the room in which the conditioned response had initially been learned. Two months later, just prior to Albert being adopted, he was tested one last time and again expressed considerable fear toward the same objects.

In addition to this study's demonstrating stimulus generalization, an equally important reason why it still is widely discussed today is the serious ethical issues it raises. Essentially, Watson and Rayner induced a phobia in Albert (see Section 6.1d), a practice that would not be tolerated by current ethical standards of psychological research. Further, the researchers made no attempt to recondition their young subject (Harris, 2002). This overall careless treatment may be partly explained by recent evidence suggesting that Albert suffered from a neurological disorder, and thus, was considered—by that era's standards—as less valuable than a healthy child (Beck et al., 2009).

Stimulus discrimination In classical conditioning, the tendency for a conditioned response not to be elicited by stimuli similar to the conditioned stimulus

While performing their conditioning studies, Pavlov and his coworkers noticed that the dogs sometimes did not exhibit a conditioned response when presented with stimuli that were somewhat similar to the conditioned stimulus. When an animal gives a conditioned response to the conditioned stimulus but not to stimuli similar to it, the opposite of stimulus generalization occurs—namely, **stimulus discrimination**. Like generalization, discrimination has survival value because slightly different stimuli can have very different consequences (Thomas, 1992). For the most part, our natural tendency is to generalize, and we need experience to teach us to discriminate. This greater tendency to generalize explains why Albert (in Closer Look 6-1) reacted to the other furry objects in the same way he had been conditioned to react to the white rat. If he had somehow been encouraged to directly experience the fact that the unconditioned stimulus did not follow the presentation of these other objects, he would have developed stimulus discrimination.

Higher-order conditioning A classical conditioning procedure in which a neutral stimulus becomes a conditioned stimulus after being paired with an existing conditioned stimulus

In addition to discovering the principles of stimulus generalization and stimulus discrimination, Pavlov (1927) learned that a conditioned stimulus could condition another neutral stimulus. This procedure is known as **higher-order conditioning** (or *second-order conditioning*), and it greatly increases the number of situations in which classical conditioning explains behavior. For example, do you know people who become so anxious upon entering a classroom to take an exam that their ability to concentrate is affected? Such anxiety is often due to higher-order conditioning (Mineka & Oehlberg, 2008). Early in their schooling, academic performance may have been a neutral event for these people. However, somehow it became associated with criticism (the UCS) from parents or teachers, which elicited anxiety (the UCR). Through conditioning, then, academic performance (the CS) acquired the ability to trigger a stress response (the CR). As these people continued taking exams, this conditioned stimulus began functioning like a UCS through higher-order conditioning. That is, the kinds of neutral stimuli that immediately precede test-taking—such as walking into a testing room or hearing test booklets being passed out—became conditioned stimuli that also elicited test anxiety. The "Psychological Applications" section in Chapter 9 discusses how to break this unpleasant kind of higher-order conditioning.

Fortunately, higher-order conditioning is equally effective at eliciting pleasant responses. For example, your cologne may spark romantic feelings in those who associate that fragrance with past loves. Likewise, complete strangers may respond warmly upon discovering that you are from their hometown. In both instances, a previously neutral stimulus (you) becomes a conditioned stimulus after being paired with an existing conditioned stimulus (cologne or hometown). As you can see, higher-order conditioning has a role in shaping a variety of advantageous—and disadvantageous—responses (Till et al., 2008). With this knowledge, are you developing a greater appreciation—perhaps, even affection—for classical conditioning principles?

Journey of Discovery

Every year, thousands of drug users die from overdoses. Those who have narrowly survived such overdoses tend to report that the setting in which they took the drug that caused the problem was different from their normal drug-taking environment (Siegel, 1984). How might classical conditioning principles explain why these different settings were more likely to be associated with drug overdoses?

6.1d *Animals Differ in What Responses Can Be Classically Conditioned.*

Pavlov and other early learning theorists assumed that the principles of conditioning were similar across all species, and thus that psychologists could just as easily study rats and pigeons as people. They further assumed that associations could be conditioned between any stimulus an organism could perceive and any response it could make. However, research conducted during the past 35 years indicates that neither of these assumptions is correct. Not only do animals often differ in what responses can be conditioned, but also some responses can be conditioned much more readily to certain stimuli than to others. The essential insight gained from this research is that an animal's biology steers it toward certain kinds of conditioning that enhance its survival (Hollis, 1997).

Taste Aversion

One of the most dramatic examples of a behavior being more easily conditioned by certain stimuli than by others is *taste aversion*. If you have ever experienced food poisoning, you are undoubtedly familiar with this concept. When you consumed the food that ultimately made you sick, there were probably many things going on around you besides the taste of the food. But if you are like most people, the lesson you learned was to avoid whatever food you had eaten and not (for example) the people you were talking to or the show you were watching on TV. Why is this so? Let us consider the results of an animal study that helps us better understand this behavior.

In a classic study of taste aversion in rats, John Garcia and Robert Koelling (1966) presented groups of rats with either flavored or plain water; however, drinking the plain water triggered a light flash and a loud click, which the researchers referred to as "bright-noisy water." After drinking, the rats received a UCS: Group A received electrical shocks to their feet that immediately produced pain, while Group B received radiation in X-rays that made them nauseated about an hour later.

According to traditional classical conditioning principles, a conditioned response occurs only if the unconditioned stimulus follows the conditioned stimulus within a very short interval. Based on this knowledge, wouldn't you predict that the Group A rats that drank the flavored water would learn to avoid it because drinking this water immediately preceded their literally shocking UCS? Wouldn't you also predict that the Group B rats should not learn to avoid drinking either kinds of water because the effects of their UCS—the radiation—were not felt until much later? As depicted in Figure 6-4, something different happened. Garcia and Koelling found that the rats exposed to the immediately painful shocks (Group A) learned to avoid the bright-noisy water but not the flavored water. In contrast, rats exposed to the delayed nausea of the radiation (Group B) learned to avoid the flavored water but not the bright-noisy water.

If you were the researchers, how would you explain these findings? Why would the rats have been conditioned to associate the shocks with the bright-noisy water but not the flavored water? Why would nausea become associated with any stimulus that preceded it so far in advance? Why did the rats learn to associate the nausea with the flavored water but not the bright-noisy water?

Garcia and Koelling argued that these constraints on learning were by-products of the rats' evolutionary history. Through the process of adapting to their environment,

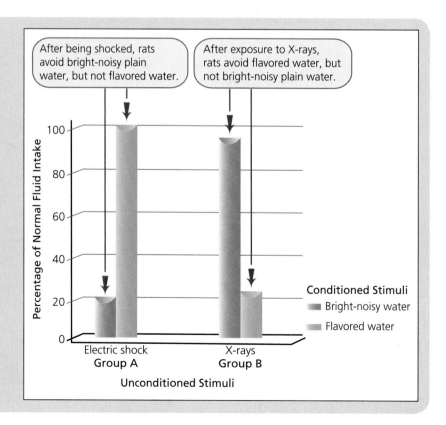

FIGURE 6-4

Biological Constraints on Taste Aversion in Rats

Rats learned to avoid plain water that was associated with a light-noise combination when it was followed by electric shock, but not when it was followed by X-rays that made the rats nauseated. In contrast, rats quickly learned to avoid flavored water when it was followed by X-rays, but they did not readily acquire an aversion to this same water when it was followed by shock. How might these constraints on learning be by-products of the rats' evolutionary history?

After being shocked, rats avoid bright-noisy plain water, but not flavored water.

After exposure to X-rays, rats avoid flavored water, but not bright-noisy plain water.

Percentage of Normal Fluid Intake

100
80
60
40
20
0

Electric shock
Group A

X-rays
Group B

Unconditioned Stimuli

Conditioned Stimuli
Bright-noisy water
Flavored water

rats—like all other creatures—evolved to learn those things crucial to their survival. The sudden pain of a shock is more likely to be caused by an external stimulus than by something the rat ingests, so it is not surprising that rats are predisposed to associate shock with a sight or a sound. Similarly, nausea is more likely to be caused by something the rat drinks or eats than by some external stimulus. Thus, it makes evolutionary sense that rats are predisposed to associate nausea with a taste. It is also adaptive that in taste aversion, strong conditioning develops despite the long delay between the CS (the taste) and the UCS (the nausea). Animals biologically equipped to associate taste stimuli with illness that occurs minutes or even hours later are more likely to survive and pass their genes on to the next generation (Seligman, 1970).

Garcia decided to apply this newfound insight into conditioned taste aversion to a practical problem: controlling predators' attacks on ranchers' livestock (Garcia et al., 1977; Gustafson et al., 1974). In one study, captured wolves were fed sheep carcasses containing lithium chloride (UCS), a chemical that causes severe nausea and vomiting (UCR). After recovering from this very unpleasant experience, these same hungry predators were placed in a pen with a live sheep. At first, the wolves moved toward the sheep (CS) in attack postures. However, as soon as they smelled their prey, they backed off and avoided further contact (CR). Based on this research, many ranchers today condition potential predators to avoid their herds by depositing lithium chloride-injected livestock carcasses near their herds. This same strategy is used to both condition predators to avoid killing endangered species and to condition free-grazing livestock not to eat toxic yet tasty plants (Gorniak et al., 2008; Nicolaus & Nellis, 1987). The flexibility of animals' aversive learning ability was recently demonstrated in a study of honeybees that learned to avoid pheromones to which they are innately attracted, when those pheromones were paired with an electrical shock (Roussel et al., 2012). In other words, aversive learning in honeybees is strong enough to override genetically preprogrammed responding.

INFO-BIT During the early stages of pregnancy, many women experience "morning sickness," which is characterized by nausea and vomiting. One study found that 60 percent of pregnant women experienced an aversion toward certain foods during the same week that they experienced their first episode of morning sickness (Bayley, Dye, Jones, DeBono, & Hill, 2002). This positive correlation between onset of nausea and onset of food aversion suggests that taste aversion learning is involved in the development of some but not all food aversions during pregnancy.

Conditioning the Immune System

Chemotherapy drugs are given to cancer patients to inhibit the growth of new cancer cells, but these drugs also inhibit the growth of immune cells, thereby weakening the body's ability to fight off illnesses. Chemotherapy drugs typically are given to patients each time in the same room in the same hospital. Thus, is it possible that these patients' immune systems become classically conditioned to negatively react in advance to stimuli in the hospital? Apparently, yes. In a study of women undergoing treatment for ovarian cancer, researchers found that following several chemotherapy sessions, the

Shutterstock

For cancer patients who have been undergoing outpatient chemotherapy at this hospital, how might the simple action of entering this setting for treatment weaken their immune system? What is the UCS? What is the UCR? What is the CS? What is the CR?

patients' immune systems were weakened as soon as they entered the hospital—in anticipation of the treatment (Bovbjerg et al., 1990). The hospital setting had become a conditioned stimulus, causing an inhibition of cellular activity.

Phobias

People who have been injured in car accidents sometimes develop an intense fear of riding in all cars. These exaggerated and irrational fears of objects or situations are known as *phobias* and are discussed more extensively in Chapter 11, Section 11.2a. Such intense fear reactions often develop through classical conditioning (Öhman & Ruck, 2007).

Although we can develop a phobia toward anything, there is evidence that some objects or situations elicit phobic reactions more easily than others. For instance, people tend to develop phobias for snakes and heights quite easily; however they seldom develop phobias for knives and electrical outlets, even though these objects are often associated with painful experiences (Kleinknecht, 1991; LoLordo & Droungas, 1989). In a series of studies investigating the development of classically conditioned fear reactions, Arne Öhman and Joaquim Soares found that when photos of various animals and plants were paired with an electric shock, participants more readily acquired fear responses to pictures of snakes and spiders than to pictures of flowers and mushrooms (Öhman & Soares, 1994). They also found that conditioned fear responses to snakes and spiders were much more resistant to extinction (Soares & Öhman, 1993).

Evolutionary theorists contend that people more easily develop phobias for certain objects or situations because those stimuli once posed a real danger to our ancestors (Buss, 1995; Seligman, 1971). During the time our ancestors lived, those individuals whose genetic makeup allowed them to quickly learn to avoid hazards were more likely to survive and reproduce. According to this perspective, then, the reason snakes and heights make many of us unduly anxious in our modern world is because the genes that trigger such anxiety are still part of our genetic makeup.

Further support for the view that we have evolved to fear certain objects and situations more than others comes from a perceptual experiment conducted by Öhman and his coworkers (2001a). In this study, either participants were shown images of a few snakes and spiders placed within a much larger environmental scene of many flowers and mushrooms, or they were shown a few flowers and mushrooms placed within a larger scene of many snakes and spiders. Their task was to quickly identify the embedded images in the larger environmental scene (similar to a *Where's Waldo?* picture). Participants were significantly faster at finding snakes and spiders against a background of mushrooms and flowers than they were at finding mushrooms and flowers against a snake and spider background. This finding is consistent with the hypothesis that humans have developed specialized neural circuitry that quickly and automatically identifies stimuli associated with threat and danger in our evolutionary past (Öhman et al., 2001b; Öhman & Mineka, 2003). This evolved neural mechanism for threat detection and fear activation

Shutterstock

Humans' evolutionary history may predispose us to be apprehensive and even fearful toward snakes. In contrast, eagles hunt and eat snakes as part of their regular diet and exhibit no such anxiety. What other common phobias might be partly primed by our evolutionary heritage?

appears to be located in the amygdala of the brain, and the fear response occurs before conscious cognitive analysis of the stimulus takes place (Man et al., 2012; Mineka & Öhman, 2002). Further discussion of how the brain coordinates these intense emotional responses can be found in Chapter 9, Section 9.5e.

In our modern world, fear of snakes serves little adaptive function because very few of us are at risk of dying from poisonous snakebites. So why do we still carry the tendency to fear snakes? One reason is the timescale of evolution. Evolutionary changes are noticeable not in a single generation, or a few generations, but over hundreds of generations. A second reason is that evolutionary pressures will not remove fear of snakes until, over the long term, the fear becomes an actual *disadvantage* (Buss et al., 1998). If the fear is merely neutral—an annoying holdover from prehistoric times, with no effect on reproductive success—it may remain part of the human condition. In other words, the fact that something is passed on through the generations implies nothing about its value in current society.

Section REVIEW

- Classical conditioning explains how organisms learn that certain events signal the presence or absence of other events; such knowledge helps the organisms prepare for future events.

- A neutral stimulus will lead to a conditioned response whenever it provides information about the upcoming occurrence of the unconditioned stimulus.

- Conditioned responses usually gradually develop over a series of presentations.

- In higher-order conditioning, a conditioned stimulus is used to condition another neutral stimulus.

- Stimulus generalization is when a conditioned response is elicited by stimuli similar to the conditioned stimulus.

- Stimulus discrimination is when a conditioned response is not elicited by other stimuli.

- An animal's biology steers it toward certain kinds of conditioning that enhance its survival.

6.2 Operant Conditioning

The type of learning that occurs due to classical conditioning helps you prepare for future events, but it seldom allows you to change those events. Thus, when Little Albert B. saw a white furry animal (the CS), he began crying (CR) in anticipation of hearing a frightening sound (UCS); however, his crying could not control the presentation of either the CS or the UCS. Now let us examine another type of learning in which you do learn that your actions, rather than conditioned stimuli, produce consequences.

6.2a *Operant Behavior Is Controlled by Consequences.*

A few years before Pavlov began watching hungry dogs salivate after being presented with food and a ticking metronome, American psychologist Edward L. Thorndike (1898)—a student of William James—was observing hungry cats trying to escape from a "puzzle box" to reach a bowl of food. To escape, the cats had to press a lever (the response), which in turn lifted a gate that allowed access to the food (the stimulus). Through trial and error, Thorndike's cats learned the correct behavior to reach the food.

The Law of Effect

How was the learning of Thorndike's cats different from the learning of Pavlov's dogs? In classical conditioning, an organism's behavior is largely determined by stimuli that *precede it*. In Pavlov's experiments, food caused the dogs to salivate. However, in Thorndike's research, behavior was influenced by stimuli that *followed it*. In addition, classical conditioning involves the learning of associations between stimuli, and the organism exerts little influence over the environment; in contrast, Thorndike's cats learned an association between behavior and its consequences and actively created a change in the environment. The cats learned to associate a response (lever-pressing) with a subsequent desirable consequence (food). Gradually, the behavior that produced these desirable consequences increased in frequency and became the dominant response when the cats were placed in the puzzle box. Thorndike (1911) called this relationship between behavior and its consequences the **law of effect** because behavior becomes more or less likely based on the *effect* it has in producing desirable or undesirable consequences.

Law of effect A basic principle of learning that states that a behavior becomes more or less likely based on its effect in producing desirable or undesirable consequences

You can see how the law of effect would be very useful to survival. Evolution works by selecting those individuals whose behavior best promotes survival in their given environment. Those animals that repeat behavior followed by desirable consequences and terminate behavior followed by undesirable consequences (if the consequences didn't terminate the animals first) would be most likely to profit from experience with their environment, and thus, survive and reproduce.

What Is Operant Conditioning?

Today Thorndike's law of effect is considered a fundamental principle of learning, but it was not at first accepted by the scientific community (Iversen, 1992). Then in the 1930s, former frustrated writer and new psychologist B. F. Skinner elaborated on the law of effect and made it the cornerstone for his influential theory of learning, **operant conditioning**. Skinner used the term *operant conditioning* because the organism's behavior is *operating* on the environment to achieve some desired goal. Operant behavior is largely *voluntary*, *goal directed*, and controlled by its *consequences*. Thus, when a rat presses a bar in a Skinner box (see Figure 6-5), it does so because it has learned that bar pressing will lead to food pellets. Likewise, when my daughters clean their rooms, they choose to engage in this behavior because they have learned that it will provide them with something highly valued, namely, permission to play with friends.

Operant conditioning A type of learning in which behavior is strengthened if followed by reinforcement and weakened if followed by punishment.

 **INFO-BIT**   Thorndike had previously called operant conditioning *instrumental conditioning* because the behavior is *instrumental* in obtaining rewards.

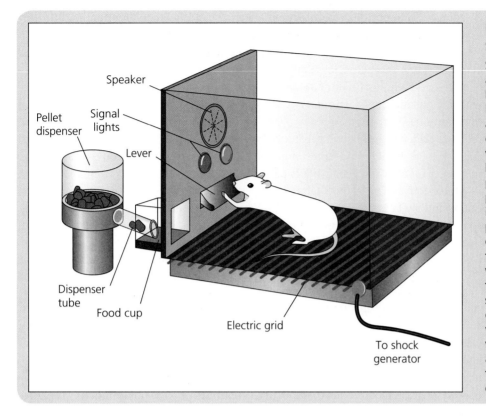

FIGURE 6-5

Skinner Box

Skinner designed an apparatus called a "Skinner box" in which animals learned to obtain food or to avoid shocks by operating on their environment within the box. In a Skinner box, the animal learns to press the bar to obtain food pellets, which are delivered into the box down the pellet tube. If the delivery of food pellets increases the frequency of bar pressing, what is the technical term for these pellets? The speaker and light allow the experimenter to manipulate visual and auditory stimuli, while the electric floor grid allows the experimenter to control aversive consequences (shock).

Labels on figure: Speaker; Signal lights; Pellet dispenser; Lever; Dispenser tube; Food cup; Electric grid; To shock generator

6.2b A Reinforcer Increases the Probability of Behavior.

As you have seen, people and other animals tend to repeat behaviors that are followed by desirable consequences. This fundamental principle of behaviorism—that rewarded behavior is likely to be repeated—is known as **reinforcement**. A **reinforcer** is any stimulus or event that increases the likelihood that the behavior preceding it will be repeated (Miller & Grace, 2003). A reinforcer may be a concrete reward, such as food, money, or attention. For example, if people laugh and pay attention to you when you tell a joke, their response is likely to make your joke-telling more likely in the future. A reinforcer could also be an activity, such as allowing children to play with friends after they clean their rooms.

How do you know whether something is a reinforcer? Simple. Observe whether it increases the behavior it follows. While "friend play" reinforces my daughters' room cleaning, I have learned that allowing them to watch a football game on television with me is not a reinforcer. Sometimes, the same stimulus is a reinforcer in one situation but not in another. For example, whereas laughter may reinforce joke-telling, my sister's laughter while teaching me to dance years ago certainly did not increase my desire to get on the dance floor! Likewise, a stimulus may be a reinforcer for one animal but not for another. Do you think the food pellets that rats in a Skinner box worked so hard to obtain would be a reinforcer for you? The lesson to be learned here is that something is a reinforcer not because of what it is, but rather because of what it does.

Reinforcement The process by which a stimulus increases the probability of the behavior that it follows

Reinforcer Any stimulus or event that increases the likelihood that the behavior preceding it will be repeated

Primary versus Secondary Reinforcers

How does a stimulus become a reinforcer? Actually, some stimuli are innately reinforcing, whereas others become reinforcing through learning. A **primary reinforcer** is innately reinforcing because it satisfies a biological need. Food, water, warmth, sex, physical activity, novel stimulation, and sleep are all examples of primary reinforcers.

Primary reinforcer Stimulus that is naturally reinforcing because it satisfies a biological need

Secondary reinforcer
Stimulus that is learned and becomes reinforcing by being associated with primary reinforcers

In contrast, a **secondary reinforcer** is learned and becomes reinforcing by being associated with a primary reinforcer.

Does this sound familiar? It should, because this learning involves classical conditioning. Through classical conditioning, a neutral stimulus becomes a conditioned stimulus (in our case, a secondary reinforcer) by being repeatedly paired with an unconditioned stimulus (the primary reinforcer) that naturally evokes an unconditioned response. An example of a secondary reinforcer is money. You value money because it has been repeatedly associated with a host of primary reinforcers, such as food, shelter, and entertainment. Likewise, attention becomes a secondary reinforcer for children because it is paired with primary reinforcers from adults, such as protection, warmth, food, and water. Other powerful secondary reinforcers are praise and success. Thus, an important element in operant conditioning—namely, secondary reinforcers—comes into existence not through operant conditioning but through classical conditioning.

Positive and Negative Reinforcers

Positive reinforcer Stimulus that strengthens a response by presenting a positive stimulus after a response

Negative reinforcer Stimulus that strengthens a response by removing an aversive or unpleasant stimulus after a response

The examples used thus far to describe reinforcers are known as positive reinforcers. A **positive reinforcer** strengthen a response by presenting a positive stimulus after a response. Another type of reinforcer is a **negative reinforcer**, which strengthens a response by *removing* an aversive or unpleasant stimulus after a response. Although negative reinforcement sounds like it means reinforcing behavior with a negative consequence, in fact it refers to removing something from the environment. (Negative consequences are a form of punishment, which is discussed in Section 6.2c.) In a Skinner box, a moderate electric shock administered through the floor grid often serves as a negative reinforcer. When the rat presses the bar, the shock is turned off. The removal of the shock strengthens the bar-pressing behavior.

Just as the rat learns that it can end an unpleasant sensation by responding in a specific way, you too have learned certain responses to escape negative reinforcers. The cold weather you avoid by going indoors is a negative reinforcer. Your parents nagging you to take out the garbage or to turn down the stereo are negative reinforcers.

Praise becomes a secondary reinforcer because it is associated with primary reinforcers, such as gentle physical contact and warmth. Can you think of other secondary reinforcers in your own life?

When you respond in the correct fashion, the noxious stimulus (the cold temperature or the nagging) is terminated. Similarly, when you clean your smelly refrigerator, the removal of the foul odor is also a negative reinforcer: It strengthens refrigerator-cleaning behavior in the future.

6.2c Punishment Decreases the Probability of Behavior.

The opposite consequence of reinforcement is **punishment**. While reinforcement always *increases* the probability of a response—either by presenting a desirable stimulus or by removing or avoiding an aversive stimulus—punishment always *decreases* the probability of whatever response it follows. Like reinforcement, there are two types of punishment. A **positive punisher** weakens a response by presenting an aversive stimulus after a response. Shocking a rat in a Skinner box for pressing a food bar and scolding a child for eating candy before dinner are examples of the use of positive punishment to reduce the future likelihood of unwanted behavior. In contrast, a **negative punisher** weakens a response by removing a positive stimulus after a response. Grounding a teenager for impolite behavior and denying an end-of-year bonus to a lazy worker are examples of negative punishment.

Do not confuse positive punishment with *negative reinforcement* (see Section 6.2b). Although both involve an aversive stimulus, remember that a reinforcer strengthens behavior. Negative reinforcement strengthens behavior by *removing* an aversive stimulus, while positive punishment weakens behavior by *presenting* an aversive stimulus. Table 6-1 distinguishes between the two types of reinforcement and the two types of punishment.

Skinner, who was enthusiastic about using reinforcement to shape behavior, was equally adamant in opposing punishment. One reason he did not recommend the use of punishment to shape behavior is that, in most instances, its implementation must conform to some very narrow guidelines. In order for punishment to have a chance of effectively reducing unwanted behaviors, three conditions must be met (Baron, 1983; Bower & Hilgard, 1981). First, the punishment must be *prompt*, administered quickly after the unwanted action. Second, it must be *relatively strong*, so that the offender duly notes its aversive qualities. And third, it must be *consistently applied*, so the responder knows that punishment is highly likely to follow future unwanted actions. Yet even if these conditions are met, reduction of the undesirable behavior is not guaranteed. For instance, punishment is often used to curb aggressive behavior. But if potential aggressors are extremely angry, threats of punishment *preceding* an attack frequently fail to inhibit aggression (Baron, 1973). Here, the strength of the anger overrides any concerns about the negative consequences of aggression. Likewise, the

Punishment The process by which a stimulus decreases the probability of the behavior it follows

Positive punisher Stimulus that weakens a response by presenting an aversive stimulus after a response

Negative punisher Stimulus that weakens a response by removing a positive stimulus after a response

TABLE 6-1 What Are the Differences Between Types of Reinforcement and Punishment?

		Effect on Behavior	
	Procedure	Strengthens	Weakens
Positive reinforcement	Presentation of stimulus	X	
Positive punishment	Presentation of stimulus		X
Negative reinforcement	Removal of stimulus	X	
Negative punishment	Removal of stimulus		X

use of punishment *following* aggression may actually provoke counteraggression in the aggressor-turned-victim, because such punishment may be frustrating and anger-producing. If the frustration and anger following punishment doesn't lead to direct aggression, it can cause *passive aggressiveness*, which is a subtle and indirect form of aggression (Vaillancourt & Sharma, 2011).

Using physical punishments, such as spankings, to reduce unwanted behavior is an especially questionable practice (Boutwell et al., 2011). As you will learn in Section 6.3, research indicates that employing physical punishment as a remedy for aggression and other undesirable behaviors may simply teach and encourage observers to copy these aggressive actions. That is, the person using physical punishment may serve as an aggressive model. This is exactly the process underlying the continuing cycle of family violence found in many societies—observing adult aggression appears to encourage rather than discourage aggression in children. For this reason, a growing number of countries are moving to enacting legal bans against spankings and other forms of physical punishment (Gershoff & Bitensky, 2007).

One alternative to punishment proposed by Skinner is to allow undesirable actions (such as a child's temper tantrums) to continue without either positive or negative consequences until they are extinguished. In other words, ignore the unwanted behavior—but immediately reinforce desirable responses when they occur. Another useful extinction technique is the "time-out," in which misbehaving children are removed for a short period of time from sources of positive reinforcement. Have you ever used these techniques? Were they effective?

6.2d *Different Reinforcement Schedules Lead to Different Learning.*

Thus far my description of the learning that occurs in operant conditioning has relied on an underlying assumption that a reinforcer follows every response. Although a **continuous reinforcement schedule** leads to the fastest learning, in most instances of daily living, we are not reinforced for every response.

The biggest problem with continuous reinforcement is that, when it ends, extinction occurs rapidly. For example, what happens when you put money into a vending machine and do not receive a soda? You might respond by inserting more coins. But if doing so does not lead to the desired beverage, you do not continue to pump money into the machine, do you? It is unlikely, because behavior regulated by continuous reinforcement is easily extinguished. The same is not true for responses that are reinforced only some of the time. Did you stop going to movies, visiting friends, or eating food because you had a few unrewarding experiences? You persist in many activities even though you are reinforced only intermittently. Thus, although continuous reinforcement allows you to *acquire* responses most quickly, once responses have been learned, a **partial reinforcement schedule** has an important effect on your continued *performance*. Being reinforced only once in a while keeps you responding vigorously for longer periods of time than does continuous reinforcement (Poling, 2010).

Skinner and his colleagues identified and studied several partial reinforcement schedules (Ferster & Skinner, 1957; Skinner, 1938). *Partial schedules* are defined in terms of number of responses or the passage of time. *Ratio schedules* mean that the first response after a specified number of responses is reinforced. *Interval schedules* mean that the first response after a specified time period is reinforced. In addition, some partial schedules are strictly *fixed*, while others are unpredictably *variable*.

A **fixed-ratio reinforcement schedule** reinforces behavior after a specified number of responses. For example, students may be given a prize after reading 20 books, or factory workers may be paid a certain amount of money for every 40

Violence and injury enclose in their net all that do such things, and generally return upon him who began.

—Lucretius, Roman philosopher and poet, 99–55 B.C.

Continuous reinforcement schedule A schedule of reinforcement in which every correct response is followed by a reinforcer

Partial reinforcement schedule A schedule of reinforcement in which correct responses are followed by reinforcers only part of the time.

Fixed-ratio reinforcement schedule A partial reinforcement schedule that reinforces a response after a specified number of nonreinforced responses

machinery pieces they assemble (a system known as "piecework"). The students read their first 19 books without reinforcement, as do the workers with their first 39 machinery pieces, because they know the payoff will occur when the last book or piece is completed in the ratio. When people and animals are placed on a fixed-ratio reinforcement schedule, it produces high response rates, with only brief pauses following reinforcement (see Figure 6-6).

Why do you think people and animals on fixed-ratio schedules take such short breaks before working again on their tasks? Quite simply, resting reduces rewards. In industry, this schedule is popular with management because it produces high productivity. However, it is unpopular with workers because it produces stress and fatigue. You might wonder why these employees do not exercise some self-restraint and simply slow down. According to behaviorists, this is unlikely because the source of control over their actions lies largely in the environment, not in the individual. They work themselves to exhaustion simply and solely because the fixed-ratio schedule reinforces energetic responding. The only way to reduce fatigue is to somehow turn off the reinforcement schedule eliciting these high response rates. Fortunately for workers, many employee unions in the United States, Canada, and Europe have done just that: They have pressured management to replace the fixed-ratio piecework pay with a fixed-interval hourly wage.

Although fixed-ratio schedules are more resistant to extinction than continuous reinforcement, the person or animal will stop responding soon after reinforcement stops. Why? Because when the reinforcer is not delivered after the required number of responses, it quickly becomes apparent that something about the schedule has changed.

What happens when a ratio schedule is not fixed, but varies? That is, a reinforcer may be delivered after the first response on trial 1, after the fourth response on trial 2, after the ninth response on trial 3, and so on. The average ratio may be one reinforcer after every six trials, but the responder never knows how many responses are needed to obtain the reinforcer on any given trial. A schedule like this that reinforces a response after a variable number of nonreinforced responses is known as a **variable-ratio reinforcement schedule**. As you can see in Figure 6-6, variable-ratio schedules

BVT *Lab*

Visit **www.BVTLab.com** to explore the student resources available for this chapter.

Variable-ratio reinforcement schedule A partial reinforcement schedule that reinforces the first response after a variable number of nonreinforced responses

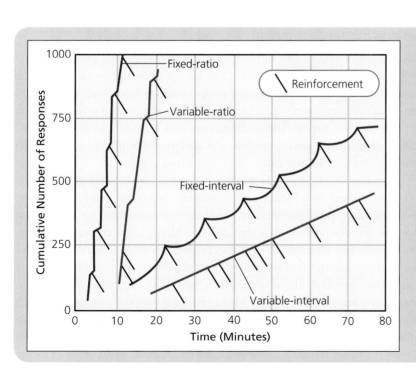

FIGURE 6-6

Schedules of Reinforcement

The predictability of fixed-ratio schedules leads to a high rate of responding, with brief pauses after each reinforcer. The unpredictability of variable-ratio schedules leads to high, steady rates of responding, with few pauses between reinforcers. The predictability of fixed-interval schedules leads to a low rate of responding until the fixed interval of time approaches, and then the rate of responding increases rapidly until the reinforcer is delivered; after that, a low rate of responding resumes. The unpredictability of variable-interval schedules produces a moderate, but steady, rate of responding.

lead to the highest rates of responding, the shortest pauses following reinforcement, and the greatest resistance to extinction. Golfing and most other sports activities are reinforced on variable-ratio schedules. Even after golfers hit balls into sand traps and overshoot the green all day, it only takes a few good (reinforced) shots to get most of them excited about playing again. Most games of chance are also based on variable-ratio schedules. The intermittent and unpredictable nature of the reinforcement is why people continue pumping money into slot machines. Their concern is that as soon as they leave, someone else will win all the money.

In a **fixed-interval reinforcement schedule**, reinforcement occurs for the first response after a fixed time interval has elapsed. As you can see in Figure 6-6, this schedule produces a pattern of behavior in which very few responses are made until the fixed interval of time approaches, and then the rate of responding increases rapidly. Researchers investigating the study patterns of college students found that they follow a fixed-interval behavior pattern when professors gave exams separated by a few weeks (Mawhinney et al., 1971). That is, when exams were given every 3 weeks, students began studying a few days before each exam, stopped studying immediately after the test, and began studying again as the next exam approached. In contrast, when professors gave daily quizzes, studying did not taper off after testing.

Unlike the predictability of fixed-interval reinforcement, a **variable-interval reinforcement schedule** reinforces the first response after a variable time interval has elapsed. As you can see in Figure 6-6, such schedules produce relatively steady rates of responding. Have you ever taken a course in which your grade was based on surprise exams that were given after a varying number of days or weeks? Because you did not know when you would be tested, you probably studied on a more regular basis in this sort of course than when exams were spread out in a fixed-interval pattern (Ruscio, 2001). Similarly, have you ever tried to connect to your Internet server but received a busy signal or a message that it was unavailable due to temporary maintenance? You know sometime in the near future that your attempt to connect will be reinforced, but you are unsure when that moment will arrive. Thus, you periodically dial up your server. You are on a variable-interval schedule of reinforcement!

6.2e *Accidental Reinforcement Can Cause Superstitious Behavior.*

As a teenager, when first asking girls out for dates, I used the phone so I could read what I wanted to say from a prepared script. One day I received a phone acceptance right after I shot 10 consecutive free throws on my driveway basketball court. After this simple coincidence, I rarely phoned another girl for a date without first shooting 10 baskets in a row. This **superstitious behavior** was learned simply because it happened to be followed by a reinforcer (the girl accepting my offer!), even though my free throw shooting was not the cause of the accepted offer.

In 1948, Skinner (1948a) was able to train superstitious responding in hungry pigeons by reinforcing them with food every 15 seconds, regardless of what they were doing. Skinner reasoned that when reinforcement occurred, it would be paired with whatever response the pigeons had just performed. Although this response had not caused the reinforcer, the fact that the reinforcer was delivered after the response would be sufficient to strengthen the response. Then, the next time food was delivered, the pigeons would be more likely than before to be engaging in that particular behavior, thereby strengthening it even further. This chain of events would continue until each individual pigeon would be spending most of its time engaging in its own particular superstitious behavior. This is exactly what happened for six out of eight pigeons. One pigeon repeatedly pecked at the floor, another turned counterclockwise, another tossed

Fixed-interval reinforcement schedule A partial reinforcement schedule that reinforces the first response after a specific number of nonreinforced responses

Variable-interval reinforcement schedule A partial reinforcement schedule that reinforces the first response after a variable time interval has elapsed

Superstitious behavior A behavior learned simply because it happened to be followed by a reinforcer, even though this behavior was not the cause of the reinforcer

What type of reinforcement schedule does the U.S. Postal Service have you on regarding your daily mail delivery?

its head about, and so on. Subsequent research has found that some of the behaviors Skinner observed in the pigeons are instinctive responses that pigeons make in preparation for food, and thus are not examples of superstitious behavior. Nevertheless, Skinner's initial reasoning bears repeating: When you are accidentally reinforced after engaging in a particular behavior, you may come to associate that desirable outcome with the preceding behavior and thus begin performing superstitious actions in the belief that this will help you receive another reinforcer.

Athletes and sports fans often engage in superstitious behavior during athletic events (Burger & Lynn, 2005). For example, athletes wear lucky socks, avoid unlucky numbers, and engage in other forms of superstitious behavior in the hopes of gaining a competitive edge (Valeo & Beyerstein, 2008). Likewise, fans that sit in particular seats just before a game-winning play may seek out that chair while watching future sporting events to "help" their team win. In all these instances, none of these actions did anything to cause the favorable outcomes; the rewards followed them purely by chance. Such instances of *accidental reinforcement* function as a partial reinforcement schedule for these people, strengthening the behavior preceding their rewards. In their minds, these actions may have caused the rewards, so it makes sense to engage in these rituals whenever they want to secure the same rewards.

Although superstitious actions do not directly influence the delivery of a reinforcer, they may sometimes have the indirect benefit of helping the superstitious person cope with anxiety and stress (Schippers & Van Lange, 2006). That is, by engaging in a ritual that you believe increases your chance of achieving success, you may gain a sense of personal control over the situation, which may help you perform better. For example, although shooting 10 consecutive free throws did not magically cause girls to go out with me, it may have lowered my anxiety level to the point where I could read my prepared script without stammering and thus come across as more poised than desperate!

The calming effect of superstitious behavior may partly explain why nearly 70 percent of college students admit to engaging in some type of superstitious action before taking an exam (Gallagher & Lewis, 2001). I was one of those "70 percent" in college. On the day of an exam, I would not take a shower lest I "wash off" the knowledge gained while studying. I usually did well on those exams, which reinforced my nonshowering behavior. Can you think of any of your own past or present behavior that might fit Skinner's definition of superstitious behavior? Does this behavior serve a useful function for you, or does it hinder your daily routine?

6.2f *Shaping Reinforces Closer Approximations to Desired Behavior.*

The reinforcement techniques discussed thus far describe how you can increase the frequency of behaviors once they occur. Suppose, however, you want to train a dog to stand on its hind legs and dance, or teach a child to write the alphabet or play the piano. These behaviors are unlikely to occur spontaneously, so instead you must employ an operant conditioning procedure that Skinner called **shaping**, or the *method of successive approximations* (Peterson, 2004).

Shaping In operant conditioning, the process of teaching a new behavior by reinforcing closer and closer approximations to the desired behavior; also known as the *method of successive approximations*

INFO-BIT

In 1948, Skinner's passions for writing and improving the world through behaviorism combined as he wrote a novel, *Walden Two* (Skinner, 1948b). In this novel, people band together and use principles of behaviorism to create a utopian society. Later, in 1967, a group of people in Twin Oaks, Virginia, founded a community based on Skinner's novel. The community is still in existence today, although in a form somewhat different from the scientifically run community Skinner conceived.

In shaping, you teach a new behavior by reinforcing behaviors that are closer and closer approximations to the desired behavior (see Table 6-2). For example, when my brother Randy taught his son Spencer to write the letter "Q," Randy first identified what Spencer was initially capable of writing. Spencer's first attempt at the letter "Q" was a circular scrawl. Randy reinforced this response with praise. After several similar reinforced responses, Randy next raised the criterion for reinforcement to a circle with any straight line, then to a circle with an intersecting straight line placed anywhere; finally, he reinforced Spencer only when he drew the correct "Q" letter. During this shaping process, when Spencer encountered difficulty at any point, Randy lowered the criterion for reinforcement to a level at which his son could perform successfully. Like Randy, all of us use praise and other reinforcers to shape successively closer approximations of desirable behavior in others. Whether it's teaching people to correct their tennis serve or improve their grammar, shaping will figure prominently in the learning process. In Chapter 12, we will examine how shaping is used in therapy

TABLE 6-2   **How to Shape Behavior**
1. Identify what the respondent can do now.
2. Identify the desired behavior.
3. Identify potential reinforcers in the respondent's environment.
4. Break the desired behavior into small substeps to be mastered sequentially.
5. Move the respondent from the entry behavior to the desired behavior by successively reinforcing each approximation to the desired behavior.

Source: Adapted from Galanter, 1962.

to change maladaptive thoughts and behavior, thus allowing people to lead more normal and happier lives.

Using shaping techniques, Skinner trained pigeons to play Ping-Pong with their beaks and to bowl in a miniature alley. During World War II, he even devised a plan to train pigeons to guide missiles toward enemy targets! Thankfully for the pigeons, this plan was never implemented. However, two former students of Skinner, Keller and Marion Breland, went into business training animals for advertising and entertainment purposes. "Priscilla, the Fastidious Pig," for example, was trained to push a shopping cart past a display case and place the sponsor's product into her cart. Today, when you go to a circus or marine park and see elephants balancing on one leg or sea lions waving "hello" to you with their flippers, you are seeing the results of shaping.

Behavior psychologists also use shaping to train monkeys to provide live-in help for people who are paralyzed, blind, or have some other physical disability. These specially trained monkeys can perform a variety of activities, including combing a person's hair, turning on lights and electronic devices, and retrieving food from the refrigerator.

Helping Hands: Monkey Helpers for the Disabled www.monkeyhelpers.org.

The operant conditioning technique of shaping is used to train monkeys to help people with disabilities live in their own homes. Here is monkey-helper Minnie assisting Craig with opening the fridge and fetching items that Craig asks for. These Capuchin monkeys are used because they have high intelligence and form a strong emotional bond with their human companions. It often takes up to two years of training for these monkeys to reliably perform the necessary help.

6.2g *Skinner Overlooked Genetic Predispositions and Cognitive Processes.*

As a traditional behaviorist, Skinner focused on observable stimulus-response relationships and overlooked the impact that genetic predispositions and cognitive processes have on learning (Kirsch et al., 2004). Therefore, it became the task of other investigators to test and revise aspects of operant conditioning that related to these two factors.

Biological Constraints on Learning

One of the early assumptions underlying operant conditioning was that animals could be trained to emit any response that they were physically capable of making. However, as with classical conditioning, it was soon learned that an animal's biology could restrict its capacity for operant conditioning. Remember the animal trainers Keller and Marion Breland? Although they could train pigs to push shopping carts past display cases and raccoons to dunk basketballs in hoops, they could not train these animals to reliably deposit silver dollars into a piggy bank (Breland & Breland, 1961). Instead, the pigs threw the coins onto the ground and pushed them about, while the raccoons in the experiment continually rubbed the coins between their paws. Both behaviors illustrate how species-specific behavior patterns can interfere with operant conditioning, a genetic constraint that the Brelands called **instinctive drift** (Breland & Breland, 1961). Through evolution, pigs have developed a foraging behavior pattern of rooting for food in the ground with their snouts, whereas raccoons' foraging behavior involves washing food objects with their paws before eating them. These instincts inhibit learning new operant responses. Thus, just as certain species can be classically conditioned to learn certain responses more easily than others, operant learning is similarly constrained by an animal's evolutionary heritage.

Instinctive drift Species-specific behavior patterns that interfere with operant conditioning

Many of the studies that have explored the principles of classical conditioning and operant conditioning were performed on animals, such as rats and pigeons. How can scientists make generalizations about the way people behave based on these studies? Why not just study people?

Latent Learning

In the journey of discovery chronicled in this book, psychologists sometimes head down wrong paths due to misguided assumptions or failure to take notice of others' discoveries. Such was the case with Skinner. Despite evidence to the contrary, he died refusing to admit that an understanding of cognitive processes was necessary to fully understand human and animal behavior (Baars, 2003; Skinner, 1990). Yet, even as Skinner was developing his learning theory in the 1930s based on reinforced behavior, Edward Tolman's research (1922, 1932) with rats indicated that learning could occur without any reinforcement, something the theory of operant conditioning assumed was not possible.

In one of Tolman's experiments, one group of rats wandered through a maze once a day for ten days without being reinforced (Tolman & Honzik, 1930). Meanwhile, another group of rats spent the same amount of time in the maze, but the rats were reinforced with food at the "goal box" in each of their ten trials. These reinforced rats quickly learned to accurately run the maze to reach the food reward; the nonreinforced rats made many errors, however, suggesting little maze learning. On the 11th day, the nonreinforced rats were suddenly rewarded with food at the goal box, and they immediately thereafter made as few errors as the other rats. A third group of control rats that still received no food reward continued making many errors (see Figure 6-7).

How would you explain these findings using operant conditioning theory? You could not, because you would have to discuss cognition. However, not being constrained in this manner, Tolman suggested that, through experience, even the rats that had received no reinforcement had formed a *cognitive map*, or mental image, of the maze. They formed these maps prior to being conditioned, which meant that learning could occur without reinforcement. The learning of these rats remained hidden or *latent* because there was no incentive to engage in the behavior that would demonstrate it until that behavior was reinforced. Tolman called such learning that is not currently manifest in behavior and occurs without apparent reinforcement **latent learning**. Based on this and other research, psychologists now overwhelmingly believe that internal cognitive processes must be considered when explaining human, as well as animal, learning (Keith & McVery, 1988). Thus, despite Skinner's denials, operant conditioning is now thought to involve the cognitive *expectancy* that a given consequence will follow a given behavior.

Latent learning Learning that occurs without apparent reinforcement and is not demonstrated until sufficient reinforcement is provided

Learned Helplessness

In the 1960s, a group of researchers studying *avoidance learning,* caused by negative reinforcers, stumbled upon an interesting and puzzling phenomenon. In these experiments, a dog was placed on one side of a box with a wire grid floor. Next, a light

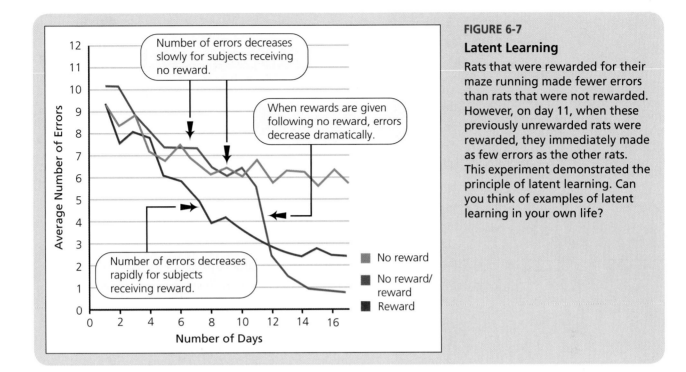

FIGURE 6-7

Latent Learning

Rats that were rewarded for their maze running made fewer errors than rats that were not rewarded. However, on day 11, when these previously unrewarded rats were rewarded, they immediately made as few errors as the other rats. This experiment demonstrated the principle of latent learning. Can you think of examples of latent learning in your own life?

came on signaling that the animal's feet would be shocked in ten seconds unless it jumped a hurdle and crossed to the other side of the box. This jumping response to the light was the avoidance learning, and the animals quickly learned to avoid the electrical shock by jumping the hurdle. In one experiment, prior to placing dogs in the box, the researchers strapped the dogs down in a harness and then classically conditioned them to fear the light by repeatedly pairing it with a mild electrical shock. To the researchers' surprise, when these dogs were later placed in the box, they did not learn the simple escape response but instead passively lay down, whimpered, and accepted the shock (Overmier & Leaf, 1965).

Why do you think exposure to inescapable shock later caused the dogs not to learn a very simple escape response? Two young graduate students, Martin Seligman and Steven Maier, offered an answer (Maier et al., 1969; Seligman & Maier, 1967). When shock is inescapable, dogs learn that they are helpless to exert control over the shock by means of any voluntary behaviors—and they expect this to be the case in the future. Because the dogs developed the *expectation* that their behavior had no effect on the outcome in the situation, they simply gave up trying to change the outcome. Seligman and Maier called this reaction **learned helplessness**. Here again, in contradiction to behaviorist theory, research demonstrated that mental processes play a significant role in learning.

In human studies, people exposed to uncontrollable bad events first feel angry and anxious. However, after repeated exposure to these uncontrollable events, they begin feeling helpless, and their anger and anxiety are replaced with depression (Bargai et al., 2007; Waschbusch et al., 2003). They have learned to think of themselves as helpless victims who are controlled by external forces. This type of learning explains why many unemployed workers who are repeatedly passed over for new jobs eventually give up. Unfortunately, by concluding that there is nothing they can do to change their job status, these individuals often overlook real employment possibilities. In Chapters 10 and 12, we will examine the role that learned helplessness plays in depression.

Learned helplessness The passive resignation produced by repeated exposure to aversive events that cannot be avoided

- The law of effect states that behavior becomes more or less likely based on the effect it has in producing desirable or undesirable consequences.

- Operant conditioning refers to learning in which behavior is strengthened if followed by reinforcement and weakened if followed by punishment.

- A reinforcer is any stimulus or event that increases the likelihood that the behavior preceding it will be repeated.

- Primary reinforcers are innately reinforcing because they satisfy some biological need, whereas secondary reinforcers are learned through classical conditioning.

- Positive reinforcers strengthen a response by presenting a positive stimulus, whereas negative reinforcers strengthen a response by removing an aversive stimulus.

- The opposite consequence of reinforcement is punishment.

- Positive punishers weaken a response by presenting an aversive stimulus, whereas negative punishers weaken a response by removing a positive stimulus.

- In order for punishment to effectively shape behavior, it must be promptly administered, relatively strong, and consistently applied.

- Continuous reinforcement results in the fastest learning, but partial reinforcement maintains vigorous responding for longer periods of time.

- Partial reinforcement schedules are defined in terms of the number of responses (ratio) or the passage of time (interval): fixed-ratio, variable-ratio, fixed-interval, or variable-interval.

- The steps in shaping behavior are as follows: (1) identify what the respondent can do, (2) identify the desired behavior, (3) identify potential reinforcers, (4) break desired behavior into small substeps, and (5) move the respondent to desired behavior by successively reinforcing each approximation to desired behavior.

- Due to accidental reinforcement, superstitious behavior may develop.

- As with classical conditioning, learning in operant conditioning is limited by an animal's evolutionary heritage.

- Cognitive processes must be taken into account in order to fully understand operant conditioning principles.

6.3 Observational Learning

Classical conditioning and operant conditioning are two ways in which we and other animals learn from experience. Both of these conditioning processes involve *direct* experience with desirable and undesirable outcomes. Yet, what about the learning that occurs without direct experience? Have you ever noticed that people and many animals learn by watching and imitating others? For example, by observing their mothers, jaguar cubs learn basic hunting techniques, as well as which prey are easiest to kill. Various bird species have also demonstrated their ability to learn by watching other birds perform specific actions (Akins et al., 2002; Baker, 2004). Similarly, today while shopping, I couldn't help but notice a mother with her son, who looked about four years of age. She was yelling at the top of her lungs, "How many times have I told you not to yell at people?!!! I've told you, YOU HAVE TO BE POLITE!!!" Where do you think the child learned his misbehavior?

6.3a   Learning Often Occurs by Observing Others' Behavior.

Just as nonreinforced learning cannot be explained within the framework of either classical or operant conditioning, neither can the fact that people and other animals learn simply through observing the behavior of others. Instead, a third form of learning, observational learning, must be introduced. **Observational learning** is learning by observing and imitating the behavior of others. These others whom we observe and imitate are called *models* because they teach us how to play social roles. Observational learning helps children learn how to behave in their families and cultures, and it also helps adults learn the skills necessary for career success.

Observational learning is the central feature of Albert Bandura's (1986) **social learning theory**, which contends that people learn social behaviors mainly through observation and cognitive processing of information, rather than through direct experience. According to this theory, when you watch others engage in some activity with which you are not familiar, a great deal of cognitive learning takes place before you yourself perform the behavior. For instance, consistent with the law of effect discussed earlier, you are most likely to imitate a model whose actions you see rewarded, and you are least likely to imitate behavior that is punished. This observational learning mechanism—in which you learn the consequences of an action by observing its consequences for someone else—is known as *vicarious conditioning*. As you can see, the only difference between this and the conditioning that occurs in operant learning is that in vicarious learning, the behavior of others is being reinforced or punished rather than your own.

A survey of 750 teenagers in Los Angeles indicated that having a role model or a mentor has a positive influence on the lives of adolescents (Yancey et al., 2002). In this study, a little over half the respondents reported that they had a role model whom they wanted to be like, with White teens (64 percent) being more likely to have role models than African American teens (53 percent) or Latino teens (54 percent). The most popular role models were parents and other relatives (32 percent); almost as many teenagers, however, identified media figures such as athletes, singers, or musicians as their role models (28 percent). Girls most often identified people whom they personally knew as role models, whereas boys were more likely to identify sports stars and other media figures.

The teenagers who identified one or more important role models in their lives earned higher grades in school and had more positive self-esteem than those who did not have a role model. Among the minority adolescents, those who had no role models had the lowest levels of ethnic identity development, whereas those who had role models they personally knew had the highest levels of ethnic identity development. As discussed in Chapter 3, Section 3.5d, higher levels of ethnic identity development not only promote a strong sense of ethnic pride that protects minority youth from internalizing negative ethnic stereotypes into their self-concepts but also help people pursue mainstream goals and participate in mainstream life. These findings, along with those of other studies (Bryant & Zimmerman, 2003; Flouri & Buchanan, 2003), demonstrate the important "role" that role models play in shaping the behavior and self-esteem of children and adolescents.

Observational learning
Learning a behavior by observing and imitating the behavior of others (models)

Social leaning theory A theory contending that people learn social behaviors mainly through observation and cognitive processing of information

Albert Bandura, b. 1925.

Photo courtesy of Albert Bandura

INFO-BIT Research suggests that observing peers who smoke influences adolescents' decisions to start smoking (Hawkins, Catalano, & Miller, 1992). Which teens do you think are most susceptible to such influence? The answer is, those who are "outsiders," meaning that they have not yet been accepted into a teen group they desire to join. If the members of the group smoke, the outsiders imitate these teens and begin smoking. Can you think of ways that this knowledge could be used in developing effective antismoking ads for teenagers?

6.3b *Mirror Neurons Play a Role in Observational Learning.*

Humans have an inborn tendency to imitate one another; and such imitation helps to form emotional bonds as well as to facilitate learning. PET scan and EEG recordings of people's brains while they observe another person performing an action find that similar neural circuits are firing in the observers' brains as are firing in the brains of those who are carrying out the action (Iacoboni, 2007). These specialized neural circuits located in the frontal lobes of the cerebral cortex are called *mirror neurons* (Gallese et al., 2007; Oberman et al., 2007). The firing of these mirror neurons probably does not directly cause imitative behavior, but the mirror neurons may serve as the basis of imitation learning. Adults and children with autism have trouble imitating other people's actions, and research suggests that they may have deficits in their mirror neuron circuits (Bernier & Dawson, 2009).

Mirror neurons not only play a role in imitating others' actions but also appear to play a role in *understanding* those actions—that is, in inferring the intentions of actions (Rizzolatti, 2005). Understanding other people's actions greatly facilitates learning because it informs the observer *why* others are doing what they are doing. Such understanding makes it easier for people to later transfer what they have learned in one context to another context.

Mirror neurons in the frontal lobes of the cerebral cortex appear to play a critical role in observational learning.

6.3c *We Often Learn Aggressive Behavior Through Observation.*

Research suggests that widespread media coverage of a violent incident is often followed by a sudden increase in similar violent crimes (Phillips, 1986). Apparently, reading and watching news accounts of violence can trigger some people to "copy" the aggression. This dangerous manifestation of observational learning has been dramatically illustrated in the rash of shootings at elementary and secondary schools since the 1999 tragedy at Columbine High School in Littleton, Colorado, which left 17 people dead and many wounded. What insights do you think psychology can bring to bear on this type of learning?

Bandura's Research on Observational Learning of Aggression

The first set of experiments demonstrating the power of observational learning in eliciting aggression were the famous *Bobo doll* studies (Bandura et al. 1961) described in Chapter 1, Section 1.3e. Likewise, in another classic study conducted by Albert Bandura and his coworkers (1963), young children watched a short film in which an aggressive adult model named Rocky takes food and toys from someone named Johnny. In one condition, children saw Johnny respond by punishing Rocky, while in another condition, children saw Rocky sing, "Hi ho, hi ho, it's off to play I go," as he pranced off with Johnny's belongings in a sack. Not surprisingly, those children who saw Rocky rewarded for his aggression behaved more aggressively than those who saw Rocky punished.

Although these findings might leave you with the impression that aggressive models who are punished have little negative impact on children's later behavior, this is not really the case. The research demonstrates that children are less likely to *imitate* the actions of punished aggressors. Does this mean these children fail to learn the aggressive behavior, or does it mean their awareness of punishment simply inhibits the expression of these behaviors?

To answer this question, in one study Bandura (1965) offered children a reward if they could imitate the aggressive behavior of the model they had previously observed. Every single one of the participants could mimic the model's aggressive actions, even those who had seen the punished model. Thus, simply observing someone being punished for aggression does not prevent the *learning* of aggression—it simply inhibits its *expression* in certain circumstances.

Bandura (1979) believes children observe and learn aggression through many avenues, but the three principal ones are the family, the culture, and the media. First, in families where adults use violence, children grow up being much more likely to use it themselves (Herrenkohl et al., 1983). Second, in communities where aggression is considered to be a sign of manhood, learning aggressive behaviors is eagerly and consciously transmitted from generation to generation, especially among males (Cohen & Nisbett, 1977). Finally, the media—principally television and the movies—unceasingly convey images of violence and mayhem to virtually all segments of society on a daily basis (Gerbner & Signorielli, 1990). Do you think such viewing can produce antisocial behavior?

Violence Depicted on Television and in Films

Numerous experimental studies indicate that exposure to media violence significantly enhances children's and adolescents' aggression (Liebert & Sprafkin, 1988; Wood et al., 1991). Further, longitudinal research conducted in a number of countries, including the United States, indicates that the early TV habits of children significantly predicts their later aggressive behavior, even after statistically controlling for their initial aggressiveness. What appears to influence children's later aggressiveness is their *identification* with aggressive TV and movie characters. That is, children who watch a lot of media violence when they are young and identify with aggressive media characters are most likely to become highly aggressive later in life (Huesmann & Hasbrouck, 1996; Huesmann & Miller, 1994).

Beyond the learning of aggressive behavior through the repeated observation of violence, another possible negative effect of such observation is emotional *blunting* or desensitization, which means simply becoming indifferent to aggressive outbursts. In a series of experiments, for example, children who had just watched a violent movie were less concerned when they observed other youngsters fighting and were slower to stop the fight than a control group of children who had not seen the movie. Similar desensitization effects were also observed in college students who watched a lot of violent TV programs. When their physiological responses were monitored, the heavy consumers had the lowest levels of arousal when observing both fictional and realistic aggression (Bartholow et al., 2006). These findings suggest that people who are exposed to a lot of media violence become habituated to violence in other areas of their lives (Carnagey et al., 2007). Being less anxious and bothered by aggressive behavior, these individuals may be less inhibited than others in responding aggressively when facing social confrontations.

Violence Depicted in Music Lyrics and Music Videos

Is there any scientific evidence that the violence often depicted in music videos and in music lyrics increases aggressive tendencies and behavior? Several studies have examined this question. In one study involving young African American men, exposure to violent rap music videos increased endorsement of violent behavior in response to a hypothetical conflict situation (Johnson et al., 1995). Similarly, college students shown rock music videos containing violence subsequently displayed a greater acceptance of antisocial behavior compared with students in a control group (Hansen & Hansen, 1990). Regarding the effects of music lyrics, numerous studies have found consistent evidence that songs with violent lyrics increase aggression-related thoughts and feelings of hostility in listeners (Anderson et al., 2003; Brummert-Lennings & Warburton, 2011). Overall, the implication of these findings is that watching and/or listening to violent music causes people to not only be more accepting of antisocial behavior but also creates an emotional mindset for them that makes aggressive responses more likely.

Does exposure to violent music lyrics actually increase aggressive behavior? Peter Fischer and Tobias Greitemeyer (2006) addressed this question in a series of studies in which male and female participants in Germany listened to popular songs containing men-hating lyrics, women-hating lyrics, or neutral song lyrics. After listening to the selected songs, participants completed various psychological tasks, including some that measured aggressive attitudes and cognitions. When the study was supposedly completed, participants were asked to briefly help assign instructions to people in an unrelated study. The experimenter explained that this other study required people to stick their left hand in freezing cold ice water while they completed intellectual tasks, and they were further told that keeping the hand in ice water could be very painful, especially when this procedure lasted longer than 25 seconds. The participants' task was to decide how long two specific individuals—one female and one male—would hold their hand in the ice water. The assigned times given to the female and male were the dependent measures of aggression in the study.

Results indicated that male participants who listened to women-hating song lyrics not only reported more aggressive thoughts but also later behaved more aggressively to the female target person, assigning her significantly longer times of ice water treatment than did men who listened to neutral or men-hating lyrics. Similarly, women who listened to men-hating song lyrics reported more aggressive cognitions and later assigned significantly longer times of ice water treatment to the male target person than did women who listened to neutral or women-hating lyrics. Overall, these findings provide some evidence that exposure to violent music provokes aggressive thoughts in listeners and increases their aggressive responses toward people who are similar to the targeted victims in the music lyrics.

Of course, the findings from these various studies do not mean that most people who regularly view or listen to media violence will begin terrorizing their schools, neighborhoods, and work settings. The relationship between viewing media violence and behaving aggressively is by no means perfect. It also does not mean that media violence is a primary cause of aggression in society. However, while exposure to such staged violence is not the primary cause of aggression, it may be the one factor that is easiest to control and reduce (Hamilton, 1998; Wilson et al., 1998).

6.3d *Positive Social Modeling Can Counteract the Negative Influence of Aggressive Models.*

Living in a culture in which violent images saturate the media, what can you do as an individual to teach children not to imitate such behavior? First, remember that just as destructive models can teach people how to act aggressively, social learning theorists contend that nonaggressive models can urge observers to exercise restraint in the face of provocation. In an experiment supporting this claim, research participants who watched a nonaggressive model exhibit restraint in administering shocks to a "victim" in a learning experiment were subsequently less aggressive than those who had observed an aggressive model (Baron & Kepner, 1970).

Besides being reduced by nonaggressive models, aggression also can be controlled if an authority figure condemns the behavior of aggressive individuals. For example, research demonstrates that when a child watches violence on television in the presence of an adult who condemns the violence, the child is less likely to later imitate this aggression (Hicks, 1968; Horton & Santogrossi, 1978). This bit of knowledge was not lost on my wife and me in raising our own children. On more than one occasion while watching television with our daughters when they were preschoolers, the screen would suddenly erupt with violent images so quickly that we did not have time to change the channel. Each time this happened, we condemned the violence. Later, while we were watching a Looney Toons cartoon, Elmer Fudd pulled out a shotgun and blew the head off Daffy Duck. Without missing a beat, Lillian, who was four years old at the time, turned to us and said, "Boy, that wasn't very nice, was it? People shouldn't be so mean."

Shutterstock

Research demonstrates that the negative effects of television violence can be reduced if adults condemn the violence when it occurs. However, for this strategy to work, adults must monitor children's television viewing and take the time to watch the shows with the children.

Finally, an essential ingredient in reducing aggressive responses is to diminish exposure to violence. A number of studies find that when children spend less time watching violent television shows and playing violent videogames their aggressive behavior is significantly reduced. For example, one study examined third- and fourth-grade students at two comparable schools over a six-month period (Robinson et al., 2001). In one of the schools, TV and videogame exposure was reduced by one-third when students and parents were encouraged to engage in alternative forms of home entertainment, while in the other school no effort was made to reduce exposure. The researchers found that children at the intervention school were subsequently less aggressive on the playground than students at the control school, especially those students who had been initially rated as most aggressive by their classmates.

Journey of Discovery

Why are the studies on observational learning now mostly based on human populations? Why does observational learning make evolutionary sense for human beings?

- Observational learning refers to learning by observing and imitating the behavior of others.

- Mirror neurons in the brain provide humans with an inborn tendency to imitate one another, and such imitation helps to form emotional bonds as well as to facilitate learning.

- Adolescents who have role models are more academically successful and have more positive self-esteem than those who have no role models.

- Watching violence on television may encourage children to become more aggressive.

- The negative effects of observing aggression can be controlled by having an authority figure condemn the aggression.

PSYCHOLOGICAL
applications

Learning How to Exercise Self-Control in Your Academic and Personal Life

- Do you have trouble getting out of bed in the morning to attend an early class?

- Do you procrastinate in studying for exams and end up cramming the night before?

- Do you tend to spend money quickly, thereby leaving yourself with little to live on until your next pay period?

- Are you having difficulty exercising on a regular basis?

- Would you like to stop smoking or cut down on your consumption of alcohol?

If you answered yes to any of these questions, the bad news is that you are struggling with issues of self-control. The good news, however, is that what you learned in this chapter can help you regain control over those troubled aspects of your academic and personal life. In most self-control issues, problems arise because we choose *short-term reinforcers* that provide immediate gratification instead of choosing *long-term reinforcers* that provide delayed gratification. For instance, we sacrifice a chance at a good grade at the end of the semester for the luxury of getting an extra hour's sleep each class session. Likewise, we choose to continue smoking because doing so gives us an immediate nicotine high, even though smoking significantly lowers our life expectancy. Why do short-term reinforcers have greater incentive value than long-term reinforcers?

The Relative Value of Short-Term and Long-Term Reinforcers

Let's consider this question by examining the problem of early-morning class attendance. When resolving to change your habit of skipping class, you consider the incentive value of both the short-term and the long-term reinforcers. In most cases, such resolutions are made when both reinforcers are relatively distant, such as just before you go to bed the night before class. At that time, the incentive value of getting a good grade is usually greater than the value of getting extra sleep, so you set your alarm for an early rising. However, as the availability of a reinforcer gets closer, its incentive value increases (Ainslie, 1975). Thus, when the alarm interrupts your sleep in the morning, the short-term reinforcer—extra sleep—is now immediately available, while the long-term reinforcer—a good grade—is still distant. Now it will be much harder to maintain your resolve and forgo the short-term reinforcement of extra sleep. If the thought of staying in your warm, comfy bed has greater incentive value than getting a good grade, you will break your nighttime resolution.

Strategies to Modify Troublesome Behavior

Now that you understand the process of shifting incentive values, what can you do to counteract the allure of these resolution-breaking short-term reinforcers? You can adopt the following six strategies to modify your problem behavior and regain self-control.

1. *Set realistic goals.* Punishment weakens the behavior it follows. Because failure to reach your goals will punish your efforts, it is important that you set goals that you can realistically achieve.

2. *Shape your behavior.* As previously noted, the delay in receiving a long-term reinforcement can weaken your resolve to change your troublesome behavior. One strategy to increase the incentive value of the long-term reinforcer is to shape your behavior. That is, give yourself modest reinforcers for achieving successive steps toward your ultimately desired goal. For example, after going for a week without missing class, reward yourself by going to a movie or spending time with friends. Similarly, if you were smoking a pack a day and wanted to stop, during the first week, you might reward yourself if you smoked only a half pack per day. Remember, a reinforcer strengthens the behavior it follows, not the behavior it precedes. Reinforce yourself only *after* you perform the desired behavior, not before. If you reward yourself before attending class or before lowering your cigarette consumption, you are not reinforcing the desired behavior.

3. *Chart your progress.* To give yourself feedback on how well you are progressing toward meeting your goals, keep a chart of your progress. For example, to support your efforts to stop smoking, the chart would track how many cigarettes you smoked each day. Place the chart in a place where you will regularly see it. Charting your progress in this manner will bring into play both positive and negative reinforcement: You will praise yourself after reaching your daily goals, and you will work harder to remove the guilt—a negative reinforcer—that follows a day in which you fail to meet your goals.

4. *Identify environmental cues that trigger undesirable behavior.* Environmental stimuli can serve as signals that we are about to have access to certain desirable, yet harmful, situations or substances. For example, if you regularly smoked after meals or when in taverns, those situations will likely trigger your urge to "light up" during the time you are trying to quit smoking. If you can identify these environmental cues, you can try to avoid putting yourself in those situations while you are trying to change your behavior (stay away from taverns for a while). If you cannot avoid the tempting situations (as will be the case in eating meals), take steps to countercondition yourself. Instead of smoking after meals, have a favorite dessert or beverage.

5. *Keep focused on the long-term reinforcer.* As previously stated, the undesirable short-term reinforcers are generally more salient than the desirable long-term reinforcers. Thus, when tempted by these more salient and troublesome reinforcers, take advantage of the cognitive aspects of learning and selectively focus on the long-term reinforcers. For example, instead of succumbing to temptation and grabbing an extra hour of sleep, imagine how good you will feel at the end of the semester when you receive a good grade in your course. Such imagining can subjectively close the gap between the present and the future goal, increasing its incentive value in the present.

6. *Select desirable role models.* Observational learning teaches us that we can learn by observing and imitating the behavior of others. Just as you may have acquired your undesirable behavior by imitating others, you can change your behavior by identifying people who possess traits and skills you desire. By observing these individuals, you not only will learn how to behave differently but also will receive inspiration by seeing someone successfully doing what you ultimately want to do.

Suggested Websites

Neuroscience: Learning and Memory

http://www.brembs.net/learning

This website presents information describing and distinguishing between classical and operant conditioning principles.

Animal Training at Sea World

http://www.seaworld.org/infobooks/Training/home.html

This Sea World website contains information about animal behavior and the training of marine animals at Sea World.

Albert Bandura

http://www.emory.edu/EDUCATION/mfp/bandurabio.html

This website at Emory University provides a biography of Albert Bandura, an overview of his theory of observational learning, and his research on modeling violence.

Key Terms

Chapter Review

Review Questions

1. The person(s) associated with classical conditioning is(are) _____.
   a. B. F. Skinner
   b. Ivan Pavlov
   c. John Watson
   d. Martin Seligman
   e. b and c

2. Which of the following is not an example of higher-order conditioning?
   a. A perfume sparks romantic feelings.
   b. A new acquaintance likes you because she knew and liked your sibling.
   c. Upon entering a room to take an exam, you experience test anxiety.
   d. You dislike Pringles™ potato chips because you once got sick from eating too many.
   e. None of the above

3. Which of the following was missing from the experiment on Little Albert B.?
   a. extinction
   b. stimulus generalization
   c. punishment
   d. all of the above
   e. a and c

4. Which of the following is true?
   a. Classical conditioning involves "mindless" automatic learning.
   b. Humans are passive in learning conditioned responses.
   c. Learning occurs when the conditioned stimulus comes after or at the same time as the unconditioned stimulus.
   d. b and c
   e. None of the above

5. Which of the following is true?
   a. Animals do not differ in what responses can be conditioned.
   b. Associations can be conditioned between all stimulus and response situations.
   c. a and b
   d. None of the above

6. Which of the following can be used to protect endangered species from predators?
   a. conditioned taste aversion
   b. extinction
   c. spontaneous recovery
   d. b and a
   e. None of the above

7. Which of these is true of operant conditioning?
   a. Behavior is determined by stimuli that precede it.
   b. Associations between behavior and consequences are learned.
   c. Behavior is largely goal oriented.
   d. b and c
   e. All of the above

8. Which of the following would likely be a reinforcer for students to study more?
   a. money
   b. less homework
   c. studying with someone you enjoy being with
   d. good grades
   e. All of the above

9. Which of the following is a primary reinforcer?
   a. food
   b. water
   c. warmth
   d. sex
   e. All of the above

10. Which type of reinforcement has the greatest long-term effects?
    a. continuous reinforcement
    b. fixed-ratio schedule
    c. variable-ratio schedule
    d. punishment
    e. None of the above

11. What is the term for something that weakens behavior by presenting an aversive stimulus?
    a. negative reinforcement
    b. shaping
    c. punishment
    d. avoidance behavior
    e. None of the above

12. Which of the following is a drawback of punishment?
    a. It doesn't teach new desirable forms of behavior.
    b. It can lead to more aggression.
    c. It encourages aggressive behavior.
    d. All of the above
    e. None of the above

13. Which of the following is true about B. F. Skinner?
    a. He assumed that latent learning was not possible.
    b. He overlooked the impact of inborn biology on learning.
    c. He elaborated on the law of effect.
    d. He was named Burrhus Frederick Skinner.
    e. All of the above

14. Which of the following applies to social learning theory?
    a. It contends that people learn social behavior through direct experience.
    b. It is inconsistent with the law of effect.
    c. It requires cognition.
    d. All of the above
    e. None of the above

15. Which of the following is true?
    a. Media are the primary cause of aggression in children.
    b. Observing someone being punished for behaving aggressively does not prevent learning aggression.
    c. Less time watching violent TV diminishes aggressive behavior.
    d. b and c
    e. All of the above

16. By applying the learning principles in Chapter 6, determine which of the following would be helpful in modifying troublesome behavior.
    a. Identifying environmental cues that trigger undesirable behavior.
    b. Keeping focused on long-term reinforcers.
    c. Selecting desirable role models.
    d. Charting your progress.
    e. All of the above

Chapter Seven

Memory

Chapter Outline

Psychological Applications: *Improving Everyday Memory*

At the Russian newspaper where reporter Solomon Shereshevskii worked, he was surprised to learn that his editor was upset with him for never writing down assignments. Shereshevskii informed his editor that he didn't need to write down assignments because he remembered everything people told him, word for word. Didn't everybody have this ability, he naively asked?

Following that innocent question, Shereshevskii soon found himself in the office of psychologist Alexander Luria, who proceeded to test his memory. Over the years, Luria discovered there was virtually no limit to what this reporter could remember. For example, he could memorize a list of 70 words in four minutes. Although this feat is not that unusual, what was extraordinary was that whenever Shereshevskii created an image in his mind, it became so vivid that he never forgot it.

God gave us memories that we might have roses in December.

—J.M. Barrie, Scottish playwright, 1860–1937

Wikimedia Commons

Russian psychologist Alexander Luria's study of reporter Solomon Shereshevskii's memory abilities led to important insights into how we learn and remember information.

Fifteen years after memorizing this word list, Luria asked him if he could recall it. Shereshevskii closed his eyes, paused, and then replied, "Yes, yes … this was a series you gave me once when we were in your apartment … You were sitting at the table and I in the rocking chair … You were wearing a gray suit and you looked at me like this … Now I can see you saying …," and then he recited the words in the exact order they were read to him so long ago (Luria, 1968).

While Shereshevskii stands out because of his amazing memory, "Ben" is noteworthy for his limited ability to remember information and events. Ben, a middle-aged businessman, happened to sit next to me during a plane trip and noticed an early draft of this memory chapter lying on my lap. "You know," he said nonchalantly, "I have no short-term memory." With that attention-grabbing opening line, Ben

Shutterstock

You store a great amount of information in memory, but how does this information get into memory? How is it stored and organized? Can you "lose" this information? These are some of the important memory questions researchers try to answer.

proceeded to tell me that four years ago he suffered damage to his short-term memory when he received insufficient oxygen during minor knee surgery. Now he has to repeat information many times before he

can remember it. If he doesn't repeat information over and over, or if he doesn't write it down immediately, it will disappear. By his own admission, Ben's moods are now much more even-keeled than before the accident. Why? Because, when he does experience emotions such as happiness, sadness, or anger, they last only until his attention is distracted and then quickly fade from consciousness, and from memory.

Despite this substantial memory handicap, Ben recently became the public relations director for a major industrial manufacturing firm. Perhaps what is most surprising about Ben's new job situation is that no one there is apparently aware of his disorder. When he was first hired, it took him a number of months to memorize the names of his office staff; and he still occasionally calls the company president "Prez" and the chief financial officer "Chief" when their names escape him. Thus far, Ben's bosses have interpreted this informality as simply an example of his winning personality.

Ben and Shereshevskii represent opposite ends of the memory spectrum. In

Memory The mental process by which information is encoded and stored in the brain, and later retrieved

most of us, **memory**—the mental process by which information is encoded and stored in the brain, and later retrieved—operates somewhere between these two extremes (Benjamin, 2006; Bransford et al., 2008). There is a close link between the subject matter of Chapter 6, learning, and the subject matter of this chapter (Healy, 2005). Memory involves the retention of what we learn. The lesson learned from Ben's current predicament is that without a well-functioning memory, learning becomes extremely problematic.

How extensive is your memory system? Well, by the time you reach your early 70s, you will have memories that would completely fill the hard drives of about eight laptop computers. That's impressive. Of course, a good deal of the information you store in memory is not very impressive, or useful. For example, have you memorized the theme songs from some very bad television shows? Despite the fact that some of your memories seem silly, you could not live a normal life without the ability to interpret, store, and later recall your life experiences.

7.1 The Nature of Memory

Until the late 1950s, most psychologists viewed memory as a single system. This perspective was largely due to the influence of behaviorism, in which remembering something was conceived of as simply due to the strength of stimulus-response pairings (see Chapter 6, Section 6.2a). If a person or animal consistently responded in the same way to the same stimulus, this meant they had formed a strong memory for the response. According to behaviorists, this single conditioning process was the extent of memory. Discussing unobservable events, such as cognition, was considered off-limits to the science of psychology. Then, because of technological advances outside the discipline, as well as scientific discoveries within, psychologists dramatically changed their views of memory (Emilien et al., 2004).

7.1a The Computer's Information-Processing System Has Been a Useful Model for Human Memory.

The event outside of psychology that served as a catalyst in changing psychologists' thinking on memory was the advent of the computer age. Like us, computers have memories. As psychologists adopted terms and concepts from computer science, they began to view memory as a kind of information-processing system that depended on three basic processes (Mayer, 2012; Norman et al., 2007). According to this **information-processing model**, in both computer and human memory, information goes through three basic processes: an input or *encoding* process, a *storage* process, and a *retrieval* process.

Information Processing

Encoding refers to the first memory process, in which incoming information is organized and transformed so that it can be entered into memory (Bauml & Aslan, 2006; Goh & Lu, 2012). In the computer, typing on the keyboard transforms information into electronic language. In the brain, sensory information from our surroundings is transformed into neural language in the various sensory cortexes. For example, when presented with the sentence "Sporminore is a town in northern Italy," if you encode the image of the letters as they appear here, you are using *visual encoding*; and the information is represented in memory as a picture. If you encode the sound of the words as if they were spoken, you are using *acoustic encoding*; and the information is represented in memory as a sequence of sounds. Finally, if you encode the fact that this sentence is referring to the birthplace of your grandfather (which for me is true), you are using *semantic encoding*; and the information is represented in memory by its meaning to you (Hargreaves et al., 2012). The type of encoding used—visual, acoustic, or semantic—can influence what is remembered. As you will discover in Section 7.1d, semantic encoding yields much better memories than visual or acoustic encoding. However, because semantic encoding involves the processing the general, underlying meaning of information, it often ignores specific details.

The second memory process is **storage**, which involves entering and maintaining information in memory for a period of time. Just as the computer can store information for either brief periods (in random access memory) or indefinitely (on a floppy or hard disk), we too have similar memory capabilities. The human memory systems that store information for relatively brief time periods are known as *sensory memory* and *short-term memory*, while the more permanent system is known as *long-term memory*.

Information-processing model A memory model concerning the sequential processing and use of information, involving encoding, storage, and retrieval

Encoding The first memory process, in which information is organized and transformed so it can be entered into memory

Storage The second memory process, in which information is entered and maintained in memory for a period of time

Retrieval The third memory process, which involves recovering stored information from memory so it can be used

Finally, the third memory process is **retrieval**, which involves recovering stored information from memory so it can be used (Kizilirmak et al., 2012). In both computers and humans, this means pulling information out of long-term memory storage and placing it into a much smaller working memory. To demonstrate for yourself how the retrieval process works, recall the name of your best friend from sixth grade. In doing so, perhaps memories of your hometown come to mind, along with images of your sixth-grade classroom and activities you engaged in with this person. Each of these memories can serve as a stimulus to help you remember your best friend's name. When the correct memories come to mind, you retrieve the name.

In a nutshell, these are the three memory processes. Encoding gets information into memory, storage keeps it in, and retrieval takes it out, just like a computer. Although the computer is by far the most popular metaphor for our memory system, as already noted, it is not a perfect metaphor. Indeed, the human brain often does not operate like a typical computer. For instance, computers are based on algorithms (see Chapter 8, Section 8.2b)—they process information sequentially, or *serially,* working on only one stream of data at a time. However, the human brain is much more complex and can process many kinds of information simultaneously, in a *parallel* fashion. Thus, the computer may not be the last and best metaphor for the human mind, but as of this writing, it is still the most convenient and popular metaphor for organizing the major findings on memory. With this caveat in mind, let us examine how psychologists, operating within this information-processing perspective, began questioning old assumptions about how we form memories.

The Identification of Three Memory Systems

A series of studies in the 1950s indicated that if people are distracted from rehearsing a small amount of information given to them, in a matter of seconds this information is often completely forgotten (Brown, 1958; Peterson & Peterson, 1959). In trying to make sense of these findings, researchers "remembered" the findings from one of the earliest memory studies. In 1885, German psychologist Hermann Ebbinghaus (1850–1909), using himself as his own subject, studied a list of nonsense syllables (such as BIW or SUW) and measured how many he later recalled. As illustrated in Figure 7-1, Ebbinghaus discovered that nonsense syllables near the beginning and end of the list were more easily remembered than the ones in the middle. The resulting U-shaped

FIGURE 7-1

The Memory Curve

Hermann Ebbinghaus (1913) found that memory is better for the first few and last few items in a string of nonsense syllables. These two memory effects were respectively called the *primacy effect* and the *recency effect*. In the 1950s, memory researchers argued that the primacy effect suggested the existence of a long-term memory system, while the recency effect suggested that there is a short-term memory system. What was the reasoning behind these assertions?

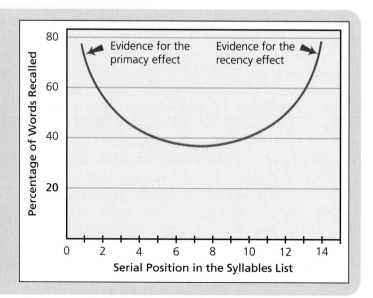

pattern was referred to as the *serial-position effect*, with the increased memory for items near the beginning called the **primacy effect** and the increased memory for the last few items called the **recency effect** (Castel, 2008; Duffy & Crawford, 2008).

In the 1950s, these serial-position findings were reinterpreted as providing evidence for the existence of two distinct memory systems, not just one. Memory researchers argued that the primacy effect occurs because people have more time to think about the earlier items than the later items; and, thus, the earlier ones are more likely to be stored in a memory system that can hold information for a long time. This memory system was labeled **long-term memory** (Tulving, 2008). Memory researchers further contended that the recency effect occurs because the last items are still in a memory system that holds information only for relatively short periods of time, up to about 18 seconds. This memory system was called **short-term memory**. Whatever you are currently thinking about or conscious of is contained within short-term memory; and some of the information actively processed here makes its way into the considerably more durable long-term memory, which has an immense capacity for information (Majerus et al., 2006). Long-term memory is the memory system containing the name of your sixth-grade friend.

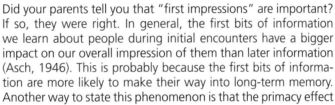

Did your parents tell you that "first impressions" are important? If so, they were right. In general, the first bits of information we learn about people during initial encounters have a bigger impact on our overall impression of them than later information (Asch, 1946). This is probably because the first bits of information are more likely to make their way into long-term memory. Another way to state this phenomenon is that the primacy effect has more influence on impression formation than does the recency effect.

Neuroimaging studies find that when participants recall items from different serial positions in Ebbinghaus's memory task, different areas of the cerebral cortex are activated (Ranganath et al., 2003; Zhang et al., 2003). The fact that different brain areas are used when recalling items at different serial positions in the memory list is further evidence of distinct memory systems.

One important point about the relationship between short-term and long-term memory is that information flows in both directions. Not only does information from short-term memory go to long-term memory (for further encoding and storage), but also a great deal of information stored in long-term memory is sent back to short-term memory (this is the retrieval process). The reason it is so difficult for Ben to memorize new information is that his short-term memory system has trouble working with this information and sending it on to long-term memory. In contrast, the reason you are able to answer the question about your sixth-grade friend is because the correct information can be retrieved from long-term memory and sent to short-term memory.

The last memory system that scientists discovered is the first memory system that typically comes into play in the memory process. A few years after identifying short-term and long-term memory, additional research demonstrated that a **sensory memory** also exists, containing a vast amount of information from the senses that decays even more quickly than short-term memory (Besle et al., 2007; Sinclair et al., 2011). Apparently, the purpose of this memory system is to retain for a split second a highly accurate record of what each of our senses has just experienced in the environment. Thus, sensory memory is like a "snapshot" of our surroundings concerning specific sensory information. Some of this sensory information is then transferred to short-term memory, where we become aware of it; and all the remaining sensory information that is not transferred fades away. This process repeats itself each

Primacy effect The increased memory for the first bits of information presented in a string of information

Recency effect The increased memory for the last bits of information presented in a string of information

Long-term memory A durable memory system that has an immense capacity for information storage

Short-term memory A limited-capacity memory system through which we actively "work" with information.

Sensory memory A memory system that very briefly stores the sensory characteristics of a stimulus

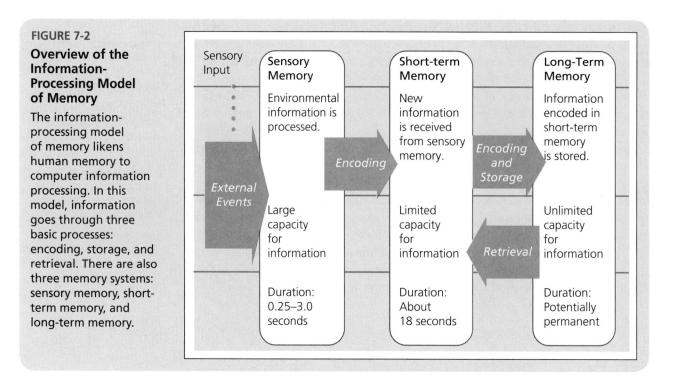

FIGURE 7-2

Overview of the Information-Processing Model of Memory

The information-processing model of memory likens human memory to computer information processing. In this model, information goes through three basic processes: encoding, storage, and retrieval. There are also three memory systems: sensory memory, short-term memory, and long-term memory.

moment, with sensory memory continuously supplying short-term memory with new information to process.

Sensory memory happens automatically, without effort and without conscious awareness. Further, unlike the two-way processing that occurs between short-term and long-term memory, information does not travel back from short-term memory to sensory memory. In other words, sensory memory is not involved in the retrieval process of memory. Thus, we cannot analyze or intentionally review a sensory memory.

Is This the Only Model of Memory?

Figure 7-2 provides an overview of the information-processing model, depicting how information is transferred between the three memory systems and how they are related to encoding, storage, and retrieval. This model has dominated research on memory for about five decades. Although psychologists traditionally divide memory up into these three systems, it is important to mention that these are *abstract* memory systems and do not actually exist as physically identifiable brain areas. It should also be noted that this model does not explain all memory processes, and there are competing memory-system theories. Later in the chapter, in Section 7.2d, I discuss a more recent approach, the *parallel distributed processing model*, in which memory is represented as a weblike network of connections that operate simultaneously rather than sequentially. For now, however, let us examine in greater detail each of these three memory systems from the traditional memory model.

7.1b *Sensory Memory Preserves Detailed Sensory Information for a Few Moments.*

Sensory memory is the doorway to memory. It serves as a holding area, storing information just long enough for us to select items for attention from the multitude transmitted from our senses every moment. Those items not transferred to short-term memory are quickly replaced by incoming stimuli and lost.

BVT *Lab*

Flashcards are available
for this chapter at
www.BVTLab.com.

Sensory information is not actually stored all together in one system but instead is saved in separate memory subsystems, each related to a different source of sensory information. The duration of sensory memory varies depending on the sense involved, but none lasts more than a few seconds. Visual sensory memory is referred to as *iconic memory* because it is the fleeting memory of an image, or icon. Auditory sensory memory is referred to as *echoic memory* because this brief memory is often experienced like an echo (Schroger, 2007).

You cannot directly access sensory memory. Try the following demonstration. Move your forefinger back and forth in front of your face. The blurred images of many fingers that you see are not the actual sensory-memory images. They are gone. What you are consciously aware of is the end result of the sensory information reaching short-term memory. How do psychologists study something that cannot be consciously accessed? George Sperling (1960), who presented participants with different displays of letters, consisting of three rows of four letters each, conducted the groundbreaking research in this area. These displays were presented for only one-twentieth of a second and looked like this:

W   K   L   P

R   B   C   U

X   V   T   D

Presenting the letters so briefly meant that participants could get only a glance at them, and most people could recall only 4 or 5 of the 12 letters. They knew they had seen more, but the fleeting image faded before they could report more than the first few letters. With this feedback, Sperling slightly modified his experiment to determine whether his participants were really seeing more of a fleeting image than they could report. The main modification involved assigning a different tone to each row of the display and then sounding one of these tones immediately after the letter pattern disappeared from view. Participants were told to report the letters in the top row if they heard a high tone, the middle row if they heard a medium tone, and the bottom row if they heard the low tone. Because the tone was not sounded until after the letter pattern disappeared, participants had to rely on their visual sensory memory, or iconic memory, to report the correct row.

With this modification, participants now correctly identified three or four letters from any given line, indicating that they had stored a fairly complete pattern of the letters in sensory memory. However, if the tone was delayed for half a second, only one or two letters were still available. At a 1-second delay, the information in their iconic memory had completely disappeared, and they could report nothing of what they saw. Now remember, as I just discussed, the participants did not directly perceive the letters in sensory memory. What they "saw" was what had been sent to short-term memory from sensory memory. Subsequent research indicated that iconic memory lasts no more than four-tenths of a second (Thurgood et al., 2011). However, the brighter the visual image, the slower it fades.

Sensory memory studies of hearing, or *echoic memory*, indicate that auditory echoes last longer than visual fleeting images—up to a few seconds. The longer duration of echoic memory explains why we hear a series of musical notes as a melody or perceive speech as a "string" of continuous words rather than as disjointed sounds. Of course, here again, we are not directly accessing echoic memory but are aware, instead, of what has been transferred from echoic memory to short-term memory.

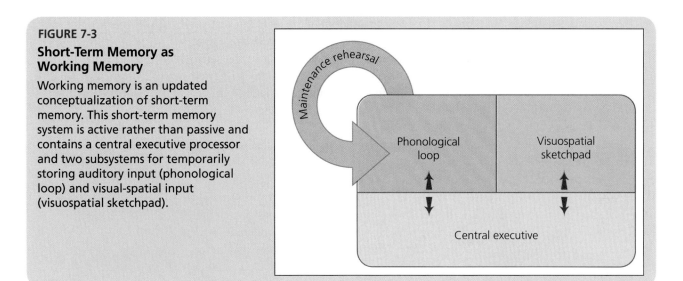

Short-Term Memory as Working Memory

Working memory is an updated conceptualization of short-term memory. This short-term memory system is active rather than passive and contains a central executive processor and two subsystems for temporarily storing auditory input (phonological loop) and visual-spatial input (visuospatial sketchpad).

7.1c   Short-Term Memory Is Conceived of as a "Working Memory" System.

Although sensory memories are brief replicas of environmental information, for us to make sense of this information and retain it for a longer time, it has to be transferred to the second memory system, namely, short-term memory. Although short-term memory was once considered a relatively passive storage area that simply held information until it faded or was transferred to long-term memory, it is now thought of as the memory area where we actively "work" with information that comes from either sensory or long-term memory (Nee et al., 2008). This more complex and expanded view of short-term memory is referred to as **working memory** (Baudouin et al., 2006).

As depicted in Figure 7-3, working memory has three basic components. The first is the *phonological loop*, which temporarily stores auditory input such as spoken words and meaningful sounds and is also used to generate and decode language. It can be "refreshed" through rehearsal. When reciting a phone number to yourself while searching for a pen to write it down, you are relying on this "inner voice." This component of working memory represents all of what we originally thought of as short-term memory. The second component is the *visuospatial sketchpad*, which temporarily stores visual and spatial images. When an architect envisions a new building design, when a choreographer imagines a dancer's movements, or when you recall the appearance of your favorite stuffed animal from childhood—all these cognitive tasks rely on the visuospatial sketchpad. Finally, the third aspect of working memory is the *central executive* that supervises and coordinates the other two components (Simmons et al., 2012). The central executive is in charge of encoding information received from sensory memory and then filtering the sufficiently important information to long-term memory. It also retrieves information from long-term memory, if this is necessary.

As you can see, the two original defining characteristics of short-term memory—small capacity and short duration—still exist in the concept of working memory. However, this new view of short-term memory assumes that it handles many more functions and is an active, rather than a passive, process (Han & Kim, 2004). In this introduction to the psychology of memory, despite the fact that some researchers make distinctions between short-term memory and working memory, I use these terms interchangeably.

Working memory The term used to describe short-term memory as an active memory system that contains a "central executive" processor and two subsystems for temporarily storing auditory and visual-spatial input

Encoding in Short-Term Memory

Encoding information in short-term memory is much more complex than what occurs in sensory memory. The two storage systems in working (short-term) memory encode information either acoustically (the phonological loop) or visually (the visuospatial sketchpad); however, acoustic encoding seems to dominate. In one study, for example, participants were presented with a list of letters and then asked to immediately repeat them (Conrad, 1964). Even though the letters were presented visually, the mistakes made in remembering the letters were overwhelmingly acoustic in nature. That is, a correct letter (such as *V*) was much more likely to be remembered as a similar-sounding letter (such as *E*) than as a similar-looking letter (such as *U*). This research suggests that although we can store information in short-term memory using both visual and acoustic codes, we rely more on acoustic encoding, perhaps because it is easier to rehearse by mentally talking to ourselves than by creating mental images.

Storage Capacity of Short-Term Memory

Before reading further, complete the exercises in Self-Discovery Questionnaire 7-1 to test the storage capacity of your short-term memory. In the 1950s, George Miller tested many people's ability to remember various lists of letters, words, and digits. He found that the capacity of short-term memory is quite limited: about seven items or *chunks* of information (plus or minus two) can be retained at any one time (Miller, 1956). Cross-cultural research indicates that this seven-item limit to short-term memory is universal (Yu et al., 1985). Some research even suggests that this number may be as low as four chunks on average (Cowan, 2001).

What happens when new information is presented to you after your short-term memory capacity is filled? Often, new information simply displaces the currently held information. However, what if you combine many discrete bits of information into a small number of meaningful groupings? This memory strategy, known as **chunking**, can greatly increase the amount of information held in short-term memory. Remember that long list of letters presented in task 2 of Self-Discovery Questionnaire 7-1? If you examine the pattern of letters closely, you will be able to chunk those 18 individual items into the following six chunks: CNN ABC CBS NBC MCI CIA. Encoding these six chunks is less likely to exceed your short-term memory capacity.

> **Chunking** Organizing items of information into a meaningful unit, or chunk, that can be stored in short-term memory

Chunking is one of the important memory strategies we learn in childhood, and these information chunks can be quite complex (Mathy & Feldman, 2012). For example, you probably can repeat the following 66-letter, 14-word sentence very easily after reading it only once: *On Tuesday, three-fisted boys run after four-legged girls to compare extra limbs.* Here, you might represent this information as the following four manageable chunks: (1) "On Tuesday" (2) "three-fisted boys" (3) "run after four-legged girls" (4) "to compare extra limbs." In this case, the reason your short-term memory is so good is because you possess a great deal of knowledge about the material, namely, the English language. The ability to create meaningful chunks largely depends on how much you know about the material that needs to be remembered. Thus, for chunking to effectively increase short-term memory capacity, it often requires the retrieval of information from long-term memory.

Maintenance Rehearsal

Although information is stored in short-term memory for only about 18 seconds, this time can be extended through **maintenance rehearsal**, which is the process of repetitively verbalizing or thinking about information. Reciting a phone number until you write it down is an example of maintenance rehearsal. If you are distracted

> **Maintenance rehearsal** The process of repetitively verbalizing or thinking about information to either extend the usual 18-second duration of short term memory or transfer the rehearsed information to long-term memory

SELF-DISCOVERY 7-1
Questionnaire

Testing Your Short-Term Memory Capacity

Complete the following two tasks to test the storage capacity of your short-term memory.

Task 1

Directions: Ask someone to read you the letters in the top row at the rate of about one per second. Then try to repeat them back in the same order. Repeat this for the next row, and the one after that, until you make a mistake. How many letters could you repeat back perfectly?

Q M R

H Z X E

X D P Q F

G N M S W R

D H W Y U N J

E P H E A Z K R

N R E F D T O Q P

U H V X G F N I K J

H F R D S X A W U G T

H E Q L I M Y D J R N K

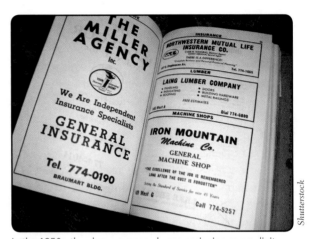

Shutterstock

In the 1950s, the phone company began assigning seven-digit phone numbers to its customers. How was this new policy shaped by George Miller's research on short-term memory capacity?

Task 2

Directions: Read the following string of letters, and then try to write them down in the correct order:

CNNA   BCCBSNB   CMCIC   IA   How many letters in each task were you able to recall?

---

before finding a pen, you will likely forget the number because it is no longer in the phonological loop of short-term memory and was not transferred to the more durable long-term memory system. Maintenance rehearsal is also important in helping you transfer information to long-term memory. This is the method you often rely on when memorizing dialogue in a play, multiplication tables, or foreign language vocabulary.

7.1d We Often Encode Information into Long-Term Memory Using Elaborative Rehearsal.

One problem with using maintenance rehearsal to transfer information to long-term memory is that information learned this way has few retrieval cues and is often not strongly integrated into long-term memory. As a result, such information is often hard to retrieve from long-term memory. A different way to encode information utilizes **elaborative rehearsal**, which involves thinking about how new information relates to information already stored in long-term memory. This rehearsal is referred to as *elaborative* because rather than merely repeating the information over and over to

Elaborative rehearsal
Rehearsal that involves thinking about how new information relates to information already stored in long-term memory

yourself, you *elaborate* on how it is related to something you already know (Richmond et al., 2011). Can you still recite many—or all—of those 18 individual letters in task 2 of Self-Discovery Questionnaire 7-1? If so, it is most likely because you elaborated on how certain of these clusters of letters represent the names of previously learned organizations (CNN, ABC, CBS, NBC, MCI, and the CIA). Similarly, one way I remember phone numbers is by associating them with the jersey numbers of football players from the Green Bay Packers (information that is in my long-term memory). So, 242-1566 becomes 242-"Bart Starr" and "Ray Nitschke." Organizational strategies such as this one are called *mnemonics* (pronounced "neh MON ix"), which are discussed in greater detail later in this chapter's "Psychological Applications" section.

"Shallow" versus "Deep" Processing

Psychologists Fergus Craik and Robert Lockhart (1972) propose that elaborative rehearsal is a more effective way of encoding new information than maintenance rehearsal because elaborative rehearsal involves a deeper level of cognitive processing. The more you think about how new information is related to existing knowledge you possess, the "deeper" the processing and the better your memory of it becomes. Craik and Lockhart believe that *shallow* processing typically involves encoding information in terms of its superficial perceptual qualities, such as its sights and sounds, whereas *deep* processing often involves encoding information in terms of its meaning, or semantics (refer back to Section 7.1a). For instance, look at the adjectives listed below for five seconds each and mentally note which contain the letter *e*:

1. curious
2. humorous
3. sensitive
4. daring
5. quiet
6. introspective
7. ambitious
8. responsible

Journey of Discovery

The finding that deep processing leads to more effective encoding and better retention of new information has many practical applications for you as a student. In your own studying, how can you process new information at a deep, rather than shallow, level?

Now, instead of scanning these words for the letter *e*, note which of these adjectives describe you as a person. Research indicates that this semantic exercise, in contrast to the previous perceptual exercise, not only triggers more activity in a part of the frontal cortex of the left cerebral hemisphere associated with language, but also leads to a greater likelihood of long-term memory storage (Gabrieli et al., 1996). What largely explains the more permanent memory storage in semantic exercises versus perceptual exercises is that semantic exercises create more associations between new memories and existing memories (Lockhart & Craik, 1990). Further, in the semantic exercise just described, you were asked to process the adjectives by associating them with a very important set of existing memories: your self-concept. When new information is processed in terms of its relevance to us, we process it at a deeper level and better remember it at a later time (Rathbone et al., 2011). Indeed, Craik and Lockhart contend that the distinction between short-term memory and long-term memory is simply a matter of the depth of the encoding process. Instead

FIGURE 7-4

Which Is the Real Penny?

Among all these coins, can you correctly identify the real penny? Our failure to encode the details of coins and other currency into long-term memory is what counterfeiters rely on in plying their trade.

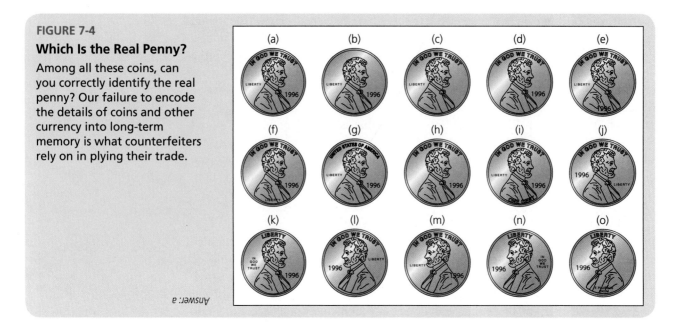

Answer: a

of describing two distinct memory systems (short and long), they prefer to describe a continuum of processing ranging from shallow to very deep. Information processed at a shallow level can be retained only briefly (in what is conventionally called short-term memory), whereas information processed at a deeper level can be kept indefinitely (in what is traditionally called long-term memory). Whether or not Craig and Lockhart's hypothesis is supported by future studies, their research is important because it informs us that the most important determinant of memory is how extensively information is encoded or processed when it is first received. Elaborative rehearsal, which relies extensively on semantic encoding, provides a much deeper level of processing than maintenance rehearsal, which relies primarily on acoustic encoding.

Semantic Encoding Errors

Because semantic encoding is the dominant encoding process for long-term memory, the types of errors we make in remembering information are often associated with the unique qualities of semantic encoding. For instance, semantic encoding often ignores details and instead encodes the general underlying meaning of information. Consider Figure 7-4. Can you identify the correct drawing of a U.S. penny?

When Americans are asked this question, most are unsuccessful, as are people from Great Britain who are asked to identify their country's coins (Nickerson & Adams, 1979; Richardson, 1993). The reason most of us are so bad at correctly identifying a familiar object, such as a penny, is because we never encoded all of its specific details into long-term memory. Our tendency to encode the general meaning of visual stimuli rather than its specific details is what counterfeiters depend on when passing fake currency. To reduce this problem, the U.S. Treasury is now using more distinctive drawings on paper money so that people will more easily recognize counterfeit currency when they see it.

Very few of us ever encode the specific details of currency notes into long-term memory. This fact allows counterfeiters to pass off fake money as real. To reduce this problem, the U.S. Treasury prints more distinctive drawings on paper money so that we will more easily recognize counterfeit money when we see it.

Shutterstock

- Computer information processing serves as a rough working model for human information processing.

- In the three basic information processes, the encoding stage transfers information into memory, the storage stage organizes and maintains information in memory for a period of time, and the retrieval stage recovers stored information from memory so it can be used.

- The three memory systems have the following characteristics: Sensory memory stores information just long enough for us to select items for attention; short-term memory (or working memory) actively works with about seven bits of information; and long-term memory has immense information capacity and durability.

- Information can be kept in short-term memory longer through rehearsal.

- Some information is encoded into long-term memory automatically, but a great deal of encoding involves conscious processing.

- Semantic encoding is the dominant encoding process for long-term memory.

7.2 What Constitutes Long-Term Memory?

The traditional information-processing model describes long-term memory as one solitary system. Yet, beginning in the late 1970s and early 1980s, some cognitive psychologists challenged this view and proposed that long-term memory consists of multiple systems that encode and store different types of information. Thus, unlike a computer, which has one internal hard drive and perhaps one external hard drive to store information for long periods of time, the current view of memory is that the brain has multiple internal "hard drives."

Memory researchers are not in agreement on how many long-term memory systems exist. In carving up long-term memory and trying to make sense of it, some cognitive psychologists distinguish among memory systems based on the types of information stored, such as specific facts, general knowledge, or habitual actions. Other researchers emphasize how information is stored in memory, such as whether or not conscious recollection is involved. In this section of the chapter, we will examine both these views of long-term memory and see how together they can provide us with a useful template for understanding the memory process.

7.2a *Long-Term Memories Can Be Explicit or Implicit.*

Memory researchers state that one way to understand the content of long-term memory is to determine whether the information can be consciously recollected or not. As you have learned throughout this textbook, experience affects how we behave. However, our memory of these past experiences can be either conscious or relatively unconscious.

Explicit Memory

For many years, psychologists primarily studied the conscious recollection of previous experiences, known as **explicit memory**. Explicit remembering can be either

Explicit memory Memory of pervious experiences that one can consciously recollect; also called *declarative memory*

intentional or unintentional. For example, you might intentionally recall an argument, or this memory might spontaneously enter your consciousness. Both instances involve explicit memory because conscious recollection takes place. Explicit memory is sometimes also referred to as *declarative memory* because, if asked, you can "declare" this information (Davachi & Dobbins, 2008). Explicit memory is often described as having two subsystems: *episodic memory* and *semantic memory*

Episodic memory is memory for factual information acquired at a specific time and place (Hasselmo, 2012). Do you remember what you had for dinner last night? Do you know when you received your first romantic kiss? Can you recall the name of the current president of the United States? Do you remember how you felt during your first day attending college? All these questions involve episodic memories. When memory researchers present participants with a list of words, numbers, or nonsense syllables—such as in Ebbinghaus's memory-curve studies—and later test their memory for this information, they are studying episodic memory.

Episodic memory for events in your own life—your personal life history—is called *autobiographical memory* (Addis et al., 2012). Autobiographical memory is not composed simply of previously experienced events; it is memory of the self, engaged in those events (Pernot-Marino et al., 2004). This memory of self-experiences creates the essence of "you" in your own mind. Research suggests that when we recall autobiographical memories that were either positive or negative, we tend to "see" the events from our own perspective, whereas we tend to "see" emotionally neutral autobiographical memories as an observer would (D'Argembeau et al., 2003).

Given our discussion in Chapter 3, Section 3.5d, concerning how culture shapes the structure of self-concept, would it surprise you to learn that your autobiographical memories are shaped by whether you grew up in a collectivist or an individualist culture? Developmental psychologist Qi Wang (2001) asked Chinese college students in Beijing and American college students in Boston to report their earliest childhood memories. His subsequent analysis indicated that the Chinese students' early memories were more likely than those of the American students to include other people and to center on routine group activities involving family or community members ("I used to play with friends … We went to the bush to pick wild fruits to eat."). In contrast, American students' early memories were more self-focused and involved more themes of individual autonomy than those of the Chinese students ("When I was four, I got stung by a bee."). These cultural differences in the content of autobiographical memories reflect Chinese culture's emphasis on interdependence and tightly knit social relationships, and American culture's emphasis on independence and loosely knit relationships. Therefore, how your culture socializes you to think of yourself in relation to your group and how it teaches you to relate to others shapes not only the structure of your self-concept but also the content of your autobiographical memories (Fivush & Nelson, 2004).

In contrast to the specific information stored in episodic memory, **semantic memory** is more general in nature. It stores general knowledge about the world that we typically do not remember acquiring at a specific time and place (Sitnikova et al., 2006). For example, do you remember when or where you learned that George Washington was the first president of the United States? Or when you learned that Santa Claus had a reindeer with a big red nose? All the countless facts that you have learned during the course of your life generally fit into this category of memory. Studies of brain-injured patients and neuroimaging studies of healthy individuals suggest that both episodic and semantic memories involve the activation of the frontal lobe, but that the right frontal lobe may play a larger role in episodic memory and that semantic memory may involve more left frontal lobe activity (Hasegawa et al., 1998; Nyberg et al., 2003). These findings provide further evidence that long-term memory consists of multiple systems (Brown & Robertson, 2007).

Episodic memory Memory for factual information acquired at a specific time and place

Semantic memory Memory for general knowledge about the world that is not associated with the time and place the information was learned

Implicit Memory

Remembering does not always involve conscious recollection. In fact, quite often we retain information that influences our thoughts and actions, without consciously remembering it. This psychological process is known as **implicit memory** and is also referred to as *nondeclarative memory* because you cannot "declare" this information (Knowlton & Foerde, 2008). How might implicit memory affect your thoughts and behavior? If a horse traumatized you as a youngster, you might feel anxious when you are around horses as an adult, even though you have no conscious memory of the childhood incident (see the discussion of repression in Section 7.4c). Similarly, feeling uneasy and irritable around a new acquaintance because she unconsciously reminds you of a disagreeable person from your past is another example of the power of implicit memory. Both these examples represent *classically conditioned memory* (see Chapter 6, section 6.1b).

To study implicit memory, psychologists often use word-completion tasks where a participant is asked to complete word stems, such as part_ _ _ _ _ _ _. Because you just saw the word earlier in the sentence, you are more likely to think of *participant* than the word *partnership*. This method of activating implicit memories is known as **priming** (P. K. Smith & Bargh, 2008). The fact that a previous experience (seeing the word *participant*) makes you more likely to respond in a certain way demonstrates that you can retain more implicit knowledge about the past than you realize.

Another type of implicit memory is **procedural memory**, which is memory of how to perform skilled motor activities—such as how to ride a bike, drive a car, do a cartwheel, or even walk. Often referred to as *habits*, these activities are so well learned that we carry them out automatically, without conscious thought. We begin forming procedural memories during infancy when we learn to walk, talk, and engage in other routine activities. It is often difficult to describe in words how to actually perform these actions. For example, when recently asked to describe how to drive using a stick shift on a car, I was at a loss for words. After a few failed attempts at verbally describing how to depress the clutch pedal while simultaneously repositioning the shifter, I sat on a chair and demonstrated the procedure by imagining myself in the driver's seat. Similarly, when one of my daughters asked for instructions on how to tie a Windsor knot on a necktie, I could not give her proper instructions until I literally undid the necktie I was wearing and retied it while describing my actions.

It is not unusual for a great deal of cognitive activity to be involved in implicit memory. For example, while reading these words, you are unconsciously remembering their meaning. Similarly, typing on a computer keyboard involves the use of implicit memories. To demonstrate the truth of this statement, complete Self-Discovery Questionnaire 7-2 before reading further.

Do you recall the story of Henry Molaison from Chapter 2? Although the surgical removal of his hippocampus destroyed Henry's ability to acquire new episodic or semantic memories, he was still able to acquire procedural memories, which involve the cerebellum and not the hippocampus (Cohen et al., 1985; Gluck & Myers, 2001). Thus, Henry Molaison was able to learn new skills, such as reading mirror writing or solving mazes and puzzles, despite being unable to remember

Implicit memory Memory of previous experiences without conscious recollection; also called *nondelcarative memory*

Priming A method of activating implicit memories, in which a recently presented bit of information facilitates—or "primes"—responses in a subsequent situation

Procedural memory Memory of how to perform skilled motor activities, which have become well-learned habits and are carried out automatically (without conscious thought)

Shutterstock

Once learned, information regarding how to perform skilled motor activities, such as bike riding, is part of your procedural memory.

SELF-DISCOVERY 7-2
Questionnaire

Do You Rely on Your Implicit Memory When Typing?

Shutterstock

Can you recite from memory the letters on a computer keyboard, starting with the bottom left row? Is this a difficult task for you? Why?

A great deal of knowledge is stored in the form of implicit memories. For example, your knowledge of how to perform skilled motor activities, what is called *procedural memory*, involves the use of implicit memories. Let's demonstrate this memory fact by considering your knowledge of computers, specifically your computer keyboard. First try reciting from memory the letters on the keys of a computer keyboard, starting with the bottom left row. Don't spread your fingers in front of you to help in recalling the letter order!

Was it difficult? Impossible? I'm betting that you could not recall all the letters in their proper order.

Now spread your fingers in front of you as if they were resting on a keyboard, and "type" your name using the imaginary keys. If you have experience typing on the computer, this is an easy task; and it demonstrates that you really do know the proper order of the keys. Thus, although it is difficult for you to consciously "declare" this information, you still can unconsciously pull it out of memory and use it to correctly type your name.

---

having done so. This fact from Molaison's life is further evidence that long-term memory is comprised of multiple subsystems.

Countless everyday situations and activities require you to use all the different types of long-term memory, both explicit and implicit. For example, when driving a car, you rely on procedural memory to steer, shift, speed up, and slow down. Remembering the rules of driving—such as stopping at red lights, yielding to pedestrians, and driving on the right side of the road—is an example of semantic memory. Recalling that you were ticketed for speeding on a particular stretch of road on your 19th birthday is an example of episodic memory. Finally, that rush of adrenaline and the sinking feeling you experience in your stomach when noticing the flashing lights of a police car behind you while driving is an example of classically conditioned memory. ("Drat! Another ticket!")

In closing this section, it should be mentioned that although some cognitive psychologists believe that explicit and implicit memories constitute separate memory systems, other memory researchers believe that these two types of memories simply involve the use of different types of encoding and retrieval processes (LeDoux, 2008). While acknowledging this difference of opinion among the experts, I organize my discussion of long-term memory by assuming, for the time being, that explicit memory and implicit memory are two separate and distinct subsystems. Operating from this assumption, Figure 7-5 categorizes episodic and semantic memories into the explicit domain, while placing classically conditioned and procedural memories

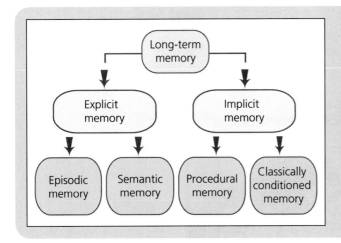

FIGURE 7-5

Types of Long-Term Memory

Long-term memory consists of two basic subsystems: Explicit memory involves memories that we can consciously recollect, and implicit memory involves memories without conscious recollection. Within explicit memory, there are two types of memory information: episodic memory, containing factual information acquired at a specific time and place, and semantic memory, containing general knowledge not associated with a specific time and place. Within implicit memory, classically conditioned and procedural memories are the most common types of memory information.

into the implicit domain. Future research will determine whether these distinctions remain useful in helping us understand the memory process.

7.2b Some Information in Long-Term Memory Is Organized into Networks.

An immense amount of information encoded into long-term memory is unique to your own personal experiences. However, other people who have had similar cultural experiences as yourself share much of the information you have encoded into long-term memory. As an illustration of this fact, complete Self-Discovery Questionnaire 7-3.

In an early study of how information is organized in long-term memory, William Bousfield (1953) asked people to memorize 60 randomly presented words that came from four semantic categories: names, animals, vegetables, and professions. Despite the random order of presentation, people later tended to recall the words in clusters corresponding to the four categories. That is, even when items on a list have little in common, we still try to impose a semantic structure (Tulving, 1962). Due to both experience and genetic predisposition, we develop the habit of organizing information into meaningful patterns or concepts to facilitate encoding, and hence, long-term memory.

In attempting to understand how knowledge is often semantically organized in long-term memory, a number of theorists have proposed that information is stored in a vast network of interrelated concepts (Grebitus & Bruhn, 2008). One of the most influential of these theories is called the **semantic network model** (Binder et al., 2009; Collins & Loftus, 1975). According to this theory, there are many kinds of memory associations we can make among concepts. A *concept* consists of a cluster of objects, ideas, or events that share common properties and are linked to other concepts in the long-term memory network. Some concepts in this network are more strongly linked than others.

Figure 7-6 depicts a small semantic network, as it might look right after you think of the concept *Santa Claus*. When you think of a concept, according to the semantic network model, your thoughts naturally go to related concepts stored in long-term memory. In Figure 7-6, this network of possible associations is represented by lines connecting the concepts. *Santa Claus* activates associations with the following concepts: *red* and *white* because *Santa Claus* has a red suit and a white beard; *snow* and *Christmas* because he visits during a specific night in winter; *reindeer* and *rooftops* because these animals fly him to the tops of houses; and *elves* and *presents* because his elf-helpers make presents that he delivers. The lengths of the lines indicate

Semantic network model A theory that describes concepts in long-term memory as being organized in a complex network of associations

SELF-DISCOVERY 7-3
Questionnaire

Are You an "April, August, December" Encoder? (I Doubt It.)

Do you know how you encoded the months of the year into long-term memory?

To experience how you encode some information into long-term memory, try this exercise: Recite the names of the 12 months of the year as fast as you can. Go!

Barring any physical problems with your brain, I'm sure that you—and everyone else reading this chapter—knew all 12 names of the months. I'm also willing to bet that everyone recited them in the following order: January, February, March, April, May, June, July, August, September, October, November, December. Am I right about your recitation? Why do you think this is so?

Now recite these same months again as fast as you can, but this time, recite them in alphabetical order. Go!

If you did indeed take up my challenge, I'm virtually certain that it took you much longer to complete the second task than the first, despite the fact that the first task allowed you to "practice" recalling the months' names. Why?

the strength of the association between the concepts. Shorter lines imply stronger associations, meaning that you will more easily recall concepts with these stronger associations. Thus, when you hear the name *Santa Claus*, you are more likely to think of the words *Christmas, red,* and *reindeer* than the words *elves* and *white.* Similarly, you are much more likely to think of the words *elves, white, snow,* and *presents* than the words *leprechauns, blue, sleet,* and *offerings.*

FIGURE 7-6

A Semantic Network Model

According to the semantic network model, information in long-term memory is organized in a complex network of memory associations. The shorter the link between concepts, the more likely it is that retrieving one concept will trigger the retrieval of the other concept.

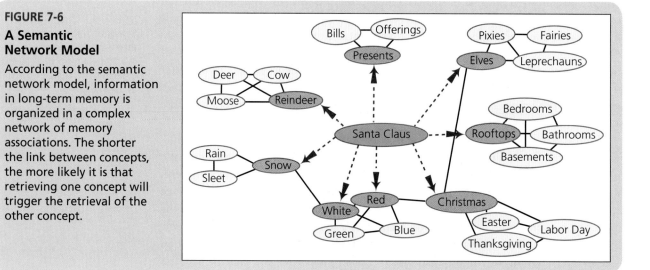

Although the semantic network model assumes that semantic networks are a universal way of organizing information, cross-cultural studies indicate that the way people use these networks is influenced by experience and education. Research in rural Liberia and Guatemala, for example, found that children who receive more schooling are more likely to use semantic categories in recalling lists of concepts than children with less schooling (Cole & Cole, 1993). This finding makes sense because semantic grouping allows for the quick learning of a lot of information, a basic requirement in academic settings. Children with less schooling have less need to memorize large amounts of information and therefore are less likely to organize information semantically. These findings do not mean that school-educated children have better memories than those with no schooling. Instead, it means that people tend to organize information in long-term memory in a way that is consistent with their life experiences and the demands of their surroundings.

7.2c Information in Long-Term Memory Can Be Organized Around Schemas.

The tendency to encode information by semantic categories doesn't mean that all stored memories are arranged in semantic networks. Semantic networks are of limited help in explaining how information is clustered into coherent wholes, called *schemas*. As discussed in Chapter 3, Section 3.3a, schemas are organized, repeatedly exercised patterns of thought or behavior. Regarding encoding and memory, research indicates that people are more likely to remember things that can be incorporated into existing schemas than things that cannot (Marshall, 1995).

John Bransford and Marcia Johnson (1972) conducted a memory experiment that demonstrated the importance of having the right schema at the right time. To understand the importance yourself, read the following story read by Bransford and Johnson's participants; and then, like them, try to recall as much of it as you can:

> *If the balloons popped, the sound wouldn't be able to carry, since everything would be too far away from the correct floor. A closed window would also prevent the sound from carrying, since most buildings tend to be well insulated. Since the whole operation depends on the steady flow of electricity, a break in the middle of the wire would also cause problems. Of course, the fellow could shout, but the human voice is not loud enough to carry that far. An additional problem is that the string could break on the instrument. Then there would be no accompaniment to the message. It is clear that the best situation would involve less distance. Then there would be fewer potential problems. With face-to-face contact, the least number of things could go wrong.*

After reading this passage, take a little break, look around your immediate surroundings, and make a mental note of ten different objects you can see. What color is each of them? What are their sizes in relation to one another?

Now that I have distracted you from thinking about the Bransford and Johnson story for more than 18 seconds, how much of it can you remember? Experimental participants remembered less than 4 of its 14 ideas when, like you, they were given *no schema* in which to understand the story. However, when participants were given a schema in which to understand the story—by being shown a cartoon similar to the one in Figure 7-7—before reading the story, they recalled twice as many ideas (about 8 out of 14). Interestingly, participants who were given the schema after the reading remembered no more than those not shown the picture at all. Apparently, seeing the picture beforehand allowed participants to make sense of what they were reading. This suggests that it is crucial to have the right schema during the encoding stage in

FIGURE 7-7

Man Serenading a Woman

Source: Reprinted from *Journal of Verbal Learning and Verbal Behavior, 11,* John D. Bransford and M. K. Johnson, "Contextual prerequisites for understanding: Some investigations of comprehension and recall," pp. 717–726, copyright © 1972. Reprinted with permission from Elsevier. This material may not be reproduced in any form or by any means without the prior written permission of the publisher.

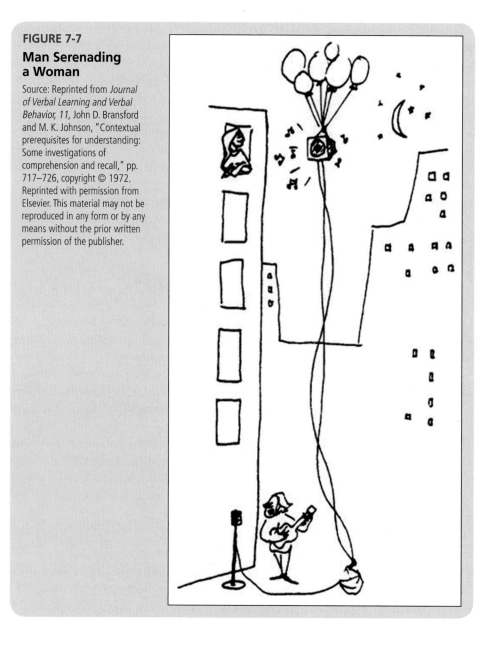

order to understand and remember complex material. Further studies indicate that schemas help us remember and organize details, speed up processing time, and fill in gaps in our knowledge (Fiske & Taylor, 1991; Hirt, 1990). The fact that schemas can fill in gaps in our knowledge explains why they sometimes contribute to memory distortions (Section 7.3d).

Because schemas develop from our experiences, it is reasonable to assume that they are significantly shaped by culture. In one study, students in the United States and the Pacific island nation of Palau read separate descriptions of funerals in the two cultures and were later asked to recall everything they could about them (Pritchard, 1991). It was hypothesized that students would better remember the funeral description from their own culture because it would more closely match their cultural schema for funerals. Results supported this hypothesis.

Further cross-cultural research indicates that *cultural utility* plays an important role in what kind of schemas develop, and thus what is remembered (Hunn, 1982, 1990; Mistry & Rogoff, 1994). For example, the Fore people of New Guinea have highly elaborate schemas for many different bird species, but they tend to group all butterflies together under one schematic category (Diamond, 1966). The reason for this schematic difference is that birds are a valued food source for the Fore, while butterflies are of little use to them. This research suggests that culture shapes schema formation and thus plays an important role in what we attend to, process, encode, and later recall from long-term memory (Malt, 1995).

7.2d *Memory May Involve Parallel Processing of Neural Units.*

Do you realize that while reading these words you are performing some amazing memory feats? You are recognizing the patterns that make up the letters of the alphabet while simultaneously recognizing how sets of these letters make up words in the English language and how these word strings make up meaningful sentences. How can you execute these different memory tasks so quickly?

As already mentioned, the traditional information-processing model assumes that the brain works sequentially, like a computer; however, such *serial processing* would occur too slowly to account for your reading of the words on this page. Rather, we know that the human brain performs many tasks simultaneously—that is, in parallel. It apparently accomplishes this *parallel processing* of information because millions of neurons distributed throughout the brain are active at once, and each neuron is communicating with thousands of other neurons. This simultaneous neural communication produces the type of cognitive complexity necessary for parallel processing. Building on this idea of simultaneous neural communication, the **parallel distributed processing model** of memory contend that what we call memory is knowledge distributed across a dense network of neural associations (McLeod et al., 2006). When this neural network is activated, different areas of the network operate simultaneously, in a parallel fashion. Such parallel processing allows us to quickly and efficiently utilize our storehouse of knowledge.

A parallel distributed processing system consists of a large network of interconnected neurons called *processing units*, which are distributed throughout our brains. Each unit is designed to work on a specific type of memory task. For example, one model suggests that for comprehending written English there might be individual processing units for 16 different letter patterns, for each of the 26 letters in the English alphabet, and for thousands of words (McClelland & Rumelhart, 1981). When you look at a book written in English, these processing units are activated at the same time, without your conscious awareness. The letter-related units recognize letters while the word units recognize words from letter combinations—and presto, you comprehend the words on the page with amazing speed and seemingly effortless cognition.

The parallel distributed processing model maintains that information in memory is not located in a specific place in the brain but resides, instead, in connections between the involved processing units in the neural network. This model better represents the actual operation of the brain than do the information-processing models and also has been used to explain perception, language, and decision making. However, the information-processing approach is still better at explaining memory for single events, as well as why learning new information can sometimes cause you to forget previously learned information (see Section 7.4b). In sizing up these two approaches, memory expert Endel Tulving (1999) advises that, at least for the present, both models are necessary for a fuller understanding of memory.

BVT *Lab*

Visit **www.BVTLab.com** to explore the student resources available for this chapter.

Parallel distributed processing model A memory model in which a large network of interconnected neurons, or processing units, distributed throughout the brain simultaneously work on different memory tasks

- Explicit memory involves conscious recollection.

- The two major types of explicit long-term memory are episodic and semantic.

- Implicit memory involves using information in long-term memory without being aware that you are doing so.

- Implicit memory involves priming, and classically conditioned and procedural memories.

- In the semantic network model, information is organized in long-term memory as a vast network of interrelated concepts.

- Schemas help us remember and organize details, speed up processing time, and fill in knowledge gaps.

- The parallel distributed processing model contends that memory is a large network of interconnected neurons, or processing units, that simultaneously work on different memory tasks.

7.3 How Do We Retrieve Information from Memory?

Encoding, storing, and organizing information in long-term memory are important cognitive processes, but they would be of no use to us if we could not later retrieve this information when we needed it. Remembering involves retrieving information from long-term memory so it resides in consciousness, or short-term memory. To appreciate firsthand the power and imperfection of memory retrieval, try answering the following questions:

- Did Abraham Lincoln fly in a spaceship to the moon?

- How many days are there in the month of April?

- What did you eat for breakfast last Monday?

- In Mexico, which national hero is considered the "father" of his country?

- Which of the following terms refers to conscious recollection of previous experiences?
  a. implicit memory
  b. explicit memory
  c. procedural memory
  d. sensory memory

7.3a *Memory Retrieval Varies in Difficulty.*

When answering the previous questions, it is likely that you found some easier than others. For instance, you probably quickly answered that Lincoln never flew to the moon, but it probably took you a bit longer to remember that there are 30 days in April. Did you remember what you ate for breakfast last Monday, and were you able to recall that Benito Juárez, Mexico's first president of Indian descent, was his country's national hero? Finally, were you able to recognize that answer "b" was the correct answer for the last question?

As this exercise hopefully illustrates, although memory retrieval can be effortless and automatic, it can also be difficult and unreliable. The effortful nature of memory retrieval might have been demonstrated when you tried to answer the "April" question. Perhaps you had to recite a rhyme learned in childhood to aid your recall: "Thirty days hath September, April, June, and November." By the way, if you could not answer the "Mexican national hero" question, it may have been because the Benito Juárez information was not stored in long-term memory. Finally, the explicit memory question might have been relatively easy because all you had to do was recognize it as the correct response.

When measuring explicit memory, psychologists typically test people's recall ability and their *recognition*

Why is it easier to recognize a familiar person's face than to recall his or her name?

Shutterstock

ability. Although **recall** requires a person to retrieve and reproduce information from memory, **recognition** simply requires a person to decide whether or not the information has been previously encountered. In most cases, recall is more difficult than recognition because recall requires more extensive mental processing (Watkins & Tulving, 1975). This is the main reason you will often *recognize* a person's face as familiar, even though you cannot *recall* her or his name (Boehm et al., 2005). Studies indicate that the cognitive capacity for recalling information from long-term memory emerges late in the first year of life, well before children have the verbal ability to describe past experiences (Bauer, 2002).

To directly test the explicit remembering of faces versus names, researchers first asked young and old high school graduates to write down the names of as many former classmates as they could remember (Bahrick et al., 1975). For all age groups, recall was poor. Recent graduates could recall only a few dozen names, and those who had graduated more than 40 years earlier recalled fewer than 20 names. Next, researchers asked these same individuals to identify the face of a former classmate from a card containing five photographs. In this recognition task, recent graduates and those who had graduated up to 35 years earlier correctly recognized classmates 90 percent of the time! Even those who had graduated 48 years earlier still recognized classmates three-fourths of the time.

In analyzing these findings, it is important to realize that they do not suggest that we are better at remembering faces than names. Instead, they indicate that recall is more difficult than recognition. Remembering faces becomes much more difficult when we have to *recall* each facial feature rather than simply *recognize* it as familiar. Similarly, our ability to recognize familiar names is equal to our ability to recognize familiar faces.

The greater difficulty of recall tasks compared with recognition tasks is one of the main reasons most students prefer true-false and multiple-choice exams to essay and fill-in-the-blank exams. The former types of questions require recognition of the correct answer, while the latter types require the retrieval and reproduction of information (Kroll et al., 2002). The different remembering required in these exams, however, doesn't necessarily mean that recognition tests are easy. As you undoubtedly know from personal experience, multiple-choice tests can be extremely challenging (you might even say "tricky") if the

Recall A measure of explicit memory in which a person must retrieve and reproduce information from memory

Recognition A measure of explicit memory in which a person need only decide whether or not something has been previously encountered

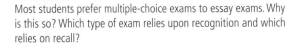

Most students prefer multiple-choice exams to essay exams. Why is this so? Which type of exam relies upon recognition and which relies on recall?

iStock

alternatives are very similar to the correct response. Sometimes the correct answer feels like it is on the "tip of your tongue"—so close you can almost taste it. Read Closer Look 7-1 for a better understanding of this memory problem.

What Do We Know about the Tip-of-the-Tongue Phenomenon?

In explicit memory, we often can retrieve some features but not enough to identify an entire concept. For example, pause for a few seconds and try to recall the names of all the dwarfs from the movie *Snow White and the Seven Dwarfs.*

How did you do? If your retrieval attempt resulted in incomplete recall, you are in good company—most people cannot recall all seven names without assistance (Miserandino, 1991). Now try this second exercise: Pick out the seven dwarf names from among the 14 names listed in alphabetical order here:

Angry, Bashful, Crummy, Doc, Dopey, Father, Grumpy, Happy, Leafy, Sleepy, Sneezy, Snowy, Sweaty, Windy

I'm guessing that the second exercise, which involves recognition rather than recall, was easier for you than the first exercise. In doing the first exercise, you may have felt that the names were just about to enter consciousness, but you were having trouble pulling them out of. About once a week, most people are unable to remember something they are absolutely certain they know. This frustrating retrieval problem is known as the **tip-of-the-tongue phenomenon** and is another demonstration of how recognition is easier than recall (Biedermann et al., 2008; Hanley & Chapman, 2008).

Listed next are some basic facts about the tip-of-the-tongue phenomenon (Brown, 1991, 2012):

- It appears to be universal, occurring in all cultures and age groups.

- It increases in frequency with age.

- It is most often triggered by names of personal acquaintances.

- When a person tries to remember the sought-after word, related words come to mind. These words usually have a similar meaning (*favoritism* instead of *nepotism*) or sound (*Greg* instead of *Craig*).

- People can guess the first letter of the sought-after word about half the time.

- About half the time, the person remembers the sought-after word within the first minute.

By the way, if you are still wondering about those dwarf names, they are *Sleepy, Grumpy, Dopey, Sneezy, Happy, Bashful,* and *Doc.*

Tip-of-the-tongue phenomenon The temporary inability to remember something you know, accompanied by the feeling that it is just beyond your conscious state

7.3b Retrieval Cues Help Trigger Recall of Stored Memories.

One of the most effective ways to facilitate remembering is to use retrieval cues. A **retrieval cue** is a stimulus that allows us to more easily recall information from long-term memory. The reason similar stimuli help us remember information is that many elements of the physical setting in which we learn are simultaneously encoded into long-term memory along with the information we are learning (Tulving & Thomson, 1973). The helpfulness of the physical setting in fostering retrieval is also

Retrieval cue A stimulus that allows us to more easily recall information from long-term memory

why students perform better on exams when tested in the classroom in which they learned the material, rather than being tested in a different setting (Saufley et al. 1985).

If you think of a memory as being held in storage by a web of associations, as in the semantic network model (see Section 7.2b), then retrieval cues would be the individual strands in the web that lead to the memory (Anderson, 1983). The more retrieval cues you have for a particular memory and the better learned these cues are, the more accessible the memory will be. You are likely to retrieve the sought-after memory if you can activate one or more of those strands.

Thus far, I have mentioned only retrieval cues originating in our external world. Yet, our internal psychological environment can also be encoded and become part of our

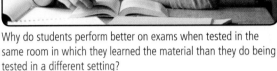

Why do students perform better on exams when tested in the same room in which they learned the material than they do being tested in a different setting?

memory strands. For example, when people learn information while in an altered state of consciousness induced by alcohol, marijuana, or some other drug, they may later recall it better when tested under the same altered state (Eich, 1989). Similar effects have been found for positive and negative moods. When in a positive mood, we tend to recall positive memories, while negative memories are more accessible when we are depressed. This tendency for retrieval from memory to be better when our *state* of mind at the time of retrieval matches our *state* at the time of initial encoding is known as **state-dependent memory** (Rezayof et al., 2008). Two factors that appear to influence the strength of state-dependent memory are *self-awareness* and *the presence of other retrieval cues*. That is, evidence for state-dependent memory is strongest when people are self-aware and thus attentive to their internal state of mind, and when other retrieval cues are weak.

As mentioned in Section 7.1d, the best retrieval cues come from associations formed when we encode information into long-term memory. A large body of evidence supports this rule of retrieval, known as the **encoding specificity principle** (Tulving & Thomson, 1973). For instance, in one study, participants were shown a long list of words and then asked either a semantic (meaning) or a rhyming question about each word (Morris et al., 1977). Thus, if the word was *dairy*, they might be asked if "*dairy* products come from cows" or if "*dairy* rhymes with *fairy*." Later, participants were asked to identify from a list those words they had been shown before. Results indicated that participants did much better at recognizing words for which semantic questions had previously been asked than they did for rhyming-word questions. The fact that semantically coded retrieval cues worked better than rhyming cues is not surprising, because as previously mentioned (Section 7.1d), long-term memories are often encoded semantically. However, when asked to identify words that *rhymed* with the ones that they had previously seen (for example, *berry*, which rhymes with *dairy*), participants did much better at recognizing words that rhymed with words for which they had been asked a rhyming question rather than a semantic question.

The importance of having the right retrieval cues for a memory task strikes close to home for every college student. In what you might perceive to be a cruel classroom demonstration of the encoding specificity principle, half the students in a college class were told that an upcoming exam would be multiple-choice (a recognition task), while the other half expected an essay exam (a recall task). Only some of the students, however, were given the exam they expected. Consistent with the encoding specificity principle, those students did much better on the exam than those who received an unexpected type of exam (D'Ydewalle & Rosselle, 1978). These results, combined with the previous study's findings, clearly indicate that the best retrieval cues are those that closely match the original encoding process.

State-dependent memory The tendency for retrieval from memory to be better when our state of mind during retrieval matches our state during encoding

Encoding specificity principle A retrieval rule stating that retrieving information from long-term memory is most likely to occur when the conditions at retrieval closely match the conditions present during the original learning

I cannot at the present moment recall what the General's Christian name was. Your poor dear mother always addressed him as "General." That I remember perfectly.

—Lady Bracknell in The Importance of Being Earnest by Oscar Wilde, Irish author and satirist, 1854–1900

7.3c *Source Confusion Can Create Memory Illusions.*

One of the primary distinctions between semantic and episodic memory involves remembering the time and place when the information in question was learned. With semantic memory the information in question is no longer associated with the time and place it was learned; with episodic memory, the information is most definitely tied to a specific time and place. Yet, sometimes we forget the true source of the episodic memory, and then we have a *memory illusion*. Memory illusions appear to be shaped by implicit remembering.

Déjà vu illusion A memory illusion in which people feel a sense of familiarity in a situation that they know they have never encountered before

A common type of memory illusion is the **déjà vu illusion** (Juan, 2006). In French, *déjà vu* literally means "already seen." About 60 percent of Americans experience déjà vu at least once in their lives. People who experience this memory illusion *subjectively* feel a sense of familiarity in a situation that they *objectively* know they have never encountered before. An example of déjà vu would be walking into a house for the very first time and experiencing a strong feeling of having been there before. Such experiences occur most often among people who regularly remember their dreams and daydream a great deal. They are also most likely to occur when one is stressed and when one is overtired (Brown, 2003). Although a popular belief is that déjà vu occurs because people are experiencing previous lives (reincarnation), a more cognitive—and less extraordinary—explanation is that people are simply implicitly remembering similar, but unidentifiable, situations they have previously experienced in their present lives. When brain scans have been able to locate the neurological source of déjà vu experiences, they tend to originate in the temporal lobes (Zeman, 2005).

Cryptomnesia A memory illusion in which people believe that some work they have done is a novel creation when, in fact, it is not original

Another type of memory illusion is **cryptomnesia**, which is also known as *unintended plagiarism*. In cryptomnesia, a person honestly believes that some work she or he has done is a novel creation, when in reality the work is not original (Brown & Murphy, 1989; Taylor, 1965). This type of memory illusion is common when people collaborate on a project. In such instances, group members recall an idea they heard from others—but they forget where and from whom they originally heard it. After a while, each of them believes it was they who came up with the brilliant idea that made the project a success. If you think of cryptomnesia as being an instance in which someone else's old idea becomes your new idea, then cryptomnesia is almost the opposite of déjà vu, in which something new seems old. With cryptomnesia, as with déjà vu, previously learned information is retained and influences our thoughts and actions without us consciously remembering it.

Accusations of cryptomnesia usually arise only after someone publicly presents the unintentionally plagiarized work as her or his own. A number of the more famous incidents—and even scandals—resulting from such public presentations have involved such well-known individuals as Sigmund Freud (founder of psychoanalysis), Helen Keller (educator and lecturer who was both deaf and blind), Friedrich Nietzsche (German philosopher and poet), Eddie Murphy (comedian and movie star), and George Harrison (former member of the Beatles). How common is cryptomnesia? The frequency of its occurrence is difficult to estimate because people in private life are rarely confronted with evidence that their ideas and works are not original. It is safe to assume, however, that cryptomnesia is not a rare product of implicit memory.

7.3d *Memories Are Often Sketchy Reconstructions of the Past.*

Based on the Chapter 4 discussion of perception, you understand that errors or misperceptions are bound to occur because our beliefs and expectations significantly influence how we perceive sensory stimuli. Similarly, our previous discussion of schemas (see Section 7.2c) demonstrated that beliefs and expectations could significantly shape what we encode and later retrieve from memory. How does this reconstructive process take place?

The scientific belief in the reconstructive nature of memory was first proposed about 70 years ago by English psychologist Sir Frederic Bartlett (1932). By testing people's memories of stories they had read, Bartlett found that accurate recollections were rare. Instead, people reconstructed the material they had learned, shortening and lengthening different aspects and changing details, overall, to better fit their own beliefs and expectations. These memory distortions became more pronounced over time, yet people were largely unaware that they had reconstructed the past. In fact, the reconstructed memories were often those aspects of the story that people most adamantly claimed to be true. Based on these findings, Bartlett concluded that information already stored in long-term memory strongly influences how we both encode and later remember new information.

One factor that influences the reconstruction of memory is age-related differences in encoding and retrieval. That is, an adult's mind is organized differently from that of a two-year-old, and, thus, the encoding and retrieval operations are different. According to the previously discussed *encoding specificity principle*, the effectiveness of a retrieval operation is determined by how well it re-creates the conditions present at the time of the original encoding. As a result, it is highly questionable whether a childhood experience that was encoded using a two-year-old's sensorimotor schemes can be accurately retrieved using an adult's formal operational schemes (Simcock & Hayne, 2002). This so-called **infantile amnesia** is one of the primary problems surrounding claims by adults concerning their recently "remembered" memories of early childhood sexual abuse (see Section 7.4c).

Infantile amnesia The inability to remember events that occurred during the early part of life (usually before the age of 3)

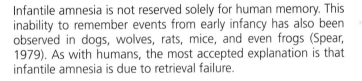

INFO-BIT Infantile amnesia is not reserved solely for human memory. This inability to remember events from early infancy has also been observed in dogs, wolves, rats, mice, and even frogs (Spear, 1979). As with humans, the most accepted explanation is that infantile amnesia is due to retrieval failure.

Another factor that can alter people's memory of past events is the *way* they are questioned about what they witnessed during those events. These distortions and alterations in memory are known as **misinformation effects**. The altered memories generated by such misinformation not only feel real to those who hold them but also often look real to observers (Schooler et al., 1986). In a famous study, Elizabeth Loftus and John Palmer (1974) demonstrated misinformation effects when they showed participants a short film of two cars colliding. Afterward, some of the participants were asked, "About how fast were the cars going when they *contacted* each other?" while others were asked, "About how fast were the cars going when they *smashed* into each other?" Those who heard the word *smashed* estimated the cars' speed at 41 miles per hour, while those who heard the word *contacted* gave a 31-mile-per-hour estimate. In addition, when questioned again a week later, the "smashed" participants were more than twice as likely as the "contacted" participants to recall seeing broken glass at the accident scene, despite the fact that no broken glass was visible in the film.

Misinformation effects Distortions and alterations in a witness' memory due to receiving misleading information during questioning

Further research indicates that altered memories are most likely to be created when misleading information is subtly introduced and when original memories have faded with the passage of time (Jaschinski & Wentura, 2002; Loftus, 1993). For example, during criminal trials, eyewitness memory distortions may occur in response to misleading questions posed by lawyers (Zaragoza et al., 2007). A witness might

Ten thousand different things that come from your memory or imagination—and you do not know which is which, which was true, which is false.

—Amy Tan, American author, b. 1952

be asked whether a mugger's glasses had plastic or wire frames, suggesting that the mugger wore glasses. The witness may not remember glasses, and the mugger may not have worn glasses; however, this question may lead the witness to now "remember" seeing glasses on the mugger's face. Currently, it is unclear whether misleading information permanently alters memory or whether true memories can be retrieved under the right conditions. Children are particularly susceptible to misinformation effects, and this fact has made the prosecution of alleged child sexual abuse cases problematic (Howe, 2008). That is, if children's memories can be literally altered through skillful questioning, then how trustworthy are their testimonies? Until more is learned about misinformation effects, distinguishing between the true and false memories of witnesses of any age—but especially those of children—will be one of the major challenges of the courts (Patterson, 2004).

Have these studies concerning the reconstructive nature of memory surprised you? Do they cause you to doubt your recollection of important life events? What about those events from your past that seem "frozen in time"? How accurate are these memories? Check out Closer Look 7-2 concerning what we know about these so-called flashbulb memories.

How Accurate Are Flashbulb Memories?

When discussing the reconstructive nature of memory, many people bring up the fact that they seem to remember certain experiences in their lives in amazing detail, as if literally frozen in time. These detailed and vivid memories of surprising and emotion-provoking events are known as **flashbulb memories** (Uttl et al., 2006). Flashbulb memories are often formed when you learn of the death of a loved one or a personally important public figure. For middle-aged and elderly Americans, the assassination of President Kennedy on 1963 created a flashbulb memory. On September 11, 2001, the terrorist attacks at New York's World Trade Center and the Pentagon created flashbulb memories for millions of people worldwide (Kvavilashvil et al., 2009).

Research suggests that self-relevance is a critical factor that interacts with surprise and emotion in producing such memories. Strong emotional reactions at the time of the event activate the amygdala—the portion of the brain that plays a key role in emotions—which in turn influences the hippocampus to create a memory (Cahill et al., 1996). Age is also important. When they asked people who were between one and seven years old in 1963 to recall how they heard about the Kennedy assassination, researchers found that the number of flashbulb memories steadily increased as age at encoding rose (Winograd & Killinger, 1983). Whereas all those who were seven years old at the time had flashbulb memories of this event, only 50 percent of the four-year-olds had such memories. Also, individuals who were older at the time of encoding had more elaborate and detailed memories. The likely reason for this increase is that a seven-year-old's encoding process is more similar than a four-year-old's to that of an adult, and thus, the seven-year-old's childhood memories are more accessible for adult retrieval.

Although people tend to express high confidence in the accuracy of their flashbulb memories, substantial evidence indicates that changes and reconstructions do occur (Terr, 1988; Wagenaar & Groeneweg, 1990). For example, one day after the space shuttle *Challenger* explosion in 1986, college students were asked to describe exactly how they heard the news. Then, three years later, many of these same students were again asked to recall their experiences (Neisser & Harsch, 1992). Despite expressing confidence in the accuracy of their memories, only about seven percent of the students demonstrated a high degree of agreement in their two reports. For instance, although 21 percent initially reported that they learned the news from television, three years later this figure had risen to 45 percent. Those who had produced false memories during the three-year period were

Flashbulb memories Detailed and vivid memories of surprising and emotion-provoking events surprised, if not amazed, when shown the handwritten reports they had produced right after the explosion. These findings suggest that flashbulb memories are not burned into our minds and fully retained but are subject to considerable change and reconstruction over time (Schmidt, 2004; Schmolck et al., 2000).

Despite the susceptibility to error of flashbulb memories, they still tend to be more accurate than other types of memories, perhaps partly because of their stronger emotional content (MacKay & Ahmetzanov, 2005). However, additional research suggests that the greater accuracy may also be due to people spending more time thinking about the content of flashbulb memories (Bohn & Berntsen, 2007). In other words, you are more likely to accurately remember something if you spend a lot of time elaboratively rehearsing it. As previously discussed in Section 7.1d, elaborative rehearsal involves a relatively deep level of cognitive processing.

Section REVIEW

- Recall requires both retrieval and reproduction of information, whereas recognition requires only a decision on whether or not the information has been previously encountered.

- A retrieval cue is a stimulus that helps us recall information from memory.

- According to the encoding specificity principle, retrieving information from long-term memory is most likely when the conditions at retrieval closely match the conditions present during the original learning.

- Déjà vu and cryptomnesia are memory illusions shaped by implicit memory.

- Information stored in long-term memory influences both encoding and later remembering of new information, and the way people are questioned about their memories can cause memory reconstruction.

7.4 How Does Forgetting Occur?

What would happen if you did not forget? Wouldn't this be an overwhelming experience? Shereshevskii, the Russian reporter whose story you read at the beginning of this chapter, could answer this question. Over the years, as his memories piled up, they began to overwhelm him. Eventually, the slightest stimulus evoked so many memories that Shereshevskii could no longer hold a job, read, or even follow a simple conversation. For Shereshevskii, not being able to forget became as problematic as Henry Molaison's condition of not being able to remember (described in Chapter 2).

7.4a *Most Forgetting Occurs Soon After Learning.*

Unlike what Shereshevskii learned, much of what the normal person learns is quickly forgotten. Do you remember Herman Ebbinghaus's research from the late 1800s discussed in Section 7.1a? After learning more than 1,200 lists of nonsense syllables and then measuring how much he recalled from 20 minutes to 31 days later, he discovered that most forgetting occurs during the first nine hours after learning. As you can see in his "forgetting curve," depicted in Figure 7-8, more than 40 percent of the material was forgotten after just 20 minutes. By nine hours, more than 60 percent was lost, but then the course of forgetting leveled off. These findings, combined with

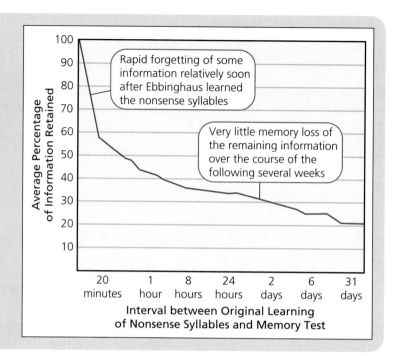

FIGURE 7-8
Ebbinghaus's Forgetting Curve
Ebbinghaus discovered that more than 60 percent of forgetting occurs during the first nine hours after learning, and then forgetting levels off. Is the "relearning" of this information generally difficult or easy, relative to information that was not previously learned?

Figure labels: Rapid forgetting of some information relatively soon after Ebbinghaus learned the nonsense syllables. Very little memory loss of the remaining information over the course of the following several weeks. Y-axis: Average Percentage of Information Retained. X-axis: Interval between Original Learning of Nonsense Syllables and Memory Test — 20 minutes, 1 hour, 8 hours, 24 hours, 2 days, 6 days, 31 days.

later research, indicate that the greatest amount of forgetting occurs in the first few hours after learning, with progressively less memory loss as time marches on (Wixted & Ebbesen, 1991).

A second important discovery made by Ebbinghaus was that although you may forget information you previously learned, this does not necessarily mean you have forgotten everything about that information. He discovered that it took less time to relearn a list of nonsense words than it did to initially learn the list. The implication of these findings is that most forgetting is not complete: You may forget something if you do not rehearse it for a period of time, but it is much easier to relearn it in the future than to learn it initially. This is good news for all of us who have not practiced our French or algebra since high-school graduation!

One reason we forget information soon after learning it is that we are not sufficiently attentive when the information is presented. Such *absentmindedness* accounts for those instances when we forget new acquaintances' names, misplace our keys, or are unsure whether we took our daily vitamins. The pervasiveness of people's daily inattentiveness was demonstrated in a clever study in which a research confederate approached people on a public street and asked them for directions (Simons & Levin, 1998). While these unsuspecting individuals were answering the confederate's query, two workers carrying a large door passed between them. During the few moments in which the participant's view was obscured, a second confederate stepped in to replace the original confederate. Would it surprise you to learn that only half the participants noticed the change? This study suggests that inattentiveness or shallow encoding can cause rapid forgetting of newly presented information.

7.4b Forgetting Often Occurs Due to Interference.

Based on Ebbinghaus's research, the popular early view of why forgetting occurs was that unless memories are periodically rehearsed, the simple passage of time causes them to fade and eventually **decay** (Thorndike, 1914). But although decay contributes to forgetting in short-term memory, research strongly suggests that decay does not significantly influence forgetting in long-term memory (Cowan, 1995).

Memories are hunting-horns whose noise dies away in the wind.

—Guillaume Apollinaire, French poet and art critic, 1880–1918

Decay Forgetting due to the passage of time

John Jenkins and Karl Dallenbach conducted an important study that discredited the decay theory of forgetting in long-term memory in 1924. They had college students learn lists of nonsense words either just after waking in the morning or just before going to sleep at night, and then tested the students' recall after one, two, four, or eight hours. For the sleeping students, this meant waking them. Despite the same amount of time passage, much more forgetting occurred when students were awake and involved in other activities than when they were asleep.

If forgetting is not due to the simple passage of time, then what is its cause? Actually, the key to this answer is contained within Jenkins and Dallenbach's findings. Do you see it? More forgetting occurred among students who had learned nonsense words early in the morning because they were exposed to more information during the day that could potentially interfere with their remembering. In contrast, the students who had learned the nonsense words before bedtime were exposed to much less potentially interfering information while they slept. These findings suggest that learning new information can act backwards in time to interfere with remembering older information. This forgetting due to interference from newly learned information is known as **retroactive interference** (Eakin & Smith, 2012). You experience retroactive interference when learning the information in this chapter interferes with your memory of information learned in a previous chapter.

The other major type of interference is **proactive interference**, which occurs when previously learned information acts forward in time to interfere with remembering more recently learned information (Makovski & Jiang, 2008). Thus, if your memory of information learned in a previous chapter of this textbook interferes with your learning of information in the current chapter, you are experiencing proactive interference. Another common example of proactive interference—that is often embarrassing—occurs when you call your current girlfriend or boyfriend by a previous partner's name. Of the two types of interference, proactive interference probably causes more forgetting than retroactive interference because we have stored up a great deal of information in long-term memory that can potentially interfere with any new information we might try to learn. Luckily, the greater potential ability of proactive interference to cause forgetting may be offset by the fact that we can also use already-stored information to elaboratively encode new information (refer back to Section 7.1d) and thus *improve* our memory.

A meta-analysis of 26 different studies (Kail, 2002) suggests that young children (age 4) are more susceptible to proactive interference than older children (age 13). In contrast, among adults, those who are older are more vulnerable to proactive interference than those who are younger (Hasher et al., 2002). A likely explanation for both sets of findings is that these age-related changes in retroactive interference are associated with age-related changes in the brain's information-processing speed. As children's brains mature, neural processing speed increases, whereas neural processing speed decreases in later adulthood. Thus, the very young and the very old are most susceptible to forgetting due to proactive interference.

For both proactive and retroactive interference, one important factor in determining how much interference will occur—at any age—is the degree of *similarity* between the old and the new information. As the degree of similarity increases, the likelihood of interference also increases. For example, as illustrated in Figure 7-9, if your new phone number at the college dorm is very similar to your old phone number at home, you may well experience retroactive interference when you call home and proactive interference when you call your dorm room.

Retroactive interference
Forgetting due to interference from newly learned information

Proactive interference
Forgetting due to interference from previously learned information

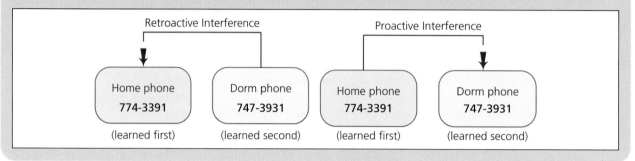

FIGURE 7-9   Interference in Memory

After learning your new college dorm phone number, you may have trouble remembering your parents' number at home (retroactive interference). However, your memory of your parents' phone number may also interfere with remembering your new dorm number (proactive interference). For both types of interference, the degree of similarity between the old and new information significantly determines how much interference occurs. More similar information causes greater interference than less similar information. Can you think of other examples of retroactive and proactive interference in your life?

Retroactive Interference

Home phone
774-3391
(learned first)

Dorm phone
747-3931
(learned second)

Proactive Interference

Home phone
774-3391
(learned first)

Dorm phone
747-3931
(learned second)

7.4c   We Are Sometimes Motivated to Forget.

In 1990 George Franklin, Sr. stood trial for the brutal 1969 murder of an eight-year-old child, Susie Nason. The major evidence provided against Franklin was the eyewitness testimony of his own daughter, Eileen, who had been Susie's best friend. What made this case so unusual was that Eileen's memory of witnessing the murder had been repressed for 20 years. Then one day, while playing with her own young daughter, she had a brief flashback of the murder—the look of betrayal in Susie's eyes just before she was killed. Later, more flashbacks occurred, including the memory of Susie begging for mercy and the images of Eileen's father sexually assaulting Susie in the back of a van and of Eileen's father raising a rock above his head just before smashing Susie's skull.

One of the problems with Eileen's memory of the murder was that it changed across various tellings. First, she told police that the murder occurred in the morning while driving to school. However, when reminded that Susie had not been missing until after school was out, Eileen said it was in the late afternoon. Initially, she also reported that her sister, Janice, was riding in the van but then was dropped off when Susie was picked up. Later, that detail disappeared from her testimony. Despite these inconsistencies, the jury was so impressed with Eileen's detailed and confident memory of the murder that it returned a guilty verdict after only a day of deliberation. This case marked the first time that the return of a repressed memory proved to be the deciding factor in convicting someone of a crime in the United States. Did Eileen really witness the murder of her best friend 20 years earlier? Could such a traumatic event be forgotten for so long and then suddenly be remembered?

What Is Motivated Forgetting?

Motivated forgetting
Forgetting due to a desire to eliminate awareness of some unpleasant or disturbing memory

Beyond the influence of interference, sometimes people forget things because they want to forget them. This is called **motivated forgetting**, and it usually occurs because a memory is unpleasant or disturbing. Sigmund Freud (1946, 1949) is generally credited with providing the theoretical framework for understanding this type of self-protective forgetting. In Freud's psychoanalytic theory, there are two types of motivated forgetting: *suppression* and *repression*.

Suppression Motivated forgetting that occurs consciously

Suppression occurs when a person *consciously* tries to forget something. For example, while preparing to execute a complicated routine during an important performance, a dancer is likely to suppress the memory of being sprawled on stage when she last attempted this number. In this situation, although the performer is aware that she failed in her previous attempt, she consciously chooses not to think about it. Freud believed that *repression*, unlike conscious forgetting, occurs when a person unconsciously "pushes" unpleasant memories out of conscious awareness. Although these memories are no longer remembered in the conventional sense, they continue to unconsciously influence the person's thoughts, feelings, and behavior. According to psychoanalytic theory, repression plays a key role both in the formation of personality and in the development of psychological disorders (as you will see in Chapters 10 and 11). Despite the assumption by psychoanalysts that repression shapes human thought and behavior, it remains a controversial topic.

Should We Trust Repressed Memories?

Many memory researchers believe it is naive to assume that people can accurately recover memories that were previously unconsciously repressed. They further contend that people can unknowingly manufacture false memories (Loftus, 2011). For ethical reasons, psychologists cannot attempt to implant false memories of murder or sexual assault in research participants. However, Elizabeth Loftus and James Coan (1995) successfully implanted less traumatic false childhood memories in five research participants ranging in age from 8 to 42. Following Loftus and Coan's instructions, trusted family members told these five individuals that, at age 5, they had been lost in a shopping mall for an extended time before being rescued by an elderly man. Following these suggestions, all participants became convinced that they indeed had been lost. One of these individuals, a 14-year-old named Chris, received this false account from his older brother. Two days later, Chris could remember the incident with strong feelings: "That day, I was so scared that I would never see my family again. I knew that I was in trouble." Within two weeks, he remembered that the man who rescued him was bald and wore glasses and a flannel shirt. When debriefed and told that his memory was false, he replied, "Really? I thought I remembered being lost... and looking around for you guys. I do remember that. And then crying, and Mom coming up and saying 'Where were you? Don't you ever do that again.'"

These and other studies demonstrate that false memories can be implanted into the minds of both children and adults (Johnson & Raye, 2000; Smith et al., 2003). In fact, research indicates that simply repeating imaginary events to people causes them to become more confident that they actually experienced these events (Begg et al., 1992; Zaragoza & Mitchell, 1996). Once constructed, these false memories may feel as real as—or even more real than—genuine memories. How are these false memories constructed? Loftus suggests that people may combine actual personal experiences—or memories of witnessing others' experiences—with their memories of the location selected by the family member in which the alleged incident occurred (Loftus et al., 1995). Although people may be confused when others first tell them about the false incidents, they soon combine previously unconnected bits of information into new—yet thoroughly false—memories.

Of course, this research does not tell us whether George Franklin's daughter, Eileen, recalled a false memory of sexual assault and murder rather than an authentic repressed memory. It does, however, raise the possibility that her repressed memory, and those of others who have come forward with similar claims, may not be real. Psychologists who conduct research on false memories readily acknowledge that childhood abuse is a major societal problem. Indeed, Elizabeth Loftus is herself a survivor of such trauma, having been molested at age 6 (without forgetting). Yet, many memory researchers are concerned that some cases involving repressed memories may reflect something other than real experiences. Certain techniques commonly used in therapy to recover childhood memories of abuse, such as hypnosis and dream interpretation, can distort

BVT *Lab*

Improve your test scores. Practice quizzes are available at www.BVTLab.com.

patients' recollections of past events and create false memories of abuse (Erdelyi, 2010). One antidote to naively accepting recovered memories of childhood trauma is to educate the public about the reconstructive nature of memory and how they can be tricked into "remembering" things that never happened (McHugh et al., 2004).

Journey of Discovery

Could you falsely reconstruct a childhood memory based on your *beliefs* about how memory works? That is, do you think that your beliefs about how memory works could affect your recollection of past events?

Section REVIEW

- Most forgetting occurs during the first nine hours after learning.

- It is much easier to relearn forgotten information than to learn new information.

- Most forgetting is caused by interference (retroactive and proactive).

- Two types of motivated forgetting are suppression and repression.

- Therapeutic techniques used to recover childhood memories of abuse can create false memories of abuse.

7.5 What Is the Biological Basis for Memories?

As mentioned at the beginning of the chapter, memory has been likened to the computer's information-processing system. In this regard, while cognitive psychologists have studied our memory "software," neuroscientists have focused their attention on its "hardware"—the biological underpinnings of memory.

7.5a Long-Term Potentiation May Be the Neural Basis for Memory.

Where is a memory physically located in the brain? Neuroscientists have searched for the place where memory "lives," or the *engram*, for more than 50 years (Lashley, 1950; Schotanus & Chergui, 2008). Although there still is no scientific consensus on what an engram is or where it is located in the brain, it appears that memories begin as electrical impulses traveling between neurons, and that the establishment of long-term memories involves changes in these neurons. Eric Kandel and James Schwartz (1982) observed such neuronal changes when studying learning in the California sea slug, *Aplysia*, which has a small number (about 20,000) of large-sized neurons. By repeatedly giving sea slugs a squirt of water (the CS) followed by a mild electric shock to the tail (the UCS), Kandel and Schwartz were able to classically condition the sea slugs to reflexively withdraw their gills when only squirted with the water (the CR). Kandel and Schwartz discovered that when the sea slug forms a new memory for this classically conditioned response, significant changes occur in both the *function* and the *structure* of its affected neurons (Kandel, 1995). Regarding function, an increase occurs in the amount of the neurotransmitters released at the synapses—the communication points—of the neurons. Regarding structure, not only does the number of synapses increase, so does the number of interconnecting branches between neurons. These structural changes make communication along this new neural circuit more efficient.

This strengthening of synaptic transmission, which is known as **long-term potentiation**, has also been found in the brains of more complex animals (Goosens & Maren, 2002). For example, when rats are raised in enriched environments containing many objects with which they can play and from which they can learn, their brains develop more elaborate neural connections than rats raised in impoverished environments (Black et al., 1990; Chang et al., 1991). Additional research supporting long-term potentiation as the neural basis for memory has found that the formation of long-term memories can be blocked if animals are given drugs that inhibit long-term potentiation (del Olmo et al., 2003). Finally, when researchers altered the genes of mice so that long-term potentiation was enhanced in the hippocampus and other areas of the brain used in memory, the mice remembered new information over longer time periods than normal mice (Tang et al., 1999). Together, this research suggests that long-term potentiation is the physiological key to memory. When a new memory is formed, functional and structural changes take place in specific neurons, creating a kind of *memory circuit*. Each time that the new memory is recalled, the neurons in this new circuit are activated, which strengthens their neural connections. As the communication links between the neurons increase in strength, the memory becomes established as a long-term memory.

The process by which neural connections become stronger and new memories become lasting, or long-term, memories is called *consolidation*. When these memories are then retrieved from long-term memory, "worked with" in working memory, and then stored again for later retrieval, this process is known as *reconsolidation* (Nader & Einarsson, 2010). As already discussed (see Section 7.3d), during the reconsolidation process a retrieved memory can be affected by new circumstances, making the reconsolidated memory different from the memory that existed before reconsolidation. Think of a memory as if it were a book in a library: when the book is checked out, used, and then returned to the library stacks, some of the book pages may be torn or stained, or there may be notes written on the pages. The book has been altered somewhat by this process. A growing number of neuroscientists studying memory believe that this process of reconsolidation may explain why our memories for events can change over time.

7.5b Several Brain Regions Are Involved in Memory Formation and Storage.

During the first half of the twentieth century, neuroscientists believed that a specific memory could be found in a specific place in the brain (Penfield, 1958). Although we now know that a specific memory cannot be tied to a specific brain site, certain types of memories appear to be stored in certain brain areas (McCarthy, 1995). Short-term memory, the type of memory where we actively "work" with information, appears to involve prefrontal regions of the cerebral cortex

Long-term potentiation The long-lasting strengthening of synaptic transmission along a specific neural circuit, which is believed to be the neural basis for long-term memory

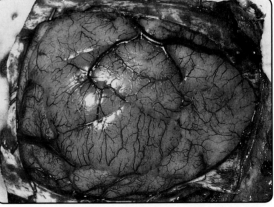

Wikimedia Commons

In the 1950s, neurosurgeons "mapped" the cerebral cortex while performing brain surgery. Surgeons would place numbered tags on the exposed brain to designate which locations induced particular memories, sensory experiences, or motor activities. Although scientists initially believed they had discovered the physical traces of memory, the engram, additional research suggested that these were not true memory traces.

(Chein et al., 2011). In long-term memory, a number of brain regions have been identified. The neocortex, striatum, and amygdala play important roles in the type of long-term memory previously identified as implicit memory. Regarding the sort of memory consolidation necessary for explicit memory, both animal and human studies reveal that several brain regions are involved, including the hippocampus and nearby portions of the cortex and the thalamus (Tsukiura et al., 2011). Of these brain regions, the hippocampus appears to be most important in the encoding of new memories and the transfer of them from short-term to long-term memory. Again, do you remember the tragic story of Henry Molaison? Because his entire hippocampus was surgically removed to control his epileptic seizures, he lost the ability to form explicit long-term memories. Or did he? Read on.

Anterograde amnesia The inability to form long-term memories due to physical injury to the brain

Retrograde amnesia The loss of information previously stored in long-term memory due to physical injury to the brain

Shutterstock

Black-capped chickadees remember the location of up to 6,000 sites where they stockpiled food during the winter. They also recall what kind of food they put at a particular site and when they put it there (Clayton & Dickinson, 1998). These birds have a much larger hippocampus than birds that do not stockpile food (Clayton, 1998).

This inability to form new memories is called **anterograde amnesia**. *Anterograde* means "forward moving." Henry Molaison's short-term memory was fine following his surgery, and he could still form implicit memories and remember events stored in long-term memory prior to his surgery. Similar memory deficits occur in monkeys when their hippocampus is surgically removed (Zola-Morgan & Squire, 1993). These findings suggest that although the hippocampus is critical for long-term memory formation, it is not involved in short-term memory activities or in the storage and retrieval of long-term memories.

While you are thinking about Henry, you should know that in his final years he was still helping memory researchers unlock the wonders of the human mind. For many years, scientists believed that Henry could no longer form new explicit memories. He was unable to learn new vocabulary words or remember people he had met. However, some psychologists wondered whether, over time, other areas of Henry's brain might have taken over some memory functions of the hippocampus so that he could have some limited ability to form explicit memories. In 2004, psychologists Gail O'Kane and her colleagues tested this hypothesis by testing Henry's knowledge of people who became famous after his brain surgery in 1953. In this testing, Henry was given the first name of 35 different famous persons and asked to say the last name that came to mind. Examples were "Ray_____ (Charles)," "Ronald_____ (Reagan)," and "Fidel_____ (Castro)." The researchers discovered that Henry was able to correctly supply the last name of about one-third of the famous people. This is clear evidence that certain areas of Henry's brain had taken on the task of creating some limited explicit memories, a testament to the brain's *plasticity* (see Chapter 2, Section 2.3h).

Another type of amnesia is **retrograde amnesia**, which is the loss of information previously stored in long-term memory (Brown, 2002; Fast & Fujiwara, 2001). People who have automobile accidents or experience some other kind of blow to the head often cannot remember the events leading up to their physical injury (Levin et al., 1984). For example, Princess Diana's bodyguard, who was the sole survivor of the car crash that claimed her life, retained no memory of the accident. In more severe cases, the person may not remember events that occurred years before. However, in

FIGURE 7-10

Anterograde and Retrograde Amnesia

In anterograde amnesia, a person is unable to form new memories after the amnesia-inducing event. In retrograde amnesia, a person is unable to retrieve information stored in long-term memory from before the amnesia-inducing event.

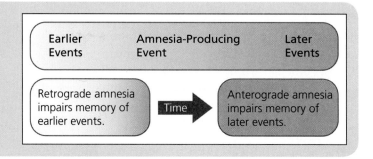

most cases, such memory loss of "distant events" is only temporary (Russell, 1971). Figure 7-10 reviews the differences between anterograde and retrograde amnesia.

When researchers discovered the role played by the hippocampus in long-term memory formation, that discovery also helped them better understand the biological basis for infantile amnesia (refer back to Section 7.3d), which is a special form of retrograde amnesia (Newcombe et al., 2000). That is, the hippocampus does not fully develop until about age 2. Thus, any memory encoding that the immature hippocampus performs is likely to be inaccessible for later conscious remembering by the mature brain.

As you see from this brief overview of the biological basis of memory, neuroscientists' insights into our memory "hardware" provide a more complete understanding of the entire memory system. As we learn more about the biopsychology of memory, we will be in a better position to treat memory deficits caused by illness and trauma, as well as enhance the memory of healthy individuals.

Section REVIEW

- Long-term potentiation appears to be the physiological key to memory.

- There is no specific location in the brain associated with a specific memory, but certain types of memories appear to be stored in certain brain areas.

PSYCHOLOGICAL applications

Improving Everyday Memory

Mnemonics are strategies to make it easier to encode, store, and/or retrieve information. This chapter has described current research and theory on memory. How can you use this knowledge to improve your ability to remember facts and other information? What follows is not an exhaustive guide, but research indicates that these ten techniques can improve your everyday memory:

> **Mnemonics** Strategies that make it easier to encode, store, and/or retrieve information

1. *Focus your attention.* When you don't pay close attention to something, you are unlikely to remember it. Distracting stimuli, such as having the television on while studying, significantly interfere with encoding information into long-term memory. Thus, to aid remembering, eliminate distractions by finding a quiet place to concentrate. If you cannot escape annoying distractions, reading aloud what you need to remember can help focus your attention (Hertel & Rude, 1991).

2. *Space out your study sessions.* One of the most common mistakes students make is waiting until a day before an exam to study. Yet Ebbinghaus's (1885) famous research on forgetting (see Section 7.1a) revealed another important truth about learning new material: Don't try to memorize by swallowing all your information in one big gulp. Studying new information over several days results in better learning than cramming your studying into one day (Bahrick et al., 1993). Such *distributed practice* is most effective if the interval between practice sessions is about 24 hours. Thus, four separate 1-hour study sessions spread out over four days will lead to better retrieval than one 4-hour session (Aamodt & Wang, 2008).

3. *Construct information in a hierarchy.* One of the most effective ways to remember information is to arrange it in a series of categories, from the most general to the most specific. For example, the topics in this chapter are organized hierarchically: first, with the general topic of the chapter ("Memory"); next, with more focused "level-A" sections (such as "The Nature of Memory") that contain even more specific "level-B" headings (such as "The Computer's Information-Processing System Has Been a Useful Model for Human Memory"); and, finally, within these level-B headings are very specific "level-C" subsection headings (such as "Information Processes," "The Identification of Three Memory Systems," and "Is This the Only Model of Memory?"). Using hierarchical systems can double the amount of information you can recall (Bower et al., 1969).

When you study, external distractions can make it difficult to encode information into long-term memory. You can minimize distractions by finding a quiet place to concentrate.

4. *Use the method of loci.* In studying the amazing Shereshevskii, Alexander Luria discovered that Shereshevskii habitually and automatically used visual imagery to encode information into long-term memory. Although we are unlikely to come close to matching Shereshevskii's memory skills, research indicates that we can better remember information if we associate it with vivid mental images. One well-known visual mnemonic technique is the *method of loci* (pronounced "LOW-sigh"), which requires you to mentally place items to be memorized in specific locations well-known to yourself, such as rooms in your house. When you want to recall these items, you simply take a mental "walk" by these locations and "see" the memorized items. Shereshevskii would often mentally place items he wanted to remember at different locations on Gorky Street in Moscow. Later, he could recall these items in reverse order by mentally "walking" down Gorky Street in the opposite direction. In using the method of loci, choose extremely familiar memory locations so they provide a vivid context for organizing the information to be memorized. If you wanted to learn a grocery list, for example, you might mentally place each food item at a specific location in your home: strawberries on your bed, milk jugs in your bathroom sink, hot dogs hanging from the kitchen door, and so on. By mentally strolling through your home, the food items pop into your mind, as illustrated in Figure 7-11.

5. *Use the peg-word method.* Another effective use of visual imagery to encode information into long-term memory is the peg-word method, which involves using a series of words that serve as "pegs" on which memories can be "hung." In one variation of this memory technique, the peg words rhyme with numbers to make the words easy to remember. For example: One is the sun, two is a shoe, three is a tree, four is a door, five is a hive, six is sticks, seven is heaven, eight is a plate, nine is twine, and ten is a pen. As illustrated in Figure 7-12, if you wanted to learn a grocery list, you might associate sun and strawberries by imagining the sun ripening strawberries. Two is a shoe, so you might imagine a shoe resting on a jug of milk. The image of hot dogs in a tree and olives on sticks might also serve as memorable images, and so on. At the grocery store, you remember the list of groceries by simply recalling the peg words associated with each number. These peg words then serve as retrieval cues for the groceries.

FIGURE 7-11

The Method of Loci

With the method of loci, you remember things by mentally placing items in specific locations well-known to yourself. To recall these items, you mentally "walk" by these locations and "see" the memorized items. In this example, you memorize a grocery list by placing each food item in separate locations at home.

Step 1: Mentally place items in specific locations.

Strawberries on your bed

Milk jugs in the bathroom sink

Hot dogs hanging from the kitchen window

Butter smeared on the refrigerator

Ice cream dripping off the stove

Olives tumbling out of the dishwasher

Flour covering the living room floor

Sugar cubes piled on the couch

Carrots on the front door

Coffee beans strewn on the front porch

Step 2: Mentally "walk" by specific location to recall the items.

FIGURE 7-12

The Peg-Word Method

Step 1: Memorize these peg words in order	Step 2: Hang new items on the peg words	Step 3: Imagine a memorable interactive image.
One is the sun.	Sun——strawberries	
Two is a shoe.	Shoe——milk	
Three is a tree.	Tree——hot dogs	
Four is a door.	Door——butter	
Five is a hive.	Hive——ice cream	
Six is sticks.	Sticks——olives	
Seven is heaven.	Heaven——flour	
Eight is a plate.	Plate——sugar cubes	
Nine is twine.	Twine——carrots	
Ten is a pen.	Pen——coffee beans	

6. *Use verbal mnemonics.* The use of verbal mnemonics can facilitate recall by giving extra meaning to concepts. One effective verbal mnemonic is an *acronym*, which is a word that consists of all the first letters of the items to be memorized. For example, you can remember the names of the Great Lakes (Huron, Ontario, Michigan, Erie, and Superior) by remembering the acronym HOMES. Similarly, an acrostic is a phrase in which the first letters of each word are used to remind you of something. In grade school, my daughters recited the phrase, "My Very Educated Mother Just Sold Us Nine Pizzas" to remember the names of the planets (Mercury, Venus, Earth, Mars, Jupiter, Saturn, Uranus, Neptune, and Pluto). Finally, another verbal mnemonic that provides an organizational structure to information is a *rhyme*. Often-used rhymes are "I before *E* except after *C*" and "Thirty days hath September …"

7. *Use external mnemonics.* External mnemonics play a leading role in helping us fortify our memories. Examples of such memory aids include the alarm clock that reminds you to get up in the morning, your lecture notes that facilitate your retrieval of classroom material, the rubber band worn on your wrist that reminds you to visit a sick friend, and the grocery list that helps you purchase the ingredients for your next meal. To effectively use these external memory aids, you must first recognize your need to use them and then select an appropriate aid for the task at hand. Ben, the public relations director with a severe short-term memory deficit, could not have survived in his job without heavily relying on external memory devices. For example, before walking into meetings, Ben would discreetly hold in his hand the business cards of those in attendance. This external memory aid helped Ben remember their names and relevant details of previous meetings. Immediately following meetings, he would write down or tape-record his recollections before they disappeared. Although Ben could not properly function without constantly relying on these external aids, his case is merely an extension of what most of us do to bolster our fairly efficient memory systems.

8. *Overlearn.* Studying information even after you think you already know it is one of the most effective ways to firmly embed it in memory. Any information that is well-learned is more likely to survive a case of the jitters than information only minimally learned.

9. *Use sleep to your advantage.* As you recall from Chapter 5, Section 5.2e, there is evidence that the cognitive processing that occurs during nighttime dreaming consolidates and stores information gathered during the day (Pavlides & Winson, 1989). In this chapter, you also discovered that due to lack of interference, things learned just before sleep are retained better than information learned earlier in the day. Together, these findings suggest that your parents' advice to get a good night's rest before a big exam—and to study just before going to sleep—is well worth heeding.

10. *Cultivate close relationships.* Finally, an intriguing way to expand your memory is to form a partnership with someone else's memory! Research reveals that people in close relationships have a shared memory system that is greater than either of their individual memories (Andersson & Rönnberg, 1997). In such collaborative memory, each person enjoys the benefits of the other's memory by taking responsibility for remembering just those items that fall clearly to him or her. For two people living together, this may involve one person assuming responsibility for remembering where the tools in the basement workroom are located, while the other assumes responsibility for remembering where the special dinnerware and napkins are stored. If you learn in a general way what the other person knows in detail, you can significantly improve your overall ability to remember things. By updating one another regarding your individual knowledge areas, each of you will further embellish your collaborative memory.

Suggested Websites

American Psychological Association

http://www.apa.org

At the American Psychological Association website, you can search for press releases and other information about recent memory research.

Mind Tools

http://www.mindtools.com/memory.html

This website contains memory techniques and mnemonics for use in everyday living, as well as links to other related websites.

Eyewitness Identification Research Laboratory

http://eyewitness.utep.edu

This website discusses research on eyewitness testimony and provides recommendations on how to correctly design and conduct police lineups and photospreads for eyewitnesses.

How Can Eyewitness Identification Research Go Wrong?

http://www.pbs.org/wgbh/pages/frontline/shows/dna/photos/

This website discusses how conducting police lineups and photospreads for eyewitnesses can inadvertently lead to incorrect identifications.

Key Terms

Anterograde amnesia, 320
Chunking, 293
Cryptomnesia, 310
Decay, 314
Déjà vu illusion, 310
Elaborative rehearsal, 294
Encoding specificity
    principle, 309
Encoding, 287
Episodic memory, 298
Explicit memory, 297
Flashbulb memories, 312
Implicit memory, 299
Infantile amnesia, 311
Information-processing
    model, 287

Long-term memory, 289
Long-term potentiation, 319
Maintenance rehearsal, 293
Memory, 286
Misinformation effects, 311
Mnemonics, 321
Motivated forgetting, 316
Parallel distributed processing
    model, 305
Primacy effect, 289
Priming, 299
Proactive interference, 315
Procedural memory, 299
Recall, 307
Recency effect, 289
Recognition, 307

Retrieval cue, 308
Retrieval, 288
Retroactive interference, 315
Retrograde amnesia, 320
Semantic memory, 298
Semantic network model, 301
Sensory memory, 289
Short-term memory, 289
State-dependent memory, 309
Storage, 287
Suppression, 316
Tip-of-the-tongue
    phenomenon, 308
Working memory, 292

Review Questions

1. When you encode information into memory using its personal meaning, which of the following are you using?
   a. visual encoding
   b. acoustic encoding
   c. semantic encoding
   d. information-processing
   e. c and d

2. If, in trying to memorize an alphabetical list of Russian states, you can remember the last two states on the list better than the middle two states on the list, you have experienced the _____ effect.
   a. serial-position
   b. primacy
   c. recency
   d. a and c
   e. b and c

3. Which of the following is true of sensory memory?
   a. It requires conscious awareness.
   b. It exists in the hippocampus.
   c. It can be studied in the laboratory.
   d. It exists in one system.
   e. It can be directly accessed.

4. Which of the following is true of short-term memory?
   a. It stores spoken words and visual and spatial images.
   b. It seems to be dominated by visual encoding.
   c. It has an unlimited capacity.
   d. It does not retrieve information from long-term memory.
   e. a and d

5. When I remember my first day as a college student, I am relying on _____ memory.
   a. episodic
   b. semantic
   c. procedural
   d. short-term
   e. working

6. Which of the following statements is true?
   a. School-educated children have better memories than those with no schooling.
   b. All stored memories are stored in semantic networks.
   c. Bransford and Johnson's research suggests that it is crucial to have the right schema during the encoding stage.
   d. Cultural utility does not play a role in how schemas develop.
   e. Parallel distributed processing models believe information in memory is located in a specific part of the brain.

7. What does the research on recognition and recall of high school classmates suggest?
   a. that we are better at remembering faces than names
   b. that recognition is more difficult than recall
   c. that recall is more difficult than recognition
   d. a and b
   e. a and c

8. If I don't like my professor because he unconsciously reminds me of a high-school teacher I disliked, which type of memory am I using?
   a. explicit
   b. recognition
   c. recall
   d. implicit
   e. priming

9. Which of the following is true of the tip-of-the-tongue phenomenon?
   a. It is another demonstration of how recognition is easier than recall.
   b. It increases in frequency with age.
   c. It appears to occur in all cultures and age groups.
   d. It has to do with explicit memory.
   e. All of the above

10. Which of the following statements is true?
    a. Implicit memories cannot be activated.
    b. Cryptomnesia is a type of tip-of-the-tongue phenomenon.
    c. Memory illusions are believed to be a direct result of implicit memory.
    d. When in a negative mood, we tend to recall positive memories.
    e. According to the encoding specificity principle, there is little problem in believing a claim by an adult that he or she has just remembered being sexually abused as a child.

11. Which of the following statements is true of forgetting?
    a. The greatest amount of forgetting occurs in the first few hours after learning.
    b. Research indicates that decay significantly influences forgetting in long-term memory.
    c. Jenkins and Dallenbach's research indicates that decay causes greater memory loss than interference.
    d. Proactive interference involves forgetting based on newly learned information.
    e. a and d

12. Which of the following is true of the memories of past events?
    a. They can be consciously or unconsciously forgotten.
    b. They can be falsely implanted in children and adults.
    c. They can be influenced by our beliefs about how memory works.
    d. They are more likely to be well remembered than completely forgotten if there is strong emotion and self-relevance.
    e. All of the above

13. Which of the following brain regions are involved in memory formation and storage?
    a. cerebral cortex and amygdala
    b. striatum and neocortex
    c. long-term memory, short-term memory, and sensory-memory systems
    d. all of the above
    e. a and b

14. Considering Ebbinghaus's research, how could you best use four hours to study for an exam?
    a. four straight hours the night before the exam
    b. two separate 2-hour sessions the day of the exam
    c. four 1-hour sessions, each 24 hours apart
    d. one 4-hour session, 24 hours before the exam
    e. none of the above

15. According to research on memory, which of the following statements is true?
    a. Hierarchical systems can double the amount of information you can recall.
    b. It is not helpful to use the method of loci when trying to recall information.
    c. Do not waste time studying information you already know.
    d. It is a myth that studying before you go to sleep will improve your recall.
    e. Individual memories are greater than collaborative memories.

Chapter Eight

Language, Thinking, and Intelligence

Chapter Outline

*I*magine an alternative reality where people are absolutely obsessed with Great Literature and where children swap author cards with the zeal that children in our world have for sports cards. Instead of seeking religious converts, missionaries show up at your door trying to convince you that Francis Bacon is the true author of Shakespeare's plays. In pubs and other social venues, "Will-Speak" machines that quote Shakespeare on command stand in place of the flashy video games of our world. However, this literature-enriched world is not without its share of problems. The Crimean War between Great Britain and czarist Russia— which ended in 1856 in our reality—is still being waged, and Wales has

The world we have created is a product of our thinking; it cannot be changed without changing our thinking.

—Albert Einstein, German physicist, 1879–1955

a communist government. An evil, multinational conglomerate, the Goliath Corporation, controls much of the world's economy and resources. And, oh yes, the Third Most Wanted criminal on the planet has somehow entered the original manuscript of Charlotte Brontë's *Jane Eyre* and kidnapped its namesake. Big problem. Suddenly, everyone reading *Jane Eyre* discovers the book's narrative is in serious disarray as the remaining characters are at a loss on how to proceed with the disrupted storyline.

Welcome to the hilariously off-kilter world of author Jasper Fforde, where fictional characters from famous and not-so-famous (and even unpublished) novels have lives beyond the stories they inhabit and occasionally cross over to the "real" world. The heroine of Fforde's novels is a smart, gun-toting literary detective named Thursday Next, who has the job of setting right that which has gone so wrong. Does this story sound like the basis for a commercially successful book? Not according to almost all the major publishing houses around

the globe. Fforde's first manuscript, *The Eyre Affair*, received 76 rejections before finally being published in 2001. Today he is a best-selling author and touted by literary critics as the "adult's J. K. Rowling" (the *Harry Potter* author).

What do Jasper Fforde and the content of his books have to do with the content of this chapter? Fforde's work represents an excellent example of the creative expression of language and the ability to envision alternative realities. This chapter examines the psychology of *language* and *cognition*, including the range of mental abilities that identify intelligence. In this regard, Fforde's work is an illustration of our chapter topics. At the outset, let us explore how our world is transformed by the ability to share the meaning of these markings on the page and the vocal utterances we emit. We will begin this journey by stepping into the past and examining the evolution of language.

Language is a complex means of communicating, involving the use of symbols and rules for combining them. In writing books, authors rely upon creative literary skills to convey their ideas to readers.

All that mankind has done, thought, gained or been: it is lying as in magic preservation in the pages of books.

—Thomas Carlyle, British author and social critic, 1795–1881

Literature is the one place in any society where within the secrecy of our own heads, we can hear voices talking about everything in every possible way.

—Salmon Rushdie, Indian-born British author, b. 1947

8.1 Language

Communication The sending and receiving of information

Language A systematic way of communicating information using symbols and rules for combining them

Speech The oral expression of language

Communication is the sending and receiving of information. Every day of our lives, we communicate hundreds, if not thousands, of bits of information to others. Some of these messages are intended, while others are not. **Language**, the primary mode of communication among humans, is a systematic way of communicating information using symbols and rules for combining them. It is a complex and sophisticated skill, and the principal tool for building human culture. **Speech** is the oral expression of language; approximately 6,500 spoken languages exist today. How did they come into being?

$8.1a$ *Human Language Evolution Had Social and Cognitive Advantages.*

The search for the origins of language begins in the brain. As noted in Chapter 2, Section 2.3e, PET scan studies indicate that the major neural mechanisms for language are located in the left hemisphere, even in most left-handed people (see Figure 8-1). A small clump of neurons near the front of the brain, known as *Broca's area*, influences brain areas that control the muscles of the lips, jaw, tongue, soft palate, and vocal cords

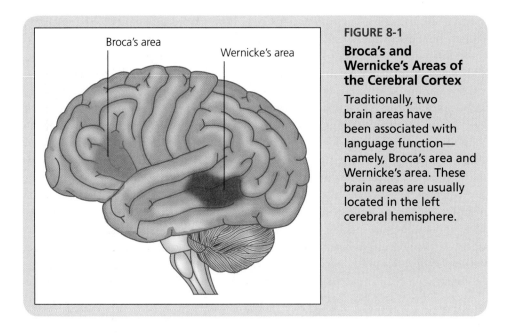

FIGURE 8-1

Broca's and Wernicke's Areas of the Cerebral Cortex

Traditionally, two brain areas have been associated with language function—namely, Broca's area and Wernicke's area. These brain areas are usually located in the left cerebral hemisphere.

during speech. Thus, Broca's area is important in *language production*. Connected by a nerve bundle to Broca's area is *Wernicke's area*, a part of the brain important for *language comprehension*, which is the ability to understand the message conveyed by words, phrases, and sentences (Hale, 2007; Hickok et al., 2011).

Even though Broca's area is primarily responsible for speech production and Wernicke's area is more involved in speech comprehension, brain scans indicate that Broca's area is also activated when a person is trying to comprehend a sentence with a complex *syntax*, which is the area of grammar dealing with the language rules for combining words into sentences. Thus, Broca's area appears to be involved when we use the grammatical rules of a language in both producing and comprehending sentences (Newman et al., 2003).

INFO-BIT

The two areas in the left temporal lobes of the brain associated with language function are named after two nineteenth-century scientists. *Broca's area* is named after a French neuroanatomist who first described how damage to this area disrupted language production. *Wernicke's area* is named after the German neurologist Carl Wernicke, who first reported how damage to this area disrupted language comprehension.

Although we can identify the major brain areas associated with language production and comprehension, answering the "when" and "why" questions of language evolution has proven to be a bigger problem (Botha, 1997). The *gradual increase theory* contends that human language is the product of a very long period of biological evolution, spanning millions of years. In contrast, the *threshold theory* asserts that human language is more a product of sudden cultural evolution. Proponents of the threshold theory believe that language is no older than 50,000 years and is closely tied to the development of tools, imagery, and art (Isaac, 1983). Genetic testing of different animal species provides evidence bolstering the threshold theory (Enard, 2011; Enard et al., 2002). This research suggests that roughly 200,000 years ago, mutations in the FOXP2 gene may have caused changes in the brains of archaic *Homo sapiens*, providing them with much finer control over their mouth and throat muscles. Within 1,000 generations, or about 20,000 years, these mutations may have played a central role in enabling modern humans to speak and, therefore, develop language about 50,000 years ago. The human and chimpanzee FOXP2 genes differ by only 2 out of their 715 amino acids, but this small difference may partly explain why chimps cannot speak.

Beyond the "when" question, one possible reason why language evolved is that it had *social significance* to humans (Bejarano, 2011; Oda, 2001). That is, it provided a way for our ancestors to more efficiently communicate in such cooperative ventures as hunting and gathering food. Support for this view comes from cross-cultural studies indicating that language is mostly used today for establishing, maintaining, and refining social relationships (Burling, 1986; Dunbar, 1993). It is also possible that language evolved because of its *cognitive significance* to humans. Throughout evolutionary history, brains have been shaped to construct a representation of the world appropriate to a species' daily life. Human brains have been shaped to facilitate reflective thought and imagery, abilities essential for complex decision making and problem solving. From this perspective, language use evolved as a means of facilitating the construction of an inner reality that we call *consciousness*. Thus, consistent with the Chapter 5 discussion (see Section 5.1b) of the evolution of consciousness, language may have evolved because it facilitated the construction of consciousness at the same time it facilitated the cooperative efforts of individuals living in groups. By sharing a common language, our ancestors could communicate about events not currently present, such as food in a distant valley, or they could conjure up ideas in the minds of fellow tribal members about alternative realities, which became the foundation for their mythologies. This ability to create pictures and thoughts in another's mind through language is the art of the writer and orator. As Jasper Fforde, author of the *Thursday Next* novels, explains the marvel of written language:

> If books and reading were invented tomorrow they would be hailed as the greatest technological advance known to mankind. No batteries, simple, portable, durable. Why bother building sets or creating convincing computer effects when the images are already there in the reader's mind? …When a reader praises an author, they should reserve 75% of that praise for themselves. (White, 2002, p. 10)

Some linguists believe that remnants of the earliest language spoken by our ancestors—referred to as *protolanguage*—are preserved in the distinctive clicking sounds still spoken by some southern and eastern African tribes. Linguists once assumed that these click languages—each with a set of four or five click sounds—were derived relatively recently from a common language. However, genetic testing of people from different click-speaking tribes who live thousands of miles apart (the Hadzabe and the !Kung) has found no evidence of any interbreeding over tens of thousands of years (Knight et al., 2003). This means that these two cultures have had no apparent contact with one another for thousands of generations. Although it is possible that the two cultures independently invented similar-sounding clicks, some linguists believe it is far more likely that these two tribes are very distant descendants of the world's earliest language users. If this is so, then these unusual click sounds may represent the remaining distinctive elements of this ancient vocabulary.

INFO-BIT

Anatomically, the evolutionary descent of the larynx in the human vocal tract increased the range of sounds that we could make. The "cost" of this anatomical change is that we now have an increased risk of choking when we eat or drink (J. M. Smith & Szathmáry, 1995).

8.1b   Language Capabilities May Not Be Unique to Humans.

Beyond searching for the reasons why we became language users, scientists have also wondered whether language and speech are uniquely human abilities. Since the 1930s, a number of attempts have been made to teach language to a few select species, such as chimpanzees, bonobos, gorillas, dolphins, and parrots (Hayes, 1951; Kellogg & Kellogg, 1933; Oelschlager, 2008).

Perhaps the most famous case is that of Washoe, a young female chimpanzee who was raised at home by Allen and Beatrix Gardner (1969) and taught sign language as though she were a deaf human child. Within four years, Washoe was using more than 100 signs, ranging from *baby*, *banana*, and *airplane* to *window*, *woman*, and *you*. She could also combine words to produce sentencelike phrases such as *gimme banana* and *open food drink*. Some of these phrases appeared to be novel constructions by Washoe, as in her combination of *water bird* to refer to a swan. Even more impressive was Washoe's apparent ability to engage in simple conversations, prompting a visiting reporter for *The New York Times* to declare, "Suddenly I realized I was conversing with a member of another species in my native tongue."

During the 1970s and 1980s, research with other chimps and gorillas using sign language or plastic shapes representing words provided further evidence of ape language ability (Premack & Premack, 1983). One female gorilla named Koko learned more than 600 words and demonstrated even more spontaneous and productive use of language than Washoe (Patterson, 1978). In one memorable incident, Koko created a new word for an object she had previously never encountered, calling a ring a *finger bracelet*.

Additional research with bonobos (or "pigmy chimps"), which are close genetic relatives of both chimpanzees and humans, provided further evidence that apes could use language. In particular, one young male bonobo, Kanzi, began using symbols at age 2 1/2 years to communicate with humans without any special training (Rumbaugh, 1990). Like human children, Kanzi learned to use symbols early in life by observing his adoptive mother use language (while she was in a training study). Eighty percent of the time, this communication occurred spontaneously, without prompting by the researchers. Kanzi learned not only how to "talk" by using hand signals and typing geometric symbols on a keyboard, but also how to comprehend the semantic nuances of spoken English. Although dogs, cats, horses, and many other species can sometimes guess what we mean when we talk to them by attending to various situational cues (for example, our tone of voice and gaze direction), Kanzi's understanding of spoken English was much more complex. For instance, when listening through earphones to a list of words spoken by a person in another room—thus eliminating situational cues—Kanzi was able to select the correct picture from among a pile of pictures. In another testing situation, when he was told to "Give the dog a shot," Kanzi picked up a toy hypodermic syringe from among a host of objects and "injected" his stuffed toy dog.

Over the years, scientists have observed Kanzi (a bonobo), Washoe (a chimp), Koko (a gorilla), and other apes not only sign spontaneously but also use their signing to let others know their likes and dislikes, just as humans do. Although these apes have not mastered human language, these animals are able to communicate with humans and even with others of their own species using a form of human language (Jensvold & Gardner, 2000). In contrast to humans, their vocabulary is small and their sentences are simple, similar to those of a 2-year-old child. Further, it takes substantially longer and requires more effort for them to learn a language than it does for human children. This suggests that the human brain must have something present at birth that is more ready to acquire language that the ape brain lacks.

BVT *Lab*

Flashcards are available for this chapter at www.BVTLab.com.

Shutterstock

Bonobos and other apes have been taught by humans to communicate with sign language. Once taught, they have been observed teaching their offspring sign language. Does this mean that these animals possess the ability to learn language, an ability once thought unique to humans?

8.1c Infants Appear to Be Born Prepared to Learn Language.

As in other areas of psychological inquiry, researchers have debated the degree to which language acquisition is simply due to experience and learning, and the degree to which it naturally unfolds due to inborn capacities (Sealey, 2000; Snow, 1999).

The Behaviorist Perspective

Until about 1960 most psychologists assumed that children's development of language ability was simply a learned response. Championing this behaviorist perspective, B. F. Skinner (1957) asserted that people speak as they do because they have been reinforced for doing so. Children, according to Skinner, begin life with a blank "language blackboard," which is then slowly filled by the experiences provided by people in their social environment. Throughout this learning process, Skinner and other behaviorists assumed that children were relatively passive; parents and other speakers were given credit for shaping their younger charges' utterances into intelligible words by selectively reinforcing correct responses.

The problem with this explanation is that it does not fit the evidence. Behaviorism cannot explain how children often produce sentences they have never heard before (Brown, 1973). Instead of saying, "Mommy went to work" or "That is my cookie"—which would be correct imitations of adult speech—children typically say "Mommy goed to work" and "That mine cookie." Perhaps more importantly, children's imitation of adult speech drops dramatically after age 2, despite the fact that language development continues. How could children continue to learn language if imitation is at the core of their learning?

Selective reinforcement and punishment also cannot explain language development. Parents rarely provide negative feedback when their young children make grammatical errors, and children's speech usually is not significantly influenced by such corrections when they do occur (Gordon, 1990). This does not mean that operant conditioning principles do not play a role in learning language; for example, anyone who remembers learning when to use "who" and when to use "whom" can attest to the influence that learning principles can have in language acquisition. Yet, contrary to earlier behaviorist assumptions, operant conditioning principles do not play the primary role in language development.

The Nativist Perspective

Standing in sharp contrast to the behaviorist view of language development is the nativist perspective, which contends that normal development proceeds according to an inborn program that is not significantly influenced by environmental factors. Nativist theories of language acquisition suggest that we learn language for the same reason that we learn to walk—because we're biologically equipped for it (Perani et al., 2011). In this vein, linguist Noam Chomsky (1957) proposed that humans are born with specialized brain structures or neural prewiring, called the **language acquisition device**, which facilitates the learning of language. According to Chomsky, thanks to this inborn capacity to acquire language, if children are exposed to it, they will learn to talk even if they are not reinforced for doing so.

Noam Chomsky, b. 1928

Language acquisition device According to Chomsky's linguistic theory, an innate mechanism that facilitates the learning of language

Although the existence of a language acquisition device remains an unconfirmed hypothesis, studies suggest that we may indeed be biologically predisposed to acquire language. For example, by studying videotapes of infants while they were engaged in babbling and nonbabbling mouth movements, Siobhan Holowka and Laura-Ann Petitto (2002) discovered that the right sides of the babies' mouths opened wider than the left sides when they babbled, but not when they nonbabbled. As you recall from Chapter 2, Section 2.3e, the right side of the body is controlled by the left side of the brain, which is where the major neural mechanisms for language are located. Holowka and Petitto contend from their findings that certain brain areas are specialized for language very early in life, and perhaps even prior to birth. These studies suggest that we have an inborn capacity for language.

The Interactionist Perspective

In the debate on language acquisition, while behaviorists emphasize environmental factors and nativists champion inborn predispositions, it appears that the most complete explanation is one that takes an interactionist perspective (Nelson et al., 2003). As the name implies, *interactionists* assume that environmental and biological factors interact to affect the course of language development.

Although children appear to be born with the capacity for language, a good deal of research suggests that their experiences during early childhood are critical in their acquiring this ability. As previously discussed in Chapter 3, Section 3.1c, there are *sensitive periods* during development after which it becomes more difficult to acquire certain abilities. For language acquisition, if children are not exposed to any human language before a certain age, their language abilities never fully develop. This sensitivity period for language begins during the first year of life and ends at about age 12 when children reach or are near puberty. Around the onset of puberty, the brain's pruning of underused neurons and overall neural wiring is at its peak; thereafter, the brain's ability to make new neural connections—its plasticity—decreases (see Chapter 2, Section 2.3h). Consistent with this notion of a language sensitivity period is the finding that when adults learn a language, they speak with a more native-like accent if they overheard the language regularly during childhood than if they did not (Au et al.,

Verbal interaction with competent language users is essential in order for children to develop language skills. Which perspective on language development does this evidence support?

2002). Apparently, early exposure to a language establishes a long-lasting mental representation of it in memory.

One environmental factor that is critical in children's language development is adult interaction. Studies of abused and neglected children who received little adult attention found that they had impaired speech comprehension and verbal expression when compared with children who received normal adult attention (Allen & Oliver, 1982; Culp et al., 1991). Unlike these language deficits, no differences were found in the children's cognitive development, leading to the conclusion that language development is particularly vulnerable in an environment lacking normal parent-child verbal interaction. Numerous studies indicate that when children are isolated from normal language interaction beyond their middle childhood, they develop irreversible language deficits (Ouellet et al., 2001). Taken together, these studies suggest that a critical component in the development of language is supportive social interaction with competent language users.

8.1d *Language Development Occurs in Distinct Stages.*

Regardless of the exact process by which language acquisition occurs, it begins shortly after birth and involves a number of distinct stages that move from simple to complex (Taylor, 2012). All human languages are composed of **phonemes**, which are the smallest significant sound units in speech. For example, to say *men*, you use three phonemes: *m*, *e*, and *n*. Linguists estimate that humans have the capacity at birth to produce about 100 phonemes, but because no language uses all these phonemes, this number is reduced to a much smaller set as children learn to speak (Maye et al., 2008). The Hindi language uses the most phonemes (over 60), and the Polynesian language uses the least (only 11). Most languages consist of between 30 and 40 phonemes; the English language uses about 40.

One step above phonemes in the language hierarchy are **morphemes**, which are the smallest units of language that carry meaning. Morphemes include prefixes and suffixes, such as the *re* in *replay* or the *s* in *plans*. The word *tourists* contains three morphemes—*tour*, *ist* (meaning "person who does something"), and *s* (indicating plural)—each of which adds to the meaning of the morpheme it follows. The average English speaker uses the available 40 phonemes to build between 50,000 and 80,000 morphemes.

In every culture throughout the world, language development begins with children using primitive-sounding phonemes. By 3 to 5 weeks of age, newborns begin a vocalization pattern known as *cooing*, in which they produce phoneme sounds such as *ooooh* and *aaaah*. Between the fourth and sixth month, infants can read lips and distinguish between the phonemes that comprise their language (Cohen et al., 1992). They also begin *babbling*, in which they spontaneously repeat phoneme combinations like *ahh-goo* and *baa-baa* (Plaut & Kello, 1999). This sequence of cooing, then babbling, occurs even among babies born deaf (Oller & Eilers, 1988).

Up until about 10 months of age, children from different cultures appear capable of discriminating between the phonemes in all existing languages. However, by about 10 months of age, many of the phonemes not in children's native language drop out, resulting in their babbling taking on a more culture-specific sound (De Boysson-Bardies et al., 1989). Because one language might not include all the phonemes found in another language, people who learn to speak another language

Phonemes The smallest significant sound units in speech

Morphemes The smallest units of language that carry meaning

often have difficulty pronouncing the novel phonemes in their second language. This is why Japanese who learn to speak English often fail to distinguish between *r* sounds and *l* sounds. Similarly, native English speakers have difficulty vocalizing the guttural Arabic *ch* or rolling the *r* sound of German.

At about age 1, most children begin uttering morpheme sounds that can be identified as words, like *mama*, *papa*, and the ever-popular *no*. This period in language acquisition is typically called the *one-word stage* because children can use only one-word phrases (Akhtar & Tomasello, 1996). These words usually relate to specific objects or concepts that children regularly encounter or use in their world. Because they still possess a fairly small vocabulary, young children often don't have words for many of the objects they want to talk about.

Throughout the world, children progress through distinct stages in developing language. During the early stages of language development, what sort of speech feedback do adults provide that facilitates children's language learning?

Consequently, they *overextend* their words to these yet unnamed objects. Thus, an 18-month-old child might use the word wawa not only for water but also for milk, juice, and any other liquid. Similarly, anything sweet might be called a *cookie*. Overextension is an application of the process of *assimilation* of children's words. As you recall from Chapter 3, Section 3.3a, assimilation is the process of using existing schemas to deal with information encountered in the world. When children call all liquids *wawa*, they are assimilating these objects into their *wawa* schema. However, when they begin calling liquids by their specific names—for example, milk is no longer wawa, but *milk*—this is an application of the process of *accommodation*, which involves the creation of new schemas.

By age 2, children enter the *two-word stage*, in which they begin using two separate words in the same sentence. During this two-word stage, a phase of **telegraphic speech** begins, in which children use multiple-word sentences that leave out all but the essential words, like in a telegrammed message (*BABY BORN. MOTHER FINE*). Thus, instead of saying "I want to go outside," children will say, "Want outside." Even when using this basic telegraphic speech, youngsters demonstrate an elementary knowledge of syntax: Words are almost always spoken in their proper order ("Want outside" instead of "Outside want").

Telegraphic speech An early speech phase in which children use short, multiple-word sentences that leave out all but the essential words, as in a telegrammed message

Journey of Discovery

Research indicates that infants have an inborn ability to detect phoneme sounds that are not a part of their culture's language repertoire. Given that you cannot ask infants questions, how do you think psychologists tested this ability in newborns? That is, how did they design an experiment to test children's inborn ability to detect phoneme sounds?

Once children move beyond using two-word sentences, they quickly produce longer phrases, and telegraphic speech is used less frequently by age 3 (Riley, 1987; Waxman, 2003). By the time children reach age 4, they are using plurals, as well as the present and past tense in sentences; however, they often *over*generalize grammatical rules. For example, in using the past tense, they will incorrectly say things like "I goed outside" or "I rided my bike." Because "goed" and "rided" are words children would not have heard from adults, their use suggests that children are naturally predisposed to pick up grammatical rules and then apply them generally (Marcus, 1996). Children also don't seem to be especially attentive to adult corrections, as illustrated in the following dialogue (quoted in Cazden, 1972):

Child: "My teacher holded the baby rabbits and we patted them."

Mother: "Did you say your teacher held the baby rabbits?"

Child: "She holded the baby rabbits and we patted them."

Mother: "Did you say she held them tightly?"

Child: "No, she holded them loosely."

Of course, children's seeming inattentiveness to adult corrections does not mean that adults are irrelevant to children's language acquisition. As noted earlier, especially during the early stages of language development, the day-to-day verbal feedback that infants receive from their caregivers plays an important role in the learning process. This **child-directed speech**—also called *motherese*—is characterized by exaggerated intonations, high pitch, clear enunciation, short sentences, repetition, and slow speech (Stumper et al., 2011). Child-directed speech may help infants recognize specific language forms and understand where utterances begin and end, skills necessary for future language learning. Adults who communicate with deaf children exhibit a similar pattern by making signs more slowly, repeating the signs, and making exaggerated gestures when signing (Sandler, 2003). Deaf infants pay more attention to this *child-directed signing* than to the more rapid, fluid signing typically used between adults.

Child-directed speech Speech to babies that is characterized by exaggerated intonations, high pitch, clear enunciation, short sentences, repetition, and slow speech; also called *motherese*

INFO-BIT   During childhood, we learn almost 5,000 words per year, which amounts to about 13 new words per day. The vocabulary of high school graduates includes about 80,000 words, while adults with excellent vocabularies retain upward of 200,000 words (G. A. Miller & Gildea, 1987)!

8.1e   *Language Can Influence Thought.*

In this chapter, in addition to examining our language system, we analyze how we think. Yet, how strong is the connection between cognition and language? Anthropologists Benjamin Lee Whorf and Edward Sapir developed the *Whorf-Sapir hypothesis*, which proposed that the structure of language *determines* the structure of thought (Whorf, 1956). The implications of this hypothesis are profound. First, if language shapes your conception of reality, without a word or phrase to describe an experience, you literally cannot think about it. Second, if language shapes reality, then no two cultures share the same understanding of the world; their thinking and their perceptions of the world differ because of differences in their languages (Pilling & Davies, 2004).

The idea that language determines thinking has been the subject of considerable debate and research over the years. In a critical test of the Whorf-Sapir hypothesis, Eleanor Rosch (1973) compared the color perceptions of the Dani people of New Guinea—who use only two words for color (*bright* and *dark*)—with those of English-speaking people—who use many different color terms. Despite these large language differences, Rosch found no differences in the way the two groups perceived color: Dani speakers made discriminations among colors as fine as the discriminations of English speakers. Other cross-cultural studies using different languages have also failed to support the hypothesis that language determines thinking (Regier et al.,

Every country has its own language, yet the subjects of which the untutored soul speaks are the same everywhere.

—Tertullian, Roman theologian, 160–240 A.D.

2010). Thus, counter to the Whorf-Sapir hypothesis, even though a language lacks terms for certain stimuli, the users of the language may still be able to perceive the various features of those stimuli. In fact, when we encounter something novel, we change our language to accommodate the need to refer to it. We manipulate our language much more than our language manipulates us.

Although the hypothesis that language determines thought in some sort of lockstep fashion has no empirical support, most psychologists do believe in a weaker version of the Whorf-Sapir hypothesis—that language can *influence* thinking (Zhang & Xiumei, 2007). This position, known as **linguistic relativism**, may not seem that unusual to you if you speak two dissimilar languages, like English and Japanese or English and Chinese (Brown, 1986). English, rooted in an individualist cultural context, has many self-focused words, while the collectivist-based Japanese and Chinese languages have many interpersonally focused words. Bilingual people report that the way they think about themselves and others is influenced by which language they happen to be using. For instance, when speaking English, bilingualists are more likely to attend to their own personal needs and desires, while social obligations are more salient in their thoughts when they speak Japanese or Chinese (Boucher & O'Dowd, 2011; Matsumoto, 1994). Beyond these particular culturally-based language influences on thought, Exploring Culture & Diversity 8-1 discusses how gender-related pronouns in language can shape people's thinking.

Linguistic relativism The idea that language can influence thinking

Exploring CULTURE & DIVERSITY 8.1

How Is Thinking Influenced by Generic Masculine Pronouns?

In English, you cannot avoid specifying gender when using pronouns like *his* or *her*. Yet, traditionally in the English language, masculine pronouns and nouns have been used to refer to all people, regardless of gender. Although the **generic masculine** is meant to include women as well as men, it does not do so in reality. For example, a number of studies indicate that people learn to associate men and women with certain activities and occupations by listening to the gendered pronouns used to describe these activities and occupations (McConnell & Fazio, 1996; Miller & Swift, 1991). When telling children what a physician does on the job, for instance, using the generic masculine ("He takes care of sick people") conveys to the child that this is an occupation for men, not women. Similarly, after reading a paragraph that describes psychologists with the generic masculine *he*, both women and men rated psychology as a less attractive profession for women than students who read a gender-neutral (*they*) description (Briere & Lanktree, 1983). Based on this research, the American Psychological Association recommends that gender-neutral language be used to reduce gender bias in people's thinking. Reading-time studies indicate that using gender-neutral terms instead of gendered terms is cognitively efficient and does not reduce reading comprehension (Foertsch & Gernsbacher, 1997). Table 8-1 lists some suggestions for avoiding gendered terms in your own language.

Generic masculine The use of masculine nouns and pronouns to refer to all people, instead of just males

In summary, then, although research does not support the original strong version of the linguistic relativity hypothesis—that language determines what we can (and cannot) think about—it does appear that language can make certain ways of thinking more or less likely. This weaker version of the original hypothesis tells us that although language is not the sole determinant of thought, it does influence thought in some meaningful ways.

TABLE 8-1   Suggestions for Reducing Gendered Terms in Language

Gendered Terms to Avoid	Alternative Gender-Neutral Terms
He, his, him	He or she, she or he, her or his, his or her, him or her, her or him, or switch to the plural they, their, them
Man, mankind	Humanity, people, human beings, humankind, the human species
Man-made	Handmade, synthetic, fabricated, constructed
Coed	Student
Freshman	First-year student, frosh
Manpower	Workers, human resources, personnel, workforce
Businessman	Businessperson
Chairman, chairwoman	Chairperson, head, chair
Saleswoman, salesgirl	Sales clerk
Foreman	Supervisor
Policeman, policewoman	Police officer
Waitress	Server
Man-to-man	Person-to-person
Forefathers	Ancestors
Housewife, househusband	Homemaker
Mothering	Parenting, caregiving, nurturing
Gunman	Shooter
Fireman	Firefighter
Mailman	Mail carrier
Caveman	Prehistoric person
Fisherman	Fisher
First baseman	First base player
Actress	Actor
Brotherhood	Kinship
Weatherman	Meteorologist

- According to the evolutionary perspective, language may have evolved because it facilitated the construction of consciousness and the cooperative efforts of group living.

- Certain nonhuman species can be taught languagelike communication.

- Three theories of how language develops in humans maintain the following: Behaviorists stress the role played by operant conditioning; nativists contend that humans are born with a capacity to acquire language; and interactionists assert that environmental and biological factors interact.

- The smallest significant sound units in speech are phonemes; morphemes are the smallest language units that carry meaning.

- Children progress through distinct stages in language development.

- Although the linguistic relativity hypothesis proposes that the structure of language determines the structure of thought, research suggests that this is not the case; however, language can make certain ways of thinking more or less likely.

8.2 Thinking

Thinking, or **cognition**, is the mental activity of knowing and the processes through which knowledge is acquired and problems are solved. While Chapter 3 examined how cognition develops in children, in this chapter section we begin by examining the building blocks of cognition, namely, *concepts*.

Cognition The mental activity of knowing and the processes through which knowledge is acquired and problems are solved

8.2a Concept Formation Is a Basic Element of Cognition.

A **concept** is a mental grouping of objects, ideas, or events that share common properties (Markman, 1999). For example, the concept *insect* stands for a class of animals that have three body divisions (head, thorax, abdomen), six legs, an external skeleton, and a rapid reproductive system. As you recall from our discussion of the semantic network model in Chapter 7, Section 7.2b, concepts enable us to store our memories in an organized fashion. When one concept in our long-term memory is activated, other closely related concepts are also activated, or *primed*.

Concept A mental grouping of objects, ideas, or events that share common properties

The primary means of coding experience by forming concepts is called **categorization** (Rakison & Oakes, 2003). As a species, we spontaneously categorize things we experience. Categorization is adaptive because it saves time and helps in making predictions about the future. I know, for example, that if I eat an object from the concept cheese, I am likely to enjoy the experience. I also know that if I need medical attention, I will likely receive it by seeking out people from either of the concepts *physician* or *nurse*. Like the heart that pumps life-giving blood throughout the body or the lungs that replenish the oxygen in this blood, humans could not survive without engaging in categorization.

Categorization The primary means of coding experience through the process of forming concepts

We form some concepts by identifying *defining features*. For instance, if an animal has three body divisions, six legs, an external skeleton, and a rapid reproductive system, I would say it was an insect; if it lacks one or more of these features, I would not think of it as an insect (Medin, 1989). The problem with forming concepts by

FIGURE 8-2

When Is This Object a "Cup," and When Is It a "Bowl"?

definition is that many familiar concepts have uncertain or *fuzzy boundaries*. This fact makes categorizing some members of familiar concepts more difficult than others. To see an illustration of this point, consider the objects included within the fuzzy boundaries of the concept *cup* in Figure 8-2. In one experiment, when people were individually shown objects like this and asked to name them, they were more likely to abandon the "cup" label and identify the object as a "bowl" as its width increased relative to its depth (Labov, 1973). However, the point at which this shift occurred was gradual, not fixed.

Findings such as these suggest that categorizing has less to do with the features that define all members of a concept and more to do with the features that characterize the typical member of a concept. This is the reason some members of familiar concepts are easier to categorize than others; they are better representatives of the concept (Olson et al., 2004; Rosch, 1978). The most representative members of a concept are known as **prototypes**. For example, most people consider a German shepherd more doglike than a Chihuahua, a robin more birdlike than a penguin, and an undergraduate more "studentlike" when she is 20 years of age versus 65. For most of us, German shepherds are "doggier," robins are "birdier," and 20-year-olds are "studentier" because they more closely resemble our prototypes for their respective concepts than the alternative choices. In fact, the Chihuahua might be mistakenly categorized as a rat because it looks more "ratty" than "doggy," and the elderly student might be mistaken for a college professor.

Our failure to correctly categorize things because they don't match our prototype for that concept can lead to errors in decision making. For instance, if certain physical symptoms don't fit our flu prototype, we may continue our normal activities, thus worsening our condition and also infecting others (Bishop, 1991). Similarly, we may turn our life savings over to a dishonest investment adviser because he looks like "Honest Abe."

Prototype The most representative member of a concept

8.2b *We Employ a Number of Problem-Solving Strategies.*

One important way we use concepts is in **problem solving**, which is the thought process you use to overcome obstacles to reach your goals (Pretz, 2008). There are a number of ways to problem-solve. A very simple strategy is **trial and error**, which involves trying one possible solution after another until one works. Do you remember Edward Thorndike's puzzle box experiments with hungry cats described in Chapter 6, Section 6.2a? Through trial and error, Thorndike's cats eventually learned how to escape from the puzzle box to reach a bowl of food. In many species, trial and error often provides responses that are important to survival. Whether you are a lion cub discovering how best to attack your prey or a teenager finding the right tone of voice to use when asking someone for a date, haphazardly trying various solutions until you stumble on one that works may be time-consuming, but it is often effective.

Unlike trial and error, which does not guarantee success, an **algorithm** is a problem-solving strategy that involves following a specific rule or step-by-step procedure that inevitably produces the correct solution. For example, recently, I needed to contact a student named John Smith. I knew he lived in Milwaukee, but I

Problem solving The thought process used to overcome the obstacles to reaching a goal

Trial and error A problem-solving strategy that involves trying one possible solution after another until one works

Algorithm A problem-solving strategy that involves following a specific rule or step-by-step procedure until you inevitably produce the correct solution

Which of these birds is more birdlike to you—the robin in (a) or the penguin in (b)? That is, which of these birds is closer to your bird prototype?

didn't know his phone number. There are 40 John Smiths in the Milwaukee telephone directory. One available strategy was to use an algorithm; that is, simply phone all the John Smiths until I found the right one. Assuming that my John Smith had a phone and that his number was listed, this strategy was guaranteed to work. The drawback to algorithms, however, is that they are inflexible. Further, like trial and error, they are time-consuming. Computers are based on algorithms, and that is the reason they are inflexible in their functioning.

Instead of trying to solve my problem of contacting John Smith by calling all the John Smiths in the phone book, I used a **heuristic**, which involves following a general rule of thumb to reduce the number of possible solutions (Gigerenzer et al., 2011). The general rule I used was that college students usually live on or near campus. Now, the number of phone numbers to call was reduced to five. Heuristics have a reasonably good chance of working, and true to form, I found my John Smith on the third call. However, unlike algorithms, they do not guarantee success. What if my John Smith had lived at home with his parents? The chief advantage of heuristics is that they usually save time. Learning to use these short-cut cognitive strategies is an important skill that helps college students efficiently solve many problems in English, math, and science courses (Sharps et al., 2008).

Sometimes, we are unaware of using any problem-solving strategy at all; solutions simply pop into our heads (MacGregor & Cunningham, 2008; Ollinger et al., 2008). The sudden realization of how a problem can be solved is called **insight**. Consider the following problem that is often solved by insight:

> A man walks into a tavern and asks for a glass of water. The bartender pulls a shotgun from behind the bar and points it at the man. The man says "Thank you" and walks out.

Can you explain the behavior of these two people? This story was presented to people in an insight problem-solving study, with participants being allowed to ask yes/no questions for up to two hours (Durso et al., 1994). At several points during this problem-solving period, participants were asked to rate the degree to which different

Heuristic A problem-solving strategy that involves following a general rule of thumb to reduce the number of possible solutions

Insight A problem-solving strategy that involves a sudden realization of how a problem can be solved

pairings of 14 words were related to the problem. Some of these word pairs were explicitly stated in the story (*man, bartender*), others were implicit in the correct solution (*surprise, remedy*), and still others had no relation at all to the story (*clock, grass*). Results indicated that at first, the implicitly related words were thought by participants to be highly unrelated to the story. However, before insight was achieved, participants slowly perceived an increased association between the story and these implicitly related words. No such increase in relatedness occurred for explicitly related words or unrelated words. These results suggest that in solving problems through insight, people gradually increase their focus on those concepts important to the solution, even though they are yet unaware of the solution itself. Thus, although insight seems to happen unexpectedly, the cognitive organization necessary for this type of problem solving is built beforehand, like the slowly gathering clouds that eventually lead to the sudden lightning flash. (The solution to the problem preceding this paragraph is that the man had the hiccups.)

Brain-imaging studies find that insight involves increased activity in the right temporal lobe, specifically in the area known as the anterior cingulate cortex, and also more balanced brain activity between the right and left cerebral hemispheres (Takeuchi et al., 2010). Additional research suggests that we solve more problems with insight when we are in a good mood rather than a bad mood because good moods are more likely to increase neural activity in the anterior cingulate cortex (Subramaniam et al., 2009). Overall, brain-imaging research informs us that the analogy of insight being like a lightning bolt or a light bulb turning on are accurate depictions of this flash of right-temporal lobe activity in the brain (Jung-Beeman et al., 2004).

 **INFO-BIT**   Culture plays an important role in preserving useful problem-solving techniques across generations, even among nonhuman primates. For example, for more than a century, certain bands of chimpanzees in western Africa have used a variety of crude stone hammers to crack open calorie-rich panda nuts. Using an elaborate set of procedures, the chimps establish nut-cracking stations on battered tree roots, which they employ as anvils. It takes up to seven years for the animals to learn the precise technique for successfully extracting the nutrients from the nut's outer husk, and this technique has not been observed among chimps in central Africa, where similar nuts are available.

8.2c   *Internal Obstacles Can Impede Problem Solving.*

Despite having various strategies to solve problems, psychologists have identified a number of cognitive tendencies that act as barriers to problem solving (Stein & Burchartz, 2006). Three of the more common internal obstacles are *confirmation bias*, *mental set*, and *functional fixedness*.

Confirmation Bias

Confirmation bias The tendency to seek information that supports our beliefs while ignoring disconfirming information

When you think you have a solution to a problem, you may fall victim to **confirmation bias**, which is the tendency to seek only information that verifies your beliefs (K. Edwards & Smith, 1996). Unfortunately, such selective attention prevents you from realizing that your solution is incorrect. In one confirmation-bias study, college students were given the three-number sequence 2-4-6 and told to discover the rule used to generate it (Wason, 1960). Before announcing their beliefs about the rule (which is simply any three increasing numbers), students could make up their own number sequences, and the experimenter told them whether these sequences fit the rule. The students were instructed to announce the correct rule only after receiving feedback from enough self-generated number sequences to feel certain that they knew the solution. True to the confirmation bias, 80 percent of the students convinced themselves of an incorrect rule. Typically, they would begin with a wrong hypothesis (for example, adding by 2s) and then search only for confirming evidence (testing 8-10-12, 20-22-24, 19-21-23, and so on). Had they tried to disconfirm this hypothesis by testing other number sequences that simply increased in value (for example, 1-2-3 or 10-19-39), they would have realized their error. Experiments like this indicate that an important barrier to problem solving is our tendency to search more energetically for information that will confirm our beliefs than for information that might refute them (Klayman & Ha, 1987).

How might this tendency to seek confirming information lead to incorrect social beliefs? In one experiment, Mark Snyder and William Swann (1978) asked some participants to find out whether the person they were about to interact with was an introvert, while other participants were asked to find out whether the person was an extravert. Consistent with the confirmation bias, the questions that people asked their interaction partners were biased in the direction of the original question. If they had been asked to find out whether the person was an introvert, they asked questions such as "What do you dislike about loud parties?" In contrast, in the extravert condition, they asked questions such as "How do you liven things up at a party?" Because most people can recall both introverted and extraverted incidents from their past, the interaction partners' answers provided confirmatory evidence for either personality trait. As you can see, such confirmation seeking can easily lead to mistakes when forming impressions about individuals. Similarly, incorrect stereotypes of social groups can also be perpetuated by seeking confirmation of preexisting beliefs (Yzerbyt et al., 1996).

Mental Set

Another common obstacle to problem solving is **mental set**—the tendency to persist in using solutions that have worked in the past, even though better alternatives may exist (Luchins & Luchins, 1994). In 1942, in his "water-jar" problems study, Abraham Luchins first demonstrated the influence that a mental set can have on problem solving. Participants were asked to solve problems involving the filling of water jars. In the first task, using a 21-cup jar, a 127-cup jar, and a 3-cup jar, they were asked to measure out exactly 100 cups of water. With minimal effort, participants discovered that the solution was to fill the largest jar (B), and from it fill the second-largest jar (A) once and the smallest jar (C) twice. Try solving the remaining problems in Figure 8-3 yourself before reading further.

Like Luchins's participants, you probably ran into a mental set. That is, you probably discovered that you could use the basic algorithm B – A – 2C to solve all the remaining problems; but this caused you to miss the much simpler solutions for problem 6 (B – C) and for problem 7 (B + C). Although mental sets can lead to solutions, they can also lead to "mental ruts" when the situation changes and old methods are no longer efficient or are completely ineffective (Pashler et al., 2000). Now that you understand something about mental sets, complete Closer Look 8-1 before continuing with your reading.

Mental set The tendency to continue using solutions that have worked in the past, even though a better alternative may exist

FIGURE 8-3

The Water-Jar Problems

In each problem, what is the most efficient way of measuring out the correct amount of water using jars A, B, and/or C?

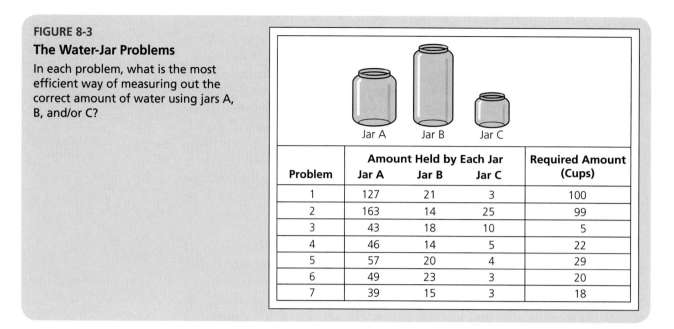

Problem	Amount Held by Each Jar			Required Amount (Cups)
	Jar A	Jar B	Jar C	
1	127	21	3	100
2	163	14	25	99
3	43	18	10	5
4	46	14	5	22
5	57	20	4	29
6	49	23	3	20
7	39	15	3	18

Can You Solve the Nine-Dot Problem?

Connect all nine dots with four straight lines without lifting your pencil from the paper. A line must pass through each point. Can you solve this problem?

Solution: To solve the nine-dot problem, you need to step out of the mental set in which you think that the four lines must remain within or on the edge of the square of dots. When you realize that the lines can extend beyond the "boundaries" of the square, you solve the problem.

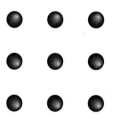

If the only tool you have is a hammer, you tend to see every problem as a nail.

—Abraham Maslow, founder of humanistic psychology, 1908–1970

FIGURE 8-4a

The Candle Problem

How would you mount a candle on a bulletin board so that it does not drip when lit? All you have to work with is a candle, a book of matches, and a box of tacks. (See the solution on page 384.)

Functional Fixedness

Finally, related to mental set is **functional fixedness**, which identifies our tendency to think of objects as functioning in fixed and unchanging ways (Furio et al., 2000). In problem solving, when you are unable to consider using familiar objects in unusual ways—for example, using a dime as a screwdriver—you are experiencing this cognitive obstacle. In one study of functional fixedness, participants were given a small cardboard box of tacks, some matches, and a candle (see Figure 8-4). Their task was to mount the candle on a bulletin board in such a way that it would burn without dripping wax on the floor (Duncker, 1945). Before reading further, try solving "The Candle Problem" in Figure 8-4.

Many participants could not solve the problem because they thought of the box as simply a container for tacks, not as a support for a candle. Later research found that when the experimenter used the term *box of tacks* rather than just *tacks* when describing the task, more solutions were obtained (Glucksberg & Danks, 1968; Glucksberg & Weisberg, 1966). This suggests that when a person hears the word *box*, numerous possible encodings of *box* may be activated from memory, thus making a solution more likely. In general, the more experience a person has with an object, the greater the likelihood that he or she will experience functional fixedness with this object.

Functional fixedness The tendency to think of objects as functioning in fixed and unchanging ways and ignoring other less obvious ways in which they might be used

8.2d *Decision-Making Heuristics Often Sidetrack Everyday Cognition.*

As discussed in the "Psychological Applications" section of Chapter 1, *critical thinking* is the process of deciding what to believe and how to act based on a careful evaluation of the evidence. Although we often may engage in systematic and rational decision making, we may also often take cognitive shortcuts. When we do engage in lazy decision making, what kind of time-saving mental shortcuts do we use? Heuristics, of course! To understand how we use specific types of heuristics, and how they can sometimes lead us astray, let us examine two heuristics identified by Amos Tversky and Daniel Kahneman (1974): *representativeness* and *availability*.

The Representativeness Heuristic

Representativeness heuristic The tendency to make decisions based on how closely an alternative matches (or represents) a particular prototype

Remember my example of being cheated out of your life savings because your investment adviser happened to look like an honest person? To judge the likelihood of things based on how closely they represent particular prototypes is to use a cognitive shortcut known as the **representativeness heuristic** (Gilovich & Savitsky, 2002; Tversky & Kahneman, 1974). The problem with this cognitive shortcut is that, being a rapid method of decision making, it doesn't take into account other important qualifying information. The most important information of this type relates to *base rates*—the frequency with which some event or pattern occurs in the general population.

The tendency to overlook base-rate information was demonstrated in a well-known study by Tversky and Kahneman (1973). Research participants were told that an imaginary person named Jack had been selected from a group of 100 men. Some participants were told that 30 of the men were engineers (a base rate for engineers of 30 percent), and others were told that 70 were engineers (a base rate of 70 percent). Half the participants were given no other information, but the other half were given a description of Jack that either fit the common stereotype of engineers (for example, practical, likes to work with numbers) or did not. They were then asked to guess the probability that Jack was an engineer. Results indicated that when participants received only information related to base rates, they were more likely to guess that Jack was an engineer when the base rate was 70 percent than when it was 30 percent. However, when they received information about Jack's personality and behavior, they tended to ignore the base-rate information and focus, instead, on whether Jack fit their prototype of an engineer. The tendency to ignore or underuse useful base-rate information and overuse personal descriptors of the individual being judged has been called the *base-rate fallacy*.

The Availability Heuristic

Availability heuristic The tendency to judge the frequency or probability of an event in terms of how easy it is to think of examples of that event

Following the terrorist attacks on September 11, 2001, many Americans were afraid to fly on commercial airlines. Instead of flying, people began driving in their cars cross-country. In nixing plane travel for car travel, they based their judgments on the **availability heuristic**, which is the tendency to judge the frequency or probability of an event in terms of how easy it is to think of examples of that event. In using the availability heuristic, the most important factor for people is not the content of their memory but the ease with which this content comes to mind (Gana et al., 2011; Vaughn & Weary, 2002). Because people could easily recall the horrible images of September 11, they decided that car travel was safer than plane travel. These judgments were made despite the fact that National Safety Council data reveal that, mile for mile, Americans are 37 times more likely to die in a vehicle crash than on a commercial flight. Indeed, if terrorists destroyed more than 50 planes per year, each containing 60 passengers, we would still be safer traveling by plane than by car. In this instance, it appears that reliance on the availability heuristic caused many Americans to actually increase their safety risks when traveling.

Wikimedia Commons

Following wide media coverage of an airline crash, some people decide to drive long distances instead of flying to their destinations because they believe it is safer. Which heuristic are these people using in deciding to drive rather than fly?

In Olympic competition, athletes who win an event receive the gold medal, those who finish in second place receive a silver medal, and third-place finishers get a bronze medal. Fourth-place finishers receive nothing. During the 1992 Olympics, bronze medalists (third-place finishers) exhibited more joy than silver medalists (second-place finishers) after their events (Medvec et al., 1995). How can this finding be explained by the availability heuristic?

The ease with which we generally recall our own characteristics and opinions from memory helps explain why we tend to believe that other people share our views and preferences to a greater extent than is actually true. This *false consensus effect* has been observed in numerous contexts: We exaggerate how common our own personalities are in the general population; we overestimate how many people smoke or do not smoke, based on our own smoking habits; we assume that most people agree with our political beliefs (Aksoy & Weesie, 2011). The ease with which we generally recall important aspects of ourselves from memory may well explain our tendency to exaggerate how common our own characteristics and opinions are in the general population. That is, perhaps we often assume others share our characteristics, habits, and opinions because these self-aspects are readily available in memory. As you can see, this type of thinking, brought about by the availability heuristic, can cause us to make misguided decisions. To gain further insight into your own tendencies to engage in effortless versus effortful thinking, examine Self-Discovery Questionnaire 8-1.

When Do We Use Heuristics?

With what frequency do we take mental shortcuts in decision making? As you have learned, frequency is partly determined by our need for cognition. Beyond this individual difference, Anthony Pratkanis (1989) has identified at least five conditions most likely to lead to the use of heuristics rather than rational decision making. The first condition in which these mental shortcuts will likely be used is when we simply don't have time to engage in systematic analysis. The second and third conditions are when we are overloaded with information, so it is impossible to process all that is meaningful and relevant, and/or when we consider the issues in question to be not very important. Finally, heuristics will often be relied on when we have little other knowledge or information to use in making a decision or when something about the situation in question calls to mind a given heuristic, making it cognitively available.

One final note: Although basing decisions on heuristics may lead to errors, relying on them may actually be adaptive under conditions where we don't have the luxury of carefully analyzing all our options (Johnston et al., 1997; Klein, 1996). For example, reacting quickly in an emergency based only on information most accessible from memory (the availability heuristic) may often be the difference between life and death. Thus, although heuristics can lead to sloppy decision making, their time-saving quality may sometimes be a lifesaver. In this regard, heuristics can be very helpful because they provide a reasonably accurate basis for making decisions under many conditions (Haselton & Nettle, 2006).

To most people, nothing is more troublesome than the effort of thinking.

—James Bryce, British statesman, 1838–1922

SELF-DISCOVERY 8-1
Questionnaire

Do We Differ in Our Need for Cognition?

An important ingredient in competent decision making is to critically analyze your options and hazards, an approach not everyone takes. John Cacioppo and Richard Petty (1982) have designed a self-report scale measuring individual differences in the motivation to think, which they call the **need for cognition**. People high in the need for cognition (high NFC) like to work on difficult cognitive tasks, analyze situations, and make subtle cognitive distinctions. In contrast, individuals with a low need for cognition (low NFC) are more likely to take mental shortcuts and avoid effortful thinking unless they are required to do so (Nair & Ramnarayan, 2000; Sommers & Kassin, 2001). Spend a few minutes answering the need for cognition items in Table 8-2 before reading further.

Need for cognition A person's preference for and tendency to engage in effortful cognitive activities

Researchers have studied how the need for cognition affects people's attention to political campaigns and their voting decisions. During the 1984 presidential and vice-presidential debates, for instance, voters high in the need for cognition were more likely to watch these events than were their low-NFC counterparts (Ahlering, 1987). The high-NFC voters also developed more beliefs about the candidates than did those low in the need for cognition, and their attitudes toward the candidates eight weeks before the November election were better predictors of their actual voting behavior (Cacioppo et al., 1986). This latter finding probably occurred because attitudes and beliefs formed due to critical analysis are more resistant to change than attitudes shaped by lazy thinking (Priluck & Till, 2004; Shestowsky et al., 1998).

Although high-NFC persons are more disposed to critically analyze information when making decisions than low-NFC persons, this is no guarantee that they will actually do so. Even people who enjoy intellectual stimulation will often engage in lazy thinking when the decisions have little relevance to their lives (Leippe & Elkin, 1987). Yet it is also true that people who are typically lazy thinkers can become critical thinkers if the decision is personally compelling and relevant. Thus, while our need for cognition will generally affect how much we critically analyze our options before making a decision, when we believe that a decision is important, we all tend to take greater care in weighing our options. Yet, because we sometimes are not aware that a decision is "important" until after the fact, the greater overall care taken by high-NFC individuals should lead to better results than the lazier decision-making style of low-NFC persons (Cacioppo et al., 1996).

TABLE 8-2 Need for Cognition Scale: Sample Items

Directions: These are sample items taken from the Need-for-Cognition Scale. If you agree with items 1, 3, 5, and 7 and disagree with items 2, 4, 6, and 8, you exhibit behaviors indicative of a person high in the need for cognition. If your responses to these items are exactly the opposite you may be low in the need for cognition. Based on your responses, which route to decision making do you think you tend to take?

1. I really enjoy a task that involves coming up with new solutions to problems.

2. Thinking is not my idea of fun.

3. The notion of thinking abstractly is appealing to me.

4. I like tasks that require little thought once I've learned them.

5. I usually end up deliberating about issues even when they do not affect me personally.

6. It's enough for me that something gets the job done; I don't care how or why it works.

7. I prefer my life to be filled with puzzles that I must solve.

8. I only think as hard as I have to.

Source: From " The Need for Cognition" by J. T. Cacioppo and R. E. Petty in *Journal of Personality and Social Psychology*, 1982, 42, 116–131 (table 1, pp. 120–121). Copyright © 1982 by the American Psychological Association. Adapted with permission.

Section
REVIEW

- Concept formation is a basic element of cognition, and the process of forming concepts is called categorization.

- Failing to correctly categorize things because they don't match our prototype can lead to errors in decision making.

- Typical problem-solving strategies include trial and error, algorithms, heuristics, and insight.

- Three common internal obstacles to problem solving are confirmation bias, mental set, and functional fixedness.

- An important ingredient in competent decision making is critical analysis, but we often rely on time-saving heuristics.

- People with a high need for cognition are likely to engage in critical thinking.

8.3 Intelligence and Intelligence Testing

Thus far, we have examined how we communicate and think. However, do we individually differ in our capacity to think in a useful, efficient, and creative manner? Let us continue our discovery journey by analyzing the nature of intelligence. **Intelligence** consists of the mental abilities necessary to adapt to and shape the environment (van Heck & Den Oudsten, 2008). This means that intelligence involves not only reacting to one's surroundings but also *actively forming* them. It also means that intelligent behavior in New York City, for example, may not be intelligent or adaptive in the jungles of South America (Detterman, 2005). These mental abilities are the keys to lifelong learning.

Intelligence The mental abilities necessary to adapt to and shape the environment

8.3a *Early Intelligence Testing Was Shaped by Racial and Cultural Stereotypes.*

Psychometrics—which literally means "to measure the mind"—is the measurement of intelligence, personality, and other mental processes. Although the psychometric approach has been extensively employed in the study of intelligence, the results have sometimes given psychology a black eye. For example, in the nineteenth century, British mathematician and naturalist Sir Francis Galton (1822–1911) believed that the wealthy families in society—like his own—were also the more intelligent because intelligence was assumed to result in success and wealth (Galton, 1869). He was so confident that families ended up either wealthy or poor because of their inherited traits that he founded the **eugenics** (the Greek word for "well-born") movement to improve the hereditary characteristics of society. Eugenics proposed not only that men and women of high mental ability—meaning upper-middle-class White individuals—should be encouraged to marry and have children, but also that those of lesser intelligence—meaning lower-class Whites and members of other races—should be discouraged (or prevented) from reproducing.

Psychometrics The measurement of intelligence, personality, and other mental processes

Eugenics The practice of encouraging supposedly superior people to reproduce, while discouraging or even preventing those judged to be inferior from doing so

How did Galton measure intelligence? Believing that intelligence is a product of how quickly and accurately people respond to stimuli, Galton's assessment battery included measurements of sensory abilities and reaction times, as well as

Wikimedia Commons

Sir Francis Galton: "If everybody were to agree on the improvement of the race of man being a matter of the very utmost importance, and if the theory of the hereditary transmission of qualities in men was as thoroughly understood as it is in the case of our domestic animals, I see no absurdity in supposing that, in some way or other, the improvement would be carried into effect."

measurements of head size and muscular strength. Unfortunately for Galton, his tests not only did not correlate with each other but also had almost no relation to accepted criteria of intellectual functioning (Sharp, 1898; Wissler, 1901).

While Galton's attempts to measure intelligence failed, across the English Channel, French psychologist Alfred Binet and physician Theodore Simon developed an inexpensive, easily administered, objective measure of intelligence that could identify lower-performing children in need of special education (Binet & Simon, 1905). In contrast to Galton's work, the resulting Binet-Simon test measured general mental ability and emphasized abstract reasoning rather than sensory skills. Today, Alfred Binet is considered to be the "father" of modern intelligence testing. He contended that cognitive development follows the same course in all children, but some learn faster and more easily than others. In intelligence testing, this means that "average" children will perform similarly to those their own chronological age, "dull" children will perform similarly to children younger than themselves, and "bright" children will perform like older children. Binet reasoned that general mental ability could be calculated by comparing children's *mental age* with their chronological age. Thus, a 12-year-old child who performs equally to the average child her chronological age would have the mental age of 12 years. Armed with this method of intellectual comparison, testers could place children into appropriate grades in school and identify those who would benefit from additional tutoring. Unlike Galton's intelligence test, the Binet-Simon test proved to be the first valid intelligence measuring instrument: That is, it accurately identified lower-performing students (Huteau, 2007).

In designing the Binet-Simon test, Binet, unlike Galton, made no assumptions about why intelligence differences exist. However, he did insist that his test did not measure inborn intelligence, and he believed that intellectual ability could be increased through education. He also realized that his test merely *sampled* intelligence and did not measure all intellectual aspects. Finally, he warned that because the test was developed in France using children with similar cultural backgrounds, it might not accurately measure intelligence in other countries. Two of his fears were that his test would be used not to help slow learners receive special help but would be used, instead, to (1) limit their educational opportunities and (2) plant the idea in their own minds that they are incapable of learning. Unfortunately, both fears were realized when his test was redesigned for use in the United States by psychologist Henry Goddard (Mayrhauser, 2002).

Despite Binet's insistence that his test did not measure inherited intelligence, Goddard, a strong advocate of Galton's eugenics movement, used Binet's test to identify the feebleminded so they could be segregated and prevented from having children (Thalassis, 2004). To describe these low-intelligence people, he coined the term *moron*, which is derived from a Greek word meaning "foolish." Goddard (1913, 1919) used the Binet-Simon test to assess newly arrived immigrants at Ellis Island in New York Harbor. Because these tests were biased toward native-born English speakers, many immigrants scored very low. These test results were later used by politicians to pass the Immigration Act of 1924, which dramatically restricted admittance of certain "undesirable" ethnic groups, especially those from eastern and southern Europe (Sedgwick, 1995). Although Goddard and most other psychologists involved in the eugenics movement later reversed their positions and argued against such discriminatory measures, this aspect of their research not only harmed the reputation of psychology as a science but also justified racist societal practices here and abroad (Leahey, 1991).

8.3b *Modern Tests of Mental Abilities Measure Either Aptitude or Achievement.*

When describing mental abilities tests, psychologists generally place them into the two categories of *aptitude* and *achievement* (Reynolds & Livingston, 2012; Russo, 2011). Intelligence tests are **aptitude tests**; they predict your capacity to learn a new skill if you are given an adequate education. In contrast to predicting what you can learn, **achievement tests** measure what you have already learned. Whenever you are given an exam in a course to determine what you have learned, you are taking an achievement test.

Although the distinctions between aptitude and achievement tests seem clear-cut, they are not. For instance, suppose two college students who have an equal capacity for learning math are given a test of mathematical aptitude. One student, however, attended a high school where he had four years of college-level math instruction, while the other student's school offered no college-level courses. Despite their equal capacity for learning math, it's likely that the student with the greater math experience will obtain a higher math aptitude score. The implication of this example is that your score on an aptitude test can be affected by your prior experience in the area being tested.

The Stanford-Binet Intelligence Test

Although Goddard introduced the Binet-Simon test to America, Lewis Terman (1877–1956), a psychology professor at Stanford University, was responsible for revising it so it could be used on American children (Terman, 1916). The resulting **Stanford-Binet Intelligence Test** employed a new scoring system known as the **intelligence quotient (IQ)**. Based on an idea of German psychologist William Stern (1914), IQ was represented as a ratio of mental age divided by chronological age, multiplied by 100:

$$IQ = \frac{\text{Mental age}}{\text{Chronological age}} \times 100$$

With this formula, a child whose mental and chronological ages were the same had an IQ of 100. However, a 10-year-old who answered questions at the level of a typical 8-year-old had an IQ of 80, and an 8-year-old who answered questions like a typical 10-year-old had an IQ of 125. The advantage of this ratio formula over the Binet-Simon scoring system was that it was more useful when comparing mental ages within a group of children who differed in their chronological ages.

Although the IQ ratio was adequate in representing children's intelligence, it proved problematic when the Stanford-Binet was redesigned to also measure adult intelligence. Because the rate of growth does not occur as rapidly in adulthood as in childhood, using the IQ ratio led to the mistaken representation that intelligence *declines* with age. For example, if Raymond had the mental age of 20 at age 15, he would have an IQ of 133, which is considered mentally gifted. However, at the age of 40, if Raymond's mental age had increased to 28, his IQ would now be only 70, which is the beginning of the intellectually disabled range. Raymond might have a successful career in a profession requiring above-average intelligence, but the ratio IQ would not accurately reflect this fact. Today, most intelligence tests, including the Stanford-Binet, no longer compute a ratio IQ. Instead, it has been replaced with a *deviation IQ*, which compares how a person's intelligence test score deviates from the average score of her or his same-age peers, which is 100 (Alfonso & Flanagan, 2007).

Aptitude test Test designed to predict a person's capacity for learning

Achievement test A test designed to assess what a person has learned

Stanford-Binet Intelligence Test The widely used American revision of the original French Binet-Simon intelligence test

Intelligence quotient (IQ) Originally, the ratio of mental age to chronological age multiplied by 100 (MA/CA × 100) that today is calculated by comparing how a person's performance deviates from the average score of her or his same-age peers, which is 100

Wikimedia Commons

Lewis Terman: "The children of successful and cultured parents test higher than children from wretched and ignorant homes for the simple reason that their heredity is better … The whole question of racial differences in mental traits will have to be taken up anew and by experimental methods. The writer predicts that when this is done, there will be discovered enormously significant racial differences in general intelligence, differences which cannot be wiped out by any scheme of mental culture." (1916, pp. 91–92, 115)

The Wechsler Intelligence Scales

The person responsible for developing the deviation IQ score was David Wechsler, one of those supposedly feebleminded eastern Europeans who immigrated to this country in the early 1900s. Today's most widely used set of intelligence tests in the United States is the **Wechsler Intelligence Scales**, named after their creator. Three separate intelligence tests have been designed—for adults (*Wechsler Adult Intelligence Scale*), for preschoolers (*Wechsler Preschool and Primary Scale of Intelligence*), and for school-age children (*Wechsler Intelligence Scale for Children*).

For all the Wechsler tests, intelligence is measured by 11 subtests—6 verbal and 5 performance—that yield a verbal IQ score, a performance IQ score, and an overall IQ score. Figure 8-5 provides sample items from the adult test for the verbal and performance subscales. As you can see, the verbal items consist of vocabulary, general information, analogies, math, comprehension, and the recall of number strings. In contrast, the performance subscales require you to locate missing picture parts, reproduce block designs, assemble jigsaw puzzles, arrange cartoons in a logical sequence, and copy symbols on paper. Because the performance subtests rely less on familiarity with words and language than do the verbal subtests, the performance subtests are less likely to be affected by the test takers' education or cultural experiences. Significant differences between the verbal and performance scores alert test administrators to

Wechsler Intelligence Scales The most widely used set of intelligence tests, containing both verbal and performance (nonverbal) subscales

---

FIGURE 8-5   Sample Items from the Wechsler Adult Intelligence Scale (WAIS)

Source: From Robert M. Thorndike. Measurement and Evaluation in Psychology and Education, 7/e. Published by Allyn and Bacon/Merrill Education, Boston, MA. Copyright © 2005 by Pearson Education. Adapted by permission of the publisher. Upper Saddle River, NJ.

VERBAL

General Information
    What day of the year is independence Day?

Similarities
    In what way are *wool* and *cotton* alike?

Arithmetic Reasoning
    If eggs cost 60 cents a dozen, what does 1 egg cost?

Vocabulary
    Tell me the meaning of corrupt.

Comprehension
    Why do people buy fire insurance?

Digit Span
    Listen carefully, and when I am through, say the numbers right after me.
              7   3   4   1   8   6
    Now I am going to say some more numbers, but I want you to say them backward.
              3   8   4   1   6

PERFORMANCE

Picture Completion
    I am going to show you a picture with an important part missing. Tell me what is missing.

'85

SUN	MON	TUE	WED	THU	FRI	SAT
1	2	3	4	5	6	7
8	9	10	11	12	13	14
15	16	17	18	19	20	21
22	23	24	25	26	27	28
29	30					

Picture Arrangement
    The pictures below tell a story. Put them in the right order to tell the story.

Block Design
    Using the four blocks, make one just like this.

Object Assembly
    If these pieces are put together correctly, they will make something. Go ahead and put them together as quickly as you can.

Digit-Symbol Substitution

possible learning problems (Edwards & Paulin, 2007; Weiss et al., 2005). For instance, a verbal score considerably lower than a performance score might indicate a reading or language disability. However, as just mentioned, it could also mean that the test taker is not very familiar with the language or customs of the larger society.

Group-Administered Tests

While the Stanford-Binet and the Wechsler tests are administered to people individually, group-administered tests can assess hundreds or thousands of people simultaneously. Group aptitude and achievement tests are widely used today, including the familiar college entrance *Scholastic Assessment Test (SAT)*, which was previously known as the Scholastic Aptitude Test. The reason for this name change is because the old name's use of the term *aptitude* implied that the SAT measures a person's capacity for learning. In reality, it measures learned verbal and mathematical skills; thus, it is more accurately considered an achievement test. As such, SAT scores are significantly influenced by the quality of the schools test takers attend. Overemphasizing SAT scores in evaluating students for college admission, therefore, can disadvantage students who attended inferior schools and also those whose main academic strengths lie in such areas as music and art. Both the verbal and math sections of the SAT have an average score of 500 and a range from 200 to 800, resulting in a total score range from 400 to 1600.

Similar tests are also used to assess students' potential for postgraduate training. For graduate school in the arts and sciences, there is the Graduate Record Exam (GRE); for graduate school in business, there is the Graduate Management Admission Test (GMAT); medical schools use the Medical College Admission Test (MCAT); and law schools use the Law School Aptitude Test (LSAT). There is sufficient evidence that, like the SAT, these exams measure not only the potential for performing well on scholastic tasks but also achievement. The practical importance of this fact for students is that studying can improve test performance. Extensive training or coaching on how to take the SAT can increase one's total score by as many as 30 to 50 points (Coyle et al., 2011; Kulik et al., 1984).

Journey of Discovery

Women who go to college after their mid-20s receive better grades than would be predicted by their scores on SAT tests taken just before entering college. Why might this be the case?

8.3c Psychological Tests Must Be Standardized, Reliable, and Valid.

All psychological tests, including the mental ability tests discussed in this chapter, are measurement instruments that must have three basic characteristics: *standardization*, *reliability*, and *validity*. The Stanford-Binet, Wechsler, and scholastic tests we have reviewed thus far all possess these characteristics.

Standardization

If you have taken the SAT or any other achievement or aptitude tests, you may recall that the testing procedures are extremely rigid. Regardless of where or when the

FIGURE 8-6

The Normal Distribution

Scores on standardized aptitude tests, such as the Wechsler Adult Intelligence Scale, tend to form a normal distribution (also known as a "bell-shaped curve"). The Wechsler scale, like other IQ tests, calls the average score 100.

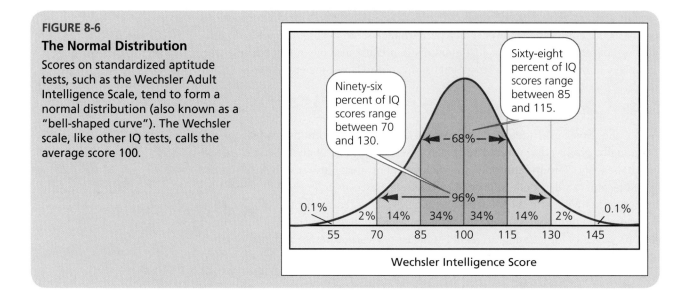

Standardization The process of establishing uniform procedures for administering a test and for interpreting its scores

Normal distribution The bell-shaped appearance of a distribution that results when the mean, median, and mode are identical in value

Flynn effect The tendency for people's performance on IQ tests to improve from one generation to the next

test is administered, everyone receives the same instructions, the same questions, and the same time limits. You may also remember that when you received your test results, your individual score was compared against those of a previously tested group of people who had followed the same testing procedures that you followed. This comparison process allowed you to convert your "raw score" into a *percentile*, which indicates the percentage of people in the standard group who scored at or below your score. This entire process of establishing uniform procedures for administering a test and interpreting its scores is known as **standardization**.

Standardized test results often show a roughly **normal distribution**, which has a bell-shaped appearance when the individual scores are placed in a graph. As you can see in Figure 8-6, in a normal distribution, most test scores cluster around the *median*, or middle score, which has a value similar to both the *mean* (the average test score) and the *mode* (the most frequent test score). As previously mentioned, the mean score on an intelligence test is 100. As we move away—in either direction—from this mean score, we find fewer test scores. Also as depicted in Figure 8-6, in a normal distribution of IQ scores, 68 percent of the scores will range between 85 and 115, and 96 percent of the scores will fall between 70 and 130. Only 2 percent of the population has IQ scores above 130, and only 2 percent has scores below 70.

Periodically, the Stanford-Binet and the Wechsler IQ tests must be restandardized to maintain the mean score of 100. This is necessary because in every single one of the 20 countries studied worldwide, each succeeding generation intellectually outperforms the previous generation (Flynn, 1987, 2007; Woodley, 2012). For restandardization purposes, this means that test items must be made more difficult to keep the average intelligence score at 100. This tendency for people's performance on IQ tests to improve from one generation to the next is known as the **Flynn effect**, after the psychologist who first noticed it.

What accounts for this rapid increase in IQ? Evolution—which occurs slowly—cannot provide an answer; and the increase certainly appears inconsistent with Galton's prediction that higher birthrates observed among those with lower IQ scores would move IQ scores lower. A likely explanation is that it is the combined effects of improvements in health, education and nutrition, greater experience with testing, and increased exposure to a broader range of information via television and the computer (Colom et al., 2005; Eppig et al., 2010).

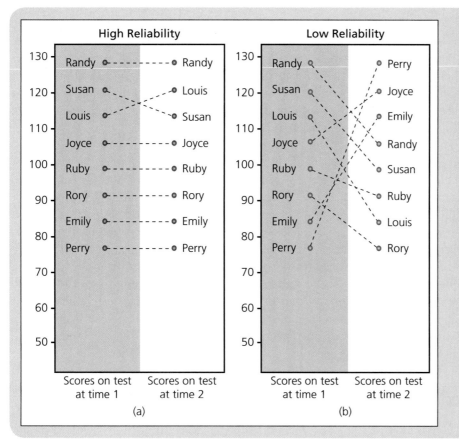

FIGURE 8-7

Determining Both Test-Retest and Alternate-Forms Reliabilities

In test-retest reliability, people take a test at time 1 and again at time 2. In alternate-forms reliability, they take one version of the test at time 1 and a slightly different version at time 2. For both of these reliability techniques, people's scores at time 1 are depicted on the left, and their scores at time 2 are depicted on the right. (*a*) When people obtain similar scores on both occasions, the test has high reliability. (*b*) If they get very different scores, the test has low reliability.

Reliability

The **reliability** of a test indicates the degree to which it yields consistent results. The most common technique for estimating this type of consistency is through *test-retest reliability*, which is checking to see how people score on the same test on two separate occasions. The drawback to this reliability technique, however, is that people tend to remember the test items when they take the test again—and this influences their performance. A solution is to use *alternate-forms reliability*, in which slightly different versions of the test are given to people on the two separate occasions. The items on the two test versions are similar in format but different enough in content that test takers' performance will not be influenced by familiarity.

Reliability estimates for both techniques are based on correlation coefficients. As you recall from Chapter 1, Section 1.3d, a *correlation coefficient* (also known by the symbol *r*) is a statistical measure of the direction and strength of the linear relationship between two variables, ranging from −1.00 to +1.00. In estimating both test-retest and alternate-forms reliability, the two variables are the two test scores obtained on two different occasions. If people's test scores at time 1 have a strong correspondence with their scores at time 2 (Figure 8-7a), the correlation coefficient will be near +1.00, meaning that the test's reliability is high, which is good news for the test developer. However, if people's scores at time 1 and time 2 do not correspond (Figure 8-7b), then the correlation coefficient will be closer to 0.00, meaning that the test's reliability is low. The contemporary intelligence tests described thus far have correlation coefficients of about +.90, which indicate high reliability (Hunt, 2011).

Reliability The degree to which a test yields consistent results

Validity

Validity The degree to which a test measures what it is designed to measure

Content validity The degree to which the items on a test are related to the characteristic the test supposedly measures

Predictive validity The degree to which a test predicts other observable behavior related to the characteristic the test supposedly measures; also known as *criterion validity*

Knowing that a test is reliable does not tell you anything about its validity. **Validity** refers to the degree to which a test measures what it is designed to measure. In our household, we have a weighing scale that is highly reliable: Everyone who steps on it consistently weighs 32 pounds. Although it is reliable, none of us believe it is a *valid* weight measure. While the invalidity of our household scale is a source of amusement for us, invalid intelligence tests are no joking matter.

How do researchers determine whether an intelligence test is valid? Typically, they analyze different aspects of the test. **Content validity** refers to the degree to which the items on a test are related to the characteristic the test supposedly measures. For example, if an intelligence test consisted of measuring a person's weight and height, we would probably conclude that it was low in content validity because these measurements seem completely unrelated to our conception of intelligence. However, if it contained items that measured abstract reasoning, we would be more inclined to believe that it had reasonable content validity.

Besides content validity, tests are analyzed in terms of **predictive validity** (also known as *criterion validity*), which is the degree to which the test results predict other observable behavior related to the characteristic the test supposedly measures. How well do contemporary intelligence tests predict behavior that is thought to be related to intelligence? It depends. The correlation between IQ scores and scholastic achievement (usually measured by students' school grades) is about +.60 to +.70 during elementary school, which is quite high. However, during the college years, this correlation drops to about +.40 to +.50.

Why does predictive validity decline from elementary school to college? More important than the greater number of social distractions in college is the fact that there is a more *restricted range* of intelligence among college students than among students in elementary school. That is, regardless of whether they are low or high in intelligence, almost all children attend elementary school. In such an environment where virtually all intelligence levels are represented, it isn't surprising that IQ scores do a pretty good job predicting school grades: The cream rises to the top. However, following high school, students with above-average intelligence—the "cream" of elementary school—are the ones most likely to attend college. In this "creamy" environment, IQ scores cannot possibly predict academic performance as well as in the "milky" elementary school environment.

Do SAT scores significantly predict whether students will actually succeed or fail in college? Yes, but similar to IQ scores, they are not strong predictors—the correlation with college grades is less than +.50 (Aiken, 1996; Coyle et al., 2011). The SAT is a better predictor of college performance for those who score at the two extremes. Very low scorers are quite likely to fail in college, while very high scorers are quite likely to succeed. A probable reason for the greater predictive power of the SAT at these two extremes has to do with the fact that college success is due to both intellectual ability and a desire to achieve. Most high SAT scorers have both of these personal qualities, while many of the low scorers have neither.

In summary, an intelligence test, like any other psychological test, is useful only to the extent that it is both reliable and valid. Does the test yield consistent scores, and does it actually predict what it supposedly measures? In general, the reliability of intelligence tests is higher than their validity.

What About Possible Cultural Bias in Testing?

Intelligence tests measure people's developed abilities at a particular point in time. As such, they detect not only innate differences in intellectual abilities but also differences due to cultural learning and experiences. Because of this fact, two people with the same innate intellectual ability will probably score differently on an intelligence test when one of them has considerably less experience with the culture in which the test was developed.

In the United States, critics of intelligence tests claim that Whites and middle- and upper-class individuals have had greater exposure than ethnic minority and lower- class individuals to the topics contained within some of the test items in the country's most commonly used IQ tests. Consider again the sample item on the Wechsler Adult Intelligence Scale in Figure 8-5, which asks why people buy fire insurance. Is it possible that this item is biased against a person who has never had enough possessions to make the cost of fire insurance relevant? Consider, also, this question on a children's IQ test: "Which is most similar to a xylophone? (violin, tuba, marimba, piano)." Are White children of well-to-do parents more likely to have attended orchestra concerts or learned about these instruments than minority children of poor parents? Could such questions explain the racial group differences in IQ test scores discussed later in this chapter (see Section 8.4c)?

It is true that some of the test items on the most frequently used IQ tests in the United States are still based on the vocabulary and experiences of the dominant middle- class culture. As such, these tests are measuring a person's achievement in acquiring knowledge valued by mainstream culture, in addition to measuring innate abilities (Coyle et al., 2011; Suzuki et al., 2008). Supporters of IQ tests respond to these charges of culture bias by pointing out that although these tests do not provide an unbiased measure of cognitive abilities in general, they do provide a fairly accurate measure of whether people are likely to succeed in school and in certain occupations. Thus, in statistically predicting academic and career success, standard intelligence tests and achievement tests are not biased. Their predictive ability is roughly the same for Blacks and Whites and for rich and poor (Neisser et al., 1996; te Nijenhuis et al., 2004).

The question of cultural bias in intelligence testing is also an issue when attempting to assess and compare the intellectual abilities of people in different cultures around the world. Intelligence researchers have attempted to construct "culture-free" tests to solve this problem, but it is now clear that no current test is completely free of cultural bias. For example, the Raven Progressive Matrices Test, which was initially touted as "culture-free," is now known to be "culturally loaded." In this test, people are presented with a number of increasingly difficult nonverbal matrix problems to solve, such as the exercise in Figure 8-8. The problem with using this test to measure intelligence cross-culturally is that, whereas matrices are repeatedly encountered in most cultures that have formal schooling, they are virtually nonexistent in cultures that lack formal schooling. Because of this difference, test takers in cultures with formal schooling perform at a higher level than test takers where formal schooling is rare (Benson, 2003). Yet, even with this culturally based problem, the Raven Progressive Matrices Test has been found to have adequate validity across a number of cultures (Rushton et al., 2004).

The problem of cultural bias does not mean that administering valid intelligence tests in other cultures is impossible. However, it does mean that simply translating a test developed in the United States into the local language of another culture is not sufficient. Instead, researchers must become very familiar with the cultures they study and design tests consistent with the needs and values of the people who will be tested (Greenfield et al., 2003; Holding et al., 2004). For example, when Ashley Maynard (2002) studied intellectual development among children in a Zinacantec Mayan village in Chiapas, Mexico, she used toy looms, spools of thread, and other common objects from the local culture. Her results indicated that the progression of children's intellectual development was comparable to that found among children

BVT *Lab*

Visit **www.BVTLab.com** to explore the student resources available for this chapter.

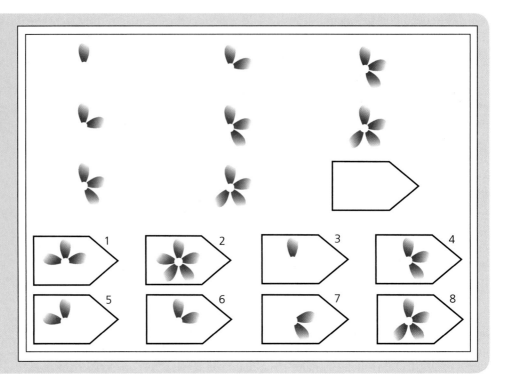

FIGURE 8-8

Raven Progressive Matrices Test

This example of an item like those on the Raven Progressive Matrices Test relies on visual-spatial ability. Which of the eight figures presented at the bottom best completes the logic of the matrix at the top?

in the United States. Maynard's research demonstrates that when psychologists use testing materials and measurement techniques associated with test takers' cultural experiences, the psychologists can be more confident in making cross-cultural comparisons of intellectual abilities.

Journey of Discovery

Imagine that you wanted to develop your own intelligence test. What are some of the pitfalls in early intelligence testing you would want to avoid?

8.3d Intelligence Encompasses Either a General Ability or Several Distinct Abilities.

As researchers began to more carefully study the nature of intelligence, one primary question concerned whether intelligence was best conceptualized as a general, unifying capacity along which people vary, or whether it should be thought of as composed of many separate and relatively independent abilities (Brody, 2000). One researcher who explored this question in the 1920s was British psychologist Charles Spearman (1863–1945). To aid him in his dissection of intelligence, Spearman helped develop a statistical technique called **factor analysis**, which allows researchers to identify clusters of test items that correlate with one another. By analyzing these correlations, researchers are in a better position to judge whether people's test performance can be accounted for by a single underlying ability (known as a *factor*) or whether multiple abilities (or *factors*) are needed. In essence, factor analysis helps researchers reduce the number of variables they are studying to a more manageable level by grouping together those that seem to be measuring the same thing. For example, if people who do well on reading tests also do well on writing and vocabulary tests, this suggests

Factor analysis A statistical technique that allows researchers to identify clusters of variables or test items that correlate with one another

that there might be an underlying "verbal ability" factor that is tapped by each of the individual performance measures. Moreover, if all the different intelligence abilities are highly correlated with one another, this might suggest that intelligence can be thought of as "one thing" rather than "many things."

Based on his factor-analytic research, Spearman (1927) concluded there was a **general intelligence factor**, or **g-factor**, underlying all mental abilities and a set of specific factors (s-factors) underlying certain individual mental abilities. However, because the g-factor could predict performance on a variety of intelligence tests measuring math ability, vocabulary, and general knowledge, Spearman asserted that the g-factor was much more important than the specific factors. He and other researchers believed that this general factor, which involves the more complex, higher-level mental functions, provided the key to understanding intelligence.

Although the g-factor's relative simplicity was appealing to many researchers, others argued that a person's intellect could not be captured by a general factor. Leading this dissenting group was Louis Thurstone (1887–1955). In the 1930s, Thurstone's (1938) own factor-analytic studies led him to conclude that there were seven clusters of *primary mental abilities*: reasoning, verbal fluency, verbal comprehension, perceptual speed, spatial skills, numerical computation, and memory (see Table 8-3). For Thurstone, just as we have games called football, baseball, soccer, basketball, hockey, tennis, and track but no game called athletics, we also have seven primary mental abilities but no general ability called intelligence.

How could the same statistical technique—namely, factor analysis—lead researchers to different conclusions? The answer is that despite its reliance on sophisticated and objective mathematical formulas, factor analysis requires researchers to make a number of highly subjective decisions concerning how their data will be organized and interpreted. As a result, researchers with different assumptions about how intelligence is organized sometimes interpret the findings of factor analysis differently.

Which of these perspectives on intelligence prevails today? The current scientific reality is that there is solid evidence for both perspectives: We have distinct mental abilities, but there is also evidence of a general intelligence factor (Johnson et al., 2004). A number of PET-scan studies find that when people perform different cognitive tasks associated with spatial reasoning, verbal abilities, or perceptual-motor skills, the same brain area, the lateral frontal cortex, is activated (Anderson, 2005; Duncan et al., 2000). The fact that these different mental abilities rely on some of

General intelligence factor (g-factor) The intelligence factor that Spearman and other researchers believed underlies all mental abilities

TABLE 8-3 Thurstone's Primary Mental Abilities

Primary Mental Ability	Description
Reasoning	Ability to find a rule or principle from a few examples
Verbal fluency	Ability to use words in special contexts, such as in solving anagrams and making rhymes
Verbal comprehension	Ability to understand words and sentences
Perceptual speed	Ability to detect visual details quickly
Spatial skills	Ability to visualize complex shapes in different orientations
Numerical computation	Ability to make mental and other mathematical computations
Memory	Ability to recall verbal material, learn pairs of related words, etc.

the same underlying neurological processes is consistent with the g-factor hypothesis. However, it is possible that the brain scans performed using current PET technology are not sensitive enough to detect activation of different subregions of the lateral frontal cortex when people are performing different cognitive tasks. In the future, a more sensitive brain-scanning device may find this different subregion activation. Such a discovery would be inconsistent with the hypothesis that the g-factor is associated with a single general cognitive process. Thus, until we can determine what different neural networks in this region of the brain are doing, the issue of the existence of a general intelligence factor remains open to debate.

In the twenty-first century, Howard Gardner (1999) is an advocate of the view that there are different kinds of intelligence. His theory of **multiple intelligences** contends that the human brain has evolved separate systems for different adaptive abilities, and what we call "intelligence" in our culture is simply a small cluster of these abilities (Gardner, 2011). Gardner proposes that intelligence consists of at least eight distinct and relatively independent intelligences, all of which are differently developed in each of us: linguistic or verbal, logical-mathematical, spatial, musical, bodily-kinesthetic, naturalist, interpersonal, and intrapersonal. The degree to which particular individuals develop these intellectual abilities largely depends on which ones are most highly valued in their culture (Furnham et al., 2002).

Table 8-4 summarizes the multiple intellectual abilities described by Gardner. The first three on this list are most highly valued in Western culture; thus, they are the ones measured by conventional intelligence tests. A person with high *linguistic intelligence*, such as an author or public speaker, would be good at communicating

Multiple intelligences
Gardner's theory contends that there are at least eight distinct and relatively independent intelligences (linguistic, logical-mathematical, spatial, musical, bodily-kinesthetic, naturalist, interpersonal, and intrapersonal)—all of which are differently developed in each of us

TABLE 8-4   Gardner's Multiple Intelligences

Type of Intelligence	Description
Linguistic intelligence	Ability to communicate through written and spoken language: author, poet, public speaker, native storyteller
Logical-mathematical intelligence	Ability to solve math problems and analyze arguments: engineer, scientist, mathematician, navigator
Spatial intelligence	Ability to perceive and arrange objects in the environment: carpenter, air traffic controller, sculptor, architect
Musical intelligence	Ability to analyze, compose, or perform music: musician, singer, composer
Bodily-kinesthetic intelligence	Ability to control body motions to handle objects skillfully: athlete, dancer, surgeon, craftsperson
Naturalist intelligence	Ability to see patterns in nature: forest ranger, ecologist, zoologist, botanist
Interpersonal intelligence	Ability to interact well socially and to reliably predict others' motives and behavior: mental health therapist, salesperson, politician, fund-raiser
Intrapersonal intelligence	Ability to gain insight into one's own motives and behavior: meditator, essayist, stand-up comic
A Possible Ninth Intelligence	
Existential intelligence	Ability to pose and ponder large philosophical questions: philosopher, clergy

through written and spoken language. A person with high *logical-mathematical intelligence*, such as an engineer or scientist, would be good at solving math problems and analyzing arguments; and a person with high *spatial intelligence*, such as a carpenter or air traffic controller, would be skilled at perceiving and arranging objects in the environment. Regarding the five less conventional forms of intelligence, *musical intelligence* entails the ability to analyze, compose, or perform music. Our gifted athletes, dancers, and surgeons display *bodily-kinesthetic intelligence*; bodily-kinesthetic intelligence is also necessary, however, in ordinary activities, such as driving a car or hammering a nail. *Naturalist intelligence*, which relates to seeing patterns in nature, is an ability that forest rangers, ecologists, and zoologists must possess. Finally, *interpersonal intelligence* identifies the ability to interact well socially and to reliably predict others' motives and behavior, while *intrapersonal intelligence* is associated with insight into one's own motives and behavior. Besides these eight basic intelligences, Gardner has also suggested a possible ninth intelligence, *existential intelligence*, which deals with the posing and pondering of large philosophical questions, such as the meaning of life (Davis et al., 2011).

Although Gardner considers these different intelligences to be separate systems located in distinct brain areas, he does believe that they often interact to produce intelligent behavior. For example, skilled politicians rely heavily on linguistic intelligence when debating issues, but they also use logical-mathematical intelligence to critically analyze these issues and interpersonal intelligence to understand what motivates voters (Bass, 2002). By combining skills in different intellectual domains, people can become competent in certain tasks or occupations, even though they may not be particularly gifted in any specific intelligence.

Shutterstock

Howard Gardner's theory of multiple intelligences proposes that we have evolved separate brain systems for different mental abilities. Musical intelligence entails the ability to analyze, compose, or perform music.

Support for Gardner's theory comes from the fact that brain damage may severely diminish one kind of mental ability but not others. Further, among healthy individuals, it is extremely rare to find the so-called Renaissance person who excels in all or several forms of intelligence. More frequently, a person with an extraordinary ability in one area will have normal abilities in the others. The existence of **prodigies**, people who easily master skills in one intellectual area, supports Gardner's hypothesis that various types of intelligence exist and are relatively independent of one another. Besides prodigies, an even greater intellectual variance can be found among **savants**, who demonstrate exceptional ability in one specific area, such as music or drawing, while having very limited mental abilities in all other areas (D. H. Feldman & Morelock, 2011). In one such case, Harriet, an autistic child who did not speak until the age of 9, could hum a classic operatic piece in perfect pitch at the age of 7 months. By age 4, she had taught herself to read music; and she had also learned to play the piano, violin, clarinet, trumpet, and French horn. As an adult, although Harriet's IQ was only 73, her proficiency in music increased dramatically. She not only could identify and provide key details about any major symphony but also could play a tune in the style and manner of the composers of these symphonies (Treffert, 1989, 1992).

Prodigies Individuals who easily master skills in a particular intellectual area

Savant Intellectually disabled individuals who demonstrate exceptional ability in one specific intellectual area

FIGURE 8-9

Sternberg's Triarchic Theory of Intelligence

According to Robert Sternberg, intelligence consists of analytical, creative, and practical abilities. You use analytical thinking to solve familiar problems, creative thinking to think about problems in new ways, and practical thinking to apply what you know to everyday situations. Of these three types of abilities, which do you think you employ most efficiently?

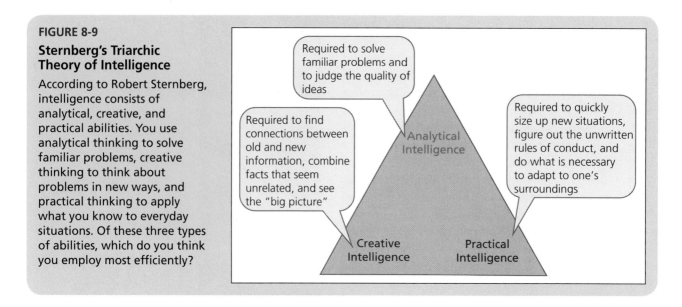

Triarchic theory of intelligence Sternberg's theory that three sets of mental abilities make up human intelligence: analytic, creative, and practical

Not everyone agrees with Gardner's theory. For instance, some critics question how athletic prowess can be considered a mental ability and instead believe it should more properly be labeled a talent (Hoberman, 1997). Others charge that Gardner's list of intelligences is arbitrary and that it is simply wrong to deny the existence of a general intelligence factor (Brody, 1992). Robert Sternberg (2005) agrees with Gardner's idea of multiple intelligences; yet his **triarchic theory of intelligence** (*triarchic* means "ruled by threes") asserts that human intelligence can be more simply described as comprising three sets of mental abilities, not eight (see Figure 8-9):

- *Analytical intelligence* is required to solve familiar problems and to judge the quality of ideas. This is the type of intelligence that is valued on tests and in the classroom; thus, people who are high in analytical intelligence tend to score high on general intelligence.

- *Creative intelligence* is required to develop new ways of solving problems (Zhang & Sternberg, 2011). People with a high degree of creative intelligence have the ability to find connections between old and new information, combine facts that appear unrelated, and see the "big picture."

- *Practical intelligence* is required to apply, utilize, and implement ideas in everyday situations. People who are high in practical intelligence have what we call "street smarts"; they are quick to size up new situations, figure out the unwritten rules of conduct, and do what is necessary to adapt to—and shape—their surroundings (Sternberg et al., 1995; Wagner, 2000).

Although some tasks require us to utilize all three intelligences, the triarchic theory does not define intelligence by how skilled we are in all three aspects. Some people are more intelligent in solving abstract, theoretical problems, whereas others are more intelligent when the problems are more concrete and practical. Sternberg contends that *successful intelligence* is knowing when and how to use analytic, creative, and practical abilities (Sternberg, 2003). People who are successfully intelligent will seek challenges that capitalize on their intellectual strengths and downplay their weaknesses. This is exactly what personnel departments try to do when selecting employees: match people's intellectual strengths with specific jobs within the organization. Successful organizations have workers who are skilled at analyzing existing problems, others who are best at using this analysis to create new ideas, and still others who can adeptly apply these new ideas as effective solutions.

TABLE 8-5   Four Theories of Intelligence

Theory	Summary
Spearman's general intelligence (g-factor)	A basic or general form of intelligence predicts our abilities in various academic areas.
Thurstone's primary mental abilities	Intelligence involves seven primary mental abilities: reasoning, verbal fluency, verbal comprehension, perceptual speed, spatial skills, numerical computation, and memory.
Gardner's multiple intelligences	Intelligence is best thought of as comprising at least eight distinct intelligences that are developed differently in each person: linguistic, logical-mathematical, spatial, musical, bodily-kinesthetic, naturalist, interpersonal, and intrapersonal.
Sternberg's triarchic theory of intelligence	Three sets of mental abilities make up intelligence: analytic, creative, and practical.

So where are we in the scientific debate concerning the existence of general intelligence versus multiple intelligences? As of this writing, research still supports both perspectives. There is solid evidence that we have distinct mental abilities, and there is also evidence of a general intelligence factor. As previously noted, brain scans indicate that when people work on tasks requiring different intellectual abilities, the same area of the frontal cortex is activated (Duncan et al., 2000). The fact that these different abilities rely on some of the same underlying neurological processes is consistent with the "g-factor" hypothesis. In an attempt to settle this controversy, many modern theories propose that although intelligence may encompass a general ability to deal with a wide variety of cognitive tasks and problems, it also can be expressed in many ways, perhaps even in the form of multiple intelligences. Table 8-5 summarizes the four theories of intelligence discussed in this chapter. Self-Discovery Questionnaire 8-2 and the end-of-chapter "Psychological Applications" section analyze two types of intelligence that fit into the multiple-intelligences viewpoint.

SELF-DISCOVERY 8-2
Questionnaire

What Does It Mean to Be Emotionally Intelligent?

Related to Gardner's idea of intrapersonal intelligence is what various researchers have called **emotional intelligence**, which is the ability to recognize and regulate our own and others' emotions (Matthews et al., 2012). Individuals with high emotional intelligence are attentive to their own feelings, can accurately discriminate between them, and can use this information to guide their own thinking and actions. For example, when they experience negative moods, emotionally intelligent people try to create a more positive state of

Emotional intelligence
The ability to recognize and regulate our own and others' emotions

mind by doing something they enjoy or by finishing a task that will bring them a reward (Tice & Baumeister, 1993). In contrast, those who are less emotionally skilled tend to be "ruled" by their emotions: They not only have quick tempers but also "stew in their own negative juices" when things don't go their way (Caprara et al., 1996). Of the two extremes of the spectrum of emotional intelligence, which do you think leads to greater happiness and success?

Emotionally intelligent people are aware not only of their own emotional states but of those of others as well (O'Sullivan, 2005). For example, in one study, participants being rated on their emotional intelligence watched a computer screen as people's faces morphed into different emotional expressions. The participants' task was to click a key as soon as they could identify the morphing expression. Results indicated that the emotionally intelligent participants were faster at identifying the expressions than their less emotionally intelligent counterparts (Petrides & Furnham, 2003).

People with emotional intelligence are those we seek out when we are troubled. Their emotional attentiveness makes them sympathetic listeners, and their skill at managing social conflict means

People with emotional intelligence are sympathetic listeners, and we seek them out when we are troubled. Are emotionally intelligent people generally happier than those who are less emotionally intelligent?

that they often provide us with good advice on how to resolve our difficulties. Due to their ability to accurately measure the "pulse" of social relationships, emotionally intelligent people get along well with others, have many friends, and often achieve great success in their careers (Salovey et al., 2003). Based on these findings, it isn't surprising that our skill at managing the emotional realm significantly determines the extent to which our lives are successful and fulfilling. Before reading further, spend a few minutes answering the items in Table 8-6.

TABLE 8-6 Measuring Your Level of Empathy for Others

Instructions: One aspect of emotional intelligence is the ability to be attentive to the feelings of others. *Empathy* is a feeling of compassion and tenderness toward those who encounter unfortunate life events. Research indicates that people differ in their levels of empathy. To discover your level of empathy or *empathic concern* for others, read each of the following items and then, using the following response scale, indicate how well each statement describes you.

0 = extremely uncharacteristic (not at all like me)
1 = uncharacteristic (somewhat unlike me)
2 = neither characteristic nor uncharacteristic
3 = characteristic (somewhat like me)
4 = extremely characteristic (very much like me)

1. When I see someone being taken advantage of, I feel kind of protective toward them.

2. When I see someone being treated unfairly, I sometimes don't feel very much pity for them.*

3. I often have tender, concerned feelings for people less fortunate than me.

4. I would describe myself as a pretty soft-hearted person.

5. Sometimes, I don't feel very sorry for other people when they are having problems.*

6. Other people's misfortunes do not usually disturb me a great deal.*

7. I am often quite touched by things that I see happen.

Scoring your responses: Three of the items on this scale are reverse-scored; that is, for these items, a lower rating actually indicates a higher level of empathic concern or personal distress. Before summing the items, recode those with an asterisk (*) so that 0 = 4, 1 = 3, 3 = 1, 4 = 0.

The mean score for female college students is about 22, and the mean score for male students is about 19 (M. H. Davis, 1996). The higher your score, the higher the level of empathic concern you have for others.

Source: From *Empathy: A Social Psychological Approach* by Mark H. Davis. Copyright © 1996. Reprinted by permission of Westview Press, a member of Perseus Books, L.L.C.

- The first useful intelligence test was developed by Alfred Binet to identify lower-performing children needing special education; however, Henry Goddard inappropriately used the Binet-Simon test to assess the intelligence of diverse groups, including immigrants.

- Intelligence tests are aptitude tests; achievement tests measure what you have already learned.

- Standardization is the process of establishing uniform procedures for administering a test and for interpreting its scores.

- Test reliability indicates the degree to which a test yields consistent results.

- Test validity indicates the degree to which a test measures what it is designed to measure.

- Reliability of intelligence tests is higher than their validity.

- Intelligence tests are not "culture-free," and care is needed when comparing people from different cultural backgrounds.

- Spearman's factor-analytic research suggested a general intelligence, or g-factor, underlying all mental abilities and a set of specific factors (s-factors) underlying certain individual mental abilities.

- Gardner's theory of multiple intelligences proposes at least eight separate abilities: linguistic, logical-mathematical, spatial, musical, bodily-kinesthetic, naturalist, interpersonal, and intrapersonal.

- According to Sternberg's triarchic theory, intelligence comprises three sets of mental abilities: analytical, creative, and practical.

- Emotional intelligence helps us achieve and maintain personal and career success.

8.4 Neurological, Hereditary, and Environmental Influences on Intelligence

We have all heard people described as "quick-witted" and "dim-witted." When individuals substantially differ in their intelligence levels, how do they differ in their neurological functioning? Further, to what degree does heredity determine intelligence, and to what degree do the physical and social environment in which we are raised determine it? Are there group differences in intellectual ability? These are some of the questions we will address in this final section of the chapter.

8.4a People Appear to Differ in Their Neural Complexity, Quickness, and Efficiency.

Is the size of people's brains an indicator of their intelligence? When magnetic resonance imaging (MRI) scans directly measure brain size and then adjust it for body size, brain size has a moderately high correlation ($r = +.44$) with IQ scores (Cairo, 2011; Rushton & Ankney, 1996). In explaining the brain size-IQ correlation, some neuroscientists point to the fact that larger brains have more neurons than do smaller brains (Olszewski-Kubilius & Lee, 2011). The higher intelligence found among those with bigger brains might be caused by these individuals having a larger number of neural connections and a correspondingly greater cognitive capacity (Vernon et al., 2000). One problem with this "greater neuron" explanation is that men, on average, have about 4 billion (or 16 percent) more neurons than women; yet men do not outscore women on IQ tests. In addition, archeological records indicate that Neanderthals had larger brains than modern humans, but no scientists have suggested that our extinct hominid cousins were more intelligent than we are. Another possibility is that the brain size–IQ correlation is related to different levels of *myelin* in the brain (Miller, 1994). As you recall from Chapter 2, Section 2.1b, the myelin sheath is the protective coating of glial cells around an axon that hastens the transmission of the neuron's electrochemical charge. The possibility that intelligence might be related to myelin is one of the reasons intelligence researchers have devoted a great deal of attention to the brain's processing speed.

A number of studies indicate that intelligence is partly based on neural complexity, quickness, and efficiency (Bassett & Gazzaniga, 2011). For example, IQ scores tend to be correlated with the complexity of electrical activity in the brain. When responding to simple stimuli, high scorers have more complex brain patterns than low scorers (Barrett & Eysenck, 1992). Regarding neural "quickness," the speed at which neural impulses travel (see Figure 8-10) is positively correlated with IQ— about +.40—suggesting that intelligent people are literally more quick-witted than the less intelligent (McGarry-Roberts et al., 1992). Finally, additional studies suggest that smarter brains are not only quick and complex but also more efficient (Jausovek & Jausovek, 2003). Using PET scans, Richard Haier and his coworkers (1992, 1995) found that people with higher intelligence tend to consume less *glucose*—a simple sugar required for brain activity—while working on problem-solving tasks. They also found evidence suggesting that the brains of intelligent people become more efficient with practice than the brains of those with less intelligence. That is, after practicing a relatively complex computer game, intelligent participants' brains subsequently consumed less glucose overall when playing this game, even though certain brain areas actually consumed more glucose. Haier and his coworkers contend that, by concentrating the processing of information in relatively small areas of their brains, intelligent people use their brains more efficiently. Although the origins of these biological differences in brain functioning could be genetic, the fact that greater efficiency is achieved with practice suggests that these differences also develop from experience. Together, these findings suggest that intelligence is a product of both our biology (*nature*) and our experience (*nurture*).

FIGURE 8-10

An Inspection Time Task

In a typical experiment measuring neural "quickness," researchers will often study how fast participants can process perceptual information presented to them. An incomplete stimulus is quickly flashed on a computer screen, but its lingering afterimage is immediately hidden (or *masked*) by another stimulus. The participant is then asked whether the long side of the original stimulus appeared on the left or right. Researchers determine how much time participants need to inspect the stimulus in order to answer such questions correctly 80 percent of the time. Participants who need less time to correctly answer these questions tend to score higher on intelligence tests.

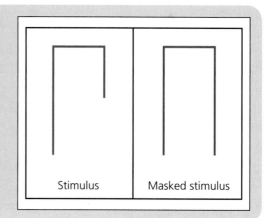

Stimulus   Masked stimulus

Extremes of Intelligence

Although intellectual performance can be improved through learning, researchers have devoted considerable time and energy to studying people who score at the two extremes of the IQ normal distribution. The diagnosis of **intellectual disability** is given to people who not only have an IQ score at or below 70, but also have difficulty adapting to the routine demands of independent living (Detterman et al., 2000). Estimates are that only about 1 to 2 percent of the population meets both criteria, with males outnumbering females by 50 percent (Toth & King, 2010). Within this designation, there are four intellectual disability categories, which vary in severity. As you can see in Table 8-7, most intellectually disabled people are only mildly disabled.

Also included among organic causes are genetic disorders, the most common being **Down syndrome**, which is caused by an extra chromosome coming from either the mother's egg (the primary source) or the father's sperm (Davis, 2008). The production of this extra chromosome is strongly related to maternal age. Among mothers under age 33, the rate of Down syndrome is only 0.9 per 1,000 live births. This rate increases to 3.8 in mothers who are age 44 or older (Grigorenko, 2000). Characteristic signs of Down syndrome are small head, nose, ears, and hands; slanting eyes; short neck; and thin hair. Individuals with this disorder have IQs that place them in the mild-to-severe range of intellectual disability. When given proper training and placed within a supportive family environment, many people with Down syndrome can care for themselves, hold a job, and lead happy, fulfilling lives.

Approximately 75 percent of intellectual disability cases cannot be linked to any organic cause; instead, they are thought to result from unfavorable social conditions or subtle and difficult-to-detect physiological effects (Handen, 1997). Most of these cases involve less-severe forms of intellectual disability, and poor children are 10 times more likely to be classified in this manner than those from the general population. Among the remaining 25 percent of cases, doctors are able to identify a specific organic cause, such as the developing fetus or infant child being exposed

Intellectual disability A diagnostic category used for people who not only have an IQ score below 70 but also have difficulty adapting to the routine demands of independent living

Down syndrome A form of intellectual disability caused by an extra chromosome in an individual's genetic makeup

TABLE 8-7   Degrees of intellectual Disability

Level	Typical IQ Scores	Percentage of the Disabled	Adaptation to Demands of Life
Mild	50–70	85%	May learn academic skills up to the sixth-grade level. With assistance, adults often can learn self-supporting social and vocational skills.
Moderate	35–49	10%	May progress to second-grade level. Within sheltered workshops, adults can contribute to their own support through manual labor.
Severe	20–34	<4%	May learn to talk and to perform simple work tasks under close supervision but are generally unable to profit from vocational training.
Profound	Below 20<	2%	Limited motor development and little or no speech. Require constant aid and supervision.

Source: Reprinted with permission from the *Diagnostic and Statistical Manual of Mental Disorders, Text Revision*, Fourth Edition. Copyright © 2000 American Psychiatric Association.

to harmful substances (for example, alcohol and lead) or trauma to the child's head (Yeargin-Allsopp et al., 1997).

INFO-BIT   When the English physician Langdon Down identified Down syndrome in 1866, it was called "Mongolism" because the slanting eyes of Down syndrome people bore some resemblance to Asian eyes in the minds of Westerners. Consistent with then existing scientific theories of White intellectual superiority, nineteenth-century European scientists claimed that Down syndrome individuals failed to develop beyond the physical and intellectual level of Asians, such as Mongolians.

At the other extreme of the IQ normal distribution is the "gifted" category. This term has commonly been reserved for those people with IQs above 130 or 135. Consistent with theories of multiple intelligences, U.S. federal law designates that giftedness should be based on superior potential in any of six areas: general intelligence, specific aptitudes (for example, math and writing), performing arts, athletics, creativity, and leadership (Callahan, 2000). Although more school districts are beginning to identify gifted students based on these broader standards, most continue emphasizing IQ scores (Dai & Renzulli, 2008; Lewis et al., 2012).

To adequately challenge gifted students in school, educators have developed two separate intervention strategies (Keen & Howard, 2002). *Acceleration* involves admitting gifted students to school early and encouraging them to skip grades. *Enrichment*, in contrast, keeps gifted students in their normal grade level but supplements their course work with advanced material, independent study projects, and other special learning experiences. Both intervention strategies can be effective; many gifted students in these programs still complain, however, that their classes move too slowly, involve too much repetition of already mastered material, and place too much emphasis on the mastery of facts rather than the use of thinking skills (Gallagher et al., 1997). One problem is that these programs are underfunded. Relative to the money provided for the education of intellectually disabled students, little money is spent on education for gifted children, especially those who are poor or live in rural areas.

Doing easily what others find difficult is talent; doing what is impossible for talent is genius.

—Henri-Frederic Amiel, Swiss critic, 1821–1881

One common belief about gifted individuals is that their "gift" is really a curse because it makes them social misfits who lead lonely, unsatisfying lives. Is this stereotype true? In 1921, in an attempt to answer this question, Lewis Terman began tracking the lives of over 1,500 California children with IQs above 135 (Terman, 1925). Over the course of the next 70 years, Terman and later researchers discovered that, by and large, these men and women led healthy, well-adjusted lives, with slightly more successful marriages and much more successful careers than the average person (Holahan & Sears, 1995; Terman & Oden, 1947). Other longitudinal studies of gifted individuals have replicated these findings. Counter to prevailing stereotypes, research clearly indicates that children with high IQs are less likely to be social misfits than their less-gifted counterparts (Lubinski et al., 2001). However, childhood giftedness does not guarantee adult eminence. For example, although the "Termanites" (as the gifted children tracked by Terman affectionately called themselves) generally grew up to be very successful adults in their chosen careers, very few became the best and brightest members of their generation (Pyryt, 1993). Thus, although IQ is an important contributor to a person's life path, it is only one factor determining a person's life accomplishments. This is certainly good news to the vast majority of us who do not fall within the lofty 1 percent upper realm of the IQ normal distribution!

iStock

Is this your stereotype of a gifted student? Does research support this stereotype? How do the lives of gifted people differ from those of the average person?

8.4b Twin and Adoption Studies Indicate That Both Genes and Environment Influence Intelligence.

Psychologists and behavior geneticists who study the heritability of intelligence express the degree to which heredity determines intelligence within a particular human group in terms of a **heritability coefficient**, which ranges from 0 to 1 (Sternberg & Kaufman, 2002). A coefficient of 0 would mean that heredity has no influence on intelligence, while a coefficient of 1 would mean that heredity is the only influence. As with most of the intelligence testing conducted today, heritability coefficient estimates are almost always based on standard IQ tests, which define intelligence primarily in terms of analytic and verbal ability. To gain a better understanding of heritability research, let us first examine studies of twins and then turn our attention to the adoption studies.

Heritability coefficient A statistical coefficient, ranging from 0 to 1, that estimates the degree to which heredity determines intelligence within a particular human group

Twin Studies

Why would researchers studying the role of genetic factors in intelligence be so interested in studying identical and fraternal twins? As you learned in Chapter 2, identical twins have identical genes, whereas fraternal twins share only about half of the same genes. The rationale for studying twins is that they normally are raised in similar environments. If the IQ scores of identical twins were more similar than those of fraternal twins, this presumably would be due to their greater genetic similarity. Or would it?

As you can see from Figure 8-11, the findings of more than 100 twin studies indicate that the average correlation of identical twins' IQ scores is .86, while that of fraternal twins is significantly lower, .60 (Bouchard & McGue, 1981; McGue et al., 1993). These results seem to support the genetic contribution to intelligence. However, these same twin studies also point to environmental effects on intelligence (Lytton & Gallagher, 2002). Fraternal twins—who are genetically no more similar than regular siblings, but who are exposed to more similar experiences due to their identical ages—have more similar IQ scores than other siblings. In addition, nontwin siblings raised together have more similar IQs ($r = .47$) than siblings raised apart ($r = .24$).

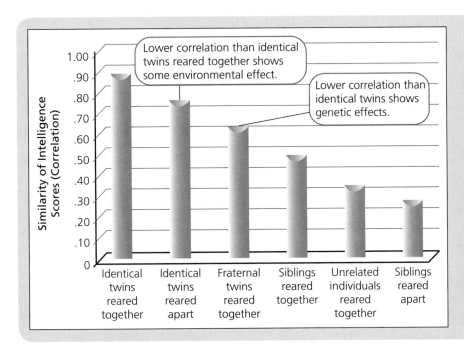

FIGURE 8-11

Studies of IQ Similarity: The Nature-Nurture Debate

The results of over 100 studies correlating the IQ scores for people with different genetic and environmental backgrounds found that the most genetically similar people had the most similar IQ scores. Do these findings suggest that intelligence is partly inherited? How do the other findings reported here support the argument that intelligence is partly determined by environmental factors?

Together, do these findings suggest that genes and environment both contribute to intelligence, but that genes have a greater influence?

That is a reasonable conclusion, but environmentally oriented researchers argue that the higher IQ correlations among identical twins than among fraternal twins may be substantially caused by environmental factors. According to this argument, parents of identical twins tend to treat them more alike than parents of fraternal twins, often even dressing them identically. As a result, fraternal twins' environments often are not as similar as are the environments of identical twins. Perhaps it is this greater environmental similarity that explains the higher IQ correlations among the identical twins than among the fraternal twins.

Genetically oriented researchers respond that identical twins raised apart still have higher IQ correlations ($r = .72$) than fraternal twins raised together ($r = .60$). Isn't this convincing evidence for genetic effects? Maybe not, say the environmentally oriented researchers. These higher IQ correlations for identical twins reared apart may be due to *prenatal environmental factors*. About two-thirds of identical twins share the same placenta and amniotic sac in the uterus, which makes their prenatal environment more alike than that of fraternal twins, who are almost always in separate sacs (Phelps et al., 1997). Twins in the same sac share the same blood, which contains chemicals that affect brain development. Perhaps the high IQ correlations among identical twins separated at birth are due to shared early environment as well as shared genes.

Adoption Studies

Given the competing ways in which twin study findings can be interpreted as supporting either genetic or environmental effects on IQ, researchers have sought further clues among adopted children. Biological parents supply these children their genes, while adoptive parents provide them their environment. If heredity matters more than environment, the children's IQ scores should correlate higher with their biological parents' IQ scores than with their adoptive parents' scores. The reverse finding should occur if environment matters more than heredity.

A number of adoption studies have found that children who were adopted within two weeks to one year of birth were later found to have higher IQ correlations with their biological parents than with their adoptive parents (Scarr & Weinberg, 1983; Turkheimer, 1991). Furthermore, many of these same studies find that as adopted children grow up, their IQ correlation with their biological parents doesn't decrease; it increases! How could this be if environment is more important than genetics in determining intelligence? These and other findings suggest that heredity makes a somewhat larger contribution than environment (Loehlin et al., 1997; Teasdale & Owen, 1984).

Although adoption studies point toward a substantial hereditary contribution to intelligence, they also report evidence of significant environmental influences. For instance, in France, the IQ scores of lower-class children adopted by upper-class families were compared with the IQ scores of their siblings who had not been adopted (Capron & Duyme, 1989; Schiff et al., 1978). Although the average adopted children's scores in these studies ranged between 104 and 111, the average scores for their brothers and sisters reared in the original lower-class households ranged between 92 and 95, a significant difference. Furthermore, when children of upper-class parents were adopted, their later average IQ score was 120 if their adoptive parents were from upper-class families, but only 108 if lower-class families adopted them.

Based on the twin and adoption studies combined, the best estimate is that heredity accounts for a little over 50 percent of the variation in intelligence, with environmental factors being responsible for a little less than 50 percent. However, this

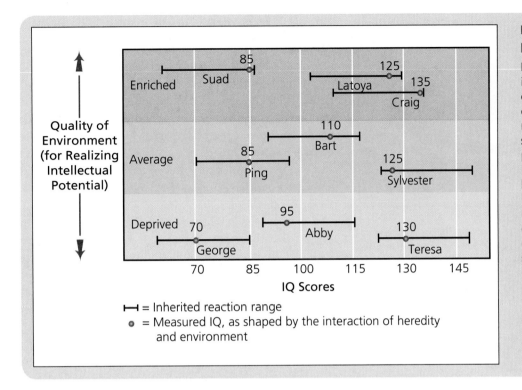

FIGURE 8-12

Reaction Range

Reaction range indicates the extent to which the environment can raise or lower IQ scores, given the preexisting hereditary limits. Each person has her or his own individual reaction range. People who grow up in enriched environments should score at the top of their reaction range, whereas those who grow up in impoverished settings should score closer to the bottom of their range.

does not mean that a little over half of *your* intelligence is inherited and a little less than half is environmentally influenced. It simply means that genetics and environmental factors are respectively responsible for a bit more and a bit less than about half of the differences among individuals in the population (R. E. Nisbett et al., 2012).

So how do genes and environment interact in determining intelligence? The concept of **reaction range** provides a possible answer (see Figure 8-12). Our genes establish a range of potential intellectual growth, and our environmental experiences interact with our genetic makeup in determining where we ultimately fall in this reaction range. For example, children with a natural aptitude for writing are more likely to spend leisure time writing and to also select writing and literature courses in high school. If their parents and teachers further nourish this natural aptitude by offering them enrichment opportunities, their skills are further enhanced. Thus, their subsequently high scores on verbal aptitude tests are due to both their natural ability and their experience. For most people in most environments, their reaction range is about a 25-point spread on an IQ test. A number of studies find that exposing children to healthy and stimulating environments can enhance their intellectual abilities (Grotzer & Perkins, 2000). For example, in a longitudinal study, inner-city children who received a great deal of intellectual stimulation at home and in day care or school had, by age 12, average IQ scores 15 to 30 points higher than those of inner-city children who were not exposed to enriching environments (Campbell & Ramey, 1994).

Reaction range A person's genetically determined range of potential intellectual growth, with environmental factors influencing where the person ultimately falls in this range.

8.4c There Are Group Differences in IQ Scores.

As discussed at the beginning of this chapter, claims about group differences in intelligence have often been used to rationalize racial, ethnic, and gender discrimination. For this reason, claims about group differences must be subjected to very careful analysis. In this section, we examine research regarding gender differences in intelligence and then focus on racial differences.

Cross-cultural studies find that although male and female IQ scores are virtually identical, females tend to outperform males on verbal aptitude tests, and males tend to do better on visual-spatial tests. What are some possible explanations for these differences?

Gender Differences

Although male and female IQ scores are virtually identical, a few differences in certain aptitudes are worth mentioning (Ardila et al., 2011; Olszewski-Kubilius & Lee, 2011). Females tend to do better on verbal aptitude tests, such as naming synonyms and verbal fluency, while males tend to do better on visual-spatial tests, such as mental rotation and tracking a moving object through space. These gender differences have been found in at least 30 countries around the world (Beller & Gafni, 1996; Vogel, 1996).

As discussed in Chapter 2, Section 2.3f, some studies suggest that these female-male differences in verbal and spatial abilities might be linked to sex differences in the organization of those areas of the cerebral hemispheres controlling verbal and spatial abilities and to hormonal fluctuations (Burgaleta et al., 2012). Other studies suggest that these differences are a product of gender socialization and the different skills taught to girls and boys (Halpern, 2012). For example, girls not only receive greater encouragement to talk during infancy and early childhood than do boys, but in school they are more likely to be praised for their reading and writing. On the other hand, boys are more often encouraged to play sports and engage in other activities that develop their visual-spatial skills.

Gender differences have also been found in mathematical ability. For example, in the 60-item SAT math test, male high-school seniors average about four more correct answers than their female counterparts (Held et al., 1993). Are these differences caused by genetics, socialization, or some combination of the two? In contrast to the substantial gender differences found in verbal and spatial abilities (about one standard deviation), a meta-analysis of 242 studies published between 1990 and 2007, representing the testing of 1,286,350 people, found no gender differences in math abilities (Lindberg et al., 2010).

Despite the fact that gender differences in math abilities seem to have disappeared, there is still a considerable disparity in the gender composition of undergraduate and graduate college programs that require extensive mathematical knowledge and skills. In fact, it is still the case that men are more likely than women to score very high or very low on tests of mathematical ability. In fact, men are much more likely than women to score in the top one percentile on math tests used for college admissions. For example, many colleges use the Physics C (Mechanics) College Board Advanced Placement Test to select incoming students for their accelerated and advanced physics and science courses and programs. However, as you can see in Figure 8-13, a much higher percentage of male students than female students achieve the highest grade (5) on this test. This means that many more men than women are being admitted to the top science and engineering programs. These gender differences probably do not reflect any innate differences between men and women; they are most likely, instead, due to cultural stereotypes and the resulting ways in which we socialize men and women to think about their mathematical abilities (Cvencek et al., 2011).

Racial Differences

In the United States, African Americans score between 10 and 15 points lower on intelligence tests than White Americans and Asian Americans, whose IQ averages are about 100 (Cosmides & Tooby, 2002; Sackett & Shen, 2010). Hispanic Americans achieve IQ scores somewhere in between those of Blacks and Whites, and Asian

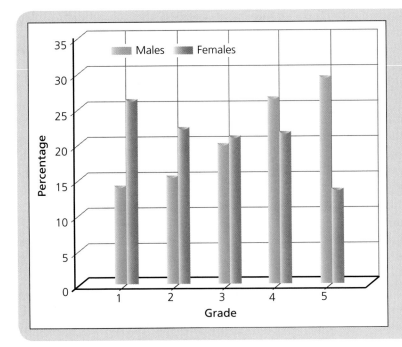

FIGURE 8-13

Gender Differences in Physics Advanced Placement Exam Grades

Colleges often use the Physics C (Mechanics) College Board Advanced Placement Test to select incoming students for their accelerated and advanced physics and science courses and programs. The highest grade level that a student can attain on this exam is a 5. How might the gender difference depicted in this figure have an impact on who is admitted to elite math and science programs in college or on who receives academic scholarships to those programs?

Source: From "Stability and change in gender-related differences on the College Board Advanced Placement and Achievement Tests" by H. Stumpf and J. C. Stanley in Current Directions in Psychological Science, 1998, 192–196.

Americans score about 5 points higher than Whites. Although research suggests that the average IQ scores for Black children have risen over the past 20 years, these group-based IQ differences persist (Hartmann et al., 2007). As mentioned in Section 8.3c, critics of conventional intelligence tests argue that these group differences are caused by culturally biased test items; however, defenders of these tests respond that these differences also occur on nonverbal test items—such as counting digits backward—that do not appear to be culturally biased against ethnic minorities.

In making sense of these findings, we must remember that group differences tell us nothing about the intellectual ability of any specific person. As you can see in Figure 8-14, tens of millions of African American and Hispanic individuals have IQs higher than those of the average White or Asian American. Yet, if heredity

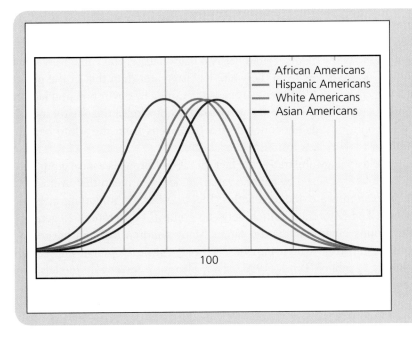

FIGURE 8-14

Racial Differences in IQ Scores

The average score of Asian Americans on IQ tests is about 3 to 5 points higher than White Americans' average score of 100. White Americans, in turn, average about 7 points higher than Hispanic Americans and 10 to 15 points higher than African Americans. However, as you can see by examining the graph, the IQ variation within these groups is much greater than the differences among their average IQ scores.

Source: Data from N. J. Mackintosh. (1998). *IQ and human intelligence.* Oxford: Oxford University Press. Neisser, U. (1998). *The rising curve: Long-term gains in IQ and related measures.* Washington, D.C.: American Psychological Association. Herrnstein, R. J., & Murray, C. (1994). *The bell curve: Intelligence and class structure in American life.* New York: The Free Press.

influences individual differences in intelligence, does it also substantially explain these group differences?

Research by Sandra Scarr is a good example of how scientists have sought answers to this question. In her first line of research, Scarr and Richard Weinberg (1976) examined the IQ of lower-class Black and White children adopted by both Black and White middle-class families. They found that adopted African-American children had an average IQ of 110, over 20 points higher than children who were raised in their original lower-class African-American families. Even when these adopted children reached adulthood, their IQ scores remained 10 points higher than those of African Americans raised in lower-class Black families (Weinberg et al., 1992). The researchers concluded that these findings suggest that Black-White IQ differences in the general population are substantially affected by environmental factors, such as unequal economic and educational conditions. Scarr and her colleagues (1977) also examined the chemical composition of blood among African Americans. Because many African Americans have European ancestors, Scarr reasoned that if Black-White IQ differences were predominantly caused by genetics, then African Americans with a greater proportion of European ancestry in their blood should have the highest IQ scores. Counter to a genetic explanation of racial differences in IQ scores, no correlation was found between IQ and racial ancestry. In fact, virtually all the studies that have sought to find the source of these Black-White IQ differences have failed to find evidence for genetic effects (Eyeferth, 1961; Loehlin et al., 1973; Nisbett, 1995). Indeed, although scientists have discovered some genes weakly associated with intelligence, they have not found that these genes are more prevalent in one racial group than another (Burdick et al., 2006). Based on these converging findings from different research avenues, the general scientific consensus is that it is "highly unlikely" that genetic differences between the races cause the observed group differences in IQ scores (Nisbett et al., 2012).

To understand group-based differences in IQ scores in the United States, think of contemporary American society as if it were a field that has large patches of both fertile and barren soil (Feldman & Lewontin, 2008). As depicted in Figure 8-15, imagine that you have corn seeds with some degree of individual genetic variation. Further imagine filling a white bag and a black bag with an equal number of these seeds. Next, plant these seeds in this field of nonuniform soil. Distribute the white bag of corn seeds so that a much higher percentage grows in the rich, fertile areas of soil than in the poor, barren soil areas. In contrast, distribute the black bag of seeds so that a much higher percentage grows in the poor, barren areas of soil than in the rich, fertile soil areas. As the plants from these two bags mature, you will observe that the average height of the plants from the white bag is greater than that of the plants from the black bag. This group difference is caused entirely by environmental factors (differences in soil nutrients). However, if you do not acknowledge the environmental differences, you would mistakenly conclude that the seeds from the white bag are genetically superior to the seeds from the black bag.

As this corn/field analogy illustrates, the fact that IQ differences *within* groups are partly or even completely caused by genetic variation does not mean that average IQ differences *between* groups are due to genetics (Block, 2002). An important question that needs to be asked before attributing between-group IQ differences to genetics is this: Are the groups' environments the same? Many children living in poverty do not receive proper nutrition, which impedes neurological development and causes attention problems at school (Brody, 1992). They also have fewer role models who can teach them skills and habits necessary to flourish academically, and they attend schools with lower-quality learning resources and lower expectations for academic

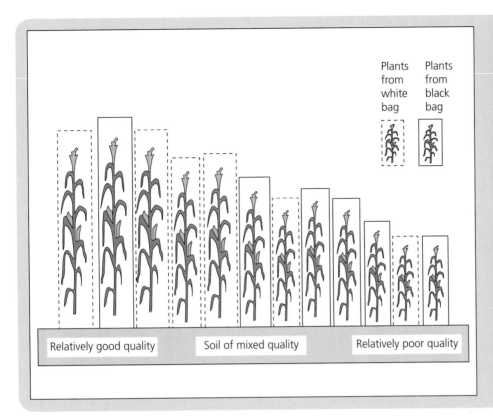

Plants from white bag   Plants from black bag

Relatively good quality   Soil of mixed quality   Relatively poor quality

FIGURE 8-15

Between-Group Variation and Environmental Impact

The same corn seeds are placed in a white bag and a black bag. They are then distributed unevenly within a field that has areas of both rich and poor soil. Some of the height variation in the grown plants may reflect genetic differences. However, the overall height difference between the corn plants that came from seeds in the black bag and those from seeds in the white bag are due to the overall differences in the environment where the "black-bag" and "white-bag" seeds grew.

achievement. Either singly or together, these aspects of an impoverished environment interfere with intellectual growth.

Due to the dissimilarity in environments, it is a mistake to assume that IQ differences between Blacks and Whites stem from genetic factors. Although intelligence researchers generally agree that individual differences in IQ scores are substantially influenced by genetic factors, there is no compelling evidence that group differences in IQ are due to genetics.

8.4d Cultural and Social Psychological Factors May Explain Group IQ Differences.

Beyond socioeconomic disadvantages accounting for lower IQ scores among Blacks and other selective minority groups, some social scientists also contend that certain cultural and psychological forces contribute to these between-group differences.

Voluntary versus Involuntary Minorities

One way to distinguish among minority groups in the United States is in terms of how they became a "minority" (Ogbu, 2004). *Voluntary minorities* are people who have freely come to this country because they perceived it as "the land of opportunity," whereas *involuntary minorities* are people who are a part of this country because their ancestors were conquered, colonized, or enslaved. Instead of seeking out the United States, the ancestors of involuntary minorities were forced against their will to become a part of this country. Involuntary minorities include Native Americans, most African Americans, early Mexicans in the Southwest, native Hawaiians, Alaskan natives, and Puerto Ricans.

Numerous studies indicate that involuntary minorities in the United States achieve lower IQ scores than voluntary minorities (Brand, 1996; Lundy & Firebaugh, 2005).

Similar findings have also been reported in Canada, Europe, India, Japan, and New Zealand. For example, in Japan the Burakumin are an involuntary minority group that comprises 2 percent of the population. They have the same ethnic and national origins as the dominant Ippan Japanese, yet they have been discriminated against for centuries. Over the past 20 years, the Japanese government has engaged in a substantial effort to improve the educational and social opportunities of the Burakumin. However, members of this involuntary minority still encounter negative stereotypes and discrimination in mainstream Japanese society. When the IQ scores of the Burakumin and the Ippan are compared, the Burakumin score 16 points lower, which is comparable to the 15-point IQ difference found between U.S. Blacks and Whites (Ikeda, 2001). Interestingly, when the Burakumin immigrate to the United States as voluntary minorities, they perform very well on IQ tests, actually doing slightly better than other Japanese immigrants (Ito, 1967).

What is it about the involuntary minority status that might cause these lower IQ scores? Two of the likely causes are (1) persisting negative cultural stereotypes within the dominant culture concerning involuntary minorities' intellectual abilities and (2) the self-protective defensive reaction many involuntary minority members subsequently develop against the rejecting mainstream culture (Shimahara & Holowinsky, 2001).

Oppositional Identities

Anthropologist John Ogbu (2002) believes that some members of stigmatized racial and ethnic groups respond to negative ethnic stereotypes and discrimination by developing an *oppositional* ethnic identity and cultural frame of reference that defensively opposes the rejecting dominant culture (see Chapter 3, Section 3.5d, for a discussion of ethnic identity development). This type of reaction makes a good deal of sense, in certain respects. If you live in a society in which your racial or ethnic group is devalued, developing an oppositional identity may help you cope with your hostile environment by clearly defining your racial or ethnic group in contrasting ways with the larger culture (Crocker & Major, 1989; Crocker et al., 1998). Although an oppositional identity can psychologically insulate you—the stigmatized person—from some of the negative effects of social injustice, such as loss of self-esteem, it can also constrict your personal identity. For example, among many African American youths with oppositional ethnic identities, committing themselves to academic excellence and learning to follow the academic standards of the school are often perceived as adopting a White American cultural frame of reference and "acting White" (Ford, 1996). Unfortunately, by rejecting these academic pursuits, not only are African Americans and other minorities more likely to score lower on IQ tests than their White counterparts, but also this rejection will hinder them from fully taking advantage of the civil rights advances that have occurred over the past 50 years (Bankston & Caldas, 1997; Fordham & Ogbu, 1986).

Stereotype Threat

In addition to the problem that oppositional identities pose to minority students' academic achievement, social psychologist Claude Steele (2011) asserts that for those minority students who do want to excel academically, negative cultural stereotypes about their supposed inferior intellectual abilities can create feelings of anxiety and vulnerability, especially when they are in the company of people outside their racial group. That is, if you are a student who is often one of only a few members of your race enrolled in a particular course, your individual performance is often looked upon by students not of your race as representing the "typical" student of your racial group. Accompanying this scrutiny is the added social stigma associated with your minority label, which often implies a suspicion of intellectual inferiority. Because these negative stereotypes are widely known throughout society, you are susceptible, as the target of such stereotyping, to developing **stereotype threat**, which is the disturbing awareness that your performance on some task might confirm the negative stereotype as something that you personally possess (Schmader et al., 2008). According to Steele, when highly motivated minority students take an intelligence test while simultaneously worrying that a low score will confirm that they fit the "mentally inferior" stereotype, this added pressure is often sufficient to significantly hinder their performance.

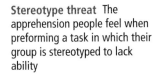

Stereotype threat The apprehension people feel when preforming a task in which their group is stereotyped to lack ability

Evidence for the stereotype threat effect among African American college students comes from a series of experiments that Steele and Joshua Aronson (1995) conducted. In one of these studies, Black and White students were given a difficult English test. In the *stereotype threat condition*, the test was described as a measure of intellectual ability, while in the *nonstereotype threat condition*, it was described as a laboratory problem solving task that didn't measure intelligence. Because one of the more salient racial stereotypes is that Blacks are intellectually inferior to Whites, the researchers presumed that describing the test as an intellectual measure would make this negative stereotype relevant to the Black students' performance. In turn, researchers also expected this stereotype relevance to establish for these Black students a fear of confirming the stereotype ("If I do poorly, my performance will reflect badly on my race and on me"). Steele and Aronson hypothesized that the anxiety created by such thinking would interfere with the Black students' performance. In contrast, when the task was described as not measuring intelligence, the researchers assumed that this would make the negative racial stereotype *irrelevant* to the Black students' performance, and therefore not arouse anxiety. Figure 8-16 shows that when the test was presented as a measure of ability, Blacks performed worse than Whites,

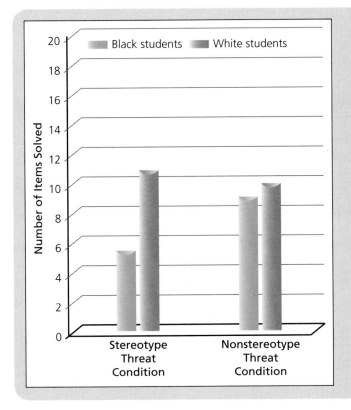

FIGURE 8-16

African American Intellectual Test Performance and Stereotype Threat

Steele and Aronson (1995) administered a difficult English test to Black and White college students. When the test was described as a measure of intellectual ability (stereotype threat condition), Blacks performed worse than Whites. However, when it was not associated with ability (nonstereotype threat condition), no significant racial differences were found. How are these findings consistent with the stereotype threat hypothesis?

consistent with the stereotype threat hypothesis. However, when it was not associated with ability, no significant racial differences were found.

One common reaction in academic settings is for those affected by stereotype threat to *disidentify* with the activity that is the source of the threat, namely, academic achievement. That is, you change your self-concept so that academic achievement is no longer very important to your self-esteem (Steele, 1992, 1997). This sort of academic disidentification is much more common among African American and other involuntary minority students than among White American and voluntary minority students (Ambady et al., 2001; Major et al., 1998). Although such disidentification protects self-esteem and is a coping response to racial prejudice and discrimination, it also is one of the psychological factors that undermines involuntary minority students' school achievement.

Academic disidentification resulting from stereotype threat also occurs among lower-class Whites and among female students of all races and ethnic categories who are in male-dominated majors, such as engineering and chemistry. For example, Steven Spencer and his colleagues (1999) found that women performed as well as men on a difficult English test where they suffered no social stigma, but women underachieved relative to men on a comparably difficult math test where they were more vulnerable to suspicions of intellectual inferiority. In a follow-up to this study, the researchers gave female and male college students a difficult math test but divided it into two halves and presented it as two distinct tests. Half the students were told that the first test was one on which men outperformed women and that the second test was one on which there were no gender differences. The other students were told the opposite—test one was described as exhibiting no gender differences, but men outperformed women on test two. Consistent with the stereotype threat hypothesis, when told that the test yielded gender differences, women performed significantly worse than men. However, when the test was described as not exhibiting any gender differences, women and men performed at the same level. This dramatic change occurred even though the two tests were the same! Similar to African American students' disidentification process described earlier, women are most likely to disidentify with math and math-related careers where negative gender stereotypes are salient (Spencer et al., 1999).

Journey of Discovery

Stereotype threat in academia can also occur among members of privileged groups, such as White middle-class men. Can you guess what ethnic group might cause White middle-class men to experience stereotype threat in academia?

Considered together, these studies inform us that negative stereotypes can create damaging self-fulfilling prophecies among members of many different social groups by inducing stereotype threat. Further, these findings raise the very real possibility that stereotype threat may partly explain both the racial differences found in intelligence testing and the gender differences found in advanced-math testing (refer back to Section 8.4c).

Valuing Academic Achievement

Thus far, we have examined cultural and social psychological factors that might depress IQ scores among selective racial and ethnic groups. Yet, why do elementary school children in Taiwan and Japan outscore American children by about 15 points (roughly one standard deviation) in math ability, and to a lesser extent, in reading skills? Interviews with the parents of these children conducted by Harold Stevenson and his coworkers (1986) found that the Chinese and Japanese parents downplayed the importance of innate intellectual ability and stressed, instead, hard work. They also considered doing well in school to be the *most important* goal for their children. In contrast, the American parents were more likely to believe that intelligence is genetically determined, and they designated academic achievement as a much lower-valued goal for their children. Follow-up studies found that the achievement differences between these Asian and American children persisted through high school (Stevenson et al., 1993). Overall, this research suggests that intellectual growth is nurtured when parents and the larger culture stress the value of education and the importance of working hard to achieve intellectual mastery (Deslandes & Bertrand, 2005; Li, 2004). In contrast, intellectual growth is stunted when cultural beliefs impress upon the child that his or her own academic success is either unlikely (due to negative cultural stereotypes) or not highly valued (due to it being incompatible with more important cultural values).

8.4e Intellectual Ability Is Shaped by Self-Fulfilling Prophecies.

In 1948, the sociologist Robert Merton introduced the concept of the **self-fulfilling prophecy** to describe a situation in which someone's expectations about a person or group actually lead to the fulfillment of those expectations. As illustrated in Figure 8-17, the self-fulfilling prophecy involves a three-step process. First, the perceiver (the "prophet") forms an impression of the target person. Second, the perceiver acts toward the target person in a manner consistent with this first impression. Third, in response, the target person's behavior changes to correspond to the perceiver's actions. Research indicates that behavior changes due to self-fulfilling prophecies can be permanent and can markedly change the course of an individual's life (Smith et al., 1999). How might self-fulfilling prophecies influence the development—for better or worse—of children's intellectual abilities?

Self-fulfilling prophecy The process by which someone's expectations about a person or group lead to the fulfillment of those expectations

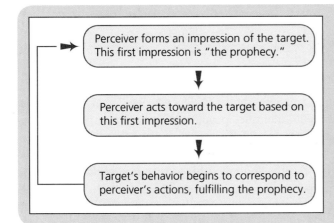

FIGURE 8-17

The Development of a Self-Fulfilling Prophecy

Self-fulfilling prophecies often involve three stages, or steps. In step 1, the perceiver forms an impression of the target. In step 2, the perceiver behaves in a manner consistent with this first impression. In step 3, the target responds to the perceiver's actions in a way that confirms the perceiver's initial impression.

Academic Achievement and the Self-Fulfilling Prophecy

Robert Rosenthal and Lenore Jacobson (1968) explored this very question by studying the academic achievement of elementary schoolchildren. Rosenthal and Jacobson first gave IQ tests to first- and second-grade children at the school and then told their teachers that the tests identified certain students as "potential bloomers" who should experience substantial IQ gains during the remaining school year. In reality, the children identified as potential bloomers had simply been randomly selected by the researchers and did not differ intellectually from their classmates. Eight months later, when the students were again tested, the potential bloomers not only exhibited improved schoolwork but also showed higher gains in their IQ scores than those who had not been identified as bloomers. Additional research indicates that teachers treat students who are positively labeled in this manner differently from others in the following ways (Jussim, 1989; Meichenbaum & Turk, 1976):

- Teachers create a warmer socioemotional climate for gifted students.

- Teachers provide gifted students with more feedback on their academic performance.

- Teachers challenge gifted students with more difficult material.

- Teachers provide gifted students with a *greater opportunity to respond* to material presented in class.

Treated in this favorable manner, positively labeled students are likely to assume either that the teacher especially likes them and has good judgment or that the teacher is a likable person. Whichever attribution is made, the positively labeled students work harder and begin thinking of themselves as high achievers. Through this behavioral and self-concept change, the prophecy is fulfilled.

Unfortunately, self-fulfilling prophecies can also cause some students' academic potential to be destroyed by negative expectations. Teachers and fellow students often treat children labeled as "troubled" or "intellectually inferior" in a way that reinforces the negative label so it is more likely to be internalized. In educational settings, this form of self-fulfilling prophecy is all too common, and over time it leads to negative self-beliefs and low self-esteem among those targeted students. The children most likely to be identified early as problem students are those from involuntary minority groups. Although similar negative expectations also occur for certain White children and those from voluntary minorities, they are more the exception than the rule. The resulting differences in how these students are treated may be small and subtle, but their cumulative effects can be profound.

Can Your Beliefs About Intelligence Affect Your Intellectual Potential?

Besides others' expectations either enhancing or diminishing our intellectual potential, research also suggests that our beliefs about intelligence itself can have similar effects. Carol Dweck (2002, 2006) identifies people who believe that intelligence is basically fixed at birth as *entity theorists*. These persons believe that life experiences cannot substantially change inborn intelligence. In contrast, Dweck identifies people who believe that intelligence is flexible and malleable as *incremental theorists*. These individuals believe that life experiences can substantially alter inborn intelligence. Dweck's research finds that entity theorists' beliefs about intelligence can handicap them in their academic pursuits.

After performing poorly on an intellectual task, entity theorists are more likely than incremental theorists to lose their motivation and give up; and they are less likely to learn from their mistakes. Incremental theorists respond very differently to academic setbacks. Believing that intelligence is malleable, they tend to work harder after failure and seek to learn from their mistakes. Achieving success after failure increases their motivation to learn new material that will make success even likelier in the future.

How might thinking of intelligence as flexible and malleable counter the negative effects of stereotype threat previously discussed in Section 8.4d? Joshua Aronson and his colleagues (2002) explored this question by teaching African American and European American college students to think of intelligence as changeable, rather than fixed. Compared to students in a control condition who did not receive this information, students in the "incremental theory" condition significantly improved their grade point averages and also more strongly believed that academic achievement was personally important. Further, the African American students benefited more from learning about the malleable nature of intelligence than did the European American students, suggesting that this intervention reduced their stereotype threat. In other words, realizing that their intellectual ability and potential could be improved through hard work might have been a potent stereotype antidote for Black students who have historically been the targets of negative stereotypes alleging limited inborn intelligence. Subsequent longitudinal studies have replicated these findings among middle-school students (Blackwell et al., 2007). Overall, this research identifies a very cost-effective method for improving students' academic motivation and achievement. In a very real sense, reteaching students to think of intelligence as being malleable and changeable is another example of the self-fulfilling prophecy.

Section REVIEW

- Intelligence is partly based on neural complexity, quickness, and efficiency.

- Seventy-five percent of intellectual disability cases result from a harmful environment or subtle physiological effects; 25 percent are linked to organic causes.

- Gifted students are less likely to be social misfits than the nongifted.

- Twin and adoption studies indicate substantial hereditary contribution to individual intelligence but also significant environmental influences.

- Females perform better on verbal aptitude tests, and males do better on visual-spatial tests.

- Little scientific evidence exists to support hereditary explanations of racial differences in IQ scores.

- In cultures throughout the world, involuntary minority groups score lower on IQ tests than do voluntary minority groups.

- Racially based IQ differences are most likely due to environmental factors such as unequal economic and educational conditions, differing cultural values surrounding education, and negative effects of racial stereotypes on minority students' self-confidence.

- Self-fulfilling prophecies can enhance or diminish intellectual ability.

- Thinking of intelligence as being malleable can short-circuit stereotype threats related to intellectual achievement.

PSYCHOLOGICAL
a p p l i c a t i o n s

How Can You "Create" a Creative Environment?

Creativity is the ability to produce novel, high-quality products or ideas (Glaveanu, 2012; Stokes, 2006). In trying to understand the creative process, psychologists have distinguished between two types of thinking: *convergent thinking* and *divergent thinking* (Guilford, 1959). **Convergent thinking** involves applying logic and conventional knowledge to arrive at (or *converge upon*) a single solution to a problem. Most formal education empha-sizes this type of thinking. For example, when teachers ask students to solve a math problem, they encourage the students to focus on one particular approach and work through a series of steps until they find the "right" answer. Traditional IQ tests primarily require the use of convergent thinking. In contrast, **divergent thinking** involves pursuing many different and often unconventional paths to generate many different solutions to a problem (Plucker et al., 2011). When engaged in this type of thinking, you often are moving away (or diverging) from the problem and considering it from a variety of perspec-tives. Groups searching for new directions and novel ideas may sometimes encourage their members to engage in divergent thinking during *brainstorming* sessions (Kurtzberg & Amabile, 2001). In these sessions, members are instructed to say the first thing that comes to mind without worrying about its logic or social acceptability. The goal in brain-storming is to generate as many different ideas as possible to help the group meet existing challenges. Unfortunately, one of the biggest obstacles to success in such brainstorming sessions is that members often censor their own creative ideas out of concern for how other group members might respond (Boddy, 2012).

Creativity The ability to produce novel, high-quality products or ideas

Convergent thinking Applying logic and conventional knowledge to arrive at (or *converge upon*) a single solution to a problem

Divergent thinking Pursuing many different and often unconventional paths to generate many different solutions to a problem

Psychologists have traditionally considered divergent thinking to be a more important ingredient in creativity than convergent thinking because people who are divergent thinkers are more likely to break out of mental sets that hinder the adoption of new ideas (see Section 8.2c). However, it is also true that successful completion of a creative project often requires frequent convergent thought as well as divergent thought. Overall, despite the contribution of convergent thinking to creative endeavors, creativity tests generally contain items that emphasize divergent thinking (Diakidoy & Spanoudis, 2002). For example, test takers might be asked to list as many white, edible things as they can think of in three minutes, or to list all the uses they can think of for a brick. Responses to such items are scored in terms of the number of unique or novel ideas generated, with higher scores indicating higher levels of creativity. Creativity is also measured by asking people to generate a creative product—a poem, a story, a drawing, or perhaps a photo—which judges then rate. Despite the obvious subjectivity of such creativity ratings, the agreement level among judges is quite high (Amabile, 1996). To give you some idea of how judges might rate the creativity of such projects, examine the two photos in Figure 8-18. How would you rate each photo's level of creativity? What criteria are you using in making your judgments? Is one photo more creative than the other?

Most creative people have an intermediate level of education—enough formal schooling to have learned the neces-sary skills to generate creative products, but not so much formal education as to stifle the creative spirit (Simonton, 2000). During the early stages of their careers, creative people tend to rely heavily on a few close friends for advice and encour-agement. However, their intense devotion to work often causes strained relationships with other people (Gardner, 1993).

Does Culture Shape Creative Expression?

Cultural values often channel creative energy into specific fields (Chiu & Kwan, 2010; Simonton & Ting, 2010). When a culture values a particular form of creative expression, it teaches its children how to express themselves in this manner. For example, the birth of the Renaissance—a period of immense artistic creativity at the beginning of the fifteenth century in Florence, Italy—was made possible due to the generous support of artists by the entire population, especially those who had wealth and power. Cultures can also restrict creativity. In the Omaha Indian culture, for instance, there is only one way to sing a song; and if anyone deviates from that format, ritual weeping occurs (Colligan, 1983). As you might guess, this response is an effective way to prevent people from taking "creative liberties" with music. A similar social norm prevents singers in the United States from engaging in too much creative expression when performing "The Star-Spangled Banner."

What is considered "creative" is also shaped by culture. An important feature of creativity in Western cultures is producing an observable product. In contrast, the Eastern view of creativity is less product-focused and more related to personal fulfillment or the expression of an inner sense of ultimate reality (Kuo, 1996). In Hinduism, creativity is thought of as entailing spiritual or religious expression rather than as providing an innovative solution to a problem (Aron & Aron, 1982). This Eastern sense of creativity has a great deal to do with what humanistic psychologists in the West refer to as *self-actualization*, or the process of achieving one's full potential (see Chapter 9, Section 9.1f).

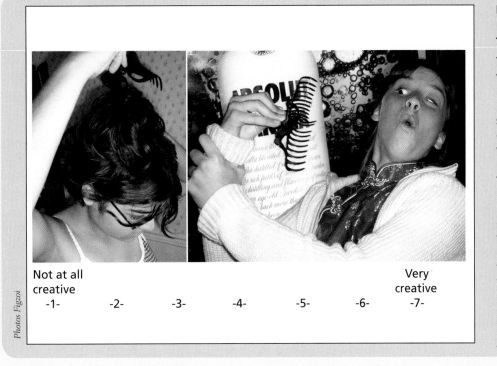

Photos Figzoi

Not at all creative   Very creative

-1-   -2-   -3-   -4-   -5-   -6-   -7-

FIGURE 8-18

How Creative Are These Photos?

The assignment here was to take a photo in which a common hair clip was the subject of focus. No other instructions were given to the participants. Using the scale provided below the photos, rate the creativity of each photo and then ask others to do so as well. Is there agreement on which photo is more creative? What criteria did you and others use in making your judgments?

Another distinction between Western and Eastern views of creativity is the way creativity is related to traditional views. The Western approach to creativity typically involves a break with tradition. This is consistent with the Western philosophy of individualism, which values nonconformity and the expression of ideas that run counter to the group. In contrast, the Eastern approach to creativity is more likely to involve the *reinterpretation* of traditional ideas so that traditional truths come alive and become revitalized in daily activities. This conception of creativity is consistent with the Eastern philosophy of collectivism, which values conformity and the upholding of traditional values and beliefs.

As you can see, culture has an important influence on the nature of creativity, in both how it is defined and how it is channeled. You may be born with a certain degree of creative potential, but how that potential develops and is later expressed will be significantly shaped by your social reality. Yet in most cultures, creative individuals tend to share the following characteristics (Simonton, 2011):

- They have wide interests.

- They like to work hard.

- They are open to new experiences.

- They are risk takers.

- They have at least moderate intelligence.

- They are willing to tolerate rejection.

Do you remember Jasper Fforde, the best-selling author of the *Thursday Next* book series highlighted at the beginning of this chapter? Fforde embodies many of these characteristics. Although he was recognized as an intelligent child, young Fforde was disinterested in traditional schooling and thrived academically only after his parents placed him in a school with a more progressive attitude toward learning. In adulthood, Fforde pursued a wide variety of interests, including working at odd jobs, like being a cameraman in the movie industry, and flying vintage airplanes. Even during the years in which publishing houses repeatedly rejected his manuscripts, he continued to hone his skills after completing his regular workday.

Fostering Creativity

Beyond possessing important personal characteristics, to be creative you need to have a lot of things go your way (Sternberg & Lubart, 1996). For example, many highly creative artists' talents go unrecognized because their works remain obscure, through no fault of their own. In Fforde's case, his first *Thursday Next* book was never even recognized by his own literary agent as anything special until the agent was so desperate for material that he read the whole thing. This makes it sound like creativity is a fragile and illusive form of intelligence, but it's not. Creativity experts contend that you have the power to construct the necessary conditions that foster creative accomplishments. They recommend the following six steps to increase your own creativity. Accompanying each recommendation is a qualification concerning its limits.

- *Redefine problems.* As discussed in Section 8.2c, a number of cognitive tendencies act as barriers to problem solving. Although certain thinking strategies may have effectively solved problems for us in the past, creative solutions often require us to look "through" and "around" problems rather than directly at them. *Warning: Don't feel that you must "reinvent the wheel" for every new problem. Often, tried-and-true problem-solving strategies are the best tools for creative products.*

- *Make a habit out of questioning tradition.* Since childhood, we have been rewarded for conforming to the way other people think and act. Such conformity is often necessary for a society to properly function, but it does not provide a fertile environment for creative ideas. One of the defining characteristics of creative people is that they regularly question traditional ways of thinking and behaving. *Warning: Defying tradition simply because it brings you attention is not the purpose of this exercise!*

- *Find something you love to do.* Creative people, whether they are children or adults, are motivated primarily by the enjoyment, challenge, and satisfaction they derive from working on their projects, rather than from the external rewards they receive. *Warning: Being rewarded for doing things you naturally enjoy can undermine your enjoyment of those activities (see the discussion on intrinsic motivation in Chapter 9, Section 9.1e).*

- *Become an expert in your area of interest.* Case studies of 120 creative people from diverse professions found that high-quality training preceded great accomplishments (Bloom, 1985). This research suggests that you will have a much better chance of being a creative success if you have developed a good base of knowledge in your chosen interest area. By tapping your accumulated learning, you will be able to generate more ideas and make more mental connections that will ultimately lead to creative problem solving. *Warning: Don't feel you need to know everything about your area of interest before you can make a creative contribution to it.*

- *Tolerate ambiguity and take sensible risks.* Because creative ideas run against the grain of everyday thinking and often do not fit neatly into clearly defined categories, you must have sufficient confidence in your ideas so that you are not easily discouraged when others don't understand or accept what you have to offer. *Warning: Do not totally ignore feedback from others because you can profit from others' advice.*

- *Choose friends and associates who will support your creative endeavors.* Analysis of the lives of over 2,000 successful scientists and inventors found that the most creative individuals were not isolated geniuses. Rather, they had high emotional intelligence and surrounded themselves with people who encouraged them in their work (Simonton, 1992). *Warning: Do not surround yourself with "yes people" who will agree with anything you say. Blind conformity does not foster a creative environment.*

FIGURE 8-4b

Solution to The Candle Problem

The solution to The Candle Problem in Figure 8-4a (page 345) relies on realizing that the box is not just a container for the tacks, but can itself be used as part of the solution.

Suggested Websites

The Psychology of Language Page

http://www.duke.edu/~pk10/language/psych.htm

This website discusses the controversy concerning "nature versus nurture" explanations for language development.

Center for the Study of Language and Information (CSLI)

http://www-csli.stanford.edu

This website is the home page for CSLI, an independent research center at Stanford University.

History of Influences in the Development of Intelligence Theory and Testing

http://www.indiana.edu/~intell/map.shtml

This website discusses the history of intelligence testing and theory development.

Multiple Intelligences

http://www.thomasarmstrong.com/multiple_intelligences.htm

This website outlines Gardner's theory of multiple intelligences and how it might apply in educational settings.

IQ Tests

http://www.2h.com/iq-tests.html

This website contains a number of intelligence tests and brainteasers.

Key Terms

Achievement test, 353
Algorithm, 342
Aptitude test, 353
Availability heuristic, 348
Categorization, 341
Child-directed speech, 338
Cognition, 341
Communication, 330
Concept, 341
Confirmation bias, 344
Content validity, 358
Convergent thinking, 384
Creativity, 384
Divergent thinking, 384
Down syndrome, 369
Emotional intelligence, 365
Eugenics, 351
Factor analysis, 360
Flynn effect, 356
Functional fixedness, 347
General intelligence factor (g-factor), 361

Generic masculine, 339
Heritability coefficient, 371
Heuristic, 343
Insight, 343
Intellectual disability, 369
Intelligence quotient (IQ), 353
Intelligence, 351
Language acquisition device, 335
Language, 330
Linguistic relativism, 339
Mental set, 345
Morphemes, 336
Multiple intelligences, 362
Need for cognition, 350
Normal distribution, 356
Phonemes, 336
Predictive validity, 358
Problem solving, 342
Prodigies, 363
Prototype, 342
Psychometrics, 351

Reaction range, 373
Reliability, 357
Representativeness heuristic, 348
Savant, 363
Self-fulfilling prophecy, 381
Speech, 330
Standardization, 356
Stanford-Binet Intelligence Test, 353
Stereotype threat, 379
Telegraphic speech, 337
Trial an error, 342
Triarchic theory of intelligence, 364
Validity, 358
Wechsler Intelligence Scales, 354

Review Questions

1. The content and comprehension of language is associated with which area?
   a. Broca's area
   b. the right cerebral hemisphere
   c. Wernicke's area
   d. the larynx
   e. the location of the hippocampus

2. A weaker version of Whorf's linguistic relativity hypothesis is supported by which of the following?
   a. research showing that bilinguists focus on personal needs when speaking English and social needs when speaking Japanese
   b. Rosch's research on cross-cultural color perception, showing that the Dani people have only two words for color
   c. research showing that the structure of language determines the structure of thought
   d. the finding that Chinese languages have many self-focused words
   e. research showing that language does not influence thinking in collectivist cultures

3. The way language calls attention to an individual's gender, and the use of generic masculine pronouns and nouns support which of the following notions?
   a. Language determines thought.
   b. Cultural thinking can influence people's style of language.
   c. Gender-neutral language erases females from our thinking.
   d. Collectivist cultures exhibit more gender bias than individualist cultures.
   e. Language influences thought.

4. Categorizing, or forming concepts, is accomplished by which of the following?
   a. identifying features that define all members of a concept
   b. learning specific concept formation rules
   c. learning the fixed boundaries between objects' properties
   d. identifying features that define typical members of a concept
   e. learning the specific rules that define the meaning of fuzzy boundaries

5. Which of the following is true about trial-and-error problem-solving strategies?
   a. They guarantee success because you can keep guessing until you get it right.
   b. They are faster and more efficient than using complex algorithms.
   c. They are slower than heuristic strategies.
   d. They follow a systematic and methodical step-by-step procedure.
   e. They involve a gradually increasing focus on concepts important to the solution.

6. Confirmation bias leads to problem-solving errors _____.
   a. because we seek only information that confirms our beliefs
   b. only when we waste time testing alternative hypotheses rather than seeking confirming evidence
   c. only when we pursue information that disconfirms our beliefs
   d. when we fail to rely on solutions that worked in the past
   e. because we tend to confirm what experts tell us

7. Research on decision-making strategies and shortcuts indicates which of the following?
   a. Representative heuristics are the best way to eliminate the base-rate fallacy.
   b. Only people with a low need for cognition take shortcuts in their decision making strategies.
   c. A useful decision-making strategy that can narrow our choices is to rely on the ease with which previous examples of an event are recalled.
   d. Heuristics are complex cognitive processes used primarily by those with a high need for cognition.
   e. Heuristics are used more frequently when we are in a hurry than when we have time to think about our choices.

8. Intelligence has been assessed or scored in a variety of ways since Galton's measures of sensory abilities and head size. Most intelligence tests today rely on a scoring method known as _____.
    a. ratio IQ
    b. deviation IQ
    c. an intelligence quotient
    d. mental age/chronological age (x 100)
    e. verbal IQ

9. Standardization, or establishing rigid test administration and interpretation procedures, typically results in which of the following?
    a. a reliable test
    b. a standard test
    c. a valid test
    d. a normal distribution of scores
    e. the Flynn effect

10. Research investigating the nature of intelligence has supported all except which of the following
    a. Intelligence consists of a single general factor, referred to as g.
    b. Intelligence consists of several specific factors.
    c. The same areas of the frontal cortex "light up" for different intellectual tasks.
    d. Seven clusters of primary mental abilities are needed to explain intelligence.
    e. Factor analysis consistently indicates five factors of intelligence.

11. Which of the following is true of research evidence for multiple intelligences?
    a. It is lacking.
    b. It is provided by the existence of savants.
    c. It is negated by the existence of prodigies.
    d. It contradicts Thurstone's approach to understanding intelligence.
    e. It has shown that athletic ability is not a talent but a specific type of intelligence.

12. According to Sternberg's triarchic theory of intelligence, which of the following is true?
    a. Creative intelligence is the type valued in academic settings.
    b. Practical intelligence is superior to creative intelligence.
    c. Intelligence is defined by how skilled an individual is in all three aspects of intelligence.
    d. Successful intelligence is knowing how and when to use analytical, creative, and practical intelligence.
    e. Analytical intelligence is related to nonconformity, risk-taking, and openness to new experiences.

13. An individual with high emotional intelligence would likely exhibit all except which of the following?
    a. an ability to read their own emotions, but not others' emotions
    b. a tendency to finish rewarding tasks
    c. an ability to discriminate between different feelings
    d. success in their career
    e. reliance on their emotions to guide their thinking and actions.

14. Research by neuroscientists on the relationship between intelligence and the brain has shown which of the following?
    a. The strong relationship between head size and intelligence supports Galton's views.
    b. Women have more neurons than men, on average.
    c. Larger brains may be associated with higher intelligence because they have more myelin.
    d. There is no relationship between intelligence and mental quickness.
    e. the brains of more intelligent people use more glucose, explaining their intelligence and the larger size of their brains.

15. Research on intelligence has relied extensively on twin and adoption studies, which have indicated which of the following?
    a. Identical twins raised apart have similar IQ correlations to fraternal twins raised together.
    b. Reaction range refers to the range of similarity in twins' IQ scores.
    c. Prenatal environmental factors have been discounted as a source of IQ differences among twins.
    d. Heredity has a slightly larger effect on intelligence than environment.
    e. Adopted infants' IQ scores are more similar to their adopted parents' IQ scores than to their biological parents' IQ scores.

16. Research on group differences in intelligence has indicated which of the following?
    a. It is highly unlikely that Black-White IQ score differences are due to genetic differences.
    b. Gender differences in math abilities have been growing larger.
    c. Gender socialization of boys and girls fully explains differences in verbal and spatial abilities.
    d. Individual abilities can be predicted by examining group differences in ability.
    e. The strong correlation between IQ and racial ancestry supports Jensen's view of racial differences in intelligence.

17. Developing an oppositional ethnic identity may do what?
    a. eliminate the constriction of personal identity
    b. help explain racial and ethnic differences in IQ scores
    c. expose the individual to increased negative effects of social injustice
    d. cause a loss of self-esteem
    e. lead Blacks to identify with White cultural values, thus increasing their IQ scores

Chapter Nine
Motivation and Emotion

Chapter Outline

Psychological Applications: *How Can You Manage Your Emotions and Control Test Anxiety?*

When I was eleven, my family and I had just returned home from a weeklong trip to the big city of Chicago. I brought back a model airplane kit for my best friend Pete, and I was about to run the gift over to his house when the phone rang. As my mother talked on the phone, I realized something was wrong. When she hung up she called for my father, ushered him into the bedroom, and closed the door. A few minutes later, the door opened and they called for my teenaged sister and me. I couldn't recall later who said the words "Gramma died," but I distinctly remembered their effect. I felt as if the thoughts and feelings in my head were swimming past but not quite catching hold. Gramma … Gramma who taught me French … Gramma who made me polenta and torta … Gramma who gave me treats—and even a little wine—when I would spend the night at her house. Dead?

Then there was a knock at the door. It was Pete, coming over to play. I went outside to talk to Pete, but I couldn't talk about what I was thinking and feeling. As I stood there mumbling clipped responses to the many questions Pete had about the trip, I suddenly realized I was holding the model airplane kit in my hands. I gave it to my friend; and as Pete opened it, my father, who had been listening to our conversation from behind the screen door, asked me whether I was going to tell Pete about my Gramma. I looked at my father, my Gramma's son, and saw that his eyes looked hurt, but were dry, nonetheless. With

that look, I knew I couldn't tell Pete anything; if I did, the tears would come. Feeling trapped, I choked out the two-word phrase "I can't!" and ran back into the house, past my crying mother and sister, and into my room.

During the time leading up to the funeral, I did cry, but only when I was by myself. Although my father's eyes were red throughout that time, I never saw tears flow down his cheeks. I also don't remember seeing any males in the family crying during this whole ordeal. Even though I felt the pain, I knew I wasn't supposed to show it to others.

Why did I think and act the way I did upon hearing the news of my grandmother's death? Why did my mother and sister respond differently than my father and I? Surely, it wasn't a matter of us not loving Gramma. It wasn't a matter of love, but rather a matter of what motivates men and women to express—or not express—certain emotions.

In this chapter, you will examine what motivates people's behavior. You will learn about different approaches to identifying and understanding the cognitive, physiological, social, and environmental factors that shape our various needs and desires. Then you will explore three different motivational issues—eating, sex, and striving for achievement. Finally, you will learn more about a topic that is integral to a full understanding of motivation, the psychology of emotion.

9.1 Motivation

You do things. You not only do things, you also often feel irrepressible urges to initiate certain actions. Sometimes you feel "pushed" to behave, while at other times you feel "pulled." This "push" or "pull" to act in certain ways or achieve particular goals is the topic of our discovery quest in this section of the chapter.

9.1a Motivation Is a Dynamic Process.

Motivation An inner state that energizes behavior toward the fulfillment of a goal

Motivation is an inner state that energizes behavior toward the fulfillment of a goal (King, 2008). The study of motivation is essentially the study of motion—of what moves a person or other animal to act in a particular way. As such, motivation is best regarded as a dynamic process, one in which motivational states are constantly changing due to changes both outside and inside the person and due to responses made toward the motivated state itself.

To better understand how motivation is a dynamic process, imagine that you have a strong desire to be a painter. Due to the positive feelings associated with this desire, you enroll as a student at a famous art institute. Your subsequent successes and failures at the institute—combined with conflicting goals related to your desire for wealth, romance, and children—might change the intensity of your motivation toward this goal. Due to this dynamic quality, motivation is not easily measured or quantified. Psychologists often measure it by looking for changes in intensity and direction of desire or need—and at what caused those changes.

In making sense of this moving target, theories of motivation focus on what influences behavior at any given time, and on either internal or external sources for that influence. *Internal theories* assume that something about the organism pushes it toward (or away from) some object. In contrast, *external theories* focus more on attributes of the goal or the environment that *pull* the organism in a certain direction. Clearly, no matter which emphasis is given, both internal and external issues need to be addressed when studying motivation (Hogan, 2005).

9.1b   *Genes May Shape Our Motivation.*

At the beginning of the twentieth century, many psychologists were fascinated by Charles Darwin's (1871) theory of evolution. Extending his theory, they proposed that humans, like other animals, have instincts. An **instinct** is an unlearned, relatively fixed pattern of behavior that is essential to a species' survival. William McDougall (1908) was an early proponent of the view that much of human behavior is controlled by instincts; and he generated a list of 18 human instincts, including greed, self-assertion, and gregariousness. In subsequent years, other instinct theorists expanded this list into the thousands. The argument became that if a behavior is seen, it must be instinctual. Of course, one problem with such reasoning is that it is circular. An observed behavior (for example, *aggression*) is attributed to an instinct (*aggressiveness*), which in turn is inferred from the behavior. A second problem with instinct theory is that it cannot accommodate the role of learning that early behaviorists were demonstrating in their research (see Chapter 6). Simply put, many so-called instinctual behaviors are learned and shaped by experience.

Although instinct theory collapsed due to its false assumptions, we have seen in our study of other topics in psychology that genes may predispose the human species— as well as other species—to engage in certain patterns of behavior. This contemporary evolutionary perspective states that we do, indeed, inherit adaptive genetic traits, but these traits express themselves more as predispositions for behaviors rather than as a predetermined set of actions (Barrett et al., 2002). For example, early instinct theorists would have explained alcoholism as being directly caused by an inherited instinct. In contrast, modern evolutionary theorists acknowledge that there may be a genetic predisposition for such behavior, but they reject the notion that some genetic code predetermines that someone will become an alcoholic. Instead, they contend that genes might affect how the body responds to alcohol or what emotional responses a person might have to certain environmental cues associated with drinking. Such predispositions might increase the likelihood of excessive drinking, but they would not predetermine the behavior or the addiction.

Instinct An unlearned, relatively fixed pattern of behavior that is essential to a species' survival

9.1c   *We Are Sometimes Motivated to Reduce Arousal.*

When the original instinct theory fell out of scientific favor, many psychologists sought to explain motivation by turning to **drive-reduction theory** (Hull, 1943), which is based on the concept of homeostasis. **Homeostasis** is the tendency for organisms to keep physiological systems internally balanced by adjusting them in response to change. An example of homeostasis is the body's temperature-regulation system: A dip or rise in body temperature causes various physiological responses (for example, constriction of blood vessels and sweating), which return the body's temperature to the desired level.

Drive-reduction theory The idea that an imbalance in homeostasis creates a physiological need, which in turn produces a drive that motivates the organism to satisfy the need

Homeostasis The tendency of organisms to keep physiological systems internally balanced by adjusting them in response to change

FIGURE 9-1

Drive-Reduction Theory

Drive-reduction theory contends that we are motivated to keep physiological systems internally balanced, a state called homeostasis. For example, when deprived of liquids you experience a physiological need, which produces a drive to find and consume liquids to satisfy this need. When the need is satisfied, the drive is reduced; and homeostasis is restored.

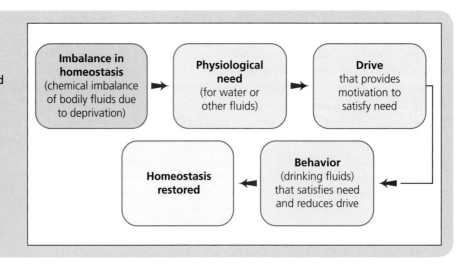

Drive A physiological state of arousal that moves an organism to meet a need

According to drive-reduction theory, an imbalance in homeostasis creates a physiological need, which in turn produces a **drive**, defined as a physiological state of arousal that moves the organism to meet the need. Once the need is met, the drive is reduced and the behavior that was initiated in response to the drive ceases. For example, as depicted in Figure 9-1, if you were deprived of water or other liquids for an extended period of time, the chemical balance of your bodily fluids would become disturbed, initiating a "thirst drive," marked by arousal and discomfort, pushing you to seek liquid to alleviate the discomfort. After you consumed a sufficient amount of liquid, homeostasis would be achieved, the drive would be reduced, and you would stop drinking.

Part of the difference between instinct theory and drive-reduction theory is that drive-reduction theory, by distinguishing between primary and secondary drives, recognizes the importance of learning in motivation. *Primary drives* are unlearned drives that arise from basic biological needs, such as the need for food and water. *Secondary drives* are acquired drives that are learned by being associated with primary drives. For example, the need to acquire money is a learned, secondary drive that can develop into a strong influence on behavior. By recognizing the existence of secondary drives, drive-reduction theory can explain a much wider range of behavior than instinct theory.

Despite its advantages over instinct theory, drive-reduction theory ran into problems because people engage in many behaviors—such as riding roller coasters, watching scary movies, or taking drugs—that seem designed to increase arousal. Due to the fact that drive-reduction theory could not account for all areas of motivation, psychologists concluded that it was incomplete.

 **INFO-BIT**   As you recall from Chapter 6, Section 6.2b, food, water, and other stimuli that satisfy primary drives are called primary reinforcers, while stimuli that satisfy secondary drives are known as secondary reinforcers.

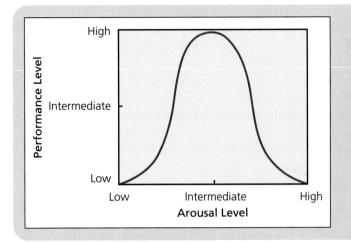

FIGURE 9-2

The Yerkes-Dodson Law

According to the Yerkes-Dodson law, we perform best when we are at an intermediate level of arousal. How might this psychological principle explain our inability to think when we are either nearly asleep or overexcited?

9.1d We Are Sometimes Motivated to Maintain an Optimal Level of Arousal.

Contrary to drive-reduction theory, research indicates that levels of arousal that are too low are as uncomfortable as those that are too high. For example, when research participants were placed in an artificial environment that deprived them of sensory stimulation, they reported difficulties in thinking and within hours became increasingly irritable and began having vivid daydreams and hallucinations (Heron, 1957). Overall, it appears that we seek to achieve and maintain an *optimum* level of bodily arousal—not too much and not too little. This preference conforms to the **Yerkes-Dodson law**, which is named after the researchers who discovered it. As depicted in Figure 9-2, this law contends that when we are underaroused or overaroused, we perform below our abilities. Why? When underaroused, we tend to be bored and sluggish, whereas overarousal makes us nervous and tense. Our best performance occurs when we are at an intermediate level of arousal (Teigen, 1994). Thus, instead of motivation simply being tied to reducing arousal, it appears that motivation is associated with *regulating* arousal.

Not surprisingly, people differ in their optimal arousal. Those who enjoy high arousal tend to listen to loud music, socialize a great deal, eat spicy foods, drink alcohol, smoke tobacco, engage in frequent sexual activity, and do things that are risky or novel (Trimpop & Kirkcaldy, 1997). Individuals with lower optimal arousal seek less intense stimulation and take fewer risks in life. Biology and blood chemistry appear to explain many of these individual differences.

Yerkes-Dodson law The idea that we perform best when we are at an intermediate level of arousal

9.1e Incentive Theory Examines How External Factors Motivate Behavior.

Unlike instinct, drive, or other physiological theories, **incentive theory** focuses on the role of external factors in motivation—how things in our environment *pull* us in certain directions (Balleine, 2005). Developed from the insights gained from classical and operant conditioning research (see Chapter 6), this theory proposes that any stimulus that we learn to associate with positive or negative outcomes can serve as an incentive for our behavior. An **incentive** is a positive or negative stimulus in the environment that attracts or repels us. According to this theory, we will be motivated to behave in certain ways when we expect to gain positive incentives and/or avoid negative incentives through our actions.

Incentive theory A theory of motivation stating that behavior is directed toward attaining desirable stimuli, called positive incentives, and avoiding undesirable stimuli, called negative incentives

Incentive A positive or negative environmental stimulus that motivates behavior

The value of an incentive can change over time and across situations. For example, gaining praise from your parents may have had greater incentive value for you during different periods of your childhood and adolescence (Pomerantz et al., 2005). In certain situations, such as when you were with your teenaged friends, you may have gone out of your way to avoid receiving parental praise, which was a negative incentive. Biology also influences the value of an incentive. That is why food is a stronger motivator when you are hungry than when you are full.

The idea that a great deal of motivation can be explained in terms of incentives has led researchers to further distinguish between two types of motivation that are tied to whether incentives are either *intrinsic* or *extrinsic* to the behavior being performed (Harackiewicz et al., 2005). A behavior or an activity that a person perceives as a valued goal in its own right represents a source of **intrinsic motivation**. On the other hand, a behavior or an activity may be valued because engaging in it leads to the receipt of a reward separate from what the act itself provides (Seifert et al., 2012). The classic example is doing work for pay. In such instances, the work itself may not provide pleasure, but it does provide access to another outcome—money—that does bring pleasure. The type of motivation that leads a person to engage in a behavior or an activity for external reasons is known as **extrinsic motivation**.

In general, we value behaviors and activities that are intrinsically motivating more highly than we value those that are extrinsically motivating. In explaining this value difference, various psychologists have proposed that intrinsic motivation is based on our need to control our own behavior (Deci, 2004; Guofang & Qinglin, 2004). From this perspective, the primary reason certain activities are intrinsically motivating— and more valued—is that they satisfy our need to feel that we are competent beings who control our own lives. Of course, it is not always possible to determine whether we engage in a behavior because of intrinsic or extrinsic rewards. In fact, both sources of motivation often operate simultaneously. For example, a child may read a lot, not simply because she enjoys the activity for its own sake, but also because doing so earns praise from adults and better grades in school.

As you undoubtedly already know, there is less need to use extrinsic motivators to convince people to do tasks that they already enjoy. Yet did you also know that using extrinsic motivators sometimes increases or decreases people's intrinsic motivation (Deci, 1975)? On the one hand, receiving external rewards for a task may reinforce our sense of competence and thus enhance intrinsic motivation (R. M. Ryan & Deci, 2000). However, as we learned in Chapter 6, Section 6.2b, rewards are often used to control people's behavior. If the controlling aspect of a reward is salient when it is given to us for performing a task that we enjoy, we may perceive that our behavior is more motivated by the reward (extrinsic motivation) than by our enjoyment of the task (intrinsic motivation). Self-Discovery Questionnaire 9-1 discusses how you can use rewards without undermining intrinsic motivation.

Intrinsic motivation
Motivation to engage in a behavior or an activity because one finds it interesting or enjoyable for its own sake

Extrinsic motivation
Motivation to engage in a behavior or an activity because of the external rewards it can provide

[Tom] had discovered a great law of human action...namely, that Work consists of whatever a body is obliged to do, and that Play consists of whatever a body is not obliged to do.

—Mark Twain, American author, in The Adventures of Tom Sawyer (1876)

 **INFO-BIT**   In a longitudinal study of businesspersons, those who had an extrinsic motivation toward work when they were in graduate school were happier with their lives and jobs nine years later, when they earned more money rather than less. This is not surprising. However, businesspersons who had an intrinsic motivation toward work when they were in graduate school were less satisfied with their lives nine years later if they were earning a lot of money (Malka & Chatman, 2003). This research suggests that how people react to being very well compensated on the job may be at least partly shaped by whether they chose their careers because of their "love of the work" or their "love of the money."

SELF-DISCOVERY 9-1
Questionnaire

How Can You Use Rewards Without Undermining Intrinsic Motivation?

Many psychologists argue that American society has become so dependent on the use of extrinsic motivators (rewards and punishments) that it has seriously reduced people's intrinsic motivation for many activities (Deciet al., 1999). For example, in one study, preschoolers, who normally chose to spend a lot of time drawing, were asked to draw a picture (Lepper et al., 1973). Preschoolers in one condition of the experiment were told that they would receive a reward for the picture, while those in another condition were not told of any reward but were given one after completing the picture. Finally, preschoolers in a third condition were not told about any rewards and not given any rewards. Results indicated that those who had expected and received a reward drew the least when later given the opportunity to do so. Other studies have found that students' involvement in math tends to decrease when rewards are emphasized at school or at home (Vansteenkiste et al., 2004), and overall academic achievement and interest decrease when parents use rewards, such as money, for good grades (Ginsburg & Bronstein, 1993; Gottfried et al., 1994).

Does this mean that external rewards always undermine intrinsic motivation? No. Although psychologists disagree on how much damage external rewards can cause to intrinsic motivation, they also can be beneficial. As previously mentioned, positive reinforcement, properly presented, can increase feelings of personal autonomy and competence and can reduce many of the negative effects that failure inflicts on intrinsic motivation. However, for these good effects to occur, rewards need to be given in response to specific performance standards and/or because the recipient surpasses the performance of others. Simply rewarding someone for participating in a task or

Shutterstock

Most people in the performing arts make very little money and have an intrinsic motivation toward their craft. Do you believe that you will have a similar level of intrinsic motivation for the profession you choose?

for meeting some vague or meaningless objective ("Good breathing, Timmy!") often undermines intrinsic motivation. Further, tangible rewards, such as money or treats, are much more likely to undermine intrinsic motivation than verbal praise, which often increases intrinsic motivation by bolstering our confidence that we are capable individuals. Perhaps the key ingredient in determining whether rewards enhance or undermine intrinsic motivation for a task is the degree to which the rewards convey to recipients that they are their "own masters" rather than being "pawns" of others' desires.

Journey of Discovery

Sometimes, when athletes are paid large sums of money to play their sport, they seem to lose their love for the game and become less motivated. How could this change in athletic motivation be explained by intrinsic and extrinsic motivation?

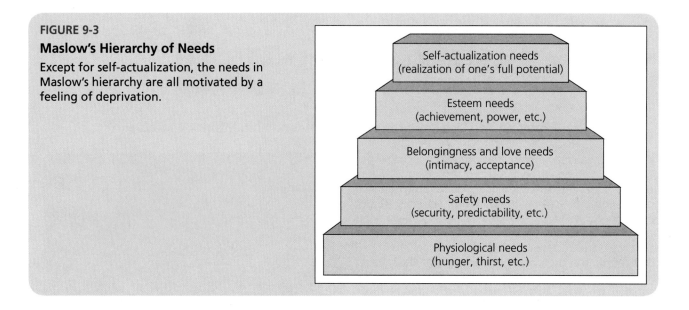

FIGURE 9-3
Maslow's Hierarchy of Needs
Except for self-actualization, the needs in Maslow's hierarchy are all motivated by a feeling of deprivation.

Self-actualization needs
(realization of one's full potential)

Esteem needs
(achievement, power, etc.)

Belongingness and love needs
(intimacy, acceptance)

Safety needs
(security, predictability, etc.)

Physiological needs
(hunger, thirst, etc.)

9.1f *Maslow Proposed That Needs Are Organized in a Hierarchy.*

Out of the humanistic tradition, Abraham Maslow (1970) developed another approach to understanding motives. As first discussed in Chapter 1, Section 1.2b, the humanistic view, in general, and Maslow's theory of motivation, in particular, assumed that people have a basic need for personal growth—to fulfill their potential. As illustrated in Figure 9-3, Maslow proposed that we are born with a **hierarchy of needs**, meaning that basic needs must be sufficiently satisfied before we are motivated to satisfy higher-level needs. The needs further up the hierarchy are considered less basic because we can survive without satisfying them.

The most basic of these needs are physiological, such as hunger and thirst. Once these *physiological needs* are adequately satisfied, they recede into the motivational hierarchy; and the next set of needs, *safety needs*, is activated. These needs involve striving for a sense of safety, security, and predictability in life. Regarding these first two need levels, Maslow contended that when food and safety are difficult to attain, they dominate people's lives; then, higher-level needs have little motivational power. But if these two levels of needs are reasonably satisfied, the person becomes motivated by more social needs. The first social needs activated are the *belongingness* and *love needs*, which involve the desire for intimacy, love, and acceptance from others. Next on the hierarchy are *esteem needs*, which involve the desire for achievement, power, and recognition and respect from others.

Up to this point in the hierarchy, Maslow believed that people are motivated by a desire to overcome their feelings of being deprived of some kind of physical or psychological need. Thus, all the needs in the first four levels of the hierarchy are *deficiency needs*, which if absent, inhibit our personal growth. In contrast, the needs in the upper reaches of the hierarchy are *self-actualization* needs that move the person toward fulfilling her or his potential. **Self-actualization** is the ultimate goal of human growth, although Maslow hypothesized that it is only a significant motive for a few of us. Why? The primary reason is that most of us are preoccupied throughout our lives with trying to make up for deficiencies lower in the hierarchy (Maslow, 1971; Vittersø, 2004).

Hierarchy of needs Maslow's progression of human needs, in which those that are the most basic—namely, physiological needs—must be sufficiently satisfied before higher-level safety needs and then psychological needs become activated

According to Maslow's theory of motivation, what needs are likely motivating the thinking and behavior of a homeless person?

Self-actualization The ultimate goal of growth, being the realization of one's full potential

The simplicity of Maslow's needs hierarchy made it an appealing theory of motivation in such diverse fields as philosophy, business, and education (Banwell, 2004; Trigg, 2004). Despite this interest, the simplicity of the theory proved to be its primary problem. Although research generally suggests that the motives lower in Maslow's hierarchy do take precedence over those higher in the hierarchy, safety needs remain high in importance for all age groups; and there is no clear evidence that met needs become less important than unmet needs in motivating people's behavior (Baumeister & Leary, 1995; Reiss & Havercamp, 2005). Research also finds cultural differences in emphasizing self-actualization, with individualist societies, like the United States, valuing this motive more than collectivist societies in Southeast Asia, where harmony and belongingness are more highly valued. Despite these shortcomings and limitations, the theory provides a comprehensive and organized framework for discussing human motives.

Section REVIEW

- Studying motivation involves exploring how behavior is energized toward the fulfillment of a goal.

- According to instinct theories, motivated behaviors are genetically determined; this theory cannot account for motivation affected by experience and learning.

- According to drive-reduction theory, motivation originates from attempts to reduce unpleasant drive states and return the body to homeostasis.

- The Yerkes-Dodson law states that people are motivated to seek an optimal level of arousal.

- In incentive theory, only externally produced consequences determine motivation, and the theory distinguishes between extrinsic and intrinsic motivation.

- Maslow's needs hierarchy reflects a prioritization of goals, ranging from basic survival goals to the ultimate goal of self-actualization.

9.2 Hunger and Eating

Having explored some of the underlying factors in motivation, let us now turn to specific motives, such as eating (Michaelidou et al., 2012). We first explore the biological mechanisms that underlie this most basic of human needs; and then we discuss various theories related to hunger, eating, and **satiety** (pronounced "sa-TY-a-tee"), which means being full to satisfaction.

Satiety Being full to satisfaction—in this case, with food

9.2a *Various Biological Mechanisms Control Hunger and Eating.*

Due to its importance for survival, it is not surprising that the controls over hunger, eating, and satiety are complex and represent several independent and interacting bodily systems. Three of the major control systems are the stomach, the bloodstream, and the brain.

The Stomach

It seems logical that the stomach should play some role in whether we feel hungry or full. In one early investigation of this body organ, A. L. Washburn, working with Walter Cannon, swallowed a long tube with a balloon that was then inflated (Cannon & Washburn, 1912). Whenever Washburn's stomach contracted, the corresponding changes in the balloon's air pressure were recorded. Although stomach contractions corresponded to Washburn's perceptions of hunger, later research demonstrated that these contractions do not cause hunger pangs (Rozin et al., 1998). In fact, you can still feel hungry even after your stomach has been surgically removed! Although the stomach doesn't cause the sensation of hunger, the sensation of food satiety at least partly originates in this body organ. As the stomach becomes swollen from eating, sensory neural signals reflecting satiety are sent from the stomach—and the small intestine and liver—to the brain. The stomach also releases the hormone gastrin, which, among other actions, signals the pancreas to begin releasing insulin, a hormone that, among other things, decreases appetite (Masaki et al., 2004).

The Bloodstream

The blood is the pathway for many eating-related signals that flow to the brain. The brain monitors two main types of blood signals: those dealing with the level of food nutrients that the stomach has supplied to the bloodstream and those dealing with hormone levels in the bloodstream related to those nutrients. When the brain receives signals that the level of food nutrients in the blood is low, we feel hungry. The two major types of food nutrients are *fatty acids* and the blood sugar glucose, which is converted into energy that can be stored and later used by cells throughout the body, including the brain. The blood hormone *insulin* is essential in this conversion process. High insulin production leads to cells taking in more glucose than they can use, with the excess being converted into fat. As previously mentioned, increased levels of insulin lead to decreased hunger, while drops in the levels of insulin result in increased hunger.

One blood signal that tells the brain that eating should start or stop comes from *cholecystokinin (CCK)*, which is released from the small intestine as a hormone and from the brain as a neurotransmitter. CCK not only aids digestion but also regulates how much we eat by decreasing hunger. Administering CCK to food-deprived humans and other animals reduces hunger and eating but doesn't affect thirst or water consumption. If receptors in the brain for CCK are blocked, animals continue eating even after consuming their normal amount of food.

The Brain

The *hypothalamus*, which is a small structure buried deep within the brain, plays a significant role in regulating eating behavior. As noted in Chapter 2, Section 2.3b, the hypothalamus is primarily responsible for homeostatic regulation. A major part of maintaining homeostasis is balancing the body's energy demands with energy availability. About 60 years ago, studies on rats suggested that two small parts of the hypothalamus were the primary centers for coordinating hunger and satiety. The lateral (side) area of the hypothalamus (LH) was thought to be the "hunger on" center (Stellar, 1954), and the ventromedial (bottom center) area of the hypothalamus (VMH) appeared to be the "hunger off" center (Hetherington & Ranson, 1942). The reason for these beliefs was the discovery that making small lesions (holes) in the VMH led to massive increases in eating, whereas lesioning the LH led to finicky eating. Although these two areas of the hypothalamus play an important role in hunger and satiety, later studies indicated that the "hunger on-off" labels were too simplistic because the LH and VMH interact with many other brain systems to produce their effects.

Today, scientists believe that another part of the hypothalamus, the *paraventricular nucleus (PVN)*, plays a more important role in hunger regulation by having neural circuitry that responds to various neurotransmitters. For instance, the neurotransmitter *neuropeptide Y* has a marked effect at the PVN and greatly increases carbohydrate eating, whereas the neurotransmitter *serotonin* inhibits carbohydrate consumption (Mori et al., 2004). Thus, rather than describing the hypothalamus as having hunger on and hunger off areas, it is more accurate to state that it has some neurons that fire when blood nutrient levels are low and others that fire when nutrients are at high levels and should be released. These neurons act less like on-off hunger switches and more like sensors that provide information to the frontal lobes of the brain, which then decide eating behavior (Winn, 1995).

Another problem with the idea of a hunger on switch in the brain is that it doesn't make sense from an evolutionary perspective. If humans and other animals were motivated to seek food only after a drop in their blood nutrient levels flipped the hunger switch, they would be in a weakened, energy-depleted state. Then they would need to hunt and kill their food (or shop for and cook it) before finally eating. A more adaptive approach would be to *anticipate* the energy demands, thus completing eating and beginning the process of digestion *prior* to a drop in homeostatic balance. (Collier, 1986) Such anticipation of hunger requires the intervention of the frontal lobes' higher-order thinking.

Early studies with rats found that destruction of the ventromedial area of the hypothalamus resulted in massive eating and gross obesity. How did later research refine our understanding of the role that the hypothalamus plays in hunger regulation?

Source: P. Teitelbaum, Appetite, Proceedings of the American Philosophical Society, 108, *1964, 464–473*

9.2b *Our Environment Also Controls Hunger and Eating.*

The fact that there is more to hunger than the operation of our physiological states was demonstrated by Paul Rozin and his colleagues (1998) when they tested two brain-damaged patients who—similar to Henry Molaison in Chapter 2—had no recollection of events occurring more than a few minutes ago. After eating a normal meal, these patients ate a second and sometimes a third full meal when evidence of the prior meal had been cleared away. This suggests that knowing when to eat is not simply a function of body chemistry and hypothalamic activity but also involves external cues and memory of when we last ate.

Anticipation has a significant influence on hunger and eating. Do you recall Ivan Pavlov's digestion studies of dogs from Chapter 6, Section 6.1a? In conducting his studies, Pavlov (1927) would place meat powder on a dog's tongue to elicit reflexive salivation. One thing he noticed was that, over time, dogs began salivating *before* any food reached their mouths and even before they smelled the food—in other words, in anticipation of the meal. Since Pavlov's time, many studies have shown that physiological responses that prepare the body for food (for example, a surge in insulin) occur in response to cues normally related to eating. These cues are such things as the sight or smell of appealing food, the time of day, other people eating, and the clattering of dishes. This means that hunger is also a response to environmental cues that indicate food is on the way, rather than simply being a response to specific changes occurring within the body.

Another control over eating is related to the incentive value of food. Although the early phases of eating depend on the taste of food, as you continue eating the same food, its positive incentive value declines (Rolls, 1986). In other words, the first taste of barbecued ribs may be wonderful, but they lose their "scrumptiousness" with each bite. Accordingly, you will tend to consume many more calories when there are a variety of foods available rather than just one kind. The body's monitoring of fat or glucose content cannot explain this effect. Simply put, taste variety matters in how much you eat.

Restrained eaters expend a considerable amount of their self-regulatory resources controlling what and how much they eat. When such people are under stress, how might they react when encountering an array of delicious food like that displayed in this photo? Why are they more likely than unrestrained eaters to go on high-calorie eating binges?

Finally, one other factor that affects eating behavior has to do with how you think about food in relation to yourself. If you are chronically worrying about and trying to control what and how much you eat, you are a *restrained eater*, whereas if you are relatively unconcerned about controlling your eating you are an *unrestrained eater* (Herman & Polivy, 2004; Johnson & Wardle, 2005). Restrained eaters put constant limits on the amount of food they allow themselves to consume, and they are perpetual dieters. Restrained eaters also tend to be heavily influenced by what the situation says is correct about eating rather than by what their body signals are telling them. The constant monitoring of food consumption requires great self-control on the part of restrained eaters. However, when stressed by daily events, they are much more likely than unrestrained eaters to go on high-calorie binges when they "let their guard down" (Tanaka, 2002). Despite their constant dieting, restrained eaters have more difficulty than unrestrained eaters avoiding "forbidden" yet desirable food, such as chocolate (Stirling & Yeomans, 2004). The apparent cause of these self-control lapses by restrained eaters is that stressful events temporarily deplete their ability to regulate and control their eating desires.

Research indicates that at any given time of the day people have only limited amounts of energy available for self-regulation (Rudasill, 2011). This is true regardless of whether a person is a restrained or an unrestrained eater. Yet restrained eaters are constantly using some of their limited, self-regulatory energy to control their eating, whereas unrestrained eaters are not. However, when restrained eaters need to focus energy on one task, such as studying for a big exam or handling conflict in a romantic relationship, they may not have enough self-regulatory energy left to keep themselves from consuming that half-gallon of ice cream in the freezer. This research suggests that people who are constantly trying to lose weight by controlling their eating may unintentionally be creating circumstances that actually cause them to gain weight.

9.2c The Body May Be "Set" to Maintain Weight Within a Limited Range.

Set point A level of weight that the body works to maintain

Research investigating the effects of both starvation and overeating suggest that the body has a **set point** for weight, meaning a level of body weight that it works to maintain (Hallschmid et al., 2004). Although this physiological process is only partly understood, it appears that the body monitors fat-cell levels to keep them relatively stable (Friedman, 2000). When the body's fat cells rise above this set point, they release the hormone leptin. *Leptin*, which in Greek (*leptos*) means "thin," has the effect of decreasing hunger by altering neural activity in the hippocampus (Balthasar et al., 2004; Denis et al., 2004). In essence, releasing leptin is the fat cells' way of telling the brain to stop eating because there is enough fat already in the body. In contrast, when fat-cell levels fall below the set point, the body compensates in the opposite direction by increasing hunger and decreasing metabolism. This constant compensation due to fluctuations in the body's fat-cell levels keeps your weight within a limited range.

Some set-point theorists propose that our weight and fat content are preprogrammed for us genetically and that this set point can be altered only under extreme circumstances, if at all. The practical implication of this assumption is that even after extensive dieting or overeating, we are genetically destined to eventually return to our original weight. What specifically determines our set point may have something to do with our *number* of fat cells. Research indicates that when people gain or lose weight, they do not also gain or lose fat cells. Instead, their existing fat cells increase or decrease in average *size* (Hirsch et al., 1989). According to the reasoning of set-point theorists, if you have many more fat cells than the average person, you also have a correspondingly higher set point, which greatly increases your chances of becoming overweight. On the other hand, if you have relatively few fat cells, your set point is lower, and you are likely to be relatively thin.

Some researchers have criticized the idea that we have a genetically determined set point, saying that it is inconsistent with the increasing prevalence of obesity in countries where food supplies exceed need. For example, The Centers for Disease Control and Prevention report that the percent of obese American adults increased from 13 percent of the population in 1962 to 36 percent today (a whopping 50 percent of African American women are obese). How can a genetically fixed set point explain this increase? It would either have to be the case that genetically programmed set points are rising at a rapid rate—which is virtually impossible—or that our natural set points are at a level that is pathologically too high—which means that they really haven't been controlling the weight levels of many people at all.

Faced with this problem, most researchers share the prevailing view that set points are not genetically fixed. However, this does not mean that people don't differ in their set points or that genetics doesn't significantly shape set-point levels. What it means is that your set point can change over time. Unfortunately, the change usually is upward, not downward. Research suggests that long-term overeating can gradually raise your set point, but it is much more difficult to lower your set point (Bolles, 1980; Keesey, 1995). These results don't mean that if you are obese you have no control over your weight. Instead, they suggest that you must make permanent changes in your eating habits to lose weight and maintain it at a healthy level. Weight change can be brought about by a *lifestyle* change, not just a fad diet.

9.2d *Friends and Family Influence Body Weight.*

Over the years, social psychologists have discovered that people who regularly interact with one another become more similar in their attitudes, beliefs, and lifestyle habits than those who have less contact (Harton & Bullock, 2007). In essence, the *social impact* that these individuals have on one another appears to increase their similarity. Given this mutual influence, is it possible that our friends and family members will have a significant impact on our eating habits, and thus, on our body weight?

In an attempt to answer this question, Nicholas Christakis and James Fowler (2007) analyzed the social networks of more than 12,000 people over a 32-year period, examining whether weight gain in one person was associated with weight gain in her or his friends, siblings, spouse, and neighbors. Their results found that a person's probability of becoming obese was not related to neighbors' obesity, but likelihood of obesity increased by 57 percent if she or he had a friend who became obese. Among pairs of adult siblings, if one sibling became obese, the likelihood that the other would become obese increased by 40 percent. If one spouse became obese, the likelihood that the other spouse would become obese increased by 37 percent. Persons of the same sex had relatively greater influence on each other than those of the other sex. Christakis and Fowler believe that obesity often spreads through

People who regularly interact with one another become more similar in their eating habits and obesity levels, most likely because they compare themselves to one another regarding acceptable weight levels. How might health professionals use people's social networks to promote healthier eating habits and weight levels?

families and friendship networks because individuals in these social networks compare themselves to one another and collectively begin to believe that being overweight is acceptable and not very worrisome ("I'm doing okay weight-wise compared to my friends and family"). The researchers speculated that neighbors' obesity levels were not associated because, unlike family members and friends, neighbors were less likely to be comparison targets in evaluating one's own acceptable weight and eating habits.

The importance that social influence has on the spread of obesity in social networks suggest that health professionals can potentially harness this influence to slow the spread of obesity (Smith & Christakis, 2008). Convincing a few people in the same social network to adopt healthy eating habits should increase the likelihood that others in the network will adopt these healthier eating norms. In other words, what we say and how we behave in our social networks may have a ripple effect throughout the network, influencing our friends, our friends' friends, and even our friends' friends' friends.

Section REVIEW

- The three major biological control systems in hunger and eating are the stomach, bloodstream, and brain.

- Hunger is also a response to environmental cues, anticipation, and the incentive value of food.

- Restrained eaters chronically worry about controlling what and how much they eat and may unintentionally create circumstances that cause them to gain weight.

- The body has a set point for weight, but this set point may not be genetically fixed.

- People's social networks reinforce and shape eating habits, and establish either healthy or unhealthy weight levels.

9.3 Sexual Motivation

In 1938, at the beginning of Indiana University's fall semester, students were excited to learn that a new course on human sexuality would be taught by Professor of Zoology Alfred Kinsey. Most young adults knew very little about sex. To appreciate their experience, imagine that you had never once read or been told anything factual about human sexual behavior. Further, imagine that one of the things you were told by your parents was that holding hands was not only a sexual act but also a mortal sin, and that masturbation caused nervous disorders and even madness. Now, imagine that during your first class sessions with Professor Kinsey, you are lectured in detail about the physiology of sex and shown slides of the penis, clitoris, and various positions for sexual intercourse. You are also told that sexual ignorance causes mental anguish and that sexual liberation is the key to a strong marriage and a happy life.

Despite strong protests from other professors and the public, who were horrified by the content of Kinsey's course, he argued that scientific research should be used to dispel the myths about sex being taught by schools and religious institutions. In fact, Kinsey and his colleague, Walter Pomeroy, began questioning 18,000 people on this most intimate subject. Using interviews and surveys to obtain participants' sexual histories, they provided evidence indicating that sexual fantasies, masturbation, premarital and extramarital sex, and same-sex sexual contacts were fairly common among Americans (Kinsey et al., 1948, 1953). Despite some flaws in the methodology, their research remains an important contribution to the understanding of human sexual behavior, which, like hunger, is another basic, primary motive.

Engaging in sexual behavior is essential for the continuation of a species. From an evolutionary perspective, it follows that reproduction would be more likely to occur if the process were pleasurable, which it is. In fact, research suggests that the reinforcing properties of sex may well involve the same brain structures and neurotransmitter systems that are so strongly stimulated by cocaine and other addictive drugs (Walsh, 1993).

Motives for sexual behavior also include nonphysical factors such as peer approval, the need to feel valued, the need for intimacy, stress reduction, the need for power, and procreation desires. Understanding this powerful human motivator has proven to be a puzzle. In this section of the chapter, we will put some of the pieces together.

9.3a   *Men Seek Greater Sexual Variety than Do Women.*

A nationwide study of American sexual behaviors provides a fairly detailed look at what Americans do sexually, with whom, and how often (Laumann et al., 1994). As you can see from Figure 9-4, the most appealing sexual activity among heterosexual Americans is vaginal intercourse, followed by watching one's partner undress, and then oral sex. Do you notice an overall gender difference in the data? Put simply, men report enjoying every activity more than women. This is consistent with other studies indicating that

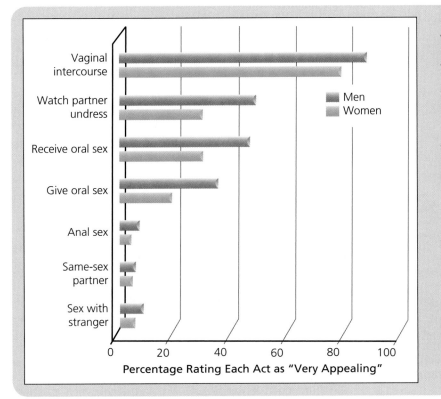

FIGURE 9-4

What Sexual Acts Do Americans Find Very Appealing?

A random survey of almost 3,500 U.S. adults has increased our understanding of U.S. sexual practices and desires. Why do you think men report enjoying every activity on this graph more than do women (Laumann et al., 1994)?

Shutterstock

Sex sells!!! If you read magazines, watch television, or go to the movies, you know that sexual content is readily available for viewing. As with other animals, humans find sex to be a very powerful motivating force in everyday living. Do men and women differ in their interest in sex?

Sexual script A learned preconception about how a series of events, perceived as sexual, is likely to occur

men are much more likely than women to masturbate frequently and to desire more sexual partners (Fletcher, 2002; Oliver & Hyde, 1993). Indeed, a cross-cultural survey of over 16,000 people in 52 nations across North and South America, Europe, the Middle East, Africa, Asia, and the Pacific Islands found that gender differences in the desire for sexual variety are universal (Schmitt, 2003). Men want sex more than do women at the start of the relationship, in the middle of it, and even after many years in the relationship (Impett & Peplau, 2003). Why might this be so?

One possibility has to do with the different sexual scripts men and women learn while growing up (Laumann & Gagnon, 1995; Ross & Coleman, 2011). A **sexual script** is a preconception about how a series of events, perceived as being sexual, is likely to occur. In North American culture and many other cultures, the traditional sexual script taught to women is to downplay interest in sex and resist sexual advances. Men, in contrast, are conventionally taught to freely express sexual interest, brag about sexual exploits, and sometimes even persist in sexual advances despite a partner's protests. See Exploring Culture & Diversity 9-1 for more discussion of sexual scripts.

Exploring CULTURE & DIVERSITY 9.1

Acquaintance rape Forced sexual intercourse that occurs either on a date or between people who are acquainted or romantically involved; also known as *date rape*

Rape myth The false belief that deep down, women enjoy forcible sex and find it sexually exciting

How Do Traditional Sexual Scripts Contribute to Acquaintance Rape?

Forced sexual intercourse that occurs either on a date or between people who are acquainted or romantically involved is known as **acquaintance rape**. On American college campuses, acquaintance rapes account for 84 percent of all rapes or attempted rapes (Koss, 1993). Further, one in five women report that they have been forced to do something sexual (Laumann et al., 1994). One factor contributing to these sexual assaults is the **rape myth**, which is the false belief that, deep down, women enjoy forcible sex and find it sexually exciting (Zurbriggen & Yost, 2004). Not surprisingly, men are much

TABLE 9-1 Rape Myth Acceptance Scale

Directions: There are 19 items on this scale. For items 1–11, use the following 7-point scale to indicate your degree of agreement or disagreement:

Strongly disagree 1 2 3 4 5 6 7 Strongly agree

1. A woman who goes to the home or apartment of a man on their first date implies that she is willing to have sex.

2. Any female can get raped.

3. One reason that women falsely report a rape is that they frequently have a need to call attention to themselves.

4. Any healthy woman can successfully resist a rapist if she really wants to.

5. When women go around braless or wearing short skirts and tight tops, they are just asking for trouble.

6. In the majority of rapes, the victim is promiscuous or has a bad reputation.

7. If a woman engages in necking or petting and she lets things get out of hand, it is her own fault if her partner forces sex on her.

8. Women who get raped while hitchhiking get what they deserve.

9. A woman who is stuck-up and thinks she is too good to talk to guys on the street deserves to be taught a lesson.

10. Many women have an unconscious wish to be raped and may then unconsciously set up a situation in which they are likely to be attacked.

11. If a woman gets drunk at a party and has intercourse with a man she's just met there, she should be considered "fair game" to other males at the party who want to have sex with her too, whether she wants to or not.

Note: For questions 12 and 13, use the following scale:

1 = About 0%, 2 = About 25%, 3 = About 50%, 4 = About 75%, 5 = About 100%

12. What percentage of women who report a rape would you say are lying because they are angry and want to get back at the man they accuse?

13. What percentage of reported rapes would you guess were merely invented by women who discovered they were pregnant and wanted to protect their own reputations?

Note: For items 14–19, read the statement, and use the following scale to indicate your response:

1 = Always, 2 = Frequently, 3 = Sometimes, 4 = Rarely, 5 = Never

A person comes to you and claims s/he was raped. How likely would you be to believe the statement if the person were a/an:

14. best friend?

15. Indian woman?

16. neighborhood woman?

17. young boy?

18. black woman?

19. white woman?

Note: Once you have indicated your response to each item, reverse the scoring for item 2 (1 = 7, 2 = 6, 3 = 5, 5 = 3, 6 = 2, 7 = 1). Then add up your total score. The higher your total score is, the greater is your belief in the rape myth. The mean total score in Burt's (1980) original sample of 598 American adults (average age of 42 years) was 86.6, with a standard deviation of 11.9. How does your total score compare with Burt's original sample? Are you more or less likely to believe in the rape myth than these American adults? Have your friends complete this scale as well. How do your beliefs about the rape myth compare to their beliefs?

Total score: _____

Source: From "Cultural Myths and Supports for Rape" by Martha Burt in *Journal of Personality and Social Psychology, 38,* 1980, pp. 217–230. Copyright © 1980 by the American Psychological Association. Adapted with permission

more likely to endorse this myth than are women. One consequence of men adhering to the rape myth is that they are more likely to believe that women don't really mean it when they say "no" to sexual advances (Littleton & Axsom, 2003). Spend a few minutes responding to the items in Table 8-1 related to the rape myth.

Traditional sexual scripts—in which the woman's role is to act resistant to sex and the man's role is to persist in his sexual advances—foster both the rape myth and acquaintance rape. These sexual scripts are reinforced throughout society, including in popular culture. For example, a recent 20-year study of the 1.36 billion dollar romance novel industry found that most depictions of sexuality in romance novels conform to traditional sexual scripts (Menard & Cabrera, 2011). This is unfortunate because the complementary male predator script and female resistor script reflect the dominance and control men exert over women in patriarchal societies (see Chapter 3, Section 3.2e) and is a symptom of cultural sexism. Despite increased gender equality between women and men over the past 35 years, traditional sexual scripts persist in many dating relationships (Eaton & Rose, 2011). Numerous studies indicate that acquaintance rape is much more likely to occur when the resistant female sexual script is combined with the male sexual script of predator (Peterson & Muehlenhard, 2004). A victim following the resistant female sexual script often does not clearly communicate the limits of acceptable behavior to the person who persists after initial sexual advances have been discouraged. Instead of employing the highly effective tactic of declaring to her attacker, "This is rape and I'm calling the cops," a victim of acquaintance rape is often nonassertive or in the habit of giving mixed messages. In following the resistant female sexual script, the victim has problems with forcefully conveying a clear message of "no" and is later less likely than other women to acknowledge her experience as rape.

Despite this lack of assertiveness by the female victim, it in no way justifies forced sex. It cannot be stressed enough that acquaintance rape occurs when a man refuses to stop his sexual aggression (Ryan, 2011). Such men tend to be more sexually active than other men; they enjoy exerting dominance in sexual encounters, and they treat women as property rather than people (Chiroro et al., 2004). Generally, an acquaintance rapist also has a history of antisocial behavior and displays a lot of anger toward women. Because he believes that women often need a little force to enjoy sex, the victimizer does not believe that acquaintance rape is rape, even after he has committed this crime.

Although the definition of the rape myth is framed to include only women as targets, a similar myth exists for gay men. That is, some people falsely believe that gay men have an unconscious desire to be raped (Davies et al., 2010). As with the traditional rape myth, heterosexual men are most likely to endorse rape myths regarding gay men; gay men are least likely to endorse such beliefs (Chapleau et al., 2007; Davies & McCartney, 2003).

So what can we learn from this research? First, learning and practicing sexual scripts in which men act as "predators" and women play the "resistant" role promotes sexual aggression and acquaintance rape. Second, people who are sexually attracted to one another should put aside these traditional, limiting gender roles and engage in open, honest communication. In such exchanges, a refusal of sexual intimacy should be accepted as such.

Instead of supporting a sociocultural explanation, some psychologists believe that these gender differences reflect the different evolutionary pressures exerted on women and men (Buss, 1999; Pedersen et al., 2002). A starting point in this evolutionary explanation is the following question: When a man and a woman have sex, which of them is most likely to bear responsibility for any resulting offspring? The answer is the woman. Furthermore, unlike a man, a woman can have only one pregnancy at a time, and her reproductive years are relatively short. These biological limitations mean that to maximize the probability that her genes will be passed on to future generations through her offspring, the best sexual strategy for a woman is to adopt a cautious approach. Such a strategy will better allow her to identify men with the best genes and those most likely to help care for offspring. In contrast to this cautious approach, it is to a man's advantage to establish sexual intimacy as quickly as possible in a relationship and have frequent sexual encounters with many different women (Pedersen et al., 2002). According to evolutionary theorists, over thousands of generations, men who seek frequent sex and prefer many mates produce more offspring than men with a weaker sex drive and weaker preference for sexual variety. Thus, a higher sex drive and a preference for sexual variety have become common among men. High sex drive and a preference for variety have not become widespread among women because such desires among women do not necessarily produce more children (Schmitt et al., 2001).

 **INFO-BIT** A sex difference in sexual variety preferences is also observed in other animal species. In most species, males show more interest in more partners than do females. However, this sex difference reverses in a few species (such as the sandhill crane), in which the females abandon their eggs (and their mates) and seek other reproductive partners. In such instances, the males care for the eggs and later offspring. Thus, this parental investment theory is not about males always having more interest in low-cost, indiscriminate sex than females. Instead, it is a theory about how sex differences in mating behavior are caused by differences in the parents' investment obligations to their young (Buss & Schmitt, 1993).

Which of these two explanations—evolutionary or sociocultural—is correct? Although I have contrasted the two viewpoints, they may often complement rather than compete with one another. Perhaps the ultimate "best" explanation for gender differences in preferences for sexual variety may describe how evolutionary pressures faced by our prehuman ancestors shaped certain patterns of social behavior—including those related to sex—leaving modern women and men with certain *capacities* to possibly react differently to sex. Yet the degree to which we actually manifest these inherited capacities today may be decided by how we are raised and taught to behave in our current social surroundings. In other words, culture and social learning either enhance or override these inherited capacities.

9.3b Sex and Love May Be More Fused for Women than for Men.

Consistent with our previous discussion of evolutionary explanations for different sexual motivation in women and men, some social scientists have suggested that sexual desire and romantic love have evolved to meet different human needs (Diamond, 2003). These theorists propose that sexual desire is governed by the *sexual mating system*, in which the goal is to sexually reproduce and thereby pass one's genes on to the next generation. In contrast, romantic love is governed by the *attachment system*, in which the goal is to establish and maintain a strong emotional bond between two people. As discussed in Chapter 3, Section 3.2a attachment is a part of our evolutionary heritage that developed to foster childrearing. In childrearing, the function of the attachment bond between infant and caregiver is to maximize the newborn's survival. Parents who love their babies will feed and protect them. Similarly, infants who become emotionally attached to their parents are more likely to remain physically close, thereby decreasing the likelihood of being killed by predators during their most vulnerable stage of life. Likewise, in childrearing, the attachment bond between the two parents also maximizes the newborn's survival. Parents who love one another are more likely to stay together to raise their children, and there is strength in numbers. According to this perspective, then, sexual desire fuels the sexual mating system, ensuring that a new generation is born into this world. In turn, romantic love fuels the attachment system, ensuring that enough members of the new generation will survive childhood.

When examining the causal link between sexual desire and romantic love, psychologists have traditionally assumed that sexual desire leads to the formation of an emotional bond, or romantic love, and not the other way around. In other words, you meet someone who is sexually appealing, and this initial sexual interest motivates you to seek out this person and become better acquainted. As this sexually charged relationship develops, you fall in love. Sound familiar? Yet there are numerous examples from everyday life of people developing sexual desires for a particular person *after* developing a strong emotional attachment to her or him (Rose & Zand, 2000). Based on our discussion thus far, would it surprise you to learn that women appear more likely than men to feel sexually attracted toward someone only after feeling romantically attracted to him?

When college students were asked what they thought caused sexual desire, both sexes strongly agreed that the causes were often different for women and men (Peplau & Garnets, 2000; Regan et al., 2000). The most widely endorsed causes of female sexual desire were interpersonal experiences related to romantic love, whereas the most widely endorsed causes of male desire were biological processes and a physical "need" for sex. Thus, it appears that women tend to emphasize emotional intimacy as more of a necessity for sexuality than men. The same gender difference exists among homosexual adults. Like heterosexual women, lesbians are less likely than gay and heterosexual men to desire or engage in casual sex (Peplau et al., 2004).

Thinking about these gender differences within the contexts of the sexual mating system and the attachment system, we see that men appear more focused than women on the sexual mating aspect of this process, whereas women appear more focused than men on the attachment aspect. For women more than men, the goal of sex is intimacy; and the best context for pleasurable sex is a committed relationship. For men, this is less true (Peplau, 2003). Of course, this does not mean that women are not interested in casual sex and that men do not seek committed romantic relationships. It simply means that gender differences in motivational tendencies regarding sex and intimacy appear to exist. However, these are only tendencies, and many women and men do not fit these general patterns. That is, some women show high levels of interest in casual sex, and some men seek sex only in committed relationships.

Finally, in considering how evolutionary and sociocultural factors may shape sexuality, growing evidence indicates that men and women differ in the malleability of their sexual motivation. For example, findings from the previously discussed national survey of Americans indicate that men of all educational and socioeconomic levels are about equally interested in sexual variety and experimentation, but that women's sexual desires and behaviors depend significantly on social factors such as education and religion (Laumann et al., 1994). Highly educated women are much more likely than uneducated women to engage in oral sex, anal sex, homosexual activity, and other types of sexual experimentation. Similarly, women's interest in sexual experimentation is sharply curbed if they are members of socially conservative religions. Further evidence that women's sexual motivation is more influenced by situational factors than men's is revealed in how the two sexes respond to a romantic breakup. Although women and men may have frequent sex with their partners while involved in an intimate relationship, following a breakup, women are much more likely than men to have no sex at all—including masturbation—for several months (Peplau, 2003). Roy Baumeister (2000) believes such findings suggest that compared to men, women have higher *erotic plasticity*, meaning that their sexual motivation is more easily shaped by social, cultural, and situational factors.

9.3c The Sexual Response Cycle Is Very Similar in Men and Women.

Women and men may differ in what influences their sexual motivation, but they do not substantially differ in how they experience the sexual act itself (Halaris, 2003). This fact became apparent in the mid-1960s when William Masters and Virginia Johnson (1966) published their pioneering work on the human sexual response. By monitoring 382 female and 312 male volunteers as they masturbated or had intercourse, Masters and Johnson determined that women's and men's physiological changes as they approach and achieve orgasm are remarkably similar, and that the physiological expression of an orgasm is similar regardless of how it is achieved.

The **sexual response cycle** the body passes through during sexual activity involves the following four stages:

1. *Excitement* The initial stage when the body becomes aroused (for example, the skin becomes flushed, the penis and clitoris become enlarged, and vaginal lubrication increases).

2. *Plateau* The stage of full arousal (the penis enlarges even more, and the outer third of the vagina becomes engorged with blood).

3. *Orgasm* The stage involving muscle contractions throughout the body (men ejaculate sperm-filled semen, and women's vaginal contractions facilitate conception by helping propel semen from the penis up into the vagina).

4. *Resolution* The stage when the body gradually returns to an unaroused state (muscles relax, and the engorged genital blood vessels release excess blood).

One thing to remember about the stages in the sexual response cycle is that they blend into one another with no clear divisions. During a given cycle, a woman may experience no orgasm, one orgasm, or multiple orgasms. In contrast, a man experiences only one orgasm but can achieve orgasm again following a rest—or *refractory*—period. This refractory period can last from a few minutes to a day or more, with the length of the rest period typically becoming longer with age. The intensity of orgasms varies, both in individuals and in situations. Sometimes you might experience it as something like a sigh, while at other times it might feel like your entire body is simultaneously celebrating all the holidays of the year!

Some people cannot complete the sexual response cycle. For men, this might involve being unable to have or maintain an erection. Fortunately, the drug sildenafil (trade name Viagra) has helped such men achieve and maintain an erection by increasing blood flow to the penis. About 10 percent of women and a few men remain at the plateau stage without experiencing orgasm, and some men experience premature ejaculation. Such sexual disorders can sometimes be traced to physiological or psychological causes, but often the cause is unknown.

Not surprisingly, cognitive factors influence sexual arousal (Scepkowski et al., 2004; Sewell, 2005). For example, men who have problems getting and maintaining an erection tend to be less aware of how aroused they are. Further, men who can become aroused fairly easily are relatively unconcerned by occasions when they cannot get or maintain an erection. In such instances, they tend to attribute their nonarousal to external events, such as something they ate or excessive fatigue. In contrast, men with arousal problems are more likely to make damaging internal attributions. They believe that their nonarousal is caused by long-term physiological or psychological problems.

Testosterone, a male sex hormone found in both men and women, has a positive influence on sexual desire, although the effect is stronger in men than women (Harding & Velotta, 2011). Despite this positive effect, eliminating testosterone production does

Sexual response cycle The four stages of sexual responding—excitement, plateau, orgasm, and resolution; first identified by Masters and Johnson

Testosterone A male sex hormone found in both men and women that has a positive influence on sexual desire; the additional testosterone in males stimulates the growth of the male sex organs in the fetus and the development of the male sex characteristics during puberty.)

not eliminate desire; and heightened levels of this hormone do not affect desire to the same extent as psychological factors, such as the quality of the partners' relationship. Many other hormonal and neurological systems are involved with sexual desire, responses, and behaviors; none alone, however, adequately explains why people are so driven to achieve sexual satisfaction, or the varied approaches sexual behaviors take. Turning sexual behaviors "on" or "off" is dramatically simpler among most animals other than humans and a few species of nonhuman primates (De Waal, 2000).

9.3d Sexual Orientation Is a Continuum.

Do you recall the moment when you decided you were going to be sexually attracted to women, men, or both? It is a pretty safe bet that your answer is no. Instead of choosing what kind of person sexually attracts you, like most people, you probably discovered your sexual attractions while growing up. **Sexual orientation** is the degree to which we are sexually attracted to persons of the other sex and/or to persons of our own sex. The dawning awareness of our sexual orientation usually occurs by adolescence, typically about three years before we become sexually active (Bell et al., 1981). This finding suggests that we generally realize to what sex we are attracted, not because of our sexual behavior, but because of our sexual feelings. In other words, at some time during childhood and adolescence, we typically discover that we have sexual feelings toward members of the other sex, our own sex, or both sexes. These sexual feelings—rather than actual sexual behavior—are what primarily determines whether we identify ourselves as heterosexual, homosexual, or bisexual.

In studying sexual orientation, behavioral scientists conceptualize it as a continuum, with **heterosexuality** at one end, **homosexuality** at the other end, and **bisexuality** somewhere in between (Haslam, 1997). To characterize individuals' sexual orientation from this continuum perspective, Alfred Kinsey and his coworkers (1948) devised a 7-point scale, which is depicted in Figure 9-5. On this scale, if you are attracted exclusively to persons of the other sex and you engage in sexual behavior only with such persons, you are at the heterosexual end of the continuum

Sexual orientation The degree to which a person is sexually attracted to persons of the other sex and/or to persons of the same sex

Heterosexuality The sexual orientation in which a person is sexually attracted primarily to members of the other sex

Homosexuality The sexual orientation in which a person is sexually attracted primarily to members of the same sex

Bisexuality The sexual orientation in which a person is sexually attracted to members of both sexes

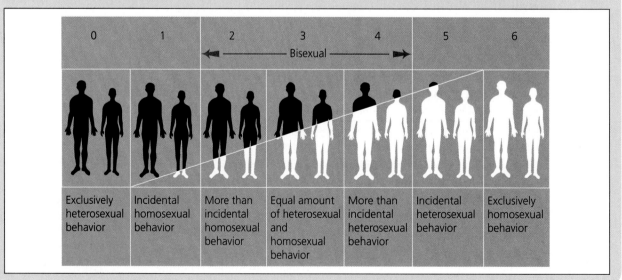

FIGURE 9-5 Sexual Orientation as a Continuum

Kinsey designed this seven-point scale to describe sexual orientation as a continuum, with heterosexuality and homosexuality at the ends and bisexuality in the middle.

0	1	2	3	4	5	6
		←	Bisexual	→		
Exclusively heterosexual behavior	Incidental homosexual behavior	More than incidental homosexual behavior	Equal amount of heterosexual and homosexual behavior	More than incidental heterosexual behavior	Incidental heterosexual behavior	Exclusively homosexual behavior

(category 0). In contrast, if you are attracted exclusively to persons of your own sex and you engage in sexual behavior only with such persons, you are at the homosexual end of the continuum (category 6). Finally, if you fall somewhere between these two extremes (categories 2–4), you are usually defined as bisexual. This scientific viewpoint stands in sharp contrast to the conventional view that sexual orientation is an all-or-none distinction.

To more fully appreciate the complexity and diversity of human sexuality, it is useful to distinguish sexual orientation from sexual identity. **Sexual identity** refers to the identity a person organizes around his or her sexual orientation. North American culture, as well as many other cultures, has a fairly rigid notion of sexual identity: You can be "heterosexual," "gay," "lesbian," or "bisexual." Yet more recently, a noticeable number of individuals in our culture (estimates of less than 1 percent of the population) identify themselves as *asexual*, meaning they lack sexual attraction to others. Such individuals cannot be placed on Kinsey's continuum of sexual orientation because his conception of sexual orientation assumes that a person has some identifiable sexual attraction.

In considering Kinsey's continuum concept of sexual orientation, it is important to note that your sexual orientation does not always coincide with your sexual identity. For example, you could experience sexual attraction toward members of both sexes but not identify yourself as bisexual. Similarly, you could be attracted to members of your own sex but still think of yourself as heterosexual. In fact, three different people could have the same distribution of sexual behavior on Kinsey's scale—for example, a score of 4—but have three different sexual identities: homosexual (gay or lesbian), bisexual, or heterosexual. To further complicate matters, while the vast majority of people's gender identities match the sex to which they were assigned at birth (see Chapter 3, Section 3.2e), a *transgendered* person is born with an "assigned sex" but feels that her or his gender identity is that of the other sex (Pollock & Eyre, 2012). A transgender identity is not related to any specific form of *sexual orientation*; in adolescence and adulthood, when sexual identity becomes an important defining feature of personal identity, transgender individuals may identify as heterosexual, homosexual, bisexual, or asexual. The "take-away message" here is that we socially construct our sexual identity just as we do our gender identity (see Chapter 3, Section 3.4e), with the help of others. Because people in most cultures are strongly socialized to think of themselves and others as sexually attracted to members of the other sex, it generally takes a longer time for people with a homosexual or bisexual orientation to cognitively pull themselves out of the heterosexual identity category and recategorize themselves as gay, lesbian, or bisexual. The same degree of complexity faces those individuals who have a transgender identity because this gender identity is out-of-step with the typical gender identity categories of male or female.

Many people who define themselves as heterosexual, gay, or lesbian have had sexual experiences outside their sexual identities (Diamond, 1998; Diamond & Savin-Williams, 2000). Indeed, cross-cultural research indicates that homosexual behavior is quite common (Minturn et al., 1969). For example, one cross-cultural study found that homosexual behavior of some sort was considered normal and socially acceptable for at least some individuals in almost two-thirds of the 76 societies investigated (Ford & Beach, 1951). Even in cultures with the most restrictive views about same-sex sexual relations, homosexual behavior still takes place (Balthazart, 2012). Yet, remember, behavior does not equal identity. What is the prevalence of heterosexual, gay, lesbian, and bisexual identities in the general population?

Sexual identity The identity a person organizes around his or her sexual orientation, typically labeled "heterosexual," "gay," "lesbian," or "bisexual"

Many years ago I chased a woman for almost two years, only to discover that her tastes were exactly like mine: we both were crazy about girls.

—Groucho Marx, American comedian, 1895–1977

Have you ever wondered about the origin of the derogatory word faggot, which is used by bigots when referring to homosexual persons? The dictionary defines faggot as a bundle of sticks for firewood. During the European Inquisition, when accused "witches" were burned at the stake, people condemned to death for homosexual behavior were often set aflame ahead of time to act as kindling for the "witches" flames.

Heterosexism A system of cultural beliefs, values, and customs that exalts heterosexuality and denies, denigrates, and stigmatizes any nonheterosexual form of behavior or identity

We must make it clear that a platform of "I hate gay men and women" is not a way to become president of the United States.

Jimmy Carter, 39th President of the United States, b. 1924

Journey of Discovery

What are the similarities and differences between the terms *sexual identity* and *gender identity*?

Frequency of Different Sexual Identities

Heterosexuality has clearly been the most practiced form of sexuality in all cultures throughout history (Bullough, 1980). Yet homosexual and bisexual activities have also occurred throughout these same time periods. Fantasies about, and sexual behaviors between, people of the same sex are far more common than identifying oneself as gay, lesbian, or bisexual. The *National Health and Social Life Survey* of American sexual behaviors found that 9 percent of men and 4 percent of women have had some form of sexual contact with a person of the same sex after puberty (Laumann et al., 1994). In this survey, only about 1.4 percent of women identified themselves as lesbians, and only 2.8 percent of men identified themselves as gay. About half as many women and men reported a bisexual identity. The rates in this survey are comparable to those in other surveys in the United States and in Europe (Balthazart, 2012; Sandfort et al., 2001). Of course, these percentages are likely to underestimate the actual percentage of people with homosexual and bisexual identities. Can you guess why?

The answer is **heterosexism**, which is a system of cultural beliefs, values, and customs that exalts heterosexuality and denies, denigrates, and stigmatizes any nonheterosexual form of behavior or identity (Silverschanz et al., 2008). How does heterosexism manifest itself? Open and blatant expression of antigay attitudes by heterosexuals, such as calling another person a "faggot" or a "dyke," is certainly an example of heterosexism. Similarly, denying gay and lesbian couples the right to legally marry—only seven states and the District of Columbia currently recognize same-sex marriage—is a manifestation of heterosexism. However, heterosexism can also operate on a more subtle level. Like the fish that doesn't realize it is wet, heterosexual individuals are so used to defining heterosexual behaviors as normal and natural that they cease to think of them as a manifestation of sexuality. For instance, although heterosexual persons may hardly notice a man and woman kissing in public, they often react with disgust or even hostility if the couple is of the same sex. Such condemnation of nonheterosexual behavior can make it dangerous for homosexual and bisexual individuals to do anything in public that would identify them as nonheterosexual individuals, a fact underscored by the high rate of gay hate crimes committed each year (Herek et al., 2002). In such an intolerant social environment, it is likely that some gay, lesbian, and bisexual survey respondents are reluctant to tell a stranger (even anonymously) about their true sexual identity and sexual orientation. Exploring Culture & Diversity 9-2 discusses the process of "coming out" in a heterosexist society.

Exploring CULTURE & DIVERSITY 9-2

What Is the Typical "Coming Out" Process in a Heterosexist Society?

Gay, lesbian, and bisexual individuals who have not publicly revealed their sexual identity to those with whom they interact on a daily basis often describe feeling as if they are hiding their "true selves" or "living a lie." Imagine talking to friends or coworkers over dinner and not being able to share with them the many wonderful things you did with your boyfriend or girlfriend that weekend. Or imagine not feeling free to bring this person home to meet your parents and grandparents because you are afraid of facing possible disapproval and hostility. On those rare occasions when you vaguely refer to this special person in conversation, you are careful to replace "she" or "he" with the romantically appropriate pronoun. Engaging in such conscious concealment of your sexual identity will likely make you feel psychologically distant from your friends, coworkers, and family members. It also will likely harm your mental health and lower your self-esteem (Fergusson et al., 1999; Sandfort et al., 2001).

The alternative to concealing this central part of your personal identity is to "come out of the closet" and publicly switch your sexual identity. *Coming out* is the process by which people acknowledge that they are gay, lesbian, or bisexual, or in some cases that they are simply questioning their sexual orientation. Most individuals make this acknowledgment first to themselves and later to others. Although coming out is often thought of as a one-time event, it is more properly considered a continual process that gay, lesbian, and bisexual persons experience throughout their lives. For instance, the person who acknowledges to himself and his close friends that he is gay while a sophomore in college may not come out to his family and hometown friends until his senior year. Then, after moving to another city following graduation, he may have to repeat the coming-out process at his new job and with his new friends. Coming out often creates stress because you are never sure how others will react due to heterosexism in the mainstream culture. Yet studies indicate that coming out promotes better psychological adjustment and overall mental health (Goldman, 2008; Strickland, 1995).

Nonheterosexual teenagers and young adults are much more likely to publicly switch their sexual identities while in college than in high school (Laumann et al., 1994). One reason for this timing is that college comes after high school, and students are simply more likely to realize they have a homosexual or bisexual orientation as they mature. However, a second reason is that the antigay prejudice permeating many aspects of mainstream society is generally less pronounced on college campuses than in high schools. Gay history courses, gay/lesbian/bisexual/straight alliances, and gay awareness weeks are now a normal part of the college experience for many students in the United States. With social norms promoting acceptance of diversity, college is often a place where many gay men, lesbians, and bisexuals feel comfortable enough to be themselves. Yet, even in a relatively tolerant social environment, it is still important for people to "test the waters" before coming out to everyone in their lives. Although there is no perfect formula for coming out, it is often best to first reveal your sexual identity to one or two friends who are likely to be accepting and supportive. If successful, this initial disclosure and subsequent social support can help buffer the negative effects of possible future rejections from family members, friends, or acquaintances.

9.3e *Biology Plays a Substantial Role in Determining Sexual Orientation.*

Whenever discussion focuses on the possible causes of sexual orientation, it is often phrased in terms of "What causes homosexuality?" Yet this question is scientifically misconceived because it falsely assumes either that heterosexuality needs no explanation or that its causes are already known. So what does cause sexual orientation?

Some researchers have examined whether specific brain areas might be associated with sexual orientation (Cohen, 2002). For example, a small part of the hypothalamus—no bigger than a grain of sand—has been found to be twice as large in the brains of heterosexual men as in those of homosexual men (LeVay, 1991, 2007). A similar difference has been found in a section of the fibers of the corpus callosum that connect the right and left brain hemispheres. However, here, this brain area is one-third larger in homosexual men than in heterosexual men (Allen & Gorski, 1992). Both of these brain differences are similar to the differences found between heterosexual men and heterosexual women. Together, they may indicate that brain development affects sexual orientation. However, it is equally possible that these brain differences may not be the cause of sexual orientation, but rather they may be the effect of behaviors associated with these two different sexual orientations (Breedlove, 1997). In other words, certain differences in the life experiences of gay and heterosexual men may cause this part of the hypothalamus to develop differently. Until further research is conducted, both of these interpretations are plausible.

The finding that all three "points" on the sexual orientation continuum—heterosexuality, bisexuality, and homosexuality—exist throughout the world has bolstered the view that sexual orientation is substantially determined by our genes. As in studies on the inheritance of intelligence (see Chapter 8, Section 8.4b), research on the inheritance of sexual orientation has focused on twins (Kendler et al., 2000). One study found that among gay men who were identical twins, over half of their twin brothers were also gay, compared with less than one-quarter of fraternal twin brothers (Bailey & Pillard, 1991, 1995). Similar findings were also obtained with lesbian twins (J. Bailey et al., 1993).

Although early attempts to identify social developmental causes of sexual orientation claimed that a smothering mother, absent father, sexual abuse, or "deviant" homosexual role models caused homosexuality, research did not support any of these claims (Storms, 1983). For example, sons of gay men are not more likely to become gay if they live with their father, and over 90 percent of children of lesbian mothers develop a heterosexual orientation (Bailey et al., 1995; Golombok & Tasker, 1996). Thus, unlike contagious diseases, you cannot "catch" a sexual orientation. The only early childhood experience that predicts the development of a homosexual versus a heterosexual orientation in adulthood for both women and men is *gender nonconformity*.

When 1,500 homosexual and heterosexual women and men were interviewed about earlier life experiences, lesbians and gay men were significantly more likely to report that they had preferred play activities traditionally associated with the other sex and were more likely to have had other-sex friends (Bell et al., 1981). They also were less likely to have had a traditional gender role (masculine for boys and feminine for girls). Describing their childhood using labels derived from a heterosexist culture, the lesbians had acted more like "tomboys" and the gay men had acted more like "sissies" than did their heterosexual counterparts.

These gender nonconformity findings have been replicated in other studies, and a growing number of psychologists believe that they are due to one or more of the previously discussed biological factors (Bailey & Zucker, 1995; Lippa, 2002). Of course, it is important to remember that we are discussing group differences here, and there are many exceptions to these general findings. In other words, many heterosexuals prefer activities traditionally associated with the other sex, and many gay men and lesbians prefer traditional gender activities. Thus, despite these findings of group differences, you cannot reliably identify people's sexual orientation based on whether they like to play baseball versus perform gymnastics.

So where are we in our understanding of the causes of sexual orientation? There is good evidence of genetic or other biological influences on sexual orientation, but the nature of these influences is still an open question. It is clear that, in almost all instances, we don't consciously choose our sexual orientation. As an active creator of the social reality in which you live, you can use the information in this chapter to dispel many people's misconceptions about sexual orientation issues and thereby reduce heterosexism. Remember, in the journey of discovery, knowledge is power.

- Evolutionary and sociocultural factors may jointly explain the greater desire that men appear to have for sexual variety when compared with women.

- Women and men are similar in their sexual arousal response.

- Regarding human sexual motivation, men may be more focused than women on the sexual mating aspect of this process, whereas women may be more focused than men on the attachment aspect.

- Women's sexual motivation may be more easily shaped by social, cultural, and situational factors than is men's sexual motivation.

- Sexual orientation is a continuum, with heterosexuality at one end, homosexuality at the other end, and bisexuality somewhere in between. A person's sexual orientation does not always coincide with her or his sexual identity.

- Heterosexism is a system of cultural beliefs, values, and customs that exalts heterosexuality and denies, denigrates, and stigmatizes any nonheterosexual form of behavior or identity.

- Genetic and other biological factors influence sexual orientation.

9.4 Belongingness and Achievement Motivation

Belongingness and achievement are two social motives that figure prominently in Maslow's hierarchy of needs. The need to belong was identified as the first psychological need activated when physiological needs have been adequately satisfied. How do you know when you need the company of others? Why do some people need to socialize more than others? What about your need to achieve, which Maslow identified as being at the next level in his hierarchy? Why do people differ in their need for achievement?

Need to belong The need to interact with others and be socially accepted (also known as the *need for affiliation*)

$9.4a$ People Differ in Their Need to Seek the Company of Others.

The need to interact with others and be socially accepted is called the **need to belong** (also known as the *need for affiliation*). For most of us, this need is as real as our need for food. When this need is denied due to rejection, we often react with increased stress, anxiety, anger, jealousy, sadness, and decreased physical health (DeWall et al., 2011; Gere & MacDonald, 2010). The popularity of rejection-based television shows such as *American Idol* and *Dancing with the Stars* is substantially based on the importance of belongingness and our fascination with how others handle rejection.

Shutterstock

If you are a fan of reality TV shows such as *American Idol* or *Dancing with the Stars,* do you think your fascination is at least partly based on the human need to belong and the corresponding fear of being rejected?

Why Is Social Rejection Painful?

Evidence of the importance of belongingness comes from brain-imaging studies indicating that the same area in the brain's frontal lobes that triggers the emotional pain following rejection also triggers the emotional distress associated with physical pain (Eisenberger, 2011). Why would your brain react to social rejection and physical injury in a similar way? Neuroscientists suggest that the pain experienced following both social rejection and physical injury is your brain's attempt to send a warning signal that your survival is being threatened (Taylor & Gonzaga, 2007). Evolutionary psychologists suggest that during the course of primate evolution, the social attachment "alarm" system came under the control of the same brain area involved in pain detection because this promoted the goal of social connectedness. In other words, our tendency to seek out others, to make friends, and to form enduring close relationships is an inherited trait that has helped our species survive and reproduce.

If social rejection aches like physical pain, can it be treated like physical pain? To find out, C. Nathan DeWall and his coworkers (2010, 2011) asked research participants to take an over-the-counter pain drug (acetaminophen, brand name Tylenol) or a placebo daily for three weeks while also keeping a diary of their daily activities and social interactions. Participants who were taking acetaminophen reported significantly fewer episodes of hurt feelings than those taking the placebo. A follow-up study also found that people who had taken acetaminophen for three weeks showed less neural activity in their pain-related frontal lobes after being socially rejected while playing a computer game than did participants who had taken a placebo for three weeks. Despite this evidence, I don't recommend that you take two Tylenol pills to reduce the pain of social rejection. Instead, research suggests that seeking positive social interactions with friends and family following rejection releases mood-enhancing *endorphins* in the brain, which ease hurt feelings (see Chapter 2, Section 2.1d). If friends and family aren't readily available, physical exercise also naturally produces these beneficial neurotransmitters.

One last point bears mentioning. Beyond seeking emotional relief after being rejected, it also may be important for you to pay attention to why your social attachment "alarm" system has been activated. Is it possible that the social snub you experienced is due to your behaving badly? Being snubbed may be a clue that you need to change your ways. It is also possible that the hurt you are feeling is a signal that you should avoid those who are snubbing you and cultivate new, healthier social relationships. In both instances, the sting of rejection can motivate you to seek positive changes in your life.

Differences in the Need to Belong

Just as some of us enjoy eating more than others, we also differ in our desire to seek the company of others. Studies find that people with a high need to belong seek out warm social relationships and want to be liked by others. In contrast, people with a low need to belong tend to be loners who are not very interested in or comfortable with socializing with others (Carvallo & Gabriel, 2006). Spend a few minutes responding to the items in Self-Discovery Questionnaire 9-2 to learn more about your desire and need for close relationships.

Whether you have a high or a low need to belong is strongly shaped by your life experiences. For example, in the United States and many other countries, girls are more likely than boys to be raised to think and act in ways that stress their emotional connectedness to other individuals. This might explain why women are more likely than men to remember birthdays, anniversaries, who said what during important conversations with friends or loved ones, and even what casual acquaintances sound and look like (Schmid Mast & Hall, 2006). Of course, this does not mean that all women have a higher need to belong than all men. There are many boys and men who have higher affiliation needs than the average girl and woman. There are also many girls and women who are less interested in seeking out others for close relationships than the average boy and man.

SELF-DISCOVERY 9-2
Questionnaire

How Important Are Your Close Relationships in Defining You?

Instructions: Below is a series of statements about your attitudes and beliefs about having close relationships with other people. Please read each statement and indicate the extent to which you agree or disagree with it using the following scale:

Strongly disagree 1 2 3 4 5 6 7 Strongly agree

1. My close relationships are an important reflection of who I am. ___

2. When I feel very close to someone, it often feels to me like that person is an important part of who I am. ___

3. I usually feel a strong sense of pride when someone close to me has an important accomplishment. ___

4. I think one of the most important parts of who I am can be captured by looking at my close friends and understanding who they are. ___

5. When I think of myself, I often think of my close friends or family also. ___

6. If a person hurts someone close to me, I feel personally hurt as well. ___

7. In general, my close relationships are an important part of my self-image. ___

8. Overall, my close relationships have very little to do with how I feel about myself.* ___

9. My close relationships are unimportant to my sense of what kind of person I am.* ___

10. My sense of pride comes from knowing who I have as close friends. ___

11. When I establish a close friendship with someone, I usually develop a strong sense of identification with that person. ___

Directions for Scoring: Two of the items are reverse-scored; that is, for these items a lower rating actually indicates a higher level of relational-interdependence. Before summing the items for a total score, recode those with an asterisk ("*") so that 1 = 7, 2 = 6, 3 = 5, 5 = 3, 6 = 2, and 7 = 1.

When Susan Cross and her colleagues developed this questionnaire, the mean score for 2,330 female students was about 57, while the average score for 1,819 male students was about 53, indicating differences between women and men. Higher scores indicate greater interest in developing close, committed social relationships.

SOURCE: Cross, S. E., Bacon, P. L., & Morris, M. L. (2000). The relational-interdependent self-construal and relationships. *Journal of Personality and Social Psychology, 78,* 791–808.

9.4b Individuals Differ in Their Need for Achievement.

The motives examined thus far—sex, hunger, and belongingness—are observed in many other species. However, achievement motivation may be unique to humans (Epstein, 1998). Some people seem to be more driven to succeed than others—to achieve their goals—sometimes at the expense of other pleasures. Others seem to avoid challenges out of fear of failing. Are these inborn traits? Do these tendencies develop out of experience?

The **need for achievement (n-Ach)** is a desire to overcome obstacles and meet high standards of excellence (Murray, 1938). Although several methods have been devised to study the need for achievement, researchers have traditionally measured the strength of this motive by examining people's fantasies. One of the most popular tools used to measure n-Ach in this manner is the **Thematic Apperception Test (TAT)**, which we will examine again in Chapter 10, Section 10.6a. The TAT consists of a series of ambiguous pictures similar to the one shown in Figure 9-6. Persons taking the test are asked to make up stories about the ambiguous pictures. These stories are then scored for the presence of a number of motives (for example, *need for power* and *need for affiliation*), including the n-Ach. In evaluating n-Ach, trained scorers

Need for achievement (n-Ach) A desire to overcome obstacles and meet high standards of excellence

Thematic Apperception Test (TAT) A test in which people "project" their inner feelings and motives through the stories they make up about ambiguous pictures

FIGURE 9-6   Measuring the Need for Achievement with the Thematic Apperception Test (TAT)

People taking the TAT tell or write stories about what is happening in a scene, such as this one showing two elderly women closely examining a letter. The following story illustrates strong achievement motivation: "Two older women are looking at a letter addressed to their granddaughter and are very curious about its contents, because they know she is waiting to learn whether she has won a national writing contest. This young woman desperately wants to attend college to pursue her writing career, and winning this contest will provide her with enough money to do so. Her grandmothers taught her to read and write but don't have any money to send her to college. When the young woman arrives home and opens the letter, she learns that she achieved the top prize in this nationwide competition. Many prestigious universities recruit her. The woman grows up to become a famous writer. Now, whenever she is faced with a difficult challenge and doubts her abilities, the woman thinks about her grandmothers and realizes that, by working hard, she will succeed."

Richard F. Stone, A Bad Case of Curiosity, watercolor on board, 15.5 × 16.75 inches.

look for the presence of achievement-related imagery and themes in the stories. For instance, if you were shown this picture of two elderly women looking at a letter and responded by saying this was a letter for their granddaughter informing her that she had won a national writing contest, your response would be scored as indicating achievement desires. If your TAT stories consistently contained such themes, you would be regarded as having a high n-Ach. Research suggests that the TAT does a moderately good job of measuring individual differences in n-Ach (McGrath & Carroll, 2012; Tuerlinckx et al., 2002).

High n-Ach people have an intrinsic *desire to succeed*. This desire is assumed not to develop from biological or genetic sources but to come from experience and parental encouragement. David McClelland (1985) contends that n-Ach develops when children *internalize* achievement values displayed by their parents and other important role models. Such internalization comes about by children observing adults engaging in achievement tasks and by themselves being placed in achievement situations that they can master. These challenges, however, cannot be so easy that the person doesn't feel some sense of satisfaction and accomplishment.

Some people's achievement needs are less determined by a desire to achieve greatness than by a fear of appearing foolish, lazy, or stupid. Thus, an important component in understanding n-Ach is the additional motivational push we receive from *fear of failure* (Atkinson, 1957; Bjornebekk et al., 2011). If your desire for success is considerably stronger than your fear of failure, you will have a high n-Ach. However, if your fear of failure is considerably stronger than your desire for success, you will have a low n-Ach.

Do high n-Ach people approach all achievement challenges with equal desire? Not at all. In fact, high n-Ach individuals are more likely to choose tasks that are moderately difficult and challenging (those tasks with about a 50/50 chance of success) than tasks that are either extremely difficult or easy (Atkinson, 1977; Slade & Rush, 1991). This is so because their desire for success is stronger than their fear of failure. Thus, these people are attracted to achievement situations that they can master if they work hard and precisely apply their skills (McClelland, 1995). When they succeed at these tasks, high n-Ach people are generally perceived as being talented, hardworking, and deserving of praise and rewards. This positive feedback serves to both satisfy and further strengthen their achievement desires. In contrast, extremely difficult and easy tasks are not nearly as appealing to those with a high n-Ach because the probability of success is either very low ("Why waste my time?") or virtually guaranteed ("Where is the challenge?"). Further, if they do succeed at a virtually impossible task, their achievement is likely to be dismissed by others as sheer "dumb luck."

People with a high need for achievement are those whose desire to succeed is much stronger than their fear of failure.

What about low n-Ach individuals? Do they completely avoid achievement situations? Again, the answer is no. They tend to pick achievement situations that are either very easy so that success is guaranteed or extremely difficult so that they have a good excuse for failing (McClelland, 1985). The key fact to remember about low n-Ach people is that their fear of failure is stronger than their desire for success. As a result, they pick achievement situations that will protect them against either failing or being blamed for failing. However, such situations also virtually guarantee that they cannot take credit for any success that they achieve. Thus, while they may protect themselves from embarrassment and loss of self-esteem, they have little hope of winning praise or enhancing their self-esteem. As a result, achievement situations are unlikely to ever be very rewarding to those with low n-Ach.

This desire to meet high standards of excellence in achievement situations causes many people to experience high levels of anxiety as they prepare to demonstrate their skills. Such anxiety can sabotage achievement desires. The "Psychological Applications" section at the end of this chapter examines the psychological aspects of high anxiety in academic testing situations and offers tips on how to control such anxiety.

9.4c *Certain Strategies Can Increase Achievement Motivation.*

We are not born with the motivation to achieve. Instead, we acquire it through parents and others encouraging and helping us discover the rewards of mastering challenging tasks while surviving failures (Vallerand et al., 1997). Yet how can we foster achievement motivation in people who typically avoid achievement situations?

One effective strategy is to get people to emotionally identify with the achievement task, so they become intrinsically motivated (see Section 9.1e). If you can convince people that they are working on a task because it is important to them, they will work harder and do better work, even if they are low n-Ach individuals. Second, you should also take steps to increase the value of achieving (for example, emphasize feelings of pride and accomplishment) while decreasing the negative effects of failing (for example, downplay feelings of shame and guilt). By providing realistic models of success with positive outcomes, while introducing examples of failure within a supportive environment, the emotional responses and expectations related to both can be shifted (Corker & Donnellan, 2012). Experience with failing—and finding that the world does not end in the absence of success—can lessen the fear and help one to cope with difficult challenges.

If people confine themselves to tasks that are too easy, they gain little satisfaction when they succeed. On the other hand, if they regularly are asked to work on tasks well beyond their capabilities, achievement situations will become associated with disappointment and a feeling of inferiority. Thus, a third important factor in increasing achievement motivation is to place people in achievement situations that are moderately difficult but that can be mastered if they exert themselves (Locke & Latham, 1990). Children are much more likely to develop a high need for achievement if they have parents who accurately assess their abilities and then place them in achievement situations where the children's abilities will often lead to success, if they work hard (Boon, 2007). Such children develop a positive incentive value for such achievement situations.

Finally, a fourth factor is to be careful how people are given feedback when working on achievement tasks. Frequent feedback is more helpful when success is being demonstrated and something is being gained. However, giving less-frequent feedback and keeping long-term outcomes in mind are better when progress on achieving the task goal is slow or uneven (Cochran & Tesser, 1996). This less-frequent feedback shifts people's attention away from their immediate frustrations and toward the desired end state of success.

Section **REVIEW**

- Need for achievement (n-Ach) is a desire to overcome obstacles and meet high standards of excellence; it is assumed to develop from experience and parental encouragement.

- High n-Ach persons seek out achievement tasks that are moderately difficult, while low n-Ach persons choose either very easy or extremely difficult tasks.

- Achievement motivation can be enhanced through various intervention strategies.

9.5 Emotion

In my chapter-opening story, why do you think I tried so hard to hide my tears? According to incentive theory, I must have perceived a negative incentive in my social environment, which caused me to not publicly display my grief in such a vulnerable manner. My childhood experience illustrates the fact that incentives in the social environment can shape the expression of emotions. In fact, it is difficult to imagine the pushes and pulls of motivation not shaping in some manner such emotions as fear, anxiety, love, desperation, or loathing. It is equally difficult to think of a strong emotion that doesn't serve to either push or pull us toward or away from some goal. In many respects, motivation and emotion are two sides of the same coin, with emotions both reflecting and inciting our motives. Let us now examine the character of emotions and the various theories that have been developed to explain them.

9.5a *Emotions Are Positive or Negative Feeling States.*

Visualize the following experiences, pausing between each one and carefully paying attention to how you would feel:

- You're walking down the street, a car comes up fast from behind, and the driver blows the horn just as the car reaches you.

- You're walking down the street and see your heart's greatest desire, not just walking toward you, but also looking at you and smiling.

- You're walking down the street and see that thoroughly annoying person who makes your life miserable stumble and fall face-first into a mud puddle.

These incidents would probably induce different emotional responses. What makes up an emotion? Choose any one of the preceding situations. In response to this change in environment, would there be changes in how your body felt? Would you feel your heart race? Muscles tense or relax? Would your attention, or what you were thinking about, change along with the emotion? What changes in body posture and/or facial expression would occur? Would there be any changes in behavior?

Go back to the situation of seeing "your heart's greatest desire"—but now add into the vision that he or she is walking hand in hand with another person, both gazing longingly into each other's eyes. The primary "thing" in the environment is still the "greatest desire," but the context (and therefore meaning) has changed—and so has the way your body feels and how you might behave.

These examples illustrate the complexity of **emotions**. For our purposes, we define emotion as a positive or negative feeling state (or *evaluative response*) that typically includes some combination of physiological arousal, cognitive appraisal, and behavioral expression. Although many theories have been developed to explain emotions, most consider that all emotions have the following unifying characteristics:

Emotion A positive or negative feeling state that typically includes some combination of physiological arousal, cognitive appraisal, and behavioral expression

- Emotions involve the reactions of many bodily systems.

- Expressions of emotion are based on genetically transmitted mechanisms but are altered by learning and interpretation of events.

- Emotions communicate information between people.

- Emotions help individuals respond and react to changes in their environment.

In short, an emotion is an experience that is felt as happening to the self. It is generated partly by a cognitive appraisal of a situation and is accompanied by reflexive physiological changes (for example, an increase in blood pressure and heart rate) and behavioral responses (for example, facial expressions and postural changes).

9.5b *Emotions Facilitate Survival.*

Humans, like other animals, signal their readiness to fight, flee, mate, and attend to each other's needs through a variety of facial and bodily nonverbal expressions (Buck, 1984). These adaptive response patterns include emotions (Bonanno et al., 2002). Evolutionary theories have emphasized the survival value of emotions, not only because they tend to motivate us to avoid what is harmful and approach what is beneficial, but also because emotional expressions and behaviors foster communication with others (Oehman, 2002).

After observing that a number of facial expressions of emotion appeared to be universal, Charles Darwin (1872) proposed that facial expressions are inborn and that the expressions we see today are those that allowed our ancestors to most effectively communicate to one another their inner states and behavioral intentions. Consistent with Darwin's evolutionary view of emotional expressiveness, cross-cultural research indicates that similar facial expressions are readily displayed and accurately interpreted by people from differing cultures (Ekman & Friesen, 1971; Matsumoto et al., 1988). Although this research indicates substantial cross-cultural agreement in both the experience and the expression of emotions, certain emotions are easier to distinguish from one another than others. For example, people from all cultures can easily tell the difference between happiness and anger, but it is harder for them to distinguish adoration from desire. This finding has led to the belief that certain emotions are more basic, or *primary*, than others (Ekman & Friesen, 1971; Izard, 1989). Most classification lists include the following seven primary emotions: *anger, disgust, fear, happiness, surprise, contempt,* and *sadness* (Ekman, 1993). The possible reason these seven primary emotions are most accurately "read" is because the facial expressions associated with each emotion are relatively unique to that emotion (Smith et al., 2005). According to this explanation, the human brain has evolved to efficiently transmit signals to the facial muscles associated with specific emotions and also to "read" those facial signals on human faces. Further, the human face has evolved to accurately transmit facial expressions associated with specific emotions. Check out Self-Discovery Questionnaire 9-3 to determine how accurate you are in identifying the emotion conveyed in different facial expressions.

This does not mean, however, that people throughout the world always express emotions in the same way. Given the important role that emotions play in human interactions, it makes abundant sense that cultures would develop social rules for when and how different emotions are expressed (Mesquita & Frijda, 1992). For example, the cultural belief systems of individualism and collectivism have shaped norms related to the acceptability of acting in ways that might threaten group harmony. That is, collectivists are much more likely than individualists to monitor their behavior so that it does not disrupt the smooth functioning of the group. Regarding emotions, research suggests that although people from collectivist and individualist cultures do not differ in publicly displaying positive emotions, collectivists are much more uncomfortable about publicly expressing negative emotions (Stephan et al., 1996).

Does this mean that people from collectivist cultures feel negative emotions differently than individualists feel them? In an attempt to answer this question, Paul Ekman (1970) unobtrusively recorded the facial expressions of Japanese and Americans while they individually watched either an emotionally neutral film or one depicting body mutilation. In this "viewing alone" condition, Ekman found a very strong, positive correlation between the Japanese and American participants' displayed facial expressions ($r = +.88$), indicating clear agreement in their expression of such emotions as anger, disgust, surprise, and fear. However, when someone else entered the viewing room while a participant was watching a film, the Japanese, unlike the Americans, tended to display polite smiles rather than expressing their authentic emotions of the moment. These findings suggest that collectivism influences whether people publicly express negative feelings, but not whether they privately experience them. In other words, there is no evidence that collectivists feel emotions differently than do individualists.

Returning to the notion that emotions have survival value, further studies indicate that as people immerse themselves in satisfying friendships and romantic relationships, they experience an *emotional convergence* with their partners. That is, the emotions of the two people become increasingly similar over time (Anderson et al., 2003). When

What are the feelings of men? They are joy, anger, sadness, fear, love, disliking, and liking. These seven feelings belong to men without their learning them.

—From The Li Chi, first-century Chinese encyclopedia

SELF-DISCOVERY 9-3
Questionnaire

Can You Match the Seven Primary Emotions with Their Correct Facial Expressions?

Cross-cultural research has determined that the seven primary emotions are anger, disgust, fear, happiness, surprise, contempt, and sadness. In identifying these emotions as "primary," social scientists mean that people find them easier to distinguish from one another than other emotions. Examine each of the seven facial expressions here. Can you identify the correct emotion to each expression? Answers are listed below.

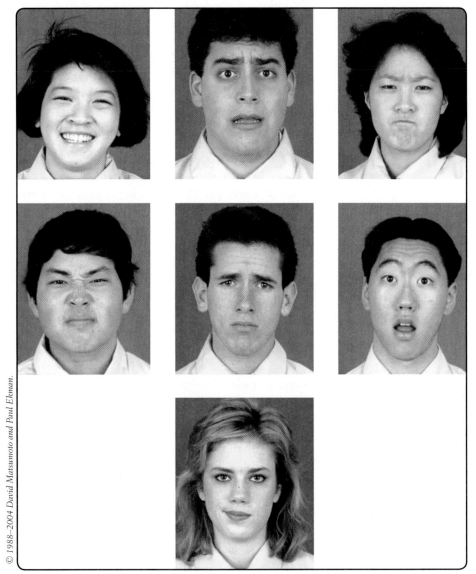

© 1988–2004 David Matsumoto and Paul Ekman.

Answers: Top row, left to right: happiness, fear, anger. Middle row, left to right: disgust, sadness, surprise. Bottom row: contempt.

one person reacts to a situation with fear, laughter, or sadness, her or his partner's emotions are likely to correspond. The benefit of such emotional convergence is that people's thoughts and behaviors become more coordinated (Keltner & Haidt, 2003). They emotionally respond as a "team," supporting each other's definition of the situation. Such partner support not only increases people's confidence that they are accurately reacting to events around them—after all, there is strength in numbers—but also might at times have real, immediate survival value. For example, if one person reacts fearfully to an approaching stranger, her or his partner is also likely to be on guard. This ability to quickly construct a united defensive front when facing possible danger provides safety not afforded those couples who are emotionally out of synch.

9.5c Emotions Result in Bodily Responses.

Can you imagine riding a roller coaster and not feeling your heart pounding or your blood pressure rising? What if there were no anticipatory "butterflies" in your stomach prior to an important date? The emotional impact of these events would be blunted without the physiological feedback. The *autonomic nervous system* produces the bodily responses integral to emotion. As discussed in Chapter 2, Section 2.2a, the autonomic nervous system is the part of the peripheral nervous system that commands movement of involuntary, nonskeletal muscles—such as the heart, lung, and stomach muscles—over which we have little or no control. The autonomic nervous system is further divided into two separate branches—the *sympathetic* and *parasympathetic* nervous systems (Figure 9-7)—that tend to work in opposition to each other in order to keep the body's vital systems in a state of homeostasis (see the earlier discussion in Section 9.1c).

As you recall, the sympathetic nervous system is geared toward energy expenditure—getting the body ready to respond (the "fight or flight" response) by moving blood to the muscles and releasing stored energy. This system not only is activated to meet physical demands but also functions when you experience strong emotions. In contrast, the parasympathetic nervous system is geared toward energy conservation and "refueling" by stimulating digestion and decreasing blood flow to the muscles. Although this system has not traditionally been associated with emotion to the same degree as the sympathetic system, its role in emotions has received additional attention. For example, *emotional fainting* is likely a symptom of an overreaction by the parasympathetic system (Vingerhoets, 1985). In addition, *worrying* is characterized by low parasympathetic activity combined with a relatively inflexible autonomic response (Borkovec et al., 1998).

 **INFO-BIT**   Studies using magnetic resonance imaging have found evidence that women's brains tend to be better organized to perceive and remember emotions than men's brains (Canli et al., 2002). These results might partly explain why women are twice as likely as men to experience clinical depression (see Chapter 11, Section 11.2b).

9.5d Two Theories Dispute Whether Physiological Responses Precede Emotions.

In 1884, William James and Danish physiologist Carl Lange independently proposed that our subjective emotional experiences are automatically caused by specific physiological changes in the autonomic nervous system that in turn are caused by

FIGURE 9-7 The Dual Functions of the Autonomic Nervous System

The sympathetic and parasympathetic divisions of the autonomic nervous system often stimulate opposite effects in the body's organs. The sympathetic nervous system prepares your body for action, while the parasympathetic nervous system calms the body. Can you explain how these two systems respond to threat?

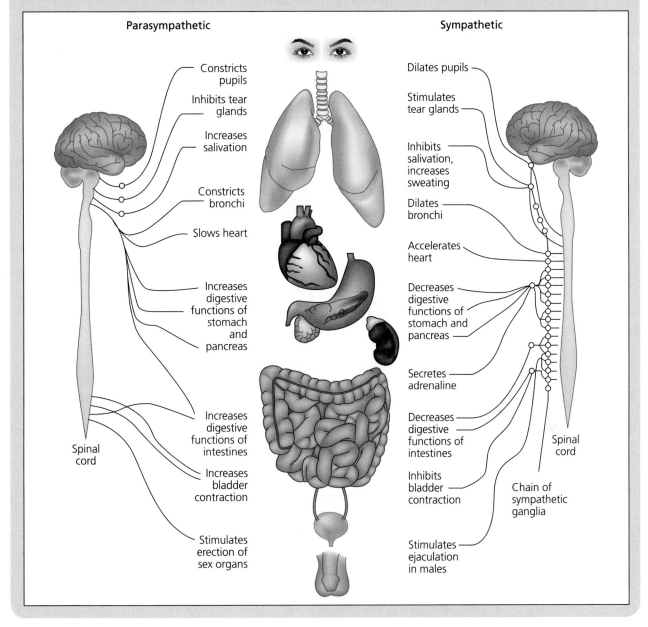

environmental stimuli. According to James, "we feel sorry because we cry, angry because we strike, and afraid because we tremble" (1890, p. 1066).

Consider the example of a car honking at you unexpectedly. The **James-Lange theory** predicts that your heart would pound and your body would tremble *before* you felt fear. According to the theory, your brain would perceive the physiological responses to the horn honking as being the emotion of fear. Similarly, the palm sweating, heart fluttering, and stomach churning responses upon seeing your "greatest desire" would be perceived as "longing" or "love." All emotions are considered the product of different physiological changes that the brain automatically interprets, all of which occur in response to environmental stimuli.

James-Lange theory A theory stating that emotion-provoking events induce specific physiological changes in the autonomic nervous system, which our brain automatically interprets as specific emotions

FIGURE 9-8

Two Contrasting Theories of Emotion

While the James-Lange theory proposes that physiological reactions cause emotions, the Cannon-Bard theory contends that these two processes occur simultaneously in response to emotion-provoking events.

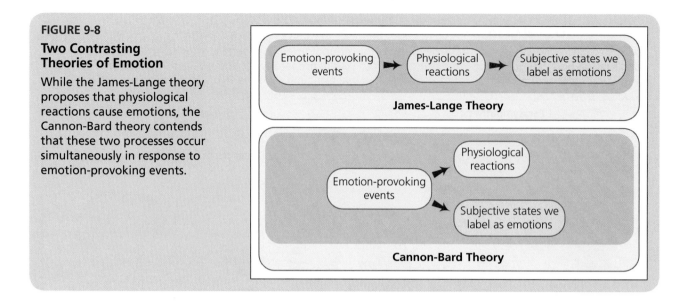

Cannon-Bard theory A theory that emotion-provoking events simultaneously induce both physiological responses and subjective states that are labeled as emotions

In contrast to this view, physiologists Walter Cannon (1927) and Philip Bard (1934) offered what is now called the **Cannon-Bard theory**, which proposes that feedback from bodily organs cannot be the source for our emotions because autonomic processes are typically too slow (taking 1–2 seconds) to explain the almost instantaneous experience of emotions. This theory further asserts that because many different emotional states are associated with the same autonomic responses, arousal is too general to directly cause specific emotions. Instead, emotion-provoking events simultaneously induce both physiological responses and subjective states that we label as emotions. This occurs because information concerning the emotion-inducing event is transmitted simultaneously to the brain's cortex—which causes the subjective awareness of emotion—and to the autonomic nervous system—which causes the physiological arousal. From this perspective, then, when the car's horn sounds, this event causes your heart to race as you experience a feeling you call "fear." Figure 9-8 illustrates how these two theories view the process of emotion differently.

Which theory is more accurate? Actually, research partially supports both theories. First, the contention by Cannon and Bard that autonomic responses occur too slowly to account for many emotional responses still appears to be valid. However, consistent with the James-Lange theory, research over the past decade suggests that different emotions do appear to be associated with distinct autonomic responses. For example, anger and fear produce greater heart rate acceleration than happiness, and they are also autonomically distinguishable from each other. Cross-cultural research further indicates that these associations between specific bodily changes and specific emotional experiences are universal, suggesting that they may be "hardwired" into the brain (Levenson et al., 1992). Although these findings suggest that emotional reactions can be generated by changes in our bodily states, most researchers agree with the Cannon-Bard proposition that our subjective experience of emotion also involves cognition.

Facial feedback hypothesis A theory of emotion proposing that specific facial expressions trigger the subjective experience of specific emotions

One variation of James's theory is the **facial feedback hypothesis**, which proposes that specific facial expressions trigger the subjective experience of specific emotions (Laird, 1974). In one experiment testing this hypothesis, the German psychologist Fritz Strack and his colleagues (1988) asked college students to hold a pen in their mouths while they looked at a series of amusing cartoons. Participants in the *lips condition* were instructed to hold the pen tightly with their lips, while those in the *teeth condition* were told to hold the pen with their front teeth (see photo on this page). In a control condition, participants were told to hold the pen in their nondominant hand. After reading the cartoons, all students rated how funny they were using a 10-point scale. You can tell by looking at the photograph that holding a pen with the teeth causes a person to smile, while holding it with the lips produces a frown. Did this manipulation of facial expressions cause participants to experience different emotions? Yes. Those participants who held the pen between their teeth found the cartoons to be the most amusing, followed by those who held it in their hand. Students who held the pen in their lips gave the cartoons the lowest ratings of amusement. The way this phenomenon may work is that our facial muscles send feedback signals to the brain, producing neurological changes that trigger specific emotions, even though the emotions triggered may not be exactly the same as when we are genuinely happy or sad (Ekman & Davidson, 1993). If you would like to further

Photo courtesy of Figzoi

The facial feedback hypothesis states that changes in facial expression can lead to corresponding changes in emotion. In an experiment testing this hypothesis, Fritz Strack and his colleagues (1988) asked participants to read cartoons while holding a pen in their mouths. People who were told to hold the pen between their teeth thought the cartoons were funnier than those who held the pen between their lips. Do these findings support the facial feedback hypothesis?

explore whether there is more to the experience of emotion than simply reading our physiology, check out Closer Look 9-1 on the accuracy of lie detectors.

Closer
LOOK *9-1*

Is There Such a Thing as an Accurate Lie Detector?

Because the sympathetic nervous system is associated with emotional arousal, scientists have reasoned that if they can obtain measurements of various autonomic responses they should be better able to determine whether people are lying. Why? Because usually when people are trying to cover up lies, they become anxious. The **polygraph** is the most common "lie detector" (Craig, 2012). This mechanical device measures a variety of autonomic responses, typically respiration, heart rate, blood pressure, and galvanic skin response (palm perspiration). Each of these physiological responses is affected by the sympathetic nervous system. Therefore, increases in heart rate, breathing, blood pressure, and palm sweating are interpreted as signs of lying when responding to appropriate questions. As depicted in Figure 9-9, a polygrapher will monitor physiological responses to control questions (for example, "What is your favorite color?") and compare those responses to ones relevant to the investigation ("Have you ever taken property from an employer?"). Larger responses to key questions, reflecting greater sympathetic nervous system response, are considered "consistent" with lying.

Polygraph A machine that measures several of the physiological responses accompanying emotion (such as respiration, heart rate, blood pressure, and palm perspiration)

Is a polygraph a true "lie detector"? No. It is really a detector of sympathetic nervous system activity. Researcher David Lykken (1998) made that very point when demonstrating the numerous ways in which a polygraph can lead to inaccurate conclusions about a person's guilt or innocence. It is true (I'm not lying!) that trained polygraph experts can accurately identify lying as much as 80 to 98 percent of the time. However, accuracy in identifying a person as *innocent* still suffers under this technique, with error rates as high as 55 percent (Honts & Perry, 1992; Lykken, 1984).

Further, because a polygraph is measuring sympathetic nervous system activity and not actual lying, a person being tested who consciously elevates his or her physiological responses while answering neutral questions can also fool the machine. This can be done by biting the tongue or squeezing the anal sphincter muscles. These falsely high physiological responses to neutral questions will later mask the elevated physiological responses to the important questions, resulting in lies being more likely to go undetected. Aldrich Ames, convicted of espionage that led to the deaths of at least ten CIA agents, passed

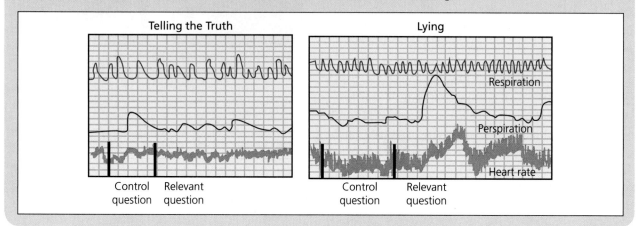

FIGURE 9-9   Detecting Lying with the Polygraph

In the polygraph test, the polygrapher compares physiological responses to control and relevant questions. The polygraph responses on the left are from a person who responded less strongly to a question relevant to a crime than to an emotionally arousing control question not relevant to the crime. This comparison of the physiological responses indicates that the person is likely being truthful. In contrast, the polygraph responses on the right are from a person who responded more strongly to a question relevant to the crime than to an emotionally arousing question not relevant to the crime. This comparison indicates that the person is likely lying. How might such polygraph methods sometimes lead to errors in detecting liars?

two lie-detector tests by taking advantage of polygraph weaknesses in this area (Weiner et al., 1995).

Due to its inability to actually detect lies, the polygraph is inadmissible as evidence in almost all courts of law. However, polygraph tests are becoming increasingly common for employment screening and as part of criminal investigations. This increased use is occurring despite the fact that a majority of experts in the field of psychophysiology believe the polygraph is an invalid and theoretically unsound approach to lie detection (Iacono & Lykken, 1997).

Are there more accurate alternatives to the polygraph? Measurements of brain activity obtained by electroencephalograph (EEG) machines and the more elaborate functional magnetic resonance imaging (fMRI) scanners have been studied as possible deception detectors, but their reliability and validity outside the laboratory have not been adequately tested (Lee et al., 2002). At this time, a truly accurate way to detect lying does not exist. The polygraph, properly administered by a trained professional, can work as one possible tool for investigation but should not be regarded by itself as providing enough evidence to determine guilt, innocence, or deception.

9.5e   *The Brain Coordinates Emotional Responses.*

Ultimately, the brain is what controls the body's responses to emotional stimuli. While no single brain region controls emotion, three regions are of particular importance: the hypothalamus, the limbic system, and the frontal lobes of the cerebral cortex. Investigations of these brain regions have provided insights into (1) how we can experience emotion before cognition (as proposed by the James-Lange theory) and (2) how the frontal lobes interpret emotion (as proposed by the Cannon-Bard theory).

The Hypothalamus

Just as the hypothalamus is vital in the regulation of eating (see Section 9.2a), it also provides a vital link between higher-order cognitive activities in the forebrain and activities controlled by more primitive areas of the lower brain and is involved with homeostatic control of the body. It does so by converting emotional signals generated in the forebrain into autonomic and endocrine responses. Thus, when something angers or frightens you, the hypothalamus will activate the autonomic nervous system's "fight or flight" responses and the release of hormones by the endocrine system.

The Limbic System

A key component in human emotional responses is the *limbic system*, which is a set of interrelated neural structures located at the border of the brain's "older parts" and the cerebral cortex (see Chapter 2, Section 2.3b). Although different structures in the limbic system relate to different aspects of emotion, the structure that has received the most attention is the *amygdala*, which is thought to be the first processor of human emotional responses (Hamann et al., 2002).

Two distinct neural circuits involving the amygdala appear to produce emotional responses, particularly fear (Cunningham & Brosch, 2012). The first circuit is very primitive and consists of the amygdala quickly evaluating incoming sensory information from the thalamus—the brain's sensory relay station—and eliciting an immediate emotional response by activating the hypothalamus. This emotional response does not entail any higher-order processing by the frontal lobes of the cerebral cortex. The fear you experience when surprised by someone jumping out at you from the shadows is an example of this first-circuit emotional response. Emotional responses acquired through classical conditioning are also a function of this primitive neural circuit, and the emotional responses that the James-Lange theory best explains arise through this first emotional circuit as well.

When the thalamus sends sensory information to the amygdala, it also simultaneously sends this information to the frontal lobes of the cerebral cortex for further processing. This second neural circuit involves slower processing because it requires more complex cognitive appraisal by the frontal lobes of the cerebral cortex, involving the use of acquired knowledge and consideration of motives and goals. Following this appraisal, information is then transmitted to the amygdala, and a second emotional response occurs when the hypothalamus is activated. The subsequent changes that occur in the autonomic and endocrine systems are relayed back to the frontal lobes for analysis and interpretation. Complex emotions such as love, happiness, sorrow, and guilt are most likely due to this second emotional circuit. The operation of this second neural circuit resembles what the Cannon-Bard theory hinted at in its proposal that the frontal lobes cause the subjective awareness of emotion. Both neural circuits are illustrated in Figure 9-10.

The Frontal Lobes of the Cerebral Cortex

While the limbic system is important for processing emotions, as already stated, the frontal lobes of the cerebral cortex are important for the *subjective experience* of emotions. As you recall from Chapter 2, Section 2.3d, the cerebral cortex is divided into two rounded halves, called the *cerebral hemispheres*, and the frontal lobes in the cerebral cortex govern higher mental processes. Overall, the right frontal lobe seems to be more active than the left frontal lobe during the expression of emotions and when processing emotional cues from others (Oatley & Jenkins, 1996). Because the right hemisphere controls the left side of the body, and the left hemisphere controls the right side, this means that the left side of the face is somewhat more involved in emotional expression than the right side.

FIGURE 9-10   Two Neural Circuits for Processing Emotion

Two distinct neural circuits process emotional responses. Activation of both circuits begins with sensory information being relayed from the thalamus. In the first circuit (purple arrows), the amygdala processes this sensory information and immediately elicits an emotional response without higher-order processing. In the second circuit (red arrows), the frontal lobes of the cerebral cortex receive the sensory information from the thalamus and engage in more complex cognitive appraisal before transmitting a signal to the amygdala. Then a second emotional response occurs. Both circuits activate the hypothalamus, which produces autonomic and endocrine changes. These changes are also sent back (outline brown arrows) to the frontal lobes, where they are analyzed and interpreted.

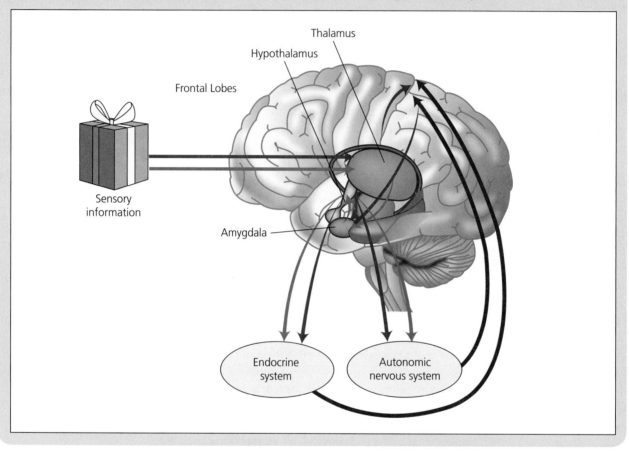

Research further suggests that each of the cerebral cortex's two frontal lobes is related to one type of emotion more than another. For example, activation of the left frontal lobe is associated with approach-related emotions, whereas activation of the right frontal lobe is associated with aversion-related emotions (Sutton & Davidson, 1997). Apparently, this hemispheric difference is inborn: Infants as young as 3 to 4 days show more active left hemispheres when given sweet-tasting sucrose and more right hemisphere activity when given sour-tasting citric acid. Similarly, 10-month-old babies with more active left hemispheres tend to be more placid and become less upset upon separation from their mothers than babies with more active right hemispheres (R. Davidson & Fox, 1989). Among adults, individuals with damage to the left frontal lobe tend to express intense negative affect, such as pathological crying, while those with damage to the right frontal lobe often display pathological laughing (Davidson, 2005). Together, these findings suggest that the left cerebral hemisphere is somewhat more involved in expressing positive emotions, while the right hemisphere is more involved in expressing negative emotions. Before reading the next section, complete Self-Discovery Questionnaire 9-4 to gain some insight into whether you exhibit more activation of your right or left frontal lobe.

SELF-DISCOVERY 9-4
Questionnaire

Which Side of Your Brain Is More Active during Emotional Situations?

People differ in which frontal lobe of their cerebral hemisphere is most active during emotional experiences, and this difference is related to what emotions they experience. One way to evaluate individual differences in frontal lobe activation is to measure the direction of a person's gaze after asking them an emotion-laden question. In a right-handed person, if the eyes move to the left, this is associated with right frontal lobe activation, whereas if the eyes move to the right, it signifies left frontal lobe activation. Researchers have used items similar to those listed below to measure frontal lobe activation (Schwartz et al. 1975). Ask a friend to read these items to you and have her or him note the direction of your first eye movement following each question. If on seven or more of the items your eyes move in the same direction, this suggests that you have more activation on one side of your brain than the other. Seven or more eye movements to the left indicate right frontal lobe activation, whereas seven or more eye movements to the right indicate left frontal lobe activation. This test is meant only for right-handed individuals, because left-handers have a more complicated pattern of hemispheric activation for which this eye-movement test is not a good measure.

Item 1: Tell me how you feel when you are nervous.

Item 2: Visualize and describe the most upsetting movie you have seen.

Item 3: Imagine that you are relaxing on a warm, sunny beach as you watch the sun set in the westward sky. Your friend is sitting nearby with his back toward your right side. Toward approximately what direction is your friend looking?

Item 4: When you visualize your father's face, what is the first emotion you experience?

Item 5: Make up a sentence using the words *alarm* and *anger*.

Item 6: Visualize and describe the most pleasurable scene in which you recently have been.

Item 7: Describe how you feel when annoyed.

Item 8: Imagine that you are a surgeon and must make a long and deep incision upon a patient's body. You must cut a straight line from the person's left eye to his right shoulder. Visualize making the incision, telling me through what areas of the patient's face you would cut.

Item 9: Visualize and describe the most beautiful photo you have recently seen.

Item 10: Construct a sentence using the words *bliss* and *delight*.

Keep in mind that this is not a conclusive measure of which frontal lobe in the cerebral cortex is more active during emotional situations. Also keep in mind that most people do not show consistent eye movements in one or the other direction. If your eye-movement responses are in the range of seven or more in one direction, you can decide whether you believe that you are more vulnerable to positive or negative emotions. As noted, research suggests that people who consistently look to the left should be more likely to experience negative emotions, while people who consistently look to the right should be more likely to experience positive emotions.

9.5f The Two-Factor Theory Emphasizes the Role of Cognition in Emotions.

The James-Lange theory hypothesizes that physiological arousal precedes the experience of emotion. The Cannon-Bard theory hypothesizes that our emotions are physiologically similar. Taking these different hypotheses from the competing theories, Stanley Schachter and Jerome Singer (1962) proposed that if people are emotionally aroused but not sure what they are feeling, they look for cues in their surroundings. If others are happy, they are likely to interpret their arousal as happiness. If others are anxious, they too are likely to feel anxious. In other words, they will perceive themselves experiencing the emotion that their surroundings tell them they should be experiencing. Thus, according to Schachter and Singer, emotions are based on two factors: *physiological arousal* and *cognitions* about what that arousal means. They named their theory the **two-factor theory** of emotions.

Two-factor theory A theory of emotion suggesting that our emotional states are sometimes determined by experiencing physiological arousal and then attaching a cognitive label to the arousal

In one field experiment testing this theory, male hikers walking across a park bridge were asked by an attractive female research assistant to write an imaginative story in response to a TAT picture while standing on the bridge (Dutton & Aron, 1974). In one condition, the bridge was very sturdy and stood only a few feet above the ground. In another condition, the bridge was 5 feet wide, 450 feet long, and constructed of wooden boards attached to wire cables that were suspended 230 feet above a rocky gorge! It was assumed that the men who encountered the assistant on the high suspension bridge would be more physiologically aroused than those who met her on the low sturdy bridge. Based on the two-factor theory, it was predicted that the men on the high bridge would interpret their arousal as being caused by sexual interest toward the assistant rather than fear of heights. Consistent with the theory, the men on the high bridge not only told TAT stories with significantly higher sexual imagery than the men on the low bridge but also were more likely to call the assistant for a date! Additional research has demonstrated that the attributions we make concerning our physiological responses to a particular stimulus will often, but not always, determine our emotional reactions (Schachter, 1959, 1966).

Journey of Discovery

Imagine that you are going out on a date with someone, and you would like this person to fall in love with you. Up to this point in your relationship, this person likes you only "as a friend." Based on your knowledge of the two-factor theory of emotions, what sort of activities might you plan for the date to increase the likelihood that the object of your affections will experience a similar emotion toward you?

9.5g   One Emotion May Trigger an Opposite Emotion.

As you learned in Section 9.5c, once the sympathetic nervous system activates the body's energy resources in response to a threat, the parasympathetic system responds by conserving these resources. Noting how the body often responds in this counterbalancing fashion, psychologist Richard Solomon (1980) suggested that our experience of emotion often occurs in a similar manner. For example, have you experienced elation after succeeding at some task only to have that feeling soon replaced by a sense of despondency? Or have you felt angry and then afterward felt a sense of calm? Solomon's **opponent-process theory** contends that every emotion triggers an opposite emotion. In addition, the theory proposes that repetition of an experience causes the initial emotional reaction to weaken and the opposing emotional reaction to strengthen (Solomon & Corbit, 1974).

Opponent-process theory A theory of emotion suggesting that every emotion triggers an opposite emotion

According to opponent-process theory, every emotion triggers an opposite emotion.

Shutterstock

Consider how the opponent-process theory would explain your emotional reaction to skydiving. During your first parachute jump, you would probably experience considerable fear as you prepared to leap from the plane. This fear would undoubtedly subside and give way to exhilaration upon your landing safely on the ground. According to the theory, your "rebound" exhilaration would become greater and start earlier with each successive jump. Eventually, your fear could diminish to the point where the entire experience was pleasurable.

TABLE 9-2 Four Theories of Emotion

Theory	Basic Assumptions
James-Lange theory	Emotion-provoking events induce physiological reactions that then cause the subjective states that we label as emotions.
Cannon-Bard theory	Emotion-provoking events simultaneously induce physiological reactions and subjective states that we label as emotions.
Two-factor theory	Emotion-provoking events induce physiological reactions that increase arousal, which we then identify as a particular emotion based on situational cues.
Opponent-process theory	An emotional reaction to an event is automatically followed by an opposite emotional reaction. Repeated exposure to the same event weakens the initial emotion while strengthening the opposing emotion.

The opponent-process theory also provides insights into drug abuse. Initially, drug use often provides intense pleasure, which is followed by unpleasant withdrawal symptoms. With repeated drug use, these unpleasant aftereffects become stronger, while the initial pleasure diminishes. Eventually, taking the drug is motivated less by the fleeting pleasure it provides and more by the desire to extinguish the pain of withdrawal. Table 9-2 summarizes the four theories of emotion discussed in this section of the chapter. After reviewing this table, check out Exploring Culture & Diversity 9-3, which examines how the social meaning of emotions may be shaped by gender.

INFO-BIT The opponent-process theory of emotion is similar to the opponent-process principle of color vision discussed in Chapter 4, Section 4.2e. This principle states that when you stare at a particular color and then look away, the opposing color is seen as an afterimage due to a "rebound effect" in opponent cells. Richard Solomon believed that the same principle holds for emotions.

Exploring **CULTURE & DIVERSITY 9-3**

How Does Gender Shape the Social Meaning of Emotion?

As children mature, they learn an *emotion culture*, which consists of the informal norms governing what emotions are appropriate in different circumstances for particular people. These norms often vary from culture to culture (see Section 9.5b).

Stephanie Shields (2002, 2005) describes two contrasting emotional styles in North American culture that are linked to gender. Both are expressed by women and men, but each is expected more of one sex than the other. *Extravagant expressiveness* is an open style of experiencing and communicating emotion that is associated with femininity. This form of emotion is evident in nurturing and is the form linked in our culture to intimacy.

This is the kind of emotion we expect when we say, "Don't just tell me that you love me; say it like you really mean it!" The second emotional style telegraphs intense emotion under control; Shields labels this emotional style *manly emotion* because of its connection to a particular version of White, heterosexual masculinity. This is the kind of emotion we have come to expect from male movie leads—think of Christian Bale in *The Dark Knight Rises*, Robert DeNiro in *Being Flynn*, or Gary Oldman in *Tinker, Tailor, Soldier, Spy*.

These two emotional styles convey different messages to those witnessing their expression. The strongly felt—yet controlled—emotion expressed in manly emotion conveys the message that the person is independent and powerful: "I can control my emotion (and, thereby, my *self*), and I can harness it to control the situation." The underlying message of extravagant expressiveness involves nurturance: "My emotion (and, thereby, my *self*) is at your service." Shields contends that in our culture manly emotion is ultimately considered more important than extravagant emotion because it is believed to express rational behavior. In contrast, while the feminine emotional standards underlying emotional expressiveness foster many socially desirable behaviors (such as tenderness and selflessness), these behaviors are culturally tainted because of their association with emotion out of control. Shields also asserts that control of emotion is more central to the masculine standards than expressiveness because control is associated with power and dominance. Historically being considered the ones who hold power in society, men are assumed to possess greater ability to control their emotions than women.

There is no scientific evidence of a gender difference in emotional control—and, of course, there is more than one way to define *control*. Research conducted by Shields and other emotion researchers does find that boys are encouraged to express emotions—such as anger, contempt, and pride—that reflect a sense of entitlement to power in society. In contrast, this same research suggests that girls are encouraged to express emotions associated with satisfaction, powerlessness, and service to others, such as happiness, fear, and empathy (Saarni, 1999; Shields, 2005). Consistent with this encouragement, women are not only better nonverbal communicators of happiness than men but are also better at masking disappointment with a positive expression (Davis, 1995).

Beyond gender differences in expressing emotions, meta-analytic studies indicate that women are significantly more adept than men in *decoding* nonverbal emotional signals. For example, in a review of seventy-five studies testing the ability of men and women to decode nonverbal behavior, Judith Hall (1978) found that 68 percent of the investigations reported superior female performance. Later meta-analyses found that this gender difference is greatest for decoding facial expressions, next largest for body cues, and smallest for correctly interpreting voice tone (Hall, 1984). The studies further suggest that this gender difference is not isolated in adult samples but can also be found in adolescents and children. Although these gender differences vary in size from study to study, women appear to be consistently better than men at decoding nonverbal cues signifying emotions (Brody & Hall, 2010).

As with emotional expression, psychologists principally explain these gender differences in reading nonverbal emotional cues by examining the different social roles played by women and men. Because the social roles played by women tend to have lower status relative to male roles, it is more important for women to learn to be accommodating and polite (Hall & Mast, 2008). Thus, by being more skilled at nonverbal communication, women of all ages are better able to understand people's feelings and thus increase their interpersonal comfort. This explanation is consistent with research indicating that regardless of gender, those who have less powerful social roles are more sensitive to the feelings of their superiors than vice versa (Hecht & LaFrance, 1998).

Section REVIEW

- Emotions are positive or negative feeling states.

- Evolutionary theories emphasize the survival value of emotions; they motivate us to avoid what is harmful and approach what is beneficial. Emotional expressions and behaviors also foster communication with others.

- The James-Lange theory and the Cannon-Bard theory disagree on whether physiological responses precede emotions.

- Emotions reflecting approach or avoidance can occur automatically and prior to conscious interpretation.

- Three brain regions are central in controlling emotions: the hypothalamus, the limbic system, and the cerebral cortex's frontal lobes.

- Cognitive appraisals help broaden the emotional experience, creating further definition and interpretation of the initial approach or avoidance response.

- One emotional experience may trigger an opposite emotional experience.

PSYCHOLOGICAL
applications

How Can You Manage Your Emotions and Control Test Anxiety?

As you read in Section 9.4b, our desire for success and our fear of failure can trigger high levels of anxiety in achievement situations. In academic achievement settings, test anxiety can seriously undermine our ability to demonstrate our intellectual skills (Seipp, 1991). Such anxiety is generally acknowledged to be a multidimensional problem, typified by worry over performance, emotional symptoms, and distracted thoughts.

Two prevailing views about the cause of test anxiety include (1) heightened anxiety blocking retrieval of learned information (Sarason et al., 1990) and (2) poor encoding and organizing skills leading to poorer preparation, and thus anxiety resulting from this realization (Birenbaum & Pinku, 1997). These two sources of performance decrements could act independently or interact. That is, poor preparation could affect performance, whether in evaluative situations or not; but worry about performance could further hinder performance under evaluative situations.

Therefore, given adequate preparation, test-anxious students have been found to perform worse than non-test-anxious students under evaluative conditions but comparably well under nonevaluative, nonthreatening conditions (Birenbaum & Pinku, 1997). This means that when information is asked for directly—as is the case when taking exams—anxiety can interfere with performance or retrieval.

How can test anxiety, or its effects on performance, be reduced? Regardless of the source of test anxiety, adequate preparation is crucial: Students must develop good study skills. Some common suggestions for improving preparation include the following:

- Go to all your classes, find out what you're expected to know, and find out when the exams are scheduled.

- Study and read as the course goes along to avoid "cramming" for exams.

- Have a study schedule that makes it easier to avoid more enjoyable distractions. Study where you can concentrate, get interested in the material, and give it your complete attention.

- Make flashcards and review them often.

- Learn how to take good notes by comparing your notes with those of others or by going over them with your instructor. Go over them right after class and review periodically.

- Make outlines and summary sheets. Ask yourself, "What is the important information?" Reciting the material in your own words will help you encode the material more deeply.

- Join a study group with motivated classmates; this is often helpful.

- Use your college's academic assistance center. (Most colleges have these centers to help improve students' study and test-taking skills; free tutoring is also usually available.)

Here are some tips to handle the "anxiety" aspects of preparing for and taking tests:

- *Keep tests in perspective.* You're more than just a test taker or a student. Often, people with the greatest test anxiety assume themselves a failure if they have not done well on an earlier exam. A test is only a test—dwelling on past mistakes will only keep you from focusing on the current or next challenge.

- *Break tasks down into more manageable bits.* By setting more realistic goals in terms of the level and extent of what can be accomplished, you can make your emotional response less severe than it might be otherwise. Time management will help with this.

- *Relax while preparing for an exam.* If you find yourself becoming "worked up" over an upcoming exam, find ways to counteract the emotions (for example, try progressive relaxation, described in Chapter 12). Your anxious emotions will interfere with encoding information. Additionally, get plenty of sleep.

- *Practice relaxation during the test, taking a moment to breathe deeply and close your eyes.* Read through the entire exam, just to get a sense of what's there; and then begin with the "friendly" questions—the ones you readily know the answers to. Focus your attention by not allowing yourself to worry, "What if I fail this exam?" Relax again and focus only on the task at hand.

Most of these suggestions require practice and time. If your anxiety about tests is disrupting your performance and is a concern to you, go to your college's counseling services center. Have them assess your test anxiety and provide you with help on trying to handle it.

Suggested Websites

Thematic Apperception Test Research

http://web.utk.edu/~wmorgan/tat/tattxt.htm

At this website, you can discover the history of the TAT.

Procrastination Research Group

http://www.carleton.ca/~tpychyl

This website contains information on the psychology of procrastination.

Emotional Intelligence Information

http://www.unh.edu/emotional_intelligence

This is a review by John D. Mayer of the scientific literature on emotional intelligence, including sections on managing emotions and controversies surrounding emotional intelligence theories.

Study Skills Self-Help Information

http://www.ucc.vt.edu/stdysk/stdyhlp.html

This website provides time management strategies for improving academic performance.

Key Terms

Acquaintance rape, 408
Bisexuality, 414
Cannon-Bard theory, 430
Drive, 396
Drive-reduction theory, 395
Emotion, 425
Extrinsic motivation, 398
Facial feedback hypothesis, 430
Heterosexism, 416
Heterosexuality, 414
Hierarchy of needs, 400
Homeostasis, 395
Homosexuality, 414

Incentive, 397
Incentive theory, 397
Instinct, 395
Intrinsic motivation, 398
James-Lange theory, 429
Motivation, 394
Need for achievement
   (n-Ach), 421
Need to belong, 419
Opponent-process theory, 436
Polygraph, 431
Rape myth, 408
Satiety, 401

Self-actualization, 400
Set point, 404
Sexual identity, 415
Sexual orientation, 414
Sexual response cycle, 413
Sexual script, 408
Testosterone, 413
Thematic Apperception Test
   (TAT), 421
Two-factor theory, 435
Yerkes-Dodson law, 397

Review Questions

1. What is one of the clear advantages of the drive-reduction theory of motivation over instinct theory?
   a. Drive-reduction theory explains why people engage in behaviors that do not reduce a drive.
   b. Drive-reduction theory accounts for low levels of arousal as well as high levels of arousal.
   c. Drive-reduction theory explains a much wider range of behavior than instinct theory.
   d. Drive-reduction theory accounts for all areas of human motivation.
   e. Drive-reduction theory does not rely on the role of learning in motivation.

2. Which of the following is true of the Yerkes-Dodson law?
   a. It describes the fixed level of optimal arousal at which all humans respond best.
   b. It claims that arousal levels vary according to environmental factors, suggesting that individuals exhibit no consistency in arousal levels.
   c. It states that individuals strive to maintain consistently low levels of arousal.
   d. It states that individuals strive to maintain consistently high levels of arousal.
   e. It states that individuals strive to maintain intermediate levels of arousal.

3. Research on intrinsic motivation indicates which of the following?
   a. The best method for enhancing a child's motivation for doing chores is a tangible reward such as money.
   b. Rewards based on verbal praise are less likely than those based on candy treats to undermine intrinsic motivation.
   c. There is little support for incentive theory, which focuses on the role of internal states in motivation.
   d. Intrinsic motivation leads a person to engage in behavior to obtain incentives.
   e. The principal reason certain activities are intrinsically motivating is that they allow the person to achieve homeostasis.

4. According to research on sexual motivation, which of the following is true?
   a. Men report enjoying different types of sexual activity more than do women.
   b. Women desire more frequent sexual partners than men because it helps ensure that they will bear offspring.
   c. Sex is motivated exclusively by physiological needs such as the pleasure instinct.
   d. Sex is motivated exclusively by socioemotional needs, including the need for intimacy.
   e. Evolutionary and sociocultural explanations for sexual motivation contradict one another.

5. Sociocultural explanations for gender differences in sexual behavior emphasize traditional sexual scripts that do which of the following?
   a. describe playful approaches to sexual behavior that enhance motivation
   b. are generally the same for men and women
   c. are learned behaviors that emphasize male dominance (for example, bragging) and female resistance to sexual advances
   d. have been found helpful in reducing acquaintance rape but not the rape myth
   e. are not harmful and may even be beneficial in the context of consensual sexual relations.

6. Sexual orientation has been found to be associated with all except which of the following?
   a. differences in the size of the hypothalamus and the corpus callosum
   b. childhood preferences for same-sex or opposite-sex activities
   c. sexual orientation of identical twins
   d. sexual orientation of parents and/or primary caregivers
   e. childhood gender role and same-sex or other-sex friends

7. The regulation of eating behavior is not associated with which of the following?
   a. the presence of CCK in the blood.
   b. a hunger on-off switch located in the hypothalamus
   c. external cues such as the rattling of dishes
   d. neurotransmitters such as serotonin
   e. the self-esteem of restrained eaters

8. What have researchers studying the effects of food deprivation and overeating found?
   a. The number of fat cells individuals have may be related to their set point.
   b. When the body's fat cells fall below a certain limit, they release leptin, which increases hunger.
   c. When people gain or lose weight, they also gain or lose fat cells.
   d. The percentage of Americans 30 percent or more above their ideal body weight has decreased since 1991.
   e. It is not possible to change your body's set point.

9. Which of the following is likely to be true of individuals with a high need for achievement?
   a. They may be motivated by either a fear of failure or a desire for success.
   b. They approach all achievement challenges with equally strong desires for success.
   c. They choose extremely difficult or challenging tasks.
   d. They choose extremely easy tasks to ensure the success they desire.
   e. They have an intrinsic desire to succeed.

10. Which of the following may enhance achievement motivation?
    a. reducing emotional identification with the achievement task
    b. frequent feedback when progress on the task is slow
    c. convincing people that the task is something important to them
    d. protecting the individual from experience with failure
    e. providing easy tasks that guarantee success

11. Emotions, defined as positive or negative feeling states or evaluative responses, share all, except which, of the following characteristics?
    a. The expression of emotions is not altered by learning or culture.
    b. Emotions communicate information between people.
    c. Emotions involve a variety of physiological reactions.
    d. Emotions help individuals respond to changes in the environment.
    e. Emotions are partly generated by cognitive appraisals of situations.

12. Cross-cultural research on emotions indicates which of the following?
    a. Collectivist cultures experience emotions differently from individualist cultures.
    b. Individualist cultures can accurately read more emotions than collectivist cultures.
    c. Ten primary emotions have been identified across all cultures.
    d. Support for the notion that facial expressions of emotion vary according to cultural beliefs.
    e. There are no differences among cultures in the facial expression of emotions.

13. Which of the following findings supports the James-Lange theory of emotion ?
    a. Associations between specific physiological changes and emotional experiences vary by culture.
    b. Emotional changes cannot be generated by changes in bodily states.
    c. The subjective experience of emotion involves cognition.
    d. Anger and fear produce greater heart rate acceleration than does happiness.
    e. The experience of emotion precedes the physiological changes that automatically occur in response to environmental stimuli.

14. Which of the following statements is true regarding how the brain coordinates emotional responses?
    a. A key component in human emotional responses is the hippocampus.
    b. The limbic system is important for processing emotions and the frontal lobes are important for experiencing emotions.
    c. The left frontal lobe is associated with aversion-related emotions and the right frontal lobe is associated with approach-related emotions.
    d. After eating, the ability to experience strong emotions is compromised because the hypothalamus not only regulates strong emotions, it also regulates eating.
    e. The brain areas that first process emotional responses are the left and right frontal lobes, with more complex processing later occurring in the amygdala.

15. According to Solomon's opponent-process theory of emotion, which of the following is true?
    a. Repeating an experience weakens the initial emotional reaction and strengthens the subsequent emotional reaction.
    b. The craving associated with drug abuse is motivated by the pleasure it provides.
    c. Men who encountered an attractive female on a high bridge interpreted their arousal as being caused by fear rather than sexual attraction.
    d. The interpretation of emotional arousal in ambiguous situations will be influenced by cues in the immediate environment.
    e. Repeating an experience strengthens the initial emotional reaction and weakens the subsequent emotional reaction.

Chapter Ten

Personality

Chapter Outline

"It is totally me, Dad!"

This was my daughter Amelia's reaction a few years ago upon reading the "personality profile" she received from the handwriting analysis machine at Michigan's Upper Peninsula State Fair. After Amelia slipped her signature into the "Data Entry" slot (and paid a $2 fee to the cashier), the lights on the graphology machine's cardboard façade flashed furiously before the machine spit out its evaluation. As Amelia marveled at the accuracy of her personality profile, I noticed a partially hidden worker placing a fresh stack of pretyped profiles into the "Completed Profile" slot behind the machine. At that moment, a scene from *The Wizard of Oz* ran through my mind. It was the scene where Dorothy returns to Oz and presents the dead witch's broom to the all-powerful Wizard. As the huge, disembodied head of the Wizard blusters and bellows at Dorothy, her dog, Toto, pulls back a curtain revealing that the Wizard is really just an ordinary man manipulating people's impressions with smoke and mirrors.

That day at the fair, I decided not to tell Amelia about the man behind the machine. Sometime later, however, we talked a bit about the validity of handwriting analysis, palm reading, and horoscopes. Put simply, these techniques that claim to assess personality have no scientific validity (Beyerstein & Beyerstein, 1992; Kelly, 1997). They provide assessments that appear remarkably accurate in divining our unique characteristics because they are either flattering to our egos or generally true of everybody (Forer, 1949). For example, consider the following generic description of personality:

You are an independent thinker, but you have a strong need to be liked and respected by others. At times, you are outgoing and extraverted, while at other times, you are reserved and introverted. You have found it unwise to be too frank in revealing yourself to others. While you have some personality weaknesses, you can generally compensate for them. You tend to be critical of yourself. You have a great deal of potential, but you have not yet fully harnessed it. Some of your aspirations are pretty unrealistic.

When college students were provided with personality assessments similar to this one and told that an astrologer had prepared the profiles just for them, almost all the students evaluated the accuracy of these descriptions as either "good" or "excellent" (Davies, 1997; Glick et al., 1989). Further, after receiving their assessments, students were more likely to believe that astrology was a valid way to assess personality. This tendency to accept global and ambiguous feedback about oneself—even if the source of the information lacks credibility—is known as the *Barnum effect*, in honor of master showman P. T. Barnum. Barnum credited his success in the circus industry to the fact that "there's a sucker born every minute."

Now I am not suggesting that my daughter and the majority of college students are "suckers" waiting to be fleeced of their money by unscrupulous fortune hunters. I am suggesting that there is a more accurate—and, yes, more ethical—way to understand our personalities. It is through the application of the scientific method. In this chapter, we continue our journey of discovery through psychology by venturing behind the scientific "curtain" of personality theory and research. I think you will find that this particular journey reveals much more than the smoke and mirrors effects typically created by graphologists, palm readers, and astrologers.

Cute is when your personality shines through your looks. Like, when you see someone's personality in the way they walk and you just feel like hugging them every time you see them.

—Natalie Portman, American actress, b. 1981

10.1 The Nature of Personality

Before reading further, spend a few minutes identifying certain recurring ways in which you respond across a variety of situations. In addition, identify ways in which you think, feel, or behave that set you apart from many other people. Which of these personal qualities help you successfully meet life's challenges?

10.1a *Consistency and Distinctiveness Define Personality.*

One important quality of personality is *consistency* in thinking, feeling, and acting. We consider people to be consistent when we see them responding in the same way in a variety of situations and over an extended period of time. Of course, people do not respond with consistency entirely; but in order for us to notice that they have a characteristic way of thinking, feeling, and behaving, they must respond consistently across many situations and over time. For instance, you may have a friend who argues at the drop of a hat. This aspect of his interaction style is consistent enough that you have a pretty good idea how he will act around others, regardless of whether they are friends, relatives, or strangers.

Distinctiveness is another important quality of personality because it is used to explain why everyone does not act the same in similar situations. Return to the example of your argumentative friend. Because most people generally try to find points of agreement when interacting with others, your friend's argumentative style is distinctive, setting him apart from most people.

Overall, then, when we study personality, we are studying how people are consistent across situations and how they differ from one another. For our purposes, **personality** is defined as the *consistent* and *distinctive* thoughts, feelings, and behaviors in which an individual engages. This definition has its roots in philosophy as much as in science. For that reason, parts of this chapter may seem like they are describing a different kind of psychology—a more speculative and less data-driven psychology—than other parts of the chapter. You will most likely notice this during the discussion of psychoanalytic and humanistic approaches to personality. During the second half of the twentieth century, the study of personality followed the rest of the field of psychology and moved away from broad theorizing to scientifically testing hypotheses about personality functioning. Modern personality theorists tend to be much more limited and narrow in their approach to the field. This more modest approach has allowed for clearer descriptions of *personality styles*, though the more overarching and comprehensive descriptions that were present earlier have been lost (Magnavita, 2002). In the later sections of the chapter, these more modern approaches to studying personality functioning are represented by the trait and social-cognitive theories. We also examine various means of assessing or describing personality.

Personality The consistent and distinctive thoughts, feelings, and behaviors in which an individual engages

10.1b *Culture and Evolutionary Processes Shape Personality.*

Personality psychology was developed and has flourished in the North American and Western European social climate of *individualism*. This philosophy of life conceives of people as being unique, independent entities, separate from their social surroundings. In contrast, *collectivism* emphasizes group needs and desires over those of the individual

Consistency and distinctiveness are important qualities of personality. What are your consistent and distinctive personal qualities?

(Singelis et al., 1995). During the past 25 years, as psychology has become more of an international science, personality theorists in individualist societies have devoted more attention to investigating how personality is a product of the individual's interaction with her or his social settings. In adopting this approach, personality theorists are thinking about human behavior in a way similar to that of collectivists (Triandis & Suh, 2002). This *interactionist* perspective on personality is discussed at various points in this chapter (see Sections 10.4d and 10.5a).

In addition to the influence that cultural beliefs can have on the study of personality, research further suggests that cultural beliefs can actually shape personality development (Church & Ortiz, 2005). For example, people from collectivist Latin cultures are often taught to have *simpatía*, which is a way of relating to others that is empathic, respectful, and unselfish and maintains harmonious social relationships (Varela et al., 2007). Likewise, the Chinese concept of *ren qin* (relationship orientation) and the Japanese concept of *amae* (indulgent dependence) emphasize social ties and dependence on others (Yu, 2007). Individuals who internalize these social norms will develop a personality style that is characteristic of their social group and may be relatively uncommon in other cultures (Ho et al., 2001).

Although personality styles may be associated with particular cultures, most personality researchers strive to identify universal aspects of personality. In this regard, a growing number of social scientists are beginning to examine how certain aspects of personality have been shaped over the course of our species' evolutionary history (Ridley et al., 2005). According to this viewpoint, because the evolutionary process is the only known creative process capable of producing complex organisms, all theories of human nature, including personality theories, must consider the basic principles of evolution by natural selection (see Chapter 1, Section 1.2e). Consistent with this viewpoint, in this chapter we periodically offer an evolutionary account of personality.

Section **REVIEW**

- Personality research examines how people are consistent across situations and how they differ from one another.

- Not only does culture influence how personality is studied, but also many contemporary psychologists study how both cultural and evolutionary forces shape personalities.

10.2 **The Psychoanalytic Perspective**

The most recognizable person in the field of psychology—Sigmund Freud—was not trained as a psychologist. Freud (1856–1939) grew up in Austria, was trained as a physician in Vienna, and aspired to become a university professor. Early in his professional career as a medical doctor, he studied the nervous system in the hope of applying newly discovered principles of physics and chemistry to the functioning of the human mind. In addition to teaching and doing laboratory work, Freud worked with patients (mostly women) who complained about problems with the functioning of their nervous systems. However, he frequently discovered that their symptoms seemed to originate from emotional trauma. Over time, Freud developed the idea that the young science of psychology held answers to many of these perplexing disorders (Freud, 1917).

An example of the kind of medical problem that set Freud on his journey of discovery into psychology was a strange neurological-like condition referred to as *glove*

FIGURE 10-1 Glove Anesthesia

Glove anesthesia describes numbness in the entire hand, ending at the wrist. The skin areas served by nerves in the arm are shown in (a). Glove anesthesia, depicted in (b), cannot be caused by nerve damage. The realization that such a condition was likely caused by emotional trauma led Freud to develop psychoanalytic theory, which emphasized unconscious conflict.

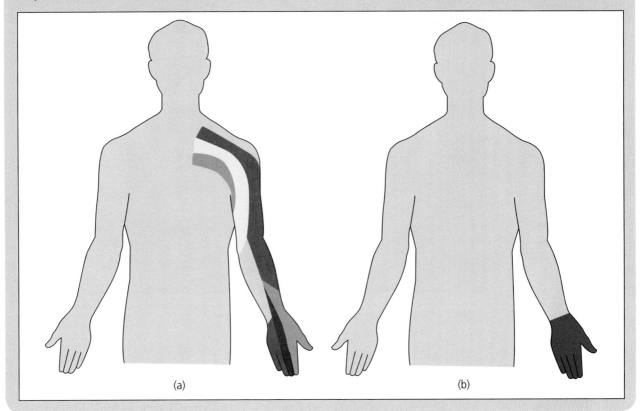

(a)   (b)

anesthesia (see Figure 10-1). In this condition, the patient has no feeling from the wrists to the tips of the fingers but does have feeling in the forearms. Glove anesthesia is not consistent with the way the nervous system functions, which suggested to Freud that its cause was not physiological but psychological (Freud, 1895/1966). As you will see, this idea revolutionized the study of personality in the early 1900s.

10.2a Psychoanalytic Theory Asserts That the Unconscious Controls Behavior.

When Freud suspected that some of the medical problems of his patients were in fact caused by emotional disturbances, he sought the advice of French neurologist Jean Charcot, who was treating such patients using hypnosis (Gay, 1998). Freud was also impressed by psychiatrist Joseph Breuer's "talking cure" therapy, in which patients with emotional problems were told to report whatever came to mind. Adapting these two techniques, Freud encouraged his patients to talk about their symptoms and what was occurring when the symptoms emerged. As they did this, Freud developed the idea that their symptoms were psychologically related to some sort of problem or dilemma they were experiencing. For instance, the previously described glove anesthesia of one of his young patients developed soon after she became aware of her emerging sexual urges. Stimulating herself with her hand was simultaneously very pleasurable and extremely anxiety-inducing. Freud believed that to prevent the expression of this

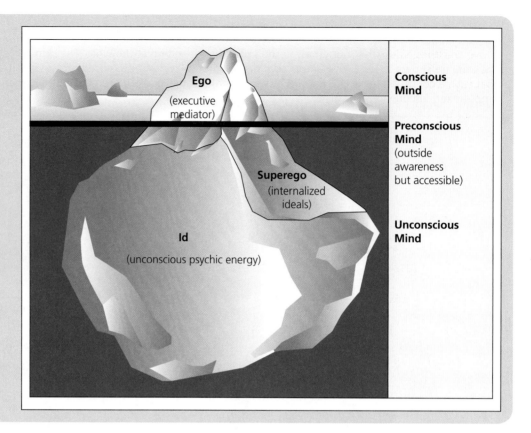

FIGURE 10-2

Freud's Model of Personality Structure

In Freud's theory of personality, the mind is likened to an iceberg: the conscious mind is the small part of the iceberg visible above the water line and the unconscious mind is that part of the iceberg below the surface. The ego includes part of the conscious mind and part of the unconscious mind. The same is true of the superego, whereas the id is completely unconscious.

Ego
(executive mediator)

Superego
(internalized ideals)

Id
(unconscious psychic energy)

Conscious Mind

Preconscious Mind
(outside awareness but accessible)

Unconscious Mind

Conscious mind According to Freud, the relatively small part of our minds that we are aware of at the moment

Preconscious mind According to Freud, those mental processes that are not currently conscious but could become so at any moment

Unconscious mind According to Freud, the thoughts, desires, feelings, and memories that are not consciously available to us but that nonetheless shape our everyday behavior

unacceptable urge to sexually gratify herself, the woman unconsciously "deadened" her hand, making it unusable. Piecing together his patients' accounts of their lives while under hypnosis, Freud believed that he had discovered the unconscious mind.

Freud's model of the mind proposed that it was mostly hidden, like an iceberg (S. Freud, 1917). As depicted in Figure 10-2, our **conscious mind** is the relatively small part of our mind that we are aware of at the moment, like the tip of the iceberg that is visible above the surface of the water. Right now, your conscious processes include (I hope!) the material from the previous sentences, perhaps an awareness of certain stimuli in your surroundings, and maybe the thought that you would like to be doing something else other than reading this book. Immediately below the surface of the conscious mind resides the **preconscious mind**, which consists of those mental processes that are not currently conscious but could become so at any moment. Examples of preconscious material might include your parents' phone number, hopefully some of the material from previous sections of this book, and a conversation you had yesterday with a friend. Below this preconscious level resides the **unconscious mind**, which is like the huge section of the iceberg that is hidden in the water's depths. The unconscious mind is driven by biological urges that have been shaped by our evolutionary history, and it contains thoughts, desires, feelings, and memories that are not consciously available to us but that nonetheless shape our everyday behavior. Examples of unconscious material are painful, forgotten memories from childhood, hidden feelings of hostility toward someone you profess to like (or even love), and sexual urges that would create intense anxiety if you became aware of them.

Freud's theory of the mind was an important milestone in the history of psychology because it challenged the prevailing notion that our consciousness was the determining factor in the management and control of behavior. As you will see in later sections of this chapter, opposition to Freud's perspective on what determines human behavior spawned a number of competing personality theories.

10.2b *Freud Divided Personality into the Id, the Ego, and the Superego.*

As Freud continued treating patients with psychological problems, he proposed another dimension to his theory of the mind, which came to be called the *structural model*. According to Freud, personality consisted of three subcomponents, or structures: the *id*, the *ego*, and the *superego*. Each structure has different operating principles and different goals, and frequently the goals of one component conflict with the goals of another component. This model of the mind is sometimes called a *conflict model* because it attempts to explain how psychological conflicts determine behavior.

The **id**—which in Latin means "it"—is an entirely unconscious portion of the mind. It contains the basic drives for reproduction, survival, and aggression. The id operates on the **pleasure principle**, meaning that it consistently wants to satisfy, as quickly and directly as possible, whatever desire is currently active. The id's agenda, as directed by the pleasure principle, might be summarized by the statement "if it feels good, do it." Freud believed that newborn infants represent the purest form of id impulses, crying whenever their needs are not immediately satisfied. He further proposed that a part of our personality continues to function like those newborns—wanting needs met immediately—throughout our lives.

 **INFO-BIT**

Hollywood has incorporated Freud's personality theory into many of its movies. For example, in the 1956 science-fiction classic, *Forbidden Planet*, an Earth scientist living on a distant planet greatly expands the power of his mind—and unknowingly, his id—by using alien technology. When a space cruiser from planet Earth visits, his id—externalized as an invisible monster—destroys anyone who expresses sexual interest in the scientist's lovely daughter.

Id An unconscious part of the mind that contains our sexual and aggressive drives

Pleasure principle The process by which the id seeks to immediately satisfy whatever desire is currently active

Ego The part of our minds that includes our consciousness and that balances the demands of the id, the superego, and reality

Reality principle The process by which the ego seeks to delay gratification of id desires until appropriate outlets and situations can be found

Superego The part of our minds that includes our conscience and counterbalances the more primitive demands of the id

One of life's realities is that our needs are seldom immediately satisfied. Freud asserted that as infants, whenever immediate gratification does not occur, we experience distress and anxiety. As a way to cope with this infantile stress, the **ego**—which in Latin means "I"—develops out of the id. Its function is to be the decision-making part of the personality that satisfies id impulses in socially acceptable ways. In performing this function, the ego is both partially conscious and partially unconscious. The conscious part of the ego is in contact with external reality, while the unconscious part is in contact with the id. In seeking id satisfaction, the ego is guided by the **reality principle**, which is the process by which it seeks to delay gratification of id desires until appropriate outlets and situations can be found. The ego is interested in achieving pleasure but learns that this will more likely occur if the constraints of reality are taken into account.

The **superego**—which in Latin means "over the I"—develops later in childhood, around age 4 or 5. The superego has several functions, including the task of overseeing the ego and making sure that it acts morally. As such, the superego is concerned not just with what is acceptable but also with what is ideal. It provides us with a conscience, making us feel guilty when we do "wrong" and instilling pride when we do "right." Essentially,

Imagine how you might behave if you had no ego and simply acted, instead, on your id desires. How long do you think you would remain healthy, acting on impulse and unchecked by ego restraint?

the superego represents the internalization of cultural norms and values into the individual mind. Not surprisingly, the superego and the id are frequently at odds about the proper course of action in a given situation. The ego balances the demands of the id and superego, along with those of external reality, to generate behavior that will still bring pleasure.

Although this description of the three personality components appears to suggest that the ego (our conscious self) is controlling our behavior, Freud contended that this is largely an illusion. Throughout our daily activities, we are generally unaware of the unconscious compromises that our ego makes to create a particular outcome. For example, a college sophomore may agree to spend hours tutoring a group of first-year students, unaware of how his sexual attraction to one member of the group figured in his decision. He may be conscious of feeling altruistic about helping these students, and thus his superego is satisfied; however, he is largely unaware of how his ego has unconsciously allowed his id to be gratified as well.

10.2c *Personality Development Occurs in Psychosexual Stages.*

Psychosexual stages The fixed sequence of childhood developmental stages during which the id primarily seeks sexual pleasure by focusing its energies on distinct erogenous zones

Fixation A tendency to persist in pleasure-seeking behaviors associated with an earlier psychosexual stage during which conflicts were unresolved

As Freud listened to his patients during therapy, they repeatedly mentioned significant events from their childhood that left them with emotional scars. Based on his patients' reconstruction of their lives, Freud created a theory about how personality develops and how the ego and superego come into existence (Stern, 1985). Consistent with the idea that personality involves a degree of consistency, his psychoanalytic theory proposed that children pass through a fixed sequence of **psychosexual stages**. Each stage is characterized by a part of the body, called an *erogenous zone*, through which the id primarily seeks sexual pleasure. Critical elements of the personality are formed during each of these stages (see Table 10-1). If children experience conflicts when seeking pleasure during a particular psychosexual stage, and if these conflicts go unresolved, the children will become psychologically "stuck"—or *fixated*—at that stage. **Fixation** is a tendency to persist in pleasure-seeking behaviors associated with an earlier psychosexual stage where conflicts were unresolved. One important point to keep in mind about fixation is that the conflicts that trigger fixation can be caused by either too little or too much gratification of id desires.

TABLE 10-1   Freud's Stages of Psychosexual Development

Stage	Approximate Age	Erogenous Zone	Key Tasks and Experiences
Oral	0–1	Mouth (sucking, biting)	Weaning (from breast or bottle)
Anal	2–3	Anus (defecating)	Toilet training
Phallic	4–5	Genitals (masturbating)	Coping with Oedipal/Electra conflict and identifying with same-sex parent
Latency	6–11	None (sexual desires repressed)	Developing same-sex contacts
Genital	Puberty onward	Genitals (being sexually intimate)	Establishing mature sexual relationships

Journey of Discovery

An increasing number of contemporary personality theorists pay attention to how culture and evolutionary forces shape personality. Is there any evidence in Freud's theory of personality that he considered the impact that culture and evolution had on personality?

Oral Stage

The first stage of psychosexual development, which encompasses the first year of life, is referred to as the **oral stage**. During this stage, infants are totally dependent on those around them to care for their needs, especially nourishment. Freud believed that the id derives intense sexual pleasure by engaging in oral activities such as sucking, biting, and chewing. Adults with fixations at the oral stage are often extremely clingy and emotionally dependent on others. In attempting to satisfy oral needs, they might smoke excessively and/or spend a great deal of time eating and thinking about eating.

Oral stage In Freud's theory, the first stage of psychosexual development, during which the child derives pleasure by engaging in oral activities

Anal Stage

The **anal stage** follows the oral stage, as the focus of erotic pleasure shifts from the mouth to the process of elimination. This psychosexual stage begins at about age 2, when toilet training becomes an area of conflict between children and parents. Freud argued that from the child's point of view, toilet training represents the parents' attempt at denying the child's primary pleasure by exerting control over where and when urination and defecation occur. Fixation at this stage, caused by overly harsh toilet-training experiences, produces children who too closely conform to the demands of parents and other caretakers. As adults, they will be excessively neat and orderly (this is the source of the term *anal retentive*). Overly relaxed toilet-training experiences can also cause fixation, with individuals forever being messy and having difficulty complying with authority and keeping their behavior under control (*anal expulsive*). Successful negotiation of this stage results in a capacity to engage in directed work without being dominated by the need to perform perfectly.

Anal stage In Freud's theory, the second stage of psychosexual development, during which the child derives pleasure from defecation

Phallic Stage

At about age 4, children enter the **phallic stage**, which is characterized by a shift in the erogenous zone to the genitals and pleasure being derived largely through self-stimulation. According to Freud, accompanying this interest in genital stimulation is the association of this pleasure with the other-sex parent. Freud asserted that boys develop an erotic attachment to their mothers and girls develop a similar attachment to their fathers. Soon, however, children realize that they are in competition with their same-sex parents for the attention and affection of their other-sex parents.

Phallic stage In Freud's theory, the third stage of psychosexual development during which the child derives pleasure from masturbation

Among boys, Freud related this dilemma to a character in ancient Greek literature, Oedipus Rex, who became king by unknowingly marrying his mother after murdering his father. This *Oedipus complex* arouses fear in boys that their fathers will punish them for their sexual desires for the mother. Freud asserted that this fear of the loss of genital pleasure is psychologically represented as *castration anxiety*, which is the fear that the father will cut off the penis.

Among girls, instead of being afraid that their mothers will harm them, Freud believed that they are likely to express anger because they believe that their mothers have already inflicted the harm: by removing their penis. This "mother conflict" is known as the *Electra complex*, after another Greek character that had her mother killed. Freud asserted that the penis envy that girls experience during this stage stems from their belief that this anatomical "deficiency" is evidence of their inferiority to boys.

Successful negotiation of the phallic stage requires that children purge their sexual desires for their other-sex parents and bury their fear and anger toward their same-sex parents. Children accomplish these dual feats by identifying with the competitive parents. According to Freud, this process of identification is critical for the development of a healthy adult personality because this is how children internalize their parents' values. This internalization of parental values—which generally mirror larger societal values—is critical in the development of the superego. Less-successful negotiation of this stage can cause people to become chronically timid because they fear that they do not "measure up" to their rivaled same-sex parent.

Latency Stage

Latency stage In Freud's theory, the fourth stage of psychosexual development during which the child is relatively free from sexual desires and conflict

From about ages 6 to 11, children are in a psychological period of relative calm, called the **latency stage**. During this time, the content of the dramatic struggles in the oral, anal, and phallic stages is forgotten by the ego. Although the ego is relatively free from interference by the id, sexual, aggressive, and other id impulses are still present and must be managed. Often this is accomplished by channeling these desires into socially acceptable activities in school, sports, and the arts.

Genital Stage

Genital stage In Freud's theory, the last stage of psychosexual development during which mature sexual feelings toward others begin to emerge, and the ego learns to manage and direct these feelings

Latency is followed by puberty and the onset of the **genital stage**. During adolescence, many of the issues of the earlier stages re-emerge and can be reworked to a certain extent. Mature sexual feelings toward others also begin to emerge, and the ego learns to manage and direct these feelings. Of all the stages, Freud spent the least amount of time discussing the psychological dynamics of the genital stage. This was probably due to his belief that personality was largely determined by age 5.

10.2d *Defense Mechanisms Reduce or Redirect Unconsciously Caused Anxiety.*

Repression In Freud's theory, a very basic defense mechanism in which people move anxiety-arousing thoughts from the conscious mind into the unconscious mind

Defense mechanism In Freud's theory, the ego's method of keeping threatening and unacceptable material out of consciousness and thereby reducing anxiety

When Freud was first developing his theory of the mind, he proposed that people managed to move anxiety-arousing thoughts into the unconscious through the use of a very basic defense mechanism that he called **repression**. As Freud's model developed from a relatively simple one to one with greater levels of complexity, he developed the idea that the ego uses a variety of more-sophisticated **defense mechanisms** to keep threatening and unacceptable material out of consciousness and thereby reduce anxiety (Freud, 1926). His daughter, Anna Freud (1936), later more fully described how these ego defense mechanisms reduce anxiety.

Defense mechanisms are important features of psychoanalytic theory because they explain why humans—whom Freud believed are essentially driven by sexual and aggressive urges—can become civilized. Furthermore, Freud asserted that the particular defense mechanisms that people rely on most often in adapting to life's challenges become distinguishing features of their personalities. Thus, Freud would tell us that although we have probably used most of the defense mechanisms described in Table 10-2 at least once in our lives, our personality could be described

TABLE 10-2   Major Ego Defense Mechanisms

Repression	Pushing high-anxiety-inducing thoughts out of consciousness and keeping them unconscious; the most basic of the defense mechanisms
Rationalization	Offering seemingly logical self-justifying explanations for attitudes, beliefs, or behavior in place of the real unconscious reasons
Reaction formation	Preventing unacceptable feelings or ideas from being directly expressed by expressing opposing feelings or ideas
Displacement	Discharging sexual or aggressive urges toward objects that are more acceptable than those that initially created the arousal
Projection	Perceiving one's own sexual or aggressive urges not in oneself but in others
Regression	Psychologically retreating to an earlier developmental stage where psychic energy remains fixated

by that configuration of defenses on which we rely most heavily. He would also say that under extreme stress, we might begin to use more powerful defenses, which are also more primitive and associated with psychological disorders.

Rationalization is probably one of the more familiar defense mechanisms. It involves offering seemingly logical self-justifying explanations for our attitudes, beliefs, or behavior in place of the real, unconscious reasons. For instance, we might say that we are punishing someone "for her own good," when in reality the punishment primarily serves to express our anger at the person. Have you ever been romantically rejected and then convinced yourself that you never really cared for the person in the first place? Freud might say this was your ego's attempt to defend you against feelings of worthlessness.

Reaction formation allows us to express an unacceptable feeling or idea by consciously expressing its exact opposite. Thus, if we are interested in sex (and according to Freud we all are) but are uncomfortable with this interest, we might devote ourselves to combating pornography. Such action allows us to think about sex but in an acceptable way. Of course, there are nondefensive reasons to oppose pornography or to engage in other activities that could indicate a reaction formation. In fact, one of Freud's primary ideas is that all human actions are *multiply determined*, meaning that each behavior has many causes.

Displacement is a defense mechanism that diverts our sexual or aggressive urges toward objects that are more acceptable than the one actually stimulating our feelings. This is commonly referred to as the "kick the dog" defense, when we unconsciously vent our aggressive impulses toward a threatening teacher, parent, or boss on a helpless creature, such as the family pet. Similarly, we might displace sexual feelings away from a parent because that is unacceptable and date, instead, someone who is remarkably like dear old mom or dad.

Projection is one of the more powerful defense mechanisms and can involve quite serious distortions of others' motivations. In projection, we perceive our own aggressive or sexual urges, not in ourselves, but in others. Thus, an insecure person may falsely accuse other people of being insecure while not recognizing this characteristic in her own personality. Freud contended that we are more likely to use projection when we are feeling strongly threatened, either by the strength of our feelings or the particularly stressful situation we are in. Soldiers in combat, for instance, may begin to see everyone around them as potential enemies who could hurt them.

Rationalization A defense mechanism in which people offer logical, self-justifying explanations for their actions in place of the real, more anxiety-producing, unconscious reasons

Reaction formation A defense mechanism that allows people to express unacceptable feelings or ideas by consciously expressing the exact opposite

Displacement A defense mechanism that diverts people's sexual or aggressive urges toward objects that are more acceptable than those that actually stimulate their feelings

Projection A powerful defense mechanism in which people perceive their own aggressive or sexual urges, not in themselves, but in others

Regression A defense mechanism in which people faced with intense anxiety psychologically retreat to a more infantile developmental stage where some psychic energy remains fixated

Another powerful defense mechanism is **regression**, which occurs when we cannot psychologically function in our current surroundings due to anxiety; and we psychologically retreat to a more infantile developmental stage where some psychic energy remains fixated. For example, following the birth of a younger sibling who threatens an older child's sense of "place" in the family, that older child may lose control of bowel or bladder functions, or return to thumb sucking. When this occurs in adults, it may be a relatively contained regression, such as talking like a baby when working with an authority figure.

10.2e *There Are Many Variations of Psychoanalytic Theory.*

In the 100 years since Freud began developing his personality theory, we have learned a great deal about human behavior, and many psychologists have worked to adapt Freud's theories to what we have learned about how people function. Yet the process of revising Freud's ideas actually began during his lifetime. Three of his closest coworkers—Alfred Adler, Carl Jung, and Karen Horney—disagreed about the central role of sexual drives in the determination of people's personalities (Mayer, 2002). Freud, an authoritarian individual, who demanded strict obedience from his followers, reacted very negatively to such criticism. Let us briefly examine the ideas of some of those individuals who refused to follow Freud's lead. These personality theories, along with Freud's original theory of psychoanalysis, are often given the general label of the **psychodynamic perspective**.

Psychodynamic perspective A diverse group of theories descending from the work of Sigmund Freud that asserts that behavior is controlled by unconscious forces

Adler's Individual Psychology

As a youngster, Alfred Adler (1870–1937) was sickly; and these early illnesses may have shaped his later views of personality development. In 1902 he joined Freud's inner circle of "disciples" who were expected to carry on their master's work while adhering to its basic theoretical principles. However, Adler soon began developing his own ideas about how personality developed, which led to arguments and tension between him and Freud. Adler's view of personality stressed social factors more than did Freud's theory. For example, concerning family dynamics, he felt that Freud focused so much attention on the mother-child-father bonds that he neglected the important influence that siblings can have on personality development. In this regard, Adler was one of the first theorists to write about how birth order shapes personality, and he coined the term *sibling rivalry*.

In 1911, the Freud-Adler relationship ended when Adler proposed his *individual psychology*, which downplayed the importance of sexual motivation and, instead, asserted that people strive for superiority. By this, Adler meant that children generally feel weak and incompetent compared with adults and older children. In turn, these feelings of inferiority motivate them to acquire new skills and develop their untapped potential. Adler (1929) called this process of striving to overcome feelings of inferiority *compensation*. However, for some individuals, such striving can lead to *overcompensation* if the sense of inferiority is excessively strong. Instead of mastering new skills, these people simply seek to obtain outward symbols of status and power, such as money and expensive possessions. By flaunting their success, they try to hide their continuing sense of inferiority.

Jung's Analytical Psychology

Carl Jung (pronounced "Yoong"; 1875–1961), a native of Switzerland and the son of a Protestant pastor, was inspired to become a psychoanalyst by reading Freud's

The Interpretation of Dreams (Freud, 1900/1953). After corresponding with Freud through letters, Jung met Freud for the first time in 1906; and the two men talked nonstop for 13 hours! They quickly became close friends, and Freud viewed his younger protégé as the person most capable of carrying on his work. However, in 1914, after Jung challenged some of Freud's central ideas concerning personality development, their friendship abruptly ended.

Carl Jung, founder analytical psychology

Jung (1916) called his approach *analytical psychology*. Like Adler, Jung de-emphasized the sex motive in his version of psychoanalysis. Instead, he asserted that people are motivated by a desire for psychological growth and wholeness, which he called the *need for individuation*. Jung's idea that humans are motivated to engage in a quest for personal growth later became the central focus of the *humanistic perspective* (see Section 10.3).

Unlike Adler, who also de-emphasized the influence of the unconscious on behavior, Jung agreed with Freud that the unconscious mind has a powerful effect on people's lives. Yet, for Jung, the unconscious was less a reservoir for repressed childhood conflicts and more a reservoir of images from our species' evolutionary past. In studying different cultures and religions, he noticed certain universal images and themes, which were also strikingly similar to the images and themes in his patients' dreams. Based on these observations, Jung asserted that besides our *personal unconscious*, we also have a **collective unconscious**, which is that part of the unconscious mind containing inherited memories shared by all human beings. Jung (1963, 1964) called these inherited memories **archetypes**, and he believed they reveal themselves when our conscious mind is distracted (as in fantasies or art) or inactive (as in dreams). He further believed that archetypes are represented in the religious symbols found throughout the world. Key archetypal figures are *mother*, *father*, *shadow*, *wise old person*, *God*, and *the hero*. Jung also claimed that the feminine and masculine qualities that everyone possesses were represented by the male feminine archetype, anima, and the female masculine archetype, animus. However, the most important archetype is the *self*, which Jung described as the ultimate unity of the personality, symbolized in religions by the circle, the cross, and the mandala.

Although Jung's idea of the collective unconscious has generally been dismissed in mainstream psychology, it has had considerably greater influence in other disciplines, such as anthropology, art, literature, and religious studies (Tacey, 2001). However, one aspect of his personality theory that has been incorporated into mainstream personality theories is the idea that we are born with tendencies to direct our psychological energies either into our inner self or into the outside world (Jung, 1921). **Introverts** are preoccupied with the inner world and tend to be hesitant and cautious when interacting with people. In contrast, **extraverts** are focused on the external world and tend to be confident and socially outgoing.

Collective unconscious In Jung's personality theory, the part of the unconscious mind containing inherited memories shared by all human beings

Archetypes In Jung's personality theory, inherited images that are passed down from our prehistoric ancestors and that reveal themselves as universal symbols in dreams, religion, and art

Introvert A person who is preoccupied with his or her inner world and tends to be hesitant and cautious when interacting with people

Extravert A person who is focused on the external world and tends to be confident and socially outgoing

Carl Jung proposed that universally shared memories within the collective unconscious reveal themselves in religion, art, and popular culture as various archetypal figures. For example, Jung might suggest artist Karl Priebe's dreamlike painting, *Mayor of Tehuantepec*, depicts the archetype of the "wise old person."

Horney's Neo-Freudian Perspective

German physician Karen Horney (pronounced "HOR-nigh"; 1885–1952) was the first influential female psychoanalyst. Like Adler, Horney (1945) believed that social factors played a much larger role in personality development than sexual influences. Instead of personality problems being caused by fixation of psychic energy, Horney believed that problems in interpersonal relationships during childhood created anxiety; this anxiety caused later personality problems. Developmental psychologists later expanded on these ideas by studying how parent-child emotional attachments shape children's personalities (see Chapter 3, Section 3.2a).

Horney was also instrumental in confronting some of Freud's assertions concerning female personality development (W. B. Smith, 2007). Whereas Freud proposed that gender differences in behavior were due to biological factors, Horney proposed social and cultural explanations. Although conceding that women often felt inferior to men, Horney (1926/1967) claimed that this is not due to penis envy but is rather because of the sexism that denied women equal opportunities. What women really envied was the social power and privilege that men enjoyed in the larger society.

An Overall Evaluation of Freud's Legacy

Freud's impact on psychology cannot be dismissed. Indeed, his influence extends into other disciplines that study humans and their behavior, such as anthropology, sociology, literature, and history. Indeed, psychoanalytic theory today may have more influence outside of psychology than within it. For example, a content analysis of 150 highly ranked American colleges and universities found that psychoanalytic ideas are represented somewhere in the curricula of most schools, but significantly more courses feature psychoanalytic ideas outside psychology departments than within them (Redmond & Shulman, 2008).

Despite Freud's influence on the social sciences and the larger culture, a major limitation of his theory is that it is not based on carefully controlled scientific research. Indeed, Freud's entire theory is based on his own self-analysis and a handful of cases from his clinical practice that do not constitute a representative sampling of the human population. As you know from our discussion of scientific methods in Chapter 1, Section 1.3a, a theory's usefulness is difficult to determine if the research sample does not represent the population of interest. Further, reexaminations of Freud's case notes suggest that he may have distorted some of his patients' histories so that they conformed to his view of personality (Esterson, 1993). Related to these criticisms is the fact that Freud did not welcome anyone questioning or challenging his ideas (Gardner, 1993). Such a stance does not advance scientific understanding.

Another criticism of Freud's theory is that many of its psychological processes—such as the id—cannot be observed, much less measured. If aspects of his theory cannot be scientifically tested, then of what use are they to the science of psychology? Further, when scientific studies have tested some of Freud's concepts, they have found little evidence to support the existence of the Oedipal/Electra complex, penis envy, or many of Freud's ideas on sexual and aggressive drives (Crews, 1998).

Despite the inability to test certain portions of Freud's personality theory, and despite the lack of evidence for other portions that have been scientifically tested, a new scientific movement has developed in recent years to bridge the gap between Freud's theory and science. Employing brain-imaging techniques and other neuroscientific methods, researchers in the field of *neuropsychoanalysis* claim that at least the following four general ideas concerning personality have received empirical support (Olds, 2012; Panksepp & Solms, 2012):

1. Unconscious processes shape human behavior.

2. Childhood experiences shape adult personality.

3. Learning to regulate impulses is critical for healthy development.

4. Some dreams are associated with wish fulfillment.

Given these continuing contributions, psychoanalysis still deserves recognition as an important, albeit flawed, perspective on personality. As long as psychoanalysis continues to generate interest among scientists who employ cutting-edge technology to test its theoretical arguments, this perspective on personality will continue to enrich and thereby illuminate our understanding of the human mind.

Section REVIEW

- Freud believed that the unconscious mind largely determines human behavior.

- Freud's three personality structures are the id (the entirely unconscious part of the personality that contains our sexual and aggressive urges), the ego (the part of the personality that balances the demands of the id, the superego, and reality), and the superego (the part of the personality that counterbalances the more primitive id demands).

- Psychosexual stages include the oral stage, anal stage, phallic stage, latency stage, and genital stage.

- The conscious part of the ego is protected from awareness of disturbing id impulses because defense mechanisms transform raw id desires into more acceptable actions.

- Later psychodynamic theorists departed from Freud's personality theory: Alfred Adler emphasized personal striving to overcome feelings of inferiority. Carl Jung emphasized how our thoughts and actions are influenced by a collective unconscious. Karen Horney stressed how social and cultural factors influence female personality.

- Psychoanalytic theory has two major limitations: (1) it is not based on carefully controlled scientific research; and (2) many of its concepts cannot be measured.

- Acknowledging these limitations, researchers in the new area of neuropsychoanalysis are using cutting-edge technology to scientifically test various aspects of psychoanalytic theory.

10.3 The Humanistic Perspective

As discussed in Chapter 1, Section 1.2b, due to many psychologists' dissatisfaction with both the behaviorists' and the psychoanalysts' views of human nature, in the 1950s a new perspective developed in psychology. This "third wave" in psychology, known as the *humanistic perspective*, emphasized people's innate capacity for personal growth and their ability to consciously make choices. Carl Rogers and Abraham Maslow were the primary architects of humanistic psychology, and they both contended that psychologists should study people's unique subjective mental experience of the world. This stance represented a direct challenge to behaviorism and was instrumental in focusing renewed attention on the self. Further, by emphasizing the possibilities for positive change that people can make at any point in their lives, the humanistic perspective stood in sharp contrast to the more pessimistic tone of the psychoanalytic perspective (Lambert & Erekson, 2008).

10.3a Rogers's Person-Centered Theory Emphasizes Self-Realization.

Carl Rogers (1902–1987) believed that people are basically good and that we all are working toward becoming the best that we can be. Rogers (1961) asserted that, instead of being driven by sexual and aggressive desires, we are motivated by a wish to be good, and that we would achieve our potential if we were given **unconditional positive regard**. Unfortunately, according to Rogers, many of us are frustrated in our potential growth because important people in our lives often provide us with positive regard only if we meet their standards. Being the recipient of this **conditional positive regard** stunts our personal growth because, in our desire to be regarded positively, we lose sight of our *ideal self*, which is the person whom we would like to become. Rogers stated that as we continue to adjust our lives to meet others' expectations, the discrepancy between our *actual self*, which is the person we know ourselves to be now, and our ideal self becomes greater.

Rogers's theory of personality is as much about how people change as it is about how people are at any given moment (Kirschenbaum, 2004). For him, the dilemma of personality involves how people's thwarted growth potential can be released. The answer to this dilemma is for people with damaged selves, or low self-esteem, to find someone who will treat them with unconditional positive regard. The assumption here is that when people are accepted for who they are, they will eventually come to accept themselves as well. With this self-acceptance, people can then put aside others' standards that are false for them and get back on track in developing their true selves. Conveying unconditional positive regard to others involves the following three characteristics: *genuineness* (being open and honest), *warmth* (being caring and nurturing), and *empathy* (accurately identifying what the person is thinking and feeling).

Unconditional positive regard An attitude of complete acceptance toward another person regardless of what she or he has said or done; based on the belief in that person's essential goodness

Conditional positive regard An attitude of acceptance toward another person only when she or he meets your standards

Peak experiences Fleeting but intense moments when a person feels happy, absorbed, and extremely capable

Shutterstock

Carl Rogers's person-centered theory of personality considers receiving unconditional positive regard an essential ingredient in healthy personal growth. Parents are the primary providers of this affection to children.

10.3b Maslow's Self-Actualization Theory Stresses Maximizing Potential.

Like Rogers, Abraham Maslow (1908–1970) was interested in people's ability to reach their full potential. As discussed in Chapter 9, Section 9.1f, this process of fulfilling one's potential was what Maslow (1970) called *self-actualization*. Like Rogers and Freud, Maslow used the case-study method in developing his theory. However, unlike Rogers and Freud, Maslow studied healthy, creative people rather than those who were troubled and seeking therapy. He chose as his subjects people who had led or were leading rich and productive lives, including outstanding college students, faculty, professionals in other fields, and historical figures, such as Abraham Lincoln, Thomas Jefferson, and Eleanor Roosevelt.

Maslow found that self-actualized people were secure in the sense of who they were and not paralyzed, therefore, by others' opinions. They were also loving and caring; and they often focused their energies on a particular task, one they often regarded as a life mission. Maslow also reported that these people had experienced personal or spiritual **peak experiences**, which are fleeting but intense moments of joy, ecstasy, and absorption, in which people feel extremely capable. A peak experience can occur while a person is engaging in a religious activity or service, while performing athletically, while listening to music, or while relating to a lover (Ravizza, 2007). Some women report their childbirth experiences to be peak experiences. Although anyone can have peak experiences, Maslow's group of self-actualizing people reported both more peak experiences and that the quality of those experiences was richer than the experiences reported by others whom he studied. These peak experiences have a lasting effect on those who experience them, enriching their outlook and causing them to become more open to the experiences of others.

10.3c   *The Humanistic Perspective Has Been Criticized as Being Overly Optimistic.*

Like Freud, humanistic psychologists have had a significant impact on popular culture. If you look in the self-help section in any bookstore, you will find numerous titles emphasizing the control you have over changing your life and achieving your full potential. However, in trying to correct for Freud's gloomy outlook on human nature, the humanistic perspective on personality may have overshot the mark and failed to acknowledge that many people engage in mean-spirited and even cruel behavior on a fairly regular basis. The truth is that people have the capacity to act in a wide variety of ways. Further, some of the forces that shape our behavior are outside our conscious awareness.

Although humanistic psychology has helped revitalize attention to the self, one of its major limitations is that it has not produced a substantial body of testable hypotheses for its personality theories. Like Freud before them, humanistic psychologists have not clearly defined their concepts and have often rejected the use of carefully controlled scientific studies to test the validity of their theories. As a result, most of the scientific investigations of the self have come from outside the humanistic perspective, especially the social-cognitive perspective (see Section 10.5c) and the closely related perspective of positive psychology (see Section 10.4d).

Section
REVIEW

- The humanistic perspective assumes that human nature is essentially good.

- Carl Rogers proposed that being provided with unconditional positive regard allows people to heal the split between their actual and their ideal selves.

- According to Abraham Maslow, in order to self-actualize, people must be motivated to become the best person they can be.

10.4 The Trait Perspective

During the summer of 1919, 22-year-old psychology student Gordon Allport was traveling through Europe when he boldly decided to ask the world-famous Sigmund Freud to meet with him. Upon arriving at Freud's office, the young Allport was at a loss in explaining the purpose of his visit. In truth, he simply wanted to meet this great man. After a strained silence, Allport told a story about a boy he saw on the train to Vienna who pleaded with his meticulously dressed mother to keep dirty passengers from sitting near him. When Allport finished telling the story, Freud paused and then asked in a soft voice, "And was that little boy you?" Allport was mortified. Freud had mistakenly perceived this "icebreaker" story as a window into the young man's unconscious. Later, after reflecting on Freud's assumption, Allport decided that psychoanalysis was not the best way to understand personality. Instead of searching for hidden, unconscious motives in people's behavior, he thought that personality psychologists should first try to describe and measure the basic factors of personality (Allport, 1967). This set him on a path of research that culminated in the development of the *trait perspective*.

10.4a Trait Theories Describe Basic Personality Dimensions.

Trait perspective A descriptive approach to personality that identifies stable characteristics that people display over time and across situations

Trait A relatively stable tendency to behave in a particular way across a variety of situations

The **trait perspective** conceives of personality as consisting of stable characteristics that people display over time and across situations (Nicholson, 2002). A **trait** is a relatively stable tendency to behave in a particular way. As an approach to understanding personality, the trait perspective is more concerned with describing *how* people differ from one another than in explaining *why* they differ. The way psychologists typically measure traits is similar to the way everyone assesses other people's personalities. They observe them over time and in various situations, or they ask them how they typically behave. For example, if a friend is always prompt, you come to rely on that as characteristic of her. From the trait perspective, we would propose that your friend is consistently on time because of an underlying trait that predisposes her to act in this manner. This may seem a little circular, and to a certain extent it is. However, like so much else in personality psychology, traits cannot be measured directly but instead are inferred from behavior.

In studying traits, Gordon Allport and his colleague Henry Odbert (1936) began by combing through a dictionary and making a list of words that described people's personal characteristics. From this initial list of 18,000 words, they reduced it to about 200 clusters of related words, which became the original traits in Allport's personality theory (Allport, 1937). Allport's perspective on personality had a good deal in common with those of humanistic psychologists in that he emphasized that the whole human being should be the focus of study. Like humanistic psychologists, he further asserted that behaviorism was seriously mistaken when it explained human behavior as no different from that of rats and pigeons. In addition to being influenced by his humanistic associations, Allport was influenced by Gestalt psychology. As you recall from Chapter 4, Section 4.5a, the Gestalt perspective contends, "the whole is different from the sum of its parts." Similarly, Allport (1961) argued that personality was not simply a collection of traits but that, instead, these traits seamlessly fit together to form a dynamic and unique personality.

Allport's contemporary, Henry Murray (1938, 1948), was also a trait psychologist who appreciated humanistic psychology's emphasis on the total person. However, Murray's personality approach was also influenced by Jung's and Freud's theories of unconscious motivation. As a result, he focused on traits that are relatively irrational, passionate, and laden with conflict and emotion. Ironically, both men were doing their research at about the same time in the same place: Harvard.

How can a single perspective—the trait perspective—contain theorists who take such different positions about the nature of personality? Actually, the trait approach is not based on specific assumptions about human nature. Traits are viewed as the small building blocks of personality; and a theorist can fit them together in a variety of ways, just as a landscaper can lay bricks into a walk in a variety of patterns. Whereas psychoanalytic and humanistic theorists have definite beliefs about whether human beings are basically rational, aggressive, or unconsciously motivated, the trait approach assumes that people differ in the degree to which they possess personality traits. For example, instead of taking a position that people are basically aggressive or nonaggressive, trait theorists contend that people differ in the degree to which they possess aggressive traits (McCrae, 2005).

10.4b Factor Analysis Is Used to Identify Personality Traits.

Allport's work in identifying a list of traits was a necessary first step in the development of a scientific trait approach to personality, yet his list of 200-some traits needed to be reduced to a more manageable level. Researchers achieved this by relying on factor analysis. As you recall from Chapter 8, Section 8.3d, *factor analysis* is a statistical technique that allows researchers to identify clusters of variables that are related to—or *correlated* with—one another. When a group of traits correlates in factor analysis, this suggests that a more general trait is influencing them. For example, several studies have found that people who describe themselves as outgoing also describe themselves as talkative, active, and optimistic about the future. This cluster of traits has been identified as consisting of the more general trait of *extraversion*.

Raymond Cattell (1965, 1986) was one of the first trait theorists to use factor analysis to identify these general traits, which he called source traits. First he collected people's ratings of themselves on many different traits, and then he identified clusters of related traits using factor analysis. Based on this procedure, Cattell concluded that you could understand an individual's personality by identifying the degree to which she or he possessed each of the 16 source traits listed in Table 10-3. To measure these traits, Cattell developed the *Sixteen Personality Factor Questionnaire (16PF)*, which is widely used for career counseling, marital counseling, and evaluating employees and executives (H. E. P. Cattell, 2001; Tango & Kolodinsk, 2004).

TABLE 10-3 Cattell's 16 Basic Personality Traits

Reserved	←→	Outgoing
Trusting	←→	Suspicious
Relaxed	←→	Tense
Less intelligent	←→	More intelligent
Stable	←→	Emotional
Assertive	←→	Humble
Happy-go-lucky	←→	Sober
Conscientious	←→	Expedient
Venturesome	←→	Shy
Tender-minded	←→	Tough-minded
Imaginative	←→	Practical
Shrewd	←→	Forthright
Apprehensive	←→	Placid
Experimenting	←→	Conservative
Self-sufficient	←→	Group-tied
Controlled	←→	Casual

Cattell was a pioneer in the use of factor analysis to study personality. He also demonstrated the importance of testing personality traits in applied settings—in business organizations, in schools, in clinical work—and then using that information to better understand the traits. Testing personality theories in applied settings and then refining the theories based on what is learned has become an important part of modern trait approaches to personality.

British psychologists Hans Eysenck and Sybil Eysenck (pronounced "EYE-zink") also used factor analysis to describe personality functioning. However, unlike Cattell, the Eysencks believed that personality researchers should rely on other evidence besides the findings of factor analysis when identifying the basic dimensions of personality. Specifically, they believed that researchers should also consider the biological bases of personality. Based on thousands of studies conducted over five decades, the Eysencks concluded that there are three genetically influenced dimensions of personality: *extraversion* (which included Cattell's factors of outgoingness and assertiveness), *neuroticism* (which included Cattell's factors of emotional instability and apprehensiveness), and *psychoticism* (which included Cattell's factors of tough-mindedness and shrewdness).

So how many basic traits are there in personality? Are there 16 source traits, as Cattell proposed, or are there the much more modest three dimensions proposed by the Eysencks? Before reading further, complete Closer Look 10-1.

Can You Perform an Intuitive Factor Analysis of Personality Traits?

In the 1930s, well before the widespread use of factor analysis in research, Gordon Allport and Henry Odbert (1936) relied upon their intuitive judgment to reduce an initial list of 18,000 personality traits to about 200 clusters of related traits. To gain some appreciation of their effort, examine carefully the 30 traits listed below and sort them into five groups of related traits, each containing six traits. In forming each grouping, keep in mind that the traits in each group are assumed to "go together," so that people who have one of the traits in the group are also likely to have the other traits. After you have finished sorting the 30 traits, identify what it is they have in common. Can you attach an overall trait name to each of the five groups of traits? Finally, for each group, how would people who possess an abundance of the overall trait differ from people who possess very little of this overall trait?

Achievement-oriented	Eccentric	Positive emotions
Action-oriented	Excitement seeking	Rich emotional life
Altruistic	Full of energy	Rich fantasy life
Anxious	Hostile	Self-conscious
Assertive	Idiosyncratic	Self-disciplined
Competent	Impulsive	Straightforward
Compliant	Modest	Tender-minded
Deliberate	Novel ideas	Trusting
Depressed	Orderly	Vulnerable
Dutiful	Outgoing	Warm

When other college students have completed a similar task (Sneed et al., 1998), more than 70 percent classified 30 traits similar to those in this exercise so that at least five of the six items in each grouping fell into clusters similar to the following: (1) *rich fantasy life, rich emotional life, action-oriented, novel ideas, eccentric, idiosyncratic;* (2) *competent, orderly, dutiful, self-disciplined, deliberate, achievement-oriented;* (3) *outgoing, positive emotions, assertive, full of energy, excitement seeking, warm;* (4) *trusting, straightforward, compliant, modest, tender-minded, altruistic;* (5) *anxious, self-conscious, depressed, hostile, impulsive, vulnerable.* Did your own clustering conform to this pattern?

10.4c *The Five-Factor Model Specifies Five Basic Personality Traits.*

Over the past 25 years, the consensus among most personality trait researchers is that there are five key factors or dimensions of personality, known as the **Five-Factor Model** (Hong et al., 2008). These five basic traits are *openness, conscientiousness, extraversion, agreeableness,* and *neuroticism* (use the acronym *OCEAN* to remember these five traits). As shown in Table 10-4, each of the five factors represents a clustering of more specific traits. For example, people who score high on neuroticism tend to be anxious, self-conscious, depressed, hostile, impulsive, and vulnerable. These lower-order traits are called *facets* in the Five-Factor Model (Wiggins, 1996).

With only slight variations, the five basic traits that make up the Five-Factor Model have consistently emerged in studies of children, college students, and the elderly (McCrae et al., 1999). Further, these traits have been found in societies as diverse as those of the United States, Bangladesh, Brazil, Japan, Canada, Finland, Spain, Germany, Poland, China, and the Philippines (Gorostiaga et al., 2011; McCrae et al., 2011; McCrae et al., 199). This is especially impressive when you consider the wide variety of languages used in these various studies to test for these traits. Although gender differences are small, a study of 24 cultures from five continents found that women tend to score higher than men on neuroticism and agreeableness (Costa et al., 2001).

Evolutionary theorists contend that the reason these five traits are found across a wide variety of cultures is that they reflect the most salient features of humans' adaptive behavior over the course of evolutionary history. In other words, these five traits have emerged as the basic components of personality because, as a species, we have evolved special sensitivity to variations in the ability to handle stress

Five-Factor Model A trait theory asserting that personality consists of five traits (neuroticism, extraversion, openness to experience, agreeableness, and conscientiousness)

Shutterstock

The Five-Factor Model of personality contends that there are five basic components of personality: openness to experience, conscientiousness, extraversion, agreeableness, and neuroticism. What traits do you think are strongest in your personality?

TABLE 10-4   The Five-Factor Model and Its Facets

Openness	Conscientiousness	Extraversion	Agreeableness	Neuroticism
Rich fantasy life	Competent	Outgoing	Trusting	Anxious
Rich emotional life	Orderly	Positive emotions	Straightforward	Self-conscious
Action-oriented	Dutiful	Assertive	Compliant	Depressed
Novel ideas	Self-disciplined	Full of energy	Modest	Hostile
Eccentric	Deliberate	Excitement seeking	Tender-minded	Impulsive
Idiosyncratic	Achievement-oriented	Warm	Altruistic	Vulnerable

(neuroticism), seek out others' company (extraversion), approach problems (openness to experience), cooperate with others (agreeableness), and meet our social and moral obligations (conscientiousness). In contrast, sociocultural theorists propose that the behaviors associated with these five traits are learned through the experiences that children and young adults have while mastering important social roles found in cultures throughout the world (B. Roberts et al., 2005). Instead of genetic predisposition to developing these traits, sociocultural theorists emphasize the role that learning plays in shaping the behaviors that psychologists associate with these traits. Presently, neither of these theories has received sufficient empirical support to declare it superior to the other.

Does this mean that these five traits compose an individual's entire personality? Most trait theorists would say no. Although almost any personality trait probably has a good deal in common with one of these five basic traits, the Five-Factor Model does not capture the entire essence of personality (Funder, 2001). Let us briefly examine each of these traits.

Openness to Experience

People who are particularly open to experience are adventurous—constantly searching out new ways to do things; and they are sensitive and passionate, with a childlike wonder at the world (McCrae, 1994). They can also flout traditional notions of what is appropriate or expected in terms of their behavior or ideas (McCrae & Costa, 1997; McCrae & John, 1992). As with most of the other dimensions, openness to experience is at the end of the pole that appears more desirable; in fact, however, many qualities of those who are more closed to experience are quite valuable. These individuals tend to be hardworking, loyal, down-to-earth, and proud of their traditional values. They also tend to be more politically conservative. A meta-analysis of 88 studies with over 22,000 participants found that people who scored low on openness to experience held more conservative political beliefs than those individuals who scored high on openness (Jost et al., 2003).

Conscientiousness

Conscientiousness is the measure of a person's willingness to conform to others' expectations and follow through on what she or he has agreed to do, despite more tempting options that may arise. People who score high on conscientiousness tend to be well organized, dependable, hardworking, and ambitious—whereas those who score low are more likely to be disorganized, undependable, lazy, and easygoing. This dimension is very important in career planning and workplace productivity. Adolescents who are conscientious are much more likely to spend time thinking about and planning their future career options than those who lack conscientiousness (Lounsbury et al., 2005). Similarly, conscientious employees are good workplace citizens, while nonconscientious employees are nonproductive and undermine the organization's health (Barrick & Mount, 1991; Howard & Howard, 2000).

Journey of Discovery

How do you think Freud would describe the highly conscientious person?

Extraversion

Extraversion was first identified by Carl Jung (see Section 10.2e) and has been included in virtually every personality system proposed in the last 50 years (Watson & Clark, 1997). Extraverts are people who seek out and enjoy others' company. They tend to be confident, energetic, bold, and optimistic; and they handle social situations with ease and grace. Extraverts' social skills, confidence, and take-charge attitude often make them well-suited for leadership positions (W. Johnson et al., 2004). On the opposite end of this particular personality dimension is the introverted character. Introverts tend to be shy, quiet, and reserved; and it is harder for others to connect with them (Tellegen et al., 1988).

Agreeableness

Agreeableness is a personality dimension that ranges from friendly compliance with others on one end to hostile antagonism on the other. People who score high on agreeableness tend to be good-natured, softhearted, courteous, and sympathetic—whereas those who score low tend to be irritable, ruthless, rude, and tough-minded. Agreeableness is a useful way to obtain popularity, and agreeable people are better liked than disagreeable people (Graziano & Eisenberg, 1997). However, people high in agreeableness may be too dependent on others' approval and thus ill-suited for situations requiring tough or more objective decisions. For instance, scientists, art or literary critics, and judges may be able to perform better if they are less agreeable and more "objective" in their jobs (Graziano et al., 1996).

Does being tough-minded versus good-natured affect how much money people earn in their jobs? A series of recent studies found that people who scored low on agreeableness earned 18 percent more in their jobs than those who were more agreeable (Judge et al., 2012). Interestingly, the relationship between agreeableness and income was significantly stronger for men than for women. One way to interpret these findings is that behaving counter to your sex's traditional gender role—men being softhearted and sympathetic and women being ruthless and tough-minded—causes more of a salary backlash for men than for women. The fact that being tough-minded is a masculine trait, and the finding that it is associated with higher salaries in our culture also reflect the greater value our culture places on masculine traits compared to feminine traits (see Chapter 3, Section 3.2e).

 **INFO-BIT** Agreeableness is consistent across the life span. Disagreeable boys develop into men who are described as irritable, undercontrolled, and moody (Caspi et al., 1989). Some researchers have suggested that this, in turn, may be related to the underlying temperament of individuals, and that being disagreeable may be related to an overactive sympathetic division of the autonomic nervous system (Rothbart, 1989).

Neuroticism

At the core of neuroticism is negative affect (McCrae & Costa, 1987). This personality dimension, which is sometimes labeled *emotional stability*, describes how people differ in terms of being anxious, high-strung, insecure, and self-pitying versus relaxed, calm, composed, secure, and content. Neurotics (people low in emotional stability) can either channel their worrying into a kind of compulsive success or let their anxiety lead them into recklessness. Many of the facets underlying neuroticism will be discussed more fully in Chapter 11, when we examine psychological disorders. Before reading further, check out Closer Look 10-2 to learn whether the Five-Factor Model is useful in understanding personality traits among nonhuman animals.

Do Nonhuman Animals Have Personality Traits?

Our family dog, Maizy, is trusting, curious, very energetic, somewhat absentminded, and extremely friendly. I would guess that she is low on neuroticism and high on agreeableness, extraversion, and openness to experience. Is my application of the Five-Factor Model to a canine based on any scientific evidence, or should it be dismissed as the whimsical musings of a dog lover?

Samuel Gosling and Oliver John believe that the Five-Factor Model can be used to describe the personality of many nonhuman animals, including dogs. In a review of 19 animal personality studies involving 12 different species, Gosling and John (1999) found that the personality traits of extraversion, neuroticism, and agreeableness commonly occur across species. Chimpanzees, gorillas, various other primates, mammals in general, and even guppies and octopuses exhibit individual differences that are remarkably similar to these three personality traits (Gosling, 2008; Locurto, 2007). The researchers believe that this cross-species similarity in personality traits suggests that biological mechanisms are likely responsible.

Using personality distinctions similar to those in the Five-Factor Model, comparative psychologist John Capitanio (1999) has also discovered that the behavior of adult male rhesus monkeys can be reliably predicted from personality dimensions. Over a 4 1/2-year period, Capitanio found that, compared to monkeys who scored low on these personality dimensions, highly extraverted monkeys engaged in more affiliative behavior; highly neurotic monkeys were more fearful and hypersensitive to changes in their surroundings; and highly agreeable monkeys were more easygoing in their social behavior. Like Gosling and John, Capitanio believes that biological mechanisms are shaping the expression of these personality traits.

These consistencies across species and over time further suggest that the five factors identified by trait theorists reflect some of the basic styles of behavior that are necessary for many species to best adapt to their environments (Capitanio, 2003; Smith & Blumstein, 2008). For instance, an animal that is high in neuroticism might be the most responsive to the presence of a predator, and so could act as a sentinel in a group of animals. Meanwhile, another animal that is low in neuroticism may promote group solidarity by being relaxed and calm. Together, these animals could contribute to the social functioning of their group in different ways, with the net result that both of them (and their kin) may be more likely to survive and reproduce. Thus, the genes that influence these personality styles are likely to be passed on to future generations (Adams, 2011).

So what are the important traits in a dog's personality? I wasn't far off the mark in sizing up Maizy. Factor analyses of experts' ratings of dog breeds identified traits that closely approximated four of the five traits in the Five-Factor Model: neuroticism, agreeableness, extraversion, and openness to experience. A fifth personality dimension, "dominance-territoriality," was also identified (Gosling & John, 1999; Svartberg & Forkman, 2002). Maizy, a golden retriever, would score very low in this dimension.

What about conscientiousness? Gosling and John's research found that chimpanzees were the only species other than humans that exhibited the trait of conscientiousness (it was not found among gorillas), although it was defined more narrowly in chimps than in humans. Among chimps, conscientiousness included individual behavioral variations involving lack of attention and goal directedness, unpredictability, and disorganized behavior. Because conscientiousness entails following rules, thinking before acting, and other complex cognitive functions, it is not surprising that this trait was found only in humans' closest genetic relative. These findings suggest that conscientiousness is a recent evolutionary development among hominids, the subfamily composed of humans, chimpanzees, and gorillas.

Shutterstock

The Five-Factor Model has been used to describe nonhuman personalities. Experts' ratings of dog breeds identified traits that closely matched four of the five traits in the Five-Factor Model, as well as a fifth personality dimension, "dominance-territoriality." Which personality factor do you think they found only in humans and chimpanzees?

10.4d Positive Psychologists Identify Personality Traits That Are Character Strengths.

As previously discussed in Chapter 1, Section 1.2b, positive psychology is a psychological perspective, closely related to humanistic psychology, that attempts to identify how people make their lives happy and fulfilling. Researchers who identify themselves as positive psychologists are currently studying what it means to be a well-adapted person in modern-day society, with a good deal of their research investigating personality traits associated with positive living. Christopher Peterson and Martin Seligman (2004) are two of the primary investigators who have sought to identify what they refer to as *character strengths* that consistently emerge across history and culture.

According to Peterson and Seligman, **character strength** is a special type of trait that allows optimal functioning in pursuing a virtue. A *virtue* is a core human characteristic valued, worldwide, in moral philosophies and religions. Character strengths are different from general personality traits because of their association with virtues. In their analysis of religions and philosophies around the world, Peterson and Seligman identified six broad categories of human virtues: wisdom, courage, justice, humanity, temperance, and spirituality (Dahlsgaard et al., 2005). Research suggests that these virtues are also associated with the type of personality traits identified as most desirable for romantic partners or friends to possess (Buss, 1989).

Having identified six common virtues, Peterson and Seligman next attempted to determine how each of these virtues is typically expressed. To achieve this goal, they enlisted a group of psychologists and psychiatrists to examine dozens of existing personality inventories and use designated criteria to identify character strengths. This procedure yielded 24 "strengths" of character distributed across the six virtue categories in their **Values in Action (VIA) Classification** system, which is listed in Table 10-5. Peterson and Seligman claim that the character strengths in the VIA Classification define what's best about people. For example, wisdom is a virtue, while creativity, curiosity, open-mindedness, love of learning, and perspective are character strengths that can be used to achieve wisdom. Across the 24 character strengths, the researchers assumed that there would be a wide range of individual differences in the degree to which people possess specific strengths (Peterson, 2006). They further assumed that individuals would rarely, if ever, display high degrees of all strengths.

In an Internet study of almost 118,000 adults from 54 countries, Nansook Park, Peterson, and Seligman (2006) found that three of the most commonly endorsed character strengths were kindness, integrity, and gratitude. Of the 24 character strengths, research suggests that the ones most strongly associated with life satisfaction are the strengths of gratitude, love, hope, curiosity, and zest (Park & Peterson, 2006, 2008; Peterson et al., 2007, 2008). Additional longitudinal research with over 17,000 individuals living in the United Kingdom found that as people aged, they tended to display higher degrees of their character strengths (Linley et al., 2007).

Given the challenges that life can present to people, positive psychologists have begun studying the role of character strengths in traumatic life events. For example, following the September 11, 2001 terrorist attacks in the United States, a survey of more than 4,800 Americans compared their character strengths before this national tragedy with two months after. Results indicated that, immediately following the attacks, Americans experienced an increase in the seven character strengths of gratitude, hope, kindness, leadership, love, spirituality, and teamwork. Ten months later, these character strengths were still elevated, although to a somewhat lesser degree than immediately following the attacks (Peterson & Seligman, 2003). These findings suggest that when a group experiences a dangerous external threat, individual

Character strength Trait that allows optimal functioning in pursuing a virtue

Values in Action (VIA) Classification of Strengths A positive psychology classification system of 24 universal character strengths that defines what's best about people

TABLE 10-5   Values in Action (VIA) Classification of Virtues and Strengths

Wisdom and Knowledge: cognitive strengths that are related to acquiring and using knowledge
- Creativity: Thinking of novel and productive ways to understand and do things
- Curiosity: Having an interest in things for their own sake
- Open-mindedness: Thinking things through and examining them from all sides
- Love of learning: Mastering new skills, topics, and bodies of knowledge
- Perspective: Being able to provide wise counsel to others

Courage: emotional strengths that require the exercise of willpower to accomplish goals in the face of opposition
- Bravery: Not shrinking from threat, challenge, difficulty, or pain
- Persistence: Finishing what you start
- Integrity: Speaking the truth and acting in a genuine and sincere manner
- Vitality: Approaching life with excitement and energy

Humanity: interpersonal strengths that involve tending to and befriending others
- Love: Valuing intimate relationships with others
- Kindness: Doing favors and good deeds for others
- Social intelligence: Being aware of the motives and feelings of other people and yourself

Justice: civic strengths that underlie healthy community life
- Citizenship: Working well as a member of a group or team
- Fairness: Treating all people the same according to notions of fairness and justice
- Leadership: Encouraging a group of which one is a member to get things done and at the same time maintaining good relations within the group

Temperance: strengths that protect against excess
- Forgiveness and mercy: Forgiving those who have done wrong
- Humility/Modesty: Letting one's accomplishments speak for themselves
- Prudence: Being careful about your choices
- Self-regulation: Regulating what you feel and do

Transcendence: strengths that forge connections to the larger universe and provide meaning
- Appreciation of beauty and excellence: Noticing and appreciating beauty, excellence, and/or skilled performance in various domains of life
- Gratitude: Being aware of and thankful for the good things that happen to you
- Hope: Expecting the best in the future and working to achieve it
- Humor: Liking to laugh and tease
- Spirituality: Having sound beliefs about the higher purpose and meaning of the universe

members often react by experiencing a heightened sense of communion with and gratitude for fellow group members, as well as a stronger belief in the higher purpose and meaning of life. A related study found that hope and spirituality were the two character strengths that contributed most to lower levels of depressive symptoms among American college students following the terrorist attacks (Ai & Evans-Campbell, 2006). Similarly, other studies suggest that recovering from a serious illness can be a character builder for many people (Peterson et al., 2006).

As with the Five-Factor Model, Peterson and Seligman do not contend that the VIA Classification system captures the complete picture of human personality. However, they do contend that the investigation of positive psychologists into human character strengths will provide important insights into how specific aspects of our personalities provide us with the necessary strengths to lead healthier, happier, and more fulfilling lives (Toner et al., 2012).

10.4e *Critics Challenge Whether Traits Reliably Predict Behavior.*

Personality theorists—whether they take a psychoanalytic, humanistic, or trait perspective—all have emphasized that personality is an important determinant of behavior. Yet Walter Mischel (1968, 1984) has argued that this is a misguided belief. Instead, he asserts that personality is not really stable over time and across situations and that the situation we place people in is a much stronger determinant of behavior than are their personalities. This viewpoint, which is called **situationism**, asserts that our behavior is not determined by stable traits but is strongly influenced by the situation.

Situationism The viewpoint that our behavior is strongly influenced by the situation, rather than by personality traits

In making a situationism argument, Mischel discussed an early study conducted by Hugh Hartshorne and Mark May (1928) in which they placed children in many different situations where they had the opportunity to lie, cheat, and steal. Instead of finding that the children displayed honest or dishonest traits consistently across many different situations, Hartshorne and May found that the situation was the most important determinant of how the children behaved. If kids thought they could get away with it, most of them were likely to behave dishonestly. In Mischel's own research, he found virtually no correlation between people's traits and their behavior across situations (Mischel, 1968, 1968, 1984). In other words, personality traits were not reliably predicting behavior. Based on this evidence, Mischel argued that personality traits are a figment of trait theorists' imaginations!

As you might guess, this critique stirred up considerable controversy among personality psychologists, who argued that Mischel was not seeing consistency in behavior across situations because he was not measuring enough behaviors (Epstein, 1980). For example, no one expects that your IQ score will predict whether you correctly answer a particular question on a particular test in a particular class during a particular semester. Predicting such a thing would be highly unreliable because so many factors exist that might influence your response (Were you rushed for time? Did you understand this information in class? Did you read the question correctly?). However, your IQ score will be much more accurate in predicting your average performance over many questions on several exams. Similarly, your score on an introversion-extraversion scale will not be very accurate in predicting whether you introduce yourself to that attractive person you see on campus tomorrow. However, your score will probably be much more accurate in predicting your average sociability across many situations. By and large, research supports this argument: Personality trait scores do reliably predict how people generally behave (Funder, 2001; Paunonen, 2003).

What about the assertion by situationists that personality is not stable over time? Actually, most studies find that personality traits are remarkably stable over the adult years but somewhat less so during childhood (Asendorpf & Van Aken, 2003). The most extensive study of personality trait stability at different ages was a meta-analysis of 150 studies involving almost 50,000 participants (Roberts & DelVecchio, 2000). In the various studies included in this meta-analysis, participants' personalities had been measured for at least one year. As depicted in Figure 10-3, results indicated that personality traits are least stable during childhood (correlations in the .40s), somewhat more stable in early adulthood (correlations in the .50s), and most stable after the age of 50 (correlations in the .70s). These findings do not support the situationists' claim that personality is not stable over time. Our personalities are quite stable, especially during the adult years, with most change occurring during the early years of life. Despite this trait

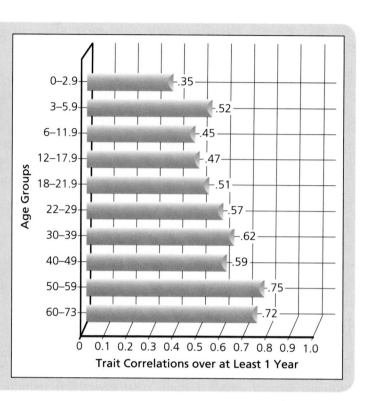

FIGURE 10-3

Stability of Personality Traits at Different Ages

A meta-analysis of 150 studies involving nearly 50,000 participants examined the stability of personality at different ages (Roberts & DelVecchio, 2000). Based on the findings depicted in this graph, at what ages is personality least stable? When is it most stable?

Source: Data from Roberts, B. W., and DelVecchio, W. F. (2000). "The rank-order consistency of personality traits from childhood to old age: A quantitative review of longitudinal studies." *Psychological Bulletin, 126,* 3–25.

stability, additional research indicates that our personalities are certainly capable of changing throughout our lives (Srivastava et al., 2003). They do not necessarily become fixed like plaster at a particular age.

One important contribution to personality theory made by situationists was their insistence that situational factors shape people's behavior. In response, many personality researchers acknowledged that situations do indeed shape behavior, and that how we behave is often determined by an *interaction* of personal and situational factors. In some situations, social norms may constrain the expression of personality traits. For example, extraverts, like everyone else, are likely to be relatively quiet and subdued at a library, in a funeral home, or during a church service. The personalities of those with whom we interact also can significantly alter our own behavior. For instance, a store clerk who is low on agreeableness may treat us very rudely, which may cause us to react in a similar fashion, despite the fact that we generally are kind and considerate. Thus, although personality traits do appear to explain a good deal of our behavior, situational forces significantly influence us (see Chapter 14).

The criticisms of the trait approach have helped to sharpen our understanding of the limits of personality as a determinant of behavior, but they have also increased our ability to predict behavior. Attending only to personality traits will not accurately predict behavior in most circumstances. Instead, many personality researchers have increasingly embraced **interactionism**, which is the study of the combined effects of both the situation and the person on human behavior (Sadler & Woody, 2003). As outlined here, Mischel's critical position toward the trait approach fueled a number of research directions that might not otherwise have been pursued. In psychology, as in all science, a critical or contrary position that is well presented frequently benefits the field by causing everyone to more clearly state (and examine) their assumptions and beliefs.

Interactionism The study of the combined effects of both the situation and the person on human behavior

- The trait perspective is a descriptive approach to personality that focuses on stable characteristics that people display over time and across situations.

- Trait theorists identify traits by relying on factor analysis.

- The Five-Factor Model, the most widely accepted trait theory, contends that personality is best described by the traits of openness to experience, conscientiousness, extraversion, agreeableness, and neuroticism.

- The Values in Action Classification of Strengths system identifies 24 universal character strengths that are related to six common virtues; these character strengths define what's best about people.

- Personality traits are most stable during later adulthood and least stable during early childhood.

- Personality traits interact with situational factors in determining behavior.

10.5 The Social-Cognitive Perspective

The perspectives examined thus far all contend that personality consists of internal psychological needs or traits that shape our thoughts, feelings, and behavior. These approaches provide a good illustration of how the ideology of *individualism* has shaped the development of many personality theories. In contrast, our fourth major approach, the **social-cognitive perspective**, has a less individualistic bias because it views personality as emerging through the process of the person interacting with her or his social environment. This perspective has its roots in the behavioral principles of *classical conditioning* and *operant conditioning*, but its closest association is with the more cognitively oriented principles of observational learning. As you recall from Chapter 6, Section 6.3a, observational learning is the central feature of Albert Bandura's (1986) *social learning theory*. Bandura proposes that people learn social behaviors primarily through observation and cognitive processing of information rather than through direct experience.

Social-cognitive perspective A psychological perspective that examines how people interpret, analyze, remember, and use information about themselves, others, social interactions, and relationships

10.5a   *Personality Is Shaped by Interactions among People's Cognitions, Behavior, and Environment.*

According to Bandura (1986), Skinner was only partly correct when he asserted that the environment determines people's behavior. Bandura pointed out that people's behavior also determines the environment. He further contended that people's thoughts, beliefs, and expectations determine and are determined by both behavior and the environment. As such, personality emerges from an ongoing mutual interaction between people's cognitions, their actions, and their environment. This basic principle of the social-cognitive perspective—which is depicted in Figure 10-4— is known as **reciprocal determinism**. Thus, while environmental factors shape our personalities, we think about what is happening to us and develop beliefs and expectations that will alter both our behavior and our environment (Makoul, 1998). In turn, these behavioral and environmental changes will influence our thoughts, which will then alter our personalities. As you can see, the idea that personality

Reciprocal determinism The social-cognitive belief that personality emerges from an ongoing mutual interaction between people's cognitions, their actions, and their environment

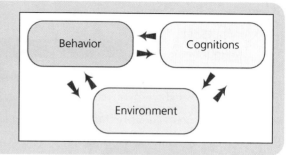

FIGURE 10-4

Reciprocal Determinism

Reciprocal determinism is the idea that personality emerges from an ongoing mutual interaction between people's cognitions, their behavior, and their environment.

emerges through reciprocal determinism does not fit into the individualist mold of traditional personality theories.

One of the most important cognitive factors in reciprocal determinism is **self-efficacy**, which is a person's belief about his or her ability to perform behaviors that should bring about a desired outcome. Perceptions of self-efficacy are largely subjective and tied to specific kinds of activities. You could have high self-efficacy for solving mathematical problems but low self-efficacy for interacting with new acquaintances. Because of these two different self-efficacies, you might approach a difficult calculus course with robust confidence, whereas you feign illness when invited to a new friend's party. Success in an activity heightens self-efficacy; failure lowers it. Further, the more self-efficacy you have at a particular task, the more likely you will pursue that task, try hard, persist in the face of setbacks, and succeed (Bandura, 1999; Pajares, 2008). Success breeds self-efficacy, which in turn breeds further success. This mutual interaction is an illustration of reciprocal determinism.

Self-efficacy A person's belief about his or her ability to perform behaviors that should bring about a desired outcome

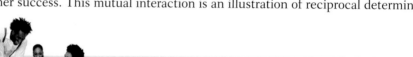

Journey of Discovery

Is self-efficacy the same thing as self-esteem?

10.5b *Life Experiences Foster Beliefs About Either Control or Helplessness.*

According to social-cognitive theorist Julian Rotter (1966, 1990), through the process of interacting with our surroundings we develop beliefs about ourselves as controlling, or controlled by, our environment. The degree to which we believe that outcomes in our lives depend on our own actions versus the actions of uncontrollable environmental forces is known as our **locus of control**. People who believe that outcomes occur because of their own efforts are identified as having an *internal locus of control*, whereas those who believe that outcomes are outside their own control are identified as having an *external locus of control*. Individuals with an internal locus of control are more likely to be achievement-oriented than are those with an external locus of control because those with an internal locus of control believe that their behavior can result in positive outcomes (Lachman & Weaver, 1998). True to these expectations, internals tend to be more successful in life than are externals. Externals are less independent than internals, and they are also more likely to be depressed and stressed (Presson & Benassi, 1996). Spend a few minutes responding to the items in Self-Discovery Questionnaire 10-1 to get an idea of whether you have an internal or external locus of control.

Locus of control The degree to which we expect that outcomes in our lives depend on our own actions and personal characteristics versus the actions of uncontrollable environmental forces

SELF-DISCOVERY 10-1
Questionnaire

Do You Have an Internal or an External Locus of Control?

Instructions: For each item, select the alternative that you more strongly believe to be true. Remember that this is a measure of your personal beliefs and that there are no correct or incorrect answers.

1. **a.** Making a lot of money is largely a matter of getting the right breaks.
    b. Promotions are earned through hard work and persistence.

2. **a.** In my experience, I have noticed that there is usually a direct connection between how hard I study and the grades I get.
    b. Many times, the reactions of teachers seem haphazard to me.

3. **a.** Marriage is largely a gamble.
    b. The number of divorces indicates that more and more people are not trying to make their marriages work.

4. **a.** When I am right, I can convince others.
    b. It is silly to think that one can really change another person's basic attitudes.

5. **a.** In our society, a person's future earning power is dependent upon his or her ability.
    b. Getting promoted is really a matter of being a little luckier than the next person.

6. **a.** I have little influence over the way other people behave.
    b. If one knows how to deal with people, they are really quite easily led.

Scoring instructions: Give yourself one point for each of the following answers: 1(a), 2(b), 3(a), 4(b), 5(b), and 6(a). Then add up your total number of points. The higher the score, the more external you are. A score of 5 or 6 suggests that you are in the high external range, while a score of 0 or 1 suggests that you are in the high internal range. Scores of 2, 3, and 4 suggest that you fall somewhere between these two extremes.

Source: Reprinted with permission from *Psychology Today* Magazine, (Copyright © 1971 Sussex Publishers, LLC.).

People who believe that external events control their lives often develop a feeling of helplessness. As discussed in Chapter 6, Section 6.2g, Martin Seligman (1975) defined this *learned helplessness* as the passive resignation produced by repeated exposure to aversive events that are believed to be unavoidable. Because people develop the expectation that their behavior has no effect on the outcome in the situation, they simply give up trying to change the outcome, even when their actions might bring rewards (Baum et al., 1998).

Learned helplessness is an example of the operation of reciprocal determinism. After repeatedly failing to achieve a desired outcome, people develop a belief that there is nothing they can do to alter their current conditions, so they stop trying. Even when the world around them changes so that success is now possible,

Persons with an internal locus of control are more achievement-oriented and successful in life than those with an external locus of control. What sort of thinking causes these differences among "internals" and "externals?"

they don't act on opportunities because they falsely believe that such action is futile. Learned helplessness explains why some people who have grown up in poverty don't take advantage of opportunities that, if pursued, could lead to economic rewards. Having developed the belief that they cannot change the cards that have been dealt them, these people remain mired in poverty and often instill these pessimistic beliefs in their children. Social welfare programs that have been successful in helping people pull themselves out of poverty specifically attack learned helplessness (Wanberg et al., 1999).

10.5c Social-Cognitive Psychologists Have Extensively Studied the Self.

In the decades of the 1950s and 1960s, humanistic psychologists' attention to the self did not generate a great deal of research; however, their self personality theories did help keep the concept alive in psychology during a time when behaviorism was the dominant perspective. Today, the self is one of the most popular areas of scientific study, and social-cognitive theorists are some of the more prominent researchers. As discussed in Chapter 3, Section 3.2d, *self-concept* is the "theory" that a person constructs about herself or himself through social interaction, whereas *self-esteem* is a person's evaluation of his or her self-concept.

Two related areas that social-cognitive psychologists have examined are whether people evaluate themselves accurately, and how they typically explain successes and failures in their lives. For example, when you receive a good grade on an exam, do you usually conclude that your success was caused by your intelligence, your hard work, or a combination of the two? What if you do poorly? Are you likely to blame your failure on the unreasonable demands of your professor or on pure bad luck? The tendency to take credit for success while denying blame for failure is known as the **self-serving bias**, and it reflects a common mode of thinking (Campbell & Sedikides, 1999). The most agreed-upon explanation for the self-serving bias is that it allows us to enhance and protect self-esteem. If we feel personally responsible for successes or positive events in our lives but do not feel blameworthy for failures or other negative events, our self-worth is likely to be bolstered.

Consistent with the self-serving bias, research suggests that when we compare our past selves to our current selves we are motivated to evaluate our past selves in a way that makes us feel good about ourselves now (Ross & Wilson, 2002, 2003). We accomplish this feat by perceiving our present self as superior to our former selves, especially in characteristics that are important to our self-concepts (Wilson & Ross, 2001). Although you might think that negatively evaluating our past selves would lower our self-esteem, past selves are not as real to us as our present self. Criticizing our past selves allows us to feel better about our current performance in relation to these important characteristics. Additional studies suggest that, regardless of our age, we tend to believe we are more superior to our peers at the present time than we were when we were younger (Wilson & Ross, 2001). Of course, it is possible that most people do learn from experience and get better with age, but it is not statistically possible for all of us to improve more than our peers! In fact, do we really improve noticeably over time? Apparently, not nearly as much as we would like to think. When people are studied longitudinally, although they perceive themselves as improving in a number of personal characteristics, there often is actually no evidence of any such improvement (Wilson & Ross, 2001). These findings suggest that wishful thinking is often an important ingredient in our self-concepts.

One point to keep in mind about these findings is that this tendency to try to enhance feelings of self-worth varies in strength across cultures. Individualist cultures are much more likely than collectivist cultures to believe that high self-esteem is essential for mental health and life satisfaction (Oishi et al., 1999). This cultural difference in the importance placed on self-esteem may explain why individualists are more likely than collectivists to exhibit the self-serving bias (Heine & Hamamura, 2007).

Self-serving bias The tendency to bolster and defend self-esteem by taking credit for positive events while denying blame for negative events

Of all the lives that I have lived, I would have to say that this one is my favorite. I am proud that I have developed into a kinder person than I ever thought I would be.

—Mary Tyler Moore, U.S. actress, b. 1936; quoted at age 60

Self-esteem and self-contempt have specific odors; they can be smelled.

—Eric Hoffer, U.S. social philosopher, 1902–1983

10.5d *The Social-Cognitive Perspective Has Difficulty Explaining Nonrational Behavior.*

Traditional behavioral theories of personality that are based primarily on the operant conditioning principles of B. F. Skinner have been criticized for assessing only how environmental factors shape personality. To its credit, the social-cognitive perspective has taken a much more complex view of human personality, while still testing its theories using the scientific method. In their reliance on carefully controlled studies, social-cognitive theories have much more in common with the trait approach to personality than with the less scientifically based theories from the humanistic and psychoanalytic perspectives.

Social-cognitive personality theories have also drawn praise for emphasizing the important role that cognitions play in personality. They have quite rightly pointed out that our behavior is significantly shaped by our beliefs and expectations, including those related to us and those related to our environment. The social-cognitive approach has also drawn praise because its scientific findings have generated useful applications in the real world concerning how to understand and help solve such problems as drug abuse, unemployment, academic underachievement, and teen pregnancy.

The social-cognitive perspective's emphasis on cognition has placed it squarely in the mainstream of contemporary psychology, and it enjoys immense popularity among many psychologists. However, by emphasizing the cognitive side of human nature, the social-cognitive perspective is best at explaining rational behavior that is thought through. Like many cognitively oriented theories, it is less able to explain behavior that is spontaneous, irrational, and perhaps sparked by unconscious motives (Schacter & Badgaiyan, 2001). Table 10-6 provides a brief summary of the four personality perspectives that we have discussed.

TABLE 10-6   The Four Perspectives on Personality

Perspective	Explanation of Behavior	Evaluation
Psychoanalytic	Personality is set early in childhood and is driven by unconscious and anxiety-ridden sexual impulses that we poorly understand.	A speculative, hard-to-test theory that has had an enormous cultural influence and a significant impact on psychology
Humanistic	Personality is based on conscious feelings about oneself and is focused on our capacity for growth and change.	A perspective that revitalized attention to the self but often did not use rigorous scientific methods
Trait	Personality consists of a limited number of stable characteristics that people display over time and across situations.	A descriptive approach that sometimes underestimates the impact that situational factors have on behavior
Social-cognitive	Personality emerges from an ongoing mutual interaction among people's cognitions, their behavior, and their environment.	An interactionist approach that tends to underestimate the impact that emotions and unconscious motives have on behavior

- In the social-cognitive perspective, personality represents the unique patterns of thinking and behavior that a person learns in the social world.

- According to the principle of reciprocal determinism, personality emerges from an ongoing mutual interaction among people's cognitions, their actions, and their environment.

- According to the concept of locus of control, by interacting with our surroundings we develop beliefs about ourselves as controlling, or being controlled by, our environment.

- Engaging in the self-serving bias allows us to enhance and protect self-esteem, which is a tendency more common in individualist cultures than in collectivist cultures.

- Social-cognitive theories are best at explaining rational behavior but are less capable of explaining irrational behavior.

10.6 Measuring Personality

Two basic assumptions underlie the attempt to understand and describe personality. The first assumption, which we just examined, is that personal characteristics shape people's thoughts, feelings, and behavior. The second assumption, which we are about to examine, is that those characteristics can be measured in some manner (Briggs, 2005). We will consider two kinds of personality tests: *projective* and *objective*.

10.6a *Projective Tests Measure Unconscious Motives.*

Projective test A psychological test that asks people to respond to ambiguous stimuli or situations in ways that will reveal their unconscious motives and desires

Projective tests are based on the assumption that if people are presented with an ambiguous stimulus or situation, the way they interpret the material will be a projection of their unconscious needs, motives, fantasies, conflicts, thoughts, and other hidden aspects of personality. In other words, when people describe what they see in ambiguous stimuli, their description will be like the image projected on the screen at the movies. In this analogy, the film in the movie projector is like the hidden personality aspects, and the responses to the test are like the images seen on the screen. Projective tests are among the most commonly used assessment devices by psychotherapists in their clinical practices. The most popular projective tests are the *Rorschach Inkblot Test* and the *Thematic Apperception Test*.

The Rorschach Inkblot Test

Rorschach Inkblot Test A projective personality test in which people are shown 10 symmetrical inkblots and asked what each might be depicting

Have you ever played the "cloud game," in which you and another person look at cloud formations and tell each other what the shapes look like? The **Rorschach Inkblot Test** has a format similar to that of the cloud game (Woods, 2008). Introduced in 1921 by the Swiss psychiatrist Hermann Rorschach (1884–1922), the test consists of ten symmetrical inkblots. Five cards are black and white, and five are colored. Rorschach purposely varied the composition of his inkblots—some of them are essentially large blobs; others are bits of ink all over the page (Mattlar, 2004). The inkblot in Figure 10-5 is similar to those developed by Rorschach.

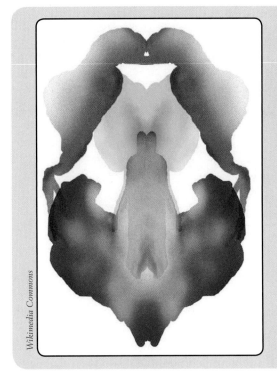

FIGURE 10-5

The Rorschach Test

Persons taking the Rorschach Inkblot Test describe what they see in a series of inkblots. The assumption of this projective personality test is that the way people interpret the inkblots will be a projection of their unconscious mind. What is one of the more serious validity problems with the Rorschach Test?

Wikimedia Commons

People's responses to the Rorschach Test are scored on three major features: the location or part of the card mentioned in the response; the content of the response; and which aspect, or *determinant*, of the card (its color or shading) prompted the response. Rorschach's original system of scoring was later revised; and by 1950 there were five separate systems for scoring and interpreting the inkblots, with none of them exhibiting good reliability or validity. In an attempt to correct these problems, James Exner (1993) integrated the five scoring systems into one system that decreased, but did not eliminate, reliability and validity concerns. One of the more serious validity problems with the Rorschach is that the current scoring system tends to misidentify mentally healthy people as having psychological problems (Daruna, 2004). Although most critics do not believe that the Rorschach is completely invalid, they believe that tests are available that are more valid and also cheaper to administer, score, and interpret. Today, many users of the Rorschach administer it as a way to start a conversation with clients seeking therapy rather than as a way to measure their personality.

Thematic Apperception Test

Another widely used projective measure is the *Thematic Apperception Test (TAT)*. As described in Chapter 9, Section 9.4b, Henry Murray developed the TAT in 1937. Administering this test involves asking a person to tell a story about several pictures the person is shown (Ephraim, 2008). In each case, the picture depicts a person or persons involved in a situation that is ambiguous. For example, in the TAT-like picture depicted in Figure 10-6, are the three people happy or sad? Is this a picture of a family, a student and teachers, or something else? The person telling the story about the TAT cards is instructed to tell about what led up to the story, what the people in the story are thinking and feeling, and how the situation resolves or comes to an end. Murray hypothesized that the issues that people are struggling with in their own lives would be perceived to be issues for the characters in the cards. He proposed that the storyteller could give the characters various needs, such as the need for nurturance

FIGURE 10-6
Thematic Apperception Test (TAT)
This picture of two adults sitting in a room focusing their attention on a child is an illustration of a TAT-like image. What sort of story do you think this picture tells? Why is the TAT referred to as a "projective" test?

Harold Edward Bryant, Evening Conversation, 1929, oil painting on canvas, 31.5 × 25.5 inches.

or the need for achievement. There would also be an opposing pressure from the environment, such as the demand to conform or to provide nurturance to others. Murray further proposed that across the stories people told, certain themes would emerge related to important issues in their lives.

Over several decades, the TAT and other variations of the test have demonstrated adequate validity in measuring need for achievement, but the test-retest reliability is relatively low. In addition, because the scenarios depicted in the TAT pictures were created for Americans, assessing the motives of people from other cultures using the TAT is often not recommended (Hofer & Chasiotis, 2004). For these reasons, the TAT is not considered to be one of the better ways to measure personality. Todazy, as with the Rorschach, psychologists using the TAT in therapy frequently employ it to help start a conversation about a client's problems.

10.6b *Objective Tests Measure Conscious Thoughts, Feelings, and Behavior.*

Objective test Personality test that asks direct, unambiguous questions about a person's thoughts, feelings, and behavior

Unlike projective tests, which are designed to trick the unconscious into revealing its contents, **objective tests** are primarily designed to assess consciously held thoughts, feelings, and behavior by asking direct, unambiguous questions. The questions can be directed toward friends and family members or toward people who have just met the person being assessed. When people evaluate themselves, the test is called a *self-report inventory*. This is the most common kind of objective personality test.

Like college exams, objective personality tests can be administered to a large group of people at the same time. Also similar to exams, objective tests usually ask true-false, multiple-choice, or open-ended questions. However, unlike exams in a college course, personality tests have no one correct answer to questions. Each respondent chooses the answer that best describes her or him. Many objective tests measure only one specific component of personality (for example, refer to the *Self-Monitoring Scale* in the end-of-chapter "Psychological Applications" section), whereas other objective tests assess several traits simultaneously.

Minnesota Multiphasic Personality Inventory (MMPI) An objective personality test consisting of true/false items that measure various personality dimensions and clinical conditions such as depression

One test that assesses several traits is the **Minnesota Multiphasic Personality Inventory (MMPI)**, which is the most extensively researched and widely used personality inventory (Butcher, 2005). Since its development in the 1940s, the MMPI has been revised so its language and content better reflect contemporary concerns and a more culturally diverse population. The more recent second edition, the MMPI-2, has 567 items, with participants responding "True," "False," or "Cannot say," The MMPI is an *empirically derived test*, meaning that the items were not selected for inclusion on a theoretical basis but were included only if they clearly distinguished one group of people from another (for example, patients with schizophrenia versus a normal comparison group). Each item had to demonstrate its usefulness by being answered differently by members of the two groups but similarly by members within each group.

The MMPI has ten *clinical scales*, which are used to identify psychological difficulties or interests; thus the groups that were used to choose the scale items were various groups of people with different psychological problems or interests. For example, the items that comprise the MMPI depression scale were those that depressed individuals endorsed more than did nondepressed people. People who score above a certain level on the depression scale are considered to have a problem with depression. Table 10-7 briefly describes the ten clinical scales for the MMPI-2.

The MMPI also contains four *validity scales*, which are item groups that detect suspicious response patterns indicating dishonesty, carelessness, defensiveness, or evasiveness (Schroeder et al., 2012). The interpretation of responses to these four scales can help psychologists understand the attitudes that someone has taken toward all the test items. For example, someone who responds "true" to items such as "I like

TABLE 10-7   MMPI-2 Clinical and Validity Scales

Scale	Description
Clinical Scales	
Hypochondriasis	Abnormal concern with bodily functions and health concerns
Depression	Pessimism, feelings of hopelessness; slowing of action and thought
Hysteria	Unconscious use of mental or physical symptoms to avoid problems
Psychopathic deviation	Disregard for social customs; emotional shallowness
Masculinity/femininity	Interests culturally associated with a particular gender
Paranoia	Suspiciousness, delusions of grandeur or persecution
Psychasthenia	Obsessions, compulsions, fears, guilt, anxiety
Schizophrenia	Bizarre thoughts and perceptions, withdrawal, hallucinations, delusions
Hypomania	Emotional excitement, overactivity, impulsiveness
Social introversion	Shyness, insecurity, disinterest in others
Validity Scales	
Cannot say	Not answering many items indicates evasiveness.
Lie	Repeatedly providing socially desirable responses indicates a desire to create a favorable impression; lying to look good.
Frequency	Repeatedly providing answers rarely given by normal people may indicate an attempt to appear mentally disordered; faking to look mentally ill.
Correction	A pattern of failing to admit personal problems or shortcomings, indicating defensiveness or lack of self-insight

every person I have ever met" and "I never get angry" may not be providing honest answers to the other test items. The four MMPI-2 validity scales are also described in Table 10-7.

The MMPI is easy to administer and score, and it has proven useful in identifying people who have psychological disorders (Bagby et al., 2005; Sellbom et al., 2012). Despite these advantages, it is often difficult to interpret MMPI scores when trying to diagnose specific disorders because people with different disorders score highly on a number of the same clinical scales. Critics also contend that the MMPI has not kept pace with advances in personality theory.

One of the most well-known objective personality tests is the Myers-Briggs Type Indicator (MBTI), created in the 1940s by Katherine Cook Briggs and her daughter, Isabel Briggs Myers. Based on Carl Jung's theory of personality (see Section 10.2e), the MBTI is widely used in many job fields and employment agencies to help people find careers that best fit their personalities (Wilde, 2011). The MBTI measures the degree to which respondents are introverted versus extraverted in their orientation toward the world, practical versus intuitive in dealing with their perceptions, analytical versus emotional in their judgments, and methodical versus spontaneous in their decision-making. When combined, these four classification preferences place a respondent into one of 16 *personality types* (Ross, 2011). Although the MBTI may be the most widely used personality measure in the world, questions remain regarding its accuracy, with some studies supporting and others questioning its validity.

Two more objective tests that represent the new wave of modern personality measures are the 243-item *Neuroticism Extraversion Openness Personality Inventory, Revised,* or *NEO-PI-R* (Costa & McCrae, 1992) and the 240-item *Values in Action Inventory of Strengths,* or *VIA-IS* (Peterson & Seligman, 2004). Unlike the MMPI, the NEO-PI-R and the VIA-IS measure personality differences that are not problematic. The NEO-PI-R is based on the Five-Factor Model, while the VIA-IS is based on positive psychology's notion of character strengths being traits that are stable over time yet changeable due to life experiences. In cultures throughout the world, both the NEO-PI-R and the VIA-IS are widely used in research and clinical therapy; they both have good validity and reliability (Gorostiaga et al., 2011; Katigbak et al., 2002; Linley et al., 2007; McCrae et al., 2011; Peterson, 2006).

Section REVIEW

- Projective testing assumes that if people are presented with ambiguous stimuli, their interpretation of it will be a projection of unconscious needs and desires.

- The two most widely used projective tests are the Rorschach Inkblot Test and the Thematic Apperception Test.

- Objective testing involves assessing consciously held thoughts, feelings, and behavior.

- The Minnesota Multiphasic Personality Inventory (MMPI) and the Myers-Briggs Type Indicator (MBTI) are two of the oldest and most widely used objective personality tests.

- The NEO-PI-R is an objective test that measures Five-Factor Model traits.

- The VIA-IS is an objective test that measures positive psychology's notion of character strengths.

10.7 Neurological and Genetic Determinants of Personality

My oldest daughter, Amelia, can be a little absentminded at times, like her father, whereas my youngest daughter, Lillian, is very organized, like her mother. Both girls are generally good-natured, ambitious, and open to new experiences—traits they share with both their parents. Did they inherit these traits from one or both of us? Or are they like one or both of us because we shaped their personalities while raising them? To what degrees do heredity and environment account for personality? Also, is there any evidence that personality traits are associated with the activation of different areas of the brain?

Identifying the biological basis of personality is a difficult task. For example, brain-imaging studies have found evidence that individual differences in four of the five personality traits in the Five Factor Model—conscientiousness, extroversion, agreeableness, and neuroticism—are correlated with individual differences in the size of specific brain areas (Canli, 2009; DeYoung et al., 2010). What do these results tell us? In examining the findings for the personality trait of conscientiousness, people who differ in conscientiousness tend to have different volumes in areas of the prefrontal cortex associated with planning and voluntary control of behavior. However, because this relationship is correlational, we don't know whether this difference in brain volume is causing the difference in conscientiousness or vice-versa. It is also possible that some unknown third variable is causing the changes in both brain volume and in conscientiousness.

10.7a *Personality Is Affected by Nervous System Arousal and Specific Brain Activity.*

The most convincing evidence that individual differences in personality are caused by biological differences among people comes from a line of research first begun by Hans Eysenck (see Section 10.4b). In studying introverts and extraverts, Eysenck (1990, 1997) suggested that these differences in personality types are caused by inherited differences in people's nervous systems, especially their brains. As you recall from Chapter 9, Section 9.1d, the Yerkes-Dodson law informs us that we seek to achieve and maintain an optimum level of bodily arousal—not too much and not too little. Yet the amount of stimulation necessary to reach the optimal level of arousal for one person is often not the same amount of stimulation needed by another person. According to Eysenck, introverts have inherited a nervous system that operates at a high level of arousal and is very sensitive to stimulation. Therefore, introverts avoid a great deal of social interaction and situational change in order to keep their arousal from reaching uncomfortable levels. Extraverts have the opposite problem. Their nervous system normally operates at a relatively low level of arousal and is much less sensitive to stimulation, and thus they seek out situations that stimulate them. Consistent with this idea of different levels of nervous system activation, researchers have found that introverted students prefer studying in quiet, socially isolated settings, whereas extraverted students prefer studying in relatively noisy settings where they can socialize with others (Campbell & Hawley, 1982). Additional studies indicate that extraverts not only choose to perform tasks in noisy settings but actually perform better, also, in such settings (Geen, 1984). Also consistent with Eysenck's arousal hypothesis are the findings that introverts are more sensitive to pain than are extraverts and that they salivate more when lemon juice is place on their tongues than do extraverts.

Some of the more inventive studies that Eysenck and his colleagues conducted to test the hypothesis that introverts have higher levels of arousal than extraverts involved classically conditioning the eye-blink response, using puffs of air to the eye as the unconditioned response (see Chapter 6, Self-Discovery Questionnaire 6-1). Eysenck

BVT *Lab*

Improve your test scores. Practice quizzes are available at www.BVTLab.com.

FIGURE 10-7

Do Introverts Have Higher Levels of Arousal Than Extraverts?

To test the hypothesis that introverts have higher levels of nervous system arousal than extraverts, numerous studies have classically conditioned the eye-blink response in these two groups of people (Eysenck, 1967; Eysenck & Levey, 1972). Results indicate that introverts show a much higher percentage of conditioned eye-blink responses to the conditioned stimulus than do extraverts. How do these findings support the hypothesis that introverts have inherited a nervous system that operates at a higher level of arousal than that of extraverts?

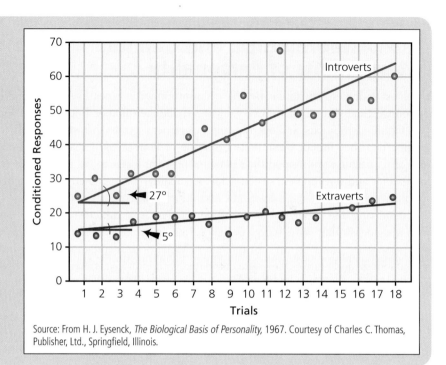

Source: From H. J. Eysenck, *The Biological Basis of Personality*, 1967. Courtesy of Charles C. Thomas, Publisher, Ltd., Springfield, Illinois.

reasoned that if introverts' nervous systems operate at a higher level of arousal than do those of extraverts, introverts' eye blinking should become conditioned faster than extraverts' to the conditioned stimulus (Eysenck & Levey, 1972). As you can see from Figure 10-7, his hypothesis was supported: Introverts exhibited a much higher percentage of conditioned eye-blink responses to the conditioned stimulus than did extraverts.

Studies employing brain-imaging technology suggest that brain structures in the frontal lobes that inhibit behavior possibly associated with danger or pain are more active among introverts than extraverts (Johnson et al., 1999). Additional research has found evidence that extraversion may be related to greater activation of dopamine pathways in the brain associated with reward and positive affect (Fishman et al., 2011; Wacker et al., 2006). Further, when introverts and extraverts are shown positive images (for example, puppies, a happy couple, or sunsets), extraverts experience greater activation of brain areas that control emotion, such as the frontal cortex and the amygdala (Canli & Amin, 2002). Together, this research suggests that introversion and extraversion are associated with distinct patterns of brain activity, and that the experience of positive affect may be a primary feature of extraversion.

Another related personality characteristic associated with a hyperactive nervous system and different brain activity is shyness, which involves feelings of discomfort and inhibition during interpersonal situations (Rubin et al., 2002). Although almost everybody feels shy at some point in their lives, about 40 percent of the population is excessively shy, which hinders them in making friends, developing romantic relationships, and pursuing other goals involving social interaction. When compared to nonshy persons, shy individuals are much more self-focused and spend an excess amount of time worrying about how others are evaluating them. Some studies show that shy children and adults are more likely to have been "high-reactive" infants, meaning they were more sensitive to environmental stimuli and thus fussier than other infants (Kagan et al., 1998; Woodward et al., 2001). Such reactivity is detectable even in the womb. Fetuses with fast heart rates are more likely to develop into shy children than are those with slow or normal heart rates.

Regarding brain activation, it appears that both the amygdala—which is involved in the emotion of fear—and the right frontal lobe—which is involved in controlling emotions—play a role in shyness. Brain scans of chronically shy adults indicate that when they are shown unfamiliar faces or when they are interacting with strangers, these shy adults experience much greater activation of the amygdala and the right frontal lobe than do nonshy persons (Birbaumer et al., 1998; McManis et al., 2002). This different level of brain activation among shy persons makes them more susceptible than others to experiencing anxious emotions.

10.7b Both Genetic and Environmental Factors Shape Personality.

Many personality theorists have long assumed that genetic predispositions influence most aspects of personality (Rowe & Van den Oord, 2005). As discussed in Chapter 8, Section 8.4b, psychologists have conducted a great deal of research comparing twins reared together versus those reared apart to better understand genetic and environmental influences on intelligence. Many of these same studies have also examined personality traits. Overall, they have found that when raised together, identical twins have more similar traits than do fraternal twins (Agrawal et al., 2004; McCrae, 1996). These findings indicate a moderate genetic influence on personality. However, this same research has found that the trait correlations for identical twins reared apart are considerably lower than for those reared together, which suggests that environment also influences trait development (Borkenau et al., 2001). Currently, the best estimates are that personality differences in the population are between 30 and 60 percent genetically determined, with the balance attributable to environment (Bouchard, 2004).

Although genetics plays an important role in shaping personality, *how* it does so is not clear. David Buss (1995) proposes that genes most likely influence personality due to their impact on physical characteristics and general predispositions toward certain temperaments associated with activity, emotionality, and sociability. These physical characteristics and temperaments then interact with environmental factors to shape personality. For example, children who inherit a healthy body and high sociability and activity levels may actively seek opportunities to play with other children. Such interactions may foster the development of important social skills and the enjoyment of social activities, which are characteristic of extraverted personalities. Of course, this does not mean that genetic predispositions will actually lead to specific personality traits for a given person. For instance, even though shyness is an inherited trait, children and older adults can consciously overcome their social inhibitions and become remarkably skilled and outgoing in a wide variety of social settings (Rowe, 1997). Parents are especially important either in diminishing children's shyness or in maintaining it into adulthood (Rubin et al., 2002). Thus, instead of genetics determining personality in some lockstep fashion, we appear to inherit the building blocks of personality from our parents; and then our interactions with our social environment create the personality that we develop (Johnson & Krueger, 2005).

Section REVIEW

- Inherited differences can be seen in introverts' and extraverts' nervous systems, especially in their brains.

- Higher levels of nervous system activity and different levels of brain activation cause shy persons to experience anxious emotions more frequently than do other people.

- Both genetic and environmental factors shape trait development.

PSYCHOLOGICAL
a p p l i c a t i o n s

Do You Have a Chameleon-Like Personality?

When studying personality, we are examining how people are consistent across situations and how they differ from one another. Yet what if I told you that personality researchers have identified a trait in which the defining characteristic is that people consistently behave inconsistently when interacting with others? Although this may sound strange to you, this trait is associated with a very normal self-presentation style that many of us exhibit. Before reading further, spend a few minutes responding to the items in Table 10.8 to better understand your association with this trait.

Self-Monitoring

In social relationships, we often try to manage the impression we make on others by carefully constructing and monitoring our self-presentations. Although we all monitor and adjust how we present ourselves to others depending on the situation and with whom we are interacting, there is a personality difference in the degree to which we make such alterations in "who we are to others." According to Mark Snyder (1987), these differences are related to a personality trait called **self-monitoring**, which is the tendency to use cues from other people's self-presentations in controlling our own self-presentations. Those of us high in self-monitoring spend considerable time learning about other people, and we tend to emphasize impression management in our social relationships (Peluchette et al., 2006).

Self-monitoring A personality trait involving the tendency to use cues from other people's self-presentations to control one's own self-presentations

In social settings, high self-monitoring persons become much less physiologically aroused than low self-monitoring persons, even while striving to project a positive self-image (Blakely et al., 2003; Hofmann, 2006). Due to their greater attention to social cues, high self-monitors are more skilled at both understanding and expressing the proper emotions in a social setting; and they often spontaneously mimic others' nonverbal behavior (Estow et al., 2007; Klein et al., 2004). For example, when trying to initiate a dating relationship, high self-monitoring men and women behave in a chameleon-like fashion, strategically and often deceptively changing their self-presentations in an attempt to appear more desirable (Rowatt et al., 1998). In contrast, low self-monitors are less attentive to situational cues, and their behavior is guided more by inner attitudes and beliefs. As a result, their behavior is more consistent across situations. Although it may appear to the casual observer that the low self-monitor has a stable personality and the high self-monitor has no identifiable personality at all, the high self-monitors' inconsistency across situations represents a stable personality trait.

Due to their greater attention to social cues, high self-monitors learn more quickly how to behave in new situations and are more likely to initiate conversations (Gangestad & Snyder, 2000). On the negative side, people high in self-monitoring have less intimate and committed social relationships; and they tend to judge people more on superficial characteristics, such as physical appearance and social activities, rather than their attitudes and values (Evans & Clark, 2012; Jamieson et al., 1987).

Self-Monitoring on the Job

Because high self-monitors' actions are guided by what they think are the appropriate behaviors in a given situation, some psychologists have wondered how this might affect their search for a job and their performance in that job (Snyder & Copeland, 1989). What about low self-monitors? Because they are guided more by their inner feelings and beliefs than social propriety, will they tend to gravitate toward and perform better in different jobs than their more socially sensitive counterparts?

Research suggests that those high in self-monitoring prefer jobs with clearly defined occupational roles. In comparison, low self-monitors tend to prefer occupational roles that coincide with their own personalities so they can "be themselves" on the job (Snyder & Gangestad, 1982). Thus, if you are high in self-monitoring, you may be more willing than those low in self-monitoring to mold and shape yourself to "fit" your chosen occupational role. You might find, for example, that occupations in the fields of law, politics, public relations, and the theater are particularly attractive. Or, considering yourself assertive, industrious, and a risk taker, you may gravitate toward careers in business or other entrepreneurial professions. In these careers, you can use your social chameleon abilities to mimic others' social expectations. In contrast, if you are low in self-monitoring and consider yourself to be warm, compassionate, and caring, you may seek out social service or "helping" occupations such as medicine, psychology, and social work.

After choosing and securing a job, your level of self-monitoring may influence your work performance. High self-monitors' social skills make them well suited for jobs that require the ability to influence others (Douglas & Gardner, 2004). One type of job that appears to be particularly suited to the skills of the high self-monitor is the so-called boundary-spanning jobs in which individuals must interact and communicate effectively with two or more parties who, because of their conflicting interests, often cannot deal directly with one another. Examples of boundary-spanning jobs

TABLE 10-8 The Self-Monitoring Scale

The personality trait of self-monitoring is measured by items on the Self-Monitoring Scale (Snyder, 1974; Snyder & Gangestad, 1982). To discover your level of self-monitoring, read each item below; and then indicate whether each statement is true or false for you.

_____ 1. I find it hard to imitate the behavior of other people.

_____ 2. At parties and social gatherings, I do not attempt to do or say things that others will like.

_____ 3. I can only argue for ideas that I already believe.

_____ 4. I can make impromptu speeches even on topics about which I have almost no information.

_____ 5. I guess I put on a show to impress or entertain others.

_____ 6. I would probably make a good actor.

_____ 7. In a group of people, I am rarely the center of attention.

_____ 8. In different situations and with different people, I often act like very different persons.

_____ 9. I am not particularly good at making other people like me.

_____ 10. I'm not always the person I appear to be.

_____ 11. I would not change my opinions (or the way I do things) in order to please someone or win their favor.

_____ 12. I have considered being an entertainer.

_____ 13. I have never been good at games like charades or improvisational acting.

_____ 14. I have trouble changing my behavior to suit different people and different situations.

_____ 15. At a party, I let others keep the jokes and stories going.

_____ 16. I feel a bit awkward in company and do not show up quite as well as I should.

_____ 17. I can look anyone in the eye and tell a lie with a straight face (if for a right end).

_____ 18. I may deceive people by being friendly when I really dislike them.

Directions for scoring: Give yourself one point for answering "True" to each of the following items: 4, 5, 6, 8, 10, 12, 17, and 18. Also give yourself one point for answering "False" to each of the following items: 1, 2, 3, 7, 9, 11, 13, 14, 15, and 16. Then add up your total number of points to arrive at your self-monitoring score.

When Snyder (1974) developed the Self-Monitoring Scale, the mean score for North American college students was about 10 or 11. The higher your score is above these values, the more of this personality trait you probably possess. The lower your score is below these values, the less of this trait you probably possess.

Source: From "The self-monitoring of expressive behavior" by Mark Snyder in _Journal of Personality and Social Psychology, 30,_ pp. 526–537. Copyright ©1974 by the American Psychological Association. Reprinted with permission.

would be the mediator in a dispute between management and labor, a real estate agent who negotiates the transfer of property from seller to buyer, and a university administrator who deals with students, faculty, and alumni. In an examination of 93 field representatives whose jobs required boundary spanning, researchers found that high self-monitors did perform better in these jobs than low self-monitors (Caldwell & O'Reilly, 1982). These findings suggest that self-monitoring skills may be particularly helpful in occupations where one must interact with people who have conflicting interests and agendas. In such work settings, high self-monitors are less likely to allow their personal feelings to affect their social interactions.

Being adept at reshaping self-presentation styles to overcome conflict on the job might be particularly useful for women who are breaking the corporate "glass ceiling" in many traditionally male-dominated occupations. For example, there is evidence that women who are business executives are less likely to experience a sexist backlash effect on the job due to their being in a traditionally masculine gender role if they are high self-monitors. One study found that over an eight-year period following graduation with an MBA degree, high self-monitoring female executives received more job promotions than did comparable low self-monitoring female executives (O'Neill & O'Reilly, 2011). The greater effectiveness of these high self-monitoring women is likely due to them being more willing and capable of shaping their self-presentations on the job, so that they overcome the underlying sexism of coworkers and thereby reduce resentment and resistance to them being in a position of power within the company.

In what type of job might you perform better if you are low in self-monitoring? The job performance of low self-monitors appears to be less influenced by their leader's behavior than that of high self-monitors,

It is not whether you really cry. It's whether the audience thinks you are crying.

—Ingrid Bergman, Swedish actress, 1915–1982

who are more sensitized to such external demands. In other words, the degree of effort that low self-monitors exert on the job is less dependent on their boss's expectations and more determined by their own intrinsic motivation. What this suggests is that if you are low in self-monitoring, you may be more effective than high self-monitors working in unsupervised settings—if you feel your work is important.

Now that you have learned about this particular personality trait, which end of the self-monitoring spectrum do you think is the desirable pole? Do you see high self-monitoring as more socially adaptive because it allows people to better negotiate in an ever-changing and complicated social world? Or do think that the chameleon-like nature of the high self-monitor suggests shallowness? Does the consistency of low self-monitoring individuals suggest "principled behavior" or "inflexibility?" The safest and perhaps wisest conclusion is that neither high nor low self-monitoring is necessarily undesirable unless it is carried to the extreme. Fortunately, pure high or low self-monitoring is rare; most of us fall somewhere on a continuum between these two extremes.

Suggested Websites

Great Ideas in Personality

http://www.personalityresearch.org

This website deals with scientific research programs in personality psychology. It provides information about personality research from a variety of perspectives, including some not covered in this chapter. It also contains a good selection of well-organized links to other personality websites.

The Society for Personality Assessment

http://www.personality.org

This Society for Personality Assessment website is intended primarily for professional use; it contains a section outlining the requirements for personality assessment credentials and telling how to go about becoming a personality psychologist.

The American Psychoanalytic Association

http://www.apsa.org

The website of the American Psychoanalytic Association is intended for both the general public and the professional psychoanalytic community. Information is provided about the current state of the psychoanalytic theoretical orientation.

Humanistic Psychology

http://www.apa.org/divisions/div32

This is the official website of the American Psychological Association's division of humanistic psychology. It provides information on upcoming APA events and information for students interested in this perspective.

QueenDom.com Complete List of Tests

http://www.queendom.com/tests/alltests.html

This website has a number of online personality tests that you can take and receive feedback on.

Key Terms

Anal stage, 453
Archetypes, 457
Character strength, 469
Collective unconscious, 457
Conditional positive regard, 460
Conscious mind, 450
Defense mechanism, 454
Displacement
Ego, 451
Extravert, 457
Five-Factor Model, 465
Fixation, 452
Genital stage, 454
Id, 451
Interactionism, 472
Introvert, 457
Latency stage, 454
Locus of control, 474

Minnesota Multiphasic
   Personality Inventory
   (MMPI), 480
Objective test, 480
Oral stage, 453
Peak experiences, 460
Personality, 447
Phallic stage, 453
Pleasure principle, 451
Preconscious mind, 450
Projection, 455
Projective test, 478
Psychodynamic perspective, 456
Psychosexual stages, 452
Rationalization, 455
Reaction formation, 455
Reality principle, 451
Reciprocal determinism, 473

Regression, 456
Repression, 454
Rorschach Inkblot Test, 478
Self-efficacy, 474
Self-monitoring, 486
Self-serving bias, 476
Situationism, 471
Social-cognitive
   perspective, 473
Superego, 451
Trait, 462
Trait perspective, 462
Unconditional positive
   regard, 460
Unconscious mind 450
Values in Action (VIA)
   Classification of
   Strengths, 469

Review Questions

1. The modern study of personality involves all except which of the following?
   a. studying how personality emerges from the interaction between the individual and his or her environment
   b. approaches that are more limited and narrow than in the first half of the twentieth century
   c. understanding how people may be generally predictable yet different from others
   d. both philosophical and scientific roots
   e. a focus on overarching and comprehensive descriptions of personality styles

2. Freud is perhaps best known for the significance of his theory of _____.
   a. glove anesthesia
   b. the nervous system
   c. the mind
   d. biological urges
   e. hypnosis

3. Regarding personality, Freud's structural model emphasized the different operating principles and goals that operated within which of the following subcomponents of the mind?
   a. the collective unconscious and archetypes
   b. id, ego, and superego
   c. id, pleasure principle, and archetypes
   d. ego, reality principle, and the collective unconscious
   e. id, superego, and reality

4. Among Freud's contributions was his theory of psychosexual stages, which included an emphasis on which of the following?
   a. five fixed stages of development in childhood and adolescence
   b. projection, which involves unresolved conflicts emerging from too little gratification of id desires
   c. the Oedipus complex, in which children develop unconditional positive regard toward their same-sex parent
   d. the oral stage, when unconscious sexual and aggressive impulses go dormant
   e. personality development after age 5

5. What does the psychoanalytic theory of defense mechanisms, or ways we control anxiety-provoking thoughts and impulses, suggest about defense mechanisms?
   a. They protect the id from unacceptable urges.
   b. They represent permanent changes in the structure of the mind.
   c. They allow us to understand our unconscious motivations.
   d. They explain why we can become civilized.
   e. They tend to be consistent, but not distinguishing, characteristics of personality.

6. An individual with a strong desire to perform immoral acts might exhibit extremely moralistic behavior and be harshly judgmental of others if he used which defense mechanism?
   a. rationalization
   b. reaction formation
   c. displacement
   d. projection
   e. regression

7. All the alternative approaches to Freud's psychoanalysis have in common which of the following notions?
   a. The collective unconscious is a fourth component of the mind's structure.
   b. Social interaction is the basis for personality.
   c. The mind can be understood only through carefully controlled scientific research.
   d. The unconscious mind is less important than Freud claimed.
   e. Sexual drives are not central in determining people's personalities.

8. The humanistic model of personality development differed from the predominant views of psychoanalysis and behaviorism primarily in which of the following?
   a. the discrepancy between Rogers's actual and feared self
   b. its exclusive focus on the development of psychologically healthy and creative people
   c. the belief that individual psychological growth is predetermined
   d. its optimistic approach to the possibilities for positive human change
   e. the scientific and testable hypotheses it generated

9. On what is the trait approach to personality primarily focused?
   a. describing how people differ from one another in specific ways
   b. Allport's view that behavior varies across situations
   c. relatively new ideas concerning the classification of people according to personality types
   d. direct measurement, rather than inference, of personality characteristics
   e. describing why people differ from one another in specific ways

10. What is the general consensus among personality researchers today about the basic personality traits?
    a. They are biologically or genetically determined.
    b. They capture the essence of individual personality.
    c. They are a result of adaptive human evolution.
    d. They vary across cultures.
    e. They include neuroticism, extraversion, openness to experience, agreeableness, and conscientiousness.

11. Which of the following is true of Mischel's controversial claim concerning the predictive ability of personality traits?
    a. Predictive ability was based on limited samples of behavior.
    b. Predictive ability was supported by personality research indicating that traits reliably predict behavior.
    c. Predictive ability led to the realization that situations do not play a role in shaping behavior.
    d. Predictive ability generated new research but did not increase the ability to predict behavior.
    e. Predictive ability indicated that children are reliably honest or dishonest across situations.

12. The social-cognitive approach describes personality as primarily based on which of the following?
    a. classical conditioning
    b. operant conditioning
    c. an individualist approach
    d. observational learning
    e. direct experience

13. What does Bandura's reciprocal determinism explain?
   a. The environment plays a more important role in behavior than the individual.
   b. Self-efficacy is stable and consistent across situations.
   c. Personality emerges from an ongoing mutual interaction between people's cognitions, actions, and environment.
   d. Individual perceptions are of little consequence in determining behavior.
   e. There is no relationship between self-efficacy and self-esteem.

14. In research on the Values In Action Classification of Strengths system, an Internet study of almost 118,000 adults from 54 countries found which of the following were three of the most commonly endorsed character strengths?
   a. creativity, curiosity, and open-mindedness
   b. forgiveness, humility, and modesty
   c. kindness, integrity, and gratitude
   d. bravery, persistence, and integrity
   e. citizenship, fairness, and leadership

15. The concept of locus of control, originated by Rotter, is associated with all except which of the following:
   a. a belief in one's ability to control the outcomes in one's life
   b. learned helplessness
   c. anger and acting-out behaviors
   d. achievement orientation
   e. success in life

16. What is the primary difference between projective and objective measures of personality?
   a. Objective measures rely on ambiguous stimuli, whereas projective measures are more direct.
   b. Projective tests assess unconscious aspects of personality, whereas objective tests assess conscious aspects of personality.
   c. Objective tests are scored on the basis of a correct answer, but there are no correct answers on projective tests.
   d. Projective tests are more reliable and valid than objective tests.
   e. Objective tests are used primarily to start conversations about a client's problems.

Chapter Eleven

Psychological Disorders

Chapter Outline

11.1 How Should We Define and Explain Psychological Disorders?
- a The Medical Model Proposes That Psychological Disorders Are Like Diseases.
- b Psychological Disorders Involve Atypical Behavior That Causes Personal Distress or Social Impairment.
- c Psychologists Rely on Different Theories to Explain Mental Illness.
- d Using Diagnostic Labels Has Both Risks and Benefits.

11.2 The Major Classes of Disorders Identified by the *DSM*
- a Anxiety Disorders Are Characterized by Distressing, Persistent Anxiety or Maladaptive Behavior.
- b Mood Disorders Are Characterized by Emotional Extremes.
- c Dissociative Disorders Involve a Loss of Contact with Portions of One's Consciousness or Memory.
- d Schizophrenia Involves Disturbances in Almost All Areas of Psychological Functioning.
- e Personality Disorders Involve Significant Impairments in Personality Functioning.

Psychological Applications: *Some Important Facts About Suicide*

During my junior year in college I rented an apartment along with two of my college friends, Tim and Doug. We were looking for another boarder to help pay the rent. After placing an ad in the local paper, we rashly accepted the first person who expressed an interest in the vacancy. Our new living companion was Jim, a quiet, frail-looking young man with long hair and a droopy mustache.

At first, other than being very quiet, Jim appeared to be your average college student. However, after a time, we noticed that he was lacking in virtually any kind of emotional expressiveness. He rarely smiled or laughed, and his actions were slow, as if he were moving through molasses. We also soon noticed that Jim regularly repeated two specific behaviors. One behavior was flicking on and off a cigarette lighter, and the other was opening and closing a small pocketknife. Both items were always in his hand or pants pocket. Strange, we thought; but was it any stranger than our roommate Tim repeatedly playing his favorite record album (yes, record, not tape or CD), the Doors' *Soft*

Parade, every single day? Was it stranger than Doug flopping down in his feather-bag chair like clockwork every day at 4:00 P.M.? Or stranger than me waking up every night and writing down my dreams in a notebook near my bed? Yes, we concluded, it was stranger than all those behaviors, but perhaps only in degree.

One group ritual that we quickly developed was returning to our apartment every day after classes to relax and watch reruns of the science fiction TV show *Star Trek* (with Captain Kirk and Spock). Although Jim would join us, he rarely spoke. Then one day, as an episode began, Tim burst out with an "Oh boy!!!" He was excited because he had never seen this episode before. To our surprise, the usually quiet Jim turned to Tim and asked, "Why did you call me a boy?" Utterly perplexed, Tim replied that he had done no such thing and was simply excited by what he was about to watch. Not satisfied with this explanation, Jim continued, "Well, if you weren't calling me a boy, then you must have been calling him a boy." He was pointing at the television. Slowly, we realized that Jim was referring to an African American actor on the screen. No amount of subsequent persuasion by Tim could convince Jim (who, by the way, was not African American) that his roommate was not being condescending to him or to minorities. Jim was convinced that Tim was "out to get him."

That same week, Doug was in charge of preparing our evening meals. After one such culinary treat, Jim confronted Doug and accused him of putting "speed" (amphetamines; see Chapter 5, Section 5.3f) in his food. Again, no amount of persuasion could convince Jim that Doug wasn't trying to poison him. After all, Jim said, what else could explain the sensations he was experiencing in his body? As with Tim following the *Star Trek* incident, Doug was now "the enemy."

About a week after these strange incidents, Tim came home from class, put his favorite album on the turntable, and settled down to relax. Yet, as the needle touched the record, it simply slid across the vinyl. No *Soft Parade*. When Tim inspected his prized record, he discovered that the vinyl grooves that produce the music had been fused together by some sort of intense heat. Immediately, the image of Jim flicking his cigarette lighter on and off popped into Tim's mind, and a chill ran down his back. Just then, Doug arrived home. Before Tim could tell him about the record, Doug plopped down in his feather-bag chair and was showered by goose down that burst from hundreds of puncture holes in the chair's fabric. Doug and Tim stared dumbfounded as feathers slowly settled on the carpeting. They must have looked like figures in a snow-globe scene. Immediately, the image of Jim opening and closing his pocketknife popped into their minds. We soon realized that, like those snow globes that captivate one's attention when shaken, our apartment had been similarly shaken, but by a powerful, invisible force beyond our understanding. We definitely had a problem. If Jim was destroying our cherished possessions as a form of distorted and misguided retribution, what was next?

* * * * *

Jim is an example of someone who experiences severe problems in his daily living, leading him (and those around him) to experience significant distress. When witnessing his bizarre thinking and behavior, those with whom Jim interacted generally were at a loss as to how to respond. Reasoning with Jim often wasn't effective, and ignoring his destructive actions was not an option. As his apartment mates, we wondered what was causing Jim to think, feel, and behave in a manner that was so dysfunctional.

Do people like Jim both interest and concern you? Such interest and concern are due to a number of factors. First, their actions are often very unusual and cry out for explanation. Second, their behavior is sometimes so strange that it is frightening. Third, you may see in them something of yourself. Haven't you, at times, become suspicious, distrustful, anxious, or depressed—or even heard or seen things that you later discovered were fabricated in your mind? Perhaps learning to understand these extreme forms of behavior in others will help you gain insight into your own behavioral oddities.

Many of the mental health problems addressed in this chapter are common; and so it is likely that some of the conditions discussed will remind you of someone you know, including yourself. Yet, even if you have not yet met people with serious psychological problems, you are likely to encounter them as your circle of acquaintances grows. Because you will eventually meet such people, it is important to have a basic understanding of the types and causes of psychological problems. The goal of this chapter is to introduce you to the topic of psychological disorders. From this introduction, you will encounter three basic questions. First, how should we define psychological disorders? Next, what are the important theoretical perspectives used to explain these disorders? Finally, how should we classify the major types of psychological disorders?

11.1 How Should We Define and Explain Psychological Disorders?

In reading the chapter-opening story of Jim and his strange behavior, you probably suspect that he had some sort of psychological disorder. How do we decide, though, when a pattern of behavior is simply "different" or "quirky" and when it is disordered? How do we explain such behavior?

11.1a The Medical Model Proposes That Psychological Disorders Are Like Diseases.

Many psychologists believe that a useful approach in organizing our thinking about mental health problems comes from the field of medicine. The **medical model** proposes that psychological disorders have a biological basis, can be classified into discrete categories, and are analogous to physical diseases. Since the late eighteenth century, the medical model has reflected the dominant way of thinking about mental disorders (Halfmann, 2012). In comparison to earlier approaches, which were largely based on superstitious beliefs that the mentally ill were possessed by demons or in league with the devil, the medical model represented an enlightened and humane orientation toward mental illness. Due to the medical model, patients were viewed with greater sympathy and less fear; and the scientific method underlying the medical model led to significant improvements in treatment.

In the late 1800s and early 1900s, Freud and other psychologically oriented therapists challenged the medical model's assumption that biological factors were the cause of all mental illness. Although not agreeing that all mental health problems have a biological basis, contemporary mainstream psychology has adopted the medical model's terminology, using such words as *illness* and *disorder* when referring to troublesome behavior patterns. As in the medical profession, in psychology a **symptom** is a departure from normal functioning or feeling that indicates the presence

We do not have to visit a madhouse to find disordered minds; our planet is the mental institution of the universe.

—Johann von Goethe, German philosopher, 1749–1832

Medical model The viewpoint from the field of medicine that psychological disorders have a biological basis and can be classified into discrete categories just as physical diseases are

Symptom A departure from normal functioning or feeling that indicates the presence of a disorder

How do we identify and label mental health problems? What symptoms do we look for in diagnosing psychological disorders?

Diagnosis The process of distinguishing one disorder from another

Etiology The initial cause that led to the development of the disorder

Prognosis A prediction about the likely course of a disorder

of a disorder, **diagnosis** involves distinguishing one disorder from another, **etiology** refers to a disorder's apparent causes and developmental history, and **prognosis** is a prediction about the likely course of a disorder.

11.1b Psychological Disorders Involve Atypical Behavior That Causes Personal Distress or Social Impairment.

One way to differentiate *disordered* from *normal* behavior is in terms of the statistical frequency of disordered behavior in the general population. Behavior that is significantly above or below the average in its frequency of occurrence is *atypical* and thus more likely to be classified as a psychological disorder. Jim's compulsive actions of repeatedly flicking on and off his lighter and opening and closing his pocketknife were certainly unusual, and they signaled an underlying psychological disorder. However, relying only on the criterion of statistical infrequency can easily lead to false judgments. For instance, the behavioral accomplishments of Nobel Prize winners and Hall of Fame athletes are statistically infrequent, but few would label these individuals as having a psychological disorder. On the other hand, some disorders, such as anxiety and depression, are statistically common in contemporary society. Thus, we cannot rely solely on deviations from the "average" in identifying psychological disorders.

Another way to differentiate between disordered and normal behavior is by determining whether the exhibited behavior violates cultural norms. For example, in mainstream American culture, reporting hallucinations is likely to raise concerns about your sanity. Yet among various Native American nations or to the Holy Ghost worshipers of Appalachia, hallucinogenic experiences are often perceived as normal and an essential ingredient in spiritual enlightenment.

Even within a given culture, shifts in norms can change people's perceptions of what is a mental disorder. As discussed in Chapter 9, Section 9.3d, homosexuality was labeled a psychological disorder by the American Psychiatric Association up until 1973, not only because it was atypical, but also because it violated prevailing standards of morality. As these examples attest, simply relying on whether or not something violates cultural norms is not adequate in determining what is disordered.

Do you consider heterosexuality a sign of mental illness? What about homosexuality? Despite the lack of any credible scientific evidence, 40 years ago, Americans exhibiting homosexual desires were considered mentally unstable. This is an example of how cultural prejudices can sometimes override scientific facts, causing widespread harm to specific groups of people in society.

INFO-BIT   Before the Civil War, many slaves in Southern states were diagnosed with mental illness because their behavior violated cultural norms (Landrine, 1988). *Drapetomania* was a psychological disorder in which a slave had an uncontrollable urge to escape from bondage, and *dysathesia aethiopica* was a disorder in which a slave was disobedient to her or his owners. Although labeling the desire to be free and the resentment of human bondage as disorders seems ludicrous, such labeling illustrates how culture can shape perceptions of mental illness.

There is more to a psychological disorder than being atypical or out of sync with cultural norms. Such behavior is much more likely to be considered disordered if it is judged *maladaptive*—disruptive or harmful—for the person or society. The inability to perform normal activities is an indication of maladaptiveness. Not leaving your house because you fear crowds, repeatedly being fired from jobs due to excessive drinking, or losing your life savings due to compulsive gambling are all examples of maladaptive behavior. Maladaptiveness is generally considered the most important criterion in defining a disorder.

Individuals who disclose that they are experiencing troubling emotions are often considered to have psychological problems. They may be able to perform normal activities, such as caring for family members and holding a job; however, they feel unreasonably fearful, anxious, guilty, angry, or depressed.

One of the advantages of this criterion is that it takes into account a person's own distress level rather than using the same standard for everyone. The problem with this criterion, however, is that some people who have psychological disorders—and who cause harm to themselves and others—are not troubled by their behavior. Further, some individuals may not be able to tell us how much distress they are experiencing because they are very young or are otherwise unable to communicate.

Cultural factors can also affect how people report personal distress. For example, Asian Americans suffering from a psychological disorder are more likely than non-Asians to report physical symptoms, such as dizziness, rather than emotional symptoms (Lin & Cheung, 1999). This is because in many Asian cultures, it is considered inappropriate to discuss one's personal feelings with others, especially non-family members. Many Hispanic Americans feel a similar reluctance to discuss psychological problems (Arredondo & Perez, 2003). Mental health professionals who are unaware of the cultural differences in how people express or present symptoms of mental illness are more likely to misdiagnose psychological disorders as physical ailments.

As you see, one of these criteria alone is usually insufficient to differentiate normal from disordered behavior. Although psychologists sometimes rely on only one criterion in making their diagnoses, they are more confident when more than one of these indicators is present and valid. Further, when making diagnoses, psychologists try to understand people's symptoms within the larger social context of their lives, in order to distinguish psychological disorders from other problems in living (Hsieh & Kirk, 2005).

In the end, diagnoses of psychological disorders often involve value judgments about what behaviors cross the bounds of normality. All four criteria are useful in arriving at a diagnosis, but they are not completely objective; and thus they can be influenced by the psychologist's value judgments (Whaley, 2004).

Drawing a line that clearly separates normality from abnormality is often difficult because, in reality, these distinctions represent two ends of a continuum. In this chapter, a **psychological disorder** is defined as a pattern of atypical behavior that results in personal distress or significant impairment in a person's social or occupational functioning. Using this definition, we see that Jim would definitely be classified as having a mental disorder. He certainly was experiencing considerable anxiety and distress, his repetitive actions were very unusual, and his physical symptoms and the nature of his social interactions were definitely interfering with normal daily living.

Every year about one quarter of adults in the United States—almost 59 million people—suffer from a psychological disorder. Among these individuals, about 14 million—approximately 6 percent of the adult population—suffer from a seriously debilitating mental illness. Over the course of their lives about half of all Americans (46 percent) will suffer from at least one psychological disorder, and more than half

BVT *Lab*

Flashcards are available for this chapter at **www.BVTLab.com**.

Psychological disorder
A pattern of atypical behavior that results in personal distress or significant impairment in a person's social or occupational functioning

There's a very fine line between a groove and a rut; a fine line between eccentrics and people who are just plain nuts.

—Christine Lavin, American singer and songwriter, b. 1952

The only difference between me and a madman is that I'm not mad.

—Salvador Dali, Spanish artist, 1904–1989

of those individuals will be diagnosed with two or more disorders at the same time (Kessler et al., 2005). The occurrence of two or more disorders at the same time is called *comorbidity*.

Worldwide, about 400 million people have psychological disorders; and it is predicted that mental health problems will soon account for 15 percent of the global burden of disease, just below that caused by heart disorders. Women and men are equally likely to experience psychological disorders during their lifetimes, and the prevalence of mental health problems in most countries is fairly stable over time (de Graaf et al., 2012).

 **INFO-BIT**   Contrary to earlier research indicating that psychological disorders occur more often among African Americans than among White Americans, more recent findings point to lower rates of mental illness among African Americans and higher rates among Hispanic Americans (Kessler et al., 2005; Sue & Chu, 2003).

11.1c   *Psychologists Rely on Different Theories to Explain Mental Illness.*

There are five primary perspectives in psychology from which to understand mental illness. The most recognizable approach is the *psychodynamic perspective*, which asserts that disordered behavior, like normal behavior, is not freely chosen; rather, unconscious forces that have been largely shaped by childhood experiences control it. The founding father of the psychodynamic perspective, Sigmund Freud, contended that early traumatic events leave the individual with troubling feelings and memories. Because this material is painful, the individual represses it to the unconscious. Once this material is unconscious, the individual does not experience the anxiety that would result if the painful material were faced directly. However, although this painful material is beyond conscious awareness, it continues to influence the person's behavior and is often expressed indirectly through defense mechanisms. This idea of how the unconscious mind shapes people's everyday actions formed the basis for Freud's theory of psychoanalysis (see Chapter 10, Sections 10.2a and 10.2b).

While the psychodynamic perspective assumes that "what you see is not what you get" when you analyze mental illness, the *behavioral perspective* assumes that disordered behavior is caused by readily identifiable factors in the person's environment and is the product of learning. As you recall from Chapter 6, behaviorists believe that learning occurs through *conditioning*. In classical conditioning, a previously neutral stimulus is paired with a stimulus that automatically elicits a reflexive response, the unconditioned stimulus. Through repeated pairing of the neutral and unconditioned stimuli, the neutral stimulus comes to elicit a response similar to the reflexive response. Classical conditioning can explain the development of several reflexive responses, including those that might lead to a psychological disorder.

The other basic form of conditioning is operant conditioning, which is driven by reinforcement and punishment (see Chapter 6, Section 6.2a). As you recall, behaviors followed by reinforcement will increase in frequency, whereas those followed by punishment will decrease in frequency. Operant conditioning explains why some individuals develop troubling behaviors (for example, a child's misconduct is reinforced), and also why some people fail to develop appropriate behaviors (for example, a child fails to learn appropriate social skills). According to the behavioral perspective, the etiology (initial cause) of disordered behavior is conditioning, whereas the maintaining cause is either the problem behavior itself or the environment that continues to condition the behavior.

Cognition is important in understanding psychological disorders because, as you will soon learn, many disorders involve severe cognitive disturbances. Indeed, the *cognitive perspective* (see Chapter 1, Section 1.2c) holds that ineffective or inaccurate thinking is the root cause of mental illness (Beck, 1991). According to this viewpoint, the person's faulty cognitive style is acquired through learning, perhaps from observing how one's parents interpret their experiences or from interpreting and attempting to understand one's own experiences. This ineffective way of thinking leads the person to experience troubling emotions or behave ineffectively. Cognitive theorists believe that the etiology of a psychological problem is learning and that the maintaining cause is the faulty cognitive style.

Theorists from the *sociocultural perspective* (see Chapter 1, Section 1.2f) propose that mental illness is the product of broad social and cultural forces. For example, within a given culture, the rates of psychological disorders are higher in poor urban settings than in other segments of the population. Further, as unemployment increases, psychiatric hospital admissions and suicides tend to increase similarly (Pines, 1993). Based on these sorts of findings, sociocultural researchers believe that social forces—such as poverty, urbanization, and inequality—may be the primary causes of many mental health problems (Jefferis et al., 2011; Lott, 2002).

Cross-culturally, although certain psychological disorders are universally encountered—such as depression and schizophrenia—others are limited to specific societies or cultural areas and have no known physiological causes (Watters, 2010). For example, in certain Mediterranean and Middle-Eastern cultures people occasionally suffer from *mal de ojo*, or "the evil eye," in which they experience fitful sleep, unexplained crying, diarrhea, vomiting, and fever. Similarly, only among the Arctic and sub-Arctic Eskimos do we find the *pibloktoq* disorder, which involves an abrupt break with reality, violence, and hyperexcitability, followed by seizures and coma. Mental health experts have not yet determined whether these *culture-bound syndromes* are distinct from the more established psychological disorders or whether they are variations of them (Gureje, 2008), but their existence demonstrates that a complete understanding of psychological disorders must consider people's sociocultural contexts.

While the previous perspectives primarily focus on the relationship between the mind and the social environment, biological researchers focus on the relationship between the mind and the body. This *biological perspective*—which includes the neuroscience and evolutionary perspectives first introduced in Chapter 1, Sections 1.2d and 1.2e—proposes that psychological disorders are caused by biological conditions, such as genetics, hormone levels, or neurotransmitter activity in the brain (McClenon, 2011). Biological irregularities related to mental illness are also shaped by many other factors, including illness and response to environmental stressors; and they often can be treated through medical intervention and drug therapies (see Chapter 12, Section 12.7).

Table 11-1 summarizes the five theoretical approaches to understanding mental illness. Over the years, as researchers have attempted to identify the origins of psychological disorders, they have discovered that adequate one-perspective explanations are rare. As a result, many current explanations of psychological disorders combine the various perspectives into one overall account.

One such interdisciplinary approach is the **diathesis-stress model** (Wagner et al., 2007), illustrated in Figure 11-1. A *diathesis* (pronounced "dye-A-thuh-sis") is an underlying vulnerability or predisposition that may be caused by genetic inheritance, biological processes, or early learning experiences. A person with a diathesis is susceptible to developing a problem later, when experiencing stress. Without the diathesis, stress alone may not be sufficient to produce a disorder (Martin et al., 2010). For example, a person may have inherited neural problems that are associated with

All are lunatics, but he who can analyze his delusion is called a philosopher.

—Ambrose Pierce, American satirist, 1842–1914

Diathesis-stress model A predisposition to a given disorder (diathesis) that combines with environmental stressors to trigger a psychological disorder

TABLE 11-1 The Etiology of Psychological Disorders by Theoretical Perspective

Perspective	Etiology
Psychodynamic	Unconscious conflict from childhood experiences
Behavioral	Conditioning from the environment
Cognitive	Learning ineffective or inaccurate thinking
Sociocultural	Broad social and cultural forces
Biological	Genetics, hormone levels, neurotransmitter activity

panic disorder. Further, overprotective parents may have taught the person to closely monitor his or her physiological reactions, a behavior that is also associated with panic disorder. Yet these predispositions may be expressed as a panic disorder only when the individual is experiencing high levels of stress in life. If such stress is infrequent, or if the person has learned how to adequately cope with such stressful events, he or she may never have a panic attack or he or she may have one that is relatively mild. Thus, the diathesis-stress model proposes that the *interaction* of both the predisposition for a disorder (diathesis) and environmental stressors is what causes the psychological disorder. Periodically throughout this chapter, I discuss how the diathesis-stress model can provide additional insight into how the other perspectives might interact in explaining a particular psychological disorder.

11.1d Using Diagnostic Labels Has Both Risks and Benefits.

Regardless of which theoretical perspective is used to understand psychological disorders, diagnostic labels can harm individuals in several ways. First, the label may dehumanize patients by encouraging mental health practitioners to treat them as labels rather than as unique individuals with problems. Further, labeled individuals may experience discrimination if job, housing, or other social opportunities are limited due to negative stereotypes about people with mental illness (see Exploring Culture & Diversity 11-1). Such labeling may also cause people to expect those labeled to behave abnormally, and thus to misperceive normal behavior as disordered.

FIGURE 11-1

The Diathesis-Stress Model

The diathesis-stress model proposes that a predisposition to a psychological disorder (diathesis) interacts with environmental stressors to cause the disorder. According to this model, the diathesis alone or the stressors alone are unlikely to trigger the disorder.

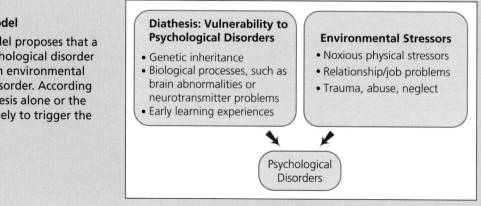

Diathesis: Vulnerability to Psychological Disorders
- Genetic inheritance
- Biological processes, such as brain abnormalities or neurotransmitter problems
- Early learning experiences

Environmental Stressors
- Noxious physical stressors
- Relationship/job problems
- Trauma, abuse, neglect

Psychological Disorders

Exploring CULTURE & DIVERSITY **11-1**

How Pervasive Is the Stigma Surrounding Mental Illness?

All available evidence strongly indicates that people identified as having psychological disorders are stigmatized in the United States and in other Western and Asian cultures (Brohan et al., 2012). A **stigma** is an attribute that serves to discredit a person in the eyes of others. In the United States, a national survey found that Americans viewed people with psychological disorders as dangerous and as less capable than the average person of handling daily affairs (Pescosolido et al., 1999). Such stigmatization is fostered and strengthened by selective news reporting of violent incidents involving people with psychological disorders and the highly negative portrayals of mentally ill people in popular culture (Angermeyer & Matschinger, 1996). For example, a content analysis of U.S. television programs found that people with psychological disorders are the most stigmatized group on the small screen; they are typically portrayed as either helpless victims or evil and violent villains (Gerbner, 1993). While 5 percent of "normal" television characters played the role of a murderer, 20 percent of "mentally ill" characters were portrayed as murderers. Similarly, whereas 40 percent of "normal" characters engaged in some form of aggression (a very high number in itself!), 70 percent of the "mentally ill" characters were violent.

Stigma An attribute that serves to discredit a person in the eyes of others

Faced with this social stigma and the fear of being negatively evaluated, people with psychological problems often conceal their symptoms and avoid seeking therapy (Wahl, 2012). In many Asian countries, the stigma of mental illness is so severe that it can damage the reputation of the family lineage and thereby significantly reduce the marriage and career prospects of other family members (Ng, 1997). This stigma is also pervasive among Asian Americans in the United States (Moon & Cho, 2012). For example, a mental health survey in Los Angeles (Zhang et al., 1998) found that Asian Americans were less than half as likely as White Americans to mention their mental health problems to a friend or relative (12 percent versus 25 percent), and only 4 percent stated that they would seek help from a psychiatrist or psychotherapist (compared to 26 percent of White Americans). In addition to preventing people from seeking help for their psychological problems, the stigma of mental illness lowers self-esteem while increasing a sense of social isolation and hopelessness.

So what is the truth underlying one of the most common stereotypes of the mentally ill—namely, that they are more violent than the average person? One study monitored the behavior of more than 1,000 individuals during the year after they had been discharged from psychiatric hospitals (Steadman et al., 1998). Results found no significant difference in the incidence of violence between the former patients and a control group of people living in the same neighborhoods with no history of serious mental health problems. Other research indicates that heightened violence is only slightly more likely among people with severe psychological disorders who are currently experiencing extreme psychological symptoms, such as bizarre delusional thoughts and hallucinated voices (Link et al., 1992). All other individuals with a psychological disorder that are not experiencing these severe symptoms are no more likely than the average person to be violent. Thus, the research

Shutterstock

The stigma surrounding psychological disorders causes many people to avoid seeking help. What is one of the most common stereotypes about people with mental illness?

clearly indicates that the cultural stereotype associating mental illness with violence is grossly exaggerated and largely unfounded. However, until such negative stereotypes surrounding psychological disorders are reduced, the stigma of the mental illness label will remain the most formidable obstacle to future progress in the area of mental health.

Despite the drawbacks associated with diagnostic labels, mental health professionals continue to use them because they serve several important functions (Andreasen & Black, 2006). The first benefit is that a label summarizes the patient's symptoms or problems. Rather than listing each patient's entire set of symptoms, clinicians can communicate a great deal of information about a patient with a single word.

A second benefit is that a diagnostic label conveys information about possible causes of the disorder. For some psychological disorders, research has identified clear causal and maintaining factors; and so the diagnostic label carries much useful information that helps the psychologist understand the individual's condition. In other disorders for which the etiology and maintaining causes are still unclear, the diagnostic label may suggest to the psychologist a range of possible causes to consider when working with the patient.

A third benefit is that a diagnostic label conveys information about the patient's prognosis, or expected future course. An important aspect of the prognosis is the patient's likely response to treatment.

Thus, although diagnostic labels may sometimes lead to aversive consequences for people who have psychological disorders, these labels also convey important information about the nature, probable causes, and likely treatments of the problem. Because of these benefits, psychologists continue to use diagnostic labels while being mindful of the potential risks.

In arriving at a diagnosis, the vast majority of psychologists, psychiatrists, and other mental health professionals rely upon the ***Diagnostic and Statistical Manual of Mental Disorders (DSM),*** published by the American Psychiatric Association. This system has been updated several times, with the newest and fifth edition version, *DSM-5*, published in 2013. The *DSM* differs from previous diagnostic systems in several ways. First, this classification system is descriptive rather than explanatory, meaning that it is not based on a particular theory concerning what causes psychological disorders. Rather, it is atheoretical. Thus, diagnoses are based more on observable symptoms than on the clinician's judgment about the underlying cause of these symptoms. Second, the *DSM* provides clearer directions to clinicians concerning the number, duration, and severity of symptoms that are necessary to assign a diagnosis. By recognizing that two patients with the same disorder may substantially differ from one another, clinicians are much more likely to acknowledge the uniqueness of all patients.

These improvements address many of the criticisms of diagnostic labels, and numerous studies indicate that *DSM* diagnoses are, in fact, more reliable than previous diagnostic systems. However, critics still contend that the *DSM* incorrectly views many normal behaviors as indicating a psychological disorder. For example, an irrational fear of embarrassment is considered a symptom of social anxiety disorder, while a habitual tendency to violate rules at home or in school is a symptom of conduct disorder. In response, ongoing research seeks to improve the reliability and validity of *DSM* diagnoses and to address criticisms of specific sections of the diagnostic system. As research identifies new disorders or more reliable ways of diagnosing a disorder, these results are incorporated into new versions of the *DSM*. The newest version, *DSM-5*, uses broader categories of disorders than previous versions; it also recognizes the substantial overlap between similar disorders (Elhai et al., 2012; Fusar-Poli & Yung, 2012). As you can see, the *DSM* will always be a "work in progress," continuously shaped by the insights of ongoing research, which is the hallmark of good science.

Diagnostic and Statistical Manual of Mental Disorders (DSM) The manual of psychological disorders published by the American Psychiatric Association and used for descriptive diagnoses

The *Diagnostic and Statistical Manual of Mental Disorders (DSM)* is the classification scheme used by most mental health professionals to diagnose psychological disorders. This classification scheme has been updated several times, with the latest version being its fifth-edition revision, or *DSM-5*.

- The medical model views psychological disorders like physical diseases.
- The criteria for differentiating disordered behavior from normal behavior include the following:
  1. Behavior is atypical.
  2. Behavior violates cultural norms.
  3. Behavior is maladaptive.
  4. Behavior involves personal distress.
- Psychologists employ multiple perspectives in studying psychological disorders.
- The diathesis-stress model proposes that the predisposition for a psychological disorder (diathesis) interacts with environmental stressors to cause the disorder to emerge.
- Two risks in using diagnostic labels are that (1) mental health professionals may become biased in interpreting normal behavior as disordered in persons labeled mentally ill, and (2) labeled individuals may be stigmatized by others and subject to discrimination.
- Using labels does have benefits. For example, diagnostic labels communicate valuable information, including possible causes of the disorder, its likely course, and possible treatment.
- Most clinicians rely on the *Diagnostic and Statistical Manual of Mental Disorders (DSM)* when diagnosing psychological disorders.

11.2 The Major Classes of Disorders Identified by the *DSM*

The remainder of this chapter introduces you to the major classes of psychological disorders. Each class of disorders is defined according to the most severe or most prominent of the patient's symptoms. While reading about these disorders, keep in mind that you may have experienced some of these symptoms yourself at some time. In recognizing yourself, you may begin to worry that you have one (or more) of these disorders. Don't become alarmed. The truth is that many of the described symptoms are fairly common in the general population. On numerous occasions throughout your life, you will experience sadness and euphoria, unrealistic anxiety and fear, and interpersonal problems. Only when these symptoms significantly disrupt your functioning or your sense of well-being are they indicative of a possible psychological disorder. In such instances, you should seek the help of a mental health professional for proper diagnosis and treatment.

11.2a Anxiety Disorders Are Characterized by Distressing, Persistent Anxiety or Maladaptive Behavior.

Everybody experiences anxiety. However, anxiety disorders are distinguished from "normal" anxiety by the severity of the emotional distress and the degree to which the anxiety disrupts daily functioning. **Anxiety disorders**, which are characterized by distressing, persistent anxiety or maladaptive behavior, are the most common

Anxiety disorders Disorder characterized by distressing, persistent anxiety or maladaptive behavior

psychological disorders (Daitch, 2011). About 25 percent of us will experience one of these disorders in our lifetime (Skaer et al., 2008). Anxiety disorders occur across the life span and commonly co-occur with many other disorders, such as depression and substance abuse. In this section, we discuss six anxiety disorders: panic disorder, specific phobias, social anxiety disorder, generalized anxiety disorder, obsessive-compulsive disorder, and post-traumatic stress disorder.

Panic Disorder (and Agoraphobia)

Panic disorder An anxiety disorder characterized by episodes of intense fear and dread that usually occur suddenly and unexpectedly

Maya is a 28-year-old hairstylist who has **panic disorder**, which is characterized by episodes of intense anxiety without an apparent reason. When having these attacks, Maya feels dizzy. Her heart races, she sweats and has tremors, and she may even faint. Besides these physiological symptoms, her psychological symptoms may include fear of dying, fear of suffocating, fear of "going crazy," and fear of losing control and doing something drastic, such as killing herself or others.

Panic episodes have a clear beginning and end, and they are relatively brief, usually lasting no more than about 10 minutes; they sometimes come and go over a period of an hour or more. As you can imagine, such episodes are extremely frightening; the symptoms of sympathetic nervous system arousal often lead sufferers like Maya to seek immediate medical attention out of concern that they are having a heart attack or some other serious life-threatening episode. About 3 percent of the general population worldwide experience panic disorder during their lifetimes (Weissman et al., 1997). In general, this anxiety disorder occurs more often in young adults than in older adults, with about twice as many women (5 percent) suffering from it as men (2 percent).

Agoraphobia Acute anxiety in situations where it is perceived to be difficult or embarrassing to escape, generally public settings or wide-open places

People often take extreme steps to limit the panic episodes. For example, Maya is embarrassed about having a panic episode in public, so she limits her social activities. She also avoids locations where she has experienced previous panic episodes, and so she has stopped going to shopping malls and restaurants. As you can see, like many people with panic disorder, Maya has significantly restricted her social activities outside her home. Such restriction of activities in an attempt to limit panic episodes can lead to a related psychological disorder called **agoraphobia**, which involves acute anxiety in situations where it is perceived to be difficult or embarrassing to escape. These situations are generally public settings or wide-open places. As its name implies, agoraphobia was originally classified as a phobia (see next subsection); yet more recent studies suggest that it is often a complication of panic disorder (Wittchen et al., 2010). One reason agoraphobia was not recognized earlier as developing from panic disorder was that those who experienced it rarely came to clinics for treatment due to their avoidance of outside activities. About one third of individuals who suffer from panic disorder also suffer from agoraphobia.

Specific Phobias

Specific phobias A group of disorders characterized by strong irrational fears of specific objects or situations

Another anxiety disorder is **specific phobias**; these are characterized by strong, irrational fears of specific objects or situations. The *DSM* classifies phobias into subtypes based on the object of fear. The most common subtypes in the United States involve fear and avoidance of particular objects and situations, such as heights, animals, enclosed spaces, blood, and automobile or air travel. Specific phobias affect about 10 percent of the population, but women are diagnosed with this disorder about twice as often as men (Narrow et al., 2002); and they tend to develop phobic symptoms earlier (age 10 for females and age 14 for males).

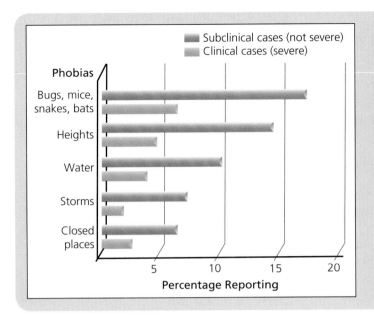

FIGURE 11-2

Frequency of Specific Phobias

Many people experience fear when exposed to these stimuli. In most of these cases, the fear represents a "subclinical" phobia, meaning that it would not be indicative of a psychological disorder.

Different types of phobias tend to have different courses. For example, fears of strangers, doctors, storms, and the dark are more common in children than in adults, whereas fears of cancer and the death of a loved one are more common in adults. Interestingly, phobias have a moderate tendency to run in families, so that individuals with phobias tend to have close relatives with similar kinds of phobias.

When analyzing phobias, it is important to distinguish them from rational fears that occur in the presence of a realistic threat. For example, it is normal to experience fear when encountering a mugger or when riding in a car that skids off the road. It is also important to distinguish clinical phobias from *subclinical phobias*, which are mild, irrational fears that do not interfere with daily functioning. You may experience fear when you encounter a huge spider in your basement while washing clothes. If you continue to use the basement for normal activities despite your fear, you have a subclinical phobia. In contrast, if you are so afraid of seeing the spider in your basement that you start taking your clothes to a laundromat, you may have a clinical phobia. Figure 11-2 shows the frequency of some common specific phobias. Before reading further, complete Closer Look 11-1.

What Do You Most Fear?

We all fear something. Fear of animals is most common during the elementary school years. Blood phobia tends to appear at about age 12, and social phobias and claustrophobia are most pronounced in later adolescence or early adulthood.

1. What is it that you fear most? _____

2. At what age did you first become aware of this fear? _____

3. How strong is this fear? Mild fear 1 2 3 4 5 6 7 8 9 10 Paralyzing fear

4. Does this fear cause a major disruption in your life? Yes ___   No ___

5. Based on what you have read about phobias, do you think this fear is

   —merely a normal reaction to a source of anxiety? _____

   —sufficiently intense to be a subclinical phobia? _____

   —sufficiently intense to be a clinical phobia? _____

Social Anxiety Disorder

Social anxiety disorder An anxiety disorder involving intense fear of being humiliated in the presence of others

Social anxiety disorder (also known as *social phobia*) involves intense fear of being humiliated in the presence of others (LeBeau et al., 2010; Yoon & Joormann, 2012). Physical symptoms often associated with this disorder include excessive blushing, sweating, trembling, difficulty breathing, nausea, stammering, and rapid speech. A person suffering from social anxiety disorder may also experience panic attacks.

For about half of those suffering from social anxiety disorder, a specific social incident can be identified as triggering the social phobia. For example, during a 1967 concert in New York's Central Park, singer Barbara Streisand suddenly forgot the lyrics to a song, triggering intense anxiety that made it impossible for her to perform in public for nearly another three decades. About 5 percent of the population suffers from social anxiety disorder, with women having only slightly higher rates than men (Narrow et al., 2002; Wong et al., 2012). Social phobia often occurs alongside major depressive disorder; and individuals suffering from social phobia may use alcohol or other drugs to reduce their anxiety, which can lead to substance abuse.

Wikimedia Commons

Singer Barbara Streisand has been diagnosed with social anxiety disorder, which is the primary reason she only rarely performs in public. Why might social anxiety disorder also be related to depression?

Generalized Anxiety Disorder

Generalized anxiety disorder (GAD) An anxiety disorder characterized by a constant state of moderate anxiety

Generalized anxiety disorder (GAD) is characterized by a constant state of moderate anxiety. This anxiety differs from normal anxiety that occurs in response to actual stressful events or situations (Huppert et al., 2008). For example, if you are a full-time college student who works 20 hours a week and maintains an active social life, it is normal to experience stress and anxiety throughout the semester. Further, the anxiety experienced in GAD differs from the anxiety felt in phobic disorder because in GAD, there is no clear object or situation that causes the anxiety. Instead, the anxiety is "free floating." GAD also differs from panic disorder in that the anxiety does not occur in discrete, relatively brief episodes but is constant.

GAD occurs in about 5 percent of the general population in their lifetime—about twice as often in women as men, and more often among those over the age of 24. GAD often occurs in association with other problems, including other anxiety disorders and depression (Ritter et al., 2010). The director and actor Woody Allen is perhaps the most famous living person who suffers from generalized anxiety disorder. In his films, Allen often portrays a character who is constantly worrying about something, and he admits that creatively expressing this anxiety on the silver screen helps him cope with this disorder.

Obsessive-Compulsive Disorder

Obsessive-compulsive disorder (OCD) An anxiety disorder characterized by persistent, unwanted, and distressing actions and/or thoughts

Obsessive-compulsive disorder (OCD) is an anxiety disorder characterized by repetitive, unwanted, and distressing actions and/or thoughts. *Obsessions* are persistent thoughts or ideas that cause distress or interfere significantly with ongoing activity. For example, some people with OCD may be bothered by thoughts of killing themselves or others, even though they have no history of, and are not truly at risk for, suicide or homicide. *Compulsions* are repetitive actions or behaviors that people feel compelled to perform in order to prevent or reduce anxiety. Most OCD rituals can be classified as *cleaning* or *checking*. For example, some people with OCD engage in hand-washing rituals, cleaning their hands hundreds of times a day, while others feel compelled to repeatedly check the locks on their doors before they leave the house. Still other individuals save newspapers and tin cans for years, to the point that it becomes difficult to navigate through their houses (Stewart et al., 2008).

In some cases, compulsions serve to control obsessions. For example, a man may have persistent thoughts about sex and try to control these thoughts and reduce the anxiety these thoughts induce by compulsively reciting a prayer. Unfortunately, this compulsive ritual lowers his anxiety only temporarily, and soon the man must repeat it or add to its length.

Most rituals are not indicators of mental illness. For example, prayer beads are used by members of various religions in counting the repetitions of prayers, chants or devotions. Similarly, komboloi, or "worry beads," are part of a ritual in traditional Greek and Cyprus culture used to relieve stress, keep hands and fingers occupied, and generally pass the time.

Psychologists today recognize that this disorder is more common than had been thought in the past. The lifetime prevalence of OCD is from 2 to 3 percent, with females having a somewhat higher risk than men (Torres et al., 2004). This disorder tends to develop in adolescence or young adulthood although it may not be diagnosed until years later. Those having OCD usually are embarrassed about their symptoms and try to hide them from others. Thus, it may be years before the symptoms become so intense that they can no longer be hidden. Research indicates there is at least a moderate genetic influence on OCD (Pato et al., 2002).

Post-Traumatic Stress Disorder

Post-traumatic stress disorder (PTSD) occurs in some individuals who have experienced or witnessed life-threatening or other traumatic events. Following such trauma, some people experience intense emotional distress, re-experiencing the event (say, through nightmares or flashbacks) and avoiding situations or persons that trigger flashbacks. When these symptoms occur long after the original trauma and significantly interfere with normal daily functioning, the individual is said to have PTSD (Lamprecht & Sack, 2002).

Post-traumatic stress disorder (PTSD) An anxiety disorder characterized by flashbacks and recurrent thoughts of life-threatening or other traumatic events

Almost 8 percent of the general population experience PTSD symptoms during some period in their lifetime. Although highly dramatic events, such as warfare and natural disasters, can lead to this disorder, most PTSD patients have experienced more common types of trauma, such as rape, child abuse, family illness, or witnessing violence (Bromet & Havenaar, 2002; Kazak et al., 2004). It appears that trauma due to crime is more likely to trigger PTSD than trauma due to natural disaster. Risk also varies with the nature and severity of the trauma (Koren et al., 2005). For example, the lifetime risk for PTSD following rape is about 35 percent, while the lifetime risk following automobile accidents ranges from 8 to 41 percent, depending on the severity of the accident (Keppel-Benson, 2002; Stallard et al., 2004). In general, as the severity of the traumatic event increases, the risk for PTSD increases.

Although only about 4 percent of the U.S. population experiences PTSD at any given time, the rates are much higher for combat veterans, inner-city residents, and recent immigrants from countries in turmoil (Kagee, 2004; Yehuda, 2000). For example, some survey studies of refugees from Vietnam, Cambodia, and Laos find rates of PTSD symptoms as high as 70 percent. Further, in a study of more than 1,000 recently immigrated schoolchildren in Los Angeles, 32 percent reported PTSD

AP Wide World Photo

Following the terrorist attacks on the World Trade Center and the Pentagon, many survivors developed post-traumatic stress disorder, which involves intense emotional distress, nightmares or flashbacks, and avoidance of situations or persons that trigger flashbacks.

symptoms in the clinical range, which is comparable to the estimated percent of children and adolescents suffering from PTSD in some war-torn Middle-Eastern countries (Dimitry, 2012; Jaycox et al., 2002).

Etiology of Anxiety Disorders

Several biological factors appear to influence the development of anxiety disorders. As discussed in Chapter 6, Section 6.1d, our genetic heritage may predispose us to more easily develop phobic reactions toward certain objects and situations, such as snakes and heights, because they once posed real dangers to our ancestors (Buss, 1995; Kleinknecht, 1991). According to this evolutionary explanation, snakes and heights make many of us unduly anxious and are the source of phobic reactions because the genes that trigger such anxiety are still part of our biological makeup.

Genetics also plays a contributory role in other anxiety disorders (Pato et al., 2002). For example, panic disorder is more likely to be shared by identical twins than fraternal twins; agoraphobia occurs at a higher frequency among family members; and family, twin, and adoption studies indicate that OCD is at least moderately influenced by genetics (Billett et al., 1998).

At the level of brain functioning, brain-imaging studies have found evidence that obsessions are at least partly caused by a malfunctioning neural structure in the *basal ganglia*, a brain region located below the cerebral cortex (Hansen et al., 2002; Saxena & Rauch, 2000). Normally, this structure—the *caudate nucleus*—terminates recurrent thoughts before they become obsessions, but in people with OCD, it does not operate correctly. Evidence also indicates that people with panic disorder are more likely to have a limbic system (most notably, the amygdala) that is more easily activated by mental imagery of traumatic events versus nontraumatic events (Shin et al., 1997). As you recall from Chapter 2, Section 2.3b, a malfunctioning amygdala can trigger intense fear.

The fact that certain drugs can alleviate anxiety symptoms and other drugs can induce those same symptoms further suggests that biology plays a role in anxiety disorders (Hansen et al., 2002). Brain scans also reveal that people who have anxiety disorders respond differently to danger signals than those who do not (Gorman, 2002). These and other findings suggest that some people are simply biologically predisposed to respond more intensely to stressful events than other people, and this stronger stress reaction puts them at greater risk for developing anxiety disorders.

As discussed in Chapter 6, behavioral or conditioning factors have also been implicated in anxiety disorders (Hopko et al., 2001; Watson & Rayner, 1920). In such cases, classical conditioning can produce emotional responses to previously neutral stimuli. After these conditioned emotional responses have been initiated, people's avoidance of the feared objects may be reinforced, because as they move away from the objects, their anxiety decreases. In other words, classical conditioning may be involved in instilling conditioned emotional responses; and operant conditioning may reinforce—and so, maintain—the person's avoidance responses. This *two-process conditioning model* has been an influential and useful way to understand anxiety disorders. Consistent with this perspective is the finding from one study that 44 percent of those with social anxiety disorder could identify a traumatic conditioning event in their past that was associated with their anxiety (Stemberger et al., 1995).

Finally, cognitive factors also play an important role in anxiety disorders (Kley et al., 2012). People who have panic disorder often closely monitor their physiological reactions because they want to detect the onset of another panic episode. However, they often misinterpret and exaggerate the significance of their physiological symptoms, perhaps because panic episodes are so distressing. Their hypervigilance regarding the onset of panic episodes may actually contribute to the condition they want to avoid (Beck, 1997). This "fear of fear" is one of the fundamental problems that must be addressed in treating panic disorder.

It is easy to see how biological, behavioral, and cognitive factors interact to cause anxiety disorders. Consider, again, panic disorder. People with panic disorder may have a biological predisposition to this problem; and biological stressors, such as breathing a carbon-dioxide-rich mixture of air, can trigger panic episodes (Rapee, 1995). Through conditioning, panic is associated with certain situations so that eventually these situations alone can trigger panic attacks. Finally, people who have panic disorder become so fearful of panic episodes that they are hypervigilant to signs of a panic attack and thus may actually frighten themselves into a panic attack. Given these possible multiple triggers, what is the ultimate cause of panic disorder? Is it biological, behavioral, or cognitive? Most likely, it is some combination of all three.

11.2b Mood Disorders Are Characterized by Emotional Extremes.

Have you ever had "the blues"? Most people have had days when they felt sad, lethargic, and uninterested in their usual activities. These are some of the symptoms of depression, the most common mood disorder. In general, **mood disorders** are characterized by emotional extremes that cause significant disruption in daily functioning (Kupfer et al., 2012). These symptoms are relatively common; almost 30 percent of the general population reports experiencing depressed mood for at least two weeks at some time in their lives. However, to qualify as a mood disorder, such emotional extremes must persist for a long time.

Mood disorders Psychological disorder characterized by emotional extremes that cause significant disruption in daily functioning

Depression

Major depressive disorder A mood disorder characterized by extreme and persistent negative moods and the inability to experience pleasure from activities previously enjoyed

The most common mood disorder is **major depressive disorder** (often referred to simply as *depression*), which is characterized by extreme and persistent negative moods and the inability to experience pleasure by participating in activities one previously enjoyed (Kristensen et al., 2012; Riso et al., 2003). Depressed individuals often experience physiological problems, such as lack of appetite, weight loss, fatigue, and sleep disorders. In addition, depressed individuals often experience behavioral symptoms, such as slowed thinking and acting (called *psychomotor retardation*), social withdrawal, and decreased rate of activity. Finally, depressed people exhibit cognitive symptoms, including low self-esteem, thinking about death and/or suicide, and having little hope for the future. When these symptoms are severe, persistent, and interfere with daily functioning, the person is diagnosed as having major depressive disorder. When these symptoms are mild but persistent, lasting for more than two years, the individual is diagnosed with dysthymia (Subodh et al., 2008). The average duration of **dysthymia** is about five to ten years.

Dysthymia Chronic low-level depression lasting more than two years

Because major depressive disorder is so common—the lifetime likelihood is about 17 percent, with an annual rate of 6.5 percent—it has been termed the "common cold" of mental illness (Kaelber et al., 1995). Further, people who experience major depressive disorder often have multiple recurrences (Solomon et al., 2004). Table 11-2 lists some well-known individuals who have struggled with this disorder during their lives. Cross-culturally, depression occurs about twice as frequently in women as in men, but significant variations are seen between cultures (see Figure 11-3). Depression is also associated with age (Weissman et al., 1996). In the general population, the risk of having a major depressive episode in a given year is highest (almost 4 percent) among people between the ages of 30 and 44 years. Although depression does occur in children, the risk among those younger than 10 years is much lower than that among adolescents and adults. Check out Self-Discovery Questionnaire 11-1, which contains a self-report questionnaire that assesses cognitive symptoms of depression.

One of the major dangers of depression is suicide; about half of all suicide victims kill themselves during a depressive episode (Kokkevi et al., 2012; Overholser et al., 2012). While the lifetime risk of suicide in the general population is 0.5 percent, it is eight times higher (4.0 percent) among people with mood disorders. In the United States about 33,000 people commit suicide annually, or about 11 per 100,000, making it the 11th leading cause of death in the country. Women are twice as likely as men to attempt suicide; but because men typically use more lethal methods (such as guns

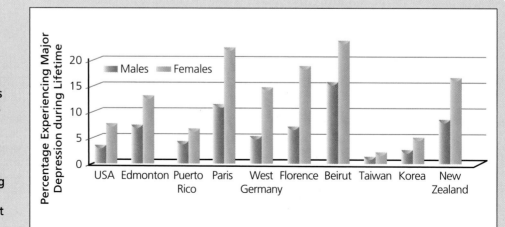

FIGURE 11-3

Gender and Depression

Interviews with 38,000 women and men in ten countries found that women's risk of experiencing major depression is double that of men's. Lifetime risk of depression among adults varies by culture (Weissman et al., 1996).

TABLE 11-2 Well-Known People Who Have Struggled with Depression

Historical Figures

John Adams	American president
Agatha Christie	British crime author
Winston Churchill	British prime minister
Charles Dickens	British author
William James	American psychologist and philosopher
Abraham Lincoln	American president
Martin Luther	German theologian
Gustav Mahler	Austrian composer
Isaac Newton	British physicist
Sylvia Plath	American writer
Edgar Allen Poe	American author and poet
Leo Tolstoy	Russian writer
Virginia Woolf	British writer

Contemporary Figures

Buzz Aldrin	American astronaut
Terry Bradshaw	American football player
Jim Carrey	Canadian actor and comedian
Sheryl Crow	American singer-songwriter
Harrison Ford	American actor
Ken Griffey, Jr.	American baseball player
Beyoncé Knowles	American singer-songwriter
Ewan McGregor	Scottish actor
Gwyneth Paltrow	American actor
J. K. Rowling	British writer
Amy Tan	American writer
Uma Thurman	American actor
Oprah Winfrey	American talk-show host

SELF-DISCOVERY 11-1
Questionnaire

What Are Some Cognitive Symptoms of Depression?

The Automatic Thoughts Questionnaire

The Automatic Thoughts Questionnaire, or ATQ (Hollon & Kendall, 1980), addresses common negative thoughts that occur when people are experiencing depressed mood. You may find it interesting to read the items of the ATQ and rate your own negative thoughts. Read each thought carefully and indicate how frequently, if at all, the thought occurred to you *over the last week*, using the following scale:

1 = not at all   2 = sometimes   3 = moderately often
4 = often   5 = all the time

____ 1. I feel like I'm up against the world.

____ 2. I'm no good.

____ 3. Why can't I ever succeed?

____ 4. No one understands me.

____ 5. I've let people down.

____ 6. I don't think I can go on.

____ 7. I wish I were a better person.

____ 8. I'm so weak.

____ 9. My life's not going the way I want it to.

____ 10. I'm so disappointed in myself.

____ 11. Nothing feels good anymore.

____ 12. I can't stand this anymore.

____ 13. I can't get started.

____ 14. What's wrong with me?

____ 15. I wish I were somewhere else.

____ 16. I can't get things together.

____ 17. I hate myself.

____ 18. I'm worthless.

____ 19. I wish I could just disappear.

____ 20. What's the matter with me?

____ 21. I'm a loser.

____ 22. My life is a mess.

____ 23. I'm a failure.

____ 24. I'll never make it.

____ 25. I feel so hopeless.

____ 26. Something has to change.

____ 27. There must be something wrong with me.

____ 28. My future is bleak.

____ 29. It's just not worth it.

____ 30. I can't finish anything.

To score the ATQ, simply add the ratings for all 30 items. The average score in a college student population is about 49, whereas the average score in a depressed sample is about 80. Keep in mind that this exercise is not meant to diagnose depression in those who answer these questions, but rather to give you an idea of the common negative thoughts that occur when people are depressed. If you experience many of these thoughts on a regular basis, you might consider consulting a mental health professional.

Source: From "Cognitive self-statements in depression: Development of an Automatic Thoughts Questionnaire" by S. D. Hollon and P. C. Kendall in *Cognitive Therapy and Research, 4*, 1980, pp. 383–395. Copyright © 1980. Reprinted by permission of Kluwer Academic/ Plenum Publishers and the authors.

---

instead of pills), men are four times more likely to actually kill themselves (18.4 versus 4.7 per 100,000). Although age was once a significant factor in predicting suicide—the elderly were five times more likely to commit suicide than young adults, 60 years ago—this is no longer the case. Over the past 60 years, suicide rates among the elderly have dropped 50 percent while rates among young adults have doubled. Since 2000, suicide rates for both age groups have remained about the same (12.1 for young adults versus 14.6 for the elderly per 100,000).

Figure 11-4 depicts the suicide rates per 100,000 people in various ethnic groups in the United States. The highest rates of suicide are among the various Native American tribes (14.6), followed by European Americans (14.4), Asian Americans (6.2), Hispanic Americans (5.4), and African Americans (5.1). Because European

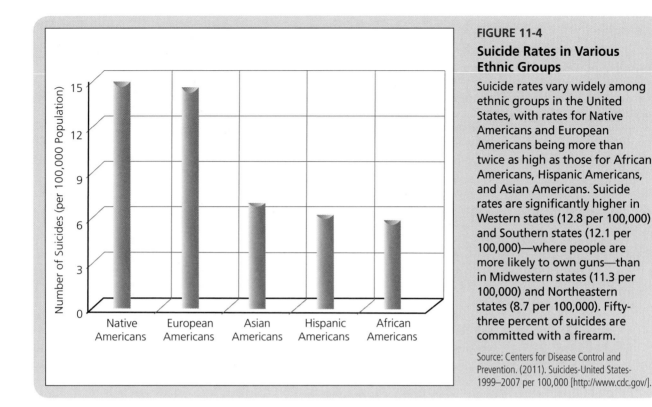

FIGURE 11-4

Suicide Rates in Various Ethnic Groups

Suicide rates vary widely among ethnic groups in the United States, with rates for Native Americans and European Americans being more than twice as high as those for African Americans, Hispanic Americans, and Asian Americans. Suicide rates are significantly higher in Western states (12.8 per 100,000) and Southern states (12.1 per 100,000)—where people are more likely to own guns—than in Midwestern states (11.3 per 100,000) and Northeastern states (8.7 per 100,000). Fifty-three percent of suicides are committed with a firearm.

Source: Centers for Disease Control and Prevention. (2011). Suicides-United States-1999–2007 per 100,000 [http://www.cdc.gov/].

Americans far outnumber Native Americans in the general population, they have a higher number of suicides than any other ethnic group. Firearms are the most common method of suicide used by both men and women in the United States, with the risk of suicide being five times greater for households having guns (Grossman et al., 2005; Rosenberg et al., 1999).

Worldwide, the annual death toll from suicide varies by country and geographic region, with some Asian (e.g., South Korea, Japan, and China) and northern European countries (e.g., Lithuania, Kazakhstan, and Hungary) having annual death rates as high as 25–34 per 100,000 (World Health Organization, 2011). Sociocultural factors, including religion, age, sex, ethnicity, and marital and employment status, are related to suicide risk. For example, countries with suicide rates as low as 4 per 100,000—nations of the Middle East (e.g., Syria, Egypt, Jordan), and Central and South America (Guatemala, Paraguay, Venezuela), as well as Greece and Mexico—have strong religious prohibitions against taking one's own life. The "Psychological Applications" section at the end of this chapter presents additional information about suicide.

Bipolar Disorder

It is clear that depression poses serious problems in a person's life, but what about the opposite mood? *Mania* is an excessively elated, active emotional state. Persons in manic states experience buoyant, exuberant mood and such boundless energy that they do not feel the need for sleep. They often have increased appetites and thus overindulge in food, alcohol, drugs, and sexual activity. Manic individuals speak and move rapidly, often going from activity to activity with endless optimism and self-confidence. Do you think that such an exaggerated emotional state could be problematic?

At first glance, manic symptoms may not seem very troublesome. They do not appear as severe as depressive symptoms, which often are accompanied by suicidal thoughts and torturous feelings. However, a person in a manic state can engage in

FIGURE 11-5

Brain Activity in Bipolar Disorder

PET scans of persons with bipolar disorder show substantial changes in brain activity when they cycle between mania and depression. Here, the top and bottom sets of brain scans were taken during times when the bipolar patient was depressed, while the middle set of brain scans was taken during a manic period. The red areas indicate a high level of neural activity.

Source: Phelps, M. E., & Maziotta, J. C. (1985). Positron-emission tomography: Human brain function and biochemistry. *Science, 228,* 799–809. Courtesy of Drs. Lewis Baxter and Michael Phelps, UCLA School of Medicine.

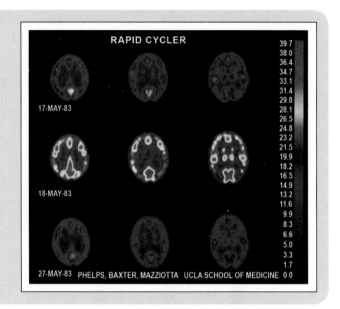

very destructive behavior (Dilsaver et al., 1999). For example, they may go to a casino and lose the family's life savings in a single session at the roulette wheel, or they may feel so "on top of the world" that they drive their car 100 miles per hour, oblivious to the danger to themselves and others. Manic persons may also experience such an increase in physical appetites that they engage in unprotected sex with a dozen people in a day. All these activities can destroy a person's life as decisively as a suicide attempt by a depressed person.

The double tragedy for those who experience such excessively elated, active emotional states is that they will also plunge into the depths of depression. Individuals with high levels of manic symptoms followed by high levels of depressive symptoms that persist for weeks and significantly interfere with daily functioning are diagnosed as having **bipolar disorder** (previously called *manic depression*). Individuals who experience mild manic and depressive symptoms that persist for a long time are diagnosed with *cyclothymic disorder*.

Bipolar disorder is less common than major depressive disorder, occurring in about 1 percent of the population (Thomas, 2004). Unlike major depression, bipolar disorder occurs about equally in men and women and tends to occur earlier in life than major depression. Although bipolar patients usually experience episodes of severe depression as well as bouts of mania, their depressive episodes are more severe than those experienced in major depression, are accompanied by higher suicide risks, and show a distinct pattern of brain activity during sleep. This evidence suggests that bipolar disorder and major depressive disorder are distinct conditions. Further, as depicted in Figure 11-5, brain scans of bipolar patients indicate that manic periods are associated with unusually high levels of brain activity. The symptoms of manic and depressive states are summarized in Table 11-3.

Bipolar disorder A mood disorder characterized by swings between the emotional extremes of mania and depression

INFO-BIT

A number of well-known artists have suffered from bipolar disorders, including such classical composers as G. F. Handel, Hector Berlioz, Gustav Mahler, and Robert Schuman (Jamison, 1995). Berlioz described his two contrasting moods as "passionate" and "morose." Schuman created pieces that contrasted an impulsive and high-spirited style with one that was melancholy and inwardly directed.

TABLE 11-3 Symptoms of Manic and Depressive States

Type of Symptom	Depressive State	Manic State
Emotional	Sad mood	Elated mood
	Lack of pleasure	
Physiological	Fatigue	Increased energy
	Sleep difficulty	Lack of need for sleep
	Decreased appetite	Increased appetite
	Decreased interest in sex	Increased interest in sex
Behavioral	Slowed pace	Increased pace
	Decreased activity level	Increased activity level
Cognitive	Low self-esteem	Increased self-esteem
	Thoughts of death	Lack of perception of danger
	Negative view of world	Positive view of world

Etiology of Mood Disorders

When seeking explanations of mood disorders, it is important to consider bipolar disorder and major depressive disorder separately. Bipolar disorder clearly has a genetic influence, and most psychologists consider it a biological disorder (G. W. Brown, 2012). Why? The risk for mood disorder in family members of bipolar disorder patients is more than 30 percent, which is very high (Sevy et al., 1995). Exactly what is inherited that may predispose an individual to bipolar disorder is as yet unclear; one possible cause, however, is imbalances in neural circuits that use serotonin, norepinephrine, and other neurotransmitters (Pinto et al., 2011). Brain-imaging studies have also found evidence that the amygdala—which plays a role in regulating mood and accessing emotional memories—may be enlarged in people who have bipolar disorder (Strakowski et al., 2002).

Major depressive disorder, unlike bipolar disorder, can be explained through several approaches (Nantel-Vivier & Pihl, 2008). First, biology does have some influence on this disorder (Rosso et al., 2005). Family, twin, and adoption studies indicate at least a moderate genetic influence on depression. For example, with identical twins, both individuals are four times more likely to experience depression at some time in their lives than are fraternal twins (Kendler et al., 1999). Thus, some individuals may be biologically predisposed to this disorder, and onset of the illness may have little relation to their psychosocial experiences. Such cases tend to be severe and are properly treated using antidepressant medications such as Prozac and Paxil.

One subtype of depression that appears to have a biological basis is **seasonal affective disorder (SAD)**. SAD is characterized by symptoms of depression at particular times of the year, especially during the winter months, when daylight hours are reduced (C. Thompson et al., 2004). Figure 11-6 shows a direct relationship between depression and the length of daylight during the year (Rosenthal et al., 1984). Of course, some cases of winter depression may be due solely to psychosocial influences, such as decreased activity due to poor weather and increased stress brought on by holiday preparations. Yet evidence that SAD is a distinct disorder comes from

Seasonal affective disorder (SAD) A subtype of depression characterized by depressive symptoms during the winter months, when daylight hours are reduced

FIGURE 11-6

Depression and Length of Daylight

People who suffer from seasonal affective disorder (SAD) experience periods of depression corresponding to the shorter days of winter.

Source: Data from Rosenthal, N. E., et al. (1984). Depression and length of daylight in seasonal affective disorder. *Archives of General Psychiatry, 41*, 72–80.

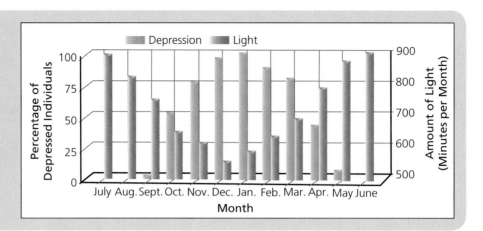

studies demonstrating that people with SAD have unusually high metabolic rates, as well as physiological differences from other depressed patients (Sher, 2002). One therapy that is quite effective in alleviating SAD is exposure to full-spectrum light for two hours a day. Research suggests that this light therapy restores brain levels of the neurotransmitter serotonin to normal, since a low serotonin level is one of the likely biological causes of depression (Gordijn et al., 2012).

Journey of Discovery

How could you explain seasonal affective disorder and its treatment using light therapy from an evolutionary perspective?

Beyond pure biological explanations, the psychodynamic perspective (Freud, 1909/1957) explains depression as caused by experiencing a "lost loved object" in childhood. As an adult, when the individual experiences subsequent losses, she or he becomes depressed. Rather than express anger outwardly toward whatever environmental circumstances contributed to the loss, the individual experiences "anger turned inward," blaming the self. Although this explanation of depression has not received much empirical support, it has been a popular approach for psychotherapists who treat depressed patients.

As you might expect, cognitive theory suggests that depression is a thinking disorder (Beck et al., 1979; Riso et al., 2003). Depressed persons have negative views of themselves, the world, and the future, and they misinterpret their daily experiences so their negative outlook is supported (Beck, 1967). In contrast, the behavioral perspective holds that depression results from low social reinforcement, which may be due to skill deficits (such as the inability to solve problems or to interact successfully with others) or to decreased opportunities to interact with others. Consistent with the diathesis-stress model, research indicates that individuals with such predisposing cognitive and behavioral conditions are more likely to become depressed following stressful events in their lives (Peterson & Seligman, 1984; Teri & Lewinsohn, 1985).

Finally, why does depression occur more frequently among women than men? Some psychologists believe that this gender difference is due to biological factors. For example, there are modest relationships between depressed mood in women and biological factors such as stage of menstrual cycle and use of oral contraceptives. However, other psychologists contend that social and cultural factors related to sexism are the more likely cause.

According to this sociocultural argument, because women have fewer educational and occupational opportunities, receive less money for their work, and experience more violence due to their gender, the world is simply more "depressing" for them than for men. Some sociocultural theorists also contend that the reported gender difference in depression may be a statistical mistake, reflecting gender differences in seeking help and clinician bias in diagnosis (Bogner & Gallo, 2004). For example, women may seek help for depression more frequently than men, not because they suffer more from this disorder, but because they are more likely than men to seek help for their problems. Further, the mental health profession may have a bias that leads to different diagnoses for women and men, even though they present identical symptoms, with the women labeled as depressed while the men are diagnosed with other conditions. Biological differences? Sociocultural differences? Gender differences in help seeking, or clinician bias? Perhaps the best explanation for this gender difference involves some combination of these perspectives.

11.2c *Dissociative Disorders Involve a Loss of Contact with Portions of One's Consciousness or Memory.*

Anxiety disorders and mood disorders involve symptoms that are familiar to most college students. However, the next category of disorders may be less familiar to you. **Dissociative disorders** are characterized by disruptions in consciousness, memory, sense of identity, or perception (Spiegel et al., 2011). As the label indicates, the primary feature of this class of disorders is *dissociation*, meaning that significant aspects of experience are kept separate—disassociated—in consciousness and memory. Dissociation usually occurs when a situation becomes overwhelmingly stressful, and the person psychologically escapes by separating his or her consciousness from the painful situational memories, thoughts, and feelings. Dissociative disorders generally involve severe symptoms as well as a higher use of mental health treatment compared with other psychiatric disorders, and thus, are very costly to treat and involve a great deal of emotional suffering by those afflicted (Brand et al., 2012).

Dissociative disorders Psychological disorders characterized by disruptions in consciousness, memory, sense of identity, or perception

Dissociative Amnesia

The type of dissociative disorder most often suffered by victims of natural disasters is called **dissociative amnesia**; it involves the inability to recall important personal information, usually of a traumatic or stressful nature. Of course, some cases of amnesia are due to organic causes, such as a head injury or a brain tumor. However, when there are no known organic causes and the person's memory loss is isolated to information threatening to the self, the amnesia is considered dissociative.

Dissociative amnesia A dissociative disorder characterized by the inability to recall important personal information, usually of a traumatic or stressful nature

There are two primary forms of dissociative amnesia: (1) localized amnesia for a specific event or events; and (2) *dissociative fugue*, which is generalized amnesia for identity and life history, and which may be accompanied by the person abruptly leaving home or work and assuming a new identity—without realizing that this identity is not the one that she or he had in the past. It may be hard for you to imagine how this can happen, but it does. One such case involved a "Mr. X," who experienced occasional fugue states over a period of several decades. During one episode, Mr. X married a woman, much to the chagrin of the wife he already had and whom he did not remember. In addition to dealing with the consequences of dissociative fugue, Mr. X soon faced legal charges of bigamy.

Dissociative Identity Disorder

Dissociative identity disorder (DID) A dissociative disorder characterized by the presence of two or more distinct identities or personalities that take turns controlling the person's behavior; also known as *multiple personality disorder*

By far, the dissociative disorder that has received the most attention is **dissociative identity disorder (DID)**, also known as *multiple personality disorder* (Lilienfeld & Lynn, 2003). This condition is characterized by the presence of two or more distinct identities or personalities, which take turns controlling the person's behavior. At least one of the personalities is unaware of what transpired when it was not in control. The symptoms of DID are bizarre and extreme. One personality may be that of a 6-year-old child, while another may be that of an infirm grandparent. One personality may be male, while another may be female. Because of the fascinating nature of its symptoms, DID has received a great deal of attention from popular culture, ranging from the 1950s non-fictional book and movie *The Three Faces of Eve* (Thigpen & Cleckley, 1957) to the 1990s fictional novel and film *Fight Club* (Palahniuk, 1996).

Prior to 1980, DID was considered one of the rarest forms of psychological disorder, with only about two cases reported per decade from 1930 to 1960 (McHugh, 1995). Yet, in the 1980s, over 20,000 cases were reported! Skeptics doubted that this increase was due to better diagnosis. Instead, they suggested it was caused both by the media coverage of multiple personalities and by psychotherapists' use of hypnosis and other suggestive techniques that can sometimes elicit DID-like symptoms in patients. According to this argument, psychotherapists may first wonder whether a patient's chaotic and unpredictable behavior is due to DID. Then, during therapy sessions, they ask leading questions that suggest the possibility of DID. Further, they may use hypnosis to try to draw out the multiple personalities. However, one of the unfortunate consequences of hypnosis is that it can lead its subjects to produce "memories" that are not true (see Chapter 5, Section 5.3a). Because these patients are distressed and looking for ways to understand their problems, they may come to accept the multiple personality explanation (Lilienfeld et al., 1999; Nogrady et al., 1985).

Research since 1980 has shown that DID is more common than was once believed (Gleaves, 1996). Although it is likely that some cases are manufactured in therapy sessions, most psychologists believe that the research evidence suggests this disorder is rare, but real (Boysen, 2011; Hopper et al., 2002). Women are about three times more likely to suffer from DID than are men, and more than 90 percent of people with DID have histories of childhood physical and sexual abuse (Schmidt, 2004).

Etiology of Dissociative Disorders

Psychodynamic theory suggests that dissociation results from the individual's attempt to repress some troubling event. If this event is associated with intense emotion, a corresponding high degree of repression may be required to keep this material in the unconscious. While repressing the memory of the troubling event, the individual also inadvertently represses other memories, including memory of identity. In the case of fugue and DID, individuals develop an alternative identity or identities as a way to avoid facing the stress that would occur upon recognizing that they had lost memory of their identity and other personal information.

Invoking a biological explanation, some psychologists suggest that dissociative disorder patients may have an undetected neurological problem (Bergmann, 2008). Research has shown that individuals with dissociative disorders have high rates of epilepsy and that those with epilepsy have high rates of dissociative disorders (Bob et al., 2002; Willerman & Cohen, 1990). As intriguing as this biological explanation may be, it cannot account for all cases of dissociative disorders because most DID patients

AP Wide World Photo

In the 1970s, the book and movie, *Sybil*, created an international sensation in its depiction of the real-life story of Shirley Ardell Mason who was diagnosed with sixteen different personalities. Mason's story was very influential in focusing the public's attention on dissociative identity disorder. In 2011, evidence came to light suggesting that Mason made up the multiple personalities for attention and excitement (Nathan, 2011).

do not have the hallmark abnormal brain wave patterns found among epileptic sufferers. Still, it is possible that at least some individuals with dissociative disorders have neurological disorders that have not yet been detected.

Another explanation of dissociative disorders comes from the cognitive perspective. This approach holds that individuals learn to dissociate as a way of coping with intense distress. When a child is exposed to prolonged, intense stress (such as torturous abuse), dissociation may be used so frequently that it becomes automatic. Consistent with this idea, several cognitive techniques have been effective in helping to limit pain and emotional distress. For example, distraction (thinking of something other than the stressful stimulus, such as the lyrics to a song), fantasy (imagining oneself as another person, such as James Bond resisting torture), and imagery (imagining oneself in a peaceful situation other than the current stressful one)—have all been shown to reduce subjective pain (Meichenbaum & Turk, 1976). Perhaps a child who experiences repeated abuse learns to cope using these cognitive techniques. Over time, the child's use of these cognitive pain-management techniques becomes automatic, even in the presence of mild stressors. At this point, the individual's dissociation no longer serves the function of protecting her or him from stress but is a problem that interferes with daily functioning in and of itself. Psychophysiological studies of DID patients provide some support for this hypothesis. When subjected to intense stress that precipitates a dissociated state, DID patients also experience a reduction in nervous system arousal (Williams et al., 2003). These results support the idea that the dissociated state functions as a protective mechanism for the person.

11.2d *Schizophrenia Involves Disturbances in Almost All Areas of Psychological Functioning.*

Do you remember Jim, from my chapter-opening story? Following the record and pillow incidents, Jim's psychological condition rapidly deteriorated. His previously quiet, sleepy demeanor gave way to episodes of whooping and hollering while he danced frenetically around the apartment jingling his ring of keys in the air. This behavior so scared us that we called his parents and only then learned that Jim had been released from a psychiatric hospital just prior to answering our ad. By the end of the day, Jim was readmitted to the hospital with a preliminary diagnosis of **schizophrenia**, which is one of the most severe forms of psychological disorder (Falkai & Moller, 2012). This disorder is so severe that it is considered a *psychosis*, meaning that the person is out of touch with reality. People with this disorder may not be aware of what is going on around them and may not be able to interact effectively with the world.

Schizophrenia A psychological disorder characterized by severe impairments in thinking, such as hallucinations, delusions, or loose associations

INFO-BIT Prior to 1911, schizophrenia was called *dementia praecox* because it was thought to be a degenerative disease of the brain (dementia) that began at a young age (praecox). Swiss psychologist Eugene Bleuler (1857–1939) challenged this view, arguing that the disorder was not always degenerative. Bleuler coined the term *schizophrenia* to refer to what he regarded as the essential characteristic of the disorder—a splitting (schiz) or lack of integration among the person's normal psychological functions.

Schizophrenia is characterized by severe impairments in thinking, including hallucinations, delusions, or loose associations. With *hallucinations*, some schizophrenic patients hear or see things that are not there. For example, they may hear voices that they attribute to aliens or demons. Some schizophrenic patients experience *delusions,* or irrational belief systems. For instance, they may believe that they are Jesus, a CIA agent, the president of the United States, a robot, their shadow, or some other unusual entity. Often, schizophrenic patients experience delusions and hallucinations that support and strengthen one another. Patients with schizophrenia may hear voices, which they attribute to God and which lead them to believe that they have been selected for a spiritual mission. Schizophrenic patients often experience *loose associations,* meaning that their thoughts are disconnected from one another and from the world around them. Schizophrenic patients can be so disorganized in their thinking that they are unable to speak in complete sentences and can only babble. Some patients' thoughts jump from topic to topic so rapidly that they cannot speak clearly. These hallucinations, delusions, and loose associations are called *positive symptoms* of schizophrenia because they are symptoms that do not typically occur in other people.

Individuals with schizophrenia also display *negative symptoms,* meaning that they do not exhibit behaviors that most other people do. For example, many schizophrenic patients are socially withdrawn, unmotivated to engage in common social or recreational activities, and emotionally unresponsive. This emotional unresponsiveness is called *flat* or *blunt affect.* Schizophrenic patients may walk around a hospital ward as though they are zombies, completely uninvolved with what is going on around them.

Finally, *cognitive symptoms* of schizophrenia involve problems with working memory, attention, verbal and visual learning and memory, reasoning and problem solving, speed of processing, and disordered speech (Abbott et al., 2012). One example of a cognitive symptom is speech that is referred to as *word salad* because spoken sentences may follow grammatical rules but the content makes little sense; words and ideas appear to be tossed around. The following is an illustration of such speech in answer to the question, "Why do you think people believe in God?"

> … I don't know why, let's see, balloon travel. He holds it up for you, the balloon. He don't let you fall out, your little legs sticking down through the clouds. He's down to the smokestack, looking through the smoke trying to get the balloon up you know. Way they're flying on top that way, legs sticking out … (Chapman & Chapman, 1973, p. 3)

Schizophrenia is diagnosed when symptoms persist for at least six months, are not due to some other condition (such as substance use or severe depression), and cause significant impairment in daily functioning. Because schizophrenics experience such severe problems in thinking, they often cannot work, manage a home or apartment successfully, or care for their basic needs. Schizophrenic individuals usually require assistance to care for themselves, either from their family or a treatment center. In the absence of such assistance, many schizophrenic individuals end up living on the streets.

Schizophrenia occurs in about 1 percent of the world's population, with roughly equal frequency among men and women; and it tends to begin more often in adolescence and young adulthood than in middle and late adulthood. Although the disorder can occur in children, it is rare in those younger than age 10. The average age at the first psychotic episode is about 21 years for men and 27 years for women. About one-third of people with schizophrenia will attempt suicide, with 1 in 10 eventually succeeding (Andreasen & Black, 2006).

Etiology of Schizophrenia

The current consensus is that schizophrenia has a strong genetic basis (Akbarian, 2010; Chen et al., 2005). For example, although 1 percent of the general population develops schizophrenia in their lifetime, from 10 to 15 percent of first-degree relatives (parents, children, siblings) of a schizophrenic patient also develop schizophrenia (Willerman & Cohen, 1990). This holds true whether a person is reared in the same household as the schizophrenic person or in an adoptive, nonschizophrenic home. Perhaps most convincing is the evidence from twin studies. Among fraternal-twin pairs in which one member displays schizophrenia, the other member has about a 15 percent risk of also developing the disorder, about the same as for non-twin siblings. However, among identical twins, the risk jumps to about 50 percent (Tsuang, 2000). Figure 11-7 depicts these findings.

What biological condition is inherited that may predispose for the development of schizophrenia? Most antipsychotic medications that control the symptoms of schizophrenia have the effect of decreasing the amount and/or activity of dopamine, a neurotransmitter that facilitates movement and influences thought and emotion (see Chapter 2, Section 2.1d). Amphetamines and other medications that increase the amount or activity of dopamine can induce symptoms that mimic those of schizophrenia (Green, 1998). Further, autopsies of schizophrenic patients often reveal an unusually high number of dopamine receptors in the brain (Seeman et al., 1993). Thus, compelling evidence indicates that increased dopamine activity is related to schizophrenia. According to this *dopamine hypothesis*, schizophrenic patients see and hear things that are not there and have racing thoughts they cannot control because the dopamine pathways in their brains are overactive.

Another biological explanation for schizophrenia is that it is caused by abnormalities in brain structure (Brown & Thompson, 2010). As illustrated in Figure 11-8, brain scans of some schizophrenic patients show enlarged ventricles (brain cavities filled with cerebrospinal fluid) in the cerebral cortex and a corresponding shrinkage in temporal lobes and frontal lobes, as well as abnormal blood flow in certain brain areas (Wright et al., 2000). What might have triggered this shrinkage of the cerebral cortex? Because schizophrenia often develops at about the same time that rapid changes are occurring in the adolescent brain (see Chapter 3, Section 3.5b), some neuroscientists suggest that this disorder is caused by excessive pruning of neurons and their interconnections (Thompson et al., 2001). Evidence supporting this theory comes from MRI studies indicating that while average adolescents lose about 15 percent of

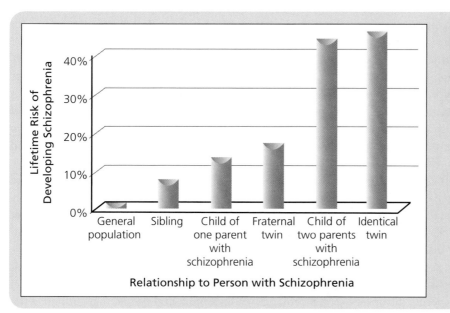

FIGURE 11-7

Risk of Developing Schizophrenia

The lifetime risk of developing schizophrenia increases with genetic closeness to relatives with schizophrenia.

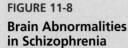

FIGURE 11-8

Brain Abnormalities in Schizophrenia

The hollow cavities in the brain (ventricles) are filled with cerebrospinal fluid. Brain scans suggest that schizophrenics may have enlarged ventricles, as shown here, which is consistent with additional findings that schizophrenics have fewer brain neurons than do normal individuals. This shrinkage of the brain may be caused by the excessive destruction of neurons and their interconnections that occurs during adolescent brain maturation.

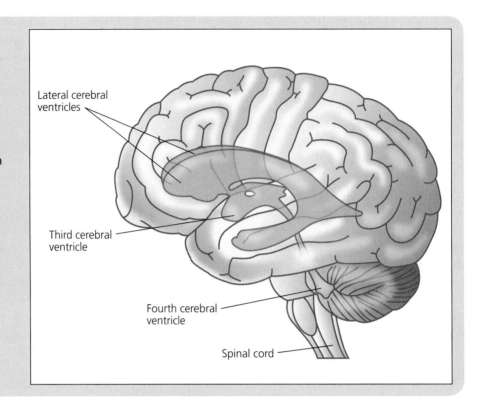

their neural mass during this important stage of brain maturation, those who develop schizophrenia lose as much as 25 percent (Gogtay et al., 2004; Keller et al., 2003). Related to these findings are studies suggesting that some of the hormones flooding the brain during puberty may activate previously dormant "vulnerability genes" that cause the type of abnormal brain development associated with schizophrenia (E. Walker & Bollini, 2002). Thus, the development of schizophrenia may be at least partially caused by an overzealous process of brain sculpting during the teen years (Selemon et al., 2005).

Brain sculpting earlier in life—during fetal development—is also a possible contributing factor in the later development of schizophrenia. As previously discussed in Chapter 3, Section 3.1c, a fetus' brain produces about 250,000 new neurons per minute. With such rapid brain growth in the womb, any kind of disease or toxic substance experienced by the mother can have a profound impact on the fetus' developing brain. A number of studies have found evidence that increased risk of schizophrenia is related to prenatal exposure to such infections and diseases as influenza, rubella, and herpes (A. S. Brown, 2006). One theory is that maternal infections and diseases adversely affect genes that regulate how neurons in the frontal lobes of the cerebral cortex communicate with one another, causing the disordered brain activity typical of schizophrenia (Bassett et al., 2008).

Regarding behavioral explanations for schizophrenia, during the 1950s some theorists proposed that the disorder might directly result from disturbed family interactions that teach children to communicate in a confusing fashion (Bateson et al., 1956; Mednick, 1958). By the 1970s, this "disturbed family" explanation had been disproven due to lack of empirical support. Although family or social factors do not cause schizophrenia, the diathesis-stress model suggests that environmental factors such as acute poverty and poor parenting may interact with biological factors in triggering the onset of the disorder. Such environmental factors may influence the course of the disorder by increasing the stress level of individuals who are biologically predisposed for schizophrenia (Walker & Diforio, 1998). By contrast, individuals who face similar environmental stressors but do not have the necessary biological vulnerability (the diathesis) will not develop schizophrenia.

Currently, the diathesis-stress model, which considers the interaction of both biological and environmental factors, provides the best explanation of this highly complex psychological disorder. This disorder does have a strong genetic component, but what is inherited is not the disorder itself but a state of vulnerability manifested as neuropsychological impairment (Byrne et al., 2003).

11.2e *Personality Disorders Involve Significant Impairments in Personality Functioning.*

A final category of psychological problems is composed of the personality disorders. **Personality disorders** differ from the other psychological disorders considered so far in that personality disorders are not associated with specific symptoms that cause distress or interfere with daily functioning (Samuel et al., 2012; Shedler & Westen, 2004). Instead, they are characterized by general styles of living that are ineffective and lead to problems for the person and for others. Personality disorders develop by adolescence or young adulthood and typically persist for a long time. They are associated with personality traits that are extreme and inflexible, and that ultimately lead the person to have problems in daily functioning. Often, individuals with personality disorder do not consider their personality to be a problem but instead blame others for their problems. Table 11-4 lists, and briefly describes, six personality disorders. To illustrate this category of disorders, let us examine a bit more extensively three of these disorders.

Two of the more common personality disorders are borderline personality and narcissistic personality. *Borderline personality disorder* is characterized by unstable personal relationships, self-concept, and emotions. Because individuals suffering from this disorder tend to see things in terms of extremes, such as things being either all good or all bad, their perceptions of events and other people often change quickly.

BVT *Lab*

Improve your test scores. Practice quizzes are available at www.BVTLab.com.

Personality disorders A category of disorders characterized by general styles of living that are ineffective and that can lead to problems

TABLE 11-4 Personality Disorder Types and Their Symptoms

Type	Major Symptoms
Antisocial	Disregard for, and violation of, the rights of others
Avoidant	Social inhibition, feelings of inadequacy, and hypersensitivity to negative evaluation
Borderline	Instability of interpersonal relationships, self-concept, and emotion
Narcissistic	Grandiosity, need for admiration, and lack of empathy
Obsessive-compulsive	Preoccupation with orderliness, perfectionism, and control (Note: Obsessive-compulsive personality disorder is different from obsessive-compulsive disorder, which is an anxiety disorder.)
Schizotypal	Cognitive and perceptual distortions and eccentricities of behavior

A person who is looked up to one day may be looked down on the next day. *Narcissistic personality disorder* is characterized by an extremely positive, self-centered, and arrogant self-concept with little empathy for others. Individuals suffering from this disorder crave constant admiration from others. Their overblown sense of self-importance and egocentric focus make them feel entitled to special privileges without any kind of reciprocation (Corbitt, 2002). As with the other personality disorders, individuals with these two disorders are extremely difficult to live with on an everyday basis.

Antisocial Personality Disorder

Antisocial personality disorder A personality disorder characterized by a persistent pattern of disregard for, and violation of, the rights of others

By far, the personality disorder that has received the most attention is the **antisocial personality disorder**, which is quite similar to the term *psychopathy*, a diagnostic category that is not used in the *DSM* (Bateman & Fonagy, 2012). Individuals with antisocial personality disorder exhibit a persistent pattern of disregard for, and violation of, the rights of others. They repeatedly exhibit antisocial behavior across all realms of life, often lying, cheating, stealing, and manipulating others to get what they want (Ermer & Kiehl, 2010; Goldstein et al., 2008). When other people catch them in their deceit, they fail to take responsibility and do not exhibit remorse. In addition to their lack of remorse and empathy toward others, they often engage in risky and irresponsible actions.

Although this description sounds nasty, people with antisocial personality disorder are, surprisingly, often charming and likable. They have learned how to manipulate people to get what they want and can lie without hesitation or guilt. In the movie *Pacific Heights*, actor Michael Keaton portrays a person who wickedly manipulates a young couple, first charming them into leasing an apartment and then taking advantage of them for monetary gain. When the couple realizes his deceit, Keaton's character convinces the police and others in the legal system that he is in the right. Although only about 3 percent of the population has antisocial personality disorder—with men outnumbering women 3 to 1—some studies suggest that at least half of male prison inmates have this disorder (Arboleda-Florez, 2007). At present, there is no effective treatment for antisocial personality disorder, mainly because individuals who demonstrate true psychopathic tendencies tend to view themselves as normal and not needing treatment.

AP Wide World Photo

Determining whether individuals who commit crimes are suffering from a psychological disorder has important implications for their prosecution and sentencing. On July 22, 2011, Anders Behring Brevik killed eight people with a bomb in Oslo, Norway, before carrying out a mass shooting at a Norwegian youth camp where he killed another 69 people, mostly teenagers. Although Brevik's callous lack of empathy and remorse on that day and during his trial is typical of people with antisocial personality disorder, he was judged to be mentally competent.

Etiology of Personality Disorders

Research since the 1970s suggests that personality disorders have a genetic component, perhaps related to abnormal brain development or chronic underarousal of both the autonomic and central nervous systems (Irle et al. 2005; Sundram et al., 2012). Most of this research has focused on the possible causes of antisocial personality disorder. One study of 14,000 adoptions found that adopted-away sons of fathers with a criminal background are themselves at increased risk for experiencing legal problems as adults, even when reared by noncriminal adoptive fathers (Hutchings & Mednick, 1977; Mednick et al., 1987). Further, this study found that the more habitual the criminal history of the father, the more likely that the adopted-away son will engage in criminal behavior. Similarly, large-scale twin studies indicate that identical twins resemble one another with respect to various types of antisocial behavior more than do fraternal twins (Kendler et al., 2012; Lykken, 1995).

At the brain activity level, research suggests that individuals with antisocial personality disorder tend to have smaller amygdala than normal individuals (Marsh et al., 2011). As discussed in Chapter 2, Section 2.3b, this brain area is associated with fear and emotional learning. Additional research finds that individuals with antisocial personality disorder have higher pain thresholds and do not experience fear or anxiety nearly to the same degree as the average person (Lykken, 1995). This research suggests that individuals with antisocial personality disorder have a lower overall level of nervous system arousal, which may partly explain why they engage in sensation-seeking behavior and do not learn from punishment.

The current thinking about antisocial personality disorder is that both biological and environmental factors interact to cause the problem (Hiatt & Dishion, 2008). For instance, there may be a biological predisposition, such as a neurological influence on impulse control. Children with this predisposition who are reared in chaotic households may not learn to control their impulses and so behave in ways to maximize their benefit, even if this means violating social rules. On the other hand, children with this predisposition who are reared in more stable homes are more likely to acquire self-control techniques so they do not act to satisfy their immediate impulses.

Every normal man must be tempted at times to spit upon his hands, hoist the black flag, and begin slitting throats.

—H. L. Mencken, American political commentator, 1880–1956

Good people do not need laws to tell them to act responsibly, while bad people will find a way around the laws.

—Plato, Greek philosopher, 427–347 B.C.

Section REVIEW

- The *DSM* lists major classes of psychological disorders.

- Anxiety disorders are characterized by distressing, persistent anxiety, or maladaptive behavior.

- Mood disorders are characterized by emotional extremes that cause significant disruption in daily functioning.

- Dissociative disorders are characterized by disruptions in consciousness, memory, sense of identity, or perception.

- Schizophrenia is characterized by severe impairment in thinking, such as hallucinations, delusions, or loose associations.

- For individuals with personality disorders, their general styles of living are ineffective and lead to problems.

PSYCHOLOGICAL
a p p l i c a t i o n s

Some Important Facts About Suicide

There are many misconceptions about suicide. In this section, let me address five commonly asked questions concerning this important issue and provide information that may prove helpful to you now or in the future (Goldston, 2003; Neuner et al., 2008).

- *Does suicide run in families?* Not exactly. People who have major mood disorders, such as severe depression and bipolar disorder, are at increased risk for suicide. It is possible to find families that have histories of suicide across generations (Egeland & Sussex, 1985), but the genetic influence appears to be related to the mood disorder rather than to suicide itself.

- *Is it true that people who talk about suicide never commit suicide?* No! This is a dangerous misconception. One of the best predictors of suicide risk is a stated threat to commit suicide. In fact, some form of warning precedes 80 percent of all suicides (Schneidman, 1987). Psychologists therefore take every threat of suicide seriously, at least until they can conduct a thorough evaluation of risk in the individual case. Some threats may be veiled. For example, a person may give away her prized possessions or talk about "getting away to end my problems." Observers should be sensitive to such hints of suicidal thinking and should ask direct questions about the person's intentions.

- *Does every person who attempts suicide truly want to die?* No! Some suicide attempts are designed more to get attention and help than to die. For example, a person who takes a half-bottle of baby aspirin or who scratches his wrist with nail clippers may not truly have intended to die. Such nonlethal attempts are called "suicidal gestures" and are considered cries for help. However, psychologists must be careful when working with clients who have histories of suicidal gestures because such clients are often not thinking in a rational manner (Jollant et al., 2005). The fact that a person has made several suicidal gestures in the past does not mean that she or he will not make a more lethal attempt in the future (Cooper et al., 2005). Also, some persons who make suicidal gestures make a mistake and inadvertently kill themselves, even though that may not have been their true intention.

- *Why do men have a higher suicide rate than women?* Even though women attempt suicide more often than men, men have a higher suicide rate. The explanation for this gender difference is complex. Men attempt suicide by using guns, hanging, and leaping from high places more frequently than do women (Rosenberg et al., 1999). Thus, men tend to use methods that are more lethal and less reversible than do women, who more frequently use pills. Although you can kill yourself with pills, they take time to work; and thus people have more time to change their minds or be found and saved. Now, why do men and women use these different methods? Perhaps men have more familiarity with and accessibility to firearms than do women, which leads men to select this more lethal method. Or perhaps men are less willing than women to call for help, and so men are less likely to make a suicidal gesture.

- *What should I do if a friend is talking about suicide?* It is important that you take the threat seriously because providing those at high risk with help and social support can prevent many suicide attempts (Joiner, 1999). However, it is also important to recognize that you are not a mental health professional; thus you are not equipped to evaluate suicide risk or provide psychotherapy. As a friend, you can listen and provide appropriate comfort and support; however, it is important to encourage your friend to seek professional help. You can convey the information that depression is not a sign of weakness or craziness but instead is recognized as a mental illness. You can convey the information that depression is well understood by the mental health profession and that there are effective treatments for it. However, it will be up to the mental health professional—not you—to provide this treatment. If your friend does not take your advice, perhaps you can find someone important in your friend's life—a family doctor, a member of the clergy, a family member—who can convince your friend to see a mental health professional. As a last resort, a suicidal individual may be committed against his or her will to a psychiatric hospital for treatment. Commitment procedures vary across states; and they usually require the request of a relative and the opinion of one or more physicians that the individual is dangerous to himself or herself, or dangerous to others, and unable to make decisions in his or her best interest. Although commitment may seem a drastic step, it is far better to commit someone to treatment than lose them through suicide.

Suggested Websites

National Institute of Mental Health (NIMH)

http://www.nimh.nih.gov/

This website, intended for both the general public and mental health professionals, includes information on various psychological disorders.

The Anxiety Panic Internet Resource

http://www.algy.com/anxiety/

This website is a self-help network that provides information and support for people who suffer from anxiety disorders.

Depression Central

http://www.psycom.net/depression.central.html

This website provides information on mood disorders.

Schizophrenia.com

http://www.schizophrenia.com/

This website provides not only information on schizophrenia but also discussion and support groups.

Key Terms

Agoraphobia, 504
Antisocial personality disorder, 524
Anxiety disorders, 503
Bipolar disorder, 514
Diagnosis, 495
Diagnostic and Statistical Manual of Mental Disorders (DSM), 502
Diathesis-stress model, 499
Dissociative amnesia, 517
Dissociative disorders, 517

Dissociative identity disorder (DID), 518
Dysthymia, 510
Etiology, 496
Generalized anxiety disorder (GAD), 506
Major depressive disorder, 510
Medical model, 495
Mood disorders, 509
Obsessive-compulsive disorder (OCD), 506
Panic disorder, 504

Personality disorders, 523
Post-traumatic stress disorder (PTSD), 507
Prognosis, 496
Psychological disorder, 497
Schizophrenia, 519
Social anxiety disorder, 506
Specific phobias, 504
Stigma, 501
Symptom, 495

Review Questions

1. The diagnosis of psychological disorders relies on specific criteria that distinguish normal from abnormal behavior. Which of the following is one of the most important of these criteria?
   a. an uncontrollable urge for freedom
   b. behavior that is disruptive or harmful to the individual or others
   c. behavior that is infrequent in the "normal" population
   d. extremely odd or eccentric behavior
   e. personal distress

2. A variety of theories attempt to explain the etiology of psychological disorders. How does the cognitive approach primarily explain mental illness?
   a. as behavior that has been conditioned through reinforcement and punishment
   b. as resulting from a diathesis-stress model of vulnerability interacting with environmental stressors
   c. as associated with broad sociocultural forces
   d. as a product of unconscious forces shaped by childhood experiences
   e. as a learned pattern of faulty thinking or maladaptive interpretations

3. The use of diagnostic labels carries both risks and benefits to the patient, including all except which of the following?

   a. confirmation bias, in which expectations of certain behaviors lead to diagnoses that may not exist

   b. the ability to summarize information concerning the patient's presenting problems

   c. dehumanization of patients by treating them as "labels" rather than individuals

   d. a clear association with specific and reliable etiologic factors for all psychological diagnoses

   e. the suggestion that researchers have identified optimal methods of treatment

4. What is the term for an attribute that serves to discredit a person in the eyes of others?

   a. stereotype
   b. stigma
   c. schema
   d. schemata
   e. socialization

5. Negative attributions surrounding mental illness can result in which of the following?

   a. avoiding seeking treatment
   b. lowered self-esteem
   c. hopelessness
   d. social isolation
   e. all of the above

6. What has research on the association between violence and mental illness found?

   a. that there are no differences between the mentally ill and the general population

   b. that there are significant differences between the mentally ill and the general population

   c. that, except for extreme cases of severe psychopathology, there are no differences between the mentally ill and the general population

   d. that violence levels among the mentally ill and the general population are disturbingly high

   e. that evidence has been inconclusive

7. Why is the *Diagnostic and Statistical Manual of Mental Disorders* considered, primarily, a work in progress?

   a. Ongoing research seeks to continually improve the reliability and validity of *DSM* diagnoses.

   b. The manual is currently undergoing its first classification revision.

   c. There is a lack of agreement among insurance companies concerning how the *DSM* classifies mental illness.

   d. The etiological descriptions provided by the *DSM* are considered tentative.

   e. The criteria specified for diagnosing mental disorders are vague and unclear.

8. Panic disorder is characterized primarily by which one of the following symptoms?

   a. extended periods of excessive fear lasting for several days at a time

   b. avoidance of places where previous attacks have or have not occurred

   c. brief attacks of intense anxiety that occur for no apparent reason

   d. strong, irrational fears of specific objects or situations

   e. subclinical phobias that do not interfere with normal functioning

9. Obsessive-compulsive disorder is unique in that two relatively distinct types of symptoms are experienced. They are which of the following?

   a. obsessions, which are unwanted, repetitive thoughts; and compulsions, which are repetitive behaviors that may disrupt daily functioning

   b. obsessions, which are urges to stalk or kill others, and compulsions, which are urges to overeat

   c. obsessions, such as repeated hand washing, and compulsions, such as fear of contamination.

   d. obsessions, which are urges to perform some type of repetitive or ritualistic behavior; and compulsions, which are repetitive, intrusive thoughts.

   e. obsessions and compulsions, which are rarely recognized as abnormal by the individual.

10. After the terrorist attacks on September 11, 2001, many people experienced symptoms of post-traumatic stress disorder, generally considered a "normal" or expected reaction to a trauma of such magnitude. However, a more serious disturbance might be indicated if an individual had which of the following?
    a. repeated intrusive thoughts or images of the attack scene
    b. made efforts to avoid all reminders of the attacks
    c. experienced flashbacks or nightmares
    d. symptoms that continued for a long period after the attacks, and if the symptoms significantly interfered with the individual's daily functioning.
    e. begun to question his or her essential beliefs concerning the nature of good and evil or the just-world phenomenon

11. Despite the similarities in many of the symptoms of anxiety disorders, a variety of theories have been proposed to explain their causes, including which of the following?
    a. conditioning explanations for the initial onset of generalized anxiety disorder
    b. hypervigilance as a cause of PTSD
    c. "fear of fear" explanations for generalized anxiety disorder
    d. sociological causes of social anxiety disorder
    e. genetic or evolutionary causes of phobias

12. Mood disorders may involve all except which of the following symptoms?
    a. a prolonged feeling of sadness and lethargy
    b. a change in sleep patterns
    c. repetitive lying or dishonesty
    d. difficulties concentrating
    e. thoughts of suicide

13. Which of the following is true of bipolar disorder, which is less common than depression.
    a. It affects only about 9 percent of the population.
    b. It is probably caused by the same etiological factors as depression.
    c. It follows the same symptom and behavior pattern in all individuals with the disorder.
    d. It involves manic behavior, which may be destructive in its consequences.
    e. It involves only mild symptoms of mania and depression, but over extended periods.

14. Etiological explanations for depression and bipolar disorder tend to be quite different, although there is some degree of overlap. Bipolar disorder is typically explained by which one of the following?
    a. misinterpretations of daily experiences
    b. a genetic or biological disturbance leading to imbalances in neural circuits
    c. low social reinforcement
    d. childhood loss, with subsequent anger turned against oneself
    e. negative views of oneself, the world, and the future

15. Researchers have determined that there are distinct gender differences in the experience of depression. These have been explained by all except which of the following?
    a. a lack of social support for men, who are less intimate in their friendships than women
    b. female hormones, which have been associated with depression
    c. social and cultural factors related to sexism
    d. statistical error, reflecting greater help seeking by women
    e. clinicians' gender bias in diagnosing depression

16. Of all the psychological diagnoses, dissociative disorder is probably the most fascinating, because the symptoms tend to be so unusual. For example, some characteristic symptoms include which of the following?
    a. a split personality consisting of two personalities, each of whom is aware of what occurs while the other is in control
    b. the gradual assumption of a new identity, with no awareness by the individual involved, and in dissociative fugue conditions, no return to the previous identity
    c. a gradual loss of memories threatening to the self, known as dissociative amnesia
    d. a permanent "dazed" state following a trauma or tragedy
    e. both male and female personalities, in dissociative identity disorder

17. Which of the following is true of schizophrenia?
    a. It is classified as a psychosis.
    b. It tends to begin in later adulthood.
    c. It involves positive symptoms.
    d. It occurs in about 10 percent of the world's population.
    e. Both a and c

18. What has research investigating the etiology of schizophrenia shown?
    a. little family risk beyond that for identical twins, which is very high
    b. that dopamine-enhancing drugs may cause schizophrenic-like symptoms, suggesting an overactive dopamine system
    c. an enlargement of the cerebral cortex and corresponding shrinkage of cerebral ventricles
    d. that disturbed family communication is directly responsible for some types of schizophrenia
    e. no evidence for prenatal etiologies

19. How do personality disorders differ from other psychological disorders?
    a. They appear to be caused by the interaction of genetic factors, such as temperament or impulse control, and environmental influences, such as family functioning.
    b. They are almost always attributable to a single cause.
    c. They are associated with maladaptive personality traits and result in longstanding problems with living rather than extreme distress or dysfunction.
    d. Individuals with personality disorders are universally unlikable.
    e. Personality disorders involve affective, cognitive, and behavioral systems of functioning.

20. Which of the following is a common misconception about suicide?
    a. Women attempt suicide more often than men, but men have a higher suicide rate.
    b. Some suicide attempts are designed more to get attention and help than to die.
    c. People who have major mood disorders are at increased risk of suicide.
    d. People who talk about suicide never commit suicide.
    e. Some suicide threats may be veiled; for example, a person may give away her prized possessions or talk about getting away to end her problems.

Answers: 1. b 2. e 3. d 4. b 5. e 6. c 7. a 8. c 9. a 10. d 11. e 12. c 13. d 14. b 15. a 16. e 17. e 18. b 19. c 20. d

Chapter Twelve

Therapy

Chapter Outline

*I*f you watch the *Dr. Phil* TV show, you might have a misperception about contemporary psychological therapies. On his show, Dr. Phil McGraw, who is not a licensed psychologist, usually diagnoses problems and formulates solutions for his TV clients within 12 minutes of meeting them, just in time for a commercial break. When he has particularly troubling cases, Dr. Phil may ask his TV clients to take a polygraph test to determine whether they are being truthful (not the best way to build trust with a person!). He also often spends a great deal of time lecturing TV clients with his "tell-it-like-it-is" style: "There's nowhere to run, nowhere to hide. You're going to get real about fat, or you're going to get real fat!" Dr. Phil also gives advice in the form of obscure proverbs that often make little sense: "You don't need a pack of wild horses to learn how to make a sandwich."

Dr. Phil's "tell-it-like-it-is" style of offering help to TV clients with mental health problems transformed him into a national celebrity, while earning him millions of dollars in merchandising deals. Yet does the mental health advice that he offers on his TV show accurately represent contemporary psychotherapy?

12.1 Who Offers Therapies for Psychological Disorders?

Although the *Dr. Phil* show may have entertainment value for many viewers, the people who appear on the show suffering from painful psychological problems are not receiving psychological therapy from this TV celebrity (Levenson, 2005). Dr. Phil does not accurately represent the therapeutic practice of psychology. Yet what are the therapeutic methods employed by mental health professionals to help individuals deal with psychological problems?

12.1a There Are Both Psychological and Biomedical Therapies.

Just as there are different types of psychological disorders for which people seek therapy (see Chapter 11), there are many types of therapists and therapeutic methods. In beginning our examination of the treatment of psychological disorders, I first identify two main categories of therapy and then describe the types of therapists who are trained as mental health professionals.

In treating psychological disorders, the two broad categories of therapy are psychological and medical. As discussed in Chapter 7, Section 7.1a, if you think of the mind as being like a computer, then mental health problems can originate in either the brain's software or its hardware. Psychologically oriented therapies typically seek solutions for what are believed to be "software" problems, while medically oriented therapies try to repair "hardware" problems. Psychological therapy, or **psychotherapy**, employs psychological methods that include a personal relationship between a trained therapist and a client. Its focus is to change the disordered thoughts, behaviors, and emotions associated with specific psychological disorders. In contrast, **biomedical**

Psychotherapy The treatment of psychological disorders by employing psychological methods that include a personal relationship between a trained therapist and a client

Biomedical therapies The treatment of psychological disorders by altering brain functioning with physical or chemical interventions

therapies treat psychological disorders by altering brain functioning through use of physical or chemical interventions.

12.1b Three Primary Mental Health Professions Provide Therapy.

The three mental health professions that provide most of the therapy to people with psychological disorders are psychiatry, social work, and psychology (Haskett et al., 2008). Psychiatrists are medical doctors (MDs) who have received subsequent training in treating mental and emotional disorders. As physicians, psychiatrists can prescribe medications, and thus biomedical therapy is an important aspect of their practice. They also receive training in psychotherapy and so may provide various kinds of "talk" therapy.

Most social workers have obtained a master's degree in social work (MSW) in a two-year graduate program after completing their undergraduate work; a smaller number have a doctorate (DSW). Clinical and psychiatric social workers provide psychotherapy and coordinate with social support agencies that may offer assistance—such as shelter, vocational training, or financial aid—to clients. They often explain problems in terms of how clients interact with their family and social surroundings.

Finally, psychologists have earned either a master's or a doctoral degree. Most frequently, a psychologist's doctoral degree is the doctorate in philosophy (PhD). However, some doctoral degrees in psychology are the doctorate in psychology (Psy.D.) or the doctorate in education (Ed.D.). In contrast to social workers and medical doctors, psychologists who receive training in psychotherapy also receive extensive training in conducting scientific research (less true for the Psy.D.).

Two specialty areas in psychology—clinical psychology and counseling psychology—provide psychotherapy. Clinical psychology is the field that works with psychological disorders—their assessment, explanation, and treatment. Counseling psychology is the field that works with essentially "normal" individuals who experience problems in living and so could benefit from educational, vocational, or personal counseling. The fields of clinical and counseling psychology overlap in that both specialties provide outpatient psychotherapy for mildly disturbed clients (Plante, 2005; Shakow, 2002).

Given the reality of managed care today, mental health providers often work together as a team to treat individuals with psychological disorders. An individual case is likely to be referred from a primary care physician to a psychiatrist, who then refers the client to a psychologist and/or a clinical social worker. Particularly for more serious conditions, such as schizophrenia and drug addiction, a social worker is often involved in training the client in basic life skills, a psychologist has numerous "talk therapy" sessions with the client, and a psychiatrist monitors and adjusts medications.

Section REVIEW

- The two broad categories of mental health therapies are psychotherapies (which employ psychological theories in treating disorders) and biomedical therapies (which involve altering brain function by means of physical or chemical interventions).

- Therapy is primarily provided by three mental health professions: psychiatry, social work, and psychology.

- Two specialty areas in psychology—clinical psychology and counseling psychology—provide psychotherapy.

12.2 Psychodynamic Therapies

Psychodynamic therapies are a diverse group of therapies, descended from the work of Sigmund Freud, which assert that psychological disorders stem primarily from unconscious forces. All these variations of Freudian therapy are included under the heading *psychodynamic therapy* because, like Freud, they stress the importance of understanding the *psychological dynamics* underlying behavior (Richards & Lynch, 2008).

12.2a   Psychoanalysis Laid the Groundwork for Psychodynamic Therapies.

Psychoanalysis dominated the field of psychotherapy throughout the first half of the 1900s. Many of the leading figures in other theoretical schools of therapy—such as Carl Rogers, Frederick Perls, Albert Ellis, and Aaron Beck, all of whose ideas on therapy are discussed later in this chapter—were originally trained in psychoanalysis.

As previously discussed, Freud asserted that some traumatic childhood event, often sexual or aggressive in nature, leaves people with troubling memories or feelings. To manage the resulting anxiety, people repress the troubling material. Although this material is now unconscious, it continues to have a powerful effect on their functioning and eventually causes psychological symptoms. According to Freud, since the cause of the patient's problem is unconscious, the goal of therapy is to bring the troubling material into conscious awareness. This process of helping clients understand their own psychological processes is called *insight* (McCabe & Quayle, 2002). For this reason, psychodynamic therapy is often called *insight-oriented*.

When clients gain insight into the underlying troubling material, they can then express the emotional energy associated with this unconscious material. This release of pent-up emotion, called *catharsis*, is an important aspect of psychodynamic therapy. In addition to discharging the emotions associated with the previously unconscious troubling material, clients can now deal with this troubling material in a conscious, rational, and more effective manner.

12.2b   Free Association Is the Primary Psychodynamic Technique.

The primary technique used in psychodynamic therapy is **free association**, in which the clients say aloud whatever comes to mind, making no deliberate attempt to inhibit their speech. According to Freud, free association gives unconscious troubling material the opportunity to come forth, perhaps allowing clients to suddenly recall important events from childhood. Free association may yield important information in other ways as well. For instance, while freely associating, clients may be unable to think of a word or finish a sentence. They may also suddenly change topics or begin to stammer. According to Freud, such responses often occur when clients are close to achieving insight concerning sensitive unconscious subjects, and their defense mechanisms attempt to block this therapeutic breakthrough.

The psychodynamic therapist also draws inferences from special types of slips of the tongue, known as *Freudian slips*, which are instances when the client means to say one thing but actually says something else. For example, if the client means to say, "I love my wife" but actually says, "I leave my wife," the therapist would interpret this slip as communicating an unconscious desire.

The therapist also interprets the underlying meaning in other forms of expression: dreams, daydreams, artwork, poetry, and so on. Freud thought that almost everything we do is caused by unconscious influences. Through interpreting the symbols in the client's dreams and artwork, the therapist may come to understand the client's unconscious.

According to psychodynamic therapy, the client often develops strong positive or negative feelings for the therapist, which is called **transference** (Scaturo, 2005). Feeling admiration and even romantic love for the therapist are common forms of positive transference, while feeling resentment and anger are common forms of negative transference. Freud interpreted transference as representing feelings that the client experienced toward others early in life. If the client becomes dependent on the therapist, this may mean that the client was overly dependent on parents during childhood. If the client resents the authority of the therapist, perhaps the client was resentful of his or her parents as a child.

Freud also warned therapists that they might, in turn, develop similarly strong feelings for their clients. This **countertransference** represents feelings that the therapist experienced toward others early in life (Bernard, 2005). Freud strongly recommended that therapists attend to these feelings so that they gain greater insight into their unconscious desires, and thereby make these feelings less likely to interfere with treatment of clients.

Another important aspect of the client-therapist relationship in Freudian therapy is resistance. **Resistance** is anything the client does that interferes with therapeutic progress. Over the course of therapy, the client may begin to sabotage therapy by missing or coming late to sessions, talking only about trivial issues, or bringing up significant issues only at the very end of a session so there is no time to address them. According to Freud, the cause of the client's problem is some troubling material in the unconscious. When the client starts making inroads toward identifying this troubling material, the material becomes even more threatening. Thus, even though the client wants to improve, the mind raises its defenses to keep this troubling material unconscious. When this occurs, the therapist's task is to focus the client's attention toward personal issues of which they are not currently aware and then help them make connections between current behavior and childhood experiences.

Transference The process by which the client develops feelings for the therapist that are presumed to reflect the client's feelings for significant others early in life

Countertransference The process by which the therapist develops feelings for the client that are presumed to reflect feelings the therapist had for others early in life

Resistance Anything the client does to interfere with therapeutic progress

12.2c *Psychodynamic Therapy Is Lengthy and Expensive.*

One of the primary criticisms of psychodynamic therapy is that it is too lengthy and expensive for all but the very wealthy. At one to three sessions a week at $150 a session, a client would pay between $40,000 and $120,000 after five years. A second criticism is that its interpretations can never be disproved. For example, if a therapist interprets a client's tardiness for an appointment as a sign of resistance, the client's attempt to disagree may be perceived as further proof of the initial interpretation. With its high costs and the availability of other psychotherapeutic techniques that are at least as effective as psychodynamic therapy, classic psychoanalysis is not widely practiced today. However, as discussed in Chapter 10, Section 10.2e, followers of Freud have modified his theory and therapy. Some disagreed with the more extreme aspects of psychoanalysis, while others altered his therapeutic approach to make therapy briefer and more accessible to a wider range of clients.

Alfred Adler was a contemporary of Freud and an early leader in the psychoanalytic movement. In contrast to Freud, Adler considered early family social interactions

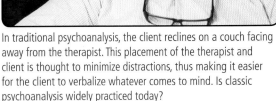

In traditional psychoanalysis, the client reclines on a couch facing away from the therapist. This placement of the therapist and client is thought to minimize distractions, thus making it easier for the client to verbalize whatever comes to mind. Is classic psychoanalysis widely practiced today?

to be more important influences on the developing personality than unconscious sexual conflicts. For example, he held that birth order shaped people's interactions with their parents and siblings and so was an important influence on personality and psychological problems. As a result, Adlerian therapists place more emphasis on the ego's conscious, rational processes than on the id's unconscious processes.

Carl Jung, Freud's most cherished pupil, was also an early leader in the psychoanalytic movement. Like Adler, Jung de-emphasized sex as the major motivation for human behavior and criticized psychoanalysis as being too negative. He also strongly disagreed with Freud's belief that adult personality is determined by early childhood experiences and argued, instead, that behavior is primarily influenced by future goals. As a result, Jungian therapists emphasize their clients' future possibilities, rather than clients' past experiences. They also compare therapy to a spiritual exercise, in which clients must first "confess" their weaknesses before they can improve.

In general, the psychodynamic approach has had an enormous impact on the way mental health professionals "do" psychotherapy (Shedler, 2010). First, this perspective has helped demythologize psychological disorders by arguing that "sane" and "insane" behaviors have their psychological roots in the same mental processes. Second, even therapists who reject Freud's theoretical basis for mental illness often still use his therapeutic technique of developing a one-to-one, therapist-client relationship aimed at increasing client insight.

Section REVIEW

- The goal of psychodynamic therapy is insight into unconscious, troubling material.

- Free association is the primary technique of psychodynamic therapy.

- Psychodynamic therapy is lengthy and expensive.

- Many current variations of Freud's classic psychoanalysis de-emphasize sex as the primary motivator of behavior; they also tend to downplay the importance of the unconscious and early childhood experiences.

12.3 Behavior Therapies

Unlike the psychodynamic perspective, behaviorists do not believe in the unconscious; and thus, for behaviorists, insight is not important in the treatment of psychological disorders. Instead, psychological disorders and "healthy" behavior both are thought to develop through learning. Thus, in **behavior therapies**, disordered behaviors are unlearned and replaced by more appropriate alternative behaviors. In treating clients, behavior therapists employ principles of classical conditioning, operant conditioning, and observational learning.

12.3a *Some Behavior Therapies Rely upon Classical Conditioning.*

The most widely used form of psychotherapy that is based on classical conditioning is **counterconditioning**, which involves conditioning new responses to stimuli that trigger unwanted behaviors. Three specific counterconditioning techniques are *systematic desensitization*, *response prevention*, and *aversive conditioning*.

Behavior therapies
Psychotherapies that apply learning principles to the elimination of unwanted behaviors

Counterconditioning A behavior therapy procedure based on classical conditioning that involves conditioning new responses to stimuli that trigger unwanted behaviors

Systematic desensitization is commonly used to treat people with phobias by gradually exposing the phobic client to the feared object without arousing anxiety and fear (Buchanan & Houlihan, 2008). Behaviorists hold that the phobia was initially acquired through classical conditioning. That is, the phobic object was originally a neutral stimulus that was then paired with something that naturally elicited fear. A phobia conditioned in this way can be counterconditioned by pairing the feared object with relaxation or another physiological state incompatible with anxiety and fear.

For example, suppose a client has a fear of snakes. The client and therapist begin by constructing a *desensitization hierarchy*, which consists of a sequence of increasingly anxiety-provoking situations related to snakes (see Table 12-1). The therapist then trains the client in relaxation exercises, such as slow breathing or muscle relaxation. The first step of the hierarchy is then introduced (imagining seeing a snake). If the client can handle this without experiencing anxiety, the next step is introduced. Whenever the client experiences anxiety, the stimulus is removed and the client is given time to relax. After the client relaxes, a less threatening object on the hierarchy is reintroduced and the client and therapist again proceed along the hierarchy. In a relatively short time, the client often can face the highest object on the hierarchy—handling a snake—without distress.

Systematic desensitization A counterconditioning technique that is commonly used to treat phobias, in which the client is gradually exposed to the feared object while remaining relaxed

---

TABLE 12-1   A Sample Desensitization Hierarchy

The scenes in this hierarchy are typical of those used in the systematic desensitization to snakes. The numbers to the left of each statement represent one patient's subjective rating of how anxiety provoking a situation is, on a scale from 0 ("not at all anxious") to 100 ("uncontrollable anxiety").

Fear Level	Scene
10	I imagine seeing a snake.
20	I see a line drawing of a snake.
25	I see a photograph of a small, harmless garden snake.
30	I see a photograph of a large python.
40	I hold a rubber snake in my hands.
50	I watch a nature video on snakes.
60	I am in the same room with a snake in a cage.
70	I am standing next to the snake cage.
80	I am looking into the top of the snake cage with the lid open.
90	I am standing next to a person holding a snake.
95	I touch a snake held by someone else.
100	I am holding a snake.

A review of 375 therapy outcome studies indicates that systematic desensitization is the most effective therapy for treating phobias (M. L. Smith & Glass, 1977). Other reviews have concluded that desensitization is also effective in treating other problems that may occur as a result of anxiety, such as sexual dysfunction (Emmelkamp, 1986).

With advancements in computer technology, clients can now go through the hierarchy by wearing virtual-reality equipment that allows them to gradually experience more and more intense anxiety-provoking 3-D situations without ever leaving the therapist's office (Reger & Holloway, 2011). This *virtual-reality graded exposure* technique is especially useful in treating acrophobia (fear of heights) because it removes any danger of clients panicking while standing on a high structure. Before reading further, work on Closer Look 12-1.

Can You Systematically Desensitize Your Greatest Fear?

In Chapter 11's Closer Look 11-1, I asked you to identify your greatest fear. Now I would like you to use the counterconditioning technique of systematic desensitization to reduce and possibly even eliminate this fear. First construct a desensitization hierarchy consisting of a list of increasingly anxiety-provoking situations related to your fear (refer to Table 12-1 as a guide). Next, find a quiet place with no distractions, sit in a comfortable reclining chair, and progressively relax all the muscles of your body (you might be able to relax better if you read Explore It Exercise 13-2 in Chapter 13). While relaxed, imagine the first, easiest scene in your fear hierarchy. When you can imagine this scene without experiencing anxiety, move on to the next scene. Whenever you experience anxiety, stop imagining the scene and give yourself time to relax. After relaxing, imagine the previous, less threatening, scene in the hierarchy and then gradually reintroduce the more threatening scene. Do not try to go through the entire hierarchy in one session. Space your sessions out over time.

Response prevention A counterconditioning technique, commonly used in the treatment of obsessive-compulsive disorder, in which clients are exposed to the situation where they previously exhibited a compulsive behavior but now are not permitted to engage in the ritual

A counterconditioning technique closely related to desensitization is **response prevention**, which is often used to treat compulsive behaviors (Abramowitz, 2002). Remember that in obsessive-compulsive disorder, people experience distressing repetitive thoughts (such as worries about catching illness by being exposed to germs) followed by ritualistic compulsive behaviors (such as washing their hands hundreds of times daily). In response prevention therapy, clients are exposed to situations that trigger the distressing thoughts and feelings (for example, touching an object that fell on the floor). In the past, the clients' distress decreased after they engaged in compulsive behaviors, and so the compulsions were reinforced. However, in this treatment, clients are prevented from engaging in the compulsive behaviors, thus shutting off their usual, troublesome escape route to anxiety reduction. In all cases, response prevention causes an initial buildup of anxiety, but over time the client's distress tends to diminish. Numerous studies indicate that response prevention is effective in treating obsessive-compulsive disorder, with about 50 percent of clients showing substantial improvement and another 25 percent showing moderate improvement (Barlow & Lehman, 1996; Steketee, 1993).

Aversive conditioning A counterconditioning technique in which a classically conditioned aversive response is conditioned to occur in response to a stimulus previously associated with an undesired behavior

One last counterconditioning technique is **aversive conditioning**, in which people are classically conditioned to react with aversion to a harmful or undesirable stimulus (Hermann et al., 2002). For example, as depicted in Figure 12-1, a client who abuses alcohol may be given a favorite drink laced with *Antabuse*, a drug that induces severe vomiting. The objective is to replace the alcoholic's positive reaction to alcohol with a decidedly negative response. After repeated pairings of alcohol with vomiting, the alcohol alone begins eliciting nausea.

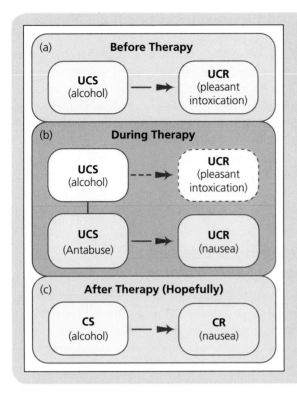

FIGURE 12-1

Aversive Conditioning for Alcoholism

(a) Initially, alcohol is an unconditioned stimulus for alcoholics, naturally evoking a pleasant unconditioned response. (b) During therapy, the Antabuse drug is mixed with alcohol and given to the alcoholic, causing severe nausea. (c) After repeated pairings, the alcohol becomes a conditioned stimulus, evoking the conditioned response (nausea). What might weaken this conditioned response following therapy so that the treatment is ultimately ineffective in promoting abstinence?

Alcoholics treated with this form of aversion therapy tend to achieve about a 60 percent abstinence rate up to one year after treatment (Rimmele et al., 1995). However, after three years, only about one-third remain abstinent. The problem with this therapy is that alcohol is an unconditioned stimulus that naturally evokes a pleasant state of intoxication, which is an unconditioned response. Alcoholics know that if they drink outside the therapist's office, they will not experience the immediate nausea but instead will experience a pleasant alcoholic "high."

As you can imagine, aversive conditioning is both distressing and messy, and many clients and therapists prefer other treatments. Aversive conditioning is typically used only after other methods have failed, and the client provides informed consent to participate in such a difficult process. Even when this procedure is used, therapists almost always combine it with another treatment, often one involving operant conditioning, our next topic of discussion.

12.3b Operant Conditioning Is Used in Token Economies.

As you recall from Chapter 6, Section 6.2, *operant conditioning* involves learning through reinforcement and punishment. Because virtually every voluntary behavior can be punished or reinforced, operant conditioning is a very flexible approach to modifying behavior. One important therapeutic application of operant conditioning principles is the **token economy**, which uses reward and punishment to modify the behavior of groups of people, often in institutional settings such as psychiatric hospitals or prisons (Correia et al., 2005; Kopelowicz et al., 2002). In this technique, desirable behaviors are reinforced with tokens (such as poker chips or checks on a card), and undesirable behaviors are punished by the loss of tokens. People whose behavior is being modified with token economies accumulate and later exchange the tokens for other forms of reinforcement (such as television privileges or field trips). Research has shown that the token economy technique is effective in shaping desirable behavior not only in psychiatric hospitals and prisons but also in school

Token economy A technique often used to modify the behavior of severely disturbed people in institutional settings; involves reinforcing desirable behaviors with tokens that can be exchanged for other forms of reinforcement, such as snacks or television privileges

classrooms, structured play activities, and homes for juvenile delinquents (Kazdin, 1982; Reitman et al., 2001).

Is there a downside to using the token economy? Critics charge that this type of *behavior modification* makes people too dependent on the external rewards earned in the token economy. Why is this a problem? Well, when was the last time someone gave you a token when you did something nice or took a token from you when you behaved badly? One of the problems with token economies is that the desirable behaviors learned through this technique are likely to be quickly extinguished when people are outside the institution. Proponents of the token economy respond that such a possibility can be considerably reduced if, prior to leaving the institution, people are slowly shifted from a token-economy reward system to rewards more likely to be encountered outside the institution, such as social approval.

12.3c *Observational Learning Is Used in Modeling and Social Skills Training.*

Observational learning is the central feature of Albert Bandura's (1986) *social learning theory*, which contends that people learn social behaviors mainly through observation and cognitive processing of information, rather than through direct experience (see Chapter 6, Section 6.3a). Specifically, *observational learning* occurs by observing and imitating the behavior of others, who are called *models*. The therapeutic application of observational learning principles is called **modeling**, and it has been especially helpful in teaching clients useful social behaviors and coping skills.

In *participatory modeling*, the therapist or someone else models more effective ways of behaving; gradually, the client is invited to participate in the behavior. For example, a person suffering from snake phobia might first watch the therapist handling snakes without the therapist expressing fear or being harmed. After watching this snake handling a few times, the client is gently coaxed into holding a snake. Participatory modeling is a very effective treatment for phobias and other fears.

Another therapeutic technique that involves observational learning is **social skills training**, which teaches clients who are inept or who act inappropriately in social situations how to interact with others more comfortably and effectively (Hersen & Bellack, 1999). Social skills training programs employ various learning techniques, including the previously discussed modeling by socially skilled trainers, as well as role-playing various problematic social encounters. The social skills taught in these training sessions cover such areas as initiating conversations, giving and receiving compliments, reacting nonviolently to conflict, nonverbal methods of communication, and actively listening to what others have to say in conversation. Training is usually conducted in groups.

Modeling A behavioral method of psychotherapy in which desirable behaviors are demonstrated as a way of teaching them to clients

Social skills training A behavioral method of psychotherapy in which clients are taught how to interact with others more comfortably and effectively

INFO-BIT

Social skills training has been shown to be effective for individuals suffering from schizophrenia, especially when used in conjunction with a drug therapy program (Kurtz & Mueser, 2008). Impulsive and hyperactive children, who often have problems interacting with others, are also regularly placed in social skills therapy programs.

In a typical session, the therapist might show a videotape of a model starting a conversation inappropriately or aggressively responding to a disagreement. The group might then discuss ways in which the model could have acted more appropriately. Following this discussion, group members might view another videotape in which the model performs more effectively. Each person in the training group might then role-play a conversation while others observe and then provide feedback. This role-playing might even be videotaped so group members can see exactly how they interacted. The session might end with a homework assignment that requires group members to work on some specific social behavior during the following week. A number of studies indicate that people who participate in such training exercises show improvements in their social skills and an increased level of social satisfaction (Erwin, 1994; Wert & Neisworth, 2003).

Journey of Discovery

Suppose a male college student seeks therapy because he is shy and has been unsuccessful in his attempts to talk to women. He reports that he stammers and has trouble thinking of anything to say. He does not initiate conversations, even to make small talk, with women classmates. When he starts to make a phone call to ask someone out, he hesitates and talks himself out of calling. How might a behavior psychotherapist use modeling and social skills training to treat this student's shyness?

Section REVIEW

- Behavior therapies use conditioning and observational learning techniques to modify problem behaviors.

- Therapy techniques based on classical conditioning include systematic desensitization (gradually exposing the phobic client to the feared object without arousing anxiety and fear); response prevention (exposing clients to situations in which they previously exhibited a compulsive behavior, but not permitting them to engage in the ritual); and aversive conditioning (an aversive response is conditioned to occur in response to a stimulus previously associated with an undesired behavior).

- Therapy techniques based on operant conditioning and observational learning include token economies (used in institutions to modify the behavior of groups of people); modeling (desirable behaviors are demonstrated as a way of teaching them to clients); and social skills training (learning how to interact with others more comfortably and effectively).

12.4 Cognitive Therapies

As discussed in Chapter 11, Section 11.1c, the cognitive perspective suggests that the immediate cause of psychological problems is inaccurate or ineffective thinking. Hassles become crises because people do not accurately evaluate the situations they encounter, and thus they do not arrive at effective solutions. Because dysfunctional thinking is considered by this perspective to be the source of psychological problems, **cognitive therapies** seek to identify and then modify these faulty cognitive processes. Like behavior therapies—and unlike psychodynamic therapies—cognitive therapies tend to be short-term, problem-focused, and highly directive.

Cognitive therapies
Psychotherapies that focus on identifying and then modifying dysfunctional patterns of thought

12.4a Rational-Emotive Behavior Therapy Confronts Clients' Irrational Assumptions.

Rational-emotive behavior therapy (REBT) The cognitive therapy of Albert Ellis, in which people are confronted with their irrational beliefs and persuaded to develop a more realistic way of thinking

Albert Ellis (1962, 1999) developed a form of cognitive therapy called **rational-emotive behavior therapy (REBT)**, which assumes that mental distress is caused not by objective events in people's lives but rather by the irrational thinking people have about those events. For example, a person might say he is depressed because he did not receive a promotion at work. However, Ellis would contend that the real cause of the depression is the person's assumption that this event means something negative about himself ("My boss does not respect me"). The goal of REBT is to help people identify problems in the way they think about their general experiences and then try to modify these cognitions. The irrational beliefs that cause emotional problems are based on what Ellis called "all-or-none" types of thinking. For instance, people who think they must be loved or approved by everyone, or that they must be successful in everything they do, are likely to feel unhappy much of the time. By setting unreachable goals, they experience frequent disappointment.

What makes REBT so unconventional is the way these therapists respond to their clients' irrational beliefs (Ellis, 2002). Instead of allowing clients to state their beliefs without evaluative comment (as happens in classical psychoanalysis), REBT therapists directly attack clients' irrational ways of thinking, pointing out how they are inevitably self-defeating and persuading them to develop a more realistic way of evaluating their lives. Of all the therapies discussed in this chapter, REBT is the one most similar to Dr. Phil's interpersonal style with his TV clients. Like Dr. Phil, REBT therapists are often blunt and confrontational in challenging clients' negative and unrealistic assessments of their present conditions. The following are typical responses therapists might make to clients' emotional woes:

"So you didn't get the promotion. Where is it written that life has to be fair?"

"Why do you always have to look on the dark side of things?"

"So what if your father didn't love you. That's his problem!"

Clients are also encouraged to "step out of character" and try new behaviors that directly challenge their irrational beliefs (Ellis et al., 2002). For example, if a woman is afraid others won't like her if she disagrees with them, her therapist might instruct her to forcefully disagree with five people during the next week. The objective in such an exercise is for the woman to discover that her world doesn't end following such exchanges.

The effectiveness of REBT is difficult to determine. There are no specific psychological disorders that are best treated by REBT, and it is unclear how much clients benefit from this form of therapy. Studies suggest, however, that it does have some positive effects on clients' later adjustment and well-being (Blackburn, 2005; Moeller & Steel, 2002).

12.4b Cognitive-Behavior Therapy Focuses on Emotional Problems.

Cognitive-behavior therapy (CBT) The cognitive therapy of Aaron Beck that identifies and then changes negative thinking and behavior by using both cognitive and behavioral principles

Like Ellis, Aaron Beck (1967) originally developed his **cognitive-behavior therapy (CBT)** to treat depression—which he considers to be a cognitive disorder—but he later applied his treatment to anxiety and other emotional problems (Beck & Emery, 1985). According to Beck, depressed people have negative views of themselves, the world, and their future; and they misinterpret everyday events to support these negative views (Beck et al., 1979). For example, they tend to exaggerate negative outcomes while downplaying positive outcomes, and they jump to overly pessimistic conclusions based on a single event. These thinking errors may occur so frequently that they become automatic.

CBT involves identifying and then changing both the client's negative thinking patterns and negative behavior patterns (Blenkiron, 2005). To do so, therapists instruct clients to keep a diary of their thoughts before and after sad episodes. Therapists then discuss these episodes with the clients and help them develop new thinking patterns that are more positive, accurate, and effective. The reason this therapy has the term *behavior* in its title is that the methods used to help clients develop new patterns of thinking often involve basic conditioning techniques. Research has shown that CBT is relatively effective in treating depression (Bourne, 2003), anxiety disorder (Durham et al., 2003), bulimia (Fairburn et al., 1997), and borderline personality disorders (Linehan, 1993). Because CBT typically requires fewer than 16 sessions, insurance providers, who often pay for a substantial portion of people's mental health services, find this form of psychotherapy very appealing in managing their health care costs.

Shutterstock

If your current life situation could be described as a glass half-filled with sweet nectar, cognitive-behavior therapists would encourage you to focus on the fact that it is half full, not half empty. If your current life situation is more aptly described as a half-filled glass of bitter medicine, you are encouraged to focus on the fact that the glass is already half empty and you can look forward to better times.

Section REVIEW

- Cognitive therapy is based on the assumption that troubling emotions and behaviors result from inaccurate or ineffective thinking.

- Cognitive therapies are short-term, active, and problem-focused.

- In rational-emotive behavior therapy, clients are bluntly confronted with their irrational beliefs and persuaded to develop a more realistic way of thinking.

- In cognitive-behavior therapy, clients' negative thinking and behavior are modified, using both cognitive and behavioral principles.

12.5 Humanistic Therapies

As discussed in Chapter 10 Section 10.3, humanistic psychology focuses on positive aspects of human experience, such as love, creativity, and spirituality. **Humanistic therapies** focus on helping people get in touch with their feelings, with their "true selves," and with their purposes in life. Humanists believe that psychological problems develop when outside forces stifle people's natural tendency to seek personal growth. One of the primary goals of humanistic therapies is to help clients actualize their basically good natures.

Humanistic therapies Psychotherapies that help people get in touch with their feelings, with their "true selves," and with their purposes in life

12.5a Client-Centered Therapy Focuses on Clients' Conscious Self-Perceptions.

The psychologist who has had the strongest influence on humanistic psychotherapy is Carl Rogers (1959, 1961), the developer of **client-centered therapy**. In articulating how therapists should view their function in treating psychological disorders, Rogers argued that they should not assume the role of "detective," as in psychodynamic therapy, or the role of "active director," as in behavior and cognitive therapies. Instead, Rogers believed that therapists should be *facilitators* of personal growth by providing a supportive environment in which clients can discover their "true selves." This emphasis on the client's own conscious self-perceptions, rather than on the

Client-centered therapy A humanistic therapy in which the client, rather than the therapist, directs the course of therapy

therapist's interpretations of those perceptions, is the reason Rogers's therapeutic approach is titled "client-centered."

A central assumption underlying client-centered therapy is that psychopathology results because people have received *conditional positive regard* from loved ones, which involves being loved and socially accepted only when meeting others' standards (Rogers, 1951). Put another way, people are accepted as worthy individuals in their own right only when they meet or conform to others' wishes and desires.

To counteract the negative effects of this conditional acceptance, Rogers proposed that psychotherapy be built around the principle of *unconditional positive regard*. That is, clients should be accepted unconditionally—treated with warmth, kindness, and caring—regardless of what they have said or done. The assumption here is that when therapists accept clients for who they are, clients will eventually come to accept themselves as well. When this self-acceptance occurs, clients can put aside the standards of others that are false for them and once again get on track in developing their true selves. Key ingredients in unconditional positive regard are *genuineness* (being open and honest), *warmth* (being caring and nurturing), and *empathy* (accurately identifying what the client is thinking and feeling).

In expressing unconditional positive regard, client-centered therapists typically use the techniques of *open-ended statements, reflection,* and *paraphrasing* (Geldard & Geldard, 2008). For instance, consider the question "Did you have a good week?" This is a closed-ended question because it can be answered with a single word, and it suggests that the client should evaluate the week. On the other hand, "Tell me about your week" is open-ended because clients can say as much or as little about the week as they choose. Open-ended statements encourage clients to speak, without limiting the topic of conversation.

With reflection, the therapist acknowledges some emotion that the client has expressed verbally or nonverbally. For example, when the client says that the week has been hard, the therapist reflects this by saying, "This has been a tough week for you." Finally, with paraphrasing, the therapist summarizes the expressed verbal content of the client. For example, when the client is distressed but does not express herself or himself clearly, the therapist may summarize what the client has said by stating, "Let me see if I am understanding the situation you faced this week. You said that …"

Therapists from many theoretical schools use some or all of these client-centered techniques to build rapport with clients. Such wide use of client-centered techniques probably explains why fellow psychotherapists often identify Carl Rogers as the person having had the biggest influence on how therapy is practiced (Smith, 1982). Further, reviews of almost 1,100 therapeutic outcome studies conducted over a 35-year period support Rogers's contention that a positive client-therapist relationship is an essential factor in determining the effectiveness of therapy (Orlinsky & Howard, 1987). Exploring Culture & Diversity Box 12-1 discusses how failure to establish rapport may partly explain the higher dropout rates among minority group members in the United States.

Exploring **CULTURE & DIVERSITY 12.1**

Why Do Certain Minorities Underutilize Therapeutic Services?

Ethnic minorities in the United States are less likely to seek mental health treatment and more likely to drop out of therapy than Whites (Moon & Cho, 2012; Neighbors et al.,

2012). For example, a nationwide survey found that African Americans and Hispanics are only half as likely to seek treatment for psychological problems as White Americans (Kessler et al., 2005).As mentioned in Chapter 11, Section 11.1b, one factor influencing a person's willingness to seek psychotherapy is the belief system in that person's culture. Partly because most modern psychotherapies were developed in Western cultures that have an individualist orientation, the primary thrust of contemporary therapies involves focusing on the client's emotions and personal needs. However, in collectivist Asian cultures, talking about personal feelings or even focusing on oneself individually is generally considered socially inappropriate (Russell & Yik, 1996). Instead, being emotionally nonexpressive and relying on oneself to cope with distress are often interpreted as signs of emotional strength and maturity (Narikiyo & Kameoka, 1992). Thus, one of the possible obstacles Asian Americans face when seeking help for psychological problems is that the conventional Western psychotherapeutic approach may appear to them to be an unwise path for finding mental health.

What are some factors that explain the relative underutilization of psychotherapy among ethnic minority groups in the Unites States?

Another reason ethnic minorities in the United States are less likely than Whites to seek mental health treatment is that a history of institutionalized discrimination based on race and ethnicity has made minorities more mistrustful of the medical and mental health professions. For example, surveys find that African Americans, Hispanic Americans, and Native Americans are much more likely than White Americans to believe that their doctors or health providers judge them unfairly or treat them with disrespect because of their race or ethnic background (Brown et al., 2000; LaVeist et al., 2000). Instead of taking advantage of conventional mental health therapy, many ethnic minorities turn to more culturally comfortable sources of help when they experience prolonged psychological distress. For example, Native Americans and Alaska Natives may rely on traditional healers, while African Americans may seek out their church ministers and rely on them, spirituality, to help cope with symptoms of psychological disorders (Trujillo, 2000). Further, partly due to the stigma surrounding mental illness, when they do seek professional help, ethnic minorities are more likely than Whites to consult primary care physicians and nurses rather than mental health specialists. Unfortunately, one of the consequences of this decision is that minority individuals are less likely than Whites to have their psychological problems accurately diagnosed and treated (Borowsky et al., 2000).

What might explain the higher therapy dropout rates among Asian Americans, Hispanic Americans, African Americans, and Native Americans, as compared to the rates for White Americans? Some of these differences might be due to the fact that dropout rates are higher among poorer clients, and ethnic minorities are overrepresented in lower-income groups. Another likely factor in explaining these differences is that although ethnic minorities make up about one-fourth of the population, only about 10 percent of mental health providers are ethnic minorities. Research indicates that clients feel more comfortable when their therapists are similar to themselves rather than dissimilar, and this may be especially true in regard to race and ethnicity. Thus, the higher dropout rates among minorities may be at least partly due to problems in establishing rapport with White therapists. A related issue for some Hispanic and Asian clients is a language barrier. Many bilingual minority clients find it easier to discuss their emotions and memories in their native language, something that English-only therapists cannot accommodate (Altarriba, 2003; Biever et al., 2002).

Faced with these cultural divisions that can impede therapeutic effectiveness, an increasing number of psychotherapists of all races and ethnicities now receive special training to help them work more effectively with clients from other cultural backgrounds (Davis-Russel, 2003). Research finds that this cultural training does improve the therapeutic process and reduces the dropout rate of minority clients (Fraga et al., 2004). In fact, in a study of Hispanic students receiving therapy from a university counseling center, researchers found that satisfaction with a therapist was not predicted by the therapist's ethnicity but depended, instead, on the degree to which the Hispanic clients believed their therapists understood their culture (Dingfelder, 2005).

Although cultural understanding appears to be more important than cultural similarity in establishing client-therapist rapport, the American Psychological Association and other mental health organizations have made concerted efforts to recruit and train more ethnic minority therapists.

As the ranks of minority mental health professionals grow in the coming years, this should persuade even more minority students to pursue careers in counseling and clinical psychology.

12.5b *Gestalt Therapy Encourages Clients to Get in Touch with Their Feelings.*

Gestalt therapy A humanistic psychotherapy that stresses awareness of feelings in the here and now

Another influential humanistic therapy is **Gestalt therapy**, which was developed by the former psychoanalyst Frederick ("Fritz") Perls, along with his wife, Laura (Perls, 1969; Perls et al., 1951). *Gestalt* is the German word for "pattern" or "whole." Perls named his approach Gestalt therapy because he said that he treated the "whole" person. To Perls, a major cause of mental illness is people's lack of awareness of their true feelings or some other important aspect of the self.

In contrast to the nondirective style typical of client-centered therapists, Gestalt therapists employ a directive approach, often putting clients on a figurative "hot seat" to encourage them to become aware of feelings and impulses they have disowned and to abandon feelings and ideas that are not their own (Bowman & Brownell, 2000). For example, if a client frowns following a comment by the therapist, the therapist might confront this directly by stating, "Are you aware of your facial expression? What does this mean to you?"

Empty-chair technique A Gestalt technique in which clients engage in emotional expression by imagining that the person to whom they would like to speak is sitting in an empty chair facing them

Perhaps the most popular technique used in Gestalt therapy to help clients gain insight into their true feelings is the **empty-chair technique**, in which the therapist places an empty chair facing the seated client and then asks the client to imagine that an important person from her or his past or present—a parent, spouse, or friend—is sitting in the chair. In this "safe" environment, the client can express her or his feelings by "talking" with the imagined person and hopefully gaining insight into those feelings. Research suggests that this technique may indeed help clients deal with the emotional turmoil that led them to seek therapy in the first place (Paivio & Greenberg, 1995). Before reading further, complete Explore it Exercise 12-1, which recreates in more detail this Gestalt technique.

Section
REVIEW

- Client-centered therapy is a form of humanistic therapy based on unconditional positive regard; it focuses on the client's self-perceptions and is nondirective.

- Gestalt therapy stresses awareness of feelings in the here and now and uses active and directive techniques, such as confrontation, to enhance awareness.

SELF-DISCOVERY 12-1
Questionnaire

Can Imaginary Conversations Resolve Conflict?

Gestalt therapists often help clients resolve conflicted feelings toward loved ones by guiding the clients through an imaginary conversation with these persons. One therapeutic procedure used to accomplish this task is known as the empty-chair technique. To help you understand how this technique works, explore it yourself by following these four steps:

1. Think of someone with whom you have had a recent conflict. Choose a conflict that is not very serious, because in this exercise I am more interested in your understanding the process of this technique rather than your resolving a major personal problem.

2. Set two chairs facing each other. Sit in one of these chairs and visualize your "target" person sitting in the other chair. Speak out loud to this absent person, describing the situation and/or behavior that created the conflict, how it makes you feel, and how you would like to resolve it.

3. Sit in the "target" person's chair and assume his or her point of view, imagining yourself sitting in the chair you just occupied. Respond to your previous statements as you think the "target" person would respond. How do the "target" person's imagined comments make you feel?

In the empty-chair technique, clients are asked to imagine having a conversation with an important person from their past or present who is sitting in the chair. The goal is to gain insight into their true feelings.

4. When you complete this exercise, reflect on its usefulness. Did you find that participating in this technique helped you better understand your "target" person's point of view? Do you see how this technique might help people resolve emotional conflicts in their lives?

12.6 Other Forms of Psychotherapy

Most forms of psychotherapy were originally developed for use with individual adult clients. However, it is important to remember that psychotherapy is often provided in other formats. In this section, we examine *child therapy*, *group therapy*, and *family/couples therapy*.

12.6a Child Therapies Use Techniques Designed for Younger Minds.

Approximately 12 percent of the children and adolescents in the United States experience significant behavioral or emotional problems, with about 2.5 million of them receiving some form of therapy (Siskind, 2005). However, due to the limitations of children's concrete thinking and language, they may be less able than adults to respond to verbal and insight-oriented therapies. Thus, therapists may have to rely more on behavioral observations and the reports of third parties (such as parents or teachers) than they would with adult clients. In some cases, the

Play therapy A therapeutic technique in which the therapist provides children with toys and drawing materials on the assumption that whatever is troubling them will be expressed in their play

parents may be recruited as "co-therapists," using at-home techniques taught to them by the therapist.

A common approach taken by therapists when working with children is **play therapy** (Homeyer & DeFrance, 2005). Here, the child plays with puppets, blocks, crayons, and other common toys, while the therapist plays with or simply observes the child. Psychodynamic therapists consider play therapy to be a childhood form of free association, a technique they believe allows the client's unconscious material to come forth (Klein, 1932). In contrast, client-centered therapists consider play therapy a perfect vehicle in which to practice their warm, nondirective approach (Axline, 1947). During play, the therapist provides the child with unconditional positive regard, thereby activating the therapeutic process. Cognitive and behavior therapists also find play therapy useful because it provides a means of helping the child acquire new cognitive or behavioral skills. In both approaches, therapy is basically an educational enterprise. By playing with the child, the therapist can demonstrate new skills, reinforce the child's successful efforts, and modify efforts that are only partly correct.

12.6b Group Therapy Involves Clients Discussing, Collectively, Their Problems with a Therapist.

Group therapy The simultaneous treatment of several clients under the guidance of a therapist

Psychotherapy can also be conducted with groups of clients (Saakvitne, 2005). **Group therapy** refers to the simultaneous treatment of several clients under the guidance of a therapist. Some therapy groups are composed of relatively well-functioning clients in outpatient settings, while other therapy groups consist of severely disturbed patients in hospital settings. Many groups are organized around one kind of problem (such as alcoholism or depression) or one kind of client (such as adolescents or police officers). The group usually consists of between 5 and 10 people who meet with a therapist about once a week for two hours. Today, all major theoretical schools of psychotherapy have some sort of group format.

Although the increased use of group therapy over the past 30 years is partly due to economics—it is more cost-effective than individual therapy—the group format has some real advantages over the individual format (Fuhriman & Burlingame, 1994). One advantage is that group therapy helps clients realize that others also struggle with many of the same problems they are working to solve. A related advantage is that a group format provides clients with the opportunity to compare themselves to others like themselves and exchange information on how to become more mentally healthy. A third advantage is that group members can become an important support network for one another, boosting self-confidence and providing acceptance. Finally, a fourth advantage is that the group setting allows the therapist to observe clients interacting with one another, which often helps the therapist better understand how to treat individual members.

Self-help group Several people regularly meeting and discussing their problems with one another without the guidance of a therapist

One variation of group therapy is the **self-help group**, which consists of several people regularly meeting and discussing their problems with one another without the guidance of a therapist. One of the oldest and best-known self-help groups is Alcoholics Anonymous (AA), which has more than 70,000 chapters and more than 2 million members worldwide (Tonigan et al., 2000). Such self-help groups appear to provide moderate to substantial benefits (Tonigan & Connors, 2008). Many therapists who treat clients in an individual or group format often also urge them to participate in self-help groups as part of their recovery process. The primary limitation of such groups is that the lack of guidance from a trained therapist can sometimes lead members to oversimplify the causes and remedies for their problems.

12.6c Family and Couples Therapies Try to Change Dysfunctional Interaction Patterns.

Research suggests that when people who have been hospitalized for a psychological disorder return home to their families, they often suffer a relapse (Hazelrigg et al., 1987). One possible cause for such setbacks is the dysfunctional nature of their family relationships. Such an occurrence is consistent with the *diathesis-stress model* (see Chapter 11, Section 11.1c), which contends that stress may trigger the onset or relapse of a disorder for people who have an underlying vulnerability (a *diathesis*) for that disorder. In an attempt to prevent such relapses, all the major theoretical schools of psychotherapy have adapted their ideas to the treatment of families. These **family therapies** are designed to constructively modify the dysfunctional relationships among family members.

Often, family therapists base their work on systems theory, a theoretical approach important in both biology and cybernetics and based on the assumption that "the whole is greater than the sum of its parts" (Wysocki et al., 2008). Systems theory readily applies to families because the family itself is a system, with each member an interacting element in that system. According to **family systems therapy**, the family acts in specific ways to maintain itself, both in terms of the interactions among the members and in terms of how the family interacts with its outside environment (Lebow, 2012). As such, an individual family member's problems cannot be understood and treated in isolation but must be examined and treated within the family system. With the therapist's guidance, family members can develop constructive communication and problem-solving skills, thereby reducing conflicts and emotional distress and improving the quality of their relationships.

Finally, a variant of family therapy is **couples therapy**, which focuses on the problematic communication and behavior patterns of romantic partners. Over half the couples entering therapy state that their number-one problem involves faulty communication (O'Leary et al., 1992). This is true for both other-sex and same-sex romantic partners (Kurdek, 1994; Miller, 1997). Due to the pervasiveness of this problem, establishing an honest dialogue between the two partners is crucial in virtually all couples therapies.

Couples therapists with a cognitive and/or behavioral orientation use various techniques to teach positive communication skills. For example, couples may keep a diary of their weekly interactions, participate in positive role-playing exercises, and even watch videotapes of them discussing their relationship. Humanistic therapies often focus on getting the partners to express their emotions toward one another and to reveal what kind of new relationship they would like to build. Finally, psychodynamic therapists emphasize helping couples gain insight into the underlying motives in their relationships and the ways they may be reacting to one another based on how they related to their own parents as children.

Overall, couples and family therapies appear to be relatively successful (Hazelrigg et al., 1987; Shadish et al., 1993). In fact, an increasing number of therapists who regularly treat married or cohabiting clients for depression on an individual basis now believe that the couples format is more effective (Beach et al., 1994).

Family therapies Therapies designed to constructively modify the dysfunctional relationships among family members

Family systems therapy A form of family therapy in which the family is treated as a dynamic system, with each member an important interacting element in that system

Couples therapy Therapy designed to help couples improve the quality of their relationship

A common problem addressed in couples therapy is faulty communication between partners. How effective is this form of therapy, compared to individual therapy, in reducing romantic relationship problems?

INFO-BIT   A growing number of therapists are interacting with their clients—and providing actual therapy—through the Internet (Bambling et al., 2008). Online therapy can be effective for certain mental health problems, such as binge eating, restrictive eating, and subclinical depression (Jacobi et al., 2012; Mackinnon et al., 2008).

Section REVIEW

- Play therapy is often used with children, even though the various therapeutic formats have different assumptions regarding its usefulness.

- Major forms of psychotherapy were originally developed for use with individual adults but have been adapted for use with children, families, couples, and groups.

- Alternative therapy formats are often as effective as, or superior to, individual therapy formats.

12.7 Biomedical Therapies

Today in the United States, the number of people who are full-time residents of psychiatric hospitals is less than one-third of the number hospitalized during the 1950s. The primary reason for this sharp decrease in hospitalization is the widespread use of drug therapies to treat psychological disorders such as schizophrenia and the mood disorders (Soliman et al., 2008). Figure 12-2 shows that by 1995, more than 90 percent of the people diagnosed with a psychological disorder were receiving drugs as part of their treatment program (Nietzel et al., 1998). This high percentage of drug therapy is due not only to its effectiveness but also to the fact that this form of therapy is often less expensive than psychological therapies. In this section, we examine some of these drugs and their effects and then discuss two controversial biomedical procedures that are sometimes used to treat severe cases of mental illness—namely, *electroconvulsive therapy* and *psychosurgery*.

FIGURE 12-2

Use of Drugs in Treating Psychological Disorders

The percentage of people diagnosed with a psychological disorder who are receiving drug therapy has increased sharply since the 1970s.

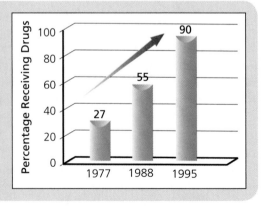

12.7a Antipsychotic Drugs Affect Dopamine Neurotransmitters.

One of the earliest successes in using medication to treat psychological disorders was the discovery in the 1950s that certain drugs used for other medical purposes reduced the positive, "uncontrollable," psychotic symptoms of schizophrenia, such as auditory hallucinations and paranoia (Lehman et al., 1998). The first of these **antipsychotic drugs**, *chlorpromazine*, is in a class of drugs called the *phenothiazines* and is marketed under the trade name Thorazine. As you recall from Chapter 11, Section 11.2d, research suggests that schizophrenia is associated with an overactive central dopamine system in the brain. Chlorpromazine and other antipsychotic medications are thought to work by blocking dopamine receptor sites in the brain, thereby reducing dopamine activity (Snyder et al., 2008).

Antipsychotic medications do not actually "cure" schizophrenia—they merely help control its severe symptoms. These patients still have schizophrenia. They often continue to experience problems in living although they may now be able to function outside the hospital, such as in their family home or a halfway house. Because antipsychotic drugs cannot cure the disorder, it is important that schizophrenic patients who receive these drugs also receive appropriate aftercare services so they do not simply move from the back wards of hospitals to the back alleys of our cities.

While they reduce positive schizophrenic symptoms, antipsychotic drugs are much less effective in relieving negative symptoms—such as the absence of emotional expression, immobility, and social withdrawal—which may be related to structural defects in the brain. These drugs also have some very unpleasant side effects, including Parkinson's disease-like muscular tremors, stiffness, sluggishness, and loss of control over voluntary movements. Even the newer antipsychotic drug *clozapine* (Clozaril), which does not have these undesirable side effects, can cause a fatal blood disorder in about 2 percent of patients who take it (LaGrenade et al., 2001). Medical advances have led to the development of even newer replacement drugs, such as *risperidone* (Risperdal), that do not appear to have some of these dangerous side effects (Ravasia, 2001). However, even these new drugs are not risk free. For example, prescribing Risperdal to elderly adults increases their risk of stroke.

Antipsychotic drugs Drugs that are effective in treating the delusions, hallucinations, and loose associations of schizophrenia by blocking dopamine receptors and thereby reducing dopamine activity

12.7b Antidepressant Drugs Affect Serotonin and Norepinephrine Neurotransmitters.

A second psychological disorder successfully treated with medication since the 1950s is depression. **Antidepressant drugs** include *iproniazid*, which is in a class of drugs called the *monoamine oxidase inhibitors (MAOI)* and was the first drug used in this way. Although initially developed to treat tuberculosis, physicians observed that iproniazid significantly improved patients' mood and energy. Iproniazid and the other MAOI drugs work by inhibiting the monoamine oxidase (MAO) enzyme involved in breaking down the neurotransmitters norepinephrine and serotonin. When MAO is inhibited, the available supply of norepinephrine and serotonin is increased, which has the effect of elevating mood. Despite these benefits, MAOI drugs can produce dangerous side effects, including virtually eliminating REM sleep (see Chapter 5, Section 5.2d) and causing a sudden increase in blood pressure—and thus, an increased likelihood of stroke—if mixed with certain foods, such as red wine, beer, and aged cheeses (Julien, 2001). In response to this health issue, a newer type of MAOI drug, *moclobemide*, is now available that is less likely to have this negative food interaction (Cheung et al., 2008).

Antidepressant drugs Drug that relieve depression by increasing the supply of norepinephrine and/or serotonin at the neuron's receptor sites

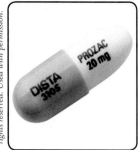

Prozac, a *selective serotonin reuptake inhibitor (SSRI)* drug, is the most widely prescribed antidepressant in the world. Why might the SSRI drugs have milder side effects than other antidepressants?

A second class of antidepressant medications that have less severe side effects and seem to work somewhat better than the MAOI drugs is composed of the *tricyclics*. These drugs increase the available supply of serotonin and norepinephrine by decreasing their reuptake at the neuron's receptor sites (see Chapter 2, Section 2.1). Among the tricyclics, *amitriptyline* (Elavil), *desipramine* (Norpramin), and *imipramine* (Tofranil) are widely used. Some of the common side effects of tricyclics are drowsiness, sleep disturbances, constipation, dry mouth, and blurred vision. These antidepressants can also affect a person's blood pressure and heart rate.

Finally, the most popular antidepressants are those that affect only serotonin—namely, the *selective serotonin reuptake inhibitors (SSRIs)*. As their name implies, SSRIs inhibit the reuptake of the neurotransmitter serotonin, which increases the available supply of serotonin in the body, making it easier for neural impulses to be transmitted along serotonin pathways in the brain (Politis et al., 2008). Among the SSRIs, *fluoxetine* (Prozac), *fluvoxetine* (Luvox), *paroxetine* (Paxil), and *sertraline* (Zoloft) are all widely used. Prozac is by far the most popular, with 54 million people using this drug worldwide. Prozac is also sometimes used to treat certain anxiety disorders and eating disorders (Julien, 2001). Controlled studies indicate that the SSRIs are as effective as the tricyclics in treating depression; the SSRIs, however, tend to have milder side effects, perhaps because they act only on one neurotransmitter (Ziegelstein, 2012).

Bipolar disorder, like depression, is a mood disorder that can be treated effectively with medication (Ketter & Wang, 2002). Since 1969, when a mineral salt of the element *lithium* was approved for use in the United States, the drug lithium has helped about 75 percent of the bipolar patients for whom it has been prescribed (Vieta et al., 2008). Without lithium, bipolar patients have a manic episode about every 14 months. With lithium, manic attacks occur as infrequently as once every 9 years. However, despite its effectiveness, lithium can cause delirium and even death if excessive doses are taken. Exactly how lithium works is unclear. Yet, because it takes at least a week of regular use before the drug shows any benefits, lithium's effects probably occur through some long-term adaptation of the nervous system. Although lithium has long been regarded as the "treatment of choice" for bipolar disorder, new mood stabilizers, such as *depakote*, have been developed and are now being used along with lithium (Gavin et al., 2008).

12.7c *Antianxiety Drugs Are the Most Widely Used Legal Drugs.*

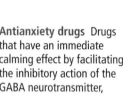

Antianxiety drugs Drugs that have an immediate calming effect by facilitating the inhibitory action of the GABA neurotransmitter, thereby reducing nerve impulse transmission

As presented in Chapter 11, Section 11.2a, one of the most common types of psychological problems is anxiety. The oldest drug treatment for anxiety is alcohol, which has been available as a tranquilizer for thousands of years. However, given the recognized negative side effects of alcohol (see Chapter 5, Section 5.3e), physicians no longer prescribe it as an anxiety treatment. Instead, a class of **antianxiety drugs**—the *benzodiazepines*—is the most frequently prescribed anxiety medication in the United States. Among the benzodiazepines are *oxazepam* (Serax), *lorazepam* (Ativan), *alprazolam* (Xanax), and *diazepam* (Valium). These drugs seem to produce their effects by facilitating the action of the neurotransmitter *gamma-aminobutyric acid (GABA)*, which has an inhibitory effect on the central nervous system (Pinna & Rasmusson, 2012). That is, when receptor sites on the neuron take up GABA, it becomes more difficult for the neuron to be stimulated to transmit a nerve impulse. In this way, antianxiety agents help "slow down" the transmission of nerve impulses and thus reduce the physiological and psychological changes that occur when a person is under stress.

Benzodiazepines are dangerous when combined with alcohol; and their side effects include lightheadedness, slurred speech, and impaired psychomotor and mental functioning. These drugs can also lead to physical dependence. Thus, when use is discontinued, the patient experiences withdrawal symptoms. Therefore, patients who discontinue their antianxiety medication should do so gradually. A newer drug, *buspirone* (*Buspar*) is effective in controlling anxiety by increasing serotonin levels in the brain without causing physical dependence or interacting negatively with alcohol. However, Buspar is slower acting than the benzodiazepines, taking up to several weeks to have an effect. Because Buspar takes time to reduce anxiety, some patients stop taking the drug because they think it has no effect other than dizziness and headache.

As you see from my overview, these drugs can be remarkably effective in treating serious psychological disorders. Of course, all drug therapies have side effects, some more serious than others.

BVT Lab

Improve your test scores. Practice quizzes are available at www.BVTLab.com.

12.7d Electroconvulsive Therapy Is Sometimes Used to Treat Depression.

Another medical treatment used to manipulate the brain is much more controversial than drug therapies and has been in use for a much longer period of time. **Electroconvulsive therapy (ECT)** was first used in the 1930s as a possible treatment for schizophrenia. Subsequent research indicated that although ECT may help reduce certain symptoms of schizophrenia (Zervas et al., 2012), it is most helpful in cases of severe depression, with about 80 percent of patients showing marked improvement (Gilman, 2008). Controlled treatment studies have found that ECT is about as effective as antidepressant medications in treating this mood disorder (Fava & Rosenbaum, 1995).

In a typical ECT procedure, patients are first given drugs both to render them unconscious and to induce profound muscle relaxation. Next, with two electrodes placed on either one side or both sides of the patient's temples, a 70- to 130-volt charge of electricity is administered for about 1 second. These shocks are continued until the patient has a seizure—a muscle contraction of the entire body—that lasts for at least 20 seconds. This treatment is repeated at least once a week for two to four weeks.

Although ECT is effective in treating severe depression, no one knows for sure why it works (Okamoto et al., 2008). Evidence suggests that ECT may be effective in treating severe depression by promoting new cell growth in the brain. Studies with rats demonstrate that ECT increases neural growth in the hippocampus, a brain area critical for the production of new memories (Hellsten et al., 2004). Additional research indicates that ECT also increases non-neuron cell growth in the frontal lobes of the cerebral cortex, which is responsible for higher mental processes (Madsen et al., 2005). This new cell growth in the frontal lobes involves two different types of cells: (1) cells that coat the inside of blood vessels and increase the efficiency of blood flow; and (2) cells that produce the myelin sheath, which insulates the axons of neurons and hastens synaptic transmission. Thus, the effectiveness of ECT in alleviating severe depression may be due to its ability to induce cell growth in areas of the brain that play a central role in the creation of new memories and complex thinking.

Electroconvulsive therapy (ECT) A physiological treatment for severe depression in which a brief electrical shock is administered to the brain of an anesthetized patient

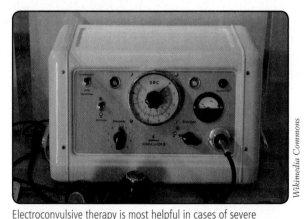

Wikimedia Commons

Electroconvulsive therapy is most helpful in cases of severe depression, with about 80 percent of patients showing significant improvement. What are some theories on why this biomedical therapy is effective?

Despite ECT's effectiveness as a treatment for depression, it has several temporary negative side effects, including confusion, loss of memory, and impaired motor coordination (O'Connor et al., 2008). In most instances, any memory loss for events preceding treatment is recovered within a few months. Due to these side effects, ECT is generally used only when severely depressed patients either cannot tolerate or have not responded to drug therapy. In some cases, it may also be used when severely depressed patients are at immediate risk for suicide because ECT has an almost immediate effect, while benefits from antidepressant medications usually take at least 10 days.

12.7e Psychosurgery Removes Portions of the Brain.

Psychosurgery A rarely used type of procedure to treat psychological disorders in which brain tissue, thought to be the cause of the disorder, is destroyed

By far the most radical and controversial method of treating psychological disorders is **psychosurgery**, which involves destroying brain tissue thought to be the cause of these disorders. In 1949, the Portuguese psychiatrist Antonio Egas Moñiz received the Nobel Prize in Medicine for his psychosurgical technique known as *prefrontal lobotomy*. In this medical procedure, two small holes are drilled in the skull; and a sharp instrument is inserted and moved from side to side, severing the neural connections between the prefrontal lobes and the rest of the brain (Egas Moñiz, 1948). At the time that Egas Moñiz was using this technique to treat psychotic patients, it was thought that destroying the prefrontal lobes would relieve the crippling emotional reactions experienced by many schizophrenics. The medical profession was so taken by Egas Moñiz's technique that during the 1940s and early 1950s more than 35,000 lobotomies were performed in the United States to treat schizophrenia, aggressiveness, anxiety, and depression.

Lobotomies did reduce the incidence of some undesirable behaviors, but patients paid a heavy price. In many cases, the treatment profoundly altered their personalities, with some becoming extremely apathetic and others becoming excitable and impulsive. Due to these very negative and irreversible effects, most physicians stopped using the procedure. Then, with the advent of antipsychotic drugs in the late 1950s, lobotomies were virtually extinguished as a medical intervention (Swayze, 1995). Today, MRI-guided precision psychosurgery is performed only in extreme cases when other types of treatment have been ineffective, and it focuses on much smaller brain areas than those involved in lobotomies.

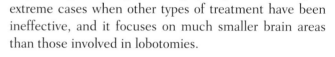

The danger of psychosurgery is illustrated by the life of Rosemary Kennedy, sister of President Kennedy. Rosemary had a history of mental deficiencies, epilepsy, and violent tantrums. In 1942, at the age of 23, Rosemary was admitted to a hospital where she had a prefrontal lobotomy, which left her permanently paralyzed on one side of her body. She spent the rest of her life in institutions.

12.7f Electrodes Implanted in the Brain Provide Deep Brain Stimulation.

In the late 1980s, physician Alim Louis Benabid developed a far less destructive surgical technique that stimulated specific brain regions affected by a disorder surgically implanting electrodes into the brain and then using mild electrical stimulation in these affected regions. Although it is still unclear how brain stimulation alters neurological processes, *deep brain stimulation (DBS)* has been effective in treating many of the movement problems associated with Parkinson's disease and is now being tested for treating other disorders, including psychological disorders (Vedam-Mai et al., 2012). In almost all instances of persons who receive DBS for a psychological disorder, they have already tried both psychotherapy and drug therapy without achieving any significant improvement in their mental health.

In treating severe depression, neurosurgeons insert electrodes into an area of the prefrontal cortex that has been found to function abnormally in persons suffering from major depressive disorder. A host of studies have found that DBS is effective in significantly reducing depressive symptoms in at least half of the individuals suffering from severe depression, with some patients experiencing immediate relief as soon as the affected brain region was stimulated by the electrodes (Puigdemont et al., 2012). DBS has also been found to provide benefits to individuals suffering from obsessive-compulsive disorder (Holtzheimer & Mayberg, 2011). One tentative conclusion to draw from this recent work is that recent advances in the medical sciences now provide the very real hope that certain new forms of psychosurgery may no longer have such serious cognitive costs to individuals who undergo these procedures.

Section REVIEW

- Antipsychotic drugs reduce positive schizophrenic symptoms, but do not relieve negative symptoms.

- Antidepressant drugs relieve depression by increasing the supply of norepinephrine and/or serotonin at the neuron's receptor sites.

- Antianxiety drugs have an immediate calming effect by facilitating the inhibitory action of the GABA neurotransmitter, thereby reducing nerve impulse transmission.

- Electroconvulsive therapy is an infrequently used physiological treatment for severe depression in which a brief electric shock is administered to an anesthetized patient's brain.

- Psychosurgery is the most radical treatment for psychological disorders and involves destruction of the brain tissue thought to cause the disorder.

- Deep brain stimulation is often effective in reducing depressive symptoms.

PSYCHOLOGICAL
applications

How Do You Select a Psychotherapist?

Americans who have mental illness are more likely to seek treatment now than they were 20 years ago. This is encouraging news, because the rate of mental illness has remained the same during this time period. Yet, given the variety of psycho-therapies available, how should you go about selecting a therapist? Working with a therapist on a psychological problem is a sensitive and personal exercise—that is, a therapist who is very successful for one client may not be as helpful for the next client. There are several important questions you can ask when considering seeing a therapist.

First, you should ask whether you actually need a therapist. As noted in Chapter 11, on psychological disorders, many people experience mild or "subclinical" levels of a symptom that only in more extreme form may qualify as a psychological disorder. For example, many people have mild, irrational fears or periods of "the blues" that would not meet diagnostic standards for a psychological disorder. When judging the severity of your symptoms, it is useful to consider the degree to which your daily functioning has been impaired. A person whose symptoms are mildly distressing but not significantly interfering with daily activities probably does not have a clinical disorder. This individual might benefit from speaking with a psychotherapist, but the therapy would likely be relatively brief. The therapist may provide information about the nature of clinical disorders, provide reassurance that this particular problem is not severe, and make a few suggestions concerning how to better manage the symptoms.

If you determine that your symptoms are producing significant impairment, you must then judge whether you have sufficient resources to cope. When facing a significant stressor, many people muster the resources to cope satisfactorily. Just because the symptoms are beginning to interfere with your functioning does not mean that the only way to solve the problem is through the help of a psychotherapist. If a problem is of recent origin, if you have successfully solved compa-rable problems before, or if you still have many ideas about how to cope with the problem, it may not be necessary to see a therapist. However, if you have exhausted your personal coping resources and no longer have confidence that you can manage the problem on your own, it may well be appropriate to seek professional help.

When shopping for a therapist, it is also useful to ask several questions. First identify the problem you would like to change: Do you want to reduce your depression? Do you want to stop drinking alcohol? Do you want to be able to go through the school day without having to wash your hands dozens of times? Do you want to get along better with your boyfriend or girlfriend? If you can identify a clear treatment goal, you will be in a better position to select a therapist and an approach to therapy. Clearly, many prospective clients do not have a clear idea of what they would like to change. This may be a part of the problem—they are dissatisfied with their lives but do not know what would help them feel better. In such cases, a psychotherapist can help the client clarify the treatment goal, although this identification process may require some time before actual therapy can begin.

Once you have identified a goal, you can consider the kind of therapy to seek. Some prospective clients have a prefer-ence for a specific form of therapy. They may have learned, from previous therapy experiences or from other information about psychotherapy, that they would like cognitive therapy or insight-oriented therapy. In these cases, it makes sense to shop for a therapist who can provide the kind of therapy that fits this preference.

Some psychological disorders have been shown to respond well to particular treatments (Nathan & Gorman, 2002). For example, bipolar disorder is almost always treated with mood-stabilizing medication. Panic disorder has been treated very successfully using cognitive-behavior therapy. Depression has been treated very successfully using cognitive therapy. If you are seeking help for one of these problems, it may be useful to look for a therapist who can provide the treat-ment that is considered most effective. Several resources are available to help you learn what therapies may be most effective for a particular kind of problem. For example, Martin Seligman (2007) has compiled a consumer guide to psychotherapy (*What You Can Change and What You Can't: The Complete Guide to Successful Self-Improvement*) that summarizes research on which therapies are generally recommended for which disorders. Also, the National Institutes of Mental Health, various advocacy groups devoted to specific disorders (such as the Obsessive-Compulsive Foundation), and psychology departments at local universities can provide useful information about the current status of available therapies for a particular disorder.

Again, even if you do not have a clear idea about the kind of problem you have or the kind of therapy that may be helpful, this should not prevent you from seeing a psychotherapist. The therapist can—following an assessment of the problem—suggest one or more possible treatments.

Given that most treatment today is paid for by a third party, such as an insurance company or a social welfare agency, you should check your insurance package to determine whether there are any limits on your mental health coverage. As discussed, many managed care systems list preferred providers, and so your choice of professionals or agencies may be limited. Also as noted, most insurance plans have an upper limit on the number of therapy sessions or the total funds available for mental health services, which may dictate selecting a therapist who provides short-term forms of psychotherapy.

You should also ask some basic questions of prospective therapists: What is the therapist's degree? Is the therapist licensed in the state? Does the therapist have experience in treating problems like the one you have? Does the therapist have a particular theoretical preference? What is the cost of therapy sessions? The receptionist can usually answer these questions before you make an appointment to see the therapist. If the therapist will not allow the receptionist to answer these questions, you might seriously consider calling another therapist.

You can obtain referrals from many sources, including your family doctor, a clergy member, a lawyer, friends, and family members. Many cities have resources to refer mental health patients to psychotherapists, such as a chapter of the Mental Health Association. Local chapters of patient advocacy groups (such as CHADD—Children and Adults with Attention-Deficit/Hyperactivity Disorder) can help steer individuals to experts in the area. Psychology departments at local universities often help people learn about practitioners in the area who may specialize in treating various disorders.

Suggested Websites

Psychology Information Online

http://www.psychologyinfo.com/

This site provides helpful tips on searching for a psychotherapist.

National Register of Health Service Providers in Psychology

http://www.nationalregister.com/

This site can help prospective clients find a registered psychologist in their area.

A Guide to Psychology and Its Practice

http://www.guidetopsychology.com/

This site provides information about psychology in general, including various forms of therapy that may be helpful for specific disorders.

Key Terms

Antianxiety drugs, 554

Antidepressant drugs, 553

Antipsychotic drugs, 553

Aversive conditioning, 540

Behavior therapies, 538

Biomedical therapies, 534

Client-centered therapy, 545

Cognitive-behavior therapy (CBT), 544

Cognitive therapies, 543

Counterconditioning, 538

Countertransference, 537

Couples therapy, 551

Electroconvulsive therapy (ECT), 555

Empty-chair technique, 549

Family systems therapy, 551

Family therapies , 551

Free association, 536

Gestalt therapy, 548

Group therapy, 550

Humanistic therapies, 545

Modeling, 542

Play therapy, 550

Psychodynamic therapies, 536

Psychosurgery, 556

Psychotherapy, 534

Rational-emotive behavior therapy (REBT), 544

Resistance, 537

Response prevention, 540

Self-help group, 550

Social skills training, 542

Systematic desensitization, 539

Token economy, 541

Transference, 537

Review Questions

1. Before Freud developed psychoanalysis, treatment for mental illness emphasized all except which of the following methods?
   a. hypnosis
   b. altering the brain's functioning with chemical interventions
   c. terrorizing the patient by threatening to have him or her killed
   d. emotional support
   e. draining excess blood from the body

2. Which of the following mental health professionals deal with psychological disorders and receive extensive training in conducting scientific research?
   a. counseling psychologists with a Psy.D.
   b. psychiatric social workers
   c. psychiatrists
   d. clinical psychologists.
   e. psychologists with a PhD or EdD

3. Although there are several varieties of psychodynamic therapies, what is one thing they all have in common?
   a. a disregard for insight.
   b. an emphasis on sex as the major motivation for human behavior
   c. the view that psychological disorders stem primarily from unconscious forces
   d. encouraging resistance as a form of free association
   e. the view that, to be effective, psychotherapy requires at least 5 years of twice-weekly sessions

4. Psychodynamic therapists often interpret transference as involving which of the following?
   a. feelings that the client experienced toward others early in life
   b. anything the client does that interferes with therapeutic progress
   c. only negative feelings clients develop toward their therapist
   d. the release of pent-up emotion
   e. free association and Freudian slips

5. The primary techniques used in behavior therapies are all based on which of the following?
   a. unconscious learning and insight
   b. observational learning
   c. desensitization hierarchies
   d. principles of learning
   e. behavior modification

6. What is the most effective technique for treating phobias?
   a. sudden and prolonged exposure to the feared object
   b. response prevention
   c. reinforcement and punishment
   d. aversive conditioning
   e. systematic desensitization.

7. Cognitive therapies may include all except which of the following?
   a. analysis of the meaning underlying dreams
   b. confronting all-or-none types of thinking
   c. trying new behaviors that directly challenge irrational beliefs
   d. highly directive, problem-focused therapeutic techniques
   e. identifying patients' negative views of themselves, the world, and their future

8. Cognitive therapy techniques used by Beck and Ellis differ with respect to which of the following?
   a. their emphasis on faulty thinking.
   b. their use of behavior techniques as well as cognitive techniques
   c. the therapeutic goal of modifying cognitions
   d. their response to clients' irrational beliefs
   e. the overall length of therapy

9. Why is Carl Rogers often identified as having the biggest influence on how therapy is practiced?
   a. He emphasized the facilitation of personal growth.
   b. His client-centered techniques are widely used by therapists of many theoretical orientations.
   c. His principles of conditional positive regard are so effective.
   d. He formulated a highly directive form of therapy used by behavior and cognitive therapists.
   e. Most therapists already used his emphasis on closed-ended statements.

10. Which of the following is true of the humanistic technique of paraphrasing?
    a. It involves analyzing the meaning underlying clients' verbal statements.
    b. It acknowledges a client's nonverbal emotions.
    c. It is a confrontational challenge of dysfunctional thoughts.
    d. It is seen in therapist responses such as "Go on" and "I see."
    e. It involves the therapist summarizing the expressed verbal content of clients' statements.

11. Gestalt therapy emphasizes all except which of the following?
    a. focusing on current feelings
    b. nondirective, client-centered approaches
    c. the empty-chair technique
    d. body awareness exercises to stimulate emotional reactions
    e. the development of self-awareness or insight

12. Which of the following is true of humanistic therapy that deals with finding meaning in life?
    a. It was developed by Perls.
    b. It emphasizes resolving past issues.
    c. It is based on Skinner's approach to operant conditioning.
    d. It has good empirical support.
    e. It emphasizes treating the whole person.

13. Children's play therapy involves all except which of the following?
    a. a form of free association
    b. a nondirective approach
    c. an educational approach to learning new skills
    d. directly challenging cognitive distortions
    e. the use of unconditional positive regard

14. What is one of the advantages of group therapy?
    a. It is less expensive than individual therapy because it doesn't last as long.
    b. It helps clients see that others share similar problems.
    c. Therapists are never used, which reduces the cost.
    d. It is based on monthly sessions rather than weekly sessions.
    e. It is more effective than couples therapy in reducing romantic relationship problems.

15. Which of the following is true of antidepressant drugs that affect only serotonin?
    a. They are called SSRIs, and they increase the availability of serotonin by inhibiting its reuptake.
    b. They are tricyclic antidepressants, a class of benzodiazepines.
    c. They are part of a class of drugs called phenothiazines.
    d. They include MAOIs.
    e. They are useful only for depression.

16. Most antianxiety drugs do which of the following?
    a. They facilitate the action of the neurotransmitter gamma-aminobutyric acid (GABA).
    b. They speed up the transmission of nerve impulses.
    c. They are safe to use with alcohol.
    d. They do not lead to physical dependence.
    e. They increase the physiological and psychological changes that occur when a person is under stress.

17. Which of the following is a possible obstacle to ethnic minorities' use of therapeutic services?
    a. belief systems of one's culture
    b. history of institutionalized discrimination
    c. greater comfort with culturally specific help
    d. stigma surrounding mental health services
    e. All of the above

18. What is one of the consequences of ethnic minorities underutilizing therapeutic services?
    a. Mental illness among ethnic minorities is underdiagnosed.
    b. Higher rates of mental illness are assumed among ethnic minorities.
    c. There is a higher mortality rate among ethnic minorities.
    d. Stereotypes are reinforced about mental illness among ethnic minorities.
    e. None of the above

19. Which of the following is not true regarding the representation of ethnic minorities in the field of professional psychology and the treatment of these populations?
    a. Only 10 percent of psychologists are from ethnically diverse backgrounds.
    b. Special training is being implemented to increase effectiveness with patients with diverse backgrounds.
    c. The poor, a category which consists disproportionately of ethnic minorities, have higher therapy dropout rates.
    d. Ethnic minorities receive special benefits to receive therapy but often do not use them.
    e. All of the above

Chapter Thirteen

Stress, Coping, and Health

Chapter Outline

Psychological Applications: *Who Is Happy and Why?*

Many of you reading this chapter are nearing the end of the semester in your college studies. This is the time in the school year when you have many demands on your time, including the final push to complete term papers and prepare for final exams. For a few of you, the semester has been a breeze, with only minor worries and concerns. For others, events have challenged the limits of your mental and physical endurance. You may now personally understand how sleep deprivation (see Chapter 5, Section 5.2d) can harm learning and creativity, or how the tip-of-the-tongue phenomenon (see Chapter 7, Section 7.4b) can mean the difference between a passing and a failing grade on an important exam. So perhaps it is timely that this chapter in our journey of discovery brings us to the psychology of stress and coping—stress caused not only by the demands of college life

and other everyday events, but also stress caused by personal and group hardships and catastrophes.

By understanding more about the causes and consequences of stress, you will be better prepared to manage major stressful events in your life, as well as the minor hassles that comprise daily living. This exploration of stress will lead you into a broader examination of the psychology of health. Do you know what it means to be healthy? Is being healthy different from being disease-free?

The psychologists and physicians whose work forms the bulk of this chapter are in the interdisciplinary field of **behavioral medicine**, which integrates behavioral and medical knowledge and then applies it to health and illness. Psychologists

Behavioral medicine An interdisciplinary field of science that integrates behavioral and medical knowledge and then applies it to health and illness

563

who study the effects of behavior and mental processes on health and illness are called **health psychologists** (Kazak et al., 2012). In studying the causes and consequences of health and illness, scientists rely on the **biopsychosocial model**, which assumes that health and overall wellness are influenced by a complex interaction between biological, psychological, and sociocultural factors.

Health psychologists Psychologists who study the effects of behavior and mental processes on health and illness

Biopsychosocial model An interdisciplinary model that assumes that health and overall wellness are caused by a complex interaction between biological, psychological, and sociocultural factors

13.1 What Causes Stress?

The process by which you perceive and respond to the challenges of college life falls under the general topic that we call stress. I define **stress** as our response to events that disturb, or threaten to disturb, our physical or psychological equilibrium (Segerstrom & O'Connor, 2012). The events that disrupt our equilibrium are known as **stressors** (Gilboa et al. 2008). For most of us, flunking out of college, experiencing the death of a loved one, or being sexually assaulted would be very stressful events. Yet most stressors are not of this magnitude, and not all stressors are unpleasant.

Stress Our response to events that disturb, or threaten to disturb, our physical or psychological equilibrium

Stressors External or internal events that challenge or threaten us

13.1a Stressors Can Be Positive or Negative, as Well as Large or Small.

Stressors come in various forms. The most obvious are life-threatening situations. Natural disasters or *major cataclysmic events*, such as the 2004 Southeast Asian tsunami that killed more than 300,000 people, are easily recognized as stressors, as are *major personal events*, such as being a victim of a crime or having a death in the family. Other stressors involve feeling frustrated, pressured, or conflicted while engaging in regular daily activities. Some stressors may be short-term and acute (for example, surgery to remove a benign tumor or ending a romantic relationship), while others may be more chronic in nature (for example, chemotherapy to treat cancer or long-standing conflicts with family members). Traumatic major events may even cause *post-traumatic stress disorder (PTSD)*, which can appear months or even years after experiencing the stressor (see Chapter 11, Section 11.2a). Symptoms of PTSD include anxiety, social withdrawal, survivor guilt, and flashbacks of the event. PTSD is also associated with an increased risk of physical illness.

 **INFO-BIT**

Caring for a sick loved one can cause serious health problems. A 9-year longitudinal study of 518,240 elderly married couples found that the increased stress due to the illness or death of a spouse could harm the partner's health and contribute to her or his own death (Christakis & Allison, 2006).

Even positive events tax your body's resources and cause stress. For example, the birth of a child is one of the happiest and most anticipated events in many people's lives, but studies of married couples have found that the arrival of a child dramatically increases stress and contributes to dissatisfaction with the relationship (Cowan & Cowan, 2000). More rarely, among art lovers, exposure to extraordinary art can induce acute stress, sometimes to such an extent that hospitalization is required. This uncommonly intense stress reaction to an overwhelmingly positive experience is known as *Stendhal's syndrome*, named after nineteenth-century French novelist

SELF-DISCOVERY 13-1
Questionnaire

The College of Undergraduate Stress Scale: What Is Your Degree of Life Stress?

Life Event	Stress Rating	Life Event	Stress Rating
Being raped	100	Difficulties with parents	73
Finding out that you are HIV positive	100	Talking in front of class	72
Being accused of rape	98	Lack of sleep	69
Death of a close friend	97	Change in housing situation (hassles, moves)	69
Death of a close family member	96	Competing or performing in public	69
Contracting a sexually transmitted disease (other than AIDS)	94	Getting in a physical fight	66
Concerns about being pregnant	91	Difficulties with a roommate	66
Finals week	90	Job changes (applying, new job, work hassles)	65
Concerns about your partner being pregnant	90	A class you hate	62
Oversleeping for an exam	89	Drinking or use of drugs	61
Flunking a class	89	Confrontations with professor	60
Having a boyfriend or girlfriend cheat on you	85	Starting a new semester	58
Ending a steady dating relationship	85	Going on a first date	57
Serious illness in a close friend or family member	85	Registration	55
		Maintaining a steady dating relationship	55
Financial difficulties	84	Commuting to campus or work, or both	54
Writing a major term paper	83	Peer pressures	53
Being caught cheating on a test	83	Being away from home for the first time	53
Drunk driving	82	Getting sick	52
Sense of overload in school or work	82	Concerns about your appearance	52
Two exams in one day	80	Getting straight A's	51
Cheating on your boyfriend or girlfriend	77	A difficult class that you love	48
Getting married	76	Making new friends, getting along with friends	47
Negative consequences of drinking or drug use	75	Fraternity or sorority rush	47
Depression or crisis in your best friend	73	Falling asleep in class	40
		Attending an athletic event	20

Directions for scoring: Sum the stress rating scores for all events that have happened to you during the past year to compute your personal life stress score. The average score for college students is 1,247 points, with a range from 182 to 2,571. Higher scores indicate higher levels of stress.

Interpretation: One drawback to the College of Undergraduate Stress Scale is that people view similar events differently. For example, while some people might find that speaking in front of a class is very stressful, others may not. Despite the fact that people can respond with different stress levels to the same event, this and other stress scales do relate to both mental and physical health.

Source: M. J. Renner and R. S. Mackin (1998). A life stress instrument for classroom use, *Teaching of Psychology, 25*, 46–48.

Stendhal, who visited Florence, Italy, and was overwhelmed by the city's rich legacy of art and history (Amancio, 2005). Yet, despite the ability of positive life events to increase stress levels, research indicates that negative events generally induce more stress than do neutral or positive events. Over the years, various researchers have developed "stress scales" based on having people rate the magnitude of readjustment required by each of many life events found to be associated with the onset of illness (Bitsika et al., 2010; Holmes & Rahe, 1967). Complete the College of Undergraduate Stress Scale (CUSS: Renner & Mackin, 2002) in Self-Discovery Questionnaire 13-1 to assess your stressful events during the past year.

Wikimedia Commons

Stendhal's syndrome is named after the nineteenth-century French novelist who was overcome with emotion upon viewing the artwork in Florence, Italy. Stendhal described his experience in the following way: "I was in a sort of ecstasy, from the idea of being in Florence, close to the great men whose tombs I had seen. … I reached the point where one encounters celestial sensations … Life was drained from me."

As disruptive as major events are to your life, they often reflect only a fraction of the stressors that affect your health and well-being. In between each of these major stressful "boulders" occur myriad *hassles* and minor stressful "pebbles," such as losing your keys, arguing with a roommate, or getting a traffic ticket. The more daily hassles you experience, the more your mental and physical health tends to suffer (Pandey et al., 2011; Safdar & Lay, 2003). The negative effects of daily hassles, however, can be alleviated by positive daily experiences.

Exploring CULTURE & DIVERSITY 13.1

What Type of Stressor Do Many Minority Group Members Regularly Experience?

One type of stressor that often takes the form of a hassle is the subtle prejudice and negative stereotyping that many minority-group members experience during their regular daily activities (Brandolo et al., 2011). Whether it is a Muslim woman receiving less than polite service while wearing the hijab at a restaurant, an African American youth being watched suspiciously while shopping, or a lesbian couple drawing disapproving stares for holding hands in public, such negative attention due to social identity is a source of stress that members of privileged majority groups—such as White, heterosexual, Christian Americans—rarely encounter.

Numerous studies in both the United States and abroad find that experiencing prejudice and/or discrimination often causes heightened levels of anxiety, worry, and bodily stress symptoms (Hansen & Sorlie, 2012). The fact that this sort of stressor is largely invisible to majority group members often results in members of privileged groups falsely believing that societal prejudices are "no big deal."

Which type of stressor (boulder or pebble) is worse for you? As mentioned, both classes of events can lead to health problems. Accumulating pebbles can leave you more vulnerable to major events when they occur. Similarly, major events can leave you unable to deal with the daily hassles of life, causing them to pile up and overwhelm you. Researchers have found that people with high stress levels during the previous year were more than twice as likely to become ill when compared to those who experienced lower levels of stress (Bieliauskas et al., 1995; Holmes & Rahe, 1967).

Finally, one of the key potential benefits of stress is that it can foster positive growth in your life. Stressful events can force you to develop effective ways of meeting a wide variety of life's challenges. In doing so, you become more capable of not only adapting to your environment but also actively shaping your surroundings, so that they better meet your needs and allow you to flourish (Yanez et al., 2011). In essence, this is how smart and attentive parents foster high need for achievement in their children (refer back to Chapter 9, Section 9.4b). That is, they place their children in achievement situations that match their abilities, so that if their children work hard, they have a good chance of succeeding (Boon, 2007). Such achievement situations will often induce stress in the children; yet when they meet the challenge and succeed at the task, their self-confidence and desire to succeed in future achievement situations is strengthened.

Wikimedia Commons

"Driving While Black," or DWB, is a word play on the term for a real crime, "Driving While Intoxicated", or DWI. The implication underlying the DWB phrase is that Black motorists are often pulled over by police officers simply because they are black, and then questioned, searched, and/or charged with a trivial offense. Such racial profiling is an example of the daily stressors that some individuals face due to their minority group status.

13.1b Selye Viewed Stress as a Specific Set of Responses to Demands.

As discussed in Chapter 2, Section 2.2a, the *sympathetic nervous system* activates the body's energies to deal with threatening situations. If something angers or frightens you, the sympathetic nervous system will prepare you for "fight or flight" by slowing your digestion, accelerating your heart rate, raising your blood sugar, and cooling your body with perspiration. If the threatening situation continues, you will remain in this state of heightened arousal. Such a scenario will likely cause serious health problems because your body continues to divert resources away from the everyday maintenance that is essential in keeping you healthy.

General Adaptation Syndrome

One scientist who was instrumental in providing greater insight into how our bodies react to stress was physician Hans Selye (1907–1982). In the 1930s, Selye stumbled upon some of the physiological mechanisms of stress while trying to discover new sex hormones. In his experiments with rats, Selye (1936) noticed that exposing the animals to a wide range of physical stressors (cold, heat, swimming, injections) caused their bodies to respond in two ways. The first response was specific to the stressor itself, such as shivering when exposed to cold and sweating when exposed to heat. In contrast, the second response was not specific to any particular stressor but was, instead, a general response geared toward energizing and protecting the body from harm. This second response is what Selye (1956) called the *stress response*, and he saw it as occurring in reaction to any significant demand on the body. If the demand

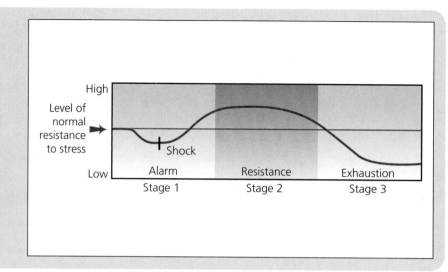

FIGURE 13-1

General Adaptation Syndrome

Hans Selye's research suggests that physical reactions to stress include three stages. During the alarm stage, the body's resistance temporarily drops below normal due to the shock of the stressor. The body is at its highest state of resistance to stress during the resistance stage, but resistance declines as the body's resources become depleted in the exhaustion stage.

General adaptation syndrome (GAS) Selye's model of stress, in which an event that threatens an organism's well-being (a stressor) leads to a three-stage bodily response: alarm, resistance, and exhaustion

continues, particular changes in the body begin to occur. He referred to this stress response, and the resulting changes in the body, as **general adaptation syndrome (GAS)**, which consists of three stages: alarm, resistance, and exhaustion. Figure 13-1 depicts these three stages in the body's response to stress.

In stage 1, upon encountering a stressor, the body first reacts with *alarm*, which is essentially the reaction previously referred to as the fight-or-flight response (Uchino et al., 2007). The alarm reaction produces an initial shock phase, during which the hypothalamus and lower brain structures (such as the amygdala) activate the sympathetic nervous system and the endocrine system to prepare you for action by slowing your digestion, accelerating your heart rate, raising your blood sugar, and cooling your body with perspiration. The adrenal gland's release of the stress hormones *epinephrine* (also called adrenaline) and *norepinephrine* (also called noradrenaline) trigger these rapid and intense physiological changes (Sher, 2003). Your body's resources are now mobilized.

No organism can survive for long in the state of heightened arousal exhibited during the alarm stage. Homeostasis must be achieved, even if the stressor persists. During stage 2, *resistance*, the parasympathetic nervous system returns many physiological functions—such as respiration and heart rate—to normal levels, even while the body focuses its resources against the continuing stressor. Although many stress hormone levels continue to circulate throughout the body at elevated levels, the outward appearance of the organism generally seems entirely normal. However, the body remains on red alert.

If the stressor continues beyond the body's capacity, the organism exhausts its resources and becomes susceptible to disease and death. This is the third stage of general adaptation syndrome, *exhaustion*. Selye described it as "a kind of premature aging due to wear and tear" (Selye, 1956, p. 31). Organs such as the heart are the first to break down during this stage.

Prolonged Stress and the HPA Axis

Selye's description of general adaptation syndrome emphasized that the same biological changes that help us deal with stress in the short run can become hazardous to our health in the long run. As described, during the alarm stage of general adaptation syndrome, the hypothalamus sends messages along a neural pathway, signaling the adrenal glands to release epinephrine and norepinephrine, which sharply heighten

FIGURE 13-2   Two Stress Pathways

Under stress, the hypothalamus signals the adrenal glands to secrete hormones using two neural pathways. Pathway 1 activates the sympathetic division of the autonomic nervous system, which produces physiological changes associated with the "fight-or-flight" response. If the stress response is prolonged, a second pathway, known as the HPA axis, is activated. The HPA axis increases the body's energy resources, enhances muscle tone in the heart and blood vessels, and protects the body's tissues from inflammation.

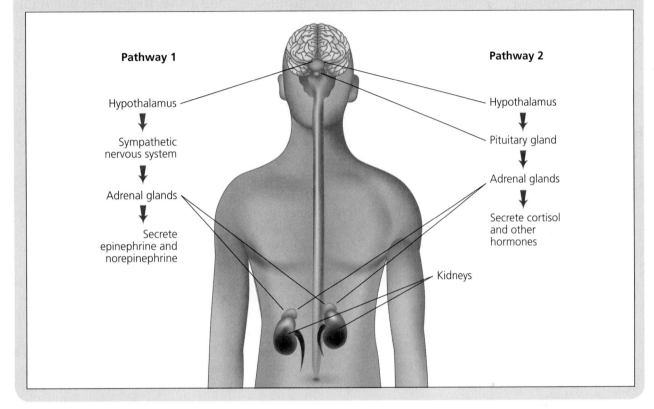

physiological arousal (Linthorst & Reul, 2008). This initial fight-or-flight response is illustrated in pathway 1 of Figure 13-2.

Later research revealed that after this initial stress response, if the threat persists, the hypothalamus plays a second important role using a different neural pathway (pathway 2 in Figure 13-2). Following prolonged stress, the hypothalamus sends messages along a neural pathway called the *HPA axis*, which stands for hypothalamus (H); pituitary gland (P); and adrenal cortex, the outer part of the adrenal glands (A). Using this second pathway, the hypothalamus signals the pituitary gland, which in turn signals the adrenal cortex to secrete *cortisol* and other hormones. The introduction of these stress hormones into the bloodstream increases the body's energy resources, enhances muscle tone in the heart and blood vessels, and protects body tissues from inflammation (Rose et al., 2010).

The increased energy due to HPA axis activation is crucial in helping the body continue resisting or coping with stressors. However, if cortisol and other stress hormones remain high for too long, they can weaken crucial body systems, causing increases in blood pressure, formation of blood clots and clogged arteries, and overall damage to the body's ability to defend itself against disease (see Section 13.1d). Elevated cortisol levels also cause increased consumption of fatty foods, which contributes to weight problems (Nieuwenhuizen & Rutters, 2008). Prolonged stress can also lead to chronic anxiety, depression, and other psychological disorders (see Chapter 11).

13.1c The "Fight-or-Flight" Stress Response May Be Gender-Specific.

Although Selye's original work assumed that the GAS-type response pattern was the same for men and women, in the past decade some researchers have questioned whether women typically respond with fight-or-flight tendencies in the initial alarm stage. Such questioning was prompted by findings indicating that in response to stress, the pituitary gland releases significantly higher levels of the oxytocin hormone in females than in males (Pedersen, 2004). As you recall from Chapter 2, Section 2.2c, the release of oxytocin is associated with increased affiliative and nurturing behaviors. The higher levels of oxytocin released in women compared with men during the stress response have led Shelley Taylor to propose that when women are exposed to stressors, instead of experiencing the fight-or-flight response, they are more likely to experience a *tend-and-befriend response* (Taylor & Master, 2011). This response involves women taking action to protect their offspring or befriend members of their social group to reduce their vulnerability.

Sociocultural theorists suggest that these differences are due to gender socialization. Traditionally, the way in which children are raised in North American culture fosters the construction of an *independent* self-concept among men and a *relational* self-concept among women (Cross & Madson, 1997). As such, girls are more likely than boys to be raised to think, act, and define themselves in ways that emphasize their emotional connectedness to other individuals (Chen et al., 2011; (Cross et al., 2000). This may lead women to respond to stress with nurturance and affiliation, tending to their offspring and seeking out others for comfort and protection. In contrast, men's tendency to exhibit fight-or-flight responses to threat may be due to their being raised to be independent and self-sufficient.

An alternative explanation is that these gender differences in stress responses are the by-products of the different mating strategies of males and females. According to this evolutionary explanation, males of many species, including our own, are more aggressive and have a stronger social-dominance orientation than females because aggression and dominance-seeking have been the primary ways males have gained sexual access to females (Buss, 1999; Buss & Schmitt, 1993). Perhaps by physically intimidating—and sometimes even killing—less aggressive males, the more aggressive males became socially dominant and thus were more likely to sexually reproduce. Unlike males, females' reproductive success did not depend on their level of aggression but depended instead on their ability to successfully nurture and protect offspring. Evolutionary psychologists contend that over many generations, the importance of aggression in male reproductive success and the importance of nurturance in female reproductive success led to genetically based differences in male and female responses to stress: Men prepare to fight or flee, while women prepare to tend and befriend (Eisler & Levine, 2002; St. Claire et al., 2010).

At this point, available evidence does not support one view over the other, and both perspectives could explain different aspects of gender differences in stress responses. Consistent with the evolutionary viewpoint, women and men may have evolved different stress responses due to differences in their mating strategies. In turn, consistent with the sociocultural perspective, this genetic tendency may be heightened or weakened by existing socialization patterns in contemporary society.

13.1d *Psychophysiological Illnesses Are Stress Related.*

Medical experts estimate that stress plays a role in 50 to 70 percent of all physical illnesses (Wolkowitz & Rothschild, 2003). These stress-related physical illnesses are referred to as **psychophysiological disorders**. The two body systems that have received the most attention from researchers studying stress-related diseases are the *cardiovascular system* and the *immune system*.

The Cardiovascular System

The cardiovascular system, made up of the heart and all the blood vessels that bring blood to and from the heart, is essential for life. However, this system is also associated with the primary causes of death—namely, heart attacks and stroke. In addition, the cardiovascular system is strongly affected by the emotional responses related to stress. People have long believed that strong emotional distress can cause sudden death from cardiac events. Converging evidence from correlational, longitudinal, and animal studies has confirmed such a connection (Rice, 2012). For example, heart attacks and deaths from cardiovascular events were elevated in the weeks that followed air strikes in Tel Aviv during the 1991 Gulf War (Meisel et al., 1991). In particular, stressful events involving anger have been related to heart attacks.

High blood pressure (or *hypertension*) and diseases of the arteries that nourish the heart are primary risk factors behind heart attacks and sudden death. Increased sympathetic nervous system activity raises heart rate and blood pressure, placing more strain on the cardiovascular system and damaging the arteries that nourish the heart. The majority of instances of *ischemia*, a condition in which the heart does not receive sufficient blood, occur during times of daily mental strain that follow anger-inducing stressors, in particular (Hughes, 2004). In addition to this physical strain, when threatening situations persist for extended time periods, stress hormones remain at high levels in the body, which can cause blood clots, artery damage, and heart attacks.

The Immune System

Another way in which stress responses work with other physical states to place us at greater risk for disease is through their effect on the immune system, our body's primary defense against disease (Anisman & Kusnecov, 2005). The **immune system** is a complex surveillance system of specialized cells, tissues, and organs that react to and destroy microorganisms determined not to be part of the body. Although you might not think of your skin as part of your immune system, it is. Skin tissue prevents many dangerous microorganisms from entering and infecting the body.

The immune system was once thought to act independently of the nervous system, but we now know that the immune system and the brain are in close communication and influence each other's actions. This communication means that the activity of one system affects the activity of the other. One pathway is through the stress response. The interdisciplinary field that studies the relationship between psychological factors and illness, especially the effects of stress on the immune system, is known as **psychoneuroimmunology**.

The foreign cells that the immune system seeks to destroy are known as antigens. In understanding how the immune system attacks these invading microorganisms, it is useful to distinguish between two immune system responses: natural immunity and specific immunity (Benjamini et al., 2000). *Natural immunity* is created by the body's natural barriers (such as the skin and protective substances in the mouth) and by specialized cells that provide a fast, all-purpose assault on a number of different invading antigens that can cause disease. The largest group of cells involved in natural immunity is the *granulocytes*, which are white blood cells that patrol the body and literally eat antigens and anything else suspicious that they find in the bloodstream, tissues, or lymphatic system. Another cell involved in natural immunity is the *natural*

Psychophysiological disorders Physical conditions, such as high blood pressure and migraine headaches, that are caused or aggravated by psychological factors such as stress

Immune system A complex surveillance system of specialized cells, tissues, and organs that is the body's primary defense against disease

Psychoneuroimmunology The interdisciplinary field that studies the relationship between psychological factors and physical illness

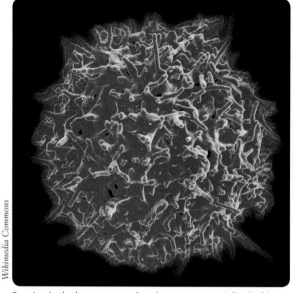

Wikimedia Commons

Forming in the bone marrow, lymphocytes are specialized white blood cells that move into certain organs and circulate throughout the bloodstream as an essential part of the body's specific immune response. The type of lymphocyte shown in this photo is a T cell. Some T cells attack and destroy invading microorganisms, whereas other T cells regulate the immune system by directing immune responses.

killer cell, which destroys antigens that are causing the early phases of viral infections and tumors, as well as infected body cells (Mihara et al., 2008).

Natural immunity defense is present at birth, but *specific immunity* (also known as *acquired immunity*) develops from the body being exposed to specific antigens that are "remembered" by the immune system. Later, when these antigens reenter the body, the immune system "remembers" exactly how to respond and produces specific protective white blood cells, called *lymphocytes*. Although the specific immune response creates a population of lymphocyte cells that protects the body against specific antigens, it often takes several days before these cells can effectively fight the infection. The two types of lymphocytes chiefly responsible for the specific immune response to infections are *B lymphocytes* (often simply called *B cells*) and *T lymphocytes* (likewise, called *T cells*). B cells get their name from the fact that they form and mature in the bone marrow and produce *antibodies*, which are protein molecules that attach themselves to antigens and mark them for destruction (Weill & Reynaud, 2005). Although T cells also form in the bone marrow, their name comes from the fact that they mature in the thymus. Some T cells directly attack cancer cells, viruses, and other antigens, whereas other T cells regulate the immune system by directing immune responses (Krogsgaard & Davis, 2005). On occasion, the lymphocytes overreact and attack harmless material, which can trigger allergic reactions to pollen and ragweed, cause the body's rejection of transplanted organs, and lead to *autoimmune diseases*, such as multiple sclerosis and rheumatoid arthritis (Bernard, 2005).

A meta-analysis of 293 stress studies involving almost 19,000 individuals found that acute, short-term stressors have different effects on the immune system than do chronic, long-term stressors (Segerstrom & Miller, 2004). It appears that when stressors are of the fight-or-flight variety (acute and of short duration), the natural immune system kicks into high gear and adaptively redistributes granulocytes and natural killer cells to fight possible infection and/or injury. This hyperactivation of natural immunity requires only minimal time and energy, but it also causes the body's resources to be directed away from the specific immune response. This suppression of the specific immune system makes evolutionary sense because during periods of challenge when quick action is necessary, suppressing immune responses that require considerable time and energy increases the efficiency of the fight-or-flight response, thus increasing chances of survival (Maier et al., 1994). Following acute stress, the immune system returns to normal. Immune system problems arise, however, when stress is prolonged, because our body's defenses are not designed to efficiently handle long-term challenges. Put simply, chronic stress dramatically reduces the efficiency of the immune system, making the body more susceptible to disease (Moynihan & Stevens, 2001). The longer the stress lasts, the more likely we are to become ill.

Chronic stress may also hasten the aging process. A study of women who were the primary caregivers for a child suffering from a serious chronic illness found that the women had body cells that looked ten years older than their chronological age (Epel et al., 2004). Further, the degree of cellular aging was highest in the women who had been caring for a disabled child the longest. One explanation for these findings is that chronic stress disrupts the normal process of cell division in the body, causing damage to cell DNA beyond what normally occurs due to natural aging. Eventually, this DNA damage no longer allows the cell to divide, and it prematurely dies. Researchers are as yet unsure how, precisely, chronic stress affects cell division and aging, but they believe that chemicals known as *free radicals* are involved in the cell damage (Moreira et al., 2008).

One form of chronic stress is bereavement, which is grief following the loss of a loved one. Bereavement is associated with decreased natural killer cell and T-cell activity (Segerstrom & Miller, 2004). When grieving spouses were studied over a two-year period, they were found to be more susceptible to illness and physical ailments and more likely to die than a comparison group of similar adults. These negative health consequences were

The stress of living in crowded urban environments can contribute to a variety of illnesses, including strokes and heart attacks. Does everyone react in the same manner to environmental stressors?

especially true for the grieving men (Stroebe et al., 2001). Chronic environmental stressors, such as poverty and noisy living conditions, are associated with irritability, fatigue, and high blood pressure, which can lead to a variety of illnesses, including strokes and heart attacks (Adler & Snibbe, 2003; Leather et al., 2003). Even the relatively short-term stressor of final exams can lower the overall effectiveness of the immune system, resulting in greater health risks among college students (Kiecolt-Glaser & Glaser, 2001).

Before complaining to your professors that exams can be hazardous to your health, keep in mind that stress is a subjective experience. While one person may perceive a particular situation as highly threatening, another person may perceive it as only mildly stressful (see Section 13.2a). In this regard, it might be useful to recall the discussion in Chapter 11, Section 11.1c, concerning how a predisposition toward a psychological disorder can lead to its onset following stressful events. This *diathesis-stress model*—which is an excellent example of the biopsychosocial perspective—helps in understanding psychophysiological illnesses. According to the model, several elements are necessary in order for disease to occur. In particular, a *predisposition*, or vulnerability, for a type of disease must exist. In addition, whether or not the disease is allowed to develop will be affected by exposure to something that lowers resistance—notably, stress. This view can help explain not only why different people develop different illnesses following stress but also why rates of illness change over time (Brannon & Feist, 2000).

Section REVIEW

- Stress is our response to events that disturb, or threaten to disturb, our physical or psychological equilibrium; stressors can be either positive or negative events, with negative events generally inducing more stress.

- According to Selye's general adaptation syndrome, threat first causes the body to react with alarm, then with resistance, and finally with exhaustion as the threat continues.

- There may be gender differences in the initial alarm stage.

- Stress can lead to decreased immune system effectiveness and contribute to a variety of diseases.

- Natural immunity involves the immune system's natural barriers and specialized body cells that make a fast, all-purpose assault on invading microorganisms.

- Specific immunity involves a slower defensive response, in which the immune system creates specific protective cells to attack specific invading microorganisms that the body was exposed to at a previous time.

13.2 What Moderates Stress?

Just because you are exposed to a stressor does not mean that you will become ill. Instead, the way you react to a stressor is shaped by how you perceive it. Your reactions to stress will be moderated by a number of factors, including the *predictability* of the stressor, *perceptions* of control, your *personality*, and the availability of *social support*.

13.2a   Cognitive Appraisal Is an Important Part of the Stress Response.

Because of Selye's model, stress was catapulted to near the top of the medical community's list of factors contributing to health problems. Yet his theory was developed before most scientists had approached the study of illness from a biopsychosocial perspective. Instead, illness was considered a purely biological phenomenon. Although the GAS easily fit into accepted medical views of the time, by focusing exclusively on the body, this theory all but ignored the role of the mind in the stress response. However, as more research was conducted, evidence emerged that *psychological awareness of the stressor* was a necessary component in the stress response. Realizing that purely biological explanations were inadequate in explaining the stress response was an important step in the development of the biopsychosocial model.

Cognitive Appraisal

Richard Lazarus (1993) was one of the first researchers to examine how we interpret and evaluate stressors in our lives, a process he called *cognitive appraisal*. Cognitive appraisal is essential in defining whether a situation is a threat, and in determining how big a threat it is, and what resources you have to deal with the threat (R. S. Lazarus & Lazarus, 1994). Some stressors, such as being a crime victim or undergoing surgery, are experienced as threats by almost everyone. However, many other events are defined differently depending on the individuals, their past experiences with similar stressors, and their feelings of competence in dealing with the stressors' demands. For example, starting a new job can fill one person with excitement, while it causes another person to feel apprehensive and overwhelmed. Context is also important. For instance, prior to the anthrax scare of 2001, you probably would not have been alarmed to find powder traces inside a letter you received in the mail. Yet today, with so much concern about biological terrorism, powdered letters are likely to prompt a 911 call.

Lazarus identified two stages in the cognitive appraisal process: primary appraisal and secondary appraisal. *Primary appraisal* involves an initial evaluation of the situation. Here, you assess what is happening, whether it is threatening, and whether you should take some action in response to the threat. If you conclude that some action is necessary, *secondary appraisal* begins. In this second stage of the cognitive appraisal process, you assess whether you have the ability to cope with the stressor. The more competent you perceive yourself to be in dealing with the stressor, the less stress you will experience (Baum & Posluszny, 1999).

Problem-Focused versus Emotion-Focused Coping

In contrast to Selye's model, which viewed the person as a passive recipient of stressors, Lazarus's model conceives of the person as an active participant in evaluating and responding to stressors. Consistent with this activist perspective, Lazarus and Susan Folkman (1984) identified two general coping strategies that people employ during secondary appraisal.

Problem-focused coping is a strategy aimed at reducing stress by overcoming the source of the problem. For example, if you fail your first exam in an important class, engaging in problem-focused coping might involve such actions as talking to your professor about extra-credit work, changing your study habits, and comparing your class notes with those of someone doing well in the class.

A second approach is **emotion-focused coping**, in which you try to manage your emotional reactions to stressors rather than trying to change the stressors themselves (Auerbach & Gramling, 1998). Engaging in this type of coping when faced with class problems might involve trying not to cry when speaking to your professor, seeking sympathy from your friends, or immersing yourself in some other activity to take your mind off your academic troubles. By controlling how you feel, you may be better able to take control of situations, thus limiting the emotional toll of the stressor. Consistent with this idea, research finds that college students experience less daily stress and better physical health if they regularly engage in leisure activities during the school year (Iwasaki, 2003).

We tend to take the active, problem-focused approach to handling stress when we think we have the resources to overcome the problem; we resort to an emotion-focused strategy, however, when we think the problem is beyond our control (Hagger & Orbell, 2003). Of course, at times we employ both types of coping. For example, while devising a plan of action to improve your class performance, you may try to emotionally distance yourself from anxiety by reminding yourself that this is just one exam out of four in the course. Table 13-1 lists some of the specific problem-focused and emotion-focused strategies that people use (Kim et al., 2003).

Problem-focused coping A coping strategy designed to reduce the stress by overcoming the source of the problem

Emotion-focused coping A coping strategy designed to manage the emotional reactions to stressors rather than trying to change the stressors themselves

TABLE 13-1 Problem-Focused and Emotion-Focused Coping

Coping Skills	Example
Problem-Focused Coping	
Confronting	Assert yourself and fight for what you want.
Planful problem solving	Develop a plan of action and implement it.
Seeking social support	Seek out others who have information about the stressor.
Emotion- Focused Coping	
Distancing	Redirect your attention to other things, or try to downplay the importance of the stressor.
Self-controlling	Keep your feelings to yourself.
Escape/avoidance	Fantasize about the stressor going away (wishful thinking).
Positive reappraisal	Think about positive aspects of yourself not related to the stressor.
Accepting responsibility	Realize that you are responsible for this problem.

INFO-BIT

What could be the evolutionary benefit of the body suppressing immune functioning during stress? The answer is two-fold: immune responses use up a lot of energy, and a full-blown immune response can greatly reduce attention to other tasks. Thus, suppression of the immune system may make your fight-or-flight response more efficient, thus increasing your chances of survival (Maier et al., 1994).

Journey of Discovery

Problem-focused coping is generally not useful in situations over which a person has no personal control. Yet a situation that appears on its surface to be uncontrollable may still have controllable aspects. Consider people caring for loved ones with terminal illnesses. During the weeks leading up to death, what sort of problem-focused coping might caregivers engage in to increase their positive moods and lower their stress?

13.2b Predictability and Control Can Moderate the Stress Response.

Whether an event will become a harmful stressor is often determined by its *predictability*. If you know that a stressor is coming but are uncertain when it will occur, you tend to experience greater stress (Boss, 1999). This effect is especially true when the stressors are intense and occur for relatively brief periods (Parkes & Weiss, 1983).

A host of studies indicate that *perceived control* over a stressor is one of the most important factors moderating the relationship between stress and illness. If people believe that they have some control over a stressor, they usually feel less stressed (Christensen et al., 1998; Theorell, 2003). For example, in one study, elderly nursing home patients who were given greater control over their daily activities experienced fewer health problems and lived longer than those who were not given much control (Rodin, 1986). Similarly, people who work at demanding jobs are least likely to develop coronary heart disease when they believe they have some control over job stressors.

Neurologically, when a stressor is judged to be controllable, a region in the prefrontal cortex involved in thinking and avoidance learning inhibits an acute stress response (Bland et al., 2005). As neuroscientist Steven Maier explains, "It's as if the prefrontal cortex says, 'Cool it brainstem. We have control over this, and there is no need to get so excited' " (Kohn, 2005). However, when the stressor is judged to be uncontrollable, the prefrontal cortex activates the brainstem, which triggers a strong fear response.

People differ in their tendency to perceive events as controllable (or uncontrollable). As discussed in Chapter 10, Section 10.5b, the tendency to assume that outcomes occur because of our own efforts is referred to as an *internal locus of control*, whereas an *external locus of control* reflects a belief that outcomes are outside our control (Rotter, 1966, 1990). A person's locus of control appears to emerge early in life and is a fairly stable personality trait. Through experience, it is also possible to develop either a sense of mastery or a sense of helplessness toward stressors. Through experiencing success when attempting to alleviate stressors, you are likely to become more confident that you can gain control over future challenges. Alternatively, repeatedly failing to eliminate stressors can lead to more generalized assumptions of being helpless (Seligman, 1975). This *learned helplessness* could cause you to falsely believe that you have no control over a stressor, thus increasing the likelihood that you will take no action to reduce the threat (Baum et al., 1998).

When people doubt their ability to assert control over a stressor, they are more likely to engage in emotion-focused coping strategies (see Section 13.2a). *Procrastination,* which involves delaying the start and completion of planful *problem solving,* is an example of the emotion-focused coping strategy of *escape-avoidance* (refer back to Table 13-1). Approximately one out of five adults regularly procrastinates when faced with a stressor, especially when it is severe (Harriot & Ferrari, 1996). These habitually indecisive individuals are easily distracted, have low self-confidence, and have an external locus of control (Ferrari & Dovidio, 2001). Far from reducing stress, however, such delays in tackling problems tend to increase stress and lead to health problems (Ferrari & Tice, 2000). For example, at the beginning of the semester in a health psychology class, researchers identified college students who were either habitually high or low in procrastination (Tice & Baumeister, 1997). As you can see in Figure 13-3, although procrastinators reported slightly fewer symptoms of physical illness than did nonprocrastinators early in the semester, procrastinators had significantly greater symptoms later in the semester as term paper deadlines came due. True to form, procrastinators not only turned their assignments in later than nonprocrastinators, but they also obtained lower grades on those papers.

13.2c *Hostile and Pessimistic Persons Are Very Reactive to Stressors.*

The fact that stressors become less worrisome and more manageable when we perceive them as predictable and controllable highlights how our thinking about events shapes our behavioral responses. Additional research indicates that some people's consistent and distinctive ways of thinking, feeling, and behaving—that is, their personalities— cause them to react negatively to stressors, whereas others respond positively (Williams & Lawler, 2001). Two personality dimensions that significantly influence stress responses are (1) *Type A behavior pattern versus Type B behavior pattern* and (2) *pessimistic explanatory style versus optimistic explanatory style.*

BVT *Lab*

Visit **www.BVTLab.com** to explore the student resources available for this chapter.

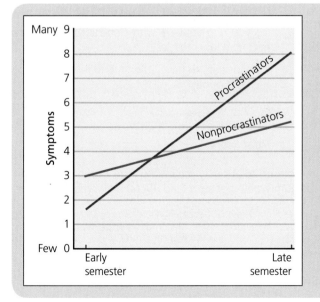

FIGURE 13-3

Procrastination and Health

At the beginning of the semester, college students who were identified as procrastinators reported slightly fewer physical illness symptoms than did nonprocrastinators. As the semester progressed and class deadlines approached, all students reported more symptoms. However, procrastinators missed more deadlines and reported more illness symptoms than nonprocrastinators.

Source: From "Longitudinal study of procrastination, performance, stress, and health: The costs and benefits of dawdling" by D. M. Tice and R. F. Baumeister in *Psychological Science, 8,* 1997, pp. 454–458.

Type A behavior pattern A complex pattern of behaviors and emotions characterized by competitiveness, impatience, ambition, hostility, and a hard-driving approach to life

Type B behavior pattern A pattern of behaviors and emotions characterized by a patient, relaxed, easygoing, approach to life, with little hurry or hostility

Type A and Type B Behavior Patterns

During the 1950s, two cardiologists, Ray Rosenman and Meyer Friedman, noted an oddity about their coronary patients: The way these patients sat on the chairs in the cardiologists' waiting room caused the chair upholstery to be worn more in the front than in the back—as if their patients were sitting on the edge of their seats. This observation, coupled with the cardiologists' later findings that many of these same people were also impatient workaholics, led Rosenman and Friedman to identify what they called the **Type A behavior pattern** (Rosenman, 1993; Rosenman et al., 1975). This complex pattern of behaviors and emotions—which is associated with increased risk of heart disease—is characterized by competitiveness, impatience, ambition, cynicism, hostility, and a hard-driving approach to life (Le Melledo et al., 2003; Song et al., 2007). The direct opposite of this personality style is the **Type B behavior pattern**, which is characterized by a patient, relaxed, easygoing approach to life, with little hurry or hostility. These individuals are only half as likely to develop coronary heart disease as their Type A counterparts (Lyness, 1993). Spend a few minutes answering the items in Self-Discovery Questionnaire 13-2 to assess your propensity for the Type A behavior pattern.

SELF-DISCOVERY 13-2
Questionnaire

Do You Have a Type A Personality?

Directions: Indicate how often each of the following applies to you in daily life, using the following three-point scale:

1 = never or seldom   2 = sometimes   3 = usually or always

___ Do you find yourself rushing your speech?

___ Do you hurry other people's speech by interrupting them with "umha, umhm" or by completing their sentences for them?

___ Do you hate to wait in line?

___ Do you seem to be short of time to get everything done?

___ Do you detest wasting time?

___ Do you eat fast?

___ Do you drive over the speed limit?

___ Do you try to do more than one thing at a time?

___ Do you become impatient if others do something too slowly?

___ Does your concentration sometimes wander while you think about what's coming up later?

___ Do you find yourself overcommitted?

___ Do you jiggle your knees or tap your fingers?

___ Do you think about other things during conversations?

___ Do you walk fast?

___ Do you hate dawdling after a meal?

___ Do you become irritable if kept waiting?

___ Do you detest losing in sports and games?

___ Do you find yourself with clenched fists or tight neck and jaw muscles?

___ Do you seem to have little time to relax and enjoy the time of day?

___ Are you a competitive person?

___ ***Total Score***

A score of 20–34 may mean low Type A behavior, 35–44 medium Type A behavior, and 45–60 high Type A behavior.

Source: From *Stress Management for Wellness,* 2nd edition, by W. Schafer. Copyright © 1992. Reprinted with permission of Brooks/Cole, an imprint of the Wadsworth Group, a division of Thomson Learning. Fax 800/730-2215.

Based on numerous studies, *cynical hostility* appears to be the toxic component of the Type A pattern (Dembroski et al., 1985; Fredrickson et al., 2000). Specifically, people who mistrust and think the worst of others and use anger as a typical response to interpersonal problems appear to be at greatest risk for heart disease (Vahtera et al., 2000). From a physiological point of view, cynical hostility appears to cause chronic overarousal of the body's stress responses (Everson et al., 1997). From a psychosocial point of view, cynical hostility contributes to poor health habits and tense social relationships (T. Smith, 1992).

Because of the health problems associated with the Type A behavior pattern, it makes sense to try to convince Type A persons to change their hostile, impatient approach to life. However, one major obstacle to orchestrating such change is that many Type A persons are not unhappy with their behavior. After all, North American culture respects and rewards this hard-driving, hostile lifestyle. (Rush Limbaugh, Donald Trump, and most of the successful contestants on TV reality shows are prototypes of the Type A person.) Yet, for people motivated to reduce their hostility and "smell the roses" in their daily lives, behavior modification and cognitive therapy (see Chapter 12, Sections 12.3 and 12.4) have been successful in changing Type A behavior (Zolnierczyk, 2004). Before reading further, check out Closer Look 13-1, on how to alter the Type A behavior pattern.

Type A individuals are competitive, impatient, ambitious, hostile, and hard-driving. Which of these characteristics is the "toxic component" of the Type A pattern?

Closer LOOK 13-1

What Are Some Strategies to Modify Time Urgency and Cynical Hostility?

Based on his research on the Type A behavior pattern, Meyer Friedman (1996) recommends a number of intervention strategies to help Type A persons slow down and reduce their free-floating hostility. Listed next are some of these exercises, plus a few of my own, that you can try during the next week to alter problematic Type A behavior patterns.

Strategies to Modify Time Urgency

Type A persons' habit of always being on the go and thinking of the things they need to accomplish causes them to pay little heed to their current surroundings. Thus, they often fail to notice and appreciate many important people or things in their lives. Here are some exercises you can do to slow down your day and become more present-time oriented:

Exercise 1: *Eat more slowly.* Linger over your meal. Enjoy the various tastes and smells of your food and drink. What do you notice about your meal that you were not aware of before?

Exercise 2: *Take periodic 15-minute breaks from work and notice something beautiful around you.* How does your mood change as you attend to your surroundings?

Exercise 3: *Walk more slowly.* How does this slower pace make you feel? Impatient? Relaxed? Maintain this

One recommendation that helps Type A individuals alter their impatient, hard-driving approach to life is to have them take "time-outs" during their busy daily schedules to appreciate the beauty around them, which they generally fail to notice.

slower walking pace for at least a week, noticing any changes in your thoughts and feelings over time.

Exercise 4: *Listen to every person who speaks to you without interrupting them, even if you think you have something useful to interject.* How difficult is this for you?

Strategies to Reduce Cynical Hostility

Type A persons' habit of criticizing others is so ingrained that they rarely praise other people. As a result, they rarely receive compliments themselves. Type A persons' free-floating hostility often results in their frowning more than smiling when with others, which often causes people to reciprocate with unfriendly facial expressions and avoidance. Here are some exercises you can do to reverse these negative behavior patterns:

Exercise 1: *Compliment at least two persons during a conversation.* Be sincere and notice their facial expressions as they receive the compliment. How do you feel?

Exercise 2: *Practice smiling as you remember two to three happy events from the past, and then purposely smile while speaking to others.* How do their facial expressions change as you smile?

Exercise 3: *Ask friends or family members about their daily activities, showing genuine interest in what they tell you, asking questions, and avoiding criticisms in your comments.* How do they respond to your expression of interest?

Exercise 4: *Just as you are about to criticize someone, try to avoid doing so.* If you must say something critical, first count to 10—or 20, or 30. Is this a difficult task for you?

Pessimists versus Optimists

Another personality dimension related to health issues is *explanatory style*—a person's degree of pessimism or optimism—regarding negative life events (Cole et al., 2008; Peterson & Steen, 2002). As outlined by Christopher Peterson and Martin Seligman, individuals with a **pessimistic explanatory style** explain uncontrollable negative events as being caused by internal factors ("It's my fault") that are stable ("It won't ever change") and global ("This affects everything"). Not surprisingly, people who fit this pattern are susceptible to depression (Lyubomirsky et al., 2011). In contrast, people with an **optimistic explanatory style** explain uncontrollable negative events as due to external factors ("It is not my fault") that are unstable or changeable ("It won't happen again") and specific ("This affects only one thing").

Research over the past 20 years indicates that people with an optimistic perspective on life are healthier and more resistant to illness than those with a pessimistic orientation (Peterson & Park, 2007; Scheier & Carver, 2000). Additional research suggests that these health differences may be partly explained by the fact that optimists seem to have better immune systems than pessimists. For example, one study found that optimists have higher numbers of helper T cells that mediate immune reactions to infection than do pessimists (Segerstrom et al., 1998).

Fortunately, individuals with a pessimistic explanatory style can be taught to change their way of thinking through cognitive therapy (see Chapter 12, Section 12.4b). Typically, this involves people keeping a diary of daily successes and failures, and identifying how they contributed to their successes and how external factors caused their failures. Essentially, pessimists are being trained to do what most of us do naturally: take credit for our successes and deny blame for our failures! As discussed in Chapter 10, Section 10.5c, this beneficial way of explaining your positive and negative outcomes is known as the *self-serving bias*. In a very real sense, research

Pessimistic explanatory style The habitual tendency to explain uncontrollable negative events as caused by one's own stable personal qualities, which affect all aspects of one's life; this pessimistic style is associated with health problems and premature death.

Optimistic explanatory style The habitual tendency to explain uncontrollable negative events as caused by temporary factors external to oneself that do not affect other aspects of one's life; this optimistic style is associated with good health and longevity.

SELF-DISCOVERY 13-3
Questionnaire

Are You Typically an Optimist or a Pessimist?

The Revised Life Orientation Test developed by Michael Scheier and Charles Carver (1994) measures people's tendencies to believe that they will generally experience good or bad outcomes in their lives. Read the 10 statements below and indicate the degree to which you personally agree with each statement, using the following scale:

0 = Strongly disagree
1 = Disagree
2 = Neutral (neither disagree nor agree)
3 = Agree
4 = Strongly agree

Try to be as accurate and honest as possible, and try not to let your opinion for one item influence your opinion on other items. There are no correct or incorrect answers.

_____ 1. In uncertain times, I usually expect the best.

_____ 2. It's easy for me to relax.

_____ 3. If something can go wrong for me, it will.

_____ 4. I'm always optimistic about my future.

_____ 5. I enjoy my friends a lot.

_____ 6. It's important for me to keep busy.

_____ 7. I hardly ever expect things to go my way.

_____ 8. I don't get upset too easily.

_____ 9. I rarely count on good things happening to me.

_____ 10. Overall, I expect more good things to happen to me than bad.

Scoring Instructions

_____ **Step 1**: Items #3, #7, and #9 are reverse scored, so subtract each of your scores on these items from 4.

_____ **Step 2**: Add these corrected scores for items #3, #7, and #9, and record the total here.

_____ **Step 3**: Add your scores for items #1, #4, and #10, and record the total score here.

_____ **Step 4**: Add the totals from steps 2 and 3 to obtain your overall score, which will range from 0 to 40.

Interpretation

Lower scores indicate more pessimism, while higher scores indicate more optimism. In a sample of more than 2,000 college students, the average score was 14.3, with a standard deviation of 4.3. If your score is 10 or lower, this indicates that you tend to be more pessimistic than the average college student. If your score is higher than 10 but lower than 19, this suggests that you tend to have the same level of optimism-pessimism as the average college student. If your score is 19 or higher, this suggests that you tend to be more optimistic than the average college student.

Source: M. F. Scheier, C. S. Carver, & M. W. Bridges, "Distinguishing optimism from neuroticism (and trait anxiety, self-mastery, and self-esteem): A reevaluation of the life orientation test," *Journal of Personality and Social Psychology, 67,* 1073. Copyright 1994 by the American Psychological Association.

on pessimists and optimists points to the important role that people's interpretations of events have on their health and behavior. Check out Self-Discovery Questionnaire 13-3 to explore your own tendencies toward optimism versus pessimism.

13.2d Social Support Has Therapeutic Effects.

The findings from positive psychology underscore the fact that stressful and traumatic events often draw people together in support of one another. Do you recall what you did when you first learned about the terrorist attacks? If you are like most people, during that time of anxiety, grief, and uncertainty, you sought the companionship of others similarly affected by this tragedy. Our desire to seek out others during times of stress and uncertainty is substantially fueled by the need to compare our emotional state with that of others ("How should I be feeling?") and also to appraise the stressful situation itself ("How much of a threat is this stressor?").

The optimist sees the rose and not its thorns; the pessimist stares at the thorns, oblivious to the rose.

—Kahlil Gibran, Lebanese poet, 1883–1931

Social support The helpful coping resources provided by friends and other people

The helpful coping resources provided by friends and other people when you are confronting a stressful situation are referred to as **social support**. An overwhelming amount of evidence indicates that having supportive people in our lives provides both psychological and physical benefits (Clark, 2003). For example, in a longitudinal study of almost 7,000 residents of Alameda County, California, researchers discovered that people lived longest when they had many social and community ties (Berkman & Syme, 1979). This was true of men and women, rich and poor, and people from all racial and ethnic backgrounds. Other studies have found that being socially isolated is, statistically, just as predictive of an early death as high cholesterol or smoking (Rogers, 1995). Physiologically, having strong social support networks is associated with a stronger immune response to stress (Glaser et al., 1992). For example, a meta-analysis of 81 studies found that having social support during times of stress lowers blood pressure, lessens the secretion of stress hormones, and strengthens immune responses (Uchino et al., 1996).

As mentioned, one common psychological benefit of social support is increased knowledge about the stressor. That is, associating with others often provides us with information about how to understand and emotionally respond to stressful events (Van der Zee et al., 1998). The people who tend to provide us with the most useful information are similar to us in some characteristic related to the stressor (Schachter, 1959). This is the rationale underlying therapeutic support groups for drug abusers, sexual assault victims, and cancer patients (see Chapter 12, Section 12.6b). In these therapy sessions, people who have experienced the same stressful events can compare themselves with one another, while they also provide and receive emotional support.

Social support during stressful times can also provide us with opportunities to simply express our feelings, which in turn can lead to physical benefits (Kelly, 1999; Pennebaker et al., 1990). In one relevant experiment, college students spent 15 minutes on each of four consecutive nights writing to the experimenter about a traumatic event in their lives. These students subsequently reported fewer illnesses over the next six months compared to students who had written to the experimenter about unimportant topics (Pennebaker & Beall, 1986). In general, while "letting out" our feelings about a traumatic event can temporarily upset and arouse us, it lowers our stress and improves our health, in the long run.

Shutterstock

People with more extensive social support networks are happier, have stronger immune systems, and live longer than those who are socially isolated. What are some of the reasons that social connections are so therapeutic?

INFO-BIT

Owning a pet can have stress-buffering effects, resulting in fewer illnesses among people who experience negative life events (Siegel, 1990).

As with most things that are good for you, however, too much social support (or support given improperly) can cause negative side effects. For example, receiving overzealous support can reduce both the recipient's sense of control over a stressor and his or her self-confidence. Receiving social support can also make a person feel beholden to the giver, turning the support into a burden (Greenberg & Frisch, 1972; Gross & Latané, 1974). When providing support to another person, the key is to convey caring for the recipient in a manner that provides real benefits, keeps him or her involved in the solution to the problem (rather than it just being "taken care of"), and avoids an inferiority-superiority relationship (Dakof & Taylor, 1990; Dunkel-Schetter et al., 1992). Exploring Culture & Diversity 13-2 discusses how women and men sometimes differ in providing social support in romantic relationships.

Exploring CULTURE & DIVERSITY **13-2**

Are There Gender Differences in Providing Social Support in Romantic Relationships?

People involved in long-term romantic relationships often view their partner as their best friend and as the person they would turn to in times of need (Pasch et al., 1997). Receiving such support has four important benefits: the *stress decreases* for those in need, which, in turn, has a positive effect on their *physical health*, while simultaneously increasing their *satisfaction* and *commitment* to the relationship (Coyne et al., 2001; Sprecher et al., 1995). In heterosexual romance, men rely more on their partners for social support than do women, who also depend on a variety of other sources, including friends, relatives, and neighbors (Cutrona, 1996). However, a woman's psychological well-being is still closely linked to the support she receives from her partner. For example, a longitudinal study of married couples found that lower levels of depression were associated with both women and men receiving a good deal of *emotional support* (tenderness and understanding) and *information support* (advice and guidance) from their partners during the previous six months (Cutrona & Suhr, 1994).

Unfortunately for women involved in heterosexual romantic relationships, their skill in providing social support during stressful times—recall the "tend-and-befriend" discussion in Section 13.1c—is generally greater than that of their male partners (Fritz et al., 2003; Vinokur & Vinokur-Kaplan, 1990). The most likely explanation for this gender difference is the greater childhood training girls receive in the caregiving role and in emotional attentiveness (Belle, 1982). While female socialization fosters the development of these *relationship-enhancing* behaviors, male socialization is more likely to promote the development of *individual-enhancing* behaviors, such as independence and control. This gender difference may explain why marriage is more beneficial to men than to women: Men marry people who, on average, have been taught to provide care and nurturance, while women marry people who, on average, have spent a lot of time learning how to be independent of others!

How does this gender socialization difference influence social support between members of lesbian or gay couples? A five-year longitudinal study suggests that while the "double dose" of relationship-enhancing skills that lesbians bring to romantic relationships is associated with slightly higher intimacy than is found among heterosexual couples and gay couples, it doesn't lead to greater relationship satisfaction (Kurdek, 1998).

13.2e   *Religion and Spirituality Can Positively Influence Health and Longevity.*

Between 80 and 85 percent of the world's population (more than 6 billion people) is affiliated with some form of religion, with the most popular religions being Christianity, Islam, Hinduism, and Buddhism. For many people, organized religion helps them cope with stress (Jackson & Bergeman, 2011). Those who regularly attend religious services are somewhat happier and less anxious and depressed, and live about seven years longer (82 years versus 75 years), than those who do not regularly attend such services (McCullough et al., 2000).

A number of studies point to lifestyle variables as largely accounting for the longevity difference. For example, Americans who regularly attend religious services drink less, smoke less, and exercise more than those who do not (Strawbridge et al., 2001). Similarly, Japanese Zen monks—who live significantly longer than the typical Japanese man—smoke less, consume less meat, and live in less crowded parts of the country than the rest of the population (Ogata et al., 1984). Thus, it may well be that the greater longevity of religious persons is substantially due to their healthier lifestyles compared with those of nonreligious persons and also due, perhaps, to the social support religious people receive from their fellow worshipers. However, might there be something else contributing to this longevity difference besides health behaviors and social support?

People (especially women) who identify themselves as highly religious tend to be healthier and live longer than those who are not very religious. What might explain these health and longevity differences?

A 60-year longitudinal study of more than 2,500 women and men found that women who identified themselves as highly religious at the age of 30 years regularly reported being in better health and having a slower decline in overall health throughout their lives compared to women who identified themselves as not being very religious (McCullough & Laurenceau, 2005). This was true even after controlling for health behaviors, social support, and social activity. In contrast, religiousness had no significant association with any aspect of men's reported health, which is consistent with the findings from other studies indicating that the religiousness-health/longevity link is stronger among women than among men (McCullough et al., 2000). The reason this link is stronger for women may be due to the fact that women are, on average, more religious than are men in nearly all cultures and throughout most of their lives (Stark, 2002).

What about people who describe themselves as religious but do not participate in formalized religious services? Do they also experience health benefits? A six-year study of nearly 4,000 people found that those who engaged in some sort of private spiritual practice—such as meditation, prayer, or Bible study—were less likely to die during the course of the study than those who did not engage in such activities, even after controlling for their health behaviors and their levels of social support (Helm et al., 2000).

What about individuals suffering from illnesses and diseases? Is there any evidence that religion or spirituality provide health benefits to the seriously ill? Among women

Shutterstock

battling breast cancer, one study found that those who had strong religious beliefs had better coping skills than those with weaker religious beliefs (Johnson & Spilka, 1991). Other studies have found that cancer patients who perceived God or Allah as having control over their disease coped better than patients without such beliefs (Ginsburg et al., 1995; Roberts et al., 1997). Finally, among older adults who had coronary bypass surgery, those with strong religious beliefs were less likely to die during the six-month period following surgery than those with weak beliefs, even after controlling for age, severity of heart problem, and level of social participation (Oxman et al., 1995). One important factor underlying highly religious individuals' greater coping skills in handling the stress of illness and disease appears to be their greater sense of hope and optimism about life and the future (Plante et al., 2000; Salsman et al., 2005).

Of course, religion is certainly not blemish free in promoting health. The biggest negative consequences associated with formal religions are the violence, wars, and intergroup intolerance actively sponsored by some religious leaders and followers (Fontana, 2003). Indeed, formal religions can play a significant— and often negative—role in prejudice and discrimination, which can result in extremely unfortunate physical and mental health consequences for those who are the targets of this intolerance (Levin, 2004; McCann, 1999). It is also true that certain fundamentalist religious groups reject important medical interventions, such as childhood vaccinations and blood transfusions, and that this rejection can have serious health consequences. Finally, although a number of studies indicate that highly religious individuals have better mental health than those who are less religious, this relationship is reversed for certain religious traditions. Several studies indicate that Catholics' religiousness is actually associated with poorer mental health, possibly due to greater feelings of guilt instilled by Roman Catholic Church traditions compared to Protestant traditions (Alferi et al., 1999; Tix & Frazier, 2005). Of course, this finding does not mean that the Catholic religious tradition is somehow worse than Protestant traditions, but it does suggest that Catholics who actively "live their faith" might confront somewhat greater mental health challenges than do highly religious Protestants (Pargament, 2002).

Despite these qualifications, scientific studies indicate that religiousness has real health benefits. People with strong religious beliefs appear to have a buffer against stress that is independent of the social support they might receive from fellow worshipers. While many of these health benefits are undoubtedly due to healthier lifestyles, the belief in the ultimate power and control of a Supreme Being may also produce health-inducing thoughts and emotions.

Section REVIEW

- Current views of human stress maintain that it is a continually changing process determined by how a threat is cognitively appraised, what resources (both within and outside the person) are available, and how the person copes with the stressor.

- Events that are predictable and those over which we perceive we have some degree of control are less stressful than unpredictable events that we view as out of our control.

- Hostile and pessimistic individuals are more reactive than others to stressors.

- Strong versus weak social support is associated with a stronger immune response to stress and with better physical and psychological health; women tend to provide better social support than do men.

- Strong religious beliefs are generally beneficial to health, but sometimes religion can be detrimental.

13.3 What Behaviors Hurt or Help Our Health?

Although stress can take a toll on physical and psychological well-being, as you have learned, both situational and personal factors can buffer many of these negative effects. In this section of the chapter, we will examine how specific behaviors are associated with health and illness.

13.3a   *Knowing about "Safer Sex" Is Not Enough.*

Do you know how HIV (the virus that causes AIDS) is passed from one person to another? Can you name at least two ways to keep from acquiring a sexually transmitted disease? If you are like most college students, you already know that HIV is spread through body fluids, such as semen and blood, and not through casual contact (including kissing, unless open sores are present) or by mosquitoes. It also is probably not news to you that HIV and other sexually transmitted diseases can be prevented by abstaining from sex, or if you are sexually active, by practicing safer sex behaviors, such as consistently using a condom (or other barrier), limiting sexual partners, and knowing the sexual histories of your partners (Emmers-Sommer et al., 2005; Ruan et al., 2008).

The fact that nearly all college students (and the vast majority of other young adults) can correctly answer these questions speaks to the success of educational programs in informing the public about HIV over the past 25 years. However, this knowledge has little relationship to whether or not unmarried adolescents or adults remain abstinent or practice safer-sex behaviors. Instead, college students engage in a number of risky sexual behaviors, including high numbers of sexual partners, one-night stands with casual acquaintances, and frequent condomless sex (Bancroft et al., 2004). Even though 1 in 6 sexually active adults reports having had at least one sexually transmitted disease (such as chlamydia, gonorrhea, genital herpes, genital warts, syphilis, or HIV), as many as 9 out of 10 do not use condoms consistently (Michael et al., 1994). Often, the riskier behaviors occur in combination with the use of alcohol or other drugs (Ratliff-Crain et al., 1999).

If knowledge about the risks doesn't promote safer behaviors, what does? Additionally, what motivates people to choose unsafe behaviors over those that are safer? Getting people to practice safer-sex behaviors, such as using condoms, takes much more than simply telling them that condoms prevent disease and that they should use them (Bryan et al., 2005; Kalichman, 2005). Here are some of the more common reasons why people don't use condoms:

- *Buying condoms can be embarrassing.* This is the case especially for people who are extremely uncomfortable discussing their sexuality. Also, the use of condoms may be inconsistent with an individual's personal or cultural values, diminishing use even further (Locke et al., 2005). Men and women who are comfortable talking about their sexual histories and about safer sex are about 6 times more likely to use condoms than those who are uncomfortable (Catania et al., 1992). Programs that make condoms freely available to everyone often eliminate these barriers to safer sex.

- *Condom use education emphasizes fear and disease prevention.* Sex education programs that use fear of AIDS as the primary focus have been shown to increase awareness, but not to change behaviors (Chesney & Coates, 1990). One reason such programs do not lead to safer sexual behavior is that people often associate condoms with disease, thus lowering their motivation to use condoms. In response, advertisers have begun depicting condoms in a more sexual manner, treating them as a desirable part of the sexual experience rather than as objects associated with disease. If condoms are not part of people's sexual scripts (see Chapter 9, Section 9.3), they are less likely to be used in the "heat of the moment."

- *Riskier sexual behaviors are more likely with alcohol consumption.* Alcohol does not necessarily cause people to lose their sexual inhibitions, but it does make them less likely to engage in logical reasoning (Coates et al., 1988). When people's ability to critically think is disrupted, they are much less apt to consider the possible consequences of their behavior (Bryan et al., 2005). When intoxicated with alcohol, people's immediate sexual arousal will be uppermost in their minds rather than any thought that sexual activity may put them at risk for a disease.

- *Low self-esteem persons are more likely than others to engage in risky sexual behaviors.* Low self-esteem persons are more vulnerable to negative events in their lives than are high self-esteem persons (Smith & Petty, 1992). When experiencing negative moods, they also have a heightened need to avoid rejection from others (Heatherton & Vohs, 2000). These reactions to negative events may explain why people with low self-esteem are more likely than high self-esteem persons to have sex without using a condom when they are in a negative mood (MacDonald & Martineau, 2002).

The research findings summarized in the preceding list suggest that effective prevention programs must focus on multiple areas of a person's life in order to increase safer sexual behaviors. Such programs need broader interventions—including discussions of nonsexual motivations for seeking intimacy, assertiveness training to help people feel comfortable stating their own preferences with a sexual partner, reducing barriers to obtaining condoms, and providing models and examples of situations in which safer sex is still exciting sex (Coates, 1990).

13.3b Obesity and Eating Disorders Are Shaped by Internal and External Forces.

As discussed in Chapter 9, Section 9.2, eating is one of our basic, primary motivated behaviors. You also learned that feelings of hunger and eating behaviors are controlled by much more than what our stomachs tell us. A complex array of physiological, psychological, and social/environmental factors combine to create our motivation to eat.

What Is Obesity?

According to the Centers for Disease Control and Prevention (CDC), **obesity**, which is the excessive accumulation of body fat, has become an epidemic in the

BVT *Lab*

Improve your test scores. Practice quizzes are available at www.BVTLab.com.

Obesity The excessive accumulation of body fat; medically, a body mass index (BMI) over 30

United States. More than one-third of American adults are obese, and almost 17% of children and adolescents fit this category (Saguy & Almeling, 2008). In diagnosing obesity, physicians calculate a *body mass index (BMI)*, which is defined as weight in kilograms divided by height in meters squared (30 kg/m2). A ratio over 25 is considered overweight; over 30, obese; over 40, extremely obese. Using the BMI, a 5-foot-4-inch tall woman weighing 174 pounds or more, or a 5-foot-10-inch tall man weighing 207 pounds or more, would be considered obese.

INFO-BIT   To calculate your BMI using pounds and inches, multiply your weight in pounds by 700, divide by your height in inches, and then divide by your height again.

Healthwise, the ideal BMI differs across racial categories. For example, African Americans' healthiest BMI score, which is around 27, is higher than that for European Americans, which is around 24 to 25 (Brannon & Feist, 2000).

Although being slightly overweight poses no health risks, obesity is closely related to numerous chronic health conditions, including high blood pressure, heart disease, diabetes, arthritis, and sleep disorders (Kiessling et al., 2008). As depicted in Figure 13-4, a 14-year longitudinal study of over 1 million Americans found that extreme obesity is a clear risk for premature death (Calle et al., 1999). Further evidence suggests that *changes* in weight due to repeated dieting and weight-gain cycles place people at higher risk for numerous diseases (Rexrode et al., 1997).

What Causes Obesity?

Ample evidence shows that people are born with tendencies to be lighter or heavier. Indeed, as much as 70 percent of individual differences in weight are due to genetics (Bulik et al., 2003). Still, genetics alone cannot explain the rapid increases in obesity in the U.S. Weight gain occurs when energy intake (through food and drink) exceeds energy expenditure (through body functions and activity), and research strongly indicates that changes in American diet and eating habits account for a substantial

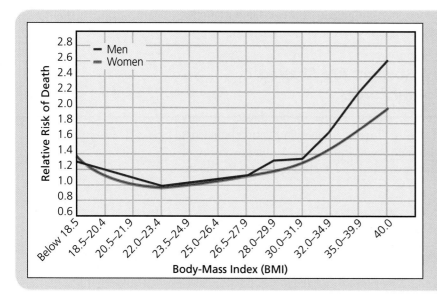

FIGURE 13-4

Obesity and Mortality

A 14-year study of over 1 million Americans found that men and women with a BMI of 40 were at least two times more likely to have died by the end of the 14-year period than were those with a BMI of 23.

Source: M. J. Thun, J. M. Petrelli, C. Rogriguez, & C. W. Health, Jr. (1999). Body-mass index and mortality in a prospective cohort of U.S. adults. *New England Journal of Medicine,* 1999, 341, 1097–1105.

portion of the national weight gain (Mokdad et al., 1999). Americans' daily diet has increased by 300 calories when compared to 15 years ago, and almost one-third of these total calories come from junk food and alcoholic beverages with little nutritional value. Once digested, these highly refined grains and sugars break down quickly to the sugar glucose in the blood, causing the pancreas to produce extra insulin to process the extra sugar. When sugar levels drop, people feel depleted of energy and experience hunger; and the eating cycle repeats itself. Over time, this cycle leads to excess weight gain (Drewnowski & Levine, 2003).

Weight loss through dieting is a common approach for trying to control weight. Although the dieting industry receives over $30 billion per year from Americans trying to lose weight, dieting is largely ineffective in achieving long-term weight loss (Stice et al., 2005). Several factors work against effective weight loss. First, as discussed in Chapter 9, Section 9.2, it is difficult to change your weight once a set point has been established. Second, many people who diet are already at or below normal weight and therefore shouldn't be dieting. Increased activity in the form of exercise may be the best predictor for long-term weight loss, both before and after dieting (Foreyt et al., 1996). As with other lifestyle changes related to health, effective long-term weight loss for people who are overweight is often achieved only after much work and many failures. Yet medical experts remind us that shedding excess weight will significantly lower our risk of premature death, chronic disease, and lower quality of life (Boyd, 2008).

On a national level, one major challenge in fighting the epidemic of obesity will be to improve the activity levels of children and adults (Goris & Westerterp, 2008). Television viewing and computer use, for example, have been pinpointed as major contributors to sedentary lifestyles and obesity (Vines, 1995). On average, 10- to 13-year-old girls spend 2½ hours a day watching television or playing video games, and boys spend 3½ hours on these same sedentary activities. If these children also spend 8 hours sleeping, they are spending almost half their day virtually motionless. One study suggests that simply reducing the amount of time children spend watching TV or playing video games is sufficient to greatly reduce their weight problems (Robinson, 1999). This reduction in weight occurred even though the children did not decrease their high-fat food intake. As we will discuss in Section 13.3c, encouraging increased physical activity may promote better health and well-being, as well as preventing obesity and related health concerns.

Finally, the food industry can play an important role in combating obesity, without necessarily lowering sales and profits. In the summer of 2003, Kraft Foods, the maker of hundreds of different snacks and packaged meals, announced that it would encourage healthier eating by reducing portion sizes for some of its products. In addition to reducing the amount of food offered to the public, research indicates that food manufacturers can promote healthier eating by selectively lowering the price of healthy foods. For example, in one study of consumer food purchases, epidemiologist Simone French (2003) found that, while highlighting the low-fat content of products had little influence on their popularity, dropping their price by

Does research suggest that reducing the price of fresh vegetables and fruit increases people's consumption of these healthy foods?

The Japanese have the longest life expectancy in the world. Not coincidentally, their diet is high in fiber and vitamins and low in fat. How does the typical Japanese diet different from the American diet?

even a nickel increased sales. Further, a 50 percent price reduction on fresh fruit and baby carrots caused a fourfold increase in fresh fruit sales and a twofold increase in baby carrot sales. This study suggests that the food industry can actually be a positive force in reducing obesity and promoting healthier eating among consumers without losing profit margins. In this sense, they can figuratively "have their cake and eat it, too."

Cultural Thinness Standards

Being significantly overweight is not just a health problem. In North American culture, obese individuals are often perceived as unattractive, lazy, weak-willed, sloppy, mean, unskilled, and slow (Bacardi-Gascon et al., 2007; Crandall, 1994). In longitudinal studies of obese women and men, researchers find that they are less likely to be hired and tend to start at lower salaries and receive lower raises than their normal-weight counterparts (Frieze et al., 1991; Gortmaker et al., 1993). Other studies suggest that weight discrimination is more pervasive and widely condoned than race and gender discrimination (A. M. Myers & Rothblum, 2005). Obesity is such a strong stigmatizing characteristic in our culture that it even affects how people evaluate individuals seen with obese persons. For example, Michelle Hebl and Laura Mannix (2003) found that male job applicants were rated more negatively when seen with an overweight woman prior to their job interviews than when seen with a woman of normal weight.

Although many people think that shaming overweight people will motivate them to lose weight, the exact opposite appears to be the case. When people are stigmatized because of their weight, they are more likely to engage in unhealthy behaviors, such as binge eating and unhealthy weight-control practices. The result is that they actually eat more and engage in less physical activity

Underlying weight discrimination is a social climate that pressures people to reach certain body ideals. Although men are the target of some social pressure in this regard, the female ideal stresses difficult-to-attain thinness standards that actually endanger women's health if they pursue these standards. One consequence of this cultural obsession with female weight is that women of all age groups are more likely to view their bodies as *objects* of others' attention; and women, on average, evaluate their bodies more negatively than men (Strelan et al., 2003). By adulthood, women are more likely to habitually experience what researchers identify as *social physique anxiety*, which is anxiety about others observing or evaluating their bodies (Fredrickson et al., 1998). Curiously, women's evaluation of their own bodies is often more negative than their perceptions of how others' evaluate their bodies—women are their own harshest critics (Dijkstra & Barelds, 2011; Franzoi et al., 2012). The women most likely caught in this hypercritical "beauty trap" are those who are most attentive to cultural beauty standards (Vartanian & Hopkinson, 2010). Spend a few minutes completing the Body Esteem Scale in Self-Discovery Questionnaire 13-4.

Although women in North American culture generally experience less positive body esteem than men, evidence

Shutterstock

Fifty years ago, department store mannequins had body shapes very similar to those of the average American woman. Today, mannequins are extremely thin, with an average hip circumference of 31 inches, compared with the 37-inch average for young adult women. If these mannequins were real, their body fat would be so low that they probably would not menstruate. Are certain women more susceptible to these cultural beauty standards than other women?

SELF-DISCOVERY 13-4
Questionnaire

What Is Body Esteem?

A person's attitudes toward her or his body are referred to as **body esteem**. Following is a list of 35 body parts and

Body esteem A person's attitudes toward her or his body

body functions that make up the *Body Esteem Scale* (Franzoi & Shields, 1984). Please read each item, and indicate how you feel about this part or function of your own body, using the following response categories:

1 = Have strong negative feelings
2 = Have moderate negative feelings
3 = Have no feeling one way or the other
4 = Have moderate positive feelings
5 = Have strong positive feelings

___ 1. body scent		___ 19. arms
___ 2. appetite		___ 20. chest or breasts
___ 3. nose		___ 21. appearance of eyes
___ 4. physical stamina		___ 22. cheeks/cheekbones
___ 5. reflexes		___ 23. hips
___ 6. lips		___ 24. legs
___ 7. muscular strength		___ 25. figure or physique
___ 8. waist		___ 26. sex drive
___ 9. energy level		___ 27. feet
___ 10. thighs		___ 28. sex organs
___ 11. ears		___ 29. appearance of stomach
___ 12. biceps		___ 30. health
___ 13. chin		___ 31. sex activities
___ 14. body build		___ 32. body hair
___ 15. physical coordination		___ 33. physical condition
___ 16. buttocks		___ 34. face
___ 17. agility		___ 35. weight
___ 18. width of shoulders		

Dimensions of Female and Male Body Esteem

As you recall from Chapter 8, Section 8.3d, factor analysis is a statistical technique that allows researchers to identify clusters of variables that are related to—or *correlated* with—one another. In studying body esteem, researchers have asked many people to evaluate different aspects of their own bodies, such as these 35 body items. When these evaluations have been factor analyzed, the findings suggest that body esteem is not one "thing" but at least three different "things" (Franzoi & Shields, 1984). In other words, when people evaluate their bodies, they do so by evaluating

different dimensions or aspects. These dimensions differ for women and men, meaning that they think about their bodies differently. For example, whereas women are more likely to think about their appetite, waist, and thighs in terms of *weight concern* (how their body looks), men are more likely to think about how these body items affect their *physical condition* (how their body moves).

The Body Esteem Scale identifies three different body esteem dimensions for both sexes. For women, the Sexual Attractiveness subscale measures attitudes toward aspects and functions of the body associated with facial attractiveness and sexuality (especially those that can be enhanced cosmetically); the Weight Concern subscale includes those body parts that can be altered by controlling functions associated with food intake; and the Physical Condition subscale measures attitudes toward stamina, agility, and strength. For men, the Physical Attractiveness subscale measures attitudes toward facial features and aspects of the physique that influence judgments of attractiveness; the Upper-Body Strength subscale measures attitudes toward the upper body (especially those that can be enhanced through anaerobic exercise); and the Physical Condition subscale measures attitudes toward stamina, agility, and general body strength.

Scoring Instructions and Standards

To determine your score for each of the subscales for your sex, simply add up your responses to the items corresponding to each body esteem dimension. For example, for women, to determine self-judgments for the weight concern dimension of body esteem, add up the responses to the 10 items comprising this subscale. For men, the items of "physical coordination" and "figure or physique" are on both the upper-body strength and the physical condition dimensions. The subscale items, plus the means and standard deviations for 964 college men and women (Franzoi & Shields, 1984), are given in the following list:

Women

Sexual attractiveness: Body scent, nose, lips, ears, chin, chest or breasts, appearance of eyes, cheeks/cheekbones, sex drive, sex organs, sex activities, body hair, face (Mean = 46.9, SD = 6.3)

Weight concern: Appetite, waist, thighs, body build, buttocks, hips, legs, figure or physique, appearance of stomach, weight (Mean = 29.9, SD = 8.2)

Physical condition: Physical stamina, reflexes, muscular strength, energy level, biceps, physical coordination, agility, health, physical condition (Mean = 33.3, SD = 5.7)

Men

Physical attractiveness: Nose, lips, ears, chin, buttocks, appearance of eyes, cheeks/cheekbones, hips, feet, sex organs, face (Mean = 39.1, SD = 5.7)

Upper-body strength: Muscular strength, biceps, body build, physical coordination, width of shoulders, arms, chest or breasts, figure or physique, sex drive (Mean = 34.0, SD = 6.1)

Physical condition: Appetite, physical stamina, reflexes, waist, energy level, thighs, physical coordination, agility, figure or physique, appearance of stomach, health, physical condition, weight (Mean = 50.2, SD = 7.7)

Source: From "The Body Esteem Scale: Multidimensional structure and sex differences in a college population" by S. L. Franzoi and S. A. Shields in *Journal of Personality Assessment, 48,* 1984, pp. 173–178. Copyright © 1984. Reprinted by permission of Lawrence Erlbaum Associates.

shows that minority women and lesbians feel less pressure than White heterosexual women to conform to the unrealistic standards of thinness in the larger culture (Franzoi & Chang, 2002). As a result, they are less concerned about dieting and weight loss. This healthier perspective appears to be partly due to a greater valuing of large body sizes in minority and lesbian cultures, but it also may be a by-product of a more general tendency to reject White and heterosexual cultural standards (Grabe & Hyde, 2006).

Despite the fact that minority heterosexual women appear to have greater body satisfaction than White heterosexual women, this does not mean they are unconcerned about weight issues (Stephens & Few, 2007). In general, they are still more dissatisfied with their bodies—particularly their weight—than are heterosexual minority men (Harris, 1995). Similar ambivalent feelings describe lesbian body attitudes (Beren et al., 1997). These findings suggest that Black and lesbian cultural values are often not enough to overcome the dominant White heterosexual cultural standard of female thinness.

What Are Eating Disorders?

As noted, female body dissatisfaction is fairly common in North American culture, with most of the dissatisfaction focused on weight issues. Sometimes this concern with body weight is taken to such extremes that individuals develop *eating disorders* (Polivy et al., 2005). One eating disorder, **anorexia nervosa**, is diagnosed when a person is significantly underweight but still expresses an intense fear of gaining weight or becoming fat. Another related eating disorder is **bulimia nervosa**, which involves recurrent episodes of binge eating—periods of intense, out-of-control eating—followed by drastic measures to compensate for bingeing, such as vomiting, using laxatives, or exercising excessively. A person who is anorexic may also be bulimic. Both eating disorders occur 10 times more frequently among women than men, with about 0.5 to 1.0 percent of women in late adolescence and early adulthood being anorexic and 1 to 3 percent being bulimic (American Psychiatric Association, 1994). Because the body is being systematically starved, both disorders pose severe health risks, including death, if left untreated. Table 13-2 contains information on warning signs of the possible development of an eating disorder.

Because anorexia nervosa and bulimia nervosa occur mostly in women and mostly in weight-conscious cultures, psychologists suspect that sociocultural factors significantly shape these disorders. Anorexia always begins as an attempt to lose weight, and the self-induced vomiting typical of bulimia almost always occurs after a person fails to follow the eating restrictions of a weight-loss diet. Further, adolescent girls who suffer from eating disorders tend to be emotionally insecure and have mothers who obsess about both their own weight and their daughters' weight and appearance (Turner et al., 2005).

No woman can be too slim. …

—Wallis Simpson, the Duchess of Windsor, 1896–1986

Besides being young, a desirable sex partner—especially a woman—should also be fat.

—Observations of the seminomadic Siriono Indians of Bolivia, 1946

Anorexia nervosa An eating disorder in which a person is significantly underweight but still expresses an intense fear of gaining weight or becoming fat

Bulimia nervosa An eating disorder in which a person engages in recurrent episodes of binge eating followed by drastic measures to purge the body of the consumed calories

TABLE 13-2	**Warning Signs of the Development of an Eating Disorder**

- Increased picky eating or food restriction, especially eating only "healthy foods" and becoming a vegetarian
- Regularly fasting and skipping meals, and engaging in dieting behavior involving calorie counting or portion control (weighing and measuring food amounts)
- Reluctance or refusal to eat with others and/or refusing to allow others to prepare foods
- Going to the bathroom immediately after eating, or taking a shower following eating (toilets and showers are the most common sites to purge food)
- Unusual number of episodes described as "stomach flu" (provides an excuse for both food restriction and purging)
- Large amounts of food missing (evidence of bingeing, which often follows food restriction)
- Strong interest in diet books and Internet Web sites related to eating disorders, especially pro-anorexia Web sites that encourage eating-disordered thinking and behavior

Note: If one or more of these warning signs are present, the person in question may be developing—or already has—an eating disorder. Encourage the person to consult both a physician and a mental health professional. This usually means someone besides a family physician because most doctors have had little training or experience with eating disorders. However, a family physician can provide a preliminary medical examination; and if not an expert in this area, the physician often can make referrals to specialists. Listed below is a Web site containing relevant information on eating disorders.

National Eating Disorders Association
http://www.nationaleatingdisorders.org
This not-for-profit organization works to prevent eating disorders and provides treatment referrals to those suffering from anorexia, bulimia, and binge-eating disorder and those concerned with body esteem and weight issues.

The highly critical scrutiny that women with eating disorders direct toward their own and other women's bodies can be described as selective attention to what is perceived as "beautiful" and "ugly." When evaluating themselves, eating-disordered women pay more attention to their "ugly" body parts and less attention to their "beautiful" body parts, which is opposite to the pattern found in healthy women (Jansen et al., 2005). This selective attention is reversed when eating-disordered women evaluate other women's bodies. They are much more likely to notice other women's attractive physical qualities rather than these women's unattractive physical characteristics. Again, healthy women reverse this pattern of selective attention. Thus, women with eating disorders engage in a type of selective attention that reinforces their body dissatisfaction.

What about genetic and motivational influences on eating disorders? A number of studies have found that identical twins are much more likely than fraternal twins to share an eating disorder; and evidence indicates that people with these disorders may have abnormally high levels of certain neurotransmitters that increase their susceptibility to anxiety, depression, and obsessive-compulsive disorder (Hannon-Engel, 2012). The possible association of obsessive-compulsive disorder with eating disorders suggests to some psychologists that the desire to achieve *psychological control* over one's life may influence disordered eating (Bruch, 1982). That is, for some individuals suffering from eating disorders, extreme dieting may represent an attempt to control one important factor in life—weight—and this control becomes a source of power and pride. Related to this motivational explanation is the finding that eating disorders are often associated with a history of sexual, physical, or emotional abuse (Dubosc et al., 2012). Here again, disordered eating may represent abuse victims' attempts to reassert control over their own bodies and lives.

The most important conclusion in understanding eating disorders may be that they are likely determined by multiple factors. Therefore, successful treatment of these disorders should involve multiple interventions, including appropriate medical

Taught from infancy that beauty is women's scepter, the mind shapes itself to the body, and roaming round its gilt cage, only seeks to adorn its prison.

—Mary Wollstonecraft, British author and feminist, 1759–1797

attention, family therapy, individual therapy, group therapy, and behavioral training (Grilo et al., 2012).

13.3c *Aerobic Exercise Can Increase Both Physical and Mental Health.*

Aerobic exercises Sustained exercise that increases heart and lung fitness

Thus far, we have focused on harmful behaviors. What can you do to reduce the likelihood of illness while simultaneously improving your psychological health? **Aerobic exercise**, which is sustained exercise that increases heart and lung fitness, not only has a positive effect on physical health but also provides benefits to mental health (Puetz et al., 2008).

The image that aerobic exercise calls to mind tends to be of rows of sweaty people jazzercising or jogging. However, any activity that increases heart rate into a certain range (defined by your age and maximum possible heart rate) for at least 12 to 20 minutes fits this definition. Thus, vigorous walking, cross-country skiing, in-line skating, dancing, and even strenuous yard work all qualify as aerobic exercise. Accumulating 30 minutes of aerobic exercise three times per week has been recommended for reducing risk for chronic disease and enhancing quality of life (Pate et al., 1995). Consistent with this recommendation, physiological studies indicate that such exercise strengthens the heart, lowers blood pressure, and facilitates the metabolism of fats and carbohydrates. Further, adults who exercise regularly live longer than those who are less active (Hillman et al., 2008).

Does exercise also improve mental health? Based on the results from over 100 studies, mental health experts believe that exercise can be effective in reducing tension and eliminating depressed moods (Blumenthal et al., 2008). For example, in one representative study, 156 adults with major depression were randomly assigned to one of the following regimens: four months of aerobic exercise, treatment with an antidepressant medication, or a combination of both exercise and medication (Babyak et al., 2000). Although a similar number of patients in each group showed mood improvements in the first four months, only those in the exercise groups maintained their improvement after ten months. One possible reason for this beneficial effect is that aerobic exercise heightens the body's supply of mood-enhancing neurotransmitters such as norepinephrine, serotonin, and the endorphins (Salmon, 2001). It is also possible that these mood benefits are partly a side effect of the muscular relaxation and sounder sleep that often follow aerobic exercise (Brannon & Feist, 2000).

Shutterstock

If you want to feel happier, sleep better, and live longer, engage in some form of aerobic exercise for 30 minutes three times per week.

Despite the benefits of regular exercise, it is possible to overdo a good thing. Some athletes *overtrain* to the point where they begin to experience negative effects such as fatigue and depression (O'Connor, 1997). Other people can become obsessed with exercising and feel anxious and uncomfortable if unable to engage in the activity. Such individuals who feel compelled to exercise often have other unhealthy concerns about weight control and body image (Slay et al., 1998).

13.3d *Relaxation Training Is Effective in Reducing Stress and Improving Health.*

Because stress is associated with physiological arousal, many psychologists recommend relaxation training as an effective stress antidote. Two effective relaxation techniques are hypnosis and meditation, discussed in Chapter 5, Sections 5.3b and 5.3c. However, the most basic relaxation technique is **progressive relaxation**, which was developed in the 1920s by Edmund Jacobson (1924). Jacobson started with the observation that it is not possible to be physiologically tense and relaxed at the same time. Although his original technique often required months of training, later modifications by Herbert Benson made progressive relaxation far simpler (Benson, 1975; Benson & Stuart, 1992). Once people develop some skill with this technique, they can use it to calm themselves down anywhere and any time (Bernstein et al., 2007; Klein, 2008).

Progressive relaxation A stress-reducing technique that involves the successive tensing and relaxing of each of the major muscle groups of the body

Progressive relaxation techniques have been used to help heart attack patients manage their stress. For instance, in one study, survivors of a first heart attack were randomly assigned to one of two experimental conditions (Friedman & Ulmer, 1984). In the *medical advice condition*, patients received medical advice about drugs, exercise, work, and diet, whereas in the *relaxation condition*, they were also taught how to relax. Three years after this intervention, the relaxation patients had suffered only half as many repeat heart attacks as those who had only received the standard medical advice. Research suggests that one physiological benefit of relaxation training is an improved immune system (Hewson-Bower & Drummond, 1996; Lowe et al., 2001). In one such experiment, blood samples were taken from college students one month prior to midterm exams and again on the day of the exams (Kiecolt-Glaser et al., 1985). Half the students had been trained in progressive relaxation techniques; the other half received no training. The students who received the relaxation training exhibited much less of a decrease during the testing period in activity of natural killer cells which fight viruses and tumors. Explore It Exercise 13-2 describes the progressive relaxation procedure.

S E L F - D I S C O V E R Y 13-5
Q u e s t i o n n a i r e

How Can You Practice Progressive Relaxation?

Progressive relaxation is an effective technique in managing stress. As originally developed by Edmund Jacobson (1924) and later refined by Herbert Benson (1975), you progressively relax muscle groups in your body, usually starting at the head and slowly moving down to the legs and feet. With practice, you can use this technique to relax quickly and with minimal effort. Practice this technique once or twice daily, but not within two hours after eating a meal, because digestion can interfere with the relaxation response.

Step 1 Sit or lie comfortably with your eyes shut and your arms and legs bent at a comfortable angle. Take a deep breath, hold it, and exhale slowly.

Repeat several times, saying the word *relax* to yourself with each exhale. Step by step, begin tensing different muscle groups one at a time— holding the tension for five seconds, concentrating on how that feels, followed by slowly releasing the tension.

Step 2 Start with your arms by clenching your fists while tensing the muscles in your upper arms. Hold. Slowly release. Inhale and exhale slowly. Maintain a passive attitude and permit relaxation to occur at its own pace. When distracting thoughts occur, do not dwell on them; simply return to repeating *relax* to yourself.

Step 3   Next, tense the thigh and calf muscles in your legs by straightening your legs and pointing your toes downward. Hold. Slowly release. Inhale and exhale slowly.

Step 4   Tense your stomach muscles; at the same time, press your palms together over your chest in order to tighten your chest muscles. Hold. Slowly release. Inhale and exhale slowly.

Step 5   Arch your back and pull your shoulders back (not too far) to tense these muscles. Hold. Slowly release. Inhale and exhale slowly.

Step 6   Tense your jaw and neck muscles by drawing the corners of your mouth back. You may also want to bend your neck first to one side and then the other. Hold. Slowly release. Inhale and exhale slowly.

Step 7   Tense your forehead by pulling your eyebrows together and wrinkling your brow. Hold. Slowly release. Inhale and exhale slowly.

Step 8   Continue to concentrate on your breathing, breathing comfortably into your abdomen (not your chest). Think *relax* with each exhale. Continue this exercise for 10 to 20 minutes. You may open your eyes to check the time, but do not use an alarm. When finished, sit or lie quietly for a few minutes, first with your eyes closed and later with your eyes opened.

Source: Adapted from *The Relaxation Response* by Herbert Benson, M.D., © 1975. Used with permission of the author.

Journey of Discovery

Based on your readings, what tactics can you employ to manage your stress and reduce stress-related ailments?

Shutterstock

Tai chi is a Chinese mind-body relaxation exercise consisting of a series of gentle movements and simple postures. Many elderly adults practice tai chi, which has been shown to be effective in preventing falling injuries due to a loss of balance.

An activity that combines both exercise and relaxation is the ancient Chinese martial arts form of meditation known as *tai chi*. This mind-body relaxation exercise consists of a series of gentle movements and simple postures designed to improve coordination, relieve stress, promote overall well-being, and strengthen the immune system. Typically, these exercise sequences are performed in a slow, relaxed manner over a 30-minute period, with participants focusing their attention on directing life energy ("chi") through the body and mind. In China, many people begin their day by meeting in public places to collectively practice this relaxation exercise. Tai chi is an especially effective exercise activity for elderly adults, and it is becoming increasingly popular in the Untied States. Various studies have found that older adults who participate in tai chi classes show improvements in their breathing, body balance, and overall physical functioning, which reduces their fear of falling (Li et al., 2012).

Section REVIEW

- Altering behaviors can prevent premature death and increase life quality.

- Young adults engage in a variety of risky sexual behaviors that jeopardize their health and well-being.

- Obesity is related to numerous chronic health conditions, including heart disease, diabetes, arthritis, and sleep disorders.

- Body dissatisfaction can lead to eating disorders.

- Reducing meal portions and increasing activity levels can help reduce societal obesity levels.

- Aerobic exercise and progressive relaxation techniques offer many positive influences on health and well-being.

PSYCHOLOGICAL
applications

Who Is Happy and Why?

In 1776, Thomas Jefferson's penning of the Declaration of Independence was a bold assertion that individuals have the inalienable rights of life, liberty, and "the pursuit of happiness." Well over 200 years after this declaration, researchers who promote the scientific study of positive psychology (see Chapter 1, Section 1.2b) have been investigating **happiness**, which is often defined as a predominance of positive over negative emotions, and satisfaction with life as a whole (Gamble & Garling, 2012). These studies indicate that happier people have high self-esteem, are optimistic and outgoing, are physically healthy, and have close friendships or satisfying marriages. When researchers compare very happy people with average and very unhappy people, they find that the very happy are more extraverted, more agreeable, and less neurotic, and they have stronger romantic and social relationships. Among college students, the most common characteristics shared by the 10 percent of the young adults with the highest happiness and the fewest signs of depression were their strong ties to friends and family and their commitment to spending time with them (Diener & Seligman, 2002). Before reading further, complete Self-Discovery Questionnaire 13-5.

Happiness A predominance of positive over negative affect (emotion) and satisfaction with life as a whole

> *Though I am grateful for the blessings of wealth, it hasn't changed who I am. My feet are still on the ground. I'm just wearing better shoes.*
>
> —Oprah Winfrey, American talk-show host, b. 1954

SELF-DISCOVERY 13-6
Questionnaire

How Satisfied Are You with Your Life?

Satisfaction with Life Scale

Directions: Below are five statements that you may agree or disagree with. Using the 1–7 scale below, indicate your agreement with each item by placing the appropriate number on the line following that item. Please be open and honest in your responses.

    1 = Strongly disagree
    2 = Disagree
    3 = Slightly disagree
    4 = Neither agree nor disagree
    5 = Slightly agree
    6 = Agree
    7 = Strongly agree

1. In most ways my life is close to my ideal.____

2. The conditions of my life are excellent.____

3. I am satisfied with my life.____

4. So far I have gotten the important things I want in life.____

5. If I could live my life over, I would change almost nothing. ____

Scoring and Interpretation of the Scale

Add up your answers to the five items and use the following normative score information to help in the interpretation:

Score	Interpretation
5–9	Extremely dissatisfied with your life
10–14	Very dissatisfied with your life
15–19	Slightly dissatisfied with your life
20	About neutral
21–25	Somewhat satisfied with your life
26–30	Very satisfied with your life
31–35	Extremely satisfied with your life

Most Americans score in the 21–25 range. A score above 25 indicates that you are more satisfied than most people. A 22-year study of American men found that life satisfaction peaks at age 65 and then declines, with extraverts having the most stable high levels of happiness (Mroczek & Spiro, 2005). In general, life satisfaction is fairly stable, although a good deal of fluctuation tends to take place around each person's happiness set point (Fujita & Diener, 2005).

Techniques to Increase Your Happiness

Now that you know your life satisfaction score, listed below are four concrete, easy-to-follow, and research-tested techniques to increase your happiness (Snyder et al., 2011; Toepfer et al., 2012).

1. **Develop a hobby.** People are happiest when doing something they enjoy, and sometimes you need a break from even the work that you love. So, develop a hobby or hobbies that engage either your existing skills or skills that you would like to develop.

2. **Count your blessings.** People who keep regular track of their daily "blessings" tend to be happier, healthier, and more energized than those who do not. So, keep a "Gratitude Journal" in which you reflect on your blessings each week.

3. **Act like a happy person.** The facial feedback hypothesis (see Chapter 9, Section 9.5d) contends that your facial expressions can shape your moods. To feel happier, put on a happy face, literally! Consciously smiling and consciously straightening your posture so that it is upright should increase your mood.

4. **Thank your heroes.** Letting others know that you are grateful to them not only makes them feel good but increases your happiness, also. In the next week, write a letter or an email of gratitude to someone who has had a positive impact on your life but whom you have never thanked.

Source for Satisfaction With Life Scale: E. Diener, R. Emmons, J. Larson, & S. Griffin, "The satisfaction with life scale," *Journal of Personality Assessment, 49* (1985): 71–75.

In studying happiness, psychologists have tried to determine what affects both our temporary feelings of happiness and our long-term life satisfaction (Boehm et al., 2011; Lyubomirsky et al., 2011a). Not surprisingly, our moods brighten when we succeed at daily tasks, when others compliment or praise us, and when we feel healthy; however, our moods darken when we fall short of goals, are criticized by others, or feel sick. We also tend to be happier on days associated with weekend leisure activities, such as Fridays and Saturdays, rather than on those associated with work, such as Mondays and Tuesdays (Larsen & Kasimatis, 1990). On average, we experience our most positive moods during the middle of the day (noon to 6:00 P.M.) and our most negative moods in the early morning and late evening (Watson et al., 1999). These mood fluctuations coincide with fluctuations in our circadian rhythms (see Chapter 5, Section 5.2a): We are happiest when at our highest levels of physiological alertness.

How is happiness affected by dramatic events? Although experiencing the death of a loved one or being the victim of a serious accident, illness, or crime can cause extreme emotional conflict, we usually recover most of our previous levels of day-to-day happiness within a year or two (Diener, 2008). This is also the case for dramatically positive events. For example, after the euphoria of winning a state lottery wears off, people usually discover that their overall happiness is unchanged (Brickman et al., 1978). Such research raises the question of whether you can buy happiness. As you can see in Figure 13-5, people in richer countries are happier than people in poorer countries (Myers & Diener, 1995). However, within any given country, the happiness differences between wealthy and middle-income people are modest (Diener et al., 1999). Further, a meta-analysis of 111 independent samples from 54 economically developing countries found that the correlation between people's economic status and their happiness was strongest in low-income, developing countries (Howell & Howell, 2008). Taken together, this research suggests that money matters in increasing happiness, for the most part, only if people do not have enough of it to cover the basic needs of food, safety, and shelter (Diener et al., 1993; Ryan & Deci, 2001). Thus, while having adequate resources to be nourished and safe is essential for happiness, once you meet your basic needs, increasing your wealth does not make you appreciably happier.

One interesting research finding regarding wealth and happiness is that people who strongly desire wealth after satisfying their basic needs tend to be less happy than the average person (Nickerson et al., 2003). This result has been confirmed in developed countries such as the United States and Germany and in less developed countries such as India and Russia (Ryan et al., 1999; Schmuck et al., 2000). Why might this be the case? One possibility is that placing too much importance on material possessions—which do not in themselves satisfy basic psychological needs—takes time and energy away from activities that do satisfy those needs. Thus, overall happiness will be lowered when people pursue their love of money rather than romantic, friendship, or familial love. In addition, people with a high desire to accumulate wealth tend to lose their sense of personal autonomy. Their pursuit of wealth makes them feel controlled by external circumstances.

Another possible explanation for why wealth is not a better predictor of happiness—and also why dramatic life events don't permanently alter levels of day-to-day happiness—is that happiness is a fairly stable trait that is substantially determined by our biology. That is, we may each have a biologically determined baseline level of happiness toward which we gravitate (DeNeve, 1999). For example, in a study of more than 2,000 identical and fraternal twins, David Lykken and Auke Tellegen (1996) analyzed the extent to which identical twins and fraternal twins exhibited similar levels of happiness. The twins' happiness levels were measured by self-report questionnaires that asked them to respond to questions such as: "Taking the good with the bad, how happy and contented are you on the average now, compared with other people?"

FIGURE 13-5

Gross National Product and Happiness

In a 24-nation study, happiness was strongly correlated with gross national product, which is a measure of national prosperity (Myers & Diener, 1995). Additional research indicates that after meeting basic needs, those who still strongly desire wealth tend to be relatively unhappy. So, does money make you happy?

Source: From "Who is Happy?" by D. Myers and E. Diener in *Psychological Science, 6,* 1995, pp. 10–19. Reprinted by permission of Blackwell Publishing Ltd.

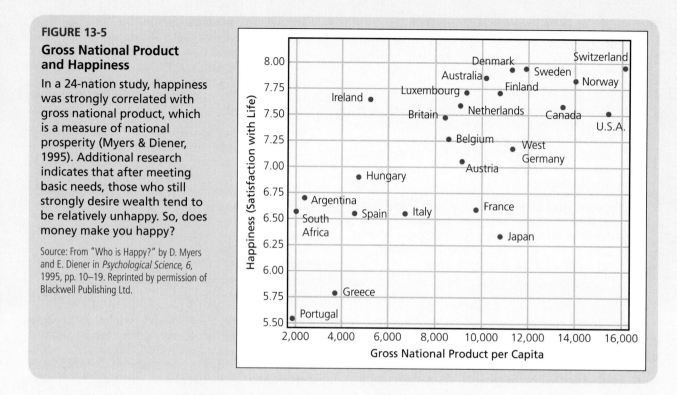

When the twins' happiness scores were correlated, levels of happiness were much more strongly correlated (positively) for the identical twins than for the fraternal twins. Overall, twin studies suggest that between 40 and 50 percent of the variability in happiness can be accounted for by genetics.

Finally, numerous studies indicate that people in individualist cultures report greater levels of happiness than people from cultures with more collectivist orientations (Myers & Diener, 1995). Although some researchers have speculated that these differences are due to quality-of-life factors, others point out that Japan, an economically powerful collectivist country, reports much lower happiness levels than Ireland, an individualist country with a much lower gross national product (Inglehart, 1990). It is possible that people from individualist cultures have been raised to better identify personal, positive feelings that do not rely on the group's well-being (Diener & Diener, 1995). It is also possible that this cultural happiness difference is simply due to the fact that happiness measures have been operationally defined according to individualist standards, such as self-esteem and perceived control over one's life (Lu & Gilmour, 2004). Perhaps people in collectivist cultures are more likely than those in individualist cultures to base their happiness on the extent to which they feel valued by others. Thus, happiness in collectivist cultures may be related more to collectivist values, such as harmony, social integration, and human heartedness, than in individualist cultures (Lu et al., 2001). So, which type of culture is happier? The answer may well depend on how the questions are asked.

If only we'd stop trying to be happy we'd have a pretty good time.

—Edith Wharton, American novelist, 1862–1937

There is no duty we so much underrate as the duty of being happy. By being happy, we sow anonymous benefits upon the world.

—Robert Louis Stevenson, Scottish novelist and poet, 1850–1894

Suggested Websites

Stress by Jim's Big Ego

http://www.bigego.com/index.php?page=songs&display=315&category=noplace_like_nowhere

For an entertaining, musical version of stress, visit this site by Jim's Big Ego, a band from Boston, Massachusetts. (A fast-Internet connection is recommended.)

Something Fishy

http://www.something-fishy.com/

This website focuses on eating disorders, including anorexia, bulimia, overeating, compulsive eating, binge eating, and more, with links to the Eating Disorder FAQ and with poems and stories from others suffering from bulimia and anorexia. The site is updated frequently.

The Medical Bases of Stress, Depression, Anxiety, Sleep Problems, and Drug Use

http://www.teachhealth.com/

This site offers information on recognizing stress in your life, as well as a stress scale, stress tolerance techniques, and links to other related websites.

Body Mass Index

http://www.halls.md/body-mass-index/bmi.htm

The Body Mass Index website allows you to calculate your BMI and compare yourself to other women and men of the same height and age.

Key Terms

Aerobic exercises, 596
Anorexia nervosa, 594
Behavioral medicine, 565
Biopsychosocial model, 566
Body esteem, 593
Bulimia nervosa, 594
Emotion-focused coping, 577
General adaptation syndrome (GAS), 570

Happiness, 600
Health psychologists, 566
Immune system, 573
Obesity, 589
Optimistic explanatory style, 582
Pessimistic explanatory style, 582
Problem-focused coping, 577

Progressive relaxation, 597
Psychoneuroimmunology, 573
Psychophysiological disorders, 573
Social support, 584
Stressors, 566
Stress, 566
Type A behavior pattern, 580
Type B behavior pattern, 580

Review Questions

1. Stressors are events that have been associated with all except which of the following?
   a. threats to our equilibrium
   b. positive events such as childbirth
   c. major cataclysmic events, such as the September 11, 2001, terrorist attacks
   d. strengthening our ability to maintain equilibrium over time
   e. daily hassles

2. What does Selye's general adaptation syndrome describe?
   a. the "fight-or-flight" response
   b. emotional responses to stress
   c. a three-stage physical reaction to stress
   d. the reduction in cortisol that occurs in response to stress
   e. the body's ability to successfully adapt to stress over time

3. Concerning gender differences in the response to stress, which one of the following statements is true?
    a. Men show higher levels of oxytocin released from the pituitary gland than do women.
    b. According to evolutionary theorists, women needed to respond to stress aggressively to protect their children.
    c. Sociocultural theorists argue that girls are raised to think "flight" instead of "fight."
    d. Women more often use a "tend and befriend" response to stress than do men.
    e. After experiencing a stressor, men are more likely than women to seek out members of their own gender to compare experiences.

4. Research on stress-related disease has indicated all except which of the following?
    a. Stress can reduce the efficiency of the immune system.
    b. Strong emotional distress can cause sudden death from heart attacks.
    c. Suppression of the immune system during stress makes your response less efficient.
    d. Anger-inducing stressors may contribute to ischemia.
    e. Both vulnerability and stress are required components of the diathesis-stress model of illness.

5. Which of the following is true of the biopsychosocial perspective?
    a. It was favored by medical researchers in the 1940s.
    b. It fails to consider the role of cognitive appraisal in stress.
    c. It was the foundation of Selye's GAS.
    d. It was discounted by research showing that psychological awareness of stressors is a necessary component in the stress response.
    e. It assumes that stress-related illness is caused by a complex interaction of factors.

6. What does research on stress responses show about cognitive appraisal of stressful events?
    a. It is an unconscious decision-making process.
    b. It involves both primary and secondary appraisal processes.
    c. It is universal and not affected by individuals' feelings of competence.
    d. It occurs after having determined that a threat exists.
    e. It results in taking appropriate action in threatening or stressful situations.

7. In general, stress-related research has found all except which of the following to be true?
    a. The negative effects of stress are cumulative.
    b. Men and women generally have different responses to stress.
    c. Individuals with low self-esteem are likely to use a problem-focused coping strategy.
    d. Focusing on the controllable aspects of uncontrollable situations such as caregiving helps reduce stress.
    e. Communication between the immune system and the brain plays a major role in the response to stressful events.

8. On what does the success of a particular coping strategy depend?
    a. the stressor's controllability
    b. using a problem-focused strategy rather than an emotion-focused strategy
    c. taking an active approach to removing the source of the threat
    d. controlling one's emotional response first, followed by controlling one's cognitive response
    e. its consistency; that is, you should choose one strategy and seek to perfect it

9. Which of the following has research on stress and personality found?
    a. Optimistic explanatory styles are detrimental because they lead to denial of real threats.
    b. Mistrust of others is more harmful to one's health than anger.
    c. There is no difference in functioning between optimists' and pessimists' immune systems.
    d. Pessimists explain uncontrollable negative events as due to external factors and positive events as due to internal factors.
    e. Type A behavior patterns are toxic because they often include a component of cynical hostility.

10. Having a strong base of social support has been associated with all except which of the following?
    a. beneficial effects on self-esteem related to being taken care of by others
    b. a stronger immune response to stress
    c. gaining information concerning how to understand and emotionally respond to stressors
    d. reduced control over the stressor due to increased dependence on others
    e. benefits related to expressing our feelings

11. Which of the following is true regarding religion and health?
    a. Religious beliefs are not related to health.
    b. Cancer fatality rates are actually higher among those who believe in God.
    c. Religious people have greater optimism than others, which helps them handle stress better.
    d. Only people who follow a monotheistic religion experience better health.
    e. All of the above

12. When does weight gain occur?
    a. when energy intake exceeds energy expenditure
    b. when energy expenditure exceeds energy intake
    c. only when there is a genetic predisposition to obesity
    d. only when there is a lack of will power
    e. None of the above is true—weight control is arbitrary.

13. Which of the following has contributed to the increase in food intake and ultimately obesity rates in the United States?
    a. Restaurants are using larger plates than in the past.
    b. Cookbooks are specifying fewer portions than in the past for the same recipe.
    c. Cup holders in cars are larger than in the past.
    d. Restaurant servings are 2 to 5 times larger than in the past.
    e. All of the above

14. Which of the following is true about eating disorders such as anorexia nervosa and bulimia nervosa?
    a. They occur 3 times more often in women than men.
    b. Both involve the body being systematically starved.
    c. They are associated more with low self-esteem than with sociocultural factors.
    d. They represent learned behaviors; there is no evidence to suggest a genetic component.
    e. They are completely separate disorders; they never occur together in the same individual.

16. Which of the following is true about physiological methods of decreasing stress?
    a. They are less effective than relaxation, meditation, or hypnosis.
    b. They are effective only if they contain an aerobic exercise component.
    c. They include relaxation, associated with a huge decrease in natural killer cell activity.
    d. Those such as moderate aerobic exercise and progressive relaxation are highly effective.
    e. They do not work as well as standard medical advice in reducing heart attacks.

17. What has research on happiness found?
    a. The pursuit of wealth may decrease one's sense of autonomy.
    b. Happiness is a highly unstable characteristic, substantially determined by our environment.
    c. Dramatic life events permanently alter one's characteristic level of happiness.
    d. People in collectivist cultures report greater levels of happiness than those in individualistic cultures.
    e. Happiness is based on biological factors; thus, faith and optimism do not generate greater levels of happiness.

Answers: 1. d 2. c 3. d 4. c 5. e 6. b 7. c 8. a 9. e 10. a 11. c 12. e 13. e 14. e 15. b 16. d 17. a

Shutterstock

Chapter Fourteen

Understanding Social Behavior

Chapter Outline

Psychological Applications: *How Can You Cope with Jealousy?*

"Your lecture saved my life!"

*I*t isn't often—make that it's *almost never*—that a college professor hears these words from a student and can take them as literal truth. Yet I had this experience last year during final-exams week. While working in my office, I looked up to see one of my introductory psychology students standing there, visibly shaken, as she made this pronouncement after having had a life-threatening encounter over the weekend. My student, Ferris, had been waiting at a bus stop not far from campus on a Saturday evening when a neatly dressed man walked up to her, put a gun to her stomach, and demanded that she hand over her purse. She was stunned and paralyzed with fear. When she didn't immediately respond, the assailant put the gun to her head and repeated his demand. Ferris noticed that people waiting across the street at another bus stop were watching her plight, but no one was taking action to help. In that moment Ferris recalled the last five minutes of my semester-ending lecture the previous morning, when I'd said to the assembled students, "And now I'm going to tell you something that may one day save your life."

Now, in my office, Ferris said that when I'd ended my lecture with this five-minute recitation of "life-saving" instructions, she dutifully wrote down the information because she thought I might test the class on it during our final exam the following week. However, she hadn't put much stock into the advice. What I'd told students was how bystanders often react—or don't react—when they witness an emergency in which a stranger needs help. My information was based on a series of social psychological experiments conducted in the 1960s by John Darley and Bibb Latané (see Section 14.4d). Listening to the lecture, Ferris had scoffed to herself, "People wouldn't just stand around when someone needs help!" Luckily, however, she continued listening as I told the class what these two social psychologists had discovered about the social dynamics of emergency situations and what was necessary to encourage others to intervene when help was needed. It was this

knowledge that Ferris drew upon that Saturday night in the moments when the mugger's gun was pointed at her head. And it is this knowledge that Ferris believes probably saved her life.

Now, I am not claiming that this chapter will similarly affect your life, but I am telling you that the reason I love the field of social psychology is that it attempts to understand the social dynamics of everyday living with other people. **Social psychology** is the scientific study of how people's thoughts, feelings, and behavior are influenced by others. Here, perhaps more than in any other leg of this discovery journey in psychology, you can seek answers to a number of questions that you have probably pondered on your own personal journey of discovery. First, you will examine how we judge our social world (social perception and prejudice). Second, you will study how we develop attitudes toward people and events. Third, you will analyze how those around us shape us (social influence). Fourth, you will learn about the factors that either strengthen or weaken our antisocial and prosocial behaviors (aggression and helping). And finally, you will be introduced to some scientific insights about interpersonal attraction and romantic love. Along the way, I promise to tell you what I told Ferris and her fellow students on our last day of class. Let's begin.

> **Social psychology** The scientific discipline that attempts to understand and explain how the thoughts, feelings, and behavior of individuals are influenced by others

14.1 Social Perception

> **Social perception** The way we seek to know and understand other persons and events; also known as *social cognition*

The way we seek to understand other people and events is known as **social perception**, and it can be roughly classified into two areas: impression formation and attribution. This section examines both of these social perception processes.

14.1a The First Step in Impression Formation Is Categorizing People into Groups.

Imagine that you are walking down a dark city street at night with no one in sight. Suddenly, you notice the outline of a person walking toward you, three blocks away. At a distance of one block, you can tell that this person is a man. In less than a minute, your paths will cross. Are you in danger?

Every day you judge people, and often you must react to them based on very little information. How do you "size up" others during initial encounters? As on the hypothetical dark street, the process of gathering information about others can be

> *Labels are devices for saving talkative persons the trouble of thinking.*
>
> —John Morley, English statesman and author, 1838–1923

of vital importance to your health and safety. **Impression formation** is the process by which you combine various sources of information about a person into an overall judgment. It is like developing a theory of a person and then using this theory as a guideline in your actions toward her or him.

In our hypothetical nighttime dilemma, the way you respond to the person approaching you will be determined by how you categorize him (Gawronski et al., 2003). As discussed in Chapter 8, Section 8.2a, human beings are categorizing creatures. That is, we identify objects—including other people—according to features that distinguish them from other objects. In social categorization, physical features such as race, sex, age, and attractiveness are the most common ways to classify people, especially during first encounters. Because these categories are used so often, labeling others according to superficial physical features becomes automatic, often occurring without conscious thought or effort (Dijksterhuis, 2010).

14.1b Categorizing People into Groups Can Lead to Stereotyping.

Not only do we group people into different categories, but we also develop beliefs about them. These social beliefs, which are often learned from others, are called **stereotypes** (Jussim et al., 2009). Stereotypes are fixed sets of beliefs about people that put them into categories and don't allow for individual variation. In a very real sense, stereotypes are "shortcuts to thinking" that provide us with information about individuals we do not personally know. Returning to our nighttime example, your stereotypical beliefs about encountering a strange man on a dark, deserted city street would probably result in greater apprehension than if the stranger were a woman or a child.

Although stereotyping people can speed up our social judgments, these cognitive shortcuts can also inhibit our thinking, especially when those who are stereotyped are not members of our ingroup. An **ingroup** is a group to which we belong and that forms a part of our social identity, whereas an **outgroup** is any group with which we do not share membership. Research and everyday experience inform us that we are much more likely to stereotype outgroup members.

For example, in one study, Galen Bodenhausen (1988) asked mostly White college students to act as mock jurors in a court case. Some students were told that the defendant's name was Carlos Ramirez, and others were told that his name was Robert Johnson. The researchers assumed that students would categorize Carlos Ramirez as an outgroup member, while categorizing the Anglo-sounding Robert Johnson as an ingroup member. Half the students in each of these experimental conditions were given information about the case before learning the defendant's name, whereas the other half were given the information afterward. Bodenhausen predicted that hearing the Hispanic-sounding name "Carlos Ramirez" before receiving the evidence would activate students' ethnic stereotypes and that this activation would bias their processing of the information. In other words, instead of "weighing the facts," these students were expected to pay more attention to stereotype-consistent information than to stereotype-inconsistent information. This is exactly what Bodenhausen found. The imaginary Carlos Ramirez was found guilty more often than the imaginary Robert Johnson only when students had learned the name before receiving the evidence. Bodenhausen also found that stereotypes influence information processing by increasing the amount of attention to and rehearsal of stereotype-consistent information.

Impression formation The process of integrating various sources of information about a person into an overall judgement

Stereotypes Fixed sets of beliefs about people that put them into categories and don't allow for individual variation

Ingroup A group to which we belong and that forms a part of our social identity

Outgroup Any group with which we do not share membership

This study, along with others, suggests that one of the important reasons why stereotyping often results in fast yet false social judgments is that filtering social perceptions through a stereotype causes us to ignore information that is relevant but inconsistent with the stereotype. Other studies found that when stereotypes are evoked from memory, they can lead to creation of false memories consistent with the stereotypes (Lenton et al., 2001). Thus, in addition to inhibiting thinking, stereotypes can also promote thinking that leads to false judgments. Together, these studies inform us that although stereotyping may often help us when we need to make quick decisions, the cost is that we may sometimes make faulty judgments about whomever we stereotype.

14.1c *There Is a Physical Attractiveness Stereotype*

As mentioned, when we first meet someone, their physical appearance is generally the first thing we notice, especially if they somehow look different from the average person. Despite the frequently quoted folk saying "You can't judge a book by its cover," we tend to ignore the wisdom contained within this phrase. Instead, research indicates that we perceive physically attractive people as more sociable, dominant, sexually attractive, mentally healthy, intelligent, and socially skilled than those who are unattractive (Feingold, 1992; Jackson et al., 1995). The appeal of physical attractiveness can even be observed in brain-scan studies where those who are shown photos of attractive faces have greater activation in brain areas associated with more positive emotions compared to when they are shown photos of unattractive faces (Karraker & Stern, 1990; Principe & Langlois, 2011).

This **physical attractiveness stereotype** is not reserved solely for adults but is found in all age groups (Karraker & Stern, 1990). As a species, we are drawn to physically attractive people, like bees to honey (Buss, 1987; Davis, 1990). This is especially true for men (Marcus & Miller, 2003). However, in initial encounters or when considering a one-night stand, women, like men, tend to place a high value on physical attractiveness (Bryan et al., 2011; Luo & Zhang, 2009).

Physical attractiveness stereotype The belief that physically attractive individuals possess socially desirable personality traits and lead happier, more fulfilling lives than less attractive persons do

Shutterstock

Individuals who are physically attractive are often assumed to possess more socially desirable personality traits than those who are physically unattractive. Is this physical attractiveness stereotype accurate?

INFO-BIT The physical attractiveness stereotype also occurs in collectivist cultures, but somewhat different cultural values shape its content (Chen et al., 1997). For example, like physically attractive people in individualist cultures, physically attractive Koreans are perceived to be more sexually warm, mentally healthy, intelligent, and socially skilled than unattractive Koreans. However, consistent with the emphasis on harmonious relationships in collectivist cultures, physically attractive Koreans are also assumed to have higher integrity and be more concerned for others than those who are physically unattractive (Wheeler & Kim, 1997).

Within a given culture and during a given time period, people generally agree on what defines physical attractiveness. What is beautiful also often conforms to the current standards of the dominant social group. For example, fine facial features and light skin have been standards for physical attractiveness in North American culture for many generations, and ethnic minority groups have generally mirrored these larger cultural preferences (Hill, 2002; Bond & Cash, 1992).

What shapes beauty standards besides the dominant cultural values? Evolutionary theorists believe that the traits valued as desirable and attractive in men and women are those that increase their ability to produce offspring (Buss, 1988; Kenrick & Trost, 1987). Researchers have identified two beauty standards that may be related to reproductive fitness: Weight, and its relationship to waist-to-hip ratios, influences perceptions of female attractiveness, and facial features influence both sexes but in different ways.

Regarding weight and waist-to-hip ratios, cross-cultural studies find that men worldwide are generally attracted to women who have a lower waist-to-hip ratio, meaning that the circumference of their waist is smaller than that of their hips (Furnham et al., 2003). The most desirable waist-to-hip ratio appears to be 0.7, so a desirable woman with a waist of 25 inches would have a 35-inch hip size, or a desirable woman with a 35-inch waist would have 50-inch hips (Streeter & McBurney, 2003). Evolutionary psychologists contend that this 0.7 waist-to-hip ratio is universally perceived as attractive because it is a biologically accurate indicator that the woman is young and fertile but currently not pregnant—and therefore sexually available. According to this argument, over the course of human evolution, those men who mated with women with a waist-to-hip ratio of about 0.7 were most likely to successfully conceive an offspring. Consistent with this reasoning, research indicates that deviations from the 0.7 ratio are associated with decreases in fertility (Van Hooff et al., 2000).

Cross-cultural research suggests that, in addition to the waist-to-hip ratio, there may be universal standards of facial attractiveness (Cunningham et al., 2002; Zebrowitz & Rhodes, 2002). Among heterosexuals, possessing youthful or slightly *immature* facial features (large eyes, small nose, full lips, small chin, delicate jaw) enhances female attractiveness, while *mature* facial characteristics related to social dominance (small eyes, broad forehead, thick eyebrows, thin lips, large jaw) increase attractiveness of males. In commenting on these preferences for mature facial features in males and slightly immature features in females, various social scientists have argued that it suggests a dominant-submissive preference in heterosexual beauty standards. Essentially, heterosexual women and men engage in a *looks-for-status exchange*, in which women exchange their beauty for their mate's social power, and men exchange their social power for their partner's beauty (Fletcher et al., 2004).

In searching for an explanation for this looks-for-status exchange, evolutionary theorists contend that what is valued as desirable and attractive in men and women

In the Old Testament, the older and powerful King David pursues and ultimately possesses the young and beautiful Bathsheba. Throughout history and in cultures around the globe, mate selection has involved this sort of youth-for-status exchange. What explanations do evolutionary and sociocultural theorists offer for this gender difference?

is that which increases their probability of producing offspring who will carry their genes to the next generation (Wade, 2003). Given the biological fact that women have a shorter time span to reproduce than do men, evolution predisposes men to perceive women who *look young* as being most desirable (that is, more physically attractive), because youth implies high reproductive potential. Using this same evolutionary logic, women are much more likely to value maturity over youthfulness in a mate, because a somewhat older man is generally a better provider for his children than is a young man, while still being functionally fertile (Buss, 1989, 1990). Male status, ambition, and other signs of *social dominance* trump youthful male looks.

In contrast to this evolutionary explanation, other social scientists maintain that men seek beauty in a woman and women seek power in a man because of the widely different social statuses they have historically held in society. This sociocultural explanation argues that women have been excluded from power and are viewed by men as objects of exchange in the social marketplace (Eagly & Wood, 1999). Men place a premium on the quality or the beauty of this exchange object, and that is why physical attractiveness is sought in a woman. Because of their historically low status and their restricted ability to socially advance based on their own individual skills, women have been forced to tie their social advancement with the status of their mate. Thus, women seek men who are socially dominant and can be "good providers."

Which of these perspectives provides the best explanation is currently a hotly debated question. If the sociocultural perspective is correct, recent social advances made by many women in North American and European countries (higher pay and increased social status) may cause shifts in the attractiveness preferences of both women and men. Women may look for more "beauty" in men, and men may look for more "economic status" in women.

A handful of studies suggest that such changes may be taking place. For example, in Spain, a content analysis of personal ads in newspapers found that while the overall preferences in what men and women seek in a mate are consistent with predictions from evolutionary theory, there was an age difference in women's preferences consistent with sociocultural predictions (Gil-Burmann et al., 2002). Unlike older Spanish women, those younger than age 40 sought mainly physical attractiveness in men, not socioeconomic status. These changes in mate preferences among younger women may be at least partly caused by the financial independence these women were enjoying due to their own careers. Similarly, in the United States researchers examined male mate preferences by posting four "female seeking male" personal ads on Internet bulletin boards (Strassberg & Holty, 2003). Results indicated that the ad that described a woman as "financially independent ... successful [and] ambitious" generated over 50 percent more responses than the ad that described a woman as "lovely ... very attractive and slim."

If future research provides additional evidence that mate preferences are indeed changing, this would not necessarily mean that evolutionary forces don't shape perceptions of attractiveness. It may simply mean that, in this instance, more powerful cultural forces have overridden inherited tendencies.

14.1d *Prejudice Is an Attitude and Discrimination Is an Action.*

The physical attractiveness stereotype illustrates how we treat people differently based on the degree to which their physical appearance matches our standards of beauty. When the stereotypes associated with a particular group of people—such as the physically unattractive—are negative and condescending, they can form the basis for prejudice and discrimination. **Prejudice** is defined as an attitude toward members of a specific group that directly or indirectly suggests they deserve an inferior social status (Jackson, 2011; Ufkes et al., 2012). Disliking, disrespecting, and/or resenting people because of their group membership are examples of prejudice. In contrast, **discrimination** is a negative and/or patronizing action toward members of a specific social group. Failing to hire people for jobs because of their group membership is an example of discrimination (Hebl et al., 2002). As its intensity heightens, discrimination may produce actions resulting in violence and death (Hepworth & West, 1988).

How Does Intergroup Competition Cause Prejudice?

Social psychologists have investigated various factors that cause prejudice and discrimination. One social cause is competition between groups. According to **realistic group conflict theory**, when two groups compete for scarce resources such as jobs, housing, consumer sales, or even food, this competition creates a breeding ground for prejudice (Gaunt, 2011; Levine & Campbell, 1972). Realistic group conflict theory contends that when groups are in conflict, two important changes occur in each group. The first change involves increased hostility toward the opposing outgroup, and the second change involves an intensification of ingroup loyalty. This pattern of behavior is referred to as **ethnocentrism** (Cohen et al., 2006).

One of the first studies to test the hypotheses derived from realistic group conflict theory was the Robbers' Cave study conducted by Muzafer Sherif and his colleagues in the summer of 1954 at the Robbers' Cave State Park in Oklahoma (Sherif et al., 1961; Sherif & Sherif, 1956).

Prejudice Attitudes toward members of specific groups that directly or indirectly suggest they deserve an inferior social status

Discrimination A negative and/or patronizing action toward members of a specific social group

Realistic group conflict theory A theory of prejudice contending that when two groups compete for scarce resources, this competition creates a breeding ground for prejudice

Ethnocentrism A pattern of increased hostility toward outgroups, accompanied by increased loyalty to one's ingroup

If we accept and acquiesce in the face of discrimination, we accept the responsibility ourselves and allow those responsible to salve their conscience by believing that they have our acceptance and concurrence. ... We should, therefore, protest openly everything ... that smacks of discrimination.

—Mary McLeod Bethune, U.S. educator and civil rights activist, 1875–1955

Since September 11, 2001, individuals identified as Muslim have been targeted with both prejudice and discrimination in the United States. What is the distinction between prejudice and discrimination?

Participants were twenty White, middle-class, well-adjusted, 11- and 12-year-old boys that had never met one another. In advance, the researchers divided the boys into two groups, with one group leaving by bus for the camp a day before the other group. Upon arrival, each group was assigned a separate cabin out of sight of the other, and thus, neither knew of the other's existence. The camp counselors were actually the researchers who unobtrusively observed and recorded day-to-day camp events as the study progressed.

The study had three phases. The first phase was devoted to creating ingroups, the second was devoted to *instilling intergroup competition*, and the third involved *encouraging intergroup cooperation*. During the first week of ingroup creation, each group separately engaged in cooperative camp activities and developed its own unique identity. One group named itself the "Rattlers" and spent a good deal of time cursing and swearing, while the other group called itself the "Eagles" and instituted a group norm forbidding profanity. As the first week drew to a close, each group became aware of the other's existence; and that's when ingroup-outgroup tensions flared: *"They* better not be in *our* swimming hole!" *"Those* guys are using *our* baseball diamond again!"

During the study's second phase, Sherif tested his hypothesis that intergroup competition would cause prejudice by creating a weeklong tournament between the two groups, consisting of 10 athletic events such as baseball, football, and tug-of-war. True to expectations, the intergroup conflict transformed these normal, well-adjusted boys into what a naive observer would have thought were "wicked, disturbed, and vicious" youngsters (Sherif, 1966, p. 58). The researchers observed a sudden increase in ethnocentrism by both groups. The number of unflattering names used to refer to outgroup members increased (for example, "pig" and "cheater"), while negative attitudes that previously existed between some ingroup members were now redirected toward the outgroup. Soon, intergroup hostility escalated from name calling to acts of physical aggression.

The third phase of the study was designed to reverse the hostility, a task that proved to be much more difficult to accomplish than the others. Simple noncompetitive contact between the groups did not ease tensions. For example, when the two groups were brought together for a meal, food was more likely to be thrown at opposing group members than eaten! Sherif and his colleagues hypothesized that to reduce intergroup conflict they needed to introduce what they called a *superordinate goal*, which is a mutually shared goal that can be achieved only through intergroup cooperation. To test this hypothesis, the researchers arranged for a series of problem situations to develop over the course of the next six days, such as the failure of the camp's water supply or the breakdown of the camp bus. At first, the groups responded to these emergencies by trying to solve the problem on their own, without the other group's assistance. However, when they discovered that intergroup cooperation was necessary, they began to work together, which resulted in a gradual easing of tensions and new friendships forming between the previously competing group members.

The Robbers' Cave study is an excellent example of how ethnocentrism can develop when two groups compete for scarce resources. It also demonstrates that having a superordinate goal can lead to peaceful coexistence between previously

Figure 3, Chapter 5, in Sherif, M., Harvey, O. J., White, B. J., Hood, W. R., & Sherif, C. (1961). Intergroup conflict and cooperation: The Robbers' Cave experiment. Norman, OK: Oklahoma Book Exchange.

The Robbers' Cave study created intergroup hostility between two groups of boys at a summer camp by having them compete against one another. What theory explains how prejudice formed between these two groups due to their competitive relationship?

antagonistic groups. Although this study used children as participants, similar results have been obtained with adult samples (Jackson, 1993; Zárate et al., 2004).

Is There Such a Thing as Unconscious Prejudice?

Intergroup competition often results in open expression of prejudicial feelings, but many instances of prejudice are subtle and difficult to detect. One reason for this is that people who hold prejudicial attitudes often do not openly express them because they realize that such attitudes are socially unacceptable. So, instead, they consciously conceal their biases from others and publicly express nonprejudiced views. However, on occasion, when their social guard is down and they behave spontaneously, they may unintentionally reveal these prejudices (Crandall & Eshleman, 2003; Vezzali et al., 2012).

Although some people consciously attempt to deceive others about their prejudice, other people's prejudice may be relatively unconscious, meaning they harbor prejudicial attitudes without being aware of it (Dovidio, 2001). *Explicit prejudice* involves consciously holding prejudicial attitudes toward a group; *implicit prejudice* involves unconsciously holding those attitudes. Individuals with implicit prejudicial attitudes may honestly believe they are not prejudiced, even while they react negatively toward people in the target group. In most instances, individuals who are implicitly prejudiced have explicit attitudes toward the target group that are relatively positive (Wilson et al., 2000).

How is it possible to react in a prejudiced manner toward others without realizing you are doing so? During such interactions, these individuals consciously focus on their positive attitudes toward the target group and actively monitor and regulate their behavior to convey warmth and friendliness. Simultaneously, they try to ignore the feelings of discomfort induced by their implicit prejudice.

How do people from the target group react while conversing with individuals who are implicitly prejudiced? Based on past interactions with such individuals, people from the target group may have learned to attend not only to these individuals' consciously constructed self-presentations but also to their nonverbal behavior for evidence of implicit prejudice. Nonverbal behaviors related to negative arousal and tension in face-to-face interactions may include excessive blinking, gaze aversion, and forced smiles. When people from the target group detect these behaviors, they feel more uncomfortable and less satisfied with the interaction than the implicitly prejudiced individuals (Vorauer & Kumhyr, 2001).

Examining both sides of this social exchange, it is understandable why the two conversational partners often have very different reactions (Hyers & Swim, 1998). Implicitly prejudiced individuals pay the most attention to their consciously held positive attitudes and overtly friendly self-presentations. As a result, they often walk away feeling relieved that things "went well" and comforted in the knowledge that they indeed are not prejudiced. In contrast, their partners from the target group pay the most attention to the others' less consciously controlled—and less friendly—nonverbal behaviors, and often walk away feeling angry and certain that they have just encountered another prejudiced person.

Can We Break the Prejudice Habit?

The research discussed thus far suggests that stereotyping and prejudice are social problems that are often difficult to change. Yet change can and does occur for those of us who want to reduce our prejudicial responding. For example, imagine that Virginia, a young White woman, has grown up being taught that Black people are intellectually

BVT *Lab*

Flashcards are available for this chapter at **www.BVTLab.com**.

inferior to Whites and has developed prejudicial views based on this upbringing. However, during the course of her life, Virginia has also been exposed to a number of people who do not fit this racial stereotype. Because of these experiences, she may begin to adopt a more accepting view of Blacks. Although Virginia no longer accepts the negative racial stereotype, she has not eliminated it from her memory. Quite the contrary. During her relearning process, the stereotype may well be more frequently activated from memory than her newly adopted beliefs. In a very real sense, for a person like Virginia who wants to be less prejudiced, censoring the negative stereotype and guarding against prejudicial thinking takes conscious and deliberate attention—like breaking a bad habit.

Take a look at Figure 14-1, which outlines how self-awareness and self-regulation may play a role in reducing prejudiced responses. Whenever Virginia encounters a Black person, the racial stereotype is likely to be involuntarily activated. If she does not consciously monitor her thoughts, she may automatically slip back into acting as though Blacks were intellectually inferior (a discrepant response). Becoming aware of this discrepancy in her actions, Virginia will feel guilty. In turn, this guilt will motivate her to heighten her self-awareness and search her memory for the situations that trigger these prejudiced responses (Iyer et al., 2003). Through such attentiveness,

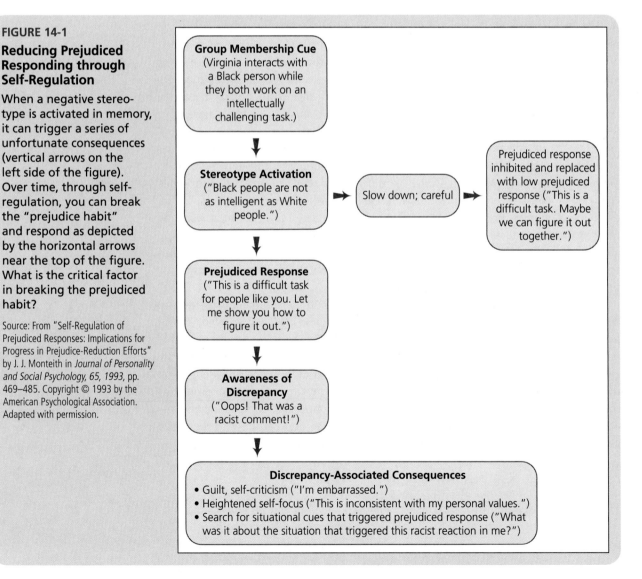

FIGURE 14-1

Reducing Prejudiced Responding through Self-Regulation

When a negative stereotype is activated in memory, it can trigger a series of unfortunate consequences (vertical arrows on the left side of the figure). Over time, through self-regulation, you can break the "prejudice habit" and respond as depicted by the horizontal arrows near the top of the figure. What is the critical factor in breaking the prejudiced habit?

Source: From "Self-Regulation of Prejudiced Responses: Implications for Progress in Prejudice-Reduction Efforts" by J. J. Monteith in *Journal of Personality and Social Psychology, 65, 1993*, pp. 469–485. Copyright © 1993 by the American Psychological Association. Adapted with permission.

Group Membership Cue
(Virginia interacts with a Black person while they both work on an intellectually challenging task.)

Stereotype Activation
("Black people are not as intelligent as White people.")

Slow down; careful

Prejudiced response inhibited and replaced with low prejudiced response ("This is a difficult task. Maybe we can figure it out together.")

Prejudiced Response
("This is a difficult task for people like you. Let me show you how to figure it out.")

Awareness of Discrepancy
("Oops! That was a racist comment!")

Discrepancy-Associated Consequences
- Guilt, self-criticism ("I'm embarrassed.")
- Heightened self-focus ("This is inconsistent with my personal values.")
- Search for situational cues that triggered prejudiced response ("What was it about the situation that triggered this racist reaction in me?")

Virginia will slowly be able to monitor and control her prejudicial responding (Monteith, 1993).

The lesson here is that you can avoid prejudiced responding if low-prejudiced standards are central to your self-concept and you bring these standards to mind before acting (Macrae et al., 1998). Although the activation of stereotypes from memory makes nonprejudiced responding difficult, you can inhibit such intolerance by consciously and carefully paying attention to what you are thinking. The crucial factor is the strength of your motivation: How committed are you to thinking and acting in a nonprejudiced manner?

14.1e *Explanations of People's Behavior Hinge on Either Internal or External Attributions.*

Imagine going shopping and encountering a clerk who does not smile or talk to you while she adds up your purchases. What explains her behavior? The process by which we use information to make inferences about the causes of behavior or events is called **attribution**. Why are we so interested in making attributions about other people's behavior? Put simply, if we think we know why people behave the way they do, we will be much more likely to view the world as coherent and controllable than if we have no clue as to their intentions and dispositions (Heider, 1958).

In making attributions, the most important judgment concerns whether we attribute a given action to internal qualities of the person or to external factors of the situation. An **internal attribution** consists of any explanation that locates the cause as inside the person, such as personality traits, moods, attitudes, abilities, or effort. An **external attribution** consists of any explanation that locates the cause as outside the person, such as the actions of others, the nature of the situation, or luck. When a clerk at a store doesn't smile at you, you may infer that she is rude and unfriendly (an internal attribution), or you may infer that she is distracted or having a bad day (an external attribution). The attribution you make will guide your future actions toward this person.

Harold Kelley (1967) developed an influential theory of how people make attributions about the actions of others (whom Kelley called *actors*). According to his **covariation model**, human beings are rational and logical observers, behaving much like naive scientists in the way they test their hypotheses about the behavior of actors. Just as a scientist arrives at a judgment of causality by noticing that a particular variable is associated with a particular effect across a number of different conditions, Kelley asserted that people make causal judgments about everyday events. For example, imagine being grilled by your parents when you tell them that you are going out for the evening with your friend Bart Simpson. Why are they so concerned? What explains their behavior?

In making an attribution for their behavior toward you spending time with Bart, the covariation model predicts that you would rely on the *covariation principle*, which states that for something to be the cause of a particular effect, it must be present when the effect occurs and absent when it does not occur. In other words, the presumed cause (Bart) and the observed effect (parents' grilling) must "covary." Whenever a particular effect (parents' grilling) has several possible causal explanations, you are much less likely to attribute the event to any particular cause (Morris & Larrick, 1995).

How do you narrow down the possible causal explanations? In assessing covariation, Kelley stated that people rely on three basic kinds of information. *Consensus* information deals with the extent to which other people (for example, other parents or your other friends) react in the same way to the stimulus object (Bart), as do the actors (your parents). *Consistency* information concerns the extent to which the actors react to this stimulus object in the same way on other occasions.

Attribution The process by which people use information to make inferences about the causes of behaviors or events

Internal attribution An attribution that identifies the cause of behavior as factors internal to the person, such as personality traits, moods, attitudes, abilities, or effort

External attribution An attribution that identifies the cause of behavior as factors external to the person, such as luck, other people, or the situation

Covariation model A theory of attribution asserting that people rely on consensus, consistency, and distinctiveness information when assigning causes for events

FIGURE 14-2   Why Did My Parents React Negatively to My Spending Time with Bart Simpson?

Available Information			What is the likely Attribution?
Low Consensus No one else is suspicious of Bart.	+ **High Consistency** My parents are always suspicious of Bart.	+ **Low Distinctiveness** My parents are suspicious of all my friends. =	**Internal Attribution** My parents' suspicions are caused by something within them: They are distrustful, suspicious people.
High Consensus Everybody is suspicious of Bart.	+ **High Consistency** My parents are always suspicious of Bart.	+ **High Distinctiveness** My parents are not suspicious of any of my other friends. =	**External Attribution** My parents' suspicions are caused by something outside them: Bart is not a trustworthy person.
Low Consensus No one else is suspicious of Bart.	+ **Low Consistency** My parents have never been suspicious of Bart before.	+ **High Distinctiveness** My parents are not suspicious of any of my other friends. =	**External Attribution** My parents' suspicions are caused by something outside them: Bart may have done something recently to raise my parents' suspicions.

Finally, *distinctiveness* information refers to the extent to which the actors react in the same way to other, different stimulus objects (for example, your other friends).

In Figure 14-2, I've outlined how Kelley's theory might predict specific attributions about your parents' behavior. For consensus, you would look at the behavior of other people: Is everybody suspicious and wary of Bart Simpson (high consensus), or is it only your parents who react this way (low consensus)? For consistency, you would consider your parents' past reactions to your spending time with Bart: Have your parents always been reluctant for you to be around Bart (high consistency), or have they been receptive to him in the past (low consistency)? For distinctiveness, you would think about your parents' reactions to your spending time with other friends: Are your parents suspicious and distrustful toward only Bart (high distinctiveness), or do they react this way toward all your friends (low distinctiveness)? According to the covariation model, you are most likely to attribute your parents' behavior to internal causes—such as the personality of your parents—when consensus and distinctiveness are low but consistency is high. On the other hand, external attributions are most likely when consensus and consistency are low and distinctiveness is high, or when all three kinds of information are high. Exploring Culture & Diversity 14-1 discusses how culture can influence our attributions.

Exploring CULTURE & DIVERSITY 14-1

How Universal Is the Fundamental Attribution Error?

Fundamental attribution error The tendency to make internal attributions rather than external attributions in explaining the behavior of others

When explaining others' actions, people from individualist cultures tend to make internal attributions rather than external attributions, a bias known as the **fundamental attribution error** (Ross, 1977). In a study that documented these cultural differences in attributional style, Joan Miller (1984) asked groups of American and Asian-Indian citizens

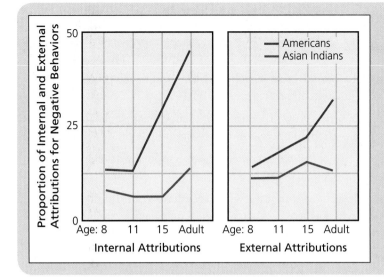

FIGURE 14-3

Is the Fundamental Attribution Error Only an Individualist Bias?

In explaining the causes of positive and negative behaviors, individualist American adults made more internal than external attributions than did collectivist Asian-Indian adults. However, no such fundamental attribution error was found among the younger children in these two cultures. What might explain these age differences?

Source: From J. G. Miller, "Culture and the Development of Everyday Social Explanation," *Journal of Personality and Social Psychology, 46* (1987): 961–978.

of varying ages to explain the causes of positive and negative behaviors they had seen in their own lives. As Figure 14.3 shows, in the youngest children of the two cultures (8- to 11-year-olds), there were no significant attribution differences. However, as the age of the participants increased, the Americans made more internal attributions, and the Asian Indians made more external attributions. This study and others strongly suggest that the fundamental attribution error is more common in individualist cultures than in collectivist cultures and that it is learned through socialization (Lee et al., 1996; Norenzayan & Nisbett, 2000).

Why is the fundamental attribution error more common in individualist cultures than in collectivist cultures? Research indicates that collectivists are just as likely as individualists to take into account people's dispositions when explaining their behavior (Krull et al., 1999). Where they differ is in their awareness of the power of the situation. Collectivists are more attentive to how situational or external factors may influence people's behavior, and that is apparently why they are less susceptible than individualists to the fundamental attribution error (Choi & Nisbett, 1998; Choi et al., 1999).

This cultural difference in making attributions appears to be rooted in different views of the self. As stated in Chapter 3, Section 3.2d, individualists view the self as internally driven and relatively uninfluenced by situational forces. In contrast, collectivists view the self as dependent upon the group and strongly influenced by social obligations. The collectivist self-view seems to foster a greater appreciation of how personal and situational factors interact in shaping behavior, which is essentially how social psychology understands social behavior. Based on these findings, some social psychologists suggest that the rules members of collectivist cultures develop in making social judgments about other people often lead to more accurate attributions than those typically developed in individualist cultures (Choi et al., 1999).

People from collectivist cultures, like Japan, are more attentive than people from individualist cultures to how situational factors may influence people's behavior. Why would this greater situational attentiveness make collectivists less susceptible to the fundamental attribution error?

- We group people into different social categories and develop beliefs about them that are known as stereotypes.

- Stereotyping can bring greater speed and efficiency to our social judgments, but it also inhibits thought and can promote prejudice and discrimination.

- Physically attractive people are assumed to possess socially desirable personality traits.

- Women are judged most attractive when they have youthful or immature facial features, whereas male attractiveness is increased with mature facial characteristics related to social dominance.

- Prejudice involves attitudes toward members of specific groups that directly or indirectly suggest they deserve an inferior social status.

- Realistic group conflict theory contends that when two groups compete for scarce resources, this competition creates a breeding ground for prejudice.

- People can hold prejudiced attitudes without being aware of them, but prejudiced thinking can be reduced through self-awareness and self-regulation.

- We attribute others' actions to either internal or external causes.

- The covariation model explains attributions as derived from consensus, consistency, and distinctiveness information.

- People from individualist cultures underestimate the influence of the situation, a judgmental bias known as the fundamental attribution error.

14.2 Attitudes

Thus far, we have discussed how we form impressions and try to explain others' actions. Through our observations of people and events, we also develop **attitudes**, which are positive or negative evaluations of objects. "Objects" include people, things, events, and issues. When we use such words as *like, dislike, love, hate, good,* and *bad*, we are describing our attitudes.

Attitudes Positive or negative evaluation of an object

14.2a *Repeated Exposure and Conditioning Shape Attitudes.*

We seem to naturally develop positive attitudes toward objects repeatedly presented to us, be they the unknown students we regularly see in class or the soft drink advertised on television (Zajonc, 1968). This tendency is called the **mere exposure effect**, and it was demonstrated in an interesting experiment conducted by Theodore Mita and his colleagues (1977). They reasoned that people are more commonly exposed to their mirrored facial images than to their true facial images and, thus, should have more positive attitudes toward the former than the latter. To test this hypothesis, they photographed students on campus and later showed them and their close friends their picture along with a mirror image print. When asked to indicate which of the two prints they "liked better," the students preferred the mirror print, while their close friends preferred the actual picture. Overall, the mere exposure effect illustrates how attitudes sometimes develop outside the realm of conscious awareness.

Mere exposure effect The tendency to develop more positive feelings toward objects and individuals the more frequently we are exposed to them

Attitudes can also be formed through operant and classical conditioning, both of which we considered in Chapter 6, Sections 6.1 and 6.2. In operant conditioning, if you are praised and encouraged when learning how to dance, for example, you are likely to develop a positive attitude toward this activity. However, if others tease and make fun of your initial awkwardness, you are likely to form a negative attitude. Similarly, in classical conditioning, attitudes may form by pairing a previously neutral stimulus with another stimulus that naturally evokes a positive or negative response in a person. For example, children may develop prejudicial attitudes toward certain groups because the children have heard their parents continuously using negatively evaluated words such as *stupid*, *lazy*, *dishonest*, and *dirty* when referring to these people (Cacioppo et al., 1992; Staats & Staats, 1958). By repeatedly pairing the social group's previously neutral name (the conditioned stimulus) with these negative adjectives (the unconditioned stimulus), children can acquire prejudicial attitudes (the conditioned response) toward these people.

Think about the mere exposure effect the next time you gaze into a mirror. You're probably the only person who knows you well who prefers that image of your face staring back at you!

14.2b *People Take One of Two Cognitive Routes in Processing Persuasive Messages.*

Not only do we form attitudes, but we also change attitudes. In fact, every day we are targets of messages to change our attitudes. Turn on the television, and commercial spokespersons will try to convince you that their products are better than all others. Go to your doctor's office for your annual physical exam, and your doctor may try to change your attitudes toward salt, fatty foods, and exercise. This process of consciously attempting to change attitudes through the transmission of a particular message is known as **persuasion** (Albarracín & Vargas, 2010).

One of the most influential persuasion theories is Richard Petty and John Cacioppo's (1986) **elaboration likelihood model**. The term *elaboration likelihood* refers to the probability that a person who receives a persuasive message will elaborate on—that is, carefully analyze and attempt to comprehend—the information contained in the message. According to the model, we tend to engage in either high or low elaboration when processing persuasive messages (Tormala & Petty, 2007). When motivated and able to think carefully about the message content (high elaboration), we take the *central route* to persuasion and are influenced by the strength and quality of the arguments.

When unable or unwilling to analyze the message, we take the peripheral route to persuasion, whereby we pay attention to cues irrelevant to the content or quality of the communication (low elaboration), such as the attractiveness of the communicator or the sheer amount of information presented. By attending to these peripheral cues, we can evaluate a message (for example, "Does the persuader look honest?" "Does she sound knowledgeable?") without engaging in any extensive thinking about the actual issues under consideration. This means that when you take the peripheral route, it isn't necessary to comprehend the message: Attitude change can occur without comprehension. Figure 14-4 depicts these two persuasion routes.

Attitude change can occur through either the thoughtful mode of central processing or the lazy mode of peripheral processing. However, attitudes formed via the lazy route are weaker, less resistant to counterarguments, and less predictive of actual behavior than those formed through the thoughtful route (Petty et al., 1995; Wagner & Petty, 2011). An analogy might be this: If attitudes are like houses, then attitudes changed by the peripheral route are like houses made from straw or sticks—they require little effort to develop and are extremely vulnerable to destruction. In contrast, attitudes changed by the central route are like houses made of bricks—they take a good deal of effort to construct and are strong and durable. This is the

Persuasion The process of consciously attempting to change attitudes through the transmission of some message

Elaboration likelihood model A theory that there are two ways in which persuasive messages can cause attitude change, each differing in the amount of cognitive effort or elaboration they require

We are not won by arguments that we can analyze but by tone and temper, by the manner which is the man himself.

—Samuel Butler, English author, 1835–1902

FIGURE 14-4

Two Routes to Persuasion

The elaboration likelihood model describes how people evaluate a persuasive message based on their ability and motivation to analyze its content. As the likelihood of thinking about the attitude-object increases, central-route processing is more likely to determine whether attitude change occurs. In contrast, as the likelihood of thinking about the attitude-object decreases, peripheral-route processing becomes more likely. Of the two routes to persuasion, which secures the most enduring attitude change?

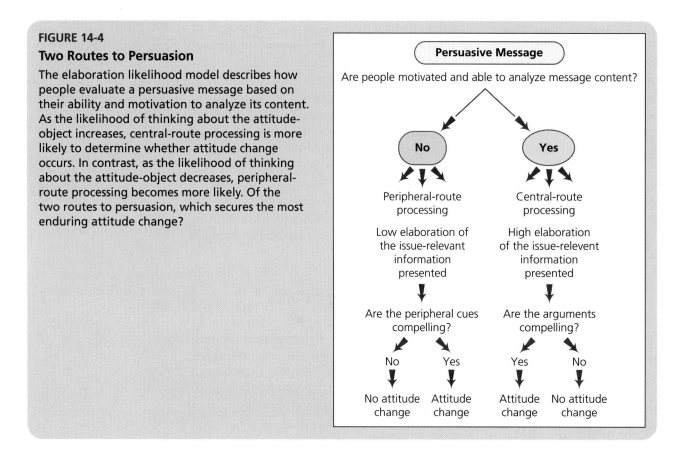

reason our psychological journey of discovery has placed so much importance on critical thinking. Such thinking results in a stronger foundation for our knowledge about the world.

14.2c Cognitive Dissonance Can Motivate Attitude Change.

Imagine that young Jack tells his grade-school friends that he dislikes girls, but later he is seen walking up a hill with Jill. How might Jack respond to this inconsistency between his attitude ("I don't like girls") and his behavior (walking with Jill)?

According to Leon Festinger's (1957) cognitive dissonance theory, when aware of an inconsistency between our attitudes and actions, we experience an unpleasant psychological state called *cognitive dissonance*. **Cognitive dissonance** is a feeling of discomfort caused by performing an action that is inconsistent with our attitudes. To relieve this feeling of discomfort, we often change our attitudes so they are in line with our behavior. Thus, if no one forced Jack to walk up the hill with Jill, then he should experience discomfort due to his dissonant thoughts ("I dislike girls, but I walked with a girl") and could be motivated to change his attitude ("Gee, maybe girls aren't that bad after all").

Since Festinger proposed this attitude theory in the 1950s, hundreds of studies have supported many of its basic principles. When people behave in ways inconsistent with their attitudes and become aware of the discrepancy, they are likely to change their attitudes so their attitudes are consistent with their behavior (Cooper, 2007).

You may have experienced what Festinger called *post-decision dissonance* soon after buying an expensive product, such as a new entertainment system, a computer, or an automobile. If you are like most people, before buying such a pricey item,

Cognitive dissonance A feeling of discomfort caused by performing an action inconsistent with one's attitudes

you read the sales brochures for all the potential choices, weighing each of their advantages and disadvantages. Your final choice probably had more of the qualities you wanted in the product than did the others, but it most likely did not beat its competitors in all areas. Because of this fact, your final choice was, to some extent, inconsistent with some of your beliefs about what you wanted in this item. That is, as soon as you *committed* yourself and purchased one of the products, the attractive aspects of the unchosen alternatives and the unattractive aspects of your choice were inconsistent with your final decision.

How did you reduce this dissonance? Like most people, you may have lowered your dissonance by not thinking about all the good qualities in the products you did not buy (you tossed out their brochures) and by thinking only about the good qualities in your chosen product (you kept this brochure and read it repeatedly). Such after-the-fact, altered perceptions are regularly found in the behavior of consumers following product choices, in voters on election day, and even in bettors at a racetrack (Knox & Inkster, 1968; Murphy & Miller, 1997). Because votes, bets, and many product purchases cannot be changed once a decision has been made, people who commit themselves are motivated to reduce post-decision dissonance. In these circumstances, the only way for people to reduce their dissonance is to convince themselves that they made the right choice.

An initial assumption of cognitive dissonance theory was that everyone has an equal desire to think and act consistently. Yet later research suggested that this desire for consistency is more common in individualist cultures than in those with a collectivist orientation (Heine & Lehman, 1997; Hoshino-Brown et al., 2005). That is, because people from collectivist cultures are socialized to think of group needs before their own needs, it is more acceptable for them to behave in a manner inconsistent with their attitudes than it is for individualists. As a result, people from collectivist cultures are less concerned than individualists about maintaining cognitive consistency. Thus, what many North Americans and other individualists consider psychologically unpleasant—namely, believing one thing but saying something else—may not be as troubling to people from cultures with a collectivist orientation. However, it is important to note that there are exceptions to this collectivist-individualist dissonance distinction. Japanese citizens living on Hokkaido, the country's northern island with a frontier tradition and a spirit of independence, exhibit cognitive dissonance similar to that of North Americans and unlike Japanese in other areas who have more collectivist leanings (Takemura & Arimoto, 2008).

If you are from an individualist culture, you might be thinking to yourself, "I don't often get upset with acting inconsistently. Why is this so?" Beyond cultural considerations, one possibility is that some of us generally tolerate cognitive inconsistencies better than others do. Spend a few minutes completing Self-Discovery Questionnaire 14-1, which measures individual differences in the preference for consistency.

Research employing this measure has found that people with a high consistency preference are motivated to behave in line with their attitudes, as predicted by cognitive dissonance theory. In contrast, those with a low preference for consistency are not bothered much by inconsistent actions and instead appear open and oriented to flexibility in their behavior (R. Cialdini et al., 1995). People who are high in the personality trait of self-monitoring (see "Psychological Applications" in Chapter 10) are such individuals. Thus, in summary, at least two factors can derail expected cognitive dissonance effects: A person's cultural upbringing may make attitude-discrepant behavior an appropriate and acceptable option, or a person's underlying personality may reduce the aversiveness of attitude-discrepant acts.

Consistency, madam, is the first of Christian duties.

—Charlotte Brontë, British author, 1816–1855

Consistency is the last refuge of the unimaginative.

—Oscar Wilde, Irish author, 1854–1900

SELF-DISCOVERY 14-1
Questionnaire

Do You Have a Preference for Consistency?

Instructions: To take the Preference for Consistency Scale (PCS), read each of the following items and then indicate how well each statement describes you, using the following scale:

1 = strongly disagree
2 = disagree
3 = somewhat disagree
4 = slightly disagree
5 = neither agree nor disagree
6 = slightly agree
7 = somewhat agree
8 = agree
9 = strongly agree

____ 1. It is important to me that those who know me can predict what I will do.

____ 2. I want to be described by others as a stable, predictable person.

____ 3. The appearance of consistency is an important part of the image I present to the world.

____ 4. An important requirement for any friend of mine is personal consistency.

____ 5. I typically prefer to do things the same way.

____ 6. I want my close friends to be predictable.

____ 7. It is important to me that others view me as a stable person.

____ 8. I make an effort to appear consistent to others.

____ 9. It doesn't bother me much if my actions are inconsistent.

Directions for scoring: The last PCS item (number 9) is reverse-scored; that is, for this item a lower rating actually indicates a higher level of consistency preference. Before summing the items, recode item 9 so that 1 = 9, 2 = 8, 3 = 7, 4 = 6, 6 = 4, 7 = 3, 8 = 2, 9 = 1. To calculate your preference for consistency score, add up your responses to the nine items.

When Cialdini and his colleagues developed the PCS, the mean score for college students was about 48. The higher your score is above this value, the greater your preference for consistency. The lower your score is below this value, the less of this preference you probably possess.

Source: From "Preference for consistency: The development of a valid measure and the discovery of surprising behavioral implications" by R. Cialdini, M. Trost, and J. Newsom in *Journal of Personality and Social Psychology*, 1995, 69, 318–328 (Appendix, p. 328). Copyright © 1995 by the American Psychological Association. Adapted with permission.

Section REVIEW

- Attitudes are formed by various means, including mere exposure, operant conditioning, and classical conditioning.

- The elaboration likelihood model describes how attitudes can be changed through either effortful or lazy thinking. Attitudes changed via the lazy route are weaker, less resistant to counterarguments, and less likely to predict later behavior.

- Cognitive dissonance theory explains how attitudes can be changed as a way to maintain cognitive consistency.

- Individualists desire to keep their attitudes and behaviors consistent, while collectivists are more likely to tolerate cognitive inconsistencies.

14.3 Social Influence

Social influence involves the exercise of social power by a person or group to change the attitudes or behavior of others in a certain direction (Cialdini & Goldstein, 2004). *Social power* refers to the force available to the influencer to motivate this change. This power can originate from having access to certain resources (for example, rewards, punishments, information) or from being liked and admired by others (Cook et al., 2006). The three main behavioral consequences of social influence are *conformity*, *compliance*, and *obedience*.

14.3a Asch's Research Demonstrates the Power of Conformity Pressure.

Can you recall incidents from your past when you behaved a certain way because everyone else was behaving that way? For instance, did you ever join in on Halloween pranks simply because it was "the thing to do"? If not, perhaps you cut classes, took drugs, or volunteered for a local charity drive because others did so. If you engaged in these activities due to perceived group pressure, you were conforming. In **conformity**, our behavior or beliefs become more similar to those of the group. Conformity is not necessarily a bad thing. In fact, if we didn't abide by most of the formal and informal rules of the social groups to which we belong, there would be social chaos.

Once conform, once do what other people do because they do it, and a lethargy steals over all the finer nerves and faculties of the soul. She becomes all outer show and inward emptiness; dull, callous, and indifferent.

—Virginia Woolf, British novelist, 1882–1941

The fish dies because it opens its mouth.

—Spanish proverb

Asch's Line Judgment Studies

In a set of classic conformity studies, Solomon Asch (1951, 1952, 1956) had male college students take part in what was described as a group visual perception experiment. Over a series of trials, six to eight men told Asch which of three comparison lines was equal in length to a standard line (see Figure 14-5). Although this task may seem easy, there was a catch. Only one person in each group was an actual participant—the rest were confederates of Asch who had been given prior instructions to pick the wrong line. The students made a total of 18 different line judgments and announced them

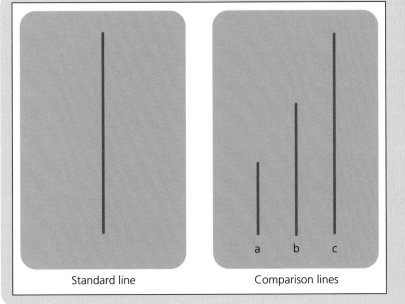

FIGURE 14-5

Asch's Line Judgment Task

In this example of Asch's classic conformity experiments, participants were asked to judge which of the three comparison lines was equal in length to the standard line.

Standard line   Comparison lines

out loud, with the actual participant giving his opinion second to last. What would the participant do when faced with this dilemma? Would he conform and also pick the incorrect line? What would you do?

Participants conformed on one-third of the critical trials by naming the same incorrect line as that named by the confederates. In contrast, when participants in a control condition made their judgments privately, less than 1 percent conformed (Asch, 1951). What Asch's research and other studies (Tanford & Penrod, 1984) demonstrate is that we often find it easier to conform than to challenge the unanimous opinions of others.

Factors That Influence Conformity

What types of social settings and personal characteristics make us more or less susceptible to others' influence? Some of the more important factors that affect conformity are listed here:

- *Group size*   As group size increases, so does conformity, but only up to a point. After the number of people exerting conformity pressure goes beyond three or four, the tendency to yield to the group does not increase (Asch, 1955).

- *Group cohesiveness*   In general, groups with a strong sense of togetherness elicit greater conformity than less cohesive groups (Christensen et al., 2004). For example, we are more likely to accept our friends' influence than that of others due to our respect for our friends' opinions, our desire to please them, and our fear of rejection (Crandall, 1988).

- *Social support*   A person who has the support of another is less likely to conform to the influence of the group (Allen & Levine, 1971). In the line judgment studies, Asch (1956) found that when one of the confederates picked the correct line, conformity dropped dramatically—to one-fourth the level shown by participants faced with a unanimous majority.

- *Desire for personal control*   Sometimes we resist social influence simply in order to feel that we control our own actions (Brehm & Brehm, 1981). Individuals with a high desire for personal control tend to resist conformity more than do those with a low desire for control (Burger, 1987).

- *Culture*   People from collectivist cultures are more concerned than individualists with gaining the approval of their group, and they feel shameful if they fail to get it (Triandis, 1989; (Wall et al., 2010) A person from an individualist culture, on the other hand, has a higher desire for personal control (see the preceding point on this list) and a need to feel unique. As a result of these different orientations, people from collectivist cultures are more conforming to their own group than are individualists (Bond & Smith, 1996). This yielding to the group by collectivists is not considered a sign of weakness as it is in individualist cultures; rather, it is believed to indicate self-control, flexibility, and maturity.

14.3b *Compliance Involves Gentle Social Influence.*

Compliance Publicly acting in accord with a direct request

In trying to "get our way" with others, the most direct route is to simply ask them to do what we desire. **Compliance** is publicly acting in accord with a direct request. When complying, you may privately agree or disagree with the action the other person is engaging in, or you may have no opinion about the behavior. For example, do you think about what passing the salt to a dinner companion implies about your relationship with this person or your own values? Probably not. You comply out of habit. However, have you ever granted someone's request to copy your answers in an exam, even though you believed it was wrong? This *external compliance*—acting in accord with a direct request despite privately disagreeing with it—often occurs due to concern about how others might respond if we refuse them. On the other hand, you may often comply with a request because you have a personal allegiance to the values and principles associated with it. Agreeing to donate money to a charity consistent with your own values is an instance of *internal compliance*.

One factor that can build the proper atmosphere for compliance is a good mood. Others are more likely to comply with our requests when they are in a good mood, especially if the request involves helping someone in need (Forgas, 1998). Because of this general awareness that good moods aid compliance, we often try to flatter people before making a request. Those we "butter up" in this manner may be suspicious of our motives after receiving our requests, but the flattery is still often effective in securing compliance (Kacmar et al., 1992).

A second factor that increases compliance is appealing to a powerful social norm that people in all cultures follow, namely, the **reciprocity norm**. This norm states that one should return a favor or a good deed, and it is based on maintaining fairness in social relationships (Gouldner, 1960). Although this norm helps ensure that social exchanges will be roughly equitable between two parties, it can also be used to exert influence over others. For example, how often have you had someone come up to you in a public place and offer you a small gift such as a flower, pencil, or flag, and then ask you to donate money to their organization? In such instances, the gift giver is hoping that the small token will make you feel obligated to return the favor and give them money (Burger et al., 1997).

Reciprocity norm The expectation that one should return a favor or a good deed

Finally, compliance can also be secured by simply providing a reason why the request should be granted. Ellen Langer and her colleagues (1978) found evidence for the power of reason-giving when they had confederates try to cut in line ahead of others at a photocopying machine. In one condition the confederates gave no reason, merely asking, "May I use the photocopying machine to make five copies?" Sixty percent of those waiting complied with this "no reason" request. Interestingly, when confederates provided a pseudoreason that provided no explanation at all but merely restated their desire to make copies ("May I use the photocopying machine to make five copies because I have to make copies?"), 94 percent complied, identical to the compliance when an actual reason was given ("I'm in a hurry").

Langer (1989) believes that such pseudoreasons work because we often mindlessly assume the requester would not ask if the request was illegitimate. When my daughter Lillian was two years old, she had already learned the importance of giving reasons when seeking compliance from her parents. In asking to go outside, she would say, "Can I go outside? … Because I have to go outside." Based on Langer's findings we see that, when it came to securing compliance, Lillian had already developed sufficient social skills to do quite nicely in the adult world. Before reading further, check out Self-Discovery Questionnaire 14-2.

14.3c *Milgram's Research Demonstrates That People Often Obey Destructive Orders.*

Unlike the rather subtle social pressures of compliance, **obedience**, which is the performance of an action in response to a direct order, is easily recognized as an exercise of power. Usually the order comes from a person of high status or authority. Because people are often instructed from a very young age to respect and obey those in positions of authority (for example, parents, teachers, and police officers), obedience to those of higher status is common and often perceived as a sign of proper

Obedience The performance of an action in response to a direct order

SELF-DISCOVERY 14-2
Questionnaire

Can You Persuade Others to Comply with a "Reasonable" Request?

Shutterstock

People are more likely to grant requests if the requests are accompanied by a reason. Why might this be so?

Ellen Langer's research found that people would often comply with a request if given some reason for making the request, even when the given reason is simply a restatement of the request. Apparently, people often mindlessly grant requests accompanied by a reason because they assume the requester would not ask if the request were illegitimate.

Test this hypothesis yourself the next time you are in line at a grocery store; ask the person in front of you if you can cut ahead of them to pay for your items "because I have to pay for these items." Do they comply? Try to gain compliance in similar situations without giving a reason for going ahead of others. Is this strategy less effective, as it was in Langer's research?

socialization. To understand how situational factors increase or decrease obedience to authority, let's explore the most discussed social-psychological study ever conducted.

Milgram's Original Obedience Research

Imagine that you volunteer to participate in an experiment investigating the effects of punishment on the learning of word pairs. You will be the teacher, and a 50-year-old man will be the learner. The experimenter explains that you will deliver increasing levels of electrical shock each time the learner makes a mistake. Once the study begins, the learner, who is in an adjacent room, makes many mistakes. Once you have delivered 75 volts of electricity, you hear through the intercom system the learner grunting and moaning in pain whenever you deliver the shocks. At 150 volts, he demands to be released, shouting that his heart is bothering him. Do you stop participating in the study at this point?

Let's imagine that you continue. At 180 volts, the learner shouts that he can no longer stand the pain. Do you now stop delivering the shocks? Why or why not?

Let's imagine that you don't stop. At 300 volts, the learner says that he absolutely refuses to provide any more answers. Now the experimenter turns to you and orders you to treat the absence of a response as equivalent to an error and deliver the appropriate level of shock. Do you do so?

Let's imagine that you obey the experimenter's commands and continue. Now, even though the learner no longer gives answers to your questions, you continue to hear from the adjoining room his screams of agony whenever your finger flips the shock-generator switch. Are these developments now sufficient for you to stop participating in the experiment?

Let's imagine that you continue, despite the learner's pleas to stop. When you surpass the 330-volt switch, the learner falls silent, not to be heard from again. As you continue to increase the shock intensity, you realize that you are getting closer to the last switch, the 450-volt switch. If you hesitate in delivering a shock, the experimenter first tells you, "Please continue," and then says, "The experiment requires that you continue," and then, "It is absolutely essential that you go on," and finally, "You have no other choice; you must go on!" What do you do?

From imagining your responses in this hypothetical situation, when do think you would have disobeyed the experimenter's commands? Would it have been following the learner's first protest? The second? The third? Is it possible that you would have continued, despite the intensity of the learner's pleas?

I am guessing your prediction is that you would have disobeyed the experimenter's orders well before the 450-volt limit was reached. If this is the case, you are in good company, for widespread disobedience is exactly what was predicted by college students, middle-class adults, and psychiatrists who were presented with this hypothetical scenario (Milgram, 1963).

When Stanley Milgram conducted this research in the early 1960s, no one actually received electrical shocks. The learner was a confederate of the experimenter. Even the learner's screams of protest and pain were prerecorded, and all participants heard exactly the same thing. To Milgram's surprise, 65 percent of the participants (26 out of 40) obeyed the experimenter completely, despite the convincing cries of agony from the learner (Milgram, 1965).

Because the findings were so unexpected, Milgram carried out a number of variations of his experiment to better understand the conditions under which obedience and disobedience would be most likely. As illustrated in Figure 14-6, these studies found that obedience increased as the distance between the teacher and the learner increased, or as the distance between the teacher and the experimenter decreased. In addition, when college students and women served as participants, the same level of destructive obedience was found (Milgram, 1974). Different researchers also obtained similar results in several other countries, suggesting that these high levels of obedience were not solely an American phenomenon (Kilham & Mann, 1974; Shanab & Yahya, 1977). The participants in these studies were not closet sadists who enjoyed their destructive obedience—in fact, their actions caused them a good deal of stress, although no enduring psychological damage (Elms, 1995; Elms & Milgram, 1966).

14.3d Recent Studies Provide New Insights into Milgram's Findings.

Four decades after Milgram's research, two separate investigations reanalyzed the data from his original studies and discovered additional insights. First, François Rochot and his coworkers (2000) analyzed the audio recordings of one of Milgram's obedience studies to better understand how participants behaved over the course of the experiment. Seeking similar answers, Dominic Packer (2008) conducted a meta-analysis of data from eight of Milgram's studies involving 320 participants. Both investigations found that an important factor in resisting the destructive commands of authority figures is an early and firm statement of opposition.

In Milgram's studies, all participants were initially obedient, but this changed at the 150-volt level as the learner began complaining and made his first demand for release.

The person who never submits to anything will soon submit to a burial mat.

—Nigerian proverb

Obedience to the law is demanded as a right; not asked as a favor.

—Theodore Roosevelt, U.S. president, 1858–1919

… far more, and far more hideous, crimes have been committed in the name of obedience than have ever been committed in the name of rebellion.

—C. P. Snow, English novelist, 1905–1980

In schools all over the world, little boys learn that their country is the greatest in the world, and the highest honor that could befall them would be to defend it heroically someday. The fact that empathy has traditionally been conditioned out of boys facilitates their obedience to leaders who order them to kill strangers.

—Myriam Miedzian, U.S. author, 1991

FIGURE 14-6

Some Factors That Influence Obedience and Disobedience to Authority

To determine what factors increase or decrease obedience, Milgram varied the location of the experiment, the participant's proximity to the victim and the experimenter, and the presence of obedient or disobedient confederates. All these factors influenced obedience levels.

Source: Data from S. Milgram, *Obedience to Authority: An Experimental View,* Harper and Row, Publishers, Inc., 1974; and S. Milgram, *The Individual in a Social World: Essays and Experiments,* Addison-Wesley Publishing Company, 1992.

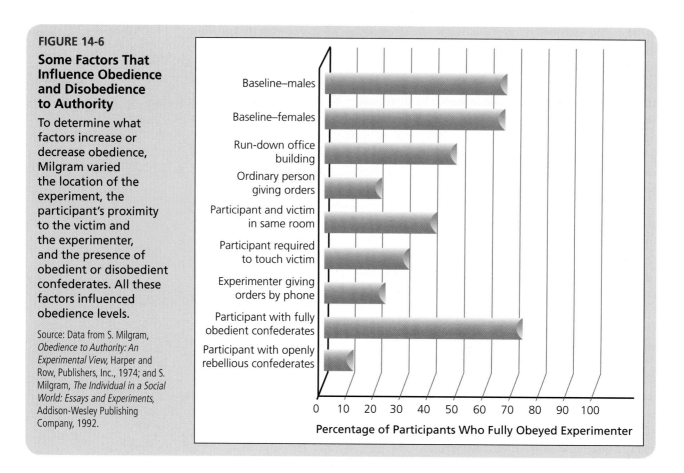

This was the point of no return regarding obedience. Rochot's analysis of the audio recordings revealed that those who firmly verbally opposed the experimenter by 150 volts all ended up defying his authority by disobeying. In contrast, if participants began their verbal challenges after 150 volts, only about half of them ever disobeyed. Packer's (2008) meta-analysis similarly found that participants who did not disobey when the learner first demanded his release at the 150-volt level were generally nonresponsive to his escalating expressions of pain as the session proceeded. As Packer explains it, the 150-volt level was the first point in Milgram's study where participants realized that there was a conflict between the experimenter's orders and the desires of the learner. The experimenter's quick dismissal of the learner's demand for release signaled to participants that in the experimenter's mind, the learner's pain and his freedom of choice were not important. For the obedient participants, after accepting the experimenter's definition of the situation at the 150-volt level, the learner's apparent agony no longer exerted much influence over their willingness to obey the experimenter's commands.

What about the disobedient participants? The crucial factor in them disobeying was an early and firm questioning of the experimenter's authority. These participants' verbal questioning signaled their refusal to passively accept the experimenter's definition of reality in this emotionally charged and conflicted situation.

When describing the situation confronting the participants in the obedience studies, I asked earlier whether you would have fully obeyed the experimenter's commands in the same circumstances. Most people believe they would resist the destructive commands and openly rebel. Of course, ethical concerns prevent a complete replication of this study, but in 2009 Jerry Burger conducted a partial replication of the Milgram procedure based on the fact that the 150-volt level was largely a point of no return in the original studies. In Milgram's study, nearly four out of five participants who obeyed the experimenter's instructions at the 150-point level continued to obey his commands all the way to 450 volts. Burger reasoned that knowing how Milgram's participants responded up to and including the 150-volt level allows us to reasonably estimate what they would do if allowed to complete the entire study. Stopping the study immediately after participants decide what to do at the 150-volt level also avoids exposing them to the extreme stress often experienced in the original studies.

What did Burger find in his partial replication of Milgram's research? Seventy percent of his 40 participants obeyed up to and at the 150-volt level and were prepared to read the next item of the test when the experimenter stopped the study. This obedience rate was slightly lower than the percentage that continued beyond this point in Milgram's study (82.5 percent), but the difference was not statistically significant. There were also no gender, age, or ethnicity differences in willingness to obey. While this study is not a definitive test of the durability of Milgram's findings, it provides no evidence that people's willingness to obey the destructive commands of authority figures has diminished in the twenty-first century.

In thinking about Milgram's study, this more recent partial replication, and whether you would follow the destructive commands of an authority figure, consider again the fundamental attribution error described in Section 14.1e. This tendency to assume that others' actions are caused by internal dispositions rather than by external forces results in underestimating the power of the situation to shape behavior. Such misrepresentation of how the social world actually operates leaves us vulnerable to manipulation by the very social forces we underestimate. If we were to develop a greater appreciation of how we can be influenced by the wishes, desires, and dictates of others, we might be better able to recognize when we are in danger of falling prey to social manipulation. Before reading further, try Closer Look 14-1 to demonstrate how people are influenced by others' actions.

LOOK 14-1

iStock

If you passed by this person on the left, do you think you would copy his behavior and look up? Do you think you might be more likely to look up if there were five people gazing into the sky rather than just one? Why?

What's Up?

We often conform to other people's actions, even in subtle and trivial ways. Test this social fact by enlisting a group of your friends to try to get other people to copy their behavior. Have your friends stand together in a public setting, looking up in the air. Tell them to simply tilt their heads up and look skyward. Do not have them point skyward with their arms. Watch passersby from a short distance. Do they look up? How long do they linger? Do they ask your friends any questions? If they do look up, approach them and ask why they looked up in the air. Also ask them if they think their behavior of looking up is an example of conformity. How do they respond?

Section REVIEW

- Social influence is the exercise of social power to change the attitudes or behavior of others in a certain direction.

- Conformity increases as group size and group togetherness increase; it decreases when you have a social supporter.

- Individualists are less conforming to their own groups than are collectivists.

- Compliance is most likely to be secured if you put a person in a good mood, do them a favor, or give them a reason for granting your request.

- Milgram's obedience experiments demonstrated that we will often obey the destructive commands of an authority figure.

- A 2009 partial replication of Milgram's original study finds no evidence that obedience levels have diminished in the past 40 years.

14.4 Hurting and Helping Others

Anger is a short madness.

—Quintus Horatius Flaccus,
Roman poet, 65–8 B.C.

Although obedience doesn't necessarily result in harm to others, the concept of aggression is directly associated with pain and destruction. **Aggression** is any form of behavior intended to harm another living being. In contrast, **helping** entails voluntary behavior that is carried out to benefit another person. Let us examine these two fundamental aspects of human behavior.

14.4a There Are Gender Differences in Styles of Aggression.

A widespread belief in our culture is that men are more aggressive than women. Does research support this cultural belief? Would it surprise you to learn that the answer is both yes and no?

Men and women do differ in one important kind of aggression: physical aggression. That is, men (and boys) are more likely than women (and girls) to engage in aggression that produces pain or physical injury (Archer, 2004). This gender difference in willingness to cause physical injury is more pronounced (1) among children than adults, and (2) for unprovoked aggression than for provoked aggression (Bettencourt & Miller, 1996). In contrast, men and women are similar to one another in their verbal aggression and in expressing feelings of anger toward members of the other sex, but men are slightly more likely than women to express verbal aggression toward same-sex persons (Archer & Côté, 2005).

Not only do men and women typically differ in their level of physical aggression, but they also appear to experience physical aggression differently (Astin et al., 2003; Campbell & Muncer, 1987). Among North Americans, women tend to view their physical aggression as stress induced, precipitated by a loss of self-control, and a negative experience. Men, in contrast, tend to perceive this type of aggression as an exercise of control over others, provoked by challenges to their self-esteem or integrity, and a positive experience (see the discussion of sexual aggression in Chapter 9, Section 9.3a). A similar gender difference pattern has been found in some European countries (Campbell et al., 1992; Fraczek, 1992).

One form of aggression often overlooked is indirect aggression—a form of social manipulation in which the aggressor attempts to harm another person without a face-to-face encounter (Archer & Coyne, 2005). Gossiping, spreading bad or false stories about someone, telling others not to associate with a person, and revealing someone's secrets are all examples of indirect aggression. Field studies among adolescents in Europe and North America (see Figure 14-7) find that girls are more likely than boys to use indirect aggression (Björkqvist et al., 1992; Vaillancourt, 2005). One explanation

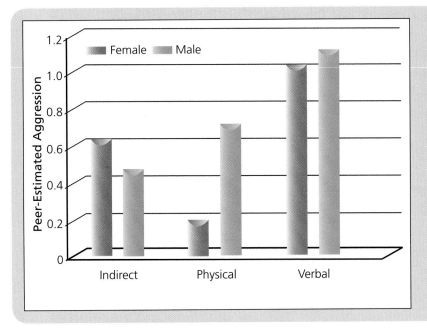

FIGURE 14-7

Gender Comparisons in Aggressive Strategies

In a study of the aggressive styles used by adolescents in Finland, Björkqvist and his colleagues (1992) found that verbal aggression is the type most commonly used by both boys and girls. However, boys display significantly more physical aggression, while girls utilize significantly more indirect forms of aggression.

for this gender difference is that girls tend to be discouraged more than boys from engaging in direct acts of aggression. As a result, they may employ indirect aggression simply because it is more socially acceptable. This research further indicates that, whereas male physical aggression decreases significantly during adolescence, teenage girls continue to exhibit higher levels of indirect aggression at all age levels (Theron et al., 2000). Can you think why this might be so? One possibility is that indirect aggression is harder to detect and punish than physical aggression.

When discussing gender differences in aggression, it is natural to ask what accounts for these differences. In most cases, social psychologists search for social or cultural explanations. However, besides these causes, some evidence indicates that biological factors also play a role in the heightened physical aggression among males. Hormones in the bloodstream clearly influence human aggression, especially testosterone, which is the most important male sex hormone (Johnson et al., 2007).

Studies find that testosterone appears to affect thinking and decision making in ways that provoke anger and inhibit empathy and fear (Van Honk & Schutter, 2007). When encountering angry faces, most people immediately detect a possible threat, consciously experience some degree of fear, and quickly respond in a nonthreatening way that reduces the likelihood of aggression in the situation. Similarly, when encountering fearful faces, most individuals consciously experience empathy and thereby are less likely to attack these fearful people (Toates, 2006). However, these typical responses are not found among individuals with high levels of testosterone. When confronted by an angry person, individuals with high levels of testosterone are more likely to behave aggressively because they experience more anger and less fear. Similarly, when in the presence of a fearful person, individuals with high levels of testosterone behave more aggressively because they feel less empathy. Together, this evidence suggests that biological factors, in addition to social and cultural factors, might help account for gender differences in aggression.

No man can think clearly when his fists are clenched.

—George Jean Nathan, American critic and writer, 1882–1958

The wish to hurt, the momentary intoxication with pain, is the loophole through which the pervert climbs into the minds of ordinary men.

—Jacob Bronowski, British scientist, 1908–1974

Men are more physically aggressive than women; however, women tend to engage in more indirect aggression, such as spreading bad or false stories about others or revealing someone's secrets. What might explain these gender differences?

14.4b *Aggressive Impulses Can Be Modified by Higher-Order Thinking.*

What occurs cognitively to trigger or defuse aggressive impulses? Leonard Berkowitz (1984, 1989) developed the **cognitive-neoassociationist model** to explain how aggression is often triggered by circumstances that arouse negative affect, such as frustration, pain, extreme temperatures, and encountering people whom we dislike.

 **INFO-BIT**   There is a common belief that people can purge themselves of aggressive urges by punching a pillow or playing some aggressive game. However, numerous studies (Bushman, 2002; Bushman et al., 1999) clearly indicate that "letting off steam" in this manner does not reduce aggressive urges—it increases them!

Cognitive-Associative Networks

Berkowitz named his theory the *cognitive-neoassociationist model* because he believes that when we experience negative affect due to some unpleasant event, this affect is encoded into memory and becomes cognitively associated with specific types of negative thoughts, emotions, and reflexive behaviors. Although these cognitive-associative networks are initially weak, the more they are activated, the stronger they become. When these associations are sufficiently strong, activating any one of them will likely activate the others, a process known as *priming* (see Chapter 7, Section 7.2a). Thus, simply remembering a past occasion when we were angry can prime hostile thoughts, angry feelings, and even reflexive actions, such as clenched fists and gritted teeth. The implication of Berkowitz's notion of priming these negative memories is that even when our surroundings don't elicit negative affect, simply thinking about aggression can activate it (Dodge, 2011).

It should be noted that this conditioning process involves the activation of our sympathetic nervous system in the fight-or-flight response, which is also the *alarm* stage in Hans Selye's general adaptation syndrome (see Chapter 13, Section 13.1b). Whether we react to negative affect with "fight" or with "flight" depends on (1) our biologically inherited aggressive tendencies, (2) our prior conditioning and learning, and (3) our attention to aspects of the situation that facilitate or inhibit aggression. Figure 14-8 depicts Berkowitz's model. Because our present objective is to understand how aversive events often lead to aggression, we will concentrate on the fight-response side of the model (the left side of Figure 14-8).

"Unthinking" Aggressive Responses

Up to this point in Berkowitz's theory of aggressive responses, the cognitions and feelings we experience due to the aversive event are simply impulsive reactions to negative affect and represent only the potential first stage in aggression. The negative thoughts, emotions, and reflexive actions evoked in the cognitive-associative networks at this stage are primitive and have not yet been shaped and developed by higher-order cognitive thinking. If such aggressive tendencies do not come under the control of more sophisticated thinking, they may cause us to spontaneously lash out with anger or aggression. Berkowitz (1994) states that this impulsive aggression is most likely when we are performing highly routine activities and thus are not consciously monitoring our thoughts, feelings, or actions. Pushing, shoving, or hitting someone

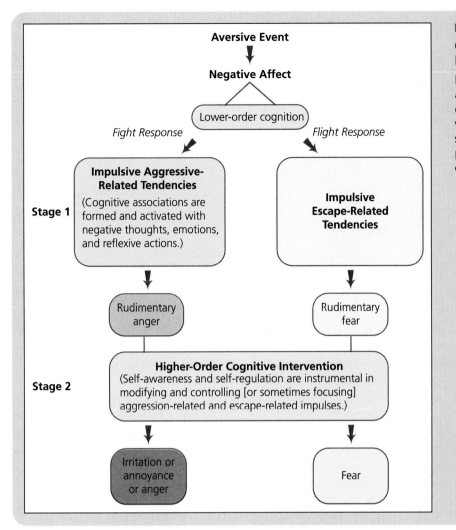

FIGURE 14-8

Cognitive-Neoassociationist Model of Aggression

Leonard Berkowitz's theory of aggression states that aversive events produce negative affect, which stimulates our aggressive inclinations. How does he propose that we can "short-circuit" this aggression?

after being repeatedly jostled in a crowd at a music concert or sporting event is an example of how negative affect can erupt into an aggressive response.

Journey of Discovery

"Road rage" has become an all-too-familiar term describing violent outbursts by people driving cars on our nation's highways. Beyond harsh penalties, what strategies might public officials employ to reduce road rage?

Higher-Order Cognitive Intervention

If we don't blindly lash out when experiencing negative thoughts, feelings, and impulses during stage 1, Berkowitz contends that higher-order cognitive processes are activated. This represents stage 2 in the aggressive response. When subjected to higher-level thinking, aggression-related tendencies are often modified and controlled.

What causes the aggression-related tendencies in stage 1 to come under the control of the more complex cognitive processes of stage 2? Research suggests that *self-awareness* and *self-regulation* are crucial in modifying and controlling our aggressive impulses (Mischel et al., 1996). Thus, when angered, we may try to make sense of our negative feelings before acting. If we conclude that no one is to blame for the aversive event, our anger will likely subside. Alternatively, we may assign blame to a particular person but still conclude that retaliation is an inappropriate response.

People who regularly consider the future consequences of their behavior tend to be less likely to act aggressively than others when angered (Joireman et al., 2003). Because of these cognitive control mechanisms in higher-order thinking, negative affect does not always lead to aggression.

Of course, after thinking things over, people may still strike out at those they blame. In fact, research indicates that when people believe that aggression will make them feel better, they are more likely to behave aggressively (Bushman et al., 2001). This finding underscores the fact that higher-order thinking does not guarantee a nonaggressive response, but it does make it more likely.

14.4c *Helping Others Is Largely a Learned Response.*

Just as all of us have had personal experiences with aggression, we have also helped and been helped by others. Consider again the chapter-opening story of my student, Ferris, needing help when confronted by a gun-wielding mugger. Would you have gone to her aid if you had been an onlooker?

Although our inclination to help those in need undoubtedly has a genetic basis (especially if those in need are blood relatives), it is substantially strengthened or weakened by our upbringing (McAndrew, 2002). As we mature, parents, teachers, and peers are extremely influential in shaping our personal norms for helping (Knafo & Plomin, 2006). If helping others becomes an important self-defining value, we will feel proud when responding to others' suffering and ashamed when ignoring them.

As you might guess, observational learning or modeling (refer back to Chapter 6, Section 6.3) has a powerful effect on our willingness to help (Eisenberg & Valiente, 2002). For example, an international study of people who rescued Jews in Nazi-occupied territory during World War II revealed that the rescuers were more likely than nonrescuers to say that they had learned generosity and caring from their parents (Oliner & Oliner, 1988). Similar findings have been obtained in studies of civil rights activists in the United States (Rosenhan, 1970). These studies suggest that parents who not only preach helping but also let their prosocial actions serve as guidelines for their children's behavior are more likely to foster helping habits in the next generation.

When anger rises, think of the consequences.

—Confucius, Chinese philosopher,
551–479 BC

Journey of Discovery

Many of you will be—or currently are—parents. Based on what you have learned about helping, what sort of cultural role models might influence the "helping habits" of boys and girls? How might greater gender-role flexibility influence male and female helping tendencies?

Do you think male bystanders would be more likely than female bystanders to intervene in an emergency like the one confronting my student in the chapter-opening story? The answer appears to be yes. Research indicates that men are more likely than women to help when the situation involves an element of danger and when there is an audience (Eagly & Crowley, 1986). In addition, men more frequently provide help to women than to other men, especially if the women are attractive (West & Brown, 1975). These findings suggest that the help typically offered by men is consistent with the male gender role: It is heroic and chivalrous, and generally directed toward the benefit of female victims.

Women helpers, in contrast, do not show a gender bias in terms of whom they help. Further, although men help more frequently in dangerous situations, women appear to be more helpful than men when assistance is consistent with the female gender role—that is, when the situation involves empathy and devotion. For example, women are more likely than men to provide social and emotional support to others (Shumaker & Hill, 1991), are more likely to volunteer for community service (Trudeau & Devlin, 1996), and are also more likely to take on the caretaking role for children and elderly people (Unger & Crawford, 1992).

14.4d Deciding to Help Often Involves a Series of Decisions.

In March 1964, people were stunned to learn the details surrounding the brutal murder of a woman outside her New York City apartment building. The victim, Kitty Genovese, was attacked by her assailant over a period of 45 minutes. News reports described neighbors ignoring Ms. Genovese's cries for help during the attack. Based on this tragic incident, two social psychologists, John Darley and Bibb Latané, decided to study the reactions of bystanders to potential emergencies. The *model of bystander intervention* that emerged from their inquiry contended that being helpful during an emergency involves not just one but a series of five decisions (Darley & Latané, 1968). As you can see from Figure 14-9, at each point in this five-step process of deciding whether or not to help, a "No" decision results in no help being given, while a "Yes" decision takes the person one step closer to helping.

According to this model, the first thing you must do as a potential helper is notice that something unusual is happening. Unfortunately, in many social settings, countless sights and sounds distract you, and thus a cry for help may go unnoticed. This is one of the possible reasons why there is a negative correlation between population density and helping (Levine et al., 1994). That is, because of all the distracting sights and sounds, residents of a crowded city are less likely to notice when someone needs help than are those who live in less densely populated urban centers.

As a bystander to an emergency, if you do indeed notice that something unusual is happening, Latané and Darley (1968, 1970) contend that you move to the second step in the decision making process—namely, deciding whether something is wrong and help is needed. For instance, if you pass an unconscious man lying on the grass in a park, you may ask yourself, "Did he suffer a heart attack, or is he merely sleeping?" This is an extremely important decision, because if you decide he is merely sleeping, you will continue on your way, having defined this as a nonemergency. Yet what if you are mistaken?

When you define the situation as an emergency, the bystander intervention model states that the third decision you must make is to determine the extent to which you have a responsibility to help. Failure to assume responsibility results in no helping, while feeling a sense of obligation moves you to the fourth step in Latané and Darley's model.

If you assume responsibility for helping, your next decision is to settle on the appropriate form of assistance to render. Yet, in the heat of the moment, what if you aren't sure what to do? You may become paralyzed with uncertainty. Unable to decide,

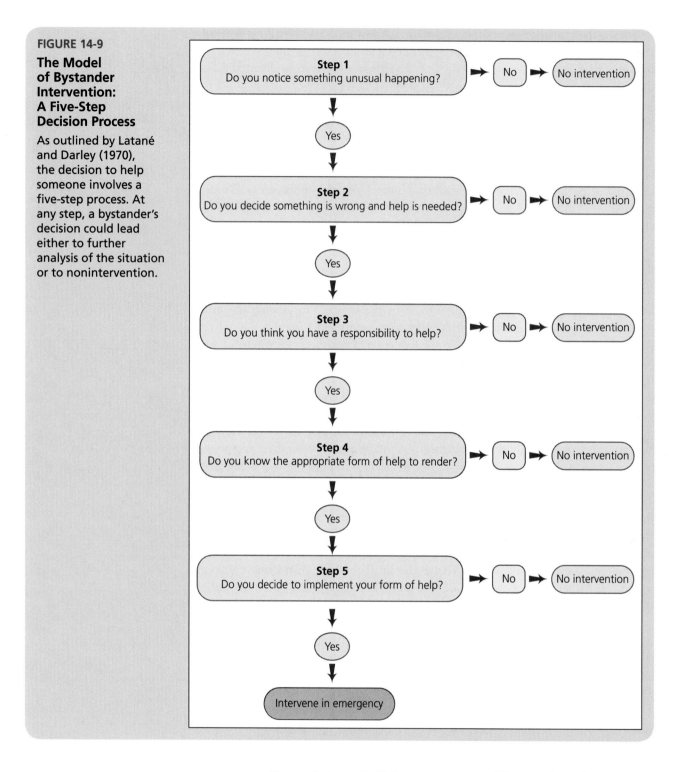

FIGURE 14-9

The Model of Bystander Intervention: A Five-Step Decision Process

As outlined by Latané and Darley (1970), the decision to help someone involves a five-step process. At any step, a bystander's decision could lead either to further analysis of the situation or to nonintervention.

you may not offer any help at all. If, however, you are able to make a choice in step 4, then in the fifth and final step, you must decide to carry out the helpful behavior.

Because many emergency situations are not clearly defined as such, when a group of people witness a possible emergency, each person's reactions will be based partly or exclusively on the reaction of the others. Unfortunately, due to our concern with how others might evaluate us, we often pretend to be calm while witnessing a possible emergency. Acting cool and calm, we then observe others' behavior for a clue as to how to define what we all are witnessing. Yet, because everyone else is also acting cool and nonchalant, we tend to underestimate the seriousness of the situation and define it as a nonemergency. Thus, in ambiguous emergency situations, the fear of being negatively evaluated, combined with the tendency to look to others for further information, results in the **audience inhibition effect**.

Inhibition in seeking information due to fear of embarrassment is one reason we sometimes don't help in emergencies. What about those situations in which someone clearly needs help, yet no one intervenes? Darley and Latané believe that the realization that others could also help diffuses bystanders' feelings of individual responsibility (step 3 in the model). They call this response to others' presence the **diffusion of responsibility**—the belief that the presence of other people in a situation makes one less personally responsible for events that occur.

More than 50 laboratory and naturalistic studies have confirmed this effect (Latané & Nida, 1981). On average, in studies where participants believed they were the only bystander to an emergency, 75 percent helped, compared with only 53 percent who helped in the presence of others. Diffusion of responsibility also occurs when people need help on the Internet (Barron & Yechiam, 2002; Blair et al., 2005). In one 30-day study involving over 4,800 chat room participants, diffusion of responsibility increased as the number of people present in a computer-mediated chat group increased. However, this bystander effect was virtually eliminated—and help was received much more quickly—when help was requested by specifying a chat room bystander's name (Markey, 2000). When a specific bystander is singled out of the crowd to help, it is virtually impossible for that individual to diffuse responsibility.

Despite the clear evidence that the presence of others influences our decisions to help, most of us deny that other bystanders have any effect on our actions (or inactions). As discussed, this underestimation of the effect that others have on our own behavior makes it all the more likely that we will fall prey to its influence. After all, how can we guard against being unhelpful when we don't recognize how the simple presence of others not only can inhibit our ability to identify emergencies accurately but also can change our feelings of personal responsibility for helping?

The good news for you, the reader of this textbook, is that knowledge really is power. My student, Ferris, discovered the power of this social psychological knowledge when she implemented the strategies suggested by the bystander intervention model. Indeed, research indicates that people are less likely to fall victim to these bystander effects in emergencies if they have previously learned about them in a psychology course (Beaman et al., 1978). This finding suggests that simply knowing about the social barriers to helping can free one from their antisocial effects. Closer Look 14-2 for specific suggestions on what to do if you need help in an emergency.

iStock

If bystanders define a situation as an emergency, how might the presence of others inhibit intervention?

Audience inhibition effect A situation in which people are inhibited from helping due to fear of being negatively evaluated by other bystanders if they do intervene and it turns out not to be an emergency

Diffusion of responsibility The belief that the presence of others in a situation makes one less personally responsible for events that occur in that situation

How Can You Increase Your Chances of Receiving Help in an Emergency?

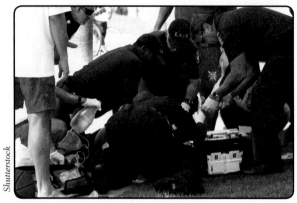

Shutterstock

Social psychological research on bystander effects in helping suggests that people can increase the likelihood of receiving help if they follow a few recommendations. Following these guidelines might save your life someday.

There is a strong likelihood that at some point in your life you will need help in an emergency. Based on what you now know about the bystander intervention model, how can you increase the probability of receiving aid? Here is the gist of the recommendations I told Ferris and my other psychology students; they are based on the insights provided by the experiments conducted by John Darley and Bibb Latané. Learn these guidelines and implement them when you are in need of help.

Guideline 1: A general point to keep in mind is that deciding to intervene in a possible emergency often involves a complex set of decisions. If bystanders make an incorrect decision at any point in this process, they will not intervene. As the victim, you must *attack and neutralize the psychological factors that cause nonintervention.*

Guideline 2: The first psychological hurdle is the audience inhibition effect, in which the fear of being negatively evaluated, combined with the tendency to look to others for further information, leads bystanders to misidentify emergencies as nonemergencies. You can eliminate this inhibition by *clearly letting everyone know that this is an emergency and you need help.* (Remembering this information while facing her assailant, Ferris began loudly screaming that she was being robbed and needed help. The mugger was so flustered at suddenly becoming the focus of public attention that he fled. However, I told Ferris that if anyone ever again tries to rob her, she should immediately relinquish her belongings. In this instance, she was initially too frightened to comply with the mugger's demand.)

Guideline 3: Even after clearing the audience inhibition hurdle, you must next *attack the diffusion of responsibility,* which is bystanders' tendency to believe they are less personally responsible for helping when others are present. Here, you should implore specific people to help you because it's hard to deny assistance when singled out. (After the mugger fled, Ferris asked specific people nearby to help her, and they complied. Most other bystanders who were not singled out by Ferris proceeded on their way.)

Guideline 4: Finally, because some people may want to help but are unsure what to do, you can overcome this last hurdle by *specifically giving bystanders instructions.*

Using your most authoritative voice will further increase obedience. And obedience is exactly what you are seeking here. (Ferris asked a specific bystander with a cell phone to call the police for assistance, and the police were on the scene within minutes.)

This Closer Look is a bit unconventional, because I am certainly not recommending that you go out and place yourself in dangerous situations to test these guidelines. However, I strongly suggest that you remember these guidelines—they really could help save your life someday.

Section REVIEW

- Men are more likely than women to engage in physical aggression, whereas women are more likely than men to engage in indirect aggression.

- Observational learning has a powerful effect on willingness to help.

- Men are more likely than women to help in dangerous situations, while women are more helpful than men in situations requiring empathy and devotion.

- The bystander intervention model contends that being helpful during an emergency involves a series of five decisions; if bystanders make incorrect decisions at any point in this process, they will not intervene.

- Two factors that make helping less likely when others are present are the audience inhibition effect and diffusion of responsibility.

14.5 Interpersonal Attraction and Love

Now that we have examined the psychology of harming and helping others, let's turn our attention to interpersonal attraction and love. We are social creatures by nature, and this is most clearly demonstrated in our desire to seek out others and form lasting close relationships.

14.5a Proximity and Similarity Often Lead to Attraction.

What determines our attraction to others? Social scientists have identified a number of factors that increase the likelihood that close relationships will take root. Two of the most important situational factors that attract us to others are how physically close we are to them (proximity) and the degree to which we share beliefs, attitudes, and other important characteristics (similarity).

Proximity

One of the most powerful factors in determining whether you develop a relationship with another person is his or her proximity to you (Back et al. 2008; Festinger et al., 1950). For example, spend a minute or two thinking about with whom you played as a child. Chances are, most of your friends were neighbors living nearby. Why does proximity promote liking? As your own childhood experiences suggest, it's easier to develop friendships with those who live close to you simply because they are more accessible. Yet another reason involves the mere exposure effect discussed in Section 14.2a: Proximity tends to be associated with repeated exposure, and such familiarity leads to greater liking.

Beyond proximity, another ingredient in attraction is similarity. Numerous studies indicate that we choose as friends and lovers those who are similar to us in race, age, social class, education, and attitudes (Whitbeck & Hoyt, 1994). Our belief that similarity attracts is the principal reason why, when trying to match up others as potential friends, we pay close attention to their shared characteristics. This tendency to be attracted to similar others is known as the **matching hypothesis** (Galupo, 2007).

One reason we might seek the company of similar others is because of our desire for social comparison (Festinger, 1954). That is, we are drawn to people with whom we can compare ourselves. The more similar they are to us, the more likely it is that the resulting comparison will provide information we can use in better understanding ourselves and our future plans (Miller, 1984). For example, imagine that you are deciding whether to take a certain college course. You know three people who were previously enrolled in the course: Juan, who always is the top student in every course he takes; Vanessa, who usually receives grades similar to yours; and Sarah, who always seems to be on academic probation. Whom would you seek out for information about the course? Most likely, you would go to Vanessa because of her academic similarity to yours. Her opinions and observations about the course—and her actual final grade—would be more useful in predicting your own performance than information obtained from Juan or Sarah.

Although research indicates that the similarity of people's attitudes is more important in determining their attraction toward one another than the similarity of their personalities (Crandall et al., 2007; Montoya & Horton, 2004), the long-term durability of the relationship is another matter. Satisfaction over time in both friendships and marriages is more influenced by personality similarity rather than attitudinal similarity (Gonzaga et al., 2007; Luo & Klohnen, 2005). In other words, we are attracted to others who share our attitudes, values, and beliefs. We may even enter into committed relationships with these individuals based on this similarity. Yet having committed ourselves to these relationships, people with similar personalities are better able than those with different personalities to coordinate their daily activities and thereby avoid the friction and conflict that lower relationship satisfaction.

14.5b *Romantic Love Consists of Both Passionate and Companionate Love.*

Just knowing that proximity and similarity may attract us to one another does not tell us about the psychological nature of romantic love. What can psychologists tell us that poets have not already revealed?

Some psychologists theorize that romantic love involves both passionate and companionate love (Hendrick & Hendrick, 2003). **Passionate love** is a state of intense longing for union with another that we typically experience most intensely during the early stages of a romantic relationship. It is a type of love that we feel with our bodies—a warm tingling, body-rush, stomach-in-a-knot kind of love. According to Ellen Berscheid and Elaine Hatfield (1974), passionate love is produced, or at least enhanced, during these first romantic encounters due to a rather interesting transference of arousal from one stimulus to another. Drawing on Schachter's (1964) two-factor theory of emotion described in Chapter 9, Section 9.5f, Berscheid and Hatfield contend that passionate love is likely to occur when the following three conditions are met:

Matching hypothesis The proposition that people are attracted to others who are similar to them in certain characteristics, such as attitudes and physical attractiveness

Passionate love A state of intense longing for union with another that we typically experience most intensely during the early stages of a romantic relationship

1. You must learn what love is and come to expect that you will eventually fall in love.

2. You must meet someone who fits your preconceived beliefs of an appropriate lover.

3. While in this person's presence, you must experience a state of physiological arousal.

How does the arousal that develops under these conditions become passionate love? Recall that Schachter's theory of emotion asserts that we use external cues to label our arousal states. According to this two-factor explanation, when arousal occurs in the presence of an appropriate love object, we may well interpret this arousal as romantic and sexual attraction (see Figure 14-10).

One reason the emotional roller-coaster ride of early love slows over time to a more smooth and steady experience is that passion generally burns less intensely as a relationship matures (Hatfield et al., 2007). As we settle into a romantic relationship, the emotional freshness and uncertainty of passionate love are replaced by a more certain and dependable type of love—if love survives at all (Knobloch, 2007). Some social scientists explain this lowering of passion as genetically predetermined. According to this perspective, passion is adaptive early in a relationship because it frequently results in children; yet, once children are born, the parents becoming less obsessed with one another aid the infants' survival.

This less impassioned, more enduring **companionate love** is the affection we feel for those with whom our lives are deeply entwined (Hatfield & Rapson, 1996). Companionate love exists between close friends as well as between lovers. It develops out of a sense of certainty in one another's love and respect, as well as a feeling of genuine mutual understanding (Sprecher, 1999).

Another difference between passionate love and companionate love lies in the beliefs we have about our partner. In the early stages of romantic relationships, when passions run high, we tend to see our partners through rose-colored glasses (Brehm, 1988). They are "perfect," the "ideal man" or "ideal woman," our "dream come true." As passion fades and we develop companionate love, this idealization of our beloved gives way to a more realistic view (see Section 14.5d). In addition, culture affects our approach to romantic love, as depicted in Exploring Culture & Diversity 14-2.

Companionate love forms the basis for long-term romantic relationships and friendships. It is the affection we feel for those with whom our lives are deeply entwined.

Love and eggs are best when they are fresh.

—Russian proverb

Companionate love The affection we feel for those with whom our lives are deeply entwined

---

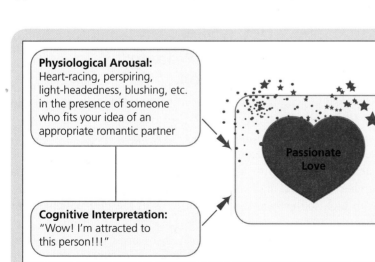

Physiological Arousal:
Heart-racing, perspiring, light-headedness, blushing, etc. in the presence of someone who fits your idea of an appropriate romantic partner

Passionate Love

Cognitive Interpretation:
"Wow! I'm attracted to this person!!!"

FIGURE 14-10

The Two-Factor Theory of Emotion and Passionate Love

According to the two-factor theory of emotion, when we experience physiological arousal in the presence of someone who fits our idea of a suitable romantic partner, we are likely to cognitively interpret this arousal as romantic and sexual attraction. This is the beginning of passionate love.

Exploring CULTURE & DIVERSITY **14-2**

People in collectivist cultures place less emphasis than those in individualist cultures on romantic love as a primary basis for marriage. Instead, they emphasize whether the potential spouse will "fit in" to their extended family. How might this emphasis on family cohesion over personal love lead to more enduring marriages than those found in individualist cultures?

Do Beliefs About Love and Marriage Differ Across Cultures?

Conceptions of love differ cross-culturally. For example, a study by Robert Levine and his colleagues (1995) examined the importance of love as a basis for marriage in both individualist and collectivist cultures. Results indicate that there are strong cross-cultural differences in the perceived importance of love. Individualist countries such as the United States, England, and Australia placed great importance on love in marriage, while collectivist countries such as India, Pakistan, Thailand, and the Philippines rated it as much less important. These beliefs appear to have behavioral consequences as well. Those countries placing great importance on love had higher marriage rates, lower fertility rates, and higher divorce rates. Other studies indicate that collectivists tend to select mates who will best "fit in" to the extended family, while individualists are more likely to select a mate who is physically attractive or has an "exciting" personality. This doesn't mean, however, that love is not a part of a collectivist marriage. Instead, in collectivist cultures, it is more common for people first to get married and then to fall in love.

One question raised by the researchers was whether there is an inherent conflict between individualist values and the interdependence necessary to maintain romantic love. That is, if you were raised to be autonomous and independent, wouldn't you tend to have difficulty maintaining an intimate relationship that is defined by partners depending on each other? The curious irony is that although individualists are more likely to marry due to romantic love, the way they've been socialized may make it less likely that their marriages will survive and their love will be nurtured.

14.5c *Positive Illusions and "Mind Reading" Increase Romantic Satisfaction.*

There is scientific evidence indicating that if you want happiness in love, you should allow your desire to feel good about your romantic relationship to dominate your desire to critically analyze the imperfections in that relationship (Gagné & Lydon, 2001). In other words, an important component of a satisfying, stable romantic relationship is the ability to mix positive illusion with sober reality when perceiving one's partner. A number of studies indicate that just as there is a *self-serving bias* that leads people with high self-esteem to see themselves in the best possible light (see Chapter 10, Section 10.5c), people in happy romantic relationships tend to attribute their partner's positive behaviors to dispositional causes (their "wonderful personality") and their negative behaviors to situational factors (a "bad day").

This *partner-enhancing bias* not only makes lovers feel better and increases relationship trust, but it also can create a self-fulfilling prophecy. In longitudinal studies, married and dating couples who idealized one another more during the initial stages of their romance reported greater increases in satisfaction and decreases in conflicts and doubts over the course of a year than couples who saw each other in a more realistic light (Murray & Holmes, 1997; Murray et al., 1996). Further, during the year, the targets of these positive illusions actually incorporated these idealized images into their own self-concepts. These studies suggest that by taking a "leap of faith" and seeing imperfect relationships in somewhat idealized ways, people not only satisfy their need to feel that their relationships are better than most other relationships, but they also create the conditions necessary for their positive illusions to be realized.

Although positive illusions might reinforce the belief that you have found your "perfect match," couldn't there also be benefits to accurately reading your partner's thoughts and feelings? In other words, can accuracy in reading your partner coexist with positive illusions about your partner? New Zealand social psychologists Geoff Thomas and Garth Fletcher (1997) have investigated the ability of relationship partners to read each other's thoughts and feelings, an interpersonal skill they call *mind reading* (also known as *empathic accuracy*).

In one of Thomas and Fletcher's typical studies, either married or dating couples are videotaped while they discuss two serious problems in their relationship. Couples are instructed to try to resolve the problems during this 10-minute discussion. After completing this task, couples are separated and partners independently review a videotape of the discussion, stopping the tape at points in time when they recall experiencing a thought or emotion and then writing it down. Next, the researchers give each partner the time points the other partner had noted and ask each person to review the tape a second time, but this second time giving their best guess as to what their partner was thinking and feeling at the indicated time points. Raters later assess the similarity between the pairs of statements from the two partners to determine each one's accuracy in reading the other's thoughts and feelings. For comparison purposes, friends of the couple and strangers also review these tapes and guess what each person was thinking and feeling at the selected time points. The central findings from these studies are that couples are more accurate in assessing what their partners were thinking and feeling than are friends of the dating partners.

More importantly, superior mind reading is related to higher relationship satisfaction (Thomas & Fletcher, 2003). Additional research suggests that superior mind readers have higher verbal skills and engage in more complex and effortful thinking when making attributions of others' behavior than inferior mind readers. In other words, people who regularly critically analyze social interaction and are also adept at verbal interaction are more accurate in reading their partners' thoughts and feelings, which appears to benefit the relationship. Not surprisingly, women are superior mind readers compared to men. On the neurological level, elevated levels of oxytocin appear to improve mind reading ability (Domes et al., 2007).

Is superior mind reading always a good thing for romantic relationships? Maybe not. Individuals in highly committed romantic relationships are sometimes motivated to inaccurately read their partners' minds, such as when they avoid acknowledging that their lover is subtly "checking out" an attractive person while in their presence (Simpson et al., 2003). In such instances, engaging in positive illusions may protect relationship harmony and satisfaction. Overall, it appears that accurate mind reading in romance increases intimacy and satisfaction with the relationship when the partners' thoughts and feelings are not threatening to the relationship. However, when these thoughts and feelings pose a potential danger, positive illusions protect relationship happiness.

Things become better when you expect the best instead of the worst.

—Norman Vincent Peale, minister and author, 1899–1993

- Two factors determining interpersonal attraction are proximity and similarity.

- Passionate love is often experienced during the early stages of romance and is associated with an idealized perception of one's romantic partner, while companionate love is a more enduring kind of love than passionate love; it exists between lovers, as well as between close friends, and is associated with a more realistic view of one's partner.

- Individualists are more likely to marry due to romantic love than are collectivists.

- Positive illusions generally enhance relationship happiness, but accurate mind reading in romance is also important.

PSYCHOLOGICAL
a p p l i c a t i o n s

How Can You Cope with Jealousy?

What Is Jealousy?

One emotion that threatens love is jealousy. **Jealousy** is the negative emotional reaction you feel when a real or imagined rival threatens a relationship important to your self-concept (Harris, 2004). Although some people believe jealousy is a healthy sign in romantic relationships, research indicates that it is actually related to strong feelings of dependence and relationship insecurity (Stieger et al., 2012). It also triggers many negative feelings and behaviors and tend to lower self-esteem.

Jealousy The negative emotional reaction experienced when a real or imagined rival threatens a relationship important to one's self-concept

Ways to Reduce Jealousy

Because jealousy is so destructive to intimate relationships, social scientists and mental health therapists have sought to develop strategies for coping constructively with the "green-eyed monster." What we know is that the people most susceptible to jealousy are those who are highly dependent on the relationship and have few alternative avenues for expressing intimacy (White & Mullen, 1989).

> "O! Beware my lord, of jealousy; It is the green-eyed monster which doth mock."
>
> — From Othello, by William Shakespeare, English dramatist and poet, 1564–1616

What type of coping strategies—both constructive and destructive varieties—do we employ in contending with jealousy? All jealousy coping strategies boil down to two major goals: (1) trying to maintain the relationship; and (2) trying to maintain self-esteem (Marelich & Holt, 2006).

As you can see from Table 14-1, these two goals can be either present or absent in the coping strategy adopted. If you are jealous and desire to maintain both the relationship and your self-esteem, you will probably try to reach a mutually satisfying solution with your partner. However, if you desire to maintain your romantic relationship regardless of any harm to your self-esteem, you may swallow your pride and put up with the part of your partner's behavior that elicits the jealousy. In contrast to these relationship-maintaining strategies, you may use verbal and physical attacks against your partner or your rival when you are more concerned with maintaining self-esteem than with maintaining the relationship. Finally, when you are not principally attempting to either maintain the relationship or bolster your self-esteem, you may engage in self-destructive behavior.

> Let's say I committed this crime [the murder of ex-wife Nicole Brown Simpson]. Even if I did do this, it would have to have been because I loved her very much, right?
>
> —O. J. Simpson, athlete and infamous celebrity, b. 1947

In commenting on these different coping strategies, Sharon Brehm (1992) brings up a good point: When jealous, before acting you should think about both the short-term and the long-term consequences of your coping responses. For example, verbally or physically attacking partners may temporarily intimidate them into not leaving, but this strategy will most likely hasten their exit from the relationship. Similarly, begging and pleading with a partner to end another romance may succeed in the short run, but such emotional clinging not only will threaten self-esteem but probably will also reduce the partner's attraction to the relationship.

The best antidotes to the "green-eyed monster" are to contain emotional outbursts, maintain daily routines, and reevaluate the importance of the relationship (Salovey & Rodin, 1988). Further, to reduce your depression and anger, you should engage in self-bolstering, which involves thinking positively about yourself and doing nice things for yourself. Making new friends and pursuing positive goals in other areas of your life are part of the self-bolstering process; and such activities will increase self-esteem, which in turn will reduce jealousy.

TABLE 14-1 Different Ways of Coping with Jealousy

		Relationship-Maintaining Behaviors	
		Yes	No
Self-Esteem-Maintaining Behaviors	Yes	Negotiating a mutually acceptable solution	Verbal/physical attacks against the partner or rival
	No	Clinging to the relationship	Self-destructive behaviors

Source: Adapted from J. B. Bryson, "Situational Determinants of the Expression of Jealousy" in H. Sigall (chair), Sexual Jealousy symposium presented at the annual meeting of the American Psychological Association, San Francisco, 1977.

Suggested Websites

stanleymilgram.com

http://www.stanleymilgram.com/

This website is a source of accurate information about the life and work of one of the most outstanding social scientists of our time, Stanley Milgram. His untimely death at the age of 51 on December 20, 1984, ended a life of scientific inventiveness and controversy.

What Makes Kids Care?

http://www.apa.org/topics/kidscare.html

This American Psychological Association website offers suggestions on how to raise children to be more altruistic and supports these suggestions with relevant theories.

Controlling Anger—Before It Controls You

http://www.apa.org/topics/controlanger.html

This American Psychological Association website provides recommendations for controlling anger before it leads to aggression.

Prejudice and Discrimination

http://www.colorado.edu/conflict/peace/problem/prejdisc.htm

The International Online Training Program on Intractable Conflict at the University of Colorado offers a website on prejudice and discrimination around the world, including possible solutions to these social problems.

Social Psychology Network

http://www.socialpsychology.org

This is the largest social psychology database on the Internet, with more than 5,000 links to psychology-related websites, especially those covering social-psychological topics.

Key Terms

Aggression, 632

Attitudes, 620

Attribution, 617

Audience inhibition effect, 639

Cognitive dissonance, 622

Cognitive-neoassociationist model, 634

Companionate love, 643

Compliance, 626

Conformity, 625

Covariation model, 617

Diffusion of responsibility, 639

Discrimination, 613

Elaboration likelihood model, 621

Ethnocentrism, 613

External attribution, 617

Fundamental attribution error, 618

Helping, 632

Impression formation, 609

Ingroup, 609

Internal attribution, 617

Jealousy, 647

Matching hypothesis, 642

Mere exposure effect, 620

Obedience, 627

Outgroup, 609

Passionate love, 642

Persuasion, 621

Physical attractiveness stereotype, 610

Prejudice, 613

Realistic group conflict theory, 613

Reciprocity norm, 627

Social influence, 625

Social perception, 608

Social psychology, 608

Stereotypes, 609

Review Questions

1. Stereotyping influences information-processing through all except which of the following?
   a. activation of ethnic stereotypes, which limit critical thinking
   b. increasing the amount of attention and rehearsal to stereotype-consistent information
   c. increasing attention to new information rather than old information
   d. decreasing attention to stereotype-inconsistent information
   e. creation of false memories consistent with the stereotype

2. Research on stereotypes and prejudice has found that:
   a. Prejudice is easier to change than discrimination.
   b. Reducing prejudice involves self-awareness and self-regulation.
   c. Efforts to reduce prejudicial responding are a waste of time.
   d. The strength of automatic associations is more important than motivation in reducing one's prejudices.
   e. Efforts to change one's prejudiced responding result in eliminating the prejudice from memory.

3. Which of the following is not evaluated in Kelley's covariation model when assessing an event or stimulus?
   a. consensus
   b. consistency
   c. social desirability
   d. distinctiveness
   e. all of the above

4. According to researchers, which of the following is true about the fundamental attribution error?
   a. It is learned at an early age, even before age 5.
   b. It is more widespread in collectivist cultures.
   c. It is the tendency for people from individualistic cultures to attribute others' behavior to internal causes.
   d. It causes Americans to make more external than internal attributions for negative events.
   e. It is associated with interactions between internal and external factors.

5. One of your friends has strong political beliefs, and your persuasive arguments do little to change her mind. Through which of the following would your friend's political attitudes likely have been formed?
   a. attending to the credibility of political speakers
   b. the central route to persuasion
   c. low elaboration of political arguments
   d. the peripheral route to persuasion
   e. the elaboration likelihood model

6. Which is true according to Festinger's theory of cognitive dissonance?
   a. People from collectivist cultures are more prone to feelings of cognitive dissonance than people from individualist cultures.
   b. Cognitive dissonance is shaped by conditioning.
   c. People in individualistic cultures are generally motivated to be consistent in their attitudes and behaviors.
   d. Someone who exhibits a great deal of flexibility in his or her behavior is bothered by cognitive dissonance.
   e. Saying one thing while believing something else is not aversive to individualists.

7. When you arrive at a party, you see that everyone is drinking dark ale, which you dislike. When your host brings you a bottle of ale, you accept graciously, exhibiting _____.
   a. conformity
   b. obedience
   c. compliance
   d. personal consistency
   e. cognitive dissonance

8. An individual's willingness to conform may be influenced by all except which of the following?
   a. group size
   b. the presence of a dissenter
   c. cultural norms
   d. desire for personal control
   e. being given a small gift

9. If you interpret going along with the group in question 7 as flexibility or maturity, which of the following is most likely true?
   a. You have a high need for personal control.
   b. You will experience cognitive dissonance.
   c. You are complying with the reciprocity norm.
   d. You may be from a collectivist culture.
   e. You are respecting the authority of your host.

10. What were some of the main results of Milgram's research?
    a. Only 10 percent of the participants obeyed the experimenter.
    b. Proximity to the learner had no effect on participants' conformity.
    c. Participants were found to be closet sadists, feeling no negative effects from their actions.
    d. They showed the power of the situation in determining behavior.
    e. They emphasized the power of dispositional factors.

11. With what is indirect aggression often associated?
    a. the activation of aggressive cognitive associations
    b. being motivated by the anticipation of rewards
    c. a tendency to be impulsive when angry
    d. a desire to physically hurt others
    e. gossiping about others

12. According to the cognitive-neoassociationist model of aggression, which is true?
    a. Acting aggressively makes us feel better, reinforcing aggression.
    b. Pleasant emotions are encoded into memory and help limit aggression.
    c. Aggression is most likely when we are thinking about our actions.
    d. Remembering a time when we were angry can elicit negative affect and aggression.
    e. Activation of the "fight-or-flight" response produces negative affect and aggression.

13. The model of bystander intervention describes a five-step decision-making process involving all except which of the following?
    a. deciding if help is needed
    b. assuming a sense of personal responsibility
    c. fear of being hurt
    d. observing how others respond
    e. the audience inhibition effect

14. Which of the following is false regarding love and marriage?
    a. Couples around the world universally view love as important for marriage.
    b. Countries placing greater importance on love before marriage have higher divorce rates.
    c. In collectivist cultures, mates are selected who best fit into the extended family.
    d. Lower fertility rates are associated with greater importance attached to love before marriage.
    e. There may be a conflict between individualist values and lifelong dependence on a romantic partner.

Glossary

Antidepressant drugs Drug that relieve depression by increasing the supply of norepinephrine and/or serotonin at the neuron's receptor sites, p. 553

Antipsychotic drugs Drugs that are effective in treating the delusions, hallucinations, and loose associations of schizophrenia by blocking dopamine receptors and thereby reducing dopamine activity, p. 553

Antisocial personality disorder A personality disorder characterized by a persistent pattern of disregard for, and violation of, the rights of others, p. 524

Anxiety disorders Disorder characterized by distressing, persistent anxiety or maladaptive behavior, p. 503

Aphasia The inability to recognize or express language as a result of damage to brain tissue, such as after a stroke, p. 71

Applied psychologists Psychologists who use existing psychological knowledge to solve and prevent problems, p. 17

Aptitude test Test designed to predict a person's capacity for learning, p. 353

Archetypes In Jung's personality theory, inherited images that are passed down from our prehistoric ancestors and that reveal themselves as universal symbols in dreams, religion, and art, p. 457

Assimilation The process of absorbing new information into existing schemas, p. 116

Attachment The strong emotional bond a young child forms with its primary caregiver, p. 101

Attitudes Positive or negative evaluation of an object, p. 620

Attribution The process by which people use information to make inferences about the causes of behaviors or events, p. 617

Audience inhibition effect A situation in which people are inhibited from helping due to fear of being negatively evaluated by other bystanders if they do intervene and it turns out not to be an emergency, p. 639

Audition The sense of hearing, p. 163

Authoritarian parent Parent who imposes many rules, demands strict obedience, and harshly punishes his or her children for rule breaking or even questioning the parent's decisions , p. 109

Authoritative parent Parent who sets rules for proper conduct for her or his children, consistently enforces those rules, yet allows the children a fair amount of freedom, p. 108

Autonomic nervous system A division of the peripheral nervous system that controls the movement of nonskeletal muscles, such as the heart and lung muscles, over which people have little or no voluntary control, p. 52

Availability heuristic The tendency to judge the frequency or probability of an event in terms of how easy it is to think of examples of that event, p. 348

Aversive conditioning A counterconditioning technique in which a classically conditioned aversive response is conditioned to occur in response to a stimulus previously associated with an undesired behavior, p. 540

Axon An extension of the soma that sends information in the form of electrochemical impulses to other neurons, p. 43

• • B • • • • • • • • • • • • • • • • •

Barbiturates Powerful depressants that reduce anxiety and promote sleep, and in milder doses produce relaxation, slight euphoria, and reduced inhibitions, p. 229

Behavioral medicine An interdisciplinary field of science that integrates behavioral and medical knowledge and then applies it to health and illness, p. 565

Behavior genetics The study of how the genotype and the environment of an organism influence its behavior, p. 78

Behaviorism An approach to psychology that studies observable behavior rather than hidden mental processes; also referred to as the *behavioral perspective*, p. 7

Behavior therapies Psychotherapies that apply learning principles to the elimination of unwanted behaviors, p. 538

Beta waves Very fast, low-amplitude brain waves associated with an active, alert state of mind, p. 210

Binocular cues Depth cues that require information from both eyes, p. 180

Biomedical therapies The treatment of psychological disorders by altering brain functioning with physical or chemical interventions, p. 534

Biopsychosocial model An interdisciplinary model that assumes that health and overall wellness are caused by a complex interaction between biological, psychological, and sociocultural factors, p. 566

Bipolar disorder A mood disorder characterized by swings between the emotional extremes of mania and depression, p. 514

Bisexuality The sexual orientation in which a person is sexually attracted to members of both sexes, p. 414

Blind spot The area on the retina where the optic nerve leaves the eye; contains no receptor cells, p. 156

Body esteem A person's attitudes toward her or his body, p. 593

Bottom-up processing The idea that perception is a process of building a perceptual experience from smaller pieces of information, p. 148

Bulimia nervosa An eating disorder in which a person engages in recurrent episodes of binge eating followed by drastic measures to purge the body of the consumed calories, p. 594

C

Cannon-Bard theory A theory that emotion-provoking events simultaneously induce both physiological responses and subjective states that are labeled as emotions, p. 430

Case study A descriptive scientific method involving in-depth analysis of a single subject, usually a person, p. 26

Categorization The primary means of coding experience through the process of forming concepts, p. 341

Central nervous system That portion of the nervous system located in the bony central core of the body and consisting of the brain and spinal cord, p. 52

Cerebellum A part of the hindbrain that regulates and coordinates basic motor activities and may also play a role in learning, p. 61

Cerebral cortex The largest structure in the forebrain; largely responsible for higher-order mental processes, p. 64

Cerebral hemispheres The two main parts of the cerebral cortex: the left and right hemispheres, p. 65

Cerebral lateralization The degree to which the right or left hemisphere controls various cognitive and behavior functions, p. 67

Cerebrospinal fluid A clear, cushioning fluid secreted by the brain and circulated inside and around the brain and spinal cord, p. 52

Character strength Trait that allows optimal functioning in pursuing a virtue, p. 469

Child-directed speech Speech to babies that is characterized by exaggerated intonations, high pitch, clear enunciation, short sentences, repetition, and slow speech; also called *motherese*, p. 338

Chromosomes Threadlike structures carrying genetic information that are found in every cell of the body, p. 76

Chunking Organizing items of information into a meaningful unit, or chunk, that can be stored in short-term memory, p. 293

Circadian rhythms Internally generated behavior and physiological changes that occur on a daily bases, p. 208

Classical conditioning A type of learning in which a neutral stimulus acquires the capacity to elicit a response after being paired with another stimulus that naturally elicits that response, p. 247

Client-centered therapy A humanistic therapy in which the client, rather than the therapist, directs the course of therapy, p. 545

Cloning The process of making a genetically identical organism through nonsexual means, p. 80

Cochlea The coiled, fluid-filled tube in the inner ear that contains the hairlike auditory receptors, p. 165

Cognition The mental activity of knowing and the processes through which knowledge is acquired and problems are solved, p. 341

Cognitive-behavior therapy (CBT) The cognitive therapy of Aaron Beck that identifies and then changes negative thinking and behavior by using both cognitive and behavioral principles, p. 544

Cognitive dissonance A feeling of discomfort caused by performing an action inconsistent with one's attitudes, p. 622

Cognitive-neoassociationist model A theory of aggression stating that aversive events produce negative affect, which stimulates the inclination to aggress, p. 634

Cognitive psychology An approach to psychology that attempts to understand behavior by studying how the mind organizes perceptions, processes information, and interprets experiences, p. 10

Cognitive therapies Psychotherapies that focus on identifying and then modifying dysfunctional patterns of thought, p. 543

Collective unconscious In Jung's personality theory, the part of the unconscious mind containing inherited memories shared by all human beings, p. 457

Collectivism A philosophy of life characterized by the priority of group needs over individual needs, a preference for tightly knit social relationships, and a willingness to submit to the influence of one's group, p. 15

Color blindness A deficiency in the ability to distinguish among colors, p. 160

Communication The sending and receiving of information, p. 330

Companionate love The affection we feel for those with whom our lives are deeply entwined, p. 643

Compliance Publicly acting in accord with a direct request, p. 626

Computerized axial tomography (CAT) scan A brain-imaging technique that combines thousands of X-ray brain photographs to construct a cross-sectional picture of the brain, p. 57

Concept A mental grouping of objects, ideas, or events that share common properties, p. 341

Concrete operational stage The third stage in Piaget's theory of cognitive development (ages 7 to 11), a time when children can perform mental operations on tangible objects or events and gradually engage in logical reasoning, p. 120

Conditional positive regard An attitude of acceptance toward another person only when she or he meets your standards, p. 460

Conditioned response (CR) In classical conditioning, the learned response to a previously neutral conditioned stimulus, p. 247

Conditioned stimulus (CS) In classical condition, a previously neutral stimulus that, after repeated pairing with an unconditioned stimulus, comes to elicit a conditioned response, p. 248

Cones Receptor neurons in the eye, located near the center of the retina, which mediate color vision, p. 155

Confirmation bias The tendency to seek information that supports our beliefs while ignoring disconfirming information, p. 344

Conformity A yielding to perceived group pressure, p. 625

Conscious mind According to Freud, the relatively small part of our minds that we are aware of at the moment, p. 450

Consciousness Awareness of yourself and your environment, p. 202

Conservation The understanding that certain physical properties of an object remain unchanged despite superficial changes in the object's appearance, p. 118

Content validity The degree to which the items on a test are related to the characteristic the test supposedly measures, p. 358

Continuous reinforcement schedule A schedule of reinforcement in which every correct response is followed by a reinforcer, p. 264

Control condition The condition in an experiment in which participants are not exposed to the independent variable, p. 31

Conventional morality The second level of moral reasoning in Kohlberg's theory of moral development that is characterized by conforming to societal norms and laws, p. 124

Convergent thinking Applying logic and conventional knowledge to arrive at (or *converge upon*) a single solution to a problem, p. 384

Cornea A clear membrane covering the front of the eyeball that aids in visual acuity by bending light that falls on its surface, p. 154

Corpus callosum A thick band of nerve fibers connecting the right and left cerebral hemispheres that transmits information between them, p. 65

Correlational research Research designed to examine the nature of the relationship between two or more naturally occurring variables, p. 26

Correlation coefficient (*r*) A statistical measure of the direction and strength of the linear relationship between two variables, which can range from −1.00 to +1.00, p. 28

Counterconditioning A behavior therapy procedure based on classical conditioning that involves conditioning new responses to stimuli that trigger unwanted behaviors, p. 538

Countertransference The process by which the therapist develops feelings for the client that are presumed to reflect feelings the therapist had for others early in life, p. 537

Couples therapy Therapy designed to help couples improve the quality of their relationship, p. 551

Covariation model A theory of attribution asserting that people rely on consensus, consistency, and distinctiveness information when assigning causes for events, p. 617

Creativity The ability to produce novel, high-quality products or ideas, p. 384

Critical thinking The process of deciding what to believe and how to act based on careful evaluation of the evidence, p. 18

Cryptomnesia A memory illusion in which people believe that some work they have done is a novel creation when, in fact, it is not original, p. 310

Culture The total lifestyle of people from a particular social grouping, including all the ideas, symbols, preferences, and material objects they share, p. 13

D

Daydreaming A relatively passive state of waking consciousness that involves turning attention away from external stimuli to internal thoughts and imaginary situations, p. 205

Decay Forgetting due to the passage of time, p. 314

Defense mechanism In Freud's theory, the ego's method of keeping threatening and unacceptable material out of consciousness and thereby reducing anxiety, p. 454

Déjà vu illusion A memory illusion in which people feel a sense of familiarity in a situation that they know they have never encountered before, p. 310

Delta waves Slow, high-amplitude brain waves most typical of stage 4 deep sleep, p. 212

Dendrites Branchlike extensions of the soma that receive information from other neurons, p. 43

Deoxyribonucleic acid (DNA) The complex molecular strands of a chromosome that contain thousands of different genes, located at fixed positions, p. 76

Dependent variable The experimental variable that is measured because it is believed to depend on the manipulated changes in the independent variable, p. 30

Depressants Psychoactive drugs that slow down—or depress—the nervous system and decrease mental and physical activity, p. 226

Depth perception The ability to perceive objects three-dimensionally, p. 180

Descriptive statistics Numbers that summarize and describe the behavior or characteristics of a particular sample of participants in a study, p. 23

Development The systematic physical, cognitive, and social changes in the individual that occur between conception and death, p. 92

Diagnosis The process of distinguishing one disorder from another, p. 496

Diagnostic and Statistical Manual of Mental Disorders (DSM) The manual of psychological disorders published by the American Psychiatric Association and used for descriptive diagnoses, p. 502

Diathesis-stress model A predisposition to a given disorder (diathesis) that combines with environmental stressors to trigger a psychological disorder, p. 499

Difference threshold The smallest difference between two stimuli that can be detected half the time; also called *just-noticeable difference,* or *jnd,* p. 151

Diffusion of responsibility The belief that the presence of others in a situation makes one less personally responsible for events that occur in that situation, p. 639

Discrimination A negative and/or patronizing action toward members of a specific social group, p. 613

Displacement A defense mechanism that diverts people's sexual or aggressive urges toward objects that are more acceptable than those that actually stimulate their feelings, p. 455

Dissociative amnesia A dissociative disorder characterized by the inability to recall important personal information, usually of a traumatic or stressful nature, p. 517

Dissociative disorders Psychological disorders characterized by disruptions in consciousness, memory, sense of identity, or perception, p. 517

Dissociative identity disorder (DID) A dissociative disorder characterized by the presence of two or more distinct identities or personalities that take turns controlling the person's behavior; also known as *multiple personality disorder,* p. 518

Divergent thinking Pursuing many different and often unconventional paths to generate many different solutions to a problem, p. 384

Divided attention Attention that is split and simultaneously focused on different stimuli, p. 204

Dopamine (DA) A neurotransmitter that promotes and facilitates movement as well as influencing thought and emotion, p. 49

Down syndrome A form of intellectual disability caused by an extra chromosome in an individual's genetic makeup, p. 369

Dream A story like sequence of vivid visual images experienced during sleep, p. 215

Drive A physiological state of arousal that moves an organism to meet a need, p. 396

Drive-reduction theory The idea that an imbalance in homeostasis creates a physiological need, which in turn produces a drive that motivates the organism to satisfy the need, p. 395

Drug abuse Persistence in drug use even when impaired behavior or social functioning results, p. 225

Drug tolerance An effect of drug abuse in which greater amounts of the drug are necessary to produce the same effect once produced by a smaller dose, p. 225

Dynamic systems theory The idea that new forms of behavior emerge from the interactions between people's biology and their culture and physical environment, p. 14

Dysthymia Chronic low-level depression lasting more than two years, p. 510

E

Eardrum A thin, flexible membrane at the end of the auditory canal that vibrates in sequence with sound waves, p. 165

Egocentrism The tendency to view the world from one's own perspective without recognizing that others may have different points of view, p. 117

Ego The part of our minds that includes our consciousness and that balances the demands of the id, the superego, and reality, p. 451

Elaboration likelihood model A theory that there are two ways in which persuasive messages can cause attitude change, each differing in the amount of cognitive effort or elaboration they require, p. 621

Elaborative rehearsal Rehearsal that involves thinking about how new information relates to information already stored in long-term memory, p. 294

Electroconvulsive therapy (ECT) A physiological treatment for severe depression in which a brief electrical shock is administered to the brain of an anesthetized patient, p. 555

Electroencephalograph (EEG) A brain-imaging technique that records "waves" of electrical activity in the brain using metal electrodes placed on a person's scalp., p. 57

Embryonic stage The second stage of prenatal development, lasting from the third week through the eighth week of pregnancy, p. 93

Emerging adulthood A stage of life for some individuals from the late teens to the mid-twenties when they are relatively free from adult responsibilities and expectations, p. 128

Emotional intelligence The ability to recognize and regulate our own and others' emotions, p. 365

Emotion A positive or negative feeling state that typically includes some combination of physiological arousal, cognitive appraisal, and behavioral expression, p. 425

Emotion-focused coping A coping strategy designed to manage the emotional reactions to stressors rather than trying to change the stressors themselves, p. 577

Encoding specificity principle A retrieval rule stating that retrieving information from long-term memory is most likely to occur when the conditions at retrieval closely match the conditions present during the original learning, p. 309

Encoding The first memory process, in which information is organized and transformed so it can be entered into memory, p. 287

Endocrine system A network of glands in various parts of the body that secrete hormones directly into the bloodstream, p. 54

Endorphins A family of neurotransmitters that are similar to morphine and that play an important role in the experience of pleasure and control of pain, p. 49

Episodic memory Memory for factual information acquired at a specific time and place, p. 298

Ethnic identity A person's sense of personal identification with a particular ethnic group, p. 131

Ethnocentrism A pattern of increased hostility toward outgroups, accompanied by increased loyalty to one's ingroup, p. 613

Etiology The initial cause that led to the development of the disorder, p. 496

Eugenics The practice of encouraging supposedly superior people to reproduce, while discouraging or even preventing those judged to be inferior from doing so, p. 351

Evolutionary psychology An approach to psychology based on the principle of natural selection, p. 11

Evolution The genetic changes that occur in a species over generations due to natural selection, p. 12

Experimental condition The condition in an experiment whereby participants are exposed to different levels of the independent variable, p. 31

Experimental research Research designed to test cause-effect relationships between variables, p. 30

Explicit memory Memory of pervious experiences that one can consciously recollect; also called *declarative memory*, p. 297

External attribution An attribution that identifies the cause of behavior as factors external to the person, such as luck, other people, or the situation, p. 617

Extinction In classical condition, the gradual weakening and disappearance of the conditioned response when the conditioned stimulus is repeatedly presented without being paired with the unconditioned stimulus, p. 252

Extrasensory perception (ESP) The ability to perceive events without using normal sensory receptors, p. 192

Extravert A person who is focused on the external world and tends to be confident and socially outgoing, p. 457

Extrinsic motivation Motivation to engage in a behavior or an activity because of the external rewards it can provide, p. 398

F

Facial feedback hypothesis A theory of emotion proposing that specific facial expressions trigger the subjective experience of specific emotions, p. 430

Factor analysis A statistical technique that allows researchers to identify clusters of variables or test items that correlate with one another, p. 360

Family systems therapy A form of family therapy in which the family is treated as a dynamic system, with each member an important interacting element in that system, p. 551

Family therapies Therapies designed to constructively modify the dysfunctional relationships among family members , p. 551

Fantasy-prone personality A person who has regular, vivid fantasies and who sometimes cannot separate fantasy from reality, p. 206

Feature detectors Cells in the visual cortex that respond only to a highly specific feature of a visual stimulus, such as a straight edge, an angle, movement of a spot, or brightness, p. 158

Femininity A set of attributes, behaviors, and social roles culturally defined as being typical of or appropriate to females, p. 111

Fetal alcohol syndrome Physical and cognitive abnormalities in children that result when pregnant women consume large quantities of alcohol, p. 95

Fetal stage The last and longest stage in prenatal development, extending from the ninth week after conception until birth, p. 93

Figure-ground relationship The Gestalt principle that, when people focus on an object in their perceptual field, they automatically distinguish it from its surroundings, p. 179

Five-Factor Model A trait theory asserting that personality consists of five traits (neuroticism, extraversion, openness to experience, agreeableness, and conscientiousness), p. 465

Fixation A tendency to persist in pleasure-seeking behaviors associated with an earlier psychosexual stage during which conflicts were unresolved, p. 452

Fixed-interval reinforcement schedule A partial reinforcement schedule that reinforces the first response after a specific number of nonreinforced responses, p. 266

Fixed-ratio reinforcement schedule A partial reinforcement schedule that reinforces a response after a specified number of nonreinforced responses, p. 264

Flashbulb memories Detailed and vivid memories of surprising and emotion-provoking events, p. 312

Flynn effect The tendency for people's performance on IQ tests to improve from one generation to the next, p. 356

Forebrain Region of the brain above the midbrain that contains the thalamus, the hypothalamus, and the limbic system, p. 62

Formal operational stage The fourth and final stage in Piaget's theory of cognitive development (ages 11 and beyond), during which a person is able to reason abstractly and make predictions about hypothetical situations, p. 120

Form perception The process by which sensations are organized into meaningful shapes and patterns, p. 179

Fovea The retina's area of central focus, p. 155

Fraternal twins Twins who develop from the union of two separate sperm and eggs; also known as *dizygotic twins*, p. 78

Free association A psychodynamic therapy technique developed by Freud, in which clients say whatever comes to mind, without making any effort to inhibit their speech, p. 536

Frequency theory A theory that pitch is determined by the frequency with which the basilar membrane vibrates, p. 167

Frontal lobes One of the four major sections of the cerebral cortex, situated in the front of each cerebral hemisphere and behind the forehead; involved in the coordination of movement and higher mental processes, p. 66

Functional fixedness The tendency to think of objects as functioning in fixed and unchanging ways and ignoring other less obvious ways in which they might be used, p. 347

Functionalism An early approach to psychology that studied how the conscious mind helps humans survive and successfully adapt to their environment, p. 6

Functional magnetic resonance imaging (fMRI) A brain-imaging technique that measures, over a few seconds, the average neural activity in different brain regions by showing fluctuations in blood oxygen levels, p. 58

Fundamental attribution error The tendency to make internal attributions rather than external attributions in explaining the behavior of others, p. 618

·· **G** ··············

Gate control theory A theory of pain perception proposing that small and large nerve fibers open and close "gateways" for pain in the spinal cord, p. 175

Gender identity The knowledge that one is a male or a female and the internalization of this fact into one's self-concept, p. 112

Gender The meanings that societies and individuals attach to being female and male, p. 81

General adaptation syndrome (GAS) Selye's model of stress, in which an event that threatens an organism's well-being (a stressor) leads to a three-stage bodily response: alarm, resistance, and exhaustion, p. 570

General intelligence factor (g-factor) The intelligence factor that Spearman and other researchers believed underlies all mental abilities, p. 361

Generalized anxiety disorder (GAD) An anxiety disorder characterized by a constant state of moderate anxiety, p. 506

Generic masculine The use of masculine nouns and pronouns to refer to all people, instead of just males, p. 339

Gene The basic biochemical unit of inheritance that is located on and transmitted by chromosomes, p. 76

Genital stage In Freud's theory, the last stage of psychosexual development during which mature sexual feelings toward others begin to emerge, and the ego learns to manage and direct these feelings, p. 454

Genotype The underlying genetic composition of an organism, p. 76

Germinal stage The first two weeks of prenatal development, from conception until the zygote implants itself in the wall of the uterus, p. 93

Gestalt An organized and coherent whole, p. 178

Gestalt psychology The approach to psychology that studies how the mind actively organizes stimuli into meaningful wholes, p. 178

Gestalt therapy A humanistic psychotherapy that stresses awareness of feelings in the here and now, p. 548

Glial cells Non-neuron cells that supply the neurons with support, nutrients, and insulation, p. 45

Gonads The two sex glands, called ovaries in females and testes in males, p. 56

Group therapy The simultaneous treatment of several clients under the guidance of a therapist, p. 550

Gustation The sense of taste, p. 172

H

Hallucinogens Psychoactive drugs that distort perception and generate sensory images without any external stimulation, p. 232

Happiness A predominance of positive over negative affect (emotion) and satisfaction with life as a whole, p. 600

Health psychologists Psychologists who study the effects of behavior and mental processes on health and illness, p. 566

Helping Voluntary behavior that is carried out to benefit another person, p. 632

Heritability coefficient A statistical coefficient, ranging from 0 to 1, that estimates the degree to which heredity determines intelligence within a particular human group, p. 371

Heterosexism A system of cultural beliefs, values, and customs that exalts heterosexuality and denies, denigrates, and stigmatizes any nonheterosexual form of behavior or identity, p. 416

Heterosexuality The sexual orientation in which a person is sexually attracted primarily to members of the other sex, p. 414

Heuristic A problem-solving strategy that involves following a general rule of thumb to reduce the number of possible solutions, p. 343

Hierarchy of needs Maslow's progression of human needs, in which those that are the most basic—namely, physiological needs—must be sufficiently satisfied before higher-level safety needs and then psychological needs become activated, p. 400

Higher-order conditioning A classical conditioning procedure in which a neutral stimulus becomes a conditioned stimulus after being paired with an existing conditioned stimulus, p. 254

Hindbrain Region of the brain above the spinal cord that contains the medulla, the pons, and the cerebellum, p. 61

Homeostasis The tendency of organisms to keep physiological systems internally balanced by adjusting them in response to change, p. 395

Homosexuality The sexual orientation in which a person is sexually attracted primarily to members of the same sex, p. 414

Hormones Chemical signals, secreted into the blood by the endocrine glands, that help regulate bodily activities, p. 54

Humanistic psychology An approach to psychology that emphasizes human beings' innate capacity for personal growth and their ability to consciously make choices, p. 10

Humanistic therapies Psychotherapies that help people get in touch with their feelings, with their "true selves," and with their purposes in life, p. 545

Hypnosis A psychological state of altered attention and awareness in which a person is unusually receptive to suggestions, p. 221

Hypnotizability The degree to which a person can enter a deep hypnotic state, p. 223

Hypothalamus A part of the forebrain involved in regulating basic biological processes, such as eating, drinking, sexual activity, emotion, and a stable body temperature, p. 62

Hypothesis An educated guess or prediction about the nature of things based upon a theory, p. 20

I

Id An unconscious part of the mind that contains our sexual and aggressive drives, p. 451

Identical twins Twins who develop from the union of the same egg and sperm, and thus share exactly the same genotype; also known as *monozygotic twins*, p. 78

Imaginary audience Adolescents' belief that their thoughts, feelings, and behavior are constantly being focused on by other people, p. 130

Immune system A complex surveillance system of specialized cells, tissues, and organs that is the body's primary defense against disease, p. 573

Implicit memory Memory of previous experiences without conscious recollection; also called *nondelcarative memory*, p. 299

Impression formation The process of integrating various sources of information about a person into an overall judgement, p. 609

Incentive A positive or negative environmental stimulus that motivates behavior, p. 397

Incentive theory A theory of motivation stating that behavior is directed toward attaining desirable stimuli, called positive incentives, and avoiding undesirable stimuli, called negative incentives, p. 397

Independent variable The experimental variable that the researcher manipulates, p. 30

Individualism A philosophy of life characterized by the priority of personal goals over group goals, a preference for loosely knit social relationships, and a desire to be relatively autonomous of others' influence, p. 15

Induced movement The illusory movement of a stationary object caused by the movement of another nearby object, p. 185

Infantile amnesia The inability to remember events that occurred during the early part of life (usually before the age of 3), p. 311

Inferential statistics Mathematical analyses that are used to determine whether the data support or do not support the research hypothesis, p. 23

Information-processing model A memory model concerning the sequential processing and use of information, involving encoding, storage, and retrieval, p. 287

Ingroup A group to which we belong and that forms a part of our social identity, p. 609

Inhalants Chemicals whose vapors can be breathed in to produce a mind-altering effect, p. 235

Insight A problem-solving strategy that involves a sudden realization of how a problem can be solved, p. 343

Insomnia A common sleep disorder characterized by the chronic inability to fall or stay asleep, p. 239

Instinct An unlearned, relatively fixed pattern of behavior that is essential to a species' survival, p. 395

Instinctive drift Species-specific behavior patterns that interfere with operant conditioning, p. 269

Intellectual disability A diagnostic category used for people who not only have an IQ score below 70 but also have difficulty adapting to the routine demands of independent living, p. 369

Intelligence quotient (IQ) Originally, the ratio of mental age to chronological age multiplied by 100 (MA/CA × 100) that today is calculated by comparing how a person's performance deviates from the average score of her or his same-age peers, which is 100, p. 353

Intelligence The mental abilities necessary to adapt to and shape the environment, p. 351

Interactionism The study of the combined effects of both the situation and the person on human behavior, p. 472

Internal attribution An attribution that identifies the cause of behavior as factors internal to the person, such as personality traits, moods, attitudes, abilities, or effort, p. 617

Internalization A process of cognition in which people absorb knowledge from their social surroundings, p. 122

Interneurons Neurons that connect the sensory neurons' input signals with the motor neurons' output signals, p. 43

Intrinsic motivation Motivation to engage in a behavior or an activity because one finds it interesting or enjoyable for its own sake, p. 398

Introvert A person who is preoccupied with his or her inner world and tends to be hesitant and cautious when interacting with people, p. 457

Iris A ring of muscles in the eye that range in color from light blue to dark brown, p. 154

J

James-Lange theory A theory stating that emotion-provoking events induce specific physiological changes in the autonomic nervous system, which our brain automatically interprets as specific emotions, p. 429

Jealousy The negative emotional reaction experienced when a real or imagined rival threatens a relationship important to one's self-concept, p. 647

L

Language acquisition device According to Chomsky's linguistic theory, an innate mechanism that facilitates the learning of language, p. 335

Language A systematic way of communicating information using symbols and rules for combining them, p. 330

Latency stage In Freud's theory, the fourth stage of psychosexual development during which the child is relatively free from sexual desires and conflict, p. 454

Latent content The true meaning of the dream that is concealed from the dreamer through the symbols that make up the manifest dream content, p. 218

Latent learning Learning that occurs without apparent reinforcement and is not demonstrated until sufficient reinforcement is provided, p. 270

Law of effect A basic principle of learning that states that a behavior becomes more or less likely based on its effect in producing desirable or undesirable consequences, p. 260

Laws of grouping Simple gestalt principles describing how people tend to group discrete stimuli together into a meaningful whole, p. 179

Learned helplessness The passive resignation produced by repeated exposure to aversive events that cannot be avoided, p. 271

Learning A relatively permanent change in behavior that results from experience, p. 246

Lens An elastic, disc-shaped structure that focuses light, p. 154

Limbic system A part of the forebrain consisting of structures that influence fear and aggression (amygdala) and the acquisition and consolidation of new information in memory (hippocampus), p. 62

Linguistic relativism The idea that language can influence thinking, p. 339

Locus of control The degree to which we expect that outcomes in our lives depend on our own actions and personal characteristics versus the actions of uncontrollable environmental forces, p. 474

Longitudinal study Research in which the same people are restudied and retested over time, p. 106

Long-term memory A durable memory system that has an immense capacity for information storage, p. 289

Long-term potentiation The long-lasting strengthening of synaptic transmission along a specific neural circuit, which is believed to be the neural basis for long-term memory, p. 319

LSD A synthesized chemical that is the most potent of the hallucinogens; induces hallucinations, distortions, and a blending of sensory experiences, p. 233

Lucid dream A dream in which the dreamer is aware of dreaming and is often able to change the plot of the dream, p. 218

···M····················

Magnetic resonance imaging (MRI) A brain-imaging technique that produces three-dimensional images of the brain's soft tissues by detecting magnetic activity from nuclear particles in brain molecules, p. 57

Maintenance rehearsal The process of repetitively verbalizing or thinking about information to either extend the usual 18-second duration of short term memory or transfer the rehearsed information to long-term memory, p. 293

Major depressive disorder A mood disorder characterized by extreme and persistent negative moods and the inability to experience pleasure from activities previously enjoyed, p. 510

Manifest content The dream that is remembered by the dreamer, p. 218

Marijuana A mild hallucinogen derived from the leafy material of the hemp, or Cannabis, plant; often induces a sense of giddiness or euphoria, as well as heightened sensitivity to various stimuli, p. 234

Masculinity A set of attributes, behaviors, and social roles culturally defined as being typical of or appropriate to males, p. 111

Matching hypothesis The proposition that people are attracted to others who are similar to them in certain characteristics, such as attitudes and physical attractiveness, p. 642

Medical model The viewpoint from the field of medicine that psychological disorders have a biological basis and can be classified into discrete categories just as physical diseases are, p. 495

Meditation A variety of mental exercises that alter the normal flow of consciousness in order to enhance self-knowledge, p. 224

Medulla A part of the hindbrain that controls breathing, heart rate, swallowing, and digestion, and allows us to maintain an upright posture, p. 61

Melatonin A hormone produced by the pineal gland that induces drowsiness, p. 208

Memory The mental process by which information is encoded and stored in the brain, and later retrieved, p. 286

Menopause The ending of menstruation, p. 136

Mental set The tendency to continue using solutions that have worked in the past, even though a better alternative may exist, p. 345

Mere exposure effect The tendency to develop more positive feelings toward objects and individuals the more frequently we are exposed to them, p. 620

Meta-analysis The use of statistical techniques to sum up a body of similar studies in order to objectively estimate the reliability and overall size of the effect, p. 24

Metacognition An awareness and understanding of one's own cognitive processes, p. 123

Midbrain The region of the brain above the hindbrain that contains the reticular formation, p. 62

Midlife crisis A stressful period when adults review and reevaluate their lives, p. 135

Mindfulness A heightened state of awareness of the present moment, p. 206

Minnesota Multiphasic Personality Inventory (MMPI) An objective personality test consisting of true/false items that measure various personality dimensions and clinical conditions such as depression, p. 480

Misinformation effects Distortions and alterations in a witness' memory due to receiving misleading information during questioning, p. 311

Mnemonics Strategies that make it easier to encode, store, and/or retrieve information, p. 321

Modeling A behavioral method of psychotherapy in which desirable behaviors are demonstrated as a way of teaching them to clients, p. 542

Molecular genetics The subdiscipline in biology that studies the molecular structure and function of genes to determine how they influence behavior, p. 79

Monocular cues Depth cues that require information from only one eye, p. 181

Mood disorders Psychological disorder characterized by emotional extremes that cause significant disruption in daily functioning, p. 509

Moon illusion A perceptual illusion in which the moon appears to be larger when near the horizon than when high in the sky, p. 189

Morphemes The smallest units of language that carry meaning, p. 336

Motivated forgetting Forgetting due to a desire to eliminate awareness of some unpleasant or disturbing memory, p. 316

Motivation An inner state that energizes behavior toward the fulfillment of a goal, p. 394

Motor neurons Neurons that send commands from the brain to glands, muscles, and organs to do, cease, or inhibit something, p. 43

Müeller-Lyer illusion A perceptual illusion in which the perceived length of a line is influenced by placing inward- or outward-facing wings on the ends of the line, p. 186

Multiple intelligences Gardner's theory contends that there are at least eight distinct and relatively independent intelligences (linguistic, logical-mathematical, spatial, musical, bodily-kinesthetic, naturalist, interpersonal, and intrapersonal)—all of which are differently developed in each of us, p. 362

Myelin sheath A protective coating of fatty material around an axon that hastens the transmission of the electrochemical charge, p. 44

· · N ·

Narcolepsy A sleep disorder characterized by uncontrolled REM sleep attacks during normal waking hours, p. 238

Naturalistic observation A scientific method that describes how people or animals behave in their natural environment, p. 24

Natural selection The process by which organisms with inherited traits best suited to the environment reproduce more successfully than less well-adapted organisms over a number of generations, which leads to evolutionary changes, p. 12

Need for achievement (n-Ach) A desire to overcome obstacles and meet high standards of excellence, p. 421

Need for cognition A person's preference for and tendency to engage in effortful cognitive activities, p. 350

Need to belong The need to interact with others and be socially accepted (also known as the *need for affiliation*), p. 419

Negative punisher Stimulus that weakens a response by removing a positive stimulus after a response, p. 263

Negative reinforcer Stimulus that strengthens a response by removing an aversive or unpleasant stimulus after a response, p. 262

Neodissociation theory A theory that hypnotized persons enter an altered state in which two streams of consciousness operate simultaneously, one actively responding to suggestions and the other passively observing what is going on, p. 224

Nerve A bundle of axons from many neurons that are routed together in the peripheral nervous system, p. 51

Neurons Specialized cells in the nervous system that send and receive information, p. 43

Neuroscience perspective An approach to psychology that attempts to understand behavior and mental processes by examining the nervous system, p. 11

Neurotransmitters Chemical messengers released by the synaptic vesicles that travel across the synaptic cleft that either excite or inhibit adjacent neurons, p. 47

Night terror A sleep disorder involving panic attacks that occur during early-night stage 4 NREM sleep, p. 238

Normal distribution The bell-shaped appearance of a distribution that results when the mean, median, and mode are identical in value, p. 356

NREM sleep Non-rapid-eye-movement sleep; which is a relatively inactive phase in the sleep cycle, p. 210

· · O ·

Obedience The performance of an action in response to a direct order, p. 627

Obesity The excessive accumulation of body fat; medically, a body mass index (BMI) over 30, p. 589

Objective test Personality test that asks direct, unambiguous questions about a person's thoughts, feelings, and behavior, p. 480

Object permanence The realization that an object continues to exist even if you can't see it or touch it, p. 117

Observational learning Learning a behavior by observing and imitating the behavior of others (models), p. 273

Obsessive-compulsive disorder (OCD) An anxiety disorder characterized by persistent, unwanted, and distressing actions and/or thoughts, p. 506

Occipital lobes One of the four major sections of the cerebral cortex, located at the back of each cerebral hemisphere and primarily responsible for visual processing, p. 65

Off-line dream theory A theory that the cognitive process of dreaming consolidates and stores information gathered during the day, thus allowing us to maintain a smaller and more efficient brain, p. 219

Olfaction The sense of smell, p. 169

Olfactory epithelium A thin layer of tissue at the top of the nasal cavity that contains the olfactory receptor cells, p. 170

Operant conditioning A type of learning in which behavior is strengthened if followed by reinforcement and weakened if followed by punishment., p. 260

Operational definition A scientist's precise description of how a variable has been quantified so that it can be measured, p. 21

Opiates A category of depressant drugs, including opium, morphine, and heroine, that depress the nervous system, temporarily relieve pain, and produce a relaxed, dreamlike state, p. 229

Opponent-process theory A theory of emotion suggesting that every emotion triggers an opposite emotion, p. 436

Opponent-process theory A theory proposing that color perception depends on receptors that make opposing responses to three pairs of color, p. 160

Optic nerve The bundle of nerve cells that carries information from the retina to the brain, p. 156

Optimistic explanatory style The habitual tendency to explain uncontrollable negative events as caused by temporary factors external to oneself that do not affect other aspects of one's life; this optimistic style is associated with good health and longevity., p. 582

Oral stage In Freud's theory, the first stage of psychosexual development, during which the child derives pleasure by engaging in oral activities, p. 453

Outgroup Any group with which we do not share membership, p. 609

•••**P**••••••••••••••••••

Panic disorder An anxiety disorder characterized by episodes of intense fear and dread that usually occur suddenly and unexpectedly, p. 504

Parallel distributed processing model A memory model in which a large network of interconnected neurons, or processing units, distributed throughout the brain simultaneously work on different memory tasks, p. 305

Parapsychology The field that studies ESP and other paranormal phenomena, p. 192

Parasympathetic nervous system The part of the autonomic nervous system that acts to conserve and maintain the body's energy resources, p. 52

Parietal lobes One of the four major sections of the cerebral cortex, situated in front of the optical lobe in each cerebral hemisphere and involved in touch sensation and in monitoring the body's position in space, p. 65

Partial reinforcement schedule A schedule of reinforcement in which correct responses are followed by reinforcers only part of the time., p. 264

Participant observation A descriptive scientific method in which a group is studied from within by a researcher who records behavior as it occurs in its natural environment, p. 25

Passionate love A state of intense longing for union with another that we typically experience most intensely during the early stages of a romantic relationship, p. 642

Peak experiences Fleeting but intense moments when a person feels happy, absorbed, and extremely capable, p. 460

Perception The process that organizes sensations into meaningful objects and events, p. 148

Perceptual constancy The tendency to perceive objects as relatively stable despite continually changing sensory information, p. 183

Perceptual illusion A misperception of physical reality, often due to the misapplication of perceptual principles, p. 185

Perceptual sets Expectations that create a tendency to interpret sensory information in a particular way, p. 184

Peripheral nervous system That portion of the nervous system containing all the nerves outside the brain and spinal cord, p. 51

Permissive parent A parent who allows his/her children to set their own rules, makes few demands, and submits to the children's desires, p. 109

Personal fable The tendency for adolescents to believe that their experiences and feelings are unique, p. 130

Personality disorders A category of disorders characterized by general styles of living that are ineffective and that can lead to problems, p. 523

Personality The consistent and distinctive thoughts, feelings, and behaviors in which an individual engages, p. 447

Persuasion The process of consciously attempting to change attitudes through the transmission of some message, p. 621

Pessimistic explanatory style The habitual tendency to explain uncontrollable negative events as caused by one's own stable personal qualities, which affect all aspects of one's life; this pessimistic style is associated with health problems and premature death., p. 582

Phallic stage In Freud's theory, the third stage of psychosexual development during which the child derives pleasure from masturbation, p. 453

Phenotype The visible and measurable traits of an organism, p. 76

Pheromones Airborne chemicals that are released by animals and detected by other animals using specialized receptors and that affect the behavior of other animals of the same species, p. 171

Phonemes The smallest significant sound units in speech, p. 336

Physical attractiveness stereotype The belief that physically attractive individuals possess socially desirable personality traits and lead happier, more fulfilling lives than less attractive persons do, p. 610

Pituitary gland The body's "master" gland, located in the base of the brain, whose hormones stimulate and regulate the rest of the endocrine system, p. 55

Placebo effect A situation in which people experience some change or improvement from an empty, fake, or ineffectual treatment, p. 196

Place theory A theory that pitch is determined by which place along the cochlea's basilar membrane is most activated, p. 166

Plasticity The ability of the brain to alter its neural connections following damage, p. 73

Play therapy A therapeutic technique in which the therapist provides children with toys and drawing materials on the assumption that whatever is troubling them will be expressed in their play, p. 550

Pleasure principle The process by which the id seeks to immediately satisfy whatever desire is currently active, p. 451

Polygraph A machine that measures several of the physiological responses accompanying emotion (such as respiration, heart rate, blood pressure, and palm perspiration), p. 431

Pons A part of the hindbrain that is concerned with sleep and arousal, p. 61

Ponzo illusion A perception illusion in which the perceived lengths of horizontal lines are influenced by their placement between vertical converging lines that serve as distance cues, p. 188

Population All the members of an identifiable group from which a sample is drawn, p. 18

Positive psychology A new scientific approach to studying optimal human functioning that asserts that the normal functioning of human beings cannot be accounted for in purely negative (or problem-focused) terms, p. 10

Positive punisher Stimulus that weakens a response by presenting an aversive stimulus after a response, p. 263

Positive reinforcer Stimulus that strengthens a response by presenting a positive stimulus after a response, p. 262

Positron emission tomography (PET) scan A brain-imaging technique that measures, over several minutes, the average amount of neural activity in different brain regions by showing each region's consumption of the sugar glucose, the brain's chemical fuel, p. 58

Postconventional morality The third and final level of moral reasoning in Kohlberg's theory of moral development; characterized by making moral judgments based on abstract universal principles, p. 125

Post-traumatic stress disorder (PTSD) An anxiety disorder characterized by flashbacks and recurrent thoughts of life-threatening or other traumatic events, p. 507

Preconscious mind According to Freud, those mental processes that are not currently conscious but could become so at any moment, p. 450

Preconventional morality The first level of moral reasoning in Kohlberg's theory of moral development; characterized by avoiding punishment and seeking rewards, p. 124

Predictive validity The degree to which a test predicts other observable behavior related to the characteristic the test supposedly measures; also known as *criterion validity*, p. 358

Prejudice Attitudes toward members of specific groups that directly or indirectly suggest they deserve an inferior social status, p. 613

Prenatal development The many changes that transform a fertilized egg into a newborn baby, p. 92

Preoperational stage The second stage in Piaget's theory of cognitive development (ages 2 to 7), marked by the full emergence of representational thought, p. 117

Primacy effect The increased memory for the first bits of information presented in a string of information, p. 289

Primary reinforcer Stimulus that is naturally reinforcing because it satisfies a biological need, p. 261

Primary sex characteristics The body organs that make sexual reproduction possible, p. 128

Priming A method of activating implicit memories, in which a recently presented bit of information facilitates—or "primes"—responses in a subsequent situation, p. 299

Private speech Overt language that is not directed to others but, rather, is self-directed, p. 122

Proactive interference Forgetting due to interference from previously learned information, p. 315

Problem-focused coping A coping strategy designed to reduce the stress by overcoming the source of the problem, p. 577

Problem-solving theory A theory that dreaming provides the opportunity to creatively solve everyday problems because dreams are not hampered by logic or realism, p. 218

Problem solving The thought process used to overcome the obstacles to reaching a goal, p. 342

Procedural memory Memory of how to perform skilled motor activities, which have become well-learned habits and are carried out automatically (without conscious thought), p. 299

Prodigies Individuals who easily master skills in a particular intellectual area, p. 363

Prognosis A prediction about the likely course of a disorder, p. 496

Progressive relaxation A stress-reducing technique that involves the successive tensing and relaxing of each of the major muscle groups of the body, p. 597

Projection A powerful defense mechanism in which people perceive their own aggressive or sexual urges, not in themselves, but in others, p. 455

Projective test A psychological test that asks people to respond to ambiguous stimuli or situations in ways that will reveal their unconscious motives and desires, p. 478

Proprioceptive senses Two additional sources of sensory information that detect body position and movement, p. 176

Prototype The most representative member of a concept, p. 342

Psychiatry A branch of medicine concerned with the diagnosis and treatment of psychological disorders. (The roughly comparable specialty area in psychology is known as clinical psychology.), p. 5

Psychoactive drugs Chemicals that modify mental processes and behavior, p. 225

Psychoanalysis An approach to psychology that studies how the unconscious mind shapes behavior, p. 7

Psychodynamic perspective A diverse group of theories descending from the work of Sigmund Freud that asserts that behavior is controlled by unconscious forces, p. 456

Psychodynamic therapies A diverse group of psychotherapies based on the work of Sigmund Freud that assert that psychological disorders stem primarily from unconscious forces, p. 536

Psychological disorder A pattern of atypical behavior that results in personal distress or significant impairment in a person's social or occupational functioning, p. 497

Psychology The scientific study of mental processes and behavior, p. 5

Psychometrics The measurement of intelligence, personality, and other mental processes, p. 351

Psychoneuroimmunology The interdisciplinary field that studies the relationship between psychological factors and physical illness, p. 573

Psychophysics The study of how physical stimuli are translated into psychological experience, p. 149

Psychophysiological disorders Physical conditions, such as high blood pressure and migraine headaches, that are caused or aggravated by psychological factors such as stress, p. 573

Psychosexual stages The fixed sequence of childhood developmental stages during which the id primarily seeks sexual pleasure by focusing its energies on distinct erogenous zones, p. 452

Psychosurgery A rarely used type of procedure to treat psychological disorders in which brain tissue, thought to be the cause of the disorder, is destroyed, p. 556

Psychotherapy The treatment of psychological disorders by employing psychological methods that include a personal relationship between a trained therapist and a client, p. 534

Puberty The growth period of sexual maturation, during which a person becomes capable of reproducing, p. 128

Punishment The process by which a stimulus decreases the probability of the behavior it follows, p. 263

Pupil A hole in the center of the iris that regulates how much light enters the eye, p. 154

R

Random assignment Placement of research participants into experimental conditions in a manner that guarantees that all have an equal chance of being exposed to each level of independent variable, p. 30

Random selection A procedure for selecting a sample of people to study in which everyone in the population has an equal chance of being chosen, p. 18

Rape myth The false belief that deep down, women enjoy forcible sex and find it sexually exciting, p. 408

Rational-emotive behavior therapy (REBT) The cognitive therapy of Albert Ellis, in which people are confronted with their irrational beliefs and persuaded to develop a more realistic way of thinking, p. 544

Rationalization A defense mechanism in which people offer logical, self-justifying explanations for their actions in place of the real, more anxiety-producing, unconscious reasons, p. 455

Reaction formation A defense mechanism that allows people to express unacceptable feelings or ideas by consciously expressing the exact opposite, p. 455

Reaction range A person's genetically determined range of potential intellectual growth, with environmental factors influencing where the person ultimately falls in this range., p. 373

Realistic group conflict theory A theory of prejudice contending that when two groups compete for scarce resources, this competition creates a breeding ground for prejudice, p. 613

Reality principle The process by which the ego seeks to delay gratification of id desires until appropriate outlets and situations can be found, p. 451

Recall A measure of explicit memory in which a person must retrieve and reproduce information from memory, p. 307

Recency effect The increased memory for the last bits of information presented in a string of information, p. 289

Reciprocal determinism The social-cognitive belief that personality emerges from an ongoing mutual interaction between people's cognitions, their actions, and their environment, p. 473

Reciprocity norm The expectation that one should return a favor or a good deed, p. 627

Recognition A measure of explicit memory in which a person need only decide whether or not something has been previously encountered, p. 307

Reflexes Automatic, involuntary responses to sensory stimuli, p. 54

Regression A defense mechanism in which people faced with intense anxiety psychologically retreat to a more infantile developmental stage where some psychic energy remains fixated, p. 456

Reinforcement The process by which a stimulus increases the probability of the behavior that it follows, p. 261

Reinforcer Any stimulus or event that increases the likelihood that the behavior preceding it will be repeated, p. 261

Reliability The degree to which a test yields consistent results, p. 357

REM sleep A relatively active phase in the sleep cycle, characterized by rapid eye movements, in which dreaming occurs, p. 211

Replication Repeating a previous study's scientific procedures using different participants in an attempt to duplicate the findings, p. 24

Representativeness heuristic The tendency to make decisions based on how closely an alternative matches (or represents) a particular prototype, p. 348

Repression In Freud's theory, a very basic defense mechanism in which people move anxiety-arousing thoughts from the conscious mind into the unconscious mind, p. 454

Resistance Anything the client does to interfere with therapeutic progress, p. 537

Response prevention A counterconditioning technique, commonly used in the treatment of obsessive-compulsive disorder, in which clients are exposed to the situation where they previously exhibited a compulsive behavior but now are not permitted to engage in the ritual, p. 540

Resting potential The stable, negative charge of an inactive neuron, p. 45

Restorative theory of sleep A theory that sleep allows the body to restore itself following the rigors of daily activity, p. 213

Reticular formation A part of the midbrain involved in the regulation and maintenance of consciousness, p. 62

Retina A light-sensitive surface at the back of the eye, p. 155

Retrieval cue A stimulus that allows us to more easily recall information from long-term memory, p. 308

Retrieval The third memory process, which involves recovering stored information from memory so it can be used, p. 288

Retroactive interference Forgetting due to interference from newly learned information, p. 315

Retrograde amnesia The loss of information previously stored in long-term memory due to physical injury to the brain, p. 320

Rods Receptor neurons in the eye located at the edges of the retina that are sensitive to the brightness of light, p. 155

Rorschach Inkblot Test A projective personality test in which people are shown 10 symmetrical inkblots and asked what each might be depicting, p. 478

· **S** · · · · · · · · · · · · · · · ·

Sample A group of subjects selected to participate in a research study, p. 18

Satiety Being full to satisfaction—in this case, with food, p. 401

Savant Intellectually disabled individuals who demonstrate exceptional ability in one specific intellectual area, p. 363

Schema An organized pattern of thought or behavior that people use to understand and interpret information, p. 116

Schizophrenia A psychological disorder characterized by severe impairments in thinking, such as hallucinations, delusions, or loose associations, p. 519

Scientific methods A set of procedures used in science to gather, analyze, and interpret information in a way that reduces error and leads to dependable generalizations, p. 18

Secondary reinforcer Stimulus that is learned and becomes reinforcing by being associated with primary reinforcers, p. 262

Secondary sex characteristics The non-reproductive physical features that distinguish the two sexes from one another, p. 128

Selective attention Focused awareness on a single stimulus to the exclusion of all others, p. 203

Self-actualization The ultimate goal of growth, being the realization of one's full potential, p. 400

Self-awareness A psychological state in which you focus on yourself as an object of attention, p. 106

Self-concept The "theory" or "story" that a person constructs about herself or himself through social interaction, p. 106

Self-efficacy A person's belief about his or her ability to perform behaviors that should bring about a desired outcome, p. 474

Self-esteem A person's overall evaluation of his or her self-concept., p. 108

Self-fulfilling prophecy The process by which someone's expectations about a person or group lead to the fulfillment of those expectations, p. 381

Self-help group Several people regularly meeting and discussing their problems with one another without the guidance of a therapist, p. 550

Self-monitoring A personality trait involving the tendency to use cues from other people's self-presentations to control one's own self-presentations, p. 486

Self-serving bias The tendency to bolster and defend self-esteem by taking credit for positive events while denying blame for negative events, p. 476

Semantic memory Memory for general knowledge about the world that is not associated with the time and place the information was learned, p. 298

Semantic network model A theory that describes concepts in long-term memory as being organized in a complex network of associations, p. 301

Sensation The process that detects stimuli from our bodies and our environment, p. 148

Sensorimotor stage The first stage in Piaget's theory of cognitive development (birth to age 2), in which infants develop the ability to coordinate their sensory input with their motor actions, p. 117

Sensory adaptation The tendency for our sensory receptors to show decreasing responsiveness to stimuli that continue without change, p. 152

Sensory memory A memory system that very briefly stores the sensory characteristics of a stimulus, p. 289

Sensory neurons Neurons that send information from sensory receptors to the brain, usually by way of the spinal cord, p. 43

Separation anxiety The fear and distress that infants display when separated from their primary caregiver, p. 102

Serotonin A neurotransmitter that is important in regulating emotional states, sleep cycles, dreaming, aggression, and appetite, p. 49

Set point A level of weight that the body works to maintain, p. 404

Sex chromosomes Threadlike structures carrying genetic information that are found in every cell of the body, p. 78

Sex The biological state of being female or male, p. 81

Sexual identity The identity a person organizes around his or her sexual orientation, typically labeled "heterosexual," "gay," "lesbian," or "bisexual", p. 415

Sexual orientation The degree to which a person is sexually attracted to persons of the other sex and/or to persons of the same sex, p. 414

Sexual response cycle The four stages of sexual responding—excitement, plateau, orgasm, and resolution; first identified by Masters and Johnson, p. 413

Sexual script A learned preconception about how a series of events, perceived as sexual, is likely to occur, p. 408

Shaping In operant conditioning, the process of teaching a new behavior by reinforcing closer and closer approximations to the desired behavior; also known as the *method of successive approximations*, p. 268

Short-term memory A limited-capacity memory system through which we actively "work" with information., p. 289

Signal-detection theory The theory that explains how detection of a stimulus is influenced by observers' expectations, p. 151

Situationism The viewpoint that our behavior is strongly influenced by the situation, rather than by personality traits, p. 471

Sleep A nonwaking state of consciousness characterized by minimal physical movement and minimal responsiveness to one's surroundings, p. 207

Sleep apnea A sleep disorder in which a person repeatedly stops breathing during sleep, p. 238

Sleep spindles Bursts of rapid, rhythmic electrical activity in the brain characteristic of stage 2 sleep, p. 211

Sleepwalking A sleep disorder in which a person arises and wanders about while remaining asleep, p. 238

Social anxiety disorder An anxiety disorder involving intense fear of being humiliated in the presence of others, p. 506

Social-cognitive perspective A psychological perspective that examines how people interpret, analyze, remember, and use information about themselves, others, social interactions, and relationships, p. 473

Social influence The exercise of social power by a person or group to change the attitudes or behavior of others in a certain direction, p. 625

Socialization Learning the ways of a given society or group well enough to be able to function according to its rules, p. 106

Social leaning theory A theory contending that people learn social behaviors mainly through observation and cognitive processing of information, p. 273

Social perception The way we seek to know and understand other persons and events; also known as *social cognition*, p. 608

Social psychology The scientific discipline that attempts to understand and explain how the thoughts, feelings, and behavior of individuals are influenced by others, p. 608

Social roles Clusters of socially defined expectations that people in given situations are supposed to fulfill, such as the role of son, daughter, student, or employee, p. 109

Social skills training A behavioral method of psychotherapy in which clients are taught how to interact with others more comfortably and effectively, p. 542

Social support The helpful coping resources provided by friends and other people, p. 584

Sociocultural perspective An approach to psychology that emphasizes social and cultural influences on behavior, p. 13

Soma The cell body of the neuron which contains the nucleus and other components that preserve and nourish it, p. 43

Somatic nervous system A division of the peripheral nervous system that transmits commands to the voluntary skeletal muscles and receives sensory information from the muscles and skin, p. 51

Sound localization The ability to locate objects in space solely on the basis of the sounds they make, p. 165

Sound waves Pressure changes in a medium (air, water, solids) caused by the vibrations of molecules, p. 163

Specific phobias A group of disorders characterized by strong irrational fears of specific objects or situations, p. 504

Speech The oral expression of language, p. 330

Spinal cord The slender, tube-shaped part of the central nervous system that extends from the base of the brain down the center of the back and made up of a bundle of nerves, p. 52

Spontaneous recovery The reappearance of an extinguished response after a period of nonexposure to the conditioned stimulus, p. 253

Standardization The process of establishing uniform procedures for administering a test and for interpreting its scores, p. 356

Stanford-Binet Intelligence Test The widely used American revision of the original French Binet-Simon intelligence test, p. 353

State-dependent memory The tendency for retrieval from memory to be better when our state of mind during retrieval matches our state during encoding, p. 309

Stereotypes Fixed sets of beliefs about people that put them into categories and don't allow for individual variation, p. 609

Stereotype threat The apprehension people feel when preforming a task in which their group is stereotyped to lack ability, p. 379

Stigma An attribute that serves to discredit a person in the eyes of others, p. 501

Stimulant-induced psychosis Schizophrenic-like symptoms that can occur following prolonged and excessive use of cocaine and amphetamines, p. 231

Stimulants Psychoactive drugs that speed up—or stimulate—the nervous system and increase mental and physical activity, p. 229

Stimulus discrimination In classical conditioning, the tendency for a conditioned response not to be elicited by stimuli similar to the conditioned stimulus, p. 254

Stimulus generalization In classical conditioning, the tendency for a conditioned response to be elicited by stimuli similar to the conditioned stimulus, p. 253

Storage The second memory process, in which information is entered and maintained in memory for a period of time, p. 287

Stranger anxiety The fear and distress that infants often display when approached by an unfamiliar person, p. 102

Stressors External or internal events that challenge or threaten us, p. 566

Stress Our response to events that disturb, or threaten to disturb, our physical or psychological equilibrium, p. 566

Stroboscopic movement The illusion of movement produced by a rapid pattern of stimulation on different parts of the retina, p. 188

Structuralism An early theory in psychology that sought to identify the components of the conscious mind, p. 6

Subliminal perception The processing of information that is just below the absolute threshold of conscious awareness, p. 195

Superego The part of our minds that includes our conscience and counterbalances the more primitive demands of the id, p. 451

Superstitious behavior A behavior learned simply because it happened to be followed by a reinforcer, even though this behavior was not the cause of the reinforcer, p. 266

Suppression Motivated forgetting that occurs consciously, p. 316

Survey A structured set of questions or statements given to a group of people to measure their attitudes, beliefs, values, or behaviors, p. 26

Sympathetic nervous system The part of the autonomic nervous system that activates the body's energy resources to deal with threatening situations, p. 52

Symptom A departure from normal functioning or feeling that indicates the presence of a disorder, p. 495

Synapse The entire area composed of the terminal button of one neuron, the synaptic cleft, and the dendrite of another neuron, p. 44

Systematic desensitization A counterconditioning technique that is commonly used to treat phobias, in which the client is gradually exposed to the feared object while remaining relaxed, p. 539

T

Taste buds Sensory receptor organs located on the tongue and inside the mouth and throat that contain the receptor cells for taste, p. 172

Telegraphic speech An early speech phase in which children use short, multiple-word sentences that leave out all but the essential words, as in a telegrammed message, p. 337

Temporal lobes One of the four major sections of the cerebral cortex, located below the parietal lobe and near the temple in each cerebral hemisphere; important in audition and language, p. 66

Teratogen Any disease, drug, or other noxious agent that causes abnormal prenatal development, p. 94

Testosterone A male sex hormone found in both men and women that has a positive influence on sexual desire; the additional testosterone in males stimulates the growth of the male sex organs in the fetus and the development of the male sex characteristics during puberty.) , p. 413

Thalamus A part of the forebrain that is the brain's sensory relay station, sending messages from the senses to higher parts of the brain, p. 62

THC The major psychoactive ingredient in marijuana, p. 234

Thematic Apperception Test (TAT) A test in which people "project" their inner feelings and motives through the stories they make up about ambiguous pictures, p. 421

Theory An organized system of ideas that seeks to explain why two or more events are related, p. 19

Theory of mind The commonsense knowledge about other people's mental states that allows one to understand or predict their behavior in specific situations, p. 120

Theta waves Irregular, low-amplitude brain waves associated with stage 1 sleep, p. 211

Thyroid gland The gland located just below the larynx in the neck that controls metabolism, p. 56

Tip-of-the-tongue phenomenon The temporary inability to remember something you know, accompanied by the feeling that it is just beyond your conscious state, p. 308

Token economy A technique often used to modify the behavior of severely disturbed people in institutional settings; involves reinforcing desirable behaviors with tokens that can be exchanged for other forms of reinforcement, such as snacks or television privileges, p. 541

Top-down processing The idea that perception of the whole is based on our memories, experiences, and expectations, which shape our perception of smaller sensory features of a stimulus, p. 148

Trait A relatively stable tendency to behave in a particular way across a variety of situations, p. 462

Trait perspective A descriptive approach to personality that identifies stable characteristics that people display over time and across situations, p. 462

Transduction The process by which our sensory organs convert a stimulus's physical properties into neural impulses, p. 149

Transference The process by which the client develops feelings for the therapist that are presumed to reflect the client's feelings for significant others early in life, p. 537

Trial and error A problem-solving strategy that involves trying one possible solution after another until one works, p. 342

Triarchic theory of intelligence Sternberg's theory that three sets of mental abilities make up human intelligence: analytic, creative, and practical, p. 364

Trichromatic theory A theory of color perception proposing that three types of color receptors in the retina produce the primary color sensations of red, green, and blue, p. 159

Two-factor theory A theory of emotion suggesting that our emotional states are sometimes determined by experiencing physiological arousal and then attaching a cognitive label to the arousal, p. 435

Type A behavior pattern A complex pattern of behaviors and emotions characterized by competitiveness, impatience, ambition, hostility, and a hard-driving approach to life, p. 580

Type B behavior pattern A pattern of behaviors and emotions characterized by a patient, relaxed, easygoing, approach to life, with little hurry or hostility, p. 580

U

Unconditional positive regard An attitude of complete acceptance toward another person regardless of what she or he has said or done; based on the belief in that person's essential goodness, p. 460

Unconditioned response (UCR) In classical conditioning, the unlearned, automatic response to an unconditioned stimulus, p. 247

Unconditioned stimulus (UCS) In classical conditioning, a stimulus that naturally and automatically elicits an unconditioned response, p. 247

Unconscious mind According to Freud, the thoughts, desires, feelings, and memories that are not consciously available to us but that nonetheless shape our everyday behavior, p. 450

V

Validity The degree to which a test measures what it is designed to measure, p. 358

Values in Action (VIA) Classification of Strengths A positive psychology classification system of 24 universal character strengths that defines what's best about people, p. 469

Variable-interval reinforcement schedule A partial reinforcement schedule that reinforces the first response after a variable time interval has elapsed, p. 266

Variable-ratio reinforcement schedule A partial reinforcement schedule that reinforces the first response after a variable number of nonreinforced responses, p. 265

Volley theory A theory of pitch stating that neurons work in groups and alternate firing, thus achieving a combined frequency corresponding to the frequency of the sound wave, p. 167

W

Wavelength The distance between two peaks of adjacent waves, p. 153

Weber's law The principle that to be noticed as different, two stimuli must differ by a constant minimum percentage rather than by a constant amount, p. 151

Wechsler Intelligence Scales The most widely used set of intelligence tests, containing both verbal and performance (nonverbal) subscales, p. 354

Wisdom Expert knowledge and judgment about important, difficult, and uncertain questions associated with the meaning and conduct of life, p. 139

Working memory The term used to describe short-term memory as an active memory system that contains a "central executive" processor and two subsystems for temporarily storing auditory and visual-spatial input, p. 292

Y

Yerkes-Dodson law The idea that we perform best when we are at an intermediate level of arousal, p. 397

Z

Zone of proximal development (ZPD) The cognitive range between what a child can do on her or his own and what the child can do with the help of adults or more-skilled children, p. 122

References

••••••**A**•••••••••••

Aamodt, S., & Wang, S. (2008). *Welcome to your brain: Why you lose your car keys but never forget how to drive and other puzzles of everyday life*. New York: Bloomsbury.

Abbott, C. C., Merideth, F., Ruhl, D., Yang, Z., Clark, V. P., Calhoun, V. D., ... Mayer, A. R. (2012). Auditory orienting and inhibition of return in schizophrenia: A functional magnetic resonance imaging study. *Progress in Neuro-Psychopharmacology & Biological Psychiatry, 37*, 161–168.

Abramov, I., & Gordon, J. (1994). Color appearance: On seeing red, or yellow, or green, or blue. *Annual Review of Psychology, 45*, 451–485.

Abramowitz, J. S. (2002). Treatment of obsessive thoughts and cognitive rituals using exposure and response prevention: A case study. *Clinical Case Studies, 1*, 6–24.

Acosta, H. M. (2004). Eight factors affecting focal distance and the moon illusion. In *Dissertation Abstracts International: Section B: The Sciences & Engineering*. *U.S.*: University Microfilms International.

Adams, M. J. (2011). Evolutionary genetics of personality in nonhuman primates. In M. Inoue-Murayama, S. Kawamura, & A. Weiss (Eds.), *From Genes to Animal Behavior* (pp. 137–164). Tokyo: Springer Japan.

Addis, D. R., Knapp, K., Roberts, R. P., Schacter, D. L., Addis, D. R., Knapp, K., ... Schacter, D. L. (2012). Routes to the past: Neural substrates of direct and generative autobiographical memory retrieval. *NeuroImage, 59*, 2908–2922.

Adeyemo, S. A. (2002). Can the action of amphetamine on dopamine cause schizophrenia? *Psychology & Education: An Interdisciplinary Journal, 39*, 29–39.

Adler, N. E., & Snibbe, A. C. (2003). The role of psychosocial processes in explaining the gradient between socioeconomic status and health. *Current Directions in Psychological Science, 12*, 119–123.

Ago, Y., Nakamura, S., Baba, A., & Matsuda, T. (2005). Sulpiride in combination with fluvoxamine increases in vivo dopamine release selectivity in rat prefrontal cortex. *Neuropsychopharmacology, 30*, 43–51.

Agrawal, A., Jacobson, K. C., Prescott, C. A., & Kendler, K. S. (2004). A twin study of personality and illicit drug use and abuse/dependence. *Twin Research, 7*, 72–81.

Ahlering, R. F. (1987). Need for cognition, attitudes, and the 1984 presidential election. *Journal of Research in Personality, 21*, 100–102.

Ai, A. L., & Evans-Campbell, T. (2006). Faith, attitudes, mental health, and personal growth following the 9/11 terrorist attacks. In S. D. Ambrose (Ed.), *Religion and Psychology: New Research* (pp. 73–106). Hauppauge, NY: Nova Science Publishers.

Aiken, L. R. (1996). *Assessment of intellectual functioning* (2nd ed.). New York: Plenum.

Ainslie, G. (1975). Specious reward: A behavioral theory of impulsiveness and impulse control. *Psychological Bulletin, 82*, 463–496.

Ainsworth, M. D. S., Blehar, M., Waters, E., & Wall, S. (1978). *Patterns of attachment*. Hillsdale, NJ: Erlbaum.

Aird, E. (2008). Gather around the children. In K. K. Kline (Ed.), *Authoritative Communities: The Scientific Case for Nurturing the Whole Child* (pp. 369–374). New York: Springer.

Aitchison, C. C. E. (2007). *Sport and gender identities: Masculinities, femininities and sexualities*. New York: Routledge/Taylor & Francis Group.

Akbarian, S. (2010). Epigenetics of schizophrenia. In N. R. Swerdlow (Ed.), *Behavioral Neurobiology of Schizophrenia and Its Treatment* (pp. 611–628). New York: Springer-Verlag Publishing.

Akhtar, N., & Tomasello, M. (1996). Two-year-olds learn words for absent objects and actions. *British Journal of Developmental Psychology, 14*, 79–93.

Akins, C. K., Klein, E. D., & Zentall, T. R. (2002). Imitative learning in Japanese quail (Coturnix japonica) using the bidirectional control procedure. *Animal Learning & Behavior, 30*, 275–281.

Aksoy, O., & Weesie, J. (2011). Beliefs about the social orientations of others: A parametric test of the triangle, false consensus, and cone hypotheses. *Journal of Experimental Social Psychology*.

Al-Ansari, E. M. (2002). Effects of gender and education on the moral reasoning of Kuwait university students. *Social Behavior & Personality, 30*, 75–82.

Albarracín, D., & Vargas, P. (2010). Attitudes and persuasion: From biology to social responses to persuasive intent. In S. T. Fiske, D. T. Gilbert, & G. Lindzey (Eds.), *Handbook of Social Psychology* (5th ed., Vol. 1, pp. 394–427). Hoboken, NJ: John Wiley.

Alcock, J. E., Burns, J. E., & Freeman, A. (2003). *Psi wars: Getting to grips with the paranormal*. Charlottesville, VA: Imprint Academic.

Alexander, J. M., & Schwanenflugel, P. J. (1994). Strategy regulation: The role of intelligence, metacognitive attributions, and knowledge base. *Developmental Psychology, 30*, 709–723.

Alexander, J., Tharyan, P., Adams, C., John, T., Mol, C., & Philip, J. (2004). Rapid tranquillization of violent or agitated patients in a psychiatric emergency setting: Pragmatic randomised trial of intramuscular lorazepam v. Haloperidol plus promethazine. *British Journal of Psychiatry, 185*, 63–69.

Alferi, S. M., Culver, J. L., Carver, C. S., Arena, P. L., & Antoni, M. H. (1999). Religiosity, religious coping, and distress: A prospective study of Catholic and evangelical Hispanic women in treatment for early-stage breast cancer. *Journal of Health Psychology, 4*, 343–356.

Alfonso, V. C., & Flanagan, D. P. (2007). Best practices in the use of the Stanford-Binet Intelligence Scales, Fifth Edition (SB5) with preschoolers. In B. A. Bracken & R. J. Nagle (Eds.), *Psychoeducational Assessment of Preschool Children* (4th ed., pp. 267–296). Mahwah, NJ: Erlbaum.

Allen, L. S., & Gorski, R. A. (1992). Sexual orientation and the size of the anterior commissure in the human brain. *Proc. Natl. Acad. Sci. USA, 89*, 7199–7202.

Allen, R. E., & Oliver, J. M. (1982). The effects of child maltreatment on language development. *Child Abuse and Neglect, 6*, 299–305.

Allen, V. L., & Levine, J. M. (1971). Social support and conformity: The role of independent assessment of reality. *Journal of Experimental Social Psychology, 7*, 48–58.

Allport, G. W. (1937). *Personality: A psychological interpretation*. New York: Henry Holt.

Allport, G. W. (1961). *Pattern and Growth in Personality*. New York: Holt Rinehart & Winston.

Allport, G. W. (1967). Gordon W. Allport. In G. Lindzey (Ed.), *A History of Psychology in Autobiography* (Vol. 5).

Allport, G. W., & Odbert, H. S. (1936). Trait-names: A psycholexical study. *Psychological Monographs, 47*.

Almagor, U. (1987). The cycle and stagnation of smells: Pastoralists-fishermen relationships in an East African society. *RES, 14*, 106–121.

Alston, J. H. (1920). Spatial condition of the fusion of warmth and cold in heat. *American Journal of Psychology, 31*, 303–312.

Altarriba, J. (2003). Does caroño equal "liking"? A theoretical approach to conceptual nonequivalence between languages. *International Journal of Bilingualism, 7*, 305–322.

Amabile, T. M. (1996). *The context of creativity*. Boulder, CO: Westview.

Amancio, E. J. (2005). Dostoiévski e a síndrome de Stendhal. *Arquivos de Neuro-Psiquiatria, 63*, 1099–1103.

Amato, L., Davoli, M., Ferri, M., Gowing, L., & Perucci, C. A. (2004). Effectiveness of interventions on opiate withdrawal treatment: An overview of systematic reviews. *Drug & Alcohol Dependence, 73*, 219–226.

Amato, P. R., & Keith, B. (1991). Parental divorce and the well-being of children: A meta-analysis. *Psychological Bulletin, 110*, 26–46.

Ambady, N., Shih, M., Kim, A., & Pittinsky, T. L. (2001). Stereotype susceptibility in children: Effects of identity activation on quantitative performance. *Psychological Science, 12*, 385–390.

American Psychiatric Association. (1994). *Diagnostic and statistical manual of mental disorders* (4th ed.). Washington, DC: American Psychiatric Press.

Amsterdam, B. (1972). Mirror self-image reactions before age two. *Developmental Psychobiology, 5*, 297–305.

Anderson, C. A., & Bushman, B. J. (2001). Effects of violent video games on aggressive behavior, aggressive cognition, aggressive affect, physiological arousal, and prosocial behavior: A meta-analytic review of the scientific literature. *Psychological Science, 12*, 353–359.

Anderson, C., Keltner, D., & John, O. P. (2003). Emotional convergence between people over time. *Journal of Personality and Social Psychology, 84*, 1054–1068.

Anderson, J. R. (1983). Retrieval of information from long-term memory. *Science, 220*, 25–30.

Anderson, J. R. (1993). Problem solving and learning. *American Psychologist, 48*, 35–44.

Anderson, M. (2005). Cortex forum on the concept of general intelligence in neuropsychology. *Cortex, 41*, 99–100.

Andersson, J., & Rönnberg, J. (1997). Cued memory collaboration: Effects of friendship and type of retrieval cue. *European Journal of Cognitive Psychology, 9*, 273–287.

Andre, J., & Owens, D. A. (2003). *Visual perception: The influence of H. W. Leibowtiz. Decade of behavior* (4th ed.). Washington, DC: American Psychology Association.

Andreasen, N. C., & Black, D. W. (2006). *Introductory textbook of psychiatry* (4th ed.). Washington, DC: American Psychiatric Publishing.

Andrews, G., Clark, M., & Luszcz, M. (2002). Successful aging in the Australian Longitudinal Study of Aging: Applying the MacArthur model cross-nationally. *Journal of Social Issues, 58*, 749–765.

Angermeyer, M. C., & Matschinger, H. (1996). The effect of violent attacks by schizophrenic persons on the attitude of the public towards the mentally ill. *Social Science & Medicine, 43*, 1721–1728.

Anisman, H., & Kusnecov, A. W. (2005). Immune System. In I. Q. Whishaw & B. Kolb (Eds.), *The Behavior of the Laboratory Rat: A Handbook with Tests* (pp. 245–254). London: Oxford University Press.

Annett, M. (1985). *Left, right, hand and brain: The right shift theory.* Hillsdale, NJ: Lawrence Erlbaum Associates.

Anstis, S. M. (1978). Apparent movement. In R. Held, H. W. Leibowitz, & H. L. Teuber (Eds.), *Handbook of Sensory Physiology: Perception* (Vol. 8, pp. 655–673). Berlin: Springer-Verlag.

Arboleda-Florez, J. (2007). The psychopath in prison. In A. R. Felthous & H. Henning (Eds.), *International Handbook on Psychopathic Disorders and the Law* (Vol. 2, pp. 373–391). New York: John Wiley & Sons.

Archer, J. (2004). Sex differences in aggression in real-world settings: A meta-analytic review. *Review of General Psychology, 8,* 291–322.

Archer, J., & Côté, S. (2005). Sex differences in aggressive behavior: A developmental and evolutionary perspective. In R. E. Tremblay, W. W. Hartup, & J. Archer (Eds.), *Developmental Origins of Aggression* (pp. 425–443). New York: Guilford Press.

Archer, J., & Coyne, M. S. (2005). An integrated review of indirect, relational, and social aggression. *Personality and Social Psychology Review, 9,* 212–230.

Ardelt, M. (2009). How similar are wise men and women? A comparison across two age cohorts. *Research in Human Development, 6,* 9–26.

Ardila, A., Rosselli, M., Matute, E., & Inozemtseva, O. (2011). Gender differences in cognitive development. *Developmental Psychology, 47,* 984–990.

Argo, F., Liguori, A., Petti, F. B., Cataldo, R., Petitti, T., & Totonelli, A. (2005). Acupuncture versus pharmacological therapy in the treatment of migraine without aura: Clinical results. *Pain Clinic, 17,* 245–247.

Arking, R. (1998). *Biology of aging: Observations and principles* (2nd ed.). Sunderland, MA: Sinauer Associates.

Arnett, J. J. (1999). Adolescent storm and stress reconsidered. *American Psychologist, 54,* 317–326.

Arnett, J. J. (2002). The psychology of globalization. *American Psychologist, 57,* 774–783.

Aron, E. N., & Aron, A. (1982). An introduction to Maharishi's theory of creativity: Its empirical base and description of the creative process. *Journal of Creative Behavior, 16,* 29–49.

Aronson, J., Fried, C. B., & Good, C. (2002). Reducing the effects of stereotype threat on African American college students by shaping theories of intelligence. *Journal of Experimental Social Psychology, 38,* 113–125.

Arredondo, P., & Perez, P. (2003). Counseling paradigms and Latina/o Americans. In F. Harper & J. McFadden (Eds.), *Culture and Counseling: New Approaches* (pp. 115–132). Boston, MA: Allyn & Bacon.

Artar, M. (2007). Adolescent egocentrism and theory of mind: In the context of family relations. *Social Behavior and Personality, 35,* 1211–1220.

Asch, S. E. (1946). Forming impressions of personality. *Journal of Abnormal and Social Psychology, 41,* 258–290.

Asch, S. E. (1951). Effects of group pressure upon the modification and distortion of judgments. In H. Guetzkow (Ed.), *Groups, Leadership, and Men.* Pittsburgh, PA: Carnegie Press.

Asch, S. E. (1952). *Social psychology.* New York: Prentice Hall.

Asch, S. E. (1955). Opinions and social pressure. *Scientific American, 193*(5) 31–35.

Asch, S. E. (1956). Studies of independence and conformity: A minority of one against a unanimous majority. *Psychological Monographs, 70*(416).

Asendorpf, J. F., & Van Aken, M. A. G. (2003). Validity of big five personality judgements in childhood: A 9-year longitudinal study. *European Journal of Personality, 17,* 1–17.

Aserinsky, E. (1996). Memories of famous neuropsychologists: The discovery of REM sleep. *Journal of the History of the Neurosciences, 5,* 213–227.

Aserinsky, E., & Kleitman, N. (1953). Regularly occurring periods of eye mobility and concomitant phenomena during sleep. *Science, 118,* 273–274.

Asli, O., & Flaten, M. A. (2012). How fast is fear? Automatic and controlled processing in conditioned fear. *Journal of Psychophysiology, 26,* 20–28.

Astin, S., Redston, P., & Campbell, A. (2003). Sex differences in social representations of aggression: Men justify, women excuse? *Aggressive Behavior, 29,* 128–133.

Atkinson, A. (1995). What makes love last. In K. R. Gilbert (Ed.), *Marriage and the Family 95/96.* Guilford, CT: Dushkin/Brown & Benchmark.

Atkinson, J. (1957). Motivational determinants of risk-taking behavior. *Psychological Review, 64,* 359–372.

Atkinson, J. W. (1977). Motivation for achievement. In T. Blass (Ed.), *Personality Variables in Social Behavior.* Hillsdale, NJ: Erlbaum.

Au, T. K., Knightly, L. M., Jun, S. A., & Oh, J. S. (2002). Overhearing a language during childhood. *Psychological Science, 13,* 234–243.

Auerbach, S. M., & Gramling, S. (1998). *Stress management: Psychological foundations.* Upper Saddel River, NJ: Prentice Hall.

Axline, V. M. (1947). *Play therapy.* Boston: Houghton Mifflin.

Aznar-Casanova, J. A., Matsushima, E. H., Silva, J. A. D., & Ribeiro-Filho, N. P. (2008). Can exocentric direction be dissociated from its exocentric distance in virtual environments? *Perception & Psychophysics, 70,* 541–550.

•• B •••••••••••••••••

Baars, B. J. (2003). Reply to comments on "The double life of B. F. Skinner. *Journal of Consciousness Studies, 10,* 79–94.

Babyak, M., Blumenthal, J., Herman, S., Khatri, P., Doraiswamy, M., & et, al. (2000). Exercise treatment for major depression: Maintenance of therapeutic benefit at 10 months. *Psychosomatic Medicine, 62,* 633–638.

Bacardi-Gascon, M., Leon-Reyes, M. J., & Jimenez-Cruz, A. (2007). Stigmatization of overweight Mexican children. *Child Psychiatry & Human Development, 38,* 99–105.

Back, M., Schmukle, S. C., & Egloff, B. (2008). Becoming friends by chance. *Psychological Science, 19,* 439–440.

Backer, M., Grossman, P., Schneider, J., Michalsen, A., Knoblauch, N., Tan, L., ... Dobos, G. J. (2008). Acupuncture in migraine: Investigation of autonomic effects. *Clinical Journal of Pain, 24,* 106–115.

Badanes, L. S., Dmitrieva, J., & Watamura, S. E. (2012). Understanding cortisol reactivity across the day at child care: The potential buffering role of secure attachments to caregivers. *Early Childhood Research Quarterly, 27,* 156–165.

Bagai, A., Thavendiranathan, P., & Detsky, A. S. (2006). Does this patient have hearing impairment? JAMA: *Journal of the American Medical Association, 295,* 416–428.

Bagby, R. M., Marshall, M. B., Michael, R., Nicholson, R. A., Bacchiochi, J., & Miller, L. S. (2005). Distinguishing bipolar depression, major depression, and schizophrenia with the MMPI-2 clinical and content scales. *Journal of Personality Assessment, 84,* 89–95.

Bahrick, H. P., Bahrick, L. E., Bahrick, A. S., & Bahrick, P. E. (1993). Maintenance of foreign vocabulary and the spacing effect. *Psychological Science, 4,* 316–321.

Bahrick, H. P., Bahrick, P. O., & Wittlinger, R. P. (1975). Fifty years of memory for names and faces: A cross-sectional approach. *Journal of Experimental Psychology: General, 104,* 54–75.

Bai, L., Zimmer, S., Rickes, O., Rohleder, N., Holthues, H., Engel, L., ... Spessert, R. (2008). Daily oscillation of gene expression in the retina is phase-advanced with respect to the pineal gland. *Brain Research, 1203,* 89–96.

Bailey, J. M., Bobrow, D., Wolfe, M., & Mikach, S. (1995). Sexual orientation of adult sons of gay fathers. *Developmental Psychology, 31,* 124–129.

Bailey, J. M., & Zucker, K. J. (1995). Childhood sex-typed behavior and sexual orientation: A conceptual analysis and quantitative review. *Developmental Psychology, 31,* 43–55.

Bailey, J., & Pillard, R. (1991). A genetic study of male homosexual orientation. *Archives of General Psychiatry, 48,* 1089–1097.

Bailey, J., & Pillard, R. (1995). Genetics of human sexual orientation. *Annual Review of Sex Research, 6,* 126–150.

Bailey, J., Pillard, R., Neale, M., & Agyei, Y. (1993). Heritable factors influence sexual orientation in women. *Archives of General Psychiatry, 50,* 217–223.

Baillargeon, R., & DeVos, J. (1991). Object permanence in young infants: Further evidence. *Child Development, 62,* 1227–1246.

Baker, A., Lee, N. K., Claire, M., Lewin, T., Grant, T., Pohlman, S., ... Carr, V. J. (2004). Drug use patterns and mental health of regular amphetamine users during a reported "heroin drought." *Addiction, 99,* 875–884.

Baker, M. C. (2004). Socially learned antipredator behavior in black-capped chickadees (Poecile atricapillus). *Bird Behavior, 16,* 13–19.

Balleine, B. W. (2005). Incentive behavior. In *The behavior of the laboratory rat: A handbook with tests* (pp. 436–446). London: Oxford University Press.

Baltes, P. B., & Mayer, K. U. (2001). *The Berlin aging study: Aging from 70 to 100.* New York: Cambridge University Press.

Baltes, P. B., & Staudinger, U. (2000). Wisdom: A metaheursitic (pragmatic) to orchestrate mind and virtue toward excellence. *American Psychologist, 55,* 122–136.

Balthasar, N., Coppari, R., McMinn, J., Liu, S. M., Lee, C. E., Tang, V., ... Lowell, B. B. (2004). Leptin receptor signaling in POMC neurons is requried for normal body weight homeostasis. *Neuron, 42,* 983–991.

Balthazart, J. (2012). *The biology of homosexuality.* New York: Oxford University Press.

Bambling, M., King, R., Reid, W., & Wegner, K. (2008). Online counselling: The experience of counsellors providing synchronous single-session counselling to young people. *Counselling & Psychotherapy Research, 8,* 110–116.

Bancroft, J., Janssen, E., Carnes, L., Goodrich, D., Strong, D., & Long, J.-S. (2004). Sexual activity and risk taking in young heterosexual men: The relevance of sexual arousability, mood, and sensation seeking. *Journal of Sex Research, 41,* 181–192.

Bandura, A. (1965). Influences of models' reinforcement contingencies on the acquisition of initiative responses. *Journal of Personality and Social Psychology, 1,* 589–593.

Bandura, A. (1979). The social learning perspective: Mechanism of aggression. In H. Toch (Ed.), *Psychology of Crime and Criminal Justice.* New York: Holt, Rinehart & Winston.

Bandura, A. (1986). *Social foundations of thought and action: A social-cognitive theory.* Englewood Cliffs, NJ: Prentice Hall.

Bandura, A. (1999). A sociocognitive analysis of substance abuse: An agentic perspective. *Psychological Science, 10,* 214–218.

Bandura, A., Ross, D., & Ross, S. A. (1961). Transmission of aggression through imitation of aggressive models. *Journal of Abnormal and Social Psychology, 63,* 575–582.

Bandura, A., Ross, D., & Ross, S. A. (1963). Vicarious reinforcement and imitative learning. *Journal of Abnormal and Social Psychology, 67,* 601–607.

Bankston, C. L., III, & Caldas, S. J. (1997). The American school dilemma: Race and scholastic performance. *The Sociological Quarterly, 38,* 423–429.

Banwell, E. (2004). Balancing individual and organizational values: Walking the tightrope to success. *Journal of Managerial Psychology, 19,* 191–193.

Barber, T. X. (1979). Suggested ("hypnotic") behavior: The trance paradigm versus an alternative paradigm. In *Hypnosis: Developments in Research and New Perspectives.* New York: Aldine.

Barber, T. X. (2000). A deeper understanding of hypnosis: Its secrets, its nature, its essence. *American Journal of Clinical Hypnosis, 42,* 208–272.

Bard, P. (1934). On emotional expression after desortication with some remarks on certain theoretical views. *Psychological Review, 41*, 309–328.

Bargai, N., Ben-Shakhar, G., & Shalev, A. Y. (2007). Posttraumatic stress disorder and depression in battered women: The mediating role of learned helplessness. *Journal of Family Violence, 22*, 267–275.

Bargh, J. A., & Churchland, T. L. (1999). The unbearable automaticity of being. *American Psychologist, 54*, 462–479.

Bargh, J. A., & Mosella, E. (2008). The unconscious mind. *Perspectives on Psychological Science, 3*, 73–79.

Barlett, C. P., Harris, R. J., & Bruey, C. (2008). The effect of the amount of blood in a violent video game on aggression, hostility, and arousal. *Journal of Experimental Social Psychology, 44*, 539–546.

Barlow, D. H., & Lehman, C. L. (1996). Advances in the psychological treatment of anxiety disorders: Implications for national health care. *Archives of General Psychiatry, 53*, 727–735.

Baron, R. A. (1973). Threatened retaliation from the victim as an inhibitor of physiccal aggression. *Journal of Research in Personality, 7*, 103–115.

Baron, R. A. (1983). The control on human aggression: A strategy based on incompatible responses. In *Aggression: Theoretical and Empirical Reviews* (Vol. 2, pp. 173–190). New York: Academic Press.

Baron, R. A., & Kepner, C. R. (1970). Model's behavior and attraction toward the model as determinants of adult aggressive behavior. *Journal of Personality and Social Psychology, 14*, 335–344.

Barrett, D. (2010). *The committee of sleep: How artists and athletes use their dreams for creative problem solving and how you can too.* Oneiroi Press.

Barrett, L., Dunbar, R., & Lycett, J. (2002). *Human evolutionary psychology.* Princeton, NJ: Princeton University Press.

Barrett, P. T., & Eysenck, H. J. (1992). Brain evoked potentials and intelligence: The Hendrickson paradigm. *Intelligence, 16*, 361–381.

Barrick, M. R., & Mount, M. K. (1991). The Big Five personality dimensions and job performance: A meta-analysis. *Personnel Psychology, 44*, 1–26.

Barron, G., & Yechiam, E. (2002). Private e-mail requests and the diffusion of responsibility. *Computers in Human Behavior, 18*, 507–520.

Bartholow, B. D., Bushman, B. J., & Sestir, M. A. (2006). Chronic violent video game exposure and desensitization to violence: Behavioral and event-related brain potential data. *Journal of Experimental Social Psychology, 42*, 532–529.

Bartlett, F. C. (1932). *Remembering: A study in experimental and social psychology.* London: Cambridge University Press.

Bartoshuk, L. M., & Beauchamp, G. K. (1994). Chemical senses. *Annual Review of Psychology, 45*, 419–449.

Bartusiak, M. (1980). Beeper man. *Discover, 57.*

Baruss, I. (2003). Dreams. In I. Baruss (Ed.), Alterations of Consciousness: An Empirical Analysis for Social Scientists (pp. 79–106). Washington, DC: American Psychological Association.

Bass, B. M. (2002). Cognitive, social, and emotional intelligence of transformational leaders. In R. E. Riggio & S. E. Murphy (Eds.), *Multiple intelligences and leadership. LEA's organization and management series* (pp. 105–118). Mahwah, NJ: Erlbaum.

Bassett, D. S., & Gazzaniga, M. S. (2011). Understanding complexity in the human brain. *Trends in Cognitive Sciences, 15*, 200–209.

Bassett, E. B., Verchinski, B. A., Mattay, V. S., Weinberger, D. R., & Meyer-Lindenberg, A. (2008). Hierarchical organization of human cortical networks in health and schizophrenia. *The Journal of Neuroscience, 28*, 9239–9248.

Bateman, A. W., & Fonagy, P. (2012). Antisocial personality disorder. In A. W. Bateman & P. Fonagy (Eds.), *Handbook of mentalizing in mental health practice.* (pp. 289–308). Arlington, VA: American Psychiatric Publishing.

Bateson, G., Jackson, D. D., Haley, J., & Weakland, J. (1956). Toward a history of schizophrenia. *Behavioral Science, 1*, 252–264.

Bateson, P. (2011). Ethical debates about animal suffering and the use of animals in research. *Journal of Consciousness Studies, 18*, 86–208.

Battro, A. M. (2001). *Half a brain is enough: The story of Nico.* New York: Cambridge University Press.

Baudouin, A., Vanneste, S., Isingrini, M., & Pouthas, V. (2006). Differential involvement of internal clock and working memory in the production and reproduction of duration: A study on older adults. *Acta, 121*, 285–296.

Bauer, P. J. (2002). Long-term recall memory: Behavioral and neuro-developmental changes in the first 2 years of life. *Current Directions in Psychological Science, 11*, 137–141.

Baum, A., Gatchel, R., & Krantz, D. (1998). *An introduction to health psychology* (3rd ed.). New York: McGraw Hill.

Baum, A., & Posluszny, D. M. (1999). Health psychology: Mapping biobehavioral contributions to health and illness. *Annual Review of Psychology, 50*, 137–163.

Baumann, C. (2008). Kant and the magnitude of sensation: A neglected prologue to modern psychophysics. *Journal of the History of the Neurosciences, 17*, 1–7.

Baumeister, R. F. (2000). Gender differences in erotic plasticity: The female sex drive as socially flexible and responsive. *Psychological Bulletin, 126*, 347–374.

Baumeister, R. F. (2005). Self-concept, self-esteem, and identity. In V. J. Derlega, B. A. Winstead, & W. H. Jones (Eds.), *Personality: Contemporary Theory and Research* (3rd ed., pp. 246–280). Belmont, CA: Thomson Wadsworth.

Baumeister, R. F., & Leary, M. R. (1995). The need to belong: Desire for interpersonal attachments as a fundamental human motivation. *Psychological Bulletin, 117*, 497–529.

Bauml, K.-H., & Aslan, A. (2006). Part-list cuing can be transient and lasting: the role of encoding. *Journal of Experimental Psychology: Learning, Memory, and Cognition, 32*, 33–43.

Baumrind, D. (1991). Parenting styles and adolescent development. In J. Brooks-Gunn, R. Lerner, & A. C. Petersen (Eds.), *The encyclopedia of adolescence.* New York: Garland.

Bayley, T. M., Dye, L., Jones, S., DeBono, M., & Hill, A. J. (2002). Food cravings and aversions during pregnancy: Relationships with nausea and vomiting. *Appetite, 38*, 45–51.

Beach, S. R. H., Whisman, M. A., & O'Leary, K. D. (1994). Marital therapy for depression: Theoretical foundation, current status, and future directions. *Behavior Therapy, 25*, 345–371.

Beaman, A. L., Barnes, P. J., Klentz, B., & McQuirk, B. (1978). Increasing helping rates through information dissemination: Teaching pays. Personality and Social *Psychology Bulletin, 9*, 181–196.

Beasley, D. J., & Amedee, R. G. (2001). Hearing loss. In *Expert guide to otolaryngology* (pp. 53–74). Philadelphia: American College of Physicians.

Beck, A. T. (1967). *Depression: Clinical, experimental, and theoretical aspects.* New York: Hoeber.

Beck, A. T. (1991). Cognitive therapy: A 30-year retrospective. *American Psychologist, 46*, 368–375.

Beck, A. T. (1997). Cognitive therapy: Reflections. In J. K. Zeig (Ed.), *The evolution of psychotherapy: The third conference.* New York: Brunner/ Mazel.

Beck, A. T., & Emery, G. (1985). *Anxiety disorders and phobias: A cognitive perspective.* New York: International Universities Press.

Beck, A. T., Rush, A. J., Shaw, B. F., & Emery, G. (1979). *Cognitive therapy of depression.* New York: Guilford Press.

Beck, H. P., Levinson, S., & Irons, G. (2009). Finding Little Albert: A Journey to John B. Watson's Infant Laboratory. *American Psychologist, 64*, 605-614.

Beede, K. E., & Kass, S. J. (2006). Engrossed in conversation: The impact of cell phones on simulated driving performance. *Accident Analysis & Prevention, 38*, 415–421.

Begg, I. M., Anas, A., & Farinacci, S. (1992). Dissociation of processes in belief: Source recollection, statement familiarity, and the illusion of truth. *Journal of Experimental Psychology: General, 121*, 446–458.

Bejarano, T. (2011). *Becoming human: From pointing gestures to syntax.* Amsterdam, Netherlands: John Benjamins Publishing Company.

Békésy, G. von. (1947). The variation of phase along the basilar membrane with sinusoidal vibrations. *Journal of the Acoustical Society of America, 19*, 452–460.

Békésy, G. von. (1957). The ear. *Scientific American,* 66–78.

Békésy, G. von. (1960). *Experiments in hearing.* New York: McGraw-Hill.

Bell, A. P., Weinberg, M. S., & Hammersmith, S. K. (1981). *Sexual preference: Its development in men and women.*

Belle, D. (1982). The stress of caring: Women as providers of social support. In L. Goldberger & S. Breznitz (Eds.), *Handbook of Stress: Theoretical and Clinical Aspects* (pp. 496–505). New York: Free Press.

Beller, M., & Gafni, N. (1996). The 1991 international assessment of educational progress in mathematics and sciences: The gender differences perspective. *Journal of Educational Psychology, 88*, 365–377.

Bem, D. J. (2011). Feeling the future: Experimental evidence for anomalous retroactive influences on cognition and affect. *Journal of Personality and Social Psychology, 100*, 407–425.

Ben-Amos, I. K. (1994). *Adolescence and youth in early modern England.*

Benbow, C. P., & Stanley, J. C. (1983). Sex differences in mathematical reasoning ability: Fact or artifact? *Science, 222*, 1029–1031.

Benet-Pagès, A., Orlik, P. S., & Lorenz-Depiereux, B. (2005). An FGF23 missense mutation causes familial tumoral calcinosis with hyperphosphatemia. *Human Molecular Genetics, 14*, 385–390.

Benjamin, A. S. (2006). Multimethod approaches to the study of cognition: The evolution of concepts in research on human memory. In *Handbook of multimethod measurement in psychology* (pp. 353–369). Washington, DC: American Psychological Association.

Benjamini, E., Coico, R., & Sunshine, G. (2000). *Immunology: A short course* (4th ed.). New York: Wiley-Liss.

Benson, E. (2003). Intelligence across cultures. *Monitor on Psychology, 34*(2), 56–58.

Benson, H. (1975). *The relaxation response.* New York: Morrow.

Benson, H., & Klipper, M. Z. (1988). *The relaxation response.* New York: Avon.

Benson, H., & Stuart, E. M. (1992). *The wellness book.* New York: Simon & Schuster.

Benyamini, Y., & Lomranz, J. (2004). The relationship of activity restriction and replacement with depressive symptoms among older adults. *Psychology and Aging, 19*, 362–366.

Benyamini, Y., & Roziner, I. (2008). The predictive validity of optimism and affectivity in a longitudinal study of older adults. *Personality and Individual Differences, 44*, 853–864.

Beren, S. E., Hayden, H. A., Wilfley, D. E., & Striegel-Moore, R. H. (1997). Body dissatisfaction among lesbian college students. *Psychology of Women Quarterly, 21*, 431–445.

Bergmann, U. (2008). She's come undone: A neurobiological exploration of dissociative disorders. In C. Forgash & M. Copeley (Eds.), *Healing the heart of trauma and dissociation with EMDR and ego state therapy* (pp. 61–89). New York: Springer.

Berk, L. E. (1994). Why children talk to themselves. *Scientific American, 271*, 78–83.

Berkman, L., & Syme, S. L. (1979). Social networks, host resistance, and mortality: A nine-year follow-up study of Alameda County residents. *American Journal of Epidemiology, 109*, 186–204.

Berkowitz, L. (1994). Is something missing? Some observations prompted by the cognitive-neoassociationist view of anger and emotional aggression. In L. R. Huesmann (Ed.), *Aggressive Behavior: Current Perspectives* (pp. 35–57). New York: Plenum.

Berkowitz, M. W., Sherblom, S., Bier, M., & Battistich, V. (2006). Educating for positive youth development. In *Handbook of Moral Development* (pp. 683–701). Mahwah, NJ: Lawrence Elbaum.

Bernard, H. S. (2005). Countertransference: The evolution of a construct. *International Journal of Group Psychotherapy, 55*, 151–160.

Bernier, R., & Dawson, G. (2009). The role of mirror neuron dysfunction in autism. In J. A. Pineda (Ed.), *Mirror neuron systems: The role of mirroring processes in social cognition* (pp. 261–286). Totowa, NJ: Humana Press.

Berninger, V. W., Abbott, R. D., Abbott, S. P., Grahm, S., & Richards, T. (2002). Writing and reading: Connections between language by hand and language by eye. *Journal of Learning Diabilities, 35*, 39–56.

Bernstein, D. A., Carlson, C. R., & Schmidt, J. E. (2007). Progressive relaxation: Abbreviated methods. In P. M. Lehrer, R. L. Woolfolk, & W. E. Sime (Eds.), *Principles and practice of stress management* (3rd ed., pp. 88–122). New York: Guilford Press.

Bernstein, I. L. (1978). Learned taste aversions in children receiving chemotherapy. *Science, 200*, 1302–1303.

Berscheid, E., & Hatfield, (Walster) E. (1974). A little bit about love. In *Foundations of interpersonal attraction* (pp. 355–381). New york: Academic Press.

Besle, J. C., Anne, M. R., Delpuech, C., Lecaignard, F., Giard, M. H., & Morlet, D. (2007). Audiovisual events in sensory memory. *Journal of Psychophysiology, 21*, 231–238.

Bettencourt, B. N., & Miller, N. (1996). Gender differences in aggression as a function of provocation: A meta-analysis. *Psychological Bulletin, 119*, 422–447.

Beyer, C., Caba, M., Banas, C., & Komisaruk, B. R. (1991). Vasoactive intestinal polypeptide (VIP) potentiates the behavioral effects of substance P intrathecal administration. *Pharmacology, Biochemistry and Behavior, 39*, 695–698.

Beyerstein, B., & Beyerstein, D. (1992). *The write stuff: Evaluations of graphology.* Buffalo, NY: Prometheus Books.

Biedermann, B., Ruh, N., Nickels, L., & Coltheart, M. (2008). Information retrieval in tip of the tongue states: New data and methodological advances. *Journal of Psycholinguistic Research, 37*, 171–198.

Bieliauskas, L. A., Counte, M. A., & Glandon, G. L. (1995). Inventorying stressing life events as related to health change in the elderly. *Stress Medicine, 11*, 93–103.

Biever, J. L., Castalo, M. T., De las Fuentes, C., González, C., Servín-López, S., & Sprowls, C. (2002). The role of language in training psychologists to work with Hispanic clients. *Professional Psychology: Research and Practice, 33*, 330–336.

Billett, E. A., Richter, M. A., & Kennedy, J. L. (1998). Genetics of obsessive-compulsive disorder. In R. P. Swinson & M. M. Antony (Eds.), *Obsessive-compulsive disorder: Theory, research, and treatment* (pp. 181–206). New York: Guilford Press.

Binder, J. R., Desai, R. H., Graves, W. W., & Conant, L. L. (2009). Where is the semantic system? A critical review and meta-analysis of 120 functional neuroimaging studies. *Cerebral Cortex, 19*, 2767–2796.

Binet, A., & Simon, T. (1905). New methods for the diagnosis of the intellectual level of subnormals. In A. Binet & T. Simon (Eds.), *The development of intelligence in children.* Baltimore: Williams & Wilkins.

Birbaumer, N., Grodd, W., Diedrich, O., Klose, U., Erb, M., & Lotze, M. (1998). fMRI reveals amygdala activation to human faces in soical phobics. *Neuroreport, 9*, 1223–1226.

Birenbaum, M., & Pinku, P. (1997). Effects of test anxiety, information organization, and testing situation on performance on two test formats. *Contemporary Educational Psychology, 22*, 23–38.

Bishop, G. D. (1991). Understanding the understanding of illness: Lay disease representations. In J. A. Skelton & R. T. Croyle (Eds.), *Mental representation in health and illness.* New York: Springer-Verlag.

Bitsika, V., Sharpley, C. F., & Rubenstein, V. (2010). What stresses university students: An interview investigation of the demands of tertiary studies. *Australian Journal of Guidance & Counselling, 20*, 41–54.

Björkqvist, K., Lagerspetz, K. M. J., & Kaukiainen, A. (1992). Do girls manipulate and boys fight? Developmental trends regarding direct and indirect aggression. *Aggressive Behavior, 18.*

Bjornebekk, G., Gjesme, T., & Ulriksen, R. (2011). Achievement motives and emotional processes in children during problem-solving: Two experimental studies of their relation to performance in different achievement goal conditions. *Motivation and Emotion, 35*, 351–367.

Black, J. E., Isaacs, K. R., Anderson, B. J., Alcantara, A. A., & Greenough, W. T. (1990). Learning causes synaptogenesis, whereas motor activity causes angiogenesis in cerebellar cortex of adult rats. *Proc. Natl. Acad. Sci. USA, 87*, 5568–5572.

Blackburn, J. (2005). Rational Emotive Behaviour therapy: Theoretical developments. *Behavioural and Cognitive Psychotherapy, 33*, 122–123.

Blackmore, S. J. (1997). Probability misjudgment and belief in the paranormal: A newspaper survey. *British Journal of Psychology, 88*, 683–689.

Blackwell, L. S., Trzesniewski, K. H., & Dweck, C. S. (2007). Implicit theories of intelligence predict achievement across an adolescent transition: A longitudinal study and an intervention. *Child Development, 78*, 246–263.

Blair, C. A., Thompson, L. F., & Wuensch, K. L. (2005). Electronic helping behavior: The virtual presence of others makes a difference. *Basic and Applied Social Psychology, 27*, 171–178.

Blakely, G. L., Andrews, M. C., & Fuller, J. (2003). Are chameleons good citizens? A longitudinal study of the relationship between self-monitoring and organizational citizenship behavior. *Journal of Business & Psychology, 18*, 131–144.

Blakemore, S. J., Burnette, S., & Dahl, R. E. (2010). The role of puberty in the developing adolescent brain. *Human Brain Mapping, 31*, 926–933.

Bland, S. T., Hargrave, D., Pepin, J. L., Amat, J., Watkins, L. R., & Maier, S. F. (2005). Stressor controllability modulates stress-induced dopamine and serotonin efflux and morphine-induced serotonin efflux in the medial prefrontal cortex. *Neuropsychopharmacology, 28*, 1589–1596.

Blazer, D. G., Hays, J. C., & Musick, M. A. (2002). Abstinence versus alcohol use among elderly rural Baptists: A test of reference group theory and health outcomes. *Aging & Mental Health, 6*, 47–54.

Blenkiron, P. (2005). Stories and analogies in cognitive behaviour therapy: A clinical review. *Behavioural and Cognitive Psychotherapy, 33*, 45–59.

Bleske-Rechek, A. L., & Buss, D. M. (2001). Opposite-sex friendship: Sex differences and similarities in initiation selection and dissolution. *Personality and Social Psychology Bulletin, 27*, 1310–1323.

Block, N. (2002). How heritability misleads about race. In J. M. Fish (Ed.), *Race and Intelligence: Separating Science from Myth* (pp. 281–296). Mahwah, NJ: Lawrence Erlbaum.

Bloom, B. S. (1985). *Developing talent in young people.* New York: Ballantine.

Blum, I. D., Lamont, E. W., & Abizaid, A. (2012). Competing clocks: Metabolic status moderates signals from the master circadian pacemaker. *Neuroscience and Biobehavioral Reviews, 36*, 254–270.

Blumenthal, J. A., Sherwood, A., Babyak, M. A., Doraiswamy, P. M., & Hoffman, B. M. (2008). Exercise, pharmacotherapy, and depression: Response to letters to the editor. *Psychosomatic Medicine, 70*, 264–265.

Bob, P., Ptacek, R., & Paclt, I. (2002). Dissociative disorders and possibilities of differential diagnostics of epileptic and psychogenic non-epileptic seizures. *Ceska a Slovenska Psychiatrie, 98*, 377–381.

Boddy, C. (2012). The Nominal Group Technique: An aid to brainstorming ideas in research. *Qualitative Market Research: An International Journal, 15*, 6–18.

Bodenhausen, G. V. (1988). Stereotypic biases in social decision making: Testing process models of stereotype use. *Journal of Personality and Social Psychology, 55*, 726–737.

Boehm, J. K., Lyubomirsky, S., & Sheldon, K. M. (2011). A longitudinal experimental study comparing the effectiveness of happiness-enhancing strategies in Anglo Americans and Asian Americans. *Cognition and Emotion, 25*, 1263–1272.

Boehm, S. G., Sommer, W., & Lueschow, A. (2005). Correlates of implicit memory for words and faces in event-related brain potentials. *International Journal of Psychophysiology, 55*, 95–112.

Bogner, H. R., & Gallo, J. J. (2004). Are higher rates of depression in women accounted for by differential symptom reporting? *Social Psychiatry and Psychiatric Epidemiology, 39*, 126–132.

Bohn, A., & Berntsen, D. (2007). Pleasantness bias in flashbulb memories: Positive and negative flashbulb memories of the fall of the Berlin Wall among East and West Germans. *Memory & Cognition, 35*, 565–577.

Bolles, R. (1980). Some functionalistic thoughts about regulation. In T. Halliday (Ed.), *Analysis of motivational processes* (pp. 63–75). London: Academic Press.

Bollmann, M. D., Saugy, M., Saudan, C., Baume, N., Avois-Mateus, L., Robinson, N., ... Mangin, P. (2007). Sports. In M. D. F. Bollmann & S. B. Karch (Eds.), *Sports. Drug Abuse Handbook.* Boca Raton, FL: CRC Press.

Bonanno, G. A., Keltner, D., Noll, J. G., Putnam, F. W., Trickett, P. K., LeJeune, J., & Anderson, C. (2002). When the face reveals what words do not: Facial expressions of emotion, smiling, and the willingness to disclose childhood sexual abuse. *Journal of Personality & Social Psychology, 83*, 94–110.

Bond, R., & Smith, P. B. (1996). Culture and conformity: A meta-analysis of studies using Asch's (1952b, 1956) line judgment task. *Psychological Bulletin, 119*, 111–137.

Bond, S., & Cash, T. F. (1992). Black beauty: Skin color and body images among African-American college women. *Journal of Applied Social Psychology, 22*, 874–888.

Bondi, M. W., Jak, A. J., Delano-Wood, L., Jacobson, M. W., Delis, D. C., & Salmon, D. P. (2008). Neuropsychological contributions to the early identification of Alzheimer's disease. *Neuropsychology Review, 18*, 73–90.

Bonson, K. R., Grant, S. J., Contoreggi, C. S., Links, J. M., Metcalfe, J., Weyl, H. L., ... London, E. D. (2002). Neural systems and cue-induced cocaine craving. *Neuropsychopharmacology, 26*, 376–386.

Boon, H. J. (2007). Low- and high-achieving Australian secondary school students: Their parenting, motivations and academic achievement. *Australian Psychologist, 42*, 212–225.

Borkenau, P., Riemann, R., Angleitner, A., & Spinath, F. M. (2001). Genetic and environmental influences on observed personality: Evidence from the German observational study of adult twins. *Journal of Personality and Social Psychology, 80*, 655–668.

Borkovec, T., Ray, W., & Stoeber, J. (1998). A cognitive phenomenon intimately linked to affective, physiological, and interpersonal behavioral processes. *Cognitive Therapy & Research, 22*, 561–576.

Bornstein, R. F., Leone, D. R., & Galley, D. J. (1987). The generalizability of subliminal mere exposure effects: Influence of stimuli perceived without awareness on social behavior. *Journal of Personality and Social Psychology, 53*, 1070–1079.

Borowsky, S. J., Rubenstein, L. V., Meredith, L. S., Camp, P., Jackson-Triche, M., & Wells, K. B. (2000). Who is at risk of nondetection of mental health problems in primary care? *Journal of General Internal Medicine, 15*, 381–388.

Bosch, H., Steinkamp, F., & Boller, E. (2006). In the eye of the beholder: Reply to Wilson and Shadish (2006) and Radin, Nelson, Dobyns, and Houtkooper (2006). *Psychological Bulletin, 132*, 533–537.

Boss, P. (1999). *Ambiguous loss: Learning to live with unresolved grief.* Cambridge, MA: Harvard University Press.

Botha, R. P. (1997). Neo-Darwinian accounts of the evolution of language: Questions about their explanatory focus. *Language & Communication, 17,* 249–267.

Bouchard, T. J., Jr. (2004). Genetic influence on human psychological traits. *Current Directions in Psychological Science, 13,* 148–151.

Bouchard, T. J., Lykken, D. T., McGue, M., Segal, N. L., & Tellegen, A. (1990). Sources of human psychological differences: The Minnesota study of twins reared apart. *Science, 250,* 223–228.

Bouchard, T. J., & McGue, M. (1981). Familial studies of intelligence: A review. *Science, 212,* 1055–1059.

Boucher, H. C., & O'Dowd, M. C. (2011). Language and the bicultural dialectical self. *Cultural Diversity and Ethnic Minority Psychology, 17,* 211–216.

Bougrine, S., Mollard, R., Ignazi, G., & Coblentz, A. (1995). Appropriate use of bright light promotes a durable adaptation to night-shifts and accelerates readjustment during recovery after a period of night-shifts. *Work & Stress, 9,* 314–326.

Bourne, N. K. (2003). Cognitive psychotherapy toward a new millennium: Scientific foundations and clinical practice. *Behaviour Research & Therapy, 41,* 630–0631.

Bousfield, W. A. (1953). The occurrence of clustering in the recall of randomly arranged associates. *Journal of General Psychology, 49,* 229–240.

Boutwell, B. B., Franklin, C. A., Barnes, J. C., & Beaver, K. M. (2011). Physical punishment and childhood aggression: The role of gender and gene-environment interplay. *Aggressive Behavior, 37,* 559–568.

Bovbjerg, D. H., Redd, W. H., Maier, L. A., Holland, J. C., Lesko, L. M., Niedzwiecki, D., … Hakes, T. B. (1990). Anticipatory immune suppression in women receiving cyclic chemotherapy for ovarian cancer. *Journal of Consulting and Clinical Psychology, 58,* 153–157.

Bower, G. H., Clark, M. C., Lesgold, A. M., & Winzenz, D. (1969). Hierarchical retrieval schemes in recall of categorized word lists. *Journal of Verbal Learning and Verbal Behavior, 8,* 323–343.

Bower, G. H., & Hilgard, E. R. (1981). *Theories of learning* (5th ed.). Englewood Cliffs, NJ: Prentice Hall.

Bowes, D. E., Tamlyn, D., & Butler, L. J. (2002). Women living with ovarian cancer: Dealing with an early death. *Health Care for Women International, 23,* 135–148.

Bowlby, J. (1969). *Attachment and loss: Vol. I. Attachment.* New York: John Wiley.

Bowlby, J. (1988). *A secure base: Parent-child attachment and healthy human development.* New York: Basic Books.

Bowman, C., & Brownell, P. (2000). Prelude to contemporary Gestalt therapy. *Gestalt Journal, 4,* 118–129.

Boyd, S. T. (2008). Management through risk factor modification. *The Diabetes Educator, 34,* 42S–48S.

Boysen, G. A. (2011). The scientific status of childhood dissociative identity disorder: A review of published research. *Psychotherapy and Psychosomatics, 80,* 329–334.

Bragman, J. E., Hranilovich, J. A., Dahl, R. E., Forbes, E. E., Chen, J., Toga, A. W., … Sowell, E. R. (2011). Puberty influences medial temporal lobe and cortical gray matter maturation differently in boys than girls matched for sexual maturity. *Cerebral Cortex, 21,* 636–646.

Brand, B. L., Lanius, R., Vermetten, E., Loewenstein, R. J., & Spiegel, D. (2012). Where are we going? An update on assessment, treatment, and neurobiological research in dissociative disorders as we move toward the *DSM-5. Journal of Trauma & Dissociation, 13,* 9–31.

Brand, C. (1996). "G," genes and pedagogy: A reply to seven (lamentable) chapters. In D. K. Detterman (Ed.), *Current topics in human intelligence: Vol. 5. The Environment* (pp. 113–120). Norwood, NJ: Ablex.

Brandolo, E., Halen, N. B. V., Libby, D., & Pencille, M. (2011). Racism as a psychosocial stressor. In R. J. Contrada & A. Baum (Eds.), *The handbook of stress science: Biology, psychology, and health.* New York: Springer Publishing.

Brannon, L., & Feist, J. (2000). *Health psychology: An introduction to behavior and health* (4th ed.). Belmont, CA: Wadsworth/Thomson Learning.

Bransford, J. D., Brown, A. L., & Cocking, R. R. (2008). Mind and brain. In M. H. Immordino-Yang & H. Mary (Eds.), *The Jossey-Bass reader on the brain and learning* (pp. 89–105). San Francisco, CA: Jossey-Bass.

Bransford, J. D., & Johnson, M. K. (1972). Contextual prerequisites for understanding: Some investigations of comprehension and recall. *Journal of Verbal Learning and Verbal Behavior, 11,* 717–726.

Braun, A. R. (2001). Ecstasy on trial: Seeking insight by prescription. *Cerebrum, 3,* 10–21.

Breedlove, S. M., Rosenzweig, M. R., & Watson, N. V. (2007). *Biological psychology: An introduction to behavioral, cognitive, and clinical neuroscience* (5th ed.). Sunderland, MA: Sinauer Associates.

Brehm, S. S. (1988). Passionate love. In R. J. Sternberg & M. L. Barnes (Eds.), *The Psychology of Love* (pp. 232–263). New Haven, CT: Yale University Press.

Brehm, S. S. (1992). *Intimate relationships.* New York: McGraw-Hill.

Brehm, S. S., & Brehm, J. W. (1981). *Psychological reactance: A theory of freedom and control.* New York: Academic Press.

Breland, K., & Breland, M. (1961). The misbehavior of organisms. *American Psychologist, 16,* 681–684.

Brickman, P., Coates, D., & Janoff-Bulman, R. J. (1978). Lottery winners and accident victims: Is happiness relative? *Journal of Personality and Social Psychology, 36,* 917–927.

Briere, J., & Lanktree, C. (1983). Sex-role related effects of sex bias in language. *Sex Roles, 9,* 625–632.

Briggs, S. R. (2005). Personality measurement. In V. J. Derlega, B. A. Winstead, & W. H. Jones (Eds.), *Personality: Contemporary Theory and Research* (3rd ed., pp. 27–62). Belmont, CA: Thomson Wadsworth.

Bril, B. (1986). Motor development and cultural attitudes. In H. T. A. Whiting & M. G. Wade (Eds.), *Themes in Motor Development.* Dordrecht, Netherlands: Martinus Nijhoff.

Broberg, D. J., & Bernstein, I. L. (1987). Candy as a scapegoat in the prevention of food aversions in children receiving chemotherapy. *Cancer, 60,* 2344–2347.

Brody, L. R., & Hall, J. A. (1993). Gender and emotion. In M. Lewis & J. M. Haviland (Eds.), *Handbook of emotions* (pp. 447–460). New York: Guilford.

Brody, L. R., & Hall, J. A. (2010). Gender, emotion, and socialization. In J. C. Chrisler & D. R. McCreary (Eds.), *Handbook of gender research in psychology, Vol 1: Gender Research in General and Experimental Psychology* (pp. 429–454). New York: Springer.

Brody, N. (1992). *Intelligence* (2nd ed.). San Diego, CA: Academic Press.

Brody, N. (2000). History of theories and measurements of intelligence. In *handbook of intelligence* (pp. 16–33). Cambridge, England: Cambridge University Press.

Brohan, E., Henderson, C., Wheat, K., Malcolm, E., Clement, S., Barley, E. A., … Thornicroft, G. (2012). Systematic review of beliefs, behaviours and influencing factors associated with disclosure of a mental health problem in the workplace. *BMC psychology, 12,* 11.

Bromberger, J. T., Kravitz, H. M., Chang, Y.-F., Cyranowski, J. M., Brown, C., & Matthews, K. A. (2011). Major depression during and after the menopausal transition: Study of Women's Health Across the Nation (SWAN). *Corrigendum Psychological Medicine: A Journal of Research in Psychiatry and the Allied Sciences, 41,* 1879–1888.

Bromet, E. J., & Havenaar, J. M. (2002). Mental health consequences of disasters. In N. Sartorius & W. Gaebel (Eds.), *Psychiatry in society* (pp. 241–261). New York: Wiley.

Brown, A. D., & Murphy, D. R. (1989). Cryptomnesia: Delineating inadvertent plagiarism. *Journal of Experimental Psychology: Learning, Memory, & Cognition, 15,* 432–442.

Brown, A. S. (1991). A review of the tip-of-the-tongue experience. *Psychological Bulletin, 109,* 204–223.

Brown, A. S. (2002). Consolidation theory and retrograde amnesia in humans. *Psychonomic Bulletin & Review, 9,* 403–425.

Brown, A. S. (2003). A review of the déjà vu experience. *Psychological Bulletin, 129,* 394–413.

Brown, A. S. (2006). Prenatal infection as a risk factor for schizophrenia. *Schizophrenia Bulletin, 32,* 200–202.

Brown, A. S. (2012). *The tip of the tongue state.* New York: Psychology Press.

Brown, E. R., Ojeda, V. D., Wyn, R., & Levan, R. (2000). Racial and ethnic disparities in access to health insurance and health care. Log Angeles, CA: UCLA Center for Health Policy Research and The Henry J. Kaiser Family Foundation.

Brown, G. G., & Thompson, W. K. (2010). Functional brain imaging in schizophrenia: Selected results and methods. In N. R. Swerdlow (Ed.), *Behavioral neurobiology of schizophrenia and its treatment* (pp. 181–214). New York: Springer-Verlag Publishing.

Brown, G. W. (2012). The promoter of the serotonin transporter genotype, environment and depression: A hypothesis supported? *Journal of Affective Disorders, 137,* 1–3.

Brown, J. (1958). Some tests of the decay theory of immediate memory. *Quarterly Journal of the Behavioral Sciences, 11,* 342–349.

Brown, R. (1973). *A first language: The early stages.* Cambridge, MA: Harvard University Press.

Brown, R. (1986). Linguistic relativity. In S. H. Hulse & B. F. Green Jr. (Eds.), *One hundred years of psychological research in America.* Baltimore, MD: John Hopkins University Press.

Brown, R. M., & Robertson, E. M. (2007). Off-line processing: Reciprocal interactions between declarative and procedural memories. *Journal of Neuroscience, 27,* 10468–10475.

Brown, W. S. (2005). Discussion: Seven Pillars of the House of Wisdom. In R. J. Sternberg & J. Jordan (Eds.), *A handbook of wisdom: Psychological perspectives* (pp. 353–368). New York: Cambridge University Press.

Bruch, H. (1982). Anorexia nervosa: Therapy and theory. *American Journal of Psychiatry, 139,* 1531–1538.

Brummert-Lennings, H. I., & Warburton, W. A. (2011). The effect of auditory versus violent media exposure on aggressive behavior: The role of song lyrics, video clips and musical tone. *Journal of Experimental Social Psychology, 47,* 794–799.

Bryan, A. D., Webster, G. D., & Manaffiey, A. L. (2011). The big, the rich and the powerful: Physical, financial, and social dimensions of dominance in mating and attraction. *Personality and Social Psychology Bulletin, 37,* 363–382.

Bryan, A., Rocheleau, C. A., Robbins, R. N., & Hutchinson, K. E. (2005). Condom use among high-risk adolescents: Testing the influence of alcohol use on the relationship of cognitive correlates of behavior. *Health Psychology, 24,* 133–142.

Bryant, A. L., & Zimmerman, M. A. (2003). Role models and psychosocial outcomes among African American adolescents. *Journal of Adolescent Research, 18,* 36–67.

Bryck, R. L., & Fisher, P. A. (2012). Training the brain: Practical applications of neural plasticity from the intersection of cognitive neuroscience, developmental psychology, and prevention science. *American Psychologist, 67,* 87–100.

Bubar, M. J., McMahon, L. R., Deurwaerdere, P. D., Spampinato, U., & Cunningham, K. A. (2003). Selective serotonin reuptake inhibitors enhance cocaine-induced locomotor activity and dopamine release in the nucleus accumbens. *Neuropharmacology, 44,* 342–353.

Buchanan, J. A., & Houlihan, D. (2008). The use of in vivo desensitization for the treatment of a specific phobia of earthworms. *Clinical Case Studies, 7,* 12–24.

Buck, R. (1984). *The communication of emotion.* New York: Guilford Press.

Budney, A. J., Hughes, J. R., Moore, B. A., & Novy, P. L. (2001). Marijuana abstinence effects in marijuana smokers maintained in their home environments. *Archives of General Psychiatry, 58,* 917–924.

Budney, A. J., Moore, B. A., & Vandrey, R. (2008). Health consequences of marijuana use. In J. Brick (Ed.), *Handbook of the medical consequences of alcohol and drug abuse* (2nd ed., pp. 251–301). New York: The Haworth Press.

Buhusi, C. V., & Schmajuk, N. A. (1999). Timing in simple conditioning and occasion setting: A neural network approach. *Behavioural Processes, 45,* 33–57.

Bulik, C. M., Sullivan, P. F., & Kendler, K. S. (2003). Genetic and environmental contributions to obesity and binge eating. *International Journal of Eating Disorders, 33,* 293–298.

Bullinger, M., Hygge, S., Evans, G. W., Meis, M., & Von Mackensen, S. (1999). The psychological cost of aircraft noise for children [Psychologische Beeinträchtigung von Kindern durch Fluglärm]. Aentralblatt für Hygiene und Umweltmedizin, 202, 127–138.

Bullough, V. (1980). The Kinsey scale in historical perspective. In S. A. Sanders & J. M. Reinisch (Eds.), *Homosexuality/heterosexuality: Concepts of sexual orientation.* New York: Oxford University Press.

Burdick, K. E., Lencz, T., Funke, B., Finn, C. T., Szeszko, P. R., & J. M. Kane, et al. (2006). Genetic variation in dtnbp1 influences general cogntitive ability. *Human Molecular Genetics, 15,* 1563–1568.

Bureau, J.-F., Beliveau, M.-J., Moss, E., & Lepine, S. (2006). Association between mother-child attachment and attachment narratives during the school-age years. *Canadian Journal of Behavioral Science, 38,* 50–62.

Burgaleta, M., Head, K., Alvarez-Linera, J., Martinez, K., Escorial, S., Haier, R., & Colom, R. (2012). Sex differences in brain volume are related to specific skills, not to general intelligence. *Intelligence, 40,* 60–68.

Burger, J. M. (1987). Desire for control and conformity to a perceived norm. *Journal of Personality and Social Psychology, 53,* 355–360.

Burger, J. M., Horita, M., Kinoshita, L., Roberts, K., & Vera, G. (1997). Effects of time on the norm of reciprocity. *Basic and Applied Social Psychology, 19,* 91–100.

Burger, J. M., & Lynn, A. L. (2005). Superstitous Behavior Among Amreican and Japanese Professional Baseball Players. *Basic and Applies Social Psychology, 27,* 71–76.

Burling, R. (1986). The selective advantage of complex language. *Ethology & Sociobiology, 1,* 1–16.

Burnham, M. M., Goodlin-Jones, B. L., Gaylor, E. E., & Anders, T. F. (2003). Use of sleep aids during the first year of life. *Journal of the American Academy of Child & Adolescent Psychiatry, 42,* 92.

Bushman, B. J., Baumeister, R. F., & Phillips, C. M. (2001). Do people aggress to improve their mood? Catharsis beliefs, affect regulation, opportunity, and aggressive responding. *Journal of Personality and Social Psychology, 81,* 17–33.

Buske-Kirschbaum, A., Kirschbaum, C., Stierle, H., Jabaij, L., & Hellhammer, D. (1994). Conditioned manipulation of natural killer (NK) cells in humans using a discriminative learning protocol. *Biological Psychology, 38,* 143–155.

Buss, D. H. (1999). *Evolutionary psychology.* Boston, MA: Allyn & Bacon.

Buss, D. M. (1987). Sex differences in human mate selection criteria: An evolutionary perspective. In C. Crawford, M. Smith, & D. Krebs (Eds.), *Sociobiology and psychology: Ideas, issues and applications* (pp. 335–351). Hillsdale, NJ: Erlbaum.

Buss, D. M. (1988). The evolution of human intrasexual competition: Tactics of mate attraction. *Journal of Personality and Social Psychology, 54,* 616–628.

Buss, D. M. (1989). Sex differences in human mate preferences: Evolutionary hypotheses tested in 37 cultures. *Behavioral and Brain Sciences, 12,* 1–49.

Buss, D. M. (1990). Evolutionary social psychology: Prospects and pitfalls. *Motivation and Emotion, 14,* 265–286.

Buss, D. M. (1995). Evolutionary psychology: A new paradigm for psychological science. *Psychological Inquiry, 6,* 1–31.

Buss, D. M., Haselton, M. G., Shackelford, T. K., Bleske, A. L., & Wakefield, J. (1998). Adaptations, exaptations, and spandrels. *American Psychologist, 53,* 533–548.

Buss, D. M., & Schmitt, D. P. (1993). Sexual strategies theory: An evolutionary perspective on human mating. *Psychological Review, 100,* 204–232.

Buss, D. M., & Schmitt, D. P. (2011). Evolutionary psychology and feminism. *Sex Roles, 64,* 768–787.

Butcher, J. N. (2005). *A beginner's guide to the MMPI-2* (2nd ed.). Washington, DC: American Psychological Association.

Butler, A. B. (2008). Evolution of brains, cognition, and consciousness. *Brain Research Bulletin, 75,* 442–449.

Butterworth, G. (1992). Origins of self-perception in infancy. *Psychological Inquiry, 3,* 103–111.

Buzzi, G. (2011). False awakenings in light of the dream protoconsciousness theory: A study in lucid dreamers. *International Journal of Dream Research, 4,* 110–116.

Byrne, M., Clafferty, B. A., Cosway, R., Grant, E., Hodges, A., Whalley, H. C., … Johnstone, E. C. (2003). Neuropsychology, genetic liability, and psychotic symptoms in those at high risk of schizophrenia. *Journal of Abnormal Psychology, 112,* 38–48.

C

Cacchione, P. Z. (2008). Sensory changes. In E. Capezuti, D. Zwicker, M. DeAnne, T. T. Fulmer, & D. Gray-Miceli (Eds.), *Evidence-based geriatric nursing Protocols for best practice* (3rd ed., pp. 477–502). New York: Springer.

Cacioppo, J. T., Marshall-Goodell, B. S., Tassinary, L. G., & Petty, R. E. (1992). Rudimentary determinants of attitudes: Classical conditioning is more effective when prior knowledge about the attitude stimulus is low than high. *Journal of Experimental Social Psychology, 28,* 207–233.

Cacioppo, J. T., & Petty, R. E. (1982). The need for cognition. *Journal of Personality and Social Psychology, 42,* 116–131.

Cacioppo, J. T., Petty, R. E., Feinstein, J. A., & Jarvis, W. B. G. (1996). Dispositional differences in cognitive motivation: The life and times of individuals varying in need for cognition. *Psychological Bulletin, 119,* 197–253.

Cacioppo, J. T., Petty, R. E., Kao, C. F., & Rodriguez, R. (1986). Central and peripheral routes to persuasion: An individual differences perspective. *Journal of Personality and Social Psychology, 51,* 1032–1043.

Cahill, L., Haier, R. J., Fallon, J., Alkire, M. T., Tang, C., Keator, D., … McGaugh, J. L. (1996). Amygdala activity at encoding correlated with long-term free recall of emotional information. *Proceedings of the National Academy of Sciences, USA, 93,* 8016–8021.

Cain, W. (1978). The odoriferous environment and the application of olfactory research. In *Handbook of perception* (pp. 277–304). New York: Academic Press.

Cairo, O. (2011). External measures of cognition. *Frontiers in Human Neuroscience, 5.*

Caldwell, D. F., & O'Reilly, C. A., III. (1982). Boundary spanning and individual performance: The impact of self-monitoring. *Journal of Applied Psychology, 67,* 124–127.

Callaghan, J. (2005). Competing devotions: Career and family among women executives. *Feminism & Psychology, 15,* 359–361.

Callahan, C. M. (2000). Intelligence and giftedness. In R. J. Sternberg (Ed.), *Handbook of intelligence* (pp. 159–175). Cambridge: Cambridge University Press.

Calle, E. E., Thun, M. J., Petrelli, J. M., Rogriguez, C., & Health, C. W., Jr. (1999). Body-mass index and mortality in a prospective cohort of U.S. Adults. *New England Journal of Medicine, 341,* 1097–1105.

Calvin, W. H. (1996). *How brains think.* New York: Basic Books.

Campbell, A., & Muncer, S. (1987). Models of anger and aggression in the social talk of women and men. *Journal of the Theory of Social Behaviour, 17,* 489–511.

Campbell, A., Muncer, S., & Coyle, E. (1992). Social representation of aggression as an explanation of gender differences: A preliminary study. *Aggressive Behavior, 18,* 95–108.

Campbell, F. A., & Ramey, C. T. (1994). Effects of early intervention on intellectual and academic achievement: A follow-up study of children from low-income families. *Child Development, 65,* 684–698.

Campbell, W. K., & Sedikides, C. (1999). Self-threat magnifies the self-serving bias: A meta-analytic integration. *Review of General Psychology, 3,* 23–43.

Campos, J. L., Langer, A., & Krowitz, A. (1970). Cardiac responses on the visual cliff in prelocomotor human infants. *Science, 170,* 196–197.

Canli, T. (2009). Neuroimaging of personality. In P. J. Corr & G. Matthews (Eds.), *The Cambridge handbook of personality psychology* (pp. 305–322). New York: Cambridge University Press.

Canli, T., & Amin, Z. (2002). Neuroimaging of emotion and personality: Scientific evidence and ethical considerations. *Brain & Cognition, 50,* 414–431.

Canli, T., Desmond, J. E., Zhao, A., & Gabrieli, J. D. E. (2002). Gender and memory. *Proceedings of the National Academy of Sciences, 10,* 1073.

Cannon, W. B. (1927). The James-Lange theory of emotion: A critical examination and an alternative theory. *American Journal of Psychology, 39,* 106–124.

Cannon, W. B., & Washburn, A. (1912). An explanation of hunger. *American Journal of Physiology, 29,* 441–454.

Capitanio, J. P. (1999). Personality dimensions in adult male rhesus macaques: Prediction of behaviors across time and situation. *American Journal of Primatology, 47,* 299–320.

Capitanio, J. P. (2003). Intra- and interspecific variation in personality. In W. Kaumanns (Ed.), *How societies arise: The Macaque model.* Cambridge: Cambridge University Press.

Capone, G. T., & Kaufmann, W. E. (2008). Human brain development. In P. J. Accardo (Ed.), Capute and Accardo's Neurodevelopmental *Disabilities in infancy and childhood: Vol 1: Neurodevelopmental diagnosis and treatment* (pp. 27–59). Baltimore, MD: Paul H Brookes Publishing.

Cappelletti, M., Fregni, F., Shapiro, K., Pascual-Leone, A., & Caramazza, A. (2008). Processing nouns and verbs in the left frontal cortex: A transcranial magnetic stimulation study. *Journal of Cognitive Neuroscience, 20,* 707–720.

Caprara, G. V., Barbaranelli, C., & Zimbardo, P. G. (1996). Understanding the complexity of human aggression: Affective, cognitive, and social dimensions of individual differences in propensity toward aggression. *European Journal of Personality, 10,* 133–155.

Capron, C., & Duyme, M. (1989). Assessment of effects of socioeconomic status on IQ in a full cross-fostering study. *Nature, 340,* 552–553.

Card, N. A. (2012). *Applied meta-analysis for social science research.* New York: Guilford Press.

Carmona, R. H. (2004). *The health consequences of smoking: A report of the Surgeon General.* Dept. of Health and Human Services, Centers for Disease Control and Prevention, National Center for Chronic Disease Prevention and Health Promotion, Office on Smoking and Health; Washington, DC: For sale by the Supt. of Docs., U.S. G.P.O.

Carnagey, N. L., Anderson, C. A., & Bushman, B. J. (2007). The effect of video game violence on physiological desensitization to real-life violence. *Journal of Experimental Social Psychology, 43,* 489–496.

Carter, P. L. (2003). "Black" cultural capital, status positioning, and schooling conflicts for low-income African American youth. *Social Problems, 50,* 136–155.

Cartwright, R. D. (1977). *Night life: Explorations in dreaming.* Englewood Cliff, NJ: Prentice Hall.

Cartwright, R. D. (1989). Dreams and their meaning. In M. H. Dryger, T. Roth, & W. C. Dement (Eds.), *Principles and practice of sleep medicine.* San Diego: Harcourt Brace Jovanovich.

Cartwright, R. D. (1991). Dreams that work: The relation of dream incorporation to adaptation to stressful events. *Dreaming, 1,* 3–9.

Carvalho, C., Mazzoni, G., Kirsch, I., Meo, M., & Santandrea, M. (2008). The effect of posthypnotic suggestion, hypnotic suggestibility, and goal intentions on adherence to medical instructions. *International Journal of Clinical and Experimental Hypnosis, 56,* 143–155.

Carvallo, M., & Gabriel, S. (2006). No man is an island: The need to belong and dismissing avoidant attachment style. *Personality and Social Psychology Bulletin, 32,* 697–709.

Case, R. (1992). Neo-Piagetian theories of child development. In R. J. Sternberg & C. A. Berg (Eds.), *Intellectual development* (pp. 161–196). New York: Cambridge University Press.

Caspi, A., Bem, D. J., & Elder, G. H., Jr. (1989). Continuities consequences of interactional styles across the life course. *Journal of Personality, 57,* 375–406.

Castel, A. D. (2008). Metacognition and learning about primacy and recency effects in free recall: The utilization of intrinsic and extrinsic cues when making judgments of learning. *Memory & Cognition, 36,* 429–437.

Catania, J., Coates, T., Kegeles, S., Thompson-Fullilove, M., Peterson, J., Marin, B., ... Hully, S. (1992). Condom use in multi-ethnic neighborhoods of San Francisco: The population-based AMEN study. *American Journal of Public Health, 82,* 284–287.

Cattell, H. E. P. (2001). The Sixteen Personality Factor (16PF) Questionnaire. In W. I. Dorfman & M. Hersen (Eds.), *Understanding psychological assessment: Perspectives on individual differences* (pp. 187–215). Dordrecht, Netherlands: Kluwer Academic Publishers.

Cattell, R. B. (1965). *The scientific analysis of personality.* Chicago, IL: Aldine.

Cattell, R. B. (1986). The 16 PF personality structure and Dr. Eysenck. *Journal of Social Behavior and Personality, 1,* 153–160.

Cazden, C. (1972). *Child language and education.* New York: Holt.

Chang, F. I. F., Isaacs, K. R., & Greenough, W. T. (1991). Synapse formation occurs in association with the induction of long-term potentiation in two-year-old rat hippocampus in vitro. *Neurobiology of Aging, 12,* 517–522.

Chao, J., & Nestler, E. J. (2004). Molecular neurobiology of drug addiction. *Annual Review of Medicine, 55,* 113–132.

Chao, R. K. (1992). Beyond parental control and authoritarian parenting style: Understanding Chinese parenting through the cultural notion of training. *Child Development, 65,* 1111–1119.

Chapleau, K. M., Oswald, D. L., & Russell, B. L. (2007). How ambivalent sexism toward women and men support rape myth acceptance. *Sex Roles, 57,* 131–136.

Chapman, L. J., & Chapman, J. P. (1973). *Disordered thought in schizophrenia.* New York: Appleton-Century-Crofts.

Chase-Lansdale, P. L., Cherlin, A. J., & Kiernan, K. E. (1995). The long-term effects of parental divorce on the mental health of young adults: A developmental perspective. *Child Development, 66,* 1614–1634.

Chaves, J. F. (1999). Applying hypnosis in pain management: Implications of alternative theoretical perspectives. In *Clinical Hypnosis and Self-regulation: Cognitive-behavioral Perspectives. Dissociation, Trauma, Memory, and Hypnosis Book Series* (pp. 227–247). Washington, DC: American Psychological Association.

Chein, J. M., Moore, A. B., & Conway, A. R. A. (2011). Domain-general mechanisms of complex working memory span. *NeuroImage, 54,* 550–559.

Chen, A. H., Zhou, Y., Gong, H. Q., & Liang, P. J. (2004). Firing rates and dynamic correlated activities of ganglion cells both contribute to retinal information processing. *Brain Research, 1017,* 13–20.

Chen, L. M., Turner, G. H., Friedman, R. M., Zhang, N., Gore, J. C., Roe, A. W., & Avison, M. J. (2007). High-resolution maps of real and illusory tactile activation in primary somatosensory cortex in individual monkeys with functional magnetic resonance imaging and optical imaging. *Journal of Neuroscience, 27,* 9181–9191.

Chen, S., Boucher, H., & Kraus, M. W. (2011). The relational self. In V. L. Vignoles (Ed.), *Handbook of identity theory and research* (Vol. 1–2, pp. 149–175). New York: Springer Science + Business Media.

Cherry, E. C. (1953). Some experiments on the recognition of speech, with one and with two ears. *Journal of the Acoustical Society of America, 25,* 975–979.

Chesney, M., & Coates, T. (1990). Health promotion and disease prevention: AIDS put the models to the test. In S. Petro, P. Franks, & T. Wolfred (Eds.), *Ending the HIV epidemic: Community strategies in disease prevention and health promotion* (pp. 48–62). Santa Cruz, CA: ETR Associates.

Cheung, A., Sacks, D., Dewa, C. S., Pong, J., & Levitt, A. (2008). Pediatric prescribing practices and the FDA black-box warning on antidepressants. *Journal of Developmental & Behavioral Pediatrics, 29,* 213–215.

Chiroro, P., Bohner, G., Viki, G. T., & Jarvis, C. I. (2004). Rape myth acceptance and rape proclivity: Expected dominance versus expected arousal as mediators in acquaintance-rape situations. *Journal of Interpersonal Violence, 19,* 427–441.

Chiu, C. Y., & Kwan, L. Y. Y. (2010). Culture and creativity: A process model. *Management and Organization Review, 6,* 447–461.

Choi, I., & Nisbett, R. E. (1998). Situational salience and cultural differences in the correspondence bias and in the actor-observer bias. Personality and Social Psychology Bulletin, 24, 949–960.

Choi, I., Nisbett, R. E., & Norenzayan, A. (1999). Causal attribution across cultures: Variation and universality. *Psychological Bulletin, 125,* 47–63.

Chomsky, N. (1957). *Syntactic structures.* South Holland: The Hague: Mouton.

Christakis, N. A., & Allison, P. D. (2006). Mortality after the hospitalization of a spouse. *New England Journal of Medicine, 354,* 719–730.

Christakis, N. A., & Fowler, J. H. (2007). The spread of obesity in a large social network over 32 years. The *New England Journal of Medicine, 357,* 370–379.

Christensen, K. A., Stephens, M. A. P., & Townsend, A. L. (1998). Mastery in women's multiple roles and well-being: Adult daughters providing care to impaired parents. *Health Psychology, 17,* 163–171.

Christensen, P. N., Rothberger, H., Wood, W., & Matz, D. C. (2004). Social norms and identity relevance: A motivational approach to normative behavior. *Personality and Social Psychology Bulletin, 30,* 1295–1309.

Church, A. T., & Ortiz, F. A. (2005). Culture and personality. In V. J. Derlega, B. A. Winstead, & W. H. Jones (Eds.), *Personality: Contemporary theory and research* (3rd ed., pp. 420–456). Belmont, CA: Thomson Wadsworth.

Cialdini, R. B., & Goldstein, N. J. (2004). Social influence: Compliance and conformity. *Annual Review of Psychology, 55,* 591–621.

Cialdini, R., Trost, M., & Newsom, J. (1995). Preference for consistency: The development of a valid measure and the discovery of surprising behavioral implications. *Journal of Personality and Social Psychology, 69,* 318–328.

Cicchetti, D. (2002). How a child builds a brain: Insights from normality and psychopathology. In W. Hartup & R. A. Weinberg (Eds.), Child Psychology in Retrospect and Prospect: In Celebration of the 75th Anniversary of the Institute of Child Development. *The Minnesota Symposia on Child Psychology* (Vol. 32, pp. 23–71). Mahwah, NJ: Erlbaum.

Civin, C. I., Gewirtz, A. M., Hawley, R. G., & Goodell, M. A. (2005). Advancing the fast-paced field of stem cell research: STEM CELLS increases from 6 to 10 issues in its 23rd year of publication. *Stem Cells, 23,* 1–2.

Clark, K. B., & Clark, M. P. (1939). The development of self and the emergence of racial identification in Negro preschool children. *Journal of Social Psychology, 10,* 591–599.

Clark, R. (2003). Self-reported racism and social support predict blood pressure reactivity in Blacks. *Annals of Behavioral Medicine, 25,* 127–136.

Clarke, T.-K., Treutlein, J., Zimmermann, U. S., Kiefer, F., Skowronek, M. H., Rietschel, M., ... Schumann, G. (2008). HPA-axis activity in alcoholism: Examples for a gene-environment interaction. *Addiction Biology, 13,* 1–14.

Classen, C. (1993). *Worlds of sense: Exploring the senses in history and across cultures.* New York: Routledge.

Classen, C., Howes, D., & Synnott, A. (1994). *Aroma: The cultural history of smell.* London: Routledge.

Coates, T. (1990). Strategies for modifying sexual behavior for primary and secondary prevention of HIV disease. *Journal of Consulting and Clinical Psychology, 58,* 57–69.

Coates, T., Stall, R., Catania, J., & Kegeles, S. (1988). Behavioral factors in the spread of HIV infection. *AIDS, 2 (Suppl 1):* S239–S246.

Cobb, J. M., Fluster, Z., Leder, G., Seaver, A., Hendrick, J. L., & Hokanson, J. F. (2010). Information processing demands while texting on a simulated driving task. *Journal of Sport & Exercise Psychology, 32,* S72.

Coch, D. (2007). Neuroimaging research with children: Ethical issues and case scenarios. *Journal of Moral Education, 36,* 1–18.

Cochran, W., & Tesser, A. (1996). The "what the hell" effect: Some effects of goal proximity and goal framing on performance. In L. Martin & A. Tesser (Eds.), *Striving and feeling: Interactions among goals, affect, and self-regulation* (pp. 99–120). Mahwah, NJ: Erlbaum.

Coderre, T. J., Mogil, J. S., & Bushnell, M. C. (2003). The biological psychology of pain. In *Handbook of psychology: Biological psychology* (Vol. 3, pp. 237–268). New York: John Wiley & Sons.

Cohen, D., & Nisbett, R. E. (1977). Field experiments examining the culture of honor: The role of institutions in perpetuating norms about violence. *Personality and Social Psychology Bulletin, 23,* 1188–1199.

Cohen, K. M. (2002). Relationships among childhood sex-atypical behavior, spatial ability, handedness, and sexual orientation in men. *Archives of Sexual Behavior, 31,* 129–143.

Cohen, L. B., Diehl, R. L., Oakes, L. M., & Loehil, J. L. (1992). Infant perception of /aba/versus/apa: Building a quantitative model of infant categorical discrimination. *Developmental Psychology, 28,* 261–272.

Cohen, N. J., Eichenbaum, H., Deacedo, B. S., & Corkin, S. (1985). Different memory systems underlying acquisition of procedural and declarative knowledge. *Annals of the New York Academy of Sciences, 444,* 54–71.

Cohen, T. R., Montoya, R. M., & Insko, C. A. (2006). Group morality and intergroup relations: Cross-cultural and experimental evidence. *Personality and Social Psychology Bulletin, 32,* 1559–1572.

Cojan, Y., Waber, I., Schwartz, S., Rossier, I., Forster, A., & Vuilleumier, P. (2009). The brain under self-control: Modulation of inhibitory and monitoring cortical networks during hypnotic paralysis. *Neuron, 62,* 862–875.

Cole, D. A., Ciesla, J. A., Dallaire, D. H., Jacquez, F. M., Pineda, A. Q., LaGrange, B., ... Felton, J. W. (2008). Emergence of attributional style and its relation to depressive symptoms. *Journal of Abnormal Psychology, 117,* 16–31.

Cole, M. (1992). Culture in development. In M. H. Bornstein & M. E. Lamb (Eds.), *Developmental psychology: An advanced textbook* (3rd ed.). Hillsdale, NJ: Erlbaum.

Cole, M., & Cole, S. R. (1993). *The development of children* (2nd ed.). New York: Freeman.

Collier, G. (1986). The dialogue between the house economist and the resident physiologist. *Nutrition and Behavior, 3,* 9–26.

Colligan, J. (1983). Musical creativity and social rules in four cultures. *Creative Child and Adult Quarterly, 8,* 39–47.

Collins, A. M., & Loftus, E. F. (1975). A spreading-activation theory of semantic processing. *Psychological Review, 82,* 407–428.

Collins, D., Pan, Z., Johnson, K., Crouser, M., & Shamblen, S. (2008). Individual and contextual predictors of inhalant use among 8th graders: A multilevel analysis. *Journal of Drug Education, 38* (193–210).

Colom, R., Lluis-Font, J. M., & Andres-Pueyo, A. (2005). The generational intelligence gains are caused by decreasing variance in the lower half of the distribution: Supporting evidence for the nutrition hypothesis. *Intelligence, 33,* 83–91.

Colrain, I. M. (2011). Sleep and the brain. *Neuropsychology Review, 21,* 1–4.

Conrad, R. (1964). Acoustic confusions in immediate memory. *British Journal of Psychology, 55,* 75–84.

Cook, K. S., Cheshire, C., & Gerbasi, A. (2006). Power, dependence, and social exchange. In P. Burke (Ed.), *Contemporary Social Psychological Theories.* Stanford, CA: Stanford University Press.

Cooper, B. Y., Vierck, C. J., Jr., & Yeomans, D. C. (1986). Selection reduction of second pain sensations by systemic morphine in humans. *Pain, 24,* 93–116.

Cooper, D. B. (Ed.). (2000). *Alcohol use.* Oxford, UK: Radcliffe Medical Press.

Cooper, J. (2007). *Cognitive dissonance: Fifty years of a classic theory.* Thousand Oaks, CA: Sage.

Cooper, J., Kapur, N., Webb, R., Lawlor, M., Guthrie, E., Mackway-Jone, K., & Appleby, L. (2005). Suicide after deliberate self-harm: A 4-year cohort study. *American Journal of Psychiatry, 162,* 297–303.

Coppola, K. M., & Trotman, F. K. (2002). Dying and death: Decisions at the end of life. In F. K. Trotman, C. M. Brody, & M. Claire (Eds.), *Psychotherapy and counseling with older women: Cross-cultural, family, and end-of-life issues.* Springer Series, Focus on Women (pp. 221–238). New York: Springer.

Corbitt, E. M. (2002). Narcissism from the perspective of the five-factor model. In P. T. Costa Jr. & T. A. Widiger (Eds.), *Personality Disorders and the Five-factor Model of Personality* (2nd ed., pp. 293–298). Washington, DC: American Psychological Association.

Coren, S. (1989). Left-handedness and accident-related injury risk. *American Journal of Public Health, 79,* 1–2.

Coren, S. (1992). *The left-hander syndrome: The causes and consequences of left-handedness.* New York: Free Press.

Coren, S., & Aks, D. J. (1990). Moon illusion in pictures: A multimechanism approach. *Journal of Experimental Psychology: Human Perception & Performance, 16,* 365–380.

Coren, S., & Halpern, D. F. (1991). Left-handedness: A marker for decreased survival fitness. *Psychological Bulletin, 109,* 90–106.

Coren, S., Porac, C., & Theodor, L. H. (1987). Set and subjective contour. In S. Petry & G. E. Meyer (Eds.), *The Perception of Illusory Contours* (pp. 237–245). New York: Springer-Verlag.

Corker, K. S., & Donnellan, M. B. (2012). Setting lower limits high: The role of boundary goals in achievement motivation. *Journal of Educational Psychology, 104,* 138–149.

Corkin, S. (1984). Lasting consequences of bilateral medial temporal lobectomy: Clinical course and experimental findings in H. M. Seminars in *Neurology, 4,* 249–259.

Cornejo, C. (2001). Piaget, Vygotski and Maturana: Three voices, two constructivisms. *Psykhe: Revista de la Escuela de Psicologia, 10,* 87–96.

Correia, C. J., Sigmon, S. C., Silverman, K., Bigelow, G., Stitzer, & Maxine, L. (2005). A comparison of voucher-delivery schedules for the initiation of cocaine abstinence. *Experimental and Clinical Psychopharmacology, 13,* 253–258.

Cosmides, L., & Tooby, J. (2002). unraveling the enigma of human intelligence: Evolutionary pscyhology and the multimodular mind. In *The evolution of intelligence* (pp. 145–198). Mahwah, NJ: Erlbaum.

Costa, P. T., Jr., & McCrae, R. R. (1992). NEO Personality Inventory-Revised (NEO PI-R) and NEO Five-Factor Inventory (NEO-FFI). *Professional Manual.* Odessa, FL: Psychological Assessment Resources.

Costa, P. T., Jr., Terracciano, A., & McCrae, R. R. (2001). Gender differences in personality traits across cultures: Robust and surprising findings. *Journal of Personality and Social Psychology, 81,* 322–331.

Courage, M. L., & Adams, R. J. (1990). Visual acuity assessment from birth to three years using the acuity card procedures: Cross-sectional and longitudinal samples. *Optometry and Vision Science, 67,* 713–718.

Cowan, C. P., & Cowan, P. (2000). *When partners become parents: The big life change for couples.* Mahwah, NJ: Erlbaum.

Cowan, N. (1995). *Attention and memory: An integrated framework.* New York: Oxford University Press.

Cowan, N. (2001). The magical number 4 in short-term memory: A reconsideration of mental storage capacity. *Behavioral and Brain Sciences, 24,* 87–114.

Cowart, B. J. (1981). Development of taste perception in humans: Sensitivity and preference through the lifespan. *Psychological Bulletin, 90,* 43–73.

Coyle, T., Snyder, A., Pillow, D., & Kochunov, P. (2011). SAT predicts GPA better for high ability subjects: Implications for Spearman's Law of Diminishing Returns. *Personality and Individual Differences, 50,* 470–474.

Coyne, J. C., Rohrbaugh, M. J., Shoham, V., Sonnega, J. S., Nicklas, J. M., & Cranford, J. A. (2001). Prognostic importance of marital quality for survival of congestive heart failure. *American Journal of Cardiology, 88,* 526–529.

Crabtree, B. F., & Miller, W. L. (Eds.). (1992). *Doing qualitative research: Multiple strategies.* Thousand Oaks, CA: Sage.

Craig, L. A. (2012). Review of The use of the polygraph in assessing, treating and supervising sex offenders. *Criminal Justice and Behavior, 39,* 220–221.

Craik, F. I. M., & Lockhart, R. S. (1972). Levels of processing: A framework for memory research. *Journal of Verbal Learning and Verbal Behavior, 11,* 671–684.

Crandall, C. S. (1988). Social contagion of binge eating. *Journal of Personality and Social Psychology, 55,* 588–598.

Crandall, C. S. (1994). Prejudice against fat people: Ideology and self-interest. *Journal of Personality and Social Psychology, 66,* 882–894.

Crandall, C. S., & Eshleman, A. (2003). A justification-suppression of the expression and experience of prejudice. *Psychological Bulletin, 129,* 414–446.

Crandall, C. S., Silvia, P. J., N'Gbala, A. N., Tsang, J.-A., & Dawson, K. (2007). Balance theory, unit relations, and attribution: The underlying integrity of Heiderian theory. *Review of General Psychology, 11,* 12–30.

Crews, F. C. (1998). *Unauthorized Freud: Doubters confront a legend.* New York: Viking Penguin Inc.

Crocker, J., & Major, B. (1989). Social stigma and self-esteem: The self-protective properties of stigma. *Psychological Review, 96,* 608–630.

Crocker, J., Major, B., & Steele, C. (1998). Social stigma. In *The handbook of social psychology* (4th ed.). New York: McGraw-Hill.

Cross, S. E., Bacon, P. L., & Morris, M. L. (2000). The relational-interdependent self-construal and relationships. *Journal of Personality and Social Psychology, 78,* 791–808.

Cross, S. E., & Gore, J. S. (2004). The relational self-construal and the construction of closeness. In A. Aron & D. Mashek (Eds.), *The handbook of closeness and intimacy* (pp. 229–245). Hillsdale, NJ: Lawrence Earlbaum Associates, Inc.

Cross, S. E., & Madson, L. (1997). Models of the self: Self-construals and gender. *Psychological Bulletin, 122,* 5–37.

Cross, W. E., & Cross, T. B. (2008). Theory, research, and models. In S. M. Quintana & C. McKown (Eds.), *Handbook of race, racism, and the developing child* (pp. 154–181). Hoboken, NJ: John Wiley & Sons Inc.

Culp, R. E., Watkins, R. V., Lawrence, H., & Letts, D. (1991). Maltreated children's language and speech development: Abused, neglected, and abused and neglected. *First Language, 11,* 377–389.

Cunningham, M. R., Barbee, A. P., & Philhower, C. L. (2002). Dimensions of facial physical attractiveness: The intersection of biology and culture. In G. Rhodes & L. A. Zebrowitz (Eds.), *Facial attractiveness: evolutionary, cognitive, and social perspectives. Advances in visual cognition* (Vol. 1, pp. 193–238). Westport, CT: Ablex.

Cunningham, S., Scerbo, M. W., & Freeman, F. G. (2000). The electrocortical correlates of daydreaming during vigilance tasks. *Journal of Mental Imagery, 24,* 61–72.

Cunningham, W. A., & Brosch, T. (2012). Motivational salience: Amygdala tuning from traits, needs, values, and goals. *Current Directions in Psychological Science, 21,* 54–59.

Cuper, P. F., & Lynch, T. R. (2008). When is fantasy proneness associated with distress? An examination of two models. *Imagination, Cognition and Personality, 28,* 251–268.

Cutler, W. B., Friedmann, E., & McCoy, N. L. (1998). Pheromonal influences on sociosexual behavior in men. *Archives of Sexual Behavior, 27,* 1–3.

Curtiss, S., De Bode, S., & Mathern, G. W. (2001). Spoken language outcomes after hemispherectomy: Factoring in etiology. *Brain & Language, 79,* 379–396.

Cutrona, C. E. (1996). *Social support in couples.* Thousand Oaks, CA: Sage.

Cutrona, C. E., & Suhr, J. A. (1994). Social support communication in the context of marriage: An analysis of couples' supportive interactions. In B. B. Burleson, T. L. Albrecht, & I. G. Sarason (Eds.), *Communication of social support: messages, relationships, and community* (pp. 113–135). Thousand Oaks, CA: Sage.

Cvencek, D., Meltzoff, A. N., & Greenwald, A. G. (2011). Math-gender stereotypes in elementary school children. *Child Development, 82,* 766–779.

• • D •

D'Ydewalle, G. (2000). Sensation/perception, information processing, attention. In *International handbook of psychology* (pp. 79–99). London: Sage.

D'Ydewalle, G., & Rosselle, H. (1978). Text expectations in text learning. In M. M. Gruneberg, P. E. Morris, & R. N. Sykes (Eds.), *Practical aspects of memory.* Orlando, FL: Academic Press.

D'Argembeau, A., Comblain, C., & Van der Linden, M. (2003). Phenomenal characteristics of autobiographical memories for positive, negative, and neutral events. *Applied Cognitive Psychology, 17,* 281–294.

Dade, L. A., Zatorre, R. J., & Jones-Gotman, M. (2002). Olfactory learning: Convergent findings from lesion and brain imaging studies in humans. *Brain, 125,* 86–101.

Dahlsgaard, K., Peterson, C., & Seligman, M. E. P. (2005). Shared virtue: The convergence of valued human strengths across culture and history. *Review of General Psychology, 9,* 203–213.

Dai, D. Y., & Renzulli, J. S. (2008). Snowflakes, living systems, and the mystery of giftedness. *Gifted Child Quarterly, 52,* 114–130.

Daitch, C. (2011). *Anxiety disorders: The go-to guide for clients and therapists.* New York: W. W. Norton.

Dakof, G., & Taylor, S. (1990). Victims' perceptions of social support: What is helpful from whom? *Journal of Personality and Social Psychology, 58,* 80–89.

Dambrun, M., Duarte, S., & Guimond, S. (2004). Why are men more likely to support group-based dominance than women? The mediating role of gender identification. *British Journal of Social Psychology, 43,* 287–297.

Daniell, H. W. (1971). Smoker's wrinkles: A study in the epidemiology of "Crow's feet." *Annals of Internal Medicine, 75,* 873–880.

Darley, J. M., & Latané, B. (1968). Bystander intervention in emergencies: Diffusion of responsibility. *Journal of Personality and Social Psychology, 8,* 377–383.

Daruna, J. H. (2004). The Rorschach Test challenges science with the complexity of imagination. *Journal of Psychopathology & Behavioral Assessment, 26,* 147–149.

Darwin, C. (1871). *The descent of man.* London: John Murray.

Darwin, C. (1872). *Expression of emotion in man and animals.* London: John Murray.

Das Gupta, M. D., & Mari Bhat, P. N. (1997). Fertility decline and increased manifestation of sex bias in India. *Population Studies, 51,* 307–315.

Dasen, P. R. (1994). Culture and cognitive development from a Piagetian perspective. In W. J. Lonner & R. Malpass (Eds.), *Psychology and culture* (pp. 145–149). Boston, MA: Allyn & Bacon.

Davachi, L., & Dobbins, I. G. (2008). Declarative memory. *Current Directions in Psychological Science, 17,* 112–118.

Davidson, R., & Fox, N. (1989). Frontal brain asymmetry predicts infants' response to maternal separation. *Journal of Abnormal Psychology, 98,* 127–131.

Davidson, R. J. (2005). Affective neuroscience and psychophysiology: Towards synthesis. *Psychophysiology, 40,* 655–665.

Davidson, R. J., Kabat-Zinn, J., Schumacher, J., Rosenkrantz, M., Muller, D., & Santorelli. (2003). Alterations in brain and immune function produced by mindfulness meditation. *Psychosomatic Medicine, 65,* 564–570.

Davies, M. F. (1997). Positive test strategies and confirmatory retrieval processes in the evaluation of personality feedback. *Journal of Personality and Social Psychology, 73,* 574–583.

Davies, M., & McCartney, S. (2003). Effects of gender and sexuality on judgments of victim blame and rape myth acceptance in a depicted male rape. *Journal of Community & Applied Social Psychology, 13,* 391–398.

Davies, M., Walker, J., Archer, J., & Pollard, P. (2010). A comparative study of long-term psychological functioning in male survivors of stranger and acquaintance rape. *Journal of Aggression, Conflict and Peace Research, 2,* 25–33.

Davis, A. S. (2008). Children with Down syndrome: Implications for assessment and intervention in the school. *School Psychology Quarterly, 23,* 271–281.

Davis, J. M. (2006). The choice of drugs for schizophrenia. *New England Journal of Medicine, 354,* 518–520.

Davis, M. H. (1996). *Empathy: A social psychological approach.* Boulder, CO: Westview Press.

Davis, S. (1990). Men as success objects and women as sex objects: A study of personal advertisements. *Sex Roles, 23,* 43–50.

Davis, T. L. (1995). Gender differences in ¬masking negative emotions: Ability or motivation? *Developmental Psychology, 31,* 660–667.

Davis-Russel, E. (2003). Intergrating multicultural issues into graduate clinical psychology training. In K. Quina (Ed.), *Teaching gender and multicultural awareness: Resources for the psychology classroom* (pp. 339–346). Washington, DC: American Psychological Association.

Dawson, E., Gilovich, T., & Regan, D. T. (2002). Motivated reasoning and performance on the Wason Selection Task. *Personality & Social Psychology Bulletin, 28,* 1379–1387.

De Boysson-Bardies, B., Halle, P., Sagart, L., & Durand, C. (1989). A cross linguistic investigation of vowel formats in babbling. *Journal of Child Language, 16,* 1–17.

De Graaf, R., Ten Have, M., Van Gool, C., & Van Dorsselaer, S. (2012). Prevalence of mental disorders and trends from 1996 to 2009. Results from the Netherlands mental health survey and incidence study-2. *Social Psychiatry and Psychiatric Epidemiology, 47,* 203–213.

De Pascalis, V. (1999). Psychophysiological correlates of hypnosis and hypnotic susceptibility. *International Journal of Clinical and Experimental Hypnosis, 47,* 117–143.

De Valois, R. L., Abramov, I., & Jacobs, G. H. (1966). Analysis of response patterns of LGN cells. *Journal of the Optical Society of America, 56,* 966–977.

De Valois, R. L., & Jacobs, G. H. (1984). Neural mechanisms of color vision. In I. Darian-Smith (Ed.), *The Nervous System* (Vol. 3). Baltimore, MD: Williams & Wilkins.

De Waal, F. B. M. (2000). Primates—A natural heritage of conflict resolution. *Science, 289,* 586–590.

Debener, S., Hine, J., Bleeck, S., & Eyles, J. (2008). Source localization of auditory evoked potentials after cochlear implantation. *Psychophysiology, 45,* 20–24.

DeCasper, A. J., & Fifer, W. P. (1980). Of human bonding: Newborns prefer their mothers' voices. *Science, 208,* 1174–1176.

DeCasper, A. J., & Sigafoos, A. D. (1983). The intrauterine heartbeat: A potent reinforcer for newborns. *Infant Behavior and Development, 6,* 19–25.

DeCasper, A. J., & Spence, M. J. (1986). Prenatal maternal speech influences newborns' perception of speech sounds. *Infant Behavior and Development, 9,* 133–150.

Deci, E. (1975). *Intrinsic motivation.* New York: Plenum.

Deci, E., Koestner, R., & Ryan, R. (1999). A meta-analytic review of experiments examining the effects of extrinsic rewards on intrinsic motivation. *Psychological Bulletin, 125,* 627–668.

Deci, E. L. (2004). Promoting intrinsic motivation and self-determination in people with mental retardation. In N. Switzky (Ed.), *Personality and motivational systems in mental retardation* (Vol. 28, pp. 1–29). San Diego, CA: Elsevier Academic Press.

Deci, E. L., Driver, R. E., Hotchkiss, L., Robbins, R. J., & Wilson, I. M. (1993). The relation of mothers' controlling vocalizations to children's intrinsic motivation. *Journal of Experimental Child Psychology, 55,* 151–162.

Deckman, M. (2002). Holy ABCs! The impact of religion on attitudes about education policies. *Social Science Quarterly, 83,* 472–487.

DeHart, T., Pelham, B. W., & Tennen, H. (2006). What lies beneath: Parenting style and implicit self-esteem. *Journal of Experimental Social Psychology, 42,* 1–17.

Deikman, A. J. (2000). A functional approach to mysticism. In *Cognitive models and spiritual maps: Interdisciplinary explorations of religious experience* (pp. 75–91). Thorverton, England: Imprint Academic.

Del Olmo, N., Handler, A., Alvarez, L., Bustamante, J., Del Rio, R. M., & Solis, J. M. (2003). Taurine-induced synaptic potentiation and the late phase of long-term potentiation are related mechanistically. *Neuropharmacology, 44,* 26–39.

Dembroski, T., MacDougall, J., Williams, R., Haney, T., & Blumenthal, J. (1985). Components of Type A, hostility, and anger in relationship to angiographic findings. *Psychosomatic Medicine, 47,* 219–233.

Dement, W. (1960). The effect of dream deprivation. *Science, 131,* 1705–1707.

Dement, W. (1978). *Some must watch while some must sleep.* New York: Norton.

Dement, W. C. (1999). *The promise of sleep.* New York: Delacorte Press.

Dement, W. C., Greenberg, S., & Klein, R. (1966). The effect of partial REM sleep deprivation and delayed recovery. *Journal of Experimental Psychology, 53,* 339–346.

Dement, W. C., & Wolpert, E. (1958). The relation of eye movements, body motility, and external stimuli to dream content. *Journal of Experimental Psychology, 55,* 543–553.

DeNeve, K. M. (1999). Happy as an extraverted clam? The role of personality for subjective well-being. *Current Directions in Psychological Science, 124,* 197–229.

Denis, R. G., Bing, C., Brocklehurst, S., Harrold, J. A., Vernon, R. G., & Williams, G. (2004). Diurnal changes in hypothalamic neuropeptide and SOCS-3 expression: Effects of lactation and relationship with serum leptin and food intake. *Journal of Endocrinology, 183,* 173–181.

Dennis, T. (2006). Emotional self-regulation in preschoolers: The interplay of child approach reactivity, parenting, and control capacities. *Developmental Psychology, 42,* 84–97.

Deregowski, J. B. (1989). Real space and represented space: Cross-cultural perspectives. *Brain and Behavioral Sciences, 12,* 51–119.

Deslandes, R., & Bertrand, R. (2005). Motivation of parent involvement in secondary-level schooling. *Journal of Educational Research, 98,* 164–175.

Detterman, D. K. (2005). International handbook of intelligence. *Intelligence, 33,* 107–108.

Detterman, D. K., Gabriel, L. T., & Ruthsatz, J. M. (2000). Intelligence and mental retardation. In *Handbook of intelligence* (pp. 141–158). Cambridge, England: Cambridge University Press.

DeVries, R. (2000). Vygotsky, Piaget, and education: A reciprocal assimilation of theories and educational practices. *New Ideas in Psychology, 18,* 187–213.

DeWall, C. A., Deckman, T., Pond, R. S., Jr., & Bonser, I. (2011). Belongingness as a core personality trait: How social exclusion influences social functioning and personality expression. *Journal of Personality, 79,* 979–1012.

DeWall, C., MacDonald, G., Webster, G. D., Masten, C. L., Baumeister, R. F., Powell, C., … Eisenberger, N. I. (2010). Acetaminophen reduces social pain: Behavioral and neural evidence. *Psychological Science, 21,* 931–937.

DeYoung, C. G., Hirsh, J. B., Shane, M. S., Papademetris, X., Rajeevan, N., & Gray, J. R. (2010). Testing predictions from personality neuroscience. *Psychological Science, 21,* 820–828.

Di Lazzaro, V., Pilato, F., Dileone, M., Profice, P., Capone, F., Ranieri, F., … Tonali, P. A. (2008). Modulating cortical excitability in acute stroke: A repetitive TMS study. *Clinical Neurophysiology, 119,* 715–723.

Diakidoy, I. A. N., & Spanoudis, G. (2002). Domain specificity in creativity testing: A comparison of performance on a general divergent-thinking test and a parallel, content-specific test. *Journal of Creative Behavior, 36,* 41–61.

Diamond, A. (1985). The development of the ability to use recall to guide action, as indicated by infants' performance on AB. *Child Development, 56,* 868–883.

Diamond, J. (1966). Classification system of primitive people. *Science, 151,* 1102–1104.

Diamond, L. M. (1998). Development of sexual orientation among adolescent and young adult women. *Developmental Psychology, 34,* 1085–1095.

Diamond, L. M. (2003). What does sexual orientation orient? A biobehavioral model distinguishing romantic love and sexual desire. *Psychological Review, 110,* 173–192.

Diamond, L. M., & Savin-Williams, R. C. (2000). Explaining diversity in the development of same-sex sexuality among young women. *Journal of Social Issues, 56,* 297–313.

Diamond, M. C. (1988). *Enriching heredity: The impact of environment on the anatomy of the brain.* New York: Free Press.

DiCamillo, K. (2003). *The Tale of Despereaux.* Somerville, MA: Candlewick Press.

Diener, E. (2008). Myths in the science of happiness, and directions for future research. In M. Eid & R. J. Larsen (Eds.), *The science of subjective well-being* (pp. 493–514). New York:: Guilford Press.

Diener, E., & Diener, M. (1995). Cross-cultural correlates of life-satisfaction and self-esteem. *Journal of Personality and Social Psychology, 68,* 653–663.

Diener, E., Sandvik, E., Seiditz, L., & Diener, M. (1993). The relationship between income and subjective well-being: Relative or absolute? *Social Indicators Research, 28,* 195–223.

Diener, E., & Seligman, E. P. (2002). Very happy people. *Psychological Science, 13,* 81–84.

Diener, E., Suh, E. M., Lucas, R. E., & Smith, H. L. (1999). Subjective well-being: Three decades of progress. *Psychological Bulletin, 125,* 276–302.

Dijksterhuis, A. (2010). Automaticity and the unconscious. In S. T. Fiske, D. T. Gilbert, & G. Lindzey (Eds.), *Handbook of social psychology* (5th ed., Vol. 1, pp. 228–267). Hoboken, NJ: John Wiley.

Dijkstra, P., & Barelds, D. P. H. (2011). Women's metaperceptions of attractiveness and their relations to body image. *Body Image, 8,* 74–77.

DiLorenzo, P., & Youngentob, S. L. (2003). Olfaction and taste. In M. Gallagher & R. J. Nelson (Eds.), *Handbook of psychology: Biological psychology* (Vol. 3, pp. 269–297). New York: John Wiley & Sons.

Dilsaver, S. C., Chen, Y. R., Shoaib, A. M., & Swann, A. C. (1999). Phenomenology of mania: Evidence for distinct depressed, dysphoric, and euphoric presentations. *American Journal of Psychiatry, 156,* 426–430.

Dimitry, L. (2012). A systematic review on the mental health of children and adolescents in areas of armed conflict in the Middle East. *Child: Care, Health and Development, 38,* 153–161.

Dingfelder, S. F. (2005). Hispanic psychology: Closing the gap for Latino patients. *Monitor on Psychology, 36*(1), 68–69.

Dodds, C. M., Bullmore, E. T., Henson, R. N., Christensen, S., Miller, S., Smith, M., … Nathan, P. J. (2011). Effects of donepezil on cognitive performance after sleep deprivation. *Human Psychopharmacology: Clinical and Experimental, 26,* 578–587.

Dodge, K. A. (2011). Social information processing patterns as mediators of the interaction between genetic factors and life experiences in the development of aggressive behavior. In P. R. Shaver & M. Mikulincer (Eds.), *Human aggression and violence: Causes, manifestations, and consequences* (pp. 165–185). Washington, DC: American Psychological Association.

Doll, E., Gittler, G., & Holzinger, B. (2009). Dreaming, lucid dreaming and personality. *International Journal of Dream Research, 2,* 52–57.

Domes, G., Heinrichs, M., Michel, A., Berger, C., & Herpertz, S. C. (2007). Oxytocin improves "mind-reading" in humans. *Biological Psychiatry, 61,* 731–733.

Domhoff, G. W. (2003). *The scientific study of dreams: Neural networks, cognitive development, and content analysis.* Washington, DC: American Psychological Association.

Domjan, M. (2005). Pavlovian conditioning: A functional perspective. *Annual Review of Psychology, 56,* 179–206.

Donnellan, M. B., Burt, S. A., Levendosky, A. A., & Klump, K. L. (2008). Genes, personality, and attachment in adults: A multivariate behavioral genetic analysis. *Personality and Social Psychology Bulletin, 34,* 3–16.

Doty, R. L., Green, P. A., Ram, C., & Tandeil, S. L. (1982). Communication of gender from human breath odors: Relationship to perceived intensity and pleasantness. *Hormones and Behavior, 16,* 13–22.

Douglas, C., & Gardner, W. L. (2004). Transition to self-directed work teams: Implications of transition time and self-monitoring for managers' use of influence tactics. *Journal of Organizational Behavior, 25,* 47–65.

Dovidio, J. F. (2001). On the nature of contemporary prejudice: The third wave. *Journal of Social Issues, 57,* 829–849.

Dow, B. M. (2002). Orientation and color columns in monkey visual cortex. *Cerebral Cortex, 12,* 1005–1015.

Dowling, G. A., Burr, R. L., Van Someren, E. J. W., Hubbard, E. M., Luxenberg, J. S., Mastick, J., & Copper, B. A. (2008). Melatonin and bright-light treatment for rest-activity disruption in institutionalized patients with Alzheimer's disease. *Journal of the American Geriatrics Society, 56,* 239–246.

Dowling, J. E. (1992). *Neurons and networks: An introduction to neuroscience.* Cambridge, MA: Harvard University Press.

Drayna, D. (2006). Is our behavior written in our genes? *New England Journal of Medicine, 354,* 7–9.

Drewnowski, A., & Levine, A. S. (2003). Sugar and fat: From genes to culture. *Journal of Nutrition, 133,* 829–830.

Dubosc, A., Capitaine, M., Franko, D. L., Bui, E., Brunet, A., Chabrol, H., & Rodgers, R. F. (2012). Early adult sexual assault and disordered eating: The mediating role of posttraumatic stress symptoms. *Journal of Traumatic Stress, 25,* 50–56.

Duffy, S., & Crawford, L. E. (2008). Primacy or recency effects in forming inductive categories. *Memory & Cognition, 36,* 567–577.

Dunbar, R. I. M. (1993). Coevolution of neocortical size, group size and language in humans. *Behavioral and Brain Sciences, 16,* 681–735.

Dunbar-Hall, P. (2011). Children's learning of music and dance in Bali: An ethnomusicological view of the cultural psychology of music education. In M. S. Barrett (Ed.), *A cultural psychology of music education* (pp. 17–40). New York: Oxford University Press.

Duncan, J., Seitz, R. J., Kolodny, J., Bor, D., Herzog, H., Ahmed, A., … Emslie, H. (2000). A neural basis for general intelligence. *Science, 289,* 457–460.

Duncker, K. (1945). On problem solving. *Psychological Monographs, 5*(270), 58.

Dunkel-Schetter, C., Blasband, D., Feinstein, L., & Herbert, T. (1992). Elements of supportive interactions: When are attempts to help effective? In S. Spacapan & S. Oskamp (Eds.), *Helping and being helped: Naturalistic studies* (pp. 83–114). Newbury Park, CA: Sage.

Duquette, M., Roy, M., Lepore, F., Peretz, I., & Rainville, P. (2008). Cerebral mechanisms involved in the interaction between pain and emotion. *Revue Neurologique, 163,* 169–179.

Durham, R. C., Chambers, J. A., MacDonald, R. R., Power, K. G., & Major, K. (2003). Does cognitive-behavioural therapy influence the long-term outcome of generalized anxiety disorder? An 8–14 year follow-up of two clinical trials. *Psychological Medicine, 33,* 499–509.

Durso, F. T., Rea, C. B., & Dayton, T. (1994). Graph-theoretic confirmation of restructuring during insight. *Psychological Science, 5,* 94–98.

Dutton, D. G., & Aron, A. (1974). Some evidence for heightened sexual attraction under conditions of high anxiety. *Journal of Personality and Social Psychology, 30,* 510–517.

Dweck, C. I. S. (2002). Beliefs that make smart people dumb. In R. J. Sternberg (Ed.), *Why smart people can be so stupid* (pp. 24–41). New Haven CT: Yale University Press.

Dweck, C. S. (2006). *Mindset: The new psychology of success.* New York: Random House.

· · · · · · · **E** · · · · · · · · ·

Eagly, A. H., & Crowley, M. (1986). Gender and helping behavior: A meta-analytic review of the social psychological literature. *Psychological Bulletin, 100,* 283–308.

Eagly, A. H., & Wood, W. (1999). The origins of sex differences in human behavior. *American Psychologist, 54,* 408–423.

Eakin, D. K., & Smith, R. (2012). Retroactive interference effects in implicit memory. *Journal of Experimental Psychology: Learning, Memory, and Cognition.*

Earleywine, M. (2002). *Understanding marijuana: A new look at the scientific evidence.* New York: Oxford University Press.

Eaton, A. A., & Rose, S. (2011). Has dating become more egalitarian? A 35 year review using Sex roles. *Sex Roles, 64,* 843–862.

Ebbinghaus, H. (1885). Über das gedächtnis: Untersuchungen zur experimentellen psychologie. In H. A. Ruger & C. E. Byssenine (Trans.), *Memory: A contribution to experimental psychology.* New York: Dover, 1913.

Ebbinghaus, H. (1913). Über das gedächtnis: Untersuchugen zur experimentellen psychologie. Leipzig: Dunker & Humbolt. *Memory: A contribution to experimental psychology.* (H. A. Ruger & C. E. Byssenine, Trans.). New York: Dover. (Original work published 1885).

Eccles, J., Brown, B. V., & Templeton, J. (2008). A developmental framework for selecting indicators of well-being during the adolescent and young adult years. In B. V. Brown (Ed.), *Key indicators of child and youth well-being: Completing the picture* (pp. 197–236). Mahwah, NJ: Lawrence Erlbaum.

Eccles, J. C. (1989). *Evolution of the brain: Creation of the self.* London: Routledge.

Eccles, J., Templeton, J., Barber, B., & Stone, M. (2003). Adolescence and emerging adulthood: The critical passage ways to adulthood. In M. H. Bornstein & L. Davidson (Eds.), *Well-being: Positive Development Across the Life Course. Crosscurrents in Contemporary Psychology* (pp. 383–406). Mahwah, NJ: Lawrence Erlbaum.

Echterling, L. G., & Whalen, J. (1995). Stage hypnosis and public lecture effects on attitudes and beliefs regarding hypnosis. *American Journal of Clinical Hypnosis, 38,* 13–21.

Edwards, K., & Smith, E. E. (1996). A disconfirmation bias in the evaluation of arguments. *Journal of Personality and Social Psychology, 71,* 5–24.

Edwards, O. W., & Paulin, R. V. (2007). Referred students' performance on the Reynolds Intellectual Assessment Scales and the Wechsler Intelligence Scale for Children–Fourth Edition. *Journal of Psychoeducational Assessment, 25,* 334–340.

Egas Moñiz, A. (1948). How I came to perform prefrontal leucotomy. *Proceedings of the First International Congress of Psychosurgery.* Lisbon: Edicos Atica.

Egeland, J. D., & Sussex, J. N. (1985). Suicide and family loading for affective disorders. *Journal of the American Medical Association, 254,* 915–918.

Eich, J. E. (1989). Theoretical issues in state dependent memory. In F. I. M. Craik (Ed.), *Varieties of memory and consciousness: Essays in honour of Endel Tulving* (pp. 331–354). Hillsdale, NJ: Erlbaum.

Eimer, M., & Schlaghecken, F. (In Press). Links between conscious awareness and response inhibition: Evidence from masked priming. *Psychonomic Bulletin & Review.*

Eisenberg, N., & Valiente, C. (2002). Parenting and children's prosocial and moral development. In M. H. Bornstein (Ed.), *Handbook of parenting:* Vol. 5. Practical Issues in Parenting (2nd ed., pp. 111–142). Mahwah, NJ: Erlbaum.

Eisenberger, N. I. (2011). Social pain: Experiential, neurocognitive, and genetic correlates. In A. Todorov, S. T. Fiske, & D. A. Prentice (Eds.), *Social neuroscience: Toward understanding the underpinnings of the social mind* (pp. 229–248). New York: Oxford University Press.

Eisler, R., & Levine, D. S. (2002). Nurture, nature, and caring: We are not prisoners of our genes. *Brain & Mind, 3,* 9–52.

Ekman, P. (1970). Universal facial expressions of emotion. *California Mental Health Research Digest, 8,* 151–158.

Ekman, P. (1993). Facial expression and emotion. *American Psychologist, 48,* 384–392.

Ekman, P., & Davidson, R. J. (1993). Voluntary smiling changes regional brain activity. *Psychological Science, 4,* 342–345.

Ekman, P., & Friesen, W. V. (1971). Constants across cultures in the face and emotion. *Journal of Personality and Social Psychology, 17,* 124–129.

Elhai, J. D., Miller, M. E., Ford, J. D., Biehn, T. L., Palmieri, P. A., & Frueh, B. C. (2012). Posttraumatic stress disorder in DSM-5: Estimates of prevalence and symptom structure in a nonclinical sample of college students. *Journal of Anxiety Disorders, 26,* 58–64.

Elkind, D., & Bowen, R. (1979). Imaginary audience behavior in children and adolescents. *Developmental Psychology, 15,* 38–44.

Elliott, M. A., & Ainsworth, K. (2012). Predicting university undergraduates' binge-drinking behavior: A comparative test of the one- and two-component theories of planned behavior. *Addictive Behaviors, 37,* 92–101.

Ellis, A. (1962). *Reason and emotion in psychotherapy.* New York: Lyle Stuart.

Ellis, A. (1999). Why rational emotive therapy to rational emotive behavior therapy? *Psychotherapy, 36,* 154–159.

Ellis, A. (2002). *Overcoming resistance: A rational emotive behavior therapy integrated approach* (2nd ed.). New York: Springer.

Ellis, A., Shaughnessy, M. F., & Mahan, V. (2002). An interview with Albert Ellis about Rational Emotive Behavior Therapy. *North American Journal of Psychology, 4*, 355–366.

Ellis, B. J., & Boyce, W. T. (2008). Biological sensitivity to context. *Current Directions in Psychological Science, 17*, 183–187.

Ellis, B. J., & Essex, M. J. (2007). Family environments, adrenarche, and sexual maturation: A longitudinal test of a life history model. *Child Development, 78*, 1799–1817.

Elms, A. C. (1995). Obedience in retrospect. *Journal of Social Issues, 51*, 21–31.

Elms, A. C., & Milgram, S. (1966). Personality characteristics associated with obedience and defiance toward authoritative command. *Journal of Experimental Research in Personality, 1*, 282–298.

Elsesser, K., & Peplau, L. A. (2006). The glass partition: Obstacles to cross-sex friendships at work. *Human Relations, 59*, 1077–1100.

Emilien, G., Durlach, C., Antoniadis, C., Van der Linden, M., & Maloteaux, J.-M. (2004). Memory Neurological, imaging, and psychopharmacological perspectives. London: Psychology Press.

Emmelkamp, P. M. G. (1986). Behavior therapy with adults. In S. L. Garfield & A. E. Bergin (Eds.), *Handbook of psychotherapy and behavior change* (3rd ed., pp. 385–442). New York: Wiley.

Emmers-Sommer, T. M., Allen, M., & Duck, S. (Eds.). (2005). *Safer sex in personal relationships: The role of sexual script in HIV infection and prevention.* Mahwah, NJ: Lawrence Erlbaum.

Enard, W. (2011). FOXP2 and the role of cortico-basal ganglia circuits in speech and language evolution. *Current Opinion in Neurobiology, 21*, 415–424.

Enard, W., Przeworski, M., Fisher, S. E., Lai, C. S. L., Wiebe, V., Kitano, T., ... Paaebo, S. (2002). Molecular evolution of FOXP2, a gene involved in speech and language. *Nature, 418*, 869–872.

Epel, E., Blackburn, E. H., Lin, J., Dhabar, F., Adler, N., Morrow, J., & Cawthon, R. (2004). *Organismal stress and telomeric aging: An unexpected connection.* Proc. Natl. Acad. Sci. USA, 101, 17312–17315.

Ephraim, D. (2008). Psychocultural system manual. In S. R. Jenkins (Ed.), *A handbook of clinical scoring systems for thematic apperceptive techniques* (pp. 739–760). Mahwah, NJ: Lawrence Erlbaum.

Eppig, C., Fincher, C. L., & Thornhill, R. (2010). Parasite prevalence and the worldwide distribution of cognitive ability. *Proceedings of the Royal Society B: Biological Sciences, 277*, 3801–3808.

Epstein, S. (1980). The stability of behavior: II. Implications for psychological research. *American Psychologist, 35*, 790–806.

Epstein, S. (1998). Cognitive-experiential self-theory. In D. F. Barone & M. Hersen (Eds.), *Advanced personality: The plenum series in social/clinical psychology* (pp. 211–238). New York: Plenum.

Erdelyi, M. H. (2010). The ups and downs of memory. *American Psychologist, 65*, 623–633.

Erel, O., Oberman, Y., & Yirmiya, N. (2000). Maternal versus nonmaternal care and seven domains of children's development. *Psychological Bulletin, 126*, 727–747.

Erikson, E. H. (1950). *Childhood and society.* New York: W. W. Norton: W. W. Norton.

Ermer, E., & Kiehl, K. A. (2010). Psychopaths are impaired in social exchange and precautionary reasoning. *Psychological Science, 21*, 1399–1403.

Ertekin-Taner, N., Ronald, J., Feuk, L., Prince, J., Tucker, M., Younkin, L., ... Younkin, S. G. (2005). Elevated amyloid \ss protein (A\ss42) and late onset Alzheimer's disease are associated with single nucleotide polymorphisms in the urokinase-type plasminogen activator gene. *Human Molecular Genetics, 14*, 447–460.

Erwin, P. G. (1994). Effectiveness of social skills training with children: A meta-analytic study. *Counseling Psychology Quarterly, 7*, 305–310.

Espeseth, T., Westlye, L. T., Fjell, A. M., Walhovd, K. B., Rootwelt, H., & Reinvang, I. (2008). Accelerated age-related cortical thinning in healthy carriers of apolipoprotein E epsilon 4. *Neurobiology of Aging, 29*, 329–340.

Esterson, A. (1993). *Seductive mirage: An exploration of the work of Sigmund Freud.* Chicago: Open Court.

Estow, S., Jamieson, J. P., & Yates, J. R. (2007). Self-monitoring and mimicry of positive and negative social behaviors. *Journal of Research in Personality, 41*, 425–433.

Eun, B. (2010). From learning to development: A sociocultural approach to instruction. *Cambridge Journal of Education, 40*, 401–418.

Evans, A. T., & Clark, J. K. (2012). Source characteristics and persuasion: The role of self-monitoring in self-validation. *Journal of Experimental Social Psychology, 48*, 383–386.

Evans, M. (2001). Cognitive and contextual factors in the emergence of diverse belief systems: Creation versus evolution. *Cognitive Psychology, 42*, 217–266.

Evans, S., Ferrando, S., Findler, M., Stowell, C., Smart, C., & Haglin, D. (2008). Mindfulness-based cognitive therapy for generalized anxiety disorder. *Journal of Anxiety Disorders, 22*, 716–721.

Everson, S., Kauhanen, J., Kaplan, G., Goldberg, D., Julkunen, J., Tuomilehto, J., & Salonen, J. (1997). Hostility and increased risk of mortality and acute myocardial infarction: The mediating role of behavioral risk factors. *American Journal of Epidemiology, 146*, 142–152.

Ewbank, M. P., Smith, W. A. P., Hancock, E. R., & Andrews, T. J. (2008). The M170 reflects a viewpoint-dependent representation for both familiar and unfamiliar faces. *Cerebral Cortex, 18*, 364–370.

Exner, J. E. (1993). *The Rorschach: A comprehensive system* (3rd ed., Vol. 1). New York: John Wiley.

Eyeferth, K. (1961). Leistengen vershiedener Gruppen von Beastzungskindern in Hamburg-Wechsler Intelligenztest für Kinder (HAWIK). *Archir für die Gesamte Psychologie, 113*, 224–241.

Eysenck, H. J. (1967). *The biological basis of personality.* Springfield, IL: Charles C. Thomas.

Eysenck, H. J. (1990). Biological dimensions of personality. In L. A. Pervin (Ed.), *Handbook of personality: Theory and research* (pp. 244–276). New York: Guilford Press.

Eysenck, H. J. (1997). Personality and experimental psychology: The unification of psychology and the possibility of a paradigm. *Journal of Personality and Social Psychology, 73*, 1224–1237.

Eysenck, H. J., & Levey, A. (1972). Conditioning introversion-extraversion and the strength of the nervous system. In V. Nebylitsyn & J. Gray (Eds.), *Biological basis of individual behavior* (pp. 206–220). New York: Academic Press.

F

Fagerskiold, A. (2008). A change in life as experienced by first-time fathers. *Scandinavian Journal of Caring Sciences, 22*, 64–71.

Fairburn, C. G., Welch, S. L., Doll, H. A., Davies, B. A., & O'Connor, M. E. (1997). Risk factors for bulimia nervosa. *Archives of General Psychiatry, 54*, 509–511.

Falck, R. S., Wang, J., & Carlson, R. G. (2008). Depressive symptomatology in young adults with a history of MDMA use: A longitudinal analysis. *Journal of Psychopharmacology, 22*, 47–54.

Falkai, P., & Moller, H. J. (2012). Neurobiology of schizophrenia: From outcome to pathophysiological insights. *European Archives of Psychiatry and Clinical Neuroscience, 262*, 93–94.

Fanselow, M. S., & Poulos, M. A. (2005). The neuroscience of mammalian associative learning. *Annual Review of Psychology, 56*, 207–234.

Farahany, N. (2008). Tomorrow's technology. *Milwaukee Journal Sentinel*, 9A. Retrieved from www.JSOnline. com

Fast, K., & Fujiwara, E. (2001). Isolated retrograde amnesi. *Neurocase, 7*, 269–272.

Fauber, J. (2004). Beauty and the brain: Doctors foresee demand for treatment to enhance abilities. *Milwaukee Journal Sentinel*, 1A. Retrieved from www.JSOnline. com

Fava, M., & Rosenbaum, J. F. (1995). Pharmacotherapy and somatic therapies. In *Handbook of depression* (2nd ed., pp. 280–301). New York: Guilford Press.

Faymonville, M. E., Laureys, S., Degueldre, C., DelFiore, G., Luxen, A., & Franck, G. (2000). Neural mechanisms of antinociceptive effects of hypnosis. *Anesthesiology, 92*, 1257–1267.

Fechner, G. T. (1966). *Elements of psychophysics.* (H. E. Alder, Trans.). New York: Holt, Rinehart & Winston. (Original work published 1860).

Federmeier, K. D., & Kutas, M. (2002). Picture the difference: Electrophysiological investigations of picture processing in the two cerebral hemispheres. *Neuropsychologia, 40*, 730–747.

Feingold, A. (1992). Good-looking people are not what we think. *Psychological Bulletin, 111*, 304–341.

Feldman, D. H., & Morelock, M. J. (2011). Prodigies and savants. In R. J. Sternberg & S. B. Kaufman (Eds.), *The Cambridge handbook of intelligence* (pp. 210–234). New York: Cambridge University Press.

Feldman, M. W., & Lewontin, R. C. (2008). Race, ancestry, and medicine. In *Revisiting race in a genome age* (pp. 89–101). Piscataway, NJ: Rutgers University Press.

Fenigstein, A., Scheier, M. F., & Buss, A. H. (1975). Public and private self-consciousness: Assessment and theory. *Journal of Consulting and Clinical Psychology, 43*, 522–527.

Fergusson, D. M., Horwood, L. J., & Beautrais, A. L. (1999). Is sexual orientation related to mental health problems and suicidality in young people? *Archives of General Psychiatry, 56*, 876–880.

Fernandez, E., & Turk, D. C. (1989). the utility of cognitive coping strategies for altering pain perception: A meta-analysis. *Pain, 38*, 123–135.

Fernandez-Castillo, N., Orejarena, M. J., Ribases, M., Blanco, E., Casas, M., Robledo, P., ... Cormand, B. (2012). Active and passive MDMA ('ecstasy') intake induces differential transcriptional changes in the mouse brain. *Genes, Brain & Behavior, 11*, 38–51.

Fernberger, S. W. (1933). Wundt's doctorate students. *Psychological Bulletin, 30*, 80–83.

Ferrari, J. R., & Dovidio, J. F. (2001). Behavioral information search by indecisives. *Personality and Individual Differences, 30*, 1–21.

Ferrari, J. R., & Tice, D. M. (2000). Procrastination as a self-handicap for men and women: A task avoidance strategy in a laboratory setting. *Journal of Research in Personality, 34*, 73–83.

Ferster, C. S., & Skinner, B. F. (1957). *Schedules of reinforcement.* New York: Appleton-Century-Crofts.

Festinger, L. (1954). A theory of social comparison processes. *Human Relations, 7*, 117–140.

Festinger, L. (1957). *A theory of cognitive dissonance.* Stanford, CA: Stanford University Press.

Festinger, L., Riecken, H. W., & Schachter, S. (1956). *When prophecy fails.* Minneapolis, MN: University of Minnesota Press.

Festinger, L., Schachter, S., & Back, K. (1950). *Social pressures in informal groups: A study of a housing community.* New York: Harper.

Finger, S., & Wade, N. J. (2002). The neuroscience of Helmholtz and the theories of Johannes Müller: Part 2: Sensation and perception. *Journal of the History of the Neurosciences, 11*, 234–254.

Fischer, P., & Greitemeyer, T. (2006). Music and aggression: The impact of sexual-aggressive song lyrics on aggression-related thoughts, emotions, and behavior toward the same and the opposite sex. *Personality and Social Psychology Bulletin, 32*, 1165–1176.

Fish, J. M. (2002). The myth of race. In J. M. Fish (Ed.), *Race and intelligence: Separating science from myth* (pp. 113–141). Mahwah, NJ: Lawrence Erlbaum.

Fisher, C. B., Vacanti-Shova, K., Knapp, S. J., Gottlieb, M. C., Handelsman, M. M., & VandeCreek, L. D. (2012). The responsible conduct of psychological research: An overview of ethical principles, APA Ethics Code standards, and federal regulations. In *APA handbook of ethics in psychology, Vol 2: Practice, teaching, and research* (pp. 335–369). Washington, DC: American Psychological Association.

Fishman, I., Ng, R., & Bellugi, U. (2011). Do extraverts process social stimuli differently from introverts? *Cognitive Neuroscience, 2*, 67–73.

Fiske, S. T., & Taylor, S. E. (1991). *Social cognition* (2nd ed.). New York: McGraw-Hill.

Fivush, R., & Nelson, K. (2004). Culture and language in the emergence of autobiographical memory. *Psychological Science, 15*, 573–577.

Flavell, J. H. (1992). Cognitive development: Past present, and future. *Developmental Psychology, 28*, 998–1005.

Flavell, J. H. (1999). Cognitive development: Children's knowledge about the mind. *Annual Review of Psychology, 50*, 21–45.

Fletcher, G. (2002). *The new science of intimate relationships.* Malden, MA: Blackwell.

Fletcher, G. J. O., Tither, J. M., O'Loughlin, C., Friesen, M., & Overall, N. (2004). Warm and homely or cold and beautiful? Sex differences in trading off traits in mate selection. *Personality and Social Psychology Bulletin, 30*, 659–672.

Flouri, E., & Buchanan, A. (2003). The role of father involvement in children's later mental health. *Journal of Adolescence, 26*, 63–78.

Flynn, J. R. (1987). Massive IQ gains in 14 nations: What IQ tests really measure. *Psychological Bulletin, 101*, 171–191.

Flynn, J. R. (2007). *What is intelligence? Beyond the Flynn effect.* New York: Cambridge University Press.

Foertsch, J., & Gernsbacher, M. A. (1997). In search of gender neutrality: Is singular they a cognitively efficient substitute for generic he? *Behavior Therapy, 16*, 292–302.

Fontana, D. (2003). *Psychology, religion, and spirituality.* Oxford, UK: Blackwell.

Ford, C. S., & Beach, F. A. (1951). *Patterns of sexual behavior.* New York: Harper & Brothers.

Ford, D. Y. (1996). *Reversing underachievement among gifted Black students: Promising practices and programs.* New York: Teachers College Press.

Fordham, S., & Ogbu, J. U. (1986). Black students' school success: Coping with the "burden of 'acting white'." *The Urban Review, 18*, 176–206.

Forer, B. R. (1949). The fallacy of personal validation: A classroom demonstration of gullibility. *Journal of Abnormal and Social Psychology, 44*, 118–123.

Foreyt, J., Walker, S., II, C. P., & Goodrick, G. (1996). Future directions in obesity and eating disorders. *Addictive Behaviors, 21*, 767–778.

Forgas, J. P. (1998). Asking nicely? The effects of mood on responding to more or less polite requests. *Personality and Social Psychology Bulletin, 24*, 173–185.

Fowers, A. F., & Fowers, B. J. (2010). Social dominance and sexual self-schema as moderators of sexist reactions to female subtypes. *Sex Roles, 62*, 468–480.

Fox, B. A. (1988). *Cognitive and interactional aspects of correction in tutoring* (Tech. Rep. No. 88-2). Boulder: University of Colorado, Institute of Cognitive Science.

Fox, E., Derakshan, N., & Standage, H. (2011). The assessment of human attention. In K. C. Klauer, A. Voss, & C. Stahl (Eds.), *Cognitive methods in social psychology* (pp. 15–47). New York: Guilford Press.

Fraczek, A. (1992). Patterns of aggressive-hostile behavior orientation among adolescent boys and girls. In K. Björkqvist & P. Niemelä (Eds.), *Of mice and women: Aspects of female aggression* (pp. 107–112). San Diego, CA: Harcourt Brace Jovanovich.

Fraga, E. D., Atkinson, D. R., & Wampold, B. E. (2004). Ethnic group preferences for multicultural counseling competencies. *Cultural Diversity and Ethnic Minority Psychology, 10*, 53–65.

Frankenberger, K. D. (2000). Adolescent egocentrism: A comparison among adolescents and adults. *Journal of Adolescence, 23*, 343–354.

Franzoi, S. L., & Chang, Z. (2002). The body esteem of Hmong and Caucasian young adults. *Psychology of Women Quarterly, 26*, 89–91.

Franzoi, S. L., Davis, M. H., & Young, R. D. (1985). The effects of private self-consciousness and perspective-taking on satisfaction in close relationships. *Journal of Personality and Social Psychology, 48*, 1584–1594.

Franzoi, S. L., & Shields, S. A. (1984). The Body Esteem Scale: Multidimensional structure and sex differences in a college population. *Journal of Personality Assessment, 48*, 173–178.

Franzoi, S. L., Vasquez, K., Sparapani, E., Frost, K., Martin, J., & Aebly, M. (2012). Exploring body comparison tendencies: Women are self-critical whereas men are self-hopeful. *Psychology of Women Quarterly, 36*, 99–109.

Fredrickson, B. L., Maynard, K. E., Helms, M. J., Haney, T. L., Siegler, I. C., & Barefoot, J. C. (2000). Hostility predicts magnitude and duration of blood pressure response to anger. *Journal of Behavioral Medicine, 23*, 229–243.

French, S. A. (2003). Pricing effects on food choices. *Journal of Nutrition, 133*, 841–843.

Freud, A. (1936). *The writings of Anna Freud: The ego and the mechanics of defense.* Madison CT: International Universities Press.

Freud, S. (1895). Project for a scientific psychology. In *The standard edition of the complete psychological works of Sigmund Freud* (Vol. 1, pp. 292–398). London: Hogarth Press.

Freud, S. (1900a). *The interpretation of dreams.* In Vols. 4 And 5 of the standard edition. London: Hogarth.

Freud, S. (1900b). The interpretation of dreams. In *The standard edition of the complete psychological works of Sigmund Freud* (Vol. 4–5). London: Hogarth.

Freud, S. (1909). Analysis of a phobia in a five-year-old boy. In J. Strachey (Ed.), *The standard edition of the complete psychological works of Sigmund Freud* (Vol. 10, pp. 3–149). London: Hogarth.

Freud, S. (1917). Introductory lectures on psychoanalysis. Part III. General theory of the neurosis. In *The standard edition of the complete psychological works of Sigmund Freud* (Vol. 16, pp. 243–496). London: Hogarth Press.

Freud, S. (1926). Inhibitions, symptoms, and anxiety. In *The standard edition of the complete psychological works of Sigmund Freud* (Vol. 20, pp. 89–174). London: Hogarth Press.

Freud, S. (1946). *The ego and the mechanisms of defense.* New York: International Universities Press.

Freud, S. (1949). *A general introduction to psychoanalysis.* New York: Penguin.

Freund, A. M., & Ritter, J. O. (2009). Midlife crisis: A debate. *Gerontology, 55*, 582–591.

Friedman, D., Nessler, D., Johnson, R., Jr., Ritter, W., & Bersick, M. (2008). Age-related changes in executive function: An event-related potential (ERP) investigation of task-switching. *Aging, Neuropsychology, and Cognition, 15*, 1–34.

Friedman, J. M. (2000). Obesity in the new millennium. *Nature, 404*, 632–634.

Friedman, L. J. (2001). Erik Erikson on identity, generativity, and pseudospeciation: A biographer's perspective. *Psychoanalysis & History, 3*, 179–192.

Friedman, M. (1996). *Type A behavior: Its diagnosis and treatment.* New York: Plenum.

Friedman, M., & Ulmer, D. (1984). *Treating Type A behavior—and your heart.* New York: Knopf.

Frieze, I. H., Olson, J. E., & Russell, J. (1991). Attractiveness and income for men and women in management. *Journal of Applied Social Psychology, 21*, 1039–1057.

Fritz, H. L., Nagurney, A. J., & Helgeson, V. S. (2003). Social interactions and cardiovascular reactivity during problem disclosure among friends. *Personality and Social Psychology Bulletin, 29*, 713–725.

Fuchs, C. S., Stampfer, M. J., & Colditz, G. A. (1995). Alcohol consumption and mortality among women. *New England Journal of Medicine, 332*, 1245–1250.

Fuhrman, A., & Burlingame, G. M. (1994). Group psychotherapy: Research and practice. In A. Fuhriman & G. M. Burlingame (Eds.), *Handbook of group psychotherapy.* New York: Wiley.

Fujita, F., & Diener, E. (2005). Life satisfaction set point: Stability and change. *Journal of Personality and Social Psychology, 88*, 158–164.

Funder, D. C. (2001). Personality. *Annual Review of Psychology, 52*, 197–221.

Furio, C., Calatayud, M. L., Barcenas, S. L., & Padilla, O. M. (2000). Functional fixedness and functional reduction as common sense reasonings in chemical equilibrium and in geometry and polarity of molecules. *Science & Education, 84*, 545–565.

Furnham, A., McClelland, A., & Omer, L. (2003). A cross-cultural comparison of ratings of perceived fecundity and sexual attractiveness as a function of body weight and waist-to-hip ratio. *Psychology Health and Medicine, 8*, 219–230.

Furnham, A., Moutafi, J., & Baguma, P. (2002). A cross-cultural study on the role of weight and waist-to-hip ratio on female attractiveness. *Personality and Individual Differences, 32*, 729–745.

Furumoto, L., & Scarborough, E. (2002). Placing women in the history of psychology: The first American women psychologists. In W. E. Pickren & D. A. Dewsbury (Eds.), *Evolving Perspectives on the history of psychology* (pp. 527–543). Washington, DC: American Psychological Association.

Fusar-Poli, P., & Yung, A. R. (2012). Should attenuated psychosis syndrome be included in *DSM-5*? *The Lancet, 379*, 591–592.

G

Gabrieli, J. D. E., Desmond, J. E., Demb, J. B., Wagner, A. D., Stone, M. V., Vaidya, C. J., & et, al. (1996). Functional magnetic resonance imaging of semantic memory processes in the frontal lobes. *Psychological Science, 7*, 278–283.

Gafner, G., & Benson, S. (2003). *Hypnotic techniques: For standard psychotherapy and formal hypnosis.* New York: Norton.

Gagné, F. M., & Lydon, J. E. (2001). Mindset and relationship illusions: The moderating effects of domain specificity and relationship commitment. *Personality and Social Psychology Bulletin, 27*, 1144–1155.

Gagneux, P., Boesch, C., & Woodruff, D. S. (1999). Female reproductive strategies, paternity and community structure in wild West African Chimpanzees. *Animal Behavior, 57*, 9–12.

Gaivoronskaia, G., & Solem, K. E. (2004). Genetic testing: Affected parties and decision making. *Journal of Risk Research, 7*, 481–493.

Gallagher, J., Harradine, C. C., & Coleman, M. R. (1997). Challenge or boredom? Gifted student's views on their schoolings. *Roeper Review, 19*, 132–141.

Gallagher, T. J., & Lewis, J. M. (2001). Rationalists, fatalists, and the modern superstitious: Test-taking in introductory sociology. *Sociological Inquiry, 71*, 1–12.

Gallese, V., Eagle, M. N., & Migone, P. (2007). Intentional attunement: Mirror neurons and the neural underpinnings of interpersonal relations. *Journal of the American Psychoanalytic Association, 55*, 131–176.

Galton, F. (1869). *Hereditary genius: An inquiry into its laws and consequences.* New York: Appleton.

Galupo, M. P. (2007). Friendship patterns of sexual minority individuals in adulthood. *Journal of Social and Personal Relationships, 24*, 139–151.

Gamble, A., & Garling, T. (2012). The relationships between life satisfaction, happiness, and current mood. *Journal of Happiness Studies, 13*, 31–45.

Gana, K., Lourel, M., Trouillet, R., Fort, I., Mezred, D., Blaison, C., … Ledrich, J. (2011). Judgment of riskiness: Impact of personality, naïve thinking, and heuristic thinking among female students. *Psychology & Health, 25*, 131–147.

Gander, P. H., Marshall, N. S., James, I., & Le Quesne, I. (2006). Investigating driver fatigue in truck crashes: Trial of a systematic methodology. *Transportation Research Part F: Traffic Psychology and Behavior, 9*, 65–76.

Gandevia, S. C., McCloskey, D. I., & Burke, D. (1992). Kinesthetic signals and muscle contraction. *Trends in Neurosciences, 15,* 62–65.

Gangestad, S. W., & Snyder, M. (2000). Self-monitoring: Appraisal and reappraisal. *Psychological Bulletin, 126,* 530–555.

Gantz, B. J., & Turner, C. W. (2003). *Combining acoustic and electric hearing.* Laryngoscope, 1726–1730.

Garcia, J., & Koelling, R. A. (1966). Relation of cue to consequence in avoidance learning. *Psychonomic Science, 4,* 123–124.

Garcia, J., Rusniak, K. W., & Brett, L. P. (1977). Conditioning food-illness aversions in wild animals: Caveat Canonici. In H. Davis & H. M. B. Hurwitz (Eds.), *Operant-Pavlovian interactions.* Hillsdale, NJ: Erlbaum.

Gardner, B. T. (1969). Teaching sign language to a chimpanzee. *Science, 165,* 664–672.

Gardner, H. (1993). *Creating minds: An anatomy of creativity seen through the lives of Freud, Einstein, Picasso, Stravinsky, Elliot, Graham, and Gandhi.* New York: Basic Books.

Gardner, H. (1999). *Intelligence reframed: Multiple intelligences for the 21st century.* New York: Basic Books.

Gardner, H. (2011). The theory of multiple intelligences. In M. A. Gernsbacher, R. W. Pew, L. M. Hough, & J. R. Pomerantz (Eds.), *Psychology and the real world: Essays illustrating fundamental contributions to society* (pp. 122–130). New York: Worth.

Gatchel, R. J., & Turk, D. C. (Eds.). (1999). *Psychosocial factors in pain: Critical perspectives.* New York: Guilford Press.

Gaunt, R. (2011). Effects of intergroup conflict and social contact on prejudice: The mediating role of stereotypes and evaluations. *Journal of Applied Social Psychology, 41,* 1340–1355.

Gauvain, M., Beebe, H., & Zhao, S. (2011). Applying the cultural approach to cognitive development. *Journal of Cognition and Development, 12,* 121–133.

Gavin, D. P., Kartan, S., Chase, K., Grayson, D. R., & Sharma, R. P. (2008). Reduced baseline acetylated histone 3 levels, and a blunted response to HDAC inhibition in lymphocyte cultures from schizophrenic subjects. *Schizophrenia Research, 103,* 330–332.

Gawronski, B., Ehrenberg, K., Banse, R., Zukova, J., & Klauer, K. C. (2003). It's in the mind of the beholder: The impact of stereotypic associations on category-based and individuating impression formation. *Journal of Experimental Social Psychology, 39,* 16–30.

Gay, P. (1998). *Freud: A life for our time.* New York: Norton.

Gazzaniga, M. S. (1967). The split brain in man. *Scientific American, 217,* 24–29.

Gazzaniga, M. S. (1988). *Mind matters: How mind and brain interact to create our conscious lives.* Boston, MA: Houghton Mifflin.

Gazzaniga, M. S. (Ed.). (2000). *The new cognitive neuroscience.* (2nd ed.). Cambridge, MA: The MIT Press.

Geen, R. G. (1984). Preferred stimulation levels in introverts and extroverts: Effects on arousal and performance. *Journal of Personality & Social Psychology, 46,* 1303–1312.

Geldard, K., & Geldard, D. (2008). *Personal counseling skills: An integrative approach.* Springfield, IL: Charles C. Thomas.

Gelfand, S. A. (1981). *Hearing.* New York: Marcel Dekker.

Genovesio, A., & Ferraina, S. (2004). Integration of retinal disparity and fixation-distance related signals toward an egocentric coding of distance in the posterior parietal cortex of primates. *Journal of Neurophysiology, 91,* 2670–2684.

Gerbner, G. (1993). Images that hurt: Mental illness in the mass media. *Journal of the California Alliance for the Mentally Ill, 4,* 17–20.

Gerbner, G., & Signorielli, N. (1990). *Violence profile 1967 through 1988–89: Enduring patterns.* Unpublished manuscript. Anneberg School of Communications, University of Pennsylvania.

Gere, J., & MacDonald, G. (2010). An update of the empirical case for the need to belong. *The Journal of Individual Psychology, 66,* 93–115.

Gerhardsson, L., Lundh, T., Londos, E., & Minthon, L. (2011). Cerebrospinal fluid/plasma quotients of essential and non-essential metals in patients with Alzheimer's disease. *Journal of Neural Transmission, 118,* 957–962.

Gershoff, E. T., & Bitensky, S. H. (2007). The case against corporal punishment of children: Converging evidence from social science research and international human rights law and implications for U.S. Public policy. *Psychology, Public Policy, and Law, 13,* 231–272.

Getzmann, S. (2003). A comparison of the contrast effect in sound localization in the horizontal and vertical planes. *Experimental Psychology, 50,* 131–141.

Ghazvini, A., & Mullis, R. L. (2002). Center-based care for young children: Examining predictors of quality. *Journal of Genetic Psychology, 163,* 112–125.

Gibson, E. J., & Walk, R. D. (1960). The "visual cliff." *Scientific American,* 64–71.

Gigerenzer, G., Hertwig, R., & Pachur, T. (Eds.). (2011). *Heuristics: The foundations of adaptive behavior.* New York: Oxford University Press.

Gilbert, A. (2008). *What the nose knows: The science of scent in everyday life.* New York: Crown Publishers.

Gilboa, S., Shirom, A., Fried, Y., & Cooper, C. (2008). A meta-analysis of work demand stressors and job performance. *Personnel Psychology, 61,* 227–271.

Gil-Burmann, C., Pelaez, F., & Sanchez, S. (2002). Mate choice differences according to sex and age: An analysis of personal advertisements in Spanish newspapers. *Human Nature, 13,* 493–508.

Gilligan, C. (1982). *In a different voice: Psychological theory and women's development.* Cambridge, MA: Harvard University Press.

Gilligan, C. (1990). Teaching Shakespeare's sister. In C. Gilligan, N. Lyons, & T. Hanmer (Eds.), *Making connections: The relational worlds of adolescent girls at Emma Willard School.* Cambridge, MA: Harvard University Press.

Gilman, S. L. (2008). Electrotherapy and mental illness: Then and now. *History of Psychiatry, 19,* 339–357.

Gilovich, T., & Savitsky, K. (2002). Like goes with like: The role of representativeness in erroneous and pseudo-scientific beliefs. In T. Gilovich, D. Griffin, & D. Kahneman (Eds.), *Heuristic and biases: The psychology of intuitive judgment* (pp. 617–624). New York: Cambridge University Press.

Ginsburg, G., & Bronstein, P. (1993). Familyl factors related to children's intrinsic/extrinsic motivational orientation and academic motivation orientation and performance. *Child Development, 64,* 1461–1474.

Ginsburg, M. L., Quirt, C., Ginsburg, A. D., & MacKillop, W. J. (1995). Psychiatric illness and psychosocial concerns of patients with newly diagnosed lung cancer. *Canadian Medical Association Journal, 152,* 701–708.

Glaser, R., Kiecolt-Glaser, J., Bonneau, R., Malarkey, W., Kennedy, S., & Hughes, J. (1992). Stress-induced modulation of the immune response to recombinant hepatitis B vaccine. *Psychosomatic Medicine, 54,* 22–29.

Glaveanu, V. P. (2012). Habitual creativity: Revising habit, reconceptualizing creativity. *Review of General Psychology, 16,* 78–92.

Gleaves, D. H. (1996). The sociocognitive model of dissociative identity: A reexamination of evidence. *Psychological Bulletin, 120,* 42–59.

Glick, P., & Fiske, S. T. (1996). The abivalent sexism inventory: differentiating hostile and benevolent sexism. *Journal of Personality and Social Psychology, 70,* 491–512.

Glick, P., Gottesman, D., & Jolton, J. (1989). The fault is not in the stars: Susceptibility of skeptics and believers in astrology to the Barnum effect. *Personality and Social Psychology Bulletin, 15,* 417–429.

Glover, S., & Dixon, P. (2002). Dynamic effects of the Ebbinghaus illusion in grasping: Support for a planning/control model of action. *Perception & Psychophysics, 64,* 266–278.

Gluck, M. A., & Myers, C. E. (2001). *Gateway to memory: An introduction to neural network modeling of the hippocampus and learning.* Cambridge, MA: MIT Press.

Glucksberg, S., & Danks, J. (1968). Effects of discriminative labels and of nonsense labels upon availability of novel function. *Journal of Verbal Learning and Verbal Behavior, 7,* 72–76.

Glucksberg, S., & Weisberg, R. W. (1966). Verbal behavior and problem solving: Some effects of labeling in a functional fixedness problem. *Journal of Experimental Psychology, 71,* 659–664.

Goddard, H. H. (1913). The Binet tests in relation to immigration. *Journal of Psycho-Asthenics, 18,* 105–107.

Goddard, H. H. (1919). *Psychology of the normal and submormal.* New York: Dodd, Mead.

Goel, N. (2011). Genetics of sleep timing, duration, and homeostasis in humans. *Sleep Medicine Clinics, 6,* 171–182.

Gogtay, N., Sporn, A., Clasen, L. S., Nugent, T. F., Iii, G., Nicolson, R., … Rappoport, J. L. (2004). Comparison of progressive cortical gray matter loss in childhood-onset schizophrenia with that in childhood-onset atypical psychoses. *Archives of General Psychiatry, 61,* 17–22.

Goh, W. D., & Lu, S. H. X. (2012). Testing the myth of the encoding-retrieval match. *Memory & Cognition, 40,* 28–39.

Goldberg, C. (2003). Privacy an issue in brain imaging: Machines can track unconscious preferences, fear. *Boston Globe.*

Goldberg, E. (2001). *The executive brain: Frontal lobes and the civilized mind.* New York: Oxford University Press.

Goldman, L. (2008). *Coming out, coming in: Nurturing the well-being and inclusion of gay youth in mainstream society.* New York: Routledge.

Goldstein, R. B., Grant, B. F., Ruan, W. J., Smith, S. M., & Saha, T. D. (2008). Antisocial personality disorder with childhood- versus adolescence-onset conduct disorder: Results from the National Epidemiologic Survey on Alcohol and Related Conditions: Erratum. *Journal of Nervous and Mental Disease, 196,* 263.

Goldston, D. B. (2003). Assessing risk of suicidal behaviors: Multitiered screening assessments. In D. B. Goldston (Ed.), *Measuring suicidal behavior and risk in children and adolescents* (pp. 205–220). Washington, DC: American Psychological Association.

Golombok, S., & Tasker, F. (1996). Do parents influence the sexual orientation of their children? Findings from a longitudinal study of lesbian families. *Developmental Psychology, 32,* 3–11.

Gonzaga, G. C., Campos, B., & Bradbury, T. (2007). Similarity, convergence, and relationship satisfaction in dating and married couples. *Journal of Personality and Social Psychology, 93,* 34–48.

Goode, E. (1999). *Tales of midlife crisis found greatly exaggerated.* New York Times.

Goodman, N. (2002). The serotonergic system and mysticism: Could LSD and the nondrug-induced mystical experience share common neural mechanisms? *Journal of Psychoactive Drugs, 34,* 263–272.

Goodnow, J. J. (1988). Children's household work: Its nature and function. *Psychological Bulletin, 103,* 5–26.

Goosens, K. A., & Maren, S. (2002). Long-term potentiation as a substrate for memory: Evidence from studies of amygdaloid plasticity and Pavlovian fear conditioning. *Hippocampus, 12,* 592–599.

Gopnik, A. (1996). The post-Piaget era. *Psychological Science, 7,* 221–225.

Gorassini, D. R. (1996). Conviction management: Lessons from hypnosis research about how self-images of dubious validity can be willfully sustained. In N. P. Spanos & B. Wallace (Eds.), *Hypnosis and imagination: Imagery and human development series* (pp. 177–198). Amityville, NY: Baywood.

Gordijn, M. C. M., T' Mannetje, D., & Meesters, Y. (2012). The effects of blue-enriched light treatment compared to standard light treatment in seasonal affective disorder. *Journal of Affective Disorders, 136,* 72–80.

Gordon, P. (1990). Learnability and feedback. *Developmental Psychology, 26,* 217–220.

Goris, A. H. C., & Westerterp, R. K. (2008). Physical activity, fat intake and body fat. *Physiology & Behavior, 94,* 164–168.

Gorman, C. (2002). The science of anxiety. *Time*, 46–54.

Gorniak, S. L., Pfister, J. A., Lanzonia, E. C., & Raspantini, E. R. (2008). A note on averting goats to a toxic but palatable plant, Leucaena leucocephala. *Applied Animal Behaviour Science, 111*, 396–401.

Gorostiaga, A., Balluerka, N., Alonso-Arbiol, I., & Haranburu, M. (2011). Validation of the Basque Revised NEO Personality Inventory (NEO PI-R). *European Journal of Psychological Assessment, 27*, 193–205.

Gortmaker, S. L., Must, A., Perrin, J. M., Sobol, A. M., & Dietz, W. H. (1993). Social and economic consequences of overweight in adolescence and young adulthood. *New England Journal of Medicine, 329*, 1008–1012.

Gosling, S. D. (2008). Personality in non-human animals. *Social and Personality Psychology Compass, 2*, 985–1001.

Gosling, S. D., & John, O. P. (1999). Personality dimensions in nonhuman animals: A cross-species review. *Current Directions in Psychological Science, 8*, 69–75.

Gottfried, A. W., Gottfried, A. E., Bathurst, K., & Guerin, D. W. (1994). *Gifted IQ: Early developmental aspects: The Fullerton longitudinal study*. New York: Plenum Press.

Gould, E., Reeves, A. J., Graziano, M. S., & Gross, C. G. (1999). Neurogenesis in the neocortex of adult primates. *Science, 286*, 548–552.

Gould, E., Tanapat, P., Rydel, T., & Hastings, N. (2000). Regulation of hippocampal neurogenesis in adulthood. *Biological Psychiatry, 48*, 715–720.

Gouras, P. (1991). Color vision. In *Principles of neural science* (3rd ed., pp. 467–480). New York: Elsevier.

Grabe, S., & Hyde, J. S. (2006). Ethnicity and body dissatisfaction among women in the United States: A meta-analysis. *Psychological Bulletin, 132*, 622–640.

Grant, B. F., & Dawson, D. A. (1997). Age at onset of alcohol use and its association with DSM-IV alcohol abuse and dependence: Results from the National Longitudinal Alcohol Epidemiologic Survey. *Journal of Substance Abuse, 9*, 103–110.

Grant, J. A., Courtemanche, J., Duerden, E. G., Duncan, G. H., & Rainville, P. (2010). Cortical thickness and pain sensitivity in Zen meditators. *Emotion, 10*, 43–53.

Graves, F. C., & Hennesy, M. B. (2000). Comparison of the effects of the mother and an unfamiliar adult female on cortisol and behavioral responses of pre- and postweaning guinea pigs. *Developmental Psychobiology, 36*, 91–100.

Graziano, W. G., & Eisenberg, N. (1997). Agreeableness: A dimension of personality. In R. Hogan, J. Johnson, & S. Briggs (Eds.), *Handbook of personality psychology* (pp. 795–824). San Diego: Academic Press.

Graziano, W. G., Jensen-Campbell, L. A., & Hair, E. C. (1996). Perceiving interpersonal conflict and reacting to it: The case for agreeableness. *Journal of Personality and Social Psychology, 70*(4).

Grebitus, C., & Bruhn, M. (2008). Analyzing semantic networks of pork quality by means of concept mapping. *Food Quality and Preference, 19*, 86–96.

Gredler, M. E., & Shields, C. C. (2008). *Vygotsky's legacy: A foundation for research and practice*. New York: Guilford Press.

Green, J. T., & Woodruff-Pak, D. S. (2000). Eyeblink classical conditioning: Hippocampal formation is for neutral stimulus associations as cerebellum is for association response. *Psychological Bulletin, 126*, 138–158.

Green, M. F. (1998). *Schizophrenia from a neurocognitive perspective: Probing the impenetrable darkness*. Boston, MA: Allyn & Bacon.

Greenberg, M., & Frisch, D. (1972). Effects of intentionality on willingness to reciprocate a favor. *Journal of Experimental Social Psychology, 21*, 61–72.

Greenfield, P. M. (1994). Independence and interdependence as developmental scripts: Implications for theory, research, and practice. In P. M. Greenfield & R. R. Cocking (Eds.), *Cross-cultural roots of minority child development* (pp. 1–37). Hillsdale, NJ: Erlbaum.

Greenfield, P. M., Keller, H., Fuligni, A., & Maynard, A. (2003). Cultural pathways through universal development. *Annual Review of Psychology, 54*, 461–490.

Greenfield, P. M., & Lave, J. (1982). Cognitive aspects of informal education. In D. A. Wagner & H. W. Stevenson (Eds.), *Cultural perspectives on child development*. San Francisco: W. H. Freeman.

Greenstein, V. C., Holopigian, K., Seiple, W., Carr, R. E., & Hood, D. C. (2004). Atypical multifocal ERG responses in patients with diseases affecting the photoreceptors. *Vision Research, 44*, 2867–2876.

Greenwald, A. G., Spangenberg, E. R., Pratkanis, A. R., & Eskenazi, J. (1991). Double-blind tests of subliminal self-help audiotapes. *Psychological Science, 2*, 119–122.

Gregory, R. I. (1998). *Eye and brain: The psychology of seeing* (5th ed.). Princetown, NJ: Princeton University Press.

Grigorenko, E. L. (2000). Heritability and intelligence. In R. J. Sternberg (Ed.), *Handbook of intelligence* (pp. 53–91). Cambridge, England: Cambridge University Press.

Grilo, C. M., White, M. A., Wilson, G. T., Gueorguieva, R., & Masheb, R. M. (2012). Rapid response predicts 12-month post-treatment outcomes in binge-eating disorder: Theoretical and clinical implications. *Psychological Medicine: A Journal of Research in Psychiatry and the Allied Sciences, 42*, 807–817.

Grinker, J. A. (1982). Physiological and behacioral basis for human obesity. In *The physiological mechanisms of motivation*. New York: Springer-Verlag.

Gross, A., & Latané, J. (1974). Receiving help, reciprocating, and interpersonal attraction. *Journal of Applied Social Psychology, 4*, 210–223.

Grossman, D. C., Mueller, B. A., Riedy, C., Dowd, M. D., Villaveces, A., Prodzinski, J., … Harruff, R. (2005). Gun storage practices and risk of youth suicide and unintentional firearm injuries. *Journal of the American Medical Association, 293*, 707–714.

Grotzer, T. A., & Perkins, D. N. (2000). Teaching intelligence: A performance conception. In R. J. Sternberg (Ed.), *Handbook of intelligence* (pp. 492–515). Cambridge, England: Cambridge University Press.

Guilford, J. P. (1959). Traits of creativity. In *Creativity and its cultivation* (pp. 142–161). New York: Harper & Row.

Gulick, W. L., Gescheider, G. A., & Frisina, R. D. (1989). *Hearing: Physiological acoustics, neural coding, and psychoacoustics*. New York: Oxford University Press.

Gunn, S. R., & Gunn, W. S. (2007). Are we in the dark about sleepwalking's dangers? In C. A. Read (Ed.), *Cerebrum 2007: Emerging ideas in brain science* (pp. 71–84). Washington, DC: Dana Press.

Guofang, R., & Qinglin, Z. (2004). Three viewpoints on the relationship between praise and intrinsic motivation. *Psychological Science (China), 27*, 1002–1004.

Gupta, S. (2006). Sleep deprived. *Time*, 66.

Gureje, O. (2008). Review of culture and mental health. A comprehensive textbook. *British Journal of Psychiatry, 192*, 237–238.

Guthrie, J. P., Ash, R. A., & Bendapudi, V. (1995). Additional validity evidence for a measure of morningness. *Journal of Applied Psychology, 80*, 186–190.

• • • • **H** • • • • • • • • • • • •

Hackett, T. A., & Kaas, J. H. (2003). Auditory processing in the primate brain. In M. Gallagher & R. J. Nelson (Eds.), *Handbook of psychology: Biological psychology* (Vol. 3, pp. 187–210). New York: John Wiley & Sons.

Hagenauer, M. H., King, A. F., Possidente, B., McGinnis, M. Y., Lumia, A. R., Peckham, E. M., & Lee, T. M. (2011). Changes in circadian rhythms during puberty in Rattus norvegicus: Developmental time course and gonadal dependency. *Hormones and Behavior, 60*, 46–57.

Hagger, M. S., & Orbell, S. (2003). A meta-analytic review of the common-sense model of illness representations. *Psychology & Health, 18*, 141–184.

Haier, R. J., Chueh, D., Touchette, P., Lott, I., Buchsbaum, M. S., MacMillan, D., … Sosa, E. (1995). Intelligence and changes in regional cerebral glucose metabolic rate following learning. *Intelligence, 16*, 415–426.

Haier, R. J., Siegel, B. V., Tang, C., Abel, L., & Buchsbaum, M. S. (1992). Intelligence and changes in regional cerebral glucose metabolic rate following learning. *Intelligence, 16*, 415–426.

Halaris, A. (2003). Neurochemical aspects of the sexual response cycle. CNS Spectrums, 8, 211–216.

Hale, S. (2007). *The man who lost his language: A case of aphasia* (rev. Ed.). London, England: Jessica Kingsley Publishers.

Halfmann, D. (2012). Recognizing medicalization and demedicalization: Discourses, practices, and identities. *Health: An Interdisciplinary Journal for the Social Study of Health, Illness and Medicine, 16*, 186–207.

Hall, J. A. (1978). Gender effects in decoding nonverbal cues. *Psychological Bulletin, 85*, 845–875.

Hall, J. A. (1984). *Nonverbal sex differences: Communication accuracy and expressive style*. Baltimore, MD: Johns Hopkins University Press.

Hall, J. A., & Mast, M. S. (2008). Are women always more interpersonally sensitive than men? Impact of goals and content domain. *Personality and Social Psychology Bulletin, 34*, 144–155.

Hall, J. J., Neal, T. J., & Dean, R. S. (2008). Lateralization of cerebral functions. In A. M. H. Jr & D. Wedding (Eds.), *The Neuropsychology handbook* (pp. 183–214). New York: Springer.

Hallberg, L. R.-M., Ringdah, A., Holmes, A., & Carver, C. (2005). Psychological general well-being (quality of life) in patients with cochlear implants: Importance of social environment and age. *International Journal of Audiology, 44*, 706–711.

Hallschmid, M. S., Benedict, C., Born, J., Fehm, H.-L., & Kern, W. (2004). Manipulating central nervous mechanisms of food intake and body weight regulation by intranasal administration of neuropeptides in man. *Physiology and Behavior, 83*, 55–64.

Halpern, D. F. (2012). *Sex differences in cognitive abilities* (4th ed.). New York: Psychology Press.

Hamann, S. B., Ely, T. D., Hoffman, J. M., & Kilts, C. D. (2002). Ecstasy and agony: Activation of the human amygdala in positive and negative emotion. *Psychological Science, 13*, 135–141.

Hamilton, J. T. (1998). *Channeling violence: The economic market for violent television programming*. Princeton, NJ: Princeton University Press.

Hamilton, M. E., Voris, J. C., Sebastian, P. S., Singha, A. K., Krejci, L. P., Elder, I. R., … Hernandez, L. L. (1997). Money as a tool to extinguish conditioned responses to cocaine in addicts. *Journal of Clinical Psychology, 54*, 211–218.

Han, S.-H., & Kim, M.-S. (2004). Visual search does not remain efficient when executive working memory is working. *Psychological Science, 15*, 623–628.

Handen, B. L. (1997). Mental retardation. In *Assessment of childhood disorders* (3rd ed., pp. 369–407). New York: Guilford Press.

Haney, M., Hart, C. L., Ward, A. S., & Foltin, R. W. (2003). Nefazodone decreases anxiety during marijuana withdrawal in humans. *Psychopharmacology, 165*, 157–165.

Hanley, J. R., & Chapman, E. (2008). Partial knowledge in a tip-of-the-tongue state about two- and three-word proper names. *Psychonomic Bulletin & Review, 15*, 156–160.

Hannon-Engel, S. (2012). Regulating satiety in bulimia nervosa: The role of cholecystokinin. *Perspectives in Psychiatric Care, 48*, 34–40.

Hansen, C. H., & Hansen, R. D. (1990). Rock music videos and antisocial behavior. *Basic and Applied Social Psychology, 11*, 357–369.

Hansen, E. S., Hasselbalch, S., Law, I., & Bolwig, T. G. (2002). The caudate nucleus in obsessive-compulsive disorder. Reduced metabolism following treatment with paroxetine: A PET study. *International Journal of Neuropsychopharmacology, 5*, 1–10.

Hansen, K. L., & Sorlie, T. (2012). A study of Sami and non-Sami populations in Norway. *Transcultural Psychiatry, 49,* 26–50.

Harackiewicz, J. M., Durik, A. M., & Barron, K. E. (2005). Multiple goals, optimal motivation, and the development of interest. In J. P. Forgas, K. P. Williams, & S. M. Lahan (Eds.), *Social motivation: conscious and unconscious processes.* (pp. 21–39). New York: Cambridge University Press.

Harder, D., Maggio, J., & Whitney, G. (1989). Assessing gustatory detection capabilities using preference procedures. *Chemical Senses, 14,* 547–564.

Harding, S. M., & Velotta, J. P. (2011). Comparing the relative amount of testosterone required to restore sexual arousal, motivation, and performance in male rats. *Hormones and Behavior, 59,* 666–673.

Hargreaves, I. S., White, M., Pexman, P. M., Pittman, D., & Goodyear, B. G. (2012). The question shapes the answer: The neural correlates of task differences reveal dynamic semantic processing. *Brain and Language, 120,* 73–78.

Harlow, H. F., & Harlow, M. K. (1962). Social deprivation in monkeys. *Scientific American, 200,* 68–74.

Harlow, H. F., & Zimmermann, R. R. (1959). Affectional responses in the infant monkey. *Science, 130,* 421–432.

Harriot, J., & Ferrari, J. R. (1996). Prevalence of procrastination among samples of adults. *Psychological Bulletin, 78,* 611–616.

Harris, B. (2002). What ever happened to little Albert? In W. E. Pickren & D. A. Dewsbury (Eds.), *Evolving perspectives on the history of psychology* (pp. 237–254). Washington, DC: American Psychological Association.

Harris, C. R. (2004). The evolution of jealousy. *American Scientist, 92,* 62–71.

Harris, D. L. I. (2011). Infertility and reproductive loss. In D. L. Harris (Ed.), *Counting our losses: Reflecting on change, loss, and transition in everyday life* (pp. 171–118). New York: Routledge/Taylor & Francis Group.

Hart, A. J., Whalen, P. J., Shin, L. M., McInerney, S. C., Fischer, H., & Rauch, S. L. (2000). Differential response in the human amygdala to racial outgroup vs. ingroup face stimuli. *Neuroreport, 11,* 2351–2355.

Harter, S. (1988). Developmental processes in the construction of the self. In *Integrative processes and socialization: Early to middle childhood.* Hillsdale, NJ: Erlbaum.

Hartley, W. S. (1970). *Manual for the twenty statements problem.* Kansas City, MO: Department of Research Greater Kansas City Mental Health Foundation.

Hartman, E. (1978). *The sleeping pill.* New Haven, CT: Yale University Press.

Hartmann, P., Kruuse, N. H. S., & Nyborg, H. (2007). Testing the cross-racial generality of Spearman's hypothesis in two samples. *Intelligence, 35,* 47–57.

Harton, H. C., & Bullock, M. (2007). Dynamic social impact: A theory of the origins and evolution of culture. *Social and Personality Psychology Compass, 1,* 521–540.

Hartshorne, H., & May, M. A. (1928). Studies in deceit. New York: Macmillan.

Harvey, A. G., & Tang, N. K. Y. (2012). (Mis)perception of sleep in insomnia: A puzzle and a resolution. *Psychological Bulletin, 138,* 77–101.

Harvey, P. H., & Krebs, J. R. (1990). Comparing brains. *Science, 249,* 140–145.

Harwerth, R. S., Fredenburg, P. M., & Smith, E. (2003). Temporal integration for stereoscopic vision. Temporal integration for stereoscopic vision. *Vision Research, 43,* 505–517.

Hasegawa, I., Fukushima, T., Ihara, T., & Miyashita, Y. (1998). Callosal window between prefrontal cortices: Cognitive interaction to retrieve long-term memory. *Science, 281,* 814–818.

Haselton, M. G., & Buss, D. M. (2000). Error management theory: A new perspective on biases in cross-sex mind reading. *Journal of Personality and Social Psychology, 78,* 81–91.

Haselton, M. G., & Nettle, D. (2006). The paranoid optimist: An integrative evolutionary model of cognitive biases. *Personality and Social Psychology Review, 10,* 47–66.

Hasher, L., Chung, C., May, C. P., & Foong, N. (2002). Age, time of testing, and proactive interference. *Canadian Journal of Experimental Psychology, 56,* 200–207.

Haskett, M. E., Scott, S. S., Nears, K., & Grimmett, M. A. (2008). Lessons from Katrina: Disaster mental health services in the Gulf Coast region. *Professional Psychology: Research and Practice, 39,* 93–99.

Haslam, N. (1997). Evidence that male sexual orientation is a matter of degree. *Journal of Personality and Social Psychology, 73,* 862–870.

Hasselmo, M. E. (2012). *How we remember: Brain mechanisms of episodic memory.* Cambridge, MA: MIT Press.

Hasselmo, M. E., & Bower, J. M. (1993). Acetylcholine and memory. *Trends in Neurosciences, 16,* 218–222.

Hatfield, E., & Rapson, R. (1996). *Love and sex: Cross-cultural perspectives.* Boston, MA: Allyn & Bacon.

Hatfield, E., Rapson, R. L., & Martel, L. D. (2007). Passionate love and sexual desire. In K. Shinobu & D. Cohen (Eds.), *Handbook of cultural psychology* (pp. 760–779). New York: Guilford Press.

Hauri, D. D., Lieb, C. M., Rajkumar, S., Kooijman, C., Sommer, H. L., & Roosli, M. (2011). Direct health costs of environmental tobacco smoke exposure and indirect health benefits due to smoking ban introduction. *European Journal of Public Health, 21,* 316–322.

Haw, J. (2011). Improving psychological critical thinking in Australian university students. *Australian Journal of Psychology, 63,* 150–153.

Hawkins, D. R. (1986). The importance of dreams. *Harvard Medical School Mental Health Letter,* 5–7.

Hawkins, J. D., Catalano, R. F., & Miller, J. Y. (1992). Risk and protective factors for alcohol and other drug problems in adolescence and early adulthood: Implications for substance abuse prevention. *Psychological Bulletin, 112,* 64–105.

Hayes, C. (1951). *The ape in our house.* New York: Harper.

Hayes, N. (2002). *Psychology in perspective* (2nd ed.). Basingstoke, England: Palgrave.

Hayflick, L. (1965). The limited in vitro lifetime of human diploid cell strains. *Experimental Cell Research, 37,* 614–636.

Hazan, C., & Shaver, P. (1987). Romantic love conceptualized as an attachment process. *Journal of Personality and Social Psychology, 52,* 511–524.

Hazelrigg, M. D., Cooper, H. M., & Borduin, C. M. (1987). Evaluating the effectiveness of family therapies: An integrative review and analysis. *Psychological Bulletin, 101,* 428–442.

He, H.-G., Polkki, T., vehvilainen-Julkunen, K., & Pietila, A.-M. (2005). Chinese nurses' use of non-pharmacological methods in children's postoperative pain relief. *Journal of Advanced Nursing, 51,* 335–342.

Healy, A. F. (Ed.). (2005). *Experimental cognitive psychology and its applications.* Washington, DC: American Psychological Association.

Heatherton, T. F., & Vohs, K. D. (2000). Interpersonal evaluations following threats to self: Role of self-esteem. *Journal of Personality and Social Psychology, 78,* 725–736.

Hebl, M. R., Foster, J. B., Mannix, L. M., & Dovidio, J. F. (2002). Formal and interpersonal discrimination: A field study of bias toward homosexual applicants. *Personality and Social Psychology Bulletin, 28,* 815–825.

Hebl, M. R., & Mannix, L. M. (2003). The weight of obesity in evaluating others: A mere proximity effect. *Personality & Social Psychology Bulletin, 29,* 28–38.

Hecht, M. A., & LaFrance, M. (1998). License or obligation to smile: The effect of power and sex on amount and type of smiling. *Personality and Social Psychology Bulletin, 24,* 1332–1342.

Heider, F. (1958). *The psychology of interpersonal attraction.* New York: Wiley.

Heine, S. J., & Hamamura, T. (2007). In search of East Asian self-enhancement. *Personality and Social Psychology Review, 11,* 4–27.

Heine, S. J., & Lehman, D. R. (1997). Culture, dissonance, and self-affirmation. *Personality and Social Psychology Bulletin, 23,* 389–400.

Held, J. D., Alderton, D. E., Foley, P. P., & Segall, D. O. (1993). Arithmetic reasoning gender differences: Explanations found in the Armed Services Vocational Aptitude Battery (ASVAB). *Learning and Individual Differences, 5,* 171–186.

Hellman, K., Hernandez, P., Park, A., & Abel, T. (2010). Genetic evidence for a role for protein kinase A in the maintenance of sleep and thalamocortical oscillations. *Sleep: Journal of Sleep and Sleep Disorders Research, 33,* 19–28.

Hellsten, J., Wennström, M., Bengzon, J., Mohapel, P., & Tingström, A. (2004). Electroconvulsive seizures induce endothelial cell proliferation in adult rat hippocampus. *Biological Psychiatry, 55,* 420–427.

Helm, H., Hays, J. C., Flint, E., Koenig, H. G., & Blazer, D. G. (2000). Does private religious activity prolong survival? A six-year follow-up study of 3,851 older adults. *Journal of Gerontology, 55A,* M400–M405.

Helmholtz, H. von. (1863). *On the sensations of tone as a physiological basis for the theory of music* (A. J. Ellis, Trans.). New York: Dover.

Helson, R., & Srivastava, S. (2002). Creative and wise people: Similarities, differences, and how they develop. *Personality and Social Psychology Bulletin, 28,* 1430–1440.

Hendrick, C., & Hendrick, S. S. (2003). Romantic love: Measuring cupid's arrow. In S. J. Lopez & C. R. Snyder (Eds.), *Positive psychological assessment: A handbook of models and measures* (pp. 235–249). Washington, DC: American Psychological Association.

Henningfield, D. R., Schuh, L. M., & Jarvik, M. E. (1995). Pathophysiology of tobacco dependence. In F. E. Bloom & D. J. Kupfer (Eds.), *Psychopharmacology: The fourth generation* (pp. 1715–1729). New York: Raven Press.

Henriques, J. B., & Davidson, R. (1990). Regional brain electrical asymmetries discriminate between previously depressed and healthy control subjects. *Journal of Abnormal Psychology, 99,* 22–31.

Henry, K. R. (1984). Cochlear damage resulting from exposure to four different octave bands of noise at three different ages. *Behavioral Neuroscience, 1,* 107–117.

Hepworth, J. T., & West, S. G. (1988). Lynchings and the economy: A time-series reanalysis of Hovland and Sears (1940). *Journal of Personality and Social Psychology, 55,* 239–247.

Herek, G. M., Cogan, J. C., & Gillis, J. R. (2002). Victim experiences in hate crimes based on sexual orientation. *Journal of Social Issues, 58,* 319–339.

Herman, C. P., & Polivy, J. (2004). The self-regulation of eating: Theoretical and practical problems. In R. F. Baumeister & K. D. Vohs (Eds.), *Handbook of self-regulation: Research, theory, and applications* (pp. 492–508). New York: Guilford Press.

Hermann, C., Ziegler, S., Birbaumer, N., & Flor, H. (2002). Psychophysiological and subjective indicators of aversive Pavlovian conditioning in generalized social phobia. *Biological Psychiatry, 52,* 328–337.

Heron, W. (1957). The pathology of boredom. *Scientific American, 196,* 52–56.

Herrenkohl, E. C., Herrenkohl, R. C., & Toedter, L. J. (1983). Perspectives on the intergenerational transmission of abuse. In D. Finkelhor, R. J. Gelles, G. T. Hotaling, & M. A. Straus (Eds.), *The dark side of families* (pp. 305–316). Beverly Hills, CA: Sage.

Herrera, R. S., & DelCampo, R. L. (1995). Beyond the superwoman syndrome: Work satisfaction and family functioning among working-class Mexican American women. *Hispanic Journal of Behavioral Sciences, 17,* 49–60.

Hersen, M., & Bellack, S. A. (Eds.). (1999). *Handbook of comparative interventions for adult disorders* (2nd ed.). New York: Wiley.

Hershenson, M. (1982). Moon illusion and spiral aftereffect: Illusions due to the loom-zoom system? *Journal of Experimental Psychology, 111,* 423–440.

Hershenson, M. (2003). A trick of the moonlight: Review of H. Ross & C. Plug, The mystery of the moon illusion. *Nature, 421,* 695.

Hertel, P. T., & Rude, S. S. (1991). Depressive deficits in memory: Focusing attention improves subsequent recall. *Journal of Experimental Psychology: General, 120,* 301–309.

Hess, E. H. (1975). The role of pupil size in communication. *Scientific American, 110–112,* 116–119.

Hetherington, A. W., & Ranson, S. W. (1942). The spontaneous activity and food intake of rats with hypothalamic lesions. *American Journal of Physiology, 136,* 609–617.

Hewson-Bower, B., & Drummond, P. D. (1996). Secretory immunoglobulin A increases during relaxation in children with and without recurrent upper respiratory tract infections. *Journal of Developmental and Behavioral Pediatrics, 17,* 311–346.

Hiatt, K. D., & Dishion, T. J. (2008). Antisocial personality development. In T. P. Beauchaine & S. P. Hinshaw (Eds.), *Child and adolescent psychopathology.* (pp. 370–404). Hoboken, NJ: John Wiley.

Hickman, R., McCoy, S. W., Long, T. M., & Rauh, M. J. (2011). Applying contemporary developmental and movement science theories and evidence to early intervention practice. *Infants & Young Children, 24,* 29–41.

Hickok, G., Costanzo, M., Capasso, R., & Miceli, G. (2011). The role of Broca's area in speech perception: Evidence from aphasia revisited. *Brain and Language, 119,* 214–220.

Hicks, D. (1968). Short- and long-term retention of affectively-varied modeled behavior. *Psychonomic Science, 11,* 369–370.

Higgins, E. T. (2004). Making a theory useful: Lessons handed down. *Personality and Social Psychology Review, 8,* 138–145.

Highstein, S. M., Fay, R. R., & Popper, A. N. E. (2004). *The vestibular system.* New York: Springer.

Hilgard, E. R. (1965). *Hypnotic susceptibility.* New York: Harcourt Barce Jovanovich.

Hilgard, E. R. (1986). *Divided consciousness: Multiple controls in human thought and action.* New York: Wiley.

Hilgard, E. R. (1992). Dissociation and theories of hypnosis. In E. Fromm & M. R. Nash (Eds.), *Contemporary Hypnosis Research* (pp. 69–101). New York: Guilford Press.

Hill, C. L. M., & Updegraff, J. A. (2012). Mindfulness and its relationship to emotional regulation. *Emotion, 12,* 81–90.

Hill, M. E. (2002). Skin color and the perception of attractiveness among African Americans. Does gender make a difference? *Social Psychology Quarterly, 65,* 77–91.

Hill, P. (1993). Recent advances in selected areas of adolescent development. *Journal of Child Psychology and Psychiatry, 34,* 69–99.

Hillman, C. H., Erickson, K. I., & Kramer, A. F. (2008). Be smart, exercise your heart: Exercise effects on brain and cognition. *Nature Reviews Neuroscience, 9,* 58–65.

Hilts, P. J. (1995). *Memory's ghost: The strange tale of Mr. M. and the nature of memory.* New York: Simon & Schuster.

Hirsch, H. V. B., & Spinelli, D. N. (1970). Visual experience modifies distribution of horizontally and vertically oriented receptive fields in cats. *Science, 168,* 869–871.

Hirsch, J., Fried, S. K., Edens, N. K., & Leibel, R. L. (1989). The fat cell. *Medical Clinics of North America, 73,* 83–96.

Hirt, E. R. (1990). Do I see only what I expect? Evidence for an expectancy-guided retrieval model. *Journal of Personality and Social Psychology, 58,* 937–951.

Ho, D. Y. F., Peng, S. Q., Lai, A. C., & Chan, S. F. (2001). Indigenization and beyond: Methodological relationalism in the study of personality across cultural traditions. *Journal of Personality, 69,* 925–953.

Hoberman, J. (1997). *Darwin's athletes: How sport has damaged Black America and preserved the myth of race.* Boston, MA: Houghton Mifflin.

Hobson, J. A. (1999). *Consciousness.* New York: Scientific American Library.

Hobson, J. A., Stickgold, R., & Pace-Schott, E. F. (1998). The neuropsychology of REM sleep dreaming. *NeuroReport, 9*(3), R1–R14.

Hock, R. R. (1992). *Forty studies that changed psychology: Explorations into the history of psychological research.* Englewood Cliffs, NJ: Prentice Hall.

Hodos, W., & Butler, A. B. (2001). Sensory system evolution in vertebrates. In *Brain evolution and cognition* (pp. 113–133). New York: John Wiley.

Hofer, J., & Chasiotis, A. (2004). Methodological considerations of applying a TAT-type picture-story test in cross-cultural research. *Journal of Cross-Cultural Psychology, 35,* 224–241.

Hoffman, L., & Thelen, M. (2010). William James and the fight for science. *Journal of Humanistic Psychology, 50,* 430–439.

Hofmann, S. G. (2006). The emotional consequences of social pragmatism: The psychophysiological correlates of self-monitoring. *Biological Psychology, 73,* 169–174.

Hogan, J. A. (2005). Motivation. In J. J. Bolhuis (Ed.), *The behavior of animals: Mechanisms, function, and evolution* (pp. 41–70). Malden, MA: Blackwell Publishers.

Holahan, C. K., & Sears, R. R. (1995). *The gifted group in later maturity.* Palo Alto, CA: Stanford University Press.

Holding, P. A., Taylor, H. G., Kazungu, S. D., Mkala, T., Gona, J., Mwamuye, B., … Stevenson, J. (2004). Assessing cognitive outcomes in a rural African population: Development of a neuropsychological battery in Kilifi District, Kenya. *Journal of the International Neuropsychological Society, 10,* 246–260.

Hollis, K. L. (1997). Contemporary research on Pavlovian conditioning: A "new" functional analysis. *American Psychologist, 52,* 956–965.

Hollon, S. D., & Kendall, P. C. (1980). Cognitive self-statements in depression: Development of an automatic thoughts questionnaire. *Cognitive Therapy and Research, 4,* 383–395.

Holman, W. D. (2001). Reaching for integrity: An Eriksonian life-cycle perspective on the experiences of adolescents being raised by grandparents. *Child & Adolescent Social Work Journal, 18,* 21–35.

Holmes, T., & Rahe, R. (1967). The Social Readjustment Rating Scale. *Journal of Psychosomatic Research, 11,* 213–218.

Holowka, S., & Petitto, L.-A. (2002). Left hemisphere cerebral specialization for babies while babbling. *Science, 297,* 1515.

Holtzheimer, P. E., & Mayberg, H. S. (2011). Deep brain stimulation for psychiatric disorders. *Annual Review of Neuroscience, 34,* 289–307.

Homeyer, L. E., & DeFrance, E. (2005). Play therapy. In C. A. Malchiodi (Ed.), *Expressive therapies* (pp. 141–161). New York: Guilford Press.

Hong, R. Y., Paunonen, S. V., & Slade, H. P. (2008). Big five personality factors and the prediction of behavior: A multitrait-multimethod approach. *Personality and Individual Differences, 45,* 160–166.

Honts, C., & Perry, M. (1992). Polygraph admissibility: Changes and challenges. *Law and Human Behavior, 16,* 357–379.

Hopko, D. R., McNeil, D. W., Zvolensky, M. J., & Eifert, G. H. (2001). The relation between anxiety and skill in performance-based anxiety disorders: A behavioral formulation of social phobia. *Behavior Therapy, 32,* 185–207.

Hoppe, R. B. (1988). In search of a phenomenon: Research in parapsychology. [Review of Foundations of parapsychology.]. *Contemporary Psychology, 33,* 129–130.

Hoptman, M. J., & Davidson, R. J. (1994). How and why do the two cerebral hemispheres interact? *Psychological Bulletin, 116,* 195–219.

Horney, K. (1926). *Feminine psychology.* New York: Norton.

Horney, K. (1945). *Our inner conflicts.* New York: Norton.

Hornsey, M. J., Jetten, J., McAuliffe, B. J., & Hogg, M. A. (2006). The impact of individualist and collectivist group norms on evaluations of dissenting group members. *Journal of Experimental Social Psychology, 42,* 57–68.

Hornyak, L. M., & Green, J. P. (Eds.). (2000). *Healing from within: The use of hypnosis in women's health care.* Washington, DC: American Psychological Association.

Horton, R. W., & Santogrossi, D. A. (1978). The effect of adult commentary on reducing the influence of televised violence. *Personality and Social Psychology Bulletin, 4,* 337–340.

Hoshino-Brown, E., Zanna, A. S., Spencer, S. J., Zanna, M. P., Kitayama, S., & Lackenbauer, S. (2005). On the cultural guises of cognitive dissonance: The case of Easterners and Westerners. *Journal of Personality and Social Psychology, 89,* 394–310.

Hough, J. V., Matthews, P., Wood, M. W., & Dyer, R. (2002). Middle ear electromagnetic semi-implantable hearing device: Results of the phase II SOUNDTEC direct system clinical trail. *Otolaryngology Neurotology, 23,* 895–903.

Howard, M. O., & Perron, B. E. (2009). *A survey of inhalant use disorders among delinquent youth: Prevalence, clinical features, and latent structure of DSM-IV diagnostic criteria, 9*(ArtID 8).

Howard, P. J., & Howard, J. M. (2000). *The owner's manual for personality at work.* Austin, TX: Bard Press.

Howe, M. L. (2008). Visual distinctiveness and the development of children's false memories. *Child Development, 79,* 65–79.

Howell, K. K., Coles, C. D., & Kable, J. A. (2008). The medical and developmental consequences of prenatal drug exposure. In J. Brick (Ed.), *Handbook of the medical consequences of alcohol and drug abuse* (2nd ed., pp. 219–249). New York: The Haworth Press.

Howell, R. T., & Howell, C. J. (2008). The relation of economic status to subjective well-being in developing countries: A meta-analysis. *Psychological Bulletin, 134,* 536–550.

Hsieh, D. K., & Kirk, S. A. (2005). The limits of diagnostic criteria: The role of social context in clinicians' judgments of mental disorder. In S. A. Kirk (Ed.), *Mental disorders in the social environment: Critical perspectives. Foundations of social work knowledge* (pp. 45–61). New York: Columbia University Press.

Hubel, D. H. (1996). A big step along the visual pathway. *Nature, 380,* 197–198.

Hubel, D. H., & Wiesel, T. N. (1965a). Receptive fields and functional architecture in two non-striate visual areas (18 and 19) of the cat. *Journal of Neurophysiology, 28,* 229–289.

Hubel, D. H., & Wiesel, T. N. (1965b). Binocular interaction in striate cortex of kittens reared with artificial squint. *Journal of Neurophysiology, 28,* 1041–1059.

Huesmann, L. R., & Hasbrouck, J. E. (1996). Television violence: Implications for violence prevention. *School Psychology Review, 25,* 134–151.

Huesmann, L. R., & Miller, L. S. (1994). Long-term effects of repeated exposure to media violence in childhood. In L. R. Huesmann (Ed.), *Aggressive behavior: Current perspectives* (pp. 153–186). New York: Plenum.

Huffman, S., Zehner, E., Harvey, P., Martin, P., Piwoz, E., Ndure, K., … Quinn, V. (2001). *The LINKAGES Project.* Retrieved from www.linkagesproject.org/

Hughes, J. R. (2007). A review of sleepwalking (somnambulism): The enigma of neurophysiology and polysomnography with differential diagnosis of complex partial seizures. *Epilepsy & Behavior, 11,* 483–491.

Hughes, T. (2004). Ischemic cerebrovascular disease. *Cognitive Neuropsychology, 21,* 2783.

Hull, C. L. (1943). *Principles of behavior: An introduction to behavior theory concerning the individual organism.* New Haven, CT: Yale University Press.

Humphrey, N. K. (1992). *A history of the mind.* New York: Simon & Schuster.

Hunn, E. (1982). The utilitarian factor in folk biological classification. *American Anthropologist, 84,* 830–847.

Hunn, E. (1990). *Nch'i-Wana "The Big River": Mid-Columbia Indians and their land.* Seattle, WA: University of Washington Press.

Hunt, E. (2011). *Human intelligence.* New York: Cambridge University Press.

Hunt, R. W. G. (1998). *Measuring colour* (3rd ed.). London: Fountain Press.

Huppert, J. D., Strunk, D. R., Ledley, D. R., Davidson, J. R. T., & Foa, E. B. (2008). Generalized social anxiety disorder and avoidant personality disorder: Structural analysis and treatment outcome. *Depression and Anxiety, 25,* 441–448.

Hutchings, B., & Mednick, S. A. (1977). Criminality in adoptees and their adoptive and biological parents: A pilot study. In S. A. Mednick & K. O. Christiansen (Eds.), *Biosocial bases of criminal behavior* (pp. 124–141). New York: Plenum Press.

Huteau, M. (2007). The study of intelligence: Novelty and impact of Alfred Binet's work. *Bulletin de Psychologie, 60,* 357–370.

Hyers, L., & Swim, J. (1998). A comparison of the experiences of dominant and minority group members during an inter-group encounter. *Group Process and Intergroup Relations, 1,* 143–163.

Hygge, S., Evans, G. W., & Bullinger, M. (2002). A prospective study of some effects of aircraft noise on cognitive performance in school children. *Psychological Science, 13,* 469–474.

Hyman, R. (1994). Anomaly or artifact? Comments on Bem and Honorton. *Psychological Bulletin, 115,* 19–24.

Hyman, R. (1996). Evaluation of the military's twenty-year program on psychic spying. *The Skeptical Inquirer, 27,* 21–23.

Iaccino, J. F. (1993). *Left brain-right brain differences: Inquiries, evidence, and new approaches.* NJ: Erlbaum.

Iacoboni, M. (2007). Face to face: The neural basis of social mirroring and empathy. *Psychiatric Annals, 37,* 236–241.

Iacono, W., & Lykken, D. (1997). The validity of the lie detector: Two surveys of scientific opinion. *Journal of Applied Psychology, 82,* 426–433.

Ichikawa, M., & Saida, S. (2002). Integration of motion parallax with binocular disparity specifying different surface shapes. *Japanese Psychological Research, 44,* 34–44.

Ikeda, H. (2001). Buraku students and cultural identity: The case of a Japanese minority. In I. Z. Holowinsky (Ed.), Ethnicity, race, and nationality in education: A global perspective. *The Rutgers Invitational Symposium on Education Series* (pp. 81–100). Piscataway, NJ: Rutgers University Press.

Impett, E., & Peplau, L. A. (2003). Sexual compliance: Gender, motivational, and relationship perspectives. *Journal of Sex Research, 40,* 87–100.

Ingbar, D. H., & Gee, J. B. L. (1985). Pathophysiology and treatment of sleep apnea. *Annual Review of Medicine, 36,* 369–395.

Inglehart, R. (1990). *Culture shift in advanced industrial society.* Princeton, NJ: Princeton University Press.

Inglehart, R., & Oyserman, D. (2004). Individualism autonomy and self-espression: The human development syndrome. In *Comparing cultures: dimensions of culture in a comparative perspective* (pp. 74–96). Leiden, The Netherlands: Brill.

Inhelder, B., & Piaget, J. (1958). *The growth of logical thinking from childhood to adolescence.* New York: Basic Books.

Irle, E., Lange, C., & Sachsse, U. (2005). Reduced size and abnormal asymmetry of parietal cortex in women with borderline personality disorder. *Biological Psychiatry, 57,* 173–182.

Irwin, M. R., Cole, J. C., & Nicassio, P. M. (2006). Comparative meta-analysis of behavioral interventions for insomnia and their efficacy in middle-aged adults and in older adults 55+ years of age. *Health Psychology, 25,* 3–14.

Isaac, G. L. (1983). Aspects of human evolution. In D. S. Bendall (Ed.), *Evolution from molecules to men.* Cambridge: Cambridge University Press.

Isada, N. B., & Grossman, J. H. (1991). Perinatal infections. In S. G. Gabbie, J. R. Niebyl, & J. L. Simpson (Eds.), *Obstetrics: Normal and problem pregnancies.* New York: Churchill Livingstone.

Ishikawa, A., Kanayama, Y., Matsumura, H., Tsuchimochi, H., Ishida, Y., & Nakamura, S. (2006). Selective rapid eye movement sleep deprivation impairs the maintenance of long-term potentiation in the rat hippocampus. *European Journal of Neuroscience, 24,* 243–248.

Ito, H. (1967). Japan's outcasts in the United States. In G. A. DeVos & H. Wagatsuma (Eds.), *Japan's invisible race.* Berkeley, CA: University of California Press.

Ito, T. A., Miller, N., & Pollock, V. E. (1996). Alcohol and aggression: A meta-analysis on the moderating effects of inhibitory cues, triggering effects, and self-focused attention. *Psychological Bulletin, 120,* 60–82.

Iversen, I. (1992). Skinner's early research: From reflexology to operant conditioning. *American Psychologist, 47,* 1318–1328.

Iwasaki, Y. (2003). Roles of leisure in coping with stress among university students: A repeated-assessment field study. *Anxiety, Stress, & Coping, 16,* 31–57.

Iyer, A., Leach, C. W., & Crosby, F. (2003). White guilt and racial compensation: The benefits and limits of self-focus. *Personality and Social Psychology Bulletin, 29,* 117–129.

Izard, C. (1989). The structure and functions of emotions: Implications for cognition, motivation, and personality. In *The G. Stanley Hall Lecture Series* (Vol. 9, pp. 39–73). Washington, DC: American Psychological Association.

Jablonski, N. G. (1998). Ultraviolet light-induced neural tube defects in amphibian larvae and their implications for the evolution of melanized pigmentation and declines in amphibian populations. *Journal of Herpetology, 32,* 455–457.

Jackson, B. R., & Bergeman, C. S. (2011). How does religiosity enhance well-being? The role of perceived control. *Psychology of Religion and Spirituality, 3,* 149–161.

Jackson, J. W. (1993). Realistic group conflict theory: A review and evaluation of the theoretical and empirical literature. *Psychological Record, 43,* 395–413.

Jackson, L. A., Hunter, J. E., & Hodge, C. N. (1995). Physical attractiveness and intellectual competence: A meta-analytic review. *Social Psychology Quarterly, 58,* 108–122.

Jackson, L. M. (2011). Ideology and prejudice. In L. M. Jackson (Ed.), *The psychology of prejudice: From attitudes to social action* (pp. 65–80). Washington, DC: American Psychological Association.

Jacobi, C., Volker, U., Trockel, M. T., & Taylor, C. B. (2012). Effects of an internet-based intervention for subthreshold eating disorders: A randomized controlled trial. *Behaviour Research and Therapy, 50,* 93–99.

Jacobs, R. A. (2002). Visual cue integration for depth perception. In R. P. N. Rao & B. A. Bruno (Eds.), *Probabilistic models of the brain: Perception and neural function. Neural information processing series* (pp. 61–76). Cambridge, MA: The MIT Press.

Jacobson, E. (1924). The technique of progressive relaxation. *Journal of Nervous and Mental Disease, 60,* 568–578.

Jaffe, J. H. (1990). Drug addiction and abuse. In *Goodman and Gilman's the pharmacological basis of therapeutics* (8th ed.). New York: Pergamon.

Jaffee, S., & Hyde, J. S. (2000). Gender differences in moral orientation: A meta-analysis. *Psychological Bulletin, 126,* 703–726.

James, W. (1890). *The principles of psychology* (Vol. 2). New York: Henry Holt.

Jamieson, D. W., Lydon, J. E., & Zanna, M. P. (1987). Attitude and activity preference similarity: Differential bases of interpersonal attraction for low and high self-monitors. *Journal of Personality and Social Psychology, 53,* 1052–1060.

Jamison, K. R. (1995). Manic-depressive illness and creativity. *Scientific American, (2),* 62–67.

Jansen, A., Nederkoorn, C., & Mulkens, S. (2005). Selective visual attention for ugly and beautiful body parts in eating disorders. *Behaviour Research and Therapy, 43,* 183–196.

Jaschinski, U., & Wentura, D. (2002). Misleading postevent information and working memory capacity: An individual differences approach to eyewitness memory. *Applied Cognitive Psychology, 16,* 223–231.

Jasinski, D. R., Faries, D. E., Moore, R. J., Schuh, L. M., & Allen, A. J. (2008). Abuse liability assessment of atomoxetine in a drug-abusing population. *Drug and Alcohol Dependence, 95,* 140–146.

Jausovek, N., & Jausovek, K. (2003). Spatiotemporal brain activity related to intelligence: A low resolution brain electromagnetic tomography study. *Cognitive Brain Research, 16,* 267–272.

Jaycox, L. H., Stein, B. D., Kataoka, S. H., Wong, M., Fink, A., Escudero, P., & Zaragoza, C. (2002). *Journal of the American Academy of Child Adolescent. Psychiatry, 41,* 1104–1110.

Jefferis, B. J., Nazareth, I., Marston, L., Moreno-Kustner, B., Bellon, J. A., Svab, I., ... King, M. (2011). Associations between unemployment and major depressive disorder: Evidence from an international, prospective study (the predict cohort). *Social Science & Medicine, 73,* 1627–1634.

Jensen, M. S., & Mathewson, K. E. (2011). Simultaneous perception of both interpretations of ambiguous figures. *Perception, 40,* 1009–1011.

Jensvold, M. L. A., & Gardner, R. A. (2000). Interactive use of sign language by cross-fostered chimpanzees (Pan troglodytes). *Journal of Comparative Psychology, 114,* 335–346.

Jiang, Y., Luo, Y. J., & Parasuraman, R. (2002). Neural correlates of perceptual priming of visual motion. *Brain Research Bulletin, 57,* 211–219.

Johnson, D. L., Wiebe, J. S., Gold, S. M., Andreasen, N. C., Hichwa, R. D., Watkins, G. L., & Et al. (1999). Cerebral blood flow and personality: A positron emission tomography study. *American Journal of Psychiatry, 156,* 252–257.

Johnson, F., & Wardle, J. (2005). Dietary restraint, body dissatisfaction, and psychological distress: A prospective analysis. *Journal of Abnormal Psychology, 114,* 119–125.

Johnson, H. D., Brady, E., Mcnair, R., Congdon, D., Niznik, J., & Anderson, S. (2007). Identity as a moderator of gender differences in the emotional closeness of emerging adults' same- and cross-sex friendships. *Adolescence, 42,* 1–23.

Johnson, J. D., Jackson, L. A., & Gatto, L. (1995). Violent attitudes and deferred academic aspirations: Deleterious effects of exposure to rap music. *Basic and Applied Social Psychology, 16,* 27–41.

Johnson, J. D., Noel, N. E., & Sutter-Hernandez, J. (2000). Alcohol and male acceptance of sexual aggression: The role of perceptual ambiguity. *Journal of Applied Social Psychology, 30,* 1186–1200.

Johnson, M. K., & Raye, C. L. (2000). Cognitive and brain mechanisms of false memories and beliefs. In E. Scarry (Ed.), *Memory, brain, and belief* (pp. 35–86). Cambridge, MA: Harvard University Press.

Johnson, R. T., Burk, J. A., & Kirkpatrick, L. A. (2007). Dominance and prestige as differential predictors of aggression and testosterone levels in men. *Evolution and Human Behavior, 28,* 345–351.

Johnson, S. C., & Spilka, B. (1991). Outcome research and religious psychotherapies: Where are we and where are we going? *Journal of Psychology and Theology, 21,* 297–308.

Johnson, W., Bouchard, T. J., Jr., Krueger, R. F., McGue, M., & Gottesman, I. I. (2004). Just one g: Consistent results from three test batteries. *Intelligence, 32,* 95–107.

Johnson, W., & Krueger, R. F. (2005). Higher perceived life control decreases genetic variance in physical health: Evidence from a national twin study. *Journal of Personality and Social Psychology, 88,* 165–173.

Johnston, K. L., & White, K. M. (2003). Binge-drinking: A test of the role of group norms in the theory of planned behaviour. *Psychology & Health, 18,* 63–77.

Johnston, T. D., & Edwards, L. (2002). Genes, interactions, and the development of behavior. *Psychological Review, 109,* 26–34.

Joiner, T. (1999). The clustering and containing of suicide. *Current Directions in Psychological Science, 8,* 89–92.

Joireman, J., Anderson, J., & Strathman, A. (2003). The aggression paradox: Understanding links among aggression, sensation seeking, and the consideration of future consequences. *Journal of Personality and Social Psychology, 84,* 1287–1302.

Jollant, F., Bellivier, F., Leboyer, M., Astruc, B., Torres, S., Verdier, R., … Courtet, P. (2005). Impaired decision making in suicide attempters. *American Journal of Psychiatry, 162,* 304–310.

Joseph, R. (2000). The evolution of sex differences in language, sexuality, and visual-spatial skills. *Archives of Sexual Behavior, 29,* 35–66.

Jost, J. T., Glaser, J., Kruglanski, A. W., & Sulloway, F. J. (2003). Political conservatism as motivated social cognition. *Psychological Bulletin, 129,* 339–375.

Juan, S. (2006). *The odd brain: Mysteries of our weird and wonderful brains explained.* Kansas City, MO: Andrews McMeel Publishing.

Judge, T. A., Livingston, B. A., & Hurst, C. (2012). Do nice guys—and gals—really finish last? The joint effects of sex and agreeableness on income. *Journal of Personality and Social Psychology, 102,* 390–407.

Julien, R. M. (2001). *A primer of drug action: Nontechnical guide to the actions, uses, and side effects of psychoactive drugs* (9th ed.). New York: Freeman.

Jung, C. G. (1916). *Analytical psychology.* New York: Moffat.

Jung, C. G. (1921). *Psychological types.* New York: Harcourt Brace.

Jung, C. G. (1963). *Memories, dreams, reflections.* New York: Random House.

Jung, C. G. (1964). *Man and his symbols.* New York: Dell.

Jung-Beeman, M., Bowden, E. M., Haberman, J., Frymiare, J. L., Arambel-Liu, S., & Greenglatt, R. (2004). Neural activity when people solve verbal problems with insight. *PLOS Biology, 2,* 500–510.

Jussim, L. (1989). Teacher expectations: Self-fulfilling prophecies, perpetual biases, and accuracy. *Journal of Personality and Social Psychology, 57,* 469–480.

Jussim, L., Cain, T. R., Crawford, J. T., Harber, K., & Cohen, F. (2009). The unbearable accuracy of stereotypes. In T. D. Nelson (Ed.), *Handbook of prejudice, stereotyping, and discrimination* (pp. 199–227). New York: Psychology Press.

K

Kaas, J. H. (2008). The evolution of the complex sensory and motor systems of the human brain. *Brain Research Bulletin, 75,* 384–390.

Kacmar, K. M., Delery, J. E., & Ferris, G. R. (1992). Differential effectiveness of applicant impression management tactics on employment interview decisions. *Journal of Applied Social Psychology, 22,* 1250–1272.

Kaechele, H. (2006). Dream work in therapy: Facilitating exploration, insight, and action. *Psychotherapy Research, 16,* 140–141.

Kaelber, C. T., Moul, D. E., & Farmer, M. E. (1995). Epidemiology of depression. In E. E. Beckham & W. R. Leber (Eds.), *Handbook of depression* (2nd ed., pp. 3–35). New York: Guilford Press.

Kaeppler, C., & Hohagen, F. (2003). Psychosocial aspects of insomnia: Results of a study in general practice. *European Archives of Psychiatry & Clinical Neuroscience, 253,* 49–52.

Kagan, J., Snidman, N., & Arcus, D. (1998). Childhood derivatives of high and low reactivity in infancy. *Child Development, 69,* 1483–1493.

Kagan, S., & Knight, G. P. (1979). Cooperation-competition and self-esteem: A case of cultural relativism. *Journal of Cross-Cultural Psychology, 10,* 457–467.

Kagee, A. (2004). Present concerns of survivors of human rights violations in South Africa. *Social Science and Medicine, 59,* 625–635.

Kâgitçibasi, C. (1994). A critical appraisal of individualism and collectivism: Toward a new formulation. In U. Kim, H. C. Triandis, C. Kâgitçibasi, S. Choi, & G. Yoon (Eds.), *Individualism and collectivism: Theory, method, and applications* (pp. 52–65). Thousand Oaks, CA: Sage.

Kail, R. (2002). Developmental change in proactive interference. *Child Development, 73,* 1703–1714.

Kail, R. V. (2007). Cognitive development includes global and domain-specific processes. In G. W. Ladd (Ed.), *Appraising the human developmental sciences: Essays in honor of Merrill-Palmer Quarterly* (pp. 56–66). Detroit, MI: Wayne State University Press.

Kalichman, S. C. (2005). The other side of the healthy relationships intervention: Mental health outcomes and correlates of sexual risk behavior change. *AIDS Education and Prevention, 17,* 66–75.

Kalish, R. (1985). The social context of death and dying. In R. H. Binstock & E. Shanas (Eds.), *Handbook of aging and the social sciences* (2nd ed.). New York: Van Nostrand Reinhold.

Kalmbach, B. E., & Mauk, M. D. (2012). Multiple sites of extinction for a single learned response. *Journal of Neurophysiology, 107,* 226–238.

Kanagawa, C., Cross, S. E., & Markus, H. R. (2001). "Who am I?" The cultural psychology of the conceptual self. *Personality and Social Psychology Bulletin, 27,* 90–103.

Kandel, E. R. (1995). Cellular mechanisms of learning and memory. In E. R. Kandel, J. H. Schwartz, & T. M. Jessell (Eds.), *Essentials of neural science and behavior.* Norwalk, CT: Appleton & Lange.

Kandel, E. R., & Schwartz, J. H. (1982). Molecular biology of learning: Modulation of transmitter release. *Science, 218,* 433–443.

Karim, S., Minhas, H. M., Bhattacharya, S., Sein, K., Nayar, B., Morris, J., … Burns, A. (2011). The symptomatology of Alzheimer's disease: A cross-cultural study. *International Journal of Geriatric Psychiatry, 26,* 415–422.

Karpov, Y. V. (2005). *The Neo-Vygotskian approach to child development.* New York: Cambridge University Press.

Karraker, K. H., & Stern, M. (1990). Infant physical attractiveness and facial expression: Effects on adult perceptions. *Basic and Applied Social Psychology, 11,* 371–385.

Karraker, K. H., Vogel, D. A., & Lake, M. A. (1995). Parents' gender-stereotyped perceptions of newborns: The eye of the beholder revisited. *Sex Roles, 33,* 687–701.

Karremans, J. C., Stroebe, W., & Claus, J. (2006). Beyond Vicary's fantasies: The impact of subliminal priming and brand choice. *Journal of Experimental Social Psychology, 42,* 792–798.

Katigbak, M. S., Church, A. T., Guanzon-Lapena, M. A., Carlota, A. J., & Del Pilar, G. H. (2002). Are indigenous personality dimensions culture specific? Philippine inventories and the five-factor model. *Journal of Personality and Social Psychology, 82,* 89–101.

Katkin, E. S., Wiens, S., & Ohman, A. (2001). Nonconscious fear conditioning, visceral perception, and the development of gut feeling. *Psychological Science, 12,* 366–370.

Katz, P. (1986). Gender identity: Development and consequences. In R. Ashmore & F. D. Boca (Eds.), *The social psychology of female-male relations* (pp. 21–67). Orlando, FL: Academic Press.

Katzenberg, D., Young, T., Finn, L., Lin, L., King, D. P., Takahashi, J. S., & Mignot, E. (1998). A CLOCK polymorphism associated with human diurnal preference. *Sleep, 21,* 569–576.

Kaufman, A. S., Kaufman, J. C., Chen, T. H., & Kaufman, N. L. (1996). Differences on six horn abilities for 14 age groups between 15–16 and 75–94 years. *Psychological Assessment, 8,* 161–171.

Kaufman, L., & Rock, I. (1962). The moon illusion (Vol. 1). *Science, 136,* 953–961.

Kaut, K. P. (2002). Religion, spirituality, and existentialism near the end of life. *American Behavioral Scientist, 46,* 220–234.

Kawamoto, K., Ishimoto, S., Minoda, R., Brough, D. E., & Raphael, Y. (2003). Math1 gene transfer generates new cochlear hair cells in mature guinea pigs in vivo. *Journal of Neuroscience, 23,* 4395–4400.

Kayumov, L., Rotenberg, V., Buttoo, K., Auch, C., Pandi-Perumal, S. R., & Shapiro, C. M. (2000). Interrelationships between nocturnal sleep, daytime alertness, and sleepiness: Two types of alertness proposed. *Journal of Neuropsychiatry & Clinical Neurosciences, 12,* 86–90.

Kazak, A. E., Alderfer, M., Rourke, M. T., Simms, S., Streisand, R., & Grossman, J. R. (2004). Posttraumatic stress disorder (PTSD) and posttraumatic stress symptoms (PTSS) in families of adolescent childhood cancer survivors. *Journal of Pediatric Psychology, 29,* 211–219.

Kazak, A. E., Bosch, J., & Klonoff, E. A. (2012). Health Psychology special series on health disparities. *Health Psychology, 31,* 1–4.

Kazdin, A. E. (1982). The token economy: A decade later. *Journal of Applied Behavior Analysis, 15,* 431–445.

Keen, C., & Howard, A. (2002). Experiential learning in Antioch College's work-based learning program as a vehicle for social and emotional development for gifted college students. *Journal of Secondary Gifted Education, 13,* 130–140.

Keesey, R. E. (1995). A set-point model of weight regulation. In K. D. Brownell & C. G. Fairburn (Eds.), *Eating disorders and obesity* (pp. 46–50). New York: Guilford Press.

Keith, J. R., & McVery, K. M. (1988). Latent place learning in a novel environment and the influences of prior training in rats. *Psychobiology, 16,* 146–151.

Keller, A., Castellanos, F., Vaituzis, A. C., Jeffries, N. O., Giedd, J. N., & Rapoport, J. L. (2003). Progressive loss of cerebellar volume in childhood-onset schizophrenia. *American Journal of Psychiatry, 160,* 128–133.

Kelley, H. H. (1967). Attribution theory in social psychology. In D. L. Vine (Ed.), *Nebraska symposium on motivation.* Lincoln, NE: University of Nebraska Press.

Kellogg, W. N., & Kellogg, L. A. (1933). *The ape and the child.* New York: McGraw-Hill.

Kelly, A. E. (1999). Revealing personal secrets. *Current Directions in Psychological Science, 8,* 105–109.

Kelly, B. D. (2008). Meditation, mindfulness, and mental health. *Irish Journal of Psychological Medicine, 25,* 3–4.

Kelly, I. W. (1997). Modern astrology: A critique. *Psychological Reports, 81,* 1035–1066.

Keltner, D., & Haidt, J. (2003). Approaching awe, a moral, spiritual, and aesthetic emotion. *Cognition & Emotion, 17,* 297–314.

Kendler, K. S., Aggen, S. H., & Patrick, C. J. (2012). A multivariate twin study of the DSM-IV criteria for antisocial personality disorder. *Biological Psychiatry, 71,* 247–253.

Kendler, K. S., Gardner, C. O., & Prescott, C. A. (1999). Clinical characteristics of major depression that predict risk of depression in relatives. *Archives of General Psychiatry, 56,* 322–327.

Kendler, K. S., Neale, M. C., Thornton, L. M., Aggen, S. H., Gilman, S. E., & Kessler, R. C. (2002). Cannabis use in the last year in a U.S. National sample of twin and sibling pairs. *Psychological Medicine, 32,* 551–554.

Kendler, K. S., Thornton, L. M., Gilman, S. E., & Kessler, R. C. (2000). Sexual orientation in U.S. National sample of twin and nontwin sibling pairs. *American Journal of Psychiatry, 157,* 1843–1846.

Kenrick, D. T., & Trost, M. R. (1987). A biosocial theory of heterosexual relationships. In K. Kelly (Ed.), *Females, males, and sexuality.* Albany, NY: State University of New York Press.

Keppel-Benson, J. M. (2002). Post-traumatic stress in children following motor vehicle accidents. (T. H. Ollendick & M. J. Benson, Eds.) *Journal of Child Psychology & Psychiatry & Allied Disciplines, 43,* 203–212.

Kessler, R. C., Berglund, P. A., Demler, O., Jin, R., & Walters, E. E. (2005). Lifetime prevalence and age-of-onset distributions of DSM-IV disorders in the National Comorbidity Survey Replication (NCS-R). *Archives of General Psychiatry, 62,* 593–602.

Ketter, T. A., & Wang, P. W. (2002). Predictors of treatment response in bipolar disorders: Evidence from clinical and brain imaging studies. *Journal of Clinical Psychiatry, 63,* 21–25.

Keune, P., & Forintos, D. P. (2010). Mindfulness meditation: A preliminary study on meditation practice during everyday life activities and its association with well-being. *Psihologijske Teme, 19,* 373–386.

Key, W. B. (1989). *The age of manipulation.* New York: Holt.

Kiecolt-Glaser, J. K., & Glaser, R. (2001). Psychological stress and wound healing. *Advances in Mind-Body Medicine, 17,* 15–17.

Kiecolt-Glaser, J. K., Glaser, R., Williger, D., Stout, J., Messick, G., Sheppard, S., … Donnerberg, R. (1985). Psychosocial enhancement of immunocompetence in a geriatric population. *Health Psychology, 4,* 25–41.

Kiessling, S. G., McClanahan, K. K., & Omar, H. A. (2008). Obesity, hypertension, and mental health evaluation in adolescents: A comprehensive approach. *International Journal of Adolescent Medicine and Health, 20,* 5–15.

Kilham, W., & Mann, L. (1974). Level of destructive obedience as a function of transmitter and executant roles in the Milgram obedience paradigm. *Journal of Personality and Social Psychology, 29,* 696–702.

Kim, A. (2009). Early experimental psychology. In J. P. Symons (Ed.), *The Routledge companion to philosophy of psychology* (pp. 41–58). New York: Routledge/Taylor & Francis Group.

Kim, H.-W., Greenberg, J. S., Seltzer, M. M., & Krauss, M. W. (2003). The role of coping in maintaining the psychological well-being of mothers of adults with intellectual disability and mental illness. *Journal of Intellectual Disability Research, 47,* 313–327.

Kim, N.-G. (2008). The moon illusion and the size-distance paradox. In S. Cummins-Sebree, M. A. Riley, & K. Shockley (Eds.), *Studies in perception and action IX: Fourteenth International Conference on Perception and Action* (pp. 210–213). Mahwah, NJ: Lawrence Erlbaum.

Kim, S. S., Reed, P. G., D. Hayward, R., & Koenig, H. G. (2011). Spirituality and psychological well-being: Testing a theory of family interdependence among family caregivers and their elders. *Research in Nursing & Health, 34,* 103–115.

Kimura, D. (1992). Sex differences in the brain. *Scientific American, 267,* 81–87.

King, L. A. (2008). Personal goals and life dreams: Positive psychology and motivation in daily life. In J. Y. Shah & W. L. Gardner (Eds.), *Handbook of motivation science* (pp. 518–530). New York: Guilford Press.

Kingery, P. M., Alford, A. A., & Coggeshall, M. B. (1999). Marijuana use among youth: Epidemiologic evidence from the U.S. and other nations. *School Psychology International, 20,* 9–21.

King-Smith, P. E. (2005). Threshold nonlinearities and signal detection theory. *Perception, 34,* 941–946.

Kinsey, A., Pomeroy, W., & Martin, C. (1948). *Sexual behavior in the human male.* Philadelphia, PA: Saunders.

Kinsey, A., Pomeroy, W., Martin, C., & Gebhard, P. (1953). *Sexual behavior in the human female.* Philadelphia, PA: Saunders.

Kiple, K. F., & Ornelas, K. C. (2001). Experimental animals in medical research: A history. In *Why animal experimentation matters: The use of animals in medical research. New studies in social policy* (pp. 23–48). New Brunswick, NJ: Transaction Publishers.

Kirsch, I., & Braffman, W. (2001). Imaginative suggestibility and hypnotizability. *Current Directions in Psychological Science, 10,* 57–61.

Kirsch, I. L., Steven, J., Vigorito, M., & Miller, R. R. (2004). The role of cognition in classical and operant conditioning. *Journal of Clinical Psychology, 60,* 369–392.

Kirschenbaum, H. (2004). Carl Rogers's life and work: An assessment on the 100th anniversary of his birth. *Journal of Counseling and Development, 82,* 116–124.

Kirschner, S. R., & Martin, J. (Eds.). (2010). *The sociocultural turn in psychology: The contextual emergence of mind and self.* New York: Columbia University Press.

Kizilirmak, J. M., Rosler, F., & Khader, P. H. (2012). Control processes during selective long-term memory retrieval. *NeuroImage, 59,* 1830–1841.

Klatzky, R. L., & Lederman, S. J. (2008). Object recognition by touch. In J. J. Rieser, D. H. Ashmead, F. F. Ford, & A. L. Corn (Eds.), *Blindness and brain plasticity in navigation and object perception* (pp. 185–207). Mahwah, NJ: Lawrence Erlbaum.

Klayman, J., & Ha, Y.-W. (1987). Confirmation, disconfirmation, and information in hypothesis testing. *Psychological Review, 94,* 211–228.

Klein, G. (1996). The effect of acute stressors on decision making. In E. Salas (Ed.), *Stress and human performance* (pp. 49–88). Mahwah, NJ: Erlbaum.

Klein, M. (1932). *The psycho-analysis of children.* London: Hogarth.

Klein, O., Snyder, M., & Livingston, R. W. (2004). Prejudice on the stage: Self-monitoring and the public expression of group attitudes. *British Journal of Social Psychology, 43,* 299–314.

Klein, R. J. (2008). Ready..., Set ..., Relax!: Relaxation strategies with children and adolescents. In C. A. Malchiodi (Ed.), *Creative interventions with traumatized children* (pp. 302–320). New York: Guilford Press.

Klein, S. B. (2012). *Learning: Principles and applications* (6th ed.). Thousand Oaks, CA: Sage Publications.

Kleinknecht, R. A. (1991). *Mastering anxiety: The nature and treatment of anxious conditions.* New York: Plenum.

Kley, H., Heinrichs, N., Bender, C., & Tuschen-Caffier, B. (2012). Predictors of outcome in a cognitive-behavioral group program for children and adolescents with social anxiety disorder. *Journal of Anxiety Disorders, 26,* 79–87.

Knafo, A., & Plomin, R. (2006). Parental discipline and affection and children's prosocial behavior: Genetic and environmental links. *Journal of Personality and Social Psychology, 90,* 147–164.

Knight, A., Underhill, P. A., Mortensen, H. M., Zhivotovsky, L. A., Lin, A. A., Henn, B. M., … Mountain, J. L. (2003). African Y chromosome and mtDNA divergence provides insight into the history of click languages. *Current Biology, 13,* 464–473.

Knobloch, L. K. (2007). Perceptions of turmoil within courtship: Associations with intimacy, relational uncertainty, and interference from partners. *Journal of Social and Personal Relationships, 24,* 363–384.

Knowlton, B. J., & Foerde, K. (2008). Neural representations of nondeclarative memories. *Current Directions in Psychological Science, 17,* 107–111.

Knox, R. E., & Inkster, J. A. (1968). Postdecision dissonance at post-time. *Journal of Personality and Social Psychology, 8,* 319–323.

Knyazev, G. G., Savostyanov, A. N., & Levin, E. A. (2006). Alpha synchronization and anxiety: Implications for inhibition vs. alertness hypotheses. *International Journal of Psychophysiology, 59,* 151–158.

Koester, J. (1995). Membrane potential. In E. R. Kandel, J. H. Schwartz, & T. M. Jessell (Eds.), *Essentials of neural science and behavior.* Norwalk, CT: Appleton & Lange.

Kohlberg, L. (1981). *Essays on moral development.* New York: Harper & Row.

Kohlberg, L. (1984). The psychology of moral development: The nature and validity of moral stages. In *Essays on moral development* (Vol. 2). New York: Harper & Row.

Kohn, C. K. (2005). Rat brain's executive hub quells alarm center if stress is controllable. *Mental Health Weekly Digest, 7.*

Kokkevi, A., Rotsika, V., Arapaki, A., & Richardson, C. (2012). Adolescents' self-reported suicide attempts, self-harm thoughts and their correlates across 17 European countries. *Journal of Child Psychology and Psychiatry, 53,* 381–389.

Kolb, B., & Whishaw, I. Q. (1998). *Fundamentals of human neuropsychology* (3rd ed.). New York: Freeman.

Konisberg, R. D. (2011). *The truth about grief: The myth of its five stages and the new science of loss.* New York: Simon & Schuster.

Kopelowicz, A., Liberman, R. P., & Zarate, R. (2002). Psychosocial treatments for schizophrenia. In P. E. Nathan & J. M. Gorman (Eds.), *A guide to treatments that work* (2nd ed., pp. 201–228). London: Oxford University Press.

Koren, D., Norman, D., Cohen, A., Berman, J., & Klein, E. M. (2005). Increased PTSD risk with combat-related injury: A matched comparison study of injured and uninjured soldiers experiencing the same combat events. *American Journal of Psychiatry, 162,* 276–282.

Koss, M. (1993). Rape: Scope, impact, interventions, and public policy responses. *American Psychologist, 48,* 1062–1069.

Kossoff, E. H., Vining, E. P. G., Pillas, D. J., Pyzik, P. L., Avellino, A. M., Carson, B. S., & Freeman, J. M. (2003). Hemispherectomy for intractable nihemispheric epilepsy: Etiology vs. outcome. *Neurology, 61,* 887–890.

Kotzer, A. M. (2000). Factors predicting postoperative pain in children and adolescents following spine fusion. *Issues in Comprehensive Pediatric Nursing, 23,* 83–102.

Kozulin, A. (2009). Review of Vygotsky's legacy: A foundation for research and practice and Key to learning: The technology of child development—Vygotskian approach to early education. *Journal of Cognitive Education and Psychology, 8,* 216–221.

Krefting, L. A. (2003). Intertwined discourses of merit and gender: Evidence from academic employment in the USA. *Gender, Work and Organization, 10,* 260–278.

Kribbs, N. B. (1993). Siesta. In M. A. Carskadon (Ed.), *Encyclopedia of sleep and dreaming.* New York: Macmillan.

Kringelbach, M. L., O'Doherty, J., Rolls, E. T., & Andrews, C. (2003). Activation of the human orbitofrontal cortex to a liquid food stimulus is correlated with its subjective pleasantness. *Cerebral Cortex, 13,* 1064–1071.

Kristensen, P., Weisaeth, L., & Heir, T. (2012). Bereavement and mental health after sudden and violent losses: A review. *Psychiatry: Interpersonal and Biological Processes, 75,* 76–97.

Krogsgaard, M., & Davis, M. M. (2005). How T cells "see" antigen. *Nature Immunology, 6,* 239–245.

Kroll, N. E. A., Yonelinas, A. P., Dobbins, I. G., & Frederick, C. M. (2002). Separating sensitivity from response bias: Implications of comparisons of yes-no and forced-choice tests for models and measures of recognition memory. *Journal of Experimental Psychology: General, 131,* 241–254.

Krull, D. S., Loy, M. H.-M., Lin, J., Wang, C.-F., Chen, S., & Zhao, X. (1999). The fundamental attribution error: Correspondence bias in individualist and collectivist cultures. *Personality and Social Psychology Bulletin, 25,* 1208–1219.

Kryger, M. H., Roth, T., & Dement, W. C. (Eds.). (2000). *Principles and practice of sleep medicine* (4th ed.). Philadelphia, PA: Saunders.

Kübler-Ross, E. (1969). *On death and dying.* New York: Macmillan.

Kübler-Ross, E. (1981). *Living and dying.* New York: Macmillan.

Kulik, J. A., Bangert-Downs, R. L., & Kulik, C. (1984). Effectiveness of coaching for aptitude tests. *Psychological Bulletin, 95,* 179–188.

Kunzendorf, R. G., Treantafel, N., Taing, B., Flete, A., Savoie, S., Agersea, S., & Williams, R. (2006). The sense of self in lucid dreams: "Self as subject" vs. "Self as agent" vs. "Self as object." *Imagination, Cognition and Personality, 26,* 303–323.

Kuo, T. B. J., Shaw, F.-Z., Lai, C., Lai, C.-W., & Yang, C. C. H. (2004). Changes in sleep patterns in spontaneously hyperactive rats. *Sleep: Journal of Sleep & Sleep Disorders Research, 27,* 406–412.

Kuo, Y.-Y. (1996). Taoistic psychology of creativity. *Journal of Creative Behavior, 30,* 197–212.

Kupfer, D. J., Frank, E., & Phillips, M. L. (2012). Major depressive disorder: New clinical, neurobiological, and treatment perspectives. *The Lancet, 379,* 1045–1055.

Kurdek, L. A. (1994). Conflict resolution styles in gay, lesbian, heterosexual non-parent, and heterosexual parent couples. *Journal of Marriage and the Family, 56,* 705–722.

Kurdek, L. A. (1995). Lesbian and gay couples. In A. R. D'Augelli & C. J. Patterson (Eds.), *Lesbian, Gay, and Bisexual Identities over the Lifespan: Psychological Perspectives* (pp. 243–261). New York: Oxford University Press.

Kurdek, L. A. (1998). Relationship outcomes and their predictors: Longitudinal evidence from heterosexual married, gay cohabiting, and lesbian cohabiting couples. *Journal of Marriage and the Family, 60,* 553–568.

Kurtz, M. M., & Mueser, K. T. (2008). A meta-analysis of controlled research on social skills training for schizophrenia. *Journal of Consulting and Clinical Psychology, 76,* 491–505.

Kurtzberg, T. R., & Amabile, T. M. (2001). From Guilford to creative synergy: Opening the black box of team-level creativity. *Creativity Research Journal, 13,* 285–294.

Kvavilashvil, L., Mirani, J., Schlagman, S., Foley, K., & Kornbrot, D. E. (2009). Consistency of flashbulb memories of September 11 over long delays: Implications for consolidation and wrong time slice hypotheses. *Journal of Memory and Language, 61,* 556–572.

Kyjonkova, H., & Lacinova, L. (2010). Private speech and activity type in preschool children. *Ceskoslovenska Psychologie, 54,* 342–356.

L

LaBerge, S. (2007). Lucid dreaming. In D. Barrett & P. McNamara (Eds.), *The new science of dreaming: Volume 2. Content, recall, and personality correlates* (pp. 307–328). Westport, CT: Praeger Publishers.

Labov, W. (1973). The boundaries of words and their meanings. In R. W. Shiny (Ed.), *New ways of analyzing variations in English* (Vol. 1). Washington, DC: Georgetown University Press.

Lachman, M. E., & Weaver, S. L. (1998). The sense of control as a moderator of social class differences in health and well-being. *Journal of Personality and Social Psychology, 74,* 763–773.

Ladd-Franklin, C. (1929). *Colour and colour theories.* New York: Harcourt, Brace & Company.

LaGrenade, L., Graham, D., & Trontell, A. (2001). *Myocarditis and cardiomyopathy associated with clozapine use in the United States.* New England Journal of Medicine, 345, 224–225.

Laing, D. G., Prescott, J., Bell, G. A., & Gillmore, R. (1993). A cross-cultural study of taste discrimination with Australians and Japanese. *Chemical Senses, 18,* 161–168.

Laird, J. D. (1974). Self-attribution of emotion: The effects of expressive behavior on the quality of emotional experience. *Journal of Personality and Social Psychology, 29,* 475–486.

Lamb, M. E., Pleck, J. H., Charnov, E. L., & Levine, J. A. (1987). A biosocial perspective on paternal behavior and involvement. In *Parenting across the lifespan: biosocial perspectives.* Hawthrone, NY: Aldine de Gruyter.

Lamb, M., Sternberg, K. J., & Prodromidis, M. (1992). Nonmaternal care and the security of the infant-mother attachment: A reanalysis of the data. *Infant Behavior and Development, 15,* 71–83.

Lambert, M. J., & Erekson, D. M. (2008). Positive psychology and the humanistic tradition. *Journal of Psychotherapy Integration, 18,* 222–232.

Laming, D. (1985). Some principles of sensory analysis. *Psychological Review, 92,* 462–485.

Lamprecht, F., & Sack, M. (2002). Posttraumatic stress disorder revisited. *Psychosomatic Medicine, 64,* 222–237.

Land, E. H. (1986). Recent advances in retinex theory. *Vision Research, 675,* 7–21.

Landrine, H. (1988). Revising the framework of abnormal psychology. In P. Bronstein & K. Quina (Eds.), *Teaching a psychology of people.* Washington, DC: American Psychological Association.

Langer, E. J. (1989). Minding matters: The consequences of mindlessness-mindfulness. In L. Berkowitz (Ed.), *Advances in experimental social psychology* (Vol. 22, pp. 137–173). San Diego, CA: Academic Press.

Langer, E. J., Blank, A., & Chanowitz, B. (1978). The mindlessness of ostensibly thoughtful action. *Journal of Personality and Social Psychology, 36,* 635–642.

Langford, P. E. (2005). *Vygotsky's developmental and educational psychology.* New York: Psychology Press.

Larsen, R. J., & Kasimatis, M. (1990). Individual differences in entrainment of mood to the weekly calendar. *Journal of Personality and Social Psychology, 58,* 164–171.

Lashley, K. S. (1950). In search of the engram. *Symposium of the Society for Experimental Biology, 4,* 454–482.

Latané, B., & Darley, J. M. (1968). Group inhibition of bystander intervention in emergencies. *Journal of Personality and Social Psychology, 10,* 216–221.

Latané, B., & Darley, J. M. (1970). *The unresponsive bystander: Why doesn't he help?* Englewood Cliffs, NJ: Prentice Hall.

Latané, B., & Nida, S. (1981). Ten years of research on group size and helping. *Psychological Bulletin, 89,* 308–324.

Laumann, E., & Gagnon, J. (1995). A sociological perspective on sexual action. In *Conceiving sexuality: approaches to sex research in post-modern world.* New York: Routledge.

Laumann, E., Gagnon, J., Michael, R., & Michaels, S. (1994). *The social organization of sexuality: Sexual practices in the United States.* Chicago, IL: University of Chicago Press.

LaVeist, T. A., Diala, C., & Jarrett, N. C. (2000). Social status and perceived discrimination: Who experiences discrimination in the health care system, how, and why? In C. Hogue, M. Hargraves, & K. Scott-Collins (Eds.), *Minority health in America* (pp. 194–208). Baltimore, MD: Johns Hopkins University Press.

Lavond, D. G., & Steinmetz, J. E. (2003). *Handbook of classical conditioning.* Dordrecht, Netherlands: Kluwer Academic Publishers.

Lazar, S. W., Bush, G., Gollub, R. L., Fricchione, G. L., Khalsa, G., & Benson, H. (2000). Functional brain mapping of the relaxation response and meditation. *Neuroreport: For Rapid Communication of Neuroscience Research, 11,* 1581–1585.

Lazarus, R., & Folkman, S. (1984). *Stress, appraisal, and coping.* New York: Springer.

Lazarus, R. S. (1993). From psychological stress to the emotions: A history of changing outlooks. *Annual Review of Psychology, 44,* 1–21.

Lazarus, R. S., & Lazarus, B. N. (1994). *Passion and reason: Making sense of our emotions.* New York: Oxford University Press.

Le Melledo, J. M., Arthur, H., Dalton, J., Woo, C., Lipton, N., Bellavance, F., ... Bradwejn, J. (2003). The influence of Type A behavior pattern on the response to the panicogenic agent CCK-4. *Journal of Psychosomatic Research, 51,* 513–520.

Leahey, T. H. (1991). *A history of modern psychology.* Englewood Cliffs, NJ: Prentice Hall.

Leak, G. K., DeNeve, K. M., & Greteman, A. J. (2007). The relationship between spirituality, assessed through self-transcendent goal strivings, and positive psychological attributes. *Research in the Social Scientific Study of Religion, 18,* 263–279.

Leather, P., Beale, D., & Sullivan, L. (2003). Noise, psychosocial stress and their interaction in the workplace. *Journal of Environmental Psychology, 23,* 213–222.

LeBeau, R. T., Glenn, D., Liao, B., Wittchen, H.-U., Beesdo-Baum, K., Ollendick, T., & Craske, M. G. (2010). Specific phobia: A review of *DSM-IV* specific phobia and preliminary recommendations for *DSM-V. Depression & Anxiety, 27,* 148–167.

Lebow, J. L. (2012). Listening to many voices. *Family Process, 51,* 1–7.

LeDoux, J. E. (2008). Remembrance of emotions past. In M. H. Immordino-Yang (Ed.), *The Jossey-Bass reader on the brain and learning* (pp. 151–179). San Francisco, CA: Jossey-Bass.

Lee, F., Hallahan, M., & Herzog, T. (1996). Explaining real-life events: How culture and domain shape attributions. *Personality and Social Psychology Bulletin, 22,* 732–741.

Lee, J. H., Cheng, R., Honig, L. S., Vonsattel, J.-P. G., Clark, L., & Mayeux, R. (2008). Association between genetic variants in SORL1 and autopsy-confirmed Alzheimer disease. *Neurology, 70,* 887–889.

Lee, T. M. C., Liu, H.-L., Tan, L.-H., Chan, C. C. H., Mahankali, S., Feng, C.-M., ... Gao, J.-H. (2002). Lie detection by functional magnetic resonance imaging. *Human Brain Mapping, 15,* 157–164.

Lehman, A. F., Steinwachs, D. M., Dixon, L. B., Goldman, H. H., Osher, F., Postrado, L., ... Zito, J. (1998). Translating research into practice: The schizophrenia patient outcomes research team (PORT) treatment recommendations. *Schizophrenia Bulletin, 24,* 1–10.

Lehman, D. R., Lempert, R. O., & Nisbett, R. E. (1988). The effects of graduate training on reasoning. *American Psychologist, 43,* 431–442.

Leippe, M. R., & Elkin, R. A. (1987). When motives clash: Issue involvement and response involvement as determinants of persuasion. *Journal of Personality and Social Psychology, 52,* 269–278.

Leitenberg, H., & Henning, K. (1995). Sexual fantasy. *Psychological Bulletin, 117,* 469–496.

Lemonick, M., & Dorfman, A. (2002). Father of us all? *Time,* 40–47.

Lenartowicz, A., Verbruggen, F., Logan, G. D., & Poldrack, R. A. (2011). Inhibition-related activation in the right inferior frontal gyrus in the absence of inhibitory cues. *Journal of Cognitive Neuroscience, 23,* 3388–3399.

Lenton, A. P., Blair, I. V., & Hastie, R. (2001). Illusions of gender: Stereotypes evoke false memories. *Journal of Experimental Social Psychology, 37,* 3–14.

Lepper, M., Greene, D., & Nisbett, R. (1973). Undermining children's intrinsic interest with extrinsic rewards: A test of the overjustification hypothesis. *Journal of Personality and Social Psychology, 23,* 129–137.

Lerner, A. G., Gelkopf, M., Skladman, I., Rudinski, D., Nachshon, H., & Bleich, A. (2003). Clonazepam treatment of lysergic acid diethylamide-induced hallucinogen persisting perception disorder with anxiety features. *International Clinical Psychopharmacology, 18,* 101–105.

Lerner, R., & Steinberg, L. (Eds.). (2004). Handbook of adolescent psychology (2nd ed.). New York: Wiley.

Leslie, A. M., German, T. P., & Polizzi, P. (2005). Belief-desire reasoning as a process of selection. *Cognitive Psychology, 50,* 45–85.

Letendre, J. (2007). "Sugar and spice but not always nice": Gender socialization and its impact on development and maintenance of aggression in adolescent girls. *Child & Adolescent Social Work Journal, 24,* 353–368.

Lettori, D., Battaglia, D., Sacco, A., Veredice, C., Chieffo, D., Massimi, L., ... Guzzetta, F. (2008). Early hemispherectomy in catastrophic epilepsy A neuro-cognitive and epileptic long-term follow-up. *Seizure, 17,* 49–63.

LeVay, S. (1991). A difference in hypothalamic structure between heterosexual and homosexual men. *Science, 253,* 1034–1037.

LeVay, S. (2007). A difference in hypothalamic structure between heterosexual and homosexual men. In G. Einstein (Ed.), *Sex and the Brain* (pp. 721–724). Cambridge, MA: MIT Press.

Levenson, R. W. (2005). Presidential column: Desperately seeking Phil. *Observer, 18,* 4.

Levenson, R. W., Ekman, P., Heider, K., & Friesen, W. V. (1992). Emotion and autonomic nervous system activity in the Minangkabau of West Sumatra. *Journal of Personality and Social Psychology, 62,* 972–988.

Levin, H. S., Papanicolaou, A., & Eisenberg, H. (1984). Observations on amnesia after nonmissle head injury. In *Neuropsychology of memory*. New York: Guilford Press.

Levin, S. (2004). Perceived group status differences and the effects of gender, ethnicity, and religion on social dominance orientation. *Political psychology, 25,* 31–48.

Levine, H. G. (1992). Temperance cultures: Alcohol as a problem in Nordic and English-speaking cultures. In *The nature of alcohol and drug-related problems* (pp. 16–36). New York: Oxford University Press.

Levine, R. A., & Campbell, D. T. (1972). *Ethnocentrism.* New York: Wiley.

Levine, R., & Norenzayan, A. (1999). The pace of life in 31 countries. *Journal of Cross-Cultural Psychology, 26,* 554–571.

Levine, R. V., Martinez, T. S., Brase, G., & Sorenson, K. (1994). Helping in 36 U.S. Cities. *Journal of Personality and Social Psychology, 67,* 69–82.

Levine, R. V., Sata, S., Hashimoto, T., & Verma, J. (1995). Love and marriage in eleven cultures. *Journal of Cross-Cultural Psychology, 26,* 554–571.

Levinoff, E. J., Phillips, N. A., Verret, L., Babins, L., Kelner, N., Akerib, V., & Chertkow, H. (2006). Cognitive estimation impairment in Alzheimer Disease and mild cognitive impairment. *Neuropsychology, 20,* 123–132.

Levy, J. (1972). Lateral specialization of the human brain: Behavioral manifestations and possible evolutionary basis. In J. A. Kiger (Ed.), *The biology of behavior.* Corvallis: Oregon State University.

Levy, J., Heller, W., Banich, M., & Burton, L. A. (1983). Asymmetry of perception in free viewing of chimeric faces. *Brain and Cognition, 2,* 404–419.

Lewin, R. (1993). *The origin of modern humans.* New York Scientific American Library.

Lewis, L. C., Rivera, A., & Roby, D. (2012). *Identifying and serving culturally and linguistically diverse gifted students.* Waco, TX, USA: Prufrock Press.

Lewis, M., & Brooks, J. (1978). Self-knowledge in emotional development. In M. Lewis & L. Rosenblum (Eds.), *The development of affect* (pp. 205–226). New York: Plenum.

Lewis, M., & Weintraub, M. (1979). Origins of early sex-role development. *Sex Roles, 5,* 135–153.

Li, F., Harrner, P., Fitzgerald, K., Eckstrom, E., Stock, R., Galver, J., … Batya, S. S. (2012). Tai chi and postural stability in patients with Parkinson's disease. *The New England Journal of Medicine, 366,* 511–519.

Li, J. (2004). Highabilities and excellence: A cultural perspective. In Beyond Knowledge: Extracognitive Aspects of Developing High Ability. *The Educational Psychology Series* (pp. 187–208). Mahwah, NJ: Lawrence Erlbaum.

Liebert, R. M., & Sprafkin, J. (1988). *The early window* (3rd ed.). New York: Pergamon Press.

Liegeois, F. J., & Morgan, A. T. (2012). Neural bases of childhood speech disorders: Lateralization and plasticity for speech functions during development. *Neuroscience and Biobehavioral Reviews, 36,* 439–458.

Lilienfeld. S. O., Kirsch, I., Sarvin, T. R., Lynn, S. J., Chaves, J. F., Ganaway, G. K., & Powell, R. A. (1999). Dissociative identity disorder and the sociocognitive model: Recalling the lessons of the past. *Psychological Bulletin, 125,* 507–523.

Lilienfeld, S. O., & Lynn, S. J. (2003). Dissociative identity disorder: Multiple personalities, multiple controversies. In S. O. Lilienfeld & S. J. Lynn (Eds.), *Science and pseudoscience in clinical psychology* (pp. 109–142). New York: Guilford Press.

Lin, K. M., & Cheung, F. (1999). Mental health issues for Asian Americans. *Psychiatric Services, 50,* 774–780.

Lindberg, S. M., Hyde, J. S., Petersen, J. L., & Linn, M. C. (2010). New trends in gender and mathematics performance: A meta-analysis. *Psychological Bulletin, 136,* 1123–1135.

Linehan, M. M. (1993). *Cognitive-behavioral treatment of borderline personality disorder.* New York: Guilford Press.

Link, B. G., Andrews, H., & Cullen, F. T. (1992). The violent and illegal behavior of mental patients reconsidered. *American Sociological Review, 57,* 275–292.

Linley, M., Wood, J., Harrington, P. C., & Seligman, M. (2007). Character strengths in the United Kingdom: The VIA inventory of strengths. *Personality and Individual Differences, 42,* 341–351.

Linthorst, A. C. E., & Reul, J. M. (2008). Stress and the brain: Solving the puzzle using microdialysis. *Pharmacology, Biochemistry and Behavior, 90,* 163–173.

Lipman, J. J., Miller, B. E., Mays, K. S., & Miller, M. N. (1990). Peak B endorphin concentration in cerebrospinal fluid: Reduced in chronic pain patients and increased during the placebo response. *Psychopharmacology, 102,* 112–116.

Lippa, R. A. (2002). Gender-related traits of heterosexual and homosexual men and women. *Archives of Sexual Behavior, 21,* 83–98.

Lippa, R. A. (2005). Sex and gender. In V. J. Derlega, B. A. Winstead, & W. H. Jones (Eds.), *Personality: contemporary theory and research* (3rd ed., pp. 332–365). Belmont, CA: Thomson Wadsworth.

Littleton, H. L., & Axsom, D. (2003). Rape and seduction scripts of university students: Implications for rape attributions and unacknowledged rape. *Sex Roles, 49,* 465–475.

Livianos, L., Sierra, P., Arques, S., Garcia, A., & Rojo, L. (2012). Is melatonin an adjunctive stabilizer? *Psychiatry and Clinical Neurosciences, 66,* 82–83.

Locke, E., & Latham, G. (1990). *A theory of goal setting and task performance.* Englewood Cliffs, NJ: Prentice Hall.

Locke, T. F., Newcomb, M. D., & Goodyear, R. K. (2005). Childhood experiences and psychosocial influences on risky sexual behavior, condom use, and HIV attitudes-behaviors among Latino males. *Psychology of Men and Masculinity, 6,* 25–38.

Lockhart, R. S., & Craik, F. I. (1990). Levels of processing: A retrospective commentary on a framework for memory research. *Canadian Journal of Psychology, 44,* 87–112.

Locurto, C. (2007). Individual differences and animal personality. *Comparative Cognition & Behavior Review, 2,* 67–78.

Loehlin, J. C., Horn, J. M., & Willerman, L. (1997). Heredity, environment, and IQ in the Texas Adoption Project. In R. J. Sternberg & E. L. Grigorenko (Eds.), *Intelligence, heredity, and environment* (pp. 105–125). Cambridge, England: Cambridge University Press.

Loehlin, J. C., Vandenberg, S., & Osborne, R. (1973). Blood group genes and negro-white ability differences. *Behavior Genetics, 3,* 263–270.

Loftus, E. F. (1993). The reality of repressed memories. *American Psychologist, 48,* 518–537.

Loftus, E. F. (2011). Crimes of memory: False memories and societal justice. In M. A. Gernsbacher, R. W. Pew, L. M. Hough, & J. R. Pomerantz (Eds.), *Psychology and the real world: Essays illustrating fundamental contributions to society* (pp. 83–88). New York: Worth Publishers; US.

Loftus, E. F., & Coan, D. (1995). The construction of childhood memories. In D. Peters (Ed.), *The child witness in context: Cognitive, social and legal perspectives.* New York: Kluwer.

Loftus, E. F., Feldman, J., & Dashiell, R. (1995). The reality of illusory memories. In D. L. Schacter (Ed.), *Memory distortion: How minds, brains, and societies reconstruct the past* (pp. 47–68). Cambridge, MA: Harvard University Press.

Loftus, E. F., & Palmer, J. C. (1974). Reconstruction of automobile destruction: An example of the interaction between language and memory. *Journal of Verbal Learning and Verbal Behavior, 13,* 585–589.

Logvinenko, A. D., Epelboim, J., & Steinman, R. M. (2002). The role of vergence in the perception of distance: A fair sest of Bishop Berkeley's claim. *Spatial Vision, 15,* 77–79.

LoLordo, V. M., & Droungas, A. (1989). Selective associations and adaptive specializations: Taste aversions and adaptive specializations: Taste aversions and phobias. In S. B. Klein & R. R. Mower (Eds.), *Contemporary learning theories: Instrumental conditioning and the impact of biological constraints on Learning.* Hillsdale, NJ: Erlbaum.

Loring, D. W., Meador, K., Lee, G., Murro, A., Smith, J., Flanigin, H., … King, D. (1990). Cerebral language lateralization: Evidence from intracarotid amobarbital testing. *Neuropsychologia, 28,* 831–838.

Lott, B. (2002). Cognitive and behavioral distancing from the poor. *American Psychologist, 57,* 100–110.

Lotto, R. B., & Purves, D. (2002). The empirical basis of color perception. *Consciousness & Cognition, 11,* 609–629.

Lounsbury, J. W., Hutchens, T., & Loveland, J. M. (2005). An investigation of Big Five personality traits and career decidedness among early and middle adolescents. *Journal of Career Assessment, 13,* 25–39.

Lourenço, O., & Machado, A. (1996). In defense of Piaget's theory: A reply to 10 common criticisms. *Psychological Review, 103,* 143–164.

Lovibond, P. F. (2004). Cognitive processes in extinction. *Learning and Memory, 11,* 495–500.

Lowe, G., Bland, R., Greenman, J., Kirkpatrick, N., & Lowe, G. (2001). Progressive muscle relaxation and secretory immunoglobulin A. *Psychological Reports, 88,* 912–914.

Lu, L., & Gilmour, R. (2004). Culture and conceptions of happiness: Individual oriented and social oriented SWB. *Journal of Happiness Studies, 5,* 269–291.

Lu, L., Gilmour, R., Kao, S., Weng, T., Hu, C., Chern, J., … Shih, J. (2001). Two ways to achieve happiness: When the East meets the West. *Personality and Individual Differences, 30,* 1161–1174.

Lubinski, D., Webb, R. M., Morelock, M. J., & Benbow, C. P. (2001). Top 1 in 10,000: A 10-year follow-up of the profoundly gifted. *Journal of Applied Psychology, 86,* 718–729.

Lucas, W. (1985). Police use of psychics: A waste of resources and tax money. *Campus Law Enforcement Journal, 15,* 15–21.

Luchins, A. S., & Luchins, E. H. (1994). the water jar experiments and Einstellung effects: II. Gestalt psychology and past experience. *Gestalt Theory, 16,* 205–259.

Lucidi, F., Russo, P. M., Mallia, L., Devoto, A., Lauriola, M., & Violani, C. (2006). Sleep-related car crashes: Risk perception and decision-making processes in young drivers. *Accident Analysis & Prevention, 38,* 302–309.

Lundy, G. F., & Firebaugh, G. (2005). Peer Relations and School Resistance: Does Oppositional Culture Apply to Race or to Gender? *Journal of Negro Education, 74,* 233–245.

Luo, M., Fee, M. S., & Katz, L. C. (2003). Encoding pheromonal signals in the accessory olfactory bulb of behaving mice. *Science, 299,* 1196–1201.

Luo, S., & Klohnen, E. C. (2005). Assortative mating and marital quality in newlyweds: A couple-centered approach. *Journal of Personality and Social Psychology, 88,* 304–326.

Luo, S., & Zhang, G. (2009). What leads to romantic attraction: Similarity, reciprocity, security, or beauty? Evidence from a speed-dating study. *Journal of Personality, 77,* 933–964.

Luria, A. R. (1968). *The mind of a mnemonist: A little book about a vast memory.* (L. Solotaroff, Trans.). New York: Basic Books.

Lykken, D. T. (1984). Polygraph interrogation. *Nature, 307,* 681–684.

Lykken, D. T. (1995). *The antisocial personalities.* Hillsdale, NJ: Erlbaum.

Lykken, D. T. (1998). *A tremor in the blood: Uses and abuses of the lie detector.* New York: Plenum.

Lykken, D. T., & Tellegen, A. (1996). Happiness is a stochastic phenomenon. *Psychological Science, 65,* 56–68.

Lynch, M. (1994). Developmental psychology. In *People: psychology from a cultural perspective* (pp. 65–81). Grove, CA: Brooks/Cole.

Lyness, S. A. (1993). Predictors of differences between Type A and Type B individuals in heart rate and blood pressure reactivity. *Psychological Bulletin, 114,* 266–295.

Lynn, S. J., & Kirsch, I. (2006). Questions and Contoversies. In *Essentials of clinical hypnosis: An evidence-based approach* (pp. 197–213). Washington, DC: American Psychological Association.

Lynn, S. J., Neufeld, V. A., Green, J. P., & Sandberg, D. (1996). Daydreaming, fantasy, and psychopathology. In B. Wallace (Ed.), *Hypnosis and imagination. imagery and human development series.* Amityville, NY: Baywood.

Lytton, H., & Gallagher, L. (2002). Parenting twins and the genetics of parenting. In *Handbook of parenting: Vol. 1. Children and parenting* (pp. 227–253). Mahwah, Nj: Erlbaum.

Lyubomirsky, S., Dickerhoof, R., Boehm, J. K., & Sheldon, K. M. (2011). Becoming happier takes both a will and a proper way: An experimental longitudinal intervention to boost well-being. *Emotion, 11,* 391–402.

Lyvers, M., Brooks, J., & Matica, D. (2004). Effects of caffeine on cognitive and autonomic measures in heavy and light caffeine consumers. *Australian Journal of Psychology, 56,* 33–41.

M

Maas, J. B. (1998). *The sleep advantage: Preparing your mind for peak performance.* New York: Villard.

Maccoby, E. E. (1990). Gender and relationships: A developmental account. *American Psychologist, 45,* 513–520.

MacDonald, T. K., & Martineau, A. M. (2002). Self-esteem, mood, and intentions to use condoms: When does low self-esteem lead to risky health behaviors? *Journal of Experimental Social Psychology, 38,* 299–306.

MacFarlane, A. (1975). Olfaction in the development of social preferences in the human neonate. *CIBA Foundation Symposium 33: Parent-infant interaction.* Amsterdam, The Netherlands: Elsevier.

MacGregor, J. N., & Cunningham, J. B. (2008). Rebus puzzles as insight problems. *Behavior Research Methods, 40,* 263–268.

MacKay, D. G., & Ahmetzanov, M. V. (2005). Emotion, memory, and attention in the Taboo Stroop Paradigm. *Psychological Science, 16,* 25–32.

Mackinnon, A., Griffiths, K. M., & Christensen, H. (2008). Comparative randomised trial of online cognitive-behavioural therapy and an information website for depression: 12-Month outcomes. *British Journal of Psychiatry, 192,* 130–134.

Macrae, C. N., Bodenhausen, G. V., & Milne, A. B. (1998). Saying no to unwanted thoughts: Self-focus and the regulation of mental life. *Journal of Personality and Social Psychology, 74,* 578–589.

Madigan, S., & O'Hara, R. (1992). Short-term memory at the turn of the century. *American Psychologist, 47,* 170–174.

Madsen, T. M., Yeh, D. D., Valentine, G. W., & Duman, R. S. (2005). Electroconvulsive seizure treatment increases cell proliferation in rat frontal cortex. *Neuropsychopharmacology, 30,* 27–34.

Maier, S. F., Seligman, M. E. P., & Solomon, R. L. (1969). Pavlovian fear conditioning and learned helplessness: Effects on escape and avoidance behavior of (a) the CS-US contingency, and (b) the independence of the US and voluntary responding. In B. A. Campbell & R. M. Church (Eds.), *Punishment and aversive behavior.* New York: Appleton-Century-Crofts.

Maier, S. F., Watkins, L. R., & Fleshner, M. (1994). Psychoneuroimmunology: The interface between behavior, brain, and immunity. *American Psychologist, 49,* 1004–1017.

Majerus, S., Poncelet, M., Greffe, C., & Van Der Linden, M. (2006). Relations between vocabulary development and verbal short-term memory: The relative importance of short-term memory for serial order and item information. *Journal of Experimental Child Psychology, 93,* 95–119.

Major, B., Spencer, S., Schmader, T., Wolfe, C., & Crocker, J. (1998). Coping¬ with negative stereotypes about intellectual performance: The role of psychological disengagement. *Personality and Social Psychology Bulletin, 24,* 34–50.

Makin, J. W., & Porter, R. H. (1989). Attractiveness of lactating females' breast odors to neonates. *Child Development, 60,* 803–810.

Makoul, G. (1998). Perpetuating passivity: Reliance and reciprocal determinism in physician-patient interaction. *Journal of Health Communication, 3,* 233–259.

Makovski, T., & Jiang, Y. V. (2008). Proactive interference from items previously stored in visual working memory. *Memory & Cognition, 36,* 43–52.

Malka, A., & Chatman, J. A. (2003). Intrinsic and extrinsic work orientations as moderators of the effect of annual income on subjective well being: A longitudinal study. *Personality and Social Psychology Bulletin, 29,* 737–746.

Mallick, B. N., Madan, V., & Jha, S. K. (2008). Rapid eye movement sleep regulation by modulation of the noradrenergic system. In J. M. Monti, S. R. Pandi-Perumal, & C. M. Sinton (Eds.), *Neurochemistry of sleep and wakefulness* (pp. 59–81). New York: Cambridge University Press.

Malnic, B., Hirono, J., Sato, T., & Buck, L. B. (1999). Combinatorial receptor codes for odors. *Cell, 96,* 713–723.

Malone, S. M., Taylor, J., Marmorstein, N. R., McGue, M., & Iacono, W. G. (2004). Genetic and environmental influences on antisocial behavior and alcohol dependence from adolescence to early adulthood. *Development and Psychopathology, 16,* 943–966.

Malt, B. C. (1995). Category coherence in cross-cultural perspective. *Cognitive Psychology, 29,* 85–148.

Man, M.-S., Mikheenko, Y., Braesicke, K., Cockcroft, G., & Roberts, A. C. (2012). Serotonin at the level of the amygdala and orbitofrontal cortex modulates distinct aspects of positive emotion in primates. *International Journal of Neuropsychopharmacology, 15,* 91–105.

Marcincuk, M. C., & Roland, P. S. (2002). Geriatric hearing loss: Understanding the causes and providing appropriate treatment. *Geriatrics Advisor, 57,* 44–59.

Marcus, B. H., Lewis, B. A., King, T. K., Albrecht, A. E., Hogan, J., Bock, B., … Abrams, D. B. (2003). Rationale, design, and baseline data for Commit to Quit II: An evaluation of the efficacy of moderate-intensity physical activity as an aid to smoking cessation in women. *Preventive Medicine, 36,* 479–492.

Marcus, D. K., & Miller, R. S. (2003). Sex differences in judgments of physical attractiveness: A social relations analysis. *Personality and Social Psychology Bulletin, 29,* 325–335.

Marcus, G. F. (1996). Why do children say "breaked"? *Current Directions in Psychological Science, 5,* 81–85.

Marelich, W. D., & Holt, T. (2006). Salvaging the self and romantic jealousy response. In A. P. Prescott (Ed.), *The concept of self in psychology* (pp. 167–181). Hauppauge, NY: Nova Science Publishers.

Margolskee, R. (1995). Receptor mechanisms in gustation. In R. L. Doty (Ed.), *Handbook of olfaction and gustation.* New York: Marcel Dekker.

Markman, A. B. (1999). *Knowledge representation.* Mahwah, NJ: Erlbaum.

Marsh, A. A., Finger, E. C., Schechter, J. C., Jurkowitz, I. T. N., Reid, M. E., & Blair, R. J. R. (2011). Adolescents with psychopathic traits report reductions in physiological responses to fear. *Journal of Child Psychology Psychiatry, 52,* 834–841.

Marsh, H. W., Craven, R. G., & Debus, R. (1991). Self-concepts of young children 5 to 8 years of age: Measurement and multidimensional structure. *Journal of Educational Psychology, 83,* 377–392.

Marshall, N. L. (2004). The quality of early child care and children's development. *Current Directions in Psychological Science, 13,* 165–168.

Marshall, S. P. (1995). *Schemas in problem solving.* Cambridge, England: Cambridge University Press.

Martin, A. L., Halket, E., Asmundson, G. J. G., Flora, D. B., & Katz, J. (2010). Posttraumatic stress symptoms and the diathesis-stress model of chronic pain and disability in patients undergoing major surgery. *The Clinical Journal of Pain, 26,* 518–527.

Martin, B. R. (1995). Marijuana. In F. E. Bloom & D. J. Kupfer (Eds.), *Psychopharmacology: The fourth generation* (pp. 1757–1765). New York: Raven Press.

Masaki, T., Chiba, S., Noguchi, H., Yasuda, T., Tobe, K., Suzuki, R., … Yoshimatsu, H. (2004). Obesity in insulin receptor substrate-2-deficient mice: Disrupted control of arcuate nucleus neuropeptides. *Obesity Research, 12,* 878–885.

Maslow, A. (1970). *Motivation and personality* (2nd ed.). New York: Harper & Row.

Maslow, A. (1971). *The farther reaches of human nature.* New York: Viking Press.

Mason, D. J., Humphreys, G. W., & Kent, L. (2004). Visual search, singleton capture, and the control of attentional set in ADHD. *Cognitive Neuropsychology, 21,* 661–687.

Mason, W. A. (1997). A historical review of the stress field. *Journal of Human Stress, 52,* 713–720.

Masters, W., & Johnson, V. (1966). *Human sexual response.* Boston: Little, Brown.

Mathy, F., & Feldman, J. (2012). What's magic about magic numbers? Chunking and data compression in short-term memory. *Cognition, 122,* 346–362.

Matsumoto, D. (1994). *People: Psychology from a cultural perspective.* Pacific Grove, CA: Brooks/Cole.

Matsumoto, D., Kudoh, J., Scherer, K., & Wallbott, H. (1988). Antecedents and reactions to emotions in the United States and Japan. *Journal of Cross-Cultural Psychology, 19,* 267–286.

Matthews, G., Zeidner, M., & Roberts, R. D. (2012). *Emotional intelligence 101.* New York: Springer Publishing.

Mattlar, C.-E. (2004). The Rorschach comprehensive system is reliable, valid, and cost-effective. In A. Andronikof (Ed.), *Rorschachiana XXVI: Yearbook of the international Rorschach society* (pp. 158–186). Ashland, OH: Hogrefe & Huber Publishers.

Mattson, S. N., Crocker, N., & Nguyen, T. T. (2011). Fetal alcohol spectrum disorders: Neuropsychological and behavioral features. *Neuropsychology Review, 21,* 81–101.

Matusov, E., & Hayes, R. (2000). Sociocultural critique of Piaget and Vygotsky. *New Ideas in Psychology, 18,* 215–239.

Mawhinney, V. T., Boston, D. E., Loaws, O. R., Blumenfeld, G. T., & Hopkins, B. L. (1971). A comparison of students' studying behavior produced by daily, weekly, and three-week testing schedules. *Journal of Applied Behavior Analysis, 4,* 257–264.

Maye, J., Weiss, D. J., & Aslin, R. N. (2008). Statistical phonetic learning in infants: Facilitation and feature generalization. *Developmental Science, 11,* 122–134.

Mayer, E. L. (2002). Freud and Jung: The boundaried mind and the radically connected mind. *Journal of Analytical Psychology, 47,* 91–99.

Mayer, R. E. (2012). Information processing. In K. R. Harris, S. Graham, T. Urdan, C. McCormick, G. M. Sinatra, & J. Sweller (Eds.), *APA educational psychology handbook, Vol 1: Theories, constructs, and critical issues* (pp. 85–99). Washington, DC: American Psychological Association.

Maynard, A. E. (2002). Cultural teaching: The development of teaching skills in Maya sibling interactions. *Child Development, 73,* 969–982.

Mayrhauser, R. T. V. (2002). The mental testing community and validity: A prehistory. In W. E. Pickren & D. A. Dewsbury (Eds.), *Evolving perspectives on the history of psychology* (pp. 303–324). Washington, DC: American Psychological Association.

McAdams, D. P. (1988). Personal needs and personal relationships. In *Handbook of personal relationships: Theory, research and intervention* (pp. 7–22). New York: Wiley.

McAndrew, F. T. (2002). New evolutionary perspectives on altruism: Multilevel-selection and costly-signaling theories. *Current Directions in Psychological Science, 11,* 79–82.

McBride, R. E., Xiang, P., & Wittenburg, D. (2002). Dispositions toward critical thinking: The preservice teacher's perspective. *Teachers & Teaching: Theory & Practice, 8,* 29–40.

McCabe, R., & Quayle, E. (2002). Knowing your own mind. *Psychologist, 15,* 14–16.

McCann, S. J. H. (1999). Threatening times and fluctuations in American church memberships. *Personality and Social Psychology Bulletin, 25,* 325–336.

McCarthy, G. (1995). Functional neuroimaging of memory. *The Neuroscientist, 1,* 155–163.

McCarthy, R. E. (1992). *Secrets of Hollywood: Special effects.* Stoneham, MA: Focal Press.

McCaul, K. D., & Malott, J. (1984). Distraction and coping with pain. *Psychological Bulletin, 95,* 516–533.

McClain, C. S., Rosenfeld, B., & Breitbart, W. (2003). The influence of spirituality on end-of-life despair among terminally ill cancer patients. *Lancet, 361,* 1603–1607.

McClelland, D. C. (1985). *Human motivation.* Glenview, IL: Scott, Foresman.

McClelland, D. C. (1995). Achievement motivation in relation to achievement-related recall, performance, and urine flow, a marker associated with release of vasopressin. *Motivation and Emotion, 19,* 59–76.

McClelland, J. L., & Rumelhart, D. E. (1981). An interactive activation model of context effects in letter perception: Part I. An account of basic findings. *Psychological Review, 102,* 375–407.

McClenon, J. (2011). Evolutionary Theories of Schizophrenia: An Experience-Centered Review. *Journal of Mind and Behavior, 32,* 135–150.

McClintock, M. K. (1971). Menstrual synchrony and suppression. *Nature, 229,* 244–245.

McConnell, A. R., & Fazio, R. H. (1996). Women as men and people: Effects of gender-marked language. *Personality and Social Psychology Bulletin, 22,* 1004–1013.

McCoy, J. G., & Strecker, R. E. (2011). The cognitive cost of sleep lost. *Neurobiology of Learning and Memory, 96,* 564–582.

McCrae, R. R. (1994). Openness to experience: Expanding the boundaries of Factor V. European *Journal of Personality, 13,* 39–55.

McCrae, R. R. (1996). Social consequences of experiential openness. *Psychological Bulletin, 52,* 509–516.

McCrae, R. R. (2005). Personality structure. In V. J. Derlega, B. A. Winstead, & W. H. Jones (Eds.), *Personality: Contemporary theory and research* (3rd ed., pp. 192–216). Belmont, CA: Thomson Wadsworth.

McCrae, R. R., & Costa, P. T., Jr. (1987). Validation of a five-factor model of personality across instruments and observers. *Journal of Personality and Social Psychology, 52,* 81–90.

McCrae, R. R., & Costa, P. T., Jr. (1997). Personality structure as a human universal. *American Psychologist, 52,* 509–516.

McCrae, R. R., Costa, P. T., Jr., Lirna, M. P. de, Simoes, A., Ostendorf, F., Angleitner, A., ... Piedmont, R. L. (1999). Age differences in personality across the adult life span: Parallels in five cultures. Developmental Psychology, 35, 466–477.

McCrae, R. R., & John, O. P. (1992). An introduction to the five-factor model and its applications. *Journal of Personality, 60,* 175–215.

McCrae, R. R., Jr, P. T. C., Pilar, G. H. del, Rolland, J. P., & Parker, W. D. (1998). Cross-cultural assessment of the five-factor model: The revised NEO personality inventory. *Journal of Cross-Cultural Psychology, 29,* 171–188.

McCrae, R. R., Kurtz, J. E., Yamagata, S., & Terracciano, A. (2011). Internal consistency, retest reliability, and their implications for personality scale validity. *Personality and Social Psychology Review, 15,* 28–50.

McCready, D. (1999). *The moon illusion explained.* Retrieved from miles to illusion researchers and placed on the website http://facstaff.uww.edu/mccreadd/. Revised December 2002

McCullough, M. E., Hoyt, W. T., Larson, D. B., Koenig, H. G., & Thoresen, C. E. (2000). Religious involvement and mortality: A meta-analytic review. *Health Psychology, 19,* 211–222.

McCullough, M. E., & Laurenceau, J.-P. (2005). Religiousness and the trajectory of self-rated health across adulthood. *Personality and Social Psychology Bulletin, 31,* 560–573.

McDougall, I., Brown, F. H., & Fleagle, J. G. (2005). Stratigraphic placement and age of modern humans from Kibish, Ethiopia. *Nature, 433,* 733–736.

McDougall, W. (1908). *Introduction to social psychology.* London: Methuen & Co.

McGarry-Roberts, P. A., Stelmack, R. M., & Campbell, K. B. (1992). Intelligence, reaction time, and event-related potentials. *Intelligence, 16,* 289–313.

McGee, M. T. (1989). *Beyond ballyhoo: Motion picture promotion and gimmicks.* Jefferson, NC: McFarland.

McGlone, J. (1978). Sex differences in functional brain asymmetry. *Cortex, 14,* 122–128.

McGrath, R. E., & Carroll, J. E. (2012). The current status of "projective" tests." In H. Cooper, P. M. Camic, D. L. Long, A. T. Panter, D. Rindskopf, & K. J. Sher (Eds.), *APA handbook of research methods in psychology, Vol 1: Foundations, planning, measures, and psychometrics* (pp. 329–348). Washington, DC: American Psychological Association.

McGue, M., Bouchard, T. J., Jr., Iacono, W. G., & Lykken, D. T. (1993). Behavioral genetics of cognitive ability: A life-span perspective. In G. E. McClearn (Ed.), *Nature, nurture and psychology.* Washington, DC: American Psychological Association.

McGuire, W. J. (1999). *Constructing social psychology: Creative and critical processes.* Cambridge: Cambridge University Press.

McHugh, P. R., Lief, H. I., Freyd, P. P., & Fetkewicz, J. M. (2004). From refusal to reconciliation: Family relationships after an accusation based on recovered memories. *Journal of Nervous & Mental Disease, 192,* 525–531.

McKinnon, J. W. (1976). The college student and formal operations. In J. W. Renner, D. G. Stafford, A. E. Lawson, J. W. McKinnon, F. E. Friot, & D. H. Kellog (Eds.), *Research training and learning with the Piaget model* (pp. 110–129). Norman, OK: University of Oklahoma Press.

McLean, J. H., & Shipley, M. T. (1992). Neuroanatomical substrates of olfaction. In *Science of olfaction* (pp. 126–171). New York: Springer-Verlag.

McLeod, P., Plunkett, K., & Rolls, E. T. (2006). The attraction of parallel distributed processing for modelling cognition. In J. L. Bermudez (Ed.), *Philosophy of psychology: Contemporary readings* (pp. 182–202). New York: Routledge/Taylor & Francis Group.

McManis, M. H., Kagan, J., Snidman, N. C., & Woodward, S. A. (2002). EEG asymmetry, power, and temperament in children. *Developmental Psychobiology, 41,* 169–177.

McMillan, B., Sherlock, K., & Conner, M. (2003). Expanding the traditional user versus non-user dichotomy amongst ecstasy users. *Journal of Community & Applied Social Psychology, 13,* 15–28.

McNamara, P., McLaren, D., Smith, D., Brown, A., & Stickgold, R. (2005). A "Jekyll and Hyde" within: Aggressive versus friendly interactions in REM and non-REM dreams. *Psychological Science, 16,* 130–136.

McNaughton, B. L., Barnes, C. A., Battaglia, F. P., Bower, M. R., Cowen, S. L., Ekstrom, A. D., ... Sutherland, G. R. (2003). Off-line reprocessing of recent memory and its role in memory consolidation: A progress report. In R. Stickgold (Ed.), *Sleep and brain plasticity* (pp. 225–246). Oxford, UK: Oxford University Press.

McNulty, J. K., & Fincham, F. D. (2012). Beyond positive psychology? Toward a contextual view of psychological processes and well-being. *American Psychologist, 67,* 101–110.

Mebert, C., & Michel, G. (1980). Handedness in artists. In J. Herron (Ed.), *Neuropsychology of left handedness.* New York: Academic Press.

Medin, D. L. (1989). Concepts and conceptual structure. *American psychologist, 44,* 1469–1481.

Mednick, S. A. (1958). A learning theory approach to research in schizophrenia. *Psychological Bulletin, 55,* 316–327.

Mednick, S. A., Gabrielli, W. F., & Hutchings, B. (1987). Genetic factors in the etiology of criminal behavior. In S. A. Stacks (Ed.), *The causes of crime: New biological approaches* (pp. 267–291). Cambridge, MA: Cambridge University Press.

Medvec, V. H., Madley, S. F., & Gilovich, T. (1995). When less is more: Counterfactual thinking and satisfaction among Olympic medallists. *Journal of Personality and Social Psychology, 69,* 603–610.

Meichenbaum, D., & Turk, D. (1976). The cognitive-behavioral management of anxiety, anger, and pain. In P. O. Davidson (Ed.), *The behavioral management of anxiety, depression and pain* (pp. 1–34). New York: Brunner/Mazel.

Meikle, L., McMullen, J. R., Sherwood, M. C., Lader, A. S., Walker, V., Chan, J. A., & Kwiatkowski, D. J. (2005). A mouse model of cardiac rhabdomyoma generated by loss of Tsc1 in ventricular myocytes. *Human Molecular Genetics, 14,* 429–435.

Meisel, S., Kutz, I., & Dayan, K. (1991). Effect of Iraqi missile war on incidence of acute myocardial infarction and sudden death in Israeli civilians. *Lancet, 338,* 660–661.

Meltzoff, A. N., & Moore, M. K. (1989). Imitation in newborn infants: Exploring the range of gestures imitated and the underlying mechanisms. *Developmental Psychology, 25,* 954–962.

Melzack, R. (1973). *The puzzle of pain.* New York: Basic Books.

Melzack, R. (1986). Neurophysiological foundations of pain. In *The psychology of pain* (pp. 1–24). New York: Raven Press.

Melzack, R. (1992). Phantom limbs. *Scientific American, 266,* 120–126.

Melzack, R., & Wall, P. D. (1982a). *The challenge of pain.* Harmondsworth, England: Penguin.

Melzack, R., & Wall, P. D. (1982b). Pain mechanisms: A new theory. *Science, 13,* 971–979.

Menard, A. D., & Cabrera, C. (2011). "Whatever the approach, Tab B still fits into Slot A": Twenty years of sex scripts in romance novels. *Sexuality & Culture: An Interdisciplinary Quarterly, 15,* 240–255.

Mendoza, J. E., & Foundas, A. L. (2008). *Clinical neuroanatomy: A neurobehavioral approach.* New York: Springer.

Menzel, R., & Backhaus, W. (1989). Color vision in honey bees: Phenomena and physiological mechanisms. In D. G. Stavenga & R. C. Hardie (Eds.), *Facets of vision* (pp. 281–297). Berlin: Springer-Verlag.

Mercer, J. (2006). *Understanding attachment: Parenting, child care, and emotional development.* Westport, CT: Praeger.

Mercier, C., Aballea, A., Vargas, C. D., Paillard, J., & Sirigu, A. (2008). Vision without proprioception modulates cortico-spinal excitability during hand motor imagery. *Cerebral Cortex, 18,* 272–277.

Merikle, P. M., & Skanes, H. E. (1992). Subliminal self-help audiotapes: A search for placebo effects. *Journal of Applied Psychology, 77,* 772–776.

Mesquita, B., & Frijda, N. (1992). Cultural variations in emotions: A review. *Psychological Bulletin, 112,* 179–204.

Michael, R., Gagnon, J., Laumann, E., & Kolata, G. (1994). *Sex in America.* New York: Little, Brown.

Michaelidou, N., Christodoulides, G., & Torova, K. (2012). Determinants of healthy eating: A cross-national study on motives and barriers. *International Journal of Consumer Studies, 36,* 17–22.

Middlebrooks, J. C., & Green, D. M. (1991). Sound locilzation by human listeners. *Annual Review of Psychology, 42,* 135–159.

Miguens, M., Olmo, N. D., Higuera-Matas, A., Torres, I., Garcia-Lecumberri, C., & Ambrosio, E. (2008). Glutamate and aspartate levels in the nucleus accumbens during cocaine self-administration and extinction: A time course microdialysis study. *Psychopharmacology, 196,* 303–313.

Mihara, T., Nakashima, M., Kuroiwa, A., Akitake, Y., Ono, K., Hosokawa, M., ... Takahashi, M. (2008). Natural killer cells of Parkinson's disease patients are set up for activation: A possible role for innate immunity in the pathogenesis of this. *Parkinsonism & Related Disorders, 14*, 46–51.

Mikko, H., Hakola, T., Kandolin, I., Sallinen, M., Virkkala, J., Bonnefond, A., & Mutanen, P. (2006). A controlled intervention study on the effects of a very rapidly forward rotating shift system on sleep-wakefulness and well-being among young and elderly shift workers. *International Journal of Psychophysiology, 59*, 70–79.

Mikulincer, M., & Erev, I. (1991). Attachment style and the structure of romantic love. *British Journal of Social Psychology, 30*, 273–291.

Milgram, S. (1963). Behavioral study of obedience. *Journal of Abnormal and Social Psychology, 67*, 371–378.

Milgram, S. (1965). Some conditions of obedience and disobedience to authority. *Human Relations, 18*, 57–76.

Milgram, S. (1974). *Obedience to authority: An experimental view.* New York: Harper & Row.

Miller, C., & Swift, K. (1991). *Words and women.* New York: HarperCollins.

Miller, E. M. (1994). Intelligence and brain myelination: A hypothesis. *Personality and Individual Differences, 17*, 803–832.

Miller, G. A. (1956). The magical number seven, plus or minus two: Some limits on our capacity to process information. *Psychological Review, 63*, 81–97.

Miller, G. A., & Gildea, P. M. (1987). How children learn words. *Scientific American, 257*, 94–99.

Miller, J. G. (1984). Culture and the development of everyday social explanation. *Journal of Personality and Social Psychology, 46*, 961–978.

Miller, J. G. (2007). Cultural psychology of moral development. In S. Kitayama & D. Cohen (Eds.), *Handbook of cultural psychology* (pp. 477–499). New York: Guilford Press.

Miller, L. C., Berg, J. H., & Archer, R. L. (1983). Openers: Individuals who elicit intimate self-disclosure. *Journal of Personality and Social Psychology, 44*, 1234–1244.

Miller, N. E. (1985). The value of behavior research on animals. *American Psychologist, 40*, 423–440.

Miller, R. R., & Grace, R. C. (2003). Conditioning and learning. In *Handbook of psychology: Experimental psychology* (Vol. 4, pp. 357–397). New York: John Wiley & Sons.

Miller, R. S. (1997). We always hurt the ones we love: Aversive interactions in close relationships. In *Aversive interpersonal behaviors* (pp. 11–29). New York: Plenum Press.

Miller, W. I. (1997). *The anatomy of disgust.* Cambridge, MA: Harvard University Press.

Mills, S. L., & Catania, K. C. (2004). Identification of retinal neurons in a regressive rodent eye (the naked mole-rat). *Visual Neuroscience, 21*, 107–117.

Milner, B., Corkin, S., & Teuber, H. L. (1968). Further analysis of the hippocampal amnesic syndrome: 14-Year follow-up study of H. M. *Neuropsychologia, 6*, 317–338.

Mineka, S., & Oehlberg, K. (2008). The relevance of recent developments in classical conditioning to understanding the etiology and maintenance of anxiety disorders. *Acta Psychologica, 127*, 567–580.

Mineka, S., & Öhman, A. (2002). Phobias and preparedness: The selective, automatic, and encapsulated nature of fear. *Biological Psychiatry, 52*, 927–937.

Minton, H. (2000). Psychology and gender at the turn of the century. *American Psychologist, 55*, 613–615.

Minturn, L., Grosse, M., & Haider, S. (1969). Cultural patterning of sexual beliefs and behavior. *Ethnology, 8*, 301–313.

Mintzer, M. Z., & Griffiths, R. R. (2003). Triazolam-amphetamine interaction: Dissociation of effects on memory versus arousal. *Journal of Psychopharmacology, 17*, 17–29.

Mischel, W. (1968). *Personality and assessment.* New York: Wiley.

Mischel, W. (1984). Convergences and challenges in the search for consistency. *American Psychologist, 39*, 351–364.

Mischel, W., Cantor, N., & Feldman, S. (1996). Principles of self-regulation: The nature of willpower and self-control. In *Social psychology: Handbook of basic principles* (pp. 329–360). New York: Guilford.

Miserandino, M. (1991). Memory and the seven dwarfs. *Teaching of Psychology, 18*, 169–171.

Mistry, J., & Rogoff, B. (1994). Remembering in a cultural context. In W. J. Lonner & R. S. Malpass (Eds.), *Psychology and Culture.* Boston, MA: Allyn & Bacon.

Mita, T. H., Dermer, M., & Knight, J. (1977). Reversed facial images and the mere-exposure hypothesis. *Journal of Personality and Social Psychology, 35*, 597–601.

Mitchell, B. A. (2006). *The boomerang age: Transitions to adulthood in families.* New Brunswick, NJ: Aldine Transaction.

Mitchell, C. M., Novins, D. K., & Holmes, T. (1999). Marijuana use among American Indian adolescents: A growth curve analysis from ages 14 through 20 years. *Journal of the American Academy of Child & Adolescent Psychiatry, 38*, 72–78.

Mitchell, D. E. (1980). The influence of early visual experience on visual perception. In C. S. Harris (Ed.), *Visual coding and adaptability.* Hillsdale, NJ: Erlbaum.

Moeller, A. T., & Steel, H. R. (2002). Clinically significant change after cognitive restructuring for adult survivors of childhood sexual abuse. *Journal of Rational-Emotive & Cognitive Behavior Therapy, 20*, 49–64.

Mogg, K., & Bradley, B. P. (1999). Orienting of attention to threatening facial expressions presented under conditions of restricted awareness. *Cognition and Emotion, 12*, 713–740.

Mokdad, A., Serdula, M., Dietz, W., Bowman, B., Marks, J., & Koplan, J. (1999). The spread of obesity epidemic in the United States, 1991–1998. *Journal of the American Medical Association, 282*, 1519–1522.

Moll, N. M., Rietsch, A. M., Thomas, S., Ransohoff, A. J., Lee, J.-C., Fox, R., ... Fisher, E. (2011). Multiple sclerosis normal-appearing white matter: Pathology-imaging correlations. *Annals of Neurology, 70*, 764–773.

Mollon, J. D. (1990). The club-sandwich mystery. *Nature, 343*, 16–17.

Mondloch, C. J., Lewis, T. L., Budreau, D. R., Maurer, D., Dannemiller, J. L., Stephens, B. R., & Kleiner-Gathercoal, K. A. (1999). Face perception during early infancy. *Psychological Science, 10*, 419–422.

Monsour, M. (1997). Communication and cross-sex friendship across the lifecycle: A review of the literature. *Communication Yearbook, 20*, 375–414.

Monteith, M. J. (1993). Self-regulation of prejudiced responses: Implications for progress in prejudice-reduction efforts. *Journal of Personality and Social Psychology, 65*, 469–485.

Montgomery, T. R. (2008). The dysmorphology examination. In P. J. Accardo (Ed.), *Capute and Accardo's Neurodevelopmental disabilities in infancy and childhood: Vol 1: Neurodevelopmental diagnosis and treatment* (pp. 311–320). Baltimore, MD: Paul H Brookes Publishing.

Montoya, R. M., & Horton, R. S. (2004). On the importance of cognitive evaluation as a determinant of interpersonal attraction. *Journal of Personality and Social Psychology, 86*, 696–712.

Moon, A., & Cho, I. (2012). Psychology of Asian American older adults: Status, challenges, and strengths. In E. C. Chang & C. A. Downey (Eds.), *Handbook of race and development in mental health* (pp. 189–206). New York: Springer Science + Business Media.

Moore, T. E. (1995). Subliminal self-help auditory tapes: An empirical test of perceptual consequences. *Canadian Journal of Behavioural Science, 27*, 9–20.

Moreira, P. I., Santos, M. S., Oliveira, C. R., Shenk, J. C., Nunomura, A., Smith, M. A., ... Perry, G. (2008). Alzheimer disease and the role of free radicals in the pathogenesis of the disease. *CNS & Neurological Disorders–Drug Targets, 7*, 3–10.

Mori, R. C., Telles, M. M., Guimaraes, R. B., Novo, N. F., Juliano, Y., Nascimento, C. M., & Ribeiro, E. B. (2004). Feeding induced by increasing doses of neuropeptide Y: Dual effect on hypothalamic serotonin release in normal rats. *Nutritional Neuroscience, 7*, 235–239.

Morikawa, K. (2003). An application of the Mueller-Lyer illusion. *Perception, 32*, 121–123.

Morin, C. M., Rodrigue, S., & Ivers, H. (2003). Role of stress, arousal, and coping skills in primary insomnia. *Psychosomatic Medicine, 65*, 259–267.

Morone, N. E., Greco, C. M., & Weiner, D. K. (2008). Mindfulness meditation for the treatment of chronic low back pain in older adults: A randomized controlled pilot study. *Pain, 134*, 310–319.

Morris, C. D., Bransford, J. D., & Franks, J. J. (1977). Levels of processing versus transfer appropriate processing. *Journal of Verbal Learning and Verbal Behavior, 16*, 519–533.

Morris, M. W., & Larrick, R. P. (1995). When one cause casts doubt on another: A normative analysis of discounting in causal attribution. *Psychological Review, 102*, 331–355.

Moses, L. J., & Chandler, M. J. (1992). Traveler's guide to children's theories of mind. *Psychological Inquiry, 3*, 286–301.

Moses, P., & Stiles, J. (2002). The lesion methodology: Contrasting views from adult and child studies. *Developmental Psychobiology, 40*, 266–277.

Moss, E., Bureau, J.-F., Cyr, C., Mongeau, C., & Laurent, S. D. (2004). Correlates of attachment at age 3: Construct validity of the preschool attachment classification system. *Developmental Psychology, 40*, 323–334.

Mouritsen, H., & Frost, B. J. (2002). Virtual migration in tethered flying monarch butterflies reveals their orientation mechanisms. *Proc. Natl. Acad. Sci. USA, 99*, 10162–10166.

Moynihan, J., & Stevens, S. (2001). Mechanisms of stress-induced modulation of immunity in animals. In R. Ader, D. Felten, & N. Cohen (Eds.), *Psychoneuroimmunology* (3rd ed., Vol. 2, pp. 227–250). San Diego, CA: Academic Press.

Mozell, M. M., Smith, B. P., Smith, P. E., Sullivan, R. L., & Swender, P. (1969). Nasal chemoreception in flavor identification. *Archives of Otolaryngology, 90*, 131–137.

Mroczek, D. K., & Spiro, A. (2005). Change in life satisfaction during adulthood: Findings from the Veterans Affairs Normative Aging Study. *Journal of Personality and Social Psychology, 88*, 189–202.

Murphy, P. L., & Miller, C. T. (1997). Postdecisional dissonance and the commodified self-concept: A cross-cultural examination. *Personality and Social Psychology Bulletin, 23*, 50–62.

Murray, G. K., Corlett, P. R., Clark, L., Pessiglione, M., Blackwell, A. D., Honey, G., ... Fletcher, P. C. (2008). How dopamine dysregulation leads to psychotic symptoms. Abnormal mesolimbic and mesostriatal prediction error signalling in psychosis. *Molecular Psychiatry, 13*, 239.

Murray, G. K., Veijola, J., Moilanen, K., Miettunen, J., Glahn, D. C., Cannon, T. D., ... Isohanni, M. (2006). Infant motor decleopment is associated with adult cognitive categorisation in a logitudinal birth cohort study. *Journal of Child Psychology and Psychiatry, 47*, 25–29.

Murray, H. A. (1938). *Explorations in personality: A clinical and experimental study of fifty men of college age, by the workers at the Harvard Psychological Clinic.* New York: Oxford University Press.

Murray, H. A. (1948). *Assessment of men.* New York: Science Editions.

Murray, S. L., & Holmes, J. G. (1997). A leap of faith? Positive illusions in romantic relationships. *Personality and Social Psychology Bulletin, 23*, 586–604.

Murray, S. L., Holmes, J. G., & Griffin, D. W. (1996). The benefits of positive illusions: Idealization and the construction of satisfaction in close relationships. *Journal of Personality and Social Psychology, 70*, 78–98.

Musikantow, R. (2011). Thinking in circles: Power and responsibility in hypnosis. *American Journal of Clinical Hypnosis, 54*, 83–85.

Myers, A. M., & Rothblum, E. D. (2005). Coping with prejudice and discrimination based on weight. In J. L. Chin (Ed.), *The psychology of prejudice and discrimination: Disability, religion, physique, and other traits, Vol. 4. Race and ethnicity in psychology* (pp. 112–134). Westport, CT: Praeger/Greenwood.

Myers, D., & Diener, E. (1995). Who is happy? *Psychological Science, 6,* 10–19.

N

Nader, K., & Einarsson, E. O. (2010). Memory reconsolidation: An update. *Annals of the New York Academy of Sciences, 1191,* 27–41.

Nair, K. U., & Ramnarayan, S. (2000). Individual differences in need for cognition and complex problem solving. *Journal of Research in Personality, 34,* 305–328.

Nakajima, M., Nakajima, S., & Imada, H. (2000). General learned irrelevance and its prevention. *Learning and Motivation, 30,* 265–280.

Nakiyingi, J. S., Bracher, M., Whitworth, J. A. G., Ruberantwari, A., Busingye, J., Mbulaiteye, S. M., & Zaba, B. (2003). *Child survival in relation to mother's HIV infection and survival: Evidence from a Ugandan cohort study. AIDS, 17,* 1827–1834.

Nantel-Vivier, A., & Pihl, R. O. (2008). Biological vulnerability to depression. In J. R. Z. Abela & B. L. Hankin (Eds.), *Handbook of depression in children and adolescents* (pp. 103–123). New York: Guilford Press.

Nardi, P. M., & Sherrod, D. (1994). Friendship in the lives of gay men and lesbians. *Journal of Social and Personal Relationships, 11,* 185–199.

Narikiyo, T. A., & Kameoka, V. A. (1992). Attributions of mental illness and judgments about help seeking among Japanese-American and white American students. *Journal of Counseling Psychology, 39,* 363–369.

Narrow, W. E., Rae, D. S., Robins, L. N., & Regier, D. A. (2002). Revised prevalence based estimates of mental disorders in the United States: Using a clinical signficance criterion to reconcile 2 surveys' estimates. *Archives of General Psychiatry, 59,* 115–123.

Nathan, P. (1982). *The nervous system* (2nd ed.). Oxford, UK: Oxford University Press.

National Opinion Research Center. (2003). *General Social Survey.* Retrieved from www.norc.org/

National Sleep Foundation. (2002). *2001 Sleep in America Poll.* Retrieved from http://www.sleepfoundation.org/atf/cf/%7BF6BF2668-A1B4-4FE8-8D1A-A5D39340D9CB%7D/2001poll.pdf

Nee, D. E., Berman, M. G., Moore, K. S., & Jonides, J. (2008). Neuroscientific evidence about the distinction between short- and long-term memory. *Current Directions in Psychological Science, 17,* 102–106.

Neely, C. L. (2008). Reviews of Indian feminisms: Law, patriarchies, and violence in India and body evidence: Intimate violence against South Asian women in America. *Violence Against Women, 14,* 496–501.

Neighbors, H. W., Hudson, D. L., & Bullard, K. M. (2012). The challenge of understanding the mental health of African Americans: The risks and rewards of segregation, support, and John Henryism. In C. A. Downey (Ed.), *Handbook of race and development in mental health* (pp. 45–66). New York: Springer Science + Business Media.

Neisser, U., Boodoo, G., Jr, T. J. B., Boykin, A. W., Brody, N., Ceci, S. J., ... Urbina, S. (1996). Intelligence: Knowns and unknowns. *American Psychologist, 51,* 77–101.

Neisser, U., & Harsch, N. (1992). Phantom flashbulbs: False recollections of hearing the news about Challenger. In E. Winograd & U. Neisser (Eds.), *Affect and accuracy in recall: Studies of "flashbulb" memories* (pp. 9–31). New York: Cambridge University Press.

Nelson, K., Skwerer, D. P., Goldman, G. S., Henseler, S., Presler, N., & Walkenfeld, F. F. (2003). Entering a community of minds: An experiential approach to "theory of mind." *Human Development, 46,* 24–46.

Nelson, L., Badger, S., & Wu, B. (2004). The influence of culture in emerging adulthood: Perspectives of Chinese college students. *International Journal of Behavioral Development, 28,* 26–36.

Nestor, P. G., & Schutt, R. K. (2012). *Research methods in psychology: Investigating human behavior.* Thousand Oaks, CA: Sage.

Neuner, T., Schmid, R., Wolfersdorf, M., & Spiessl, H. (2008). Predicting inpatient suicides and suicide attempts by using clinical routine data? *General Hospital Psychiatry, 30,* 324–330.

Newberg, A. B., D'Aquili, E. G., & Rause, V. (2001). *Why God won't go away: Brain science and the biology of belief.* New York: Ballantine Books.

Newcombe, N. S., Drummey, A. B., Fox, N. A., Lie, E., & Ottinger-Alberts, W. (2000). Remembering early childhood: How much, how, and why (or why not). *Current Directions in Psychological Science, 9,* 55–58.

Newman, S. D., Just, M. A., Keller, T. A., Roth, J., & Carpenter, P. A. (2003). Differential effects of syntactic and semantic processing on the subregions of Broca's area. *Cognitive Brain Research, 16,* 297–307.

Newport, F., & Strausberg, M. (2001). Americans' belief in psychic and paranormal phenomena is up over last decade. *The Gallup Organization.* Retrieved from http://www.gallup.com/poll/4483/Americans-Belief-Psychic-Paranormal-Phenomena-Over-Last-Decade.aspx)

Neyens, D. M., & Boyle, L. N. (2008). The influence of driver distraction on the severity of injuries sustained by teenage drivers and their passengers. *Accident Analysis & Prevention, 40,* 254–259.

Nicholls, J. G., Martin, A. R., Fuchs, P. A., Brown, D. A., Diamond, M. E., & Weisblat, D. A. (2012). *From neuron to brain* (5th ed.). Sunderland, MA: Sinauer Associates.

Nicholson, A. N., Pascoe, P. A., Spencer, M. B., Stone, B. M., Roehis, T., & Roth, T. (1986). Sleep after transmeridian flights. *Lancet, 2,* 1205–1208.

Nicholson, I. A. M. (2002). Gordon Allport, character, and the "Culture of Personality." In W. E. Pickren & D. A. Dewsbury (Eds.), *Evolving perspectives on the history of psychology* (pp. 324–345). Washington, DC: American Psychological Association.

Nickell, J. A. (1996). Fantasy proneness in the thirteen cases of alleged encounters in John Mack's Abduction. *Skeptical Inquirer, 54,* 18–20.

Nickerson, C., Schwarz, N., Diener, E., & Kahneman, D. (2003). Zeroing on the dark side of the American dream: A closer look at the negative consequences of the goal for financial success. *Psychological Science, 41,* 531–536.

Nickerson, R. S. (2000). Null hypothesis significance testing: A review of an old continuing controversy. *Psychological Methods, 5,* 241–301.

Nickerson, R. S., & Adams, M. J. (1979). Long-term memory for a common object. Cognitive Psychology, 11, 287–307.

Nicolaus, L. K., & Nellis, D. W. (1987). The first evaluation of the use of conditioned taste aversion to control predation by mongooses upon eggs. Applied Animal Behaviour Science, 17, 329–346.

Nietzel, M. T., Speltz, M. L., McCauley, E. A., & Bernstein, D. A. (1998). Abnormal psychology. Boston, MA: Allyn & Bacon.

Nieuwenhuizen, A. G., & Rutters, F. (2008). The hypothalamic-pituitary-adrenal-axis in the regulation of energy balance. Physiology & Behavior, 94, 169–177.

Nijhawan, R. (1991). Three-dimensional Müeller-Lyer illusion. Perception & Psychophysics, 49, 333–341.

Nisbet, M. (1998). Psychic telephone networks profit on yearning, gullibility. The Skeptical Inquirer, 5–6.

Nisbett, R. (1995). Race, IQ, and scientism. In The Bell Curve Wars: Race, Intelligence and the Future of America (pp. 36–57). New York: Basic Books.

Nisbett, R. E., Aronson, J., Blair, C., Dickens, W., Flynn, J., Halpern, D. F., & Turkheimer, E. (2012). Group differences in IQ are best understood as environmental in orgin. American Psychologist, 67, 503–504.

Nisbett, R. E., & Wilson, T. D. (1977). Telling more than we can know: Verbal reports on mental processes. Psychological Review, 84, 231–259.

Noben-Trauth, K., Zheng, Q. Y., & Johnson, K. R. (2003). Association of Cadherin 23 with polygenic inheritance and genetic modification of sensorineural hearing loss. Nature Genetics, 35, 21–23.

Nogrady, H., McConkey, K., & Perry, C. (1985). Enhancing visual memory: Trying hypnosis, trying imagination, and trying again. Journal of Abnormal Psychology, 94, 195–204.

Norenzayan, A., & Nisbett, R. E. (2000). Culture and causal cognition. Current Directions in Psychological Science, 9, 132–135.

Norman, G. J., Hawkley, L. C., Cole, S. W., Berntson, G. G., & Cacioppo, J. T. (2012). Social neuroscience: The social brain, oxytocin, and health. Social Neuroscience, 7, 18–29.

Norman, K. A., Newman, E. L., & Detre, G. (2007). A neural network model of retrieval-induced forgetting. Psychological Review, 114, 887–953.

Norwich, K. H. (1987). On the theory of Weber fractions. Perception & Psychophysics, 42, 286–298.

Nyberg, I., Marklund, P., Persson, J., Cabeza, R., Forkstam, C., Petersson, K. M., & Ingvar, M. (2003). Common prefrontal activations during working memory, episodic memory. Neuropsychologia, 41, 371–377.

Nygard, L. (2004). Responses of persons with dementia to challenges in daily activities: A synthesis of findings from empirical studies. American Journal of Occupational Therapy, 58, 435–445.

O

O'Connor, K. J., Cunningham, W. A., Funayama, E. S., Gatenby, J. C., Gore, J. C., & Banaji, M. R. (2000). Performance on indirect measures of race evaluation predicts amygdala activation. Journal of Cognitive Neuroscience, 12, 729–738.

O'Connor, M., Lebowitz, B. K., Ly, J., Panizzon, M. S., Elkin-Frankston, S., Dey, S., ... Pearlman, C. (2008). A dissociation between anterograde and retrograde amnesia after treatment with electroconvulsive therapy: A naturalistic investigation. Journal of ECT, 24, 146–151.

O'Connor, P. (1997). Overtraining and staleness. In W. Morgan (Ed.), Physical Activity and Mental Health (pp. 145–160). Washington, DC: Taylor & Francis.

O'Farrell, T., & Murphy, C. M. (1995). Marital violence before and after alcoholism treatment. Journal of Consulting and Clinical Psychology, 63, 256–262.

O'Keeffe, F. E., Scott, S. A., Tyers, P., O'Keeffe, G. W., Dalley, J. W., Zufferey, R., & Caldwell, M. A. (2008). Induction of A9 dopaminergic neurons from neural stem cells improves motor function in an animal model of Parkinson's disease. Brain: A Journal of Neurology, 131, 630–641.

O'Leary, K. D., Vivian, D., & Malone, J. (1992). Assessment of physical aggression in marriage: The need for multimodal assessment. Behavioral Research and Therapy, 14, 1–10.

O'Neill, O. A., & O'Reilly, C. A. (2011). Reducing the backlash effect: Self-monitoring and women's promotions. Journal of Occupational and Organizational Psychology, 84, 825–832.

O'Sullivan, M. (2005). Emotional intelligence and deception detection: Why most people can't "read" others, but a few can. In R. S. Feldman & S. Robert (Eds.), Applications of Nonverbal Communication (pp. 215–253). Mahwah, NJ: Lawrence Erlbaum.

Oatley, K., & Jenkins, J. (1996). Understanding emotions. Cambridge, MA: Blackwell.

Oberman, L. M., Pineda, J. A., & Ramachandran, V. S. (2007). The human mirror neuron system: A link between action observation and social skills. Social Cognitive and Affective Neuroscience, 2, 62–66.

Oda, R. (2001). Lemur vocal communication and the origin of human language. In T. Matsuzawa (Ed.), Primate Origins of Human Cognition and Behavior (pp. 115–134). New York: Springer-Verlag.

Oehman, A. (2002). Automaticity and the amygdala: Nonconscious responses to emotional faces. Directions in Psychological Science, 11, 62–66.

Oelschlager, H. H. A. (2008). The dolphin brain–A challenge for synthetic neurobiology. Brain Research Bulletin, 75, 450–459.

Offit, K., Groeger, E., Turner, S., Wadsworth, E. A., & Weiser, M. A. (2004). The "duty to warn" a patient's family members about hereditary disease risks. Journal of the American Medical Association, 292, 1469–1473.

Ogata, M., Ikeda, M., & Kuratsune, M. (1984). Mortality among Japanese Zen priests. Journal of Epidemiology and Community Health, 38, 161–166.

Ogbu, J. U. (2002). Cultural amplifiers of intelligence: IQ and minority status in cross-cultural perspective. In J. M. Fish (Ed.), Race and Intelligence: Separating Science from Myth (pp. 241–278). Mahwah, NJ: Lawrence Erlbaum.

Ogbu, J. U. (2004). Collective Identity and the Burden of "Acting White" in Black History, Community, and Education. The Urban Review, 36, 1–35.

Oghalai, J. S. (2005). Cochlear hearing loss. In R. Jackler & D. Brackmann (Eds.), Neurotology (2nd ed.). Philadelphia: Mosby.

Öhman, A., Flykt, A., & Esteves, F. (2001). Emotion drives attention: Detecting the snake in the grass. Journal of Experimental Psychology: General, 130, 466–478.

Öhman, A., Lundqvist, D., & Esteves, F. (2001). The face in the crowd revisited: A threat advantage with schematic stimuli. Journal of Personality and Social Psychology, 80, 381–396.

Öhman, A., & Mineka, S. (2003). The malicious serpent: Snakes as a prototypical stimulus for an evolved module of fear. Current Directions in Psychological Science, 12, 5–9.

Öhman, A., & Ruck, C. (2007). Four principles of fear and their implications for phobias. In J. Rottenberg & S. L. Jonathan (Eds.), Emotion and psychopathology: bridging affective and clinical science (pp. 167–189). Washington, DC: American Psychological Association.

Öhman, A., & Soares, J. J. F. (1994). "Unconscious anxiety": Phobic responses to masked stimuli. Journal of Abnormal Psychology, 103, 231–240.

Oishi, S., Diener, E. F., Lucas, R. E., & Shu, E. M. (1999). Cross-cultural variations in predictors of life satisfaction: Perspectives from needs and values. Personality and Social Psychology Bulletin, 25, 980–990.

Okamoto, T., Yoshimura, R., Ikenouchi-Sugita, A., Hori, H., Umene-Nakano, W., Inoue, Y., ... Nakamura, J. (2008). Efficacy of electroconvulsive therapy is associated with changing blood levels of homovanillic acid and brain-derived neurotrophic factor (BDNF) in refractory depressed patients: A pilot study. Progress in Neuro-Psychopharmacology & Biological Psychiatry, 32, 1185–1190.

Okamura, H. (2008). Brain comes to light. Nature, 452, 294–295.

Olausson, H., Lamarre, Y., Backlund, H., Morin, C., Wallin, B. G., Starck, G., ... Bushnell, M. C. (2002). Unmyelinated tactile afferents signal touch and project to insular cortex. Nature Neuroscience, 5, 900–904.

Oldfield, R. C. (1971). The assessment and analysis of handedness: The Edinburgh Inventory. Neuropsychologia, 9, 97–114.

Olds, D. D. (2012). Psychoanalysis and the neurosciences. In G. O. Gabbard, B. E. Litowitz, & P. Williams (Eds.), Textbook of Psychoanalysis (2nd ed., pp. 445–459). Arlington, VA: American Psychiatric Publishing.

Oliner, S. P., & Oliner, P. M. (1988). The altruistic personality: Rescuers of Jews in Nazi Europe. London: Free Press.

Oliver, M. B., & Hyde, J. S. (1993). Gender differences in sexuality: A meta-analysis. Psychological Bulletin, 114, 29–51.

Oller, D. K., & Eilers, R. E. (1988). The role of audition in infant babbling. Child Development, 59, 441–449.

Ollinger, M., Jones, G., & Knoblich, G. (2008). Investigating the effect of mental set on insight problem solving. Experimental Psychology, 55, 269–282.

Olson, K. R., Lambert, A. J., & Zacks, J. M. (2004). Graded structure and the speed of category verification: On the moderating effects of anticipatory control for social vs. Non-social categories. Journal of Experimental Social Psychology, 40, 239–246.

Olszewski-Kubilius, P., & Lee, S.-Y. (2011). Gender and other group differences in performance on off-level tests: Changes in the 21st century. Gifted Child Quarterly, 55, 54–73.

Ong, A. D., & Dulmen, M. H. M. V. (Eds.). (2007). Oxford handbook of methods in positive psychology. New York: Oxford University Press.

Orlinsky, D. E., & Howard, K. I. (1987). The relation of process to outcome in psychotherapy. In Handbook of psychotherapy and behavior change (3rd ed., pp. 311–381). New York: Wiley.

Orsini, C. A., Kim, J. H., Knapska, E., & Maren, S. (2011). Hippocampal and prefrontal projections to the basal amygdala mediate contextual regulation of fear after extinction. The Journal of Neuroscience, 31, 17269–17277.

Ossorio, P., & Duster, T. (2005). Race and genetics: Controversies in biomedical, behavioral, and forensic sciences. American Psychologist, 60, 115–128.

Oswald, F., Wahl, H.-W., Schilling, O., Nygren, C., Fange, A., Sixsmith, A., ... Iwarsson, S. (2007). Relationships between housing and healthy aging in very old age. The Gerontologist, 47, 96–107.

Ouellet, C., Norman, M.-T. L., & Cohen, H. (2001). Language evolution in children with cochlear implants. Brain & Cognition, 46, 231–235.

Overholser, J. C., Braden, A., & Dieter, L. (2012). Understanding suicide risk: Identification of high-risk groups during high-risk times. Journal of Clinical Psychology, 68, 334–348.

Overmier, J. B., & Leaf, R. C. (1965). Effects of discriminative Pavlovian fear conditioning upon previously or subsequently acquired avoidance responding. Journal of Comparative and Physiological Psychology, 60, 213–218.

Oxman, T. E., Freeman, D. H., & Manheimer, E. D. (1995). Lack of social participation or religious strength and comfort as risk factors for death after cardiac surgery in the elderly. Psychosocial Medicine, 57, 5–15.

Oyama, T., & Goto, T. (2007). Editorial: Studies on optical illusions in Japan. Japanese Psychological Research, 49, 1–6.

Oyserman, D., Coon, H. M., & Kemmelmeier, M. (2002). Rethinking individualism and collectivism: Evaluation of theoretical assumptions and meta-analyses. Psychological Bulletin, 128, 3–72.

Oyserman, D., & Lee, S. W. S. (2008). Does culture influence what and how we think? Effects of priming individualism and collectivism. Psychological Bulletin, 134, 311–342.

• • • • **P** • • • • • • • • • • • • • •

Packer, D. J. (2008). Identifying systematic disobedience in Milgram's obedience experiments: A meta-analytic review. Perspectives on Psychological Science, 3, 301–304.

Paivio, S. C., & Greenberg, L. S. (1995). Resolving "unfinished business": Efficacy of experiential therapy using empty-chair dialogue. Journal of Consulting and Clinical Psychology, 63, 419–425.

Pajares, F. (2008). Motivational role of self-efficacy beliefs in self-regulated learning. In D. H. Schunk & B. J. Zimmerman (Eds.), Motivation and Self-regulated Learning: Theory, Research, and Applications (pp. 111–139). Mahwah, NJ: Lawrence Erlbaum.

Pandey, A., Quick, J. A., Rossi, A. M., Nelson, D. L., & Martin, W. (2011). Stress and the workplace: 10 Years of science. 1997-2007. In R. J. Contrada & A. Baum (Eds.), The Handbook of Stress Science: Biology, Psychology, and Health. New York: Springer Publishing.

Panksepp, J., & Solms, M. (2012). What is neuropsychoanalysis? Clinically relevant studies of the minded brain. Trends in Cognitive Sciences, 16, 6–8.

Pargament, K. I. (2002). The bitter and the sweet: An evaluation of the costs and benefits of religiousness. Psychological Inquiry, 13, 168–181.

Park, N., & Peterson, C. (2006). Character strengths and happiness among young children: Content analysis of parental descriptions. Journal of Happiness Studies, 7, 323–341.

Park, N., & Peterson, C. (2008). The cultivation of character strengths. In M. Ferrari & G. Potworowski (Eds.), Teaching for Wisdom (pp. 57–75). Mahwah, NJ: Erlbaum.

Park, N., Peterson, C., & Seligman, M. E. P. (2006). Character strengths in fifty-four nations and the fifty US states. The Journal of Positive Psychology, 1, 118–129.

Parke, R. D., & Buriel, R. (1998). Socialization in the family: Ethnic and ecological perspectives. In W. Damon & N. Eisenberg (Eds.), Handbook of child psychology: Vol. 3. Social, emotional, and personality development (5th ed., pp. 463–552). New York: Wiley.

Parker, S. T., Parker, S. T., Langer, J., & McKinney, M. L. (2000). Homo erectus infancy and childhood: The turning point in the evolution of behavioral development in hominids. In Biology, brains, and behavior: The evolution of human development (pp. 279–318). School of American Research Advanced Seminar Series.

Parkes, C. M. P., & Weiss, R. S. (1983). Recovery from bereavement. New York: Basic Books.

Parkinson Study Group. (2002). Dopamine transporter brain imaging to assess the effects of pramipexole vs. levodopa on Parkinson disease progression. JAMA: Journal of the American Medical Association, 287, 1653–1661.

Pasch, L. A., Bradbury, T. N., & Sullivan, K. T. (1997). Social support in marriage: An analysis of intraindividual and interpersonal components. In G. R. Pierce, B. Lakey, I. G. Sarason, & B. R. Sarason (Eds.), Sourcebook of Social Support and Personality (pp. 229–256). New York: Plenum.

Pashler, H., Johnston, J. C., & Ruthruff, E. (2000). Attention and performance. Annual Review of Psychology, 52, 629–651.

Passman, R. H., & Weisberg, P. (1975). Mothers and blankets as agents for promoting play and exploration by young children in a novel environment: The effects of social and nonsocial attachment objects. Developmental Psychology, 11, 170–177.

Pate, R., Pratt, M., Blair, S., Haskell, W., Macera, C., & et, al. (1995). Physical activity and public health: A recommendation from the Centers for Disease Control and Prevention and the American College of Sports Medicine. Journal of the American Medical Association, 273, 402–407.

Patenaude, A. F. (2005). Children and genetic testing. In A. F. Patenaude (Ed.), Genetic testing for cancer: psychological approaches for helping patients and families (pp. 229–250). Washington, DC: American Psychological Association.

Pato, M. T., Pato, C. N., & Pauls, D. L. (2002). Recent findings in the genetics of OCD. Journal of Clinical Psychiatry, 63, 30–33.

Patrick, A., & Durndell, A. (2004). Lucid dreaming and personality: A replication. Dreaming, 14, 234–239.

Patterson, B. W. (2004). The "Tyranny of the eyewitness". Law & Psychology Review, 28, 195–203.

Patterson, F. (1978). Conversations with a gorilla. National Geographic, 438–465.

Paulus, E. V., & Mintz, E. M. (2012). Developmental disruption of the serotonin system alters circadian rhythms. Physiology & Behavior, 105, 257–263.

Paunonen, S. V. (2003). Big five factors of personality and replicated predictions of behavior. Journal of Personality and Social Psychology, 84, 411–424.

Paus, T. (2005). Mapping brain maturation and cognitive development during adolescence. Trends in Cognitive Sciences, 9, 60–68.

Pavlov, I. P. (1927). Conditioned reflexes (G.V. Anrep, Trans.). London: Oxford University Press.

Pavlov, I. P. (1997). Excerpts from The work of the digestive glands. American Psychologist, 52, 936–940.

Pearson, J., Brandeis, L., & Cuello, A. C. (1982). Depletion of substance P-containing axons in substantia gelatinosa of patients with diminished pain sensitivity. *Nature, 295,* 61–63.

Pearson, N. J., Johnson, L. L., & Nahin, R. L. (2006). Insomnia, trouble sleeping, and complementary and alternative medicine: Analysis of the 2002 National Health Interview Survey data. *Archives of Internal Medicine, 166,* 1775–1782.

Pedersen, C. A. (2004). *Biological aspects of social bonding and the roots of human violence.* Ann. N.Y. Acad. Sci., 1036, 106–127.

Pedersen, W. C., Miller, L. C., Putcha-Bhagavatula, A. D., & Yang, Y. (2002). Evolved sex differences in the number of partners desired? The long and the short of it. *Psychological Science, 13,* 157–161.

Pederson, D. R., Moran, G., Sitko, C., Campbell, K., Ghesquire, K., & Acton, H. (1990). Maternal sensitivity and the security of infant-mother attachment: A q-sort study. *Child Development, 61,* 1974–1983.

Peele, S. (1996). Utilizing culture and behaviour in epidemiological models of alcohol consumption and consequences for Western nations. *Alcohol & Alcoholism, 32,* 51–64.

Peluchette, J. V., Karl, K., & Rust, K. (2006). Dressing to impress: Beliefs and attitudes regarding workplace attire. *Journal of Business and Psychology, 21,* 45–63.

Penfield, W. W. (1958). *The excitable cortex in conscious man.* Springfield, IL: Charles Thomas.

Penfield, W. W., & Milner, B. (1968). Memory deficit produced by bilateral lesions in the hippocampal zone. A.M.A. *Archives of Neurology and Psychiatry, 79,* 475–497.

Pennebaker, J. W., & Beall, S. (1986). Confronting a traumatic event: Toward an understanding of inhibition and disease. *Journal of Abnormal Psychology, 95,* 274–281.

Pennebaker, J. W., Colder, M., & Sharp, L. K. (1990). Accelerating the coping process. *Journal of Personality and Social Psychology, 58,* 528–537.

Peplau, L. A. (2003). Human sexuality: How do men and women differ? *Current Directions in Psychological Science, 12,* 37–40.

Peplau, L. A., Fingerhut, A., & Beals, K. (2004). Sexuality in the relationships of lesbians and gay men. In J. Harvey, A. Wenzel, & S. Sprecher (Eds.), *Handbook of sexuality in close relationships.* Mahwah, NJ: Erlbaum.

Peplau, L. A., & Garnets, L. D. (2000). A new paradigm for understanding women's sexuality and sexual orientation. *Journal of Social Issues, 56,* 329–350.

Peplau, L. A., & Taylor, S. E. (Eds.). (1997). *Sociocultural perspectives in social psychology: Current readings.* Upper Saddle River, NJ: Prentice Hall.

Perakh, M. (2004). *Unintelligent design.* Thousand Oaks, CA: Prometheus Books.

Perani, D., Saccuman, M. C., Scifo, P., Awander, A., Spada, D., Baldoli, C., ... Friederici, A. D. (2011). Neural language networks at birth. *Proc. Natl. Acad. Sci. USA, 108,* 16056–16061.

Pereira-Pasarin, L. P., & Rajaram, S. (2011). Study repetition and divided attention: Effects of encoding manipulations on collaborative inhibition in group recall. *Memory & Cognition, 39,* 968–976.

Perlman, D. (2007). The best of times, the worst of times: The place of close relationships in psychology and our daily lives. *Canadian Psychology, 48,* 19–23.

Perls, F. S. (1969). *Gestalt therapy verbatim.* Lafayette, CA: Real People Press.

Perls, F. S., Heffertine, R. F., & Goodman, P. (1951). *Gestalt therapy.* New York: Julian Press.

Pernot-Marino, E., Danion, J.-M., & Hedelin, G. (2004). Relations between emotion and conscious recollection of true and false autobiographical memories: An investigation using lorazepam as a pharmacological tool. *Psychopharmacology, 175,* 60–67.

Pert, C. B. (2002). The wisdom of the receptors: Neuropeptides, the emotions, and bodymind. *Advances in Mind-Body Medicine, 18,* 30–35.

Pesant, N., & Zadra, A. (2006). Dream content and psychological well-being: a longitudinal study of the continuity hypothesis. *Journal of Clinical Psychology, 62,* 111–121.

Pescosolido, B. A., Monahan, J., Link, B. G., Stueve, A., & Kikuzawa, S. (1999). The public's view of the competence, dangerousness, and need for legal coercion of persons with mental health problems. *American Journal of Public Health, 89,* 1339–1345.

Peterson, C. (2006). The Values in Action (VIA) Classification of Strengths: The un-DSM and the real DSM. In M. Csikszentmihalyi & I. Csikszentmihalyi (Eds.), *A life worth living: Contributions to positive psychology* (pp. 29–48). New York: Oxford University Press.

Peterson, C., & Park, N. (2007). Explanatory style and emotion regulation. In J. Gross & J. James (Eds.), *Handbook of emotion regulation* (pp. 159–179). New York: Guilford Press.

Peterson, C., Park, N., Pole, N., D'Andrea, W., & Seligman, M. E. P. (2008). Strengths of character and posttraumatic growth. *Journal of Traumatic Stress, 21,* 214–217.

Peterson, C., Park, N., & Seligman, M. E. P. (2006). Greater strengths of character and recovery from illness. *The Journal of Positive Psychology, 1,* 17–26.

Peterson, C., Ruch, W., Beermann, U., Park, N., & Seligman, M. E. P. (2007). Strengths of character, orientations to happiness, and life satisfaction. *The Journal of Positive Psychology, 2,* 149–156.

Peterson, C., & Seligman, E. M. (1984). Causal explanations as a risk factor for depression: Theory and evidence. *Psychological Review, 91,* 347–374.

Peterson, C., & Seligman, M. E. P. (2003). Character strengths before and after September 11. *Psychological Science, 14,* 381–384.

Peterson, C., & Seligman, M. E. P. (2004). *Character strengths and virtues: A handbook and classification.* Washington, D. American Psychological Association.

Peterson, C., & Steen, T. A. (2002). Optimistic explanatory style. In C. R. Snyder & S. J. Shane (Eds.), *Handbook of positive psychology* (pp. 244–256). London: Oxford University Press.

Peterson, G. B. (2004). A day of great Illumition: B. F. Skinner's discovery of shaping. *Journal of the Experimental Analysis of Behavior, 82,* 317–328.

Peterson, G. W., Steinmetz, S. K., & Wilson, S. M. (2005). *Parent-youth relations: Cultural and cross-cultural perspectives.* New York: Haworth Press.

Peterson, L. R., & Peterson, M. J. (1959). Short-term retention of individual verbal items. *Journal of Experimental Psychology, 58,* 193–198.

Peterson, Z. D., & Muehlenhard, C. L. (2004). Was it rape? The function of women's rape myth acceptance and definitions of sex in labeling their own experiences. *Sex Roles, 51,* 129–144.

Peto, R., Lopez, A. D., Boreham, J., & Thun, M. (1992). Morality from tobacco in developed countries: Indirect estimation from national vital statistics. *Lancet, 339,* 1268–1278.

Petrides, K. V., & Furnham, A. (2003). Trait emotional intelligence: Behavioural validation in two studies of emotion recognition and reactivity to mood induction. *European Journal of Personality, 17,* 39–57.

Petty, R. E., & Cacioppo, J. T. (1986). *Communication and persuasion: Central and peripheral routes to attitude change.* New York: Springer-Verlag.

Petty, R. E., Haugtvedt, C. P., & Smith, S. M. (1995). Elaboration as a determinant of attitude strength: Creating attitudes that are persistent, resistant, and predictive of behavior. In R. E. Petty & J. A. Krosnick (Eds.), *Attitude strength: Antecedents and consequences.* Hillsdale, NJ: Erlbaum.

Pezze, M. A., Feldon, J., & Murphy, C. A. (2002). Increased conditioned fear response and altered balance of dopamine in the shell and core of the nucleus accumbens during amphetamine withdrawal. *Neuropharmacology, 42,* 633–643.

Pfaffmann, C. (1978). The vertebrate phylogeny, neural code, and integrative process of taste. In *Handbook of perception* (Vol. 6A). New York: Academic Press.

Phelps, J. A., Davis, J. O., & Schartz, K. M. (1997). Nature, nurture, and twin research strategies. *Current Directions in Psychological Science, 6,* 117–121.

Phillips, D. P. (1986). Natural experiments on the effects of mass media violence on fatal aggression: Strengths and weaknesses of a new approach. In L. Berkowitz (Ed.), *Advances in experimental social psychology* (Vol. 19, pp. 207–250). Orlando, FL: Academic Press.

Phillips, D. P., & Brugge, J. F. (1985). Progress in neurophysiology of sound localization. *Annual Review of Psychology, 36,* 245–274.

Phinney, J., & Kohatsu, E. (1997). Ethnic and racial identity and mental health. In J. Schulenberg, J. Maggs, & K. Hurrelmann (Eds.), *Health risks and developmental transitions during adolescence* (pp. 420–443). New York: Cambridge University Press.

Phinney, J. S. (1993). A three-stage model of ethnic identity development. In M. Bernal & G. Knight (Eds.), *Ethnic identity: Formation and transmission among hispanics and other minorities* (pp. 61–79). Albany, NY: State University of New York Press.

Phinney, J. S., Cantu, C. L., & Kurtz, D. A. (1997). Ethnic and American identity and self-esteem. *Journal of Youth and Adolescence, 26,* 165–185.

Piaget, J. (1972a). *The child's conception of the world.* Totowa, NJ: Littlefield, Adams.

Piaget, J. (1972b). Intellectual evolution from adolescence to adulthood. *Human Development, 15,* 1–12.

Piaget, J., & Inhelder, B. (1956). *The child's conception of space.* (F. J. Langdon & J. L. Lunzer, Trans.). London: Routledge & T. K. Paul.

Piaget, J., & Inhelder, B. (1969). *The psychology of the child.* New York: Basic Books.

Picchioni, D., Horovitz, S. G., Fukunaga, M., Carr, W. S., Meltzer, J. A., Balkin, T., ... Braun, A. R. (2011). Infraslow EEG oscillations organize large-scale cortical-subcortical interactions during sleep: A combined EEG/fMRI study. *Brain Research, 1374,* 63–72.

Piccione, C., Hilgard, E. R., & Zimbardo, P. G. (1989). On the degree of stability of measured hypnotizability over a 25-year period. *Journal of Personality and Social Psychology, 56,* 289–295.

Pickering, G. J., & Robert, G. (2006). Perception of mouthfeel sensations elicited by red wine are associated with sensitivity to 6-N-propylthiouracil. *Journal of Sensory Studies, 21,* 249–265.

Pilling, M., & Davies, I. R. L. (2004). Linguistic relativism and colour cognition. *British Journal of Psychology, 95,* 429–455.

Pines, A. M. (1993). Burnout. In L. Goldberger & S. Breznitz (Eds.), *Handbook of stress: Theoretical and clinical aspects.* New York: Free Press.

Pinna, G., & Rasmusson, A. M. (2012). Up-regulation of neurosteroid biosynthesis as a pharmacological strategy to improve behavioural deficits in a putative mouse model of post-traumatic stress disorder. *Journal of Neuroendocrinology, 24,* 102–116.

Pinto, C., Souza, R. P., Lioult, D., Semeralul, M., Kennedy, J. L., Warsh, J. J., ... Luca, V. (2011). Parent of origin effect and allelic expression imbalance of the serotonin transporter in bipolar disorder and suicidal behaviour. *European Archives of Psychiatry and Clinical Neuroscience, 261,* 533–538.

Pisoni, D. B. (2008). Speech perception in deaf children with cochlear implants. In D. B. Pisoni & R. E. Remez (Eds.), *The handbook of speech perception* (pp. 494–523). Malden, MA: Blackwell Publishing.

Plack, C. J. (2005). *The sense of hearing.* Mahwah, NJ: Lawrence Erlbaum.

Plante, T. G. (2005). *Contemporary clinical psychology* (2nd ed.). New York: John Wiley.

Plante, T. G., Yancey, S., Sherman, A., & Guertin, M. (2000). The association between strength of religious faith and psychological functioning. *Pastoral Psychology, 38,* 405–412.

Plaut, D. C., & Kello, C. T. (1999). The emergence of phonology from the interplay of speech comprehension and production: A distributed connectionist approach. In B. MacWhinney (Ed.), *The emergence of language* (pp. 381–415). Mahwah, NJ: Erlbaum.

Plomin, R. (1984). Childhood temperamnet. In *Advances in clinical child psychology* (Vol. 6). New York: Plenum.

Plomin, R., & Crabbe, J. (2000). DNA. *Psychological Bulletin, 128.*

Plomin, R., DeFries, J. C., McClearn, G. E., & Rutter, M. (1997). *Behavioral genetics* (3rd ed.). New York: Freeman.

Plucker, J. A., Qian, M., & Wang, S. (2011). Is originality in the eye of the beholder? Comparison of scoring techniques in the assessment of divergent thinking. *The Journal of Creative Behavior, 45,* 1–22.

Pokorny, J., Shevell, S. K., & Smith, V. C. (1991). Colour appearance and colour constancy. In *The perception of colour: Vol 6. Vision and visual dysfunction* (pp. 43–61). Boca Raton, FL: CRC.

Poling, A. (2010). Progressive-ratio schedules and applied behavior analysis. *Journal of Applied Behavior Analysis, 43,* 347–349.

Politis, A. M., Papadimitriou, G. N., Theleritis, C. G., Psarros, C., & Soldatos, C. R. (2008). Combination therapy with amisulpride and antidepressants: Clinical observations in case series of elderly patients with psychotic depression. *Progress in Neuro-Psychopharmacology & Biological Psychiatry, 32,* 1227–1230.

Polivy, J., Herman, C.-P., & Boivin, M. (2005). Eating Disorders. In J. E. Maddux & B. A. Winstead (Eds.), *Psychopathology: Foundations for a contemporary understanding* (pp. 229–254). Mahwah, NJ: Lawrence Erlbaum.

Pollock, L., & Eyre, S. L. (2012). Growth into manhood: Identity development among female-to-male transgender youth. *Culture, Health & Sexuality, 14,* 209–222.

Pomerantz, E. M., Wang, Q. N., & Florrie, F.-Y. (2005). Mothers' affect in the homework context: The importance of staying positive. *Developmental Psychology, 41,* 414–427.

Porter, F. L., Porges, S. W., & Marshall, R. E. (1988). Newborn pain cries and vagal tone: Parallel changes in response to circumcision. *Child Development, 59,* 495–505.

Porter, R. H. (1991). Human reproduction and the mother-infant relationship. In *Taste and Smell in Health and Disease.* New York: Raven Press.

Porter, R. H., & Moore, J. D. (1981). Human kin recognition by olfactory cues. *Physiology and Behavior, 27,* 493–495.

Poulsen, A. (2010). Adolescence in developmental psychology. *Psyke & Logos, 31,* 45–63.

Pratkanis, A. R. (1989). The cognitive representation of attitudes. In A. R. Pratkanis, S. J. Breckler, & A. G. Greenwald (Eds.), *Attitude structure and function* (pp. 71–98). Hillsdale, NJ: Erlbaum.

Premack, D., & Premack, A. (1983). *The mind of an ape.* New York: Norton.

Prepeliczay, S. (2003). Socio-cultural and psychological aspects of contemporary LSD use in Germany. *Journal of Drug Issues, 32,* 431–458.

Presson, P. K., & Benassi, V. A. (1996). Locus of control and depressive symptomatology: A meta-analysis. *Journal of Social Behavior and Personality, 11,* 201–212.

Pretz, J. E. (2008). Intuition versus analysis: Strategy and experience in complex everyday problem solving. *Memory & Cognition, 36,* 554–566.

Priluck, R., & Till, B. D. (2004). The role of contingency awareness, involvement, and need for cognition in attitude formation. *Journal of the Academy of Marketing Science, 32,* 329–344.

Principe, D. P., & Langlois, J. H. (2011). Faces differing in attractiveness elicit corresponding affective responses. *Cognition and Emotion, 25,* 140–148.

Priori, A., Mameli, F., Cogiamanian, F., Marceglia, S., Tiriticco, M., Mrakic-Sposta, S., ... Sartori, G. (2008). Lie-specific involvement of dorsolateral prefrontal cortex in deception. *Cerebral Cortex, 18,* 451–455.

Pritchard, R. (1991). The effects of cultural schemata on reading processing strategies. *Reading Research Quarterly, 24,* 273–293.

Provins, K. A. (1997). Handedness and speech: A critical reappraisal of the role of genetic and environmental factors in the cerebral lateralization of function. *Psychological Review, 104,* 544–571.

Puetz, T. W., Flowers, S. S., & Connor, P. J. O. (2008). A randomized controlled trial of the effect of aerobic exercise training on feelings of energy and fatigue in sedentary young adults with persistent fatigue. *Psychotherapy and Psychosomatics, 77,* 167–174.

Pugh, E. N., Jr. (1988). Vision: Physics and retinal physiology. In *Steven's handbook of experimental psychology* (Vol. 1). New York: Wiley.

Puigdemont, D., Perez-Egea, R., & Portella, M. J. (2012). Deep brain stimulation of the subcallosal cingulate gyrus: Further evidence in treatment-resistant major depression. *International Journal of Neuropsychopharmacology, 15,* 121–133.

Pyryt, M. C. (1993). The fulfillment of promise revisited: A discriminant analysis of factors predicting success in the Terman study. *Roeper Review, 15,* 178–179.

Q

Qin, Y., Carter, C. S., Silk, E. M., Stenger, V. A., Fissell, K., Goode, A., & Anderson, J. R. (2004). The change of the brain activation patterns as children learn algebra equation solving. *Proc. Natl. Acad. Sci. USA, 101,* 5686–5691.

Querido, J. G., Warner, T. D., & Eyberg, S. M. (2002). Parenting styles and child behavior in African American families of preschool children. *Journal of Clinical Child Psychology, 31,* 272–277.

Quinn, P. C., Westerlund, A., & Nelson, C. A. (2006). Neural makers of categorization in 6-month-old infants. *Psychological Science, 17,* 59–66.

R

Rabin, M. D., & Cain, W. S. (1986). Determinants of measured olfactory sensitivity. *Perception & Psychophysics, 39,* 281–286.

Rackett, P., & Holmes, B. M. (2010). Enhancing the attachment relationship: A prenatal perspective. *Educational and Child Psychology, 27,* 33–50.

Radhakrishnan, R., & Sluka, K. A. (2005). Deep tissue afferents, but not cutaneous afferents, mediate transcutaneous electrical nerve stimulation-induced antihyperalgesia. *Journal of Pain, 6,* 673–680.

Raffaelli, M., & Ontai, L. L. (2004). Gender socialization in Latino/a families: Results from two retrospective studies. *Sex Roles, 50,* 287–299.

Rahn, E. J., & Hohmann, A. G. (2009). Cannabinoids as pharmacotherapies for neuropathic pain: From the bench to the bedside. *Neurotherapeutics, 6,* 713–737.

Raithatha, N., & Smith, R. (2004). Disclosure of genetic tests for health insurance: Is it ethical not to? *Lancet, 363,* 395–396.

Rajimehr, R., Vaziri-Pashkam, M., Afraz, S.-R., & Esteky, H. (2004). Adaptation to apparent motion in crowding condition. *Vision Research, 44,* 925–931.

Rakison, D. H., & Oakes, L. M. (2003). *Early category and concept development: Making sense of the blooming, buzzing confusion.* London: Oxford University Press.

Ramachandran, V. S. (1992). Blind spots. *Scientific American,* 102–109.

Randi, J. (1980). *Flim-flam.* New York: Lippincott.

Ranganath, C., Johnson, M. K., & D'Esposito, M. (2003). Prefrontal activity associated with working memory and episodic long-term memory. *Neuropsychologia, 41,* 378–389.

Rao, S. M., Huber, S. J., & Bornstein, R. A. (1992). Emotional changes with multiple sclerosis and Parkinson's disease. *Journal of Consulting and Clinical Psychology, 9,* 59–74.

Rapee, R. M. (1995). Psychological factors influencing the affective response to biological challenge procedures in panic disorder. *Journal of Anxiety Disorders, 9,* 59–74.

Rathbone, C. J., Conway, M. A., & Moulin, C. J. A. (2011). Remembering and imagining: The role of the self. *Consciousness and Cognition: An International Journal, 20,* 1175–1182.

Ratliff-Crain, J., Donald, K., & Ness, J. (1999). The relative impact of knowledge, beliefs, peer norms, and past behaviors on current risky sexual behaviors among college students. *Psychology and Health, 14,* 625–641.

Ravasia, S. (2001). Risperidone-induced edema. *Canadian Journal of Psychiatry, 46,* 453–454.

Ravizza, K. (2007). Peak experiences in sport. In M. Bar-Eli (Ed.), *Essential readings in sport and exercise psychology* (pp. 122–125). Champaign, IL: Human Kinetics.

Ream, G., Benoit, E., Johnson, B. D., & Dunlap, E. (2008). Smoking tobacco along with marijuana increases symptoms of cannabis dependence. *Drug and Alcohol Dependence, 95,* 199–208.

Redmond, J., & Shulman, M. (2008). Access to psychoanalytic ideas in American undergraduate institutions. *Journal of the American Psychoanalytic Association, 56,* 391–408.

Regan, D., & Beverley, K. I. (1984). Figure-ground segregation by motion contrast and by luminance contrast. *Journal of the Optical Society of America A, 1,* 433–442.

Regan, P. C., Levin, L., Sprecher, S., Christopher, F. S., & Cate, R. (2000). Partner preferences: What characteristics do men and women desire in their short-term sexual and long-term romantic partners? *Journal of Psychology & Human Sexuality, 12,* 1–21.

Reger, G. M., & Holloway, K. M. (2011). Virtual reality exposure therapy. In B. A. Moore & W. E. Penk (Eds.), *Treating PTSD in military personnel: A clinical handbook* (pp. 90–106). New York: Guilford Press.

Regier, T., Kay, P., Gilbert, A., & Ivry, R. (2010). Language and thought: Which side are you on, anyway? In B. C. Malt & P. Wolff (Eds.), *Words and the mind: How words capture human experience* (pp. 165–182). New York: Oxford University Press.

Reiser, M. (1982). *Police psychology: Collected papers.* Los Angeles, CA: Lehi Publishing Company.

Reiss, S., & Havercamp, S. M. (2005). Motivation in developmental context: A new method for studying self-actualization. *Journal of humanistic psychology, 45,* 41–53.

Reitman, D., Hupp, S. D. A., O'Callaghan, P. M., Gulley, V., & Northup, J. (2001). The influence of a token economy and methylphenidate on attentive and disruptive behavior during sports with ADHD-diagnosed children. *Behavior Modification, 25,* 305–323.

Renner, J. W., Abraham, M. R., Grzybowski, E. B., & Marek, E. A. (1990). Understandings and misunderstandings of eighth graders of four physics concepts found in textbooks. *Journal of Research in Science in Teaching, 27,* 35–54.

Renner, M. J., & Mackin, R. S. (2002). A life stress instrument for classroom use. (R. A. Griggs, Ed.) *Handbook for teaching introductory psychology: Vol. 3: With an emphasis on assessment,* 236–238.

Rescorla, R. A. (1968). Probability of shock in the presence and absence of CS in fear conditioning. *Journal of Comparative and Physiological Psychology, 66,* 1–5.

Rescorla, R. A., & Wagner, A. R. (1972). A theory of Pavlovian conditioning: Variations in the effectiveness of reinforcement and nonreinforcement. In A. H. Black & W. F. Perokasy (Eds.), *Classical conditioning II: Current theory.* New York: Appleton-Century-Crofts.

Ressler, K. J., Sullivan, S. L., & Buck, L. B. (1994). A molecular dissection of spatial patterning in the olfactory system. *Current Opinion in Neurobiology, 4,* 588–596.

Reuter-Lorenz, P. A., & Miller, A. C. (1998). The cognitive neuroscience of human laterality: Lessons from the bisected brain. *Current Directions in Psychological Science, 7*(15–20).

Rexrode, K., Carey, V., Hennekens, C., Walters, E., Colditz, G., Stampher, M., ... Manson, J. (1997). A prospective study of body mass index, weight change, and risk of stroke in women. *Journal of the American Medical Association, 277,* 1539–1545.

Reynolds, C. R., & Livingston, R. B. (2012). *Mastering modern psychological testing: Theory and methods.* Upper Saddle River, NJ: Pearson Education.

Rezayof, A., Alijanpour, S., Zarrindast, M.-R., & Rassouli, Y. (2008). Ethanol state-dependent memory: Involvement of dorsal hippocampal muscarinic and nicotinic receptors. *Neurobiology of Learning and Memory, 89,* 441–447.

Rhine, J. B. (1934). Extra-sensory perception of the clairvoyant type. *Journal of Abnormal and Social Psychology, 29,* 151–171.

Ricard, M. (2011). This is your brain on mindfulness. In B. Boyce & S. Shambhala (Eds.), *The mindfulness revolution: Leading psychologists, scientists, artists, and meditation teachers on the power of mindfulness in daily life* (pp. 127–135). Boston, MA: Shambhala Publications.

Rice, M. J. (2011). The institutional review board is an impediment to human research: The result is more animal-based research. *Philosophy, Ethics, and Humanities in Medicine, 6,* ArtID–12.

Rice, V. H. (Ed.). (2012). *Handbook of stress, coping, and health: Implications for nursing research, theory, and practice* (2nd ed.). Thousand Oaks, CA: Sage.

Richards, A. D., & Lynch, A. A. (2008). The identity of psychoanalysis and psychoanalysts. *Psychoanalytic Psychology, 25,* 203–219.

Richardson, J. (1993). The curious case of coins: Remembering the appearance of familiar objects. *The Psychologist: Bulletin of the British Psychological Society, 6,* 360–366.

Richardson, J. T. E., & Zucco, G. M. (1989). Cognition and olfaction: A review. *Psychological Bulletin, 105,* 352–360.

Richmond, A. S., Carney, R. M., & Levin, J. R. (2011). Got neurons? Teaching neuroscience mnemonically promotes retention and higher-order thinking. *Psychology Learning & Teaching, 10,* 40–45.

Ridley, J., Yu, D. W., & Sutherland, W. J. (2005). Why long-lived species are more likely to be social: The role of local dominance. *Behavioral Ecology, 16,* 358–363.

Riley, L. R. (1987). *Psychology of language development: A primer.* Toronto: C. J. Hogrefe.

Rimmele, C. T., Howard, M. O., & Hilfrink, M. L. (1995). Aversion therapies. In R. K. Hester & W. R. Miller (Eds.), *Handbook of alcoholism treatment approaches: Effective alternatives* (2nd ed., pp. 134–147). Boston, MA: Allyn & Bacon.

Riso, L. P., Du Toit, P. L., Blandino, J. A., Penna, S., Dacey, S., Duin, J. S., ... Ulmer, C. S. (2003). Cognitive aspects of chronic depression. *Journal of Abnormal Psychology, 112,* 72–80.

Ritter, M. R., Blackmore, M. A., & Heimberg, R. G. (2010). Generalized anxiety disorder. In D. McKay, J. S. Abramowitz, & S. Talor (Eds.), *Cognitive-behavioral therapy for refractory cases: Turning failure into success* (pp. 111–137). Washington, DC: American Psychological Association.

Rizzolatti, G. (2005). The mirror neuron system and its function in humans. *Anatomy and Embryology, 210,* 419–421.

Roberts, B. W., & DelVecchio, W. F. (2000). The rank-order consistency of personality traits from childhood to old age: A quantitative review of longitudinal studies. *Psychological Bulletin, 126,* 3–25.

Roberts, B., Wood, D., & Smith, J. L. (2005). Evaluating Five Factor Theory and social investment perspectives on personality trait development. *Journal of Research in Personality, 39,* 166–184.

Roberts, J. A., Brown, D., Elkins, T., & Larson, D. B. (1997). Factors influencing views of patients with gynecologic cancer about end-of-life decisions. *American Journal of Obstetrics and Gynecology, 176,* 166–172.

Robinson, D. N. (2008). *Consciousness and mental life.* New York: Columbia University Press.

Robinson, T. (1999). Reducing children's television viewing to prevent obesity: A randomized controlled trial. *Journal of the American Medical Association, 282,* 1561–1567.

Robinson, T. N., Wilde, M. L., Navracruz, L. C., Haydel, K. F., & Varady, A. (2001). Effects of reducing children's television and video game use on aggressive behavior: A randomized controlled trial. *Archives of Pediatrics and Adolescent Medicine, 155,* 17–23.

Roche-Labarbe, N., Aarabi, A., Kongolo, G., Gondry-Jouet, C., Dumpelmann, M., Grebe, R., & Wallois, F. (2008). High-resolution electroencephalography and source localization in neonates. *Human Brain Mapping, 29,* 167–176.

Rochot, F., Maggioni, O., & Modigliani, A. (2000). The dynamics of obeying and opposing authority: A mathematical model. In T. Blass (Ed.), *Obedience to authority: Current perspectives on the Milgram paradigm.* Mahwah, NJ:: Erlbaum.

Rodin, J. (1986). Aging and health: Effects of the sense of control. *Science, 233,* 1271–1276.

Rogers, C. R. (1951). *Client-centered therapy: Its current practice, implications, and theory.* Boston, MA: Houghton Mifflin.

Rogers, C. R. (1959). A theory of therapy, personality, and interpersonal relationships as developed in the client-centered framework. In S. Koch (Ed.), *Psychology: A study of a science* (Vol. 3, pp. 184–256). New York: McGraw-Hill.

Rogers, C. R. (1961). *On becoming a person.* Boston, MA: Houghton Mifflin.

Rogers, L. (2001). *Sexing the brain.* London: Weidenfeld & Nicolson.

Rogers, R. G. (1995). Marriage, sex, and mortality. *Journal of Marriage and the Family, 57,* 515–526.

Rogoff, B. (1990). *Apprenticeship in thinking: Cognitive development in a social context.* New York: Oxford University Press.

Rolls, A., & Deco, G. (2002). *Computational neuroscience of vision.* London: Oxford University Press.

Rolls, B. (1986). Sensory-specific satiety. *Nutrition Reviews, 44,* 93–101.

Rosch, E. H. (1973). Natural categories. *Cognitive Psychology, 4,* 328–350.

Rosch, E. H. (1978). Principles of categorization. In E. Rosch & B. L. Lloyd (Eds.), *Cognition and categorization.* Hillsdale, NJ: Erlbaum.

Rose, A. J., Vegiopoulos, A., & Herzig, S. (2010). Role of glucocorticoids and the glucocorticoid receptor in metabolism: Insights from genetic manipulations. *Journal of Steroid Biochemistry & Molecular Biology, 122,* 10–20.

Rose, S., & Zand, D. (2000). Lesbian dating and courtship from young adulthood to midlife. *Journal of Gay and Lesbian Social Services, 11,* 77–104.

Rosen, K. S., & Rothbaum, F. (1993). Quality of parental caregiving and security of attachment. *Developmental Psychology, 29,* 358–367.

Rosenberg, M. (1965). *Society and the adolescent self-image.* Princeton, NJ: Princeton University Press.

Rosenberg, M. L., Mercy, J. A., & Potter, L. B. (1999). Firearms and suicide. *New England Journal of Medicine, 341,* 1609–1611.

Rosenhan, D. L. (1970). The natural socialization of altruistic autonomy. In J. Macaulay & L. Berkowitz (Eds.), *Altruism and helping behavior.* New York: Academic Press.

Rosenman, R. H. (1993). Relationships of the Type A behavior pattern with coronary heart disease. In L. Goldberger & S. Breznitz (Eds.), *Handbook of stress: theoretical and clinical aspects* (2nd ed.). New York: Free Press.

Rosenman, R. H., Brand, R. J., Jenkins, C. D., Freidman, M., Straus, R., & Wurm, M. (1975). Coronary heart disease on the Western collaborative group study: Final follow-up experience of 8 1/2 years. *Journal of the American Medical Association, 233,* 872–877.

Rosenthal, R., & Jacobson, L. (1968). *Pygmalion in the classroom: Teacher expectation and pupils' intellectual development.* New York: Holt.

Ross, C. R. J. (2011). Jungian typology and religion: A perspective from North America. *Research in the Social Scientific Study of Religion, 22,* 65–191.

Ross, H. E. (2000). Sensation and perception. In *Psychology for psychiatrists* (pp. 20–40). London: Whurr Publishers.

Ross, H., & Plug, C. (2002). *The mystery of the moon illusion.* Oxford, UK: Oxford University Press.

Ross, J. N., & Coleman, N. M. (2011). Gold Digger or Video Girl: The salience of an emerging hip-hop sexual script. *Culture, Health & Sexuality, 13,* 157–171.

Ross, L. (1977). The intuitive psychologist and his shortcomings: Distortions in the attribution process. In L. Berkowitz (Ed.), *Advances in experimental social psychology* (Vol. 10, pp. 174–221). New York: Academic Press.

Ross, M., & Wilson, A. E. (2002). It feels like yesterday: Self-esteem, valence of personal past experiences, and judgments of subjective distance. *Journal of Personality and Social Psychology, 82,* 792–803.

Ross, M., & Wilson, A. E. (2003). Autobiographical memory and conceptions of self: Getting better all the time. *Current Directions in Psychological Science, 12,* 66–69.

Rossini, P. M., & Pauri, F. (2000). Neuromagnetic integrated methods tracking human brain mechanisms of sensorimotor areas' "plastic" reorganization. *Brain Research Reviews, 33,* 131–154.

Rosso, I. M., Cintron, C. M., Steingard, R. J., Renshaw, P. F., Young, A. D., & Yurgelum-Todd, D. A. (2005). Amygdala and hippocampus volumes in pediatric major depression. *Biological Psychiatry, 57,* 21–26.

Roth, R. M., Koven, N. S., & Pendergrass, J. C. (2008). An introduction to structural and functional neuroimaging. In D. Wedding (Ed.), *The Neuropsychology Handbook* (pp. 217–250). New York: Springer.

Rothbart, M. K. (1989). Biological process in temperament. In *Handbook of temperament in childhood* (pp. 77–110). Sussex, England: Wiley.

Rothbaum, F., Weisz, J., Pott, M., Miyake, K., & Morelli, G. (2000). Attachment and culture: Security in the United States and Japan. *American Psychologist, 55,* 1093–1104.

Rotter, J. (1966). Generalized expectancies for internal versus external control of reinforcement. *Psychological Monographs, 80.*

Rotter, J. (1990). Internal versus external control of reinforcement: A case history of a variable. *American Psychologist, 45,* 489–493.

Roussel, E., Padie, S., & Giurfa, M. (2012). Aversive learning overcomes appetitive innate responding in honeybees. *Animal Cognition, 15,* 135–141.

Rowatt, W. C., Cunningham, M., & Druen, P. B. (1998). Deception to get a date. *Personality and Social Psychology Bulletin, 24,* 1228–1242.

Rowe, C. C., & Van den Oord, E. J. C. G. (2005). Genetic and environmental influences. In W. H. Jones (Ed.), *Personality: Contemporary theory and research* (3rd ed., pp. 63–97). Belmont, CA: Thomson Wadsworth.

Rozin, P., Dow, S., Moscovitch, M., & Rajaram, S. (1998). What causes humans to begin and end a meal? A role for memory for what has been eaten, as evidenced by a study of multiple meal eating in amnesic patients. *Psychological Science, 9,* 392–396.

Ruan, S., Yang, H., Zhu, Y., Ma, Y., Li, J., Zhao, J., ... Raymond, H. F. (2008). HIV prevalence and correlates of unprotected anal intercourse among men who have sex with men, Jinan, China. *AIDS and Behavior, 12,* 469–475.

Rubin, K. H., Burgess, K. B., & Coplan, R. J. (2002). Social withdrawl and shyness. In C. H. Hart (Ed.), *Blackwell handbook of childhood social development* (pp. 330–352). Malden, MA: Blackwell.

Rudasill, K. M. (2011). Review of Self and social regulation: Social interaction and the development of social understanding and executive functions. *Developmental Neuropsychology, 36,* 403–404.

Rumbaugh, D. M. (1990). Comparative psychology and the great apes: Their competency in learning, language, and numbers. *Psychological Record, 40,* 15–39.

Ruscio, J. (2001). Administering quizzes at random to increase students' reading. *Teaching of Psychology, 28,* 204–206.

Rushton, J. P., & Ankney, C. D. (1996). Brain size and cognitive ability: Correlations with age, sex, social class, and race. *Psychonomic Bulletin and Review, 3,* 21–36.

Rushton, J. P., Skuy, M., & Bons, T. A. (2004). Construct validity of Raven's Advanced Progressive Matrices for African and Non-African engineering students in South Africa. *International Journal of Selection and Assessment, 12,* 220–229.

Russell, J. A., & Yik, S. M. (1996). Emotions among the Chinese. In *The handbook of Chinese psychology.* Hong Kong, China: Oxford University Press.

Russell, W. R. (1971). *The traumatic amnesics.* London: Oxford University Press.

Russo, M. (2011). Aptitude testing over the years. *Interpreting, 13,* 5–30.

Rustemeyer, R., & Fischer, N. (2007). Paradigms of self-concept research with focus on gender identity. In A. J. Lauber (Ed.), *Gender identity, psychology and lifestyle* (pp. 1–35). Hauppauge, NY: Nova Science Publishers.

Rustin, M. (2011). In defence of infant observational research. *European Journal of Psychotherapy and Counselling, 13,* 153–167.

Rutishauser, U. (2008). Polysialic acid in the plasticity of the developing and adult vertebrate nervous system. *Nature Reviews Neuroscience, 9,* 26–35.

Ruys, K. I., & Stapel, D. A. (2008). How to heat up from the cold: Examining the preconditions for (unconscious) mood effects. *Journal of Personality and Social Psychology, 94,* 777–791.

Ryan, C. S., Hemmes, N. S., & Brown, B. L. (2011). Effects of conditioning history on selective stimulus control by elements of compound discriminative stimuli. *Behavioural Processes, 87,* 291–301.

Ryan, K. M. (2011). The relationship between rape myths and sexual scripts: The social construction of rape. *Sex Roles, 65,* 774–782.

Ryan, R. M., Chirkov, V. I., Little, T. D., Sheldon, K. M., Timoshina, E., & Deci, E. L. (1999). The American dream in Russia: Extrinsic aspirations in two cultures. *Personality and Social Psychology Bulletin, 25,* 1509–1524.

Ryan, R. M., & Deci, E. L. (2000). When rewards compete with nature: The undermining of intrinsic motivation and self-regulation. In C. Sansone & J. M. Harackiewicz (Eds.), *Intrinsic and Extrinsic Motivation: The Search for Optimal Motivation and Performance* (pp. 13–78). San Diego, CA: Academic Press.

Ryan, R. M., & Deci, E. L. (2001). On happiness and human potentials: A review of research on hedonic and eudaimonic well-being. *Annual Review of Psychology, 52,* 141–166.

• • • **S** • • • • • • • • • • • • • • • • • •

Saakvitne, K. W. (2005). Holding hope and humanity in the face of trauma's legacy: The daunting challenge for group therapists. *International Journal of Group Psychotherapy, 55,* 137–149.

Saarni, C. (1999). *The development of emotional competence.* New York: Guilford.

Sackett, P. R., & Shen, W. (2010). Subgroup differences on cognitive tests in contexts other than personnel selection. In J. L. Outtz (Ed.), *Diverse impact: implications for organizational staffing and high stakes selection* (pp. 323–346). New York: Routledge/Taylor & Francis Group.

Sadler, P., & Woody, E. (2003). Is who you are who you're talking to? Interpersonal style and complementarity in mixed-sex interactions. *Journal of Personality & Social Psychology, 84,* 80–95.

Safdar, S., & Lay, C. H. (2003). The relations of immigrant-specific and immigrant-nonspecific daily hassles to distress controlling for psychological adjustment and cultural competence. *Journal of Applied Social Psychology, 33,* 299–320.

Sage, C., Huang, M., Karimi, K., Gutierrez, G., Vollrath, M. A., Zhang, D.-S., ... Chen, Z.-Y. (2005). Proliferation of functional hair cells in vivo in the absence of the retinoblastoma protein. Retrieved from www.sciencemag.org

Saguy, A. C., & Almeling, R. (2008). Fat in the fire? Science, the news media, and the "obesity epidemic." *Sociological Forum, 23,* 53–83.

Salmon, P. (2001). Effects of physical exercise on anxiety, depression, and sensitivity to stress: A unifying theory. *Clinical Psychology Review, 21,* 33–61.

Salovey, P., Mayer, J. D., Caruso, D., & Lopes, P. N. (2003). Measuring emotional intelligence as a set of abilities with the Mayer-Salovey-Caruso Emotional Intelligence Test. In S. J. Lopez & C. R. Snyder (Eds.), *Positive psychological assessment: A handbook of models and measures* (pp. 251–265). Washington, DC: American Psychological Association.

Salovey, P., & Rodin, J. (1988). Coping with envy and jealousy. *Journal of Social and Clinical Psychology, 7,* 15–33.

Salsman, J. M., Brown, T. L., Brechting, E. H., & Carlson, C. R. (2005). The link between religion and spirituality and psychological adjustment: The mediating role of optimism and social support. *Personality and Social Psychology Bulletin, 31,* 522–535.

Samuel, D. B., Lynam, D. R., Widiger, T. A., & Ball, S. A. (2012). An expert consensus approach to relating the proposed DSM-5 types and traits. *Personality Disorders: Theory, Research, and Treatment, 3,* 1–16.

Sanders, G., Sjodin, M., & De Chastelaine, M. (2002). On the elusive nature of sex differences in cognition: Hormonal influences contributing to within-sex variation. *Archives of Sexual Behavior, 31,* 145–152.

Sandfort, T. G. M., De Graaf, R., Bijl, R. V., & Schnabel, P. (2001). Same-sex sexual behavior and psychiatric disorders. *Archives of General Psychiatry, 58,* 85–91.

Sandler, W. (2003). On the complementarity of signed and spoken languages. In Y. Levy & J. Schaeffer (Eds.), *Language competence across populations: Toward a definition of specific language impairment* (pp. 383–409). Mahwah, NJ: Lawrence Erlbaum.

Saracho, O. N., & Spodek, B. (2007). Challenging the stereotypes of Mexican American fathers. *Early Childhood Education Journal, 35,* 223–231.

Sarason, I., Sarason, B., & Pierce, G. (1990). Anxiety, cognitive interference, and performance. *Journal of Social Behavior and Personality, 5,* 1–18.

Saufley, W. H., Otaka, S. R., & Bavaresco, J. L. (1985). Context effects: Classroom tests and context independence. *Memory & Cognition, 13,* 522–528.

Savic, I., Berglund, H., & Lindstrom, P. (2005). Brain response to putative pheromones in homosexual men. *Proceedings of the National Academies of Science, 102,* 7356–7361.

Savic, I., Berglund, H., & Lindstrom, P. (2007). Brain response to putative pheromones in homosexual men. In G. Einstein (Ed.), *Sex and the brain* (pp. 731–738). Cambridge, MA: MIT Press.

Saxena, S., & Rauch, S. L. (2000). Functional neuroimaging and the neuroanatomy of obsessive-compulsive disorder. *Psychiatric Clinics of North America, 23,* 563–586.

Scarr, S., Pakstis, A. J., Katz, S. H., & Barker, W. B. (1977). The absence of a relationship between degree of white ancestry and intellectual skills within a black population. *Human Genetics, 39,* 69–86.

Scarr, S., & Weinberg, R. A. (1976). IQ test performance of black children adopted by white families. *American Psychologist, 31,* 726–739.

Scarr, S., & Weinberg, R. A. (1983). The Minnesota adoption studies: Genetic differences and malleability. *Child Development, 54,* 260–267.

Scaturo, D. J. (2005). Transference, countertransference, and resistance: Unconscious determinants of dilemmas. In D. J. Scaturo & J. Douglas (Eds.), *Clinical dilemmas in psychotherapy: A transtheoretical approach to psychotherapy integration* (pp. 127–142). Washington, DC: American Psychological Association.

Scepkowski, L. A., Wiegel, M., Bach, A. K., Weisberg, R. B., Brown, T. A., & Barlow, D. H. (2004). Attributions for sexual situations in men with and without erectile disorder: Evidence from a sex-specific Attributional Style Measure. *Archives of Sexual Behavior, 33,* 559–569.

Schachter, S. (1959). *The psychology of affiliation: Experimental studies of the sources of gregariousness.* Stanford, CA: Stanford University Press.

Schachter, S. (1964). The interaction of cognitive and physiological determinants of emotional state. In L. Berkowitz (Ed.), *Advances in experimental social psychology* (Vol. 1, pp. 49–80). New York: Academic Press.

Schachter, S. (1966). The interaction of cognitive and physiological determinants of emotional state. In C. Spielberger (Ed.), *Anxiety and behavior.* New York: Academic Press.

Schachter, S., & Singer, J. (1962). Cognitive, social, and physiological determinants of emotional state. *Psychological Review, 69,* 379–399.

Schachtman, T. (2004). Pavlovian conditioning: Basic associative processes. *International Journal of Comparative Psychology, 17,* 14–15.

Schacter, D. L., & Badgaiyan, R. D. (2001). Neuroimaging of priming: New perspectives on implicit and explicit memory. *Current Directions in Psychological Science, 10,* 1–4.

Schaie, K. W. (1996). Intellectual development in adulthood. In J. E. Birren, K. Schaie, R. P. Abeles, M. Gatz, & T. A. Salthouse (Eds.), *Handbook of the psychology of aging* (4th ed., pp. 266–286). San Diego, CA: Academic Press.

Scharf, C. (1983). Loudness. In *Hearing Research and Theory* (pp. 1–56). New York: Academic Press.

Schedlowski, M., & Pacheco-Lopez, G. (2010). The learned immune response: Pavlov and beyond. *Brain, Behavior, and Immunity, 24,* 176–185.

Scheier, M., & Carver, C. (2000). Optimism, coping, and health: Assessment and implications of generalized outcome expectancies. *Health Psychology, 4,* 219–247.

Scheier, M. F., Carver, C. S., & Bridges, M. W. (1994). Distinguishing optimism from neuroticism (and trait anxiety, self-mastery, and self-esteem): A reevaluation of the Life Orientation Test. *Journal of Personality and Social Psychology, 67,* 1063–1078.

Schenck, C. H. (2007). *Sleep: The mysteries, the problems, and the solutions.* New York: Penguin.

Schiff, M., Duyme, M., Dumaret, A., Steward, J., Tomkiewicz, S., & Feingold, J. (1978). Intellectual status of working class children adopted early into upper middle-class families. *Science, 200,* 1503–1504.

Schiffman, S. S. (1997). Taste and smell losses in normal aging and problem disease. *Journal of the American Medical Association, 278,* 1357–1363.

Schippers, M. C., & Van Lange, P. A. M. (2006). The psychological benefits of superstitious rituals in top sport: A study among top sportspersons. *Journal of Applied Social Psychology, 36,* 2532–2553.

Schmader, T., Johns, M., & Forbes, C. (2008). An integrated process model of stereotype threat effects on performance. *Psychological Review, 115,* 336–356.

Schmajuk, N. A., & Larrauri, J. A. (2006). Experimental challenges to theories of classical conditioning: Application of an attentional model of storage and retrieval. *Journal of Experimental Psychology: Animal Behavior Processes, 32,* 1–20.

Schmelter, A., Jansen, P., & Heil, M. (2009). Empirical evaluation of virtual environment technology as an experimental tool in developmental spatial cognition research. *European Journal of Cognitive Psychology, 21,* 724–739.

Schmid Mast, M. S., & Hall, J. A. (2006). Women's advantage at remembering others' appearance: A systematic look at the why and when of a gender difference. *Personality and Social Psychology Bulletin, 32,* 353–364.

Schmid, R. E. (2008). Humans might have faced extinction, study suggests. *Milwaukee Journal Sentinel,* 12A. Retrieved from www.JSOnline.com

Schmidt, S. J. (2004). Developmental needs meeting strategy: A new treatment approach applied to dissociative identity disorder. *Journal of Trauma and Dissociation, 5,* 55–78.

Schmitt, D. P., Shackelford, T. K., Duntley, J., Tooke, W., & Buss, D. M. (2001). The desire for sexual variety as a key to understanding basic human mating strategies. *Personal Relationships, 8,* 425–455.

Schmolck, H., Buffalo, E. A., & Squire, L. R. (2000). Memory distortions develop over time: Recollections from the O. J. Simpson trial verdict after 15 and 32 months. *Psychological Science, 11,* 39–45.

Schmuck, P., Kasser, T., & Ryan, R. M. (2000). The relationship of well-being to intrinsic and extrinsic goals in Germany and the U.S. *Social Indicators Research, 50,* 225–241.

Schneider, B. (1985). Organizational behavior. *Annual Review of Psychology, 36,* 573–611.

Schneidman, E. S. (1987). A psychological approach to suicide. In *Cataclysms, cries, and catastrophes: Psychology in action* (Vol. 6, pp. 147–183). Washington, DC: American Psychological Association.

Schnicker, K., Legenbauer, T., & Hiller, W. (2011). Therapy effects and response rates of patients with eating disorders: A naturalistic study. *Verhaltenstherapie, 21,* 31–38.

Schooler, J. W., Gerhard, D., & Loftus, E. F. (1986). Qualities of the unreal. *Journal of Experimental Psychology: Learning, Memory, and Cognition, 12,* 171–181.

Schotanus, S. M., & Chergui, K. (2008). Dopamine D1 receptors and group I metabotropic glutamate receptors contribute to the induction of long-term potentiation in the nucleus accumbens. *Neuropharmacology, 54,* 837–844.

Schroeder, R. W., Baade, L. E., Peck, C. P., VonDran, E. J., Brockman, C. J., Webster, B. K., & Heinrichs, R. J. (2012). Validation of MMPI-2-RF Validity Scales in criterion group neuropsychological samples. *The Clinical Neuropsychologist, 26,* 129–146.

Schroger, E. (2007). Mismatch negativity: A microphone into auditory memory. *Journal of Psychophysiology, 21,* 138–146.

Schwartz, G. E., Davidson, R. J., & Maer, F. (1975). Right hemisphere lateralization for emotion in the human brain: Interactions with cognition. *Science, 190,* 286–288.

Schwartz, S., & Maquet, P. (2002). Sleep imaging and the neuro-psychological assessment of dreams. *Trends in Cognitive Sciences, 6,* 23–30.

Scott, A. J. (1994). Chronobiological considerations in shiftworker sleep and performance and shiftwork scheduling. *Human Performance, 7,* 207–233.

Sealey, A. (2000). Child language: Children, language and the social world. Harlow, Endlang: Pearson.

Sebastian, C., Burnett, S., & Blakemore, S. J. (2008). Development of the self-concept during adolescence. *Trends in Cognitive Sciences, 12,* 441–446.

Sedgwick, J. (1995). Inside the Pioneer Fund. In R. Jacoby & N. Glauberman (Eds.), *The Bell Curve debate: History, documents, opinions* (pp. 144–161). New York: Random House.

Seeman, P., Guan, H., & Hubert, H. (1993). Dopamine D4 receptors elevated in schizophrenia. *Nature, 365,* 441–445.

Segall, M. H., Campbell, D. T., & Herskovits, M. J. (1966). *The influence of culture on visual perception.* Indianapolis, IN: Bobbs-Merri¬l.

Segall, M. H., Dasen, P. R., Berry, J. W., & Poortinga, Y. H. (1990). *Human behavior in global perspective: An introduction to cross-cultural psychology.* New York: Pergamon.

Segerstrom, S. C., & Miller, G. E. (2004). Psychological stress and the human immune system: A meta-analytic study of 30 years of inquiry. *Psychological Bulletin, 130,* 601–630.

Segerstrom, S. C., & O'Connor, D. B. (2012). Stress, health and illness: Four challenges for the future. *Psychology & Health, 27,* 128–140.

Segerstrom, S. C., Taylor, S., Kemeny, M., & Fahey, J. (1998). Optimism is associated with mood, coping, and immune change in response to stress. *Journal of Personality and Social Psychology, 74,* 1646–1655.

Seifer, R., Schiller, M., Sameroff, A. J., Resnick, S., & Riordin, A. J. (1996). Attachment, maternal sensitivity, and infant temperament during the first year of life. *Developmental Psychology, 32,* 12–25.

Seifert, C. M., Chapman, L. S., Hart, J. K., & Perez, P. (2012). Enhancing intrinsic motivation in health promotion and wellness. *American Journal of Health Promotion, 26,* 3–10.

Seiler, C. B., Jones, K. E., Shera, D., & Armstrong, C. L. (2011). Brain region white matter associations with visual selective attention. *Brain Imaging and Behavior, 5,* 262–273.

Seipp, B. (1991). Anxiety and academic performance: A meta-analysis of findings. *Anxiety Research, 4,* 27–41.

Sekuler, R., & Blake, R. (1994). *Perception* (3rd ed.). New York: McGraw-Hill.

Seldon, H. L. (2005). Does brain white matter growth expand the cortex like a balloon? Hypothesis and consequences. *Laterality: Asymmetries of Body, Brain and Cognition, 10,* 81–95.

Selemon, L. D., Wang, L., Nebel, M. B., Csernansky, J. G., Goldman-Rakic, P. S., & Rakic, P. (2005). Direct and indirect effects of fetal irradiation on cortical gray and white matter volume in the Macaque. *Biological Psychiatry, 57,* 83–90.

Seligman, M. E. P. (1970). On the generality of laws of learning. *Psychological Review, 77,* 406–418.

Seligman, M. E. P. (1971). Phobias and preparedness. *Behavior Therapy, 2,* 307–321.

Seligman, M. E. P. (1975). *Helplessness: On depression, development, and death.* San Francisco, CA: Freeman.

Seligman, M. E. P. (2007). *What you can change and what you can't: The complete guide to successful self-improvement.* London: Random House/Vintage Books.

Seligman, M. E. P., & Maier, S. F. (1967). Failure to escape traumatic shock. *Journal of Experimental Psychology, 74,* 1–9.

Sellbom, M., Ben-Porath, Y. S., Patrick, C. J., Wygant, D. B., Gartland, D. M., & Stafford, K. P. (2012). Development and construct validation of MMPI-2-RF indices of global psychopathy, fearless-dominance, and impulsive-antisociality. *Personality Disorders: Theory, Research, and Treatment, 3,* 17–38.

Selye, H. (1936). A syndrome produced by nocuous agents. *Nature, 138,* 32.

Selye, H. (1956). *The stress of life.* New York: McGraw-Hill.

Sémon, M., Mouchiroud, D., & Duret, L. (2005). Relationship between gene expression and GC-content in mammals: Statistical significance and biological relevance. *Human Molecular Genetics, 14,* 421–427.

Sevy, S., Mendlewicz, J., & Mendelbaum, K. (1995). Genetic research in bipolar illness. In *Handbook of depression* (2nd ed., pp. 203–212). New York: Guilford Press.

Sewell, K. W. (2005). The experience cycle and the sexual response cycle: Conceptualization and application to sexual dysfunctions. *Journal of Constructivist Psychology, 18,* 3–13.

Shadish, W. R., Montgomery, L. M., Wilson, P., Wilson, M. R., Bright, I., & Okwumabua, T. (1993). Effects of family and marital psychotherapies: A meta-analysis. *Journal of Consulting and Clinical Psychology, 61,* 992–1002.

Shakow, D. (2002). Clinical psychology seen some 50 years later. In W. E. Pickren & D. A. Dewsbury (Eds.), *Evolving perspectives on the history of psychology* (pp. 433–451). Washington, DC: American Psychological Association.

Shamay-Tsoory, S. G. (2007). Impaired empathy following ventromedial prefrontal brain damage. In P. Woodruff (Ed.), *Empathy in mental illness* (pp. 89–110). New York: Cambridge University Press.

Shanab, M. E., & Yahya, K. A. (1977). A behavioral study of obedience in children. *Journal of Personality and Social Psychology, 35,* 530–536.

Shanahan, T. L., Kronauer, R. E., Duffy, J. F., Williams, G. H., & Czeisler, C. A. (1999). Melatonin rhythm observed throughout a three-cycle bright-light stimulus designed to reset the human circadian pacemaker. *Journal of Biological Rhythms, 14,* 237–253.

Sharp, S. E. (1898). Individual psychology: A study of psychological method. *American Journal of Psychology, 10,* 329–391.

Sharps, M. J., Hess, A. B., Price-Sharps, J. L., & Teh, J. (2008). Heuristic and algorithmic processing in English, mathematics, and science education. *Journal of Psychology: Interdisciplinary and Applied, 142,* 71–88.

Shaywitz, B. A., Shaywitz, S. E., Pugh, K. R., Constable, R. T., Skudlarski, P., Fulbright, R. K., ... Gore, J. C. (1995). Sex differences in the functional organization of the brain of language. *Nature, 373*(607-609).

Shaywitz, J., & Liebowitz, M. R. (2003). Antiepileptic treatment of anxiety disorders. *Primary Psychiatry, 10,* 51–56.

Shedler, J. (2010). The efficacy of psychodynamic psychotherapy. *American Psychologist, 65,* 98–109.

Shedler, J., & Westen, D. (2004). Refining personality disorder diagnosis: Integrating science and practice. *American Journal of Psychiatry, 161,* 1350–1365.

Sher, L. (2002). Suicidal behaviour and seasonality. *Nordic Journal of Psychiatry, 56,* 67.

Sher, L. (2003). Daily hassles, cortisol, and depression. *Australian & New Zealand Journal of Psychiatry, 37,* 383–384.

Sherif, M. (1966). *In common predicament: Social psychology of intergroup conflict and cooperation.* Boston: Houghton Mifflin.

Sherif, M., Harvey, O. J., White, B. J., Hood, W. R., & Sherif, C. (1961). *Intergroup conflict and cooperation: The Robbers' Cave experiment.* Norman, OK: Oklahoma Book Exchange.

Sherif, M., & Sherif, C. W. (1956). *An outline of social psychology.* New York: Harper & Brothers.

Shestowsky, D., Wegener, D. T., & Fabrigar, L. R. (1998). Need for cognition and interpersonal influence: Individual differences in impact on dyadic decisions. *Journal of Personality and Social Psychology, 74,* 1317–1328.

Shields, S. A. (2002). *Speaking from the heart: Gender and the social meaning of emotion.* Cambridge, England: Cambridge University Press.

Shields, S. A. (2005). The politics of emotion in everyday life: "Appropriate" emotion and claims on identity. *Review of General Psychology, 9,* 3–15.

Shigematsu, N., Yamamoto, K., Higuchi, S., & Fukuda, T. (2008). An immunohistochemical study on a unique colocalization relationship between substance P and GABA in the central nucleus of amygdala. *Brain Research, 1198,* 55–67.

Shimahara, K. N., & Holowinsky, I. Z. (2001). Ethnicity, race, and nationality in education: A global perspective. In K. N. Shimahara & I. Z. Holowinsky (Eds.), *The Rutgers Invitational Symposium on Education Series* (pp. 81–100). Piscataway, NJ: Rutgers University Press.

Shin, L. M., Kosslyn, S. M., McNally, R. J., Alpert, N. M., Thompson, W. L., Raush, S. L., ... Pitman, R. K. (1997). Visual imagery and perception in posttraumatic stress disorder: A positron emission tomographic investigation. *Archives of General Psychiatry, 54,* 233–241.

Shin, Y. K., Yoon, I. Y. H., No, Y. M., Hong, M. C., Yun, Y. D., Jung, B. K., ... Hong, S. C. (2008). Prevalence of narcolepsy-cataplexy in Korean adolescents. *Acta Neurologica Scandinavica, 117,* 273–278.

Shumaker, S. A., & Hill, D. R. (1991). Gender differences in social support and physical health. *Health Psychology, 10,* 102–111.

Sicotte, N. L., Woods, R. P., & Mazziotta, J. C. (1999). Handedness in twins: A meta-analysis. *Laterality, 4,* 265–286.

Sidanius, J., Levin, S., Liu, J., & Pratto, F. (2000). Social dominance orientation, anti-egalitarianism and the political psychology of gender: An extension and cross-cultural replication. *European Journal of Social Psychology, 30,* 41–67.

Siegel, J. M. (1990). Stressful life events and use of physician services among the elderly: The moderating role of pet ownership. *Journal of Personality and Social Psychology, 58,* 1081–1086.

Siegel, J. M. (2003). Why we sleep. *Scientific American,* 92–97.

Silber, M. H. (2001). Sleep disorders. *Neurology Clinics, 19,* 173–186.

Silverschanz, P., Cortina, L., Konik, J., & Magley, V. J. (2008). Slurs, snubs, and queer jokes: Incidence and impact of heterosexist harassment in academia. *Sex Roles, 58,* 179–191.

Simcock, G., & Hayne, H. (2002). Breaking the barrier? Children fail to translate their preverbal memories into language. *Psychological Science, 13,* 225–231.

Simmons, F. R., Willis, C., & Adams, A.-M. (2012). Different components of working memory have different relationships with different mathematical skills. *Journal of Experimental Child Psychology, 111,* 139–155.

Simons, D. J., & Levin, D. T. (1998). Failure to detect changes to people during a real-world interaction. *Psychonomic Bulletin and Review, 5,* 644–649.

Simonton, D. K. (1992). The social context of career success and course for 2,026 scientists and inventors. *Personality and Social Psychology Bulletin, 18,* 452–463.

Simonton, D. K. (2000). Creative development as acquired expertise: Theoretical issues and an empirical test. *Developmental Review, 20,* 283–318.

Simonton, D. K. (2011). Exceptional talent and genius. In S. von Stumm & A. Furnham (Eds.), *The Wiley-Blackwell handbook of individual differences* (pp. 635–655). Hobeken, NJ: Wiley-Blackwell.

Simonton, D. K., & Ting, S.-S. (2010). Creativity in eastern and western civilizations: The lessons of historiometry. *Management and Organization Review, 6,* 329–350.

Simpson, J. A., Rholes, W. S., Campbell, L., & Wilson, C. L. (2003). Changes in attachment orientations across the transition to parenthood. *Journal of Experimental Social Psychology, 39,* 317–331.

Sinclair, R. J., Dixit, S., & Burton, H. (2011). Recognition memory for vibrotactile rhythms: An fMRI study in blind and sighted individuals. *Somatosensory & Motor Research, 28,* 48–62.

Singelis, T. M., Triandis, H. C., Bhawuk, D. S., & Gelfand, M. (1995). Horizontal and vertical dimensions of individualism and collectivism: A theoretical and measurement refinement. *Cross-Cultural Research, 29,* 240–275.

Singer, J. A., Singer, J. L., & Zittel, C. (2000). Personality variations in autobiographical memories, self-representations, and daydreaming. In R. G. Kunzendorf & B. Wallace (Eds.), *Individual Differences in Conscious Experience: Advances in Consciousness Research* (Vol. 20, pp. 269–307). Amsterdam, Netherlands: John Benjamins.

Singh, A., & Selesnick, S. H. (2005). Meningiomas. In *Neurology* (2nd ed.). Philadelphia, PA: Lippincott, Williams & Wilkins.

Siskind, D. (2005). Psychotherapy with children and parents during divorce. In P. Hymowitz (Ed.), *A handbook of divorce and custody: Forensic, developmental, and clinical perspectives* (pp. 331–341). Hillsdale, NJ: Analytic Press.

Sitnikova, T., West, W. C., Kuperberg, G. R., & Holcomb, P. J. (2006). The neural organization of semantic memory: Electrophysiological activity suggests feature-based segregation. *Biological Psychology, 71,* 326–340.

Skaer, T. L., Sclar, D. A., & Robison, L. M. (2008). Trend in anxiety disorders in the USA 1990-2003. *Primary Care & Community Psychiatry, 13,* 1–7.

Skinner, B. F. (1938). The behavior of organisms. New York: Appleton-Century-Crofts.

Skinner, B. F. (1948a). "Superstition" in the pigeon. *Journal of Experimental Psychology, 38,* 168–172.

Skinner, B. F. (1948b). *Walden two.* New York: Macmillan.

Skinner, B. F. (1957). *Verbal behavior.* New York: Appleton-Century-Crofts.

Skinner, B. F. (1990). Can psychology be a science of the mind? *American Psychologist, 45,* 1206–1210.

Slade, L. A., & Rush, M. C. (1991). Achievement motivation and the dynamics of task difficulty choices. *Journal of Personality and Social Psychology, 60,* 165–172.

Slaughter, M. (1990). The vertebrate retina. In *Science of Vision.* New York: Springer-Verlang.

Slay, H., Hayaki, J., Napolitano, M., & Brownell, K. (1998). Motivations for running and eating attitudes in obligatory versus nonobligatory runners. *International Journal of Eating Disorders, 23,* 267–275.

Slotkin, T. A. (2008). If nicotine is a developmental neurotoxicant in animal studies, dare we recommend nicotine replacement therapy in pregnant women and adolescents? *Neurotoxicology and Teratology, 30,* 1–19.

Smallwood, J. (2011). The footprints of a wandering mind: Further examination of the time course of an attentional lapse. *Cognitive Neuroscience, 2,* 91–97.

Smedley, A., & Smedley, B. D. (2005). Race as biology is fiction, racism as a social problem is real: Anthropological and historical perspectives on the social construction of race. *American Psychologist, 60,* 16–26.

Smith, A. E., Jussim, L., & Eccles, J. (1999). Do self-fulfilling prophecies accumulate, dissipate, or remain stable over time? *Journal of Personality and Social Psychology, 77,* 548–565.

Smith, B. R., & Blumstein, D. T. (2008). Fitness consequences of personality: A meta-analysis. *Behavioral Ecology, 19,* 448–455.

Smith, D. (1982). Trends in counseling and psychotherapy. *American Psychologist, 37,* 802–809.

Smith, E. J., Partridge, J. C., Parsons, K. N., White, E. M., Cuthill, I. C., Bennett, A. T. D., & Church, S. C. (2002). Ulraviolet vision and mate choice in the guppy (Poecilia reticulata). *Behavioral Ecology, 13,* 1–19.

Smith, J. M., & Szathmáry, E. (1995). *The major transitions in evolution.* Oxford, UK: W. H. Freeman.

Smith, K. P., & Christakis, N. A. (2008). Social networks and health. *Annual Review of Sociology, 34,* 405–429.

Smith, L., Totterdell, P., & Folkard, S. (1995). Shiftwork effects in nuclear power workers: A field study using portable computers. *Work & Stress, 9,* 235–244.

Smith, M. L., Cottrell, G. W., Gosselin, F., & Schyns, P. G. (2005). Transmitting and decoding facial expressions. *Psychological Science, 16,* 184–189.

Smith, M. L., & Glass, G. V. (1977). Meta-analysis of psychotherapy outcome studies. *American Psychologist, 32,* 752–760.

Smith, P. K., & Bargh, J. A. (2008). Nonconscious effects of power on basic approach and avoidance tendencies. *Social Cognition, 26,* 1–24.

Smith, S. M., & Petty, R. E. (1992). Personality moderators of mood congruency effects on cognitions: The role of self-esteem and negative mood regulation. *Journal of Personality and Social Psychology, 68,* 1092–1107.

Smith, T. (1992). Hostility and health: Current status of a psychosomatic hypothesis. *Health Psychology, 11,* 139–150.

Smith, T. B., McCullough, M. E., & Poll, J. (2003). Religiousness and depression: Evidence for a main effect and the moderating influence of stressful life events. *Psychological Bulletin, 129,* 614–636.

Smith, W. B. (2007). Karen Horney and psychotherapy in the 21st century. *Clinical Social Work Journal, 35,* 57–66.

Smith-Rohrberg, D., Bruce, R., & Altice, F. L. (2004). Research note - Review of corrections-based therapy for opiate-dependent patients: Implications for buprenorphine treatment among correctional populations. *Journal of Drug Issues, 34,* 451–480.

Snarey, J. R. (1985). Cross-cultural universality of social-moral development: A critical review of Kohlbergian research. *Psychological Bulletin, 97,* 202–233.

Snow, C. E. (1999). Social perspectives on the emergence of language. In B. MacWhinney (Ed.), The Energence of Language (pp. 257–276). Mahwah, NJ: Erlbaum.

Snyder, C. R., Lopez, S. J., & Pedrotti, J. T. (2011). *Positive psychology: The scientific and practical explorations of human strengths.* Thousand Oaks, CA: Sage.

Snyder, M. (1974). The self-monitoring of expressive behavior. *Journal of Personality and Social Psychology, 30,* 526–537.

Snyder, M. (1987). Public appearances/private realities: *The psychology of self-monitoring.* New York: Freeman.

Snyder, M., & Copeland, J. (1989). Self-monitoring processes in organizational settings. In R. A. Giacalone & P. Rosenfeld (Eds.), *Impression management in the organization* (pp. 7–19). Hillsdale, NJ: Erlbaum.

Snyder, M., & Gangestad, S. (1982). Choosing social situations: Two investigations of self-monitoring processes. *Journal of Personality and Social Psychology, 43,* 123–135.

Snyder, M., & Swann, W. B. (1978). Hypothesis-testing processes in social interaction. *Journal of Personality and Social Psychology, 36,* 1202–1212.

Snyder, S., Greenberg, D., & Yamamura, H. I. (2008). Antischizophrenic drugs and brain cholinergic receptors: Affinity for muscarinic sites predicts extrapyramidal effects. In S. H. Snyder (Ed.), Science and Psychiatry: Groundbreaking Discoveries in Molecular Neuroscience (pp. 137–146). Arlington, VA: American Psychiatric Publishing.

Soares, J. F. J., & Öhman, A. (1993). Preattentive processing, preparedness and phobias: Effects of instruction on conditioned electrodermal responses to masked and non-masked fear-relevant stimuli. *Behavior Research and Therapy, 31,* 87–95.

Soliman, M., Santos, A. M., & Lohr, J. B. (2008). Emergency, inpatient, and residential treatment. In D. V. Jeste (Ed.), *Clinical handbook of schizophrenia* (pp. 339–353). New York: Guilford Press.

Solomon, D. A., Leon, A. C., Endicott, J., Mueller, T. I., Coryell, W., Shea, M. T., & Keller, M. B. (2004). Psychosocial impairment and recurrence of major depression. *Comprehensive Psychiatry, 45,* 423–430.

Solomon, R. L. (1980). The opponent-process theory of acquired motivation: The costs of pleasure and the benefits of pain. *American Psychologist, 35,* 691–712.

Solomon, R. L., & Corbit, J. D. (1974). An opponent-process theory of motivation: I. Temporal dynamics of affect. *Psychological Review, 81,* 119–145.

Sommers, S. R., & Kassin, S. M. (2001). On the many impacts of inadmissible testimony: Selective compliance, need for cognition, and the overcorrection bias. *Personality and Social Psychology Bulletin, 27,* 1368–1377.

Song, Y. H., Terao, T., & Nakamura, J. (2007). Type A behaviour pattern is associated with cynicism and low self-acceptance in medical students. *Stress and Health: Journal of the International Society for the Investigation of Stress, 23,* 323–329.

Sowell, E. R., Thompson, P. M., & Toga, A. W. (2004). Mapping changes in the human cortex throughout the span of life. *Neuroscientist, 10,* 372–392.

Spanos, N. P., Flynn, D. M., & Niles, J. (1989). Rapport and cognitive skill training in the enhancement of hypnotizability. *Imagination, Cognition, and Personality, 9,* 245–262.

Spear, N. E. (1979). Experimental analysis of infantile amnesia. In F. J. Evans (Ed.), *Functional disorders of memory* (pp. 75–102). Hillsdale, NJ: Erlbaum.

Spearman, C. E. (1927). *The abilities of man.* London: Macmillan.

Spencer, S. J., Steele, C. M., & Quinn, D. M. (1999). Stereotype threat and women's math performance. *Journal of Experimental Social Psychology, 35,* 4–28.

Sperling, G. (1960). The information available in brief visual presentation. *Psychological Monographs: General and Applied, 74,* 1–29.

Spiegel, D., Loewenstein, R. J., Lewis-Fernandez, R., Sar, V., Simeon, D., Vermetten, E., ... Dell, P. F. (2011). Dissociative disorders in *DSM-5. Depression and Anxiety, 28,* E17–E45.

Sprecher, S. (1999). "I love you more today than yesterday": Romantic partners' perceptions of changes in love and related affect over time. *Journal of Personality and Social Psychology, 76,* 46–53.

Sprecher, S., Metts, S., Burleson, B., Hatfield, E., & Thompson, A. (1995). Domains of expressive interaction in intimate relationships: Associations with satisfaction and commitment. *Family Relations, 44,* 1–8.

Springer, S. P., & Deutsch, G. (1998). *Left brain, right brain: Perspectives from cognitive neuroscience* (5th ed.). New York: W. H. Freeman.

Srivastava, S., John, O. P., Gosling, S. D., & Potter, J. (2003). Development of personality in early and middle adulthood: Set like plaster or persistent change? *Journal of Personality & Social Psychology, 84,* 1041–1053.

Sroufe, A., & McIntosh, J. (2011). Divorce and attachment relationships: The longitudinal journey. *Family Court Review, 49,* 464–473.

St. Claire, L., Hayward, R. C., & Rogers, P. J. (2010). Interactive effects of caffeine consumption and stressful circumstances on components of stress: Caffeine makes men less, but women more effective as partners under stress. *Journal of Applied Social Psychology, 40,* 3106–3129.

Staats, A. W., & Staats, C. K. (1958). Attitudes established by classical conditioning. *Journal of Abnormal and Social Psychology, 57,* 37–40.

Stallard, P., Salter, E., & Velleman, R. (2004). Posttraumatic stress disorder following road traffic accidents: A second prospective study. *European Child and Adolescent Psychiatry, 13,* 172–178.

Stamos, D. N. (2008). *Evolution and the big questions: Sex, race, religion, and other matters.* Malden, MA: Blackwell Publishing.

Stapel, D. A., & Koomen, W. (2006). The flexible unconscious: Investigating the judgemental impact of varieties of unaware perception. *Journal of Experimental Social Psychology, 42,* 112–119.

Stark, R. (2002). Physiology and faith: Addressing the "universal" gender difference in religious commitment. *Journal for the Scientific Study of Religion, 41,* 495–507.

Steadman, H. J., Mulvey, E. P., Monahan, J., Robbins, P. C., Appelbaum, P. S., Grisso, T., … Silver, E. (1998). Violence by people discharged from acute psychiatric inpatient facilities and by others in the same neighborhoods. *Archives of General Psychiatry, 55,* 393–401.

Stebbins, W. C. (1980). The evolution of hearing in the mammals. In R. R. Fay (Ed.), *Comparative Studies of Hearing in Vertebrates* (pp. 421–436). New York: Springer-Verlag.

Steele, C. M. (1992). Race and the schooling of Black Americans. *The Atlantic Monthly,* 68–78.

Steele, C. M. (1997). A threat in the air: How stereotypes shape intellectual identity and performance. *American Psychologist, 52,* 613–629.

Steele, C. M. (2011). Foreword: Pursuing effective integrated education. *Journal of Social Issues, 67,* 431–434.

Steele, C. M., & Aronson, J. (1995). Stereotype threat and the intellectual test performance of African Americans. *Journal of Personality and Social Psychology, 69,* 797–811.

Steele, C. M., & Josephs, R. A. (1988). Drinking your troubles away: I. The psychology of drunken excess. *Journal of Personality and Social Psychology, 48,* 18–34.

Steil, J. M. (1994). Equality and entitlement in marriage. In *Entitlement and the affectional bond: Justice in close relationships* (pp. 229–285). New York: Plenum Press.

Stein, E. A., Pankiewicz, J., Harsch, H. H., Cho, J.-K., Fuller, S. A., & Hoffmann, R. G. (1998). Nicotine-induced limbic cortical activation in the human brain: A functional MRI study. *American Journal of Psychiatry, 155,* 1009–1015.

Stein, M., & Burchartz, B. (2006). The invisible wall project: Reasoning and problem solving process of primary and lower secondary students. *Mathematical Thinking and Learning, 8,* 65–90.

Steinberg, J. (1995). The graying of the senses. *Journal of NIMH Research, 7,* 32–33.

Steinberg, L. (2007). Risk taking in adolescence: New perspectives from brain and behavioral science. *Current Directions in Psychological Science, 16,* 55–59.

Steinberg, L., Dornbusch, S. M., & Brown, B. B. (1992). Ethnic differences in adolescent achievement: An ecological perspective. *American Psychologist, 47,* 723–729.

Steketee, G. S. (1993). *Treatment of obsessive-compulsive disorder.* New York: Guilford.

Stellar, E. (1954). The physiology of motivation. *Psychological Review, 61,* 5–22.

Stemberger, R. T., Turner, S. M., Beidel, D. C., & Calhoun, K. S. (1995). Social phobia: An analysis of possible developmental factors. *Journal of Abnormal Psychology, 104,* 526–531.

Stener-Victorin, E., Kruse-Smidje, C., & Jung, K. (2004). Comparison between electro-acupuncture and hydrotherapy, both in combination with patient education and patient education alone, on the symptomatic treatment of osteoarthritis of the hip. *Clinical Journal of Pain, 20,* 179–185.

Stephan, W., Stephan, C., & De Vargas, M. (1996). Emotional expression in Costa Rica and the United States. *Journal of Cross-Cultural Psychology, 27,* 147–160.

Stephens, D. P., & Few, A. L. (2007). The effects of images of African American women in hip hop on early adolescents' attitudes toward physical attractiveness and interpersonal relationships. *Sex Roles, 56,* 251–264.

Stern, D. (1985). *The interpersonal world of the infant: A view from psychoanalysis and developmental psychology.* New York: Basic Books.

Stern, W. (1914). *The psychological methods of testing intelligence.* Baltimore, MD: Warwick & York.

Sternbach, R. A. (1963). Congenital insensitivity to pain: A review. *Psychological Bulletin, 60,* 252–264.

Sternberg, R. J. (2003). Construct validity of the theory of successful intelligence. In J. Lautrey & T. I. Lubart (Eds.), *Models of intelligence: International perspectives* (pp. 55–77). Washington, DC: American Psychological Association.

Sternberg, R. J. (2005). The importance of converging operations in the study of human intelligence. *Cortex, 41,* 243–244.

Sternberg, R. J., & Kaufman, J. C. (2002). *The evolution of intelligence.* Mahwah, NJ: Erlbaum.

Sternberg, R. J., & Lubart, T. I. (1996). Investing in creativity. *American Psychologist, 51,* 677–688.

Sternberg, R. J., Wagner, R. K., Williams, W. M., & Horvath, J. (1995). Testing common sense. *American Psychologist, 50,* 913–927.

Stevens, J. C. (1989). Food quality reports from noninstitutionalized aged. *Annals of the New York Academy of Sciences, 561,* 87–93.

Stevens, S. S. (1955). The measurement of loudness. *Journal of the Acoustical Society of American, 27,* 815–819.

Stevenson, H. W., Chen, C., & Lee, S. (1993). Mathematics achievement of Chinese, Japanese, and American children: Ten years later. *Science, 259,* 53–58.

Stevenson, H. W., Lee, S., & Stigler, J. W. (1986). Mathematics achievement of Chinese, Japanese, and American children. *Science, 231,* 693–699.

Stevenson, H. W., & Zusho, A. (2002). Adolescence in China and Japan: Adapting to a changing environment. In B. B. Brown, R. Larson, & T. S. Saraswathi (Eds.), *The world's youth: Adolescence in eight regions of the globe* (pp. 141–170). New York: Cambridge University Press.

Stewart, K. T., Hayes, B. C., & Eastman, C. I. (1995). Light treatment for NASA shiftworkers. *Chronobiology International, 12,* 141–151.

Stewart, S. E., Beresin, C., Haddad, S., Stack, D., Egan, F., & Jeanne, J. M. (2008). Predictors of family accommodation in obsessive-compulsive disorder. *Annals of Clinical Psychiatry, 20,* 65–70.

Stice, E., Presnell, K., Shaw, H., & Rohde, P. (2005). Psychological and behavioral risk factors for obesity onset in adolescent girls: A prospective study. *Journal of Consulting and Clinical Psychology, 73,* 195–202.

Stieger, S., Preyss, A. V., & Voracek, M. (2012). Romantic jealousy and implicit and explicit self-esteem. *Personality and Individual Differences, 52,* 51–55.

Stirling, L. J., & Yeomans, M. R. (2004). Effect of exposure to a forbidden food on eating in restrained and unrestrained women. *International Journal of Eating Disorders, 35,* 59–68.

Stokes, P. D. (2006). *Creativity from constraints: The psychology of breakthrough.* New York: Springer.

Storms, M. D. (1983). *Development of sexual orientation.* Washington, DC: Office of Social and Ethical Responsibility, American Psychological Association.

Strack, F., Martin, L. L., & Stepper, S. (1988). Inhibiting and facilitating conditions of facial expressions: A nonobtrusive test of the facial feedback hypothesis. *Journal of Personality and Social Psychology, 54,* 768–777.

Strakowski, S. M., Adler, M. C., & DelBello, M. P. (2002). Volumetric MRI studies of mood disorders: Do they distinguish unipolar and bipolar disorder? *Bipolar Disorders, 4,* 80–88.

Strassberg, D. S., & Holty, S. (2003). An experimental study of women's internet personal ads. *Archives of Sexual Behavior, 32,* 253–260.

Strausfeld, N. J. (2001). Insect brain. In *Brain evolution and cognition* (pp. 367–400). New York: Wiley.

Strawbridge, W. J., Sjema, S. J., Cohen, R. D., & Kaplan, G. A. (2001). Religious attendance increases survival by improving and maintaining good health behaviors, mental health, and social relationships. *Annals of Behavioral Medicine, 23,* 68–74.

Strayer, D. L., & Johnston, W. A. (2001). Driven to distraction: Dual-task studies of simulated driving and conversing on a cellular phone. *American Psychological Society, 12,* 462–466.

Streeter, A. S., & McBurney, D. H. (2003). Waist-to-hip ratio and attractiveness: New evidence and a critique of a "critical test." *Evolution and Human Behavior, 24,* 88–98.

Strelan, P., Mehaffey, S. J., & Tiggemann, M. (2003). Self-objectification and esteem in young women: The mediating role of reasons for exercise. *Sex Roles, 48,* 89–95.

Strenger, C. (2009). Sosein: Active self-acceptance in midlife. *Journal of Humanistic Psychology, 49,* 46–65.

Strentz, H. (1986). Become a psychic and amaze your friends! *Atlanta Journal,* 15A.

Strickgold, R. (2003). Human studies of sleep and off-line memory reprocessing. In *Sleep and brain plasticity* (pp. 41–63). Oxford, UK: Oxford University Press.

Strickland, B. R. (1995). Research on sexual orientation and human development: A commentary. *Developmental Psychology, 31,* 137–140.

Stringer, C. (2003). Human evolution: Out of Ethiopia. *Nature, 423,* 692–695.

Stroebe, M., Stroebe, W., & Schut, H. (2001). Gender differences in adjustment to bereavement: An empirical and theoretical review. *Review of General Psychology, 5,* 62–83.

Stumper, B., Bannard, C., Lieven, E., & Tomasello, M. (2011). "Frequent frames" in German child-directed speech: A limited cue to grammatical categories. *Cognitive Science: A Multidisciplinary Journal, 35,* 1190–1205.

Stunkard, A. J., Harris, J. R., Pedersen, N. L., & McClearn, G. E. (1990). The body-mass index of twins who have been reared apart. *New England Journal of Medicine, 322,* 1483–1487.

Subodh, B. N., Avasthi, A., & Chakrabarti, S. (2008). Psychosocial impact of dysthymia: A study among married patients. *Journal of Affective Disorders, 109,* 199–204.

Subramaniam, K., Kounios, J., Parrish, T. B., & Jung-Beeman, M. (2009). A brain mechanism for facilitation of insight by positive affect. *Journal of Cognitive Neuroscience, 21,* 415–432.

Suchan, B., Gayk, A. E., Schmid, G., Koster, O., & Daum, I. (2008). *Hippocampal involvement in recollection but not familiarity across time: A prospective study.* Hippocampus, 18, 92–98.

Sue, S., & Chu, J. Y. (2003). The mental health of ethnic minority groups: Challenges posed by the supplement to the Surgeon General's report on mental health. *Culture, Medicine and Psychiatry, 27,* 447–465.

Sundram, F., Deeley, Q., Sarkar, S., Daly, E., Latham, R., Craig, M., … Murphy, D. G. M. (2012). White matter microstructural abnormalities in the frontal lobe of adults with antisocial personality disorder. *Cortex: A Journal Devoted to the Study of the Nervous System and Behavior, 48,* 216–229.

Sutton, S. K., & Davidson, R. J. (1997). Prefrontal brain symmetry: A biological substrate of the behavioral approach and inhibition systems. *Psychological Science, 8,* 204–210.

Suzuki, L. A., Prevost, L., & Short, E. L. (2008). Multicultural issues and the assessment of aptitude. In L. A. Suzuki & J. G. Ponterotto (Eds.), *Handbook of multicultural assessment: Clinical, psychological, and educational applications* (pp. 490–519). San Francisco, CA: Jossey-Bass.

Svartberg, K., & Forkman, B. (2002). Personality traits in the domestic dog (Canis familiaris). *Applied Animal Behaviour Science, 79,* 133–155.

Swann, W. B., Jr., Chang-Schneider, C., & McClarty, K. L. (2007). Do people's self-views matter? Self-concept and self-esteem in everyday life. *American Psychologist, 62,* 1–11.

Swanson, L. W. (2004). *Brain maps: Structure of the rat brain* (3rd ed.). San Diego, CA: Elsevier/Academic Press.

Swayze, V. W. (1995). Frontal leucotomy and related psychosurgical procedures in the era before antipsychotics (1935–1954): A historical overview. *American Journal of Psychiatry, 152,* 505–515.

Sweat, J. A., & Durm, M. W. (1993). Psychics: Do police departments really use them? *The Skeptical. Inquirer, 17,* 148–158.

Swerdlow, J. L. (1995). Quite miracles of the brain. *National Geographic, 187*(6), 2–41.

Swets, J. A. (1992). The science of choosing the right decision threshold in high-stakes diagnostics. *American Psychologist, 121,* 371–394.

T

Tabaee, A., Roach, M., & Selesnich, S. H. (2004). Middle ear cogential disorders. In *Current Diagnosis and Treatment in Otolaryngology-Head and Neck Surgery.* New York: McGraw Hill.

Tacey, D. (2001). *Jung and the new age.* Philadelphia, PA: Brunner-Routledge.

Takemura, K., & Arimoto, H. (2008). Independent self in Japan's "North Frontier": An experiment of cognitive dissonance in Hokkaido. *Japanese Journal of Experimental Social Psychology, 48,* 40–49.

Takeuchi, H., Taki, Y., Sassa, Y., Hashizume, H., Sekiguichi, A., Fukushima, A., & Kawashima, R. (2010). White matter structures associated with creativity: Evidence from diffusion tensor imaging. *NeuroImage, 51,* 11–18.

Tamaru, S., Kikuchi, A., Takagi, K., Wakamatsu, M., Ono, K., Horikoshi, T., ... Nakamura, T. (2011). Neurodevelopmental outcomes of very low birth weight and extremely low birth weight infants at 18 months of corrected age associated with prenatal risk factors. *Early Human Development, 87,* 55–59.

Tanaka, K. (2002). Effect of the cognitive load of being a photo-model and dieting on eating behavior. *Japanese Journal of Health Psychology, 15,* 41–48.

Tanford, S., & Penrod, S. (1984). Social influence model: A formal integration of research on majority and minority influence. *Psychological Bulletin, 95,* 189–225.

Tang, T.-P., Shimizu, E., Dube, G. R., Rampon, C., Kerchner, G. A., Zhuo, M., ... Tsien, J. Z. (1999). Genetic enhancement of learning and memory in mice. *Memory, 401,* 63–69.

Tango, R. A., & Kolodinsk, P. (2004). Investigation of placement outcomes 3 years after a job skills training program for chronically unemployed adults. *Journal of Employment Counseling, 41,* 80–92.

Tansley, K. (1965). *Vision in vertebrates.* London: Chapman & Hall.

Tattersall, I. (2007). How did modern human cognition evolve? In B. Stemmer (Ed.), *Consciousness and cognition: Fragments of mind and brain* (pp. 3–17). San Diego, CA: Elsevier Academic Press.

Taylor, F. K. (1965). Cryptomnesia and plagiarism. *British Journal of Psychiatry, 111,* 1111–1118.

Taylor, S. E., & Gonzaga, G. C. (2007). Affiliative responses to stress: A social neuroscience model. In E. Harmon-Jones & P. Winkielman (Eds.), *Social neuroscience: Integrating biological and psychological explanations of social behavior* (pp. 454–473). New York: Guilford Press.

Taylor, S. E., Klein, L. C., Lewis, B. P., Gruenewald, T. L., Gurung, R. A. R., & Updegraff, J. A. (2000). Biobehavioral responses to stress in females: Tend-and-befriend, not fight-or-flight. *Psychological Review, 107,* 411–429.

Taylor, S. E., & Master, S. L. (2011). Social responses to stress: The tend-and-befriend model. In A. Baum (Ed.), *The handbook of stress science: Biology, psychology, and health* (pp. 101–109). New York: Springer.

Taylor, T. J. (2012). Understanding others and understanding language: How do children do it? *Language Sciences, 34,* 1–12.

Te Nijenhuis, J., Tolboom, E., Resing, W., & Bleichrodt, N. (2004). Does cultural background influence the intellectual performance of children from immigrant groups? The RAKIT Intelligence Test for immigrant children. *European Journal of Psychological Assessment, 20,* 10–26.

Teasdale, T. W., & Owen, D. R. (1984). Heredity and familial environment in intelligence and educational level: A sibling study. *Nature, 309,* 620–622.

Teigen, K. H. (1994). Yerkes-Dodson: A law for all seasons. *Theory and Psychology, 4,* 525–547.

Tellegen, A., Lykken, D. T., Bouchard, T. J., Jr., Wilcox, K. J., Segal, N. L., & Rich, S. (1988). Personality similarity in twins reared apart and together. *Journal of Personality and Social Psychology, 54,* 1020–1030.

Teri, L., & Lewinsohn, P. M. (1985). Group intervention for unipolar depression. *Behavior Therapist, 8,* 109–111.

Terman, L. M. (1916). *The measurement of intelligence.* Boston, MA: Houghton Mifflin.

Terman, L. M. (1925). Genetic studies of genius: Vol. 1. *Mental and physical traits of a thousand gifted children.* Stanford, CA: Stanford University Press.

Terman, L. M., & Oden, M. H. (1947). *Genetic studies of genius: Vol. 4. The gifted child grows up: Twenty-five years' follow-up of a superior group.* Stanford, CA: Stanford University Press.

Terr, L. C. (1988). What happens to early memories of trauma? A study of 20 children under age five at the time of documented traumatic events. *Journal of the American Academy of Child and Adolescent Psychiatry, 27,* 96–104.

Thalassis, N. (2004). Measuring minds: Henry Herbert Goddard and the origins of American intelligence testing. *British Journal of Psychology, 95,* 119–123.

Thanellou, A., & Green, J. T. (2011). Spontaneous recovery but not reinstatement of the extinguished conditioned eyeblink response in the rat. *Behavioral Neuroscience, 125,* 613–625.

Theorell, T. (2003). To be able to exert control over one's own situation: A necessary condition for coping with stressors. In J. C. Quick & L. E. Tetrick (Eds.), *Handbook of occupational health psychology* (pp. 201–219). Washington, DC: American Psychological Association.

Theron, W. H., Matthee, D. D., Steel, H. R., & Ramirez, J. M. (2000). Direct and indirect aggression in women: A comparison between South African and Spanish university students. In *Cross-cultural approaches to research on aggression and reconciliation* (pp. 99–109). Huntington, NY: Nova.

Thigpen, C. H., & Cleckley, H. M. (1957). *The three faces of Eve.* New York: McGraw-Hill.

Thoman, E. B. (1999). Morningness and eveningness: Issues for study of the early ontogeny of these circadian rhythms. *Human Development, 42,* 206–212.

Thomas, D. R. (1992). Discrimination and generalization. In *Encyclopedia of learning and memory.* New York: Macmillan.

Thomas, G., & Fletcher, G. J. O. (1997). Empathic accuracy in close relationships. In W. Ickes (Ed.), *Empathic accuracy* (pp. 194–218). New York: Guilford Press.

Thomas, G., & Fletcher, G. J. O. (2003). Mind-reading accuracy in intimate relationships: Assessing the roles of the relationship, the target, and the judge. *Journal of Personality and Social Psychology, 85,* 1079–1094.

Thomas, P. (2004). The many forms of bipolar disorder: A modern look at an old illness. *Journal of Affective Disorders, 79,* S3–S8.

Thomas, R. M. (2001). *Recent theories of human development.* Thousand Oaks, CA: Sage.

Thompson, C., Thompson, S., & Smith, R. (2004). Prevalence of seasonal affective disorder in primary care: A comparison of the seasonal health questionnaire and the seasonal pattern assessment questionnaire. *Journal of Affective Disorders, 78,* 219–226.

Thompson, P. M., Vidal, C., Giedd, J. N., Gochman, P., Blumenthal, J., Nicolson, R., ... Rapoport, J. L. (2001). Mapping adolescent brain change reveals dynamic wave of accelerated gray matter loss in very early-onset schizophrenia. *Proc. Natl. Acad. Sci. USA, 98,* 11650–11655.

Thorndike, E. L. (1898). Animal intelligence: An experimental study of the associative processes in animals. *Psychological Review Monograph Supplement, 2*(8).

Thorndike, E. L. (1911). *Animal intelligence: Experimental studies.* New York: Macmillan.

Thorndike, E. L. (1914). *The psychology of learning.* New York: Teachers College.

Thorpe, M. P., & Day, R. D. (2008). Families and obesity: A family process approach to obesity in adolescents. In H. E. Fitzgerald, V. Mousouli, & H. D. Davies (Eds.), *Obesity in Childhood and Adolescence, Vol 2: Understanding Development and Prevention* (pp. 117–140). Westport, CT: Praeger.

Thurgood, C., Whitfield, T. W. A., & Patterson, J. (2011). Towards a visual recognition threshold: New instrument shows humans identify animals with only 1ms of visual exposure. *Vision Research, 51,* 966–1971.

Thurstone, L. L. (1938). *Primary mental abilities (Vol. 1).* Chicago, IL: Chicago University Press.

Tice, D., & Baumeister, R. F. (1993). Anger control. In D. Wegner & J. Pennebaker (Eds.), *Handbook of mental control.*

Tice, D. M., & Baumeister, R. F. (1997). Longitudinal study of procrastination, performance, stress, and health: The costs and benefits of dawdling. *Psychological Science, 8,* 454–458.

Till, B. D., Stanley, S. M., & Priluck, R. (2008). Classical conditioning and celebrity endorsers: An examination of belongingness and resistance to extinction. *Psychology & Marketing, 25,* 179–196.

Timberlake, W. (2004). Trends in the study of Pavlovian conditioning. *International Journal of Comparative Psychology, 17,* 119–130.

Tither, J. M., & Ellis, B. J. (2008). Impact of fathers on daughters' age at menarche: A genetically and environmentally controlled sibling study. *Developmental Psychology, 44,* 1409–1420.

Tix, A. P., & Frazier, P. A. (2005). Mediation and moderation of the relationship between intrinsic religiousness and mental health. *Personality and Social Psychology Bulletin, 31,* 395–406.

Toates, F. (2006). A model of the hierarchy of behaviour, cognition, and consciousness. *Consciousness and Cognition: An International Journal, 15,* 75–118.

Todd, J. T., & Norman, J. F. (2003). The visual perception of 3-D shape from multiple cures: Are observers capable of perceiving metric structure? *Perception & Psychophysics, 65,* 31–47.

Toepfer, S. M., Cichy, K., & Peters, P. (2012). Letters of gratitude: Further evidence for author benefits. *Journal of Happiness Studies, 13,* 187–201.

Tolman, E. C. (1922). A new formula for behaviorism. *Psychological Review, 29,* 44–53.

Tolman, E. C. (1932). *Purposive behavior in animals and men.* New York: Appleton-Century-Crofts.

Tolman, E. C., & Honzik, C. H. (1930). Insight in rats. University of California Publications in Psychology, 4, 215–232.

Tomarken, A. J., Davidson, R. J., & Henriques, J. B. (1990). Resting frontal brain asymmetry predicts affective responses to films. *Journal of Personality and Social Psychology, 59,* 791–801.

Toner, E., Haslam, N., Robinson, J., & Williams, P. (2012). Character strengths and wellbeing in adolescence: Structure and correlates of the Values in Action Inventory of Strengths for Children. *Personality and Individual Differences, 52,* 637–642.

Tonigan, J. S., & Connors, G. J. (2008). Psychological mechanisms in Alcoholics Anonymous. In M. Galanter & H. D. Kleber (Eds.), *The American Psychiatric Publishing Textbook of Substance Abuse Treatment* (4th ed., pp. 491–498). Arlington, VA: American Psychiatric Publishing.

Tonigan, J. S., Miller, W. R., & Connors, G. J. (2000). Project MATCH client impressions about Alcoholics Anonymous: Measurement issues and relationship to treatment outcome. *Alcoholism Treatment Quarterly, 18*, 25–41.

Torbeyns, J., Arnaud, L., Lemaire, P., & Verschaffel, L. (2004). Cognitive change as strategy change. In A. Demetriou & A. Raftopoulos (Eds.), *Cognitive Developmental Change: Theories, Models and Measurement* (pp. 186–216). New York: Cambridge University Press.

Tormala, Z. L., & Petty, R. E. (2007). Contextual contrast and perceived knowledge: Exploring the implications for persuasion. *Journal of Experimental Social Psychology, 43*, 17–30.

Torres, A., Rodrigues, D., Andre, M., Crepaldi, A. L., & Miguel, E. C. (2004). Obsessive-compulsive symptoms in patients with panic disorder. *Comprehensive Psychiatry, 45*, 219–224.

Toth, K., & King, B. H. (2010). Intellectual disability (mental retardation). In Dulcan's *Textbook of Child and Adolescent Psychiatry*. Arlington, VA: American Psychiatric Association.

Tower, R. K., Kelly, C., & Richards, A. (1997). Individualism, collectivism and reward allocation: A cross-cultural study in Russian and Britain. *British Journal of Social Psychology, 36*, 331–345.

Tramer, M. R., Carroll, D., Campbell, F. A., Reynolds, D. J., Moore, R. A., & McQuay, H. J. (2001). Cannabinoids for control of chemotherapyinduced nausea and vomiting: Quantitative systematic review. *British Medical Journal, 323*, 16–21.

Trappey, C. (1996). A meta-analysis of consumer choice and subliminal advertising. *Psychology and Marketing, 13*, 517–530.

Treffert, D. A. (1989). *Extraordinary people: Understanding savant syndrome*. New York: Ballantine Books.

Treffert, D. A. (1992). Savant syndrome. In *Encyclopedia of learning and memory* (pp. 573–574). New York: Macmillan.

Triandis, H. C. (1989). The self and social behavior in differing cultural contexts. *Psychological Review, 96*, 506–520.

Triandis, H. C. (1995). *Individualism & collectivism*. Boulder, CO: Westview Press.

Triandis, H. C., & Suh, E. M. (2002). Cultural influences on personality. *Annual Review of Psychology, 53*, 133–160.

Trigg, A. B. (2004). Deriving the Engel Curve: Pierre Bourdieu and the social critique of Maslow's hierarchy of needs. *Review of Social Economy, 62*, 393–406.

Trimpop, R., & Kirkcaldy, B. (1997). Personality predictors of driving accidents. *Personality & Individual Differences, 23*, 147–152.

Trudeau, K. J., & Devlin, A. S. (1996). College students and community service: Who, with whom, and why? *Journal of Applied Social Psychology, 26*, 1867–1888.

Trujillo, A. (2000). Psychotherapy with Native Americans: A view into the role of religion and spirituality. In A. E. Bergin (Ed.), *Handbook of Psychotherapy and Religious Diversity* (pp. 445–466). Washington, DC: American Psychological Association.

Trupp, M. S. (2006). Wider than the sky: The phenomenal gift of consciousness. *Journal of Nervous and Mental Disease, 194*, 66–67.

Tsai, D. F.-C. (2005). Human embryonic stem cell research debates: A confucian argument. *Journal of Medical Ethics, 31*, 635–640.

Tsuang, M. (2000). Schizophrenia: Genes and environment. *Biological Psychiatry, 47*, 210–220.

Tsukiura, T., Sekiguchi, A., Yomogida, Y., Nakagawa, S., Shigemune, Y., Kambara, T., & Kawashima, R. (2011). Effects of aging on hippocampal and anterior temporal activations during successful retrieval of memory for face-name associations. *Journal of Cognitive Neuorscience, 23*, 200–213.

Tuerlinckx, F., Boeck, P. D., & Lens, W. (2002). Measuring needs with the Thematic Apperception Test: A psychometric study. *Journal of Personality & Social Psychology, 82*(3), 448–461.

Tulving, E. (1962). Subjective organization in free-recall of "unrelated" words. *Psychological Review, 69*, 344–354.

Tulving, E. (1999). Study of memory: Processes and systems. In M. Jelicic (Ed.), *Memory: Systems, Process, or Function?* (pp. 11–30). Oxford, UK: Oxford University Press.

Tulving, E. (2008). On the law of primacy. In M. A. Gluck, J. R. Anderson, & S. M. Kosslyn (Eds.), *Memory and mind: A festschrift for Gordon H. Bower* (pp. 31–48). Mahwah, NJ: Lawrence Erlbaum.

Tulving, E., & Thomson, D. M. (1973). Encoding specificity and retrieval processes in episodic memory. *Psychological Review, 80*, 352–373.

Turiel, E. (2006). The development of morality. In W. Damon & R. M. Lerner (Eds.), *Handbook of child psychology: Vol. 3, social, emotional, and personality development* (pp. 789–857). Hoboken, NJ: John Wiley.

Turk, D. C., & Winter, F. (2006). The pain survival guide: How to to reclaim your life. Washington, DC: American Psychological Association.

Turkheimer, E. (1991). Individual and group differences in adoption studies of IQ. *Psychological Bulletin, 110*, 392–405.

Turnbull, C. (1989). *The mountain people*. London: Paladin.

Turner, H. M., Rose, K. S., & Cooper, M. J. (2005). Parental bonding and eating disorder symptoms in adolescents: The mediating role of core beliefs. Eating Behaviors, 6, 113–118.

Tversky, A., & Kahneman, D. (1973). Availability: A heuristic for judging frequency and probability. *Cognitive Psychology, 5*, 207–232.

Tversky, A., & Kahneman, D. (1974). Judgment under uncertainty: Heuristics and biases. *Science, 185*, 1124–1131.

Tyrrell, R. A., & Leibowtiz, H. W. (1990). The relation of vergence effort to reports of visual fatigue following prolonged near work. *Human Factors, 32*, 341–357.

U

Uchino, B. N., Cacioppo, J. T., & Kiecolt-Glaser, J. K. (1996). The relationship between social support and physiological processes: A review with emphasis on underlying mechanisms and implications for health. *Psychological Bulletin, 119*, 488–531.

Uchino, B. N., Smith, T. W., Holt-Lunstad, J., Campo, R., & Reblin, M. (2007). Stress and illness. In L. G. Tassinary & G. G. Berntson (Eds.), *Handbook of psychophysiology* (pp. 608–632). New York: Cambridge University Press.

Ufkes, E. G., Otten, S., Van der Zee, K. I., Giebels, E., & Dovidio, J. F. (2012). The effect of stereotype content on anger versus contempt in "day-to-day" conflicts. *Group Processes & Intergroup Relations, 15*, 57–74.

Ujike, H., & Ono, H. (2001). Depth thresholds of motion parallax as a function of head movement velocity. *Vision Research, 41*, 2835–2843.

Unger, R. K., & Crawford, M. (1992). *Women and gender: A feminist psychology*. New York: McGraw-Hill.

Uttl, B., Ohta, N., & Siegenthaler, A. L. E. (2006). *Memory and emotion: Interdisciplinary perspectives*. Malden, MA: Blackwell Publishing.

V

Vahtera, J., Kivimaeki, M., Uutela, A., & Pentti, J. (2000). Hostility and ill health: Role of psychosocial resources in two contexts of working life. *Journal of Psychosomatic Research, 48*, 89–98.

Vaidya, J. G., Block, R. I., O'Leary, D. S., Ponto, L. B., Ghoneim, M. M., & Bechara, A. (2012). Effects of chronic marijuana use on brain activity during monetary decision-making. *Neuropsychopharmacology, 37*, 618–629.

Vaillancourt, T. (2005). Indirect aggression among humans: Social construct or evolutionary adaptation? In R. E. Tremblay, W. W. Hartup, & J. Archer (Eds.), *Developmental origins of aggression* (pp. 158–177). New York: Guilford Press.

Vaillancourt, T., & Sharma, A. (2011). Intolerance of sexy peers: Intrasexual competition among women. Aggressive Behavior, 37, 569–577.

Valeo, T., & Beyerstein, L. (2008). Curses! In D. Gordon (Ed.), *Your Brain on Cubs: Inside the Heads of Players and Fans* (pp. 59, 74, 139, 140). Washington, DC: Dana Press.

Valeriani, M., Ranghi, F., & Giaquinto, S. (2003). Corrigendum to "The effects of aging on selective attention to touch: A reduced inhibitory control in elderly subjects?" *International Journal of Psychophysiology, 49*, 75–87.

Vallerand, R. J., Fortier, M. S., & Guay, F. (1997). Self-determination and persistence in a real-life setting: Toward a motivational model of high school dropout. *Journal of Personality and Social Psychology, 72*, 1161–1176.

Van der Oord, S., Prins, P. J. M., Oosterlaan, J., & Emmelkamp, P. M. G. (2008). Efficacy of methylphenidate, psychosocial treatments and their combination in school-aged children with ADHD: A meta-analysis. *Clinical Psychology Review, 28*, 783–800.

Van der Zee, K., Oldersma, F., Buunk, B. P., & Bos, D. (1998). Social comparison preferences among cancer patients as related to neuroticism and social comparison orientation. *Journal of Personality and Social Psychology, 75*, 801–810.

Van Doorn, H., Van der Kamp, J., & Savelsbergh, G. J. P. (2007). Grasping the Muller-Lyer illusion: The contributions of vision for perception in action. *Neuropsychologia, 45*, 1939–1947.

Van Geert, P. L. C., & Steenbeek, H. W. (2010). Networks as complex dynamic systems: Applications to clinical and developmental psychology and psychopathology. *Behavioral and Brain Sciences, 33*, 174–175.

Van Heck, G. L., & Den Oudsten, B. L. (2008). Emotional intelligence: Relationships to stress, health, and well-being. In I. Nyklicek, J. Denollet, & Johan (Eds.), *Emotion regulation: Conceptual and clinical issues* (pp. 97–121). New York: Springer.

Van Honk, J., & Schutter, D. J. L. G. (2007). Testosterone reduces conscious detection of signals serving social correction. *Psychological Science, 18*, 663–667.

Van Hooff, M. H., Voorhorst, F. J., Kaptein, M. B., Hirasing, R. A., Koppenaal, C., & Schoemaker, J. (2000). Insulin, androgen, and gonadotropin concentration, body mass index, and waist-to-hip ratio in the first years after menarche in girls with regular menstrual cycle, irregular menstrual cycles, or oligomenorrhea. *Journal of Clinical Endocrinology and Metabolism, 85*, 1394–1400.

Vansteenkiste, M., Simons, J., Lens, W., Sheldon, K. M., & Deci, E. L. (2004). Motivating learning, performance, and persistence: The synergistic effects of intrinsic goal contents and autonomy-supportive contexts. *Journal of Personality and Social Psychology, 87*, 246–260.

Varela, F. J., Palacios, A. G., & Goldsmith, T. H. (1993). Color vision of birds. In H. P. Ziegler & H.-J. Bishof (Eds.), *Vision, brain and behavior in birds* (pp. 77–98). Cambridge: MIT Press.

Varela, R. E., Steele, R. G., & Benson, E. R. (2007). The contribution of ethnic minority status to adaptive style: A comparison of Mexican, Mexican American, and European American children. *Journal of Cross-Cultural Psychology, 38*, 26–33.

Vargas, J. S. (2003). A commentary on "The double life of B. F. Skinner" by B. J. Baars. *Journal of Consciousness Studies, 10*, 68–73.

Vartanian, L. R., & Hopkinson, M. M. (2010). Social connectedness, conformity, and internalization of societal standards of attractiveness. *Body Image, 7,* 86–89.

Vaughn, L. A., & Weary, G. (2002). Roles of the availability of explanations, feelings of ease, and dysphoria in judgments about the future. *Journal of Social and Clinical Psychology, 21,* 686–704.

Vedam-Mai, V., Van Battum, E. Y., Kamphuis, W., Feenstra, M. G. P., Denys, D., Reynolds, B. A., ... Hoi, E. M. (2012). Deep brain stimulation and the role of astrocytes. *Molecular Psychiatry, 17,* 124–131.

Vein, A. M., Sidorov, A. A., Martazaev, M. S., & Karlov, A. V. (1991). Physical exercise and nocturnal sleep in healthy humans. *Human Physiology, 17,* 391–397.

Veresov, N. (2005). Marxist and non-Marxist aspects of the cultural-historical psychology of L. S. Vygotsky. *Critical Social Studies, 7,* 31–49.

Vernon, P. A., Wickett, J. C., Bazana, P. G., & Stelmack, R. M. (2000). The neuropsychology and psychophysiology of human intelligence. In *Handbook of intelligence* (pp. 245–264). Cambridge: Cambridge University Press.

Vezzali, L., Capozza, D., Giovannini, D., & Stathi, S. (2012). Improving implicit and explicit intergroup attitudes using imagined contact: An experimental intervention with elementary school children. *Group Processes & Intergroup Relations, 15,* 203–212.

Vieta, E., Suppes, T., Eggens, I., Persson, I., Paulsson, B., & Brecher, M. (2008). Efficacy and safety of quetiapine in combination with lithium or divalproex for maintenance of patients with bipolar I disorder (international trial 126). *Journal of Affective Disorders, 109,* 251–263.

Vines, G. (1995). Fight fat with feeling. *New Scientist,* 14–15.

Vingerhoets, A. (1985). The role of the parasympathetic division of the autonomic nervous system in stress and the emotions. *International Journal of Psychosomatics, 32*(3), 28–34.

Vining, E. P. G., Freeman, J. M., Pillas, D. J., Uematsu, S., Carson, B. S., Brandt, J., ... Zukerberg, A. (1997). Why would you remove half a brain? The outcome of 58 children after hemispherectomy—The Johns Hopkins Experience: 1968 To 1996. *Pediatrics, 100,* 163–171.

Vinokur, A. D., & Vinokur-Kaplan, D. (1990). In sickness and in health: Patterns of social support and undermining in older married couples. *Journal of Aging and Health, 2,* 215–241.

Vitterso, J. (2004). Subjective well-being versus self-actualization: Using the flow-simplex to promote a conceptual clarification of subjective quality of life. *Social Indicators Research, 65,* 299–331.

Vogel, G. (1996). School achievement: Asia and Europe top in the world, but reasons are hard to find. *Science, 274,* 1296.

Volkow, N. D., & Li, T.-K. (2007). Drugs and alcohol: Treating and preventing abuse, addiction, and their medical consequences. In M. T. Tsuang, W. S. Stone, & M. J. Lyons (Eds.), *Recognition and prevention of major mental and substance use disorders* (pp. 263–296). Washington, DC: American Psychiatric Publishing.

Vorauer, J. D., & Kumhyr, S. M. (2001). Is this about you or me? Self- versus other-directed judgments and feelings in response to intergroup interaction. *Personality and Social Psychology Bulletin, 27,* 706–719.

Vyazovskiy, V. V., & Tobler, I. (2005). Theta activity in the waking EEG is a marker of sleep propensity in the rat. *Brain Research, 105,* 64–71.

Vygotsky, L. S. (1986). *Thought and language* (A. Kozulin, Trans.). Cambridge, MA: MIT Press (Original work published 1934).

• • • • • • • • • **W** • • • • • • • • •

Waage, S., Pallesen, S., & Bjorvatn, B. (2007). Shift work and sleep disturbance. *Tidsskrift for Norsk Psykologforening, 44,* 428–433.

Wacker, J., Chavanon, M.-L., & Stemmler, G. (2006). Investigating the dopaminergic basis of extraversion in humans: A multilevel approach. *Journal of Personality and Social Psychology, 91,* 171–187.

Wade, T. J. (2003). Evolutionary theory and African American self-perception: Sex differences in body-esteem predictors of self-perceived physical and sexual attractiveness, and self-esteem. *Journal of Black Psychology, 29,* 123–141.

Wagenaar, W. A., & Groeneweg, J. (1990). The memory of concentration camp survivors. *Applied Cognitive Psychology, 4,* 77–87.

Wagner, B. C., & Petty, R. E. (2011). The elaboration likelihood model of persuasion: Thoughtful and non-thoughtful social influence. In *Theories in Social Psychology* (pp. 96–116). Hoboken, NJ: Wiley-Blackwell.

Wagner, H. (2001). Hunting in barn owls: Peripheral and neurobiological specializations and their general relevance in neural computation. In *Brain Evolution and Cognition* (pp. 205–235). New York: John Wiley.

Wagner, J., Chaney, J., Hommel, K., Andrews, N., & Jarvis, J. (2007). A cognitive diathesis-stress model of depressive symptoms in children and adolescents with juvenile rheumatic disease. *Children's Health Care, 36,* 45–62.

Wagner, R. K. (2000). Practical intelligence. In *Handbook of intelligence* (pp. 380–395). Cambridge, MA: Cambridge University Press.

Wahl, O. F. (2012). Stigma as a barrier to recovery from mental illness. *Trends in Cognitive Sciences, 16,* 9–10.

Walk, R. D. (1981). *Perceptual development.* Monterey, CA: Brooks/Cole.

Walk, R. D., & Gibson, E. J. (1961). A comparative and analytical study of visual depth perception. *Psychological Monographs,* (75).

Walker, E., & Bollini, A. M. (2002). Pubertal neurodevelopment and the emergence of psychotic symptoms. *Schizophrenia Research, 54,* 17–23.

Walker, E. F., & Diforio, D. (1998). Schizophrenia: A neural diathesis-stress model. *Psychological Review, 104,* 667–685.

Walker, M. P., & Stickgold, R. (2006). Sleep, memory, and plasticity. *Annual Review of Psychology, 57,* 139–166.

Wall, J. A. J., Beriker, N., & Wu, S. (2010). Turkish community mediation. *Journal of Applied Social Psychology, 40,* 2019–2042.

Wall, P. (2000). *Pain: The science of suffering.* New York: Columbia University Press.

Wallace, B. A., & Hodel, B. (2008). Embracing mind: *The common ground of science and spirituality.* Boston, MA: Shambhala Publications.

Wallace, P. (1977). Individual discrimination of humans by odor. *Physiology and Behavior, 19,* 577–579.

Waller, D., Loomis, J. M., Gollege, R. G., & Beall, A. C. (2002). Place learning in humans: The role of distance and direction information. *Spatial Cognition and Computation, 2,* 333–354.

Walsh, S. (1993). Cited in Toufexis, A. (1993, February 15). (A. Toufexis, Ed.) *Time,* 49–51.

Walsh, V. (2000). Hemispheric asymmetries: A brain in two minds. *Current Biology, 10,* 460–462.

Walter, L. M., Nixon, G. M., Davey, M. J., O'Driscoll, D. M., Trinder, J., & Horne, R. S. C. (2011). Sleep disturbance in pre-school children with obstructive sleep apnoea syndrome. *Sleep Medicine, 12,* 880–886.

Wanberg, C. R., Kenfer, R., & Rotundo, M. (1999). Unemployed individuals: Motives, job-search constraints as predictors of job seeking and reemployment. *Journal of Applied Psychology, 54,* 897–910.

Wang, D., & Audette, J. F. (2008). Acupuncture in pain management. In J. F. Audette & A. Bailey (Eds.), *Integrative pain medicine: The science and practice of complementary and alternative medicine in pain management* (pp. 379–416). Totowa, NJ: Humana Press.

Wang, G.-J., Volkow, N. D., Thanos, P. K., & Fowler, J. S. (2003). Positron emission tomographic evidence of similarity between obesity and drug addiction. *Psychiatric Annals, 33,* 104–111.

Wang, L. M., Schroeder, A., Loh, D., Smith, D., Lin, K., Han, J. H., ... Colwell, C. S. (2008). Role for the NR2B subunit of the N-methyl-D-aspartate receptor in mediating light input to the circadian system. *European Journal of Neuroscience, 27,* 1771–1779.

Wang, Q. (2001). Culture effects on adults' earliest childhood recollection and self-description: Implications for the relation between memory and the self. *Journal of Personality and Social Psychology, 81,* 220–223.

Waschbusch, D. A., Sellers, D. P., LeBlanc, M., & Kelley, M. L. (2003). Helpless attributions and depression in adolescents: The roles of anxiety, event valence and demographics. *Journal of Adolescence, 26,* 169–183.

Wason, P. C. (1960). On the failure to eliminate hypotheses in a conceptual task. *Quarterly Journal of Experimental Psychology, 12,* 129–140.

Wasserman, A. E., & Miller, R. R. (1997). What's elementary about associative learning? *Annual Review of. Psychology, 48,* 573–607.

Watkins, M. J., & Tulving, E. (1975). Episodic memory: When recognition fails. *Journal of Experimental Psychology: General, 104,* 5–29.

Watson, D., & Clark, L. A. (1997). Extraversion and its positive emotional core. In *Handbook of personality psychology.* San Diego, CA: Academic Press.

Watson, D., Wiese, D., Vaidya, J., & Tellegen, A. (1999). The two general activation systems of affect: Structural findings, evolutionary considerations, and psychobiological evidence. *Journal of Personality and Social Psychology, 76,* 820–838.

Watson, J. B. (1913). Psychology as the behaviorist views it. *Psychological Review, 20,* 158–177.

Watson, J. B. (1924). Behaviorism. New York: Norton.

Watson, J. B., & Rayner, R. (1920). Conditioned emotional responses. *Journal of Experimental Psychology, 3,* 1–14.

Watters, E. (2010). *Crazy like us: The globalization of the American psyche.* New York: Free Press.

Waxman, S. R. (2003). Early category and concept development: Making sense of the blooming, buzzing confusion. In L. M. Oakes (Ed.), *Early category and concept development: Making sense of the blooming, buzzing confusion* (pp. 213–241). London: Oxford University Press.

Webb, W. B. (1992). *Sleep: The gentle giant.* Bolton, MA: Anker Publishing.

Wechsler, H., Lee, J. E., Kuo, M., Seibring, M., Nelson, T. F., & Lee, H. (2002). Trends in college binge drinking during a period of increased prevention efforts: Findings for 4 Harvard Public School of Public Health College Study Surverys: 1993–2001. *Journal of American College Health, 50,* 203–217.

Weill, J. C., & Reynaud, C. A. (2005). Do developing B cells need antigen? *Journal of Experimental Medicine, 201,* 7–9.

Weinberg, R. A., Scarr, S., & Waldman, I. D. (1992). The Minnesota Trans¬racial Adoption Study: A follow-up of IQ test performance at adolescence. *Intelligence, 16,* 117–135.

Weiner, T., Johnston, D., & Lewis, N. (1995). *Betrayal: The story of Aldrich Ames, an American spy.* New York: Random House.

Weisbuch, M., Mackie, D. M., & Garcia-Marques, T. (2003). Prior source exposure and persuasion: Further evidence for misattributional processes. *Personality and Social Psychology Bulletin, 29,* 691–700.

Weisenberg, M. (1977). Pain and pain control. *Psychological Bulletin, 84,* 1008–1044.

Weiss, L. G., Saklofske, D. H., & Prifitera, A. (2005). Interpreting the WISC-IV index scores. In A. Prifitera, D. H. Saklofske, & L. G. Weiss (Eds.), *WISC-IV clinical use and interpretation: Scientist-practitioner Perspectives* (pp. 71–100). San Diego, CA: Elsevier Academic Press.

Weissman, M. M., Bland, R. C., Canino, G. J., Faravelli, C., Greenwald, S., & Hwu, H.-G. (1997). The cross-national epidemiology of panic disorder. *Archives of General Psychiatry, 54,* 305–309.

Weissman, M. M., Bland, R. C., Canino, G. J., Faravelli, C., Greenwald, S., Hwu, H.-G., ... Yeh, E.-K. (1996). Cross-national epidemiology of major depression and bipolar disorder. *Journal of the American Medical Association, 276,* 293–299.

Weitzman, E. R., Nelson, T. F., & Wechsler, H. (2003). Taking up binge drinking in college: The influences of person, social group, and environment. *Journal of Adolescent Health, 32,* 26–35.

Welsh, D. K. (1993). Timing of sleep and wakefulness. In M. A. Carskadon (Ed.), *Encyclopedia of sleep and dreaming.* New York: Macmillan.

Wert, B. Y., & Neisworth, J. T. (2003). Effects of video self-modeling on spontaneous requesting in children with autism. *Journal of Positive Behavior Interventions, 5,* 30–34.

West, S. G., & Brown, T. J. (1975). Physical attractiveness, the severity of the emergency and helping: A field experiment and interpersonal simulation. *Journal of Experimental Social Psychology, 11,* 531–538.

Wever, E. G. (1949). *Theory of hearing.* New York: Wiley.

Wever, E. G., & Bray, C. W. (1937). The perception of low tones and the resonance-volley theory. *Journal of Psychology, 3,* 101–114.

Wever, R. A. (1979). *The circadian system in man.* Berlin: Springer-Verlag.

Whaley, A. L. (2004). A two-stage method for the study of cultural bias in the diagnosis of schizophrenia in African Americans. *Journal of Black Psychology, 30,* 167–186.

Whitbeck, L. B., & Hoyt, D. R. (1994). Social prestige and assortive mating: A comparison of students from 1956 and 1988. *Journal of Social and Personal Relationships, 11,* 137–145.

White, C. E. (2002). *A conversation with Jasper Fforde.* Write: The Internet Writing Journal. Retrieved from http://www.writerswrite.com/journal/feb02/fforde.htm

White, G. L., & Mullen, P. E. (1989). *Jealousy: Theory, research, and clinical strategies.* New York: Guilford Press.

Whitehead, W. I., & Kuhn, and W. F. (1990). Chronic pain: An overview. In T. W. Miller (Ed.), *Chronic pain* (Vol. 1, pp. 5–48). Madison, CT: International Universities Press.

Whorf, B. L. (1956). Science and linguistics. In J. B. Carroll (Ed.), *Language, thought, and reality: Selected writings of Benjamin Lee Whorf.* Cambridge, MA: MIT Press.

Wickwire, E. M. J., Roland, M. M. S., Elkin, T. D., & Schumacher, J. A. (2008). Sleep disorders. In D. Reitman (Ed.), *Handbook of psychological assessment, case conceptualization, and treatment, Vol 2: Children and adolescents* (pp. 622–651). Hoboken, NJ: John Wiley & Sons Inc.

Wiesel, T. N. (1982). Postnatal development of the visual cortex and the influence of environment. *Nature, 299,* 583–591.

Wiggins, D. H. J. (1996). *The five factor model of personality: Theoretical perspectives.* New York: Guilford Press.

Wilde, D. J. (2011). *Jung's personality theory quantified.* New York: Springer-Verlag Publishing.

Willerman, L., & Cohen, D. B. (1990). *Psychopathology.* New York: McGraw-Hill.

Willford, J. A., Richardson, G. A., & Day, N. L. (2012). Sex-specific effects of prenatal marijuana exposure on neurodevelopment and behavior. In L. Kestler (Ed.), *Gender differences in prenatal substance exposure* (pp. 121–136). Washington, DC: American Psychological Association.

Williams, C. L., Haines, J., & Sale, I. M. (2003). Psychophysiological and psychological correlates of dissociation in a case of dissociative identity disorder. *Journal of Trauma & Dissociation, 4,* 101–118.

Williams, D., & Lawler, K. A. (2001). Stress and illness in low-income women: The roles of hardiness, John Henryism, and race. *Women and Health, 32,* 61–76.

Willis, W. D. (1985). *The pain system: The neural basis of nocicepetive transmission in the mammalian nervous system.* Basel: Karger.

Wills, T. A., Yaeger, A. M., & Sandy, J. M. (2003). Buffering effect of religiosity for adolescent substance use. *Psychology of Addictive Behaviors, 17,* 24–31.

Willson, A. E. (2003). Race and women's income trajectories: Employment, marriage, and income security over the life course. *Social Problems, 50,* 87–110.

Wilson, A. E., & Ross, M. (2001). From chump to champ: People's appraisals of their earlier and current selves. *Journal of Personality and Social Psychology, 80,* 572–584.

Wilson, B. J., Donnerstein, E., Linz, D., Kunkel, D., Potter, J., Smith, S. L., ... Gray, T. (1998). Content analysis of entertainment television: the importance of context. In *Television violence and public policy* (pp. 13–51). Ann Arbor, MI: University of Michigan Press.

Wilson, T. D., Lindsey, S., & Schooler, T. Y. (2000). A model of dual attitudes. *Psychological Review, 107,* 101–126.

Winn, P. (1995). The lateral hypothalamus and motivated behavior: An old syndrome reassessed and a new perspective gained. *Current Directions in Psychological Science, 4,* 182–187.

Winograd, E., & Killinger, W. A. (1983). Relating age at encoding in early childhood to adult recall: Development of flashbulb memories. *Journal of Experimental Psychology: General, 112,* 413–422.

Wiseman, R., & Greening, E. (2002). The mind machine: A mass participation experiment into the possible existence of extra-sensory perception. *British Journal of Psychology, 93,* 487–499.

Wissler, C. (1901). The correlation of mental and physical tests. *Psychological Review Monograph Supplement, 3*(6).

Wittchen, H. U., Gloster, A. T., Bessdo-Baum, K., Fava, G. A., & Craskeet, M. G. (2010). Agoraphobia: A review of the diagnostic classificatory position and criteria. *Depression and Anxiety, 27,* 113–133.

Wixted, J. T., & Ebbesen, E. B. (1991). On the form of forgetting. *Psychological Science, 2,* 409–415.

Wolkowitz, O. M., & Rothschild, A. J. (2003). *Psychoneuroendocrinology: The scientific basis of clinical practice.* Arlington, VA: American Psychiatric Publishing.

Wong, N., Sarver, D. E., & Beidel, D. C. (2012). Quality of life impairments among adults with social phobia: The impact of subtype. *Journal of Anxiety Disorders, 26,* 50–57.

Wood, D. J., Bruner, J. S., & Ross, G. (1976). The role of tutoring in problem solving. *Journal of Child Psychology and Psychiatry, 17,* 89–100.

Wood, N., & Cowan, N. (1995). The cocktail party phenomenon revisited: How frequent are attention shifts to one's name in an irrelevant auditory channel? *Journal of Experimental Psychology: Learning, Memory, and Cognition, 21,* 255–260.

Wood, W., Wong, F. Y., & Charchere, J. G. (1991). Effects of media violence on viewers' aggression in unconstrained social interaction. *Psychological Bulletin, 109,* 371–383.

Woods, J. M. (2008). The history of the Rorschach in the United States. *Rorschachiana, 29,* 64–80.

Woodward, S. A., McManis, M. H., Kagan, J., Deldin, P., Snidman, N., Lewis, M., & Kahn, V. (2001). Infant temperament and the brainstem auditory evoked response in later childhood. *Developmental Psychology, 37,* 533–538.

Woolsey, T. A., Hanaway, J., & Gado, M. H. (2008). *The brain atlas: A visual guide to the human central nervous system* (3rd ed.). Hoboken, NJ: John Wiley.

Wootton, J. (2008). Meditation and chronic pain. In J. F. Audette & A. Bailey (Eds.), *Integrative pain medicine: The science and practice of complementary and alternative medicine in pain management* (pp. 195–209). Totowa, NJ: Humana Press.

Wright, I. C., Rabe, H. S., Woodruff, P. W. R., David, S. A., Murray, M. R., & Bullmore, E. T. (2000). Meta-analysis of regional brain volumes in schizophrenia. *American Journal of Psychiatry, 157,* 16–25.

Wright, K., & Flemons, D. (2002). Dying to know: Qualitative research with terminally ill persons and their families. *Death Studies, 26,* 255–281.

Wright, P. H., & Scanlon, M. B. (1991). Gender role orientations and friendship: Some attenuation, but gender differences abound. *Sex Roles, 24,* 551–566.

Wu, Y.-T., Tsou, K.-I., Hsu, C.-H., Fang, L.-J., Yao, G., & Jeng, S.-F. (2008). Brief report: Taiwanese infants' mental and motor development—6–24 months. *Journal of Pediatric Psychology, 33,* 102–108.

Wyche, K. F. (1993). Psychology and African American women: Findings from applied research. *Applied & Preventive Psychology, 2,* 115–121.

Wysocki, T., Harris, M. A., Buckloh, L. M., Mertlich, D., Lochrie, A. S., Taylor, A., ... White, N. H. (2008). Randomized, controlled trial of behavioral family systems therapy for diabetes: Maintenance and generalization of effects on parent-adolescent communication. *Behavior Therapy, 39,* 33–46.

X

Xuei, X., Flury-Wetherill, L., Almasy, L., Bierut, L., Tischfield, J., Schuckit, M., ... Edenberg, H. J. (2008). Association analysis of genes encoding the nociceptin receptor (OPRL1) and its endogenous ligand (PNOC) with alcohol or illicit drug dependence. *Addiction Biology, 13,* 80–87.

Y

Yamaguchi, S., Hale, L. A., D'Esposito, M., & Knight, R. T. (2004). Rapid prefrontal-hippocampal habituation to novel events. *Journal of Neuroscience, 24,* 5356–5363.

Yancey, A. K., Siegel, J. M., & McDaniel, K. L. (2002). Role models, ethnic identity, and health-risk behaviors in urban adolescents. *Archives of Pediatric Adolescent Medicine, 156,* 55–61.

Yanez, B. R., Stanton, A. L., Hoyt, M. A., Tennen, H., & Lechner, S. (2011). Understanding perceptions of benefit following adversity: How do distinct assessments of growth relate to coping and adjustment to stressful events. *Journal of Social and Clinical Psychology, 30,* 699–721.

Yang, S. (2008). Real-life contextual manifestations of wisdom. *International Journal of Aging and Human Development, 67,* 273–303.

Yantis, S. (2008). The neural basis of selective attention: Cortical sources and targets of attentional modulation. *Current Directions in Psychological Science, 17,* 86–90.

Yeargin-Allsopp, M., Murphy, C. C., Cordero, J. F., & Decoufle, P. (1997). Reported biomedical causes and associated medical conditions for mental retardation among 10-year-old children. *Developmental Medicine & Child Neurology, 39,* 142–149.

Yehuda, R. (2000). The biology of post traumatic stress disorder. *Journal of Clinical Psychiatry, 61*(7), 14–21.

Yelena, P., Leo, M. A., Kroll, W., & Lieber, C. S. (2002). Effects of alcohol consumption on eight circulating markers of liver fibrosis. *Alcohol & Alcoholism, 37,* 256–260.

Yensen, R., & Dryer, D. (2007). Addiction, despair, and the soul: Successful psychedelic psychotherapy, a case study. In M. J. Winkelman & T. B. Thomas (Eds.), *Psychedelic medicine: New evidence for hallucinogenic substances as treatments* (Vol. 2, pp. 15–28). Westport, CT: Praeger Publishers.

Yoder, J. D. (1999). *Women and gender: Transforming psychology.* Upper Saddle River, NJ: Prentice Hall.

Yoder, J. D., Perry, R. L., & Saal, E. I. (2007). What good is a feminist identity?: Women's feminist identification and role expectations for intimate and sexual relationships. *Sex Roles, 57,* 365–372.

Yoon, K. L., & Joormann, J. (2012). Stress reactivity in social anxiety disorder with and without comorbid depression. *Journal of Abnormal Psychology, 121,* 250–255.

Young, L. J. (2002). The neurobiology of social recognition: Approach and avoidance. *Biological Psychiatry, 51,* 18–26.

Yousem, D. M., Maldjian, J. A., Siddiqi, F., Hummel, T., Alsop, D. C., Geckle, R. J., ... Doty, R. L. (1999). Gender effects on odor-stimulated functional magnetic resonance imaging. *Brain Research, 818,* 480–487.

Yousem, D. M., Oguz, K. K., & Li, C. (2001). Imaging of the olfactory system. *Seminars in Ultrasound, CT & MR, 22,* 456–472.

Yu, B., Zhang, W., Jing, Q., Peng, R., Zhang, G., & Simon, H. A. (1985). STM capacity for Chinese and English language materials. *Memory and Cognition, 13,* 202–207.

Yu, D. S. (2007). Review of indigenous and cultural psychology: Understanding people in context. *Pastoral Psychology, 56,* 115–119.

Yzerbyt, V. Y., Rocher, S., & Schadron, G. (1996). Stereotypes as explanations: A subjective essentialist view of group perception. In P. J. Oakes, N. Ellemers, & S. A. Haslam (Eds.), *The social psychology of stereotyping and group life.* Cambridge, MA: Blackwell.

· · **Z** ·

Zajonc, R. B. (1968). Attitudinal effects of mere exposure. *Journal of Personality and Social Psychology Monograph Supplement, 9*(2 - Part - 2), 1–27.

Zanot, E. J., Pincus, J. D., & Lamp, E. J. (1983). Public perceptions of subliminal advertising. *Journal of Advertising, 12,* 37–45.

Zaragoza, M. S., Belli, R. F., & Payment, K. E. (2007). Misinformation effects and the suggestibility of eyewitness memory. In M. Garry & H. Hayne (Eds.), *Do justice and let the sky fall: Elizabeth Loftus and her contributions to science, law, and academic freedom* (pp. 35–63). Mahwah, NJ: Lawrence Erlbaum.

Zaragoza, M. S., & Mitchell, K. J. (1996). Repeated exposure to suggestion and the creation of false memories. *Psychological Science, 7,* 294–300.

Zárate, M. A., Garcia, B., Garza, A. A., & Hitlan, R. T. (2004). Cultural threat and perceived realistic group conflict as dual predictors of prejudice. *Journal of Experimental Social Psychology, 40,* 99–105.

Zarbatany, L., Conley, R., & Pepper, S. (2007). Personality and gender differences in friendship needs and experiences in preadolescence and young adulthood. *International Journal of Behavioral Development, 28,* 299–310.

Zebrowitz, L. A., & Rhodes, G. (2002). Nature let a hundred flowers bloom: The multiple ways and wherefores of attractiveness. In L. A. Zebrowitz (Ed.), *Facial attractiveness: Evolutionary, cognitive, and social perspectives* (Vol. 1, pp. 261–293). Westport, CT: Ablex.

Zeman, A. (2005). Tales from the temporal lobes. *New England Journal of Medicine, 352,* 119–121.

Zervas, I. M., Theleritis, C., & Soldatos, C. R. (2012). Using ECT in schizophrenia: A review from a clinical perspective. *The World Journal of Biological Psychiatry, 13,* 69–105.

Zhang, D. R., Li, Z. H., Chen, X. C., Wang, Z. X., Zhang, X. C., Meng, X. M., ... Hu, X. P. (2003). Functional comparison of primacy, middle and recency retrieval in human auditory short-term memory: An event-related fMRI study. *Cognitive Brain Research, 16,* 91–98.

Zhang, F., Zhou, H., Wilson, B. C., Shi, J.-S., Hong, J.-S., & Gao, H.-M. (2012). Fluoxetine protects neurons against microglial activation-mediated neurotoxicity. *Parkinsonism & Related Disorders, 18,* 213–217.

Zhang, Q. H., & Xiumei, Z. J. (2007). A comparative study on the classification of basic color terms by undergraduates from Yi nationality, Bai nationality and Naxi nationality. *Acta Psychologica Sinica, 39,* 18–26.

Zhou, P., Shah, B., Prasad, K., & David, R. (2005). Letrozole significantly improves growth potential in a pubertal boy with growth hormone deficiency. *Pediatrics, 115,* 245–248.

Ziegelstein, R. C. (2012). Reuptake inhibitors. *Journal of Psychosomatic Research, 72,* 3–4.

Zimmer, A. C. (2006). Visual perception and theories of painting: An uneasy complementarity. In L. Albertazzi (Ed.), *Visual thought* (pp. 221–232). Amsterdam, Netherlands: John Benjamins.

Zinn, M. B., Hondagneu-Sotelo, P., & Messner, M. A. (2000). *Gender through the prism of difference* (2nd ed.). Needham Heights, MA: Allyn & Bacon.

Zola-Morgan, S., & Squire, L. R. (1993). Neuroanatomy of memory. *Annual Review of Neuroscience, 16,* 25–33.

Zrenner, E., Abramov, I., Akita, M., Cowey, A., Livingstone, M., & Valberg, A. (1990). Color perception: Retina to cortex. In J. S. Werner (Ed.), *Visual perception: The neurophysiological foundations.* San Diego, CA: Academic Press.

Zurbriggen, E. L., & Yost, M. R. (2004). Power, desire, and pleasure in sexual fantasies. *Journal of Sex Research, 41,* 288–300.

Zwislocki, J. J. (1981). Sound analysis in the ear: A history of discoveries. *American Scientist, 69,* 184–192.

Name Index

Subject Index